P9-AQG-699

50
BEST
PLAYS
OF THE
AMERICAN
THEATRE

★★★★

71-4441
v.4

812. OY
G 25

72

50
BEST
PLAYS
OF THE
AMERICAN
THEATRE

★★★★

Selected by CLIVE BARNES

with Individual Play Introductions by
JOHN GASSNER

Introduction to The Odd Couple
and Fiddler on the Roof by CLIVE BARNES

CROWN PUBLISHERS, INC., NEW YORK

WITHDRAWN
ST MARY'S COLLEGE LIBRARY
O'FALLON, MISSOURI

WITHDRAWN
SOCCS LIBRARY
4601 Mid Rivers Mall Drive
St. Peters, MO 63376

NOTE: All plays contained in this volume are fully protected under the copyright laws of the United States of America, the British Empire, including the Dominion of Canada, and all other countries of the Copyright Union. Permission to reproduce, wholly or in part, by any method, must be obtained from the copyright owners or their agents. (See notices at the beginning of each play.)

SECOND PRINTING, JANUARY, 1970

© 1969 BY CROWN PUBLISHERS, INC.
LIBRARY OF CONGRESS CATALOG CARD NUMBER: 57–12830
PRINTED IN THE UNITED STATES OF AMERICA
PUBLISHED SIMULTANEOUSLY IN CANADA BY GENERAL PUBLISHING COMPANY LIMITED

Table of Contents

71-441.

50
BEST
PLAYS
OF THE
AMERICAN
THEATRE
★★★★

Come Back, Little Sheba

BY WILLIAM INGE

First presented by The Theatre Guild at the Booth Theatre in New York on February 15, 1950, with the following cast:

DOC	Sidney Blackmer	MRS. COFFMAN	Olga Fabian
MARIE	Joan Lorring	MILKMAN	John Randolph
LOLA	Shirley Booth	MESSENGER	Arnold Schulman
TURK	Lonny Chapman	BRUCE	Robert Cunningham
POSTMAN	Daniel Reed	ED ANDERSON	Wilson Brooks
	ELMO HUSTON	Paul Krauss	

———

ACT ONE

Scene One: Morning in late spring.
Scene Two: The same evening, after supper.

ACT TWO

Scene One: The following morning.
Scene Two: Late afternoon the same day.
Scene Three: 5:30 the next morning.
Scene Four: Morning, a week later.

The action takes place in a rundown neighborhood of a Midwestern city.

———

Copyright, 1949, as an unpublished work, by WILLIAM INGE.

Copyright, 1950, by WILLIAM INGE.

Reprinted by permission of Random House, Inc. All rights reserved.

Born in Independence, Kansas, in 1913, and the holder of a B.A. from the University of Kansas and an M.A. from Peabody College of Nashville, Tennessee, William Inge is a genuine Midwesterner. His claims to that distinction—and it is a distinction in his case since the tone and quality of *Come Back, Little Sheba* cannot conceivably have been drawn from any other region!—were strengthened by his professional work. He taught at Stephens College in Columbia, Missouri, where the celebrated Maude Adams headed the theatre department during the last years of her life; and he gave an extension course in playwriting at Washington University in St. Louis, where he also filled the post of drama, film and music critic on the *St. Louis Star-Times*.

While occupying this position, Mr. Inge went to see the pre-Broadway production of Tennessee Williams' *The Glass Menagerie* in Chicago. Profoundly impressed by what he later called "the first real experience I had felt in the theatre for years," he proceeded to write his first play, *Farther Off From Heaven*. Margo Jones produced it in her Dallas arena theatre in 1947. *Come Back, Little Sheba* was his second play, and it introduced an authentic new talent to Broadway in 1950. Although that talent is as remote from the Great White Way as any that has won acclaim there for many years, it was instantly welcomed by the Theatre Guild and loyally supported by the Guild's able play editor Phyllis Anderson, whose faith in the author proved justified. At this writing, Mr. Inge has a new play, *Picnic,* scheduled for the season of 1952-1953 and resides within commuting distance of New York in Old Greenwich, Connecticut.

Both *Farther Off From Heaven* and *Come Back, Little Sheba* have in common with *The Glass Menagerie* a concern with small lives and a sparing expenditure of plot. But, unlike Tennessee Williams, Mr. Inge resolutely allowed the facts of a constricted, essentially small-town life to speak for themselves, without the accessory machinery of narrations, flashbacks, and symbolism. In this respect, too, his work, remote from literary sophistication, remained inviolately Midwestern. To *Come Back, Little Sheba,* however, the author gave a universality which he once defined by referring us to Thoreau's statement in *Walden* that "the mass of men lead lives of quiet desperation." Thoreau added, "What is called resignation is confirmed desperation," and it would be difficult to find an apter description of the first and third acts of Inge's play. *Come Back, Little Sheba* brings a large if quietly dispensed compassion to bear upon ordinary lives.

Inge's artistry may be described as Naturalism with a heart. It does not pitch the drama on the heights, but neither does it artificially inflate the human condition. It does not scintillate, but neither does it purvey the factitious glitter of verbal gymnasts. The play belongs to Main Street and Gopher Prairie, and if this is a limitation in the work, it is also evidence of its authenticity. There are too many examples of disingenuous artistry by contemporaries who think they are on Parnassus when they are merely in literary society. Inge gave the impression of being a lonely writer who was disinclined to run with any literary pack, and his play is a genuine middle-class drama that pretends to be nothing else. It does not varnish a St. Louis background with a British accent. Is it, for that reason, any the less universal?

ACT ONE

SCENE ONE

The stage is empty.

It is the downstairs of an old house in one of those semi-respectable neighborhoods in a Midwestern city. The stage is divided into two rooms, the living room at right and the kitchen at left, with a stairway and a door between. At the foot of the stairway is a small table with a telephone on it. The time is about 8:00 A.M., a morning in the late spring.

At rise of curtain the sun hasn't come out in full force and outside the atmosphere is a little gray. The house is extremely cluttered and even dirty. The living room somehow manages to convey the atmosphere of the twenties, decorated with cheap pretense at niceness and respectability. The general effect is one of fussy awkwardness. The furniture is all heavy and rounded-looking, the chairs and davenport being covered with a shiny mohair. The davenport is littered and there are lace antimacassars on all the chairs. In such areas, houses are so close together they hide each other from the sunlight. What sun could come through the window, at right, is dimmed by the smoky glass curtains. In the kitchen there is a table, center. On it are piled dirty dishes from supper the night before. Woodwork in the kitchen is dark and grimy. No industry whatsoever has been spent in making it one of those white, cheerful rooms that we commonly think kitchens should be. There is no action on stage for several seconds.

Doc comes downstairs to kitchen. His coat is on back of chair, center. He straightens chair, takes roll from bag on drainboard, folds bag and tucks it behind sink. He lights stove and goes to table, fills dishpan there and takes it to sink. Turns on water, tucks towel in vest for apron. He goes to chair and says prayer. Then he crosses to stove, takes frying pan to sink and turns on water.

Marie, a young girl of eighteen or nineteen who rooms in the house, comes out of her bedroom (next to the living room), skipping airily into the kitchen. Her hair is piled in curls on top of her head and she wears a sheer dainty negligee and smart, feathery mules on her feet. She has the cheerfulness only youth can feel in the morning.

MARIE *(goes to chair, opens pocketbook there)*. Hi!

DOC. Well, well, how is our star boarder this morning?

MARIE. Fine.

DOC. Want your breakfast now?

MARIE. Just my fruit juice. I'll drink it while I dress and have my breakfast later.

DOC *(places two glasses on table)*. Up a little early, aren't you?

MARIE. I have to get to the library and check out some books before anyone else gets them.

DOC. Yes, you want to study hard, Marie, learn to be a fine artist some day. Paint lots of beautiful pictures. I remember a picture my mother had over the mantelpiece at home, a picture of a cathedral in a sunset, one of those big cathedrals in Europe somewhere. Made you feel religious just to look at it.

MARIE. These books aren't for art, they're for biology. I have an exam.

DOC. Biology? Why do they make you take biology?

MARIE *(laughs)*. It's required. Didn't you have to take biology when you were in college?

DOC. Well . . . yes, but I was preparing to study medicine, so of course I *had* to take biology and things like that. You see —I was going to be a real doctor then— only I left college my third year.

MARIE. What's the matter? Didn't you like the pre-med course?

DOC. Yes, of course . . . I had to give it up.

MARIE. Why?

DOC *(goes to stove with roll on plate—evasive)*. I'll put your sweet roll in now, Marie, so it will be nice and warm for you when you want it.

MARIE. Dr. Delaney, you're so nice to your wife, and you're so nice to me, as a matter of fact, you're so nice to everyone. I hope my husband is as nice as you are. Most husbands would never think of getting their own breakfast.

DOC *(very pleased with this)*. . . . . uh . . . you might as well sit down now and . . . yes, sit here and I'll serve you your breakfast now, Marie, and we can eat it together, the two of us.

MARIE *(a light little laugh as she starts*

dancing away from him). No, I like to bathe first and feel that I'm all fresh and clean to start the day. I'm going to hop into the tub now. See you later. *(She goes upstairs)*

DOC *(the words appeal to him).* Yes, fresh and clean— *(Doc shows disappointment but goes on in businesslike way setting his breakfast on the table)*

MARIE *(offstage).* Mrs. Delaney.

LOLA *(offstage).* 'Mornin', honey. *(Then Lola comes downstairs. She is a contrast to Doc's neat cleanliness, and Marie's Over a nightdress she wears a lumpy kimono. Her eyes are dim with a morning expression of disillusionment, as though she had had a beautiful dream during the night and found on waking none of it was true. On her feet are worn dirty comfies)*

LOLA *(with some self-pity).* I can't sleep late like I used to. It used to be I could sleep till noon if I wanted to, but I can't any more. I don't know why.

DOC. Habits change. Here's your fruit juice.

LOLA *(taking it).* I oughta be gettin' your breakfast, Doc, instead of you gettin' mine.

DOC. I have to get up anyway, Baby.

LOLA *(sadly).* I had another dream last night.

DOC *(pours coffee).* About Little Sheba?

LOLA *(with sudden animation).* It was just as real. I dreamt I put her on a leash and we walked downtown—to do some shopping. All the people on the street turned around to admire her, and I felt so proud. Then we started to walk, and the blocks started going by so fast that Little Sheba couldn't keep up with me. Suddenly, I looked around and Little Sheba was gone. Isn't that funny? I looked everywhere for her but I couldn't find her. And I stood there feeling sort of afraid. *(Pause)* Do you suppose that means anything?

DOC. Dreams are funny.

LOLA. Do you suppose it means Little Sheba is going to come back?

DOC. I don't know, Baby.

LOLA *(petulant).* I miss her so, Doc. She was such a cute little puppy. Wasn't she cute?

DOC *(smiles with the reminiscence).* Yes, she was cute.

LOLA. Remember how white and fluffy she used to be after I gave her a bath?

And how her little hind-end wagged from side to side when she walked?

DOC *(an appealing memory).* I remember.

LOLA. She was such a cute little puppy. I hated to see her grow old, didn't you, Doc?

DOC. Yah. Little Sheba should have stayed young forever. Some things should never grow old. That's what it amounts to, I guess.

LOLA. She's been gone for such a long time. What do you suppose ever happened to her?

DOC. You can't ever tell.

LOLA *(with anxiety).* Do you suppose she got run over by a car? Or do you think that old Mrs. Coffman next door poisoned her? I wouldn't be a bit surprised.

DOC. No, Baby. She just disappeared. That's all we know.

LOLA *(redundantly).* Just vanished one day . . . vanished into thin air. *(As though in a dream)*

DOC. I told you I'd find another one, Baby.

LOLA *(pessimistically).* You couldn't ever find another puppy as cute as Little Sheba.

DOC *(back to reality).* Want an egg?

LOLA. No, just this coffee. *(He pours coffee and sits down to breakfast, Lola, suddenly)* Have you said your prayer, Doc?

DOC. Yes, Baby.

LOLA. And did you ask God to be with you—all through the day, and keep you strong?

DOC. Yes, Baby.

LOLA. Then God will be with you, Docky. He's been with you almost a year now and I'm so proud of you.

DOC *(preening himself a little).* Sometimes I feel sorta proud of myself.

LOLA. Say your prayer, Doc. I like to hear it.

DOC *(matter-of-factly).* God grant me the serenity to accept the things I cannot change, courage to change the things I can, and wisdom always to tell the difference.

LOLA. That's nice. That's so pretty. When I think of the way you used to drink, always getting into fights, we had so much trouble. I was so scared! I never knew what was going to happen.

DOC. That was a long time ago, Baby.

LOLA. I know it, Daddy. I know how you're going to be when you come home now. (*She kisses him lightly*)

DOC. *I* don't know what I would have done without you.

LOLA. And now you've been sober almost a year.

DOC. Yep. A year next month. (*He rises and goes to the sink with coffee cup and two glasses, rinsing them*)

LOLA. Do you have to go to the meeting tonight?

DOC. No. I can skip the meetings now for a while.

LOLA. Oh, good! Then you can take me to a movie.

DOC. Sorry, Baby. I'm going out on some Twelfth Step work with Ed Anderson.

LOLA. What's that?

DOC (*drying the glasses*). I showed you that list of twelve steps the Alcoholics Anonymous have to follow. This is the final one. After you learn to stay dry yourself, then you go out and help other guys that need it.

LOLA. Oh!

DOC (*goes to sink*). When we help others, we help ourselves.

LOLA. I know what you mean. Whenever I help Marie in some way, it makes me feel good.

DOC. Yah. (*Lola takes her cup to Doc and he washes it*) Yes, but this is a lot different, Baby. When I go out to help some poor drunk, I have to give him courage—to stay sober like I've stayed sober. Most alcoholics are disappointed men ... They need courage ...

LOLA. You weren't ever disappointed, were you, Daddy?

DOC (*after another evasive pause*). The important thing is to forget the past and live for the present. And stay sober doing it.

LOLA. Who do you have to help tonight?

DOC. Some guy they picked up on Skid Row last night. (*Gets his coat from back of chair*) They got him at the City Hospital. I kinda dread it.

LOLA. I thought you said it helped you.

DOC (*puts on coat*). It does, if you can stand it. I did some Twelfth Step work down there once before. They put alcoholics right in with the crazy people. It's horrible—these men all twisted and shaking—eyes all foggy and full of pain. Some

guy there with his fists clamped together, so he couldn't kill anyone. There was a young man, just a *young* man, had scratched his eyes out.

LOLA (*cringing*). Don't, Daddy. Seems a shame to take a man there just 'cause he got drunk.

DOC. Well, they'll sober a man up. That's the important thing. Let's not talk about it any more.

LOLA (*with relief*). Rita Hayworth's on tonight, out at the Plaza. Don't you want to see it?

DOC. Maybe Marie will go with you.

LOLA. Oh, no. She's probably going out with Turk tonight.

DOC. She's too nice a girl to be going out with a guy like Turk.

LOLA. I don't know why, Daddy. Turk's nice. (*Cuts coffee cake*)

DOC. A guy like that doesn't have any respect for *nice* young girls. You can tell that by looking at him.

LOLA. I never saw Marie object to any of the lovemaking.

DOC. A big, brawny bozo like Turk, he probably forces her to kiss him.

LOLA. Daddy, that's not so at all. I came in the back way once when they were in the living room, and she was kissing him like he was Rudolph Valentino.

DOC (*an angry denial*). Marie is a nice girl.

LOLA. I know she's nice. I just said she and Turk were doing some tall spooning. It wouldn't surprise me any if . . .

DOC. Honey, I don't want to hear any more about it.

LOLA. You try to make out like every young girl is Jennifer Jones in the *Song of Bernadette*.

DOC. I do not. I just like to believe that young people like her are clean and decent . . . (*Marie comes downstairs*)

MARIE. Hi! (*Gets cup and saucer from drainboard*)

LOLA (*at stove*). There's an extra sweet roll for you this morning, honey. I didn't want mine.

MARIE. One's plenty, thank you.

DOC. How soon do you leave this morning? (*Lola brings coffee*)

MARIE (*eating*) As soon as I finish my breakfast.

DOC. Well, I'll wait and we can walk to the corner together.

MARIE. Oh, I'm sorry, Doc. Turk's coming by. He has to go to the library, too.

DOC. Oh, well, I'm not going to be competition with a football player. (*To Lola*) It's a nice spring morning. Wanta walk to the office with me?

LOLA. I look too terrible, Daddy. I ain't even dressed.

DOC. Kiss Daddy good-bye.

LOLA (*gets up and kisses him softly*). Bye, bye, Daddy. If you get hungry, come home and I'll have something for you.

MARIE (*joking*). Aren't you going to kiss *me*, Dr. Delaney? (*Lola eggs Doc to go ahead*)

DOC (*startled, hesitates, forces himself to realize she is only joking and manages to answer*). Can't spend my time kissing all the girls.

(*Marie laughs. Doc goes into living room while Lola and Marie continue talking. Marie's scarf is tossed over his hat on chair, so he picks it up, then looks at it fondly, holding it in the air inspecting its delicate gracefulness. He drops it back on chair and goes out.*)

MARIE. I think Dr. Delaney is so nice.

LOLA (*she is by the closet now, where she keeps a few personal articles. She is getting into a more becoming smock*). When did you say Turk was coming by?

MARIE. Said he'd be here about 9:30. (*Doc exits, hearing the line about Turk*) That's a pretty smock.

LOLA (*goes to table, sits in chair and changes shoes*). It'll be better to work around the house in.

MARIE (*not sounding exactly cheerful*). Mrs. Delaney, I'm expecting a telegram this morning. Would you leave it on my dresser for me when it comes?

LOLA. Sure, honey. No bad news, I hope.

MARIE. Oh, no! It's from Bruce.

LOLA (*Marie's boy friends are one of her liveliest interests*). Oh, your boy friend in Cincinnati. Is he coming to see you?

MARIE. I guess so.

LOLA. I'm just dying to meet him.

MARIE (*changing the subject*). Really, Mrs. Delaney, you and Doc have been so nice to me. I just want you to know I appreciate it.

LOLA. Thanks, honey.

MARIE. You've been like a father and mother to me. I appreciate it.

LOLA. Thanks, honey.

MARIE. Turk was saying just the other night what good sports you both are.

LOLA (*brushing hair*). That so?

MARIE. Honest. He said it was just as much fun being with you as with kids our own age.

LOLA (*couldn't be more flattered*). Oh, I like that Turk. He reminds me of a boy I used to know in high school, Dutch McCoy. Where did you ever meet him?

MARIE. In art class.

LOLA. Turk take art?

MARIE (*laughs*). No. It was in a life class. He was modeling. Lots of the athletes do that. It pays them a dollar an hour.

LOLA. That's nice.

MARIE. Mrs. Delaney? I've got some corrections to make in some of my drawings. Is it all right if I bring Turk home this morning to pose for me? It'll just take a few minutes.

LOLA. Sure, honey.

MARIE. There's a contest on now. They're giving a prize for the best drawing to use for advertising the Spring Relays.

LOLA. And you're going to do a picture of Turk? That's nice. (*A sudden thought*) Doc's gonna be gone tonight. You and Turk can have the living room if you want to. (*A little secretively*)

MARIE (*this is a temptation*). O.K. Thanks. (*Exits to bedroom*)

LOLA. Tell me more about Bruce. (*Follows her to bedroom door*)

MARIE (*offstage in bedroom. Remembering her affinity*). Well, he comes from one of the best families in Cincinnati. And they have a great big house. And they have a maid, too. And he's got a wonderful personality. He makes $300 a month.

LOLA. That so?

MARIE. And he stays at the best hotels. His company insists on it. (*Enters*)

LOLA. Do you like him as well as Turk? (*Buttoning up back of Marie's blouse*)

MARIE (*evasive*). Bruce is so dependable, and . . . he's a gentleman, too.

LOLA. Are you goin' to marry him, honey?

MARIE. Maybe, after I graduate from college and he feels he can support a wife and children. I'm going to have lots and lots of children.

LOLA. I wanted children, too. When I

lost my baby and found out I couldn't have any more, I didn't know what to do with myself. I wanted to get a job, but Doc wouldn't hear of it.

MARIE. Bruce is going to come into a lot of money some day. His uncle made a fortune in men's garters. (*Exits into her room*)

LOLA (*leaning on door frame*). Doc was a rich boy when I married him. His mother left him $25,000 when she died. (*Disillusioned*) It took him a lot to get his office started and everything . . . then, he got sick. (*She makes a futile gesture; then on the bright side*) But Doc's always good to me . . . now.

MARIE (*re-enters*). Oh, Doc's a peach.

LOLA. I used to be pretty, something like you. (*She gets her picture from table*) I was Beauty Queen of the senior class in high school. My dad was awful strict, though. Once he caught me holding hands with that good-looking Dutch McCoy. Dad sent Dutch home, and wouldn't let me go out after supper for a whole month. Daddy would never let me go out with boys much. Just because I was pretty. He was afraid all the boys would get the wrong idea—*you* know. I never had any fun at all until I met Doc.

MARIE. Sometimes I'm glad I didn't know my father. Mom always let me do pretty much as I please.

LOLA. Doc was the first boy Dad ever let me go out with. We got married that spring. (*Replaces picture. Marie sits on couch, puts on shoes and socks*)

MARIE. What did your father think of that?

LOLA. We came right to the city then. And, well, Doc gave up his pre-med course and went to Chiropractor School instead.

MARIE. You must have been married awful young.

LOLA. Oh, yes. Eighteen.

MARIE. That must have made your father really mad.

LOLA. Yes, it did. I never went home after that, but my mother comes down here from Green Valley to visit me sometimes.

TURK (*bursts into the front room from outside. He is a young, big, husky, good-looking boy, nineteen or twenty. He has the openness, the generosity, vigor and health of youth. He's had a little time in the service, but he is not what one would call disciplined. He wears faded dungarees and a T-shirt. He always enters unannounced. He hollers for Marie*). Hey, Marie! Ready?

MARIE (*calling. Runs and exits into bedroom, closing door*). Just a minute, Turk.

LOLA (*confidentially*). I'll entertain him until you're ready. (*She is by nature coy and kittenish with any attractive man. Picks up papers—stuffs them under table*) The house is such a mess, Turk! I bet you think I'm an awful housekeeper. Some day I'll surprise you. But you're like one of the family now. (*Pause*) My, you're an early caller.

TURK. Gotta get to the library. Haven't cracked a book for a biology exam and Marie's gotta help me.

LOLA (*unconsciously admiring his stature and physique and looking him over*). My, I'd think you'd be chilly running around in just that thin little shirt.

TURK. Me? I go like this in the middle of winter.

LOLA. Well, you're a big husky man.

TURK (*laughs*). Oh, I'm a brute, *I* am.

LOLA. You should be out in Hollywood making those Tarzan movies.

TURK. I had enough of that place when I was in the Navy.

LOLA. That so?

TURK (*calling*). Hey, Marie, hurry up.

MARIE. Oh, be patient, Turk.

TURK (*to Lola*). She doesn't realize how busy I am. I'll only have a half hour to study at most. I gotta report to the coach at 10:30.

LOLA. What are you in training for now?

TURK. Spring track. They got me throwing the javelin.

LOLA. The javelin? What's that?

TURK (*laughs at her ignorance*). It's a big, long lance. (*Assumes the magnificent position*) You hold it like this, erect—then you let go and it goes singing through the air, and lands yards away, if you're any good at it, and sticks in the ground, quivering like an arrow. I won the State championship last year.

LOLA (*she has watched as though fascinated*). My!

TURK (*very generous*). Get Marie to take you to the track field some afternoon, and you can watch me.

LOLA. That would be thrilling.

MARIE (comes dancing in). Hi, Turk.

TURK. Hi, juicy.

LOLA (as the young couple moves to the doorway). Remember, Marie, you and Turk can have the front room tonight. All to yourselves. You can play the radio and dance and make a plate of fudge, or anything you want.

MARIE (to Turk). O.K.?

TURK (with eagerness). Sure.

MARIE. Let's go. (Exits)

LOLA. 'Bye, kids.

TURK. 'Bye, Mrs. Delaney. (Gives hed a chuck under the chin) You're a swell skirt.

(Lola couldn't be more flattered. For a moment she is breathless. They speed out the door and Lola stands, sadly watching them depart. Then a sad, vacant look comes over her face. Her arms drop in a gesture of futility. Slowly she walks out on the front porch and calls.)

LOLA. Little Sheba! Come, Little She-ba. Come back . . . come back, Little Sheba! (She waits for a few moments, then comes wearily back into the house, closing the door behind her. Now the morning has caught up with her. She goes to the kitchen, kicks off her pumps and gets back into comfies. The sight of the dishes on the drainboard depresses her. Clearly she is bored to death. Then the telephone rings with the promise of relieving her. She answers it) Hello—Oh, no, you've got the wrong number—Oh, that's all right. (Again it looks hopeless. She hears the postman. Now her spirits are lifted. She runs to the door, opens it and awaits him. When he's within distance, she lets loose a barrage of welcome) 'Morning, Mr. Postman.

POSTMAN. 'Morning, ma'am.

LOLA. You better have something for me today. Sometimes I think you don't even know I live here. You haven't left me anything for two whole weeks. If you can't do better than that, I'll just have to get a new postman.

POSTMAN (on the porch). You'll have to get someone to write you some letters, lady. Nope, nothing for you.

LOLA. Well, I was only joking. You knew I was joking, didn't you? I bet you're thirsty. You come right in here and I'll bring you a glass of cold water. Come in and sit down for a few minutes and rest your feet awhile.

POSTMAN. I'll take you up on that, lady. I've worked up quite a thirst. (Coming in)

LOLA. You sit down. I'll be back in just a minute. (Goes to kitchen, gets pitcher out of refrigerator and brings it back)

POSTMAN. Spring is turnin' into summer awful soon.

LOLA. You feel free to stop here and ask me for a drink of water any time you want to. (Pouring drink) That's what we're all here for, isn't it? To make each other comfortable?

POSTMAN. Thank you, ma'am.

LOLA (clinging, not wanting to be left alone so soon; she hurries her conversation to hold him). You haven't been our postman very long, have you?

POSTMAN (she pours him a glass of water, stands holding pitcher as he drinks). No.

LOLA. You postmen have things pretty nice, don't you? I hear you get nice pensions after you been working for the government twenty years. I think that's dandy. It's a good job, too. (Pours him a second glass) You may get tired but I think it's good for a man to be outside and get a lot of exercise. Keeps him strong and healthy. My husband, he's a doctor, a chiropractor; he has to stay inside his office all day long. The only exercise he gets is rubbin' peoples' backbones. (They laugh. Lola goes to table, leaves pitcher) It makes his hands strong. He's got the strongest hands you ever did see. But he's got a poor digestion. I keep tellin' him he oughta get some fresh air once in a while and some exercise. (Postman rises as if to go, and this hurries her into a more absorbing monologue) You know what? My husband is an Alcoholics Anonymous. He doesn't care if I tell you that 'cause he's proud of it. He hasn't touched a drop in almost a year. All that time we've had a quart of whiskey in the pantry for company and he hasn't even gone near it. Doesn't even want to. You know, alcoholics can't drink like ordinary people; they're allergic to it. It affects them different. They get started drinking and can't stop. Liquor transforms them. Sometimes they get mean and violent and wanna fight, but if they let liquor alone, they're perfectly all right, just like you and me. (Postman tries to leave) You should have seen Doc before he gave it up. He lost all his patients, wouldn't even go to the office; just wanted to stay drunk all day long and he'd come home at night and . . . You just wouldn't believe it if you saw him now. He's got his patients all back, and he's just doing fine.

POSTMAN. Sure, I know Dr. Delaney. I deliver his office mail. He's a fine man.

LOLA. Oh, thanks. You don't ever drink, do you?

POSTMAN. Oh, a few beers once in a while. *(He is ready to go)*

LOLA. Well, I guess that stuff doesn't do any of us any good.

POSTMAN. No. *(Crosses down for mail on floor center)* Well, good day, ma'am.

LOLA. Say, you got any kids?

POSTMAN. Three grandchildren.

LOLA *(getting it from console table)*. We don't have any kids, and we got this toy in a box of breakfast food. Why don't you take it home to them?

POSTMAN. Why, that's very kind of you, ma'am. *(He takes it, and goes)*

LOLA. Good-bye, Mr. Postman.

POSTMAN *(on porch)*. I'll see that you get a letter, if I have to write it myself.

LOLA. Thanks. Good-bye. *(Left alone, she turns on radio. Then she goes to kitchen to start dishes, showing her boredom in the half-hearted way she washes them. Takes water back to icebox. Then she spies Mrs. Coffman hanging baby clothes on lines just outside kitchen door. Goes to door)* My, you're a busy woman this morning, Mrs. Coffman.

MRS. COFFMAN *(German accent. She is outside, but sticks her head in for some of the following)*. Being busy is being happy.

LOLA. I guess so.

MRS. COFFMAN. I don't have it as easy as you. When you got seven kids to look after, you got no time to sit around the house, Mrs. Delaney.

LOLA. I s'pose not.

MRS. COFFMAN. But you don't hear me complain.

LOLA. Oh, no. You never complain. *(Pause)* I guess my little doggie's gone for good, Mrs. Coffman. I sure miss her.

MRS. COFFMAN. The only way to keep from missing one dog is to get another.

LOLA *(goes to sink, turns off water)*. Oh, I never could find another doggie as cute as Little Sheba.

MRS. COFFMAN. Did you put an ad in the paper?

LOLA. For two whole weeks. No one answered it. It's just like she vanished—into thin air. *(She likes this metaphor)* Every day, though, I go out on the porch and call her. You can't tell; she might be around. Don't you think?

MRS. COFFMAN. You should get busy and forget her. You should get busy, Mrs. Delaney.

LOLA. Yes, I'm going to. I'm going to start my spring house-cleaning one of these days real soon. Why don't you come in and have a cup of coffee with me, Mrs. Coffman, and we can chat awhile?

MRS. COFFMAN. I got work to do, Mrs. Delaney. I got work. *(Exit)* *(Lola turns from the window, annoyed at her rejection. Is about to start in on the dishes when the milkman arrives. She opens the back door and detains him)*

MILKMAN. 'Morning, Mrs. Coffman.

MRS. COFFMAN. 'Morning.

LOLA. Hello there, Mr. Milkman. How are you today?

MILKMAN. 'Morning, Lady.

LOLA. I think I'm going to want a few specials today. Can you come in a minute? *(Goes to icebox)*

MILKMAN *(coming in)*. What'll it be? *(He probably is used to her. He is not a handsome man but is husky and attractive in his uniform)*

LOLA *(at refrigerator)*. Well, now, let's see. You got any cottage cheese?

MILKMAN. We always got cottage cheese, Lady. *(Showing her card)* All you gotta do is check the items on the card and we leave 'em. Now I gotta go back to the truck.

LOLA. Now, don't scold me. I always mean to do that but you're always here before I think of it. Now, I guess I'll need some coffee cream, too—half a pint.

MILKMAN. Coffee cream. OK.

LOLA. Now let me see . . . Oh, yes, I want a quart of buttermilk. My husband has liked buttermilk ever since he stopped drinking. My husband's an alcoholic. Had to give it up. Did I ever tell you? *(Starts out. Stops at sink)*

MILKMAN. Yes, Lady. *(Starts to go. She follows)*

LOLA. Now he can't get enough to eat. Eats six times a day. He comes home in the middle of the morning, and I fix him a snack. In the middle of the afternoon he has a malted milk with an egg in it. And then another snack before he goes to bed.

MILKMAN. What'd ya know?

LOLA. Keeps his energy up.

MILKMAN. I'll bet. Anything else, Lady?

LOLA. No, I guess not.

MILKMAN (*going out*). Be back in a jiffy. (*Gives her slip*)

LOLA. I'm just so sorry I put you to so much extra work. (*He goes. Returns shortly with dairy products*) After this I'm going to do my best to remember to check the card. I don't think it's right to put people to extra work. (*Goes to icebox, puts things away*)

MILKMAN (*smiles, is willing to forget*). That's all right, Lady.

LOLA. Maybe you'd like a piece of cake or a sandwich. Got some awfully good cold cuts in the icebox.

MILKMAN. No, thanks, Lady.

LOLA. Or maybe you'd like a cup of coffee.

MILKMAN. No, thanks. (*He's checking the items, putting them on the bill*)

LOLA. You're just a young man. You oughta be going to college. I think everyone should have an education. Do you like your job?

MILKMAN. It's O.K. (*Looks at Lola*)

LOLA. You're a husky young man. You oughta be out in Hollywood making those Tarzan movies.

MILKMAN (*steps back. Feels a little flattered*). When I first began on this job I didn't get enough exercise, so I started working out on the bar-bell.

LOLA. Bar-bells?

MILKMAN. Keeps you in trim.

LOLA (*fascinated*). Yes, I imagine.

MILKMAN. I sent my picture in to *Strength and Health* last month. (*Proudly*) It's a physique study! If they print it, I'll bring you a copy.

LOLA. Oh, will you? I think we should all take better care of ourselves, don't you?

MILKMAN. If you ask me, Lady, that's what's wrong with the world today. We're not taking care of ourselves.

LOLA. I wouldn't be surprised.

MILKMAN. Every morning, I do forty push-ups before I eat my breakfast.

LOLA. Push-ups?

MILKMAN. Like this. (*He spreads himself on the floor and demonstrates, doing three rapid push-ups. Lola couldn't be more fascinated. Then he springs to his feet*) That's good for shoulder development. Wanta feel my shoulders?

LOLA. Why . . . why, yes. (*He makes one arm tense and puts her hand on his shoulder*) Why, it's just like a rock.

MILKMAN. I can do seventy-nine without stopping.

LOLA. Seventy-nine!

MILKMAN. Now feel my arm.

LOLA (*does so*). Goodness!

MILKMAN. You wouldn't believe what a puny kid I was. Sickly, no appetite.

LOLA. Is that a fact? And, my! Look at you now.

MILKMAN (*very proud*). Shucks, any man could do the same . . . if he just takes care of himself.

LOLA. Oh, sure, sure. (*A horn is heard offstage*)

MILKMAN. There's my buddy. I gotta beat it. (*Picks up his things, shakes hands, leaves hurriedly*) See you tomorrow, Lady.

LOLA. 'Bye.

(*She watches him from kitchen window until he gets out of sight. There is a look of some wonder on her face, an emptiness, as though she were unable to understand anything that ever happened to her. She looks at clock, runs into living room, turns on radio. A pulsating tom-tom is heard as a theme introduction. Then the announcer.*)

ANNOUNCER (*in dramatic voice*). TA-BOOoooo! (*Now in a very soft, highly personalized voice. Lola sits on couch, eats candy*) It's Ta-boo, radio listeners, your fifteen minutes of temptation. (*An alluring voice*) Won't you join me? (*Lola swings feet up*) Won't you leave behind your routine, the dull cares that make up your day-to-day existence, the little worries, the uncertainties, the confusions of the work-a-day world and follow me where pagan spirits hold sway, where lithe natives dance on a moon-enchanted isle, where palm trees sway with the restless ocean tide, restless surging on the white shore? Won't you come along? (*More tom-tom*) (*Now in an oily voice*) But remember, it's TA-BOOOOOooooo-OOO! (*Now the tom-tom again, going into a sensual, primitive rhythm melody. Lola has been transfixed from the beginning of the program. She lies down on the davenport, listening, then slowly, growing more and more comfortable.)*

WESTERN UNION BOY *(at door).* Telegram for Miss Marie Buckholder.

LOLA. She's not here.

WESTERN UNION BOY. Sign here.

(Lola does, then she closes the door and brings the envelope into the house, looking at it wonderingly. This is a major temptation for her. She puts the envelope on the table but can't resist looking at it. Finally she gives in and takes it to the kitchen to steam it open. Then Marie and Turk burst into the room. Lola, confused, wonders what to do with the telegram, then decides, just in the nick of time, to jam it in her apron pocket.)

MARIE. Mrs. Delaney! *(Turns off radio. At the sound of Marie's voice, Lola embarrassedly slips the message into her pocket and runs in to greet them)* Mind if we turn your parlor into an art studio?

LOLA. Sure, go right ahead. Hi, Turk. *(Turk gives a wave of his arm)*

MARIE *(to Turk, indicating her bedroom).* You can change in there, Turk. *(Exit to bedroom)*

LOLA *(puzzled).* Change?

MARIE. He's gotta take off his clothes.

LOLA. Huh? *(Closes door)*

MARIE. These drawings are for my life class.

LOLA *(consoled but still mystified).* Oh.

MARIE *(sits on couch).* Turk's the best male model we've had all year. Lotsa athletes pose for us 'cause they've all got muscles. They're easier to draw.

LOLA. You mean . . . he's gonna pose naked?

MARIE *(laughs).* No. The women do, but the men are always more proper. Turk's going to pose in his track suit.

LOLA. Oh. *(Almost to herself)* The women pose naked but the men don't. *(This strikes her as a startling inconsistency)* If it's all right for a woman, it oughta be for a man.

MARIE *(businesslike).* The man always keeps covered. *(Calling to Turk)* Hurry up, Turk.

TURK *(with all his muscles in place, he comes out. He is not at all self-conscious about his semi-nudity. His body is something he takes very much for granted. Lola is a little dazed by the spectacle of*

flesh). How do you want this lovely body? Same pose I took in Art Class?

MARIE. Yah. Over there where I can get more light on you.

TURK *(opens door. Starts pose).* Anything in the house I can use for a javelin?

MARIE. Is there, Mrs. Delaney?

LOLA. How about the broom?

TURK. O.K. *(Lola runs out to get it. Turk goes to her in kitchen, takes it, returns to living room and resumes pose)*

MARIE *(from her sofa, studying Turk in relation to her sketch-pad, moves his leg).* Your left foot a little more this way. *(Studying it)* O.K., hold it. *(Starts sketching rapidly and industriously. Lola looks on, lingeringly)*

LOLA *(starts unwillingly into kitchen, changes her mind and returns to the scene of action. Marie and Turk are too busy to comment. Lola looks at sketch, inspecting it).* Well . . . that's real pretty, Marie. *(Marie is intent. Lola moves closer to look at the drawing)* It . . . it's real artistic. *(Pause)* I wish *I* was artistic.

TURK. Baby, I can't hold this pose very long at a time.

MARIE. Rest whenever you feel like it.

TURK. O.K.

MARIE *(to Lola).* If I make a good drawing, they'll use it for the posters for the Spring Relays.

LOLA. Ya. You told me.

MARIE *(to Turk).* After I'm finished with these sketches I won't have to bother you any more.

TURK. No bother. *(Rubs his shoulder— he poses)* Hard pose, though. Gets me in the shoulder. *(Marie pays no attention. Lola peers at him so closely he becomes a little self-conscious and breaks pose. This also breaks Lola's concentration)*

LOLA. I'll heat you up some coffee. *(Goes to kitchen)*

TURK *(softly to Marie).* Hey, can't you keep her out of here? She makes me feel naked.

MARIE *(laughs).* I can't keep her out of her own house, can I?

TURK. Didn't she ever see a man before?

MARIE. Not a big, beautiful man like you, Turky. *(Turk smiles, is flattered by any recognition of his physical worth, takes it as an immediate invitation to lovemaking. Pulling her up, he kisses her as Doc comes up on porch. Marie pushes*

Turk away) Turk, get back in your corner. *(Doc comes in from outside)*

DOC *(cheerily)*. Hi, everyone.

MARIE. Hi.

TURK. Hi, Doc. *(Doc then sees Turk, feels immediate resentment. Goes into kitchen to Lola)* What's goin' on here?

LOLA *(getting cups)*. Oh, hello, Daddy. Marie's doin' a drawin'.

DOC *(trying to size up the situation. Marie and Turk are too busy to speak)*. Oh.

LOLA. I've just heated up the coffee, want some?

DOC. Yeah. What happened to Turk's clothes?

LOLA. Marie's doing some drawings for her *life* class, Doc.

DOC. Can't she draw him with his clothes on?

LOLA *(with coffee. Very professional now)*. No, Doc, it's not the same. See, it's a *life* class. They draw bodies. They all do it, right in the classroom.

DOC. Why, Marie's just a young girl; she shouldn't be drawing things like that. I don't care if they do teach it at college. It's not right.

LOLA *(disclaiming responsibility)*. I don't know, Doc.

TURK *(turns)*. I'm tired.

MARIE *(squats at his feet)*. Just let me finish the foot.

DOC. Why doesn't she draw something else, a bowl of flowers or a cathedral . . . or a sunset?

LOLA. All she told me, Doc, was if she made a good drawing of Turk, they'd use it for the posters for the Spring Relay. *(Pause)* So I guess they don't want sunsets.

DOC. What if someone walked into the house now? What would they think?

LOLA. Daddy, Marie just asked me if it was all right if Turk came in and posed for her. Now that's all she said, and I said O.K. But if you think it's wrong I won't let them do it again.

DOC. I just don't like it.

MARIE. Hold it a minute more.

TURK. O.K.

LOLA. Well, then you speak to Marie about it if . . .

DOC *(he'd never mention anything disapprovingly to Marie)*. No, Baby. I couldn't do that.

LOLA. Well, then . . .

DOC. Besides, it's not her fault. If those college people make her do drawings like that, I suppose she has to do them. I just don't think it's right she should have to, that's all.

LOLA. Well, if you think it's wrong . . .

DOC *(ready to dismiss it)*. Never mind.

LOLA. I don't see any harm in it, Daddy.

DOC. Forget it.

LOLA *(goes to icebox)*. Would you like some buttermilk?

DOC. Thanks. *(Marie finishes sketch)*

MARIE. O.K. That's all I can do for today.

TURK. Is there anything I can do for *you?*

MARIE. Yes—get your clothes on.

TURK. O.K., coach. *(Turk exits)*

LOLA. You know what Marie said, Doc? She said that the women pose naked, but the men don't.

DOC. Why, of course, honey.

LOLA. Why is that?

DOC *(stumped)*. Well . . .

LOLA. If it's all right for a woman it oughta be for a man. But the man always keeps covered. That's what she said.

DOC. Well, that's the way it should be, honey. A man, after all, is a man, and he . . . well, he has to protect himself.

LOLA. And a woman doesn't?

DOC. It's different, honey.

LOLA. Is it? I've got a secret, Doc. Bruce is comin'.

DOC. Is that so?

LOLA *(after a glum silence)*. You know Marie's boy friend from Cincinnati. I promised Marie a long time ago, when her fiancé came to town, dinner was on me. So I'm getting out the best china and cooking the best meal you ever sat down to.

DOC. When did she get the news?

LOLA. The telegram came this morning.

DOC. That's fine. That Bruce sounds to me like just the fellow for her. I think I'll go in and congratulate her.

LOLA *(nervous)*. Not now, Doc.

DOC. Why not?

LOLA. Well, Turk's there. It might make him feel embarrassed.

DOC. Well, why doesn't Turk clear out now that Bruce is coming? What's he hanging around for? She's engaged to marry Bruce, isn't she? *(Turk enters from bedroom and goes to Marie, starting to make advances)*

LOLA. Marie's just doing a picture of him, Doc.

DOC. You always stick up for him. You encourage him.

LOLA. Shhh, Daddy. Don't get upset.

DOC (*very angrily*). All right, but if anything happens to the girl I'll never forgive you. (*Doc goes upstairs. Turk then grabs Marie, kisses her passionately*)

CURTAIN

SCENE TWO

The same evening, after supper. Outside it is dark. There has been an almost miraculous transformation of the entire house. Lola, apparently, has been working hard and fast all day. The rooms are spotlessly clean and there are such additions as new lampshades, fresh curtains, etc. In the kitchen all the enamel surfaces glisten, and piles of junk that have lain around for months have been disposed of. Lola and Doc are in the kitchen, he washing up the dishes and she puttering around putting the finishing touches on her housecleaning.

LOLA (*at stove*). There's still some beans left. Do you want them, Doc?

DOC. I had enough.

LOLA. I hope you got enough to eat tonight, Daddy. I been so busy cleaning I didn't have time to fix you much.

DOC. I wasn't very hungry.

LOLA (*at table, cleaning up*). You know what? Mrs. Coffman said I could come over and pick all the lilacs I wanted for my centerpiece tomorrow. Isn't that nice? I don't think she poisoned Little Sheba, do you?

DOC. I never did think so, Baby. Where'd you get the new curtains?

LOLA. I went out and bought them this afternoon. Aren't they pretty? Be careful of the woodwork, it's been varnished.

DOC. How come, honey?

LOLA (*gets broom and dustpan from closet*). Bruce is comin'. I figured I had to do my spring housecleaning some time.

DOC. You got all this done in one day? The house hasn't looked like this in years.

LOLA. I can be a good housekeeper when I want to be, can't I, Doc?

DOC (*holding dustpan for Lola*). I never

had any complaints. Where's Marie now?

LOLA. I don't know, Doc. I haven't seen her since she left here this morning with Turk.

DOC (*with a look of disapproval*). Marie's too nice to be wasting her time with him.

LOLA. Daddy, Marie can take care of herself. Don't worry. (*Returns broom to closet*)

DOC (*goes into living room*). 'Bout time for Fibber McGee and Molly.

LOLA (*untying apron. Goes to closet and then back door*). Daddy, I'm gonna run over to Mrs. Coffman's and see if she's got any silver polish. I'll be right back. (*Doc goes to radio. Lola exits*) (*At the radio Doc starts twisting the dial. He rejects one noisy program after another, then very unexpectedly he comes across a rendition of Shubert's famous "Ave Maria," sung in a high soprano voice. Probably he has encountered the piece before somewhere, but it is now making its first impression on him. Gradually he is transported into a world of ethereal beauty which he never knew existed. He listens intently. The music has expressed some ideal of beauty he never fully realized and he is even a little mystified. Then Lola comes in the back door, letting it slam, breaking the spell, and announcing in a loud, energetic voice:*) Isn't it funny? I'm not a bit tired tonight. You'd think after working so hard all day I'd be pooped.

DOC (*in the living room; he cringes*). Baby, don't use that word.

LOLA (*to Doc on couch. Sets silver polish down and joins Doc*). I'm sorry, Doc. I hear Marie and Turk say it all the time, and I thought it was kinda cute.

DOC. It . . . it sounds vulgar.

LOLA (*kisses Doc*). I won't say it again, Daddy. Where's Fibber McGee?

DOC. Not quite time yet.

LOLA. Let's get some peppy music.

DOC (*tuning in a sentimental dance band*). That what you want?

LOLA. That's O.K. (*Doc takes a pack of cards off radio and starts shuffling them, very deftly*) I love to watch you shuffle cards, Daddy. You use your hands so gracefully. (*She watches closely*) Do me one of your card tricks.

DOC. Baby, you've seen them all.

LOLA. But I never get tired of them.

DOC. O.K. Take a card. *(Lola does)* Keep it now. Don't tell me what it is.

LOLA. I won't.

DOC *(shuffling cards again)*. Now put it back in the deck. I won't look. *(He closes his eyes)*

LOLA *(with childish delight)*. All right.

DOC. Put it back.

LOLA. Uh-huh.

DOC. O.K. *(Shuffles cards again, cutting them, taking top half off, exposing Lola's card, to her astonishment)* That your card?

LOLA *(unbelievingly)*. Daddy, how did you do it?

DOC. Baby, I've pulled that trick on you dozens of times.

LOLA. But I never understand how you do it.

DOC. Very simple.

LOLA. Docky, show me how you do that.

DOC *(you can forgive him a harmless feeling of superiority)*. Try it for yourself.

LOLA. Doc, you're clever. I never could do it.

DOC. Nothing to it.

LOLA. There is *too*. Show me how you do it, Doc.

DOC. And give away all my secrets? It's a gift, honey. A magic gift.

LOLA. Can't you give it to me?

DOC *(picks up newspaper)*. A man has to keep some things to himself.

LOLA. It's not a gift at all, it's just some trick you *learned*.

DOC. O.K., Baby, any way you want to look at it.

LOLA. Let's have some music. How soon do you have to meet Ed Anderson? *(Doc turns on radio)*

DOC. I still got a little time. *(Pleased)*

LOLA. Marie's going to be awfully happy when she sees the house all fixed up. She can entertain Bruce here when he comes, and maybe we could have a little party here and you can do your card tricks.

DOC. O.K.

LOLA. I think a young girl should be able to bring her friends home.

DOC. Sure.

LOLA. We never liked to sit around the house 'cause the folks always stayed there with us. *(Rises—starts dancing alone)* Remember the dances we used to go to, Daddy?

DOC. Sure.

LOLA. We had awful good times—for a while, didn't we?

DOC. Yes, Baby.

LOLA. Remember the homecoming dance, when Charlie Kettlekamp and I won the Charleston contest?

DOC. Please, honey, I'm trying to read.

LOLA. And you got mad at him 'cause he thought he should take me home afterwards.

DOC. I did not.

LOLA. Yes, you did—Charlie was all right, Doc, really he was. You were just jealous.

DOC. I *wasn't* jealous.

LOLA *(she has become very coy and flirtatious now, an old dog playing old tricks)*. You got jealous every time we went out any place and I even looked at another boy. There was never anything between Charlie and me; there never was.

DOC. That was a long time ago . . .

LOLA. Lots of other boys called me up for dates . . . Sammy Knight . . . Hand Biderman . . . Dutch McCoy.

DOC. Sure, Baby. You were the "it" girl.

LOLA *(pleading for his attention now)*. But I saved all my dates for *you*, didn't I, Doc?

DOC *(trying to joke)*. As far as *I* know, Baby.

LOLA *(hurt)*. Daddy, I did. You *got* to believe that. I never took a date with any other boy but you.

DOC *(a little weary and impatient)*. That's all forgotten now. *(Turns off radio)*

LOLA. How can you talk that way, Doc? That was the happiest time of our lives. I'll never forget it.

DOC *(disapprovingly)*. Honey!

LOLA *(at the window)*. That was a nice spring. The trees were so heavy and green and the air smelled so sweet. Remember the walks we used to take, down to the old chapel, where it was so quiet and still? *(Sits on couch)*

DOC. In the spring a young man's fancy turns . . . pretty fancy.

LOLA *(in the same tone of reverie)*. I was pretty then, wasn't I, Doc? Remember the first time you kissed me? You were scared as a young girl, I believe, Doc; you trembled so. *(She is being very soft and delicate. Caught in the reverie, he chokes a little and cannot answer)* We'd been going together all year and you were always so shy. Then for the first time you grabbed me and kissed me. Tears came to your eyes, Doc, and you said you'd love me forever and ever, Remember? You said . . . if I didn't marry you, you wanted to die . . . I remember 'cause it scared me for anyone to say a thing like that.

DOC *(in a repressed tone)*. Yes, Baby.

LOLA. And when the evening came on, we stretched out on the cool grass and you kissed me all night long.

DOC *(opens doors)*. Baby, you've got to forget those things. That was twenty years ago.

LOLA. I'll soon be forty. Those years have just vanished—vanished into thin air.

DOC. Yes.

LOLA. Just disappeared—like Little Sheba. *(Pause)* Maybe you're sorry you married me now. You didn't know I was going to get old and fat and sloppy . . .

DOC. Oh, Baby!

LOLA. It's the truth. That's what I am. But I didn't know it, either. Are you sorry you married me, Doc?

DOC. Of course not.

LOLA. I mean, are you sorry you *had* to marry me?

DOC *(goes to porch)*. We were never going to talk about that, Baby.

LOLA *(following Doc out)*. You *were* the first one, Daddy, the *only* one. I'd just die if you didn't believe that.

DOC *(tenderly)*. I know, Baby.

LOLA. You were so nice and so proper, Doc; I thought nothing we could do together could ever be wrong—or make us unhappy. Do you think we did wrong, Doc?

DOC *(consoling)*. No, Baby, of course I don't.

LOLA. I don't think anyone knows about it except my folks, do you?

DOC. Of course not, Baby.

LOLA *(follows him in)*. I wish the baby had lived, Doc. I don't think that woman knew her business, do you, Doc?

DOC. I guess not.

LOLA. If we'd gone to a doctor, she would have lived, don't you think?

DOC. Perhaps.

LOLA. A doctor wouldn't have known we'd just got married, would he? Why were we so afraid?

DOC *(sits on couch)*. We were just kids.

Kids don't know how to look after things.

LOLA *(sits on couch)*. If we'd had the baby she'd be a young girl now; then maybe you'd have *saved* your money, Doc, and she could be going to college—like Marie.

DOC. Baby, what's done is done.

LOLA. It must make you feel bad at times to think you had to give up being a doctor and to think you don't have any money like you used to.

DOC. No . . . no, Baby. We should never feel bad about what's past. What's in the past can't be helped. You . . . you've got to forget it and live for the present. If you can't forget the past, you stay in it and never get out. I might be a big M.D. today, instead of a chiropractor; we might have had a family to raise and be with us now; I might still have a lot of money if I'd used my head and invested it carefully, instead of gettin' drunk every night. We might have a nice house, and comforts, and friends. But we don't have any of those things. So what! We gotta keep on living, don't we? I can't stop just 'cause I made a few mistakes. I gotta keep goin' . . . somehow.

LOLA. Sure, Daddy.

DOC *(sighs and wipes brow)*. I . . . I wish you wouldn't ask me questions like that, Baby. Let's not talk about it any more. I gotta keep goin', and not let things upset me, or . . . or . . . *I* saw enough at the City Hospital to keep me sober for a long time.

LOLA. I'm sorry, Doc. I didn't mean to upset you.

DOC. I'm not upset.

LOLA. What time'll you be home tonight?

DOC. 'Bout eleven o'clock.

LOLA. I wish you didn't have to go tonight. I feel kinda lonesome.

DOC. Yah, so am I, Baby, but some time soon, we'll go *out* together. I kinda hate to go to those night clubs and places since I stopped drinking, but some night I'll take you out to dinner.

LOLA. Oh, will you, Daddy?

DOC. We'll get dressed up and go to the Windermere and have a fine dinner and dance between courses.

LOLA *(eagerly)*. Let's do it, Daddy. I got a little money saved up. I got about forty dollars out in the kitchen. We can take that if you need it.

DOC. I'll have plenty of money the first of the month.

LOLA (*she has made a quick response to the change of mood, seeing a future evening of carefree fun*). What are we sitting around here so serious for? (*Turns to radio*) Let's have some music. (*Lola gets a lively foxtrot on the radio, dances with Doc. They begin dancing vigorously as though to dispense with the sadness of the preceding dialogue, but slowly it winds them and leaves Lola panting*) We oughta go dancing . . . all the time, Docky . . . It'd be good for us. Maybe if I danced more often, I'd lose . . . some of . . . this fat. I remember . . . I used to be able to dance like this . . . all night . . . and not even notice . . . it. (*Lola breaks into a Charleston routine as of yore*) Remember the Charleston, Daddy? (*Doc is clapping his hands in rhythm. Then Marie bursts in through the front door, the personification of the youth that Lola is trying to recapture*)

DOC. Hi, Marie.

MARIE. What are you trying to do, a jig, Mrs. Delaney? (*Marie doesn't intend her remark to be cruel, but it wounds Lola. Lola stops abruptly in her dancing, losing all the fun she has been able to create for herself. She feels she might cry; so to hide her feelings she hurries quietly out to kitchen, but Doc and Marie do not notice. Marie notices the change in atmosphere*) Hey, what's been happening around here?

DOC. Lola got to feeling industrious. You oughta see the kitchen.

MARIE (*running to kitchen, where she is too observant of the changes to notice Lola weeping in corner. Lola, of course, straightens up as soon as Marie enters*). What got into you, Mrs. Delaney? You've done wonders with the house. It looks marvelous.

LOLA (*quietly*). Thanks, Marie.

MARIE (*darting back into living room*). I can hardly believe I'm in the same place.

DOC. Think your boy friend'll like it? (*Meaning Bruce*)

MARIE (*thinking of Turk*). You know how men are. Turk never notices things like that. (*Starts into her room blowing*) a kiss to Doc on her way. Lola comes back in, dabbing at her eyes)

DOC. Turk? (*Marie is gone; he turns to Lola*) What's the matter, honey?

LOLA. I don't know.

DOC. Feel bad about something.

LOLA. I didn't want her to see me dancing that way. Makes me feel sorta silly.

DOC. Why, you're a fine dancer.

LOLA. I feel kinda silly.

MARIE (*jumps back into the room with her telegram*). My telegram's here. When did it come?

LOLA. It came about an hour ago, honey. (*Lola looks nervously at Doc. Doc looks puzzled and a little sore*)

MARIE. Bruce is coming! "Arriving tomorrow 5:00 P.M. CST, Flight 22, Love, Bruce." When did the telegram come?

DOC (*looking hopelessly at Lola*). So it came an hour ago.

LOLA (*nervously*). Isn't it nice I got the house all cleaned? Marie, you bring Bruce to dinner with us tomorrow night. It'll be a sort of wedding present.

MARIE. That would be wonderful, Mrs. Delaney, but I don't want you to go to any trouble.

LOLA. No trouble at all. Now I insist. (*Front doorbell rings*) That must be Turk.

MARIE (*whisper*). Don't tell *him*. (*Goes to door. Lola scampers to kitchen*) Hi, Turk. Come on in.

TURK (*entering. Stalks her*). Hi. (*Looks around to see if anyone is present, then takes her in his arms and starts to kiss her*)

LOLA. I'm sorry, Doc. I'm sorry about the telegram.

DOC. Baby, people don't do things like that. Don't you understand? *Nice* people don't.

MARIE. Stop it!

TURK. What's the matter?

MARIE. They're in the kitchen. (*Turk sits with book*)

DOC. Why didn't you give it to her when it came?

LOLA. Turk was posing for Marie this morning and I couldn't give it to her while he was here. (*Turk listens at door*)

DOC. Well, it just isn't nice to open other people's mail. (*Turk goes to Marie's door*)

LOLA. I guess I'm not nice then. That what you mean?

MARIE. Turk, will you get away from that door?

DOC. No, Baby, but . . .

LOLA. I don't see any harm in it, Doc. I steamed it open and sealed it back. *(Turk at switch in living room)* She'll never know the difference. I don't see any harm in that, Doc.

DOC *(gives up)*. O.K., Baby, if you don't see any harm in it, I guess I can't explain. *(Starts getting ready to go)*

LOLA. I'm sorry, Doc. Honest, I'll never do it again. Will you forgive me?

DOC *(giving her a peck of a kiss)*. I forgive you.

MARIE *(comes back with book)*. Let's look like we're studying.

LOLA. What time'll you be home tonight?

TURK. Biology? Hot dog!

LOLA *(after Marie leaves her room)*. Now I feel better. Do you have to go now? *(Turk sits by Marie on the couch)*

DOC. Yah.

LOLA. Before you go, why don't you show your tricks to Marie?

DOC *(reluctantly)*. Not now.

LOLA. Oh, please do. They'd be crazy about them.

DOC *(with pride)*. O.K. *(Preens himself a little)* If you think they'd enjoy them . . . *(Lola, starting to living room, stops suddenly upon seeing Marie and Turk spooning behind a book. A broad, pleased smile breaks on her face and she stands silently watching. Doc is at sink)* Well . . . what's the matter, Baby?

LOLA *(in a soft voice)*. Oh . . . nothing . . . nothing . . . Doc.

DOC. Well, do you want me to show 'em my tricks or don't you?

LOLA *(coming back to center kitchen; in a secretive voice with a little giggle)*. I guess they wouldn't be interested now.

DOC *(with injured pride. A little sore)*. Oh, very well.

LOLA. Come and look, Daddy.

DOC *(shocked and angry)*. No!

LOLA. Just one little look. They're just kids, Daddy. It's sweet. *(Drags him by arm)*

DOC *(jerking loose)*. Stop it, Baby. I won't do it. It's not decent to snoop around spying on people like that. It's cheap and mischievous and mean.

LOLA *(this had never occurred to her)*. Is it?

DOC. Of course it is.

LOLA. I don't spy on Marie and Turk to be mischievous and mean.

DOC. Then why *do* you do it?

LOLA. You watch young people make love in the movies, don't you, Doc? There's nothing wrong with that. And I *know* Marie and I like her, and Turk's nice, too. They're both so young and pretty. Why shouldn't I watch them?

DOC. I give up.

LOLA. Well, why shouldn't I?

DOC. I don't know, Baby, but it's not nice. *(Turk kisses Marie's ear)*

LOLA *(plaintive)*. I think it's one of the nicest things I know.

MARIE. Let's go out on the porch. *(They steal out)*

DOC. It's not right for Marie to do that, particularly since Bruce is coming. We shouldn't allow it.

LOLA. Oh, they don't do any harm, Doc. I think it's all right. *(Turk and Marie go to porch)*

DOC. It's not all right. I don't know why you encourage that sort of thing.

LOLA. I don't encourage it.

DOC. You do, too. You like that fellow Turk. You said so. And I say he's no good. Marie's sweet and innocent; she doesn't understand guys like him. I think I oughta run him outa the house.

LOLA. Daddy, you wouldn't do that.

DOC *(very heated)*. Then you talk to her and tell her how we feel.

LOLA. Hush, Daddy. They'll hear you.

DOC. I don't care if they do hear me.

LOLA *(to Doc at stove)*. Don't get upset, Daddy. Bruce is coming and Turk won't be around any longer. I promise you.

DOC. All right. I better go.

LOLA. I'll go with you, Doc. Just let me run up and get a sweater. Now wait for me.

DOC. Hurry, Baby.

(Lola goes upstairs. Doc is at platform when he hears Turk laugh on the porch. Doc sees whiskey bottle. Reaches for it and hears Marie giggle. Turns away as Turk laughs again. Turns back to the bottle and hears Lola's voice from upstairs.)

LOLA. I'll be there in a minute, Doc. *(Enters downstairs)* I'm all ready. *(Doc turns out kitchen lights and they go into living room)* I'm walking Doc down to the bus. *(Doc sees Turk with Lola's picture. Takes it out of his hand, puts it on shelf as Lola leads him out. Doc is off-stage)* Then I'll go for a long walk in the moonlight. Have a good time. *(She exits)*

MARIE. 'Bye, Mrs. Delaney. *(Exits)*

TURK. He hates my guts. *(Goes to front door)*

MARIE. Oh, he does not. *(Follows Turk, blocks his exit in door)*

TURK. Yes, he does. If you ask me, he's jealous.

MARIE. Jealous?

TURK. I've always thought he had a crush on you.

MARIE. Now, Turk, don't be silly. Doc is nice to me. It's just in a few little things he does, like fixing my breakfast, but he's nice to everyone.

TURK. He ever make a pass?

MARIE. No. He'd never get fresh.

TURK. He'd better not.

MARIE. Turk, don't be ridiculous. Doc's such a nice, quiet man; if he gets any fun out of being nice to me, why not?

TURK. He's got a wife of his own, hasn't he? Why doesn't he make a few passes at her?

MARIE. Things like that are none of our business.

TURK. O.K. How about a snuggle, lovely?

MARIE *(a little prim and businesslike)*. No more for tonight, Turk.

TURK. Why's tonight different from any other night?

MARIE. I think we should make it a rule, every once in a while, just to sit and talk. *(Starts to sit on couch, but goes to chair)*

TURK *(restless, sits on couch)*. O.K. What'll we talk about?

MARIE. Well . . . there's lotsa things.

TURK. O.K. Start in.

MARIE. A person doesn't start a conversation that way.

TURK. Start it any way you want to.

MARIE. Two people should have something to talk about, like politics or psychology or religion.

TURK. How 'bout sex?

MARIE. Turk!

TURK *(chases her around couch)*. Have you read the Kinsey Report, Miss Buckholder?

MARIE. I should say not.

TURK. How old were you when you had your first affair, Miss Buckholder? And did you ever have relations with your grandfathei?

MARIE. Turk, stop it.

TURK. You wanted to talk about something; I was only trying to please. Let's have a kiss.

MARIE. Not tonight.

TURK. Who you savin' it up for?

MARIE. Don't talk that way.

TURK *(gets up, yawns)*. Well, thanks, Miss Buckholder, for a nice evening. It's been a most enjoyable talk.

MARIE *(anxious)*. Turk, where are you going?

TURK. I guess I'm a man of action, Baby.

MARIE. Turk, don't go.

TURK. Why not? I'm not doing any good here.

MARIE. Don't go.

TURK *(returns and she touches him. They sit on couch)*. Now why didn't you think of this before? C'mon, let's get to work.

MARIE. Oh, Turk, this is all we ever do.

TURK. Are you complaining?

MARIE *(weakly)*. No.

TURK. Then what do you want to put on such a front for?

MARIE. It's not a front.

TURK. What else is it? *(Mimicking)* Oh, no, Turk. Not tonight, Turk. I want to talk about philosophy, Turk. *(Himself again)* When all the time you know that if I went outa here without givin' you a good lovin' up you'd be sore as hell . . . Wouldn't you?

MARIE *(she has to admit to herself it's true; she chuckles)*. Oh . . . Turk . . .

TURK. It's true, isn't it?

MARIE. Maybe.

TURK. How about tonight, lovely; going to be lonesome?

MARIE. Turk, you're in training.

TURK. What of it? I can throw the old javelin any old time, *any* old time. C'mon, Baby, we've got by with it before, haven't we?

MARIE. I'm not so sure.

TURK. What do you mean?

MARIE. Sometimes I think Mrs. Delaney knows.

TURK. Well, bring her along. I'll take care of her, too, if it'll keep her quiet.

MARIE *(a pretense of being shocked)*. Turk!

TURK. What makes you think so?

MARIE. Women just sense those things. She asks so many questions.

TURK. She ever *say* anything?

MARIE. No.

TURK. Now *you're* imagining things.

MARIE. Maybe.

TURK. Well, stop it.

MARIE. O.K.

TURK (*follows Marie*). Honey, I know I talk awful rough around you at times; I never was a very gentlemanly bastard, but you really don't mind it . . . do you? (*She only smiles mischievously*) Anyway, you know I'm nuts about you.

MARIE (*smug*). Are you?

(*Now they engage in a little rough-house, he cuffing her like an affectionate bear, she responding with "Stop it," "Turk, that hurt," etc. And she slaps him playfully. Then they laugh together at their own pretense. Now Lola enters the back way very quietly, tiptoeing through the dark kitchen, standing by the doorway where she can peek at them. There is a quiet, satisfied smile on her face. She watches every move they make, alertly.*)

TURK. Now, Miss Buckholder, what is your opinion of the psychodynamic pressure of living in the atomic age?

MARIE (*playfully*). Turk, don't make fun of me.

TURK. Tonight?

MARIE (*her eyes dance as she puts him off just a little longer*). Well.

TURK. Tonight will never come again. (*This is true. She smiles*) O.K.?

MARIE. Tonight will never come again. . . . (*They embrace and start to dance*) Let's go out somewhere first and have a few beers. We can't come back till they're asleep.

TURK. O.K.

(*They dance slowly out the door. Then Lola moves quietly into the living room and out onto the porch. There she can be heard calling plaintively in a lost voice.*)

LOLA. Little Sheba . . . Come back . . . Come back, Little Sheba. Come back.

CURTAIN

ACT TWO

SCENE ONE

The next morning. Lola and Doc are at breakfast again. Lola is rambling on while Doc sits meditatively, his head down, his face in his hands.

———

LOLA (*in a light, humorous way, as though the faults of youth were as blameless as the uncontrollable actions of a puppy. Chuckles*). Then they danced for a while and went out together, arm in arm. . . .

DOC (*sitting at table, very nervous and tense*). I don't wanna hear any more about it, Baby.

LOLA. What's the matter, Docky?

DOC. Nothing.

LOLA. You look like you didn't feel very good.

DOC. I didn't sleep well last night.

LOLA. You didn't take any of those sleeping pills, did you?

DOC. No.

LOLA. Well, don't. The doctors say they're terrible for you.

DOC. I'll feel better after a while.

LOLA. Of course you will.

DOC. What time did Marie come in last night?

LOLA. I don't know, Doc. I went to bed early and went right to sleep. Why?

DOC. Oh . . . nothing.

LOLA. You musta slept if you didn't hear her.

DOC. I heard her; it was after midnight.

LOLA. Then what did you ask me for?

DOC. I wasn't sure it was her.

LOLA. What do you mean?

DOC. I thought I heard a man's voice.

LOLA. Turk probably brought her inside the door.

DOC (*troubled*). I thought I heard someone laughing. A man's laugh . . . I guess I was just hearing things.

LOLA. Say your prayer?

DOC (*gets up*). Yes.

LOLA. Kiss me 'bye. (*He leans over and kisses her, then puts on his coat and starts to leave*) Do you think you could get home a little early? I want you to help me entertain Bruce. Marie said he'd be here about 5:30. I'm going to have a lovely dinner: stuffed pork chops, twice-baked potatoes, and asparagus, and for dessert a big chocolate cake and maybe ice cream . . .

DOC. Sounds fine.

LOLA. So you get home and help me.

DOC. O.K.

(*Doc leaves kitchen and goes into living room. Again on the chair is Marie's scarf. He picks it up as before and fondles it. Then there is the sound of Turk's laughter, soft and barely audible. It sounds like the laugh of a sated Bacchus. Doc's body stiffens. It is a sickening fact he must face and it has been revealed to him in its ugliest light. The lyrical grace, the spiritual ideal of Ave Maria is shattered. He has been fighting the truth, maybe suspecting all along that he was deceiving himself. Now he looks as though he might vomit. All his blind confusion is inside him. With an immobile expression of blankness on his face, he stumbles into the table above the sofa.)*

LOLA *(still in kitchen)*. Haven't you gone yet, Docky?

DOC *(dazed)*. No . . . no, Baby.

LOLA *(in doorway)*. Anything the matter?

DOC. No . . . no, I'm all right now. *(Drops scarf, takes hat, exits. He has managed to sound perfectly natural. He braces himself and goes out. Lola stands a moment, looking after him with a little curiosity. Then Mrs. Coffman enters, sticks her head in back door.)*

MRS. COFFMAN. Anybody home?

LOLA *(on platform)*. 'Morning, Mrs. Coffman.

MRS. COFFMAN *(inspecting the kitchen's new look)*. So this is what you've been up to, Mrs. Delaney.

LOLA *(proud)*. Yes, I been busy.

(Marie's door opens and closes. Marie sticks her head out of her bedroom to see if the coast is clear, then sticks her head back in again to whisper to Turk that he can leave without being observed.)

MRS. COFFMAN. Busy? Good Lord, I never seen such activity. What got into you, Lady?

LOLA. Company tonight. I thought I'd fix things up a little.

MRS. COFFMAN. You mean you done all this in one day?

LOLA *(with simple pride)*. I said I been busy.

MRS. COFFMAN. Dear God, you done your spring housecleaning all in one day. *(Turk appears in living room)*

LOLA *(appreciating this)*. I fixed up the living room a little, too.

MRS. COFFMAN. I must see it. *(Goes into living room. Turk overhears her and ducks back into Marie's room, shutting the door behind himself and Marie)* I declare! Overnight you turn the place into something really swanky.

LOLA. Yes, and I bought a few things, too.

MRS. COFFMAN. Neat as a pin, and so warm and cozy. I take my hat off to you, Mrs. Delaney. I didn't know you had it in you. All these years, now, I've been sayin' to myself, "That Mrs. Delaney is a good for nothing, sits around the house all day, and never so much as shakes a dust mop." I guess it just shows, we never really know what people are like.

LOLA. I still got some coffee.

MRS. COFFMAN. Not now, Mrs. Delaney. Seeing your house so clean makes me feel ashamed. I gotta get home and get to work. *(Goes to kitchen)*

LOLA *(follows)*. I hafta get busy, too. I got to get out all the silver and china. I like to set the table early, so I can spend the rest of the day looking at it. *(Both laugh)*

MRS. COFFMAN. Good day, Mrs. Delaney. *(Exits)*

(Hearing the screen door slam, Marie guards the kitchen door and Turk slips out the front. But neither has counted on Doc's reappearance. After seeing that Turk is safe, Marie blows a good-bye kiss to him and joins Lola in the kitchen. But Doc is coming in the front door just as Turk starts to go out. There is a moment of blind embarrassment, during which Doc only looks stupefied and Turk, after mumbling an unintelligible apology, runs out. First Doc is mystified, trying to figure it all out. His face looks more and more troubled. Meanwhile, Marie and Lola are talking in the kitchen.)

MARIE. Boo! *(Sneaking up behind Lola at back porch)*

LOLA *(jumping around)*. Heavens! You scared me, Marie. You up already?

MARIE. Yah.

LOLA. This is Saturday. You could sleep as late as you wanted.

MARIE *(pouring a cup of coffee)*. I thought I'd get up early and help you.

LOLA. Honey, I'd sure appreciate it. You can put up the table in the living room, after you've had your breakfast. That's where we'll eat. Then you can help me set it. *(Doc closes door)*

MARIE. O.K.

LOLA. Want a sweet roll?

MARIE. I don't think so. Turk and I had so much beer last night. He got kinda tight.

LOLA. He shouldn't do that, Marie.

MARIE *(starts for living room)* Just keep the coffee hot for me. I'll want another cup in a minute. *(Stops on seeing Doc)* Why, Dr. Delaney! I thought you'd gone.

DOC *(trying to sustain his usual manner)*. Good morning, Marie. *(But not looking at her)*

MARIE *(she immediately wonders)*. Why . . . why . . . how long have you been here, Doc?

DOC. Just got here, just this minute.

LOLA *(comes in)*. That you, Daddy?

DOC. It's me.

LOLA. What are you doing back?

DOC. I . . . I just thought maybe I'd feel better . . . if I took a glass of soda water . . .

LOLA. I'm afraid you're not well, Daddy.

DOC. I'm all right. *(Starts for kitchen)*

LOLA *(helping Marie with table)*. The soda's on the drainboard. *(Doc goes to kitchen, fixes some soda, and stands a moment, just thinking. Then he sits sipping the soda, as though he were trying to make up his mind about something)* Marie, would you help me move the table? It'd be nice now if we had a dining room, wouldn't it? But if we had a dining room, I guess we wouldn't have you, Marie. It was my idea to turn the dining room into a bedroom and rent it. I thought of lots of things to do for extra money . . . a few years ago . . . when Doc was so . . . so sick. *(They set up table—Lola gets cloth from cabinet)*

MARIE. This is a lovely tablecloth.

LOLA. Irish linen. Doc's mother gave it to us when we got married. She gave us all our silver and china, too. The china's Havelin. I'm so proud of it. It's the most valuable possession we own. I just washed it. . . . Will you help me bring it in? *(Getting china from kitchen)* Doc was sorta Mama's boy. He was an only child and his mother thought the sun rose and set in him. Didn't she, Docky? She brought Doc up like a real gentleman.

MARIE. Where are the napkins?

LOLA. Oh, I forgot them. They're so nice I keep them in my bureau drawer with my handkerchiefs. Come upstairs and we'll get them.

(Lola and Marie go upstairs. Then Doc listens to be sure Lola and Marie are upstairs, looks cautiously at the whiskey bottle on pantry shelf but manages to resist several times. Finally he gives in to temp-tation, grabs bottle off shelf, then starts wondering how to get past Lola with it. Finally, it occurs to him to wrap it inside his trench coat which he gets from pantry and carries over his arm. Lola and Marie are heard upstairs. They return to the living room and continue setting table as Doc enters from kitchen on his way out.)

LOLA *(coming downstairs)*. Did you ever notice how nice he keeps his fingernails? Not many men think of things like that. And he used to take his mother to church every Sunday.

MARIE *(at table)*. Oh, Doc's a real gentleman.

LOLA. Treats women like they were all beautiful angels. We went together a whole year before he even kissed me. *(Doc comes through the living room with coat and bottle, going to front door)* On your way back to the office now, Docky?

DOC *(his back to them)*. Yes.

LOLA. Aren't you going to kiss me good-bye before you go, Daddy? *(She goes to him and kisses him. Marie catches Doc's eye and smiles. Then she exits to her room, leaving door open)* Get home early as you can. I'll need you. We gotta give Bruce a royal welcome.

DOC. Yes, Baby.

LOLA. Feeling all right?

DOC. Yes.

LOLA *(in doorway, Doc is on porch)*. Take care of yourself.

DOC *(in a toneless voice)*. Good-bye. *(He goes)*

LOLA *(coming back to table with pleased expression, which changes to a puzzled look, calls to Marie)*. Now that's funny. Why did Doc take his raincoat? It's a beautiful day. There isn't a cloud in sight.

CURTAIN

SCENE TWO

It is now 5:30. The scene is the same as the preceding except that more finishing touches have been added and the two women, still primping the table, lighting the tapers, are dressed in their best. Lola is arranging the centerpiece.

LOLA *(above table, fixing flowers)*. I just love lilacs, don't you, Marie? *(Takes one and studies it)* Mrs. Coffman was nice;

she let me have all I wanted. *(Looks at it very closely)* Aren't they pretty? And they smell so sweet. I think they're the nicest flower there is.

MARIE. They don't last long.

LOLA *(respectfully)*. No. Just a few days. Mrs. Coffman's started blooming just day before yesterday.

MARIE. By the first of the week they'll all be gone.

LOLA. Vanish . . . they'll vanish into thin air. *(Gayer now)* Here, honey, we have them to spare *now*. Put this in your hair. There. *(Marie does)* Mrs. Coffman's been so nice lately. I didn't use to like her. Now where could Doc be? He promised he'd get here early. He didn't even come home for lunch.

MARIE *(gets two chairs from bedroom)*. Mrs. Delaney, you're a peach to go to all this trouble.

LOLA *(gets salt and pepper)*. Shoot, I'm gettin' more fun out of it than you are. Do you think Bruce is going to like us?

MARIE. If he doesn't, I'll never speak to him again.

LOLA *(eagerly)*. I'm just dying to meet him. But I feel sorta bad I never got to do anything nice for Turk.

MARIE *(carefully prying)*. Did . . . Doc ever say anything to you about Turk . . . and me?

LOLA. About Turk and you? No, honey. Why?

MARIE. I just wondered.

LOLA. What if Bruce finds out that you've been going with someone else?

MARIE. Bruce and I had a very business-like understanding before I left for school that we weren't going to sit around lonely just because we were separated.

LOLA. Aren't you being kind of mean to Turk?

MARIE. I don't think so.

LOLA. How's he going to feel when Bruce comes?

MARIE. He may be sore for a little while, but he'll get over it.

LOLA. Won't he feel bad?

MARIE. He's had his eye on a pretty little Spanish girl in his history class for a long time. I like Turk, but he's not the marrying kind.

LOLA. No! Really? *(Lola, with a look of sad wonder on her face, sits on arm of couch. It's been a serious disillusionment)*

MARIE. What's the matter?

LOLA. I . . . I just felt kinda tired. *(Sharp buzzing of doorbell. Marie runs to answer it)*

MARIE. That must be Bruce. *(She skips to the mirror again, then to door)* Bruce!

BRUCE. How are you, sweetheart?

MARIE. Wonderful.

BRUCE. Did you get my wire?

MARIE. Sure.

BRUCE. You're looking swell.

MARIE. Thanks. What took you so long to get here?

BRUCE. Well, honey, I had to go to my hotel and take a bath.

MARIE. Bruce, this is Mrs. Delaney.

BRUCE *(now he gets the cozy quality out of his voice)*. How do you do, ma'am?

LOLA. How d'ya do?

BRUCE. Marie has said some very nice things about you in her letters.

MARIE. Mrs. Delaney has fixed the grandest dinner for us.

BRUCE. Now that was to be my treat. I have a big expense account now, honey. I thought we could all go down to the hotel and have dinner there, and celebrate first with a few cocktails.

LOLA. Oh, we can have cocktails, too. Excuse me, just a minute. *(She hurries to the kitchen and starts looking for the whiskey. Bruce kisses Marie)*

MARIE *(whispers)*. Now, Bruce, she's been working on this dinner all day. She even cleaned the house for you.

BRUCE *(with a surveying look)*. Did she?

MARIE. And Doc's joining us. You'll like Doc.

BRUCE. Honey, are we going to have to stay here the whole evening?

MARIE. We can't just eat and run. We'll get away as soon as we can.

BRUCE. I hope so. I got the raise, sweetheart. They're giving me new territory. *(Lola is frantic in the kitchen, having found the bottle missing. She hurries back into the living room)*

LOLA. You kids are going to have to entertain yourselves awhile 'cause I'm going to be busy in the kitchen. Why don't you turn on the radio, Marie? Get some dance music. I'll shut the door so . . . so I won't disturb you. *(Lola does so, then goes to the telephone)*

MARIE. Come and see my room, Bruce. I've fixed it up just darling. And I've got your picture in the prettiest frame right on my dresser. *(They exit and their voices are heard from the bedroom while Lola is phoning)*

LOLA *(at the phone)*. This is Mrs. Delaney. Is . . . Doc there? Well, then, is Ed Anderson there? Well, would you give me Ed Anderson's telephone number? You see, he sponsored Doc into the club and helped him . . . you know . . . and . . . and I was a little worried tonight. . . . Oh, thanks. Yes, I've got it. *(She writes down number)* Could you have Ed Anderson call me if he comes in? Thank you. *(She hangs up. On her face is a dismal expression of fear, anxiety and doubt. She searches flour bin, icebox, closet. Then she goes into the living room, calling to Marie and Bruce as she comes)* I . . . I guess we'll go ahead without Doc, Marie.

MARIE *(enters from her room)*. What's the matter with Doc, Mrs. Delaney?

LOLA. Well . . . he got held up at the office . . . just one of those things, you know. It's too bad. It would have to happen when I needed him most.

MARIE. Sure you don't need any help?

LOLA. Huh? Oh, no. I'll make out. Everything's ready. I tell you what I'm going to do. Three's a crowd, so I'm going to be the butler and serve the dinner to you two young lovebirds *(The telephone rings)* Pardon me . . . pardon me for just a minute. *(She rushes to phone, closing the door behind her)* Hello? Ed? Have you seen Doc? He went out this morning and hasn't come back. We're having company for dinner and he was supposed to be home early. . . . That's not all. This time we've had a quart of whiskey in the kitchen and Doc's never gone near it. I went to get it tonight. I was going to serve some cocktails. It was *gone*. Yes, I saw it there yesterday. No, I don't think so. . . . He said this morning he had an upset stomach but . . . Oh, would you? . . . Thank you, Mr. Anderson. Thank you a million times. And you let me know when you find out anything. Yes, I'll be here . . . yes. *(Hangs up and crosses back to living room)* Well, I guess we're all ready.

BRUCE. Aren't you going to look at your present?

MARIE. Oh, sure, let's get some scissors. *(Their voices continue in bedroom)*

MARIE *(enters with Bruce)*. Mrs. Delaney, we think you should eat with us.

LOLA. Oh, no, honey, I'm not very hun-gry. Besides, this is the first time you've been together in months and I think you should be alone. Marie, why don't you light the candles? Then we'll have just the right atmosphere. *(She goes into kitchen, gets tomato-juice glasses from icebox while Bruce lights the candles)*

BRUCE. Do we have to eat by candle-light? I won't be able to see. *(Lola returns)*

LOLA. Now, Bruce, you sit here. *(He and Marie sit)* Isn't that going to be cozy? Dinner for two. Sorry we won't have time for cocktails. Let's have a little music. *(She turns on the radio and a Viennese waltz swells up as the curtain falls with Lola looking at the young people eating.)*

CURTAIN

SCENE THREE

Funereal atmosphere. It is about 5:30 the next morning. The sky is just beginning to get light outside, while inside the room the shadows still cling heavily to the corners. The remains of last night's dinner clutter the table in the living room. The candles have guttered down to stubs amid the dirty dinner plates, and the lilacs in the centerpiece have wilted. Lola is sprawled on the davenport, sleeping. Slowly she awakens and regards the morning light. She gets up and looks about strangely, beginning to show despair for the situation she is in. She wears the same spiffy dress she had on the night before but it is wrinkled now, and her marcelled coiffure is awry. One silk stocking has twisted loose and falls around her ankle. When she is sufficiently awake to realize her situation, she rushes to the telephone and dials a number.

LOLA *(at telephone. She sounds frantic)*. Mr. Anderson? Mr. Anderson, this is Mrs. Delaney again. I'm sorry to call you so early, but I just *had* to. . . . Did you find Doc? . . . No, he's not home yet. I don't suppose he'll come home till he's drunk all he can hold and wants to sleep. . . . I don't know what else to think, Mr. Anderson. I'm scared, Mr. Anderson. I'm awful scared. Will you come right over? . . . Thanks, Mr. Anderson. *(She hangs up and goes to kitchen to make coffee. She finds some left from the night before, so turns on the fire to warm it up. She wanders around vaguely, trying to get her thoughts in order, jumping at every sound. Pours herself a cup of coffee, then takes it to living room, sits and sips it. Very quietly Doc enters through the back way into the kitchen. He carries a big bottle of whiskey which he carefully places back in the pantry, not making a sound, hangs up overcoat, then puts suitcoat on back of chair. Starts to go upstairs. But Lola speaks)* Doc? That you, Doc? *(Then Doc quietly walks in from kitchen. He is staggering drunk, but he is managing for a few minutes to appear as though he were perfectly sober and nothing had happened. His steps, however, are not too sure and his eyes are like blurred ink spots. Lola is too frightened to talk. Her mouth is gaping and she is breathless with fear)*

DOC. Good morning, honey.

LOLA. Doc! You all right?

DOC. The morning paper here? I wanta see the morning paper.

LOLA. Doc, we don't get a morning paper. *You* know that.

DOC. Oh, then I suppose I'm drunk or something. That what you're trying to say?

LOLA. No, Doc . . .

DOC. Then give me the morning paper.

LOLA *(scampering to get last night's paper from console table)*. Sure, Doc. Here it is. Now you just sit there and be quiet.

DOC *(resistance rising)*. Why shouldn't I be quiet?

LOLA. Nothin', Doc . . .

DOC *(has trouble unfolding paper. He places it before his face in order not to be seen. But he is too blind even to see)*. Nothing, Doc. *(Mockingly)*

LOLA *(cautiously, after a few minutes' silence)*. Doc, are you all right?

DOC. Of course, I'm all right. Why shouldn't I be all right?

LOLA. Where you been?

DOC. What's it your business where I been? I been to London to see the Queen. What do you think of that? *(Apparently she doesn't know what to think of it)* Just let me alone. That's all I ask. I'm all right.

LOLA *(whimpering)*. Doc, what made you do it? You said you'd be home last night . . . 'cause we were having company. Bruce was here and I had a big dinner

fixed . . . and you never came. What was the matter, Doc?

DOC *(mockingly)*. We had a big dinner for *Bruce.*

LOLA. Doc, it was for you, too.

DOC. Well . . . I don't want it.

LOLA. Don't get mad, Doc.

DOC *(threateningly)*. Where's Marie?

LOLA. I don't know, Doc. She didn't come in last night. She was out with Bruce.

DOC *(back to audience)*. I suppose you tucked them in bed together and peeked through the keyhole and applauded.

LOLA *(sickened)*. Doc, don't talk that way. Bruce is a nice boy. They're gonna get married.

DOC. He probably *has* to marry her, the poor bastard. Just 'cause she's pretty and he got amorous one day . . . Just like I had to marry *you.*

LOLA. Oh, Doc!

DOC. You and Marie are both a couple of sluts.

LOLA. Doc, please don't talk like that.

DOC. What are you good for? You can't even get up in the morning and cook my breakfast.

LOLA *(mumbling)*. I will, Doc. I will after this.

DOC. You won't even sweep the floors, till some bozo comes along to make love to Marie, and then you fix things up like Buckingham Palace or a Chinese whorehouse with perfume on the lampbulbs, and flowers, and the gold-trimmed china *my mother* gave us. We're not going to use these any more. My mother didn't buy those dishes for whores to eat off of. *(He jerks the cloth off the table, sending the dishes rattling to the floor)*

LOLA. Doc! Look what you done.

DOC. Look what I *did,* not *done.* I'm going to get me a drink. *(Goes to kitchen)*

LOLA *(follows to platform)*. Oh, no, Doc! You know what it does to you!

DOC. You're damn right I know what it does to me. It makes me willing to come home here and look at you, you two-ton old heifer! *(Takes a long swallow)* There! And pretty soon I'm going to have another, then another.

LOLA *(with dread)*. Oh, Doc! *(Lola takes phone. Doc sees this, rushes for the butcher-knife from kitchen-cabinet drawer. Not finding it, he gets a hatchet from the back porch)* Mr. Anderson? Come quick,

Mr. Anderson. He's back. He's *back!* He's got a hatchet!

DOC. God damn you! Get away from that telephone. (*He chases her into living room where she gets the couch between them*) That's right, phone! Tell the world I'm drunk. Tell the whole damn world. Scream your head off, you fat slut. Holler till all the neighbors think I'm beatin' hell outuv you. Where's Bruce now—under Marie's bed? You got all fresh and pretty for him, didn't you? Combed your hair for once—you even washed the back of your neck and put on a girdle. You were willing to harness all that fat into one bundle.

LOLA (*about to faint under the weight of the crushing accusations*). Doc, don't say any more . . . I'd rather you hit me with an axe, Doc. . . Honest I would. But I can't stand to hear you talk like that.

DOC. I oughta hack off all that fat, and then wait for Marie and chop off those pretty ankles she's always dancing around on . . . then start lookin' for Turk and fix him too.

LOLA. Daddy, you're talking crazy!

DOC. I'm making sense for the first time in my life. You didn't know I knew about it, did you? But I saw him coming outa there, I saw him. You knew about it all the time and thought you were hidin' something . . .

LOLA. Daddy, I didn't know anything about it at all. Honest, Daddy.

DOC. Then *you're* the one that's crazy, if you think I didn't know. You were running a regular house, weren't you? It's probably been going on for years, ever since we were married. (*He lunges for her. She breaks for kitchen. They struggle in front of sink*)

LOLA. Doc, it's not so; it's not so. You gotta believe me, Doc.

DOC. You're lyin'. But none a that's gonna happen any more. I'm gonna fix you now, once and for all. . . .

LOLA. Doc . . . don't do that to me. (*Lola, in a frenzy of fear, clutches him around the neck holding arm with axe by his side*) Remember, Doc. It's *me*, Lola! You said I was the prettiest girl you ever saw. Remember, Doc! It's me! Lola!

DOC (*the memory has overpowered him. He collapses, slowly mumbling*). Lola . . . my pretty Lola. (*He passes out on the floor. Lola stands now, as though in a trance. Quietly Mrs. Coffman comes creeping in through the back way*)

MRS. COFFMAN (*calling softly*). Mrs. Delaney! (*Lola doesn't even hear. Mrs. Coffman comes in*) Mrs. Delaney! Here you are, Lady. I heard screaming and I was frightened for you.

LOLA. I . . . I'll be all right . . . some men are comin' pretty soon; everything'll be all right.

MRS. COFFMAN. I'll stay until they get here.

LOLA (*feeling a sudden need*). Would you . . . would you *please*, Mrs. Coffman? (*Breaks into sobs*)

MRS. COFFMAN. Of course, Lady. (*Regarding Doc*) The doctor got "sick" again?

LOLA (*mumbling*). Some men . . . 'll be here pretty soon . . .

MRS. COFFMAN. I'll try to straighten things up before they get here. . . .
(*She rights chair, hangs up telephone and picks up the axe, which she is holding when Ed Anderson and Elmo Huston enter unannounced. They are experienced AA's. Neatly dressed businessmen approaching middle-age.*)

ED. Pardon us for walking right in, Mrs. Delaney, but I didn't want to waste a second. (*Kneels by Doc*)

LOLA (*weakly*). It's all right. . . .
(*Both men observe Doc on the floor, and their expressions hold understanding mixed with a feeling of irony. There is even a slight smile of irony on Ed's face. They have developed the surgeon's objectivity.*)

ED. Where is the hatchet? (*To Elmo as though appraising Doc's condition*) What do you think, Elmo?

ELMO. We can't leave him here if he's gonna play around with hatchets.

ED. Give me a hand, Elmo. We'll get him to sit up and then try to talk some sense into him. (*They struggle with the lumpy body, Doc grunting his resistance*) Come on, Doc, old boy. It's Ed and Elmo. We're going to take care of you. (*They seat him at table*)

DOC (*through a thick fog*). Lemme alone.

ED. Wake up. We're taking you away from here.

DOC. Lemme 'lone, God damn it. (*Falls forward, head on table*)

ELMO (to Mrs. Coffman). Is there any coffee?

MRS. COFFMAN. I think so, I'll see. (Goes to stove with cup from drainboard. Lights fire under coffee and waits for it to get heated)

ED. He's way beyond coffee.

ELMO. It'll help some. Get something hot into his stomach.

ED. If we could get him to eat. How 'bout some hot food, Doc? (Doc gestures and they don't push the matter)

ELMO. City Hospital, Ed?

ED. I guess that's what it will have to be.

LOLA. Where you going to take him? (Elmo goes to phone; speaks quietly to City Hospital)

ED. Don't know; wanta talk to him first.

MRS. COFFMAN (coming in with the coffee). Here's the coffee.

ED (taking cup). Hold him, Elmo, while I make him swallow this.

ELMO. Come on, Doc, drink your coffee. (Doc only blubbers)

DOC (after the coffee is down). Uh . . . what . . . what's goin' on here?

ED. It's me, Doc. Your old friend Ed. I got Elmo with me.

DOC (twisting his face painfully). Get out, both of you. Lemme 'lone.

ED (with certainty). We're takin' you with us, Doc.

DOC. Hell you are. I'm all right. I just had a little slip. We all have slips. . . .

ED. Sometimes, Doc, but we gotta get over 'em.

DOC. I'll be O.K. Just gimme a day to sober up. I'll be as good as new.

ED. Remember the last time, Doc? You said you'd be all right in the morning and we found you with a broken collar bone. Come on.

DOC. Boys, I'll be all right. Now lemme alone.

ED. How much has he had, Mrs. Delaney?

LOLA. I don't know. He had a quart when he left here yesterday and he didn't get home till now.

ED. He's probably been through a couple of quarts. He's been dry for a long time. It's going to hit him pretty hard. Yah, he'll be a pretty sick man for a few days. (Louder to Doc, as though he were talking to a deaf man) Wanta go to the City Hospital, Doc?

DOC (this has a sobering effect on him. He looks about him furtively for possible escape). No . . . no, boys. Don't take me there. That's a torture chamber. No, Ed. You wouldn't do that to me.

ED. They'll sober you up.

DOC. Ed, I been there; I've seen the place. That's where they take the crazy people. You can't do that to me, Ed.

ED. Well, you're crazy, aren't you? Goin' after your wife with a hatchet. (They lift Doc to his feet. Doc looks with dismal pleading in his eyes at Lola, who has her face in her hands.)

DOC (so plaintive, a sob in his voice). Honey! Honey! (Lola can't look at him. Now Doc tries to make a getaway, bolting blindly into the living room before the two men catch him and hold him in front of living room table) Honey, don't let 'em take me there. They'll believe you. Tell 'em you won't let me take a drink.

LOLA. Isn't there any place else you could take him?

ED. Private sanitariums cost a lotta dough.

LOLA. I got forty dollars in the kitchen.

ED. That won't be near enough.

DOC. I'll be at the meeting tomorrow night sober as you are now.

ED (to Lola). All the king's horses couldn't keep him from takin' another drink now, Mrs. Delaney. He got himself into this; he's gotta sweat it out.

DOC. I won't go to the City Hospital. That's where they take the crazy people. (Stumbles into chair)

ED (using all his patience now). Look, Doc. Elmo and I are your friends. You know that. Now if you don't come along peacefully, we're going to call the cops and you'll have to wear off this jag in the cooler. How'd you like that? (Doc is as though stunned) The important thing is for you to get sober.

DOC. I don't wanta go.

ED. The City Hospital or the City Jail. Take your choice. We're not going to leave you here. Come on, Elmo. (They grab hold of him)

DOC (has collected himself and now given in). O.K., boys. Gimme another drink and I'll go.

LOLA. Oh, no, Doc.

ED. Might as well humor him, ma'am. Another few drinks couldn't make much difference now. (Mrs. Coffman runs for bottle and glass in pantry and comes right *back with them. She hands them to Lola)* O.K., Doc, we're goin' to give you a drink. Take a good one; it's gonna be your last for a long, long time to come. *(Ed takes the bottle, removes the cork and gives Doc a glass of whiskey. Doc takes his fill, straight, coming up once or twice for air. Then Ed takes the bottle from him and hands it to Lola. To Lola)* That'll keep him three or four days, Mrs. Delaney; then he'll be home again, good as new. *(Modestly)* I . . . I don't want to pry into personal affairs, ma'am . . . but he'll need you then, pretty bad . . . Come on, Doc. Let's go.

(Ed has a hold of Doc's coat sleeve trying to maneuver him. A faraway look is in Doc's eyes, a dazed look containing panic and fear. He gets to his feet.)

DOC *(struggling to sound reasonable)*. Just a minute, boys . . .

ED. What's the matter?

DOC. I . . . I wanta glass of water.

ED. You'll get a glass of water later. Come on.

DOC *(beginning to twist a little in Ed's grasp)*. . . . a glass of water . . . that's all . . . *(One furious, quick twist of his body and he eludes Ed)*

ED. Quick, Elmo.

(Elmo acts fast and they get Doc before he gets away. Then Doc struggles with all his might, kicking and screaming like a pampered child. Ed and Elmo holding him tightly to usher him out.)

DOC *(as he is led out)*. Don't let 'em take me there. Don't take me there. Stop them, somebody. Stop them. That's where they take the crazy people. Oh, God, stop them, somebody. Stop them.

(Lola looks on blankly while Ed and Elmo depart with Doc. Now there are several moments of deep silence.)

MRS. COFFMAN *(clears up. Very softly)*. Is there anything more I can do for you now, Mrs. Delaney?

LOLA. I guess not.

MRS. COFFMAN *(puts a hand on Lola's shoulder)*. Get busy, Lady. Get busy and forget it.

LOLA. Yes . . . I'll get busy right away. Thanks, Mrs. Coffman.

MRS. COFFMAN. I better go. I've got to make breakfast for the children. If you want me for anything, let me know.

LOLA. Yes . . . yes . . . good-bye, Mrs. Coffman. *(Mrs. Coffman exits. Lola is too exhausted to move from the big chair. At first she can't even cry; then the tears come slowly, softly. In a few moments Bruce and Marie enter, bright and merry. Lola turns her head slightly to regard them as creatures from another planet)*

MARIE *(springing into room. Bruce follows)*. Congratulate me, Mrs. Delaney.

LOLA. Huh?

MARIE. We're going to be married.

LOLA. Married? *(It barely registers)*

MARIE *(showing ring)*. Here it is. My engagement ring. *(Marie and Bruce are too engrossed in their own happiness to notice Lola's stupor)*

LOLA. That's lovely . . . lovely.

MARIE. We've had the most wonderful time. We danced all night and then drove out to the lake and saw the sun rise.

LOLA. That's nice.

MARIE. We've made all our plans. I'm quitting school and flying back to Cincinnati with Bruce this afternoon. His mother has invited me to visit them before I go home. Isn't that wonderful?

LOLA. Yes . . . yes, indeed.

MARIE. Going to miss me?

LOLA. Yes, of course, Marie. We'll miss you very much . . . uh . . . congratulations.

MARIE. Thanks, Mrs. Delaney. *(Goes to bedroom door)* Come on, Bruce, help me get my stuff. *(To Lola)* Mrs. Delaney, would you throw everything into a big box and send it to me at home? We haven't had breakfast yet. We're going down to the hotel and celebrate.

BRUCE. I'm sorry we're in such a hurry, but we've got a taxi waiting. *(They go into room)*

LOLA *(goes to telephone, dials)*. Long-distance? I want to talk to Green Valley 223. Yes. This is Delmar 1887. *(She hangs up. Marie comes from bedroom, followed by Bruce, who carries suitcase)*

MARIE. Mrs. Delaney, I sure hate to say good-bye to you. You've been so wonderful to me. But Bruce says I can come and visit you once in a while, didn't you, Bruce?

BRUCE. Sure thing.

LOLA. You're going?

MARIE. We're going downtown and have our breakfast, then do a little shopping and catch our plane. And thanks for everything, Mrs. Delaney.

BRUCE. It was very nice of you to have us to dinner.

LOLA. Dinner? Oh, don't mention it.

MARIE *(to Lola)*. There isn't much time for good-bye now, but I just want you to know Bruce and I wish you the best of everything. You and Doc both. Tell Doc good-bye for me, will you, and remember I think you're both a coupla peaches.

BRUCE. Hurry, honey.

MARIE. 'Bye, Mrs. Delaney! *(She goes out)*

BRUCE. 'Bye, Mrs. Delaney. Thanks for being nice to my girl. *(He goes out and off porch with Marie)*

LOLA *(waves. The phone rings. She goes to it quickly)*. Hello. Hello, Mom. It's Lola, Mom. How are you? Mom, Doc's sick again. Do you think Dad would let me come home for a while? I'm awfully unhappy, Mom. Do you think . . . just till I made up my mind? . . . All right. No, I guess it wouldn't do any good for you to come here . . . I . . . I'll let you know what I decide to do. That's all, Mom. Thanks. Tell Daddy hello. *(She hangs up)*

CURTAIN

SCENE FOUR

It is morning, a week later. The house is neat again. Lola is dusting in the living room as Mrs. Coffman enters.

———

MRS. COFFMAN. Mrs. Delaney! Good morning, Mrs. Delaney.

LOLA. Come in, Mrs. Coffman.

MRS. COFFMAN *(coming in)*. It's a fine day for the games. I've got a box lunch ready, and I'm taking all the kids to the Stadium. My boy's got a ticket for you, too. You better get dressed and come with us.

LOLA. Thanks, Mrs. Coffman, but I've got work to do.

MRS. COFFMAN. But it's a big day. The Spring Relays . . . All the athletes from the colleges are supposed to be there.

LOLA. Oh, yes. You know that boy, Turk, who used to come here to see Marie —he's one of the big stars.

MRS. COFFMAN. Is that so? Come on . . . do. We've got a ticket for you. . . .

LOLA. Oh, no, I have to stay here and clean up the house. Doc may be coming home today. I talked to him on the phone. He wasn't sure what time they'd let him out, but I wanta have the place all nice for him.

MRS. COFFMAN. Well, I'll tell you all about it when I come home. Everybody and his brother will be there.

LOLA. Have a good time.

MRS. COFFMAN. 'Bye, Mrs. Delaney.

LOLA. 'Bye.

(Mrs. Coffman leaves, and Lola goes into kitchen. The mailman comes onto porch and leaves a letter, but Lola doesn't even know he's there. Then the milkman knocks on the kitchen door.)

LOLA. Come in.

MILKMAN *(entering with armful of bottles, etc.)*. I see you checked the list, lady. You've got a lot of extras.

LOLA. Yah—I think my husband's coming home.

MILKMAN *(he puts the supplies on table, then pulls out magazine)*. Remember, I told you my picture was going to appear in *Strength and Health*. *(Showing her magazine)* Well, see that pile of muscles? That's me.

LOLA. My goodness. You got your picture in a magazine.

MILKMAN. Yes, ma'am. See what it says about my chest development? For the greatest self-improvement in a three months' period.

LOLA. Goodness sakes. You'll be famous, won't you?

MILKMAN. If I keep busy on these barbells. I'm working now for "muscular separation."

LOLA. That's nice.

MILKMAN *(cheerily)*. Well, good day, ma'am.

LOLA. You forgot your magazine.

MILKMAN. That's for you. *(Exits. Lola puts away the supplies in the icebox. Then Doc comes in the front door, carrying the little suitcase she previously packed for him. His quiet manner and his serious demeanor are the same as before. Lola is shocked by his sudden appearance. She jumps and can't help showing her fright)*

LOLA. Docky! *(Without thinking she assumes an attitude of fear. Doc observes this and it obviously pains him)*

DOC. Good morning, honey. *(Pause)*

LOLA *(on platform)*. Are . . . are you all right, Doc?

DOC. Yes, I'm all right. *(An awkward*

pause. Then Doc tries to reassure her) Honest, I'm all right, honey. Please don't stand there like that . . . like I was gonna . . . gonna . . .

LOLA *(tries to relax)*. I'm sorry, Doc.

DOC. How you been?

LOLA. Oh, I been all right, Doc. Fine.

DOC. Any news?

LOLA. I told you about Marie—over the phone.

DOC. Yah.

LOLA. He was a very nice boy, Doc. Very nice.

DOC. That's good. I hope they'll be happy.

LOLA *(trying to sound bright)*. She said . . . maybe she'd come back and visit us some time. That's what she *said*.

DOC *(pause)*. It . . . it's good to be home.

LOLA. Is it, Daddy?

DOC. Yah. *(Beginning to choke up, just a little)*

LOLA. Did everything go all right . . . I mean . . . did they treat you well and . . .

DOC *(now loses control of his feelings. Tears in his eyes, he all but lunges at her, gripping her arms, drilling his head into her bosom)*. Honey, don't ever leave me. *Please* don't ever leave me. If you do, they'd have to keep me down at that place all the time. I don't know what I said to you or what I did, I can't remember hardly anything. But please forgive me . . . please . . . please . . . And I'll try to make everything up.

LOLA *(there is surprise on her face and new contentment. She becomes almost angelic in demeanor. Tenderly she places a soft hand on his head)*. Daddy! Why, of course I'll never leave you. *(A smile of satisfaction)* You're all I've got. You're all I ever had. *(Very tenderly he kisses her)*

DOC *(collecting himself now. Lola sits beside Doc)*. I . . . I feel better . . . already.

LOLA *(almost gay)*. So do I. Have you had your breakfast?

DOC. No. The food there was terrible. When they told me I could go this morning, I decided to wait and fix myself breakfast here.

LOLA *(happily)*. Come on out in the kitchen and I'll get you a nice, big breakfast. I'll scramble some eggs and . . . You see I've got the place all cleaned up just the way you like it. *(Doc goes to kitchen)* Now you sit down here and I'll get your fruit juice. *(He sits and she gets fruit juice from refrigerator)* I've got bacon this morning, too. My, it's expensive now. And I'll light the oven and make you some toast, and here's some orange marmalade, and . . .

DOC *(with a new feeling of control)*. Fruit juice. I'll need lots of fruit juice for a while. The doctor said it would restore the vitamins. You see, that damn whiskey kills all the vitamins in your system, eats up all the sugar in your kidneys. They came around every morning and shot vitamins in my arm. Oh, it didn't hurt. And the doctor told me to drink a quart of fruit juice every day. And you better get some candy bars for me at the grocery this morning. Doctor said to eat lots of candy, try to replace the sugar.

LOLA. I'll do that, Doc. Here's another glass of this pineapple juice now. I'll get some candy bars first thing.

DOC. The doctor said I should have a hobby. Said I should go out more. That's all that's wrong with me. I thought maybe I'd go hunting once in a while.

LOLA. Yes, Doc. And bring home lots of good things to eat.

DOC. I'll get a big bird dog, too. Would you like a sad-looking old bird dog around the house?

LOLA. Of course, I would. *(All her life and energy have been restored)* You know what, Doc? I had another dream last night.

DOC. About Little Sheba?

LOLA. Oh, it was about everyone and everything. *(In a raptured tone. She gets bacon from icebox and starts to cook it)* Marie and I were going to the Olympics back in our old high school stadium. There were thousands of people there. There was Turk out in the center of the field throwing the javelin. Every time he threw it, the crowd would roar . . . and you know who the man in charge was? It was my father. Isn't that funny? . . . But Turk kept changing into someone else all the time. And then my father disqualified him. So he had to sit on the sidelines . . . and guess who took his place, Daddy? You! You came trotting out there on the field just as big as you please . . .

DOC *(smilingly)*. How did I do, Baby?

LOLA. Fine. You picked the javelin up real careful, like it was awful heavy. But you threw it, Daddy, clear, *clear* up into the sky. And it never came down again. *(Doc looks very pleased with himself. Lola goes on)* Then it started to rain. And I couldn't find Little Sheba. I almost went crazy looking for her and there were so many people, I didn't even know where to look. And you were waiting to take me home. And we walked and walked through the slush and mud, and people were hurrying all around us and . . . and . . . *(Leaves stove and sits. Sentimental tears come to her eyes)* But this part is sad, Daddy. All of a sudden I saw Little Sheba . . . she was lying in the middle of the field . . . dead. . . . It made me cry, Doc. No one paid any attention . . . I cried and cried. It made me feel so bad, Daddy. That sweet little puppy . . . her curly white fur was smeared with mud, and no one to stop and take care of her . . .

DOC. Why couldn't *you?*

LOLA. I wanted to, but you wouldn't let me. You kept saying, "We can't stay here, honey; we must go on. We gotta go on." *(Pause)* Now, isn't that strange?

DOC. Dreams are funny.

LOLA. I don't think Little Sheba's ever coming back, Doc. I'm not going to call her any more.

DOC. Not much point in it, Baby. I guess she's gone for good.

LOLA. I'll fix your eggs.

(She gets up, embraces Doc, and goes to stove. Doc remains at table sipping his fruit juice. The curtain comes slowly down.)

THE FOURPOSTER

Jan de Hartog

First presented by The Playwrights' Company at the Ethel
Barrymore Theatre, New York, on October 24,
1951, with the following cast:

AGNES Jessica Tandy   MICHAEL Hume Cronyn

ACT ONE. SCENE I: 1890. SCENE II: A year later.

ACT TWO. SCENE I: 1901. SCENE II: Seven years later.

ACT THREE. SCENE I: 1913. SCENE II: Twelve years later.

Copyright, 1947, as an unpublished dramatic composition by Jan de Hartog.
© Copyright, 1952, by Jan de Hartog.
Reprinted by permission of Random House, Inc. All rights reserved.
CAUTION: Professionals and amateurs are hereby warned that THE FOURPOSTER, being fully
protected by copyright, is subject to royalty. All rights, including professional, amateur,
motion picture, talking motion picture, radio broadcasting, television, recitation, public readings,
and the rights of translation into foreign languages, are strictly reserved. All inquiries
should be addressed to the author's agent, Leah Salisbury, 234 West 44th Street, New
York, N.Y., without whose permission in writing no use of this play may be made.

JAN DE HARTOG, author of *The Fourposter*, a Dutch writer born in Haarlem in 1914, fled to England in 1943 during the German occupation of Holland and was condemned to death by the Nazis. He first attracted attention in the American theatre in 1948 with *Skipper Next to God* (previously produced in London), the drama of a sea captain who transported Jewish refugees to Palestine and refused to allow international politics to rule his conscience. It was not a play contrived for Broadway, but it attracted attention with its strenuous idealism when staged in New York with the late John Garfield in the role of the skipper. *The Fourposter* is, of course, work of a completely different character, and in the fall of 1951 it revealed a facet of the author's dramatic talent hitherto unsuspected on Broadway. Actually, Jan de Hartog who also had a fantastic drama, *This Time Tomorrow,* produced in 1947, has demonstrated considerable versatility. He is also the author of a comprehensive picaresque novel about a physician's struggles in the South Pacific, *The Spiral Road,* published in 1957, and of earlier books, praised as warm and humorous, *The Distant Shore* and *A Sailor's Life.*

Jan de Hartog has many interests. Fortunately humor is one of them, and it was a warm sense of comedy that made *The Fourposter* one of the pleasantest of Broadway plays. And the author also has a disposition to like people and to view human relationships in terms of average humanity. The background of *The Fourposter* is vividly American, but in treating married life, the author dealt with timeless traits and foibles, even while availing himself of elements of period comedy. "In cameo size," according to Brooks Atkinson, *"The Fourposter* is the story of all marriages." When the play was revived at New York's City Center on January 6, 1955, with Jessica Tandy and Hume Cronyn reenacting their original roles, it was appreciated no less than on its first appearance on Broadway proper. Dissent was possible on the grounds that the humor and sentiment were rather standardized. But a critic could be mollified on reflecting that familiarity has been a requirement of domestic comedy ever since the ancients, and the standardization of humor in De Hartog's play was certainly mitigated by the rich acting roles provided by the author.

ACT ONE

SCENE ONE

1890. Night.

Bedroom. Fourposter. Door in back wall, window to the right, washstand and low chair to the left. The room is dark. Low-burning gas lamps shimmer bluishly to the right of arch and at bed, left.

The door is opened clumsily, and HE *enters, carrying* HER *in his arms into the room out of the lighted passage.* HE *wears a top hat on the back of his head;* SHE *is in her bridal gown.* HE *stops in the moonlight, kisses her, whirls and carries her to bed.*

———

SHE. Oh, Micky, whoo! Hold me! Hold me tight! Whoo! Whoo! I'm falling. I can't . . . (HE *throws her onto the bed and tries to kiss her again.*) Michael, the door! The door! (HE *runs to the door and closes it.* SHE *gets off the bed, straightens her hat and dress.*) Oh, goodness, my hair . . . and look at my dress! (SHE *turns on the gas bracket on wall beside the bed.* HE *goes to her, takes off gloves, puts one in each pocket and kneels before her.*) What are you doing?

HE. I'm worshipping you.

SHE. Get up immediately! (*Tries to lift him up.*) Michael, get up, I say!

HE. Can't I worship you?

SHE. Are you out of your senses? If our Lord should see you . . .

HE. He could only rejoice in such happiness.

SHE. Michael, you mustn't blaspheme, you know you mustn't. Just because you've had a little too much to drink . . .

HE. I haven't drunk a thing. (*Teeters on his knees.*) If I'm drunk, I'm drunk only with happiness . . .

SHE. You wouldn't be praying with everything on if you weren't. (*Turns.*) Oh! Goodness! I think I am too.

HE. Happy?

SHE. Tipsy. Let me see if I can stand on one leg. (*Holding her hands out to him, tries and fails.*) Whoo!

HE (*rises*). Angel! (*Tries to kiss her, but* SHE *dodges.*)

SHE. Michael, that hat . . .

HE. What? Oh. (*Takes hat off.*) What have you got in your hand?

SHE. A little rose . . . a little rose from our wedding cake.

HE. Let's eat it.

SHE. No—I want to keep it—always . . . (SHE *puts it in her dress.* HE *puts hat on.*)

HE. Agnes . . . tell me that you are happy.

SHE. Please, Michael, do say something else for a change.

HE. I can't. I've only one word left to express what I feel: happy. Happy, happy, happy, happy! Happy! (*Twirls and, stumbling against dais, sprawls back against bed.*)

SHE. Are you all right?

HE. Happy!

SHE. I suddenly feel like saying all sorts of shocking things.

HE. Go on.

SHE. Listen—no, in your ear . . . (SHE *wants to whisper something but is checked by what she sees.*) Oh! Michael . . .

HE (*faces her*). What?

SHE. No, don't move. (*Looks at ear again.*) Let me see the other one. (HE *turns his head and* SHE *looks at his other ear.*) You pig!

HE. What is it?

SHE. Don't you ever wash?

HE. Every day.

SHE. All over?

HE. Oh, well—the main things.

SHE. What *are* the main things?

HE (*trying to kiss her*). My precious . . .

SHE. Your what?

HE. You are my precious. Wouldn't you like to kiss me?

SHE. I would like to go over you from top to bottom, with hot water and soap; that's what I would like to do.

HE. Please do.

SHE. Oh, well—don't let's dwell on it. (SHE *sits on trunk.*) Ouch!

HE. Sweetheart! What's the matter?

SHE. Ouch! My shoes are hurting me. I must take them off or I'll faint.

HE. Let me do it! Please . . . (SHE *puts out her foot.* HE *kneels and tenderly pulls her skirt back and kisses her shoe.*)

SHE. Michael, please, they hurt me so.

HE (*kisses her foot again; when* SHE *wants to take shoe off herself.*) No, no, dearest! Let me do it, please let me do it. (HE *takes her shoe again.*)

SHE. But you take such a long time.

HE (*untying bow on shoe*). Isn't that heaven? I could spend the whole night undressing you.

SHE. I didn't ask you to undress me. I only asked you to help me out of my shoes.

HE. I would help you out of anything you ask, dear heart. (*Takes off shoe.*)

SHE (*withdraws her foot*). Now that's one, and now . . . (*As* SHE *leans forward to take off other shoe herself, sees him, still on his knees, leaning back and staring at her.*) Please, Michael, don't look at me so creepily. Please get undre . . . Take your hat off! (HE *takes hat off, puts it on trunk.*)

HE. Agnes, do you remember what I told you when we first met?

SHE. No . . .

HE. That we had met in a former existence.

SHE. Oh, that.

HE. I am absolutely certain of it now.

SHE. Of what?

HE. That moment, just now, I suddenly had the feeling of having experienced all this before.

SHE. Did you really?

HE. You sitting here just as you are, I on my knees in front of you in a hired suit, just before we . . .

SHE. What?

HE (*putting shoe down, HE leans against her knee*). Oh, darling, I am happy.

SHE. *Must* you make me cry?

HE. You should, you know. This is a very sad occasion, really. Your youth is over.

SHE (*pushing him back and getting up*). I want to go home.

HE. What . . .

SHE. I can't! I want to go home!

HE (*still on knees*). Darling, what's the matter? What have I done?

SHE (*picks up shoe*). I want to go home. I should never have married you.

HE (*rises*). Agnes . . .

SHE. How can you! How dare you say such a thing!

HE. But what . . . I haven't said a thing all night but that I was . . .

SHE. My youth over! That's what you would like! Undressing me, the whole night long, with your hat on and unwashed ears and . . . oh! (SHE *puts her arms around his neck and weeps.*)

HE (*comforting her inexperiencedly*). That's right, darling; that's it; you cry, my dearest; that's the spirit.

SHE. That's . . . that's why you made

me drink such a lot, taking nothing yourself all the time.

HE. Why, I've had at least three bottles.

SHE. Then what did you say? What did you say, when you threw me on the bed?

HE. Threw?

SHE. "If I'm drunk, I'm drunk with happiness." That's what you said.

HE. But, darling, only a minute ago you said yourself . . .

SHE. I did not!

HE. Well, of all the . . . (*Takes her by the shoulders.*) Here—smell! (*Breathes at her with his mouth wide open.*) Ho, ho, ho!

SHE (*escaping the kiss she wants by hiding her face against his shoulder*). Oh, I'm so dizzy.

HE. I love you.

SHE. I'm so embarrassed.

HE. Why?

SHE. Because I'm so dizzy.

HE. So am I.

SHE. Dizzy?

HE. Embarrassed.

SHE. Why?

HE. Oh, well, you know. It would have been such a relief if I could have spent the whole night taking off your shoes.

SHE. And then have breakfast, straightaway, yes?

HE. Yes. Agnes, I . . . I don't revolt you, do I?

SHE. You? Why on earth should you?

HE. Well, I mean—those ears and . . . things, you know.

SHE. But, darling, I said that only because of other people. What do I care?

HE. And Agnes . . . there's something I should tell you.

SHE. Why tell it just now?

HE. You're right. (*Puts hat on.*) I'm such a fool that I . . . (SHE *frowns.* HE *takes hat off again and puts it on trunk.*) Would you like something to drink?

SHE. Heavens, no. Don't talk about drinking.

HE. A glass of water, I mean. (*Picks up glass and carafe.*) After all that champagne.

SHE. Michael, please talk about something else. I—I really couldn't just now, honestly.

HE. Well, I think I will. (*Pours glass of water.*)

SHE. Did you write a poem for tonight?

HE. No.

SHE. What a pity! I thought you would have written something beautiful for our wedding.

HE. No.

SHE. Nothing at all?

HE. No.

SHE. You're blushing. Please read it to me.

HE. I haven't got one, darling, really, I haven't.

SHE. You're lying. I can tell by your eyes that you are lying.

HE. As a matter of fact, you wouldn't like it, darling; it's rather modern. There is another one I'm writing just now . . .

SHE. I want to hear the one about our wedding.

HE. Never before in my whole life have I told anybody anything about a poem I hadn't finished . . .

SHE. Is it in your pocket? (*Starts to pick his pockets.*)

HE (*trying to keep her hands back, sits in chair*). I think it's going to be wonderful. "The Fountain of the Royal Gardens."

SHE. Why may I not hear the one about our wedding?

HE. Darling, don't you think it much more special, just now, something nobody else has ever heard before?

SHE. Has anybody heard the one about our wedding, then?

HE (*takes poems from pocket*). Listen, tell me what you think of the permutation of the consonants, the onomatopoeia, I mean: "Hissing shoots the slender shower; out of shining, slimy stone. . . ."

SHE. No.

HE. "Swaying shivers sparkling flower; rainbow shimmers in the foam." (SHE *starts toward door.*) "Flashing, dashing, splashing, crashing . . ." (SHE *hurries to the door, picking up suitcase from chest as she goes.*) Where are you going?

SHE (*opens door, taking the key from the lock*). Back in a minute. (*Exits, shuts door, locks it.*)

HE. Why are you taking your suitcase? (*Rises and runs to door; drops poems on chest as he goes.*) Agnes, darling! Agnes! Agnes! (*Tries to open the locked door.* HE *turns, sees her shoes, picks them up and smiles. Suddenly, a thought strikes him. He drops the shoes, runs onto dais, picks up suitcase there, starts to put it on bed, stops, turns, then puts suitcase on arms of chair. He opens the case, takes out night-cap and puts it on his head. He rips off his coat and vest, shirt and tie. As he starts to take his trousers off, he stops, listens, runs to door, listens again. He then takes the trousers off. He takes nightshirt from case, goes to foot of bed, throws nightshirt on bed and sits on chest and hurriedly takes off his shoes. Then he pauses, looks toward the door in embarrassment. He quickly puts the shoes back on again, gets into the nightshirt, pulls his trousers on over it; then his coat. He moves a few steps, turns, sees his vest, shirt and tie on trunk where he had thrown them. He tosses them into the suitcase, fastens it, puts suitcase in wardrobe; starts to washstand, stops, looks toward door. Then he quickly goes down to washstand, picks up towel, dampens one corner of it in pitcher of water and starts to wash his right ear.* SHE *enters. As* HE *hears door open, he sits in chair and folds his arms.* SHE *closes the door and puts the key back in the lock. Her dress is changed somehow; it looks untidier and she has taken off her wedding hat.* SHE *turns from door, spots him sitting in the chair, the collar of his jacket upturned and the night-cap on his head.*)

HE. Hullo.

SHE. What—what are you doing?

HE. Sitting.

SHE. What on earth is that?

HE. What?

SHE. On your head?

HE. Oh . . .

SHE. Do you wear a nightcap?

HE. Oh, no. Just now when there's a draft. (*Rises, takes cap off and puts it in his pocket.*)

SHE. Is that a nightshirt?

HE. What have you got on?

SHE. My father has been wearing pajamas for ages.

HE. Oh, has he really? Well, I don't.

SHE. Why have you . . . changed?

HE. Why have you?

SHE. I? Oh . . . I'm sleepy.

HE. So am I.

SHE. Well, then, shall we . . .

HE. Why, yes . . . let's.

SHE. All right. Which side do you want?

HE. I? Oh, well. . . . I don't care, really. Any side that suits you is all right with me.

SHE. I think I would like the far side. Because of the door.

HE. The door?

SHE (*turns back quilt*). Because of breakfast, and in case somebody should knock. You could answer it.

HE. I see.

SHE (*picks up "God Is Love" pillow from bed*). What's this?

HE. What?

SHE. This little pillow? Did you put that there?

HE. Of course not! What's it got written on it?

SHE. "God Is Love." Oh, how sweet! Mother must have done that. Wasn't that lovely of her? (*Puts pillow back on bed.*)

HE (*looks at door*). Yes, lovely.

(SHE *turns away and starts undressing.* HE *takes off his coat.* SHE *turns. After an embarrassing moment in which neither of them can think of anything to say.*)

SHE. Michael, please turn 'round.

HE. Oh, I'm so sorry . . . I didn't realize . . .

(HE *sits down on the edge of the chest, putting his coat beside him, and takes off his shoes and socks.* SHE *steps out of dress and hangs it in wardrobe. Goes back up onto dais.*)

SHE. It's rather a pretty bed, isn't it?

HE. Yes, it is, isn't it? It was my father's, you know.

SHE. Not your mother's?

HE. Yes, of course, my parents'. I was born in it, you know.

SHE. Michael . . .

HE (*turning toward her*). Yes, darling?

SHE (*backing up*). No, don't look! Michael?

HE (*turning away*). Yes?

SHE. Tell me how much you love me, once more.

HE. I can't any more.

SHE. What?

HE. I can't love you any more than I'm doing. I wor . . . I'm the hap . . . I'm mad about you.

SHE. That's what I am about you. Honestly.

HE. That is nice, dear.

SHE. I am so happy, I couldn't be happier.

HE. That is lovely, darling.

SHE. And I wouldn't want to be, either.

HE. What?

SHE. Happier.

HE. I see.

SHE. I wish that everything could stay as it was—before today. I couldn't stand

any more—happiness. Could you?

HE. God, no.

SHE. How coldly you say that!

HE. But what the blazing hell do you expect me to say?

SHE. Michael! Is that language for the wedding ni . . . before going to sleep? You ought to be ashamed of yourself!

HE. But damn it, Agnes . . . (*Sneezes.*) I—I've got a splitting headache and I'm dying of cold feet. (*Takes nightcap from pocket and puts it on.*)

SHE (*takes off her slippers*). Then why don't you get into bed, silly? (HE *rises.*) No! A moment! A moment! (HE *turns away.* SHE *gets into bed, the "God Is Love" pillow beneath her head.* HE *stands for a moment in embarrassment, starts to take off his trousers, then realizing that the room is still brightly lit, he goes to bracket, right of arch, and turns it off.*)

HE. May I turn 'round now?

SHE. Yes.

(HE *reaches to turn down the bracket but is stopped by her interruption.*)

SHE. Wait! It can't leak, can it? The lamp, I mean?

HE. Of course not.

SHE. But I think I smell gas.

HE (*reaches behind him and takes her hand*). Darling, listen. You are an angel, and I'm madly in love with you, and I'm embarrassed to death and so are you, and that's the reason why we . . . Good night. (HE *reaches up and turns down the bracket.*)

SHE. Good night. (HE *takes off his trousers and puts them on chair.*) Can you find your way?

HE. Yes, yes . . . (*Going back up to bed, stubs his toe.*) Ouch!

SHE. Michael! What are you doing?

HE (*on dais*). Nothing. I hurt my toe. (HE *gets into bed.*)

SHE. Oh, I'm so sorry. (*Long silence.*) Do get into bed carefully, won't you?

HE. I'm in it already.

SHE (*after another silence*). Michael?

HE. Yes?

SHE. Michael, what was it you didn't want to tell me tonight?

HE. Ah . . .

SHE. You may tell me now, if you like. I'm not embarrassed any more, somehow.

HE. Well . . .

SHE. If you tell me what it was, I'll tell you something as well.

HE. What?

SHE. But you must tell me as well. Promise me.

HE. Yes.

SHE. No, promise me first.

HE. All right. I promise.

SHE. I . . . I've never seen a man . . . before . . . completely. Never.

HE. Oh, well—you haven't missed much.

SHE. And you?

HE. Oh.

SHE. Have you ever seen) a woman before . . . completely?

HE. Well . . .

SHE. What does that mean?

HE. You know, I once had my fortune told by a gypsy.

SHE. Oh . . .

HE. She said I'd have a very happy married life, that I'd live to a ripe old age, and she said that everything would turn out all right.

SHE. And was she . . . naked?

HE. Of course not! She went from house to house with a goat.

SHE. Oh . . . Good night.

HE. Good night. (*Pause.*) Are you comfy?

SHE. Oh, yes.

HE. Not too cold?

SHE. Heavens, no. I'm simply boiling. And you?

HE. Rather cold, really.

SHE (*after a silence*). Michael!

HE. Yes?

SHE. Michael! Now I'm sure that I smell gas. (SHE *sits up.*)

HE. That must be the drink.

SHE. Do you still smell of drink that much? I can't believe it.

HE. Yes.

SHE. Let me smell your breath again.

HE. Oh, please, Agnes, let's try to go to sleep.

SHE. No, Michael, I want to smell it. If it is the gas, we may be dead tomorrow, both of us.

HE. Oh, well . . .

SHE. Oh, well! Do you want to die?

HE. Sometimes.

SHE. Now?

HE. No, no.

SHE. Please, Michael, let me have a little sniff before I go to sleep; otherwise, I won't close an eye. (*Lies down.*) Please, Michael.

HE (*sits up and leans over her*). Ho!

Ho! Ho! (*Lies back on his pillow.*) There.

SHE (*sits up and leans over him*). I don't smell a thing. Do it again.

HE. Ho! Ho!

SHE. Again?

HE. Ho, ho.

SHE. Again . . .

CURTAIN

SCENE TWO

1891. Late Afternoon.

The same bedroom. To the right, a cradle.

HE *is lying in the fourposter, with a towel wrapped around his head. The bed is strewn with books, papers, an oversized dinner bell and his dressing gown. Heaps of books and papers are on the dais at foot of bed.*

When the curtain rises, HE *awakens.*

HE (*from beneath the blankets*). Agnes! Agnes! (*Sits up.*) Agnes! (*Picks up bell and rings loudly and insistently.*)

SHE (*enters hurriedly carrying a pile of clean laundry.* SHE *is very pregnant*). Yes, yes, yes, yes, yes. What is it?

HE. I've got such a pain! (SHE *returns to door and closes it.*) I can't stand it any longer!

SHE (*putting laundry on chest*). Now, come, come, darling. Don't dramatize. I'll soak your towel again.

HE. No! It isn't my head. It's shifted to here. (*Puts his hand on his back.*)

SHE. Where?

HE. Here! (*Leans forward. Places her hand on the painful spot.*) Here! What is there? Do you feel anything?

SHE. You've got a pain there?

HE. As if I'd been stabbed. No, don't take your hand away . . . Oh, that's nice.

SHE (*suspiciously*). But what sort of pain? Does it come in—in waves? First almost nothing and then growing until you could scream?

HE. That's right. How do you know . . .

SHE. Micky, that's impossible.

HE. What's impossible? Do you think I'm shamming?

SHE. You're having labor pains!

HE. You're crazy!

SHE. And all the time . . . all the time

I've put up a brave front because I thought you were really ill!

HE. But I *am* ill! What do you think? That I lay here groaning and sweating just for the fun of it?

SHE. All the time I've been thinking of *you!*

HE. I've done nothing else, day and night, but think of *you!* How else do you think I got the pains *you're* supposed to have? (SHE *sobs.*) Oh, hell! This is driving me mad! (HE *jumps out of bed.*)

SHE. Micky! (HE *tears open the wardrobe.*) Micky, what are you doing?

HE. Where are my shoes?

SHE. Michael! You aren't running away, are you?

HE (*gets clothes from wardrobe*). I'm going to get that doctor.

SHE (*rises*). No. Michael, you mustn't.

HE (*puts clothes on chair*). If I drop dead on the pavement, I'm going to get that doctor! I'm not going to leave you in this condition a minute longer. He said so himself, the moment you got those pains . . . (*Kneels, looks under bed.*)

SHE. When *I* got them! Not when *you* got them!

HE. Don't you feel anything?

SHE. Nothing! Nothing at all.

HE. Then I don't understand why you were crying just now.

SHE. Please, darling, please go back to bed. You'll catch a cold with those bare feet and you're perspiring so freely. Please, darling.

HE. But I don't want to.

SHE (*pops him into bed*). I want you to. Uppy-pie, in you go!

HE. Anyone would think you wanted me to be ill.

SHE. No grumbling, no growling. (*Puts "God Is Love" pillow behind his head.*) There! Comfy? (*Goes to chest.*)

HE. No! (HE *throws pillow to floor.*) I'm scared.

SHE. What on earth of?

HE. Of—of the baby. Aren't you?

SHE. Good Heavens, no. Why should I? It's the most natural thing in the world, isn't it? And I'm feeling all right. (*Picks up sewing.*)

HE. You have changed a lot, do you know that?

SHE (*starts sewing*). Since when?

HE. Since you became a mother.

SHE. But I'm not a mother yet.

HE. Then you don't realize it yourself. Suddenly you have become a woman.

SHE. Have I ever been anything else?

HE. A silly child.

SHE. So that's what you thought of me when we married?

HE. When we married, my feet were off the ground.

SHE. Well, you've changed a lot, too.

HE. Of course I have. I have become a man.

SHE. Hah!

HE. Well, haven't I? Aren't I much more calm, composed . . .

SHE (*picks up rattle from bassinette and throws it to him*). You're a baby!

HE (*throws covers back and sits on edge of bed*). That's right! Humiliate me! Lose no opportunity of reminding me that I'm the male animal that's done its duty and now can be dismissed! (*Jumps out.*)

SHE. Michael!

HE. Yes! A drone, that's what I am! The one thing lacking is that you should devour me. The bees . . .

SHE. Michael, Michael, what's the matter? (*Reaches out to him.*)

HE. I'm afraid!

SHE. But I'm not, Michael, honestly, not a bit.

HE. I'm afraid of something else.

SHE. What?

HE. That I've lost you.

SHE (*rises, goes to him*). Michael, look at me . . . What did the doctor tell you?

HE. It's got nothing to do with the doctor. It's got nothing to do with you either. It's got to do with me.

SHE (*puts arms about him*). But you're going to be all right, aren't you?

HE (*breaks away*). I'd never be all right again, if I've lost you.

SHE. What are you talking about? You've got me right here, haven't you?

HE. But your heart, that's gone. I wish I was lying in that cradle.

SHE (*puts her arms around him again*). You fool . . . (*Kisses him.*) You can't be as stupid as all that. No, Michael.

HE. Listen! Before that cuckoo pushes me out of the nest, I want to tell you once more that I love you. Love you, just as you are . . . I thought I loved you when I married you, but that wasn't you at all. That was a romantic illusion. I loved a sort of fairy princess with a doll's smile and a . . . well, anyway not a princess with hiccoughs and cold feet, scratching her stomach in her sleep . . .

SHE. Michael!

HE (*takes her hand*). I thought I was marrying a princess and I woke up to find a friend, a wife . . . You know, sometimes when I lay awake longer than you, with my arm around your shoulder and your head on my chest, I thought with pity of all those lonely men staring at the ceiling or writing poems . . . pity, and such happiness that I knew at that very moment it wouldn't last. I was right, that's all.

SHE. Well, if you thought about a princess, I thought about a poet.

HE. Oh?

SHE. You didn't know that I had cold feet, and every now and again I get an attack of hiccoughs . . .

HE. You don't do anything else the whole night long.

SHE. What?

HE. Scratch your stomach and sniff and snort and smack your lips, but go on.

SHE. And you lie listening to all this without waking me up?

HE. Yes. Because I don't know anything in the world I'd rather listen to. (*Kisses her.*) Got anything to say to that?

SHE. Yes, but I won't say it.

HE. Why not?

SHE. Never mind, darling, you stay just as you are.

HE. Miserable, deserted, alone? You do nothing else all day and night but fuss over that child—eight months now! First it was knitting panties, then sewing dresses, fitting out the layette, rigging the cradle . . .

SHE. And all this time you sat quietly in your corner, didn't you?

HE. I retired into the background as becomes a man who recognizes that he is one too many.

SHE (*rises, goes to him*). Oh, angel! (*Puts her arms around his neck and kisses him.*) Do you still not understand why I love you so much?

HE. You . . . you noticed how I blotted myself out?

SHE. Did I!

HE. I didn't think you did.

SHE. You helped me more than* all model husbands put together. Without you I would have been frightened to death for eight whole months. But now I simply had

no time.

HE. I believe you're teasing me.

SHE. I love you. Do you believe that?

HE. Of course.

SHE. Must I prove it to you?

HE. Oh, no. I'm perfectly prepared to take your word for it.

SHE. All right, if you like, we'll send the child to a home.

HE. What?

SHE. And then we'll go and look at it every Sunday.

HE. Agnes, why do you tease me?

SHE. Darling, I'm not teasing you. I'm telling you the truth. Even if I were going to have twenty children, you are my husband and I'd rather leave them as foundlings . . . (SHE *grasps at her back and turns.* HE *stares at her in horror.*)

HE. Darling, what—what is it? Agnes!

SHE (*clutching the bed post*). Oh!

HE (*picks up clothes, goes to her*). The doctor! For God's sake, the doctor!

SHE. No . . . oh, oh! Don't . . . not the doctor. Stay here.

HE. Darling, darling! Angel! Agnes, my love! What must I do? For God's sake, I must do something!

SHE (*sings, convulsed by pain, loudly*). "Yankee Doodle went to town, Riding on a pony . . ."

HE. Agnes!

SHE (*sings on*). "He stuck a feather in his hat, And called it macaroni."

HE (*takes her by shoulders*). Agnes!

SHE. Oh, Micky . . . What are you doing?

HE. I—I thought you were going mad.

SHE. I? Why?

HE (*seats her on chest*). You started to sing.

SHE (*sitting*). Oh, yes. The doctor said if those pains started, I had to sing. That would help. I must have done it automatically.

HE. Are you all right now?

SHE. Oh, yes, yes.

HE. Now you just sit here quietly. I'll get the doctor.

SHE. No, Michael, you mustn't. He said we weren't to bother him until the pains came regularly.

HE. Regularly? But I won't be a minute. (*Picks up clothes.*)

SHE. Oh, please, please don't go away. Oh, I wish Mother were here.

HE (*puts clothes on bed*). Now, don't worry! This is the most natural thing in the world. You just sit here quietly. I'll put some clothes on and . . .

SHE. Oh, no, no Micky, please, please don't fuss. I wish it didn't have to happen so soon.

HE (*turns upstage with back to audience, takes off pajama pants. Puts on trousers*). Yes.

SHE (*picks up pajama pants*). I'm not nearly ready for it yet . . .

HE (*taking off robe and putting it on bed*). Well, I am. Honestly, I am. I can't wait to—to go fishing with him, if it's a boy, and—and, if it's a girl, go for walks, nature rambles. . . . (*Goes to wardrobe and gets tie.*)

SHE. But that won't happen for years. First, there will be years of crying and diapers and bottles . . .

HE (*ties tie*). I don't mind, darling. Honestly, I don't. I'll—find something to do. I'll work and—and go fishing alone. You're never going to have to worry about . . .

SHE (*in pain again*). Oh!

HE (*goes to her, kneels*). Another one?

SHE. No. No, I don't think so.

HE. Now, why don't you go to bed? (*Throws robe and coat on chest. Fixes bed linen.*) You go to bed. I'll finish dressing and make you a nice cup of tea, yes?

SHE. No, no, thank you, darling. I think I'll stay right where I am. Oh, I haven't done nearly all the things I should have done. There's still half the laundry out on the roof and . . .

HE (*stops her*). Agnes, do stop worrying. As soon as I've finished dressing, I'll go to the roof and take the washing in for you. (*Seats her on chest.*)

SHE (*puts arms about his waist*). No, please don't leave me alone.

HE (*puts his arms about her shoulders*). All right, all right. There's nothing to be afraid of. This has been going on for millions and millions of years. Now what would you like? Shall I read you something? (*Goes to the bed. Picks up books.*) Schopenhauer, *Alice in Wonderland?*

SHE. No.

HE. I know. I've started a new book. It's only half a page. Shall I read you that? Yes? (*He picks up writing pad.*)

SHE (*biting her lip*). Yes . . .

HE (*sits on foot of bed*). It's going to be a trilogy. It's called "Burnt Corn, the Story of a Rural Love." Do you like that as a title?

SHE (*biting her lips*). I think that's wonderful.

HE. Now this is how it opens . . . (*Takes hold of her hand.*) Are you all right?

SHE. Fine.

HE (*reads*). "When she entered the attic with the double bed, she bent her head, partly out of reverence for the temple where she had worshipped and sacrificed, partly because the ceiling was so low. It was not the first time she had returned to that shrine . . ." (SHE *has a pain.*) Are you all right?

SHE. Oh, Micky, I love you so. Don't, don't let's ever . . . (SHE *has another pain.* HE *drops pad and kneels before her.*)

SHE (*buries her head in his shoulder, then looks up*). Now . . . now, I think you'd better go and call him.

HE. I will, my darling. (*Puts on his coat. Goes to door, stops, returns to her.*) Now, you just sit tight. (*Goes to door, returns and kisses her. Goes back to door, turns, sees bassinette, runs to it and pulls it over close to her and exits.*)

CURTAIN

ACT TWO

SCENE ONE

1901. Night.

The same room, ten years later. The only piece of furniture left from the preceding scene is the fourposter, but it has been fitted out with new brocade curtains. Paintings hang on the walls; expensive furniture crowds the room. No washstand any more, but a bathroom to the left. Where the wardrobe stood in the preceding act, the wall has been removed and this has become an entrance to a dressing room. The whole thing is very costly, very grand and very new. Only one side of the bed has been made; there is only one pillow on the bed with the "God Is Love" pillow on top of it.

AT RISE, *there is no one in the room.* SHE *enters and slams the door behind her.* SHE *stands at the foot of the bed, removing her evening gloves. Goes to dressing table, throws gloves on the table, and is stopped by a knock at the door.* SHE *stands for a moment. The knock is repeated, more insistently.*

———

SHE (*after a pause*). Come in.

HE (*enters, closes door*). Excuse me. (*Goes to the dressing room, gets his night clothes, re-enters and crosses to door.*) Good night.

SHE (*as* HE *opens door*). You certainly were the life and soul of the party this evening, with your interminable little stories.

HE (*starts out, stops, turns*). My dear, if you don't enjoy playing second fiddle, I suggest you either quit the orchestra or form one of your own. (*Goes out and shuts door.*)

SHE (*mutters after a moment's stupefaction*). Now, I've had enough! (*Runs to door, rips it open, stands in hallway and calls off:*) Michael! (*Then bellows:*) Michael! Come here!

HE (*pops in. Has top hat and cane in hand and evening cape over arm*). Have you taken leave of your senses? The servants . . .

SHE. I don't care if the whole town hears it. (HE *exits.*) Come back, I say!

HE (*re-enters*). All right. This situation is no longer bearable! (*Closes door.*)

SHE. What on earth is the matter with you?

HE. Now, let me tell you one thing, calmly. (SHE *goes to dressing table, takes off plume, throws it on table.*) My greatest mistake has been to play up to you, plying you with presents . . .

SHE. I like that! (*Picks up gloves.*)

HE. Calmly! Do you know what I should have done? I should have packed you off to boarding school, big as you are, to learn deportment.

SHE. Deportment for what?

HE. To be worthy of *me.*

SHE. The pompous ass whose book sold three hundred thousand copies!

HE. That is entirely beside the point.

SHE. It is right to the point! Before you had written that cursed novel, the rest of the world helped me to keep you sane. Every time you had finished a book or a play or God knows what, and considered yourself to be the greatest genius since Shakespeare . . . (HE *says, "Now re-*

ally!") I was frightened to death that it might turn out to be a success. But, thank Heaven, it turned out to be such a thorough failure every time, that I won the battle with your megalomania. But now, now this book, the only book you ever confessed to be trash until you read the papers . . . Oh, what's the use!

HE. My dear woman, I may be vain, but you are making a tragic mistake.

SHE (*laughs*). Now listen! Just listen to him! To be married to a man for eleven years, and then to be addressed like a public meeting. Tragic mistake! Can't you hear yourself, you poor darling idiot, that you've sold your soul to a sentimental novel?

HE. Agnes, are you going on like this, or must I . . .

SHE. Yes, yes, you must! You *shall* hear it. (HE *pounds floor with evening cane.*) And don't interrupt me! There is only one person in this world who loves you in spite of what you are, and let me tell you . . .

HE. You are mistaken. There is a person in this world who loves me—because of what I am.

SHE. And what are you, my darling?

HE. Ask her.

SHE. Her . . .

HE. Yes.

SHE. Oh . . . (*Holds onto bed post.*) Who is she?

HE. You don't know her.

SHE. Is she . . . young? How young?

HE. No. I'll be damned if I go on with this. You look like a corpse.

SHE. A corpse?

HE. So pale, I mean. (*At door.*) Agnes, I'm not such a monster, that . . . Sit down. Please, Agnes, do sit . . . Agnes!

SHE (*turns away*). No, no . . . it's nothing. I'm all right. What do you think? That I should faint in my thirty-first year because of something so . . . so ordinary?

HE. Ordinary?

SHE. With two children? I didn't faint when Robert had the mumps, did I?

HE. Don't you think this is a little different?

SHE. No, Michael. This belongs to the family medicine chest.

HE. I love her!

SHE. So, not me any more? (HE *doesn't reply.*) I don't mean as a friend, or as . . . as the mother of your children, but as a wife? You may tell me honestly, really. Is that why you've been sleeping in the study?

HE. I haven't slept a wink.

SHE. I see. It must be Cook who snores.

HE. Since when do I snore?

SHE. Not you, dear, Cook. Every night when I went down the passage.

HE (*goes to the door, opens it*). Good night!

SHE. Sleep well.

HE. What was that?

SHE. Sleep well.

HE. Oh . . . (*Stops at door, then slams it shut.*) No! I'll be damned, I won't stand it!

SHE. What is the matter?

HE. Cook snores! Agnes, I love somebody else! It's driving me crazy! You, the children, she, the children, you . . . for three weeks I have lived through hell, and all you've got to say is "Cook snores!"

SHE. But, darling . . .

HE. No, no, no, no! You are so damned sure of yourself that it makes me sick! I know you don't take this seriously, but believe me, I love that woman! I must have that woman or I'll go mad!

SHE. Haven't you . . . had her yet?

HE. At last! Thank God, a sign of life. Why haven't you looked at me like that before? I have begged, implored, crawled to you for a little understanding and warmth, and love, and got nothing. Even my book, that was inspired by you, longing for you—right from the beginning you have seen it as a rival. Whatever I did, whatever I tried: a carriage, servants, money, dresses, paintings, everything . . . you hated that book. And now? Now you have driven me into somebody else's arms. Somebody else, who understands at least one thing clearly: that she will have to share me with my work.

SHE. Does she understand that she will have to share you with other women as well?

HE. She doesn't need to. At last I have found a woman who'll live with my work, and a better guarantee of my faithfulness nobody could have.

SHE. But how does she live with it? What does she do?

HE. She listens. She encourages me—with a look, a touch, a—well, an encouragement. When I cheer, she cheers with me, when I meditate, she meditates with me . . .

SHE. And when you throw crockery, she throws crockery with you?

HE. Haven't you understood one single word of what I have been saying? Won't you, can't you see that I have changed?

SHE. No.

HE. Then you are blind! That's all I can say. At any rate, *you've* changed.

SHE. I!

HE. No, don't let's start that.

SHE. Go on.

HE. No, it's senseless. No reason to torture you any longer, once I have . . .

SHE. Once you have tasted blood.

HE. I . . . I'm sorry it was necessary for me to hurt you. It couldn't very well have been done otherwise. I'm at the mercy of a feeling stronger than I.

SHE. Rotten, isn't it?

HE. Horrible.

SHE. And yet . . . at the same time not altogether.

HE. No. On the other hand, it's delicious.

SHE. The greatest thing a human being can experience.

HE. I'm glad you understand it so well.

SHE. Understand? Why, of course. It's human isn't it?

HE. How do you come to know that?

SHE. What?

HE. That it's—human?

SHE. Well, I'm a human being, aren't I?

HE. I never heard you talk like this before. What's the matter with you?

SHE. Well, I might have my experiences too, mightn't I? Good night.

HE. Just a minute! I want to hear a little more about this!

SHE. But I know it now, dear. .

HE. Yes, you do! But I don't! What sort of experiences are you referring to?

SHE. Now, listen, my little friend! You have dismissed me without notice, and I haven't complained once as any other housekeeper would have done. I have accepted the facts because I know a human being is at the mercy of this feeling, however horrible and at the same time delicious it may be.

HE. Agnes!

SHE. I really don't understand you. I am not thwarting you in the least, and instead of your going away happily and relieved that you are not leaving a helpless wreck behind . . .

HE. You might answer just one plain question before . . . we finish this business. Have you . . . aren't you going to be alone, if I leave you?

SHE. Alone? I've got the children, haven't I?

HE. That's not at all certain.

SHE (*after a shaky silence*). You had better leave this room very quickly now, before you get to know a side of me that might surprise you a lot.

HE. I have, I'm afraid. I demand an answer. Have you a lover?'

SHE (*goes to door, opens it*). Good night.

HE. For eleven long years I have believed in you! You were the purest, the . . .

SHE (*interrupting*). The noblest thing in my life! Good night!

HE. If you don't answer my question, you'll never see me again.

SHE. Get out of here!

HE. No.

SHE. All right. Then there's only one thing left to be done. (SHE *picks up wrap from bed and exits into dressing room*.)

HE. What? What did you want to say? (SHE *does not answer*. SHE *returns with second wrap and overnight case; puts them both on chair and opens case*.) What's the meaning of that? (SHE *picks up nightgown and negligee, packs them in case*.) Darling, believe me, I won't blame you for anything, only tell me—where are you going?

SHE (*goes to dressing table and gets brushes and comb*). Would you mind calling a cab for me?

HE. Agnes!

SHE (*packs brushes and comb in case*). Please, Michael, I can't arrive there too late. It is such an embarrassing time already. Pass me my alarm clock, will you?

HE. No, I can't have been mistaken about you that much! Only yesterday you said that I had qualities . . .

SHE. Excuse me. (*Passes him, gets her alarm clock, puts clock in case*.)

HE (*wants to stop her when she passes, but checks himself*). All right. It *is* a solution, anyhow.

SHE (*closes overnight case, picks it up, puts wrap over arm, goes around chair to him and puts out her hand*). Good-by, Michael. (HE *blocks her way*.)

HE. Do you really think I'm going to let you do this? Do you?

SHE. A gentleman does not use force when a lady wishes to leave the room.

HE. Oh, I'm so sorry. (*Steps aside*.)

SHE. Thank you. (HE *grabs her arm and pulls her back*. SHE *drops her suitcase and wrap in the struggle; HE flings her up onto the bed*.) Michael! Let me go! Let me go! I . . .

HE. Now look, I've put up with all the nonsense from you . . . (SHE *succeeds in tearing herself free, gets off the bed and kicks his shin*.) Ouch! (HE *grasps at his shinbone and limps, leans against arm of sofa*.)

SHE. Get out!

HE. Right on my scar!

SHE. Get out! (HE *takes off his coat, throws it on chair. As HE starts toward her:*) I'll scream the house down if you dare come near me! (SHE *scrambles back up onto bed*.)

HE. Where's my pillow?

SHE (*reaching for bell pull*). Get out or I'll ring the bell!

HE (*as he exits to dressing room*). Make up that bed properly.

SHE. You're the vilest swine God ever created!

HE (*re-enters carrying pillow*). If I have to make you hoarse and broken for the rest of your life, you'll know that I am a man. Make up that bed! (*Throws pillow at her*.)

SHE. I would rather . . .

HE. And shut up! Get off there!

SHE (*strikes at him with "God Is Love" pillow*). You are the silliest hack-writer I ever . . .

HE (*grabs "God Is Love" pillow and throws it*). Get off, or I'll drag you off!

SHE (*gets off bed*). And that book of yours is rubbish.

HE. What did I tell you after I finished it? Listening to me once in awhile wouldn't do you any harm. Here! (*Throws comforter at her*.) Fold that!

SHE (*throws it back*). Fold it yourself!

HE (*throws it back*). Fold it!

(SHE *goes at him and* HE *grasps her hands*. SHE *still tries to flail him*. HE *slips in the struggle and sits on dais*. SHE *tries to pound his head*. HE *regains his feet and pinions her arms behind her*.)

SHE (*as* HE *grasps her face with left hand*). I'll bite you!

HE. If you could see your eyes now, you'd close them. They're blinding.

SHE. With hatred!

HE. With love. (*gives her a quick kiss;* SHE *breaks free*. HE *gets on guard*.)

SHE (*looks at him speechless for a moment, then sits on the bed, away from him, sobbing*). I wish I were dead. I want to be dead, dead . . .

HE (*sits on edge of bed, holding shin*). Before you die, look in my eyes, just once. Look! (*Turns her to him. SHE looks.*) What do you see there?

SHE. Wrinkles!

HE (*picks up evening pumps which have come off in the scuffle and goes back onto dais*). That's how long it is since you last looked. (*Sits on bed and puts one pump on.*) What else?

SHE. But . . . what about her?

HE. I was lonely.

SHE (*stands*). You'd better go now.

HE. Weren't you?

SHE. Please go.

HE (*picks up evening coat. SHE picks up his pillow and puts it on chair. At archway, as HE puts on other pump.*) I've started writing a new book.

SHE. When?

HE. A couple of weeks ago.

SHE. And you haven't read me anything yet? Impossible.

HE. I read it to her.

SHE. Oh . . . and?

HE. She liked it all right. But she thought it a little . . . well, coarse.

SHE. You, coarse? What kind of sheep is she?

HE. Shall I go and get the manuscript?

SHE (*picks up his pillow*). Tomorrow.

HE (*moves quickly to door and puts hand on door knob*). No, now!

SHE (*goes onto dais, puts his pillow on bed*). Please . . . tomorrow.

(HE *throws coat onto bench at foot of bed and goes around onto dais and embraces her.*)

CURTAIN

SCENE TWO

1908. 4:00 A.M. to dawn.

When the curtain rises, the stage is dark. The door is opened brusquely and HE *enters, wearing an overcoat over his pajamas.* HE *is carrying a bourbon bottle and riding crop.* SHE *is asleep in the fourposter.*

———

HE (*as HE enters*). Agnes! (*Goes to dress-ing table right of arch and turns on dressing-table lamps.*) Agnes, Agnes, look at this! (*Turns on bed-table lamp.* HE *shows her brown bourbon bottle.*)

SHE (*waking up and shielding her eyes with arm*). Huh? What's the matter?

HE. In his drawer, behind a pile of junk —this!

SHE. What?

HE. He's seventeen—eighteen! And it's four o'clock in the morning! And—and now, this!

SHE (*sitting up*). What, for Heaven's sake?

HE (*hands her the bottle*). Look!

SHE (*takes bottle and looks at it*). Bourbon!

HE. Your son. The result of your modern upbringing.

SHE. But what—where . . . (*Puts bottle down on bed.*) What does all this mean? What's the time? (*Leans over and picks up clock.*)

HE (*as HE exits into bathroom*). It's time I took over his education.

SHE. But he told you he would be late tonight. He specially asked permission to go to that dance. I gave him the key myself!

HE (*re-enters and exits again into dressing room*). Where did you put that thing?

SHE. What thing?

HE. My old shaving strop.

SHE. What do you want that for? (*Lying back in bed.*) Come back to bed.

HE (*re-enters*). So you approve of all this? You think it's perfectly natural that a child boozes in his bedroom and paints the town until four o'clock in the morning?

SHE. But, darling, he told you! And surely the child has a right to a bit of gaiety.

HE. One day let me explain the difference between gaiety and delirium tremens!

SHE. What are you going to do, Michael?

HE (*turns round in the doorway*). I am going downstairs where I have been since one o'clock this morning. And when he comes home, I . . .

SHE (*climbs out of bed. Picks up robe*). I won't let you! If you are going to beat that child, you will have to do so over my dead body!

HE. Don't interfere, Agnes.

SHE. I mean it, Michael! Whatever happens, even if he has taken to opium, I will not let you beat that child!

HE. All right. In that case, we had better call the police.

SHE. But you knew he was coming in late! These children's parties go on till dawn!

HE (*with a politician's gesture of despair*). Now, in my young days, if I was told to be in at a certain hour—(*Turns to her for the beginning of a big speech.*) I— (*Sees her for the first time.*) What in the name of sanity have you got on your head?

SHE. Now, now, that's the very latest thing—everyone's wearing them—

HE. But what *is* it?

SHE. A slumber helmet.

HE. Slumber helmet! Bourbon in the bedroom, children's parties that go on till dawn and slumber helmets. All right. (*Throws riding crop on bench at foot of bed and rips off overcoat.*) I am going to bed.

SHE. Listen to me, will you?

HE (*steps out of slippers*). I have the choice between bed and the madhouse. I prefer bed. I have a life to live. Good night! (HE *gets into bed and pulls the blanket up.* SHE *goes above sofa.* HE *sits up.*) I hope you enjoy being a drunkard's mother! (*Lies back.*)

SHE. I don't want to spoil your performance as an irate father, but I can't help thinking what your attitude would be if it were not Robert, but Lizzie who stayed out late.

HE (*sits up*). Exactly the same! With this difference, that Lizzie would never do such a thing.

SHE. Ha!

HE. Because she happens to be the only sane member of this family, except me. (*Lies back.*)

SHE (*at arch*). I could tell you something about her that would . . . No, I'd better not.

HE (*sits up*). If you think that I am going to fall for that stone-age woman's trick of hinting at something and then stopping . . . That child is as straight and as sensible as—as a glass of milk. (*Lies back.*)

SHE. Milk!

HE (*finds bottle in bed, sits up, puts bottle on bed table, lies back*). At least she doesn't go to bed with a bottle of bourbon.

SHE. Mmm.

HE (*sitting up*). What—Mmm?

SHE. Nothing, nothing.

HE. Agnes, you aren't by any chance suggesting that she goes to bed with anything else, are you?

SHE. I am not suggesting anything. I am just sick and tired of your coming down like a ton of bricks on that poor boy every time, while she is allowed to do whatever she pleases.

HE. So! I have an unhealthy preference for my daughter. Is that it?

SHE. I am not saying that. I . . .

HE. All right, say it! Say it!

SHE. What?

HE. Oedipus!

SHE. Who?

HE. Oh! Leave me alone. (*Under the blankets again.*)

SHE. In his drawer, did you say?

HE. Shut up.

SHE. Darling, I know you never concern yourself with the children's education except for an occasional bout of fatherly hysteria, but I think that this time you are going a little too far, if you don't mind my saying so.

HE. What else do you want me to do? I have to spend every waking hour earning money. You are my second in command. I have to leave certain things to you; but if I see that they are obviously going wrong, it is my duty to intervene.

SHE. If that is your conception of our relationship, then you ought to think of something better than a shaving crop and a riding strop.

HE. Riding crop! And it's not a matter of thinking of something better, it's . . . (HE *stops because she has suddenly got up and gone to the window, as if she heard something.*)

SHE. Michael!

HE. Is that him? (*As* SHE *does not answer,* HE *gets out of bed and grabs his overcoat.*)

SHE (*peeking out the window*). I thought I heard the gate.

HE (*from the doorway*). Robert! (*Exits and calls offstage.*) Is that you, Robert? (*No answer, so he comes back.*) No.

SHE (*sits at dressing table, opens powder box*). Why don't you go back to bed?

HE. Because I'm worried.

SHE (*picking up hand mirror and puff and powdering her face*). Why, that's nonsense!

HE. And so are you.

SHE. What on earth gives you that idea?

HE. That you are powdering your face at four o'clock in the morning.

SHE (*puts down mirror, puff. Realizes that there is no use pretending any longer, goes to the bottle and picks it up from bed table*). What drawer was it?

HE. The one where he keeps all his junk.

SHE. I can't believe it. It can't be true.

HE. Well, there you are.

SHE. How did you find it?

HE. I was sitting downstairs waiting. I got more and more worried so I decided to go up to his room and see whether perhaps he had climbed in through the window, and then I happened to glance into an open drawer, and there it was.

SHE. But it isn't possible. A child can't be drinking on the sly without his mother knowing it.

HE. We'll have to face it, my dear. He is no longer a child. When I looked into that drawer and found his old teddy bears, his steam engine, and then that bottle, I—I can't tell you what I felt.

SHE. Suppose—of course it isn't—but suppose—it is true, whatever shall we do?

HE. I don't know—see a doctor.

SHE. Nonsense. It's perfectly natural childish curiosity. A boy has to try everything once.

HE. If that's going to be your attitude, he'll end by trying murder once. By the way, what were you going to say about Lizzie?

SHE (*smiles*). She is in love.

HE. What?

SHE. She's secretly engaged.

HE. To whom?

SHE. To the boy next door.

HE. To that—ape? To that pie face?

SHE. I think it's quite serious.

HE. The child is only . . . nonsense!

SHE. She is not a child any more. She's . . . well, the same thing Robert is, I suppose. I wouldn't be surprised if one of these days the boy came to see you to ask for her hand.

HE. If he does, I'll shoot him.

SHE. But, darling . . .

HE. But she's only sixteen! Agnes, this is a nightmare!

SHE. But, sweetheart . . .

HE. She can't be in love, and certainly not with *that!*

SHE. Why not?

HE. After spending her whole life with me, she can't fall in love with something hatched out of an egg.

SHE. Are you suggesting that the only person the child will be allowed to fall in love with is a younger edition of yourself?

HE. Of course not. Don't be indecent. What I mean is that at least we should have given them taste! They should have inherited our taste!

SHE. Well, he seems to have inherited a taste for bourbon.

HE. I don't understand how you can joke about it. This happens to be the worst night of my life.

SHE. I'm not joking, darling. I just don't think that there's much point in us sitting up all night worrying ourselves sick about something we obviously can't do anything about until the morning. Come, go back to bed.

HE. You go to bed . . . I'll wait up for him.

SHE. Shall I make you a cup of tea?

HE. Tea! Do you know that we haven't had a single crisis in our life yet for which your ultimate solution wasn't a cup of tea?

SHE. I'm sorry. I was only trying to be sensible about it.

HE. I know you are. I apologize if I've said things that I didn't mean. (*Picks up the bourbon bottle and uncorks it with his left hand.*) I think what we both need is a swig of this. Have we got any glasses up here?

SHE. Only tooth-glasses. (HE *takes a swig, then with a horrified expression thrusts the bottle and cork into her hands and runs to the bathroom.*) Michael! (SHE *smells the bottle, grimaces.*)

HE (*rushing out of bathroom with a nauseated look on his face*). What is that?

SHE. Cod liver oil!

HE. Oh! (*Runs back into bathroom.*)

SHE (*takes handkerchief from pocket, wipes bottle*). How on earth did it get into this bottle?

HE. God knows! (*Re-enters to just outside bathroom door.* HE *carries a glass of water.*) I think that little monster must have been trying to set a trap for me! (*Runs back into bathroom.*)

SHE (*holding bottle up, puzzling over*

contents). Michael, wait a minute! (SHE *is interrupted by the sound of his gargling.*) I know! Well, this is the limit!

HE (*re-enters, wiping mouth with towel*). What?

SHE. Do you remember, three years ago, that he had to take a spoonful of cod liver oil every night and that he didn't want to take it in my presence? Of course I measured the bottle every morning, but he poured it into this!

HE. Agnes, do you mean to say that that stuff I swallowed is three years old?

SHE. The little monkey! Oh, now I am going to wait till he gets home!

HE. I think perhaps we'd better call the doctor. This stuff must be putrid by now.

SHE. You'll have to speak to him, Michael. This is one time that you'll have to speak to him. I . . . (*Hears something.*) Michael, there he is! (*Rises, goes to door.* HE *rushes to door, stops, returns to bench and picks up riding crop. Starts out.* SHE *stops him.*) No, Michael, not that! Don't go that far!

HE. Three-year-old cod liver oil! (HE *whips the air with the riding crop. Exits.* SHE *listens for a moment, very worried. Then she runs into the bathroom and leaves the bottle there. Re-enters, to door, listens, goes down to bench at foot of bed and sits on end of it, all the while muttering to herself.* HE *appears in the doorway, dejectedly holding his riding crop in his hand.* HE *looks offstage, incredulously.* SHE *turns to him.*)

SHE. Well, what did you say?

HE (*closes door; distracted, turns to her*). I beg your pardon?

SHE. What did you *say* to him?

HE. Oh—er—"Good morning."

SHE. Is that all?

HE. Yes.

SHE. Well, I must say! To go through all this rigmarole and then to end up with . . . I honestly think you could have said something more.

HE (*sits on sofa*). I couldn't.

SHE. Why not?

HE. He was wearing a top hat.

(HE *makes a helpless gesture and rests his head in his hands.* SHE *laughs, crosses to him and puts her arms about him, then kisses him on the top of his head.*)

CURTAIN

ACT THREE

SCENE ONE

1913. Late afternoon.

The same bedroom. The bed canopy has been changed, as have the drapes and articles of furniture. It is all in more conservative taste now.

As the curtain rises, SHE *is seated at the dressing table, holding a wedding bouquet that matches her gown and hat. After a moment,* HE *is heard humming the Wedding March.*

———

HE (*from dressing room*). Agnes! (*Hums a bit more, then whistles for her.* HE *enters, arranging his smoking jacket. Goes to foot of bed, humming again. Sees her.*) Oh, there you are. Your hat still on? Agnes!

SHE (*starts*). Yes?

HE. Hey! Are you asleep?

SHE (*sighs and smiles absently*). Yes . . .

HE. Come on, darling. The only thing to think is: little children grow up. Let's be glad she ended up so well.

SHE. Yes . . .

HE. Thank God, Robert is a boy. I couldn't stand to go through that a second time, to see my child abducted by such a . . . Oh, well, love is blind.

SHE (*putting down bouquet*). Michael.

HE. Yes? (*Opens humidor and picks up pipe.*) What is the matter with you? The whole day long you've been so . . . so strange.

SHE. How?

HE. You aren't ill, are you?

SHE. No.

HE. That's all right then. (*Starts filling his pipe.*) What did you want to say?

SHE. Today is the first day of Lizzie's marriage.

HE. It is. And?

SHE. And the last day of ours.

HE. Beg pardon?

SHE. I waited to tell you, perhaps too long. I didn't want to spoil your fun.

HE. My *fun*?

SHE. Yes. I haven't seen you so cheerful for ages.

HE. Well . . . I'm . . . For your sake I have made a fool of myself. For your sake I have walked around all these days with the face of a professional comedian, with a flower in my buttonhole and death in my heart! Do you know what I would have liked to do? To hurl my glass in the pie face of that bore, take my child under my arm—and as for that couple of parents-in-law . . . (*Looks heavenward.*) And now you start telling me you didn't want to spoil my fun! (*Searches pockets for match.*)

SHE. With the information that I am going away.

HE. You are what . . .

SHE. I'm going away.

HE. Huh?

SHE. Away.

HE. How do you mean?

SHE. Can't you help me just a little by understanding quickly what I mean?

HE. But, darling . . .

SHE. Michael, I'll say it to you plainly once, and please try to listen quietly. If you don't understand me after having heard it once, I'll . . . I'll have to write it to you.

HE. But, darling, we needn't make such a fuss about it. You want to have a holiday now the children have left the house. What could be more sensible? No need to announce it to me like an undertaker.

SHE. Not for a holiday, Michael—forever.

HE. You want to move into another house?

SHE. I want to go away from *you*.

HE. From me?

SHE. Yes.

HE. You want to . . . visit friends, or something?

SHE. Please, darling, stop it. You knew ages ago what I meant; please don't try and play for time. It makes it all so . . . so difficult.

HE. I don't know a damned thing. What have I done?

SHE. Nothing, nothing. You are an angel. But I am . . . not.

HE. Agnes, what is the matter with you?

SHE. I would appreciate it if you would stop asking me what is the matter with me. There never has been anything the matter with me, and there couldn't be less the matter with me now. The only thing is, I can't . . .

HE. Can't what?

SHE. Die behind the stove, like a domestic animal.

HE. Good Heavens . . .

SHE. You wouldn't understand. You are a man. You'll be able to do what you like until you are seventy.

HE. But my dear good woman . . .

SHE. I won't! Today I stopped being a mother; in a few years' time, perhaps next year even, I'll stop being a woman.

HE. And that's what you don't want?

SHE. I can't help it. That happens to be the way a benevolent Providence arranged things.

HE. But, darling, then it's madness.

SHE. I want to be a woman just once, before . . . before I become a grandmother. Is that so unreasonable?

HE. But my angel . . .

SHE. For Heaven's sake, stop angeling me! You treat me as if I were sitting in a wheelchair already. I want to live, can't you understand that? My life long I have been a mother; my life long I've had to be at somebody's beck and call; I've never been able to be really myself, completely, wholeheartedly. No, never! From the very first day you have handcuffed me and gagged me and shut me in the dark. When I was still a child who didn't even know what it meant to be a woman, you turned me into a mother.

HE. But, darling, Robert is only . . .

SHE. No, not through Robert, not through Lizzie, through yourself, your selfishness, your . . . Oh, Michael. (*Puts her hand on his shoulder.*) I didn't intend to say all this, honestly, I didn't. I only wanted to be honest and quiet and nice about it, but . . . but I can't help it. I can't! The mere way you look at me, now, this very moment! That amazement, that heartbreaking stupidity . . . Don't you feel yourself that there is nothing between us any more in the way of tenderness, of real feeling, of love; that we are dead, as dead as doornails, that we move and think and talk like . . . like puppets? Making the same gestures every day, the same words, the same kisses . . . Today, in the carriage, it was sinister. The same, the same, everything was the same; the coachman's boots behind the little window, the sound of the hooves on the pavement, the scent of flowers, the . . . I wanted to throw open the door, jump out, fall, hurt myself, I don't know what . . . only to feel that I was alive! I, I, not that innocent, gay child in front, who was experiencing all this for the first time, who played the part I had rehearsed for her . . . but I couldn't. I said "yes" and "no" and "darling" and "Isn't it cold," but I heard my own voice, and saw my own face mirrored in the little window, in the coachman's boots, like a ghost, and as I put my hat straight, to prove to myself that I wasn't a ghost, driving to my own burial, I remembered how, twenty-three years ago, I had looked at myself in exactly the same way, in the same window perhaps, to see if my bridal veil . . . (HER *voice breaks;* SHE *covers her face with her hands; goes up onto dais and falls onto bed, weeping.* HE *rises, puts his pipe into his pocket, goes up onto dais and puts his hands on her waist.*) No! Don't touch me! (*Sits up, gets handkerchief from bed-table drawer and wipes her eyes.*) I don't want to, I don't want to blame you for anything. You've always been an angel to me; you've always done whatever you could, as much as you could . . . (HE *sits on bed.*) although you never opened a door for me, always got on the streetcar first, never bought me anything nice . . . Oh, yes, I know, darling, you have given me many beautiful presents. But something real —if it had only been one book you didn't want to read yourself; or one box of chocolates you didn't like yourself, but nothing. Absolutely nothing. (*Shows him her hands.*) Look, just look! Only wrinkles and a wedding ring, and a new cash book for the household every year. (HE *takes her hand, raises it to his lips, kisses the palm of her hand.*) No, Michael. That's so easy, so mean, really. You've always known how to make that one little gesture, say that one little word . . . but now it doesn't work any more. This is what I've been trying to tell you all along. It's the most difficult part of all, and I don't know if I . . . No, I can't.

HE. Say it.

SHE. I'm afraid—I think—I'm sure I don't love you any more. I don't say this to hurt you, darling, honestly I don't. I only want you to understand. Do you? Do you a little?

HE. Yes. I think so.

SHE. I even remember the moment I realized I didn't love you. One clear, terrible moment.

HE. When was that?

SHE. About a month ago, one Sunday morning, in the bathroom. I came in to bring your coffee and you were rubbing your head with your scalp lotion. I said something about that boy's poems that you had given me to read; I don't remember

what I said—and then you said, "I could tell him where to put them" . . . with both hands on your head. (*Puts hands on her head.*) And then . . . then it was suddenly as if I were seeing you for the first time. It was horrible.

HE (*after a silence*). Where had you thought of going?

SHE. Oh, I don't know. I thought a room in a boarding house somewhere.

HE. Not a trip, abroad for instance?

SHE. Good Heavens, no.

HE. Why not?

SHE. Because I don't feel like it . . . (*Turns to him.*) You don't think that I . . . that there is something the matter with me?

HE. No.

SHE. Do you understand now why I *must* go away?

HE. Well, if I were to come into the bathroom with my head full of love lyrics, like you, only to see you rubbing your face with skin food or shaving your arm pits, I don't think I'd have been overcome by any wave of tenderness for you . . . but I wouldn't go and live in a boarding house.

SHE. That was not the point. The point was what you said.

HE. "I could tell him where to put them." H'm. You're sure that was the point?

SHE. Why?

HE. Who wrote those poems you were talking about?

SHE. Well, that boy . . . that boy, who keeps asking you what you think about his work.

HE. You liked what he wrote, didn't you?

SHE. Oh, yes. I thought it young, promising . . . honestly. It had something so . . . so . . .

HE. So . . . well?

SHE. Well, what?

HE. I seem to remember this same description, twenty-three years ago.

SHE. You aren't trying to tell me that I'm . . . ? I won't say another word to you! The very idea that I, with a boy like that, such a . . . such . . . It's just that the boy has talent! At least as much as you had, when you were still rhyming about gazelles with golden horns.

HE. I was rhyming about you.

SHE. He must be rhyming about somebody as well, but . . .

HE. Of course he is. About you, too.

SHE. Me?

HE. What did he write on the title page? "Dedicated in reverent admiration to the woman who inspired my master." Well, I have been his master only insofar that I wrote him a letter: "Dear Sir, I have read your poems twice. I would advise you to do the same." Still, I don't know. Perhaps I'm growing old-fashioned. After all, he's new school and all that. I should like to read those poems again. Have you got them here?

SHE. Yes.

HE. Where are they?

SHE (*gets poems from lower drawer of bedside table; walks to foot of bed and starts to hand him the poems, then stops*). You aren't going to make fun of them, are you?

HE (*takes out glasses, puts them on, takes poems from her*). Fun? Why should I? I think this occasion is serious enough for both of us to find out what exactly we're talking about. Perhaps you're right. Perhaps I need this lesson. Well, let's have it. (*Reads the title.*) "Flashing Foam—Jetsam on the Beach of Youth." H'm. That seems to cover quite a lot. First Sonnet: "Nocturnal Embrace."

SHE. Michael, if you're going to make a fool of this poor boy who is just starting, only because you. . . .

HE. Who is doing the starting here? Me! After thirty years I'm just starting to discover how difficult it is to write something that is worth reading, and I *shall* write something worth reading one day unless . . . well, "Nocturnal Embrace." (*Reads.*)
"We are lying in the double bed,
   On the windows have thrown a net
   The dead leaves of an acorn tree."
Do you understand why it has to be an acorn tree? Why not an oak?

SHE. Because it's beautiful. Because it gives atmosphere.

HE. I see. I'm sorry. (HE *reads.*)
"From a church tower far unseen,
   A solemn bell strikes twelve."
Well, now that rhyme could definitely be improved.
"From a church tower far unseen,
   A solemn bell strikes just thirteen."
(SHE *doesn't answer.* HE *reads on.*)
"Strikes twelve,
   O'er the darkened fields,
   The silent sea.

But then we start and clasp
   A frightened, sickening gasp,
   For a foot has stopped behind the
      door."
Now this I understand. No wonder they are startled. Suppose you're just busy clasping each other, and then a foot walks along the corridor and stops right outside your door . . . (HE *shudders.*)

SHE. I'm not laughing, if that's what you're after.

HE. That's not what he was after in any case, but let's see how it ends. (HE *reads.*)
"For a foot has stopped behind the
      door.
   Silence. Thumping. It's our hearts
   Waiting with our breath . . ."
Wondering where the other foot's got to, I suppose . . .

SHE. Michael, please stop it!

HE. Why? Am I his master or am I not? And has he had the cheek to dedicate this bad pornography to my Agnes or has he not?

SHE. He meant it for the best.

HE. Oh, now, did he really? Do you call that for the best, to turn the head of a woman, the best wife any man could wish himself, at the moment when she's standing empty-handed because she imagines her job is over? To catch her at a time when she can't think of anything better to do than to become young again and wants to start for a second time fashioning the first damn fool at hand into a writer like me?

SHE. But you don't need me any more.

HE. Oh, no? Well, let me tell you something. People may buy my books by the thousands, they may write me letters and tell me how I broke their hearts and made them bawl their damn heads off, but I know the truth all right. It's *you* who make me sing . . . and if I sing like a frog in a pond, it's not my fault.

(SHE *is so amused and relieved that she cries and laughs at the same time. The laughter gets the upper hand.*)

SHE. Oh, Michael!

HE. What are you laughing at?

SHE (*sitting on sofa beside him*). Oh, Michael . . . I'm not laughing. . . . I'm not laughing. (SHE *embraces him and sobs on his shoulder.*)

HE (*comforts her like a man who suddenly feels very tired*). I'll be damned if I understand that. (HE *rests his head on her shoulder.*)

CURTAIN

SCENE TWO

1925. Dawn.

Same bedroom, twelve years later. It is apparent that they are moving out—pictures have been taken off the walls, leaving discolored squares on the wallpaper; a stepladder leans against the wall of archway; all drapes have been removed with the exception of the bed canopy and spread on the fourposter which is the only piece of furniture remaining in the room. Several large suitcases, packed and closed.

AT RISE, HE *is heard messing about in the bathroom. Then* HE *comes out, humming and carrying toilet articles.* HE *goes to the suitcases, finds them shut, carries the stuff to the bed.* HE *goes again to the suitcases, opens one. It is full.* HE *slams the lid shut and fastens the locks, at the same time noticing that a small piece of clothing is left hanging out.* HE *disregards it and drags a second case on top of the first one, opens it, finds that it is fully packed as well. However,* HE *re-arranges the contents to make room for his toilet articles. As* HE *starts back to bed, he again notices the piece of clothing hanging out of the bottom case.* HE *looks toward the door, then leans down and rips off the piece of material, puts it in his pocket and walks up onto dais.* HE *picks up his toilet articles from the bed, turns, then drops them on the floor.* HE *mutters, "Damn!" and gets down on his hands and knees to pick them up. At that moment, when* HE *is out of sight of the door,* SHE *comes in carrying the little "God Is Love" pillow. The moment* SHE *realizes he is there,* SHE *quickly hides the pillow behind her back.*

SHE. What are you doing?

HE (*rises*). Packing.

SHE (*picks up knitting bag from floor at foot of bed and puts it with the suitcases*). Well, hurry up, darling. The car comes at eight and it's almost twenty of. What have you been doing all this time?

HE. Taking down the soap dish in the bathroom.

SHE. The soap dish? What on earth for?

HE. I thought it might come in useful.

SHE. But, darling, you mustn't. It's a fixture.

HE. Nonsense. Anything that is screwed on isn't a fixture. Only things that are nailed.

SHE. That's not true at all. The agent explained it most carefully. Anything that's been fixed for more than twenty-five years is a fixture.

HE (*hands her the soap dish*). Then I'm a fixture, too.

SHE. Don't be witty, darling. There isn't time.

HE (*seeing little pillow under her arm*). Hey! (SHE *stops.*) We don't have to take that little horror with us, do we?

SHE. No. (*Exits into bathroom.*)

HE (*picks up part of his toilet things*). What about the bed?

SHE (*offstage*). What?

HE. Are you going to unmake the bed or have we sold the blankets and the sheets with it? (*Starts packing toilet things.*)

SHE (*offstage*). What is it, dear?

HE. Have we only sold the horse or the saddle as well?

SHE (*re-enters, holding the little pillow*). Horse, what horse?

HE. What's to become of those things? (SHE *still does not understand.*) Have we sold the bed clothes or haven't we?

SHE. Oh, no, dear. Only the spread. I'll pack the rest. (*Puts little pillow under arm and strips pillow cases.*)

HE. In what? These suitcases are land-mines. Why are you nursing that thing? (SHE *mumbles something and tucks little pillow more firmly under her arm.* HE *goes up to her.*) Just what are you planning to do with it?

SHE. I thought I'd leave it as a surprise.

HE. A surprise?

SHE. Yes, for the new tenants. Such a nice young couple. (*Places pillow at the head of the bed.*)

HE. Have you visualized that surprise, may I ask?

SHE. Why?

HE. Two young people entering the bedroom on their first night of their marriage, uncovering the bed and finding a pillow a foot across with "God Is Love" written on it.

SHE (*picks up rest of toilet articles and newspaper from bed. Puts them down on dais, the newspaper on top.*) You've got nothing to do with it.

HE. Oh, I haven't, have I? Well, I have.

I've only met those people once, but I'm not going to make a fool of myself.

SHE. But, darling . . .

HE. There's going to be no arguing about it, and that's final. (*Snatches pillow and throws it on trunk. Mutters.*) God Is Love!

SHE (*stripping blanket and sheets from bed*). All right. Now, why don't you run downstairs and have a look at the cellar?

HE. Why?

SHE (*stuffs bed linen in pillow case*). To see if there's anything left there.

HE. Suppose there is something left there, what do you suggest we do with it? Take it with us? You don't seem to realize that the apartment won't hold the stuff from one floor of this house.

SHE. Please, darling, don't bicker. We agreed that it was silly to stay on here with all these empty rooms.

HE. But where are we going to put all this stuff?

SHE. Now, I've arranged all that. Why don't you go down and see if there's anything left in the wine cellar?

HE. Ah, now you're talking.

(HE *goes out.* SHE *twirls the pillow case tight and leaves it by the suitcases. Picks up the "God Is Love" pillow, returns to the bed, and places it on top of the regular bed pillows, then stands back and admires it. With one hand on bedpost,* SHE *glances over the entire bed and smiles fondly. Then straightens the spread, moves around to side, smooths out the cover, goes to foot of bed, stops, hears him coming; walks around again and quickly covers the "God Is Love" pillow with spread.*)

HE (*entering with champagne bottle*). Look what I've found!

SHE (*going to foot of bed and arranging the cover there*). What?

HE. Champagne! (*Blows dust from bottle.*) Must be one that was left over from Robert's wedding.

SHE. Oh.

HE. Have we got any glasses up here?

SHE. Only the tooth glasses.

HE (*sits on edge of bed*). All right, get them.

SHE. You aren't going to drink it now?

HE. Of course. Now, don't tell me this is a fixture! (*Tears off foil from bottle.*)

SHE. But, darling, we can't drink champagne at eight o'clock in the morning.

HE. Why not?

SHE. We'll be reeling about when we get there. That would be a nice first impression to make on the landlady!

HE. I'd be delighted. I'd go up to that female sergeant major and say, "Hiya! Hah! Hah!" (*Blows his breath in her face as in the First Act. The memory strikes them both. They stay for a moment motionless.* SHE *pats his cheek.*)

SHE. I'll go get those glasses. (SHE *exits into bathroom.*)

(HE *rises, throws the foil into the wastebasket at foot of bed, goes to suitcases and puts bottle on floor. Goes back to bed and looks for the rest of his toilet articles.* HE *pulls back the spread, picks up the "God Is Love" pillow, looks under it, tosses it back, looks under the other pillows, then suddenly realizes that the "God Is Love" pillow has been put back in the bed. Picks it up and calls.*)

HE. Agnes.

SHE (*offstage*). What?

HE. Agnes.

SHE (*re-enters carrying towel and two glasses*). What? Oh . . . (SHE *is upset when she sees what it is, and very self-conscious.*)

HE. Agnes, did you put this back in the bed?

SHE (*standing at bathroom door*). Yes.

HE. Why, for Heaven's sake?

SHE. I told you . . . I wanted to leave something . . . friendly for that young couple . . . a sort of message.

HE. What message?

SHE. I'd like to tell them how happy we'd been—and that it was a very good bed . . . I mean, it's had a very nice history, and that . . . marriage was a good thing.

HE. Well, believe me, that's not the message they'll read from this pillow. Agnes, we'll do anything you like, we'll write them a letter, or carve our initials in the bed, but I won't let you do this to that boy . . .

SHE. Why not? (SHE *puts glasses and towel on floor beside knitting bag, takes little pillow from him and goes up to bed.*) When I found this very same little pillow in this very same bed on the first night of our marriage, I nearly burst into tears!

HE. Oh, you did, did you? Well, so did I! And it's time you heard about it! When, on that night, at that moment, I first saw that pillow, I suddenly felt as if I'd been caught in a world of women. Yes, women! I suddenly saw loom up behind you the biggest trade union in the world, and if I hadn't been a coward in long woolen underwear with my shoes off, I would have made a dive for freedom.

SHE. That's a fine thing to say! After all these years . . .

HE. Now, we'll have none of that. You can burst into tears, you can stand on your head, you can divorce me, but I'm not going to let you paralyze that boy at a crucial moment.

SHE. But it isn't a crucial moment!

HE. It is *the* crucial moment!

SHE. It is not! She would find it before, when she made the bed. That's why I put it there. It is meant for her, not for him, not for you, for her, from me! (*Puts little pillow on bed as before.*)

HE. Whomever it's for, the answer is NO! (HE *takes the little pillow and puts it on the trunk again.* SHE *pulls the spread up over the bed pillows.*) Whatever did I do with the rest of my toilet things?

(SHE *picks them up from floor by bed, goes to him, hands them to him, puts newspaper in wastebasket, sets basket down near arch.* HE *is very carefully packing his things. When he is finished, he closes the lid to the suitcase, tries to lock it, but doesn't succeed.*)

HE. You'll have to sit on this with me. I'll never get it shut alone. (SHE *sits down beside him.*) Now, get hold of the lock and when I say "Yes," we'll both do—that. (HE *bounces on the suitcase.*) Ready? Yes! (*They bounce.* HE *fastens his lock.*) Is it shut?

SHE (*trying to fix catch*). Not quite.

HE. What do you mean, not quite? Either it's shut or it isn't.

SHE. It isn't.

HE. All right. Here we go again. Ready? Yes! (*They bounce again.*) All right?

SHE. Yes.

HE (*picks up champagne bottle*). Now, do we drink this champagne or don't we?

SHE (*picks up glasses, towel, packs them in knitting bag*). No.

HE. All right. I just thought it would be a nice idea. Sort of round things off. (*Puts champagne bottle back on floor.*) Well, what do we do? Sit here on the suitcase till the car comes, or go downstairs and wait in the hall?

SHE. I don't know. (HE *looks at her, then at the little pillow on trunk, then smiles at her anger.*)

HE. It's odd, you know, how after you have lived in a place for so long, a room gets full of echoes. Almost everything we've said this morning we have said before . . . It's the bed, really, that I regret most. Pity it wouldn't fit. I wonder how the next couple will get along. Do you know what he does?

SHE. He's a salesman.

HE. A salesman, eh? Well, why not? So was I. Only I realized it too late. The nights that I lay awake in that bed thinking how I'd beat Shakespeare at the game . . .

SHE. Never mind, darling, you've given a lot of invalids a very nice time. (*In his reaction, as* HE *turns to reply, the doorbell rings.*)

(HE *rises and looks out window. He goes to door, opens it.* SHE *rises and turns top suitcase up.* HE *puts bed linen under left arm, picks up top suitcase in left hand.* SHE *turns up the other suitcase and* HE *picks that one up in his right hand; turns to go.* SHE *quickly gets the knitting bag, stops him and tucks it under his right arm.* HE *exits.*

SHE *picks up purse, gloves, from off of trunk, then quickly takes the little pillow and goes to bed but stops suddenly, hearing him return, and hides the pillow under her coat.* HE *goes to trunk, leans over to grasp its handle, sees that the little pillow is not there, but proceeds to drag the trunk out. At the door, as* HE *swings trunk around,* HE *looks back at her.* SHE *is standing, leaning against the bedpost, pulling on her gloves. As soon as* HE *is out of sight,* SHE *hurriedly puts the pillow back into the bed and covers it.*

HE *re-enters, wearing his hat, picks up bottle of champagne, goes up to bed, drops hat on foot of bed, flings back the covers, picks up the little pillow and throws it to her side of the bed; then throws the bottle of champagne down on the pillow on his side and flips the spread back into place.* HE *picks up his hat and goes to her. They stand there for a moment, looking about the room.* HE *puts his hat on, smiles, leans down and hesitantly, but surely, picks her up.* SHE *cries, "Michael!"* HE *stands there for a moment, kisses her, then turns and carries her out of the room.*)

CURTAIN

SCCCC - LIBRARY
WITHDRAWN
4601 Mid Rivers Mall Drive
St. Peters, MO 63376

WITHDRAWN

THE SEVEN YEAR ITCH

George Axelrod

First presented by Courtney Burr and Elliott Nugent at the
Fulton Theatre, New York, on November 20, 1952,
with the following cast:

RICHARD SHERMAN   Tom Ewell
RICKY   Johnny Klein
HELEN SHERMAN   Neva Patterson
MISS MORRIS   Marilyn Clark
ELAINE   Joan Donovan
MARIE WHATEVER-HER-NAME-WAS
Irene Moore

THE GIRL   Vanessa Brown
DR. BRUBAKER   Robert Emhardt
TOM MACKENZIE   George Keane
RICHARD'S VOICE   George Ives
THE GIRL'S VOICE   Pat Fowler

ACT ONE. SCENE I: About eight o'clock on a summer evening.

SCENE II: Immediately following.

ACT TWO. SCENE I: Evening, the following day. SCENE II: Two
hours later.

ACT THREE. The following morning.

The action of the play takes place in the   nt of the Richard
Shermans, in the Gramercy Park section of ﹏﹏ ﹏ork City. The
time is the present.

Copyright, 1952, as an unpublished work by George Axelrod.

© Copyright, 1953, by George Axelrod.

Reprinted by permission of Random House, Inc.

CAUTION: Professionals and amateurs are hereby warned that THE SEVEN YEAR ITCH, being
fully protected under the copyright laws of the United States of America, the British
Empire including the Dominion of Canada and all other countries of the Copyright Union, is
subject to royalty. All rights, including professional, amateur, motion picture, recitation,
lecturing, public readings, radio broadcasting, and the rights of translation into foreign languages
are strictly reserved. All inquiries should be addressed to the author's agent, Daniel
Hollywood Associates, 101 West 55th Street, New York, N.Y. Particular emphasis is laid on the
question of readings, permission for which must be secured from the author's agent in
writing. Inquiries about reprinting should be sent to the publishers, Random
House, Inc., 457 Madison Avenue, New York 22.

The nonprofessional acting rights of THE SEVEN YEAR ITCH are controlled exclusively by
the Dramatists Play Service, Inc., 14 East 38th Street, New York 16, N.Y., without whose
permission in writing no amate

ST. MARY'S COLLEGE LIBRARY
O'FALLON, MISSOURI

GEORGE AXELROD, the thirty-year-old New York author of *The Seven-Year Itch,* is wholly a devotee of show business. He had served the noble cause of entertainment his entire adult life by the time he saw his fabulously successful comedy on the stage. Previously, his energies had gone mainly into the channels of radio and television, to which he has contributed nearly five hundred plays or approximations of plays, although he also wrote some novels and some revue sketches for the stage. The revue, on which he had collaborated with Max Wilk, was called *Curtain Going Up.* Unfortunately it was subtitled—much too accurately, he recalls—"People Running Out." He was also occupied with a radio show called *Grand Old Opry* and a "fancy saloon show" called *All About Love,* which the young author considered "a good deal" since the management for whom the show was put on "was nice about letting us drink on the arm." After all this experience, *"Itch,"* he recalls, "was an easy one." (These *memorabilia* are taken from the author's article in the January, 1954, issue of *Theatre Arts.*)

Encouraged by the success of his first bout with Broadway showmanship, which also resulted in the successful filming of *The Seven Year Itch,* Mr. Axelrod tried his luck again. It held out rather well. Although *Will Success Spoil Rock Hunter?* collected few cheers from the New York press, the more coveted approbation of Broadway's cash customers was not slow in coming and the author had a second hit with which to replenish the United States Treasury. Mr. Axelrod's father had collaborated on variety shows at Columbia University with Oscar Hammerstein II, but had retreated to the relative security of a business career. It seemed as if his son were wholeheartedly bent upon erasing the blot upon the Axelrod scutcheon caused by this defection from the theatre.

ACT ONE

SCENE ONE

The apartment of the RICHARD SHERMANS, *about half a block from Gramercy Park in New York City.*

We see the foyer, the living room and the back terrace of a four-room apartment —the parlor floor through—in a remodeled private house.

A flight of stairs on the back wall lead to the ceiling where they stop. In one of the earlier phases of remodeling, this apartment and the one above it were a duplex. But now they are rented separately and the ceiling is boarded up.

A door, also on the back wall, leads to the kitchen. French doors, right, open onto the terrace. The terrace, while it increases the rent about thirty dollars a month, is small and rather uninviting. It looks out into the back court and because of the buildings around it you get the feeling of being at the bottom of a well. From the terrace we see some of the skyline of the city and a good deal of the backs of the buildings across the court. On the terrace there is a chaise, a table and a few shrubs.

On the left wall of the living room are high, sliding doors which lead to the bedrooms and bath. There is a fireplace in the living room. The whole apartment has a summer look. The rugs are up and the summer slip covers are on the furniture. The living room contains a piano, bookshelves, a large radio phonograph and a liquor cabinet.

When the curtain rises it is about eight o'clock on an evening in July. It is a hot, airless night. It is not yet completely dark. It grows darker gradually through the scene.

RICHARD SHERMAN, *a young-looking man of thirty-eight, is lying on the chaise on the terrace. He wears a shirt, gabardine pants, loafers and no socks.*

It is hard to know what to say about RICHARD. *He has a crew haircut. He has a good job. He's vice-president in charge of sales at a twenty-five-cent publishing house. He made eighteen thousand dollars last year. He buys his clothes at Brooks.*

At the moment, he has moved a small, portable radio out to the table on the terrace and is listening to the first game of a twi-night double header between Brooklyn and Boston. He is listening to the game and drinking unenthusiastically from a bottle of Seven-Up.

At rise we hear the ball game softly on the radio. We have come in at a rather tense moment. The bases are loaded and Hodges is up. He bunts and is thrown out. RICHARD *is disgusted. He snaps off the radio.*

———

RICHARD (*rising*). Bunt? Two runs behind, the bases loaded and they send Hodges up to bunt! (*Shaking his head, he goes into the kitchen. He reappears carrying a bottle of raspberry soda. Still appalled*) Bunt, for God's sake! Well, what are you going to do? (*He looks around aimlessly for a moment.*) I'm hungry. Well, that's what comes of having dinner at Schrafft's! Schrafft's! I wanted to have dinner in the saloon across the street—but you can't have dinner in a saloon and then not . . . They don't like it. Oh, I suppose I could have ordered a drink and then not drunk it . . . But I figure it's easier just to eat at Schrafft's. (*He drops wearily onto the chaise.*) It's hard on a man when the family goes away. It's peaceful, though, with everybody gone. It's sure as hell peaceful. (*He settles back in the chaise and grins. Music sneaks in very softly, and the light on him dims to a spot.*) Ricky was really upset this morning when they left for the station. It was very flattering. I thought the kid was going to cry . . . (*He sits, smiling, remembering the scene. Dream lighting by the front door picks up* HELEN *and* RICKY *leaving.*)

RICKY. But what about Daddy? Isn't Daddy coming with us?

HELEN. Daddy'll come up Friday night.

RICKY. But, Mommy, why can't Daddy come up with us now?

HELEN. Poor Daddy has to stay in the hot city and make money. We're going to spend the whole summer at the beach but poor Daddy can only come up week ends.

RICKY. Poor Daddy . . .

HELEN. Daddy is going to work very hard. He's going to eat properly and not smoke like Dr. Murphy told him and he's going to stay on the wagon for a while like Dr. Summers told him, to take care of his nervous indigestion . . .

(*In the spot,* RICHARD *drinks from the bottle of raspberry soda. He is somewhat awed by the taste. He looks curiously at the label and then reads it.*)

RICHARD. "Contains carbonated water, citric acid, corn syrup, artificial raspberry flavoring, pure vegetable colors and preservative." Since I've been on the wagon, I've had one continuous upset stomach. (*He looks sadly at the bottle and drinks some more.*)

HELEN. And just to make sure Daddy's all right, Mommy is going to call Daddy at ten o'clock tonight . . .

RICKY. Poor Daddy . . .

(*The music fades and so does the dream light by the door.* HELEN *and* RICKY *disappear. The lighting returns to normal.*)

RICHARD (*coming out of his reverie*). Ten o'clock! I don't even know how I'm going to stay awake till ten o'clock! (*He stares moodily off into the growing dusk. Suddenly he notices something in an apartment across the court. He is momentarily fascinated and rises for a better look.*) Hey, lady! I know it's a hot night but . . . You sit out on this terrace, it's like having a television set with about thirty channels all going at once . . . Don't give me any dirty look, lady. I pay rent for this terrace. If you don't like it, pull your blind down! (*As she apparently does so*) Oh. Well, that's life. (*He yawns. Restlessly, he rises and wanders into the living room. He yawns again and then, suddenly, in midyawn, something occurs to him.*) Helen has a lot of nerve calling me at ten o'clock. It shows a very definite lack of trust. What's she think I'm going to do? Start smoking the minute she turns her back? Start drinking? Maybe she thinks I'm going to have girls up here! . . . You know, that's a hell of a thing! . . . Seven years, we've been married. And not once have I done anything like that. Not *once!* And don't think I couldn't have, either. Because I could have. But plenty . . . (*Music sneaks in and in dream lighting we see* HELEN *seated on the couch knitting. She laughs.*) Don't laugh. There's plenty of women who think I'm *pretty* attractive, for your information!

HELEN. For instance, who?

RICHARD (*indignant*). What do you mean, for instance, who? There've been plenty of them, that's all.

HELEN. Name one. (*There is a considerable pause while he thinks about this.*) Go ahead. Just one.

RICHARD. It's hard, I mean just offhand. There're plenty of them, though. (HELEN *laughs.* RICHARD *is stung.*) Well, there's Miss Morris, for instance. She's practically thrown herself at me. You should see the way she gives me the business every time she comes into my office. . . . (MISS MORRIS, *a sexy-looking blonde in a backless summer blouse and a skirt with an exaggerated slit, drifts into the scene carrying a dictation pad and pencil.*) She wears those backless things and she's always telling me it's so hot she's not wearing any underwear . . .

HELEN. It sounds perfectly sordid. Does she sit on your lap when she takes dictation?

RICHARD. Of course not!

(MISS MORRIS *sits on his lap.*)

MISS MORRIS. Good morning, Mr. Sherman.

RICHARD. Good morning, Miss Morris. (MISS MORRIS *runs her fingers through his hair and covers his cheek and neck with little kisses.*) That will be all. (MISS MORRIS *gets up and drifts away, giving him a private wave and a wink.*) I just happened to bring her up as an example, that's all. Just an example . . .

HELEN. I'm quite sure you're a great success with the stenographers in your office.

RICHARD. I could be a great success with a couple of your high-class friends if you're going to get snooty about it. Elaine, for instance. You may not know this, but for *two years* that dame has been trying to get me into the sack . . . (ELAINE, *a luscious-looking dame in a gold-lamé evening gown, appears on the terrace. She is carrying a glass of champagne.*) The night of your birthday party, she got loaded and went after me right here on the terrace . . . (*Dream lighting on* HELEN *dims out.*)

ELAINE (*coming up behind him and draping her arms around his neck*). Do you know something, darling? I look at you and I just melt. You must know that. Men always know . . . (*Quite casually she tosses her champagne glass off the terrace and grabs him and kisses him violently.*)

RICHARD. What's the matter? Are you crazy or something?

ELAINE. Let's get out of here, darling. Come on. Nobody'll even know we're gone . . .

RICHARD. You don't know what you're

saying!

ELAINE. Oh, yes, I do! Come on, darling! Let's be a little mad! (*She drifts away, giving him the eye as she goes.*)

RICHARD. Now, Elaine may be a little mad, but she's plenty attractive! And *she's* not the only one either! You probably don't even remember that Marie whatever-her-name-was, from the UN who was staying with the Petersons in Wesport last summer . . . We went swimming together one night. Without any bathing suits. You didn't know that, did you? It was that Saturday night the MacKenzies came up and I drove over to the beach by myself . . .

(MARIE WHAT-EVER-HER-NAME-WAS *has materialized beside him. A gorgeous girl in shorts and man's shirt.*)

MARIE (*speaking in rapid but somehow sexy-sounding French. She kicks off her shorts and as she talks begins to unbutton her shirt*). Hello, Dick. You too, without doubt, like to swim at night. I like it because the wearing of a bathing costume is unnecessary . . . You see that rock over there. The men leave their bathing costumes on one side and the girls leave theirs on the other. Sometimes the bathing costumes get mixed up.

RICHARD. I don't speak very good French, but I knew what she was talking about.

MARIE. The water at night is magnificent. There is a warmness and a feeling of black velvet. Especially when one is without bathing costume . . .

RICHARD (*weakly, unable to take his eyes off the buttons*). Mais oui. Mais oui.

MARIE. Don't peek now. I am not wearing a bathing costume.

(*Her shirt is almost off. The lights dim out just in time.*)

RICHARD (*with great self-righteousness*). We didn't do anything but swim. As a matter of fact, she was plenty disappointed we didn't do anything but swim. (*The lights have dimmed back to normal.*) So, all I can say is, in the light of the circumstances, I resent your calling me at ten o'clock to check up on me. If Helen is going to start worrying about me after seven years, it's pretty ridiculous, that's all. (*He rises and begins to pace nervously.*) And she is worried too. Even if she doesn't show it. I don't know. She probably figures she isn't as young as she used to be. She's thirty-one years old. One of these days she's going to wake up and find her looks

are gone. Then where will she be? No wonder she's worried. . . . Especially since I don't look a bit different than I did when I was twenty-eight. It's not my fault I don't. It's just a simple biological fact. Women age quicker than men. I probably won't look any different when I'm sixty. I have that kind of a face. Everybody'll think she's my mother. (*He sighs a mournful sigh and sinks into chair. The downstairs door buzzer rings.*) Now who's that? (*He goes to the foyer and presses the wall button. Then he opens the front door and peers out calling.*) Hello? Hello? Who is it?

GIRL'S VOICE (*off stage*). I'm terribly sorry to bother you . . .

RICHARD. What? (*Then as he sees her, he reacts.*) Oh. Oh. Well, hello . . .

GIRL'S VOICE (*off stage*). I feel so silly. I forgot my key. I locked myself out. So I pressed your bell. I hope you don't mind.

RICHARD. No. No. I don't mind. No trouble at all.

GIRL'S VOICE (*off stage*). I'm awfully sorry.

RICHARD. Don't worry about it. Any time. It's a pleasure.

GIRL'S VOICE (*off stage*). Thank you. Well, good-by . . .

RICHARD. Good-by . . . (*He closes the door. Then, after a moment opens it again and peers out, craning his neck to see up the stairs. He comes back inside, closes the door. He is shaking his head.*)

RICHARD. Where did *that* come from? I didn't know they made them like that any more. Oh, she must be the one who sublet the Kaufmans' apartment. I should have asked her in for a drink. Oh, no, I shouldn't have. Not me, kid. (*The telephone rings.* RICHARD *glances at his watch. Then hurries to answer it.*) Hello? Oh. Hello, Helen. I wasn't expecting you to call till ten. Is everything okay? . . . Good. . . . I was just sitting here listening to the ball game. They're two runs behind and they send Hodges up to bunt. . . . Yeah, I'm sleepy too. . . . The old place is pretty empty without you. I can't wait till Friday. Ricky okay? . . . He did? Well, he hasn't done that for a long time. It was probably just the excitement . . . That's nice. No, I don't . . . Who did you meet at the A&P? . . . What's Tom MacKenzie doing up there? . . . Look, my advice to you is avoid Tom MacKenzie like the plague. If you keep meeting him at the A&P, switch to Bohack's! . . . Look, are you sure everything else is all right? Good. . . . Me too. Yeah, I'm pretty tired myself. Good night . . . Night. (*He hangs up phone.*) Well, I might as well go to sleep myself. But I'm not sleepy. I suddenly realize I am not even a little bit sleepy. Maybe I could call up Charlie Peterson. No. That's a real bad idea. Under no circumstances should I call up Charlie Peterson. . . . I'll get in bed and read. God knows I've got enough stuff here I'm supposed to read. (*Picks up brief case and begins to take out manuscripts.*) I've got a conference with Dr. Brubaker tomorrow night. It might be amusing if I'd finished his miserable book before I talk to him about it. I don't know why every psychiatrist in America feels he has to write a book. And let's see what else. *The Scarlet Letter.* I read that in school. I don't have to read that again. But I'd better. Dr. Brubaker and *The Scarlet Letter.* It looks like a big night. (*Picks up soda bottle, notices that it is empty.*) Well, one more of these for a night cap and we're all set . . . (*Sighing heavily, he goes to kitchen for a fresh bottle of soda. He walks back out to the terrace and sits for a moment on the chaise. Automatically, he switches on the radio.*)

RADIO VOICE. . . . and so as we go into the last half of the eighth inning, Boston is leading, seven to four. In the last of the eighth, for Brooklyn, it'll be Robinson, Hodges and Furillo . . .

(*RICHARD reaches over and snaps off the radio.*)

RICHARD. Frankly, I don't give a damn. (*He rises and walks to the edge of the terrace, looking hopefully toward the apartment across the court.*)

(*At that moment there is a violent crash. Apparently from the sky, an enormous iron pot with a plant in it comes plummeting down. It lands with a sickening thud on the chaise where he was sitting a moment before.*)

(*RICHARD looks at it in horror-struck silence for a moment or two.*)

RICHARD. Look at that damn thing! Right where I was sitting! I could have been killed, for God's sake! (*Cautiously, with a nervous glance upward, he leans over to examine it.*) Jes-sus! (*He darts back inside, looks wildly around for a*

cigarette, *finally finds a crumbled pack in the pocket of a raincoat hanging in the hall closet. He starts to light it. Then, stops himself.*) I forgot—I'm not smoking. Oh, the hell with *that!* (*He lights the cigarette.*) I could have been killed. Just then. Like that. Right now I could be lying out there on the lousy terrace dead. I should stop smoking because twenty years from now it might affect my goddamn lungs! (*He inhales deeply with great enjoyment.*) Oh, that tastes beautiful. The first one in six weeks. (*He lets the smoke out slowly.*) All those lovely injurious tars and resins! (*Suddenly he is dizzy.*) I'm dizzy . . . (*He sinks to the piano bench, coughing.*) Another week of not smoking and I'd really've been dead! (*He picks up the bottle of soda and starts to take a slug of that. He chokes on it.*) The hell with this stuff too! (*He goes quickly to liquor cabinet and pours an inch or two of whiskey into a glass and belts it down. Then he mixes another one and carries it onto the terrace. He sets the drink on the table and in a very gingerly fashion tries to pick up the pot. It is real heavy.*) My God! This thing weighs a ton! I could have been killed! (*Suddenly, his anger finds a direction.*) Hey, up there! What's the big idea! You want to kill somebody or something? What do you think you're doing anyway?

GIRL'S VOICE (*from terrace above*). What's the matter?

RICHARD (*yelling*). What's the matter? This goddamn cast-iron chamber pot damn near killed me, that's what's the matter. What the hell! . . . Oh. Oh. It's you. Hello.

GIRL'S VOICE. What hap———Oh, golly! The tomato plant fell over!

RICHARD. It sure did.

GIRL'S VOICE. I'm terribly sorry.

RICHARD. That's okay.

GIRL'S VOICE. I seem to be giving you a terrible time tonight. First the door and now this. I don't know what to do . . .

RICHARD. Don't worry about it. (*He drains drink.*) Hey, up there!

GIRL'S VOICE. Yes?

RICHARD. I'll tell you what you can do about it. You can come down and have a drink.

GIRL'S VOICE. But that doesn't seem . . .

RICHARD. Sure it seems . . . Come on now . . . I insist . . .

GIRL'S VOICE. Well, all right . . .

RICHARD. I'll see you in a minute.

GIRL'S VOICE. All right. I'm really terribly sorry . . .

RICHARD. That's okay. Don't worry about it. As a matter of fact, it's wonderful. See you in a minute . . .

GIRL'S VOICE. All right . . .

(RICHARD *gallops frantically into the living room. The sound of the telephone brings him up short. He goes quickly to phone and answers it.*)

RICHARD. Hi there! Oh. Oh, Helen! (*With great, if somewhat forced enthusiasm.*) Well, Helen! This *is* a surprise! And a very pleasant one if I may say so! How *are* you? . . . Sure, sure I'm all right. Why shouldn't I be all right? In what way do I sound funny? I was just out on the terrace listening to the ball game. They're two runs behind and they send Hodges up to bunt . . . What? Sure . . . Sure I will. Your yellow skirt . . . (*As she talks on the other end of the phone he is reaching around straightening up the room.*) Yes, of course I'm listening to you. You want me to send up your yellow skirt, because you're having Tom MacKenzie and some people over for cocktails. Good old Tom! How is he? . . . No. I haven't been drinking. I just had . . . What? Your yellow skirt. In the hall closet. On a wire hanger. Sure. By parcel post. The first thing in the morning. Without fail. . . . No. I don't feel a bit funny. I was just out on the terrace listening to the ball game. They're two runs behind and they send Hodges up . . . Yes . . . well, good night. Good night. Night. (*He hangs up phone. Then, galvanized into action, he starts to straighten up the place. In the middle of this he realizes he looks a little sloppy himself and he dashes off through the bedroom doors. Music swells and the lights dim out.*)

CURTAIN

SCENE TWO

The music continues through the blackout.

After a moment the curtain rises and the lights dim back up to normal.

RICHARD *reappears from the bedroom. He has put on the jacket to his pants and is frantically tying his tie.*

He is visibly agitated. He starts to arrange the room for his guest. He pauses and turns off a lamp. Catches himself and quickly turns it back on again.

RICHARD. What am I *doing* anyway! . . . This is absolutely ridiculous. The first night Helen leaves and I'm bringing dames into the apartment. . . . Now take it easy. The girl upstairs damn near kills me with a cast-iron bucket. So I ask her down for a drink. What's wrong with that? . . . If Helen was here, she'd do the same thing. It's only polite. . . . And what the hell is she doing asking Tom MacKenzie over for cocktails, for God's sake! . . . Besides, I want to get another look at that girl. She must be some kind of a model or actress or something. (*He is busily arranging things. Laying out ice and soda. Puffing cushions. Picking up his socks.*) There is absolutely nothing wrong with asking a neighbor down for a drink. Nothing. . . . I just hope *she* doesn't get the wrong idea, that's all. If this dame thinks she's coming down here for some kind of a big time or something—well, she's got a big surprise. One drink and out! That's all! I'm a happily married man, for God's sake! (*He surveys his work.*) Maybe we ought to have a little soft music, just for atmosphere. (*He goes to phonograph and starts looking through records.*) Let's see. How about the Second Piano Concerto? Maybe Rachmaninoff would be overdoing it a little. This kid is probably more for old show tunes . . . (*He finds a record: "Just One of Those Things"—it is obviously an old one with a real thirties orchestration. He puts it on and listens to it for a moment or two with great satisfaction.*) That's more like it. The old nostalgia. Never misses. . . . *Never misses? What am I trying to do?* I'll call her and tell her not to come. That's all. Why ask for trouble? (*He starts for phone—stops.*) I don't even know her phone number. I don't even know her name. What am I doing? And what the hell is she doing? She could have been down here, had her lousy drink, and gone home already! . . . She's probably getting all fixed up. She'll probably be wearing some kind of a damn evening dress! . . . Oh, my God! What have I done? (*Very quickly he has another drink.*) If anything happens, it happens. That's all. It's up to her. She looked kind of sophisticated. She must know what she's doing. . . . I'm pretty sophisticated myself. At least I used to be. I've been married so damn long I don't remember. (*Suddenly, he becomes very polished.*) Drink? . . . Thanks. (*He pours himself a drink.*) Soda? . . . A dash. (*He toasts.*) Cheers. (*He leans nonchalantly against the piano. The "real" lighting begins to dim and music: "Just One of Those Things" fades in. The front door lights up and swings majestically open flooding the room with "dream light." He moves toward the door, almost dancing. In this particular flight of fancy he is very suave, very Noel Coward.*)

(THE GIRL *is standing in the doorway. She is an extraordinarily beautiful girl in her early twenties. She wears an extravagantly glamorous evening gown. There is a wise, half-mocking, half-enticing smile on her face. She looks like nothing so much as a Tabu perfume ad.*)

THE GIRL. I came.

RICHARD. I'm so glad.

THE GIRL. Didn't you know I'd come?

RICHARD. Of course. Of course I knew. Won't you come in?

THE GIRL. Thank you. (*She comes in. The door swings closed behind her.*)

(RICHARD *turns and we suddenly notice that he is wearing a black patch over one eye.*)

RICHARD. How lovely you are! Tell me, who are you? What is your name?

THE GIRL. Does it matter?

RICHARD. No. Of course not. I was a boor to ask.

THE GIRL. Why have you invited me here?

RICHARD (*spoken—like dialogue*). Oh, it was just one of those things. Just one of those foolish things. A trip to the moon—on gossamer wings . . .

THE GIRL. How sweet! Oh—a Steinway. Do you play?

RICHARD (*somewhat wistfully. Thinking, perhaps, of other, happier days*). Just a little now—for myself . . .

THE GIRL. Play something for me . . .

RICHARD. All right. You'll be sorry you asked . . .

THE GIRL. I'm sure I'll not . . .

RICHARD (*sitting at piano*). You'll see . . . (*Very dramatically he prepares to play. His preparations, while vastly complicated, do not, however, include raising*

the lid from the keys. Finally he begins to play—or rather pantomime playing on the closed lid. We hear, however, the opening bars of the C-Sharp Minor Prelude played brilliantly.*)

RICHARD (*playing*). I'm afraid I'm a little rusty. (*She is overcome. She sinks to the piano bench beside him. He turns to her.*) Tell me, what would you think, if, quite suddenly, I were to seize you in my arms and cover your neck with kisses?

THE GIRL. I would think: What a mad impetuous fool he is!

RICHARD. And if I merely continued to sit here, mooning at you, as I have done for the last half-hour—what would you think then?

THE GIRL. I would simply think: What a fool he is!

(RICHARD *takes her dramatically in his arms. They embrace. He kisses her violently. Music sweeps in and the lights black out.*)

(*In the darkness, we hear the sound of the door buzzer. It rings twice.*)

(*The lights dim back to normal.* RICHARD *is standing where we left him, leaning against the piano, lost in reverie. The buzzer rings again and he is jarred back to reality. He puts down his drink, and falling all over himself in nervous and undignified haste dashes to the door.*)

RICHARD. Come in . . . Come in . . .

(*Revealed in the doorway is* DR. BRUBAKER. *He is a round, somewhat messy, imperious man in his middle fifties. He carries a large brief case.*)

RICHARD (*completely taken aback*). Dr. Brubaker!

DR. BRUBAKER. Good evening. I hope I'm not late. Monday is my day at the clinic plus my regular patients and of course I'm on The Author Meets the Critic Friday night. I have been preparing my denunciation. I hope I haven't kept you waiting . . .

RICHARD. Look, Dr. Brubaker. Wasn't our . . .?

DR. BRUBAKER. Your office sent me the galleys of the last five chapters. I have them here with me. They are a mass of errors. I want to go over the whole thing with you very carefully.

RICHARD. Dr. Brubaker. I'm terribly sorry. Our appointment—I believe it was for tomorrow night . . .

(DR. BRUBAKER *has opened his brief case*

and has begun to spread papers all over the table.)

DR. BRUBAKER. I understand, of course, that your firm wishes to reach as wide an audience as possible. But I must protest— and very strongly—the changing of the title of my book from *Of Man and the Unconscious* to *Of Sex and Violence* . . .

RICHARD. Dr. Brubaker, I'm terribly sorry. I know how important this is. But I'm afraid our appointment was for tomorrow night.

DR. BRUBAKER. Tomorrow night?

RICHARD. Tuesday night. I understood it was definite for Tuesday night.

DR. BRUBAKER. Good Lord!

RICHARD. And I'm afraid I have someone coming in tonight. Another appointment. With an author. And she'll be here any minute. In fact she's late.

DR. BRUBAKER. Astounding. Really incredible.

RICHARD. It's probably my fault. I probably wasn't clear on the phone.

DR. BRUBAKER. No. No. You were perfectly clear . . .

RICHARD. I can't understand how it happened.

DR. BRUBAKER. Perfectly simple. Repressed uxoricide.

RICHARD. I beg your pardon?

DR. BRUBAKER. Repressed uxoricide. I came tonight because I want to murder my wife.

RICHARD. I see . . . Yes . . . Of course . . .

DR. BRUBAKER. A perfectly natural phenomenon. It happens every day.

RICHARD. It does?

DR. BRUBAKER. Certainly. Upon leaving the clinic and being faced with the necessity of returning to my home, I felt a strong unconscious impulse to murder my wife. Naturally, not wanting to do the good woman any bodily harm, my mind conveniently changed our appointment to tonight. What could be more simple?

RICHARD. I see . . .

DR. BRUBAKER. I am most sorry to have inconvenienced you, sir . . .

RICHARD. No, no. That's quite all right . . .

DR. BRUBAKER. And I shall see you here tomorrow evening.

RICHARD. Fine, Doctor. We could just as easily have our conference tonight—except that I do have this other author coming . . .

DR. BRUBAKER. Of course. I understand perfectly. Oh . . . Have you finished reading the book?

RICHARD. Well, I got as far as Chapter Three. The Meyerholt Case.

DR. BRUBAKER. Meyer*heim*. You read very slowly. Well, sir. Good night. (*He turns and starts to go. He is almost to the door when he stops and turns back.*) Sir. I trust you will not be offended if I call to your attention the fact that you are not wearing socks . . .

RICHARD (*looking down*). Good Lord!

DR. BRUBAKER. I was interested in knowing if you were aware of it? And I gather from your expression that you were not. In Chapter Three on Gustav Meyerheim I point out that he invariably removed his socks. Before he struck.

RICHARD. Before he *struck*?

DR. BRUBAKER. Yes. Surely you recall Meyerheim. A fascinating character! A rapist! I was certain you would be amused by the coincidence. Until tomorrow then, good evening. (*The* DOCTOR *bows and exits.*)

(RICHARD *looks helplessly down at his sockless ankles, then looks wildly around, finds his socks and struggles into them, muttering angrily as he does so something that sounds vaguely like: "Damn psychiatrists—write books—make a Federal case out of everything . . . I bet his wife is a nervous wreck—every time he takes off his socks she probably hides in the closet . . .")

(*As he is fighting his way into his loafers the door buzzer sounds.*)

RICHARD. Coming . . . (*He dashes to door and opens it.* THE GIRL *is standing in the doorway. Her real-life entrance is very different from the way he imagined it. She is quite lovely but far from the exotic creature he envisioned. She wears a checked shirt and rolled dungarees. She looks at him for a moment and then smiles tentatively.*)

THE GIRL. Hi.

RICHARD (*he looks at her blankly for an instant*). Hi.

THE GIRL. Can I come in?

RICHARD. Sure . . . I mean, of course. Please do.

THE GIRL. I'm sorry I took so long but I've been watering the garden. I promised the Kaufmans I'd take good care of it, and I'm afraid I kind of neglected it. I didn't even find the hose until tonight.

RICHARD. I didn't know the Kaufmans had a garden . . .

THE GIRL. Oh, yes. They do.

RICHARD. It must be very nice.

THE GIRL. It is. But it's a lot of work. Before I found the hose I'd been using the cocktail shaker—that was the only thing I could find . . .

RICHARD. The cocktail shaker . . .

THE GIRL. Yes. They have a big glass one. It must hold about a gallon. I'm just sick about the tomato plant. Did it survive, do you think?

RICHARD. I really don't know. We could look at it, I suppose. It's out on the terrace. Right where it landed.

THE GIRL. That's awful . . . I can't figure out how it happened . . .

(RICHARD leads way to terrace.)

RICHARD. It's right there. I haven't touched it . . .

THE GIRL. Golly, look at that! I'll pay for it, of course. Do you think you could lift it up . . . ?

RICHARD. Sure. (He lifts the pot off the chaise with a great deal of effort.) This damn thing weighs a ton . . . There . . .

THE GIRL. I just thought. If you'd been sitting in that chair . . . When it fell, I mean. It might have, well—practically killed you . . .

RICHARD. That occurred to me, too.

THE GIRL. I'm really awfully sorry. It's probably criminal negligence or manslaughter or something. You could have sued somebody. Me, probably. Or your family could have. Of course I don't know what they would have collected. If they'd sued me, I mean. But anyway, they'd have had a very good case.

RICHARD. There's no use getting all upset. I wasn't sitting there, thank God, so it's all right. Look, I asked you down for a drink. Would you like one? I mean you really don't look old enough to drink . . .

THE GIRL. I do, though. I drink like a fish. Do you have Scotch?

RICHARD. Sure. At least I'm pretty sure I do. I've been drinking something for the last half hour. I'm not sure now what it was. I was a little upset . . .

THE GIRL (following him back into the living room). I don't blame you. You could have been killed, practically. I feel just terrible about it. I mean . . .

RICHARD. Let's don't start that again.

Let's just have a drink.

THE GIRL. All right. I'm glad you're taking it this way. You have every right to be just furious. I know I would be. If somebody practically dropped a tomato plant on my head.

RICHARD. Let's see, what I *was* drinking? (*Picks up glass and tastes it.*) Bourbon. But we do have Scotch around here somewhere. Yeah—here we are. How do you like it?

THE GIRL. Scotch and soda, I guess. That's what you're supposed to say, isn't it? Back home the boys drink Scotch and Pepsi-Cola a lot. Before I knew anything at all, I knew *that* was wrong.

RICHARD. That's about as wrong as you can get, yes.

THE GIRL. I knew it was. When I was very young I liked it, though. It sort of killed the taste of the Scotch.

RICHARD (*mixing drink*). I can see how it would tend to do that.

THE GIRL. Do you have a cigarette around? I left mine upstairs.

RICHARD. Oh, yes. Sure. I'm sorry. Right here. (*He takes the crumpled pack from his pocket. There is one left in it.*) It may be a little stale. I haven't been smoking. In fact, before tonight, I hadn't had a cigarette in six weeks.

THE GIRL. That's wonderful! I wish I had the will power to stop. I don't, though. I smoke like a chimney. Sometimes three packs a day.

RICHARD. My God! That's terrifying.

THE GIRL. I know. It doesn't seem to affect me, though. I guess I'm pretty healthy. What made you start aga—Oh. I'll bet you started smoking after the plant fell down. To steady your nerves.

RICHARD. Well, something like that.

THE GIRL. Now I really *do* feel awful. If I'd just had the sense to move it off the wall. Or call the janitor and have him move it. It's pretty heavy. . . . Oh, I just feel . . .

RICHARD. Please, now, that's enough. Let me get some more cigarettes. I think there's an unopened carton out in the kitchen. Excuse me a minute . . . (*He exits into the kitchen.*)

(THE GIRL *looks around the apartment then drifts over to the piano. She hits a random note or two.* RICHARD *reappears.*)

THE GIRL. Do you play the piano?

(*For one mad instant,* RICHARD *consid-*

ers the question. The faraway "Just-a-little-now-for-myself" look comes into his eye. But he quickly suppresses it.)

RICHARD (*truthfully*). I'm afraid not. I'm tone deaf. My wife plays, though . . .

THE GIRL. Oh, you're married?

RICHARD. Yes. I am.

THE GIRL. I knew it! I could tell. You *look* married.

RICHARD. I do?

THE GIRL. Mmm! It's funny. Back home practically nobody was married. And in New York everybody is. Men, I mean.

RICHARD. That's a remarkable observation.

THE GIRL. It's really true.

RICHARD. I guess so. I never really thought about it.

THE GIRL (*as he hands her drink*). Thanks. I think about it quite a lot. This is good. Do you mind if I put my feet up? I'll take my shoes off.

RICHARD. No. Of course not. Go right ahead. Make yourself comfortable.

THE GIRL. Your wife is away for the summer, isn't she?

RICHARD. Yes, as a matter of fact she is. How did you know?

THE GIRL. They all are. It's really amazing.

RICHARD. They *all* are?

THE GIRL. Mmm. Everybody's wife. Back home practically nobody goes away for the summer. Especially anybody's wife.

RICHARD. Have you been away long? In New York, that is?

THE GIRL. Oh, years. Almost a year and a half. It seems like years. I love it. Especially now that I've got my own apartment. When I lived at the club I didn't like it so much. You had to be in by one o'clock. Now I can stay out all night if I want to. I was really glad when they practically asked me to leave.

RICHARD. Why did they practically ask you to leave?

THE GIRL. It was so silly. I used to do modeling when I first came to New York and when this picture of me was published in *US Camera* they got all upset. You should have seen Miss Stephenson's face. She was the house mother.

RICHARD. What was the matter with the picture?

THE GIRL. I was nude.

RICHARD. Oh.

THE GIRL. On the beach with some drift-wood. It got honorable mention. It was called "Textures." Because you could see the three different textures. The driftwood, the sand and me. I got twenty-five dollars an hour. And it took hours and hours, you'd be surprised. And the first day the sun wasn't right and I got paid for that too.

RICHARD. That seems only fair.

THE GIRL. Sure. You get paid from the time you're called. No matter how long it takes to make the picture. But I don't do modeling any more. Since I got this steady job . . .

RICHARD. Now you have a steady job?

THE GIRL. I take in washing . . .

RICHARD. What?

THE GIRL. That's just a joke. I'm on this television program. The commercial part. First I wash my husband's shirt in *ordinary* soap flakes. Then I wash it with Trill. So when people ask me what I do I always say I take in washing. I'm on for a minute and forty-five seconds. It's really a very good part . . .

RICHARD. Oh, so you're an actress. Is that it?

THE GIRL. Mmm. It's really very interesting. People don't realize, but every time I wash a shirt on television, I'm appearing before more people than Sarah Bernhardt appeared before in her whole career. It's something to think about.

RICHARD. It certainly is.

THE GIRL. I wish *I* were old enough to have seen Sarah Bernhardt. Was she magnificent?

(RICHARD *is somewhat shaken by this question. For a moment he sits there, grinning weakly.*)

RICHARD. I really wouldn't know. I'm not quite that old myself . . .

THE GIRL. I guess you're really not, are you?

RICHARD. I am thirty-nine. Or I will be the day after tomorrow. At the moment I'm still only thirty-eight.

THE GIRL. The day after tomorrow?

RICHARD. That's right.

THE GIRL. Isn't that amazing? We were born under the same sign. I was twenty-two yesterday. I didn't do anything about it, though. I didn't even tell anyone. Oh, I did one thing. I bought a bottle of champagne. I thought I'd sit there and drink it all by myself . . .

RICHARD. That sounds absolutely sad . . .

THE GIRL. Oh, no. It would have been fun. Sitting in my own apartment drinking champagne. But I couldn't get the bottle open. You're not supposed to use a corkscrew. You're supposed to work the cork loose with your thumbs. I just couldn't seem to do it. I suppose I could have called the janitor or something. But, somehow, I didn't feel like calling the janitor to open a bottle of champagne on my birthday. Look, I got blisters on both thumbs. Well, not really blisters, but I sort of pulled the thumb part away from the nail . . .

RICHARD. It's not really a matter of brute force. It's more of a trick. (*Demonstrating with thumbs*) You kind of get one side and then the other and it finally works loose. . . . You have to have strong thumbs, though . . .

THE GIRL. I've got a wonderful idea. Let me go up and get it. It's just sitting there in the ice box. We could both drink it. Since we both have birthdays. If you can really get it open . . .

RICHARD. I'm pretty sure I could get it open—but I don't want to drink your . . .

THE GIRL. It would be fun. After I couldn't get it open I sort of lost interest in sitting up there and drinking it alone. Let me go up and get it and we'll have a double birthday party. It's very good champagne. The man said.

RICHARD. I don't really think . . .

THE GIRL. I told him to be sure and give me very good champagne. Because I couldn't tell the difference myself. Wouldn't you like to?

RICHARD. Sure. As a matter of fact, I'd love to. I think we've got some champagne glasses in the kitchen . . .

THE GIRL. Okay. I'll go up and get it. I'll be right back. Should I bring the potato chips too?

RICHARD. Sure. Let's shoot the works!

THE GIRL. That's just the way I felt. I'll be right back.

RICHARD. Okay.

THE GIRL. See you in a minute . . . (*She exits, closing the door behind her.*)

(RICHARD *stares after her, somewhat bewildered. He picks up his glass, drains it, shakes his head, picks up her glass and starts toward the kitchen. Suddenly, he stops and turns back, a reflective expression on his face.*)

RICHARD. *US Camera* . . . (*He puts down the glasses and goes to the bookshelf. He looks for a moment and then finds what he is looking for. He takes down a book. It is a very large book, very clearly marked:* US Camera. *He begins, in a casual way, to riffle through the pages. Muttering*) News events . . . Children and Animals . . . The Human Body . . . (*He turns the pages slowly and then suddenly stops. He stares. He closes the book, puts it back on the shelf, picks up the glasses and goes swiftly into the kitchen. After a moment he comes back again, carrying two champagne glasses. He polishes them, sets them down, starts for the book and stops himself. Instead he pours a little whiskey into one of the champagne glasses, gulps it down, then wipes it out with his handkerchief. Finally he pulls himself together.*) Let's see . . . Birthday party! (*He starts to fix things up a little bit. Goes to phonograph and looks through records.*) Show tunes . . . (*He puts on a record:* "Falling in Love with Love.") In seven years I never did anything like this! In another seven years I won't be able to.

(*On this sobering thought, he sits down and stares moodily into space—the music from the record fades softly down.*)

HIS VOICE. Hey, Dick. Dickie boy . . .

RICHARD. Yeah, Richard?

HIS VOICE. What do you think you're doing?

RICHARD. I don't know. I don't know what I'm doing.

HIS VOICE. This kid is just a little young, don't you think?

RICHARD. Look, let me alone, will you?

HIS VOICE. Okay. You know what you're doing.

RICHARD. No, I don't. I really don't.

HIS VOICE. Relax. You're not doing anything. Even if you wanted to—you haven't got a chance . . .

RICHARD. Oh yeah? That's what you think. She seems to like me. She seems kind of fascinated by me.

HIS VOICE. She thinks you're that nice Sarah Bernhardt fan who lives downstairs. You're getting older, boy. You got bags under your eyes. You're getting fat.

RICHARD. Fat? Where?

HIS VOICE. Under your chin there. You're getting a martini pouch. And that crewcut stuff! You're not kidding anybody. One of these mornings you're going to look in the mirror and that's all, brother.

The Portrait of Dorian Gray.

(RICHARD *examines himself nervously in the mirror. He is only slightly reassured.*)

RICHARD. Look, pal. I'm going to level with you. This is a real pretty girl—and, as we pointed out, I'm not getting any younger—so . . .

HIS VOICE. Okay, pal. You're on your own . . .

(*He stands there for a moment of nervous indecision. The buzzer sounds. He decides—and with a new briskness in his step heads gaily for the door. He opens the door, admitting the girl. She comes in. She has changed to a sophisticated cocktail dress. She carries champagne and a bag of potato chips.*)

THE GIRL. Hi. I'm sorry I took so long. I thought I ought to change. I got this dress at Ohrbach's. But I don't think you could tell, could you?

RICHARD. You look lovely. (*She reacts slightly, sensing a difference in his tone.*)

THE GIRL. Thank you. Here's the champagne. You can see where I was working on it . . .

RICHARD. Let me take a crack at it. (*He takes bottle and begins to thumb cork.*) This is a tough one . . .

THE GIRL. Should I do anything?

RICHARD. I don't think so. Just stand well back . . . (*He struggles with cork.*)

THE GIRL. We could call the janitor. He's probably got some kind of an instrument . . .

RICHARD (*through clenched teeth as he struggles*). No—let's—keep—the janitor out of this . . . Damn it . . . This thing is in here like . . .

THE GIRL. I told you. You can imagine what I went through. On my birthday and everything.

RICHARD (*he stops to rest*). You know, this is just a lot of damn chi-chi nonsense. They could put a regular cork in this stuff and you could just pull it with a corkscrew . . . (*He attacks it again.*) Come on, you stinker! . . . Hey—I think—watch out—maybe you better get a glass just in case she . . . (*The cork finally pops.*) Catch it! Catch it! (*She catches it.*)

THE GIRL. Got it! Boy, you sure have powerful thumbs . . .

RICHARD (*he is rather pleased by this*). I used to play a lot of tennis . . .

THE GIRL. Do you think it's cold enough?

I just had it sitting in the ice box . . .

RICHARD. It's fine . . . Well, happy birthday.

THE GIRL. Happy birthday. (*They touch glasses and drink.*) Is it all right? I mean is that how it's supposed to taste . . . ?

RICHARD. That's how.

(*She takes another tentative taste.*)

THE GIRL. You know, it's pretty good. I was sort of afraid it would taste like Seven-Up or something . . .

RICHARD. Hey, I forgot . . . (*He leans forward and plants a quick, nervous kiss on her forehead.*) Birthday kiss. Happy Birthday.

THE GIRL. Thank you. Same to you.

RICHARD. Maybe we ought to have some music or something. Since this a party . . .

THE GIRL. That's a good idea . . .

RICHARD. I've got about a million records here. We can probably find something appropriate. Ready for some more?

THE GIRL. Not quite yet.

(*He refills his own glass.*)

THE GIRL. I've kind of stopped buying records. I mean I didn't have a machine for so long. Now that I've got one again—or anyway the Kaufmans have one—I'm all out of the habit . . .

RICHARD. Do you like show tunes?

THE GIRL. Sure. Do you have *The King and I?*

RICHARD. I'm afraid I don't. That's a little recent for me. I've got mostly old Rodgers and Hart and Cole Porter and Gershwin. . . . How about this one? From *Knickerbocker Holiday*. (*He is offering a prized possession: the Walter Huston recording of "September Song." He puts it on and they listen for a moment in silence.*)

THE GIRL. Oh, I love that. I didn't even know it was from a show or anything. I thought it was just a song . . .

RICHARD. Walter Huston sang it. He had a wooden leg—in the show. You better have some more champagne. It's really very good. (*He puts a little more in her glass which is still half-full. He refills his own. She takes off her shoes.*)

THE GIRL. This is pretty nice . . .

RICHARD. Isn't it? It's a lot better than sitting out there listening to the ball game. Two runs behind and they send Hodges up to bunt!

THE GIRL. Is that bad?

RICHARD. It's awful.

THE GIRL. I didn't know. I was never

very good at baseball. I was going to wash my hair tonight. But after I got through with the garden I just didn't feel like it.

RICHARD. I was going to bed and read *Of Sex and Violence* and *The Scarlet Letter.* We're publishing them in the fall and I'm supposed to read them.

THE GIRL. You're a book publisher?

RICHARD. In a way. I'm the advertising manager for a firm called Pocket Classics. Two bits in any drugstore. I'm supposed to figure out a new title for *The Scarlet Letter.* They want something a little catchier . . .

THE GIRL. I think I read *The Scarlet Letter* in school . . . I don't remember much about it . . .

RICHARD. Neither do I. I sent a memo to Mr. Brady—he's the head of the company —advising him not to change the title. But we had the title tested and eighty per cent of the people didn't know what it meant. So we're changing it . . . (*He gets up and fills glass again.*) Do you know what Mr. Brady wanted to call it? (*She shakes her head.*) *I Was an Adulteress.* But he's not going to, thank God. And do you know why? Because we had *it* tested and sixty-three per cent of the people didn't know what *that* meant. I wish you'd drink some more of your champagne . . .

THE GIRL. No, thanks . . . (*She rises and drifts over to the bookcase.*) You've certainly got a lot of books . . .

RICHARD. There's cases more in the closets . . .

THE GIRL (*suddenly*). Oh! Look! You've got *US Camera!*

RICHARD (*a little flustered*). Do we? I didn't even know it. How about that! *US Camera!*

THE GIRL (*she takes it down*). I bet I bought a dozen copies of this. But I don't have a single one left. Boys and people used to keep stealing 'em . . .

RICHARD. I can't think why . . .

THE GIRL. Did you ever notice me in it? It's a picture called "Textures."

RICHARD. I'm afraid I didn't . . .

THE GIRL. I told you about it, don't you remember? See, that's me, right there on the beach. My hair was a little longer then, did you notice?

RICHARD. No, actually—I didn't . . .

THE GIRL. And of course I've taken off some weight. I weighed 124 then. Gene Belding—Gene took the picture—used to call it baby fat.

RICHARD. Baby fat?

THE GIRL. Mmm! I'm much thinner now . . .

(*They both study the picture for a moment.*)

RICHARD. This was taken at the beach?

THE GIRL. Mmm . . .

RICHARD. *What beach?*

THE GIRL. Right on Fire Island . . . Oh . . . I see what you mean. It was taken very early in the morning. Nobody was even up yet.

RICHARD. Just you and Miss Belding?

THE GIRL. *Mr.* Belding. Gene Belding. With a G . . .

RICHARD. Oh. Well, it certainly is a fine picture.

THE GIRL. I'll autograph it for you if you want. People keep asking me to . . .

RICHARD (*weakly*). That would be wonderful. . . . Maybe we'd better have some more champagne . . .

THE GIRL. Good. You know, this is suddenly beginning to feel like a party . . . (*He refills her glass which is only half-empty and fills his own all the way, emptying the bottle.*) It was awfully sweet of you to ask me down here in the first place . . . (*He drains his glass of champagne— looks at her for a moment.*)

RICHARD. Oh, it was just one of those things. Just one of those foolish things. A trip to the moon—on gossamer wings . . . Do you play the piano?

THE GIRL. The piano?

RICHARD. Yeah. Somebody should play the piano. Do you play?

THE GIRL. I really don't. Do you?

RICHARD. Just a little. For myself . . .

THE GIRL. *You* play then . . .

RICHARD. You'll be sorry you asked . . . (*He sits at piano and after a very impressive moment begins to play "Chopsticks." She listens and is delighted.*)

THE GIRL. Oh! I was afraid you could *really* play. I can play *that* too!

(*She sits on the bench beside him and they play "Chopsticks" as a duet. When they finish:*)

RICHARD. That was lovely . . . (*His manner changes.*) Tell me, what would you say if, quite suddenly, I were to seize you in my . . . Hey, come here . . . (*He reaches over and takes her in his arms.*)

THE GIRL. Hey, now wait a minute . . .

(*For a moment they bounce precariously*

around on the piano bench, then RICHARD *loses his balance and they both fall off knocking over the bench with a crash and landing in a tangle of arms and legs.*)

RICHARD (*panic-stricken*). Are you all right? I'm sorry— I don't know what happened—I must be out of my mind . . .

THE GIRL. I'm fine . . .

RICHARD. I don't know what happened . . .

THE GIRL. Well, I think I'd better go now . . . (*Putting on her shoes.*)

RICHARD. Please don't . . . I'm sorry . . .

THE GIRL. I'd better. Good night . . .

RICHARD. Please . . . I'm so sorry . . .

THE GIRL. That's all right. Good night. (*She goes, closing the door behind her.*)

(RICHARD *looks miserably at the door. Then turns and kicks viciously at the piano bench. He succeeds in injuring his toe. Sadly, still shaking his wounded foot, he limps to the kitchen and reappears a moment later with a bottle of raspberry soda. He goes to the phonograph and puts on "September Song." He listens to it with morbid fascination. In a melancholy voice he joins Mr. Huston in a line or two about what a long, long while it is from May to December. He shakes his head and crosses sadly to the terrace. He stands there—a mournful figure clutching a bottle of raspberry soda.*)

(*As he stands there, a potted geranium comes crashing down from the terrace above and shatters at his feet.*)

(*He does not even bother to look around. He merely glances over his shoulder and says:*)

RICHARD (*quietly*). Oh, now, for God's sake, let's not start that again . . .

THE GIRL'S VOICE (*from above*). Oh, golly! I was just taking them in so there wouldn't be another accident. I'm really sorry . . . I mean this is awful . . . I could have practically killed you again . . .

RICHARD. It doesn't matter . . .

THE GIRL'S VOICE (*from above*). I'm really sorry. It was an accident . . . Are you all right . . . ?

RICHARD. I'm fine.

THE GIRL'S VOICE (*from above*). Well, good night . . .

RICHARD. Good night . . .

THE GIRL'S VOICE (*from above*). Good night. See you tomorrow, maybe . . .

RICHARD. Huh? (*He straightens up.*) Yeah! I'll see you tomorrow!

THE GIRL'S VOICE (*from above*). Good night!

(*He starts to drink from the soda bottle. Stops himself. Puts it down in disgust. Then strides back to living room with renewed vigor. He goes to the liquor cabinet and begins to pour himself another drink. From the phonograph comes the happy chorus of "September Song."*)

(RICHARD, *a peculiar expression on his face, sings cheerfully with the record as:*)

THE CURTAIN FALLS

ACT TWO

SCENE ONE

The same.

It is early evening the following day. RICHARD, *back in full control and very businesslike, is deep in conference with* DR. BRUBAKER.

Both are somewhat tense and it is evident that the conference has been proceeding with difficulty. The DOCTOR *is seated amid a litter of papers and galley sheets.* RICHARD *holds a duplicate set of galleys. As the curtain rises* RICHARD *clears his throat and prepares to renew his attack.*

———

RICHARD. On page one hundred and ten, Doctor, if we could somehow simplify the whole passage . . .

DR. BRUBAKER. Simplify? In what way simplify?

RICHARD. In the sense of making it—well —simpler. Both Mr. Brady and I have gone over it a number of times, and, to be perfectly frank with you, neither of us has any clear idea of what it's actually about . . .

DR. BRUBAKER. Your Mr. Brady, sir, is, if I may also speak with frankness, a moron.

RICHARD. It is Mr. Brady's business, as an editor, to keep the point of view of the average reader very clearly in mind. If something is beyond Mr. Brady's comprehension, he can only assume that it will also be over the head of our readership.

DR. BRUBAKER. It was, I take it, at Mr. Brady's suggestion that the title of my book was changed from *Of Man and the Unconscious* to, and I shudder to say these words aloud, *Of Sex and Violence* . . .

RICHARD. That is correct. Mr. Brady felt that the new title would have a broader popular appeal.

DR. BRUBAKER. I regret to inform you, sir, that Mr. Brady is a psychopathic inferior . . .

RICHARD. Cheer up, Doctor. If you think you've got troubles, Mr. Brady wants to change *The Scarlet Letter* to *I Was an Adulteress*. I know it all seems a little odd to you—but Mr. Brady understands the twenty-five-cent book field. Both Mr. Brady and I *want* to publish worthwhile books. Books like yours. Like *The Scarlet Letter*. But you must remember that you and Nathaniel Hawthorne are competing in every drugstore with the basic writings of Mickey Spillane.

(*As* DR. BRUBAKER *is unacquainted with this author,* RICHARD's *bon mot gets no reaction.*)

DR. BRUBAKER. This is therefore why my book is to be published with a cover depicting Gustav Meyerheim in the very act of attacking one of his victims . . . (DR. BRUBAKER *has picked up a large full-color painting of the cover of his book which shows in lurid detail a wild-eyed man with a beard attempting to disrobe an already pretty-well disrobed young lady. It also bears the following line of copy: "Hotter Than the Kinsey Report." Both regard the cover for a moment.*)

RICHARD (*with a certain nervous heartiness*). I must take the responsibility for the cover myself, Doctor . . .

DR. BRUBAKER. And also for making Meyerheim's victim—all of whom incidentally, were middle-aged women—resemble in a number of basic characteristics, Miss Marilyn Monroe?

RICHARD. I'm afraid so, Doctor. Don't you think there would be something just a little bit distasteful about a book jacket showing a man attempting to attack a middle-aged lady?

DR. BRUBAKER. And it is less distasteful if the lady is young and beautiful?

RICHARD. At least, if a man attacks a young and beautiful girl, it seems more . . . Oh, my God! (*He remembers last night and shudders.*)

DR. BRUBAKER. I beg your pardon?

RICHARD. Nothing. Doctor, if you don't like the cover, I'll see if I can have it changed . . .

DR. BRUBAKER. I would be most grateful.

RICHARD. Doctor.

DR. BRUBAKER. Yes?

RICHARD. You say in the book that ninety per cent of the population is in need of some sort of psychiatric help?

DR. BRUBAKER. This is theoretically true. It is not however practical. There is the matter of cost . . .

RICHARD. With your own patients—are you very expensive?

DR. BRUBAKER (*his Third Ear has caught the direction this conversation is leading and his defenses go up immediately*). Very.

RICHARD. I'm sure you occasionally make exceptions . . .

DR. BRUBAKER. Never.

RICHARD. I mean, once in a while a case must come along that really interests you . . .

DR. BRUBAKER (*primly*). At fifty dollars an hour—all my cases interest me.

RICHARD (*undaunted*). I mean if you should run into something really spectacular. Another Gustav Meyerheim, for example . . . Doctor, tell me frankly. Do you think, just for example, that *I* need to be psychoanalyzed?

DR. BRUBAKER. Very possibly. I could recommend several very excellent men who might, perhaps, be a little cheaper.

RICHARD. How much cheaper?

DR. BRUBAKER (*considering*). Ohhhhh . . .

RICHARD. I couldn't even afford that . . .

DR. BRUBAKER. I thought not. (*He turns back to his papers.*) Now to get back to . . .

RICHARD (*seating himself casually on the couch*). I wondered if possibly you might give me some advice . . .

DR. BRUBAKER. I know. Everyone wonders that.

(*Still moving casually,* RICHARD *swings his feet onto the couch until he is lying flat on his back in the classic position.*)

RICHARD. I'm desperate, Doctor. Last night after you left, I was just sitting there listening to the ball game . . .

DR. BRUBAKER (*outmaneuvered, but still game*). This fact in itself is not really sufficient cause to undertake analysis . . .

RICHARD. No, I don't mean that. I *started out* listening to the ball game and do you know what I ended up doing?

DR. BRUBAKER. I have no idea . . .

RICHARD. I ended up attempting to commit what I guess they call criminal assault . . .

DR. BRUBAKER (*defeated, he takes a pad and pencil from his pocket*). From the way you phrase it, I assume the attempt was unsuccessful . . .

RICHARD. Thank God! All I did was knock us both off the piano bench . . .

DR. BRUBAKER (*a flicker of interest—he begins to write*). You attempted to commit criminal assault on a *piano bench?*

RICHARD. Yes.

DR. BRUBAKER. And on whose person was this obviously maladroit attempt committed?

(RICHARD *rises and goes to bookshelf. Gets* US Camera *and shows it to* DOCTOR.)

RICHARD. That's her. Her hair was a little longer then.

DR. BRUBAKER (*after a moment*). Splendid. I congratulate you on your taste. However, you ask for my advice. I give it to you. Do not attempt it again. (*A brief pause while the* DOCTOR *re-examines the photograph.*) If you *should,* however, give yourself plenty of room to work in. In any case do not attempt it precariously balanced on a piano bench. Such an attempt is doomed from the start. Now, my boy, I must go. I have many things to . . .

RICHARD. But look, Doctor—I'm married. I've always been married. Suppose this girl tells people about this. She's likely to mention it to someone. Like my wife.

DR. BRUBAKER. This is, of course, not beyond the realm of possibility. In that event I would recommend a course of vigorous denial. It would be simply your word against hers. Very possibly, if you were convincing enough, you could make it stick. And now I must really go. I thank you for your help. It is agreed that I shall make the necessary clarifications in Chapter Eight and you will devote your best efforts to making the cover of my book look less like a French postal card. I shall be in touch with your office the first of next week . . .

RICHARD. If she tells anyone about this —I'll, I'll—kill her! I'll kill her with my bare hands!

DR. BRUBAKER (*who has started to leave, turns back*). This is also a possible solution. However, I submit that murder is the most difficult of all crimes to commit successfully. Therefore, until you are able to commit a simple criminal assault, I strongly advise that you avoid anything so complex as murder. One must learn to walk before one can run. I thank you again and good night. (*He exits briskly.*)

(RICHARD *stands blankly staring after the good Doctor. He shakes his head.*)

(*Music sneaks in—he turns and there grouped about the couch and coffee table, in "dream lighting" are* HELEN, THE GIRL, MISS MORRIS, ELAINE, MARIE WHATEVER-HER-NAME-WAS *and an unidentified* YOUNG LADY *in brassiere and panties. They all brandish tea cups and in very hen-party fashion are engaged in dishing the dirt about someone. It is, after all, a figment of* RICHARD's *imagination, so the cups are raised and lowered in unison and the little clucking noises of disapproval are done in chorus.*)

THE GIRL (*very chatty*). Actually, Mrs. Sherman, it was terribly embarrassing. He seemed to go berserk. He'd been sitting playing "Chopsticks" when suddenly he grabbed me and practically tried to tear my clothes off . . .

ELAINE. My dear, the night of your birthday party he made himself perfectly obnoxious right out there on the terrace. I don't like to say this, but he attempted to take advantage of me.

(*All the girls shake their heads and make small clucking noises of shocked disapproval.*)

MISS MORRIS. It's just terrible, Mrs. Sherman. I'm positively scared to go into his office to take dictation. Why, the way that man looks at me, it makes me feel kinda naked.

(*All drink tea.*)

ELAINE. I said, Richard darling, at least have the decency not to try something like this practically in front of poor Helen's eyes!

THE GIRL. He'd been drinking heavily, of course . . . He practically guzzled a whole bottle of my champagne . . .

MARIE (*in French*). Madame! Madame! He was like a human beast! He tore off my belt, he tore off my shirt, he tore off my pants and he chased me into the sea without a bathing costume.

(*All shake heads and "Tsk-tsk." Then the unidentified* YOUNG LADY *in the bra and pants speaks up.*)

YOUNG LADY. And *me!* I'm not even safe in my own apartment! Every time I start getting ready for bed that man sits out there on the terrace—staring at me! I just hate a Peeping Tom!

HELEN. I've always suspected that Richard was not quite sane.

THE GIRL. Oh, he's sane, all right. He's just a nasty, evil-minded, middle-aged man . . .

(RICHARD *can stand it no longer.*)

RICHARD. Helen! Listen to me . . .

(*The girls raise their tea cups and vanish. Music in and out and lighting back to normal.*)

RICHARD (*in a panic, lights a cigarette*). I've got to do something. That girl's probably told fifty people about this already. If I just sent her some flowers . . . That's no good. . . . I've got to talk to her. Reason with her. Plead with her. Tell her I was drunk, which God knows I was, and beg her not to mention this to anyone or my life could be ruined . . . (*He has found telephone book and is riffling through pages.*) Twelve solid pages of Kaufman . . . Here it is . . . ORegon 3-7221. (*He lifts receiver, starts to dial, then stops.*) I can't do it. What can I possibly say to her? (*He practices—holding receiver switch down.*)

RICHARD (*with great charm*). My dear Miss— *I don't even know what the hell her name is*—My dear Young Woman— I have simply called to apologize for my absurd behavior last night. It was inexcusable, but I had been drinking. I can barely remember what happened, but I'm under the impression that I made a terrible fool of myself. I beg you to forgive me and put the whole distasteful incident out of your mind. (*Stops and puts down phone.*) No good. I can't do it. . . . And what about Helen? She hasn't called. She's probably heard about it by now. Oh, that's out of the question. How could she possibly have heard anything? But she could have. The word gets around. It's like jungle drums. . . . If she hasn't heard anything—why hasn't she called? . . . I could call her. The minute I heard her voice I could tell if she knew anything. . . . Come on. Call her. . . . Stop stalling. Pick up the telephone and call her. It's the only way you'll know. . . . Okay. Okay. (*He picks up the phone and dials the Long-Distance Operator.*) Long Distance? I want to call Cohasset. Cohasset, Massachusetts, 4-2831-J. Yeah . . . My number? ORegon 9-4437. Thank you. . . . Okay—fasten your seat belts . . . Hello? Hello, Helen? Who?

Who is this? Look, I want to talk to Mrs. Richard Sherman. Is she there? Who is this anyway? Oh. The baby sitter. Look, this is Mr. Sherman calling from New York. What do you mean she's out for the evening. With whom is she out for the evening? Mr. MacKenzie and some people? *What people?* Well, what *was* the message she left for me? . . . Oh. Oh, my God. Her yellow skirt. No, no, I didn't. Something unexpected came up. But tell her I will. The first thing in the morning. Without fail. . . . Look, I want to ask you. How did Mrs. Sherman seem? I mean did she seem upset in any way? Like she'd heard some bad news or anything like that? . . . Just about the yellow skirt. Well, good. Tell her I'll send it up the first thing in the morning. Is Ricky all right? Good. When Mrs. Sherman comes in, tell her everything is fine here and I'll talk to her tomorrow . . . Fine . . . Good-by . . . Good-by. (*He hangs up phone.*) Well, thank God! (*He sits down and lights a cigarette.*) The only thing I cannot understand is, what the hell is she doing having dinner with Tom MacKenzie. I wish she wouldn't hang around with people like that. He gets away with murder because he's a writer. Well, he's a damn lousy writer. That last book! . . . Helen should know better than to go around with people like that. She isn't even safe. . . . I know for a positive fact that he's been after her for years. Tom MacKenzie happens to be a real bum, if you want to know! And there probably aren't any other people. . . . She doesn't know what she's getting herself into. She's been married so long she forgets what it's like. . . . Helen happens to be a damned attractive woman. A man like Tom MacKenzie is perfectly capable of making a pass at her. (*By now he has begun to pace the floor.*) And don't think she doesn't know what she's doing. She's getting older. She's used to me. In many ways I'm probably very dull. And Tom MacKenzie's a writer. She probably thinks he's fascinating as hell! . . . She thought that last book of his was great! All that inwardly-downwardly-pulsating-and-afterward-her-hair-spilled-across-the-pillow crap! Strictly for little old ladies at Womrath's. . . . But Helen is just the kind of middle-aged dame who would fall for it. . . . Well, good luck! That's all! (*Brooding, he sits in easy chair, a grim expression on his face.*)

(*Music sneaks in and the "dream lighting" comes up on the far side of the stage by the fireplace. We hear the sound of wind mingled with the music. A door opens and slams shut and* TOM MACKENZIE *and* HELEN *enter, laughing.* TOM MACKENZIE *is a handsome, glamorous-type author with a mustache. He looks quite a lot like his photograph on the book jackets. He wears a tweed coat with the collar up and a hunting shirt.* HELEN *wears a sweater and skirt with a man's raincoat thrown about her shoulders. Both are very gay.*)

HELEN (*as he helps her off with raincoat*). It's been years since I took a walk on the beach in the rain . . .

TOM. I love the rain on the sea. It's so wild and untamed . . .

HELEN (*looking around*). Where are the other people?

TOM. I have a confession to make.

HELEN. Yes?

TOM. There are no other people. Don't be angry.

HELEN (*after a moment*). I'm not angry.

TOM. I hoped you wouldn't be. Come over here by the fire.

HELEN. I love an open fire.

TOM. I always say, What good is the rain without an open fire?

RICHARD (*from his chair across the room*). Oh, brother!

TOM. Let me get you a little whiskey to take out the chill . . .

HELEN. Thank you . . .

(*He pours whiskey from flask. She drinks, then hands the cup to him. He drinks—but first kisses the spot on the cup where her lips have been.*)

RICHARD (*muttering scornfully*). H. B. Warner . . .

TOM. But wait. You're shivering . . .

HELEN. It's nothing. I'll be warm in a moment . . .

TOM. No, no . . . You're soaked to the skin. You'll catch your death of cold . . .

RICHARD. Here it comes . . .

TOM. Why don't you take off your things and hang them by the fire? I'll get you something dry . . .

RICHARD (*appalled*). He used *that* in his book, for God's sake! As who didn't!

HELEN. All right. Turn your back . . .

(*He turns his back and she removes her shoes. She takes off her skirt and hangs it*

on the fire screen.*)

TOM. May I turn around now?

HELEN. If you like . . .

(*Suddenly, the mood has changed. His voice is now husky with passion.*)

TOM. Helen, darling!

HELEN. Yes, Tom?

TOM. Did anyone ever tell you that you are a very beautiful woman?

HELEN. No. Not recently anyway . . .

TOM. But surely Richard . . .

HELEN. I'm afraid Richard rather takes me for granted now . . .

TOM. That blind, utter fool!

HELEN. Oh, darling!

TOM. Darling! (*The music swells.* TOM *takes her in his arms. Murmuring as he covers her with kisses*) Inwardly, downwardly, pulsating, striving, now together, ending and unending, now, now, now! (*They are in a full mad clinch as the lights black out.*)

(*On his side of the room,* RICHARD *jumps to his feet and angrily pounds the table.*)

RICHARD. Okay! If that's the way you want it! Okay!

(*With great purpose he strides to the telephone. Gets phone book, thumbs through it, finds number and dials. He whistles softly through his teeth. . . . The tune he is whistling might, if he were not tone deaf, almost be "Just One of Those Things." After a moment someone obviously answers the phone.*)

RICHARD (*with great charm*). Hi. Did you know you left your tomato plant down here last night? I could have the janitor bring it back—or—if you want—I was thinking maybe I could . . . (*He is talking into the phone with great animation by the time the lights have dimmed and:*)

THE CURTAIN IS DOWN

SCENE TWO

The same. It is later that evening.

The apartment is empty. A single light in the foyer.

After a moment, the sound of a key in the lock and RICHARD *and* THE GIRL *enter. He switches on the lights.*

RICHARD. Well, we made it.

THE GIRL. I'm so full of steak I can

barely wobble . . .

RICHARD. Me too.

THE GIRL. I feel wonderful . . .

RICHARD. Did anyone ever tell you that you have a very, very beautiful digestive tract?

THE GIRL. Yes. But they don't usually say it like that. Mostly they just say: Boy, did you ever stuff yourself!

RICHARD. Would you like a drink or something?

THE GIRL. No, thanks. But you go ahead and have one. Don't mind me . . .

RICHARD. Not me. I'm back on the wagon again . . .

THE GIRL. This was awfully nice of you. It was enough to have you carry that heavy plant all the way upstairs. You didn't have to ask me out for dinner. I hope you didn't hurt yourself. Or strain something . . .

RICHARD. It wasn't that heavy. I was going to call the janitor to help me, but then I decided not to . . .

THE GIRL. You're in pretty good shape . . .

RICHARD. For an old man . . .

THE GIRL. You're not *that* old. You don't look a day over twenty-eight.

RICHARD. I know . . .

THE GIRL. Anyway it was very nice of you.

RICHARD. I just took a chance and called. I didn't really think you'd be home. You know, I thought you'd be out or something.

THE GIRL. No, I don't go out very much . . .

RICHARD. That's funny. I should think you'd have a line of suitors halfway round the block. Like Easter show at Radio City . . .

THE GIRL. Last night, I went to the movies by myself . . .

RICHARD. Last night?

THE GIRL (*diplomatically*). After I left here.

RICHARD (*moving the conversation past a trouble spot*). All by yourself! You must have a boy friend or something . . .

THE GIRL. I don't go out with most people who ask me. I know it sounds silly but people are always falling desperately in love with me and everything and it makes things so complicated. I mean, it's just easier to pay the fifty-five cents and go to the movies by yourself.

RICHARD. It doesn't sound very exciting . . .

THE GIRL. It is, though. This is the first time I've had my own apartment and everything.

RICHARD. You went out with me when I asked you . . .

THE GIRL. Well, that's different. I mean, it's all right going out with you. After all, you're married.

RICHARD. I see. I *think*.

THE GIRL. No. What I mean is, it's all right to have dinner with you because you're not likely to fall desperately in love with me or anything. You're more mature . . .

RICHARD. I don't feel so—mature . . .

THE GIRL. Well, you know what I mean. (*Pause.*)

RICHARD. You're absolutely sure you wouldn't like a drink?

THE GIRL. Absolutely.

RICHARD. I think maybe I'll have one. Just a little one. (*He goes to bar and fixes himself a drink.*) Not even a Coke or something?

THE GIRL. Not right now.

RICHARD. Well, happy birthday. (*Pause.*)

THE GIRL. This certainly is a beautiful apartment.

RICHARD. It's all right. It's a little ridiculous in some ways . . . The stairs, for instance . . .

THE GIRL. I think they're beautiful. I like an apartment with stairs.

RICHARD. But these don't go any place. They just go up to the ceiling and stop. They give the joint a kind of Jean Paul Sartre quality.

THE GIRL. I see what you mean. No exit. A stairway to nowhere.

RICHARD. I tried to get the landlord to take them out. See, this used to be the bottom half of a duplex. This place and the Kaufmans' were all one apartment. So when he divided them separately he just boarded up the ceiling—or in your case the floor . . .

THE GIRL. Yes, I noticed the place in the floor. I lost an orange stick down the crack. Anyway, I think the apartment's just charming . . .

RICHARD. Yeah. But we're moving into a larger place in September . . .

THE GIRL. Oh, that's too bad. But still, people in New York are always moving. You certainly have a lot of books. The last book I read was *The Catcher in the Rye* . . .

RICHARD. The last book I read was *The Scarlet Letter*. Mr. Brady thinks we can sell it. If we make it sound sexy enough.

THE GIRL. Is it sexy? I don't seem to remember.

RICHARD. No. Actually, it's kind of dull. In fact, people are going to want their quarters back. But Mr. Brady feels we can sell it if I can just figure out a way to tell people what the Scarlet Letter is.

THE GIRL. What *is* it?

RICHARD. Well, the Scarlet Letter was a big red "A." For Adultery. Anyone who was convicted of adultery had to wear it.

THE GIRL. How awful!

RICHARD. The cover will be a picture of Hester Prynne with a cigarette hanging out of her mouth. She'll be in a real tight, low-cut dress. Our big problem is—if the dress is cut low enough to sell any copies, there won't be any space on the front for a big red letter . . .

THE GIRL. The publishing business sounds fascinating.

RICHARD. Oh, it is. It is.

(*Pause.*)

THE GIRL. It's getting late. I really ought to go . . .

RICHARD. You've got plenty of time.

THE GIRL. I guess so. That's the wonderful thing about having my own apartment. I mean at the club you had to be in at one o'clock or they locked the doors.

RICHARD. It sounds barbaric . . .

THE GIRL. Oh, it practically was. It was really very funny. I mean, all the girls at the club were actresses. So naturally they were always asking each other what they called the big question . . .

RICHARD. The big question?

THE GIRL. Mmm! They were always asking each other: Would you sleep with a producer to get a part?

RICHARD. That is a big question . . .

THE GIRL. But it's so silly. If you live at the club anyway. I used to tell them, producers don't even *go* to bed before one o'clock. So the whole thing is academic, if you see what I mean. You'd be surprised how much time they spent discussing it, though.

RICHARD. I can see where they might give the matter some thought.

THE GIRL. Oh, sure. But they never dis-

cussed it in a *practical* way. When they asked me, I always used to say: It depends. How big is the part? Is the producer handsome? Things like that . . .

RICHARD. Practical things . . .

THE GIRL. Mmm! I was at the club for eight months and as far as I know no producer ever mentioned the subject to any of the girls.

RICHARD. That must have been very disappointing for them.

THE GIRL. It was.

RICHARD. But what if he was very handsome? And it was a very good part? And you didn't have to be in by one o'clock? What *would* you do?

THE GIRL. In that case . . . If I was sure he wouldn't fall desperately in love with me and ask me to marry him and everything.

RICHARD. What's so bad about that?

THE GIRL. Oh, that would spoil everything. Marrying him, I mean. It would be worse than living at the club. Then I'd have to start getting in at one o'clock again. I mean it's taken me twenty-two years to get my own apartment. It would be pretty silly if the first thing I did was get married and spoil everything. I mean, I want to have a chance to be independent first. For a few years anyway. You can't imagine how exciting it is to live by yourself—after you've had somebody practically running your life for as long as you can remember. . . . You just can't imagine . . .

(*As* RICHARD *stops listening to* THE GIRL *and gradually becomes absorbed in his own thoughts, the lights dim down till there is only a dream spot on* RICHARD.)

RICHARD. Yes, I can. As a matter of fact we have a great deal in common.

HIS VOICE (*Mockingly—imitating* HELEN's *tone*). Daddy's going to work very hard. And he's going to stay on the wagon, like Dr. Summers told him. And he's going to eat properly and not smoke, like Dr. Murphy told him. And Mommy is going to call Daddy tonight just to make sure he's all right . . . *Poor Daddy!*

RICHARD. Poor Daddy!

HIS VOICE. The girl is absolutely right. Not want to get married. You—you dope. The minute you were old enough to have any fun—the only thing you could think of to do was to get married.

RICHARD. I know. I know. It was a kind

of nervousness. But I made the best of it. I've been a pretty good husband. When I think of the chances I've had . . .

HIS VOICE. We've been through all this before . . .

RICHARD. I know. I know. I just thought I'd mention it.

HIS VOICE. Has it ever dawned on you that you're kidding yourself?

RICHARD. What do you mean by that?

HIS VOICE. All those dames you could have had if you weren't such a noble husband. The only reason you didn't do anything about 'em is that you didn't want to . . .

RICHARD. Why didn't I want to?

HIS VOICE. Laziness, pal. Laziness. It was too much trouble. You just didn't want to get involved. Elaine, for instance. It would have taken six months. And all those phone calls and taxis and excuses.

RICHARD. Yeah. (*Pause*) Why does it always have to be so complicated?

HIS VOICE. If you could answer that one, pal-pal, they'd make you President of the United States.

(RICHARD *sighs and the lights dim back to normal.* THE GIRL *is still speaking, unaware of the fact that his mind has been far away.*)

THE GIRL. . . . so when you asked me to go out for dinner with you it was all right. You're married and naturally, you don't want to fall desperately in love with anyone any more than I want anyone to fall desperately in love with me. Do you know what I mean?

RICHARD. Sure. It's too much trouble.

THE GIRL. Exactly.

RICHARD. I know just what you mean.

THE GIRL. That's right.

RICHARD. We both happen to be in positions where we can't possibly let ourselves get involved in anything . . .

THE GIRL. Mmm.

RICHARD. All the damn phone calls and taxis and everything.

THE GIRL. That's right. I mean I certainly wouldn't be sitting alone with some man in his apartment at eleven-thirty at night if he wasn't married.

RICHARD. Certainly not. (*Pause*) When you said about the producer—it would depend on if he were handsome—what did you mean by that? I mean, just out of curiosity . . . what would be your idea of handsome?

THE GIRL. Well, let's see. I really don't know. I suppose he should be tall—and kind of mature-looking . . .

RICHARD. Like me?

THE GIRL (*thoughtfully*). Mmmmm . . . (*Pause*) You're not going to start falling desperately in love with me or anything, are you?

RICHARD. No. No. Definitely not. I mean I think you're very pretty and sweet and I certainly enjoyed having dinner with you. But . . .

THE GIRL. That's just the way *I* feel about you. You're very nice-looking and charming and mature. You're someone I can be with and count on him not falling desperately in love with me . . .

RICHARD. That's right. I'm almost—well —I'm a lot older than you are. And one thing I've learned. Nothing is ever as simple as you think it's going to be. You take the simplest damn thing and, before you know it, it gets all loused up. I don't know how it happens or why it happens but it always happens . . .

THE GIRL. That's very true. You're absolutely right.

(*As* THE GIRL *stops listening to* RICHARD *and gradually becomes absorbed in her own thoughts the lights dim to a single dream spot on her.*)

HER VOICE. Well, what do you think?

THE GIRL. Mmm . . .

HER VOICE. What do you mean—mmm?

THE GIRL. I mean—I don't know . . .

HER VOICE. That's ridiculous. What is there not to know? He certainly is nice —and he's mature without being—you know—decrepit or anything . . .

THE GIRL. He certainly seems well-preserved . . .

HER VOICE. He's sweet and intelligent and married. What more do you want?

THE GIRL. I don't know.

HER VOICE. You're the one who wants to be the big-deal woman of the world. It's all your idea. It's not as if you were some kind of a virginal creature or something.

THE GIRL. Oh—shut up— I mean you make it sound so—so clinical. Besides, you certainly can't count Jerry . . .

HER VOICE. What do you mean we can't count Jerry?

THE GIRL. Well, I mean it was a big mistake—and it was so—so—and then he got all hysterical and wanted to marry me . . .

HER VOICE. It counts.

THE GIRL. I mean you can understand a person wanting to find out something about life and everything before she gets married and all settled down and has to start getting in by one o'clock again . . . Besides, what makes you think he's interested in me that way? I must seem like some kind of a juvenile delinquent to him . . .

HER VOICE. You're twenty-two years old. And he's interested.

THE GIRL. How can you tell?

HER VOICE. I can tell . . .

THE GIRL. How?

HER VOICE. I can tell. . . . What have you got to lose?

THE GIRL. Well, nothing, I guess—if you're really going to make Jerry count.

HER VOICE. He counts . . .

THE GIRL. Well, then . . .

(*The lights come back to normal.* RICHARD *is still talking, unaware that* THE GIRL'S *mind has been far away.*)

RICHARD. . . . what I'm trying to say is, that people who are really mature weigh things more carefully. They impose a discipline on themselves. They understand the cost. . . . I mean, they finally learn that sometimes something that seems very wonderful and desirable isn't really worth . . . I mean—all the hysteria it's going to cause . . . (*Pause*) Then, of course, you can over-do that line of thinking too. I mean a man—a person—anyone doesn't like to feel that he's some kind of a vegetable or something. You know. What it amounts to is this: You've got to decide which is the most painful—doing something and regretting it—or not doing something and—regretting it. Do you see what I mean?

THE GIRL. I think so . . .

RICHARD. I didn't mean to start making a speech. Look, are you sure you don't want a drink?

THE GIRL. No, thanks. Really. (*Starts to go.*)

RICHARD. Now look, really. It's not late. You don't have to go yet . . .

THE GIRL. I really should . . .

RICHARD. Well, whatever you think. Let me take you up to your door . . .

THE GIRL. No. That's all right. It's just upstairs . . .

RICHARD. Well, all right. If you have to go.

THE GIRL. I want to thank you for the dinner. It was lovely . . .

RICHARD. It was fun . . .

THE GIRL. And for carrying that heavy plant all the way upstairs . . .

RICHARD. It wasn't so heavy . . . (*They have edged almost to the door by now.*)

THE GIRL. Well, good night. And thanks —again . . .

RICHARD. Well, good night . . . (*She leans forward and kisses him lightly on the cheek.*) Well, good night . . .

(*Suddenly they move together in a tight embrace which they hold for a moment. She breaks away, then kisses him again and in the same motion goes quickly out the door closing it behind her.*)

(RICHARD *is visibly shaken. He starts after her. Stops himself. Closes the door again. And locks it. He shakes his head and then puts on the chain lock.*)

(*Comes inside, starts for the phone, stops again. Tries to pull himself together. Picks up the galley sheets and sits down on the couch and tries to work on them.*)

(*As he sits, a square in the ceiling at the top of the stairs lifts out and a moment later the girl appears. She backs down the first few steps, lowering the floor-ceiling back into place. He is oblivious to this. She turns and starts down the stairs. We see that she is carrying a small claw hammer.*)

(*Quietly she comes down into the room. She looks at him and smiles. She pauses for a moment.*)

THE GIRL. (*with a small, ineffectual wave of the hand*). Hi . . .

(RICHARD *almost jumps out of his skin. He sees her. After a moment he sees the hammer and realizes where she has come from. Then, after a long time, he smiles and makes a similar, ineffectual wave of the hand.*)

RICHARD. Hi . . .

CURTAIN

ACT THREE

The same.

It is about eight o'clock the following morning. The blinds on the French doors are drawn, but outside the sun is shining brightly. It is going to be another hot day.

As the curtain rises, RICHARD *stands by the French doors. He is in his shirt sleeves.*

He opens the blinds and then the doors. He steps out onto the terrace and breathes deeply. He comes back into the living room and notices the girl's shoes. Somewhat tentatively, he picks them up and carries them to the bedroom doors. He stops and listens for a moment. He puts the shoes back where he found them and goes to the front door. He listens again, then unlocks the door without unfastening the chain.

He kneels down and reaching around through the slightly open door fishes in milk and the newspaper. He carries the paper down to the armchair and tries to read. He can't, however.

After a moment he looks up and speaks to himself in a very reassuring voice.

RICHARD. There's not a thing in the world to worry about. Two very attractive, intelligent people happened to meet under circumstances that seemed to be —propitious--and, well, it happened. It was very charming and gay. As a matter of fact it was wonderful. But now it's over. (*He rises and starts for the bedroom.*) We'll say good-by, like two intelligent people. We'll have coffee . . . (*He knocks gently on the door. He listens. He knocks again. His calm is rapidly evaporating.*) How can she possibly sleep like that? . . . What's the matter with her anyway? Maybe she's sick or something. Maybe she's dead. . . . Maybe the excitement was too much for her and she passed away in her sleep. . . . Oh, my God! That means the police. And the reporters. "Actress found dead in publisher's apartment"! . . . (*He looks desperately around. His eye lights on the staircase.*) No. No. I'll just haul the body upstairs. That's all. Right back upstairs, nail up the floor again and that's all. They'd have no reason to suspect me. I'd wear gloves, of course. They'd never prove a thing. . . . Now stop it. You're getting hysterical again. (*Pause*) Well, if she isn't dead, why the hell doesn't she just get up and go home? It's late! It's—late—it's *really* late —it's . . . (*He picks up his wrist watch from table.*) . . . ten after eight? It seemed later than *that* . . . (*He is somewhat relieved by the time.*) Well. I'll give her another half-hour to catch up on her beauty sleep. Then, I'll very politely wake her. We'll have coffee like two intelligent

people. And then, I'll kiss her good-by. (*Confidently acting out the scene*) It's been fun, darling, but now, of course, it's over . . . No tears—no regrets . . . (*He stands waving as if she were walking up the stairs.*) Just good-by. It's been—swell . . . (*He blows a kiss upward, waves and then stands transfixed, a foolish expression on his face.*)

HIS VOICE. Pal.

RICHARD. Huh?

HIS VOICE. I don't want you to get upset or anything, but it might not be as easy as all that. You know. Be realistic.

RICHARD. What? What are you talking about?

HIS VOICE. I was just pointing out. Women don't take these things as lightly as men, you know. There *could* be complications. For example, suppose she's fallen desperately in love with you . . .

RICHARD. She can't do that. It isn't fair. She knows she can't.

HIS VOICE. After all, pal, you had a little something to do with this yourself . . .

RICHARD. Don't worry. I can handle it. Just don't worry. I can be tough if I have to. I can be pretty damn tough. If I set my mind to it, I can be a terrible heel . . .

HIS VOICE (*mocking*). Ha-ha!

RICHARD. Shut up . . . (*He stands for a moment, setting his mind to being a terrible heel. The lights dim and music sneaks in. "Dream lighting" lights up the bedroom doors. They open and the girl emerges. She is dressed like an Al Parker illustration for a story called "Glorious Honeymoon" in* The Woman's Home Companion. *She is radiant.*)

THE GIRL (*radiantly*). Good morning, my darling . . . Good morning . . . Good morning . . .

RICHARD (*very tough. He lights a cigarette and stares at her for a moment through ice-blue eyes*). Oh. It's about time you dragged your dead pratt out of the sack . . .

THE GIRL. Oh, darling, darling, darling . . . (*He exhales smoke.*) What is it, my darling, you seem troubled . . .

RICHARD. Shut up, baby, and listen to me. I got something to tell you.

THE GIRL. And I've something to tell you. I've grown older, somehow, overnight. I know now that all our brave talk of independence—our not wanting to get involved—our being—actually—*afraid* of love—it was all childish nonsense. I'm not afraid to say it, darling. I love you. I want you. You belong to me.

RICHARD. Look, baby. Let's get one thing straight. I belong to nobody, see. If some dumb little dame wants to throw herself at me—that's her lookout, see. I'm strictly a one-night guy. I've left a string of broken hearts from here to—to Westport, Connecticut, and back. Now, the smartest little move you could make is to pack your stuff and scram . . .

THE GIRL. Go? Not I! Not now! Not ever! Don't you see, my darling, after what we've been to each other . . .

RICHARD. I spell trouble, baby, with a capital "T". We're poison to each other —you and me. Don't you see that?

THE GIRL. When two people care for each other as we do . . .

RICHARD (*a little "Pal Joey" creeping in*). What do I care for a dame? Every damn dame is the same. I'm going to own a night club . . .

THE GIRL. That doesn't matter. Nothing matters. This thing is bigger than both of us. We'll *flaunt* our love. Shout it from the highest housetops. We're on a great toboggan. We can't stop it. We can't steer it. It's too late to run, the Beguine has begun . . .

RICHARD (*weakly*). Oh, Jesus Christ . . .

THE GIRL (*coolly taking charge*). Now then. Do you want to be the one to tell Helen, or shall I?

RICHARD (*with an anguished moan*). Tell Helen?

THE GIRL. Of course. We must. It's the only way . . .

RICHARD. No, no, no! You can't do that! You can't! (*He is now kneeling at her feet, pleading. She puts her arm about his shoulder. From somewhere comes the brave sound of a solo violin which plays behind her next speech.*)

THE GIRL. We can and we must. We'll face her together. Hand in hand. Proudly. Our heads held high. Oh, we'll be social outcasts, but we won't care. It'll be you and I together against the world. I'll go and dress now, darling. But I wanted you to know how I felt. I couldn't wait to tell you. Good-by, for now, my darling. I won't be long . . .

(*As the music swells, she floats off into the bedroom, waving and blowing kisses with both hands. The "dream light" fades out and the lighting returns to normal.*)

RICHARD *stands panic-stricken in the middle of the living-room floor. He shakes his head.*)

RICHARD. I'm crazy. I'm going crazy. That's all. I've run amok. Helen goes away and I run amok. Raping and looting and . . . (*He notices the cigarette in his hand.*) smoking cigarettes . . . (*He quickly puts out the cigarette.*) What have I done? What did I think I was doing? What did I possibly think I was doing? . . . Damn it! I begged Helen not to go away for the summer. I begged her! . . . What am I going to do! That girl in there undoubtedly expects me to get a divorce and marry her.

HIS VOICE. Well, why don't you?

RICHARD. Are you kidding? What about Helen?

HIS VOICE. What about her? Maybe this is all for the best. Maybe this is the best thing that could have happened to you. After all, Helen's not as young as she used to be. In a couple of years you'll look like her son.

RICHARD. Now wait a minute. Wait a minute. Helen is still pretty attractive. She happens to be a damn beautiful woman, if you want to know. And we've been through a lot together. The time I was fired from Random House. And when little Ricky was sick—and I caught the damn mumps from him. She's taken a lot of punishment from me, if you want to know. And she's been pretty nice about it . . .

HIS VOICE. The point, however is: Do you love her?

RICHARD. Love her? Well, sure. Sure, I love her. Of course I love her. I'm *used to her!*

HIS VOICE. Used to her? That doesn't sound very exciting. Of course I imagine when a man enters middle life, he doesn't want someone exciting. He wants someone comfortable. Someone he's *used* to . . .

RICHARD. Now, just a second. You've got the wrong idea. Helen's not so—*comfortable*. She's pretty exciting. You should see the way people look at her at parties and on the street and everywhere . . .

HIS VOICE. What people?

RICHARD. Men. That's what people. For instance, Tom MacKenzie, if you want to know. When Helen wears that green dress —the backless one with hardly any front— there's nothing comfortable about that at all . . . (RICHARD *sinks into chair and leans back.*) She wore it one night last spring when Tom MacKenzie was over—and you just couldn't get him out of here . . . (*Music sneaks in and the lights dim. "Dream lighting" fills the stage.*) It looked like he was going to go home about four different times but he just couldn't tear himself away . . .

(TOM *and* HELEN *appear.* HELEN *is wearing the green dress. It is everything* RICHARD *has said it is.*)

TOM. Helen, you look particularly lovely tonight . . .

HELEN. Why, thank you, Tom . . .

TOM. You're a lucky boy, Dickie, even if you don't know it.

RICHARD. I know all about it and don't call me Dickie . . .

TOM. Helen—Helen, that name is so like you. "Helen, thy beauty is to me as those Nicaean barks of yore" . . .

HELEN. Gracious . . .

TOM. No, no, I mean it. Stand there a moment. Let me drink you in. Turn around. Slowly, that's it . . . (HELEN *models dress.*) You look particularly lovely in a backless gown . . .

RICHARD (*muttering*). Backless, frontless, topless, bottomless, I'm on to you, you son of a bitch . . .

TOM (*from across the room*). What was that, old man?

HELEN (*quickly*). Don't pay any attention to Dick. You know what happens to him and martinis . . .

RICHARD. Two martinis. Two lousy martinis.

HELEN. Dr. Summers has told him time and time again that he should go on the wagon for a while till his stomach gets better . . .

TOM. That's good advice, Dick. When a man can't handle the stuff he should leave it alone completely. That's what I say. Once a year—just to test my will power—I stop everything.

RICHARD (*he starts to say something, but finally stops himself*). No comment.

HELEN (*leaping once again into the breach*). You really like this dress—do you, Tom?

TOM. I certainly do. It's a Potter original, isn't it?

HELEN. Yes—but that's wonderful! How did you know?

TOM. I'm a bit of an authority on wom-

en's clothes. You should really take me with you the next time you go shopping. We could have a bite of lunch first and really make a day of it . . . (*He has finally got to the door.*) Good night, Dick . . . (RICHARD *waves unenthusiastically.*) Good night, Helen . . . (*He kisses her.*)

HELEN. Good night, Tom . . .

TOM. I'll call you one day next week

HELEN. I'll be looking forward to it. (*She closes the door behind him.*) I thought he was never going home . . .

RICHARD (*in rather feeble imitation of* TOM). "Helen, thy beauty is to me as those Nicaean barks of yore"—is he kidding?

HELEN. You know Tom. He beats his chest and makes noises but it doesn't really mean anything . . .

RICHARD. I know. His Nicaean bark is worse than his Nicaean bite . . . (*He is pleasantly surprised by how well this came out.*) Hey, that's pretty good. That came out better than I thought it was going to. Nicaean bark—Nicaean bite . . .

HELEN (*unfractured*). Actually, in some ways, Tom is very sweet. I mean it's nice to have people notice your clothes . . .

RICHARD. Notice your clothes! He did a lot more than notice. . . . He practically . . . You know, you really ought to do something about that dress. Just the front part there . . .

HELEN. Do something about it?

RICHARD. I mean sort of . . . (*He gestures ineffectually about raising or tightening or something the front.*) I don't know. Maybe we ought to empty the ash trays or something. You should see the way he was looking at you . . .

HELEN. You should have been flattered. Don't you want people to think your wife is attractive?

RICHARD. Sure, but . . . Why don't we clean this place up a little? It looks like a cocktail lounge on West Tenth Street . . . (*He picks up an ash tray full of cigarette butts.*)

(HELEN *comes over to him.*)

HELEN. Darling . . .

RICHARD. We ought to at least empty the ash trays . . .

HELEN. Not now . . .

RICHARD (*looks at her questioningly*). Huh?

HELEN. I mean not now . . .

(*He looks at her for another moment*

and then very casually tosses away the tray full of butts and takes her in his arms.)

(The lights black out and the music swells in the darkness.)

(When the lights come on again the lighting is back to normal and RICHARD *is leaning back in the chair where we left him, a self-satisfied grin on his face.)*

HIS VOICE. Then you really do love Helen?

RICHARD. What do you want—an affidavit?

HIS VOICE. Well, good. So that leaves you with only one problem. I'm warning you, pal, it may not be as easy to get rid of this girl as you think.

RICHARD. Huh?

HIS VOICE. My dear boy, did you ever hear of a thing called blackmail?

RICHARD. *Blackmail?*

HIS VOICE. One often hears of unscrupulous young girls who prey on foolish, wealthy, middle-aged men . . .

RICHARD. Now, really . . .

HIS VOICE. You got her into bed without any great effort. Why do you suppose she was so willing?

RICHARD *(weakly)*. But she said—she told me—she went on record—she didn't want to get involved . . . (HIS VOICE *laughs coarsely.)* A minute ago you were saying she was madly in love with me . . .

HIS VOICE. *You poor, foolish, wealthy, middle-aged man.*

RICHARD. Wait a minute—in the first place I'm not wealthy . . .

HIS VOICE. Blackmail, pal, it happens every day. She'll bleed you white.

RICHARD. Oh, my God. I'll have to sell the kid's bonds. . . . Poor Ricky. Poor Helen. There's only one thing to do. Confess everything and throw myself on her mercy. We're both intelligent people. She'll forgive me.

HIS VOICE. I wouldn't be a bit surprised if she shot you dead.

RICHARD. You're out of your mind. Not Helen. If she shot anyone it would much more likely be herself. Oh, my God. She'd probably shoot us both . . . I can't go on torturing myself like this. I'll have to tell her. Oh, she'll be hurt. For a while. But she'll get over it. There's no other way. I've got to tell her and take my chances . . .

(Music and "dream lighting" in.)

RICHARD *(calling)*. Helen! Helen!

HELEN *(from kitchen)*. Yes, darling . . .

RICHARD. Can you come in here a moment, please? There's something I must tell you.

(Helen enters from the kitchen. This is the domestic, very un-green-dress HELEN. *She wears an apron and carries a bowl which she stirs with a wooden spoon.)*

HELEN *(sweetly)*. Yes, Dick? I was just making a cherry pie. I know how you hate the pies from Gristede's and I wanted to surprise you. . . .

RICHARD. I don't know how to say this to you . . .

HELEN. Yes, Dick?

RICHARD. We've been married a long time . . .

HELEN. Seven years, darling. Seven glorious years. These are sweetheart cherries . . .

RICHARD. And in all that time, I've never looked at another woman . . .

HELEN. I know that, Dick. And I want to tell you what it's meant to me. You may not know this, darling, but you're terribly attractive to women . . .

RICHARD. I am?

HELEN. Yes, you funny Richard you—you are. But in all those seven years I've never once worried. Oh, don't I know there are plenty of women who would give their eye teeth to get you. Elaine. Miss Morris. That Marie What-ever-her-name-was up in Westport. But I trust you, Dick. I always have. I always will. Do you know something?

RICHARD. What?

HELEN. I . . . Oh, I can't even say it. It's too foolish . . .

RICHARD. Go ahead. Go ahead, say it. Be foolish.

HELEN. Well—I honestly believe that if you were ever unfaithful to me—I'd know it. I'd know it instantly.

RICHARD. You would?

HELEN. Oh, yes . . .

RICHARD. How?

HELEN. Wives have ways. Little ways.

RICHARD. And what would you do?

HELEN. Oh, darling, don't be . . .

RICHARD. No. Really. I'm interested. What would you do?

HELEN. Oh, I think I'd probably shoot you dead. Afterwards, of course, I'd shoot myself. Life wouldn't be worth living after that . . .

RICHARD. Oh, no! *(A pause)* Helen . . .

HELEN. Yes?

RICHARD. Nothing. Nothing.

HELEN. Yes, there is something. I can tell.

RICHARD. No, now take it easy . . .

HELEN. I can tell. I can suddenly feel it. The vibrations—something happened while I was away this summer . . .

RICHARD. It was an accident. A crazy accident. There was this tomato . . . That is—this tomato plant fell down. It landed right out there on the terrace. But nobody was hurt, thank God. I didn't want to tell you about it. I was afraid you'd worry . . .

HELEN (*sadly*). Who was she?

RICHARD. Now, Helen—you're making this up . . .

HELEN (*turning on him*). *Who was she!*

RICHARD. Now please, really . . .

HELEN. Then it's true. It is true.

RICHARD. Look, we're both intelligent people. I knew you'd be hurt. But I know that somehow, someday, you'll forgive me. . . . (*He suddenly notices that* HELEN *is holding a revolver in her hand.*) Now put that thing down. What are you going to do?

HELEN. You've left me nothing else to do. I'm going to shoot you dead. Then I'm going to kill myself.

RICHARD. But what about—the child?

HELEN. You should have thought of that before. Good-by, Richard . . . (*She fires five times.*)

(*For a moment,* RICHARD *stands erect, weathering the hail of bullets. . . . Then slowly, tragically, in the best gangster movie tradition—clutching his middle— and making small Bogart-like sounds he sinks to the floor.*)

RICHARD (*gasping—the beads of sweat standing out on his forehead.*) Helen—I'm —going—fast . . . Give me a cigarette . . .

HELEN (*always the wife, even in times of crisis*). A cigarette! You know what Dr. Murphy told you about smoking!

RICHARD. Good-by . . . Helen . . .

(*She turns and walks sadly to the kitchen. At the door she stops, waves sadly with the wooden spoon, blows one final kiss and as the music swells she exits into kitchen. An instant later we hear the final shot.*)

(RICHARD *collapses in a final spasm of agony and the lights black out.*)

(*As the lights dim back to reality* RICH-ARD *is seated where we left him, a horror-struck expression on his face.*)

RICHARD. Oh, the hell with *that!* I'll be goddamned if I'll tell her! (*For a moment,* RICHARD *stands shaking his head.*) But I've got to . . . I've just got to . . . (*He is heading for the telephone when the sound of the door buzzer stops him.*)

(*He freezes, panic-stricken. Glances quickly at the bedroom. The buzzer sounds again. Then a third time.*)

(*When it is quite clear that whoever it is is not going to go away,* RICHARD *presses the buzzer, then opens the door a crack, still leaving the chain fastened.*)

RICHARD (*hoarsely*). Who is it?

DR. BRUBAKER (*off stage*). Once again, sir, I must trouble you . . .

RICHARD. Dr. Brubaker!

DR. BRUBAKER (*off stage*). Yes . . .

RICHARD. What it is? What can I do for you?

DR. BRUBAKER (*through door*). Last evening, after our conference, I appear to have left your apartment without my brief case.

RICHARD. No, no, Doctor. That's impossible. I'm afraid you're mistaken. I'm quite sure you had it with you. In fact, I remember quite clearly seeing . . . (*He looks wildly around the room and then sees the brief case.*) Oh. Oh, there it is. . . . You're right. Isn't that amazing? It's right there. I'm sorry I can't ask you in but the place is kind of a mess and . . . (*He is trying to get the brief case through the door without unfastening the chain. It doesn't fit. He attempts brute force, but it just isn't going to fit. He pounds at it wildly and then finally realizes that he is going to have to open the chain. He does so.*) Here you are, Doctor . . . Good-by . . .

DR. BRUBAKER (*an unstoppable force, he moves into the living room*). I thank you. If you will permit me, I'll just make sure that everything is in order . . . (*Opening the brief case and riffling through the contents*) You can see what a strong unconscious resistance this whole project has stimulated in me. . . . I cannot understand this mass compulsion on the part of the psychiatric profession to write and publish books . . .

RICHARD. Don't worry about it, Doctor. Books by psychiatrists almost always sell well. I'll talk to you again the first of the week . . .

DR. BRUBAKER. Thank you, sir. And once again I must apologize for troubling you. Particularly in the midst of such a delicate situation . . .

RICHARD. Yes. Well . . . *What?* What do you mean? What delicate situation?

DR. BRUBAKER. I meant only that, as, quite clearly, your second assault on the person of the young lady was more successful than the first, my visit could not have been more inopportune. Good-by, sir, and good luck! (DR. BRUBAKER *starts to go.* RICHARD *stops him.*)

RICHARD. Now wait a minute, Doctor. Now wait a minute. You can't just say something like that and then go . . .

DR. BRUBAKER. My boy, I have a full day ahead of me . . .

RICHARD. Look, I can't stand it. You've got to tell me. How did you know—about —what happened?

DR. BRUBAKER. In the light of our conversation of last evening, it is quite obvious. I return this morning to find you behind barred doors in an extreme state of sexomasochistic excitement bordering on hysteria . . .

RICHARD. What the hell is sexomasochistic excitement?

DR. BRUBAKER. Guilt feelings, sir. Guilt feelings. A state of deep and utter enjoyment induced by reveling in one's guilt feelings. One punishes oneself and one is pardoned of one's crime. And now, my boy, I must really go. Enjoy yourself!

RICHARD. Look, this may not seem like very much to you—you spend eight hours a day with rapists and all kinds of—but I've never done anything like this before . . .

DR. BRUBAKER. This is quite obvious.

RICHARD. This is the first time. And, by God, it's the last time . . .

DR. BRUBAKER. An excellent decision.

RICHARD. I mean, I love my wife!

DR. BRUBAKER. Don't we all? And now, sir . . .

RICHARD. If she ever finds out about this she'll—kill us both. She'll kill *herself* anyway—and I don't want her to do that. Maybe it would be better if I didn't tell her . . .

DR. BRUBAKER. Possibly . . .

RICHARD. But she'd find out some way. I know she would. What was that you said the other night? There was some phrase you used. What was it?

DR. BRUBAKER (*he has wandered over to the bookshelf and taken down the copy of* US Camera). Vigorous denial. This popular theory of omniscience of wives is completely untrue. They almost never know. Because they don't want to.

RICHARD. Yeah. Yeah. Vigorous denial. Suppose I denied it. That's all. She'd have to take my word for it. As a matter of fact, you know, it's probably a damn good thing this happened. I mean, a couple of days ago—I wasn't even sure if I did love her. Now I know I do. Helen ought to be damn glad this happened, if you want to know . . . (*He notices* DR. BRUBAKER *holding* US Camera) You can take that with you if you want to . . .

DR. BRUBAKER. No. No, thank you.

RICHARD. You know, suddenly I feel much better. Everything's going to be all right. You're absolutely right, Doctor. I just won't tell her and everything'll be fine. And if she should find out, I'll deny it . . .

DR. BRUBAKER. Vigorously.

RICHARD. Gee, Doctor—I'd like to give you fifty dollars or something . . .

DR. BRUBAKER (*considers this briefly, but rejects it*). Well . . . No, no. It will not be necessary . . . (*He is casually thumbing through* US Camera *and stops at* THE GIRL'S *picture.*) However, if the young lady should by any chance suffer any severe traumatic or emotional disturbances due to your decision to go back to your wife . . . If, in other words, she appears to be in need of psychiatric aid—I trust you will mention my name . . . Thank you once again, sir, and good day . . . (*He hands* US Camera *back to* RICHARD *and exits.* RICHARD *looks after him thoughtfully for a moment or two. Then, the doors to the bedrooms slide open and* THE GIRL *emerges. She is dressed and is bright and cheerful and very much herself.*)

THE GIRL. Hi.

RICHARD. Oh. Hi.

THE GIRL. *Golly,* I didn't know it was so late. I don't know what happened to me. I've got to be at the studio in half an hour. . . .

RICHARD. The studio . . .

THE GIRL. Sure. The television show. Forty million people are waiting to see me wash my husband's shirt in Trill—that exciting new, no-rinse detergent . . .

RICHARD. Oh.

THE GIRL. Well, I'd better go now. . . .

RICHARD. I was going to make some coffee. . . .

THE GIRL. That's all right. I'll get some on the way.

RICHARD. I don't know how to say this —but you're . . . I mean, I . . .

THE GIRL. I know. Me too . . .

RICHARD. Will I see you—again, I mean?

THE GIRL. I think better not . . .

RICHARD. This whole thing—it's been swell. Only . . .

THE GIRL. Only one thing. We mustn't forget that . . .

RICHARD. What's that?

THE GIRL. This is your birthday.

RICHARD. Gee, that's right. It is.

THE GIRL. Well, I want this to be a happy birthday . . .

RICHARD. Look. You're not upset about anything, are you?

THE GIRL. No. No, I feel fine. Are you?

RICHARD. Are you sure? I mean, well . . .

THE GIRL. No, really, I feel wonderful. . . . Only . . . Well, suddenly I feel like maybe it wouldn't be so bad to have to start getting in at one o'clock again . . .

RICHARD. Didn't you say—I mean— wouldn't that spoil everything?

THE GIRL. You don't understand—I mean it would be pretty nice to have to start getting in at one o'clock again. As soon as I find someone who's fallen desperately in love with me—someone who's sweet and intelligent and married—to me . . . I don't mean you—I mean—you know— someone who . . .

RICHARD. Someone who never saw Sarah Bernhardt?

THE GIRL. Well, yes . . . Good-by, and thanks for everything . . . (*She kisses him lightly on the cheek.*) Birthday kiss. Happy birthday, Richard.

RICHARD. Thank you . . .

(*She starts up the stairs then turns and stops.*)

THE GIRL. Hey—I forgot my hammer.

RICHARD. Yeah—you better take that . . .

(*Both laugh and are released. She goes up the stairs. The trap closes and she is gone.*)

(RICHARD *is a little awed. In a dazed way he wanders over to the bar and pours himself a glass of milk. Then, he looks at his watch, pulls himself together, picks up* US Camera *and heads for bedroom. He puts* US Camera *on shelf, starts out. Comes*

back and drops it behind the row of books, hiding it. He starts out again and the door buzzer sounds. He goes to the door and opens it. TOM MACKENZIE *is standing in the doorway.*)

TOM. Hi, there . . .

RICHARD. Hello.

TOM. How are you? Hope I didn't wake you . . .

RICHARD. What do you want?

TOM. I'm sorry to bust in on you at this ungodly hour, boy, but I'm here on business. Family business. Got any coffee?

RICHARD. No. What are you doing here? I thought you were up in the country.

TOM. I was. I just drove in this morning. Got an appointment with my agent so Helen asked me to stop by and ask you . . .

RICHARD. Oh! Oh, she did. Well, I'm damn glad she did. I want to talk to you.

TOM. What's the matter with you, boy? You're acting mighty peculiar.

RICHARD. Never mind how *I'm* acting. You think you're pretty fancy with your rain and your damn fireplaces . . .

TOM. What are you talking about? What fireplaces?

RICHARD. You know what fireplaces.

TOM. I don't even have a fireplace.

RICHARD. That's your story.

TOM. I put in radiant heat. It's the latest thing. Cost me three thousand dollars.

RICHARD. Oh, yeah?

TOM. Yeah! They take the coils and they bury them right in the floor . . . What the hell is all this about fireplaces? Are you drunk or something?

RICHARD. No, I am not drunk! (*From above comes the sound of hammering, a nail being driven into the floor.*) She had dinner with you last night, didn't she?

TOM. Sure. Sure. (*More hammering.*) What's wrong with that?

RICHARD. And she was wearing that green dress from Clare Potter wasn't she?

TOM. How the hell do I know where she bought that green dress?

RICHARD. Oh, then she *was* wearing it! Worse than I thought!

TOM. You *are* drunk. (*More hammering. This time* TOM *looks up.*) What's that?

RICHARD. That's nothing. This used to be a duplex. I just had a glass of milk!

TOM (*patiently*). Now see here, old man. Why shouldn't Helen have dinner with me? She's stuck up there in the country while you're down here doing God knows what . . .

RICHARD. What do you mean by that?

TOM. I know what happens with guys like you when their wives are away. Don't forget, I used to be married myself.

RICHARD. I got a good mind to punch you right in the nose.

TOM. Why?

RICHARD. Why—because you're too old —that's why!

TOM. Too old—what are you talking about?

RICHARD. You're getting fat—you look like the portrait of Dorian Gray!

TOM. Drunk. Blind, stinking drunk at nine o'clock in the morning. Where am I getting fat?

RICHARD. Everywhere! You know, there's something really repulsive about old men who run after young wives! Now you get out of here and get back to Helen and tell her I refuse to give her a divorce . . .

TOM. *A divorce?*

RICHARD. You heard me! You can tell her for me that I'll fight it in every court in the country!

TOM. You're crazy! Helen doesn't want a divorce . . . (*Yelling, he can no longer control himself.*) She wants her yellow skirt!

RICHARD. Her yellow skirt? Oh, my God . . .

TOM (*bellowing*). She's having people over for dinner and she needs it! (*He exits slamming the door furiously.*)

RICHARD. Her yellow skirt . . . (*He reaches into hall closet and finds it on the wire hanger. Tenderly, he folds it over his arm.*) I'll take her yellow skirt up to her myself. She needs it. She's having people over for dinner. . . . People over for dinner? *What* people? . . . *Me!* That's what people! (*Takes his hat from closet, puts it on his head at a rakish angle and with a great flourish exits out the door as:*)

THE CURTAIN FALLS

THE CRUCIBLE

(With a new scene written for the revised production of the play)

Arthur Miller

First presented by Kermit Bloomgarden at the Martin
Beck Theatre, New York, on January 22, 1953,
with the following cast:

REVEREND PARRIS Fred Stewart

BETTY PARRIS Janet Alexander

TITUBA Jacqueline Andre

ABIGAIL WILLIAMS Madeleine Sherwood

SUSANNA WALCOTT Barbara Stanton

MRS. ANN PUTNAM Jane Hoffman

THOMAS PUTNAM Raymond Bramley

MERCY LEWIS Dorothy Joliffe

MARY WARREN Jenny Egan

JOHN PROCTOR Arthur Kennedy

REBECCA NURSE Jean Adair

GILES COREY Joseph Sweeney

REVEREND JOHN HALE E. G. Marshall

ELIZABETH PROCTOR Beatrice Straight

FRANCIS NURSE Graham Velsey

EZEKIEL CHEEVER Don McHenry

MARSHAL HERRICK George Mitchell

JUDGE HATHORNE Philip Coolidge

DEPUTY GOVERNOR DANFORTH
  Walter Hampden

SARAH GOOD Adele Fortin

HOPKINS Donald Marye

NOTE: In the restaged Broadway production, which opened at the Martin Beck Theatre
on January 22, 1953, Philip Coolidge replaced Walter Hampden, and the roles of John
Proctor and his wife were played by E. G. Marshall and Maureen Stapleton.

© Copyright, 1952, 1953, by Arthur Miller.

Reprinted by permission of The Viking Press, Inc.

CAUTION: All rights reserved; no public or private performance of the play, professional
or amateur, may be given, no film, radio or television use or public reading, without
authorization from the author's representative, MCA Management, Ltd., 598 Madison
Avenue, New York 22, N.Y. For permission to reprint excerpts from the play, address
The Viking Press, 625 Madison Avenue, New York 22, N.Y.

The Crucible was actually staged twice for Broadway—once by Jed Harris, and a second time, six months later, by the author himself. For that occasion he added a new scene, a meeting between Proctor and Abigail that would strengthen the latter's motivation in precipitating the scandalous witchhunt in Salem. At the same time, in restaging the production prior to its national tour, Miller abolished the scenery and placed the action in front of drapes and an expressively lit cyclorama. In securing greater fluency for the work, he also drew attention to a timelessness of tragic implication expressed in his declaration that he wished to write a play that "would lift out of the morass of subjectivism the squirming, single defined process which would show that the sin of public terror is that it divests man of conscience, of himself."

Miller, our theatre's chief moralist, is correct in stating that "It was a theme not unrelated to those that had invested the previous plays," and that "I had grown increasingly conscious of this theme in my past work . . . ." Nor is there any doubt that the pressure upon him to turn to it directly was both personal and, given his strong sense of the responsibilities of a writer, social. He had strong feelings about the state of the public mind, and it is apparent from both the play and the explanation of it offered in his introduction to his *Collected Plays* (The Viking Press, 1957) that the political situation of the period had acquired moral and spiritual connotations for him. "It was not only the rise of 'McCarthyism' that moved me," he declares, "but something which was much more weird and mysterious. It was the fact that a political, objective, knowledgeable campaign from the far Right was capable of creating not only a terror, but a new subjective reality, a veritable mystique which was gradually assuming even a holy resonance. That so interior and subjective an emotion could have been so manifestly created from without was a marvel to me. It underlies every word in *The Crucible*." To the author's contentions, in so far as they are intended to explain *The Crucible*, it is possible to object that while it is true that Salem had no witches, it is not true that contemporary America had no Communists. But it is true that Miller's concern was with a rather different matter—namely, the matter of conscience.

The subject of "confessing" to guilt concerned him especially, in both public life and in the play, where the tragic climax revolves around whether John Proctor will validate the Salem witchhunt by signing a statement to the effect that the Devil came to him and his neighbors. Miller writes, "I saw forming [in the 1950's] a kind of interior mechanism of confession and forgiveness of sins which until now had not been rightly categorized as sins. New sins were being created monthly. It was very odd how quickly these were accepted into the new orthodoxy, quite as though they had been there since the beginning of time. . . .

"Above all, above all horrors," Miller concludes, "I saw accepted the notion that conscience was no longer a private matter but one of state administration. I saw men handing conscience to other men and thanking other men for the opportunity of doing so." Therein lies the real tragic gambit of the play, whether or not Miller played it as well as we think he should have. Miller does not say so, but this theme could have reminded him of Sophocles' *Antigone* and given him the assurance that he was speaking with the voice of high-tragic tradition.

That he did not quite do so was the result of the intrigue in the plot, as well as of a limitation of literary talent, and perhaps also of point of view. That *The Crucible* was not a warmer and less abstract play, despite the author's concentration on personal motivation, has also been noted, eliciting Miller's reply that in plays of broad social awareness emotion and private feeling should be held in check. The resistance of some of the reviewers was strong enough for them to resort to charges of "contrivance" and "melodrama," including much dependency "on a slut's malicious lie," as *Time* magazine put it. Nevertheless, the first Broadway audiences were, in the main, greatly stirred. And a London production directed by George Devine and Tony Richardson at the Royal Court Theatre on April 10, 1956, eighteen months after a rather lukewarm premiere by the Bristol Old Vic Company, roused general enthusiasm despite reservations concerning weakness of characterization and some melodrama. The London *Times* complimented the author on "generating, nevertheless, a genuine dramatic force" and the author could accept the praise in this instance without granting the reservation. He believed he was sustained by the historical record in not providing "any mitigation of the unrelieved, straightforward, and absolute dedication to evil displayed by the judges of these trials and the prosecutors . . . There was a sadism here that was breathtaking." He blamed himself, on the contrary, for mitigating the evil of Danforth in the play, whereas the record of the trials does not support any mitigation. "I believe now," he declared in his preface to *Collected Plays,* "as I did not conceive then, that there are people dedicated to evil in the world," which view carries Miller out of the camp of old-fashioned liberalism and almost into the camp of his chief antagonists, the literati of the New Conservatism. . . . He concluded with a criticism that would have surprised the Broadway critics of the play in 1953: *"The Crucible* is a tough play. My criticism of it now would be that it is not tough enough."

AUTHOR'S NOTE ON THE HISTORICAL ACCURACY
OF THIS PLAY

This play is not history in the sense in which the word is used by the academic historian. Dramatic purposes have sometimes required many characters to be fused into one; the number of girls involved in the "crying-out" has been reduced; Abigail's age has been raised; while there were several judges of almost equal authority, I have symbolized them all in Hathorne and Danforth. However, I believe that the reader will discover here the essential nature of one of the strangest and most awful chapters in human history. The fate of each character is exactly that of his historical model, and there is no one in the drama who did not play a similar—and in some cases exactly the same—role in history.

As for the characters of the persons, little is known about most of them excepting what may be surmised from a few letters, the trial record, certain broadsides written at the time, and references to their conduct in sources of varying reliability. They may therefore be taken as creations of my own, drawn to the best of my ability in conformity with their known behavior, except as indicated in the commentary I have written for this text.

ACT ONE

*A small upper bedroom in the home of
Reverend Samuel Parris, Salem, Massachusetts, in the spring of the year 1692.*

*There is a narrow window at the left.
Through its leaded panes the morning
sunlight streams. A candle still burns near
the bed, which is at the right. A chest, a
chair, and a small table are the other furnishings. At the back a door opens on the
landing of the stairway to the ground
floor. The room gives off an air of clean
spareness. The roof rafters are exposed,
and the wood colors are raw and unmel-
lowed.*

As the curtain rises, REVEREND PARRIS *is
discovered kneeling beside the bed, evidently in prayer. His daughter,* BETTY PAR-
RIS, *aged ten, is lying on the bed, inert.*

At the time of these events Parris was
in his middle forties. In history he cut a
villainous path, and there is very little
good to be said for him. He believed he
was being persecuted wherever he went,
despite his best efforts to win people and
God to his side. In meeting, he felt insulted if someone rose to shut the door
without first asking his permission. He
was a widower with no interest in children, or talent with them. He regarded
them as young adults, and until this
strange crisis he, like the rest of Salem,
never conceived that the children were
anything but thankful for being permitted
to walk straight, eyes slightly lowered,
arms at the sides, and mouths shut until
bidden to speak.

His house stood in the "town"—but we
today would hardly call it a village. The
meeting house was nearby, and from this
point outward—toward the bay or inland
—there were a few small-windowed, dark
houses snuggling against the raw Massachusetts winter. Salem had been established hardly forty years before. To the
European world the whole province was
a barbaric frontier inhabited by a sect of
fanatics who, nevertheless, were shipping
out products of slowly increasing quantity
and value.

No one can really know what their lives
were like. They had no novelists—and
would not have permitted anyone to read
a novel if one were handy. Their creed
forbade anything resembling a theater or
"vain enjoyment." They did not celebrate
Christmas, and a holiday from work
meant only that they must concentrate
even more upon prayer.

Which is not to say that nothing broke
into this strict and somber way of life.
When a new farmhouse was built, friends
assembled to "raise the roof," and there
would be special foods cooked and probably some potent cider passed around.
There was a good supply of ne'er-do-wells
in Salem, who dallied at the shovelboard
in Bridget Bishop's tavern. Probably more
than the creed, hard work kept the morals
of the place from spoiling, for the people
were forced to fight the land like heroes
for every grain of corn, and no man had
very much time for fooling around.

That there were some jokers, however,
is indicated by the practice of appointing
a two-man patrol whose duty was to "walk
forth in the time of God's worship to take
notice of such as either lye about the meeting house, without attending to the word
and ordinances, or that lye at home or in
the fields without giving good account
thereof, and to take the names of such
persons, and to present them to the magistrates, whereby they may be accordingly
proceeded against." This predilection for
minding other people's business was time-
honored among the people of Salem, and
it undoubtedly created many of the suspicions which were to feed the coming madness. It was also, in my opinion, one of
the things that a John Proctor would rebel
against, for the time of the armed camp
had almost passed, and since the country
was reasonably—although not wholly—
safe, the old disciplines were beginning to
rankle. But, as in all such matters, the
issue was not clear-cut, for danger was
still a possibility, and in unity still lay the
best promise of safety.

The edge of the wilderness was close
by. The American continent stretched end-
lessly west, and it was full of mystery for
them. It stood, dark and threatening, over
their shoulders night and day, for out of
it Indian tribes marauded from time to
time, and Reverend Parris had parishioners
who had lost relatives to these heathen.

The parochial snobbery of these people
was partly responsible for their failure to
convert the Indians. Probably they also
preferred to take land from heathens
rather than from fellow Christians. At any
rate, very few Indians were converted, and

the Salem folk believed that the virgin forest was the Devil's last preserve, his home base and the citadel of his final stand. To the best of their knowledge the American forest was the last place on earth that was not paying homage to God.

For these reasons, among others, they carried about an air of innate resistance, even of persecution. Their fathers had, of course, been persecuted in England. So now they and their church found it necessary to deny any other sect its freedom, lest their New Jersualem be defiled and corrupted by wrong ways and deceitful ideas.

They believed, in short, that they held in their steady hands the candle that would light the world. We have inherited this belief, and it has helped and hurt us. It helped them with the discipline it gave them. They were a dedicated folk, by and large, and they had to be to survive the life they had chosen or been born into in this country.

The proof of their belief's value to them may be taken from the opposite character of the first Jamestown settlement, farther south, in Virginia. The Englishmen who landed there were motivated mainly by a hunt for profit. They had thought to pick off the wealth of the new country and then return rich to England. They were a band of individualists, and a much more ingratiating group than the Massachusetts men. But Virginia destroyed them. Massachusetts tried to kill off the Puritans, but they combined; they set up a communal society which, in the beginning, was little more than an armed camp with an autocratic and very devoted leadership. It was, however, an autocracy by consent, for they were united from top to bottom by a commonly held ideology whose perpetuation was the reason and justification for all their sufferings. So their self-denial, their purposefulness, their suspicion of all vain pursuits, their hard-handed justice, were altogether perfect instruments for the conquest of this space so antagonistic to man.

But the people of Salem in 1692 were not quite the dedicated folk that arrived on the *Mayflower*. A vast differentiation had taken place, and in their own time a revolution had unseated the royal government and substituted a junta which was at this moment in power. The times, to their eyes, must have been out of joint, and to the common folk must have seemed as insoluble and complicated as do ours today. It is not hard to see how easily many could have been led to believe that the time of confusion had been brought upon them by deep and darkling forces. No hint of such speculation appears on the court record, but social disorder in any age breeds such mystical suspicions, and when, as in Salem, wonders are brought forth from below the social surface, it is too much to expect people to hold back very long from laying on the victims with all the force of their frustrations.

The Salem tragedy, which is about to begin in these pages, developed from a paradox. It is a paradox in whose grip we still live, and there is no prospect yet that we will discover its resolution. Simply, it was this: for good purposes, even high purposes, the people of Salem developed a theocracy, a combine of state and religious power whose function was to keep the community together, and to prevent any kind of disunity that might open it to destruction by material or ideological enemies. It was forged for a necessary purpose and accomplished that purpose. But all organization is and must be grounded on the idea of exclusion and prohibition, just as two objects cannot occupy the same space. Evidently the time came in New England when the repressions of order were heavier than seemed warranted by the dangers against which the order was organized. The witchhunt was a perverse manifestation of the panic which set in among all classes when the balance began to turn toward greater individual freedom.

When one rises above the individual villainy displayed, one can only pity them all, just as we shall be pitied someday. It is still impossible for man to organize his social life without repressions, and the balance has yet to be struck between order and freedom.

The witchhunt was not, however, a mere repression. It was also, and as importantly, a long overdue opportunity for everyone so inclined to express publicly his guilt and sins, under the cover of accusations against the victims. It suddenly became possible—and patriotic and holy— for a man to say that Martha Corey had come into his bedroom at night, and that, while his wife was sleeping at his side,

Martha laid herself down on his chest and "nearly suffocated him." Of course it was her spirit only, but his satisfaction at confessing himself was no lighter than if it had been Martha herself. One could not ordinarily speak such things in public.

Long-held hatreds of neighbors could now be openly expressed, and vengeance taken, despite the Bible's charitable injunctions. Land-lust which had been expressed before by constant bickering over boundaries and deeds, could now be elevated to the arena of morality; one could cry witch against one's neighbor and feel perfectly justified in the bargain. Old scores could be settled on a plane of heavenly combat between Lucifer and the Lord; suspicions and the envy of the miserable toward the happy could and did burst out in the general revenge.

REVEREND PARRIS *is praying now, and, though we cannot hear his words, a sense of his confusion hangs about him. He mumbles, then seems about to weep; then he weeps, then prays again; but his daughter does not stir on the bed.*

The door opens, and his Negro slave enters. TITUBA *is in her forties.* PARRIS *brought her with him from Barbados, where he spent some years as a merchant before entering the ministry. She enters as one does who can no longer bear to be barred from the sight of her beloved, but she is also very frightened because her slave sense has warned her that, as always, trouble in this house eventually lands on her back.*

———

TITUBA (*already taking a step backward*). My Betty be hearty soon?

PARRIS. Out of here!

TITUBA (*backing to the door*). My Betty not goin' die . . .

PARRIS (*scrambling to his feet in a fury*). Out of my sight! (*She is gone.*) Out of my—(*He is overcome with sobs. He clamps his teeth against them and closes the door and leans against it, exhausted.*) Oh, my God! God help me! (*Quaking with fear, mumbling to himself through his sobs, he goes to the bed and gently takes* BETTY's *hand.*) Betty. Child. Dear child. Will you wake, will you open up your eyes! Betty, little one . . .

(*He is bending to kneel again when his niece,* ABIGAIL WILLIAMS, *seventeen, enters —a strikingly beautiful girl, an orphan,* *with an endless capacity for dissembling. Now she is all worry and apprehension and propriety.*)

ABIGAIL. Uncle? (*He looks to her.*) Susanna Walcott's here from Doctor Griggs.

PARRIS. Oh? Let her come, let her come.

ABIGAIL (*leaning out the door to call to* SUSANNA, *who is down the hall a few steps*). Come in, Susanna.

(SUSANNA WALCOTT, *a little younger than* ABIGAIL, *a nervous, hurried girl, enters.*)

PARRIS (*eagerly*). What does the doctor say, child?

SUSANNA (*craning around* PARRIS *to get a look at* BETTY). He bid me come and tell you, reverend sir, that he cannot discover no medicine for it in his books.

PARRIS. Then he must search on.

SUSANNA. Aye, sir, he have been searchin' his books since he left you, sir. But he bid me tell you, that you might look to unnatural things for the cause of it.

PARRIS (*his eyes going wide*). No—no. There be no unnatural cause here. Tell him I have sent for Reverend Hale of Beverly, and Mr. Hale will surely confirm that. Let him look to medicine and put out all thought of unnatural causes here. There be none.

SUSANNA. Aye, sir. He bid me tell you. (*She turns to go.*)

ABIGAIL. Speak nothin' of it in the village, Susanna.

PARRIS. Go directly home and speak nothing of unnatural causes.

SUSANNA. Aye, sir. I pray for her. (*She goes out.*)

ABIGAIL. Uncle, the rumor of witchcraft is all about; I think you'd best go down and deny it yourself. The parlor's packed with people, sir. I'll sit with her.

PARRIS (*pressed, turns on her*). And what shall I say to them? That my daughter and my niece I discovered dancing like heathen in the forest?

ABIGAIL. Uncle, we did dance; let you tell them I confessed it—and I'll be whipped if I must be. But they're speakin' of witchcraft. Betty's not witched.

PARRIS. Abigail, I cannot go before the congregation when I know you have not opened with me. What did you do with her in the forest?

ABIGAIL. We did dance, uncle, and when you leaped out of the bush so suddenly, Betty was frightened and then she fainted. And there's the whole of it.

PARRIS. Child. Sit you down.

ABIGAIL (*quavering, as she sits*). I would never hurt Betty. I love her dearly.

PARRIS. Now look you, child, your punishment will come in its time. But if you trafficked with spirits in the forest I must know it now, for surely my enemies will, and they will ruin me with it.

ABIGAIL. But we never conjured spirits.

PARRIS. Then why can she not move herself since midnight? This child is desperate! (ABIGAIL *lowers her eyes.*) It must come out—my enemies will bring it out. Let me know what you done there. Abigail, do you understand that I have many enemies?

ABIGAIL. I have heard of it, uncle.

PARRIS. There is a faction that is sworn to drive me from my pulpit. Do you understand that?

ABIGAIL. I think so, sir.

PARRIS. Now then, in the midst of such disruption, my own household is discovered to be the very center of some obscene practice. Abominations are done in the forest—

ABIGAIL. It were sport, uncle!

PARRIS (*pointing at* BETTY). You call this sport? (*She lowers her eyes. He pleads.*) Abigail, if you know something that may help the doctor, for God's sake tell it to me. (*She is silent.*) I saw Tituba waving her arms over the fire when I came on you. Why was she doing that? And I heard a screeching and gibberish coming from her mouth. She were swaying like a dumb beast over that fire!

ABIGAIL. She always sings her Barbados songs, and we dance.

PARRIS. I cannot blink what I saw, Abigail, for my enemies will not blink it. I saw a dress lying on the grass.

ABIGAIL (*innocently*). A dress?

PARRIS (*—it is very hard to say*). Aye, a dress. And I thought I saw—someone naked running through the trees!

ABIGAIL (*in terror*). No one was naked! You mistake yourself, uncle!

PARRIS (*with anger*). I saw it! (*He moves from her. Then, resolved.*) Now tell me true, Abigail. And I pray you feel the weight of truth upon you, for now my ministry's at stake, my ministry and perhaps your cousin's life. Whatever abomination you have done, give me all of it now, for I dare not be taken unaware when I go before them down there.

ABIGAIL. There is nothin' more. I swear it, uncle.

PARRIS (*studies her, then nods, half convinced*). Abigail, I have fought here three long years to bend these stiff-necked people to me, and now, just now when some good respect is rising for me in the parish, you compromise my very character. I have given you a home, child, I have put clothes upon your back—now give me upright answer. Your name in the town—it is entirely white, is it not?

ABIGAIL (*with an edge of resentment*). Why, I am sure it is, sir. There be no blush about my name.

PARRIS (*to the point*). Abigail, is there any other cause than you have told me, for your being discharged from Goody Proctor's service? I have heard it said, and I tell you as I heard it, that she comes so rarely to the church this year for she will not sit so close to something soiled. What signified that remark?

ABIGAIL. She hates me, uncle, she must, for I would not be her slave. It's a bitter woman, a lying, cold, sniveling woman, and I will not work for such a woman!

PARRIS. She may be. And yet it has troubled me that you are now seven month out of their house, and in all this time no other family has ever called for your service.

ABIGAIL. They want slaves, not such as I. Let them send to Barbados for that. I will not black my face for any of them! (*With ill-concealed resentment at him.*) Do you begrudge my bed, uncle?

PARRIS. No—no.

ABIGAIL (*in a temper*). My name is good in the village! I will not have it said my name is soiled! Goody Proctor is a gossiping liar!

(*Enter* MRS. ANN PUTNAM. *She is a twisted soul of forty-five, a death-ridden woman, haunted by dreams.*)

PARRIS (*as soon as the door begins to open*). No—no, I cannot have anyone. (*He sees her, and a certain deference springs into him, although his worry remains.*) Why, Goody Putnam, come in.

MRS. PUTNAM (*full of breath, shiny-eyed*). It is a marvel. It is surely a stroke of hell upon you.

PARRIS. No, Goody Putnam, it is—

MRS. PUTNAM (*glancing at* BETTY). How high did she fly, how high?

PARRIS. No, no, she never flew—

MRS. PUTNAM (*very pleased with it*). Why, it's sure she did. Mr. Collins saw her goin' over Ingersoll's barn, and come down light as bird, he says!

PARRIS. Now, look you, Goody Putnam, she never—(*Enter* THOMAS PUTNAM, *a well-to-do, hard-handed landowner, near fifty*.) Oh, good morning, Mr. Putnam.

PUTNAM. It is a providence the thing is out now! It is a providence. (*He goes directly to the bed.*)

PARRIS. What's out, sir, what's—?

(MRS. PUTNAM *goes to the bed*.)

PUTNAM (*looking down at* BETTY). Why, her eyes is closed! Look you, Ann.

MRS. PUTNAM. Why, that's strange. (*To* PARRIS.) Ours is open.

PARRIS (*shocked*). Your Ruth is sick?

MRS. PUTNAM (*with vicious certainty*). I'd not call it sick; the Devil's touch is heavier than sick. It's death, y'know, it's death drivin' into them, forked and hoofed.

PARRIS. Oh, pray not! Why, how does Ruth ail?

MRS. PUTNAM. She ails as she must—she never waked this morning, but her eyes open and she walks, and hears naught, sees naught, and cannot eat. Her soul is taken, surely.

(PARRIS *is struck*.)

PUTNAM (*as though for further details*). They say you've sent for Reverend Hale of Beverly?

PARRIS (*with dwindling conviction now*). A precaution only. He has much experience in all demonic arts, and I—

MRS. PUTNAM. He has indeed; and found a witch in Beverly last year, and let you remember that.

PARRIS. Now, Goody Ann, they only thought that were a witch, and I am certain there be no element of witchcraft here.

PUTNAM. No witchcraft! Now look you, Mr. Parris—

PARRIS. Thomas, Thomas, I pray you, leap not to witchcraft. I know that you —you least of all, Thomas, would ever wish so disastrous a charge laid upon me. We cannot leap to witchcraft. They will howl me out of Salem for such corruption in my house.

———

A word about Thomas Putnam. He was a man with many grievances, at least one of which appears justified. Some time before, his wife's brother-in-law, James Bay-

ley, had been turned down as minister of Salem. Bayley had all the qualifications, and a two-thirds vote into the bargain, but a faction stopped his acceptance, for reasons that are not clear.

Thomas Putnam was the eldest son of the richest man in the village. He had fought the Indians at Narragansett, and was deeply interested in parish affairs. He undoubtedly felt it poor payment that the village should so blatantly disregard his candidate for one of its more important offices, especially since he regarded himself as the intellectual superior of most of the people around him.

His vindictive nature was demonstrated long before the witchcraft began. Another former Salem minister, George Burroughs, had had to borrow money to pay for his wife's funeral, and, since the parish was remiss in his salary, he was soon bankrupt. Thomas and his brother John had Burroughs jailed for debts the man did not owe. The incident is important only in that Burroughs succeeded in becoming minister where Bayley, Thomas Putnam's brother-in-law, had been rejected; the motif of resentment is clear here. Thomas Putnam felt that his own name and the honor of his family had been smirched by the village, and he meant to right matters however he could.

Another reason to believe him a deeply embittered man was his attempt to break his father's will, which left a disproportionate amount to a step-brother. As with every other public cause in which he tried to force his way, he failed in this.

So it is not surprising to find that so many accusations against people are in the handwriting of Thomas Putnam, or that his name is so often found as a witness corroborating the supernatural testimony, or that his daughter led the crying-out at the most opportune junctures of the trials, especially when—But we'll speak of that when we come to it.

———

PUTNAM (—*at the moment he is intent upon getting* PARRIS, *for whom he has only contempt, to move toward the abyss*). Mr. Parris, I have taken your part in all contention here, and I would continue; but I cannot if you hold back in this. There are hurtful, vengeful spirits layin' hands on these children.

PARRIS. But, Thomas, you cannot—

PUTNAM. Ann! Tell Mr. Parris what you have done.

MRS. PUTNAM. Reverend Parris, I have laid seven babies unbaptized in the earth. Believe me, sir, you never saw more hearty babies born. And yet, each would wither in my arms the very night of their birth. I have spoke nothin', but my heart has clamored intimations. And now, this year, my Ruth, my only— I see her turning strange. A secret child she has become this year, and shrivels like a sucking mouth were pullin' on her life too. And so I thought to send her to your Tituba—

PARRIS. To Tituba! What may Tituba—?

MRS. PUTNAM. Tituba knows how to speak to the dead, Mr. Parris.

PARRIS. Goody Ann, it is a formidable sin to conjure up the dead!

MRS. PUTNAM. I take it on my soul, but who else may surely tell us what person murdered my babies?

PARRIS (*horrified*). Woman!

MRS. PUTNAM. They were murdered, Mr. Parris! And mark this proof! Mark it! Last night my Ruth were ever so close to their little spirits; I know it, sir. For how else is she struck dumb now except some power of darkness would stop her mouth? It is a marvelous sign, Mr. Parris!

PUTNAM. Don't you understand it, sir? There is a murdering witch among us, bound to keep herself in the dark. (PARRIS *turns to* BETTY, *a frantic terror rising in him.*) Let your enemies make of it what they will, you cannot blink it more.

PARRIS (*to* ABIGAIL). Then you were conjuring spirits last night.

ABIGAIL (*whispering*). Not I, sir—Tituba and Ruth.

PARRIS (*turns now, with new fear, and goes to* BETTY, *looks down at her, and then, gazing off*). Oh, Abigail, what proper payment for my charity! Now I am undone.

PUTNAM. You are not undone! Let you take hold here. Wait for no one to charge you—declare it yourself. You have discovered witchcraft—

PARRIS. In my house? In my house, Thomas? They will topple me with this! They will make of it a—

(*Enter* MERCY LEWIS, *the Putnams' servant, a fat, sly, merciless girl of eighteen.*)

MERCY. Your pardons. I only thought to see how Betty is.

PUTNAM. Why aren't you home? Who's with Ruth?

MERCY. Her grandma come. She's improved a little, I think—she give a powerful sneeze before.

MRS. PUTNAM. Ah, there's a sign of life!

MERCY. I'd fear no more, Goody Putnam. It were a grand sneeze; another like it will shake her wits together, I'm sure. (*She goes to the bed to look.*)

PARRIS. Will you leave me now, Thomas? I would pray a while alone.

ABIGAIL. Uncle, you've prayed since midnight. Why do you not go down and—

PARRIS. No—no. (*To* PUTNAM.) I have no answer for that crowd. I'll wait till Mr. Hale arrives. (*To get* MRS. PUTNAM *to leave.*) If you will, Goody Ann . . .

PUTNAM. Now look you, sir. Let you strike out against the Devil, and the village will bless you for it! Come down, speak to them—pray with them. They're thirsting for your word, Mister! Surely you'll pray with them.

PARRIS (*swayed*). I'll lead them in a psalm, but let you say nothing of witchcraft yet. I will not discuss it. The cause is yet unknown. I have had enough contention since I came; I want no more.

MRS. PUTNAM. Mercy, you go home to Ruth, d'y'hear?

MERCY. Aye, mum.

(MRS. PUTNAM *goes out.*)

PARRIS (*to* ABIGAIL). If she starts for the window, cry for me at once.

ABIGAIL. I will, uncle.

PARRIS (*to* PUTNAM). There is a terrible power in her arms today. (*He goes out with* PUTNAM.)

ABIGAIL (*with hushed trepidation*). How is Ruth sick?

MERCY. It's weirdish, I know not—she seems to walk like a dead one since last night.

ABIGAIL (*turns at once and goes to* BETTY, *and now, with fear in her voice*). Betty? (BETTY *doesn't move. She shakes her.*) Now stop this! Betty! Sit up now!

(BETTY *doesn't stir.* MERCY *comes over.*)

MERCY. Have you tried beatin' her? I gave Ruth a good one and it waked her for a minute. Here, let me have her.

ABIGAIL (*holding* MERCY *back*). No, he'll be comin' up. Listen, now; if they be questioning us, tell them we danced—I told him as much already.

MERCY. Aye. And what more?

ABIGAIL. He knows Tituba conjured

Ruth's sisters to come out of the grave.

MERCY. And what more?

ABIGAIL. He saw you naked.

MERCY (*clapping her hands together with a frightened laugh*). Oh, Jesus!

(*Enter* MARY WARREN, *breathless. She is seventeen, a subservient, naïve, lonely girl.*)

MARY WARREN. What'll we do? The village is out! I just come from the farm; the whole country's talkin' witchcraft! They'll be callin' us witches, Abby!

MERCY (*pointing and looking at* MARY WARREN). She means to tell, I know it.

MARY WARREN. Abby, we've got to tell. Witchery's a hangin' error, a hangin' like they done in Boston two year ago! We must tell the truth, Abby! You'll only be whipped for dancin', and the other things!

ABIGAIL. Oh, *we'll* be whipped!

MARY WARREN. I never done none of it, Abby. I only looked!

MERCY (*moving menacingly toward* MARY). Oh, you're a great one for lookin', aren't you, Mary Warren? What a grand peeping courage you have!

(BETTY, *on the bed, whimpers.* ABIGAIL *turns to her at once.*)

ABIGAIL. Betty? (*She goes to* BETTY.) Now, Betty, dear, wake up now. It's Abigail. (*She sits* BETTY *up and furiously shakes her.*) I'll beat you, Betty! (BETTY *whimpers.*) My, you seem improving. I talked to your papa and I told him everything. So there's nothing to—

BETTY (*darts off the bed, frightened of* ABIGAIL, *and flattens herself against the wall*). I want my mama!

ABIGAIL (*with alarm, as she cautiously approaches* BETTY). What ails you, Betty? Your mama's dead and buried.

BETTY. I'll fly to Mama. Let me fly! (*She raises her arms as though to fly, and streaks for the window, gets one leg out.*)

ABIGAIL (*pulling her away from the window*). I told him everything; he knows now, he knows everything we—

BETTY. You drank blood, Abby! You didn't tell him that!

ABIGAIL. Betty, you never say that again! You will never—

BETTY. You did, you did! You drank a charm to kill John Proctor's wife! You drank a charm to kill Goody Proctor!

ABIGAIL (*smashes her across the face*). Shut it! Now shut it!

BETTY (*collapsing on the bed*). Mama, Mama! (*She dissolves into sobs.*)

ABIGAIL. Now look you. All of you. We danced. And Tituba conjured Ruth Putnam's dead sisters. And that is all. And mark this. Let either of you breathe a word, or the edge of a word, about the other things, and I will come to you in the black of some terrible night and I will bring a pointy reckoning that will shudder you. And you know I can do it; I saw Indians smash my dear parents' heads on the pillow next to mine, and I have seen some reddish work done at night, and I can make you wish you had never seen the sun go down! (*She goes to* BETTY *and roughly sits her up.*) Now, you—sit up and stop this!

(*But* BETTY *collapses in her hands and lies inert on the bed.*)

MARY WARREN (*with hysterical fright*). What's got her? (ABIGAIL *stares in fright at* BETTY.) Abby, she's going to die! It's a sin to conjure, and we—

ABIGAIL (*starting for* MARY). I say shut it, Mary Warren!

(*Enter* JOHN PROCTOR. *On seeing him,* MARY WARREN *leaps in fright.*)

Proctor was a farmer in his middle thirties. He need not have been a partisan of any faction in the town, but there is evidence to suggest that he had a sharp and biting way with hypocrites. He was the kind of man—powerful of body, eventempered, and not easily led—who cannot refuse support to partisans without drawing their deepest resentment. In Proctor's presence a fool felt his foolishness instantly —and a Proctor is always marked for calumny therefore.

But as we shall see, the steady manner he displays does not spring from an untroubled soul. He is a sinner, a sinner not only against the moral fashion of the time, but against his own vision of decent conduct. These people had no ritual for the washing away of sins. It is another trait we inherited from them, and it has helped to discipline us as well as to breed hypocrisy among us. Proctor, respected and even feared in Salem, has come to regard himself as a kind of fraud. But no hint of this has yet appeared on the surface, and as he enters from the crowded parlor below it is a man in his prime we see, with a quiet confidence and an unexpressed, hidden force. Mary Warren, his servant, can barely speak for embarrassment and fear. _____

MARY WARREN. Oh! I'm just going home, Mr. Proctor.

PROCTOR. Be you foolish, Mary Warren? Be you deaf? I forbid you leave the house, did I not? Why shall I pay you? I am looking for you more often than my cows!

MARY WARREN. I only come to see the great doings in the world.

PROCTOR. I'll show you a great doin' on your arse one of these days. Now get you home; my wife is waitin' with your work! (*Trying to retain a shred of dignity, she goes slowly out.*)

MERCY LEWIS (*both afraid of him and strangely titillated*). I'd best be off. I have my Ruth to watch. Good morning, Mr. Proctor.

(MERCY *sidles out. Since* PROCTOR's *entrance,* ABIGAIL *has stood as though on tiptoe, absorbing his presence, wide-eyed. He glances at her, then goes to* BETTY *on the bed.*)

ABIGAIL. Gah! I'd almost forgot how strong you are, John Proctor!

PROCTOR (*looking at* ABIGAIL *now, the faintest suggestion of a knowing smile on his face*). What's this mischief here?

ABIGAIL (*with a nervous laugh*). Oh, she's only gone silly somehow.

PROCTOR. The road past my house is a pilgrimage to Salem all morning. The town's mumbling witchcraft.

ABIGAIL. Oh, posh! (*Winningly she comes a little closer, with a confidential, wicked air.*) We were dancin' in the woods last night, and my uncle leaped in on us. She took fright, is all.

PROCTOR (*his smile widening*). Ah, you're wicked yet, aren't y'! (*A trill of expectant laughter escapes her, and she dares come closer, feverishly looking into his eyes.*) You'll be clapped in the stocks before you're twenty.

(*He takes a step to go, and she springs into his path.*)

ABIGAIL. Give me a word, John. A soft word. (*Her concentrated desire destroys his smile.*)

PROCTOR. No, no, Abby. That's done with.

ABIGAIL (*tauntingly*). You come five mile to see a silly girl fly? I know you better.

PROCTOR (*setting her firmly out of his path*). I come to see what mischief your uncle's brewin' now. (*With final emphasis.*) Put it out of mind, Abby.

ABIGAIL (*grasping his hand before he can release her*). John—I am waitin' for you every night.

PROCTOR. Abby, I never give you hope to wait for me.

ABIGAIL (*now beginning to anger—she can't believe it*). I have something better than hope, I think!

PROCTOR. Abby, you'll put it out of mind. I'll not be comin' for you more.

ABIGAIL. You're surely sportin' with me.

PROCTOR. You know me better.

ABIGAIL. I know how you clutched my back behind your house and sweated like a stallion whenever I come near! Or did I dream that? It's she put me out, you cannot pretend it were you. I saw your face when she put me out, and you loved me then and you do now!

PROCTOR. Abby, that's a wild thing to say—

ABIGAIL. A wild thing may say wild things. But not so wild, I think. I have seen you since she put me out; I have seen you nights.

PROCTOR. I have hardly stepped off my farm this sevenmonth.

ABIGAIL. I have a sense for heat, John, and yours has drawn me to my window, and I have seen you looking up, burning in your loneliness. Do you tell me you've never looked up at my window?

PROCTOR. I may have looked up.

ABIGAIL (*now softening*). And you must. You are no wintry man. I know you, John. I *know* you. (*She is weeping.*) I cannot sleep for dreamin'; I cannot dream but I wake and walk about the house as though I'd find you comin' through some door. (*She clutches him desperately.*)

PROCTOR (*gently pressing her from him, with great sympathy but firmly*). Child—

ABIGAIL (*with a flash of anger*). How do you call me child!

PROCTOR. Abby, I may think of you softly from time to time. But I will cut off my hand before I'll ever reach for you again. Wipe it out of mind. We never touched, Abby.

ABIGAIL. Aye, but we did.

PROCTOR. Aye, but we did not.

ABIGAIL (*with a bitter anger*). Oh, I marvel how such a strong man may let such a sickly wife be—

PROCTOR (*angered—at himself as well*).

You'll speak nothin' of Elizabeth!

ABIGAIL. She is blackening my name in the village! She is telling lies about me! She is a cold, sniveling woman, and you bend to her! Let her turn you like a—

PROCTOR (*shaking her*). Do you look for whippin'?

(*A psalm is heard being sung below.*)

ABIGAIL (*in tears*). I look for John Proctor that took me from my sleep and put knowledge in my heart! I never knew what pretense Salem was, I never knew the lying lessons I was taught by all these Christian women and their covenanted men! And now you bid me tear the light out of my eyes? I will not, I cannot! You loved me, John Proctor, and whatever sin it is, you love me yet! (*He turns abruptly to go out. She rushes to him.*) John, pity me, pity me!

(*The words "going up to Jesus" are heard in the psalm, and* BETTY *claps her ears suddenly and whines loudly.*)

ABIGAIL. Betty? (*She hurries to* BETTY, *who is now sitting up and screaming.* PROCTOR *goes to* BETTY *as* ABIGAIL *is trying to pull her hands down, calling "Betty!"*)

PROCTOR (*growing unnerved*). What's she doing? Girl, what ails you? Stop that wailing!

(*The singing has stopped in the midst of this, and now* PARRIS *rushes in.*)

PARRIS. What happened? What are you doing to her? Betty! (*He rushes to the bed, crying, "Betty, Betty!"* MRS. PUTNAM *enters, feverish with curiosity, and with her* THOMAS PUTNAM *and* MERCY LEWIS. PARRIS, *at the bed, keeps lightly slapping* BETTY's *face, while she moans and tries to get up.*)

ABIGAIL. She heard you singin' and suddenly she's up and screamin'.

MRS. PUTNAM. The psalm! The psalm! She cannot bear to hear the Lord's name!

PARRIS. No, God forbid. Mercy, run to the doctor! Tell him what's happened here! (MERCY LEWIS *rushes out.*)

MRS. PUTNAM. Mark it for a sign, mark it!

(REBECCA NURSE, *seventy-two, enters. She is white-haired, leaning upon her walking-stick.*)

PUTNAM (*pointing at the whimpering* BETTY). That is a notorious sign of witchcraft afoot, Goody Nurse, a prodigious sign!

MRS. PUTNAM. My mother told me that!

When they cannot bear to hear the name of—

PARRIS (*trembling*). Rebecca, Rebecca, go to her, we're lost. She suddenly cannot bear to hear the Lord's—

(GILES COREY, *eighty-three, enters. He is knotted with muscle, canny, inquisitive, and still powerful.*)

REBECCA. There is hard sickness here, Giles Corey, so please to keep the quiet.

GILES. I've not said a word. No one here can testify I've said a word. Is she going to fly again? I hear she flies.

PUTNAM. Man, be quiet now!

(*Everything is quiet.* REBECCA *walks across the room to the bed. Gentleness exudes from her.* BETTY *is quietly whimpering, eyes shut.* REBECCA *simply stands over the child, who gradually quiets.*)

———

And while they are so absorbed, we may put a word in for Rebecca. Rebecca was the wife of Francis Nurse, who, from all accounts, was one of those men for whom both sides of the argument had to have respect. He was called upon to arbitrate disputes as though he were an unofficial judge, and Rebecca also enjoyed the high opinion most people had for him. By the time of the delusion, they had three hundred acres, and their children were settled in separate homesteads within the same estate. However, Francis had originally rented the land, and one theory has it that, as he gradually paid for it and raised his social status, there were those who resented his rise.

Another suggestion to explain the systematic campaign against Rebecca, and inferentially against Francis, is the land war he fought with his neighbors, one of whom was a Putnam. This squabble grew to the proportions of a battle in the woods between partisans of both sides, and it is said to have lasted for two days. As for Rebecca herself, the general opinion of her character was so high that to explain how anyone dared cry her out for a witch—and more, how adults could bring themselves to lay hands on her—we must look to the fields and boundaries of that time.

As we have seen, Thomas Putnam's man for the Salem ministry was Bayley. The Nurse clan had been in the faction that prevented Bayley's taking office. In addition, certain families allied to the Nurses by blood or friendship, and whose farms were contiguous with the Nurse farm or close to it, combined to break away from the Salem town authority and set up Topsfield, a new and independent entity whose existence was resented by old Salemites.

That the guiding hand behind the outcry was Putnam's is indicated by the fact that, as soon as it began, this Topsfield-Nurse faction absented themselves from church in protest and disbelief. It was Edward and Jonathan Putnam who signed the first complaint against Rebecca; and Thomas Putnam's little daughter was the one who fell into a fit at the hearing and pointed to Rebecca as her attacker. To top it all, Mrs. Putnam—who is now staring at the bewitched child on the bed—soon accused Rebecca's spirit of "tempting her to iniquity," a charge that had more truth in it than Mrs. Putnam could know.

———

MRS. PUTNAM (*astonished*). What have you done?

(REBECCA, *in thought, now leaves the bedside and sits.*)

PARRIS (*wondrous and relieved*). What do you make of it, Rebecca?

PUTNAM (*eagerly*). Goody Nurse, will you go to my Ruth and see if you can wake her?

REBECCA (*sitting*). I think she'll wake in time. Pray calm yourselves. I have eleven children, and I am twenty-six times a grandma, and I have seen them all through their silly seasons, and when it come on them they will run the Devil bowlegged keeping up with their mischief. I think she'll wake when she tires of it. A child's spirit is like a child, you can never catch it by running after it; you must stand still, and, for love, it will soon itself come back.

PROCTOR. Aye, that's the truth of it, Rebecca.

MRS. PUTNAM. This is no silly season, Rebecca. My Ruth is bewildered, Rebecca; she cannot eat.

REBECCA. Perhaps she is not hungered yet. (*To* PARRIS.) I hope you are not decided to go in search of loose spirits, Mr. Parris. I've heard promise of that outside.

PARRIS. A wide opinion's running in the parish that the Devil may be among us, and I would satisfy them that they are wrong.

PROCTOR. Then let you come out and call them wrong. Did you consult the wardens before you called this minister to look for devils?

PARRIS. He is not coming to look for devils!

PROCTOR. Then what's he coming for?

PUTNAM. There be children dyin' in the village, Mister!

PROCTOR. I seen none dyin'. This society will not be a bag to swing around your head, Mr. Putnam. (*To* PARRIS.) Did you call a meeting before you—?

PUTNAM. I am sick of meetings; cannot the man turn his head without he have a meeting?

PROCTOR. He may turn his head, but not to Hell!

REBECCA. Pray, John, be calm. (*Pause. He defers to her.*) Mr. Parris, I think you'd best send Reverend Hale back as soon as he come. This will set us all to arguin' again in the society, and we thought to have peace this year. I think we ought rely on the doctor now, and good prayer.

MRS. PUTNAM. Rebecca, the doctor's baffled!

REBECCA. If so he is, then let us go to God for the cause of it. There is prodigious danger in the seeking of loose spirits. I fear it, I fear it. Let us rather blame ourselves and—

PUTNAM. How may we blame ourselves? I am one of nine sons; the Putnam seed have peopled this province. And yet I have but one child left of eight—and now she shrivels!

REBECCA. I cannot fathom that.

MRS. PUTNAM (*with a growing edge of sarcasm*). But I must! You think it God's work you should never lose a child, nor grandchild either, and I bury all but one? There are wheels within wheels in this village, and fires within fires!

PUTNAM (*to* PARRIS). When Reverend Hale comes, you will proceed to look for signs of witchcraft here.

PROCTOR (*to* PUTNAM). You cannot command Mr. Parris. We vote by name in this society, not by acreage.

PUTNAM. I never heard you worried so on this society, Mr. Proctor. I do not think I saw you at Sabbath meeting since snow flew.

PROCTOR. I have trouble enough without I come five mile to hear him preach only hellfire and bloody damnation. Take it to heart, Mr. Parris. There are many others who stay away from church these days because you hardly ever mention God any more.

PARRIS (*now aroused*). Why, that's a drastic charge!

REBECCA. It's somewhat true; there are many that quail to bring their children—

PARRIS. I do not preach for children, Rebecca. It is not the children who are unmindful of their obligations toward this ministry.

REBECCA. Are there really those unmindful?

PARRIS. I should say the better half of Salem village—

PUTNAM. And more than that!

PARRIS. Where is my wood? My contract provides I be supplied with all my firewood. I am waiting since November for a stick, and even in November I had to show my frostbitten hands like some London beggar!

GILES. You are allowed six pound a year to buy your wood, Mr. Parris.

PARRIS. I regard that six pound as part of my salary. I am paid little enough without I spend six pound on firewood.

PROCTOR. Sixty, plus six for firewood—

PARRIS. The salary is sixty-six pound, Mr. Proctor! I am not some preaching farmer with a book under my arm; I am a graduate of Harvard College.

GILES. Aye, and well instructed in arithmetic!

PARRIS. Mr. Corey, you will look far for a man of my kind at sixty pound a year! I am not used to this poverty; I left a thrifty business in the Barbados to serve the Lord. I do not fathom it, why am I persecuted here? I cannot offer one proposition but there be a howling riot of argument. I have often wondered if the Devil be in it somewhere; I cannot understand you people otherwise.

PROCTOR. Mr. Parris, you are the first minister ever did demand the deed to this house—

PARRIS. Man! Don't a minister deserve a house to live in?

PROCTOR. To live in, yes. But to ask ownership is like you shall own the meeting house itself; the last meeting I were at you spoke so long on deeds and mortgages I thought it were an auction.

PARRIS. I want a mark of confidence, is all! I am your third preacher in seven years. I do not wish to be put out like the cat whenever some majority feels the whim. You people seem not to comprehend that a minister is the Lord's man in the parish; a minister is not to be so lightly crossed and contradicted—

PUTNAM. Aye!

PARRIS. There is either obedience or the church will burn like Hell is burning!

PROCTOR. Can you speak one minute without we land in Hell again? I am sick of Hell!

PARRIS. It is not for you to say what is good for you to hear!

PROCTOR. I may speak my heart, I think!

PARRIS (*in a fury*). What, are we Quakers? We are not Quakers here yet, Mr. Proctor. And you may tell that to your followers!

PROCTOR. My followers!

PARRIS (*—now he's out with it*). There is a party in this church. I am not blind; there is a faction and a party.

PROCTOR. Against you?

PUTNAM. Against him and all authority!

PROCTOR. Why, then I must find it and join it.

(*There is shock among the others.*)

REBECCA. He does not mean that.

PUTNAM. He confessed it now!

PROCTOR. I mean it solemnly, Rebecca; I like not the smell of this "authority."

REBECCA. No, you cannot break charity with your minister. You are another kind, John. Clasp his hand, make your peace.

PROCTOR. I have a crop to sow and lumber to drag home. (*He goes angrily to the door and turns to* COREY *with a smile.*) What say you, Giles, let's find the party. He says there's a party.

GILES. I've changed my opinion of this man, John. Mr. Parris, I beg your pardon. I never thought you had so much iron in you.

PARRIS (*surprised*). Why, thank you, Giles!

GILES. It suggests to the mind what the trouble be among us all these years. (*To all.*) Think on it. Wherefore is everybody suing everybody else? Think on it now, it's a deep thing, and dark as a pit. I have been six time in court this year—

PROCTOR (*familiarly, with warmth, although he knows he is approaching the edge of* GILES' *tolerance with this*). Is it the Devil's fault that a man cannot say you good morning without you clap him for defamation? You're old, Giles, and you're not hearin' so well as you did.

GILES (*—he cannot be crossed*). John Proctor, I have only last month collected four pound damages for you publicly sayin' I burned the roof off your house, and I—

PROCTOR (*laughing*). I never said no such thing, but I've paid you for it, so I hope I can call you deaf without charge. Now come along, Giles, and help me drag my lumber home.

PUTNAM. A moment, Mr. Proctor. What lumber is that you're draggin', if I may ask you?

PROCTOR. My lumber. From out my forest by the riverside.

PUTNAM. Why, we are surely gone wild this year. What anarchy is this? That tract is in my bounds, it's in my bounds, Mr. Proctor.

PROCTOR. In your bounds! (*Indicating* REBECCA.) I bought that tract from Goody Nurse's husband five months ago.

PUTNAM. He had no right to sell it. It stands clear in my grandfather's will that all the land between the river and—

PROCTOR. Your grandfather had a habit of willing land that never belonged to him, if I may say it plain.

GILES. That's God's truth; he nearly willed away my north pasture but he knew I'd break his fingers before he'd set his name to it. Let's get your lumber home, John. I feel a sudden will to work coming on.

PUTNAM. You load one oak of mine and you'll fight to drag it home!

GILES. Aye, and we'll win too, Putnam —this fool and I. Come on! (*He turns to* PROCTOR *and starts out.*)

PUTNAM. I'll have my men on you, Corey! I'll clap a writ on you!

(*Enter* REVEREND JOHN HALE *of Beverly.*)

———

Mr. Hale is nearing forty, a tight-skinned, eager-eyed intellectual. This is a beloved errand for him; on being called here to ascertain witchcraft he felt the pride of the specialist whose unique knowledge has at last been publicly called for. Like almost all men of learning, he spent a good deal of his time pondering the invisible world, especially since he had himself encountered a witch in his parish not long before. That woman, however, turned into a mere pest under his searching scrutiny, and the child she had allegedly been afflicting recovered her normal behavior after

Hale had given her his kindness and a few days of rest in his own house. However, that experience never raised a doubt in his mind as to the reality of the underworld or the existence of Lucifer's many-faced lieutenants. And his belief is not to his discredit. Better minds than Hale's were —and still are—convinced that there is a society of spirits beyond our ken. One cannot help noting that one of his lines has never yet raised a laugh in any audience that has seen this play; it is his assurance that "We cannot look to superstition in this. The Devil is precise." Evidently we are not quite certain even now whether diabolism is holy and not to be scoffed at. And it is no accident that we should be so bemused.

Like Reverend Hale and the others on this stage, we conceive the Devil as a necessary part of a respectable view of cosmology. Ours is a divided empire in which certain ideas and emotions and actions are of God, and their opposites are of Lucifer. It is as impossible for most men to conceive of a morality without sin as of an earth without "sky." Since 1692 a great but superficial change has wiped out God's beard and the Devil's horns, but the world is still gripped between two diametrically opposed absolutes. The concept of unity, in which positive and negative are attributes of the same force, in which good and evil are relative, ever-changing, and always joined to the same phenomenon— such a concept is still reserved to the physical sciences and to the few who have grasped the history of ideas. When it is recalled that until the Christian era the underworld was never regarded as a hostile area, that all gods were useful and essentially friendly to man despite occasional lapses; when we see the steady and methodical inculcation into humanity of the idea of man's worthlessness—until redeemed—the necessity of the Devil may become evident as a weapon, a weapon designed and used time and time again in every age to whip men into a surrender to a particular church or church-state.

Our difficulty in believing the—for want of a better word—political inspiration of the Devil is due in great part to the fact that he is called up and damned not only by our social antagonists but by our own side, whatever it may be. The Catholic Church, through its Inquisition, is famous for cultivating Lucifer as the arch-fiend, but the Church's enemies relied no less upon the Old Boy to keep the human mind enthralled. Luther was himself accused of alliance with Hell, and he in turn accused his enemies. To complicate matters further, he believed that he had had contact with the Devil and had argued theology with him. I am not surprised at this, for at my own university a professor of history—a Lutheran, by the way—used to assemble his graduate students, draw the shades, and commune in the classroom with Erasmus. He was never, to my knowledge, officially scoffed at for this, the reason being that the university officials, like most of us, are the children of a history which still sucks at the Devil's teats. At this writing, only England has held back before the temptations of contemporary diabolism. In the countries of the Communist ideology, all resistance of any import is linked to the totally malign capitalist succubi, and in America any man who is not reactionary in his views is open to the charge of alliance with the Red hell. Political opposition, thereby, is given an inhumane overlay which then justifies the abrogation of all normally applied customs of civilized intercourse. A political policy is equated with moral right, and opposition to it with diabolical malevolence. Once such an equation is effectively made, society becomes a congerie of plots and counterplots, and the main role of government changes from that of the arbiter to that of the scourge of God.

The results of this process are no different now from what they were, except sometimes in the degree of cruelty inflicted, and not always even in that department. Normally the actions and deeds of a man were all that society felt comfortable in judging. The secret intent of an action was left to the ministers, priests, and rabbis to deal with. When diabolism rises, however, actions are the least important manifests of the true nature of a man. The Devil, as Reverend Hale said, is a wily one, and, until an hour before he fell, even God thought him beautiful in Heaven.

The analogy, however, seems to falter when one considers that, while there were no witches then, there are Communists and capitalists now, and in each camp there is certain proof that spies of each side are at work undermining the other. But this is a snobbish objection and not at all warranted by the facts. I have no doubt that people *were* communing with, and even worshiping, the Devil in Salem, and if the whole truth could be known in this case, as it is in others, we should discover a regular and conventionalized propitiation of the dark spirit. One certain evidence of this is the confession of Tituba, the slave of Reverend Parris, and another is the behavior of the children who were known to have indulged in sorceries with her.

There are accounts of similar *klatches* in Europe, where the daughters of the towns would assemble at night and, sometimes with fetishes, sometimes with a selected young man, give themselves to love, with some bastardly results. The Church, sharp-eyed as it must be when gods long dead are brought to life, condemned these orgies as witchcraft and interpreted them, rightly, as a resurgence of the Dionysiac forces it had crushed long before. Sex, sin, and the Devil were early linked, and so they continued to be in Salem, and are today. From all accounts there are no more puritanical mores in the world than those enforced by the Communists in Russia, where women's fashions, for instance, are as prudent and all-covering as any American Baptist would desire. The divorce laws lay a tremendous responsibility on the father for the care of his children. Even the laxity of divorce regulations in the early years of the revolution was undoubtedly a revulsion from the nineteenth-century Victorian immobility of marriage and the consequent hypocrisy that developed from it. If for no other reasons, a state so powerful, so jealous of the uniformity of its citizens, cannot long tolerate the atomization of the family. And yet, in American eyes at least, there remains the conviction that the Russian attitude toward women is lascivious. It is the Devil working again, just as he is working within the Slav who is shocked at the very idea of a woman's disrobing herself in a burlesque show. Our opposites are always robed in sexual sin, and it is from this unconscious conviction that demonology gains both its attractive sensuality and its capacity to infuriate and frighten.

Coming into Salem now, Reverend Hale conceives of himself much as a young doctor on his first call. His painfully acquired armory of symptoms, catchwords, and diagnostic procedures are now to be put to use at last. The road from Beverly is unusually busy this morning, and he has passed a hundred rumors that make him smile at the ignorance of the yeomanry in this most precise science. He feels himself allied with the best minds of Europe—kings, philosophers, scientists, and ecclesiasts of all churches. His goal is light, goodness and its preservation, and he knows the exaltation of the blessed whose intelligence, sharpened by minute examinations of enormous tracts, is finally called upon to face what may be a bloody fight with the Fiend himself.

———

(*He appears loaded down with half a dozen heavy books.*)

HALE. Pray you, someone take these!

PARRIS (*delighted*). Mr. Hale! Oh! it's good to see you again! (*Taking some books.*) My, they're heavy!

HALE (*setting down his books*). They must be; they are weighted with authority.

PARRIS (*a little scared*). Well, you do come prepared!

HALE. We shall need hard study if it comes to tracking down the Old Boy. (*Noticing* REBECCA:) You cannot be Rebecca Nurse?

REBECCA. I am, sir. Do you know me?

HALE. It's strange how I knew you, but I suppose you look as such a good soul should. We have all heard of your great charities in Beverly.

PARRIS. Do you know this gentleman? Mr. Thomas Putnam. And his good wife Ann.

HALE. Putnam! I had not expected such distinguished company, sir.

PUTNAM (*pleased*). It does not seem to help us today, Mr. Hale. We look to you to come to our house and save our child.

HALE. Your child ails too?

MRS. PUTNAM. Her soul, her soul seems flown away. She sleeps and yet she walks . . .

PUTNAM. She cannot eat.

HALE. Cannot eat! (*Thinks on it. Then, to* PROCTOR *and* GILES COREY:) Do you men have afflicted children?

PARRIS. No, no, these are farmers. John Proctor—

GILES COREY. He don't believe in witches.

PROCTOR (*to* HALE). I never spoke on witches one way or the other. Will you come, Giles?

GILES. No—no, John, I think not. I have some few queer questions of my own to ask this fellow.

PROCTOR. I've heard you to be a sensible man, Mr. Hale. I hope you'll leave some of it in Salem.

(PROCTOR *goes.* HALE *stands embarrassed for an instant.*)

PARRIS (*quickly*). Will you look at my daughter, sir? (*Leads* HALE *to the bed.*) She has tried to leap out the window; we discovered her this morning on the highroad, waving her arms as though she'd fly.

HALE (*narrowing his eyes*). Tries to fly.

PUTNAM. She cannot bear to hear the Lord's name, Mr. Hale; that's a sure sign of witchcraft afloat.

HALE (*holding up his hands*). No, no. Now let me instruct you. We cannot look to superstition in this. The Devil is precise; the marks of his presence are definite as stone, and I must tell you all that I shall not proceed unless you are prepared to believe me if I should find no bruise of hell upon her.

PARRIS. It is agreed, sir—it is agreed—we will abide by your judgment.

HALE. Good then. (*He goes to the bed, looks down at* BETTY. *To* PARRIS:) Now, sir, what were your first warning of this strangeness?

PARRIS. Why, sir—I discovered her—(*indicating* ABIGAIL)—and my niece and ten or twelve of the other girls, dancing in the forest last night.

HALE (*surprised*). You permit dancing?

PARRIS. No, no, it were secret—

MRS. PUTNAM (*unable to wait*). Mr. Parris's slave has knowledge of conjurin', sir.

PARRIS (*to* MRS. PUTNAM). We cannot be sure of that, Goody Ann—

MRS. PUTNAM (*frightened, very softly*). I know it, sir. I sent my child—she should learn from Tituba who murdered her sisters.

REBECCA (*horrified*). Goody Ann! You sent a child to conjure up the dead?

MRS. PUTNAM. Let God blame me, not you, not you, Rebecca! I'll not have you judging me any more! (*To* HALE:) Is it a natural work to lose seven children before they live a day?

PARRIS. Sssh!

(REBECCA, *with great pain, turns her face away. There is a pause.*)

HALE. Seven dead in childbirth.

MRS. PUTNAM (*softly*). Aye. (*Her voice breaks; she looks up at him. Silence.* HALE *is impressed.* PARRIS *looks to him. He goes to his books, opens one, turns pages, then reads. All wait, avidly.*)

PARRIS (*hushed*). What book is that?

MRS. PUTNAM. What's there, sir?

HALE (*with a tasty love of intellectual pursuit*). Here is all the invisible world, caught, defined, and calculated. In these books the Devil stands stripped of all his brute disguises. Here are all your familiar spirits—your incubi and succubi; your witches that go by land, by air, and by sea; your wizards of the night and of the day. Have no fear now—we shall find him out if he has come among us, and I mean to crush him utterly if he has shown his face! (*He starts for the bed.*)

REBECCA. Will it hurt the child, sir?

HALE. I cannot tell. If she is truly in the Devil's grip we may have to rip and tear to get her free.

REBECCA. I think I'll go, then. I am too old for this. (*She rises.*)

PARRIS (*striving for conviction*). Why, Rebecca, we may open up the boil of all our troubles today!

REBECCA. Let us hope for that. I go to God for you, sir.

PARRIS (*with trepidation—and resentment*). I hope you do not mean we go to Satan here! (*Slight pause.*)

REBECCA. I wish I knew. (*She goes out; they feel resentful of her note of moral superiority.*)

PUTNAM (*abruptly*). Come, Mr. Hale, let's get on. Sit you here.

GILES. Mr. Hale, I have always wanted to ask a learned man—what signifies the readin' of strange books?

HALE. What books?

GILES. I cannot tell; she hides them.

HALE. Who does this?

GILES. Martha, my wife. I have waked at night many a time and found her in a corner, readin' of a book. Now what do you make of that?

HALE. Why, that's not necessarily—

GILES. It discomfits me! Last night—mark this—I tried and tried and could not say my prayers. And then she close her book and walks out of the house, and suddenly—mark this—I could pray again!

———

Old Giles must be spoken for, if only because his fate was to be so remarkable and so different from that of all the others. He was in his early eighties at this time, and was the most comical hero in the history. No man has ever been blamed for so much. If a cow was missed, the first thought was to look for her around Corey's house; a fire blazing up at night brought suspicion of arson to his door. He didn't give a hoot for public opinion, and only in his last years—after he had married Martha—did he bother much with the church. That she stopped his prayer is very probable, but he forgot to say that he'd only recently learned any prayers and it didn't take much to make him stumble over them. He was a crank and a nuisance, but withal a deeply innocent and brave man. In court, once, he was asked if it were true that he had been frightened by the strange behavior of a hog and had then said he knew it to be the Devil in an animal's shape. "What frighted you?" he was asked. He forgot everything but the word "frighted," and instantly replied, "I do not know that I ever spoke that word in my life."

———

HALE. Ah! The stoppage of prayer—that is strange. I'll speak further on that with you.

GILES. I'm not sayin' she's touched the Devil, now, but I'd admire to know what books she reads and why she hides them. She'll not answer me, y'see.

HALE. Aye, we'll discuss it. (*To all:*) Now mark me, if the Devil is in her you will witness some frightful wonders in this room, so please to keep your wits about you. Mr. Putnam, stand close in case she flies. Now Betty, dear, will you sit up? (PUTNAM *comes in closer, ready-handed.* HALE *sits* BETTY *up, but she hangs limp in his hands.*) Hmmm. (*He observes her carefully. The others watch breathlessly.*) Can you hear me? I am John Hale, minister of Beverly. I have come to help you, dear. Do you remember my two little girls in Beverly? (*She does not stir in his hands.*)

PARRIS (*in fright*). How can it be the Devil? Why would he choose my house to strike? We have all manner of licentious people in the village!

HALE. What victory would the Devil have to win a soul already bad? It is the best the Devil wants, and who is better than the minister?

GILES. That's deep, Mr. Parris, deep, deep!

PARRIS (*with resolution now*). Betty! Answer Mr. Hale! Betty!

HALE. Does someone afflict you, child? It need not be a woman, mind you, or a man. Perhaps some bird invisible to others comes to you—perhaps a pig, a mouse, or any beast at all. Is there some figure bids you fly? (*The child remains limp in his hands. In silence he lays her back on the pillow. Now, holding out his hands toward her, he intones:*) In nomine Domini Sabaoth sui filiique ite ad infernos. (*She does not stir. He turns to* ABIGAIL, *his eyes narrowing.*) Abigail, what sort of dancing were you doing with her in the forest?

ABIGAIL. Why—common dancing is all.

PARRIS. I think I ought to say that I—I saw a kettle in the grass where they were dancing.

ABIGAIL. That were only soup.

HALE. What sort of soup were in this kettle, Abigail?

ABIGAIL. Why, it were beans—and lentils, I think, and—

HALE. Mr. Parris, you did not notice, did you, any living thing in the kettle? A mouse, perhaps, a spider, a frog—?

PARRIS (*fearfully*). I—do believe there were some movement—in the soup.

ABIGAIL. That jumped in, we never put it in!

HALE (*quickly*). What jumped in?

ABIGAIL. Why, a very little frog jumped—

PARRIS. A frog, Abby!

HALE (*grasping* ABIGAIL). Abigail, it may be your cousin is dying. Did you call the Devil last night?

ABIGAIL. I never called him! Tituba, Tituba . . .

PARRIS (*blanched*). She called the Devil?

HALE. I should like to speak with Tituba.

PARRIS. Goody Ann, will you bring her up? (MRS. PUTNAM *exits.*)

HALE. How did she call him?

ABIGAIL. I know not—she spoke Barbados.

HALE. Did you feel any strangeness when she called him? A sudden cold wind, perhaps? A trembling below the ground?

ABIGAIL. I didn't see no Devil! (*Shaking* BETTY:) Betty, wake up. Betty! Betty!

HALE. You cannot evade me, Abigail. Did your cousin drink any of the brew in that kettle?

ABIGAIL. She never drank it!

HALE. Did you drink it?

ABIGAIL. No, sir!

HALE. Did Tituba ask you to drink it?

ABIGAIL. She tried, but I refused.

HALE. Why are you concealing? Have you sold yourself to Lucifer?

ABIGAIL. I never sold myself! I'm a good girl! I'm a proper girl!

(MRS. PUTNAM *enters with* TITUBA, *and instantly* ABIGAIL *points at* TITUBA.)

ABIGAIL. She made me do it! She made Betty do it!

TITUBA (*shocked and angry*). Abby!

ABIGAIL. She makes me drink blood!

PARRIS. Blood!!

MRS. PUTNAM. My baby's blood?

TITUBA. No, no, chicken blood. I give she chicken blood!

HALE. Woman, have you enlisted these children for the Devil?

TITUBA. No, no, sir, I don't truck with no Devil!

HALE. Why can she not wake? Are you silencing this child?

TITUBA. I love me Betty!

HALE. You have sent your spirit out upon this child, have you not? Are you gathering souls for the Devil?

ABIGAIL. She sends her spirit on me in church; she makes me laugh at prayer!

PARRIS. She have often laughed at prayer!

ABIGAIL. She comes to me every night to go and drink blood!

TITUBA. You beg *me* to conjure! She beg *me* make charm—

ABIGAIL. Don't lie! (*To* HALE:) She comes to me while I sleep; she's always making me dream corruptions!

TITUBA. Why you say that, Abby?

ABIGAIL. Sometimes I wake and find myself standing in the open doorway and not a stitch on my body! I always hear her laughing in my sleep. I hear her singing her Barbados songs and tempting me with—

TITUBA. Mister Reverend, I never—

HALE (*resolved now*). Tituba, I want you to wake this child.

TITUBA. I have no power on this child, sir.

HALE. You most certainly do, and you will free her from it now! When did you compact with the Devil?

TITUBA. I don't compact with no Devil!

PARRIS. You will confess yourself or I

will take you out and whip you to your death, Tituba!

PUTNAM. This woman must be hanged! She must be taken and hanged!

TITUBA (*terrified, falls to her knees*). No, no, don't hang Tituba! I tell him I don't desire to work for him, sir.

PARRIS. The Devil?

HALE. Then you saw him! (TITUBA *weeps.*) Now Tituba, I know that when we bind ourselves to Hell it is very hard to break with it. We are going to help you tear yourself free—

TITUBA (*frightened by the coming process*). Mister Reverend, I do believe somebody else be witchin' these children.

HALE. Who?

TITUBA. I don't know, sir, but the Devil got him numerous witches.

HALE. Does he! (*It is a clue.*) Tituba, look into my eyes. Come, look into me. (*She raises her eyes to his fearfully.*) You would be a good Christian woman, would you not, Tituba?

TITUBA. Aye, sir, a good Christian woman.

HALE. And you love these little children?

TITUBA. Oh, yes, sir, I don't desire to hurt little children.

HALE. And you love God, Tituba?

TITUBA. I love God with all my bein'.

HALE. Now, in God's holy name—

TITUBA. Bless Him. Bless Him. (*She is rocking on her knees, sobbing in terror.*)

HALE. And to His glory—

TITUBA. Eternal glory. Bless Him—bless God . . .

HALE. Open yourself, Tituba—open yourself and let God's holy light shine on you.

TITUBA. Oh, bless the Lord.

HALE. When the Devil comes to you does he ever come—with another person? (*She stares up into his face.*) Perhaps another person in the village? Someone you know.

PARRIS. Who came with him?

PUTNAM. Sarah Good? Did you ever see Sarah Good with him? Or Osburn?

PARRIS. Was it man or woman came with him?

TITUBA. Man or woman. Was—was woman.

PARRIS. What woman? A woman, you said. What woman?

TITUBA. It was black dark, and I—

PARRIS. You could see him, why could you not see her?

TITUBA. Well, they was always talking; they was always runnin' round and carryin' on—

PARRIS. You mean out of Salem? Salem witches?

TITUBA. I believe so, yes, sir.

(*Now* HALE *takes her hand. She is surprised.*)

HALE. Tituba. You must have no fear to tell us who they are, do you understand? We will protect you. The Devil can never overcome a minister. You know that, do you not?

TITUBA (*kisses* HALE's *hand*). Aye, sir, oh, I do.

HALE. You have confessed yourself to witchcraft, and that speaks a wish to come to Heaven's side. And we will bless you, Tituba.

TITUBA (*deeply relieved*). Oh, God bless you, Mr. Hale!

HALE (*with rising exaltation*). You are God's instrument put in our hands to discover the Devil's agents among us. You are selected, Tituba, you are chosen to help us cleanse our village. So speak utterly, Tituba, turn your back on him and face God—face God, Tituba, and God will protect you.

TITUBA (*joining with him*). Oh, God, protect Tituba!

HALE (*kindly*). Who came to you with the Devil? Two? Three? Four? How many?

(TITUBA *pants, and begins rocking back and forth again, staring ahead.*)

TITUBA. There was four. There was four.

PARRIS (*pressing in on her*). Who? Who? Their names, their names!

TITUBA (*suddenly bursting out*). Oh, how many times he bid me kill you, Mr. Parris!

PARRIS. Kill me!

TITUBA (*in a fury*). He say Mr. Parris must be kill! Mr. Parris no goodly man, Mr. Parris mean man and no gentle man, and he bid me rise out of my bed and cut your throat! (*They gasp.*) But I tell him "No! I don't hate that man. I don't want kill that man." But he say, "You work for me, Tituba, and I make you free! I give you pretty dress to wear, and put you way high up in the air, and you gone fly back to Barbados!" And I say, "You lie, Devil, you lie!" And then he come one stormy night to me, and he say, "Look! I have *white* people belong to me." And I look—and there was Goody Good.

PARRIS. Sarah Good!

TITUBA (*rocking and weeping*). Aye, sir, and Goody Osburn.

MRS. PUTNAM. I knew it! Goody Osburn were midwife to me three times. I begged you, Thomas, did I not? I begged him not to call Osburn because I feared her. My babies always shriveled in her hands!

HALE. Take courage, you must give us all their names. How can you bear to see this child suffering? Look at her, Tituba. (*He is indicating* BETTY *on the bed.*) Look at her God-given innocence; her soul is so tender; we must protect her, Tituba; the Devil is out and preying on her like a beast upon the flesh of the pure lamb. God will bless you for your help.

(ABIGAIL *rises, staring as though inspired, and cries out.*)

ABIGAIL. I want to open myself! (*They turn to her, startled. She is enraptured, as though in a pearly light.*) I want the light of God, I want the sweet love of Jesus! I danced for the Devil; I saw him; I wrote in his book; I go back to Jesus; I kiss His hand. I saw Sarah Good with the Devil! I saw Goody Osburn with the Devil! I saw Bridget Bishop with the Devil!

(*As she is speaking,* BETTY *is rising from the bed, a fever in her eyes, and picks up the chant.*)

BETTY (*staring too*). I saw George Jacobs with the Devil! I saw Goody Howe with the Devil!

PARRIS. She speaks! (*He rushes to embrace* BETTY.) She speaks!

HALE. Glory to God! It is broken, they are free!

BETTY (*calling out hysterically and with great relief*). I saw Martha Bellows with the Devil!

ABIGAIL. I saw Goody Sibber with the Devil! (*It is rising to a great glee.*)

PUTNAM. The marshal, I'll call the marshal!

(PARRIS *is shouting a prayer of thanksgiving.*)

BETTY. I saw Alice Barrow with the Devil!

(*The curtain begins to fall.*)

HALE (*as* PUTNAM *goes out*). Let the marshal bring irons!

ABIGAIL. I saw Goody Hawkins with the Devil!

BETTY. I saw Goody Bibber with the Devil!

ABIGAIL. I saw Goody Booth with the Devil!

On their ecstatic cries

THE CURTAIN FALLS

ACT TWO

The common room of PROCTOR's *house, eight days later.*

At the right is a door opening on the fields outside. A fireplace is at the left, and behind it a stairway leading upstairs. It is the low, dark, and rather long living room of the time. As the curtain rises, the room is empty. From above, ELIZABETH *is heard softly singing to the children. Presently the door opens and* JOHN PROCTOR *enters, carrying his gun. He glances about the room as he comes toward the fireplace, then halts for an instant as he hears her singing. He continues on to the fireplace, leans the gun against the wall as he swings a pot out of the fire and smells it. Then he lifts out the ladle and tastes. He is not quite pleased. He reaches to a cupboard, takes a pinch of salt, and drops it into the pot. As he is tasting again, her footsteps are heard on the stair. He swings the pot into the fireplace and goes to a basin and washes his hands and face.* ELIZABETH *enters.*

———

ELIZABETH. What keeps you so late? It's almost dark.

PROCTOR. I were planting far out to the forest edge.

ELIZABETH. Oh, you're done then.

PROCTOR. Aye, the farm is seeded. The boys asleep?

ELIZABETH. They will be soon. (*And she goes to the fireplace, proceeds to ladle up stew in a dish.*)

PROCTOR. Pray now for a fair summer.

ELIZABETH. Aye.

PROCTOR. Are you well today?

ELIZABETH. I am. (*She brings the plate to the table, and, indicating the food.*) It is a rabbit.

PROCTOR (*going to the table*). Oh, is it! In Jonathan's trap?

ELIZABETH. No, she walked into the house this afternoon; I found her sittin' in the corner like she come to visit.

PROCTOR. Oh, that's a good sign walkin' in.

ELIZABETH. Pray God. It hurt my heart to strip her, poor rabbit. (*She sits and watches him taste it.*)

PROCTOR. It's well seasoned.

ELIZABETH (*blushing with pleasure*). I took great care. She's tender?

PROCTOR. Aye. (*He eats. She watches him.*) I think we'll see green fields soon. It's warm as blood beneath the clods.

ELIZABETH. That's well.

(PROCTOR *eats, then looks up.*)

PROCTOR. If the crop is good I'll buy George Jacobs' ·heifer. How would that please you?

ELIZABETH. Aye, it would.

PROCTOR (*with a grin*). I mean to please you, Elizabeth.

ELIZABETH (*—it is hard to say*). I know it, John.

(*He gets up, goes to her, kisses her. She receives it. With a certain disappointment, he returns to the table.*)

PROCTOR (*as gently as he can*). Cider?

ELIZABETH (*with a sense of reprimanding herself for having forgot*). Aye! (*She gets up and goes and pours a glass for him. He now arches his back.*)

PROCTOR. This farm's a continent when you go foot by foot droppin' seeds in it.

ELIZABETH (*coming with the cider*). It must be.

PROCTOR (*drinks a long draught, then, putting the glass down*). You ought to bring some flowers in the house.

ELIZABETH. Oh! I forgot! I will tomorrow.

PROCTOR. It's winter in here yet. On Sunday let you come with me, and we'll walk the farm together; I never see such a load of flowers on the earth. (*With a good feeling he goes and looks up at the sky through the open doorway.*) Lilacs have a purple smell. Lilac is the smell of nightfall, I think. Massachusetts is a beauty in the spring!

ELIZABETH. Aye, it is.

(*There is a pause. She is watching him from the table as he stands there absorbing the night. It is as though she would speak but cannot. Instead, now, she takes up his plate and glass and fork and goes with them to the basin. Her back is turned to him. He turns to her and watches her. A sense of their separation rises.*)

PROCTOR. I think you're sad again. Are you?

ELIZABETH (*—she doesn't want friction, and yet she must*). You come so late I thought you'd gone to Salem this afternoon.

PROCTOR. Why? I have no business in Salem.

ELIZABETH. You did speak of going, earlier this week.

PROCTOR (*—he knows what she means*). I thought better of it since.

ELIZABETH. Mary Warren's there today.

PROCTOR. Why'd you let her? You heard me forbid her go to Salem any more!

ELIZABETH. I couldn't stop her.

PROCTOR (*holding back a full condemnation of her*). It is a fault, it is a fault, Elizabeth—you're the mistress here, not Mary Warren.

ELIZABETH. She frightened all my strength away.

PROCTOR. How may that mouse frighten you, Elizabeth? You—

ELIZABETH. It is a mouse no more. I forbid her go, and she raises up her chin like the daughter of a prince and says to me, "I must go to Salem, Goody Proctor; I am an official of the court!"

PROCTOR. Court! What court?

ELIZABETH. Aye, it is a proper court they have now. They've sent four judges out of Boston, she says, weighty magistrates of the General Court, and at the head sits the Deputy Governor of the Province.

PROCTOR (*astonished*). Why, she's mad.

ELIZABETH. I would to God she were. There be fourteen people in the jail now, she says. (PROCTOR *simply looks at her, unable to grasp it.*) And they'll be tried, and the court have power to hang them too, she says.

PROCTOR (*scoffing, but without conviction*). Ah, they'd never hang—

ELIZABETH. The Deputy Governor promises hangin' if they'll not confess, John. The town's gone wild, I think. She speak of Abigail, and I thought she were a saint, to hear her. Abigail brings the other girls into the court, and where she walks the crowd will part like the sea for Israel. And folks are brought before them, and if they scream and howl and fall to the floor—the person's clapped in the jail for bewitchin' them.

PROCTOR (*wide-eyed*). Oh, it is a black mischief.

ELIZABETH. I think you must go to Salem, John. (*He turns to her.*) I think so. You must tell them it is a fraud.

PROCTOR (*thinking beyond this*). Aye, it is, it is surely.

ELIZABETH. Let you go to Ezekiel Cheever—he knows you well. And tell him what she said to you last week in her uncle's house. She said it had naught to do with witchcraft, did she not?

PROCTOR (*in thought*). Aye, she did, she did. (*Now, a pause.*)

ELIZABETH (*quietly fearing to anger him by prodding*). God forbid you keep that from the court, John. I think they must be told.

PROCTOR (*quietly, struggling with his thought*). Aye, they must, they must. It is a wonder they do believe her.

ELIZABETH. I would go to Salem now, John—let you go tonight.

PROCTOR. I'll think on it.

ELIZABETH (*with her courage now*). You cannot keep it, John.

PROCTOR (*angering*). I know I cannot keep it. I say I will think on it!

ELIZABETH (*hurt and very coldly*). Good, then, let you think on it. (*She stands and starts to walk out of the room.*)

PROCTOR. I am only wondering how I may prove what she told me, Elizabeth. If the girl's a saint now, I think it is not easy to prove she's fraud, and the town gone so silly. She told it to me in a room alone—I have no proof for it.

ELIZABETH. You were alone with her?

PROCTOR (*stubbornly*). For a moment alone, aye.

ELIZABETH. Why, then, it is not as you told me.

PROCTOR (*his anger rising*). For a moment, I say. The others come in soon after.

ELIZABETH (*quietly—she has suddenly lost all faith in him*). Do as you wish, then. (*She starts to turn.*)

PROCTOR. Woman. (*She turns to him.*) I'll not have your suspicion any more.

ELIZABETH (*a little loftily*). I have no—

PROCTOR. I'll not have it!

ELIZABETH. Then let you not earn it.

PROCTOR (*with a violent undertone*). You doubt me yet?

ELIZABETH (*with a smile, to keep her dignity*). John, if it were not Abigail that you must go to hurt, would you falter now? I think not.

PROCTOR. Now look you—

ELIZABETH. I see what I see, John.

PROCTOR (*with solemn warning*). You will not judge me more, Elizabeth. I have good reason to think before I charge fraud on Abigail, and I will think on it. Let you look to your own improvement before you go to judge your husband any more. I have forgot Abigail, and—

ELIZABETH. And I.

PROCTOR. Spare me! You forget nothin' and forgive nothin'. Learn charity, woman. I have gone tiptoe in this house all seven month since she is gone. I have not moved from there to there without I think to please you, and still an everlasting funeral marches round your heart. I cannot speak but I am doubted, every moment judged for lies, as though I come into a court when I come into this house!

ELIZABETH. John, you are not open with me. You saw her with a crowd, you said. Now you—

PROCTOR. I'll plead my honesty no more, Elizabeth.

ELIZABETH (*—now she would justify herself*). John, I am only—

PROCTOR. No more! I should have roared you down when first you told me your suspicion. But I wilted, and, like a Christian, I confessed. Confessed! Some dream I had must have mistaken you for God that day. But you're not, you're not, and let you remember it! Let you look sometimes for the goodness in me, and judge me not.

ELIZABETH. I do not judge you. The magistrate sits in your heart that judges you. I never thought you but a good man, John— (*with a smile—*) only somewhat bewildered.

PROCTOR (*laughing bitterly*). Oh, Elizabeth, your justice would freeze beer! (*He turns suddenly toward a sound outside. He starts for the door as* MARY WARREN *enters. As soon as he sees her, he goes directly to her and grabs her by her cloak, furious.*) How do you go to Salem when I forbid it? Do you mock me? (*Shaking her.*) I'll whip you if you dare leave this house again!

(*Strangely, she doesn't resist him, but hangs limply by his grip.*)

MARY WARREN. I am sick, I am sick, Mr. Proctor. Pray, pray, hurt me not. (*Her strangeness throws him off, and her evident pallor and weakness. He frees her.*) My insides are all shuddery; I am in the proceedings all day, sir.

PROCTOR (*with draining anger—his curiosity is draining it*). And what of these proceedings here? When will you proceed to keep this house, as you are paid nine pound a year to do—and my wife not wholly well?

(*As though to compensate,* MARY WARREN *goes to* ELIZABETH *with a small rag doll.*)

MARY WARREN. I made a gift for you today, Goody Proctor. I had to sit long hours in a chair, and passed the time with sewing.

ELIZABETH (*perplexed, looking at the doll*). Why, thank you, it's a fair poppet.

MARY WARREN (*with a trembling, decayed voice*). We must all love each other now, Goody Proctor.

ELIZABETH (*amazed at her strangeness*). Aye, indeed we must.

MARY WARREN (*glancing at the room*). I'll get up early in the morning and clean the house. I must sleep now. (*She turns and starts off.*)

PROCTOR. Mary. (*She halts.*) Is it true? There be fourteen women arrested?

MARY WARREN. No, sir. There be thirty-nine now—(*She suddenly breaks off and sobs and sits down, exhausted.*)

ELIZABETH. Why, she's weepin'! What ails you, child?

MARY WARREN. Goody Osburn—will hang!

(*There is a shocked pause, while she sobs.*)

PROCTOR. Hang! (*He calls into her face.*) Hang, y'say?

MARY WARREN (*through her weeping*). Aye.

PROCTOR. The Deputy Governor will permit it?

MARY WARREN. He sentenced her. He must. (*To ameliorate it:*) But not Sarah Good. For Sarah Good confessed, y'see.

PROCTOR. Confessed! To what?

MARY WARREN. That she—(*In horror at the memory—*) she sometimes made a compact with Lucifer, and wrote her name in his black book—with her blood—and bound herself to torment Christians till God's thrown down—and we all must worship Hell forevermore.

(*Pause.*)

PROCTOR. But—surely you know what a jabberer she is. Did you tell them that?

MARY WARREN. Mr. Proctor, in open court she near to choked us all to death.

PROCTOR. How, choked you?

MARY WARREN. She sent her spirit out.

ELIZABETH. Oh, Mary, Mary, surely you—

MARY WARREN (*with an indignant edge*). She tried to kill me many times, Goody Proctor!

ELIZABETH. Why, I never heard you mention that before.

MARY WARREN. I never knew it before. I never knew anything before. When she come into the court I say to myself, I must not accuse this woman, for she sleep in ditches, and so very old and poor. But then—then she sit there, denying and denying, and I feel a misty coldness climbin' up my back, and the skin on my skull begin to creep, and I feel a clamp around my neck and I cannot breathe air; and then—(*Entranced—*) I hear a voice, a screamin' voice, and it were my voice—and all at once I remembered everything she done to me!

PROCTOR. Why? What did she do to you?

MARY WARREN (*like one awakened to a marvelous secret insight*). So many time, Mr. Proctor, she come to this very door, beggin' bread and a cup of cider—and mark this: whenever I turned her away empty, she *mumbled*.

ELIZABETH. Mumbled. She may mumble if she's hungry.

MARY WARREN. But *what* does she mumble? You must remember, Goody Proctor. Last month—a Monday, I think—she walked away, and I thought my guts would burst for two days after. Do you remember it?

ELIZABETH. Why—I do, I think, but—

MARY WARREN. And so I told that to Judge Hathorne, and he asks her so. "Goody Osburn," says he, "what curse do you mumble that this girl must fall sick after turning you away?" And then she replies—(*Mimicking an old crone—*) "Why, your excellence, no curse at all. I only say my commandments; I hope I may say my commandments," says she!

ELIZABETH. And that's an upright answer.

MARY WARREN. Aye, but then Judge Hathorne say, "Recite for us your commandments!"—(*Leaning avidly toward them—*) and of all the ten she could not say a single one. She never knew no commandments, and they had her in a flat lie!

PROCTOR. And so condemned her?

MARY WARREN (*now a little strained, seeing his stubborn doubt*). Why, they must when she condemned herself.

PROCTOR. But the proof, the proof!

MARY WARREN (*with greater impatience with him*). I told you the proof. It's hard proof, hard as rock, the judges said.

PROCTOR (*pauses an instant then*). You will not go to court again, Mary Warren.

MARY WARREN. I must tell you, sir, I will be gone every day now. I am amazed you do not see what weighty work we do.

PROCTOR. What work you do! It's strange work for a Christian girl to hang old women!

MARY WARREN. But, Mr. Proctor, they will not hang them if they confess. Sarah Good will only sit in jail some time— (*Recalling—*) and here's a wonder for you; think on this. Goody Good is pregnant!

ELIZABETH. Pregnant! Are they mad? The woman's near to sixty!

MARY WARREN. They had Doctor Griggs examine her, and she's full to the brim. And smokin' a pipe all these years, and no husband either! But she's safe, thank God, for they'll not hurt the innocent child. But be that not a marvel? You must see it, sir, it's God's work we do. So I'll be gone every day for some time. I'm—I am an official of the court, they say, and I— (*She has been edging toward offstage.*)

PROCTOR. I'll official you! (*He strides to the mantel, takes down the whip hanging there.*)

MARY WARREN (*terrified, but coming erect, striving for her authority*). I'll not stand whipping any more!

ELIZABETH (*hurriedly, as PROCTOR approaches*). Mary, promise now you'll stay at home—

MARY WARREN (*backing from him, but keeping her erect posture, striving, striving for her way*). The Devil's loose in Salem, Mr. Proctor; we must discover where he's hiding!

PROCTOR. I'll whip the Devil out of you! (*With whip raised he reaches out for her, and she streaks away and yells.*)

MARY WARREN (*pointing at ELIZABETH*). I saved her life today!

(*Silence. His whip comes down.*)

ELIZABETH (*softly*). I am accused?

MARY WARREN (*quaking*). Somewhat mentioned. But I said I never see no sign you ever sent your spirit out to hurt no one, and seeing I do live so closely with you, they dismissed it.

ELIZABETH. Who accused me?

MARY WARREN. I am bound by law, I cannot tell it. (*To* PROCTOR:) I only hope you'll not be so sarcastical no more. Four judges and the King's deputy sat to dinner with us but an hour ago. I—I would have you speak civilly to me, from this out.

PROCTOR (*in horror, muttering in disgust at her*). Go to bed.

MARY WARREN (*with a stamp of her foot*). I'll not be ordered to bed no more, Mr. Proctor! I am eighteen and a woman, however single!

PROCTOR. Do you wish to sit up? Then sit up.

MARY WARREN. I wish to go to bed!

PROCTOR (*in anger*). Good night, then!

MARY WARREN. Good night. (*Dissatisfied, uncertain of herself, she goes out. Wide-eyed, both,* PROCTOR *and* ELIZABETH *stand staring.*)

ELIZABETH (*quietly*). Oh, the noose, the noose is up!

PROCTOR. There'll be no noose.

ELIZABETH. She wants me dead. I knew all week it would come to this!

PROCTOR (*without conviction*). They dismissed it. You heard her say—

ELIZABETH. And what of tomorrow? She will cry me out until they take me!

PROCTOR. Sit you down.

ELIZABETH. She wants me dead, John, you know it!

PROCTOR. I say sit down! (*She sits, trembling. He speaks quietly, trying to keep his wits.*) Now we must be wise, Elizabeth.

ELIZABETH (*with sarcasm, and a sense of being lost*). Oh, indeed, indeed!

PROCTOR. Fear nothing. I'll find Ezekiel Cheever. I'll tell him she said it were all sport.

ELIZABETH. John, with so many in the jail, more than Cheever's help is needed now, I think. Would you favor me with this? Go to Abigail.

PROCTOR (*his soul hardening as he senses*). What have I to say to Abigail?

ELIZABETH (*delicately*). John—grant me this. You have a faulty understanding of young girls. There is a promise made in any bed—

PROCTOR (*striving against his anger*). What promise!

ELIZABETH. Spoke or silent, a promise is surely made. And she may dote on it now —I am sure she does—and thinks to kill me, then to take my place.

(PROCTOR's *anger is rising; he cannot speak.*)

ELIZABETH. It is her dearest hope, John, I know it. There be a thousand names; why does she call mine? There be a certain danger in calling such a name—I am no Goody Good that sleeps in ditches, nor Osburn, drunk and half-witted. She'd dare not call out such a farmer's wife but there be monstrous profit in it. She thinks to take my place, John.

PROCTOR. She cannot think it! (*He knows it is true.*)

ELIZABETH (*"reasonably"*). John, have you ever shown her somewhat of contempt? She cannot pass you in the church but you will blush—

PROCTOR. I may blush for my sin.

ELIZABETH. I think she sees another meaning in that blush.

PROCTOR. And what see you? What see you, Elizabeth?

ELIZABETH (*"conceding"*). I think you be somewhat ashamed, for I am there, and she so close.

PROCTOR. When will you know me, woman? Were I stone I would have cracked for shame this seven month!

ELIZABETH. Then go and tell her she's a whore. Whatever promise she may sense —break it, John, break it.

PROCTOR (*between his teeth*). Good, then. I'll go. (*He starts for his rifle.*)

ELIZABETH (*trembling, fearfully*). Oh, how unwillingly!

PROCTOR (*turning on her, rifle in hand*). I will curse her hotter than the oldest cinder in hell. But pray, begrudge me not my anger!

ELIZABETH. Your anger! I only ask you—

PROCTOR. Woman, am I so base? Do you truly think me base?

ELIZABETH. I never called you base.

PROCTOR. Then how do you charge me with such a promise? The promise that a stallion gives a mare I gave that girl!

ELIZABETH. Then why do you anger with me when I bid you break it?

PROCTOR. Because it speaks deceit, and I am honest! But I'll plead no more! I see now your spirit twists around the single error of my life, and I will never tear it free!

ELIZABETH (*crying out*). You'll tear it free—when you come to know that I will be your only wife, or no wife at all! She has an arrow in you yet, John Proctor, and you know it well!

(*Quite suddenly, as though from the air, a figure appears in the doorway. They start slightly. It is* MR. HALE. *He is different now—drawn a little, and there is a quality of deference, even of guilt, about his manner now.*)

HALE. Good evening.

PROCTOR (*still in his shock*). Why, Mr. Hale! Good evening to you, sir. Come in, come in.

HALE (*to* ELIZABETH). I hope I do not startle you.

ELIZABETH. No, no, it's only that I heard no horse—

HALE. You are Goodwife Proctor.

PROCTOR. Aye; Elizabeth.

HALE (*nods then*). I hope you're not off to bed yet.

PROCTOR (*setting down his gun*). No, no. (HALE *comes further into the room. And* PROCTOR, *to explain his nervousness:*) We are not used to visitors after dark, but you're welcome here. Will you sit you down, sir?

HALE. I will. (*He sits.*) Let you sit, Goodwife Proctor.

(*She does, never letting him out of her sight. There is a pause as* HALE *looks about the room.*)

PROCTOR (*to break the silence*). Will you drink cider, Mr. Hale?

HALE. No, it rebels my stomach; I have some further traveling yet tonight. Sit you down, sir. (PROCTOR *sits.*) I will not keep you long, but I have some business with you.

PROCTOR. Business of the court?

HALE. No—no, I come of my own, without the court's authority. Hear me. (*He wets his lips.*) I know not if you are aware, but your wife's name is—mentioned in the court.

PROCTOR. We know it, sir. Our Mary Warren told us. We are entirely amazed.

HALE. I am a stranger here, as you know. And in my ignorance I find it hard to draw a clear opinion of them that come accused before the court. And so this afternoon, and now tonight, I go from house to house—I come now from Rebecca Nurse's house and—

ELIZABETH (*shocked*). Rebecca's charged!

HALE. God forbid such a one be charged. She is, however—mentioned somewhat.

ELIZABETH (*with an attempt at a laugh*). You will never believe, I hope, that Rebecca trafficked with the Devil.

HALE. Woman, it is possible.

PROCTOR (*taken aback*). Surely you cannot think so.

HALE. This is a strange time, Mister. No man may longer doubt the powers of the dark are gathered in monstrous attack upon this village. There is too much evidence now to deny it. You will agree, sir?

PROCTOR (*evading*). I—have no knowledge in that line. But it's hard to think. so pious a woman be secretly a Devil's bitch after seventy year of such good prayer.

HALE. Aye. But the Devil is a wily one, you cannot deny it. However, she is far from accused, and I know she will not be. (*Pause.*) I thought, sir, to put some questions as to the Christian character of this house, if you'll permit me.

PROCTOR (*coldly, resentful*). Why, we—have no fear of questions, sir.

HALE. Good, then. (*He makes himself more comfortable.*) In the book of record that Mr. Parris keeps, I note that you are rarely in the church on Sabbath Day.

PROCTOR. No, sir, you are mistaken.

HALE. Twenty-six time in seventeen month, sir. I must call that rare. Will you tell me why you are so absent?

PROCTOR. Mr. Hale, I never knew I must account to that man for I come to church or stay at home. My wife were sick this winter.

HALE. So I am told. But you, Mister, why could you not come alone?

PROCTOR. I surely did come when I could, and when I could not I prayed in this house.

HALE. Mr. Proctor, your house is not a church; your theology must tell you that.

PROCTOR. It does, sir, it does; and it tells me that a minister may pray to God without he have golden candlesticks upon the altar.

HALE. What golden candlesticks?

PROCTOR. Since we built the church there were pewter candlesticks upon the altar; Francis Nurse made them, y'know, and a sweeter hand never touched the metal. But Parris came, and for twenty week he preach nothin' but golden candlesticks until he had them. I labor the earth from dawn of day to blink of night, and I tell you true, when I look to heaven and see my money glaring at his elbows—it hurt my prayer, sir, it hurt my prayer. I think, sometimes, the man dreams cathedrals, not clapboard meetin' houses.

HALE (*thinks, then*). And yet, Mister, a Christian on Sabbath Day must be in church. (*Pause.*) Tell me—you have three children?

PROCTOR. Aye. Boys.

HALE. How comes it that only two are baptized?

PROCTOR (*starts to speak, then stops, then, as though unable to restrain this*). I like it not that Mr. Parris should lay his hand upon my baby. I see no light of God in that man. I'll not conceal it.

HALE. I must say it, Mr. Proctor; that is not for you to decide. The man's ordained, therefore the light of God is in him.

PROCTOR (*flushed with resentment but trying to smile*). What's your suspicion, Mr. Hale?

HALE. No, no, I have no—

PROCTOR. I nailed the roof upon the church, I hung the door—

HALE. Oh, did you! That's a good sign, then.

PROCTOR. It may be I have been too quick to bring the man to book, but you cannot think we ever desired the destruction of religion. I think that's in your mind, is it not?

HALE (*not altogether giving way*). I—have—there is a softness in your record, sir, a softness.

ELIZABETH. I think, maybe, we have been too hard with Mr. Parris. I think so. But sure we never loved the Devil here.

HALE (*nods, deliberating this. Then, with the voice of one administering a secret test*). Do you know your Commandments, Elizabeth?

ELIZABETH (*without hesitation, even eagerly*). I surely do. There be no mark of blame upon my life, Mr. Hale. I am a covenanted Christian woman.

HALE. And you, Mister?

PROCTOR (*a trifle unsteadily*). I—am sure I do, sir.

HALE (*glances at her open face, then at John, then*). Let you repeat them, if you will.

PROCTOR. The Commandments.

HALE. Aye.

PROCTOR (*looking off, beginning to sweat*). Thou shalt not kill.

HALE. Aye.

PROCTOR (*counting on his fingers*). Thou shalt not steal. Thou shalt not covet thy neighbor's goods, nor make unto thee any graven image. Thou shalt not take the name of the Lord in vain; thou shalt have no other gods before me. (*With some hesitation.*) Thou shalt remember the Sabbath Day and keep it holy. (*Pause. Then:*) Thou shalt honor thy father and mother. Thou shalt not bear false witness. (*He is stuck. He counts back on his fingers, knowing one is missing.*) Thou shalt not make unto thee any graven image.

HALE. You have said that twice, sir.

PROCTOR (*lost*). Aye. (*He is flailing for it.*)

ELIZABETH (*delicately*). Adultery, John.

PROCTOR (*as though a secret arrow had pained his heart*). Aye. (*Trying to grin it away—to* HALE:) You see, sir, between the two of us we do know them all. (HALE *only looks at* PROCTOR, *deep in his attempt to define this man.* PROCTOR *grows more uneasy.*) I think it be a small fault.

HALE. Theology, sir, is a fortress; no crack in a fortress may be accounted small. (*He rises; he seems worried now. He paces a little, in deep thought.*)

PROCTOR. There be no love for Satan in this house, Mister.

HALE. I pray it, I pray it dearly. (*He looks to both of them, an attempt at a smile on his face, but his misgivings are clear.*) Well, then—I'll bid you good night.

ELIZABETH (*unable to restrain herself*). Mr. Hale. (*He turns.*) I do think you are suspecting me somewhat? Are you not?

HALE (*obviously disturbed—and evasive*). Goody Proctor, I do not judge you. My duty is to add what I may to the godly wisdom of the court. I pray you both good health and good fortune. (*To* JOHN:) Good night, sir. (*He starts out.*)

ELIZABETH (*with a note of desperation*). I think you must tell him, John.

HALE. What's that?

ELIZABETH (*restraining a call*). Will you tell him?

(*Slight pause. Hale looks questioningly at* JOHN.)

PROCTOR (*with difficulty*). I—I have no witness and cannot prove it, except my word be taken. But I know the children's sickness had naught to do with witchcraft.

HALE (*stopped, struck*). Naught to do—?

PROCTOR. Mr. Parris discovered them sportin' in the woods. They were startled and took sick.

(*Pause.*)

HALE. Who told you this?

PROCTOR (*hesitates, then*). Abigail Williams.

HALE. Abigail!

PROCTOR. Aye.

HALE (*his eyes wide*). Abigail Williams told you it had naught to do with witchcraft!

PROCTOR. She told me the day you came, sir.

HALE (*suspiciously*). Why—why did you keep this?

PROCTOR. I never knew until tonight that the world is gone daft with this nonsense.

HALE. Nonsense! Mister, I have myself examined Tituba, Sarah Good, and numerous others that have confessed to dealing with the Devil. They have *confessed* it.

PROCTOR. And why not, if they must hang for denyin' it? There are them that will swear to anything before they'll hang; have you never thought of that?

HALE. I have. I—I have indeed. (*It is his own suspicion, but he resists it. He glances at* ELIZABETH, *then at* JOHN.) And you—would you testify to this in court?

PROCTOR. I—had not reckoned with goin' into court. But if I must I will.

HALE. Do you falter here?

PROCTOR. I falter nothing, but I may wonder if my story will be credited in such a court. I do wonder on it, when such a steady-minded minister as you will suspicion such a woman that never lied, and cannot, and the world knows she cannot! I may falter somewhat, Mister; I am no fool.

HALE (*quietly—it has impressed him*). Proctor, let you open with me now, for I have a rumor that troubles me. It's said you hold no belief that there may even be witches in the world. Is that true, sir?

PROCTOR (*—he knows this is critical, and is striving against his disgust with* HALE *and with himself for even answering*). I know not what I have said, I may have said it. I have wondered if there be witches in the world—although I cannot believe they come among us now.

HALE. Then you do not believe—

PROCTOR. I have no knowledge of it; the

Bible speaks of witches, and I will not deny them.

HALE. And you, woman?

ELIZABETH. I—I cannot believe it.

HALE (*shocked*). You cannot!

PROCTOR. Elizabeth, you bewilder him!

ELIZABETH (*to* HALE). I cannot think the Devil may own a woman's soul, Mr. Hale, when she keeps an upright way, as I have. I am a good woman, I know it; and if you believe I may do only good work in the world, and yet be secretly bound to Satan, then I must tell you, sir, I do not believe it.

HALE. But, woman, you do believe there are witches in—

ELIZABETH. If you think that I am one, then I say there are none.

HALE. You surely do not fly against the Gospel, the Gospel—

PROCTOR. She believe in the Gospel, every word!

ELIZABETH. Question Abigail Williams about the Gospel, not myself!

(HALE *stares at her.*)

PROCTOR. She do not mean to doubt the Gospel, sir, you cannot think it. This be a Christian house, sir, a Christian house.

HALE. God keep you both; let the third child be quickly baptized, and go you without fail each Sunday in to Sabbath prayer; and keep a solemn, quiet way among you. I think—

(GILES COREY *appears in doorway.*)

GILES. John!

PROCTOR. Giles! What's the matter?

GILES. They take my wife.

(FRANCIS NURSE *enters.*)

GILES. And his Rebecca!

PROCTOR (*to* FRANCIS). Rebecca's in the jail!

FRANCIS. Aye, Cheever come and take her in his wagon. We've only now come from the jail, and they'll not even let us in to see them.

ELIZABETH. They've surely gone wild now, Mr. Hale!

FRANCIS (*going to* HALE). Reverend Hale! Can you not speak to the Deputy Governor? I'm sure he mistakes these people—

HALE. Pray calm yourself, Mr. Nurse.

FRANCIS. My wife is the very brick and mortar of the church, Mr. Hale—(*Indicating* GILES—) and Martha Corey, there cannot be a woman closer yet to God than Martha.

HALE. How is Rebecca charged, Mr. Nurse?

FRANCIS (*with a mocking, half-hearted laugh*). For murder, she's charged! (*Mockingly quoting the warrant.*) "For the marvelous and supernatural murder of Goody Putnam's babies." What am I to do, Mr. Hale?

HALE (*turns from* FRANCIS, *deeply troubled, then*). Believe me, Mr. Nurse, if Rebecca Nurse be tainted, then nothing's left to stop the whole green world from burning. Let you rest upon the justice of the court; the court will send her home, I know it.

FRANCIS. You cannot mean she will be tried in court!

HALE (*pleading*). Nurse, though our hearts break, we cannot flinch; these are new times, sir. There is a misty plot afoot so subtle we should be criminal to cling to old respects and ancient friendships. I have seen too many frightful proofs in court—the Devil is alive in Salem, and we dare not quail to follow wherever the accusing finger points!

PROCTOR (*angered*). How may such a woman murder children?

HALE (*in great pain*). Man, remember, until an hour before the Devil fell, God thought him beautiful in Heaven.

GILES. I never said my wife were a witch, Mr. Hale; I only said she were reading books!

HALE. Mr. Corey, exactly what complaint were made on your wife?

GILES. That bloody mongrel Walcott charge her. Y'see, he buy a pig of my wife four or five year ago, and the pig died soon after. So he come dancin' in for his money back. So my Martha, she says to him, "Walcott, if you haven't the wit to feed a pig properly, you'll not live to own many," she says. Now he goes to court and claims that from that day to this he cannot keep a pig alive for more than four weeks because my Martha bewitch them with her books!

(*Enter* EZEKIEL CHEEVER. *A shocked silence.*)

CHEEVER. Good evening to you, Proctor.

PROCTOR. Why, Mr. Cheever. Good evening.

CHEEVER. Good evening, all. Good evening, Mr. Hale.

PROCTOR. I hope you come not on business of the court.

CHEEVER. I do, Proctor, aye. I am clerk

of the court now, y'know.

(*Enter* MARSHAL HERRICK, *a man in his early thirties, who is somewhat shame-faced at the moment.*)

GILES. It's a pity, Ezekiel, that an honest tailor might have gone to Heaven must burn in Hell. You'll burn for this, do you know it?

CHEEVER. You know yourself I must do as I'm told. You surely know that, Giles. And I'd as lief you'd not be sending me to Hell. I like not the sound of it, I tell you; I like not the sound of it. (*He fears* PROCTOR, *but starts to reach inside his coat.*) Now believe me, Proctor, how heavy be the law, all its tonnage I do carry on my back tonight. (*He takes out a warrant.*) I have a warrant for your wife.

PROCTOR (*to* HALE). You said she were not charged!

HALE. I know nothin' of it. (*To* CHEEVER:) When were she charged?

CHEEVER. I am given sixteen warrant tonight, sir, and she is one.

PROCTOR. Who charged her?

CHEEVER. Why, Abigail Williams charge her.

PROCTOR. On what proof, what proof?

CHEEVER (*looking about the room*). Mr. Proctor, I have little time. The court bid me search your house, but I like not to search a house. So will you hand me any poppets that your wife may keep here?

PROCTOR. Poppets?

ELIZABETH. I never kept no poppets, not since I were a girl.

CHEEVER (*embarrassed, glancing toward the mantel where sits* MARY WARREN's *poppet*). I spy a poppet, Goody Proctor.

ELIZABETH. Oh! (*Going for it:*) Why, this is Mary's.

CHEEVER (*shyly*). Would you please to give it to me?

ELIZABETH (*handing it to him, asks* HALE). Has the court discovered a text in poppets now?

CHEEVER (*carefully holding the poppet*). Do you keep any others in this house?

PROCTOR. No, nor this one either till tonight. What signifies a poppet?

CHEEVER. Why, a poppet—(*he gingerly turns the poppet over—*) a poppet may signify—Now, woman, will you please to come with me?

PROCTOR. She will not! (*To* ELIZABETH:) Fetch Mary here.

CHEEVER (*ineptly reaching toward* ELIZA-BETH). No, no, I am forbid to leave her from my sight.

PROCTOR (*pushing his arm away*). You'll leave her out of sight and out of mind, Mister. Fetch Mary, Elizabeth. (ELIZABETH *goes upstairs.*)

HALE. What signifies a poppet, Mr. Cheever?

CHEEVER (*turning the poppet over in his hands*). Why, they say it may signify that she—(*He has lifted the poppet's skirt, and his eyes widen in astonished fear.*) Why, this, this—

PROCTOR (*reaching for the poppet*). What's there?

CHEEVER. Why—(*He draws out a long needle from the poppet—*) it is a needle! Herrick, Herrick, it is a needle!

(HERRICK *comes toward him.*)

PROCTOR (*angrily, bewildered*). And what signifies a needle!

CHEEVER (*his hands shaking*). Why, this go hard with her, Proctor, this—I had my doubts, Proctor, I had my doubts, but here's calamity. (*To* HALE, *showing the needle:*) You see it, sir, it is a needle!

HALE. Why? What meanin' has it?

CHEEVER (*wide-eyed, trembling*). The girl, the Williams girl, Abigail Williams, sir. She sat to dinner in Reverend Parris's house tonight, and without word nor warnin' she falls to the floor. Like a struck beast, he says, and screamed a scream that a bull would weep to hear. And he goes to save her, and, stuck two inches in the flesh of her belly, he draw a needle out. And demandin' of her how she come to be so stabbed, she—(*to* PROCTOR *now—*) testify it were your wife's familiar spirit pushed it in.

PROCTOR. Why, she done it herself! (*To* HALE:) I hope you're not takin' this for proof, Mister!

(HALE, *struck by the proof, is silent.*)

CHEEVER. 'Tis hard proof! (*To* HALE:) I find here a poppet Goody Proctor keeps. I have found it, sir. And in the belly of the poppet a needle's stuck. I tell you true, Proctor, I never warranted to see such proof of Hell, and I bid you obstruct me not, for I—

(*Enter* ELIZABETH *with* MARY WARREN. PROCTOR, *seeing* MARY WARREN, *draws her by the arm to* HALE.)

PROCTOR. Here now! Mary, how did this poppet come into my house?

MARY WARREN (*frightened for herself,*

her voice very small). What poppet's that, sir?

PROCTOR (*impatiently, pointing at the doll in* CHEEVER's *hand*). This poppet, this poppet.

MARY WARREN (*evasively, looking at it*). Why, I—I think it is mine.

PROCTOR. It is your poppet, is it not?

MARY WARREN (*not understanding the direction of this*). It—is, sir.

PROCTOR. And how did it come into this house?

MARY WARREN (*glancing about at the avid faces*). Why—I made it in the court, sir, and—give it to Goody Proctor tonight.

PROCTOR (*to* HALE). Now, sir—do you have it?

HALE. Mary Warren, a needle have been found inside this poppet.

MARY WARREN (*bewildered*). Why, I meant no harm by it, sir.

PROCTOR (*quickly*). You stuck that needle in yourself?

MARY WARREN. I—I believe I did, sir, I—

PROCTOR (*to* HALE). What say you now?

HALE (*watching* MARY WARREN *closely*). Child, you are certain this be your natural memory? May it be, perhaps, that someone conjures you even now to say this?

MARY WARREN. Conjures me? Why, no, sir, I am entirely myself, I think. Let you ask Susanna Walcott—she saw me sewin' it in court. (*Or better still:*) Ask Abby, Abby sat beside me when I made it.

PROCTOR (*to* HALE, *of* CHEEVER). Bid him begone. Your mind is surely settled now. Bid him out, Mr. Hale.

ELIZABETH. What signifies a needle?

HALE. Mary—you charge a cold and cruel murder on Abigail.

MARY WARREN. Murder! I charge no—

HALE. Abigail were stabbed tonight; a needle were found stuck into her belly—

ELIZABETH. And she charges me?

HALE. Aye.

ELIZABETH (*her breath knocked out*). Why—! The girl is murder! She must be ripped out of the world!

CHEEVER (*pointing at* ELIZABETH). You've heard that, sir! Ripped out of the world! Herrick, you heard it!

PROCTOR (*suddenly snatching the warrant out of* CHEEVER's *hands*). Out with you.

CHEEVER. Proctor, you dare not touch the warrant.

PROCTOR (*ripping the warrant*). Out with you!

CHEEVER. You've ripped the Deputy Governor's warrant, man!

PROCTOR. Damn the Deputy Governor! Out of my house!

HALE. Now, Proctor, Proctor!

PROCTOR. Get y'gone with them! You are a broken minister.

HALE. Proctor, if she is innocent, the court—

PROCTOR. If *she* is innocent! Why do you never wonder if Parris be innocent, or Abigail? Is the accuser always holy now? Were they born this morning as clean as God's fingers? I'll tell you what's walking Salem —vengeance is walking Salem. We are what we always were in Salem, but now the little crazy children are jangling the keys of the kingdom, and common vengeance writes the law! This warrant's vengeance! I'll not give my wife to vengeance!

ELIZABETH. I'll go, John—

PROCTOR. You will not go!

HERRICK. I have nine men outside. You cannot keep her. The law binds me, John, I cannot budge.

PROCTOR (*to* HALE, *ready to break him*). Will you see her taken?

HALE. Proctor, the court is just—

PROCTOR. Pontius Pilate! God will not let you wash your hands of this!

ELIZABETH. John—I think I must go with them. (*He cannot bear to look at her.*) Mary, there is bread enough for the morning; you will bake, in the afternoon. Help Mr. Proctor as you were his daughter— you owe me that, and much more. (*She is fighting her weeping. To* PROCTOR:) When the children wake, speak nothing of witchcraft—it will frighten them. (*She caanot go on.*)

PROCTOR. I will bring you home. I will bring you soon.

ELIZABETH. Oh, John, bring me soon!

PROCTOR. I will fall like an ocean on that court! Fear nothing, Elizabeth.

ELIZABETH (*with great fear*). I will fear nothing. (*She looks about the room, as though to fix it in her mind.*) Tell the children I have gone to visit someone sick.

(*She walks out the door,* HERRICK *and* CHEEVER *behind her. For a moment,* PROCTOR *watches from the doorway. The clank of chain is heard.*)

PROCTOR. Herrick! Herrick, don't chain her! (*He rushes out the door. From outside:*) Damn you, man, you will not chain her! Off with them! I'll not have it! I will not have her chained!

(*There are other men's voices against his.* HALE, *in a fever of guilt and uncertainty, turns from the door to· avoid the sight;* MARY WARREN *bursts into tears and sits weeping.* GILES COREY *calls to* HALE.)

GILES. And yet silent, minister? It is fraud, you know it is fraud! What keeps you, man?

(PROCTOR *is half braced, half pushed into the room by two deputies and* HERRICK.)

PROCTOR. I'll pay you, Herrick, I will surely pay you!

HERRICK (*panting*). In God's name, John, I cannot help myself. I must chain them all. Now let you keep inside this house till I am gone! (*He goes out with his deputies.*)

(PROCTOR *stands there, gulping air. Horses and a wagon creaking are heard.*)

HALE (*in great uncertainty*). Mr. Proctor—

PROCTOR. Out of my sight!

HALE. Charity, Proctor, charity. What I have heard in her favor, I will not fear to testify in court. God help me, I cannot judge her guilty or innocent—I know not. Only this consider: the world goes mad, and it profit nothing you should lay the cause to the vengeance of a little girl.

PROCTOR. You are a coward! Though you be ordained in God's own tears, you are a coward now!

HALE. Proctor, I cannot think God be provoked so grandly by such a petty cause. The jails are packed—our greatest judges sit in Salem now—and hangin's promised. Man, we must look to cause proportionate. Were there murder done, perhaps, and never brought to light? Abominations? Some secret blasphemy that stinks to Heaven? Think on cause, man, and let you help me to discover it. For there's your way, believe it, there is your only way, when such confusion strikes upon the world. (*He goes to* GILES *and* FRANCIS.) Let you counsel among yourselves; think on your village and what may have drawn from heaven such thundering wrath upon you all. I shall pray God open up our eyes.

(HALE *goes out.*)

FRANCIS (*struck by* HALE's *mood*). I never heard no murder done in Salem.

PROCTOR (—*he has been reached by* HALE's *words*). Leave me, Francis, leave me.

GILES (*shaken*). John—tell me, are we lost?

PROCTOR. Go home now, Giles. We'll speak on it tomorrow.

GILES. Let you think on it. We'll come early, eh?

PROCTOR. Aye. Go now, Giles.

GILES. Good night, then.

(GILES COREY *goes out. After a moment:*)

MARY WARREN (*in a fearful squeak of a voice*). Mr. Proctor, very likely they'll let her come home once they're given proper evidence.

PROCTOR. You're coming to the court with me, Mary. You will tell it in the court.

MARY WARREN. I cannot charge murder on Abigail.

PROCTOR (*moving menacingly toward her*). You will tell the court how that poppet come here and who stuck the needle in.

MARY WARREN. She'll kill me for sayin' that! (PROCTOR *continues toward her.*) Abby'll charge lechery on you, Mr. Proctor!

PROCTOR (*halting*). She's told you!

MARY WARREN. I have known it, sir. She'll ruin you with it, I know she will.

PROCTOR (*hesitating, and with deep hatred of himself*). Good. Then her saintliness is done with. (MARY *backs from him.*) We will slide together into our pit; you will tell the court what you know.

MARY WARREN (*in terror*). I cannot, they'll turn on me—

(PROCTOR *strides and catches her, and she is repeating, "I cannot, I cannot!"*)

PROCTOR. My wife will never die for me! I will bring your guts into your mouth but that goodness will not die for me!

MARY WARREN (*struggling to escape him*). I cannot do it, I cannot!

PROCTOR (*grasping her by the throat as though he would strangle her*). Make your peace with it! Now Hell and Heaven grapple on our backs, and all our old pretense is ripped away—make your peace! (*He throws her to the floor, where she sobs, "I cannot, I cannot . . ." And now, half to himself, staring, and turning to the open door.*) Peace. It is a providence, and no great change; we are only what we always were, but naked now. (*He walks as though toward a great horror, facing the open sky.*) Aye, naked! And the wind,

God's icy wind, will blow!

And she is over and over again sobbing, "I cannot, I cannot, I cannot," as

THE CURTAIN FALLS

[The following sequence was added to Act Two by Arthur Miller for his revised version of the play, which had its first production in New York in July, 1953.]

SCENE: *A wood. Night.*

PROCTOR *appears with lantern. He enters glancing behind him, then halts, holding the lantern raised.* ABIGAIL *appears with a wrap over her nightgown, her hair down. A moment of questioning silence.*

PROCTOR (*searching*). I must speak with you, Abigail. (*She does not move, staring at him.*) Will you sit?

ABIGAIL. How do you come?

PROCTOR. Friendly.

ABIGAIL (*glancing about*). I don't like the woods at night. Pray you, stand closer. (*He comes closer to her, but keeps separated in spirit.*) I knew it must be you. When I heard the pebbles on the window, before I opened up my eyes I knew. I thought you would come a good time sooner.

PROCTOR. I had thought to come many times.

ABIGAIL. Why didn't you? I am so alone in the world now.

PROCTOR (*as a fact. Not bitterly*). Are you? I've heard that people come a hundred mile to see your face these days.

ABIGAIL. Aye, my face. Can you see my face?

PROCTOR (*holds the lantern to her face*). Then you're troubled?

ABIGAIL. Have you come to mock me?

PROCTOR (*sets lantern and sits down*). No, no, but I hear only that you go to the tavern every night, and play shovelboard with the Deputy Governor, and they give you cider.

ABIGAIL (*as though that did not count*). I have once or twice played the shovelboard. But I have no joy in it.

PROCTOR (*he is probing her*). This is a surprise, Abby. I'd thought to find you gayer than this. I'm told a troop of boys go step for step with you wherever you walk these days.

ABIGAIL. Aye, they do. But I have only lewd looks from the boys.

PROCTOR. And you like that not?

ABIGAIL. I cannot bear lewd looks no more, John. My spirit's changed entirely. I ought to be given Godly looks when I suffer for them as I do.

PROCTOR. Oh? How do you suffer, Abby?

ABIGAIL (*pulls up dress*). Why, look at my leg. I'm holes all over from their damned needles and pins. (*Touching her stomach.*) The jab your wife gave me's not healed yet, y'know.

PROCTOR (*seeing her madness now*). Oh, it isn't.

ABIGAIL. I think sometimes she pricks it open again while I sleep.

PROCTOR. Ah?

ABIGAIL. And George Jacobs . . . (*Sliding up her sleeve.*) He comes again and again and raps me with his stick—the same spot every night all this week. Look at the lump I have.

PROCTOR. Abby—George Jacobs is in the jail all this month.

ABIGAIL. Thank God he is, and bless the day he hangs and lets me sleep in peace again! Oh, John, the world's so full of hypocrites. (*Astonished, outraged:*) They pray in jail! I'm told they all pray in jail!

PROCTOR. They may not pray?

ABIGAIL. And torture me in my bed while sacred words are comin' from their mouths? Oh, it will need God himself to cleanse this town properly!

PROCTOR. Abby—you mean to cry out still others?

ABIGAIL. If I live, if I am not murdered, I surely will, until the last hypocrite is dead.

PROCTOR. Then there is no one good?

ABIGAIL (*softly*). Aye, there is one. *You* are good.

PROCTOR. Am I? How am I good?

ABIGAIL. Why, you taught me goodness, therefore you are good. It were a fire you walked me through, and all my ignorance was burned away. It were a fire, John, we lay in fire. And from that night no woman dare call me wicked anymore but I knew my answer. I used to weep for my sins when the wind lifted up my skirts; and blushed for shame because some old Rebecca called me loose. And then you burned my ignorance away. As bare as some December tree I saw them all—walking like saints to church, running to feed the sick, and hypocrites in their hearts! And God gave me strength to call them liars, and God made men to listen to me, and by God I will scrub the world clean for the love of Him! Oh, John, I will make you such a wife when the world is white again! (*She kisses his hand in high emotion.*) You will be amazed to see me every day, a light of heaven in your house, a . . . (*He rises and backs away, frightened, amazed.*) Why are you cold?

PROCTOR (*in a business-like way, but with uneasiness, as though before an unearthly thing*). My wife goes to trial in the morning, Abigail.

ABIGAIL (*distantly*). Your wife?

PROCTOR. Surely you knew of it?

ABIGAIL (*coming awake to that*). I do remember it now. (*As a duty:*) How—how—is she well?

PROCTOR. As well as she may be, thirty-six days in that place.

ABIGAIL. You said you came friendly.

PROCTOR. She will not be condemned, Abby.

ABIGAIL (*her holy feelings outraged. But she is questioning*). You brought me from my bed to speak of her?

PROCTOR. I come to tell you, Abby, what I will do tomorrow in the court. I would not take you by surprise, but give you all good time to think on what to do to save yourself.

ABIGAIL (*incredibly, and with beginning fear*). Save myself!

PROCTOR. If you do not free my wife tomorrow, I am set and bound to ruin you, Abby.

ABIGAIL (*her voice small—astonished*). How—ruin me?

PROCTOR. I have rocky proof in documents that you knew that poppet were none of my wife's; and that you yourself bade Mary Warren stab that needle into it.

ABIGAIL (*a wildness stirs in her; a child is standing here who is unutterably frustrated, denied her wish; but she is still grasping for her wits*). I bade Mary Warren . . . ?

PROCTOR. You know what you do, you are not so mad!

ABIGAIL (*she calls upwards*). Oh, hypocrites! Have you won him, too? (*Directly to him:*) John, why do you let them send you?

PROCTOR. I warn you, Abby.

ABIGAIL. They send you! They steal your honesty and . . .

PROCTOR. I have found my honesty.

ABIGAIL. No, this is your wife pleading, your sniveling, envious wife! This is Rebecca's voice, Martha Corey's voice. You were no hypocrite!

PROCTOR (*he grasps her arm and holds her*). I will prove you for the fraud you are!

ABIGAIL. And if they ask you why Abigail would ever do so murderous a deed, what will you tell them?

PROCTOR (*it is hard even to say it*). I will tell them why.

ABIGAIL. What will you tell? You will confess to fornication? In the court?

PROCTOR. If you will have it so, so I will tell it! (*She utters a disbelieving laugh.*) I say I will! (*She laughs louder, now with more assurance he will never do it. He shakes her roughly.*) If you can still hear, hear this! Can you hear! (*She is trembling, staring up at him as though he were out of his mind.*) You will tell the court you are blind to spirits; you cannot see them anymore, and you will never cry witchery again, or I will make you famous for the whore you are!

ABIGAIL (*she grabs him*). Never in this world! I know you, John—you are this moment singing secret Hallelujahs that your wife will hang!

PROCTOR (*throws her down*). You mad, you murderous bitch!

ABIGAIL (*rises*). Oh, how hard it is when pretense falls! But it falls, it falls! (*She wraps herself up as though to go.*) You have done your duty by her. I hope it is your last hypocrisy. I pray you will come again with sweeter news for me. I know you will—now that your duty's done. Good night, John. (*She is backing away, raising her hand in farewell.*) Fear naught. I will save you tomorrow. From yourself I will save you. (*She is gone.*)

PROCTOR *is left alone, amazed in terror. He takes up his lantern and slowly exits as*

THE CURTAIN FALLS

ACT THREE

The vestry room of the Salem meeting house, now serving as the anteroom of the General Court.

As the curtain rises, the room is empty, but for sunlight pouring through two high windows in the back wall. The room is solemn, even forbidding. Heavy beams jut out, boards of random widths make up the walls. At the right are two doors leading into the meeting house proper, where the court is being held. At the left another door leads outside.

There is a plain bench at the left, and another at the right. In the center a rather long meeting table, with stools and a considerable armchair snugged up to it.

Through the partitioning wall at the right we hear a prosecutor's voice, JUDGE HATHORNE's, asking a question; then a woman's voice, MARTHA COREY's, replying.

HATHORNE's VOICE. Now, Martha Corey, there is abundant evidence in our hands to show that you have given yourself to the reading of fortunes. Do you deny it?

MARTHA COREY's VOICE. I am innocent to a witch. I know not what a witch is.

HATHORNE's VOICE. How do you know, then, that you are not a witch?

MARTHA COREY's VOICE. If I were, I would know it.

HATHORNE's VOICE. Why do you hurt these children?

MARTHA COREY's VOICE. I do not hurt them. I scorn it!

GILES' VOICE (*roaring*). I have evidence for the court!

(*Voices of townspeople rise in excitement.*)

DANFORTH's VOICE. You will keep your seat!

GILES' VOICE. Thomas Putnam is reaching out for land!

DANFORTH's VOICE. Remove that man, Marshal!

GILES' VOICE. You're hearing lies, lies!

(*A roaring goes up from the people.*)

HATHORNE's VOICE. Arrest him, excellency!

GILES' VOICE. I have evidence. Why will you not hear my evidence?

(*The door opens and GILES is half carried into the vestry room by HERRICK.*)

GILES. Hands off, damn you, let me go!

HERRICK. Giles, Giles!

GILES. Out of my way, Herrick! I bring evidence—

HERRICK. You cannot go in there, Giles; it's a court!

(*Enter HALE from the court.*)

HALE. Pray be calm a moment.

GILES. You, Mr. Hale, go in there and demand I speak.

HALE. A moment, sir, a moment.

GILES. They'll be hangin' my wife!

(*JUDGE HATHORNE enters. He is in his sixties, a bitter, remorseless Salem judge.*)

HATHORNE. How do you dare come roarin' into this court! Are you gone daft, Corey?

GILES. You're not a Boston judge yet, Hathorne. You'll not call me daft!

(*Enter DEPUTY GOVERNOR DANFORTH and, behind him, EZEKIEL CHEEVER and PARRIS. On his appearance, silence falls. DANFORTH is a grave man in his sixties, of some humor and sophistication that does not, however, interfere with an exact loyalty to his position and his cause. He comes down to GILES, who awaits his wrath.*)

DANFORTH (*looking directly at GILES*). Who is this man?

PARRIS. Giles Corey, sir, and a more contentious—

GILES (*to PARRIS*). I am asked the question, and I am old enough to answer it! (*To DANFORTH, who impresses him and to whom he smiles through his strain*). My name is Corey, sir, Giles Corey. I have six hundred acres, and timber in addition. It is my wife you be condemning now. (*He indicates the courtroom.*)

DANFORTH. And how do you imagine to help her cause with such contemptuous riot? Now be gone. Your old age alone keeps you out of jail for this.

GILES (*beginning to plead*). They be tellin' lies about my wife, sir, I—

DANFORTH. Do you take it upon yourself to determine what this court shall believe and what it shall set aside?

GILES. Your excellency, we mean no disrespect for—

DANFORTH. Disrespect indeed! It is disruption, Mister. This is the highest court of the supreme government of this province, do you know it?

GILES (*beginning to weep*). Your excellency, I only said she were readin' books, sir, and they come and take her out of my house for—

DANFORTH (*mystified*). Books! What books?

GILES (*through helpless sobs*). It is my third wife, sir; I never had no wife that be so taken with books, and I thought to find the cause of it, d'y'see, but it were no witch I blamed her for. (*He is openly weeping.*) I have broke charity with the woman, I have broke charity with her. (*He covers his face ashamed.* DANFORTH *is respectfully silent.*)

HALE. Excellency, he claims hard evidence for his wife's defense. I think that in all justice you must—

DANFORTH. Then let him submit his evidence in proper affidavit. You are certainly aware of our procedure here, Mr. Hale. (*To* HERRICK:) Clear this room.

HERRICK. Come now, Giles. (*He gently pushes* COREY *out.*)

FRANCIS. We are desperate, sir; we come here three days now and cannot be heard.

DANFORTH. Who is this man?

FRANCIS. Francis Nurse, Your Excellency.

HALE. His wife's Rebecca that were condemned this morning.

DANFORTH. Indeed! I am amazed to find you in such uproar. I have only good report of your character, Mr. Nurse.

HATHORNE. I think they must both be arrested in contempt, sir.

DANFORTH (*to* FRANCIS). Let you write your plea, and in due time I will—

FRANCIS. Excellency, we have proof for your eyes; God forbid you shut them to it. The girls, sir, the girls are frauds.

DANFORTH. What's that?

FRANCIS. We have proof of it, sir. They are all deceiving you.

(DANFORTH *is shocked, but studying* FRANCIS.)

HATHORNE. This is contempt, sir, contempt!

DANFORTH. Peace, Judge Hathorne. Do you know who I am, Mr. Nurse?

FRANCIS. I surely do, sir, and I think you must be a wise judge to be what you are.

DANFORTH. And do you know that near to four hundred are in the jails from Marblehead to Lynn, and upon my signature?

FRANCIS. I—

DANFORTH. And seventy-two condemned to hang by that signature?

FRANCIS. Excellency, I never thought to say it to such a ,weighty judge, but you are deceived.

(*Enter* GILES COREY *from left. All turn to see as he beckons in* MARY WARREN *with* PROCTOR. MARY *is keeping her eyes to the ground;* PROCTOR *has her elbow as though she were near collapse.*)

PARRIS (*on seeing her, in shock*). Mary Warren! (*He goes directly to bend close to her face.*) What are you about here?

PROCTOR (*pressing* PARRIS *away from her with a gentle but firm motion of protectiveness*). She would speak with the Deputy Governor.

DANFORTH (*shocked by this, turns to* HERRICK). Did you not tell me Mary Warren were sick in bed?

HERRICK. She were, Your Honor. When I go to fetch her to the court last week, she said she were sick.

GILES. She has been strivin' with her soul all week, Your Honor; she comes now to tell the truth of this to you.

DANFORTH. Who is this?

PROCTOR. John Proctor, sir. Elizabeth Proctor is my wife.

PARRIS. Beware this man, Your Excellency, this man is mischief.

HALE (*excitedly*). I think you must hear the girl, sir, she—

DANFORTH (*who has become very interested in* MARY WARREN *and only raises a hand toward* HALE). Peace. What would you tell us, Mary Warren?

(PROCTOR *looks at her, but she cannot speak.*)

PROCTOR. She never saw no spirits, sir.

DANFORTH (*with great alarm and surprise, to* MARY). Never saw no spirits!

GILES (*eagerly*). Never.

PROCTOR (*reaching into his jacket*). She has signed a deposition, sir—

DANFORTH (*instantly*). No, no, I accept no depositions. (*He is rapidly calculating this; he turns from her to* PROCTOR.) Tell me, Mr. Proctor, have you given out this story in the village?

PROCTOR. We have not.

PARRIS. They've come to overthrow the court, sir! This man is—

DANFORTH. I pray you, Mr. Parris. Do you know, Mr. Proctor, that the entire contention of the state in these trials is that the voice of Heaven is speaking through the children?

PROCTOR. I know that, sir.

DANFORTH (*thinks, staring at* PROCTOR, *then turns to* MARY WARREN). And you, Mary Warren, how came you to cry out people for sending their spirits against you?

MARY WARREN. It were pretense, sir.

DANFORTH. I cannot hear you.

PROCTOR. It were pretense, she says.

DANFORTH. Ah? And the other girls? Susanna Walcott, and—the others? They are also pretending?

MARY WARREN. Aye, sir.

DANFORTH (*wide-eyed*). Indeed. (*Pause. He is baffled by this. He turns to study* PROCTOR's *face.*)

PARRIS (*in a sweat*). Excellency, you surely cannot think to let so vile a lie be spread in open court!

DANFORTH. Indeed not, but it strike hard upon me that she will dare come here with such a tale. Now, Mr. Proctor, before I decide whether I shall hear you or not, it is my duty to tell you this. We burn a hot fire here; it melts down all concealment.

PROCTOR. I know that, sir.

DANFORTH. Let me continue. I understand well, a husband's tenderness may drive him to extravagance in defense of a wife. Are you certain in your conscience, Mister, that your evidence is the truth?

PROCTOR. It is. And you will surely know it.

DANFORTH. And you thought to declare this revelation in the open court before the public?

PROCTOR. I thought I would, aye—with your permission.

DANFORTH (*his eyes narrowing*). Now, sir, what is your purpose in so doing?

PROCTOR. Why, I—I would free my wife, sir.

DANFORTH. There lurks nowhere in your heart, nor hidden in your spirit, any desire to undermine this court?

PROCTOR (*with the faintest faltering*). Why, no, sir.

CHEEVER (*clears his throat, awakening*). I— Your Excellency.

DANFORTH. Mr. Cheever.

CHEEVER. I think it be my duty, sir— (*Kindly, to* PROCTOR:) You'll not deny it, John. (*To* DANFORTH:) When we come to take his wife, he damned the court and ripped your warrant.

PARRIS. Now you have it!

DANFORTH. He did that, Mr. Hale?

HALE (*takes a breath*). Aye, he did.

PROCTOR. It were a temper, sir. I knew not what I did.

DANFORTH (*studying him*). Mr. Proctor.

PROCTOR. Aye, sir.

DANFORTH (*straight into his eyes*). Have you ever seen the Devil?

PROCTOR. No, sir.

DANFORTH. You are in all respects a Gospel Christian?

PROCTOR. I am, sir.

PARRIS. Such a Christian that will not come to church but once in a month!

DANFORTH (*restrained—he is curious*). Not come to church?

PROCTOR. I—I have no love for Mr. Parris. It is no secret. But God I surely love.

CHEEVER. He plow on Sunday, sir.

DANFORTH. Plow on Sunday!

CHEEVER (*apologetically*). I think it be evidence, John. I am an official of the court, I cannot keep it.

PROCTOR. I—I have once or twice plowed on Sunday. I have three children, sir, and until last year my land give little.

GILES. You'll find other Christians that do plow on Sunday if the truth be known.

HALE. Your Honor, I cannot think you may judge the man on such evidence.

DANFORTH. I judge nothing. (*Pause. He keeps watching* PROCTOR, *who tries to meet his gaze.*) I tell you straight, Mister—I have seen marvels in this court. I have seen people choked before my eyes by spirits; I have seen them stuck by pins and slashed by daggers. I have until this moment not the slightest reason to suspect that the children may be deceiving me. Do you understand my meaning?

PROCTOR. Excellency, does it not strike upon you that so many of these women have lived so long with such upright reputation, and—

PARRIS. Do you read the Gospel, Mr. Proctor?

PROCTOR. I read the Gospel.

PARRIS. I think not, or you should surely know that Cain were an upright man, and yet he did kill Abel.

PROCTOR. Aye, God tells us that. (*To* DANFORTH:) But who tells us Rebecca Nurse murdered seven babies by sending out her spirit on them? It is the children only, and this one will swear she lied to you.

(DANFORTH *considers, then beckons* HATHORNE *to him.* HATHORNE *leans in, and he speaks in his ear.* HATHORNE *nods.*)

HATHORNE. Aye, she's the one.

DANFORTH. Mr. Proctor, this morning, your wife send me a claim in which she states that she is pregnant now.

PROCTOR. My wife pregnant!

DANFORTH. There be no sign of it—we have examined her body.

PROCTOR. But if she say she is pregnant, then she must be! That woman will never lie, Mr. Danforth.

DANFORTH. She will not?

PROCTOR. Never, sir, never.

DANFORTH. We have thought it too convenient to be credited. However, if I should tell you now that I will let her be kept another month; and if she begin to show her natural signs, you shall have her living yet another year until she is delivered—what say you to that? (JOHN PROCTOR *is struck silent.*) Come now. You say your only purpose is to save your wife. Good, then, she is saved at least this year, and a year is long. What say you, sir? It is done now. (*In conflict,* PROCTOR *glances at* FRANCIS *and* GILES.) Will you drop this charge?

PROCTOR. I—I think I cannot.

DANFORTH (*now an almost imperceptible hardness in his voice*). Then your purpose is somewhat larger.

PARRIS. He's come to overthrow this court, Your Honor!

PROCTOR. These are my friends. Their wives are also accused—

DANFORTH (*with a sudden briskness of manner*). I judge you not, sir. I am ready to hear your evidence.

PROCTOR. I come not to hurt the court; I only—

DANFORTH (*cutting him off*). Marshal, go into the court and bid Judge Stoughton and Judge Sewall declare recess for one hour. And let them go to the tavern, if they will. All witnesses and prisoners are to be kept in the building.

HERRICK. Aye, sir. (*Very deferentially:*) If I may say it, sir, I know this man all my life. It is a good man, sir.

DANFORTH (—*it is the reflection on himself he resents*). I am sure of it, Marshal. (HERRICK *nods, then goes out.*) Now, what deposition do you have for us, Mr. Proctor? And I beg you be clear, open as the sky, and honest.

PROCTOR (*as he takes out several papers*). I am no lawyer, so I'll—

DANFORTH. The pure in heart need no lawyers. Proceed as you will.

PROCTOR (*handing* DANFORTH *a paper*). Will you read this first, sir? It's a sort of testament. The people signing it declare their good opinion of Rebecca, and my wife, and Martha Corey. (DANFORTH *looks down at the paper.*)

PARRIS (*to enlist* DANFORTH's *sarcasm*). Their good opinion! (*But* DANFORTH *goes on reading, and* PROCTOR *is heartened.*)

PROCTOR. These are all landholding farmers, members of the church. (*Delicately, trying to point out a paragraph:*) If you'll notice, sir—they've known the women many years and never saw no sign they had dealings with the Devil.

(PARRIS *nervously moves over and reads over* DANFORTH's *shoulder.*)

DANFORTH (*glancing down a long list*). How many names are here?

FRANCIS. Ninety-one, Your Excellency.

PARRIS (*sweating*). These people should be summoned. (DANFORTH *looks up at him questioningly.*) For questioning.

FRANCIS (*trembling with anger*). Mr. Danforth, I gave them all my word no harm would come to them for signing this.

PARRIS. This is a clear attack upon the court!

HALE (*to* PARRIS, *trying to contain himself*). Is every defense an attack upon the court? Can no one—?

PARRIS. All innocent and Christian people are happy for the courts in Salem! These people are gloomy for it. (*To* DANFORTH *directly:*) And I think you will want to know, from each and every one of them, what discontents them with you!

HATHORNE. I think they ought to be examined, sir.

DANFORTH. It is not necessarily an attack, I think. Yet—

FRANCIS. These are all covenanted Christians, sir.

DANFORTH. Then I am sure they may have nothing to fear. (*Hands* CHEEVER *the paper.*) Mr. Cheever, have warrants drawn for all of these—arrest for examination. (*To* PROCTOR:) Now, Mister, what other information do you have for us? (FRANCIS *is still standing, horrified.*) You may sit, Mr. Nurse.

FRANCIS. I have brought trouble on these people; I have—

DANFORTH. No, old man, you have not hurt these people if they are of good conscience. But you must understand, sir, that a person is either with this court or he must be counted against it, there be no road between. This is a sharp time, now, a precise time—we live no longer in the dusky afternoon when evil mixed itself with good and befuddled the world. Now, by God's grace, the shining sun is up, and them that fear not light will surely praise it. I hope you will be one of those. (MARY WARREN *suddenly sobs*.) She's not hearty, I see.

PROCTOR. No, she's not, sir. (*To* MARY, *bending to her, holding her hand, quietly:*) Now remember what the angel Raphael said to the boy Tobias. Remember it.

MARY WARREN (*hardly audible*). Aye.

PROCTOR. "Do that which is good, and no harm shall come to thee."

MARY WARREN. Aye.

DANFORTH. Come, man, we wait you.

(MARSHAL HERRICK *returns, and takes his post at the door.*)

GILES. John, my deposition, give him mine.

PROCTOR. Aye. (*He hands* DANFORTH *another paper.*) This is Mr. Corey's deposition.

DANFORTH. Oh? (*He looks down at it. Now* HATHORNE *comes behind him and reads with him.*)

HATHORNE (*suspiciously*). What lawyer drew this, Corey?

GILES. You know I never hired a lawyer in my life, Hathorne.

DANFORTH (*finishes the reading*). It is very well phrased. My compliments. Mr. Parris, if Mr. Putnam is in the court, will you bring him in? (HATHORNE *takes the deposition, and walks to the window with it.* PARRIS *goes into the court.*) You have no legal training, Mr. Corey?

GILES (*very pleased*). I have the best, sir —I am thirty-three time in court in my life. And always plaintiff, too.

DANFORTH. Oh, then you're much put-upon.

GILES. I am never put-upon; I know my rights, sir, and I will have them. You know, your father tried a case of mine— might be thirty-five year ago, I think.

DANFORTH. Indeed.

GILES. He never spoke to you of it?

DANFORTH. No, I cannot recall it.

GILES. That's strange, he give me nine pound damages. He were a fair judge, your father. Y'see, I had a white mare that time, and this fellow come to borrow the mare— (*Enter* PARRIS *with* THOMAS PUTNAM. *When he sees* PUTNAM, GILES' *ease goes; he is hard.*) Aye, there he is.

DANFORTH. Mr. Putnam, I have here an accusation by Mr. Corey against you. He states that you coldly prompted your daughter to cry witchery upon George Jacobs that is now in jail.

PUTNAM. It is a lie.

DANFORTH (*turning to* GILES). Mr. Putnam states your charge is a lie. What say you to that?

GILES (*furious, his fists clenched*). A fart on Thomas Putnam, that is what I say to that!

DANFORTH. What proof do you submit for your charge, sir?

GILES. My proof is there! (*Pointing to the paper.*) If Jacobs hangs for a witch he forfeit up his property—that's law! And there is none but Putnam with the coin to buy so great a piece. This man is killing his neighbors for their land!

DANFORTH. But proof, sir, proof.

GILES (*pointing at his deposition*). The proof is there! I have it from an honest man who heard Putnam say it! The day his daughter cried out on Jacobs, he said she'd given him a fair gift of land.

HATHORNE. And the name of this man?

GILES (*taken aback*). What name?

HATHORNE. The man that give you this information.

GILES (*hesitates, then*). Why, I—I cannot give you his name.

HATHORNE. And why not?

GILES (*hesitates, then bursts out*). You know well why not! He'll lay in jail if I give his name!

HATHORNE. This is contempt of the court, Mr. Danforth!

DANFORTH (*to avoid that*). You will surely tell us the name.

GILES. I will not give you no name. I mentioned my wife's name once and I'll burn in hell long enough for that. I stand mute.

DANFORTH. In that case, I have no choice but to arrest you for contempt of this court, do you know that?

GILES. This is a hearing; you cannot clap me for contempt of a hearing.

DANFORTH. Oh, it is a proper lawyer! Do you wish me to declare the court in full session here? Or will you give me good reply?

GILES (*faltering*). I cannot give you no name, sir, I cannot.

DANFORTH. You are a foolish old man. Mr. Cheever, begin the record. The court is now in session. I ask you, Mr. Corey—

PROCTOR (*breaking in*). Your Honor— he has the story in confidence, sir, and he—

PARRIS. The Devil lives on such confidences! (*To* DANFORTH:) Without confidences there could be no conspiracy, Your Honor!

HATHORNE. I think it must be broken, sir.

DANFORTH (*to* GILES). Old man, if your informant tells the truth let him come here openly like a decent man. But if he hide in anonymity I must know why. Now sir, the government and central church demand of you the name of him who reported Mr. Thomas Putnam a common murderer.

HALE. Excellency—

DANFORTH. Mr. Hale.

HALE. We cannot blink it more. There is a prodigious fear of this court in the country—

DANFORTH. Then there is a prodigious guilt in the country. Are *you* afraid to be questioned here?

HALE. I may only fear the Lord, sir, but there is fear in the country nevertheless.

DANFORTH (*angered now*). Reproach me not with the fear in the country; there is fear in the country because there is a moving plot to topple Christ in the country!

HALE. But it does not follow that everyone accused is part of it.

DANFORTH. No uncorrupted man may fear this court, Mr. Hale! None! (*To* GILES:) You are under arrest in contempt of this court. Now sit you down and take counsel with yourself, or you will be set in the jail until you decide to answer all questions.

(GILES COREY *makes a rush for* PUTNAM. PROCTOR *lunges and holds him.*

PROCTOR. No, Giles!

GILES (*over* PROCTOR'S *shoulder at* PUTNAM). I'll cut your throat, Putnam, I'll kill you yet!

PROCTOR (*forcing him into a chair*). Peace, Giles, peace. (*Releasing him:*) We'll prove ourselves. Now we will. (*He starts to turn to* DANFORTH.)

GILES. Say nothin' more, John. (*Pointing at* DANFORTH:) He's only playin' you! He means to hang us all!

(MARY WARREN *bursts into sobs.*)

DANFORTH. This is a court of law, Mister. I'll have no effrontery here!

PROCTOR. Forgive him, sir, for his old age. Peace, Giles, we'll prove it all now. (*He lifts up* MARY'S *chin.*) You cannot weep, Mary. Remember the angel, what

he say to the boy. Hold to it, now; there is your rock. (MARY *quiets. He takes out a paper, and turns to* DANFORTH.) This is Mary Warren's deposition. I—I would ask you remember, sir, while you read it, that until two week ago she were no different than the other children are today. (*He is speaking reasonably, restraining all his fears, his anger, his anxiety.*) You saw her scream, she howled, she swore familiar spirits choked her; she even testified that Satan, in the form of women now in jail, tried to win her soul away, and then when she refused—

DANFORTH. We know all this.

PROCTOR. Aye, sir. She swears now that she never saw Satan; nor any spirit, vague or clear, that Satan may have sent to hurt her. And she declares her friends are lying now.

(PROCTOR *starts to hand* DANFORTH *the deposition, and* HALE *comes up to* DANFORTH *in a trembling state.*)

HALE. Excellency, a moment. I think this goes to the heart of the matter.

DANFORTH (*with deep misgivings*). It surely does.

HALE. I cannot say he is an honest man; I know him little. But in all justice, sir, a claim so weighty cannot be argued by a farmer. In God's name sir, stop here; send him home and let him come again with a lawyer—

DANFORTH (*patiently*). Now look you Mr. Hale—

HALE. Excellency, I have signed seventy-two death warrants; I am a minister of the Lord, and I dare not take a life without there be a proof so immaculate no slightest qualm of conscience may doubt it.

DANFORTH. Mr. Hale, you surely do not doubt my justice.

HALE. I have this morning signed away the soul of Rebecca Nurse, Your Honor. I'll not conceal it, my hand shakes yet as with a wound! I pray you, sir, this argument let lawyers present to you.

DANFORTH. Mr. Hale, believe me; for a man of such terrible learning you are most bewildered—I hope you will forgive me. I have been thirty-two year at the bar, sir, and I should be confounded were I called upon to defend these people. Let you consider, now—(*To* PROCTOR *and the others:*) And I bid you all do likewise. In an ordinary crime, how does one defend the accused? One calls up witnesses to prove his innocence. But witchcraft is *ipso facto,* on its face and by its nature, an invisible crime, is it not? Therefore, who may possibly be witness to it? The witch and the victim. None other. Now we cannot hope the witch will accuse herself; granted? Therefore, we must rely upon her victims —and they do testify, the children certainly do testify. As for the witches, none will deny that we are most eager for all their confessions. Therefore, what is left for a lawyer to bring out? I think I have made my point. Have I not?

HALE. But this child claims the girls are not truthful, and if they are not—

DANFORTH. That is precisely what I am about to consider, sir. What more may you ask of me? Unless you doubt my probity?

HALE (*defeated*). I surely do not, sir. Let you consider it, then.

DANFORTH. And let you put your heart to rest. Her deposition, Mr. Proctor.

(PROCTOR *hands it to him.* HATHORNE *rises, goes beside* DANFORTH, *and starts reading.* PARRIS *comes to his other side.* DANFORTH *looks at* JOHN PROCTOR, *then proceeds to read.* HALE *gets up, finds position near the judge, reads too.* PROCTOR *glances at* GILES. FRANCIS *prays silently, hands pressed together.* CHEEVER *waits placidly, the sublime official, dutiful.* MARY WARREN *sobs once.* JOHN PROCTOR *touches her head reassuringly. Presently* DANFORTH *lifts his eyes, stands up, takes out a kerchief and blows his nose. The others stand aside as he moves in thought toward the window.*)

PARRIS (*hardly able to contain his anger and fear*). I should like to question—

DANFORTH (*—his first real outburst, in which his contempt for* PARRIS *is clear*). Mr. Parris, I bid you be silent! (*He stands in silence, looking out the window. Now, having established that he will set the gait:*) Mr. Cheever, will you go into the court and bring the children here? (*CHEEVER gets up and goes out upstage.* DANFORTH *now turns to* MARY.) Mary Warren, how came you to this turnabout? Has Mr. Proctor threatened you for this deposition?

MARY WARREN. No, sir.

DANFORTH. Has he ever threatened you?

MARY WARREN (*weaker*). No, sir.

DANFORTH (*sensing a weakening*). Has he threatened you?

MARY WARREN. No, sir.

DANFORTH. Then you tell me that you sat in my court, callously lying, when you knew that people would hang by your evidence? (*She does not answer.*) Answer me!

MARY WARREN (*almost inaudibly*). I did, sir.

DANFORTH. How were you instructed in your life? Do you not know that God damns all liars? (*She cannot speak.*) Or is it now that you lie?

MARY WARREN. No, sir—I am with God now.

DANFORTH. You are with God now.

MARY WARREN. Aye, sir.

DANFORTH (*containing himself*). I will tell you this—you are either lying now, or you were lying in the court, and in either case you have committed perjury and you will go to jail for it. You cannot lightly say you lied, Mary. Do you know that?

MARY WARREN. I cannot lie no more. I am with God, I am with God.

(*But she breaks into sobs at the thought of it, and the right door opens, and enter* SUSANNA WALCOTT, MERCY LEWIS, BETTY PARRIS, *and finally* ABIGAIL. CHEEVER *comes to* DANFORTH.)

CHEEVER. Ruth Putnam's not in the court, sir, nor the other children.

DANFORTH. These will be sufficient. Sit you down, children. (*Silently they sit.*) Your friend, Mary Warren, has given us a deposition. In which she swears that she never saw familiar spirits, apparitions, nor any manifest of the Devil. She claims as well that none of you have seen these things either. (*Slight pause.*) Now, children, this is a court of law. The law, based upon the Bible, and the Bible, writ by Almighty God, forbid the practice of witchcraft, and describe death as the penalty thereof. But likewise, children, the law and Bible damn all bearers of false witness. (*Slight pause.*) Now then. It does not escape me that this deposition may be devised to blind us; it may well be that Mary Warren has been conquered by Satan, who sends her here to distract our sacred purpose. If so, her neck will break for it. But if she speak true, I bid you now drop your guile and confess your pretense, for a quick confession will go easier with you. (*Pause.*) Abigail Williams, rise. (*ABIGAIL slowly rises.*) Is there any truth in this?

ABIGAIL. No, sir.

DANFORTH (*thinks, glances at* MARY, *then back to* ABIGAIL). Children, a very augur bit will now be turned into your souls until your honesty is proved. Will either of you change your positions now, or do you force me to hard questioning?

ABIGAIL. I have naught to change, sir. She lies.

DANFORTH (*to* MARY). You would still go on with this?

MARY WARREN (*faintly*). Aye, sir.

DANFORTH (*turning to* ABIGAIL). A poppet were discovered in Mr. Proctor's house, stabbed by a needle. Mary Warren claims that you sat beside her in the court when she made it, and that you saw her make it and witnessed how she herself stuck her needle into it for safe-keeping. What say you to that?

ABIGAIL (*with a slight note of indignation*). It is a lie, sir.

DANFORTH (*after a slight pause*). While you worked for Mr. Proctor, did you see poppets in that house?

ABIGAIL. Goody Proctor always kept poppets.

PROCTOR. Your Honor, my wife never kept no poppets. Mary Warren confesses it was her poppet.

CHEEVER. Your Excellency.

DANFORTH. Mr. Cheever.

CHEEVER. When I spoke with Goody Proctor in that house, she said she never kept no poppets. But she said she did keep poppets when she were a girl.

PROCTOR. She has not been a girl these fifteen years, Your Honor.

HATHORNE. But a poppet will keep fifteen years, will it not?

PROCTOR. It will keep if it is kept, but Mary Warren swears she never saw no poppets in my house, nor anyone else.

PARRIS. Why could there not have been poppets hid where no one ever saw them?

PROCTOR (*furious*). There might also be a dragon with five legs in my house, but no one has ever seen it.

PARRIS. We are here, Your Honor, precisely to discover what no one has ever seen.

PROCTOR. Mr. Danforth, what profit this girl to turn herself about? What may Mary Warren gain but hard questioning and worse?

DANFORTH. You are charging Abigail Williams with a marvelous cool plot to murder, do you understand that?

PROCTOR. I do, sir. I believe she means to murder.

DANFORTH (*pointing at* ABIGAIL, *incredulously*). This child would murder your wife?

PROCTOR. It is not a child. Now hear me, sir. In the sight of the congregation she were twice this year put out of this meetin' house for laughter during prayer.

DANFORTH (*shocked, turning to* ABIGAIL). What's this? Laughter during—!

PARRIS. Excellency, she were under Tituba's power at that time, but she is solemn now.

GILES. Aye, now she is solemn and goes to hang people!

DANFORTH. Quiet, man.

HATHORNE. Surely it have no bearing on the question, sir. He charges contemplation of murder.

DANFORTH. Aye. (*He studies* ABIGAIL *for a moment, then:*) Continue, Mr. Proctor.

PROCTOR. Mary. Now tell the Governor how you danced in the woods.

PARRIS (*instantly*). Excellency, since I come to Salem this man is blackening my name. He—

DANFORTH. In a moment, sir. (*To* MARY WARREN, *sternly, and surprised:*) What is this dancing?

MARY WARREN. I—(*She glances at* ABIGAIL, *who is staring down at her remorselessly. Then, appealing to* PROCTOR:) Mr. Proctor—

PROCTOR (*taking it right up*). Abigail leads the girls to the woods, Your Honor, and they have danced there naked—

PARRIS. Your Honor, this—

PROCTOR (*at once*). Mr. Parris discovered them himself in the dead of night! There's the "child" she is!

DANFORTH (*—it is growing into a nightmare, and he turns, astonished, to* PARRIS). Mr. Parris—

PARRIS. I can only say, sir, that I never found any of them naked, and this man is—

DANFORTH. But you discovered them dancing in the woods? (*Eyes on* PARRIS, *he points at* ABIGAIL.) Abigail?

HALE. Excellency, when I first arrived from Beverly, Mr. Parris told me that.

DANFORTH. Do you deny it, Mr. Parris?

PARRIS. I do not, sir, but I never saw any of them naked.

DANFORTH. But she have *danced*?

PARRIS (*unwillingly*). Aye, sir.

(DANFORTH, *as though with new eyes, looks at* ABIGAIL.)

HATHORNE. Excellency, will you permit me? (*He points at* MARY WARREN.)

DANFORTH (*with great worry*). Pray, proceed.

HATHORNE. You say you never saw no spirits, Mary, were never threatened or afflicted by any manifest of the Devil or the Devil's agents.

MARY WARREN (*very faintly*). No, sir.

HATHORNE (*with a gleam of victory*). And yet, when people accused of witchery confronted you in court, you would faint, saying their spirits came out of their bodies and choked you—

MARY WARREN. That were pretense, sir.

DANFORTH. I cannot hear you.

MARY WARREN. Pretense, sir.

PARRIS. But you did turn cold, did you not? I myself picked you up many times, and your skin were icy. Mr. Danforth, you—

DANFORTH. I saw that many times.

PROCTOR. She only pretended to faint, Your Excellency. They're all marvelous pretenders.

HATHORNE. Then can she pretend to faint now?

PROCTOR. Now?

PARRIS. Why not? Now there are no spirits attacking her, for none in this room is accused of witchcraft. So let her turn herself cold now, let her pretend she is attacked now, let her faint. (*He turns to* MARY WARREN.) Faint!

PARRIS. Aye, faint. Prove to us how you pretended in the court so many times.

MARY WARREN (*looking to* PROCTOR). I—cannot faint now, sir.

PROCTOR (*alarmed, quietly*). Can you not pretend it?

MARY WARREN. I—(*She looks about as though searching for the passion to faint.*) I—have no *sense* of it now, I—

DANFORTH. Why? What is lacking now?

MARY WARREN. I—cannot tell, sir, I—

DANFORTH. Might it be that here we have no afflicting spirit loose, but in the court there were some?

MARY WARREN. I never saw no spirits.

PARRIS. Then see no spirits now, and prove to us that you can faint by your own will, as you claim.

MARY WARREN (*stares, searching for the emotion of it, and then shakes her head*). I—cannot do it.

PARRIS. Then you will confess, will you not? It were attacking spirits made you faint!

MARY WARREN. No, sir, I—

PARRIS. Your Excellency, this is a trick to blind the court!

MARY WARREN. It's not a trick! (*She stands.*) I—I used to faint because I—I thought I saw spirits.

DANFORTH. *Thought* you saw them!

MARY WARREN. But I did not, Your Honor.

HATHORNE. How could you think you saw them unless you saw them?

MARY WARREN. I—I cannot tell how, but I did. I—I heard the other girls screaming, and you, Your Honor, you seemed to believe them, and I— It were only sport in the beginning, sir, but then the whole world cried spirits, spirits, and I—I promise you Mr. Danforth, I only thought I saw them but I did not.

(DANFORTH *peers at her.*)

PARRIS (*smiling, but nervous because* DANFORTH *seems to be struck by* MARY WARREN's *story.*) Surely Your Excellency is not taken by this simple lie.

DANFORTH (*turning worriedly to* ABIGAIL). Abigail. I bid you now search your heart and tell me this—and beware of it, child, to God every soul is precious and His vengeance is terrible on them that take life without cause. Is it possible, child, that the spirits you have seen are illusion only, some deception that may cross your mind when—

ABIGAIL. Why, this—this—is a base question, sir.

DANFORTH. Child, I would have you consider it—

ABIGAIL. I have been hurt, Mr. Danforth; I have seen my blood runnin' out! I have been near to murdered every day because I done my duty pointing out the Devil's people—and this is my reward? To be mistrusted, denied, questioned like a—

DANFORTH (*weakening*). Child, I do not mistrust you—

ABIGAIL (*in an open threat*). Let *you* beware, Mr. Danforth. Think you to be so mighty that the power of Hell may not turn *your* wits? Beware of it! There is— (*Suddenly, from an accusatory attitude, her face turns, looking into the air above —it is truly frightened.*)

DANFORTH (*apprehensively*). What is it, child?

ABIGAIL (*looking about in the air, clasping her arms about her as though cold*). I—I know not. A wind, a cold wind, has come. (*Her eyes fall on* MARY WARREN.)

MARY WARREN (*terrified, pleading*). Abby!

MERCY LEWIS (*shivering*). Your Honor, I freeze!

PROCTOR. They're pretending!

HATHORNE (*touching* ABIGAIL'S *hand*). She is cold, Your Honor, touch her!

MERCY LEWIS (*through chattering teeth*). Mary, do you send this shadow on me?

MARY WARREN. Lord, save me!

SUSANNA WALCOTT. I freeze, I freeze!

ABIGAIL (*shivering visibly*). It is a wind, a wind!

MARY WARREN. Abby, don't do that!

DANFORTH (*himself engaged and entered by* ABIGAIL). Mary Warren, do you witch her? I say to you, do you send your spirit out?

(*With a hysterical cry* MARY WARREN *starts to run.* PROCTOR *catches her.*)

MARY WARREN (*almost collapsing*). Let me go, Mr. Proctor, I cannot, I cannot—

ABIGAIL (*crying to Heaven*). Oh, Heavenly Father, take away this shadow!

(*Without warning or hesitation,* PROCTOR *leaps at* ABIGAIL *and, grabbing her by the hair, pulls her to her feet. She screams in pain.* DANFORTH, *astonished, cries,* "What are you about?" *and* HATHORNE *and* PARRIS *call,* "Take your hands off her!" *and out of it all comes* PROCTOR's *roaring voice.*)

PROCTOR. How do you call Heaven! Whore! Whore!

(HERRICK *breaks* PROCTOR *from her.*)

HERRICK. John!

DANFORTH. Man! Man, what do you—

PROCTOR (*breathless and in agony*). It is a whore!

DANFORTH (*dumfounded*). You charge—?

ABIGAIL. Mr. Danforth, he is lying!

PROCTOR. Mark her! Now she'll suck a scream to stab me with, but—

DANFORTH. You will prove this! This will not pass!

PROCTOR (*trembling, his life collapsing about him*). I have known her, sir. I have known her.

DANFORTH. You—you are a lecher?

FRANCIS (*horrified*). John, you cannot say such a—

PROCTOR. Oh, Francis, I wish you had some evil in you that you might know

me! (*To* DANFORTH:) A man will not cast away his good name. You surely know that.

DANFORTH (*dumfounded*). In—in what time? In what place?

PROCTOR (*his voice about to break, and his shame great*). In the proper place—where my beasts are bedded. On the last night of my joy, some eight months past. She used to serve me in my house, sir. (*He has to clamp his jaw to keep from weeping.*) A man may think God sleeps, but God sees everything. I know it now. I beg you, sir, I beg you—see her what she is. My wife, my dear good wife, took this girl soon after, sir, and put her out on the highroad. And being what she is, a lump of vanity, sir—(*He is being overcome.*) Excellency, forgive me, forgive me. (*Angrily against himself, he turns away from the Governor for a moment. Then, as though to cry out is his only means of speech left.*) She thinks to dance with me on my wife's grave! And well she might, for I thought of her softly. God help me, I lusted, and there *is* a promise in such sweat. But it is a whore's vengeance, and you must see it; I set myself entirely in your hands. I know you must see it now.

DANFORTH (*blanched, in horror, turning to* ABIGAIL). You deny every scrap and tittle of this?

ABIGAIL. If I must answer that, I will leave and I will not come back again!

(DANFORTH *seems unsteady.*)

PROCTOR. I have made a bell of my honor! I have rung the doom of my good name—you will believe me, Mr. Danforth! My wife is innocent, except she knew a whore when she saw one!

ABIGAIL (*stepping up to* DANFORTH). What look do you give me? (DANFORTH *cannot speak.*) I'll not have such looks! (*She turns and starts for the door.*)

DANFORTH. You will remain where you are! (HERRICK *steps into her path. She comes up short, fire in her eyes.*) Mr. Parris, go into the court and bring Goodwife Proctor out.

PARRIS (*objecting*). Your Honor, this is all a—

DANFORTH (*sharply to* PARRIS). Bring her out! And tell her not one word of what's been spoken here. And let you knock before you enter. (PARRIS *goes out.*) Now we shall touch the bottom of this swamp. (*To* PROCTOR:) Your wife, you say, is an honest woman.

PROCTOR. In her life, sir, she have never lied. There are them that cannot sing, and them that cannot weep—my wife cannot lie. I have paid much to learn it, sir.

DANFORTH. And when she put this girl out of your house, she put her out for a harlot?

PROCTOR. Aye, sir.

DANFORTH. And knew her for a harlot?

PROCTOR. Aye, sir, she knew her for a harlot.

DANFORTH. Good then. (*To* ABIGAIL:) And if she tell me, child, it were for harlotry, may God spread His mercy on you! (*There is a knock. He calls to the door.*) Hold! (*To* ABIGAIL:) Turn your back. Turn your back. (*To* PROCTOR:) Do likewise. (*Both turn their backs*—ABIGAIL *indignantly slow.*) Now let neither of you turn to face Goody Proctor. No one in this room is to speak one word, or raise a gesture aye or nay. (*He turns toward the door, calls:*) Enter! (*The door opens.* ELIZABETH *enters with* PARRIS. PARRIS *leaves her. She stands alone, her eyes looking for* PROCTOR.) Mr. Cheever, report this testimony in all exactness. Are you ready?

CHEEVER. Ready sir.

DANFORTH. Come here, woman. (ELIZABETH *comes to him, glancing at* PROCTOR'S *back.*) Look at me only, not at your husband. In my eyes only.

ELIZABETH (*faintly*). Good, sir.

DANFORTH. We are given to understand that at one time you dismissed your servant, Abigail Williams.

ELIZABETH. That is true, sir.

DANFORTH. For what cause did you dismiss her? (*Slight pause. Then* ELIZABETH *tries to glance at* PROCTOR.) You will look in my eyes only and not at your husband. The answer is in your memory and you need no help to give it to me. Why did you dismiss Abigail Williams?

ELIZABETH (*not knowing what to say, sensing a situation, wetting her lips to stall for time*). She—dissatisfied me. (*Pause.*) And my husband.

DANFORTH. In what way dissatisfied you?

ELIZABETH. She were—(*She glances at* PROCTOR *for a cue.*)

DANFORTH. Woman, look at me! (ELIZABETH *does.*) Were she slovenly? Lazy? What disturbance did she cause?

ELIZABETH. Your Honor, I—in that time I were sick. And I— My husband is a good and righteous man. He is never drunk as some are, nor wastin' his time at the shovelboard, but always at his work. But in my sickness—you see, sir, I were a long time sick after my last baby, and I thought I saw my husband somewhat turning from me. And this girl—(*She turns to* ABIGAIL.)

DANFORTH. Look at me.

ELIZABETH. Aye, sir. Abigail Williams—(*She breaks off.*)

DANFORTH. What of Abigail Williams?

ELIZABETH. I came to think he fancied her. And so one night I lost my wits, I think, and put her out on the highroad.

DANFORTH. Your husband—did he indeed turn from you?

ELIZABETH (*in agony*). My husband—is a goodly man, sir.

DANFORTH. Then he did not turn from you.

ELIZABETH (*starting to glance at* PROCTOR). He—

DANFORTH (*reaches out and holds her face, then*). Look at me! To your own knowledge, has John Proctor ever committed the crime of lechery? (*In a crisis of indecision she cannot speak.*) Answer my question! Is your husband a lecher!

ELIZABETH (*faintly*). No, sir.

DANFORTH. Remove her, Marshal.

PROCTOR. Elizabeth, tell the truth!

DANFORTH. She has spoken. Remove her!

PROCTOR (*crying out*). Elizabeth, I have confessed it!

ELIZABETH. Oh, God! (*The door closes behind her.*)

PROCTOR. She only thought to save my name!

HALE. Excellency, it is a natural lie to tell; I beg you, stop now before another is condemned! I may shut my conscience to it no more—private vengeance is working through this testimony! From the beginning this man has struck me true. By my oath to Heaven, I believe him now, and I pray you call back his wife before we—

DANFORTH. She spoke nothing of lechery, and this man has lied!

HALE. I believe him! (*Pointing at* ABIGAIL:) This girl has always struck me false! She has—

(ABIGAIL, *with a weird, wild, chilling cry, screams up to the ceiling.*)

ABIGAIL. You will not! Begone! Begone, I say!

DANFORTH. What is it, child? (*But* ABI-

GAIL, *pointing with fear is now raising up her frightened eyes, her awed face, toward the ceiling—the girls are doing the same—and now* HATHORNE, HALE, PUTNAM, CHEEVER, HERRICK, *and* DANFORTH *do the same.*) What's there? (*He lowers his eyes from the ceiling, and now he is frightened; there is real tension in his voice.*) Child! (*She is transfixed—with all the girls, she is whimpering open-mouthed, agape at the ceiling.*) Girls! Why do you—?

MERCY LEWIS (*pointing*). It's on the beam! Behind the rafter!

DANFORTH (*looking up*). Where!

ABIGAIL. Why?—(*She gulps.*) Why do you come, yellow bird?

PROCTOR. Where's a bird! I see no bird!

ABIGAIL (*to ceiling*). My face? My face?

PROCTOR. Mr. Hale—

DANFORTH. Be quiet!

PROCTOR. (*to* HALE). Do you see a bird?

DANFORTH. Be quiet!!

ABIGAIL (*to the ceiling, in a genuine conversation with the "bird," as though trying to talk it out of attacking her*). But God made my face; you cannot want to tear my face. Envy is a deadly sin, Mary.

MARY WARREN (*on her feet with a spring, and horrified, pleading*). Abby!

ABIGAIL (*unperturbed, continuing to the "bird"*). Oh, Mary, this is a black art to change your shape. No, I cannot, I cannot stop my mouth; it's God's work I do.

MARY WARREN. Abby, I'm *here!*

PROCTOR (*frantically*). They're pretending, Mr. Danforth!

ABIGAIL (*—now she takes a backward step, as though in fear the bird will swoop down momentarily*). Oh, please, Mary! Don't come down.

SUSANNA WALCOTT. Her claws, she's stretching her claws!

PROCTOR. Lies, lies.

ABIGAIL (*backing further, eyes still fixed above*). Mary, please don't hurt me!

MARY WARREN (*to* DANFORTH). I'm not hurting her!

DANFORTH (*to* MARY WARREN). Why does she see this vision?

MARY WARREN. She sees nothin'!

ABIGAIL (*now staring full front as though hypnotized, and mimicking the exact tone of* MARY WARREN's *cry*). She sees nothin'!

MARY WARREN (*pleading*). Abby, you mustn't!

ABIGAIL AND ALL THE GIRLS (*all transfixed*). Abby, you mustn't!

MARY WARREN (*to all the girls*). I'm here, I'm here!

GIRLS. I'm here, I'm here!

DANFORTH (*horrified*). Mary Warren! Draw back your spirit out of them!

MARY WARREN. Mr. Danforth!

GIRLS (*cutting her off*). Mr. Danforth!

DANFORTH. Have you compacted with the Devil? Have you?

MARY WARREN. Never, never!

GIRLS. Never, never!

DANFORTH (*growing hysterical*). Why can they only repeat you?

PROCTOR. Give me a whip—I'll stop it!

MARY WARREN. They're sporting. They—!

GIRLS. They're sporting!

MARY WARREN (*turning on them all hysterically and stamping her feet*). Abby, stop it!

GIRLS (*stamping their feet*). Abby, stop it!

MARY WARREN. Stop it!

GIRLS. Stop it!

MARY WARREN (*screaming it out at the top of her lungs, and raising her fists*). Stop it!!

GIRLS (*raising their fists*). Stop it!!

(MARY WARREN, *utterly confounded, and becoming overwhelmed by* ABIGAIL's—*and the girls'—utter conviction, starts to whimper, hands half raised, powerless, and all the girls begin whimpering exactly as she does.*)

DANFORTH. A little while ago you were afflicted. Now it seems you afflict others; where did you find this power?

MARY WARREN (*staring at* ABIGAIL). I— have no power.

GIRLS. I have no power.

PROCTOR. They're gulling you, Mister!

DANFORTH. Why did you turn about this past two weeks? You have seen the Devil, have you not?

HALE (*indicating* ABIGAIL *and the girls*). You cannot believe them!

MARY WARREN. I—

PROCTOR (*sensing her weakening*). Mary, God damns all liars!

DANFORTH (*pounding it into her*). You have seen the Devil, you have made compact with Lucifer, have you not?

PROCTOR. God damns liars, Mary!

(MARY *utters something unintelligible, staring at* ABIGAIL, *who keeps watching the "bird" above.*)

DANFORTH. I cannot hear you. What do you say? (MARY *utters again unintelligi-*

bly.) You will confess yourself or you will hang! (*He turns her roughly to face him.*) Do you know who I am? I say you will hang if you do not open with me!

PROCTOR. Mary, remember the angel Raphael—do that which is good and—

ABIGAIL (*pointing upward*). The wings! Her wings are spreading! Mary, please, don't, don't—!

HALE. I see nothing, Your Honor!

DANFORTH. Do you confess this power! (*He is an inch from her face.*) Speak!

ABIGAIL. She's going to come down! She's walking the beam!

DANFORTH. Will you speak!

MARY WARREN (*staring in horror*). I cannot!

GIRLS. I cannot!

PARRIS. Cast the Devil out! Look him in the face! Trample him! We'll save you, Mary, only stand fast against him and—

ABIGAIL (*looking up*). Look out! She's coming down!

(*She and all the girls run to one wall, shielding their eyes. And now, as though cornered, they let out a gigantic scream, and* MARY, *as though infected, opens her mouth and screams with them. Gradually* ABIGAIL *and the girls leave off, until only* MARY *is left there, staring up at the "bird," screaming madly. All watch her, horrified by this evident fit.* PROCTOR *strides to her.*)

PROCTOR. Mary, tell the governor what they—(*He has hardly got a word out, when, seeing him coming for her, she rushes out of his reach, screaming in horror.*)

MARY WARREN. Don't touch me—don't touch me! (*At which the girls halt at the door.*)

PROCTOR (*astonished*). Mary!

MARY WARREN (*pointing at* PROCTOR). You're the Devil's man!

(*He is stopped in his tracks.*)

PARRIS. Praise God!

GIRLS. Praise God!

PROCTOR (*numbed*). Mary, how—?

MARY WARREN. I'll not hang with you! I love God, I love God.

DANFORTH (*to* MARY). He bid you do the Devil's work?

MARY WARREN (*hysterically, indicating* PROCTOR). He come at me by night and every day to sign, to sign, to—

DANFORTH. Sign what?

PARRIS. The Devil's book? He come with a book?

MARY WARREN (*hysterically, pointing at* PROCTOR, *fearful of him*). My name, he want my name. "I'll murder you," he says, "if my wife hangs! We must go and overthrow the court," he says!

(DANFORTH's *head jerks toward* PROCTOR, *shock and horror in his face.*)

PROCTOR (*turning, appealing to* HALE). Mr. Hale!

MARY WARREN (*her sobs beginning*). He wake me every night, his eyes were like coals and his fingers claw my neck, and I sign, I sign . . .

HALE. Excellency, this child's gone wild!

PROCTOR (*as* DANFORTH's *wide eyes pour on him*). Mary, Mary!

MARY WARREN (*screaming at him*). No, I love God; I go your way no more. I love God, I bless God. (*Sobbing, she rushes to* ABIGAIL.) Abby, Abby, I'll never hurt you more! (*They all watch, as* ABIGAIL, *out of her infinite charity, reaches out and draws the sobbing* MARY *to her, and then looks up to* DANFORTH.)

DANFORTH (*to* PROCTOR). What are you? (PROCTOR *is beyond speech in his anger.*) You are combined with anti-Christ, are you not? I have seen your power; you will not deny it! What say you, Mister?

HALE. Excellency—

DANFORTH. I will have nothing from you, Mr. Hale! (*To* PROCTOR:) Will you confess yourself befouled with Hell, or do you keep that black allegiance yet? What say you?

PROCTOR (*his mind wild, breathless*). I say—I say—God is dead!

PARRIS. Hear it, hear it!

PROCTOR (*laughs insanely, then*). A fire, a fire is burning! I hear the boot of Lucifer, I see his filthy face! And it is my face, and yours, Danforth! For them that quail to bring men out of ignorance, as I have quailed, and as you quail now when you know in all your black hearts that this be fraud—God damns our kind especially, and we will burn, we will burn together!

DANFORTH. Marshal! Take him and Corey with him to the jail!

HALE (*starting across to the door*). I denounce these proceedings!

PROCTOR. You are pulling Heaven down and raising up a whore!

HALE. I denounce these proceedings, I quit this court! (*He slams the door to the outside behind him.*)

DANFORTH (*calling to him in a fury*). Mr. Hale! Mr. Hale!

THE CURTAIN FALLS

ACT FOUR

A cell in Salem jail, that fall.

At the back is a high barred window; near it, a great, heavy door. Along the walls are two benches.

The place is in darkness but for the moonlight seeping through the bars. It appears empty. Presently footsteps are heard coming down a corridor beyond the wall, keys rattle, and the door swings open. MARSHAL HERRICK enters with a lantern.

He is nearly drunk, and heavy-footed. He goes to a bench and nudges a bundle of rags lying on it.

HERRICK. Sarah, wake up! Sarah Good! (*He then crosses to the other bench.*)

SARAH GOOD (*rising in her rags*). Oh, Majesty! Comin', comin'! Tituba, he's here, His Majesty's come!

HERRICK. Go to the north cell; this place is wanted now. (*He hangs his lantern on the wall. TITUBA sits up.*)

TITUBA. That don't look to me like His Majesty; look to me like the marshal.

HERRICK (*taking out a flask*). Get along with you now, clear this place. (*He drinks, and SARAH GOOD comes and peers into his face.*)

SARAH GOOD. Oh, is it you, Marshal! I thought sure you be the devil comin' for us. Could I have a sip of cider for me goin-away?

HERRICK (*handing her the flask*). And where are you off to, Sarah?

TITUBA (*as SARAH drinks*). We goin' to Barbados, soon the Devil gits here with the feathers and the wings.

HERRICK. Oh? A happy voyage to you.

SARAH GOOD. A pair of bluebirds wingin' southerly, the two of us! Oh, it be a grand transformation, Marshal! (*She raises the flask to drink again.*)

HERRICK (*taking the flask from her lips*). You'd best give me that or you'll never rise off the ground. Come along now.

TITUBA. I'll speak to him for you, if you desires to come along, Marshal.

HERRICK. I'd not refuse it, Tituba; it's the proper morning to fly into Hell.

TITUBA. Oh, it be no Hell in Barbados. Devil, him be pleasure-man in Barbados, him be singin' and dancin' in Barbados. It's you folks—you riles him up 'round here; it be too cold 'round here for that Old Boy. He freeze his soul in Massachusetts, but in Barbados he just as sweet and —(*A bellowing cow is heard, and TITUBA leaps up and calls to the window:*) Aye, sir! That's him, Sarah!

SARAH GOOD. I'm here, Majesty! (*They hurriedly pick up their rags as HOPKINS, a guard, enters.*)

HOPKINS. The Deputy Governor's arrived.

HERRICK (*grabbing TITUBA*). Come along, come along.

TITUBA (*resisting him*). No, he comin' for me. I goin' home!

HERRICK (*pulling her to the door*). That's not Satan, just a poor old cow with a hatful of milk. Come along now, out with you!

TITUBA (*calling to the window*). Take me home, Devil! Take me home!

SARAH GOOD (*following the shouting TITUBA out*). Tell him I'm goin', Tituba! Now you tell him Sarah Good is goin' too!

(*In the corridor outside TITUBA calls on —"Take me home, Devil; Devil take me home!" and HOPKINS' voice orders her to move on. HERRICK returns and begins to push old rags and straw into a corner. Hearing footsteps, he turns, and enter DANFORTH and JUDGE HATHORNE. They are in greatcoats and wear hats against the bitter cold. They are followed in by CHEEVER, who carries a dispatch case and a flat wooden box containing his writing materials.*)

HERRICK. Good morning, Excellency.

DANFORTH. Where is Mr. Parris?

HERRICK. I'll fetch him. (*He starts for the door.*)

DANFORTH. Marshal. (*HERRICK stops.*) When did Reverend Hale arrive?

HERRICK. It were toward midnight, I think.

DANFORTH (*suspiciously*). What is he about here?

HERRICK. He goes among them that will hang, sir. And he prays with them. He sits with Goody Nurse now. And Mr. Parris with him.

DANFORTH. Indeed. That man have no authority to enter here, Marshal. Why have you let him in?

HERRICK. Why, Mr. Parris command me, sir. I cannot deny him.

DANFORTH. Are you drunk, Marshal?

HERRICK. No, sir; it is a bitter night, and I have no fire here.

DANFORTH (*containing his anger*). Fetch Mr. Parris.

HERRICK. Aye, sir.

DANFORTH. There is a prodigious stench in this place.

HERRICK. I have only now cleared the people out for you.

DANFORTH. Beware hard drink, Marshal.

HERRICK. Aye, sir. (*He waits an instant for further orders. But* DANFORTH, *in dissatisfaction, turns his back on him, and* HERRICK *goes out. There is a pause.* DANFORTH *stands in thought.*)

HATHORNE. Let you question Hale, Excellency; I should not be surprised he have been preaching in Andover lately.

DANFORTH. We'll come to that; speak nothing of Andover. Parris prays with him. That's strange. (*He blows on his hands, moves toward the window, and looks out.*)

HATHORNE. Excellency, I wonder if it be wise to let Mr. Parris so continuously with the prisoners. (DANFORTH *turns to him, interested.*) I think, sometimes, the man has a mad look these days.

DANFORTH. Mad?

HATHORNE. I met him yesterday coming out of his house, and I bid him good morning—and he wept and went his way. I think it is not well the village sees him so unsteady.

DANFORTH. Perhaps he have some sorrow.

CHEEVER (*stamping his feet against the cold*). I think it be the cows, sir.

DANFORTH. Cows?

CHEEVER. There be so many cows wanderin' the highroads, now their masters are in the jails, and much disagreement who they will belong to now. I know Mr. Parris be arguin' with farmers all yesterday—there is great contention, sir, about the cows. Contention make him weep, sir; it were always a man that weep for contention. (*He turns, as do* HATHORNE *and* DANFORTH, *hearing someone coming up the corridor.* DANFORTH *raises his head as* PARRIS *enters. He is gaunt, frightened, and sweating in his greatcoat.*)

PARRIS (*to* DANFORTH, *instantly*). Oh, good morning, sir, thank you for coming, I beg your pardon wakin' you so early. Good morning, Judge Hathorne.

DANFORTH. Reverend Hale have no right to enter this—

PARRIS. Excellency, a moment. (*He hurries back and shuts the door.*)

HATHORNE. Do you leave him alone with the prisoners?

DANFORTH. What's his business here?

PARRIS (*prayerfully holding up his hands*). Excellency, hear me. It is a providence. Reverend Hale has returned to bring Rebecca Nurse to God.

DANFORTH (*surprised*). He bids her confess?

PARRIS (*sitting*). Hear me. Rebecca have not given me a word this three month since she came. Now she sits with him, and her sister and Martha Corey and two or three others, and he pleads with them, confess their crimes and save their lives.

DANFORTH. Why—this is indeed a providence. And they soften, they soften?

PARRIS. Not yet, not yet. But I thought to summon you, sir, that we might think on whether it be not wise, to—(*He dares not say it.*) I had thought to put a question, sir, and I hope you will not—

DANFORTH. Mr. Parris, be plain, what troubles you?

PARRIS. There is news, sir, that the court —the court must reckon with. My niece, sir, my niece—I believe she has vanished.

DANFORTH. Vanished!

PARRIS. I had thought to advise you of it earlier in the week, but—

DANFORTH. Why? How long is she gone?

PARRIS. This be the third night. You see, sir, she told me she would stay a night with Mercy Lewis. And next day, when she does not return, I send to Mr. Lewis to inquire. Mercy told him she would sleep in *my* house for a night.

DANFORTH. They are both gone?!

PARRIS (*in fear of him*). They are, sir.

DANFORTH (*alarmed*). I will send a party for them. Where may they be?

PARRIS. Excellency, I think they be aboard a ship. (DANFORTH *stands agape.*) My daughter tells me how she heard them speaking of ships last week, and tonight I discover my—my strongbox is broke into. (*He presses his fingers against his eyes to keep back tears.*)

HATHORNE (*astonished*). She have robbed you?

PARRIS. Thirty-one pound is gone. I am penniless. (*He covers his face and sobs.*)

DANFORTH. Mr. Parris, you are a brainless man! (*He walks in thought, deeply worried.*)

PARRIS. Excellency, it profit nothing you should blame me. I cannot think they would run off except they fear to keep in Salem any more. (*He is pleading.*) Mark it, sir, Abigail had close knowledge of the town, and since the news of Andover has broken here—

DANFORTH. Andover is remedied. The court returns there on Friday, and will resume examinations.

PARRIS. I am sure of it, sir. But the rumor here speaks rebellion in Andover, and it—

DANFORTH. There is no rebellion in Andover!

PARRIS. I tell you what is said here, sir. Andover have thrown out the court, they say, and will have no part of witchcraft. There be a faction here, feeding on the news, and I tell you true, sir, I fear there will be riot here.

HATHORNE. Riot! Why at every execution I have seen naught but high satisfaction in the town.

PARRIS. Judge Hathorne—it were another sort that hanged till now. Rebecca Nurse is no Bridget that lived three year with Bishop before she married him. John Proctor is not Isaac Ward that drink his family to ruin. (*To DANFORTH:*) I would to God it were not so, Excellency, but these people have great weight yet in the town. Let Rebecca stand upon the gibbet and send up some righteous prayer, and I fear she'll wake a vengeance on you.

HATHORNE. Excellency, she is condemned a witch. The court have—

DANFORTH (*in deep concern, raising a hand to HATHORNE.*) Pray you. (*To PARRIS:*) How do you propose, then?

PARRIS. Excellency, I would postpone these hangin's for a time.

DANFORTH. There will be no postponement.

PARRIS. Now Mr. Hale's returned, there is hope, I think—for if he bring even one of these to God, that confession surely damns the others in the public eye, and none may doubt more that they are all linked to Hell. This way, unconfessed and claiming innocence, doubts are multiplied, many honest people will weep for them, and our good purpose is lost in their tears.

DANFORTH (*after thinking a moment, then going to CHEEVER*). Give me the list.

(CHEEVER *opens the dispatch case, searches.*)

PARRIS. It cannot be forgot, sir, that when I summoned the congregation for John Proctor's excommunication there were hardly thirty people come to hear it. That speak a discontent, I think, and—

DANFORTH (*studying the list*). There will be no postponement.

PARRIS. Excellency—

DANFORTH. Now, sir—which of these in your opinion may be brought to God? I will myself strive with him till dawn. (*He hands the list to PARRIS, who merely glances at it.*)

PARRIS. There is not sufficient time till dawn.

DANFORTH. I shall do my utmost. Which of them do you have hope for?

PARRIS (*not even glancing at the list now, and in a quavering voice, quietly*). Excellency—a dagger—(*He chokes up.*)

DANFORTH. What do you say?

PARRIS. Tonight, when I open my door to leave my house—a dagger clattered to the ground. (*Silence. DANFORTH absorbs this. Now PARRIS cries out.*) You cannot hang this sort. There is danger for me. I dare not step outside at night! (*REVEREND HALE enters. They look at him for an instant in silence. He is steeped in sorrow, exhausted, and more direct than he ever was.*)

DANFORTH. Accept my congratulations, Reverend Hale; we are gladdened to see you returned to your good work.

HALE (*coming to DANFORTH now*). You must pardon them. They will not budge.

(HERRICK *enters, waits.*)

DANFORTH (*conciliatory*). You misunderstand, sir; I cannot pardon these when twelve are already hanged for the same crime. It is not just.

PARRIS (*with failing heart*). Rebecca will not confess?

HALE. The sun will rise in a few minutes. Excellency, I must have more time.

DANFORTH. Now hear me, and beguile yourselves no more. I will not receive a single plea for pardon or postponement. Them that will not confess will hang. Twelve are already executed; the names of these seven are given out, and the village expects to see them die this morning. Postponement now speaks a floundering on my part; reprieve or pardon must cast doubt upon the guilt of them that died till now. While I speak God's law, I will not crack its voice with whimpering. If retaliation is your fear, know this—I should hang ten thousand that dared to rise against 'the law, and an ocean of salt tears could not melt the resolution of the statutes. Now draw yourselves up like men and help me, as you are bound by Heaven to do. Have you spoken with them all, Mr. Hale?

HALE. All but Proctor. He is in the dungeon.

DANFORTH (*to* HERRICK). What's Proctor's way now?

HERRICK. He sits like some great bird; you'd not know he lived except he will take food from time to time.

DANFORTH (*after thinking a moment*). His wife—his wife must be well on with child now.

HERRICK. She is, sir.

DANFORTH. What think you, Mr. Parris? You have closer knowledge of this man; might her presence soften him?

PARRIS. It is possible, sir. He have not laid eyes on her these three months. I should summon her.

DANFORTH (*to* HERRICK). Is he yet adamant? Has he struck at you again?

HERRICK. He cannot, sir, he is chained to the wall now.

DANFORTH (*after thinking on it*). Fetch Goody Proctor to me. Then let you bring him up.

HERRICK. Aye, sir. (HERRICK *goes. There is silence.*)

HALE. Excellency, if you postpone a week and publish to the town that you are striving for their confessions, that speak mercy on your part, not faltering.

DANFORTH. Mr. Hale, as God have not empowered me like Joshua to stop this sun from rising, so I cannot withhold from them the perfection of their punishment.

HALE (*harder now*). If you think God wills you to raise rebellion, Mr. Danforth, you are mistaken!

DANFORTH (*instantly*). You have heard rebellion spoken in the town?

HALE. Excellency, there are orphans wandering from house to house; abandoned cattle bellow on the highroads, the stink of rotting crops hangs everywhere, and no man knows when the harlots' cry will end his life—and you wonder yet if rebellion's spoke? Better you should marvel how they do not burn your province!

DANFORTH. Mr. Hale, have you preached in Andover this month?

HALE. Thank God they have no need of me in Andover.

DANFORTH. You baffle me, sir. Why have you returned here?

HALE. Why, it is all simple. I come to do the Devil's work. I come to counsel Christians they should belie themselves. (*His sarcasm collapses.*) There is blood on my head! Can you not see the blood on my head!!

PARRIS. Hush! (*For he has heard footsteps. They all face the door.* HERRICK *enters with* ELIZABETH. *Her wrists are linked by heavy chain, which* HERRICK *now removes. Her clothes are dirty; her face is pale and gaunt.* HERRICK *goes out.*)

DANFORTH (*very politely*). Goody Proctor. (*She is silent.*) I hope you are hearty?

ELIZABETH (*as a warning reminder*). I am yet six months before my time.

DANFORTH. Pray be at your ease, we come not for your life. We—(*Uncertain how to plead, for he is not accustomed to it.*) Mr. Hale, will you speak with the woman?

HALE. Goody Proctor, your husband is marked to hang this morning.

(*Pause.*)

ELIZABETH (*quietly*). I have heard it.

HALE. You know, do you not, that I have no connection with the court? (*She seems to doubt it.*) I come of my own, Goody Proctor. I would save your husband's life, for if he is taken I count myself his murderer. Do you understand me?

ELIZABETH. What do you want of me?

HALE. Goody Proctor, I have gone this three month like our Lord into the wilderness. I have sought a Christian way, for damnation's doubled on a minister who counsels men to lie.

HATHORNE. It is no lie, you cannot speak of lies.

HALE. It is a lie! They are innocent!

DANFORTH. I'll hear no more of that!

HALE (*continuing to* ELIZABETH). Let you not mistake your duty as I mistook my own. I came into this village like a bridegroom to his beloved, bearing gifts of high religion; the very crowns of holy law I brought, and what I touched with my bright confidence, it died; and where I turned the eye of my great faith, blood flowed up. Beware, Goody Proctor—cleave to no faith when faith brings blood. It is mistaken law that leads you to sacrifice. Life, woman, life is God's most precious gift; no principle, however glorious, may justify the taking of it. I beg you, woman, prevail upon your husband to confess. Let him give his lie. Quail not before God's judgment in this, for it may well be God damns a liar less than he that throws his life away for pride. Will you plead with him? I cannot think he will listen to another.

ELIZABETH (*quietly*). I think that be the Devil's argument.

HALE (*with climactic desperation*). Woman, before the laws of God we are as swine! We cannot read His will!

ELIZABETH. I cannot dispute with you, sir; I lack learning for it.

DANFORTH (*going to her*). Goody Proctor, you are not summoned here for disputation. Be there no wifely tenderness within you? He will die with the sunrise. Your husband. Do you understand it? (*She only looks at him.*) What say you? Will you contend with him? (*She is silent.*) Are you stone? I tell you true, woman, had I no other proof of your unnatural life, your dry eyes now would be sufficient evidence that you delivered up your soul to Hell! A very ape would weep at such calamity! Have the devil dried up any tear of pity in you? (*She is silent.*) Take her out. It profit nothing she should speak to him!

ELIZABETH (*quietly*). Let me speak with him, Excellency.

PARRIS (*with hope*). You'll strive with him? (*She hesitates.*)

DANFORTH. Will you plead for his confession or will you not?

ELIZABETH. I promise nothing. Let me speak with him.

(*A sound—the sibilance of dragging feet on stone. They turn. A pause.* HERRICK *enters with* JOHN PROCTOR. *His wrists are chained. He is another man, bearded, filthy, his eyes misty as though webs had overgrown them. He halts inside the doorway, his eye caught by the sight of* ELIZABETH. *The emotion flowing between them prevents anyone from speaking for an instant. Now* HALE, *visibly affected, goes to* DANFORTH *and speaks quietly.*)

HALE. Pray, leave them, Excellency.

DANFORTH (*pressing* HALE *impatiently aside*). Mr. Proctor, you have been notified, have you not? (*PROCTOR is silent, staring at* ELIZABETH.) I see light in the sky, Mister; let you counsel with your wife, and may God help you turn your back on Hell. (*PROCTOR is silent, staring at* ELIZABETH.)

HALE (*quietly*). Excellency, let—

(*DANFORTH brushes past* HALE *and walks out.* HALE *follows.* CHEEVER *stands and follows,* HATHORNE *behind.* HERRICK *goes.* PARRIS, *from a safe distance, offers:*)

PARRIS. If you desire a cup of cider, Mr. Proctor, I am sure I—(*PROCTOR turns an icy stare at him, and he breaks off.* PARRIS *raises his palms toward* PROCTOR.) God lead you now. (*PARRIS goes out.*)

(*Alone,* PROCTOR *walks to her, halts. It is as though they stood in a spinning world. It is beyond sorrow, above it. He reaches out his hand as though toward an embodiment not quite real, and as he touches her, a strange soft sound, half laughter, half amazement, comes from his throat. He pats her hand. She covers his hand with hers. And then, weak, he sits. Then she sits, facing him.*)

PROCTOR. The child?

ELIZABETH. It grows.

PROCTOR. There is no word of the boys?

ELIZABETH. They're well. Rebecca's Samuel keeps them.

PROCTOR. You have not seen them?

ELIZABETH. I have not. (*She catches a weakening in herself and downs it.*)

PROCTOR. You are a—marvel, Elizabeth.

ELIZABETH. You—have been tortured?

PROCTOR. Aye. (*Pause. She will not let herself be drowned in the sea that threatens her.*) They come for my life now.

ELIZABETH. I know it.

(*Pause.*)

PROCTOR. None—have yet confessed?

ELIZABETH. There be many confessed.

PROCTOR. Who are they?

ELIZABETH. There be a hundred or more, they say. Goody Ballard is one; Isaiah Goodkind is one. There be many.

PROCTOR. Rebecca?

ELIZABETH. Not Rebecca. She is one foot in Heaven now; naught may hurt her more.

PROCTOR. And Giles?

ELIZABETH. You have not heard of it?

PROCTOR. I hear nothin', where I am kept.

ELIZABETH. Giles is dead.

(*He looks at her incredulously.*)

PROCTOR. When were he hanged?

ELIZABETH (*quietly, factually*). He were

not hanged. He would not answer aye or nay to his indictment; for if he denied the charge they'd hang him surely, and auction out his property. So he stand mute, and died Christian under the law. And so his sons will have his farm. It is the law, for he could not be condemned a wizard without he answer the indictment, aye or nay.

PROCTOR. Then how does he die?

ELIZABETH (*gently*). They press him, John.

PROCTOR. Press?

ELIZABETH. Great stones they lay upon his chest until he plead aye or nay. (*With a tender smile for the old man:*) They say he give them but two words. "More weight," he says. And died.

PROCTOR (*numbed—a thread to weave into his agony*). "More weight."

ELIZABETH. Aye. It were a fearsome man, Giles Corey.

(*Pause.*)

PROCTOR (*with great force of will, but not quite looking at her*). I have been thinking I would confess to them, Elizabeth. (*She shows nothing.*) What say you? If I give them that?

ELIZABETH. I cannot judge you, John.

(*Pause.*)

PROCTOR (*simply—a pure question*). What would you have me do?

ELIZABETH. As you will, I would have it. (*Slight pause.*) I want you living, John. That's sure.

PROCTOR (*pauses, then with a flailing of hope*). Giles' wife? Have she confessed?

ELIZABETH. She will not.

(*Pause.*)

PROCTOR. It is a pretense, Elizabeth.

ELIZABETH. What is?

PROCTOR. I cannot mount the gibbet like a saint. It is a fraud. I am not that man. (*She is silent.*) My honesty is broke, Elizabeth; I am no good man. Nothing's spoiled by giving them this lie that were not rotten long before.

ELIZABETH. And yet you've not confessed till now. That speak goodness in you.

PROCTOR. Spite only keeps me silent. It is hard to give a lie to dogs. (*Pause, for the first time he turns directly to her.*) I would have your forgiveness, Elizabeth.

ELIZABETH. It is not for me to give, John, I am—

PROCTOR. I'd have you see some honesty in it. Let them that never lied die now to keep their souls. It is pretense for me, a vanity that will not blind God nor keep my children out of the wind. (*Pause.*) What say you?

ELIZABETH (*upon a heaving sob that always threatens*). John, it come to naught that I should forgive you, if you'll not forgive yourself. (*Now he turns away a little, in great agony.*) It is not my soul, John, it is yours. (*He stands, as though in physical pain, slowly rising to his feet with a great immortal longing to find his answer. It is difficult to say, and she is on the verge of tears.*) Only be sure of this, for I know it now: Whatever you will do, it is a good man does it. (*He turns his doubting, searching gaze upon her.*) I have read my heart this three month, John. (*Pause.*) I have sins of my own to count. It needs a cold wife to prompt lechery.

PROCTOR (*in great pain*). Enough, enough—

ELIZABETH (*now pouring out her heart*). Better you should know me!

PROCTOR. I will not hear it! I know you!

ELIZABETH. You take my sins upon you, John—

PROCTOR (*in agony*). No, I take my own, my own!

ELIZABETH. John, I counted myself so plain, so poorly made, no honest love could come to me! Suspicion kissed you when I did; I never knew how I should say my love. It were a cold house I kept! (*In fright, she swerves, as HATHORNE enters.*)

HATHORNE. What say you, Proctor? The sun is soon up.

(PROCTOR, *his chest heaving, stares, turns to* ELIZABETH. *She comes to him as though to plead, her voice quaking.*)

ELIZABETH. Do what you will. But let none be your judge. There be no higher judge under Heaven than Proctor is! Forgive me, forgive me, John—I never knew such goodness in the world! (*She covers her face, weeping.*)

(PROCTOR *turns from her to* HATHORNE; *he is off the earth, his voice hollow.*)

PROCTOR. I want my life.

HATHORNE (*electrified, surprised*). You'll confess yourself?

PROCTOR. I will have my life.

HATHORNE (*with a mystical tone*). God be praised! It is a providence! (*He rushes out the door, and his voice is heard calling down the corridor.*) He will confess! Proctor will confess!

PROCTOR (*with a cry, as he strides to the door*). Why do you cry it? (*In great pain he turns back to her.*) It is evil, is it not? It is evil.

ELIZABETH (*in terror, weeping*). I cannot judge you, John, I cannot!

PROCTOR. Then who will judge ,me? (*Suddenly clasping his hands:*) God in Heaven, what is John Proctor, what is John Proctor? (*He moves as an animal, and a fury is riding in him, a tantalized search.*) I think it is honest, I think so; I am no saint. (*As though she had denied this he calls angrily at her:*) Let Rebecca go like a saint; for me it is fraud!

(*Voices are heard in the hall, speaking together in suppressed excitement.*)

ELIZABETH. I am not your judge, I cannot be. (*As though giving him release:*) Do as you will, do as you will!

PROCTOR. Would you give them such a lie? Say it. Would you ever give them this? (*She cannot answer.*) You would not; if tongs of fire were singeing you, you would not! It is evil. Good, then—it is evil, and I do it!

(HATHORNE *enters with* DANFORTH, *and, with them,* CHEEVER, PARRIS, *and* HALE. *It is a businesslike, rapid entrance, as though the ice had been broken.*)

DANFORTH (*with great relief and gratitude*). Praise to God, man, praise to God; you shall be blessed in Heaven for this. (CHEEVER *has hurried to the bench with pen, ink, and paper.* PROCTOR *watches him.*) Now then, let us have it. Are you ready, Mr. Cheever?

PROCTOR (*with a cold, cold horror at their efficiency*). Why must it be written?

DANFORTH. Why, for the good instruction of the village, Mister; this we shall post upon the church door! (*To* PARRIS, *urgently:*) Where is the marshal?

PARRIS (*runs to the door and calls down the corridor*). Marshal! Hurry!

DANFORTH. Now, then, Mister, will you speak slowly, and directly to the point, for Mr. Cheever's sake. (*He is on record now, and is really dictating to* CHEEVER, *who writes.*) Mr. Proctor, have you seen the Devil in your life? (PROCTOR'S *jaws lock.*) Come, man, there is light in the sky; the town waits at the scaffold; I would give out this news. Did you see the Devil?

PROCTOR. I did.

PARRIS. Praise God!

DANFORTH. And when he come to you, what were his demand? (PROCTOR *is silent.* DANFORTH *helps.*) Did he bid you to do his work upon the earth?

PROCTOR. He did.

DANFORTH. And you bound yourself to his service? (DANFORTH *turns, as* REBECCA NURSE *enters, with* HERRICK *helping to support her. She is barely able to walk.*) Come in, come in, woman!

REBECCA (*brightening as she sees* PROCTOR). Ah, John! You are well, then, eh?

(PROCTOR *turns his face to the wall.*)

DANFORTH. Courage, man, courage—let her witness your good example that she may come to God herself. Now hear it, Goody Nurse! Say on, Mr. Proctor. Did you bind yourself to the Devil's service?

REBECCA (*astonished*).Why, John!

PROCTOR (*through his teeth, his face turned from* REBECCA). I did.

DANFORTH. Now, woman, you surely see it profit nothin' to keep this conspiracy any further. Will you confess yourself with him?

REBECCA. Oh, John—God send his mercy on you!

DANFORTH. I say, will you confess yourself, Goody Nurse?

REBECCA. Why, it is a lie, it is a lie, how may I damn myself? I cannot, I cannot.

DANFORTH. Mr. Proctor. When the Devil came to you did you see Rebecca Nurse in his company? (PROCTOR *is silent.*) Come, man, take courage—did you ever see her with the Devil?

PROCTOR (*almost inaudibly*). No.

(DANFORTH, *now sensing trouble, glances at* JOHN *and goes to the table, and picks up a sheet—the list of condemned.*)

DANFORTH. Did you ever see her sister, Mary Easty, with the Devil?

PROCTOR. No, I did not.

DANFORTH (*his eyes narrow on* PROCTOR). Did you ever see Martha Corey with the Devil?

PROCTOR. I did not.

DANFORTH (*realizing, slowly putting the sheet down*). Did you ever see anyone with the Devil?

PROCTOR. I did not.

DANFORTH. Proctor, you mistake me. I am not empowered to trade your life for a lie. You have most certainly seen some person with the Devil. (PROCTOR *is silent.*) Mr. Proctor, a score of people have already testified they saw this woman with the Devil.

PROCTOR. Then it is proved. Why must I say it?

DANFORTH. Why "must" you say it! Why, you should rejoice to say it if your soul is truly purged of any love for Hell!

PROCTOR. They think to go like saints. I like not to spoil their names.

DANFORTH (*inquiring, incredulous*). Mr. Proctor, do you think they go like saints?

PROCTOR (*evading*). This woman never thought she done the Devil's work.

DANFORTH. Look you, sir. I think you mistake your duty here. It matters nothing what she thought—she is convicted of the unnatural murder of children, and you for sending your spirit out upon Mary Warren. Your soul alone is the issue here, Mister, and you will prove its whiteness or you cannot live in a Christian country. Will you tell me now what persons conspired with you in the Devil's company? (PROCTOR *is silent*.) To your knowledge was Rebecca Nurse ever—

PROCTOR. I speak my own sins; I cannot judge another. (*Crying out, with hatred:*) I have no tongue for it.

HALE (*quickly to* DANFORTH.) Excellency, it is enough he confess himself. Let him sign it, let him sign it.

PARRIS (*feverishly*). It is a great service, sir. It is a weighty name; it will strike the village that Proctor confess. I beg you, let him sign it. The sun is up, Excellency!

DANFORTH (*considers; then with dissatisfaction*). Come, then, sign your testimony. (*To* CHEEVER:) Give it to him. (CHEEVER *goes to* PROCTOR, *the confession and a pen in hand*. PROCTOR *does not look at it*.) Come, man, sign it.

PROCTOR (*after glancing at the confession*). You have all witnessed it—it is enough.

DANFORTH. You will not sign it?

PROCTOR. You have all witnessed it; what more is needed?

DANFORTH. Do you sport with me? You will sign your name or it is no confession, Mister! (*His breast heaving with agonized breathing,* PROCTOR *now lays the paper down and signs his name.*)

PARRIS. Praise be to the Lord!

(PROCTOR *has just finished signing when* DANFORTH *reaches for the paper. But* PROCTOR *snatches it up, and now a wild terror is rising in him, and a boundless anger.*)

DANFORTH (*perplexed, but politely extending his hand*). If you please, sir.

PROCTOR. No.

DANFORTH (*as though* PROCTOR *did not understand*). Mr. Proctor, I must have—

PROCTOR. No, no. I have signed it. You have seen me. It is done! You have no need for this.

PARRIS. Proctor, the village must have proof that—

PROCTOR. Damn the village! I confess to God, and God has seen my name on this! It is enough!

DANFORTH. No, sir, it is—

PROCTOR. You came to save my soul, did you not? Here! I have confessed myself; it is enough!

DANFORTH. You have not con—

PROCTOR. I have confessed myself! Is there no good penitence but it be public? God does not need my name nailed upon the church! God sees my name; God knows how black my sins are! It is enough!

DANFORTH. Mr. Proctor—

PROCTOR. You will not use me! I am no Sarah Good or Tituba, I am John Proctor! You will not use me! It is no part of salvation that you should use me!

DANFORTH. I do not wish to—

PROCTOR. I have three children—how may I teach them to walk like men in the world, and I sold my friends?

DANFORTH. You have not sold your friends—

PROCTOR. Beguile me not! I blacken all of them when this is nailed to the church the very day they hang for silence!

DANFORTH. Mr. Proctor, I must have good and legal proof that you—

PROCTOR. You are the high court, your word is good enough! Tell them I confessed myself; say Proctor broke his knees and wept like a woman; say what you will, but my name cannot—

DANFORTH (*with suspicion*). It is the same, is it not? If I report it or you sign to it?

PROCTOR (*—he knows it is insane*). No, it is not the same! What others say and what I sign to is not the same!

DANFORTH. Why? Do you mean to deny this confession when you are free?

PROCTOR. I mean to deny nothing!

DANFORTH. Then explain to me, Mr. Proctor, why you will not let—

PROCTOR (*with a cry of his whole soul*). Because it is my name! Because I cannot have another in my life! Because I lie and sign myself to lies! Because I am not worth the dust on the feet of them that hang! How may I live without my name? I have given you my soul; leave me my name!

DANFORTH (*pointing at the confession in* PROCTOR's *hand*). Is that document a lie? If it is a lie I will not accept it! What say you? I will not deal in lies, Mister! (PROCTOR *is motionless.*) You will give me your honest confession in my hand, or I cannot keep you from the rope. (PROCTOR *does not reply.*) Which way do you go, Mister?

(*His breast heaving, his eyes staring,* PROCTOR *tears the paper and crumples it, and he is weeping in fury, but erect.*)

DANFORTH. Marshal!

PARRIS (*hysterically, as though the tearing paper were his life*). Proctor, Proctor!

HALE. Man, you will hang! You cannot!

PROCTOR (*his eyes full of tears*). I can. And there's your first marvel, that I can. You have made your magic now, for now I do think I see some shred of goodness in John Proctor. Not enough to weave a banner with, but white enough to keep it from such dogs. (ELIZABETH, *in a burst of terror, rushes to him and weeps against his hand.*) Give them no tear! Tears pleasure them! Show honor now, show a stony heart and sink them with it! (*He has lifted her, and kisses her now with great passion.*)

REBECCA. Let you fear nothing! Another judgment waits us all!

DANFORTH. Hang them high over the town! Who weeps for these, weeps for corruption! (*He sweeps out past them.* HERRICK *starts to lead* REBECCA, *who almost collapses, but* PROCTOR *catches her, and she glances up at him apologetically.*)

REBECCA. I've had no breakfast.

HERRICK. Come, man.

(HERRICK *escorts them out,* HATHORNE *and* CHEEVER *behind them.* ELIZABETH *stands staring at the empty doorway.*)

PARRIS (*in deadly fear, to* ELIZABETH). Go to him, Goody Proctor! There is yet time!

(*From outside a drumroll strikes the air.* PARRIS *is startled.* ELIZABETH *jerks about toward the window.*)

PARRIS. Go to him! (*He rushes out the door, as though to hold back his fate.*) Proctor! Proctor!

(*Again, a short burst of drums.*)

HALE. Woman, plead with him! (*He starts to rush out the door, and then goes back to her.*) Woman! It is pride, it is vanity. (*She avoids his eyes, and moves to the window. He drops to his knees.*) Be his helper!— What profit him to bleed? Shall the dust praise him? Shall the worms declare his truth? Go to him, take his shame away!

ELIZABETH (*supporting herself against collapse, grips the bars of the window, and with a cry.*) He have his goodness now. God forbid I take it from him!

(*The final drumroll crashes, then heightens violently.* HALE *weeps in frantic prayer, and the new sun is pouring in upon her face, and the drums rattle like bones in the morning air.*)

THE CURTAIN FALLS

––––––

ECHOES DOWN THE CORRIDOR

Not long after the fever died, Parris was voted from office, walked out on the highroad, and was never heard of again.

The legend has it that Abigail turned up later as a prostitute in Boston.

Twenty years after the last execution, the government awarded compensation to the victims still living, and to the families of the dead. However, it is evident that some people still were unwilling to admit their total guilt, and also that the factionalism was still alive, for some beneficiaries were actually not victims at all, but informers.

Elizabeth Proctor married again, four years after Proctor's death.

In solemn meeting, the congregation rescinded the excommunications—this in March 1712. But they did so upon order of the government. The jury, however, wrote a statement praying forgiveness of all who had suffered.

Certain farms which had belonged to the victims were left to ruin, and for more than a century no one would buy them or live on them.

To all intents and purposes, the power of theocracy in Massachusetts was broken.

TEA AND SYMPATHY

Robert Anderson

This is for
PHYLLIS
whose spirit is everywhere
in this play and in my life.

First presented by the Playwrights' Company, in association
with Mary K. Frank, at the Ethel Barrymore Theatre,
New York, on September 30, 1953, with the following cast:

LAURA REYNOLDS	Deborah Kerr	STEVE	Arthur Steuer
LILLY SEARS	Florida Friebus	BILL REYNOLDS	Leif Erickson
TOM LEE	John Kerr	PHIL	Richard Franchot
DAVID HARRIS	Richard Midgley	HERBERT LEE	John McGovern
RALPH	Alan Sues	PAUL	Yale Wexler
AL	Dick York		

In June, 1954, the principal roles were assumed by Joan Fontaine and Anthony Perkins.

ACT ONE. A dormitory in a boys' school in New England. Late afternoon of a day early in June.

ACT TWO. SCENE I: Two days later. SCENE II: Eight-thirty Saturday night.

ACT THREE. The next afternoon.

Copyrighted as an unpublished work, 1953, by Robert Woodruff Anderson.
© Copyright, 1953, by Robert Anderson.

Reprinted by permission of Random House, Inc.

CAUTION: Professionals and amateurs are hereby warned that TEA AND SYMPATHY, being
fully protected under the copyright laws of the United States, the British Empire including
the Dominion of Canada, and all other countries of the Copyright Union, is subject
to royalty. All rights including professional, amateur, motion picture, recitation, lecturing, public
reading, radio and television broadcasting, and the rights of translation into foreign
languages, are strictly reserved. Particular emphasis is laid on the question of readings, permission
for which must be obtained in writing from the author's representative. All inquiries
should be addressed to the author's representative, Audrey Wood, MCA
Management, Ltd., 598 Madison Avenue, New York, N.Y.

ROBERT ANDERSON was thirty-six when *Tea and Sympathy* had its triumphant premiere on Broadway in the early fall of 1953, and the impression he made on his producers, The Playwrights Company, resulted in their making him a member of their distinguished organization. Born in New York in 1917, Mr. Anderson received his secondary schooling at Phillips Exeter and took a bachelor's and a master's degree at Harvard in 1939 and 1940. While at Harvard he met the late Phyllis Anderson, to whose memory this book is affectionately dedicated. She headed a dramatic department at the Erskine School for girls and found it necessary to draw young Harvard men into her productions. Robert Anderson was one of them; he became her husband and she became his inspiration. She had an extraordinary talent for discovering talent and watching over it. She became play editor for the Theatre Guild and, in the last years of her lamentably brief life, was head of the play department of the powerful show-business agency, M.C.A.

Mr. Anderson abandoned a teaching career for a theatrical one. But World War II had broken out and before long he had an intermediate career as a naval officer which terminated only when the war did. But he managed to write his first play, *Come Marching Home,* while in the service, submitted it to a National Theatre Conference play contest for servicemen, and won first prize with it in 1944. The piece was produced by the University of Iowa Theatre Department in 1945. This work along with two other manuscripts also won for the author a Playwriting Fellowship from the National Theatre Conference, an organization made up of leaders of the educational theatre, and then subsidized by the Rockefeller Foundation. *Love Revisited,* a later play, was tried out at the Westport Country Playhouse in the summer of 1950, and *All Summer Long,* later seen on Broadway, was very successfully presented in Washington, D.C., in 1953, by the capital's distinguished Arena Theatre.

Tea and Sympathy, which opened its tryout tour in Hartford, Conn., got a rousing reception in New York and became the first hit of the 1953-1954 season. John Kerr, the son of June Walker, achieved stardom in the role of the misunderstood young student, and the British film star Deborah Kerr was launched upon a successful career on the American stage. Success came to *Tea and Sympathy* a second time when it was staged on April 26, 1957, in London's West End at the Comedy Theatre by the flourishing New Watergate Theatre Club. A "Club" production was needed when the Lord Chamberlain forbade a "public" performance because of the subject matter, and Mr. Anderson joined the ranks of other distinguished American playwrights whose plays proved too strong for the Lord Chamberlain's office.

In view of the argument that developed over the degree to which the author had compounded his play as an artifice, Mr. Anderson's recollection of some of the origins of his play in the September, 1954, issue of *Theatre Arts* can be instructive: He recalled a walk down the Avenue of the Americas with his wife and a friend who declared "that she was living in a theatrical boardinghouse where the landlady had the girls down for *tea and sympathy.*" He remembered a trip in 1947 to Phillips Exeter, and a visit to his first-year dormitory, "where I had been miserable and which I now found quite transformed, with a semi-private living room for the young boys presided over by a charming woman who told me that many tears were shed in that room by the younger boys." And he recalled reading Thoreau's *Walden* and marking a passage in it he considers more pertinent than the clinical question of homosexuality. The Thoreau passage reads: "If a man does not keep pace with his companions, perhaps it is because he hears a different drummer. Let him step to the music which he hears, however measured or far away." It would have been a good epigraph for the published play, even if it should not be construed as a capsule definition of the total meaning any more than the fine statement in the play that persons should give each other something more than conventional "tea and sympathy."

ACT ONE

The scene is a small old Colonial house which is now being used as a dormitory in a boys' school in New England.

On the ground floor at stage right we see the housemaster's study. To stage left is a hall and stairway which leads up to the boys' rooms. At a half-level on stage left is one of the boys' rooms.

The housemaster's study is a warm and friendly room, rather on the dark side, but when the lamps are lighted, there are cheerful pools of light. There is a fireplace in the back wall, bookcases, and upstage right double doors leading to another part of the house. Since there is no common room for the eight boys in this house, there is considerable leniency in letting the boys use the study whenever the door is left ajar.

The boys' bedroom is small, containing a bed, a chair and a bureau. It was meant to be Spartan, but the present occupant has given it a few touches to make it a little more homelike: an Indian print on the bed, India print curtains for the dormer windows. There is a phonograph on the ledge of the window. The door to the room is presumed to lead to the sitting room which the roommates share. There is a door from the sitting room which leads to the stair landing. Thus, to get to the bedroom from the stairs, a person must go through the sitting room.

As the curtain rises, it is late afternoon of a day early in June. No lamps have been lighted yet so the study is in a sort of twilight.

Upstairs in his room, TOM LEE *is sitting on his bed playing the guitar and singing softly and casually, the plaintive song, "The Joys of Love" . . .* TOM *is going on eighteen.*

He is young and a little gangling, but intense. He is wearing faded khaki trousers, a white shirt open at the neck and white tennis sneakers.

Seated in the study listening to the singing are LAURA REYNOLDS *and* LILLY SEARS. LAURA *is a lovely, sensitive woman in her mid to late twenties. Her essence is gentleness. She is compassionate and tender. She is wearing a cashmere sweater and a wool skirt. As she listens to* TOM'S *singing, she is sewing on what is obviously a period costume.*

LILLY *is in her late thirties, and in contrast to the simple effectiveness of* LAURA'S *clothes, she is dressed a little too flashily for her surroundings. . . . It would be in good taste on East 57th Street, but not in a small New England town. . . . A smart suit and hat and a fur piece. As she listens to* TOM *singing, she plays with the martini glass in her hand.*

———

TOM (*singing*).
　　The joys of love
　　Are but a moment long . . .
　　The pains of love
　　Endure forever . . .
(*When he has finished, he strums on over the same melody very casually, and hums to it intermittently.*)

LILLY (*while* TOM *is singing*). Tom Lee?

LAURA. Yes.

LILLY. Doesn't he have an afternoon class?

LAURA. No. He's the only one in the house that doesn't.

LILLY (*when* TOM *has finished the song*). Do you know what he's thinking of?

LAURA (*bites off a thread and looks up*). What do you mean?

LILLY. What all the boys in this school are thinking about. Not only now in the spring, but all the time . . . Sex! (*She wags her head a little wisely, and smiles.*)

LAURA. Lilly, you just like to shock people.

LILLY. Four hundred boys from the ages of thirteen to nineteen. That's the age, Laura. (*Restless, getting up*) Doesn't it give you the willies sometimes, having all these boys around?

LAURA. Of course not. I never think of it that way.

LILLY. Harry tells me they put saltpeter in their food to quiet them down. But the way they look at you, I can't believe it.

LAURA. At me?

LILLY. At any woman worth looking at. When I first came here ten years ago, I didn't think I could stand it. Now I love it. I love watching them look and suffer.

LAURA. Lilly.

LILLY. This is your first spring here, Laura. You wait.

LAURA. They're just boys.

LILLY. The authorities say the ages from thirteen to nineteen . . .

LAURA. Lilly, honestly!

LILLY. You sound as though you were in

the grave. How old are you?

LAURA (*smiling*). Over twenty-one.

LILLY. They come here ignorant as all get out about women and then spend the next four years exchanging misinformation. They're so cute, and so damned intense. (*She shudders again.*)

LAURA. Most of them seem very casual to me.

LILLY. That's just an air they put on. This is the age Romeo should be played. You'd believe him! So intense! These kids would die for love, or almost anything else. Harry says all their themes end in death.

LAURA. That's boys.

LILLY. Failure; death! Dishonor; death! Lose their girls; death! It's gruesome.

LAURA. But rather touching too, don't you think?

LILLY. You won't tell your husband the way I was talking?

LAURA. Of course not.

LILLY. Though I don't know why I should care. All the boys talk about me. They have me in and out of bed with every single master in the school—and some married ones, too.

LAURA (*kidding her*). Maybe I'd better listen to them.

LILLY. Oh, never with your husband, of course.

LAURA. Thanks.

LILLY. Even before he met you, Bill never gave me a second glance. He was all the time organizing teams, planning Mountain Club outings.

LAURA. Bill's good at that sort of thing; he likes it.

LILLY. And you? (LAURA *looks up at* LILLY *and smiles.*) Not a very co-operative witness, are you? I know, mind my own business. But watch out he doesn't drag his usual quota of boys to the lodge in Maine this summer.

LAURA. I've got my own plans for him. (*She picks up some vacation folders.*)

LILLY. Oh really? What?

LAURA. "Come to Canada" . . . I want to get him off on a trip alone.

LILLY. I don't blame you.

LAURA (*reflecting*). Of course I'd really like to go back to Italy. We had a good time there last summer. It was wonderful then. You should have seen Bill.

LILLY. Look, honey, you married Bill last year on his sabbatical leave, and abroad to boot. Teachers on sabbatical leave abroad are like men in uniform during the war. They never look so good again.

LAURA. Bill looks all right to me.

LILLY. Did Bill ever tell you about the party we gave him before his sabbatical?

LAURA. Yes. I have a souvenir from it. (*She is wearing a rather large Woolworth's diamond ring on a gold chain around her neck . . . She now pulls it out from her sweater.*)

LILLY. I never thought he'd use that Five-and-Dime engagement ring we gave him that night. Even though we gave him an awful ribbing, we all expected him to come back a bachelor.

LAURA. You make it sound as though you kidded him into marrying.

LILLY. Oh, no, honey, it wasn't that.

LAURA (*with meaning*). No, it wasn't. (LAURA *laughs at* LILLY.)

LILLY. Well, I've got to go. You know, Bill could have married any number of the right kind of girls around here. But I knew it would take more than the right kind of girl to get Bill to marry. It would take something special. And you're something special.

LAURA. How should I take that?

LILLY. As a compliment. Thanks for the drink. Don't tell Harry I had one when you see him at dinner.

LAURA. We won't be over to the hall. I've laid in a sort of feast for tonight.

LILLY. Celebrating something?

LAURA. No, just an impulse.

LILLY. Well, don't tell Harry anyway.

LAURA. You'd better stop talking the way you've been talking, or I won't have to tell him.

LILLY. Now, look, honey, don't you start going puritan on me. You're the only one in this school I can shoot my mouth off to, so don't change, baby. Don't change.

LAURA. I won't.

LILLY. Some day I'm going to wheedle out of you all the juicy stories you must have from when you were in the theater.

LAURA. Lilly, you would make the most hardened chorus girl blush.

LILLY (*pleased*). Really?

LAURA. Really.

LILLY. That's the sweetest thing you've said to me in days. Good-by. (*She goes out the door, and a moment later we hear the outside door close.*)

LAURA (*sits for a moment, listening to* TOM'S *rather plaintive whistling. She rises and looks at the Canada vacation literature on the desk, and then, looking at her watch, goes to the door, opens it, and calls up the stairway*). Tom . . . Oh, Tom.

(*The moment* TOM *hears his name, he jumps from the bed, and goes through the sitting room, and appears on the stairs.*)

TOM. Yes?

LAURA (*she is very friendly with him, comradely*). If it won't spoil your supper, come on down for a cup of tea.

(TOM *goes back into his room and brushes his hair, then he comes on down the stairs, and enters the study. He enters this room as though it were something rare and special. This is where* LAURA *lives.*)

LAURA (*has gone out to the other part of the house. Comes to doorway for a moment pouring cream from bottle to pitcher*). I've just about finished your costume for the play, and we can have a fitting.

TOM. Sure. That'd be great. Do you want the door open or shut?

LAURA (*goes off again*). It doesn't make any difference. (TOM *shuts the door. He is deeply in love with this woman, though he knows nothing can come of it. It is a sort of delayed puppy love. It is very touching and very intense. They are easy with each other, casual, though he is always trying in thinly veiled ways to tell her he loves her.* LAURA *enters with tea tray and sees him closing the door. She puts tray on table.*) Perhaps you'd better leave it ajar, so that if some of the other boys get out of class early, they can come in too.

TOM (*is disappointed*). Oh, sure.

LAURA (*goes off for the plate of cookies, but pauses long enough to watch* TOM *open the door the merest crack. She is amused. In a moment, she re-enters with a plate of cookies.*) Help yourself.

TOM. Thanks. (*He takes a cookie, and then sits on the floor, near her chair.*)

LAURA. Are the boys warm enough in the rooms? They shut down the heat so early this spring, I guess they didn't expect this little chill.

TOM. We're fine. But this is nice. (*He indicates low fire in fireplace.*)

LAURA (*goes back to her sewing*). I heard you singing.

TOM. I'm sorry if it bothered you.

LAURA. It was very nice.

TOM. If it ever bothers you, just bang on the radiator.

LAURA. What was the name of the song? It's lovely.

TOM. It's an old French song . . . "The Joys of Love" . . . (*He speaks the lyric.*)
    The joys of love
    Are but a moment long,
    The pain of love
    Endures forever.

LAURA. And is that true? (TOM *shrugs his shoulders.*) You sang as though you knew all about the pains of love.

TOM. And you don't think I do?

LAURA. Well . . .

TOM. You're right.

LAURA. Only the joys.

TOM. Neither, really.

(*Teapot whistles off stage.*)

LAURA. Then you're a fake. Listening to you, one would think you knew everything there was to know. (*Rises and goes to next room for tea.*) Anyway, I don't believe it. A boy like you.

TOM. It's true.

LAURA (*off stage*). Aren't you bringing someone to the dance after the play Saturday?

TOM. Yes.

LAURA. Well, there.

TOM. You.

LAURA (*reappears in doorway with teapot*). Me?

TOM. Yes, you're going to be a hostess, aren't you?

LAURA. Yes, of course, but . . .

TOM. As a member of the committee, I'm taking you. All the committee drew lots . . .

LAURA. And you lost.

TOM. I won.

LAURA (*a little embarrassed by this*). Oh. My husband could have taken me. (*She sits down again in her chair.*)

TOM. He's not going to be in town. Don't you remember, Mountain Climbing Club has its final outing this week end.

LAURA. Oh, yes, of course. I'd forgotten.

TOM. He's out a lot on that kind of thing, isn't he? (LAURA *ignores his probing.*) I hope you're not sorry that I'm to be your escort.

LAURA. Why, I'll be honored.

TOM. I'm supposed to find out tactfully and without your knowing it what color dress you'll be wearing.

LAURA. Why?

TOM. The committee will send you a corsage.

LAURA. Oh, how nice. Well, I don't have much to choose from, I guess my yellow.

TOM. The boy who's in charge of getting the flowers thinks a corsage should be something like a funeral decoration. So I'm taking personal charge of getting yours.

LAURA. Thank you.

TOM. You must have gotten lots of flowers when you were acting in the theater.

LAURA. Oh, now and then. Nothing spectacular.

TOM. I can't understand how a person would give up the theater to come and live in a school . . . I'm sorry. I mean, I'm glad you did, but, well . . .

LAURA. If you knew the statistics on unemployed actors, you might understand. Anyway, I was never any great shakes at it.

TOM. I can't believe that.

LAURA. Then take my word for it.

TOM (*after a moment, looking into the fire, pretending to be casual, but actually touching on his love for* LAURA). Did you ever do any of Shaw's plays?

LAURA. Yes.

TOM. We got an assignment to read any Shaw play we wanted. I picked *Candida*.

LAURA. Because it was the shortest?

TOM (*laughs*). No . . . because it sounded like the one I'd like the best, one I could understand. Did you ever play Candida?

LAURA. In stock—a very small stock company, way up in Northern Vermont.

TOM. Do you think she did right to send Marchbanks away?

LAURA. Well, Shaw made it seem right. Don't you think?

TOM (*really talking about himself*). That Marchbanks sure sounded off a lot. I could never sound off like that, even if I loved a woman the way he did. She could have made him seem awfully small if she'd wanted to.

LAURA. Well, I guess she wasn't that kind of woman. Now stand up. Let's see if this fits. (*She rises with dress in her hand.*)

TOM (*gets up*). My Dad's going to hit the roof when he hears I'm playing another girl.

LAURA. I think you're a good sport not

to mind. Besides, it's a good part. Lady Teazle in *The School For Scandal*.

TOM (*puts on top of dress*). It all started when I did Lady Macbeth last year. You weren't here yet for that. Lucky you.

LAURA. I hear it was very good.

TOM. You should have read a letter I got from my father. They printed a picture of me in the *Alumni Bulletin,* in costume. He was plenty peeved about it.

LAURA. He shouldn't have been.

TOM. He wrote me saying he might be up here today on Alumni Fund business. If he comes over here, and you see him, don't tell him about this.

LAURA. I won't . . . What about your mother? Did she come up for the play? (*She helps him button the dress.*)

TOM. I don't see my mother. Didn't you know? (*He starts to roll up pants legs.*)

LAURA. Why no. I didn't.

TOM. She and my father are divorced.

LAURA. I'm sorry.

TOM. You need'nt be. They aren't. I was supposed to hold them together. That was how I happened to come into the world. I didn't work. That's a terrible thing, you know, to make a flop of the first job you've got in life.

LAURA. Don't you ever see her?

TOM. Not since I was five. I was with her till five, and then my father took me away. All I remember about my mother is that she was always telling me to go outside and bounce a ball.

LAURA (*handing him skirt of the dress*). You must have done something before Lady Macbeth. When did you play that character named Grace?

TOM (*stiffens*). I never played anyone called Grace.

LAURA. But I hear the boys sometimes calling you Grace. I thought . . . (*She notices that he's uncomfortable.*) I'm sorry. Have I said something terrible?

TOM. No.

LAURA. But I have. I'm sorry.

TOM. It's all right. But it's a long story. Last year over at the movies, they did a revival of Grace Moore in *One Night of Love*. I'd seen the revival before the picture came. And I guess I oversold it, or something. But she was wonderful! . . . Anyway, some of the guys started calling me Grace. It was my own fault, I guess.

LAURA. Nicknames can be terrible. I remember at one time I was called "Beany."

I can't remember why, now, but I remember it made me mad. (*She adjusts the dress a little.*) Hold still a moment. We'll have to let this out around here. (*She indicates the bosom.*) What size do you want to be?

TOM (*he is embarrassed, but rather nicely, not obviously and farcically. In his embarrassment he looks at* LAURA's *bosom, then quickly away.*) I don't know. Whatever you think.

LAURA (*she indicates he is to stand on a small wooden footstool*). I should think you would have invited some girl up to see you act, and then take her to the dance.

TOM (*gets on stool*). There's nobody I could ask.

LAURA (*working on hem of dress*). What do you mean?

TOM. I don't know any girls, really.

LAURA. Oh, certainly back home . . .

TOM. Last ten years I haven't been home, I mean really home. Summers my father packs me off to camps, and the rest of the time I've been at boarding schools.

LAURA. What about Christmas vacation, and Easter?

TOM. My father gets a raft of tickets to plays and concerts, and sends me and my aunt.

LAURA. I see.

TOM. So I mean it when I say I don't know any girls.

LAURA. Your roommate, Al, knows a lot of girls. Why not ask him to fix you up with a blind date?

TOM. I don't know . . . I can't even dance. I'm telling you this so you won't expect anything of me Saturday night.

LAURA. We'll sit out and talk.

TOM. Okay.

LAURA. Or I could teach you how to dance. It's quite simple.

TOM (*flustered*). You?

LAURA. Why not?

TOM. I mean, isn't a person supposed to go to some sort of dancing class or something? (*He gets down from footstool.*)

LAURA. Not necessarily. Look, I'll show you how simple it is. (*She assumes the dancing position.*) Hold your left hand out this way, and put your right hand around my—(*She stops, as she sees him looking at her.*) Oh, now you're kidding me. A boy your age and you don't know how to dance.

TOM. I'm not kidding you.

LAURA. Well, then, come on. I had to teach my husband. Put your arm around me. (*She raises her arms.*)

TOM (*looks at her a moment, afraid to touch this woman he loves. Then to pass it off*). We better put it off. We'd look kind of silly, both of us in skirts.

LAURA. All right. Take it off, then. No, wait a minute. Just let me stand off and take a look . . . (*She walks around him.*) You're going to make a very lovely girl.

TOM. Thank you, ma'am . . .

(*He kids a curtsy, like a girl, and starts out of his costume.* MR. HARRIS, *a good-looking young master, comes in the hallway and starts up to Tom's room. On the landing, he knocks on Tom's door.*)

LAURA. I wonder who that is?

TOM. All the other fellows have late afternoon classes.

LAURA (*opens the door wider, and looks up the stairs*). Yes? Oh, David.

HARRIS (*turns and looks down the stairs*). Oh, hello, Laura.

LAURA. I just was wondering who was coming in.

(TOM *proceeds to get out of the costume.*)

HARRIS. I want to see Tom Lee.

LAURA. He's down here. I'm making his costume for the play.

HARRIS. I wonder if I could see him for a moment?

LAURA. Why yes, of course. Tom, Mr. Harris would like to see you. Do you want to use our study, David? I can go into the living room.

HARRIS. No, thanks. I'll wait for him in his room. Will you ask him to come up? (*He opens the door and goes in.*)

LAURA (*is puzzled at his intensity, the urgency in his voice. Comes back in the study*). Tom, Mr. Harris would like to see you in your room. He's gone along.

TOM. That's funny.

LAURA. Wait a minute . . . take this up with you, try it on in front of your mirror . . . see if you can move in it . . . (*She hands him skirt of costume.*) When Mr. Harris is through, bring the costume back.

TOM (*anxious over what* HARRIS *wants to see him about*). Yeah, sure. (*He starts out, then stops and picks up a cookie. He looks at her lovingly.*) Thanks for tea.

LAURA. You're welcome.

(TOM *goes to the door as* LAURA *turns to the desk. He stands in the door a moment and looks at her back, then he turns and shuts the door and heads upstairs.* HARRIS *has come into* TOM's *bedroom, and is standing there nervously clenching and unclenching his hands.*)

TOM (*off stage, presumably in the study he shares with his roommate*). Mr. Harris?

(LAURA *wanders off into the other part of the house after looking for a moment at the Canada vacation material on the desk.*)

HARRIS. I'm in here.

TOM (*comes in a little hesitantly*). Oh. Hello, sir.

(HARRIS *closes the door to the bedroom.* TOM *regards this action with some nervousness.*)

HARRIS. Well?

TOM (*has dumped some clothes from a chair to his bed. Offers chair to* HARRIS). Sir?

HARRIS. What did you tell the Dean?

TOM. What do you mean, Mr. Harris?

HARRIS. What did you tell the Dean?

TOM. When? What are you talking about, sir?

HARRIS. Didn't the Dean call you in?

TOM. No. Why should he?

HARRIS. He didn't call you in and ask you about last Saturday afternoon?

TOM. Why should he? I didn't do anything wrong.

HARRIS. About being with me?

TOM. I'm allowed to leave town for the day in the company of a master.

HARRIS. I don't believe you. You must have said something.

TOM. About what?

HARRIS. About you and me going down to the dunes and swimming.

TOM. Why should I tell him about that?

HARRIS (*threatening*). Why didn't you keep your mouth shut?

TOM. About what? What, for God's sake?

HARRIS. I never touched you, did I?

TOM. What do you mean, touch me?

HARRIS. Did you say to the Dean I touched you?

TOM (*turning away from* HARRIS). I don't know what you're talking about.

HARRIS. Here's what I'm talking about. The Dean's had me on the carpet all afternoon. I probably won't be reappointed next year . . . and all because I took you swimming down off the dunes on Saturday.

TOM. Why should he have you on the

carpet for that?

HARRIS. You can't imagine, I suppose.

TOM. What did you do wrong?

HARRIS. Nothing! Nothing, unless you made it seem like something wrong, did you?

TOM. I told you I didn't see the Dean.

HARRIS. You will. He'll call for you. Bunch of gossiping old busy-bodies! Well . . . (*He starts for the door, stops, turns around and softens. He comes back to the puzzled* TOM.) I'm sorry . . . It probably wasn't your fault. It was my fault. I should have been more . . . discreet . . . Good-by. Good luck with your music.

(TOM *hasn't understood. He doesn't know what to say. He makes a helpless gesture with his hands.* HARRIS *goes into the other room on his way out. Three boys, about seventeen, come in from the downstairs hall door and start up the stairs. They're carrying books. All are wearing sport jackets, khaki or flannel trousers, white or saddle rubber-soled shoes.*)

AL. I don't believe a word of it.

RALPH (*he is large and a loud-mouthed bully*). I'm telling you the guys saw them down at the dunes.

AL (*he is* TOM's *roommate, an athlete*). So what?

RALPH. They were bare-assed.

AL. Shut up, will you? You want Mrs. Reynolds to hear you?

RALPH. Okay. You watch and see. Harris'll get bounced, and I'm gonna lock my room at night as long as Tom is living in this house.

AL. Oh, dry up!

RALPH. Jeeze, you're his roommate and you're not worried.

HARRIS (*comes out the door and starts down the stairs*). Hello. (*He goes down stairs and out.*)

AL. Sir.

RALPH. Do you believe me now? You aren't safe. Believe me.

STEVE (*he is small,* RALPH's *appreciative audience. He comes in the front door*). Hey, Al, can I come and watch Mrs. Morrison nurse her kid?

RALPH. You're the loudest-mouthed bastard I ever heard. You want to give it away.

STEVE. It's time. How about it, Al?

AL (*grudgingly*). Come on.

(TOM *hears them coming, and moves to*

bolt his door, but STEVE *and* RALPH *break in before he gets to the door. He watches them from the doorway.* STEVE *rushes to bed and throws himself across it, looking out window next to bed.* RALPH *settles down next to him.*)

AL (*to* TOM *as he comes in*). Hi. These horny bastards.

STEVE. Al, bring the glasses.

(AL *goes into sitting room.*)

RALPH. Some day she's going to wean that little bastard and spoil all our fun.

STEVE. Imagine sitting in a window . . .

TOM (*has been watching this with growing annoyance*). Will you guys get out of here?

RALPH (*notices* TOM *for the first time*). What's the matter with you, Grace?

TOM. This is my damned room.

RALPH. Gracie's getting private all of a sudden.

TOM. I don't want a lot of Peeping Toms lying on my bed watching a . . . a . . .

STEVE. You want it all for yourself, don't you?

RALPH. Or aren't you interested in women?

AL (*comes back in with field glasses*). Shut up! (*Looks out window, then realizes* TOM *is watching him. Embarrassed.*) These horny bastards.

STEVE (*looking*). Jeeze!

RALPH (*a bully, riding down on* TOM). I thought you were going to play ball with us Saturday.

TOM. I didn't feel like it.

RALPH. What *did* you feel like doing, huh?

AL. Will you shut up?

STEVE. Hey, lookit. (*Grabs glasses from* AL. AL *leaves room.*)

TOM (*climbing over* STEVE *and* RALPH *and trying to pull the shade*). I told you to get out. I told you last time . . .

RALPH (*grabbing hold of* TOM, *and holding him down*). Be still, boy, or she'll see, and you'll spoil everything.

TOM. Horny bastard. Get out of here.

RALPH. Who are you calling a horny bastard? (*He grabs hold of* TOM *more forcefully, and slaps him a couple of times across the face, not trying to hurt him, but just to humiliate him.* STEVE *gets in a few pokes and in a moment, it's not in fun, but verging on the serious.*) You don't mean that now, boy, do you . . . Do you, Grace! (*He slaps him again.*)

AL (*hearing the scuffle, comes in and hauls* RALPH *and* STEVE *off* TOM). Come on, come on, break it up. Clear out. (*He has them both standing up now,* TOM *still on the bed.*)

RALPH. I just don't like that son of a bitch calling me a horny bastard. Maybe if it was Dr. Morrison instead of Mrs. Morrison, he'd be more interested. Hey, wouldn't you, Grace? (*He tries to stick his face in front of* TOM, *but* AL *holds him back.*)

AL. Come on, lay off the guy, will you? Go on. Get ready for supper.

(*He herds them out during this. When they have left the room,* TOM *gets up and goes to bureau and gets a handkerchief. He has a bloody nose. He lies down on the bed, his head tilted back to stop the blood.*)

AL (*in doorway*). You all right?

TOM. Yeah.

(RALPH *and* STEVE *go up the stairway singing in raucous voices, "One Night of Love." The downstairs outside door opens, and* BILL REYNOLDS *enters the hall with a student,* PHIL. BILL *is* LAURA's *husband. He is large and strong with a tendency to be gruff. He's wearing gray flannel trousers, a tweed jacket, a blue button-down shirt. He is around forty.*)

BILL. Okay, boy, we'll look forward to— (*He notices* RALPH *still singing. He goes to bend in the stairs and calls.*) Hey, Ralph . . . Ralph!

RALPH (*stops singing up out of sight*). You calling me, Mr. Reynolds, sir?

BILL. Yeah. Keep it down to a shout, will you?

RALPH. Oh, *yes, sir.* Sorry, I didn't know I was disturbing you, Mr. Reynolds.

BILL (*comes back and talks with* PHIL *at the bend in the stairway*). Phil, you come on up to the lodge around . . . Let's see . . . We'll open the lodge around July first, so plan to come up say, July third, and stay for two weeks. Okay?

PHIL. That'll be swell, sir.

BILL. Frank Hoctor's coming then. You get along with Frank, don't you? He's a regular guy.

PHIL. Oh, sure.

BILL. The float's all gone to pieces. We can make that your project to fix it up. Okay?

PHIL. Thanks a lot, Mr. Reynolds. (*He goes on up the stairs.*)

BILL. See you. (*He comes in and crosses to phone and starts to call.*)

LAURA (*off stage*). Tom?

(BILL *looks around in the direction of the voice, but says nothing.*)

LAURA (*comes on*). Oh, Bill. Tom was down trying on his costume. I thought . . . You're early.

BILL. Yes. I want to catch the Dean be-before he leaves his office. (LAURA *goes up to him to be kissed, but he's too intent on the phone, and she compromises by kissing his cheek.*) Hello, this is Mr. Reynolds. Is the Dean still in his office?

LAURA. What's the matter, Bill?

BILL. Nothing very pretty. Oh? How long ago? All right. Thanks. I'll give him a couple of minutes, then I'll call his home. (*Hangs up.*) Well, they finally caught up with Harris. (*He goes into the next room to take off his jacket.*)

LAURA. What do you mean, "caught up" with him?

BILL (*off stage*). You're going to hear it anyhow . . . so . . . last Saturday they caught him down in the dunes, naked.

LAURA (*crosses to close door to hall*). What's wrong with that?

BILL (*enters and crosses to fireplace and starts to go through letters propped there. He has taken off his jacket*). He wasn't alone.

LAURA. Oh.

BILL. He was lying there naked in the dunes, and one of the students was lying there naked too. Just to talk about it is disgusting.

LAURA. I see.

BILL. I guess you'll admit that's something.

LAURA. I can't see that it's necessarily conclusive.

BILL. With a man like Harris, it's conclusive enough. (*Then casually*) The student with him was—

LAURA (*interrupting*). I'm not sure I care to know.

BILL. I'm afraid you're going to have to know sooner or later, Laura. It was Tom Lee.

(TOM *rises from bed, grabs a towel and goes out up the stairs.* LAURA *just looks at* BILL *and frowns.*)

BILL. Some of the boys down on the Varsity Club outing came on them . . . or at least saw them . . . And Fin Hadley saw them too, and he apparently used his

brains for once and spoke to the Dean.

LAURA. And?

BILL. He's had Harris on the carpet this afternoon. I guess he'll be fired. I certainly hope so. Maybe Tom too, I don't know.

LAURA. They put two and two together?

BILL. Yes, Laura.

LAURA. I suppose this is all over school by now.

BILL. I'm afraid so.

LAURA. And most of the boys know.

BILL. Yes.

LAURA. So what's going to happen to Tom?

BILL (*takes pipe from mantel piece and cleans it*). I know you won't like this, Laura, but I think he should be kicked out. I think you've got to let people know the school doesn't stand for even a hint of this sort of thing. He should be booted.

LAURA. For what?

BILL. Look, a boy's caught coming out of Ellie Martin's rooms across the river. That's enough evidence. Nobody asks particulars. They don't go to Ellie's room to play Canasta. It's the same here.

LAURA (*hardly daring to suggest it*). But, Bill . . . you don't think . . . I mean, you don't think Tom is . . . (*She stops.* BILL *looks at her a moment, his answer is in his silence.*) Oh, Bill!

BILL. And I'm ashamed and sorry as hell for his father. Herb Lee was always damned good to me . . . came down from college when I was playing football here . . . helped me get into college . . . looked after me when I was in college and he was in law school . . . And I know he put the boy in my house hoping I could do something with him. (*He dials number.*)

LAURA. And you feel you've failed.

BILL. Yes. (*He pauses.*) With your help, I might say. (*Busy signal. He hangs up.*)

LAURA. How?

BILL. Because, Laura, the boy would rather sit around here and talk with you and listen to music and strum his guitar.

LAURA. Bill, I'm not to blame for everything. Everything's not my fault.

BILL (*disregarding this*). What a lousy thing for Herb. (*He looks at a small picture of a team on his desk.*) That's Herb. He was Graduate Manager of the team when I was a sophomore in college. He was always the manager of the teams, and he really wanted his son to be there in the center of the picture.

LAURA. Why are you calling the Dean?

BILL. I'm going to find out what's being done.

LAURA. I've never seen you like this before.

BILL. This is something that touches me very closely. The name of the school, it's reputation, the reputation of all of us here. I went here and my father before me, and one day I hope our children will come here, when we have them. And, of course, one day I hope to be headmaster.

LAURA. Let's assume that you're right about Harris. It's a terrible thing to say on the evidence you've got, but let's assume you're right. Does it necessarily follow that Tom—

BILL. Tom was his friend. Everyone knew that.

LAURA. Harris encouraged him in his music.

BILL. Come on, Laura.

LAURA. What if Tom's roommate, Al, or some other great big athlete had been out with Harris?

BILL. He wouldn't have been.

LAURA. I'm saying what if he had been? Would you have jumped to the same conclusion?

BILL. It would have been different. Tom's always been an off-horse. And now it's quite obvious why. If he's kicked out, maybe it'll bring him to his senses. But he won't change if nothing's done about it. (LAURA *turns away.* BILL *starts to look over his mail again.*) Anyway, why are you so concerned over what happens to Tom Lee?

LAURA. I've come to know him. You even imply that I am somewhat responsible for his present reputation.

BILL. All right. I shouldn't have said that. But you watch, now that it's out in the open. Look at the way he walks, the way he sometimes stands.

LAURA. Oh, Bill!

BILL. All right, so a woman doesn't notice these things. But a man knows a queer when he sees one. (*He has opened a letter. Reads.*) The bookstore now has the book you wanted . . . *The Rose and The Thorn.* What's that?

LAURA. A book of poems. Do you know, Bill, I'll bet he doesn't even know the meaning of the word . . . queer.

BILL. What do you think he is?

LAURA. I think he's a nice sensitive kid who doesn't know the meaning of the word.

BILL. He's eighteen, or almost. I don't know.

LAURA. How much did you know at eighteen?

BILL. A lot. (*At the desk he now notices the Canada literature.*) What are these?

LAURA. What?

BILL. These.

LAURA. Oh, nothing.

BILL (*he throws them in wastebasket, then notices her look*). Well, they're obviously something. (*He takes them out of wastebasket.*)

LAURA (*the joy of it gone for her*). I was thinking we might take a motor trip up there this summer.

BILL (*dialing phone again*). I wish you'd said something about it earlier. I've already invited some of the scholarship boys up to the lodge. I can't disappoint them.

LAURA. Of course not.

BILL. If you'd said something earlier.

LAURA. It's my fault.

BILL. It's nobody's fault, it's just—Hello, Fitz, Bill Reynolds—I was wondering if you're going to be in tonight after supper . . . Oh . . . oh, I see . . . Supper? Well, sure I could talk about it at supper. . . . Well, no, I think I'd better drop over alone. . . . All right. I'll see you at the house then . . . Good-by.

(LAURA *looks at him, trying to understand him.* BILL *comes to her to speak softly to her. Seeing him come, she holds out her arms to be embraced, but he just takes her chin in his hand.*)

BILL. Look, Laura, when I brought you here a year ago, I told you it was a tough place for a woman with a heart like yours. I told you you'd run across boys, big and little boys, full of problems, problems which for the moment seem gigantic and heartbreaking. And you promised me then you wouldn't get all taken up with them. Remember?

LAURA. Yes.

BILL. When I was a kid in school here, I had my problems too. There's a place up by the golf course where I used to go off alone Sunday afternoons and cry my eyes out. I used to lie on my bed just the way Tom does, listening to phonograph records hour after hour. (LAURA, *touched by this, kneels at his side.*) But I got over it, Laura. I learned how to take it. (LAURA

looks at him. This touches her.) When the
headmaster's wife gave you this teapot, she
told you what she tells all new masters'
wives. You have to be an interested bystander.

LAURA. I know.

BILL. Just as she said, all you're supposed to do is every once in a while give
the boys a little tea and sympathy. Do you
remember?

LAURA. Yes, I remember. It's just that . . .

BILL. What?

LAURA. This age—seventeen, eighteen—
it's so . . .

BILL. I know.

LAURA. John was this age when I married him.

BILL. Look, Laura . . .

LAURA. I know. You don't like me to
talk about John, but . . .

BILL. It's not that. It's . . .

LAURA. He was just this age, eighteen or
so, when i married him. We both were.
And I know now how this age can suffer.
It's a heartbreaking time . . . no longer a
boy . . . not yet a man . . . Bill? Bill?

BILL (*looks at her awkwardly a moment,
then starts to move off*). I'd better clean up
if I'm going to get to the Dean's for supper. You don't mind, do you?

LAURA (*very quietly*). I got things in for
dinner here. But they'll keep.

BILL (*awkwardly*). I'm sorry, Laura.
But you understand, don't you? About
this business? (LAURA *shakes her head,
"No." BILL stands over her, a little put out
that she has not understood his reasoning.
He starts to say something several times,
then stops. Finally he notices the Five-and-
Dime engagement ring around her neck.
He touches it.*) You're not going to wear
this thing to the dining hall, are you?

LAURA. Why not?

BILL. It was just a gag. It means something to you, but to them . . .

LAURA (*bearing in, but gently*). Does it
mean anything to you, Bill?

BILL. Well, it did, but . . . (*He stops
with a gesture, unwilling to go into it all.*)

LAURA. I think you're ashamed of the
night you gave it to me. That you ever let
me see you needed help. That night in
Italy, in some vague way you cried out . . .

BILL. What is the matter with you today? *Me* crying out for help. (*He heads
for the other room. A knock on the study
door is heard.*)

BILL. It's probably Tom.

(LAURA *goes to door.*)

HERB (*This is* HERBERT LEE, TOM's *father.
He is a middle-sized man, fancying himself a man of the world and an extrovert.
He is dressed as a conservative Boston
businessman, but with still a touch of the
collegiate in his attire—button-down shirt,
etc.*). Mrs. Reynolds?

LAURA. Yes?

BILL (*stopped by the voice, turns*).
Herb! Come in.

HERB (*coming in*). Hiya, Bill. How are
you, fella?

BILL (*taking his hand*). I'm fine, Herb.

HERB (*poking his finger into* BILL's
chest). Great to see you. (*Looks around
to* LAURA.) Oh, uh . . .

BILL. I don't think you've met Laura,
Herb. This is Laura. Laura this is Herb
Lee, Tom's father.

HERB (*hearty and friendly, meant to put
people at their ease*). Hello, Laura.

LAURA. I've heard so much about you.

HERB (*after looking at her for a moment*). I like her, Bill. I like her very
much. (LAURA *blushes and is a little taken
aback by this. To* LAURA) What I'd like
to know is how did you manage to do it?
(*Cuffing* BILL) I'll bet you make her life
miserable . . . You look good, Bill.

BILL. You don't look so bad yourself.
(*He takes in a notch in his belt.*)

HERB. No, *you're* in shape. I never had
anything to keep in shape, but you . . .
You should have seen this boy, Laura.

LAURA. I've seen pictures.

HERB. Only exercise I get these days is
bending the elbow.

LAURA. May I get you something? A
drink?

HERB. No, thanks. I haven't got much
time.

BILL. You drive out from Boston, Herb?

HERB. No, train. You know, Bill, I think
that's the same old train you and I used
to ride in when we came here.

BILL. Probably is.

HERB. If I don't catch the six-fifty-four,
I'll have to stay all night, and I'd rather
not.

BILL. We'd be glad to put you up.

HERB. No. You're putting me up in a
couple of weeks at the reunion. That's
imposing enough. (*There is an awkward
pause. Both men sit down.*) I . . . uh
. . . was over at the Dean's this afternoon.

BILL. Oh, he called you?

HERB. Why, no. I was up discussing Alumni Fund matters with him . . . and . . . Do you know about it?

BILL. You mean about Tom?

HERB. Yes. (*Looks at* LAURA.)

BILL. Laura knows too. (*He reaches for her to come to him, and he puts his arm around her waist.*)

HERB. Well, after we discussed the Fund, he told me about that. Thought I ought to hear about it from him. Pretty casual about it, I thought.

BILL. Well, that's Fitz.

HERB. What I want to know is, what was a guy like Harris doing at the school?

BILL. I tried to tell them.

HERB. Was there anyone around like that in our day, Bill?

BILL. No. You're right.

HERB. I tried to find the guy. I wanted to punch his face for him. But he's cleared out. Is Tom around?

LAURA. He's in his room.

HERB. How'd he get mixed up with a guy like that?

BILL. I don't know, Herb . . .

HERB. I know. I shouldn't ask you. I know. Of course I don't believe Tom was really involved with this fellow. If I believed that, I'd . . . well, I don't know what I'd do. You don't believe it, do you, Bill?

BILL. Why . . . (*Looks at* LAURA.)

HERB (*cutting in*). Of course you don't. But what's the matter? What's happened, Bill? Why isn't my boy a regular fellow? He's had every chance to be since he was knee-high to a grasshopper—boys' camps every summer, boarding schools. What do you think, Laura?

LAURA. I'm afraid I'm not the one to ask, Mr. Lee. (*She breaks away from* BILL.)

HERB. He's always been with men and boys. Why doesn't some of it rub off?

LAURA. You see, I feel he's a "regular fellow" . . . whatever that is.

HERB. You do?

LAURA. If it's sports that matter, he's an excellent tennis player.

HERB. But Laura, he doesn't even play tennis like a regular fellow. No hard drives and cannon-ball serves. He's a cut artist. He can put more damn twists on that ball.

LAURA. He wins. He's the school champion. And isn't he the champion of your club back home?

(TOM *comes down the stairs and enters his bedroom with the costume skirt and towel.*)

HERB. I'm glad you mentioned that . . . because that's just what I mean. Do you know, Laura, his winning that championship brought me one of my greatest humiliations? I hadn't been able to watch the match. I was supposed to be in from a round of golf in time, but we got held up on every hole . . . And when I got back to the locker room, I heard a couple of men talking about Tom's match in the next locker section. And what they said, cut me to the quick, Laura. One of them said, "It's a damn shame Tom Lee won the match. He's a good player, all right, but John Batty is such a regular guy." John Batty was his opponent. Now what pleasure was there for me in that?

BILL. I know what you mean.

HERB. I *want* to be proud of him. My God, that's why I had him in the first place. That's why I took him from his mother when we split up, but . . . Look, this is a terrible thing to say, but you know the scholarships the University Club sponsors for needy kids . . .

BILL. Sure.

HERB. Well, I contribute pretty heavily to it, and I happened to latch on to one of the kids we help—an orphan. I sort of talk to him like a father, go up to see him at his school once in a while, and that kid listens to me . . . and you know what, he's shaping up better than my own son.

(*There is an awkward pause. Upstairs* TOM *has put a record on the phonograph. It starts playing now.*)

BILL. You saw the Dean, Herb?

HERB. Yes.

BILL. And?

HERB. He told me the circumstances. Told me he was confident that Tom was innocently involved. He actually apologized for the whole thing. He did say that some of the faculty had suggested —though he didn't go along with this— that Tom would be more comfortable if I took him out of school. But I'm not going to. He's had nothing but comfort all his life, and look what's happened. My associates ask me what he wants to be, and I tell them he hasn't made up his mind. Because I'll be damned if I'll tell them he wants to be a singer of folk songs.

(TOM *lies on the bed listening to the music.*)

BILL. So you're going to leave him in?

HERB. Of course. Let him stick it out. It'll be a good lesson.

LAURA. Mightn't it be more than just a lesson, Mr. Lee?

HERB. Oh, he'll take some kidding. He'll have to work extra hard to prove to them he's . . . well, manly. It may be the thing that brings him to his senses.

LAURA. Mr. Lee, Tom's a very sensitive boy. He's a very lonely boy.

HERB. Why should he be lonely? I've always seen to it that he's been with people . . . at camps, at boarding schools.

BILL. He's certainly an off-horse, Herb.

HERB. That's a good way of putting it, Bill. An off-horse. Well, he's going to have to learn to run with the other horses. Well, I'd better be going up.

LAURA. Mr. Lee, this may sound terribly naïve of me, and perhaps a trifle indelicate, but I don't believe your son knows what this is all about. Why Mr. Harris was fired, why the boys will kid him.

HERB. You mean . . . (*Stops.*)

LAURA. I'm only guessing. But I think when it comes to these boys, we often take too much knowledge for granted. And I think it's going to come as a terrible shock when he finds out what they're talking about. Not just a lesson, a shock.

HERB. I don't believe he's as naïve as all that. I just don't. Well . . . (*He starts for the door.*)

BILL (*takes* HERB's *arm and they go into the hall*). I'm going over to the Dean's for supper, Herb. If you're through with Tom come by here and I'll walk you part way to the station.

HERB. All right. (*Stops on the stairs.*) How do you talk to the boys, Bill?

BILL. I don't know. I just talk to them.

HERB. They're not your sons. I only talked with Tom, I mean, really talked with him, once before. It was after a Sunday dinner and I made up my mind it was time we sat in a room together and talked about important things. He got sick to his stomach. That's a terrible effect to have on your boy . . . Well, I'll drop down. (*He takes a roll of money from his pocket and looks at it, then starts up the stairs.*)

BILL (*coming into his study*). Laura, you shouldn't try to tell him about his own son. After all, if he doesn't know the boy, who does?

LAURA. I'm sorry.

(BILL *exits into the other part of the house, pulling off his tie.* HERB *has gone up the stairs. Knocks on the study door.* LAURA *settles down in her chair and eventually goes on with her sewing.*)

AL (*inside, calls*). Come in.

(HERB *goes in and shuts the door.*)

HERB (*opens* TOM's *bedroom door and sticks his head in*). Hello, there.

TOM (*looks up from the bed, surprised*). Oh . . . Hi . . .

HERB. I got held up at the Dean's.

TOM. Oh. (*He has risen, and attempts to kiss his father on the cheek. But his father holds him off with a firm handshake.*)

HERB. How's everything? You look bushed.

TOM. I'm okay.

HERB (*looking at him closely*). You sure?

TOM. Sure.

HERB (*looking around room*). This room looks smaller than I remember. (*He throws on light switch.*) I used to have the bed over here. Used to rain in some nights. (*Comes across phonograph.*) This the one I gave you for Christmas?

TOM. Yeah. It works fine.

HERB (*turns phonograph off*). You're neater than I was. My vest was always behind the radiator, or somewhere. (*Sees part of dress costume.*) What's this?

TOM (*hesitates for a moment. Then*). A costume Mrs. Reynolds made for me. I'm in the play.

HERB. You didn't write about it.

TOM. I know.

HERB. What are you playing? (*Looks at dress.*)

TOM. You know *The School For Scandal.* I'm playing Lady Teazle.

HERB. Tom, I want to talk to you. Last time we tried to talk, it didn't work out so well.

TOM. What's up?

HERB. Tom, I'd like to be your friend. I guess there's something between fathers and sons that keeps them from being friends, but I'd like to try.

TOM (*embarrassed*). Sure, Dad. (*He sits on the bed.*)

HERB. Now when you came here, I told you to make friends slowly. I told you to make sure they were the right kind of friends. You're known by the company you keep. Remember I said that?

TOM. Yes.

HERB. And I told you if you didn't want to go out for sports like football, hockey . . . that was all right with me. But you'd get in with the right kind of fellow if you managed these teams. They're usually pretty good guys. You remember.

TOM. Yes.

HERB. Didn't you believe me?

TOM. Yes, I believed you.

HERB. Okay, then let's say you believed me, but you decided to go your own way. That's all right too, only you see what it's led to.

TOM. What?

HERB. You made friends with people like this Harris guy who got himself fired.

TOM. Why is he getting fired?

HERB. He's being fired because he was seen in the dunes with you.

TOM. Look, I don't—

HERB. Naked.

TOM. You too?

HERB. So you know what I'm talking about?

TOM. No, I don't.

HERB. You do too know. I heard my sister tell you once. She warned you about a janitor in the building down the street.

TOM (*incredulous*). Mr. Harris . . . ?

HERB. Yes. He's being fired because he's been doing a lot of suspicious things around apparently, and this finished it. All right, I'll say it plain, Tom. He's a fairy. A homosexual.

TOM. Who says so?

HERB. Now, Tom—

TOM. And seeing us on the beach . . .

HERB. Yes.

TOM. And what does that make me?

HERB. Listen, I know you're all right.

TOM. Thanks.

HERB. Now wait a minute.

TOM. Look, we were just swimming.

HERB. All right, all right. So perhaps you didn't know.

TOM. What do you mean perhaps?

HERB. It's the school's fault for having a guy like that around. But it's your fault for being a damned fool in picking your friends.

TOM. So that's what the guys meant.

HERB. You're going to get a ribbing for a while, but you're going to be a man about it and you're going to take it and you're going to come through much more careful how you make your friends.

TOM. He's kicked out because he was seen with me on the beach, and I'm telling you that nothing, absolutely nothing . . . Look, I'm going to the Dean and tell him that Harris did nothing, that—

HERB (*stopping him*). Look, don't be a fool. It's going to be hard enough for you without sticking your neck out, asking for it.

TOM. But, Dad!

HERB. He's not going to be reappointed next year. Nothing you can say is going to change anyone's mind. You got to think about yourself. Now, first of all, get your hair cut. (TOM *looks at father, disgusted.*) Look, this isn't easy for me. Stop thinking about yourself, and give me a break. (TOM *looks up at this appeal.*) I suppose you think it's going to be fun for *me* to have to live this down back home. It'll get around, and it'll affect me, too. So we've got to see this thing through together. You've got to do your part. Get your hair cut. And then . . . No, the first thing I want you to do is call whoever is putting on this play, and tell them you're not playing this lady whatever her name is.

TOM. Why shouldn't I play it? It's the best part in the play, and I was chosen to play it.

HERB. I should think you'd have the sense to see why you shouldn't.

TOM. Wait a minute. You mean . . . do you mean, you think I'm . . . whatever you call it? Do you, Dad?

HERB. I told you "no."

TOM. But the fellows are going to think that I'm . . . and Mrs. Reynolds?

HERB. Yes. You're going to have to fight their thinking it. Yes.

(TOM *sits on the bed, the full realization of it dawning.*)

RALPH (*sticks his head around the stairs from upstairs, and yells*). Hey, Grace, who's taking you to the dance Saturday night? Hey, Grace! (*He disappears again up the stairs.*)

HERB. What's that all about?

TOM. I don't know.

(LAURA, *as the noise comes in, rises and goes to door to stop it, but* AL *comes into the hall and goes upstairs yelling at the boys and* LAURA *goes back to her chair.*)

HERB (*looks at his watch*). Now . . . Do you want me to stay over? If I'm not going to stay over tonight, I've got to catch the six-fifty-four.

TOM. Stay over?

HERB. Yes, I didn't bring a change of clothes along, but if you want me to stay over . . .

TOM. Why should you stay over?

HERB (*stung a little by this*). All right. Now come on down to Bill's room and telephone this drama fellow. So I'll know you're making a start of it. And bring the dress.

TOM. I'll do it tomorrow.

HERB. I'd feel better if you did it tonight. Come on. I'm walking out with Bill. And incidentally, the Dean said if the ribbing goes beyond bounds . . . you know . . . you're to come to him and he'll take some steps. He's not going to do anything now, because these things take care of themselves. They're better ignored . . .

(*They have both started out of the bedroom, but during the above* HERB *goes back for the dress.* TOM *continues out and stands on the stairs looking at the telephone in the hall.*)

HERB (*comes out of the study. Calls back*). See you Al. Take good care of my boy here. (*Starts down stairs. Stops.*) You need any money?

TOM. No.

HERB. I'm lining you up with a counselor's job at camp this year. If this thing doesn't spoil it. (*Stops.*) You sure you've got enough money to come home?

TOM. Yes, sure. Look Dad, let me call about the play from here. (*He takes receiver off hook.*)

HERB. Why not use Bill's phone? He won't mind. Come on. (TOM *reluctantly puts phone back on hook.*) Look, if you've got any problems, talk them over with Bill —Mr. Reynolds. He's an old friend, and I think he'd tell you about what I'd tell you in a spot. (*Goes into master's study.*) Is Bill ready?

LAURA. He'll be right down. How does the costume work?

TOM. I guess it's all right, only . . .

HERB. I'd like Tom to use your phone if he may—to call whoever's putting on the play. He's giving up the part.

LAURA. Giving up the part?

HERB. Yes. I've . . . I want him to. He's doing it for me.

LAURA. Mr. Lee, it was a great honor for him to be chosen to play the part.

HERB. Bill will understand. Bill! (*He thrusts costume into* LAURA's *hand and goes off through alcove.*) Bill, what's the number of the man putting on the play. Tom wants to call him.

(LAURA *looks at* TOM *who keeps his eyes from her. She makes a move towards him, but he takes a step away.*)

BILL (*off stage*). Fred Mayberry . . . Three-two-six . . . You ready, Herb?

HERB (*off stage*). Yes. You don't mind if Tom uses your phone, do you?

BILL. Of course not.

HERB (*comes in*). When do you go on your mountain-climbing week-end, Bill?

BILL (*comes in*). This week-end's the outing.

HERB. Maybe Tom could go with you.

BILL. He's on the dance committee, I think. Of course he's welcome if he wants to. Always has been.

HERB (*holding out phone to* TOM). Tom. (TOM *hesitates to cross to phone. As* LAURA *watches him with concern, he makes a move to escape out the door.*) Three-two-six.

(TOM *slowly and painfully crosses the stage, takes the phone and sits.*)

BILL. Will you walk along with us as far as the dining hall, Laura?

LAURA. I don't think I feel like supper, thanks.

BILL (*looks from her to* TOM). What?

HERB. I've got to get along if I want to catch my train.

(TOM *dials phone.*)

BILL. Laura?

(LAURA *shakes her head, tightlipped.*)

HERB. Well, then, good-by, Laura . . . I still like you.

LAURA. Still going to the Dean's, Bill?

BILL. Yes. I'll be right back after supper. Sure you don't want to walk along with us to the dining hall?

(LAURA *shakes her head.*)

TOM. Busy.

HERB (*pats his son's arm*). Keep trying him. We're in this together. Anything you want? (TOM *shakes his head "no."*) Just remember, anything you want, let me know. (*To* LAURA) See you at reunion time . . . This'll all be blown over by then. (*He goes.*)

BILL. Laura, I wish you'd . . . Laura! (*He is disturbed by her mood. He sees it's hopeless, and goes after* HERB, *leaving door open.*)

TOM (*at phone*). Hello, Mr. Mayberry . . . This is Tom Lee . . . Yes, I know it's time to go to supper, Mr. Mayberry . . . (*Looks around at open door.* LAURA *shuts it.*) but I wanted you to know . . . (*This comes hard.*) I wanted you to know I'm not going to be able to play in the play . . . No . . . I . . . well, I just can't. (*He is about to break. He doesn't trust himself to speak.*)

LAURA (*quickly crosses and takes phone from* TOM). Give it to me. Hello, Fred . . . Laura. Yes, Tom's father, well, he wants Tom—he thinks Tom is tired, needs to concentrate on his final exams. You had someone covering the part, didn't you? . . . Yes, of course it's a terrible disappointment to Tom. I'll see you tomorrow.

(*She hangs up.* TOM *is ashamed and humiliated. Here is the woman he loves, hearing all about him . . . perhaps believing the things . . .* LAURA *stands above him for a moment, looking at the back of his head with pity. Then he rises and starts for the door without looking at her.* RALPH *and* STEVE *come stampeding down the stairway.*)

RALPH (*as he goes*). Okay, you can sit next to him if you want. Not me.

STEVE. Well, if you won't . . . why should I?

RALPH. Two bits nobody will.

(*They slam out the front door.* TOM *has shut the door quickly again when he has heard* RALPH *and* STEVE *start down. Now stands against the door listening.*)

AL (*comes out from his door, pulling on his jacket. Calls*). Tom . . . Tom! (*Getting no answer, he goes down the stairs and out.*)

LAURA. Tom . . .

TOM (*opens the study door*). I'll bet my father thinks I'm . . . (*Stops.*)

LAURA. Now, Tom! I thought I'd call Joan Harrison and ask her to come over for tea tomorrow. I want you to come too. I want you to ask her to go to the dance with you.

TOM (*turns in anguish and looks at her for several moments. Then*). You were to go with me.

LAURA. I know, but . . .

TOM. Do you think so too, like the others? Like my father?

LAURA. Tom!

TOM. Is that why you're shoving me off on Joan?

LAURA (*moving towards him*). Tom, I asked her over so that we could lick this thing.

TOM (*turns on her*). What thing? What thing? (*He looks at her a moment, filled with indignation, then he bolts up the stairs. But on the way up,* PHIL *is coming down.* TOM *feels like a trapped rat. He starts to turn down the stairs again, but he doesn't want to face* LAURA, *as he is about to break. He tries to hide his face and cowers along one side going up.*)

PHIL. What's the matter with you?

(TOM *doesn't answer. Goes on up and into the study door.* PHIL *shrugs his shoulders and goes on down the stairs and out.* TOM *comes into his own bedroom and shuts the door and leans against the doorjamb.* LAURA *goes to the partly opened door. Her impulse is to go up to* TOM *to comfort him, but she checks herself, and turns in the doorway and closes the door, then walks back to her chair and sits down and reaches out and touches the teapot, as though she were half-unconsciously rubbing out a spot. She is puzzled and worried. Upstairs we hear the first few sobs from* TOM *as the lights dim out, and*

THE CURTAIN FALLS

ACT TWO

Scene One

The scene is the same.
The time is two days later.
As the curtain rises, AL *is standing at the public telephone fastened to the wall on the first landing. He seems to be doing more listening than talking.*

AL. Yeah . . . (*He patiently waits through a long tirade.*) Yeah, Dad. I know, Dad . . . No, I haven't done anything about it, yet . . . Yes, Mr. Hudson says he has a room in his house for me next year . . . But I haven't done anything about it here yet . . . Yeah, okay, Dad . . . I know what you mean . . . (*Gets angry.*) I swear to God I don't . . . I lived with him a year, and I don't . . . All right, okay, Dad . . . No, don't *you* call. I'll do it. Right now. (*He hangs up. He stands and puts his hands in his pocket and tries to think this out. It's something he doesn't like.*)

RALPH (*comes in the house door and starts up the steps*). Hey, Al?

AL. Yeah?

RALPH. The guys over at the Beta house want to know has it happened yet?

AL. Has what happened?

RALPH. Has Tom made a pass at you yet?

AL (*reaches out to swat* RALPH). For crying out loud!

RALPH. Okay, okay! You can borrow my chastity belt if you need it.

AL. That's not funny.

RALPH (*shifting his meaning to hurt* AL). No, I know it's not. The guys on the ball team don't think it's funny at all.

AL. What do you mean?

RALPH. The guy they're supposed to elect captain rooming with a queer.

AL (*looks at him for a moment, then rejects the idea*). Aw . . . knock it off, huh!

RALPH. So you don't believe me . . . Wait and see. (*Putting on a dirty grin.*) Anyway, my mother said I should save myself for the girl I marry. Hell, how would you like to have to tell your wife, "Honey, I've been saving myself for you, except for one night when a guy—" (AL *roughs* RALPH *up with no intention of hurting him.*) Okay, okay. So you don't want to be captain of the baseball team. So who the hell cares. I don't, I'm sure.

AL. Look. Why don't you mind your own business?

RALPH. What the hell fun would there be in that?

AL. Ralph, Tom's a nice kid.

RALPH. Yeah. That's why all the guys leave the shower room at the gym when he walks in.

AL. When?

RALPH. Yesterday . . . Today. You didn't hear about it?

AL. No. What are they trying to do?

RALPH. Hell, they don't want some queer looking at them and—

AL. Oh, can it! Go on up and bury your horny nose in your *Art Models* magazine.

RALPH. At least I'm normal. I like to look at pictures of naked girls, not men, the way Tom does.

AL. Jeeze, I'm gonna push your face in in a—

RALPH. Didn't you notice all those strong man poses he's got in his bottom drawer?

AL. Yes, I've noticed them. His old man wants him to be a muscle man, and he wrote away for this course in muscle building and they send those pictures. Any objections?

RALPH. Go on, stick up for him. Stick your neck out. You'll get it chopped off with a baseball bat, you crazy bastard. (*Exits upstairs.* AL *looks at the phone, then up the way* RALPH *went. He is upset. He throws himself into a few push-ups, using the bannisters. Then still not happy with what he's doing, he walks down the stairs and knocks on the study door.*)

LAURA (*comes from inside the house and opens the door*). Oh, hello, Al.

AL. Is Mr. Reynolds in?

LAURA. Why, no, he isn't. Can I do something?

AL. I guess I better drop down when he's in.

LAURA. All right. I don't really expect him home till after supper tonight.

AL (*thinks for a moment*). Well . . . well, you might tell him just so he'll know and can make other plans . . . I won't be rooming in this house next year. This is the last day for changing, and I want him to know that.

LAURA (*moves into the room to get a cigarette*). I see. Well, I know he'll be sorry to hear that, Al.

AL. I'm going across the street to Harmon House.

LAURA. Both you and Tom going over?

AL. No.

LAURA. Oh.

AL. Just me.

LAURA. I see. Does Tom know this?

AL. No. I haven't told him.

LAURA. You'll have to tell him, won't you, so he'll be able to make other plans.

AL. Yes, I suppose so.

LAURA. Al, won't you sit down for a moment, please? (AL *hesitates, but comes in and sits down. Offers* AL *a cigarette.*) Cigarette?

AL (*reaches for one automatically, then stops*). No, thanks. I'm in training. (*He slips a pack of cigarettes from his shirt pocket to his trousers pocket.*)

LAURA. That's right. I'm going to watch you play Saturday afternoon. (AL *smiles at her.*) You're not looking forward to telling Tom, are you, Al? (AL *shakes his head, "No."*) I suppose I can guess why you're not rooming with him next year.

(AL *shrugs his shoulders*.) I wonder if you know how much it has meant for him to room with you this year. It's done a lot for him too. It's given him a confidence to know he was rooming with one of the big men of the school.

AL (*embarrassed*). Oh . . .

LAURA. You wouldn't understand what it means to be befriended. You're one of the strong people. I'm surprised, Al.

AL (*blurting it out*). My father's called me three times. How he ever found out about Harris and Tom, I don't know. But he did. And some guy called him and asked him, "Isn't that the boy your son is rooming with?" . . . and he wants me to change for next year.

LAURA. What did you tell your father?

AL. I told him Tom wasn't so bad, and . . . I'd better wait and see Mr. Reynolds.

LAURA. Al, you've lived with Tom. You know him better than anyone else knows him. If you do this, it's as good as finishing him so far as this school is concerned, and maybe farther.

AL (*almost whispering it*). Well, he *does* act sort of queer, Mrs. Reynolds. He . . .

LAURA. You never said this before. You never paid any attention before. What do you mean, "queer?"

AL. Well, like the fellows say, he sort of walks lightly, if you know what I mean. Sometimes the way he moves . . . the things he talks about . . . long hair music all the time.

LAURA. All right. He wants to be a singer. So he talks about it.

AL. He's never had a girl up for any of the dances.

LAURA. Al, there are good explanations for all these things you're saying. They're silly . . . and prejudiced . . . and arguments all dug up to suit a point of view. They're all after the fact.

AL. I'd better speak to Mr. Reynolds. (*He starts for the door.*)

LAURA. Al, look at me. (*She holds his eyes for a long time, wondering whether to say what she wants to say.*)

AL. Yes?

LAURA (*she decides to do it*). Al, what if I were to start the rumor tomorrow that you were . . . well, queer, as you put it.

AL. No one would believe it.

LAURA. Why not?

AL. Well, because . . .

LAURA. Because you're big and brawny and an athlete. What they call a top guy and a hard hitter?

AL. Well, yes.

LAURA. You've got some things to learn, Al. I've been around a little, and I've met men, just like you—same setup—who weren't men, some of them married and with children.

AL. Mrs. Reynolds, you wouldn't do a thing like that.

LAURA. No, Al, I probably wouldn't. But I could, and I almost would to show you how easy it is to smear a person, and once I got them believing it, you'd be surprised how quickly your . . . manly virtues would be changed into suspicious characteristics.

AL (*has been standing with his hands on his hips.* LAURA *looks pointedly at this stance.* AL *thrusts his hands down to his side, and then behind his back*). Mrs. Reynolds, I got a chance to be captain of the baseball team next year.

LAURA. I know. And I have no right to ask you to give up that chance. But I wish somehow or other you could figure out a way . . . so it wouldn't hurt Tom.

(TOM *comes in the hall and goes up the stairs. He's pretty broken up, and mad. After a few moments he appears in his room, shuts the door, and sits on the bed, trying to figure something out.*)

AL (*as* TOM *enters house*). Well . . .

LAURA. That's Tom now. (AL *looks at her, wondering how she knows.*) I know all your footsteps. He's coming in for tea. (AL *starts to move to door.*) Well, Al? (AL *makes a helpless motion.*) You still want me to tell Mr. Reynolds about your moving next year?

AL (*after a moment*). No.

LAURA. Good.

AL. I mean, I'll tell him when I see him.

LAURA. Oh.

AL (*turns on her*). What can I do?

LAURA. I don't know.

AL. Excuse me for saying so, but it's easy for you to talk the way you have. You're not involved. You're just a bystander. You're not going to be hurt. Nothing's going to happen to you one way or the other. I'm sorry.

LAURA. That's a fair criticism, Al. I'm sorry I asked you . . . As you say, I'm not involved.

AL. I'm sorry. I think you're swell, Mrs.

Reynolds. You're the nicest housemaster's wife I've ever ran into . . . I mean . . . Well, you know what I mean. It's only that . . . (*He is flustered. He opens the door.*) I'm sorry.

LAURA. I'm sorry too, Al. (*She smiles at him.* AL *stands in the doorway for a moment, not knowing whether to go out the hall door or go upstairs. Finally, he goes upstairs, and into the study door.* LAURA *stands thinking over what* AL *has said, even repeating to herself, "I'm not involved." She then goes into the alcove and off.*)

AL (*outside* TOM's *bedroom door*). Tom? (TOM *moves quietly away from the door.*) Tom? (*He opens the door.*) Hey.

TOM. I was sleeping.

AL. Standing up, huh? (TOM *turns away.*) You want to be alone?

TOM. No. You want to look. Go ahead. (*He indicates the window.*)

AL. No, I don't want to look, I . . . (*He looks at* TOM, *not knowing how to begin . . . He stalls . . . smiling*) Nice tie you got there.

TOM (*starts to undo tie*). Yeah, it's yours. You want it?

AL. No. Why? I can only wear one tie at a time. (TOM *leaves it hanging around his neck. After an awkward pause*) I . . . uh . . .

TOM. I guess I don't need to ask you what's the matter?

AL. It's been rough today, huh?

TOM. Yeah. (*He turns away, very upset. He's been holding it in . . . but here's his closest friend asking him to open up.*) Jesus Christ! (AL *doesn't know what to say. He goes to* TOM's *bureau and picks up his hairbrush, gives his hair a few brushes.*) Anybody talk to you?

AL. Sure. You know they would.

TOM. What do they say?

AL (*yanks his tie off*). Hell, I don't know.

TOM. I went to a meeting of the dance committee. I'm no longer on the dance committee. Said that since I'd backed out of playing the part in the play, I didn't show the proper spirit. That's what they *said* was the reason.

AL (*loud*). Why the hell don't you do something about it?

TOM (*yelling back*). About what?

AL. About what they're saying.

TOM. What the hell can I do?

AL. Jeeze, you could . . . (*He suddenly wonders what* TOM *could do.*) I don't know.

TOM. I tried to pass it off. Christ, you can't pass it off. You know, when I went into the showers today after my tennis match, everyone who was in there, grabbed a towel and . . . and . . . walked out.

AL. They're stupid. Just a bunch of stupid bastards. (*He leaves the room.*)

TOM (*following him into sitting room*). Goddamn it, the awful thing I found myself . . . Jesus, I don't know . . . I found myself self-conscious about things I've been doing for years. Dressing, undressing. . . . I keep my eyes on the floor . . . (*Re-enters his own room.*) Jeeze, if I even look at a guy that doesn't have any clothes on, I'm afraid someone's gonna say something, or . . . Jesus, I don't know.

AL (*during this,* AL *has come back into the room, unbuttoning his shirt, taking it off, etc. Suddenly he stops*). What the hell am I doing? I've had a shower today. (*He tries to laugh.*)

TOM (*looks at him a moment*). Undress in your own room, will ya? You don't want them talking about you too, do you?

AL. No I don't. (*He has said this very definitely and with meaning.*)

TOM (*looks up at his tone of voice*). Of course you don't. (*He looks at* AL *a long time. He hardly dares say this.*) You . . . uh . . . you moving out?

AL (*doesn't want to answer*). Look, Tom, do you mind if I try to help you?

TOM. Hell, no. How?

AL. I know this is gonna burn your tail, and I know it sounds stupid as hell. But it isn't stupid. It's the way people look at things. You could do a lot for yourself, just the way you talk and look.

TOM. You mean get my hair cut?

AL. For one thing.

TOM. Why the hell should a man with a crew cut look more manly than a guy who—

AL. Look, I don't know the reasons for these things. It's just the way they are.

TOM (*looking at himself in bureau mirror*). I tried a crew cut a coupla times. I haven't got that kind of hair, or that kind of head. (*After a moment*) Sorry, I didn't mean to yell at you. Thanks for trying to help.

AL (*finds a baseball on the radiator and throws it at* TOM. TOM *smiles, and throws it back*). Look, Tom, the way you walk . . .

TOM. Oh, Jesus.

AL (*flaring*). Look, I'm only trying to help you.

TOM. No one gave a goddamn about how I walked till last Saturday!

AL (*starts to go*). Okay, okay. Forget it. (*He goes out.*)

TOM (*stands there a few moments, then slams the baseball into the bed and walks out after* AL *into sitting room*). Al?

AL (*off*). Yeah?

TOM. Tell me about how I walk.

AL (*in the sitting room*). Go ahead, walk!

TOM (*walks back into the bedroom.* AL *follows him, wiping his face on a towel and watching* TOM *walk. After he has walked a bit*). Now I'm not going to be able to walk any more. Everything I been doing all my life makes me look like a fairy.

AL. Go on.

TOM. All right, now I'm walking. Tell me.

AL. Tom, I don't know. You walk sort of light.

TOM. Light? (*He looks at himself take a step.*)

AL. Yeah.

TOM. Show me.

AL. No, I can't do it.

TOM. Okay. You walk. Let me watch you. I never noticed how you walked. (*AL stands there for a moment, never having realized before how difficult it could be to walk if you think about it. Finally he walks.*) Do it again.

AL. If you go telling any of the guys about this . . .

TOM. Do you think I would? . . . (*AL walks again.*) That's a good walk. I'll try to copy it. (*He tries to copy the walk, but never succeeds in taking even a step.*) Do you really think that'll make any difference?

AL. I dunno.

TOM. Not now it won't. Thanks anyway.

AL (*comes and sits on bed beside* TOM. *Puts his arm around* TOM's *shoulder and thinks this thing out*). Look, Tom . . . You've been in on a lot of bull sessions. You heard the guys talking about stopping over in Boston on the way home . . . getting girls . . . you know.

TOM. Sure. What about it?

AL. You're not going to the dance Saturday night?

TOM. No. Not now.

AL. You know Ellie Martin. The gal who waits on table down at the soda joint?

TOM. Yeah. What about her?

AL. You've heard the guys talking about her.

TOM. What do you mean?

AL. Hell, do you want me to draw a picture?

TOM (*with disgust*). Ellie Martin?

AL. Okay. I know she's a dog, but . . .

TOM. So what good's that going to do? I get caught there, I get thrown out of school.

AL. No one ever gets caught. Sunday morning people'd hear about it . . . not the Dean . . . I mean the fellows. Hell, Ellie tells and tells and tells . . . Boy, you'd be made!

TOM. Are you kidding?

AL. No.

TOM (*with disgust*). Ellie Martin!

AL (*after a long pause*). Look, I've said so much already, I might as well be a complete bastard . . . You ever been with a woman?

TOM. What do you think?

AL. I don't think you have.

TOM. So?

AL. You want to know something?

TOM. What?

AL. Neither have I. But if you tell the guys, I'll murder you.

TOM. All those stories you told . . .

AL. Okay, I'll be sorry I told you.

TOM. Then why don't you go see Ellie Martin Saturday night?

AL. Why the hell should I?

TOM. You mean you don't have to prove anything?

AL. Aw, forget it. It's probably a lousy idea anyway. (*He starts out.*)

TOM. Yeah.

AL (*stops*). Look, about next—(*Stops.*)

TOM. Next year? Yes?

AL. Hap Hudson's asked me to come to his house. He's got a single there. A lot of the fellows from the team are over there, and . . . well . . . (*He doesn't look at* TOM.)

TOM. I understand!

AL (*looks up at last. He hates himself but he's done it, and it's a load off his chest*). See ya. (*He starts to go.*)

TOM (*as* AL *gets to door*). Al . . . (*AL

stops and looks back. Taking tie from around his neck) Here.

AL (*looks at tie, embarrassed*). I said wear it. Keep it.

TOM. It's yours.

AL (*looks at the tie for a long time, then without taking it, goes through the door*). See ya.

(TOM *folds the tie neatly, dazed, then seeing what he's doing, he throws it viciously in the direction of the bureau, and turns and stares out the window. He puts a record on the phonograph.*)

BILL (*comes in to study from the hall, carrying a pair of shoes and a slim book. As he opens his study door, he hears the music upstairs. He stands in the door and listens, remembering his miserable boyhood. Then he comes in and closes the door*). Laura. (*Throws shoes on floor near footstool.*)

LAURA (*off stage, calling*). Bill?

BILL. Yes.

LAURA (*coming in with tea things*). I didn't think you'd be back before your class. Have some tea.

BILL. I beat young Harvey at handball.

LAURA. Good.

BILL. At last. It took some doing, though. He was after my scalp because of that D minus I gave him in his last exam. (*Gives her book.*) You wanted this . . . book of poems.

LAURA (*looks at book. Her eyes shift quickly to the same book in the chair*). Why yes. How did you know?

BILL (*trying to be offhand about it*). The notice from the bookstore.

LAURA. That's very nice of you. (*She moves towards him to kiss him, but at this moment, in picking some wrapping paper from the armchair, he notices the duplicate copy.*)

BILL (*a little angry*). You've already got it.

LAURA. Why, yes . . . I . . . well, I . . . (BILL *picking it up . . . opens it.*) That is, someone gave it to me. (BILL *reads the inscription.*) Tom knew I wanted it, and . . .

BILL (*looks at her, a terrible look coming into his face. Then he slowly rips the book in two and hurls it into the fireplace*). Damn!

LAURA. Bill! (BILL *goes to footstool and sits down and begins to change his shoes.*) Bill, what difference does it make that he

gave me the book? He knew I wanted it too.

BILL. I don't know. It's just that every time I try to do something . . .

LAURA. Bill, how can you say that? It isn't so.

BILL. It is.

LAURA. Bill, this thing of the book is funny.

BILL. I don't think it's very funny.

LAURA (*going behind him, and kneeling by his side*). Bill, I'm very touched that you should have remembered. Thank you. (*He turns away from her and goes on with his shoes.*) Bill, don't turn away. I want to thank you. (*As she gets no response from him, she rises.*) Is it such a chore to let yourself be thanked? (*She puts her hands on his shoulders, trying to embrace him.*) Oh, Bill, we so rarely touch any more. I keep feeling I'm losing contact with you. Don't you feel that?

BILL (*looking at his watch*). Laura, I . . .

LAURA (*she backs away from him*). I know, you've got to go. But it's just that, I don't know, we don't touch any more. It's a silly way of putting it, but you seem to hold yourself aloof from me. A tension seems to grow between us . . . and then when we do . . . touch . . . it's a violent thing . . . almost a compulsive thing. (BILL *is uncomfortable at this accurate description of their relationship. He sits troubled. She puts her arms around his neck and embraces him, bending over him.*) You don't feel it? You don't feel yourself holding away from me until it becomes overpowering? There's no growing together any more . . . no quiet times, just holding hands, the feeling of closeness, like it was in Italy. Now it's long separations and then this almost brutal coming together, and . . . Oh, Bill, you do see, you do see. (BILL *suddenly straightens up, toughens, and looks at her.* LAURA *repulsed, slowly draws her arms from around his shoulders.*)

BILL. For God's sake, Laura, what are you talking about? (*He rises and goes to his desk.*) It can't always be a honeymoon.

(*Upstairs in his room,* TOM *turns off the phonograph, and leaves the room, going out into the hall and up the stairs.*)

LAURA. Do you think that's what I'm talking about?

BILL. I don't know why you chose a

time like this to talk about things like . . .

LAURA. . . . I don't know why, either. I just wanted to thank you for the book . . . (*Moves away and looks in book.*) What did you write in it?

BILL (*starts to mark exam papers*). Nothing. Why? Should I write in it? I just thought you wanted the book.

LAURA. Of course . . . Are you sure you won't have some tea? (*She bends over the tea things.*)

BILL. Yes.

LAURA (*straightening up, trying another tack of returning to normality*). Little Joan Harrison is coming over for tea.

BILL. No, she isn't. (LAURA *looks inquiringly.*) I just saw her father at the gym. I don't think that was a very smart thing for you to do, Laura.

LAURA. I thought Tom might take her to the dance Saturday. He's on the committee, and he has no girl to take.

BILL. I understand he's no longer on the committee. You're a hostess, aren't you?

LAURA. Yes.

BILL. I've got the mountain-climbing business this week end. Weather man predicts rain.

LAURA (*almost breaks. Hides her face in her hands. Then recovers*). That's too bad. (*After a moment*) Bill?

BILL. Yes?

LAURA. I think someone should go to the Dean about Tom and the hazing he's getting.

BILL. What could the Dean do? Announce from chapel, "You've got to stop riding Tom. You've got to stop calling him Grace?" Is that what you'd like him to do?

LAURA. No. I suppose not.

BILL. You know we're losing Al next year because of Tom.

LAURA. Oh, you've heard?

BILL. Yes, Hudson tells me he's moving over to his house. He'll probably be captain of the baseball team. Last time we had a major sport captain was eight years ago.

LAURA. Yes, I'm sorry.

BILL. However, we'll also be losing Tom.

LAURA. Oh?

BILL (*noting her increased interest*). Yes. We have no singles in this house, and he'll be rooming alone.

LAURA. I'm sorry to hear that.

BILL (*he turns to look at her*). I knew you would be.

LAURA. Why should my interest in this boy make you angry?

BILL. I'm not angry.

LAURA. You're not only angry. It's almost as though you were, well, jealous.

BILL. Oh, come on now.

LAURA. Well, how else can you explain your . . . your vindictive attitude towards him?

BILL. Why go into it again? Jealous! (*He has his books together now. Goes to the door.*) I'll go directly from class to the dining hall. All right?

LAURA. Yes, of course.

BILL. And please, please, Laura . . . (*He stops.*)

LAURA. I'll try.

BILL. I know you like to be different, just for the sake of being different . . . and I like you for that . . . But this time, lay off. Show your fine free spirit on something else.

LAURA. On something that can't hurt us.

BILL. All right. Sure. I don't mind putting it that way. And Laura?

LAURA. Yes?

BILL. Seeing Tom so much . . . having him down for tea alone all the time . . .

LAURA. Yes?

BILL. I think you should have him down only when you have the other boys . . . for his own good. I mean that. Well, I'll see you in the dining hall. Try to be on time. (*He goes out.* LAURA *brings her hands to her face, and cries, leaning against the back of the chair.* AL *has come tumbling out of the door to his room with books in hand, and is coming down stairs. Going down the hall*) You going to class, Al?

AL. Hello, Mr. Reynolds. Yes I am.

BILL (*as they go*). Let's walk together. I'm sorry to hear that you're moving across the street next year. (*And they are gone out the door.*)

TOM (*has come down the stairs, and now stands looking at the hall telephone. He is carrying his coat. After a long moment's deliberation he puts in a coin and dials*). Hello, I'd like to speak to Ellie Martin, please. (LAURA *has moved to pick up the torn book which her husband has thrown in the fireplace. She is smoothing it out, as she suddenly hears* TOM's *voice in the hall. She can't help but hear what he is saying. She stands stock still and listens, her alarm and concern showing on her face.*) Hello, Ellie? This is Tom Lee

. . . Tom Lee. I'm down at the soda fountain all the time with my roommate, Al Thompson . . . Yeah, the guys do sometimes call me that . . . Well, I'll tell you what I wanted. I wondered if . . . you see, I'm not going to the dance Saturday night, and I wondered if you're doing anything? Yeah, I guess that is a hell of a way to ask for a date . . . but I just wondered if I could maybe drop by and pick you up after work on Saturday . . . I don't know what's *in* it for you, Ellie . . . but something I guess. I just thought I'd like to see you . . . What time do you get through work? . . . Okay, nine o'clock. (LAURA, *having heard this, goes out through the alcove. About to hang up*) Oh, thanks. (*He stands for a moment, contemplating what he's done, then he slips on his jacket, and goes to the study door and knocks. After a moment, he opens the door and enters.*)

LAURA (*coming from the other room with a plate of cookies*). Oh, there you are. I've got your favorites today.

TOM. Mrs. Reynolds, do you mind if I don't come to tea this afternoon?

LAURA. Why . . . if you don't want to . . . How are you? (*She really means this question.*)

TOM. I'm okay.

LAURA. Good.

TOM. It's just I don't feel like tea.

LAURA. Perhaps, it's just as well . . . Joan can't make it today, either.

TOM. I didn't expect she would. She's nothing special; just a kid.

LAURA. Something about a dentist appointment or something.

TOM. It wouldn't have done any good anyway. I'm not going to the dance.

LAURA. Oh?

TOM. Another member of the committee will stop around for you.

LAURA. What will you be doing?

TOM. I don't know. I can take care of myself.

LAURA. If you're not going, that gives me an easy out. I won't have to go.

TOM. Just because I'm not going?

LAURA (*in an effort to keep him from going to Ellie*). Look, Tom . . . now that neither of us is going, why don't you drop down here after supper, Saturday night. We could listen to some records, or play gin, or we can just talk.

TOM. I . . . I don't think you'd better

count on me.

LAURA. I'd like to.

TOM. No, really. I don't want to sound rude . . . but I . . . I may have another engagement.

LAURA. Oh?

TOM. I'd like to come. Please understand that. It's what I'd like to do . . . but . . .

LAURA. Well, I'll be here just in case, just in case you decide to come in. (LAURA *extends her hand.*) I hope you'll be feeling better.

TOM (*hesitates, then takes her hand*). Thanks.

LAURA. Maybe your plans will change.

(TOM *looks at her, wishing they would; knowing they won't. He runs out and down the hall as the lights fade out on* LAURA *standing at the door.*)

CURTAIN

Scene Two

The time is eight-forty-five on Saturday night.

In the study a low fire is burning. As the curtain rises, the town clock is striking the three-quarter hour. LAURA *is sitting in her chair sipping a cup of coffee. The door to the study is open slightly. She is waiting for* TOM. *She is wearing a lovely but informal dress, and a single flower. In his room,* TOM *listens to the clock strike. He has just been shaving. He is putting shaving lotion on his face. His face is tense and nervous. There is no joy in the preparations. In a moment, he turns and leaves the room, taking off his belt as he goes.*

After a moment, LILLY *comes to the study door, knocks and comes in.*

LILLY. Laura?

LAURA. Oh, Lilly.

LILLY (*standing in the doorway, a raincoat held over her head. She is dressed in a low-cut evening gown, which she wears very well*). You're not dressed yet. Why aren't you dressed for the dance?

LAURA (*still in her chair*). I'm not going. I thought I told you.

LILLY (*deposits raincoat and goes immediately to look at herself in mirror next to the door*). Oh, for Heaven's sake, why not? Just because Bill's away with his loathsome little mountain climbers?

LAURA. Well . . .

LILLY. Come along with us. It's raining on and off, so Harry's going to drive us in the car.

LAURA. No, thanks.

LILLY. If you come, Harry will dance with you all evening. You won't be lonely, I promise you. (LAURA *shakes her head, "no."*) You're the only one who can dance those funny steps with him.

LAURA. It's very sweet of you, but no.

LILLY (*at the mirror*). Do you think this neck is too low?

LAURA. I think you look lovely.

LILLY. Harry says this neck will drive all the little boys crazy.

LAURA. I don't think so.

LILLY. Well, that's not very flattering.

LAURA. I mean, I think they'll appreciate it, but as for driving them crazy . . .

LILLY. After all I want to give them some reward for dancing their duty dances with me.

LAURA. I'm sure when they dance with you, it's no duty, Lilly. I've seen you at these dances.

LILLY. It's not this . . . (*indicating her bosom*) it's my line of chatter. I'm oh so interested in what courses they're taking, where they come from and where they learned to dance so divinely.

LAURA (*laughing.*) Lilly, you're lost in a boys' school. You were meant to shine some place much more glamorous.

LILLY. I wouldn't trade it for the world. Where else could a girl indulge in three hundred innocent flirtations a year?

LAURA. Lilly, I've often wondered what you'd do if one of the three hundred attempted to go, well, a little further than innocent flirtation.

LILLY. I'd slap him down . . . the little beast. (*She laughs and admires herself in mirror.*) Harry says if I'm not careful I'll get to looking like Ellie Martin. You've seen Ellie.

LAURA. I saw her this afternoon for the first time.

LILLY. Really? The first time?

LAURA. Yes. I went into the place where she works . . . the soda shop . . .

LILLY. You!

LAURA. Yes . . . uh . . . for a package of cigarettes. (*After a moment she says with some sadness*) She's not even pretty, is she?

LILLY (*turns from admiring herself at the tone in* LAURA'*s voice*). Well, honey, don't sound so sad. What difference should it make to you if she's pretty or not?

LAURA. I don't know. It just seems so . . . they're so young.

LILLY. If they're stupid enough to go to Ellie Martin, they deserve whatever happens to them. Anyway, Laura, the boys *talk* more about Ellie than anything else. So don't fret about it.

LAURA (*arranges chair for* TOM *facing fireplace. Notices* LILLY *priming*). You look lovely, Lilly.

LILLY. Maybe I'd better wear that corsage the dance committee sent, after all . . . right here. (*She indicates low point in dress*) I was going to carry it—or rather Harry was going to help me carry it. You know, it's like one of those things people put on Civil War monuments on Decoration Day.

LAURA. Yes, I've seen them.

LILLY (*indicating the flower* LAURA *is wearing*). Now that's tasteful. Where'd you get that?

LAURA. Uh . . . I bought it for myself.

LILLY. Oh, now.

LAURA. It's always been a favorite of mine and I saw it in the florist's window.

LILLY. Well, Harry will be waiting for me to tie his bow tie. (*Starts towards door.*) Will you be up when we get back?

LAURA (*giving* LILLY *her raincoat*). Probably not.

LILLY. If there's a light on, I'll drop in and tell you how many I had to slap down . . . Night-night. (*She leaves.* LAURA *stands at the closed door until she hears the outside door close. Then she opens her door a bit. She takes her cup of coffee and stands in front of the fireplace and listens.*)

TOM (*as* LILLY *goes, he returns to his room, dressed in a blue suit. He stands there deliberating a moment, then reaches under his pillow and brings out a pint bottle of whisky. He takes a short swig. It gags him. He corks it and puts it back under the pillow*). Christ, I'll never make it. (*He reaches in his closet and pulls out a raincoat, then turns and snaps out the room light, and goes out. A moment later, he appears on the stairs. He sees* LAURA'*s door partly open, and while he is putting on his raincoat, he walks warily past it.*)

LAURA (*when she hears* TOM'*s door close,*

she stands still and listens more intently. She hears him pass her door and go to the front door. She puts down the cup of coffee, and goes to the study door. She calls). Tom? *(After some moments,* TOM *appears in the door, and she opens it wide.)* I've been expecting you.

TOM. I . . . I . . .

LAURA *(opening the door wide).* Are you going to the dance, after all?

TOM *(comes in the door).* No . . . You can report me if you want. Out after hours. Or . . . *(He looks up at her finally.)* Or you can give me permission. Can I have permission to go out?

LAURA *(moving into the room, says pleasantly).* I think I'd better get you some coffee.

TOM *(at her back, truculent).* You can tell them that, too . . . that I've been drinking. There'll be lots to tell before— *(He stops.)* I didn't drink much. But I didn't eat much either.

LAURA. Let me get you something to eat.

TOM *(as though convincing himself).* No. I can't stay!

LAURA. All right. But I'm glad you dropped in. I was counting on it.

TOM *(chip on shoulder).* I said I might not. When you invited me.

LAURA. I know. *(She looks at him a moment. He is to her a heartbreaking sight . . . all dressed up as though he were going to a prom, but instead he's going to Ellie . . . the innocence and the desperation touch her deeply . . . and this shows in her face as she circles behind him to the door.)* It's a nasty night out, isn't it?

TOM. Yes.

LAURA. I'm just as glad I'm not going to the dance. *(She shuts the door gently.* TOM, *at the sound of the door, turns and sees what she has done.)* It'll be nice just to stay here by the fire.

TOM. I wasn't planning to come in.

LAURA. Then why the flower . . . and the card? "For a pleasant evening?"

TOM. It was for the dance. I forgot to cancel it.

LAURA. I'm glad you didn't.

TOM. Why? *(He stops studying the curtains and looks at her.)*

LAURA *(moving into the room again).* Well, for one thing I like to get flowers. For another thing . . . *(TOM shakes his head a little to clear it.)* Let me make you some coffee.

TOM. No. I am just about right.

LAURA. Or you can drink this . . . I just had a sip. *(She holds up the cup.* TOM *looks at the proffered coffee.)* You can drink from this side. *(She indicates the other side of the cup.)*

TOM *(takes the cup, and looks at the side where her lips have touched and then slowly turns it around to the other and takes a sip).* And for another thing?

LAURA. What do you mean?

TOM. For one thing you like to get flowers . . .

LAURA. For another it's nice to have flowers on my anniversary.

TOM. Anniversary?

LAURA. Yes.

TOM *(waving the cup and saucer around).* And Mr. Reynolds on a mountain top with twenty stalwart youths, soaking wet . . . Didn't he remember?

LAURA *(rescues the cup and saucer).* It's not that anniversary. *(TOM looks at her wondering. Seeing that she has interested him, she moves towards him.)* Let me take your coat.

TOM *(definitely).* I can't—

LAURA. I know. You can't stay. But . . . *(She comes up behind him and puts her hand on his shoulders to take off his coat. He can hardly stand her touch. She gently peels his coat from him and stands back to look at him.)* How nice you look!

TOM *(disarranging his hair or tie).* Put me in a blue suit and I look like a kid.

LAURA. How did you know I liked this flower?

TOM. You mentioned it.

LAURA. You're very quick to notice these things. So was he.

TOM *(after a moment, his curiosity aroused).* Who?

LAURA. My first husband. That's the anniversary.

TOM. I didn't know.

LAURA *(she sits in her chair).* Mr. Reynolds doesn't like me to talk about my first husband. He was, I'd say, about your age. How old are you, Tom?

TOM. Eighteen . . . tomorrow.

LAURA. Tomorrow . . . We must celebrate.

TOM. You'd better not make any plans.

LAURA. He was just your age then. *(She looks at him again with slight wonder.)* It doesn't seem possible now, looking at you . . .

TOM. Why, do I look like such a child?

LAURA. Why no.

TOM. Men are married at my age.

LAURA. Of course, they are. *He* was. Maybe a few months older. Such a lonely boy, away from home for the first time . . . and . . . and going off to war. (TOM *looks up inquiringly.*) Yes, he was killed.

TOM. I'm sorry . . . but I'm glad to hear about him.

LAURA. Glad?

TOM. Yes. I don't know . . . He sounds like someone you *should* have been married to, not . . . (*Stops.*) I'm sorry if I . . . (*Stops.*)

LAURA (*after a moment*). He was killed being conspicuously brave. He had to be conspicuously brave, you see, because something had happened in training camp . . . I don't know what . . . and he was afraid the others thought him a coward . . . He showed them he wasn't.

TOM. He had that satisfaction.

LAURA. What was it worth if it killed him?

TOM. I don't know. But I can understand.

LAURA. Of course you can. You're very like him.

TOM. Me?

LAURA (*holding out the coffee cup*). Before I finish it all? (TOM *comes over and takes a sip from his side of the cup.*) He was kind and gentle, and lonely. (TOM *turns away in embarrassment at hearing himself so described.*) We knew it wouldn't last . . . We sensed it . . . But he always said. "Why must the test of everything be its durability?"

TOM. I'm sorry he was killed.

LAURA. Yes, so am I. I'm sorry he was killed the way he was killed . . . trying to prove how brave he was. In trying to prove he was a man, he died a boy.

TOM. Still he must have died happy.

LAURA. Because he proved his courage?

TOM. That . . . and because he was married to you. (*Embarrassed, he walks to his coat which she has been holding in her lap.*) I've got to go.

LAURA. Tom, please.

TOM. I've got to.

LAURA. It must be a very important engagement.

TOM. It is.

LAURA. If you go now, I'll think I bored you, talking all about myself.

TOM. You haven't.

LAURA. I probably shouldn't have gone on like that. It's just that I felt like it . . . a rainy night . . . a fire. I guess I'm in a reminiscent mood. Do you ever get in reminiscing moods on nights like this?

TOM. About what?

LAURA. Oh, come now . . . there must be something pleasant to remember, or someone. (TOM *stands by the door beginning to think back, his raincoat in his hand, but still dragging on the floor.*) Isn't there? . . . Of course there is. Who was it, or don't you want to tell?

TOM (*after a long silence*). May I have a cigarette?

LAURA (*relieved that she has won another moment's delay*). Yes, Of course. (*Hands him a box, then lights his cigarette.*)

TOM. My seventh-grade teacher.

LAURA. What?

TOM. That's who I remember.

LAURA. Oh.

TOM. Miss Middleton . . .

LAURA. How sweet.

TOM (*drops the raincoat again, and moves into the room*). It wasn't sweet. It was terrible.

LAURA. At that time, of course . . . Tell me about her.

TOM. She was just out of college . . . tall, blonde, honey-colored hair . . . and she wore a polo coat, and drove a convertible.

LAURA. Sounds very fetching.

TOM. Ever since then I've been a sucker for girls in polo coats.

LAURA (*smiling*). I have one somewhere.

TOM. Yes, I know. (*He looks at her.*)

LAURA. What happened?

TOM. What could happen? As usual I made a fool of myself. I guess everyone knew I was in love with her. People I like, I can't help showing it.

LAURA. That's a good trait.

TOM. When she used to go on errands and she needed one of the boys to go along and help carry something, there I was.

LAURA. She liked you too, then.

TOM. This is a stupid thing to talk about.

LAURA. I can see why she liked you.

TOM. I thought she . . . I thought she loved me. I was twelve years old.

LAURA. Maybe she did.

TOM. Anyway, when I was in eighth grade, she got married. And you know what they made me do? They gave a

luncheon at school in her honor, and I had to be the toastmaster and wish her happiness and everything . . . I had to write a poem . . . (*He quotes*)
"Now that you are going to be married,
And away from us be carried,
Before you promise to love, honor and obey,
There are a few things I want to say."
(*He shakes his head as they both laugh.*) From there on it turned out to be more of a love poem than anything else.

LAURA (*as she stops laughing*). Puppy love can be heartbreaking.

TOM (*the smile dying quickly as he looks at her. Then after what seems like forever*). I'm always falling in love with the wrong people.

LAURA. Who isn't?

TOM. You too?

LAURA. It wouldn't be any fun if we didn't. Of course, nothing ever comes of it, but there are bittersweet memories, and they can be pleasant. (*Kidding him as friend to friend, trying to get him to smile again.*) Who else have you been desperately in love with?

TOM (*he doesn't answer. Then he looks at his watch*). It's almost nine . . . I'm late. (*Starts to go.*)

LAURA (*rising*). I can't persuade you to stay? (TOM *shakes his head, "no."*) We were getting on so well.

TOM. Thanks.

LAURA. In another moment I would have told you all the deep, dark secrets of my life.

TOM. I'm sorry. (*He picks up his coat from the floor.*)

LAURA (*desperately trying to think of something to keep him from going*). Won't you stay even for a dance?

TOM. I don't dance.

LAURA. I was going to teach you. (*She goes over to the phonograph and snaps on the button.*)

TOM (*opens the door*). Some other time . . .

LAURA. Please, for me. (*She comes back.*)

TOM (*after a moment he closes the door*). Tell me something.

LAURA. Yes? (*The record starts to play, something soft and melodic. It plays through to the end of the act.*)

TOM. Why are you so nice to me?

LAURA. Why . . . I . . .

TOM. You're not this way to the rest of the fellows.

LAURA. No, I know I'm not. Do you mind my being nice to you?

TOM (*shakes his head, "no"*). I just wondered why.

LAURA (*in a perfectly open way*). I guess, Tom . . . I guess it's because I like you.

TOM. No one else seems to. Why do you?

LAURA. I don't know . . . I . . .

TOM. Is it *because* no one else likes me? Is it just pity?

LAURA. No, Tom, of course not . . . It's, well . . . it's because you've been very nice to me . . . very considerate. It wasn't easy for me, you know, coming into a school, my first year. You seemed to sense that. I don't know, we just seem to have hit it off. (*She smiles at him.*)

TOM. Mr. Reynolds knows you like me.

LAURA. I suppose so. I haven't kept it a secret.

TOM. Is that why he hates me so?

LAURA. I don't think he hates you.

TOM. Yes, he hates me. Why lie? I think everyone here hates me but you. But they won't.

LAURA. Of course they won't.

TOM. He hates me because he made a flop with me. I know all about it. My father put me in this house when I first came here, and when he left me he said to your husband, "Make a man out of him." He's failed, and he's mad, and then you come along, and were nice to me . . . out of pity.

LAURA. No, Tom, not pity. I'm too selfish a woman to like you just out of pity.

TOM (*he has worked himself up into a state of confusion, and anger, and desperation*). There's so much I . . . there's so much I don't understand.

LAURA (*reaches out and touches his arm*). Tom, don't go out tonight.

TOM. I've got to. That's one thing that's clear. I've got to!

LAURA (*holds up her arms for dancing*). Won't you let me teach you how to dance?

TOM (*suddenly and impulsively he throws his arms around her, and kisses her passionately, awkwardly, and then in embarrassment he buries his head in her shoulder*). Oh, God . . . God.

LAURA. Tom . . . Tom . . . (TOM *raises his face and looks at her, and would kiss her again.*) No, Tom . . . No, I . . . (*At the first "No," TOM breaks from her and runs out the door halfway up the stairs. Calling)* Tom! . . . Tom! (TOM *stops at the sound of her voice and turns around and looks down the stairs.* LAURA *moves to the open door.)* Tom, I . . . (*The front door opens and two of the mountain-climbing boys,* PHIL *and* PAUL *come in, with their packs.)*

PHIL (*seeing* TOM *poised on the stairs).* What the hell are you doing? (TOM *just looks at him.)* What's the matter with you? (*He goes on up the stairs.)*

TOM. What are you doing back?

PAUL. The whole bunch is back. Who wants to go mountain climbing in the rain?

BILL (*outside his study door).* Say, any of you fellows want to go across the street for something to eat when you get changed, go ahead. (PHIL *and* PAUL *go up the stairs past* TOM. BILL *goes into his own room, leaving door open.)* Hi. (*He takes off his equipment and puts it on the floor.)*

LAURA (*has been standing motionless where* TOM *has left her).* Hello.

BILL (*comes to her and kisses her on the cheek).* One lousy week end a year we get to go climbing and it rains. (*Throws the rest of his stuff down.)* The fellows are damned disappointed.

LAURA (*hardly paying any attention to him).* That's too bad.

BILL (*going up to alcove).* I think they wanted me to invite them down for a feed. But I didn't want to. I thought we'd be alone. Okay? (*He looks across at her.)*

LAURA (*she is listening for footsteps outside).* Sure. (BILL *goes out through alcove.* LAURA *stoops and picks up the raincoat which* TOM *has dropped and hides it in the cabinet by the fireplace.)*

BILL (*appears in door momentarily wiping his hands with towel).* Boy it really rained. (*He disappears again.* LAURA *sadly goes to the door and slowly and gently closes it. When she is finished, she leans against the door, listening, hoping against hope that* TOM *will go upstairs. When* TOM *sees the door close, he stands there for a moment, then turns his coat collar up and goes down the hall and out. Off stage as* TOM *starts to go down the hall)* We never made it to the timberline. The rain started to come down. Another hour or so and we would have got to the hut and spent the night, but the fellows wouldn't hear of it . . . (*The door slams.*

LAURA *turns away from the study door in despair. Still off stage)* What was that?

LAURA. Nothing . . . Nothing at all.

BILL (*enters and gets pipe from mantelpiece).* Good to get out, though. Makes you feel alive. Think I'll go out again next Saturday, alone. Won't be bothered by the fellows wanting to turn back. (*He has settled down in the chair intended for* TOM. *The school bells start to ring nine.* BILL *reaches out his hand for* LAURA. *Standing by the door, she looks at his outstretched hand, as the lights fade, and*

THE CURTAIN FALLS

ACT THREE

The time is late the next afternoon.

As the curtain rises, TOM *is in his room. His door is shut and bolted. He is lying on his back on the bed, staring up at the ceiling.*

———

RALPH (*he is at the phone).* Hello, Mary . . . Ralph . . . Yeah, I just wanted you to know I'd be a little delayed picking you up . . . Yeah . . . everyone was taking a shower over here, and there's only one shower for eight guys . . . No it's not the same place as last night . . . The tea dance is at the Inn . . . (*He suddenly looks very uncomfortable.)* Look, I'll tell you when I see you . . . Okay . . . (*Almost whispers it.)* I love you . . . (STEVE, RALPH'S *sidekick, comes running in from the outside. He's all dressed up and he's got something to tell.)* Yeah, Mary. Well, I can't say it over again . . . Didn't you hear me the first time? (*Loud so she'll hear it)* Hi, Steve.

STEVE. Come on, get off. I got something to tell you.

RALPH. Mary—Mary, I'll get there faster if I stop talking now. Okay? Okay. See you a little after four. (*He hangs up.)* What the hell's the matter with you?

STEVE. Have you seen Tom?

RALPH. No.

STEVE. You know what the hell he did last night?

RALPH. What?

STEVE. He went and saw Ellie.

RALPH. Who are you bulling?

STEVE. No, honest. Ellie told Jackson over at the kitchen. Everybody knows now.

RALPH. What did he want to go and do a thing like that for?

STEVE. But wait a minute. You haven't heard the half of it.

RALPH. Listen, I gotta get dressed. (*Starts upstairs.*)

STEVE (*on the way up the stairs*). The way Ellie tells it, he went there, all the hell dressed up like he was going to the dance, and . . . (*They disappear up the stairs.* BILL *after a moment comes in the hall, and goes quickly up the stairs. He goes right into* AL *and* TOM's *main room without knocking. We then hear him try the handle of* TOM's *bedroom door.* TOM *looks at the door defiantly and sullenly.*)

'BILL (*knocks sharply*). Tom! (*Rattles door some more.*) Tom, this is Mr. Reynolds. Let me in.

TOM. I don't want to see anyone.

BILL. You've got to see me. Come on. Open up! I've got to talk to the Dean at four, and I want to speak to you first.

TOM. There's nothing to say.

BILL. I can break the door down. Then your father would have to pay for a new door. Do you want that? Are you afraid to see me? (TOM *after a moment, goes to the door and pulls back the bolt.* BILL *comes in quickly.*) Well. (TOM *goes back and sits on the bed. Doesn't look at* BILL.) Now I've got to have the full story. All the details so that when I see the Dean . . .

TOM. You've got the full story. What the the hell do you want?

BILL. We don't seem to have the full story.

TOM. When the school cops brought me in last night they told you I was with Ellie Martin.

BILL. That's just it. It seems you weren't *with* her.

TOM (*after a moment*). What do you mean?

BILL. You weren't *with* her. You couldn't be *with* her. Do you understand what I mean?

TOM (*trying to brave it out*). Who says so?

BILL. She says so. And she ought to know. (TOM *turns away.*) She says that you couldn't . . . and that you jumped up and grabbed a knife in her kitchen and tried to kill yourself . . . and she had to fight with you and that's what attracted the school cops.

TOM. What difference does it make?

BILL. I just wanted the record to be straight. You'll undoubtedly be expelled, no matter what . . . but I wanted the record straight.

TOM (*turning on him*). You couldn't have stood it, could you, if I'd proved you wrong?

BILL. Where do you get off talking like that to a master?

TOM. You'd made up your mind long ago, and it would have killed you if I'd proved you wrong.

BILL. Talking like that isn't going to help you any.

TOM. Nothing's going to help. I'm gonna be kicked out, and then you're gonna be happy.

BILL. I'm not going to be happy. I'm going to be very sorry . . . sorry for your father.

TOM. All right, now you know. Go on, spread the news. How can you wait?

BILL. I won't tell anyone . . . but the Dean, of course.

TOM. And my father . . .

BILL. Perhaps . . .

TOM (*after a long pause*). And Mrs. Reynolds.

BILL (*looks at* TOM). Yes. I think she ought to know. (*He turns and leaves the room. Goes through the sitting room and up the stairs, calling "Ralph."* TOM *closes the door and locks it, goes and sits down in the chair.*)

LAURA (*as* BILL *goes upstairs to* RALPH, *she comes into the master's study. She is wearing a wool suit. She goes to the cupboard and brings out* TOM's *raincoat. She moves with it to the door. There is a knock. She opens the door*). Oh, hello, Mr. Lee.

HERB (*coming in, he seems for some reason rather pleased*). Hello, Laura.

LAURA. Bill isn't in just now, though I'm expecting him any moment.

HERB. My train was twenty minutes late. I was afraid I'd missed him. We have an appointment with the Dean in a few minutes . . .

LAURA (*is coolly polite*). Oh, I see.

HERB. Have I done something to displease you, Laura? You seem a little . . . (HERB *shrugs and makes a gesture with his hands meaning cool.*)

LAURA. I'm sorry. Forgive me. Won't you sit down?

HERB. I remember that you were displeased at my leaving Tom in school a week ago. Well, you see I was right in a sense. Though, perhaps being a lady you wouldn't understand.

LAURA. I'm not sure that I do.

HERB. Well, now, look here. If I had taken Tom out of school after that scandal with Mr. . . . uh . . . what was his name?

LAURA. Mr. Harris.

HERB. Yes. If I'd taken Tom out then, he would have been marked for the rest of his life.

LAURA. You know that Tom will be expelled, of course.

HERB. Yes, but the circumstances are so much more normal.

LAURA (*after looking at him a moment*). I think, Mr. Lee, I'm not quite sure, but I think, in a sense, you're proud of Tom.

HERB. Well.

LAURA. Probably for the first time you're proud of him because the school police found him out of bounds with a . . .

HERB. I shouldn't have expected you to understand. Bill will see what I mean.

(BILL *starts down the stairs.*)

LAURA. Yes. He probably will.

(BILL *comes in the room.*)

HERB. Bill.

BILL. Hello, Herb.

(HERB *looks from* LAURA *to* BILL. *Notices the coldness between them.*)

BILL. I was just seeing Tom.

HERB. Yes. I intend to go up after we've seen the Dean. How is he?

BILL. All right.

HERB (*expansive*). Sitting around telling the boys all about it.

BILL. No, he's in his room alone. The others are going to the tea dance at the Inn. Laura . . . (*Sees* LAURA *is leaving the room.*) Oh, Laura, I wish you'd stay.

(LAURA *takes one step back into the room.*)

HERB. I was telling your wife here, trying to make her understand the male point of view on this matter. I mean, how being kicked out for a thing like this, while not exactly desirable, is still not so serious. It's sort of one of the calculated risks of being a man. (*He smiles at his way of putting it.*)

BILL (*preparing to tell* HERB). Herb?

HERB. Yes, Bill. I mean, you agree with me on that, don't you?

BILL. Yes, Herb, only the situation is not exactly as it was reported to you over the phone. It's true that Tom went to this girl Ellie's place, and it's true that he went for the usual purpose. However . . . however, it didn't work out that way.

HERB. What do you mean?

BILL. Nothing happened.

HERB. You mean she . . . she wouldn't have him?

BILL. I mean, Tom . . . I don't know . . . he didn't go through with it. He couldn't. (*He looks at* LAURA.) It's true. The girl says so. And when it didn't work, he tried to kill himself with a knife in the kitchen, and she struggled with him, and that brought the school cops, and that's that. (LAURA *turns away, shocked and moved.* MR. LEE *sits down in a chair bewildered.*) I'm sorry, Herb. Of course the fact that he was with Ellie at her place is enough to get him expelled.

HERB. Does everyone know this?

BILL. Well, Ellie talks. She's got no shame . . . and this is apparently something to talk about.

LAURA (*to* MR. LEE). Do you still think it will make a good smoking-car story?

BILL. What do you mean?

HERB. Why did he do it? Before, maybe he could talk it down, but to go do a thing like this and leave no doubts.

LAURA. In whose mind?

BILL. Laura, please.

LAURA (*angry*). You asked me to stay.

BILL (*flaring back at her*). Well, now you've heard. We won't keep you.

LAURA (*knowing without asking*). Why did you want me to hear?

BILL (*going to her*). I wanted you to know the facts. That's all. The whole story.

(LAURA *stands in the alcove.*)

HERB. Bill, Bill! Maybe there's some way of getting this girl so she wouldn't spread the story.

BILL. I'm afraid it's too late for that.

HERB. I don't know. Some things don't make any sense. What am I going to do now?

LAURA (*re-entering*). Mr. Lee, please don't go on drawing the wrong conclusions!

HERB. I'm drawing no conclusions. This sort of thing can happen to a normal boy. But it's what the others will think . . . Added to the Harris business. And that's all that's important. What they'll think.

LAURA. Isn't it important what Tom thinks?

BILL. Herb, we'd better be getting on over to the Dean's . . .

HERB (*indicating upstairs*). Is he in his room?

BILL. Yes.

HERB. Packing?

BILL. No.

HERB. I told him to come to you to talk things over. Did he?

BILL. No.

HERB. What am I going to say to him now?

BILL. We're expected at four.

HERB. I know. But I've got to go up . . . Maybe I should have left him with his mother. She might have known what to do, what to say . . . (*He starts out.*) You want to come along with me?

BILL (*moving to hall*). All right.

LAURA (*serious*). Bill, I'd like to talk with you.

BILL. I'll be back.

(*Goes with* HERB *to the landing.* LAURA *exits, taking off her jacket.*)

HERB. Maybe I ought to do this alone.

BILL. He's probably locked in his bedroom.

(HERB *goes up the stairs and inside the study.* BILL *stays in the hall.* TOM, *as he hears his father knocking on the bedroom door, stiffens.* HERB *tries the door handle.*)

HERB (*off, in the study*). Tom . . . Tom . . . it's Dad. (TOM *gets up, but just stands there.*) Tom, are you asleep? (*After a few moments, he reappears on the landing. He is deeply hurt that his son wouldn't speak to him.*) I think he's asleep.

BILL (*making a move to go in and get* TOM). He can't be . . .

HERB (*stops*). Yes, I think he is. He was always a sound sleeper. We used to have to drag him out of bed when he was a kid.

BILL. But he should see you.

HERB. It'll be better later, anyhow. (*He starts down the stairs, troubled, puzzled.*)

BILL. I'll go right with you, Herb. (*They re-enter the study, and* BILL *goes out through the alcove.* HERB *stays in the master's study.*)

TOM (*when his father is downstairs, he opens his bedroom door and faintly calls*). Dad?

(HERB *looks up, thinking he's heard something but then figures it must have been something else.* RALPH, STEVE *and* PHIL *come crashing down the stairs, dressed for the tea dance, ad libbing comments about the girls at the dance.* TOM *closes his door. When they have gone, he opens it again and calls "Dad" faintly. When there is no response, he closes the door, and goes and lies on the bed.*)

BILL (*re-entering*). Laura, I'm going to the Dean's now with Herb. I'm playing squash with the headmaster at five. So I'll see you at the dining room at six-thirty.

LAURA (*entering after him*). I wish you'd come back here after.

BILL. Laura, I can't.

LAURA. Bill, I wish you would.

BILL (*sees that there is some strange determination in* LAURA's *face*). Herb, I'll be with you in a minute. Why don't you walk along?

HERB. All right . . . Good-by, Laura. See you again.

BILL. You'll see her in a couple of days at the reunion.

HERB. I may not be coming up for it now . . . Maybe I will. I don't know. I'll be walking along. Good-by, Laura. Tell Tom I tried to see him. (*He goes out.*)

BILL. Now, Laura, what's the matter? I've got to get to the Dean's rooms to discuss this matter.

LAURA. Yes, of course. But first I'd like to discuss the boys who made him do this . . . the men and boys who made him do this.

BILL. No one made him do anything.

LAURA. Is there to be no blame, no punishment for the boys and men who taunted him into doing this? What if he had succeeded in killing himself? What then?

BILL. You're being entirely too emotional about this.

LAURA. If he had succeeded in killing himself in Ellie's rooms wouldn't you have felt some guilt?

BILL. I?

LAURA. Yes, you.

BILL. I wish you'd look at the facts and not be so emotional about this.

LAURA. The facts! What facts! an innocent boy goes swimming with an instructor . . . an instructor whom he likes because this instructor is one of the few who encourage him, who don't ride him . . . And because he's an off-horse, you and the rest of them are only too glad to put two and two together and get a false answer . . . anything which will let you go on and persecute a boy whom you basically don't like. If it had happened with Al or anybody else, you would have done nothing.

BILL. It would have been an entirely different matter. You can't escape from what you are . . . your character. Why do they spend so much time in the law courts on character witnesses? To prove this was the kind of man who could or couldn't commit such and such a crime.

LAURA. I resent this judgment by prejudice. He's not like me, therefore, he is capable of all possible crimes. He's not one of us . . . a member of the tribe!

BILL. Now look, Laura, I know this is a shock to you, because you were fond of this boy. But you did all you could for him, more than anyone would expect. After all, your responsibility doesn't go beyond—

LAURA. I know. Doesn't go beyond giving him tea and sympathy on Sunday afternoons. Well, I want to tell you something. It's going to shock you . . . but I'm going to tell you.

BILL. Laura, it's late.

LAURA. Last night I knew what Tom had in mind to do. I heard him making the date with Ellie on the phone.

BILL. And you didn't stop him? Then you're the one responsible.

LAURA. Yes, I am responsible, but not as you think. I did try to stop him, but not by locking him in his room, or calling the school police. I tried to stop him by being nice to him, by being affectionate. By showing him that he was liked . . . yes, even loved. I knew what he was going to do . . . and why he was going to do it. He had to prove to you bullies that he was a man, and he was going to prove it with Ellie Martin. Well . . . last night . . . last night, I wished he had proved it with me.

BILL. What in Christ's name are you saying?

LAURA. Yes, I shock you. I shock myself. But you are right. I am responsible here. I know what I should have done. I knew it then. My heart cried out for this boy in his misery . . . a misery imposed by my husband. And I wanted to help him as one human being to another . . . and I failed. At the last moment, I sent him away . . . sent him to . . .

BILL. You mean you managed to overcome your exaggerated sense of pity.

LAURA. No, it was not just pity. My heart in its loneliness . . . Yes, I've been lonely here, miserably lonely . . . and my heart in its loneliness cried out for this boy . . . cried out for the comfort he could give me too.

BILL. You don't know what you're saying.

LAURA. But I was a good woman. Good in what sense of the word? Good to whom . . . and for whom?

BILL. Laura, we'll discuss this, if we must, later on . . .

LAURA. Bill! There'll be no later on. I'm leaving you.

BILL. Over this thing?

LAURA (*after a moment*). Yes, this *thing* and all the other *things* in our marriage.

BILL. For God's sake, Laura, what are you talking about?

LAURA. I'm talking about love and honor and manliness, and tenderness, and persecution. I'm talking about a lot. You haven't understood any of it.

BILL. Laura, you can't leave over a thing like this. You know what it means.

LAURA. I wouldn't worry too much about it. When I'm gone, it will probably be agreed by all that I was an off-horse too, and didn't really belong to the clan, and it's good riddance.

BILL. And you're doing this . . . all because of this . . . this fairy?

LAURA (*after a moment*). This boy, Bill . . . this boy is more of a man than you are.

BILL. Sure. Ask Ellie.

LAURA. Because it was distasteful for him. Because for him there has to be love. He's more of a man than you are.

BILL. Yes, sure.

LAURA. Manliness is not all swagger and swearing and mountain climbing. Manliness is also tenderness, gentleness, consideration. You men think you can decide on who is a man, when only a woman can really know.

BILL. Ellie's a woman. Ask Ellie.

LAURA. I don't need to ask anyone.

BILL. What do you know about a man? Married first to that boy . . . again, a pitiable boy . . . You want to mother a boy, not love a man. That's why you never really loved me. Because I was not a boy you could mother.

LAURA. You're quite wrong about my not loving you. I did love you. But not just for your outward show of manliness, but because you needed me . . . For one unguarded moment you let me know you needed me, and I have tried to find that moment again the year we've been married . . . Why did you marry me, Bill? In God's name, why?

BILL. Because I loved you. Why else?

LAURA. You've resented me . . . almost from the day you married me, you've resented me. You never wanted to marry really . . . Did they kid you into it? Does a would-be headmaster have to be married? Or what was it, Bill? You would have been far happier going off on your jaunts with the boys, having them to your rooms for feeds and bull sessions . . .

BILL. That's part of being a master.

LAURA. Other masters and their wives do not take two boys always with them whenever they go away on vacations or week ends.

BILL. They are boys without privileges.

LAURA. And I became a wife without privileges.

BILL. You became a wife . . . (*He stops.*)

LAURA. Yes?

BILL. You did *not* become a wife.

LAURA. I know. I know I failed you. In some terrible way I've failed you.

BILL. You were more interested in mothering that fairy up there than in being my wife.

LAURA. But you wouldn't let me, Bill. You wouldn't let me.

BILL (*grabbing her by the shoulders*). What do you mean I wouldn't let you?

LAURA (*quietly, almost afraid to say it*). Did it ever occur to you that you persecute in Tom, that boy up there, you persecute in him the thing you fear in yourself? (BILL *looks at her for a long moment of hatred. She has hit close to the truth he has never let himself be conscious of. There is a moment when he might hurt her, but then he draws away, still staring at her. He backs away, slowly, and then turns to the door.*) Bill!

BILL (*not looking at her*). I hope you will be gone when I come back from dinner.

LAURA (*quietly*). I will be . . . (*Going towards him*) Oh, Bill, I'm sorry. I shouldn't have said that . . . it was cruel.

(*She reaches for him as he goes out the door.*) This was the weakness you cried out for me to save you from, wasn't it . . . And I have tried. (*He is gone.*) I have tried. (*Slowly she turns back into the room and looks at it.*) I did try. (*For a few moments she stands stunned and tired from her outburst. Then she moves slowly to* TOM's *raincoat, picks it up and turns and goes out of the room and to the stair-landing. She goes to the boys' study door and knocks.*) Tom. (*She opens it and goes in out of sight. At* TOM's *door, she calls again.*) Tom. (TOM *turns his head slightly and listens.* LAURA *opens* TOM's *door and come in.*) Oh, I'm sorry. May I come in? (*She sees she's not going to get an answer from him, so she goes in.*) I brought back your raincoat. You left it last night. (*She puts it on chair. She looks at him.*) This is a nice room . . . I've never seen it before . . . As a matter of fact I've never been up here in this part of the house. (*Still getting no response, she goes on.* TOM *slowly turns and looks at her back, while she is examining something on the walls. She turns, speaking.*) It's very cozy. It's really quite . . . (*She stops when she sees he has turned around looking at her.*) Hello.

TOM (*barely audible*). Hello.

LAURA. Do you mind my being here?

TOM. You're not supposed to be.

LAURA. I know. But everyone's out, and will be for some time . . . I wanted to return your raincoat.

TOM. Thank you. (*After a pause he sits up on the bed, his back to her.*) I didn't think you'd ever want to see me again.

LAURA. Why not?

TOM. After last night. I'm sorry about what happened downstairs.

LAURA (*she looks at him awhile, then*). I'm not.

TOM (*looks at her. Can't quite make it out*). You've heard everything I suppose.

LAURA. Yes.

TOM. Everything?

LAURA. Everything.

TOM. I knew your husband would be anxious to give you the details.

LAURA. He did. (*She stands there quietly looking down at the boy.*)

TOM. So now you know too.

LAURA. What?

TOM. That everything they said about me is true.

LAURA. Tom!

TOM. Well, it is, isn't it?

LAURA. Tom?

TOM. I'm no man. Ellie knows it. Everybody knows it. It seems everybody knew it, except me. And now I know it.

LAURA (*moves towards him*). Tom . . . Tom . . . dear. (TOM *turns away from her.*) You don't think that just because . . .

TOM. What else am I to think?

LAURA (*very gently*). Tom, that didn't work because you didn't believe in it . . . in such a test.

TOM (*with great difficulty*). I touched her, and there was nothing.

LAURA. You aren't in love with Ellie.

TOM. That's not supposed to matter.

LAURA. But it does.

TOM. I wish they'd let me kill myself.

LAURA. Tom, look at me. (TOM *shakes his head.*) Tom, last night you kissed me.

TOM. Jesus!

LAURA. Why did you kiss me?

TOM (*turns suddenly*). And it made you sick, didn't it? Didn't it? (*Turns away from her again.*)

LAURA. How can you think such a thing?

TOM. You sent me away . . . you . . . Anyway, when you heard this morning it must have made you sick.

LAURA (*sits on the edge of bed*). Tom, I'm going to tell you something. (TOM *won't turn.*) Tom? (*He still won't turn.*) It was the nicest kiss I've ever had . . . from anybody. (TOM *slowly turns and looks at her.*) Tom, I came to say goodby. (TOM *shakes his head, looking at her.*) I'm going away . . . I'll probably never see you again. I'm leaving Bill. (TOM *knits his brows, questioning.*) For a lot of reasons . . . one of them, what he's done to you. But before I left, I wanted you to know, for your own comfort, you're more of a man now than he ever was or will be. And one day you'll meet a girl, and it will be right. (TOM *turns away in disbelief.*) Tom, believe me.

TOM. I wish I could. But a person knows . . . knows inside. Jesus, do you think after last night I'd ever . . . (*He stops. After a moment, he smiles at her.*) But

thanks . . . thanks a lot. (*He closes his eyes.* LAURA *looks at him a long time. Her face shows the great compassion and tenderness she feels for this miserable boy. After some time, she gets up and goes out the door. A moment later she appears in the hall door. She pauses for a moment, then reaches out and closes it, and stays inside.*

(TOM, *when he hears the door close, his eyes open. He sees she has left his bedroom. Then in complete misery, he lies down on the bed, like a wounded animal, his head at the foot of the bed.*

(LAURA *in a few moments appears in the bedroom doorway. She stands there, and then comes in, always looking at the slender figure of the boy on the bed. She closes the bedroom door.*

(TOM *hears the sound and looks around. When he sees she has come back, he turns around slowly, wonderingly, and lies on his back, watching her.*

(LAURA *seeing a bolt on the door, slides it to. Then she stands looking at* TOM, *her hand at her neck. With a slight and delicate movement, she unbuttons the top button of her blouse, and moves towards* TOM. *When she gets alongside the bed, she reaches out her hand, still keeping one hand at her blouse.* TOM *makes no move. Just watches her.*

(LAURA *makes a little move with the outstretched hand, asking for his hand.* TOM *slowly moves his hand to hers.*)

LAURA (*stands there holding his hand and smiling gently at him. Then she sits and looks down at the boy, and after a moment, barely audible*). And now . . . nothing?

(TOM's *other hand comes up and with both his hands he brings her hand to his lips.*)

LAURA (*smiles tenderly at this gesture, and after a moment*). Years from now . . . when you talk about this . . . and you will . . . be kind. (*Gently she brings the boy's hands toward her opened blouse, as the lights slowly dim out . . . and . . .*

THE CURTAIN FALLS

THE TEAHOUSE
OF THE AUGUST MOON

John Patrick

(adapted from the novel by Vern Sneider)

The Teahouse of the August Moon opened at the Martin Beck Theatre in New York City on October 15, 1953. It was produced by Maurice Evans in association with George Schaefer and was directed by Robert Lewis. The production was designed by Peter Larkin with costumes by Noel Taylor. The cast, in order of appearance, was as follows:

SAKINI . . . . David Wayne
SERGEANT GREGOVICH   Harry Jackson
COL. WAINWRIGHT PURDY III   Paul Ford
CAPTAIN FISBY . . . . .John Forsythe
OLD WOMAN . . . . Naoe Kondo
OLD WOMAN'S DAUGHTER . . Mara Kim
THE DAUGHTER'S CHILDREN . . . . . Moy
Moy Thom, Joyce Chen
and Kenneth Wong
LADY ASTOR . . . . Saki
ANCIENT MAN . . . . Kame Ishikawa
MR. HOKAIDA . . . . .Chuck Morgan
MR. OMURA . . . . Kuraji Scida
MR. SUMATA . . . . Kaie Deei

MR. SUMATA'S FATHER   Kikuo Hiromura
MR. SEIKO . . . . Haim Winant
MISS HIGA JIGA . . . . Shizu Moriya
MR. KEORA . . . . .Yuki Shimoda
MR. OSHIRA . . . . William Hansen
VILLAGERS . . . Jerry Fujikawa, Frank
Ogawa, Richard Akagi, Laurence
Kim and Norman Chi
LADIES' LEAGUE FOR DEMOCRATIC ACTION
Vivian Thom, Naoe Kondo, Mary
Ann Reeve and Mara Kim
LOTUS BLOSSOM . . . . Mariko Niki
CAPTAIN MC LEAN . . . . . . .Larry Gates

ACT ONE. *Scene One:* Okinawa. Colonel Purdy's Office, GHQ. *Scene Two:* Outside Captain Fisby's Quarters, GHQ. *Scene Three:* Tobiki Village.

ACT TWO. *Scene One:* Tobiki Village. *Scene Two:* Colonel Purdy's Office, GHQ. *Scene Three:* Captain Fisby's Office, Tobiki. *Scene Four:* Tobiki Village.

ACT THREE. *Scene One:* The Teahouse of the August Moon. *Scene Two:* Captain Fisby's Office, Tobiki. *Scene Three:* The Teahouse of the August Moon.

Copyright 1952, by John Patrick.

The Teahouse of the August Moon is the sole property of the author and is fully protected by copyright. It may not be acted either by professionals or by amateurs without written consent. Public readings and radio or television broadcasts are likewise forbidden. All inquiries concerning rights including stock and amateur rights should be addressed to the author's agent, Miss Miriam Howell, 579 Fifth Avenue, New York 17, N. Y.

(Words from the song "Deep in the Heart of Texas" by June Hershey and Don Swander are reprinted by permission of Melody Lane Publications, Inc. The selection is owned and controlled for the territory of Australasia by Allan & Co. Pty. Ltd., Melbourne, Australia. Copyright, 1941.)

The topicality of *The Teahouse of the August Moon* was both an advantage and a disadvantage. It was a factor in the popularity of the play in New York and elsewhere. But since the political situation after World War II was everywhere unstable, the amity of the Okinawans and the American government of occupation celebrated in the play (and in the novel by Vern Sneider upon which it is based) was subjected to severe strain. Political rumblings began to shake Okinawa a few years after the play was successfully produced on Broadway, where it harvested such plums of critical approval as the New York Drama Critics award and the Pulitzer Prize in 1954. Discontent with the American occupation of Okinawa and the other Ryukyu Islands and agitation for their return to Japan had been expressed for some time before President Eisenhower's visit to the island. But his arrival there in 1960 created a particularly embarrassing climax in the history of our foreign good-will policy. Despite the elaborate precautions against violence taken by the native authorities, the President of the United States was greeted with hostile demonstrations. "When the President reached the center of town," reads the *New York Times* report of June 20, 1960, "he was confronted with about 1500 snake-dancing, shouting demonstrators. They chanted 'Go home, go home!' in English and other slogans in Japanese." The *Times* called the demonstrations only a small index of widespread disaffection among the natives and their desire to return to Japanese control, which would, it was alleged, reduce taxes, finance public improvements,* and secure social benefits for the inhabitants. Under these circumstances, it would be difficult to return to *The Teahouse of the August Moon* with the optimism that greeted the original production. It is fortunate, therefore, that the charm and liveliness of Mr. Patrick do not depend upon the unreliable international situation. The New York reviewers who called it an enchanting and amusing stage piece did not have an eye on diplomatic relations. Brooks Atkinson of the *Times* was especially sagacious in his review of the Broadway opening. Although he called the play "completely captivating," he described it as "a piece of exotic make-believe in a style as intimate as fairy-story." Mr. Atkinson declared that what the dramatist said was "interesting" but "how he says it is imaginative and original." This was certainly a just comment in so far as it pertained to the beautifully staged and designed New York production, which had David Wayne in the principal role.

John Patrick, born in 1907, a native of Carmel, California, had already won distinction as a playwright and a screenwriter when he undertook to dramatize Vern Sneider's book. Educated at Columbia and Harvard and subsequently a successful writer of radio plays for Helen Hayes, he became a "produced playwright" in 1935 with *Hell Freezes Over*, and the author of a greatly admired, if not particularly popular, drama, *The Willow and I*, in 1942. World War II, in which he participated as a captain in the American Field Service, inspired his next play, *The Hasty Heart* (1945), which was a warm and understanding character-drama as well as an admirable group picture of soldiers hospitalized behind the front lines. This play was followed by a distinctly moving historical drama, *The Story of Mary Surratt*, in which Mr. Patrick vindicated Mrs. Surratt, who was hanged for her alleged part in the assassination of Abraham Lincoln. Mr. Patrick then supplied the not altogether grateful New York public with two light comedies. *The Curious Savage* (1950) revolved

---

* In fairness to the United States, I would call attention to the following paragraphs from a March 19, 1961, *New York Times* report:

"In spite of Japan's growing economic interest in the Ryukyus, the United States contributes most of the aid given to the island. Aid given by the United States last year was estimated at $3,000,000.

"United States projects in 1960 included construction of a new electric plant, establishment of a free-trade zone, organization of unions for Ryukyu military employees, development of water systems, roads, sea walls and a port on Ishigaki Island, in the southern Ryukyus, and land reclamation.

"The United States aid also built cultural centers in different areas, a sixth radio station and a third television station on Okinawa."

around an eccentric widow, played by Lillian Gish, who invests her wealth in a so-called Happiness Fund intended to help people do the foolish things they have always wanted to do. *Lo and Behold* was a fantastic play concerning a Nobel Prize winner who dies of willful overeating and finds himself comically harassed by an odd collection of ghosts in the other world. If *The Teahouse of the August Moon* is expertly written, the credit belongs equally to the dramatist's genial sympathies and buoyant craftsmanship.

ACT ONE
Scene One

Directly behind the house curtain is a second curtain consisting of four panels of split bamboo. Each of these sections can be raised and lowered individually.

AT RISE: *As the house lights dim, the Oriental strains from a stringed instrument can be heard playing softly in the background. A pool of light picks up* SAKINI *standing framed against the bamboo backing. He wears a pair of tattered shorts and a native shirt. His shoes, the gift of a G.I., are several sizes too large. His socks are also too large and hang in wrinkles over his ankles. He is an Okinawan who might be any age between thirty and sixty. In repose his face betrays age, but the illusion is shattered quickly by his smile of childlike candor.*

With hands together in prayer-like supplication, he walks down to the footlights and bows to the audience center in solemn ritual. Then he bows from the waist—to the left and to the right.

Straightening up, he examines the audience seated before him with open curiosity. The music ceases. As it ceases, SAKINI *begins to work his jaws vigorously.*

SAKINI
Tootie-fruitie.
(He takes the gum from his mouth and, wrapping it carefully in a piece of paper, puts it in a matchbox and restores it to a pocket in his shirt.)
Most generous gift of American sergeant.
(He resumes his original posture of dignity.)
Lovely ladies, kind gentlemen:
Please to introduce myself.
Sakini by name.
Interpreter by profession.
Education by ancient dictionary.
Okinawan by whim of gods.
History of Okinawa reveal distinguished record of conquerors.
We have honor to be subjugated in fourteenth century by Chinese pirates.
In sixteenth century by English missionaries.
In eighteenth century by Japanese war lords.
And in twentieth century by American Marines.
Okinawa very fortunate.
Culture brought to us. . . . Not have to leave home for it.
Learn many things.
Most important that rest of world not like Okinawa.
World filled with delightful variation.
Illustration.
In Okinawa . . . no locks on doors.
Bad manners not to trust neighbors.
In America . . . lock and key big industry.
Conclusion?
Bad manners good business.
In Okinawa . . . wash self in public bath with nude lady quite proper.
Picture of nude lady in private home . . . quite improper.
In America . . . statue of nude lady in park win prize.
But nude lady in flesh in park win penalty.
Conclusion?
Pornography question of geography.
But Okinawans most eager to be educated by conquerors.
Deep desire to improve friction.
Not easy to learn.
Sometimes painful.
But pain makes man think.
Thought makes man wise.
Wisdom makes life endurable.
So . . .
(He crosses back to the left of the first of the panels.)
We tell little story to demonstrate splendid example of benevolent assimilation of democracy by Okinawa.
(He claps his hands, signaling the stagehand to raise the first of the four panels. Flush against the curtain is revealed a sign nailed onto a denuded palm stump. It points toward the other side of the stage and reads: COL. WAINRIGHT PURDY III.*)*
Boss by name of Colonel Purdy—Three.
Number three after name indicate he is a son of a son of a son.
(He steps to the next panel and claps again. The screen rolls up revealing a laundry line tied to a second denuded stump. As these panels are raised the background is revealed in sections. It includes a jeep parked against a pile of empty gasoline drums, trees ripped of foliage by recent gunfire—all creating an impression of general destruction. There are several articles of wearing apparel hanging on the laundry line, foremost of which is a pair of khaki pants size forty.)
Colonel Purdy, Three, displays splendid example of cleanliness for native population to follow. But native population cannot follow. Native not *have* two pairs of pants.

(He then claps for the next screen to rise, revealing more of the laundry. To the extreme right is seen the outside of Colonel Purdy's Quonset office. Nailed on the post holding the other end of the line is a sign reading: OFFICERS' LAUNDRY ONLY.*)*

Colonel Purdy put up many signs. This exceedingly civilized. Make it very easy for uncivilized to know what *not* to do. Here laundry of officer not to fraternize with laundry of enlisted man.

(SAKINI now signals for the last panel to be raised, revealing the inside of the hut. Colonel Purdy's vacant desk is beside the door. A sign denotes his proprietorship. Another sign admonishes the visitor to THINK! *The office is small and sparse. A bulletin board for "Daily Orders" hangs on the upstage wall. Against this wall is the desk of Sergeant Gregovich. Behind a sign denoting his rating sits the* SERGEANT. *His posture is frozen— as if awaiting a signal to come to life.* SAKINI *crosses down center to explain to his audience.)*

This gentleman honorable Sergeant Gregovich—assistant to Colonel Purdy. Not son of a son of a son.

(He turns toward the SERGEANT.*)*

Play has begun, Sergeant.

(GREGOVICH now comes to life. He begins to chew his gum vigorously and to look about the office. He rises and crosses down to Colonel Purdy's desk. He gets down on his hands and knees in front of the desk and reaches under it.)

Oh, you know what he is doing? Explanation. Colonel Purdy great student of history. Every month wife of Colonel Purdy send him magazine called *Adventure Magazine*. Cover has picture of pirate with black patch over eye. Everybody try to steal magazine. Colonel hide under desk so he can read first.

(GREGOVICH rises triumphantly with the magazine.)

But Sergeant always find. Smart mouse.

(GREGOVICH returns to his desk and buries himself behind the pages of the magazine. At this point COLONEL PURDY himself enters from the left. As his laundry has indicated, he is a man of proportions. The worries of the world in general and the Army of Occupation in particular weigh heavily on his shoulders. He stops to glance at the nearest official sign. He takes out a small notebook to make an entry. Sakini's presence is not recognized until indicated.)

This gentleman exalted boss—Colonel Purdy, Three. Subject of sovereign American city of Pottawattamie, Michigan.

(COLONEL PURDY hiccups and taps his chest.)

Also subject to indignity of indigestion. Colonel Purdy explain this by saying—

PURDY *(clears his throat and says to himself).* An occupational disorder of the Army of Occupation. *(He taps his chest again and puts the notebook away.)*

SAKINI. Colonel Purdy very wise man. Always hit nail on head. Every morning, look at sky—(COLONEL PURDY *puts his hands on his hips and glances skyward.)* And make prophecy.

PURDY. It's not going to rain today.

SAKINI. And you know what? Not rain. Of course, not rain here this time of year in whole history of Okinawa. But Colonel not make mistake. (COLONEL PURDY *goes down the laundry line and stops to button the top of a pair of shorts.)* Colonel Purdy gentleman of propriety. (PURDY *goes back to count articles of clothing.)* And precision. Always count laundry.

PURDY *(counts aloud).* Un—deux—trois.

SAKINI. Explanation. Army teach Colonel French for invasion of Europe. Then send to Okinawa instead.

PURDY. . . . quatre—cinq—six—sept. *(He beams with satisfaction.)*

SAKINI. Very good. Colonel count in French and not notice one pair shorts missing in Okinawa.

PURDY *(his expression quickly changes).* What? *(He goes down the line and counts again in English.)* One, two, three, four, five, six, seven! *(He inhales deeply for an explosion.)*

SAKINI *(rushes down to the footlights).* Oh—ladies please close ears unless want to hear unladylike oath. *(He puts his hands over his own ears.)*

PURDY *(explodes).* Damitohell! Damitohell! Damitohell!

SAKINI. Now Colonel yell loud for Sakini. But Sakini hide. Pretend to be asleep. *(He promptly curls up on the ground beside the office, with his back to the* COLONEL.*)*

PURDY. Sakini! (SAKINI *snores.* PURDY *strides over to tower above him.)* Sakini!

SAKINI *(rises quickly).* Oh—oh. Good

morning, boss. You sure surprise me.

PURDY. *Where* is the boy that does my laundry!

SAKINI. Bring laundry back and go home to sleep, boss.

PURDY. I want you to find out why my laundry comes back every week with one piece missing!

SAKINI. Gets lost, boss.

PURDY. I *know* it gets lost. What I want to find out is *how* it gets lost.

SAKINI. Very simple. Boy takes laundry to top of mountain stream and throws in water. Then runs down hill fast as dickens to catch laundry at bottom. Sometimes not run fast enough.

PURDY (*heaves a martyr's sigh*). No wonder you people were subjugated by the Japanese. If you're not sleeping you're running away from work. Where is your "get-up-and-go"?

SAKINI. Guess "get-up-and-go" went. (SAKINI *starts to sit on the ground.*)

PURDY. Well, get up and go over to the mess and see if Captain Fisby has arrived. If he has, tell him to report to me at once. Hurry! (*As* SAKINI *starts across the stage* PURDY *looks with annoyance at the G.I. socks that hang down over Sakini's ankles.*) Sakini!

SAKINI (*Stops*). Yes, boss?

PURDY. You're a civilian employee in the pay of the United States Army. And should dress accordingly. *Pull Your Socks Up!*

SAKINI. Yes, boss. (*He leans over and pulls up his socks— not a great improvement.*) Anything else, boss?

PURDY. That will be all. (SAKINI *ambles across the stage so slowly that the* COLONEL *explodes in exasperation.*) Is that as *fast* as you can walk!

SAKINI. Oh no, boss. But if walk any faster— socks fall down. (*As* SAKINI *exits,* COLONEL PURDY *closes his eyes and counts to ten in vehement French.* PURDY *remains arrested in this position.* SAKINI *re-enters downstage. He signals the closing of the panels left, shutting out the* COLONEL.)

SAKINI. Introduction now over. Kindly direct attention to office. (*He leans out toward the footlights and calls across stage.*) Oh, Honorable Sergeant— ready now to continue. (SERGEANT GREGOVICH *again comes to life. He glances out the office door and quickly hides the* Adventure Magazine. *He stands at attention as* COLONEL PURDY *enters.* SAKINI *exits into the wings.*)

GREGOVICH. Good morning, sir.

PURDY. At ease. (COLONEL PURDY *sits down behind his desk and begins searching through the papers on it.*) I'm thinking of getting rid of that interpreter. He doesn't set a good example.

GREGOVICH. We've got to have someone around that speaks the language, sir.

PURDY. You're quite right, Sergeant. You're quite right. It isn't often I make a mistake, but when I do—

GREGOVICH. It's a beaut?

PURDY (*stiffly*). I wasn't going to say that. I was going to say— I admit it.

GREGOVICH. Sorry, sir.

PURDY. We've got a new officer reporting this morning. He's been transferred to us from "Psychological Warfare." (*Benevolently*) I don't suppose you happen to know who *they* are?

GREGOVICH. Aren't they something at the rear of the Rear Echelon?

PURDY. They're just the cream of the Army's geniuses. They're just the brains behind the fighting heart. Every man jack of them has a mind like a steel trap. And we are lucky to be getting one of their officers.

GREGOVICH. I'll watch my step, sir.

PURDY. While we're waiting for Captain Fisby, I want you to make a note of some new signs I want painted.

GREGOVICH (*takes up a pad*). The painter hasn't finished the ones you ordered yesterday, sir.

PURDY. There's only one answer to that. Put on another sign painter. Now. I noticed the men were dancing with each other in the canteen the other night.

GREGOVICH. Yes, sir. (*He writes on his pad.*) "No dancing allowed."

PURDY (*annoyed*). I didn't say that, Gregovich! I don't object to the men dancing. I want them to enjoy themselves. But it doesn't set a good example for the natives to see noncoms dancing with enlisted men. So have a sign posted saying, "Sergeants Are Forbidden to Dance with Privates."

GREGOVICH. Yes, sir.

PURDY. Have another sign put up beside that clear pool of water just below the falls— "For Officers Only."

GREGOVICH. Where will the men bathe, sir?

PURDY. There is another pool just below it they can use.

GREGOVICH. If you'll pardon me, sir— they're not going to like that. They'll be bathing in water the officers have already bathed in.

PURDY: That's a valid objection, Gregovich. We don't want to do anything unreasonable. (*He concentrates for a moment.*) How far is the second pool below the first?

GREGOVICH. About three hundred yards.

PURDY (*satisfied*). Then it's quite all right. Water purifies itself every two hundred feet.

GREGOVICH. Do you think that will satisfy the men, sir?

PURDY. I don't see why it shouldn't. It satisfies science. Well, you might as well take those memos to the sign painter now.

GREGOVICH. Yes, sir.

(*He goes out. As soon as he is gone,* COLONEL PURDY *moves around to the front of his desk and feels under it for his* Adventure Magazine. *When he fails to find it, he kneels down on all fours to peer under the desk.* SAKINI *enters and looks around. He steps over and taps the nearest part of Colonel Purdy— his ample rear end.*)

SAKINI. Sakini here, boss.

PURDY (*glances around indignantly*). Don't *ever* put your finger on an officer!

SAKINI. Not right, boss?

PURDY. No! If you want to announce your presence—knock! (*He peers under the desk again.*) Can't you natives learn anything about custom? (SAKINI *stands unhappily a moment, then leans forward and knocks gently on the* COLONEL. PURDY *rises in wrath.*) What do you think you're doing?

SAKINI. Not know, boss. Do what you ask.

PURDY (*moves behind his desk*). Everything in this Godforsaken country conspires to annoy me. (*He turns to* SAKINI.) Well, where is Captain Fisby?

SAKINI (*points out the door*). He come now. I run ahead. (*He points to his ankles.*) Socks fall down.

(*He then steps back to allow* CAPTAIN FISBY *to enter.* CAPTAIN FISBY *is in his late twenties, nice-looking and rather on the earnest side. He is nervous and eager to make a good impression. He salutes smartly.*)

CAPTAIN FISBY. Captain Fisby reporting, sir.

PURDY (*returns the salute*). Welcome to Team 147, Captain. (*He puts out his hand.*)

FISBY (*shakes hands*). Thank you, sir.

PURDY. I can't tell you how glad I am to have you, Captain. Frankly, we're so desperate for officer personnel I'd be glad to see you even if you had two heads. (SAKINI *breaks into gales of laughter.* PURDY *turns to him icily.*) That will be all, Sakini. You can wait outside.

SAKINI (*bows*). I sit by door. Not sleep! (*He exits.*)

PURDY. Sit down, Captain, sit down. (FISBY *sits facing* PURDY.) Have you unpacked?

FISBY (*proudly*). Yes *sir!* I got in last night and unpacked at once.

PURDY. Well, that's too bad, because you'll have to pack again. I'm sending you to Tobiki at once. We need a man of your caliber up there right away. (*He laughs with forced heartiness.*)

FISBY (*forces a laugh in return*). Thank you.

PURDY. I'm informed, Captain, that you requested this transfer from "Psychological Warfare" to *my* outfit. May I say that I am honored.

FISBY. Well—in all fairness, sir— I think I should tell you . . . the information is only partly true.

PURDY (*pauses*). You *didn't* request this transfer to me?

FISBY. I was *requested* to request it, sir.

PURDY. Oh. (*He blinks to aid his digestion of this information.*) May I ask why?

FISBY. Well, my propaganda to undermine enemy morale always seemed to undermine the staff's morale instead, sir.

PURDY. *How* did you get into "Psychological Warfare" in the *first* place?

FISBY. I had been requested to request a transfer.

PURDY. From what?

FISBY. Paymaster General's office.

PURDY. What was your duty there?

FISBY. I was in charge of the payroll computation machine until— until— (*He flounders unhappily.*)

PURDY. Until *what?*

FISBY. Well, sir, machines have always been my mortal enemies. I don't think they're inanimate at all. I think they're full of malice and ill will. They—

PURDY. I *asked* you what happened, Captain.

FISBY. Well, this computation machine made a mistake of a quarter of a million dollars on the payroll. Unfortunately, the men were paid *before* the mistake was discovered.

PURDY. What did they do to you?

FISBY. For a while I was given a job licking envelopes.

PURDY. Then you asked for a transfer?

FISBY. No, sir, I developed an allergy to glue.

PURDY. How many outfits in this man's army have you been in, Captain?

FISBY. How many are there, sir?

PURDY. Never mind. I admit disappointment but not defeat. I'd thought you were given to me in recognition of my work here. Frankly, I expect to be made a general soon, and I want that star for my wife's crown. Naturally, that's very hush-hush.

FISBY (*nods*). Naturally. Maybe I just wasn't cut out to be a soldier.

PURDY. Captain, none of us was cut out to be a soldier. But we do the job. We adjust. We adapt. We roll with the punch and bring victory home in our teeth. Do you know what *I* was before the war?

FISBY (*hesitates unhappily*). A football coach?

PURDY. I was the Purdy Paper Box Company of Pottawattamie. What did I know about foreigners? But my job is to teach these natives the meaning of democracy, and they're going to learn democracy if I have to shoot every one of them.

FISBY. I'm sure your wife wouldn't want her star that way, sir.

PURDY. What did you do before the war?

FISBY. I was an associate professor at Muncie.

PURDY. What did you teach?

FISBY. The humanities.

PURDY. Captain, you are finally getting a job you're qualified by training to handle— teaching these natives how to act human.

FISBY. The humanities isn't quite that, sir.

PURDY. If you can teach one thing you can teach another. Your job at Tobiki will be to teach the natives democracy and make them self-supporting. Establish some sort of industry up there.

FISBY. Is there a general plan?

PURDY. There is a specific plan. (*He extends a document the size of a telephone book.*) Washington has drawn up full instructions pertaining to the welfare and recovery of these native villages. *This* is Plan B. Consider it your *Bible*, Captain.

FISBY. I'll study it carefully, sir. There might be some questions I'd like to ask you.

PURDY (*points to Plan B*). Washington has anticipated all your questions.

FISBY. But I was thinking—

PURDY. You don't even have to think, Captain. This document relieves you of that responsibility.

FISBY. But in dealing with the natives, sir—

PURDY (*interrupts*). It's all covered in Section Four: "Orienting the Oriental." How is your Luchuan?

FISBY. I don't know, sir. What is it?

PURDY. It's the native dialect. Well, I can see you'll need an interpreter. (*His eyes light up and he slaps his desk.*) I have just the man for you! (*He turns and calls out the door.*) Sakini!

FISBY. I could study the dialect, sir.

PURDY. No need. We won the war. I'll give you my own interpreter.

FISBY. Oh, I wouldn't want to deprive you of—

PURDY. I insist.

(SAKINI *enters. He bows—and then remembers. He leans forward and politely knocks on the desk.*)

SAKINI. Sakini present. Socks up. Not sleeping.

PURDY. Sakini, this is Captain Fisby.

FISBY. Hello, Sakini.

SAKINI (*bows, then turns to* PURDY). We meet already. (*He smiles in comradeship.*) You forget, boss?

PURDY (*covers his face, counts to ten, then looks up*). I am assigning you to Captain Fisby. He's going to take charge of a village at the top of Okinawa—a village called Tobiki.

SAKINI. Oh! Tobiki very nice place, boss. But not at top of Okinawa. At bottom.

PURDY. Don't tell me where the villages under my command are located. I happen to have looked at the map.

SAKINI. So sorry, boss. But I happen to get born in Tobiki. Is at bottom.

PURDY (*whips a map out of his desk*). Then it's time you learned where you were born. I also happen to give a course in map reading.

SAKINI (*looks at map*). So sorry, boss. But map upside down.

FISBY (*looks at map*). He's right.

PURDY (*looks at map—turns it around*). Why in hell doesn't the Army learn how to draw a map properly! (*Turns to* SAKINI.) That will be all, Sakini. Find Sergeant Gregovich and have him assign a jeep to Captain Fisby. Then load supplies and the captain's gear in the jeep. You will be leaving at once. I'll send rice rations later.

SAKINI (*takes the colonel's hand and pumps it*). Oh, thank you, boss. You very kind to send me home. I mention you in prayer to gods. (*He turns to* FISBY.) I wait at jeep for you, Captain. (*He starts to run, then slows down quickly.*) Very happy, sir. Socks up. (*He goes out.* PURDY *turns wearily to* FISBY.)

PURDY. I sometimes think we Occupation Teams have it tougher than combat troops. (*He quickly holds up a protesting hand.*) Granted they have it rough for a while. But we have the killing daily grind, with no glory in it.

FISBY. Yes, sir, I know what you mean. Life itself is a battlefield with its own obscure heroes.

PURDY (*looks at* FISBY *with surprise*). I consider that poetry, Captain.

FISBY. I'm afraid it's just prose, sir. And it isn't mine, it's Victor Hugo's.

PURDY (*corrected*). Oh, yes. Victor Hugo! How I loved *Tale of Two Cities*.

FISBY. Isn't that Dickens, sir?

PURDY. I guess I was thinking of the movie. Well! To get back to Tobiki. Your first job when you get there will be to establish a municipal government and build a school.

FISBY. A school?

PURDY. It's all in Plan B. I'll see that cement and lumber are sent down to you. Plan B calls for the schoolhouse to be pentagon-shaped.

FISBY. If you say so, sir.

PURDY. When the school is built, you will organize a Ladies' League for Democratic Action. You will deliver a series of lectures on democracy as outlined in the outline. Captain, this is a chance for you to make a name for yourself.

FISBY. I will, sir. You see, I feel that I've personally delayed victory at least a year, and I have to vindicate myself.

PURDY. That's the kind of talk I like to hear from my officers. Well, I won't detain you then. (*He rises.*) My only order to you is: Put that village on the map.

FISBY. Yes, sir.

PURDY. Send me a bimonthly Progress Report— in triplicate.

FISBY. Yes, sir.

PURDY. Don't duplicate your work.

FISBY. No, sir.

PURDY. Fire those natives with the Spirit of Occupation.

FISBY. Yes, sir.

PURDY. And remember— that the eyes of Washington are on our Occupation Teams. And the eyes of the world are on Washington.

FISBY. I'll keep the eyes in mind, sir.

PURDY. Good-bye, Captain. (FISBY *salutes smartly and goes out.* PURDY *stands for a moment, moved by the vastness of the canvas. Then he turns to his desk.*) Where the hell is my *Adventure Magazine!*

THE SCENE BLACKS OUT QUICKLY

SCENE TWO

SCENE: *Outside Captain Fisby's quarters.*

TIME: *A few minutes later.*

AT RISE: CAPTAIN FISBY *and* SAKINI *enter from left and cross before the panels, all of which are now down.*

SAKINI Everything all ready, boss. We go to Lobiki now?

FISBY. I guess so. Well, wish me luck, Sakini. I'm going out to spread the gospel of Plan B.

SAKINI. You already lucky, boss. You got me.

FISBY (*smiles*). Thanks . . . do you know the road?

SAKINI. No road, boss just path for wagon cart and goat.

FISBY. Will a jeep make it?

SAKINI. We find out, boss.

FISBY. Naturally. How long will it take us?

SAKINI. Oh— not know until we arrive, boss.

FISBY. Naturally. Well, we might as well get started. I'll drive and you give directions.

SAKINI. Oh, very happy to go home.

FISBY. Where is the jeep?

SAKINI. Right here, boss.

(*He turns and claps his hands. The panels go up. The laundry line has been removed and the jeep pulled down center. The jeep is piled with Fisby's belongings. Perched high on the top of this pyramid sits a very old and very wrinkled* NATIVE WOMAN. SAKINI *pays no attention to her as he goes around the jeep test-kicking the tires. And the* OLD WOMAN *sits disinterested and aloof from what goes on below her.*)

FISBY. Hey, wait a minute! What's she doing up there? (*He points to her. The* OLD WOMAN *sits with hands folded serenely, looking straight ahead.*)

SAKINI. She nice old lady hear we go to Tobiki village. She think she go along to visit grandson.

FISBY. Oh, she does. Well, you explain that I'm very sorry but she'll have to take a bus.

SAKINI. No buses to Tobiki. People very poor—can only travel on generosity.

FISBY. I'm sorry, but it's against regulations.

SAKINI. She not fall off, boss. She tied on.

FISBY. Well, untie her and get her down. She'll just have to find some other way to visit her grandson.

SAKINI. Her grandson mayor of Tobiki village. You make him lose face if you kick old grandmother off jeep.

FISBY. She's the mayor's grandmother?

SAKINI. Oh yes, boss.

FISBY. Well, since she's already tied on, I guess we can take her. (*He looks at the bundles.*) Are all those *mine?*

SAKINI. Oh, no. Most of bundles belong to old lady. She think she visit three or four months so she bring own bed and cooking pots.

FISBY. Well, tell her to yell out if she sees any low branches coming. (*He starts to get in.*) Let's get started.

SAKINI. Oh, can't go yet, boss.

FISBY. Why not?

SAKINI. Old lady's daughter not here.

FISBY (*glances at watch*). We can't wait for a lot of good-byes, Sakini!

SAKINI (*looking behind* FISBY). Oh, she come now—right on dot you bet.

(CAPTAIN FISBY *turns to witness a squat young* NATIVE WOMAN *come on pushing a wheelbarrow loaded with bundles. She stops long enough to bow low to* FISBY—*then begins to tie bundles onto the jeep.*)

FISBY. Sakini, can't the old lady leave some of that stuff behind?

SAKINI. Not her things, boss. Belong to daughter.

FISBY. Wait a minute. Is the daughter planning on going with us, too?

SAKINI. Old lady very old. Who take care of her on trip?

FISBY. Well, I— (*THE DAUGHTER takes the wheelbarrow and hurries off.*) Hey— you come back! Sakini—tell her to come back. We can't carry any more bundles.

SAKINI (*calmly*). Oh, she not go to get bundles, boss. She go to get children.

FISBY. Come here, Sakini. Now look— this sort of thing is always happening to me and I have to put a stop to it some place. This time I'm determined to succeed. It's not that I don't *want* to take them. But you can see for yourself, *there's no room left for kids!*

SAKINI. But daughter not go without children and old lady not go without daughter. And if old lady not go, mayor of Tobiki be mad at you.

(*Turns to see the* DAUGHTER *hurry back with three children in tow. They all bow politely to* FISBY. *Their mother then piles them on the hood of the jeep.*)

FISBY. For Pete's sake, Sakini, how does she expect me to see how to drive!

SAKINI. Old lady got very good eyesight. She sit on top and tell us when to turn.

(*At this point one of the* CHILDREN *climbs off the hood and points offstage.*)

CHILD. A! Wasureta!

DAUGHTER. Wasureta? Nanisa?

CHILD. Fija dayo.

(*The* CHILD *dashes offstage.*)

FISBY. Now, where's *he* going?

SAKINI (*to* DAUGHTER). Doshtano?

DAUGHTER. Fija turete kurendes!

SAKINI (*to* FISBY). He go to get goat.

FISBY. A goat!

SAKINI. Can't go and leave poor goat behind.

DAUGHTER (*waves gaily to the* OLD WOMAN *on top of the jeep*). Okasan daijobu! (*She climbs the pyramid of bundles to settle beside her.*)

FISBY. Well, right here is where we start seeing who's going to lose face. No goat is going to travel on this jeep.

SAKINI. You not like goats, boss?

FISBY. It has nothing to do with whether I like goats or not. I'm positive the colonel wouldn't like it.

SAKINI. But children not go without goat, mother not go without children, old lady not go without daughter—

FISBY (*repeats with* SAKINI).—and if old lady not go, the mayor of Tobiki be mad at you! (FISBY *sees the goat being led on by the* SMALL BOY.) Oh, no!

SAKINI. Everybody here, boss. Goat not got children. Goat unmarried lady goat.

FISBY. All right, all right. Put it on the hood with the kids. (*The goat is placed on the hood and held by the* CHILDREN.) We've got to get started or we'll never get off the ground.

SAKINI. All ready to go, boss. You get in now. Nobody else going.

(*But before* FISBY *can climb in an* OLD MAN *comes hurrying in and, without looking to the right or left, climbs on the back of the jeep and settles down.*)

FISBY. Now who the hell is he?

SAKINI (*looks at* OLD MAN). Now who the hell is he? (*Back to* FISBY.) Not know, boss, never see before.

FISBY. Is he a relation of theirs?

SAKINI (*to the woman on top of the jeep*). Kore dare?

MOTHER. Mitakoto nai hito desu.

SAKINI. She say she never see him before, boss.

FISBY. Well, ask him what he's doing here!

SAKINI (*goes to the* OLD MAN). Ojisan, doshtano?

OLD MAN. Washimo notte ikuyo.

SAKINI. He say he see people going somewhere on trip and he think maybe he like to go somewhere, too.

FISBY. Tell him to get off and get off quick!

SAKINI. Dame dayo, ojisan, orina, orina!

OLD MAN (*angrily*). Fija noserunnera washimo noruyo!

SAKINI. He say why not take him? You take goat. He say maybe you think he not as good as goat?

FISBY. Look, Sakini, explain to him that the eyes of the world are on Washington and the eyes of Washington are on me. I can't be responsible for—

(*But before this can be translated,* COLONEL PURDY *stalks on and comes to an abrupt halt.*)

PURDY. Captain Fisby!

FISBY. Yes, sir.

PURDY. What in the name of Occupation do you think you're doing!

FISBY. It's hard to explain, sir. . . . I, ah . . . ah . . .

(*As he founders, the* OLD LADY *on top of the bundles comes to life. She looks down and screams shrilly.*)

OLD LADY. Yakamashii oyajijana, hayo iko, iko!

PURDY. What is *she* saying?

SAKINI. She say . . . tell fat old man to shut up so we can get started! (*As* COLONEL PURDY's *jaw drops, the panels drop also.*)

BLACKOUT

SCENE THREE

SCENE: *Tobiki village.*
TIME: *Ten days later.*
AT RISE: *All the bamboo panels are down.*
SAKINI *walks in front of them to the center of the stage from the wings.*

SAKINI
  (*Bows*)
Distance from Headquarters to Tobiki village by map . . . two inches.
By horse . . . three days.
By foot . . . four days.
By jeep . . . ten days.
Explanation:
Captain want to go to Tobiki.
Children want to go ocean. Never see ocean.
We see ocean.
Captain want to go to Tobiki.
Old lady's daughter want to visit Awasi.
We go Awasi.
Old lady make second mistake.
Captain demand we go Tobiki.
Ancient man have cousin in Yatoda.
We go Yatoda.
Damn fool old lady not know one road from another.
Now we arrive Tobiki.
Tobiki welcome rice and democracy.
  (*He claps his hands for the panels to be raised, then walks into the scene. The destitute village of Tobiki is revealed with its sagging huts and its ragged villagers grouped in the square just outside of Captain Fisby's office. This is a small bamboo structure with a thatched roof. It has a makeshift desk and field telephone. There is a cot crowded against the upper wall.* FISBY, *his glasses on, sits studying Plan B. He puts the document down, and, taking off his glasses, calls to* SAKINI.)

FISBY. Sakini!

SAKINI. Right here, boss. Not asleep, boss.

FISBY. Good. According to Plan B, my first job here is to hold a public meeting.

SAKINI. Public waiting in public square . . . eager to meet new boss, boss.

FISBY. Good. Now, Plan B calls for a lecture on the ABC's of democracy. (*He turns to* SAKINI.) Make sure they understand that I come as a friend of the people. That we intend to lift the yoke of oppression from their shoulders.

SAKINI. Oh, they like that, boss. This their favorite speech.

FISBY. What do you mean, their favorite speech?

SAKINI. Oh, Japanese say same things when they come, boss. Then take everything.

FISBY. Well, we're not here to *take* anything.

SAKINI. They got nothing left to take away, boss.

FISBY (*annoyed*). Well, if they *did* have, we wouldn't take it. We're here to *give* them something.

SAKINI. Oh, not get angry, boss. We not mind. After eight centuries we get used to it. When friends come now, we hide things quick as the dickens.

FISBY (*rises, a little upset*). Well, I guess it's up to me to convince them we really are friends. Let's meet the villagers. (*He picks up his papers.*) And let them meet Plan B.

(*As they step out the door to the office, the villagers rise and bow respectfully in unison.* FISBY *surveys them.*)

SAKINI (*introducing* FISBY). Amerikano Taisho-san, Captain Fisby.

FISBY (*bows in return*). Well, we might as well get started, Sakini. (*He finds a box and stands on it. He glances into Plan B and clears his throat.*) Citizens of Tobiki village. I—

SAKINI (*interrupts him*). Sorry, boss. Can't begin lecture yet.

FISBY. Why not?

SAKINI. Not good manners. People bring you gifts. You must accept gifts first.

FISBY. But I'm here to bring gifts from my government to them.

SAKINI. Very rude to make people feel poor, boss.

FISBY. I don't want to make anyone feel poor, but—

SAKINI. You make them lose face if you refuse, boss. They not accept democracy from you.

FISBY. All right. All right, then. Say to them that I'll accept their gifts in the name of the United States Occupation Forces.

SAKINI (*turns to the* VILLAGERS). Soreja moratte okuyo!

(MR. HOKAIDA, *an enormous villager in tattered peasant clothes, steps forward.*)

MR. HOKAIDA (*bows diffidently and offers his present to* FISBY). Amerika-san, korewo dozo.

SAKINI. This Mr. Hokaida, boss. He give you fine present.

FISBY. Thank you. Thank you very much. (*He takes it and turns to* SAKINI *puzzled.*) What is it?

SAKINI. You not know?

FISBY. No.

SAKINI. Oh, where you been all your life, boss?

FISBY. Living without one of these, I guess.

SAKINI. Is very splendid cricket cage, boss.

FISBY. What's it used for?

SAKINI. Keep cricket in.

FISBY. Why?

SAKINI. So Fortune smile on you. Cricket very good luck.

FISBY. But there's no cricket in it.

SAKINI. Bad luck to give cricket. You must catch your own fortune. No one can get it for you.

FISBY (*considers this*). Thank him and tell him I'll keep my eye out for a cricket.

SAKINI. Ya, arigato. (MR. HOKAIDA *bows away as an* ANCIENT NATIVE *steps forward and bows.*) This Mr. Omura. He bring you gift of chopsticks.

MR. OMURA. Korede mainichi gochiso wo, dozo.

SAKINI. He say: May only food of gods touch your lips.

(*As* FISBY *bows,* MR. SUMATA, *a nervous citizen in a torn straw hat, pushes his way toward* SAKINI.)

MR. SUMATA. Sugu modotte kuruyo!

SAKINI. Doshtandes?

MR. SUMATA. Ima sugu presento motte kuruyo. (*He turns and runs hurriedly off stage right.*)

FISBY. What was that?

SAKINI. That Mr. Sumata. He have present at home for you. He say not go away until he get.

(*A rather handsome young Tobikian,* MR. SEIKO, *now steps forward and extends a pair of wooden sandals.*)

MR. SEIKO. Dozo korewo chakini.

SAKINI. This Mr. Seiko. He brings you geta.

FISBY. Geta?

SAKINI. Wooden sandals. Very comfortable for tired feet. He say: May you walk in prosperity.

FISBY. Tell him I shall walk in the—the cool—meadow—of—of pleasant memories. Is that all right?

SAKINI. Oh, that's very pretty, boss. (*He turns to* MR. SEIKO.) Ya, arigato, Seikosan.

MR. SEIKO (*beams, bows, and backs away*). Iya, kosi no itari desu.

SAKINI. He say you do him honor. (*Here a chunky, flat-faced, aggressive* YOUNG WOMAN *with heavy glasses pushes forward with her present.*) Oh, this Miss Higa Jiga—unmarried lady. She bring you three eggs.

FISBY. Tell her I shall eat them for breakfast. (*He bows to her.*)

SAKINI. Captain-san, daisuki desu.

MISS HIGA JIGA. Kame no tamago desu. (*She bows away.*)

SAKINI. She say she hope you enjoy turtle eggs.

FISBY (*grins and bows to her*). She'll never know.

SAKINI. You very big success. They sure like you already. (*Another* VILLAGER *steps forward and offers a gift.*) This Mr. Keora. He bring you another cricket cage. Minus cricket.

FISBY. Say to him—that my prospects of good fortune are doubled. (*He looks rather pleased with himself.*)

SAKINI. Kagowa futatsu de, un wa bai!

MR. KEORA. Hoho! Naka naka shiteki desna! (*He bows away.*)

SAKINI. He say you are inspired poet.

FISBY (*modestly*). It's all in getting the hang of it.

SAKINI (*introducing the next citizen, a very* OLD MAN *leaning on a stick*). This old man Mr. Oshira. He bring you fine lacquered cup he make himself.

FISBY. Tell him I'm forever in his debt for such a beautiful gift.

OSHIRA. You are most welcome, Captain.

FISBY (*turns to him in surprise*). You speak English!

SAKINI. Mr. Oshira teach me English when I am little boy in Tobiki.

OSHIRA. In my youth I work in Manila. How is Mr. McKinley?

FISBY (*puzzled for a moment*). Who? Oh—President McKinley. I'm afraid someone shot him.

OSHIRA. I am sad.

FISBY. It was a long time ago.

OSHIRA. Yes, a long time. (*He indicates the cup.*) May August moon fill your cup.

FISBY. May I ask, why an August moon?

OSHIRA. All moons good, but August moon little older, little wiser.

FISBY. Did Sakini say you made this cup yourself?

OSHIRA. Oh, yes. I learned from my father before me who learned from his father before him. Is our heritage.

SAKINI. Look, boss, this cup thin as paper, carved from one block of wood. Then painted many times with red lacquer.

FISBY. And did you paint the gold fish inside?

OSHIRA (*nods*). It is imperfect.

SAKINI. When Mr. Oshira little boy, he work ten years to learn how to paint gold fish exactly like his papa paint.

FISBY. It's just beautiful! Can you still make things like this?

OSHIRA. One does not forget.

FISBY. Sakini, here's an industry we can start right away. This is a lost art. (*Turns to* OSHIRA.) Is there any way we could mass-produce these?

OSHIRA. Mass-produce?

FISBY. You know—set up machines and turn them out by the gross.

OSHIRA (*shakes his head*). I take pride in making one cup at time, Captain. How can I take pride in work of machine?

FISBY. How many of these could you turn out in a day?

OSHIRA. If I work hard, maybe one or two a week.

FISBY (*disappointed*). Well, it's a start. Make as many as you can. We'll send them up to the American Post Exchange and sell them as fast as you can turn them out.

OSHIRA. I shall do my best. The swiftness of my youth has deserted me, sir. (*He bows and moves back.*) But I shall make fewer mistakes.

FISBY (*excitedly*). Sakini, tell Mr. Omura to make up a batch of chopsticks. Have everybody get to work making cricket cages, wooden sandals and—(*Pointing.*)—these straw hats. We'll put this village in the souvenir business.

SAKINI. We all make money, boss?

FISBY. If they can turn out enough of these things, I guarantee the recovery of Tobiki village. Tell them.

SAKINI. Kore dondon tskuru yoni . . .

(*There is a general exchange of chatter and approval.*) They say they make everything, fast as the dickens, boss.

FISBY. Good. We're in business. Now ask them if they'd mind postponing the rest of the gifts until later. I'd like to tell them what *we're* planning for *them.*

SAKINI. Sa, sono hanashi shiyo.

CITIZENS. No agerumono naiyo! Hanashi wo kiko.

SAKINI. They say sure. They got no more presents anyhow.

FISBY. Good. First I want to tell them about the school we're going to build for their children. All set to translate?

SAKINI. All set.

FISBY. All right. (*He consults Plan B.*) Plan B says the direct approach is most effective. This is it. (*He steps back up on a box and looks forcefully at his listeners. Then he points a dramatic finger at them.*) Do you want to be ignorant?

SAKINI (*also points a finger*). Issho bakaja dame daro?

(*The* CITIZENS *make a noise that sounds like "Hai."*)

FISBY What did they say?

SAKINI. They say "Yes."

FISBY. What do you mean, "yes"? They *want* to be ignorant?

SAKINI. No, boss. But in Luchuan "yes" means "no." They say "yes," they *not* want to be ignorant.

FISBY. Oh. (*He turns back to his rapt audience and assumes his forensic posture.*) Do you want your *children* to be ignorant?

SAKINI. Issho kodomotachi mo bakaja dame daro?

(*The* VILLAGERS *respond quickly with a noise that sounds like "Lie."*)

FISBY. What did they say then?

SAKINI. They say "No."

FISBY. "No" they do, or "No" they don't?

SAKINI. Yes, they not want no ignorant children.

FISBY. Good. (*He turns back to the* VILLAGERS.) Then this is what my government is planning to do for you. First there will be daily issues of rice for everyone.

SAKINI. Mazu kome no hykyu!

(*The* VILLAGERS *cheer.*)

FISBY. We will build a fine new school here for your children. (*Then recalling Colonel Purdy's dictum.*) Pentagon-shaped.

SAKINI. Gakko taterundayo katachi wa— (*He flounders.*) Ah— Pentagon.

(*The* CITIZENS *look at each other, puzzled.*)

MISS HIGA JIGA. Nandesutte?

SAKINI. Pentagon.

MISS HIGA JIGA. Sore wa nandesuka?

SAKINI. They say what is Pentagon? Never hear before.

FISBY. Never heard of the *Pentagon!*

SAKINI. No, boss.

FISBY. Well, they certainly do need a school here. The Pentagon is— is— (*He looks down at their eager faces.*) Well, it really means five-sided.

SAKINI. Kabega itsutsusa, ii, ni, san, yon, go. (*Holds up five fingers. There is a burst of laughter from the* CITIZENS.)

MISS HIGA JIGA (*giggling*). Ara, gokakuno kodomo nante arimasenyo.

SAKINI. They say no children in Tobiki got five-sides.

FISBY. The *school* will be five-sided— like a building in Washington.

SAKINI (*explains*). Chigauyo, chigauyo, onaji mono arundes yo, Washington ni. (*There is a decided reaction of approval.* SAKINI *turns back to* FISBY.) They very impressed.

FISBY (*continuing*). Everyone will learn about democracy.

SAKINI. Mazu minshu shugi bera-bera bera-bera.

MISS HIGA JIGA. Minshu shugi bera-bera bera-bera?

SAKINI. They say: Explain what is democracy. They know what rice is.

FISBY. Oh. (*He scratches his head.*) Well, it's a system of self-determination. It's— it's the right to make the wrong choice.

SAKINI. Machigattemo iindayo.

(*They look up blankly, silently.*)

FISBY. I don't think we're getting the point over. Explain that if I don't like the way Uncle Sam treats me, I can write the President himself and tell him so.

SAKINI. Daitoryo ni tegami kaitemo iinosa.

(*The* VILLAGERS *all laugh heartily.*)

MISS HIGA JIGA. Masaka soonakoto!

SAKINI (*triumphantly*). They say: But do you *send* the letters?

FISBY. Let's get on with the lecture. (*He turns back to the citizens and reads from Plan B.*) Tell them hereafter all men will be free and equal. . . .

SAKINI. Subete, jiyuu, to byodo, de ar, de ar.

FISBY (*increases his tempo and volume*). Without discrimination . . .

SAKINI (*taking* FISBY's *tone*). Sabetsu, taigu—haishi de ar.

FISBY. The will of the majority will rule!

SAKINI. Subete minna de kime, de ar!

FISBY (*finishing with a flourish*). And Tobiki village will take its place in the brotherhood of democratic peoples the world over!

SAKINI (*rising to new demagogic heights*). Koshite, Tobiki, jiyuu, Okinawa, byodo sabetsu, taigu—haishi, jiyuu, byodo de ar, de ar. (*A great burst of applause greets Sakini's performance. He turns to* FISBY.) We going over big, boss.

FISBY (*agrees with a nod*). Now to get this village organized. Is the mayor here?

SAKINI (*points*). Mr. Omura is mayor, boss. (MR. OMURA *steps forward.*) He only one in Tobiki with white coat.

FISBY (*glances at the worn, ragged coat*). It looks to me as if you'll have to get a new coat or a new mayor soon.

SAKINI. Better keep mayor, boss. Impossible to get white coat.

FISBY. Well, since we've got a mayor, we only have to find a Chief of Agriculture and a Chief of Police. That's going to present a problem.

SAKINI. No problem, boss. You just look over gifts and see who give you best gift. Then you give him best job.

FISBY. Sakini, that is *not* the democratic way. The people themselves must choose the man best qualified. Tell them they are to elect their own Chief of Agriculture.

SAKINI. Sah! Senkyo desu. Mazu Chief of Agriculture.

WOMEN VILLAGERS (*push* MR. SIEKO *forward shouting*). Seiko-san, Seiko-san ga ii, Seiko-san!

SAKINI. They say they elect Mr. Seiko. He best qualified for agriculture.

FISBY. He's an experienced farmer?

SAKINI. No, boss. He's artist. He draw lovely picture of golden wheat stalk with pretty green butterfly.

FISBY. Drawing pictures of wheat doesn't make him a wheat expert.

SAKINI. Wheat not grow here anyhow, boss. Only sweet potatoes.

FISBY. All right, all right! If he's their choice.

SEIKO. Ano! Watashimo shiroi koto wo.

SAKINI. He say do he get white coat like the mayor?

FISBY. Tell him I'll get him a helmet that says "Chief of Agriculture" on it.

SAKINI. Yoshi, yoshi, kammuri ageru-yo. (SEIKO *bows and backs away.*)

FISBY. Next we want to elect a Chief of Police.

SAKINI. Kondowa Chief of Police!

VILLAGERS (*clamor and push the fat* MR. HOKAIDA *forward*). Hokaida-san. Soda, soda. Hokaida-san.

FISBY. What are *his* qualifications for office?

SAKINI. People afraid of him. He champion wrestler.

(MR. HOKAIDA *flexes his muscles.*)

FISBY. Well, no one can say this isn't self-determination.

MR. HOKAIDA. Washime ano kammuri wo.

SAKINI. He say do he get helmet too?

FISBY (*nods*). I'll requisition another helmet.

SAKINI. Agemasuyo.

MR. HOKAIDA (*Bows smiling*). Ya, doomo.

FISBY. Now for the ladies. We intend to organize a Ladies' League for Democratic Action. We'll want to elect a League President.

SAKINI. Oh, ladies never vote before—they like that. (*He turns to the* LADIES.) Kondowa Ladies' League for Democratic Action!

(*This announcement is greeted by excited chatter. The* LADIES *push* MISS JIGA *forward.*)

LADIES. Higa-Jiga-san—Higa-Jiga-san!

SAKINI. They say they elect Miss Higa Jiga. They think she make classy president.

MISS HIGA JIGA (*points to her head*). Ano, watashi nimo ano booshio . . .

FISBY (*laughs*). All right, I'll see that she gets a helmet, too. Now ask them if they have any question they'd like to ask *me*.

SAKINI. Sa, nanka kikitai koto ga attara.

OLD WOMAN. Sakini-san, ima nanji kaina?

SAKINI. They say they like to know what time is it?

FISBY (*puzzled*). Time? (*Glances at his watch.*) Quarter of five, why?

SAKINI. They say they got to hurry then. They not like to miss sunset. This is time of day they sit in pine grove, sip tea and watch sun go down.

FISBY. All right, thank them and tell them they can go have tea in the pine grove.

SAKINI. Ya, minna kaette mo iiyo.

(*They bow and, chattering happily among themselves, go off right.* FISBY *gathers up his gifts.*)

FISBY. How do you think we did, Sakini?

SAKINI. They co-operate, boss. Future look very rosy.

FISBY. Where do you think I can find a cricket?

SAKINI. One come along. May have one in house now and not know it.

FISBY. Well, I'll take these things in and get started on my Progress Report. (*He goes to the office hut.*)

SAKINI. I take a little snooze then. Public speaking very exhausting.

FISBY (*as he goes inside*). *I* think I handled it pretty well.

(*He sits down at his desk. He examines his gifts and then, putting on his glasses, begins to study Plan B again. After a moment,* MR. SUMATA *enters from the right. He carries a couple of battered suitcases. He is followed by* LOTUS BLOSSOM, *a petite and lovely geisha girl in traditional costume. When they are about center stage, young* MR. SEIKO *runs up after the geisha girl. She turns to him.*)

SEIKO. Ano, chotto . . .

LOTUS BLOSSOM. Ara! Nani?

SUMATA (*steps in front of* SEIKO *and points an angry finger under his nose*). Dame, dame, atchi ike. (SEIKO *bows head and retreats.* MR. SUMATA *then turns to* SAKINI.) Amerika-san doko?

SAKINI (*indicates the office*). Asco.

SUMATA (*indicates geisha girl*). Kore tsurete kitandayo.

SAKINI. Oh? Do-sunno?

SUMATA. Kore Taisho-san ni agetainja.

(*He bows and goes off quickly, almost running. The* GEISHA *remains with* SAKINI. SAKINI *smiles and steps inside the office. He stands behind* FISBY.)

SAKINI. You busy, boss?

FISBY (*without turning around to him*). Yes, but what is it?

SAKINI. Mr. Sumata leave present for you, boss.

FISBY. Put it on the shelf where it'll be out of the way.

SAKINI (*glances back outside*). Not able to do, boss. Present get mad.

FISBY (*turns around*). What's this about, Sakini?

SAKINI (*motions to the* GEISHA, *who steps inside smiling. She bows*). Here you are, boss.

FISBY (*rising*). Who is *she!*

SAKINI. Souvenir.

FISBY. What are you talking about?

SAKINI. Present from Mr. Sumata.

FISBY. Wait a minute. Is he kidding? I can't accept a human present.

SAKINI. Oh, human present very lovely. Introducing Lotus Blossom, geisha girl first class. (*He turns to* LOTUS BLOSSOM.) Amerika-san no Captain Fisby.

LOTUS BLOSSOM (*smiling happily*). Ara, ii otokomaene! Watashi sukidawa.

SAKINI. She say she very happy to belong to handsome captain. She say she serve you well.

FISBY. She's not going to serve me at all. You get that Mr. Sumata and tell him I'm returning his present.

SAKINI. Impossible to do, boss. Mr. Sumata leave present and go up mountains to visit cousin. He say good-bye and wish you much success in Tobiki.

LOTUS BLOSSOM (*sweetly*). Watashi kokoni sumun desho?

SAKINI. She say, where do you want her to stay, boss?

FISBY. You tell her I don't care where she stays. She can't stay here.

SAKINI (*shocked*). Where she go then? She got no home. Mr. Sumata already gone away.

FISBY. Well, find her a place for the time being.

SAKINI (*grins*). Plenty of room in my house, boss. Just me and my grandpapa.

FISBY. No, I can't do that. Sit her over on that box until I can think where to put her.

SAKINI. You can put her in business, boss.

FISBY. You keep a civil tongue in your head, Sakini.

(LOTUS BLOSSOM *comes over to* FISBY, *whom she has been watching with great interest*). Okimono to ozohri motte kimasune.

SAKINI. She like to put on your sandals and kimono for you. She trained to please you, boss.

FISBY. I know what she's trained to do. And I don't need any translation. (*He sits down at his desk again.*) Sakini . . . take my supplies out of the shack and bring them over here. We'll set her up there where I can keep an eye on her.

SAKINI. Not very democratic, boss. You make her lose face if she not make you comfortable, boss. She think she bad geisha girl.

FISBY. You tell her . . . I've got some face to save, too . . . so she can just forget this Oriental hanky-panky.

SAKINI. Anta irantesa!

LOTUS BLOSSOM (*waves him away*). Ara, nani ittennoyo. Imasara ikettatte ikarenai desho.

FISBY. Well, what did she say?

SAKINI. She say for me to go on home to grandpapa . . . she first-class geisha girl . . . she know her business. Good night, boss.

(FISBY *stands eyeing* LOTUS BLOSSOM *as* SAKINI *goes out. The lights go down quickly. During the brief blackout, the two center panels are lowered, shutting out the village street. The office of Colonel Purdy is swung into place in the last panel right. The lights come up on* PURDY *twisting the bell on his field telephone.*)

PURDY. What do you mean . . . there's no answer? Well, keep trying. I'm not the kind of a man to take "no answer" for an answer.

(*The lights come up on the opposite side of the stage in Fisby's office.* FISBY *is holding onto his jacket buttons.* LOTUS BLOSSOM *stands in front of him holding out his robe. She is gently persistent and puzzled at his reticence.*)

FISBY. It's *not* a kimono . . . it's a bathrobe. And I don't *want* to put it on.

LOTUS BLOSSOM (*reaches to unbutton his jacket*). Sa! Shizukani shimasho ne.

FISBY. No, it's against regulations. (*Phone rings. He takes the robe away from* LOTUS BLOSSOM *and sits on it. Then he picks up the phone.*) Hello!

PURDY (*jumps*). You don't have to shout. I can hear you. This is Colonel Purdy.

FISBY (*leaps to his feet and pushes* LOTUS BLOSSOM *behind him as if to hide her*). Yes, sir.

PURDY. Just thought I'd check up on you. How are things going?

(LOTUS BLOSSOM *begins to fan her master.*)

FISBY. Well, everything seems to be under control at the moment.

(*He sits down and takes out a cigarette.* LOTUS BLOSSOM *promptly lights it for him.*)

PURDY. Anything *I* can do for you?

FISBY (*pauses*). I can't think of anything, sir.

PURDY. I realize it's bound to get lonely for you down there . . . so you know what I'm going to do, my boy?

FISBY (LOTUS BLOSSOM *gets the geta and kneels before him.* FISBY *watches her apprehensively and asks . . .*). What are you going to do?

PURDY. I'll tell you. I'm going to send you some of my old *Adventure Magazines*.

FISBY (*as* LOTUS BLOSSOM *starts to take off his shoes*). No, no. I don't want them. (*Into the phone.*) I mean . . . yes . . . thank you. (*He rises and twists about trying to pull his foot away from* LOTUS BLOSSOM.) I'd like something to read.

PURDY. How are you getting along with the natives?

FISBY (*his leg over the chair*). The problem here, sir, is a very old one. It seems to be a question of who's going to lose face.

PURDY. I understand. As Mrs. Purdy says, "East is East and West is West, and there can be no Twain." But you're making progress?

FISBY. Nothing I'd like to put on paper, sir.

(LOTUS BLOSSOM *gets his shoes off and slips the sandals on.*)

PURDY. Well, when things get moving down there, send in a detailed Progress Report.

FISBY. If that's what you want, sir.

(LOTUS BLOSSOM *recovers the robe. She reaches out to unbutton his jacket.*)

PURDY. You'll find these people lack the capacity for sustained endeavor. Don't hesitate to build a fire under them.

FISBY (*struggling to keep his jacket on*). That won't be necessary, sir.

PURDY. Don't forget . . . the eyes of Washington are on you, Fisby.

FISBY (*as* LOTUS BLOSSOM *tries to pull his jacket over his head*). I hope not, sir.

PURDY (*ponders*). Fisby, it just occurred to me. Have you given any thought to physical education?

FISBY. If I may say so, sir . . . (LOTUS BLOSSOM *gets one arm out.*) I consider the suggestion . . . (*He hugs the other sleeve.*) a masterpiece of timeliness. (*He gets down on one knee.*)

PURDY. Thank you, my boy. (*pauses.*) Could you use a deck of cards? Hello? Hello, Fisby . . . you're getting weak.

(*As* FISBY *looks back at the telephone and nods in complete agreement, the two scenes black out simultaneously. The panels fall. A spot picks up* SAKINI *as he steps from the wings.*)

SAKINI. Discreet place to stop now and sip soothing cup of jasmine tea.

Conclusion?

Not yet.

Continuation shortly.
Lotus Blossom not lose face!
(*He bows.*)

THE CURTAIN FALLS

ACT TWO

SCENE ONE

SCENE: *Tobiki village.*
TIME: *A few days later.*
AT RISE: *All the panels are down.* SAKINI
*enters from the wings and crosses down to the
footlights center. He bows to the audience.*

SAKINI
Lovely ladies, kind gentlemen:
Most traveled person in history of world
  is summer sun.
Each day must visit each man no matter
  where he live on globe.
Always welcome visitor.
Not bring gossip.
Not stay too long.
Not depart leaving bad taste of rude
  comment.
But summer sun never tell topside of
  world what bottomside like.
So bottomside must speak for self.
We continue with little story of Tobiki.
Center of industry.
Seat of democracy.
(*He beams.*)
Home of geisha girl.
  (*He goes to the right proscenium arch as
  all the panels are raised, revealing the
  empty street outside of Fisby's office.
  FISBY enters, starts across stage, SAKINI
  falling in step behind him.*)
Was wondering what happened to you,
boss?

FISBY (*stops*). I went down to inspect
the sweet-potato fields. Sakini, no one
was there. The potatoes were piled up,
but no one was working.
  SAKINI. Very hot day, boss.
  FISBY. But I can't find my Chief of
Agriculture. Or the Mayor, or the Chief
of Police. Where is everybody?
  SAKINI. Lotus Blossom leave belongings over at Awasi—got no way to bring
things here. So—everybody take wheelbarrow to help move Lotus Blossom to
Tobiki.

FISBY. And has she got so many things
that it takes my entire staff to move her
to this village?
  SAKINI. No, boss, but Chief of Police
not trust Chief of Agriculture, and Mayor
not trust Mr. Oshira, so all go.
  FISBY. Mr. Oshira? That old man!
  SAKINI. He's old, boss, but not dead.
  FISBY. A fine way for officials to behave!
You tell them I want to see them the
moment they come back. (*He starts for his
office.*) A fine thing!
  SAKINI. Nothing to worry about, boss.
They not beat your time. You own Lotus
Blossom.
  FISBY. I do *not* own her. It's not a question of—of—(*He sits down at his desk.*)
Well, this sort of nonsense isn't going to
stop my work. (*He shifts the papers on his
desk.*) I intend to get started on that
schoolhouse today. We've got the mate-
rials, so all we need now is some good
carpenters. (*He turns to* SAKINI, *who has
followed him inside.*) Who is the best carpenter in the village?
  SAKINI. Mr. Sumata.
  FISBY. Fine. Get hold of him. Wait a
minute! Isn't he the joker who gave me
Lotus Blossom?
  SAKINI. Mr. Sumata has finger in lots
of pies, boss.
  FISBY. Well, since he's vanished, who
is the next best carpenter?
  SAKINI. Father of Mr. Sumata.
  FISBY. Where is he?
  SAKINI. Go on vacation with Mr. Sumata.
  FISBY (*beginning to get annoyed*). Well,
who is the *third* best carpenter then?
  SAKINI. No more, boss. Only Sumata
and son. They have what you call mo-
nopoly.
  FISBY. There's something fishy about
their disappearing.
  (MISS HIGA JIGA, *wearing a red helmet with
flowers, followed by several other* LADIES,
*comes storming across the stage to the office
door.* SAKINI *hears them and goes to the door.*)
  MISS HIGA JIGA (*angrily*). Watashitachi
sabetsu taigu desyo!
  FISBY (*Goes to the door also*). What's the
matter with her?
  SAKINI. Miss Higa Jiga say do you
know what we got in this village, boss?
Discrimination.
  FISBY (*wearily*). Where?
  (SAKINI *turns to* MISS HIGA JIGA.)
  MISS HIGA JIGA (*indignantly*). Watashi-

tachi hykyu matte itara Lotus Blossom
ga kite clarku ga anata desuka ma dozo
kochirae watashitachi nijikan mo machi
mashita yo.

SAKINI. She says that Ladies' League
for Democratic Action wait in line for
rice rations. Along come Lotus Blossom
and ration clerks say, "Oh, how do you
do. Oh, please don't stand in line. You
come inside and have cup of tea." Then
clerks shut up warehouse and leave Ladies' League waiting in sun two hours.

FISBY. It's things like this that undermine the democratic ideal. You tell Miss
Higa Jiga I intend to do something about
it. (*He storms into his office.*)

SAKINI (*turns to* MISS HIGA JIGA). Nan-
toka shimasuyo.

FISBY. I can see right now we're going
to have to get rid of the disrupting factor
in our recovery. (*He picks up the field telephone and twists the handle.*) Get me Major
McEvoy at Awasi.

SAKINI (*follows* FISBY *inside*). What are
you going to do, boss?

FISBY. This village isn't big enough for
Plan B and a geisha girl.

SAKINI. Oh, boss, Tobiki never have
geisha girl before. We like very much.

FISBY. She has to go. (*Then into the telephone.*) Major McEvoy? Captain Fisby
at Tobiki. I have a request from one of
my people to transfer to your village.
Yes, it's a female citizen. Profession?
Well . . . (*He looks at* SAKINI.)

SAKINI. Oh, please not send her away,
boss. Not democratic.

FISBY. As a matter of fact her name *is*
Lotus Blossom. *How* did *you* know? What
do you mean, what am I trying to put
over on you? Oh, you did? (*He hangs up.
Then he glares at* SAKINI.)

SAKINI (*with great innocence*). He knows
Lotus Blossom, boss?

FISBY. Very well. She was at Awasi and
damn near wrecked his whole plan for
recovery. She's been booted out of every
village by every commander on the island.

SAKINI. Oh, poor little Lotus Blossom.

FISBY. Poor little Lotus Blossom my
eye. She upsets every village she's in.

SAKINI. Not her fault she beautiful,
boss.

FISBY. No wonder that Mr. Sumata
disappeared. The major paid him a
hundred yen to get her out of his village.

SAKINI (*eagerly*). You keep her now,
boss?

FISBY. I have to. (*He points a finger at*
SAKINI.) Well, she's not going to get away
with causing dissension in *my* village!

(MISS HIGA JIGA, *weary of waiting outside,
storms in.*)

MISS HIGA JIGA. Doshte itadakemasno
Daitoryo ni tegami wo kakimasawayo.

FISBY (*pleads*). Tell her to go away.

SAKINI. She say she waiting for some
democratic action. She say if she don't
get it, she thinks she write this Uncle Sam
you talk about.

FISBY. Now, look. I don't want complaints going into Headquarters. Tell
her discrimination is being eliminated.

SAKINI. Sabetsu yamemasyo.

MISS HIGA JIGA. Yamenakutemo iinoyo,
watashitachi nimo wakete itadakeba.

SAKINI. Miss Higa Jiga say please not
eliminate discrimination. She say just
give her some too.

FISBY. And just what does she means
by that?

SAKINI. She say Lotus Blossom unfair
competition.

FISBY. Granted.

SAKINI. She say you promise everybody
going to be equal.

FISBY. I intend to keep my word.

SAKINI. Well, she say she can't be equal
unless she has everything Lotus Blossom
has.

FISBY. What Lotus Blossom's got, the
Government doesn't issue.

SAKINI (*taking a piece of paper which*
MISS HIGA JIGA *waves*). She make list, boss.
Shall I read, boss?

FISBY. Go ahead.

SAKINI. She wants you to get her and
ladies in League following items: A. Red
stuff to put on lips like geisha. B. Stuff
that smell pretty—

FISBY. Now, *just* wait a minute. What
would H.Q. think if I requisitioned lipstick!

SAKINI (*hands list back to* MISS HIGA JIGA).
Dame desuyo.

MISS HIGA JIGA. Jaa Daitoryo ni tegami
wo dashimaswa.

SAKINI. She say she sorry, but now she
guess she just have to write this letter to
Uncle Samuel after all.

FISBY (*throws up his hands*). All right.
All right! Tell her I'll call up the post
exchange at Awasi and see if they have
any shaving powder and toilet water.

SAKINI. Ya, katte agemasuyo.

MISS HIGA JIGA (*beams*). Ano wasure naidene bobby pin.

SAKINI. She say, not forget bobby pins for hair.

FISBY. I think I might have been happier in the submarine command.

MISS HIGA JIGA (*stops as she is about to go*). Mohitotsu onegai watashitachi mo mina geisha ni.

SAKINI. She say one more thing. Can you get Lotus Blossom to teach Ladies' League all to be geisha girls?

FISBY (*leaps to his feet*). Teach the innocent women of this village to be— *No!* (MISS HIGA JIGA *shrugs and goes outside. As* FISBY *sinks back at his desk,* MISS HIGA JIGA *talks excitedly to the* WOMEN *gathered outside. They run off giggling.* FISBY *sits at his desk and picks up Plan B.*) Plan B! (*He thumbs through its pages.*) Let's just see if Washington anticipated *this.*

(*He buries his chin in his hands.* SAKINI *sits quietly watching him. Outside in the village street,* LOTUS BLOSSOM *enters and starts daintily toward the office. She has only gotten halfway when* SEIKO *overtakes her.*)

SEIKO (*panting*). Ano, chotto.

LOTUS BLOSSOM (*stops and looks at him archly*). Nani?

SEIKO (*takes a chrysanthemum bud from his waist*). Ano korewo dozo.

LOTUS BLOSSOM (*takes it indifferently*). Ara, so arigato.

SEIKO (*strikes his heart passionately*). Boku no, kono, hato, o.

LOTUS BLOSSOM (*flicks her finger*). Anato no hahto? Ara shinzo ne.

SEIKO (*disembowels himself with an imaginary knife*). Harakitte shinimas.

LOTUS BLOSSOM (*yawns*). Imagoro sonnano hayaranai noyo.

SEIKO (*points toward Fisby's office*). Soka Amerika-san ga iinoka?

LOTUS BLOSSOM (*haughtily*). Nandeste! Sonnakoto yokeina osowa.

SEIKO (*laughs derisively*). Nanda rashamon janaika.

LOTUS BLOSSOM (*backs him up with an angry finger*). Watashimo kotoni kansho shinaideyo.

SEIKO (*bows his head*). Gomen nasai iisugi deshta.

LOTUS BLOSSOM (*points away*). Atchi, itte. (SEIKO *sighs, turns and plods off toward the sweet-potato fields, crushed and dejected.* LOTUS BLOSSOM *tidies her hair and continues to the office. She calls in coyly.*) Fuisbee-san!

SAKINI (*rises and looks out the door*). Oh,

what do you think, boss? Lotus Blossom back. She come to see you.

FISBY. And high time. (*He turns to face the door as* LOTUS BLOSSOM *enters and bows.*) Where have *you* been all day? Never mind, I know—upsetting the agricultural horse cart.

LOTUS BLOSSOM. Fu-san no kao nikkori nasaruto totemo kawaii wa.

SAKINI. She say sun burst through the clouds now that you smile on her.

FISBY. I'm not smiling. (*She hands him Seiko's chrysanthemum bud.*)

SAKINI. Oh, boss, you know what she give you?

FISBY. The works.

SAKINI. When lady give gentleman chrysanthemum bud, in Okinawa that means her heart is ready to unfold.

FISBY. Well, this is one bud that's not going to flower.

LOTUS BLOSSOM (*offering a box she has brought*). Kore otsukemono yo. Dozo.

SAKINI. She say, you like to eat some tsukemono? Tsukemono nice thing to eat between meals.

FISBY. No.

LOTUS BLOSSOM (*takes geta and kneels beside him*). Dozo ohaki osobase.

FISBY. Tell her to *leave my feet* alone.

LOTUS BLOSSOM (*studies* FISBY). Kasa kaburu. Nisshabyo nanoyo.

SAKINI. She worried about you, boss. She say, when you go in hot sun, should wear *kasa*—that straw hat—on head.

FISBY. Tell her never mind about my feet or my head. I want her to stop interfering with the recovery program. To stop causing rebellion and making the men—ah—ah—discontented.

SAKINI (*turns to* LOTUS BLOSSOM). Jama shicha dame dayo.

LOTUS BLOSSOM (*smiles*). Fu-san ocha ikaga?

SAKINI. She say: You want some tea?

FISBY (*throwing himself down on his cot*). No.

LOTUS BLOSSOM. Shami demo hikimashoka?

SAKINI. She say: You want some music?

FISBY. No.

LOTUS BLOSSOM (*giggles*). Ara Fu-santara yaiteruno.

SAKINI. She say: You jealous, boss?

FISBY (*mirthlessly*). Ha!

LOTUS BLOSSOM. Honto ni doshita no?

SAKINI. She say: You want to tell her

your troubles, boss?

FISBY. Why should I tell her my troubles?

SAKINI. She geisha girl, that's her *business*, boss.

FISBY. Some business.

LOTUS BLOSSOM. Shoga naiwane. Mah soshite irasshai yo.

SAKINI. She say she hear about lack of co-operation here. She feel very bad. She say she want to help because you best boss she ever had. You not make her work and you not take money from her.

FISBY (*sits up on his cot*). Did the other men who owned her . . . hire her out and then take money from her?

SAKINI. Oh, sure.

FISBY. Well, where I come from we have a name for men who—who—do *that* sort of thing.

SAKINI. You have geisha business in America, too?

FISBY (*rises*). No! Sakini, you give her to understand I have no intention of putting her to—to work.

SAKINI. Why not, boss? She pay all her dues to Geisha Guild. She member in good standing.

FISBY. You mean they've got a union for this sort of thing?

SAKINI. Geisha girl have to be protected, boss. Must keep up rates.

FISBY. This is the most immoral thing I've ever heard of. Haven't you people any sense of shame?

SAKINI. We bad not to be ashamed, boss?

FISBY. Obviously, there is a fundamental difference between us that can't be reconciled. I don't say that where I I come from there's no such thing as prostitution. But, by God, we don't have unions, set rates and collect dues!

SAKINI. But geisha girl not prostitute, boss.

FISBY. At least we have the decency— (*He stops.*) What do you mean, geisha girls aren't prostitutes? Everybody knows what they do.

SAKINI. Then everybody wrong, boss.

FISBY. Well, what do they get paid for, then?

SAKINI. Hard to explain fundamental difference. Poor man like to feel rich. Rich man like to feel wise. Sad man like to feel happy. All go to geisha house and tell troubles to geisha girl. She listen politely and say, "Oh, that's too bad."

She very pretty. She make tea, she sing, she dance, and pretty soon troubles go away. Is not worth something, boss?

FISBY. And that's *all* they do?

SAKINI. Very ancient and honorable profession.

FISBY. Look, Sakini, I apologize. I guess I jumped the gun. And I'm glad you explained. It sort of puts a new light on things. (*He turns to* LOTUS BLOSSOM *and grins.*)

LOTUS BLOSSOM. Ara, kyuni nikkorisite, mada okotteru no.

SAKINI. She say: Why are you smiling at her all of a sudden? You mad or something?

FISBY. Tell her that I'm a dope. That I have a coconut for a head.

SAKINI. No use, boss. She not believe.

FISBY. Then will you ask her if she'd be kind enough to give geisha lessons to the Ladies' League for Democratic Action?

SAKINI. Odori ya shami Ladies' League ni oshiete?

LOTUS BLOSSOM. Er iiwa, demo kumiai-aga kowaiwane.

SAKINI. She say Geisha Guild closed shop, but she teach if you not report her.

(*At this point the men of the village come across the square and stop before the office.* LOTUS BLOSSOM *goes to the door. Immediately there are* ohs *and* ahs *from the men.*)

FISBY. What is that?

SAKINI. Sound like Okinawan wolf call, boss.

FISBY. Well, let's find out. (*He goes outside to face the group, followed by* SAKINI.) Ask what's the matter.

SAKINI. Doshtano?

MR. KEORA Minna gakko nanka yori chaya ga ii soda.

SAKINI. They say they just held meeting in democratic fashion and majority agree on resolution. They want you to build them cha ya.

FISBY. A what?

SAKINI. Cha ya. That's teahouse, boss.

FISBY. A teahouse?

SAKINI. Yes, boss. They say now that this village have geisha girl just like big city, they should have teahouse like big city too.

FISBY. But I can't build them a teahouse . . . I have no authority to do that.

SAKINI. But you tell them will of majority is law. You going to break law?

FISBY. They're going to get a school . . .

that's enough.

SAKINI. But majority too old to go to school . . . they want teahouse.

FISBY. There is no provision in Plan B for a teahouse.

LOTUS BLOSSOM. Ano . . . ochaya sae tatereba mondai naija nai no.

SAKINI. Lotus Blossom say teahouse in Tobiki make recovery program work. Everybody make geta and cricket cages like crazy so they can spend money at teahouse.

FISBY. I haven't got any materials to build a teahouse.

SAKINI. Zairyo ga naiyo.

LOTUS BLOSSOM. Ara, kinoo renga ya zaimoku takusan kite orimashitayo.

SAKINI. She say Army truck come yesterday and leave beautiful brick and lovely paint.

FISBY. For the new *schoolhouse*. Tell them . . . it just can't be done.

SAKINI. Dame, dame, dame desuyo!

(FISBY *looks down into the disappointed faces of the* VILLAGERS.)

VILLAGERS. Achara-san, iijiwaru dane.

SAKINI. They say you very mean to them after *all* the nice presents they give you.

FISBY. I'm sorry.

SAKINI. They very sorry too, boss. You know why?

FISBY. I think I do.

SAKINI. No, boss. When you leave here . . . Tobiki be forgotten village. Not have park, not have statue . . . not even lovely jail. Tobiki like to be proud. Teahouse give them face.

FISBY. It's going to be a fine schoolhouse. Five sides.

OSHIRA. May I speak, Captain-san?

FISBY. Of course, Mr. Oshira.

OSHIRA. There are lovely teahouses in the big cities. But the men of Tobiki have never been inside them. We are too poor and our clothes are too ragged. All of my life I have dreamed of visiting a teahouse where paper lanterns cast a light in the lotus pond and bamboo bells hanging in the pines tinkle as the breezes brush them. But this picture is only in my heart . . . I may never see it. I am an old man, sir. I shall die soon. It is evil for the soul to depart this world laden with envy or regret. Give us our teahouse, sir. Free my soul for death.

FISBY (*unhappily*). But . . . we haven't got any carpenters!

SAKINI (*calls over the heads of the group*). Oi! Daiku-san! Daiku-san! (MR. SUMATA and HIS FATHER *come trotting across the stage carrying their carpenter boxes.* SAKINI *turns to* FISBY.) Oh, what you think? Mr. Sumata and his papa just come down from mountains!

FISBY (*gives* SAKINI *a penetrating but defeated look*). All right. All right! I haven't got a chance. I guess Uncle Sam is going into the teahouse business.

(*He turns and goes back into his office, followed by* LOTUS BLOSSOM. *He picks up Plan B.* SAKINI *announces the decision from the steps.*)

SAKINI. Cha ya, tatete iiyo!

(*There is an outburst of cheers from the* VILLAGERS. *It sounds very much like* "Fisby-san, Banzai, Uncle Sam, Banzai!" *Inside* FISBY *begins tearing up Plan B.* LOTUS BLOSSOM *kneels before him, geta in hand.* FISBY *extends his feet and smiles down at her. The cheering outside continues. As the panels descend—*

THE SCENE BLACKS OUT QUICKLY

SCENE TWO

SCENE: *Colonel Purdy's office.*

TIME: *A few weeks later.*

AT RISE: *The right panel is lifted. A light picks up* COLONEL PURDY. *He sits at his desk fuming over a report. The rest of the stage remains dark. He calls* GREGOVICH *on his office inter-com.*

PURDY. Gregovich!

GREGOVICH'S VOICE. Yes, sir?

PURDY. Get me Captain Fisby at Tobiki.

GREGOVICH. Yes, sir.

(*The extreme left panel rises leaving the intervening panels lowered.* FISBY *sits with his feet propped up on his desk. He is wearing his bathrobe* "kimono." LOTUS BLOSSOM *stands at his side fanning him. Over the scene, the sound of hammering and sawing can be heard. Over this the phone can be heard to ring.* FISBY *lifts the receiver.*)

FISBY. Captain Fisby.

PURDY. Colonel Purdy.

FISBY (*over noise*). Who?

PURDY. Colonel Purdy!

FISBY. I can't hear you. Hold on a minute. (*He turns to* LOTUS BLOSSOM.) See if you can stop that hammering on the teahouse for a minute.

(*He goes through the motions.* LOTUS BLOSSOM *nods understandlingly and goes out.*)

PURDY. What's going on down there, Fisby?

FISBY (*as the noises cease*). Now, who is it?

PURDY. Colonel Purdy.

FISBY (*wraps his robe about his legs quickly*). Oh, good afternoon, Colonel.

PURDY. I want to talk to you about your Progress Report.

FISBY. I sent it in.

PURDY. I have it. I have it right in front of me. I've read it twice. Now, suppose *you* tell *me* what it says.

FISBY. What would you like to have me explain, sir?

PURDY. I'd like you to explain why there's nothing in here about the school-house. Didn't you get the lumber?

FISBY (*uneasily*). Yes, sir . . . it's being used right now. But we'll need some more, I'm afraid.

PURDY. I sent ample, according to specifications. How big a structure are you building?

FISBY. Well . . . we ought to consider expansion. Populations increase.

PURDY. We don't need to consider expansion. Our troops will be out of here by the next generation. Which brings me to another point. (*He refers to the report.*) What's this about six kids being born last week?

FISBY. Well, there wasn't much else to fill the Progress Report, sir.

PURDY. Then you've failed at your indoctrination. Don't you know yet that births are entered under "Population Increases"? They are not considered progress.

FISBY. But they weren't children, sir. They were kids . . . goats.

PURDY. There must be something wrong with this connection. It sounded just as if you said "goats."

FISBY. I did, sir. Kids . . . goats. You see, we're trying to increase the livestock herd down here. I thought . . .

PURDY. Goats! I don't care what you thought. Look here, Fisby. Suppose some congressman flew in to inspect our team. How would I explain such a report?

FISBY. Well, goats will breed, sir. Congress can't stop that. And I've been concerned with . . .

PURDY. The population of civilians alone concerns us. I want to know exactly what progress you've made as outlined in Plan B.

FISBY. Well . . . I'm getting along fine with the people.

PURDY. In other words, nothing. Listen to me. Do you realize what Major McEvoy has accomplished in his village?

FISBY. No, sir.

PURDY. Well, I'll tell you. His fourth-graders know the alphabet through "M," and his whole village can sing "God Bless America" in English.

FISBY. Yes, sir. That's real progress, sir. I wish I could say the same.

PURDY. See that you do. I don't want any rotten apples in my barrel. Now . . . I want to know exactly what you have accomplished in the five weeks you've been down there.

FISBY. Well, sir . . . I've started an industry. I'm sending our first shipment out for sale this week.

PURDY. What are you making?

FISBY (*looks down at his feet*). Oh, getas and . . .

PURDY. Wait a minute . . . what in God's name is a *geta?*

FISBY. Not "a" geta . . . *getas* . . . you have to have two.

PURDY. Are you breeding some *other* kind of animal?

FISBY. You wear them on your feet, sir. Excellent for strengthening the meta-tarsal muscles. Then . . . I have a group busy building cricket cages. . . .

PURDY. Captain Fisby!

FISBY. Yes, sir.

PURDY. What kind of cages did you say?

FISBY. Cricket. Like in cricket on the hearth. I think we'll find a great market for them. Of course, we don't supply the crickets.

PURDY. Naturally not. Captain Fisby . . . have you been taking your salt pills?

FISBY. Yes, sir . . . I take them at cha ya . . . with my tea.

PURDY. Have you been going out in the sun without your helmet?

FISBY. I wear a kasa, sir . . . it's more practical . . . wind can blow through the straw.

PURDY. I see. I see. That will be all, Captain. (*He hangs up quickly.*)

FISBY. Hello . . . hello . . .

(*He hangs up and sits looking at the phone rather puzzled. The lights go down in his office and the panel descends.* COLONEL PURDY *also sits looking at the phone in his office. He calls* SERGEANT GREGOVICH *on the inter-com.*)

PURDY. Sergeant! What is the name of that psychiatrist over at Awasi?

GREGOVICH. Captain McLean?

PURDY. Get him on the phone. My man at Tobiki has gone completely off his rocker!

THE SCENE BLACKS OUT QUICKLY

SCENE THREE

SCENE: *Captain Fisby's office.*
TIME: *A few days later.*
AT RISE: *The office is empty as the panel rises. After a moment* CAPTAIN MC LEAN *enters. He is an intense, rather wildeyed man in his middle forties. He glances about furtively, then begins to examine the papers on Fisby's desk. He makes several notes in a notebook. He picks up Fisby's cricket cage and is examining it intently when* FISBY *enters behind him. He halts upon seeing* MC LEAN. FISBY *is wearing his blue bathrobe, his geta and a native straw hat.*

FISBY. Well, who are you?

MC LEAN (*gasps in surprise*). Oh, you startled me.

FISBY. Can I do anything for you? I'm Captain Fisby.

MC LEAN. I'm Captain McLean. There was no one here . . . so I came in.

FISBY (*he looks at his insignia*). Oh, medical corps. What brings you to Tobiki?

MC LEAN. Well, I'm— I'm on leave. Thought I'd spend it making some— some— ethnological studies. (*He adds quickly.*) Of the natives.

FISBY. Well, you couldn't have come to a more interesting spot. Sit down, Captain.

MC LEAN (*sits*). Thank you. Would you have any objection to my spending a week or so making my studies, Captain?

FISBY. Not at all. Make yourself at home. I'll take that if it's in your way. (*He reaches out to relieve* MC LEAN *of the cricket cage he still holds.*)

MC LEAN (*glances at the cage in his hand and laughs awkwardly*). Oh, yes. I was just examining it.

FISBY (*pleased at his authority on the subject*). It's a cricket cage.

MC LEAN (*pauses*). You . . . like crickets?

FISBY. I haven't found one yet. But at least I've got the cage. I've got two . . . if you want one.

MC LEAN. Thank you, no. Thank you very much. (*He looks at* FISBY'S *attire.*) What happened to your uniform. Captain?

FISBY. It's around. I find getas and a kimono much more comfortable in this climate.

MC LEAN. But isn't that a bathrobe?

FISBY (*shrugs*). It passes for a kimono. Would you like to take off your shoes, Captain?

MC LEAN. Thank you . . . no. I'll keep them on if you don't mind.

FISBY. Can I offer you some tsukemono? You eat these during the day between meals. (*He extends a platter.*) Tsukemono means fragrant things.

MC LEAN. I just had a chocolate bar, thank you. (*He rises and looks out the door.*) May I ask what you're building down the road?

FISBY (*proudly*). That's my cha ya. (*He pops a few tsukemonos into his mouth.*) It's really going to be something to write home about.

MC LEAN. Cha ya?

FISBY. Well, it just so happens, Captain, that I own a geisha girl. That might sound strange to you, but you get used to these things after a while. And if you have a geisha, you've got to have a cha ya. Sure you don't want some tsukemono?

MC LEAN. I really couldn't eat a thing. (*He glances out the door again.*) May I ask what the men are doing down there wading in that irrigation ditch?

FISBY. They're not wading, they're building a lotus pond. You can't have a cha ya without a lotus pond.

MC LEAN (*sits opposite* FISBY). How have you felt lately, Fisby?

FISBY. McLean, I'll tell you something. I've never been happier. I feel reckless and free. And it all happened the moment I decided not to build that damned pentagon-shaped school.

MC LEAN. That what?

FISBY. The good colonel ordered me to build a pentagon-shaped schoolhouse down here. But the people wanted a teahouse. Believe it or not, someone gave me a geisha girl. So I'm giving this village what it wants. That must all sound pretty crazy to you, Mac.

MC LEAN. Well, yes and no.

FISBY. These are wonderful people with a strange sense of beauty. And hard-working . . . when there's a purpose. You should have seen them start out day before yesterday, great bundles of things they'd made piled high on their heads. Getas, cricket cages, lacquer ware—things to sell as souvenirs up north. Don't let anyone tell you these people are lazy.

MC LEAN. Oh. I see. I see.

FISBY. No, you don't. But you'll have a chance to study them.

MC LEAN. So you're building them a teahouse.

FISBY. Next thing I'm going to do for them is find out if this land here will grow anything besides sweet potatoes. I'm going to send for fertilizers and DDT and—

MC LEAN (*leaps to his feet*). Chemicals!

FISBY. Sure, why not?

MC LEAN. Do you want to poison these people?

FISBY. No, but—

MC LEAN. Now you've touched on a subject that is very close to me. For years I've planned to retire and buy a farm—raise specialties for big restaurants. So let me tell you this. Chemicals will kill all your earthworms, and earthworms aerate your soil.

FISBY. They do?

MC LEAN. Do you know an earthworm leaves castings eight times its own weight every day?

FISBY. That much!

MC LEAN. Organic gardening is the only thing. Nature's way—compost, manure, but no chemicals.

FISBY. Hey! You know a lot about this.

MC LEAN (*modestly*). I should. I've subscribed to all the farm journals for years.

FISBY. Say, you could help these people out while you're here—if you would. Do you think you could take over supervision—establish a sort of experimental station for them?

MC LEAN. Well, I– no—no—I haven't time.

FISBY. Take time. This is a chance for you to put some of your theories into practice.

MC LEAN (*haughtily*). They are not theories. They are proven facts.

FISBY. I'll give you a couple of men to help, and all you'd have to do is tell us how.

MC LEAN (*hesitates*). Is your soil acid or alkaline?

FISBY. Gosh, I don't know.

MC LEAN. Well, that's the very *first* thing you have to find out. Do you have bees?

FISBY. I haven't seen any.

MC LEAN (*shakes his head sadly*). People always underestimate the importance of bees for pollinating.

FISBY (*slaps him on the back*). Mac, you're just the man we've needed down here. You're a genius!

MC LEAN. I'll want plenty of manure.

FISBY. You'll get it.

MC LEAN. And I'll want to plan this program scientifically. I wish I had some of my books . . . and my seed catalogues. (*He measures from the floor.*) I've got a stack of catalogues that high.

FISBY. Why don't you make a list, and I'll get the boys over at the airstrip to fly us in seeds from the States.

MC LEAN (*the gardener fever possesses the doctor as he begins to make his list*). Every spring I've made lists of seeds and never had any soil to put them in. And now . . . I could actually germinate. (*He writes.*) Corn—Golden Bantam. (*Then adds enthusiastically:*) And Country Gentleman! Hybrid.

FISBY. Why don't I just leave you with your list while I check on the lotus pond? (MC LEAN *doesn't hear him.*) Well, I'll be back for tea. We have tea in the pine grove and watch the sun go down. (*He goes out.*)

MC LEAN (*continues with his list reading aloud*). Cucumbers— Extra Early Green Prolific. (*His enthusiasm mounts.*) Radishes—Crimson Giant! (*The telephone begins to ring; he ignores it as he writes.*) Tomatoes – Ponderosa Earliana. (*The telephone rings insistently.*) Watermelon! (*He closes his eyes ecstatically.*)

(*The panel rises on the opposite side of the stage revealing Colonel Purdy's office. The intervening panel remains down.* COLONEL PURDY *sits at his desk jiggling his telephone hook.*)

PURDY. What's the matter with this connection! Ring again!

MC LEAN (*ignores the ringing*). Watermelon— All-American Gold Medal! (*He writes it down as the phone rings. He looks up impatiently and lifts the receiver.*). Hello!

PURDY (*confidentially*). Who is this?

MC LEAN. This is Captain McLean.

PURDY. This is Colonel Purdy. Can you talk?

MC LEAN. Why not?

PURDY. I was anxious to hear your report on you-know-who.

MC LEAN. On *who?*

PURDY. *Captain Fisby!* The man I sent you down to examine.

MC LEAN. Oh. (*He weighs his problem quickly.*) Oh. Well . . . I'll have to stay down here several weeks for some . . .

PURDY. Several weeks!

MC LEAN. Rome wasn't built in a day.

PURDY. What?

MC LEAN. I said, Rome wasn't built in a day.

PURDY (*digests this*). Well . . . you're the doctor.

MC LEAN. I'll send in a report . . . from time to time. I can tell you now I expect to work miracles down here.

PURDY. Splendid . . . splendid. Is there anything I can send? Some old *Adventure Magazines* or anything?

MC LEAN. There are a couple of books I'd like, but I don't think you could get them.

PURDY (*picks up pencil*). You name them.

MC LEAN. Well . . . one is *Principles of Pea Production*, and the other is *Do's and Don'ts of Cabbage Culture.* (PURDY *starts to write . . . then stops.*) And do you think you could lay your hands on a soil test kit?

PURDY (*looks at earphone*). A what?

MC LEAN (*enunciating*). A *soil test kit.* I want to see if the soil is sour down here.

PURDY. Sour, did you say?

MC LEAN. Yes . . . if your soil is sour your seeds won't germinate. And I sure wish I had some bees.

PURDY. There *is* something wrong with this connection!

MC LEAN. I'm going to take time out here to build up the soil with manure.

PURDY (*unbelieving*). Did you say manure?

MC LEAN. I've lost faith in chemicals. You kill all your worms. I can tell you, when you kill a worm, Colonel . . . you're killing a friend. (*There is a long pause.*)

Hello . . . hello.

PURDY (*puts down the phone and turns to the squawk box*). Gregovich, where is Plan B!

GREGOVICH'S VOICE. What did you want, sir?

PURDY. I want to see who I send to analyze an analyst.

THE PANELS FALL QUICKLY ON
EACH SIDE OF THE STAGE

SCENE FOUR

SCENE: *Village square.*

TIME: *A few weeks later.*

AT RISE: *The panels rise to reveal the village square and Fisby's office. Natives are seated in the square, great bundles beside them. Others arrive and sink into positions of dejection.* FISBY *works at his desk.* SAKINI *enters and looks at the* VILLAGERS.

SAKINI (*to* MR. KEORA). Doshtano?

KEORA. Hitotsu mo unremasenna.

SAKINI. Oh, oh . . . too bad. (SAKINI *crosses and enters Fisby's office.*) Boss!

FISBY. Yes.

SAKINI. Mr. Keora and everybody back from Big Koza.

FISBY. Good. Let's see how they made out. (*He steps outside followed by* SAKINI. *He stops as he sees his* VILLAGERS *sitting dejectedly before their large bundles. He turns to* SAKINI.) What's the matter?

SAKINI. Mr. Keora very tired. Walk two days with bundle on back to sell straw hats to American soldiers at Big Koza. Nobody buy, so walk back. Too many damn hats now, boss.

FISBY. He couldn't sell *any?* (SAKINI *shakes his head.*) Why not?

SAKINI (*shrugs*). Soldiers not want. Soldiers say . . . what you think we are . . . hayseed? So come home.

FISBY (*sees old* MR. OSHIRA *and crosses to him.* OSHIRA *rises*). Mr. Oshira . . . did you take your lacquer ware to Yatoda?

OSHIRA. Oh, yes . . . but come back . . . not go again.

FISBY. But I don't understand. . . . The Navy always spends money.

OSHIRA. Sailors say, "Oh, pretty good . . . how much you want?" I say, "Twenty-five yen." They say, "Oh, too much . . . can get better in five-and-ten-cent store.

Give you one nickel."

FISBY. Did you explain how many years it took you to learn how to turn out such work?

OSHIRA (*nods*). They say, "What you want us to do, cry?"

FISBY (*angrily*). Damn stupid morons! (*He turns back to* OSHIRA.) Did you tell then that each cup was handmade?

OSHIRA. They say . . . not care. They say . . . at home have big machines that turn out ten cups every minute. They say . . . take nickel or jump in lake.

FISBY (*unhappily*). So you had to carry them all the way back?

SAKINI. Poor Mr. Oshira. No one want his lacquer ware.

FISBY. Well, he's wrong. He's a great artist and I'll buy everything he's made myself.

SAKINI. But you not able to buy everything from everybody in Tobiki, boss.

FISBY (*sits down on steps*). Tell them that they should all be proud of their work. And that I'm proud of all of them.

SAKINI. Gokro, gokro san.

FISBY. I'll think of something . . . I'll hit on an idea to bring money to this village yet.

SAKINI. Boss . . . you stop work on teahouse now?

FISBY. No! You'll get a teahouse if I give you nothing else.

SAKINI. They sure wish they could make some money to spend at teahouse, boss. Not like to go like beggars.

FISBY. Give me a little time, Sakini. (*As they sit around, each deep in his personal problems,* MC LEAN *enters. His uniform is gone. He is wearing his bathrobe, a straw hat and geta.*)

MC LEAN. Fisby! You're just the man I want to see. Can I have a couple of boys to help me? The damn Japanese beetles are eating up my Chinese peas.

FISBY (*dispiritedly*). Sure . . . I'll get a couple for you.

MC LEAN (*looks around*). What's the matter?

FISBY. There's no market for our products.

MC LEAN. Oh . . . that's too bad. What are you going to do? (*He sits down.*)

FISBY. Try to think of something.

OSHIRA. The world has left us behind. (*The* VILLAGERS *begin to rise and pick up their handiwork.*)

SEIKO. Amerika-san no seija naiyo. Sa,

sa, kaette yakezake da!

SAKINI. They say . . . tell you not your fault no one wants to buy, boss. They say guess they go home now and get drunk.

FISBY. Tell them I don't blame them. If I had anything to drink . . . I'd do the same. (*As they start to file out, both* MC LEAN *and* FISBY *have a delayed reaction. They leap to their feet together.*) Wait a minute! (*The* VILLAGERS *stop.*) What are they going to get drunk *on?*

SAKINI. They got nothing but brandy.

MC LEAN. Nothing but *brandy!*

FISBY. How did they manage to get brandy?

SAKINI. We make very fine brandy here, from sweet potatoes. Been making for generations.

FISBY. You make a brandy *yourselves?*

SAKINI. Oh, yes. We make for weddings and funerals.

FISBY (*looks at* MC LEAN). What does it taste like?

SAKINI. You want some, boss? (*He turns to* HOKAIDA.) Imozake, skoshi!

FISBY. Sakini, if this stuff is any good at all, we're in business. This is one thing I *know* our men will buy.

SAKINI. Oh . . . I think we not like to sell brandy. Only make for ceremony.

MC LEAN. It may not be any good anyhow. There are some things even the troops won't drink.

HOKAIDA (*returns with an earthen jug*). Hai, imozake. (*He hands the jug to* FISBY.)

SAKINI. There you are, boss. You like taste now?

FISBY. I'd like to smell it first. (*He gives it a sniff and jerks his head back.*)

MC LEAN. Obviously, it has a kick.

FISBY. How old is this brandy, Sakini?

SAKINI (*turns to Hokaida*). Kore itsuno?

HOKAIDA (*Holds up seven fingers*). Issukan mae dayo.

FISBY. Seven years old?

SAKINI. Oh, no, boss. He make last week.

FISBY. It couldn't smell like that in only a week.

SAKINI. Is village secret. You try now?

FISBY (*hands it to* MC LEAN). You try it, Mac. You're a medical man.

MC LEAN (*backs away*). You first.

FISBY. I insist. You're my guest.

MC LEAN. I waive the honor.

FISBY (*Turns to* SAKINI). Has anyone ever gone blind or died from this?

MC LEAN. He said they make it for

funerals.

SAKINI. Oh, no, boss. We not blind. We not dead.

FISBY. There, you see.

MC LEAN. They've worked up an immunity over the years.

FISBY. Well, I don't want to kill any of my countrymen. Couldn't you make some sort of test, Doc? (*As* MC LEAN *considers this, the bleat of a goat is heard offstage.* FISBY *and* MC LEAN *exchange looks and nod.*) Sakini, get Lady Astor. (*To* MC LEAN.) That's Miss Higa Jiga's goat. She asked me to give it a classy name

(SAKINI *goes to get* LADY ASTOR.)

MC LEAN. I'm not sure what we'll prove. Goats have hardy stomachs.

SAKINI (*returns leading a goat*). Boss, you make guinea pig of goat?

FISBY. If this passes the goat-test, it's all right. No Marine would ever admit he had a weaker stomach than a goat.

MC LEAN. May I borrow this a moment? (*He takes* MR. HOKAIDA's *red helmet and pours into it from the jug.*)

SAKINI. Lady Astor very lucky goat.

FISBY. You hold her, Sakini. Proceed, Doctor . . . in the name of science. (*The goat sniffs the contents of the helmet.*) We're either going to have an industry or goat meat for dinner.

(LADY ASTOR *begins to drink the concoction. They watch her lap up the liquor and lick her lips with relish.*)

MC LEAN (*stands back*). It doesn't seem to affect her. (*Draws his fingers back and forth in front of the goat's eyes.*) Reflexes all right.

FISBY. Let's watch her a minute. The future of Tobiki and the health of the Army are at stake here. (FISBY *and* MC LEAN *and the* VILLAGERS *stand watching the goat.* LADY ASTOR *is quite content.* FISBY *rises.*) Well, here goes. (*He takes the jug and samples the contents himself.* MC LEAN *watches him. Then he, too, tests from the jug. They look at each other and grin.*) Whee! (*He dashes for his office.*)

SAKINI (*follows*). What you going to do, boss?

FISBY. I am about to form the Cooperative Brewing Company of Tobiki. (FISBY *is followed by* SAKINI, MC LEAN, *and some of the* VILLAGERS. *He picks up the phone.*) Get me the Officers' Club at Awasi.

SAKINI. We going to make brandy, boss?

FISBY. I'll tell you in a minute. (*He turns back to telephone.*) Hello . . . Officers' Club, Awasi? This is Captain Fisby at Tobiki. Oh, hello, Major, how are you? Major, when I was with your unit, you could never keep a supply of liquor in the club, and I stumbled onto something and wondered if you'd be interested. Tobiki, as you know, is the heart of the brandy industry and— (*He takes the phone away from his ear as the word brandy is shouted back at him.*) Yes . . . brandy. . . . (*He turns to* MC LEAN.) Doc, look up the word "sweet potato" and see if it has another fancier name. (*He turns back to the phone.*) Yes . . . I'm here . . . yes . . . I could get you some if you could pay their price and keep the source secret. Oh, yes, it's been made here for generations. Why, you never tasted anything like it.

MC LEAN. The Haitian word for sweet potato is *b-a-t-a-t-a.* (*He spells it out.*)

FISBY (*into the phone*). You've heard of Seven Star Batata, haven't you? Well, Tobiki is where it's made. (*He turns to* MC LEAN.) The Seven Star did it.

SAKINI. Brandy much better if eight or ten days old, boss.

FISBY. We also have Eight Star and Ten Star. Well, naturally the Ten Star comes a little higher. It sells for— (*He looks at* SAKINI *desperately.* SAKINI *holds up ten fingers.*) A hundred occupation yen a gallon.

SAKINI. I mean *ten* yen, boss.

FISBY. Delivered. All right, we'll send up five gallons in about a week. It'll be delivered by our Department of Agriculture. You're welcome. (*He hangs up and turns to* SAKINI.) Sakini, if every family in Tobiki starts making brandy, how much can we turn out in a week?

SAKINI. Oh, maybe . . . forty . . . fifty gallons.

FISBY. Better aim for eighty. (*He lifts the receiver again.*) I'd like to get the naval base at Big Koza, Officers' Club, Commander Myers.

SAKINI. Maybe if everybody build private stills, Tobiki can turn out hundred gallon.

FISBY. I'll know better after I talk to the Navy. (*He speaks into the phone.*) Commander Myers? Captain Fisby at Tobiki. Commander, we've got a surplus of brandy down here and I was wondering . . . (*Again he takes the phone away from his ear as the word brandy is blasted back.*)

Yes. Brandy. Ten Star Batata. Well, Lady Astor won't drink anything else. Oh . . . we could supply you with as much as you want at a hundred yen a gallon. Fifteen gallons? Right! It will be delivered Horse Cart Special in ten days. (*He hangs up and turns to the others crowding into his office.*) Sakini, tell them to all start making brandy, and in a week or two everyone in this village is going to have more money than he ever dreamed of.

SAKINI. Ah, dondon kaseide sake tsukreba minna kanega mokaruyo!

MR. KEORA. Minna shiroi koto katte moii darone?

SAKINI. They say . . . if they work like the dickens, can they all have white coats like the mayor?

FISBY. Yes. I'll get the cloth somewhere. That's a promise. (*The telephone rings.*) Wait a minute. Hello? Well, word gets around fast. (*He picks up his order blank.*) Twenty gallons? PX, GHQ, C.O.D. O.K. (*He hangs up.*) Get to work, boys! (*As they turn to leave,* FISBY *suddenly leaps to his feet.*) Wait! (*They stand frozen as he crouches and starts toward them. He slaps his hand on the floor and then rises triumphantly.*) I got my cricket!

(*The* VILLAGERS *cheer for* FISBY.)

THE PANELS FALL QUICKLY

ACT THREE

SCENE ONE

SCENE: *Teahouse of the August Moon.*
TIME: *Several weeks later.*
AT RISE: *All the panels are down.* SAKINI *steps from the wings to address the audience.*

SAKINI
(*Bows*)
Ability of Americans for mass production equaled only by American capacity for consumption.
Fortune often comes in back door while we look out front window.
Prosperity not only smile on Tobiki.
Prosperity giggle like silly girl.
Very strange.
Things we do best . . . not wanted.
Things we think least of . . . wanted most.
No conclusion.

Tobiki now village of beautiful houses. But loveliest of all is Teahouse of August Moon.

(*He goes off extreme left, signaling for the panels to rise. Offstage the music of string instruments can be heard playing softly. The panels go up. The ugly thatched huts are gone. In the center of the stage, exquisite in its simplicity, stands the teahouse. Small bells tinkle from its pagoda roof. Soft lights glow through the colored paper panels. Dwarf pines edge the walk leading to a small bridge. An August moon hangs in the autumn sky. The silhouette of* LOTUS BLOSSOM *is framed in the center panel by the soft back lighting. She slides the panel open and steps into the almost bare center room of the teahouse. She crosses and lights the lanterns hanging from the eave extensions. As she goes through this ceremony, the* GUESTS *wander in. Before they enter the teahouse, they remove their shoes and rinse their fingers in the ceremonial bamboo basin. Then they enter and seat themselves on green floor mats. The* WOMEN *are dressed in silk kimonos of varying hues and the majority of the men wear spotless white suits.* LOTUS BLOSSOM *bows to them and returns through the sliding door again.* FISBY *and* MC LEAN, *followed by* SAKINI, *enter.* SAKINI *wears a white suit and the* AMERICANS *wear their bathrobes and geta. They are greeted enthusiastically by the* GUESTS.)

SAKINI. I tell Lotus Blossom you here, boss. (*He disappears through the sliding panel in the center of the teahouse.*)

FISBY (*as they walk around inspecting the grounds*). It's really something, isn't it?

MC LEAN. Where did they all get their white suits?

FISBY. They made them.

MC LEAN. Where'd they get the cloth?

FISBY. I got it from the naval base at Awasi for ten gallons of brandy. It's target cloth.

MC LEAN. Those kimonos aren't target cloth.

FISBY. Parachute silk. Six gallons' worth.

(LOTUS BLOSSOM *enters, followed by* SAKINI. *She hurries down to* FISBY *and bows. She extends a yellow chrysanthemum to him.*)

SAKINI. Chrysanthemum bud in full bloom, boss.

LOTUS BLOSSOM (*she bows as* FISBY *accepts*

the gift). Hop-pee. (*Her eyes almost disappear in a great smile of pride.*)

FISBY. What did she say?

SAKINI. I try like the dickens to teach her to say "happy birthday," but she can't say "birthday," boss.

LOTUS BLOSSOM. Hop-pee.

FISBY. Well . . . I'm floored! (*He bows to her.*) Thank you, Lotus Blossom. (*To* SAKINI.) How did you know?

MC LEAN. I gave you away.

SAKINI. Everybody in village like to show appreciation, boss.

FISBY. I should have had a kimono made. When you said "formal," I thought this would do.

LOTUS BLOSSOM. Hop-pee. Hop-pee.

FISBY. And a hop-pee hop-pee to you.

GUESTS (*murmur in the background*). Hayaku oiwai hajimeyo, soda, soda.

SAKINI. Everybody impatient to get on with the party, boss.

LOTUS BLOSSOM. Hop-pee. (*She indicates the center mat.*)

SAKINI. You sit down now, boss. Lotus Blossom going to dance in your honor.

FISBY. You hear that. . . . She's going to dance! (*Quickly sits down.*) Sit down, you farmer. . . . This is in my honor.

MC LEAN. My, my! How am I going to stall Purdy so I can stay down here?

FISBY. I'll have a relapse for you. (*They turn to watch* LOTUS BLOSSOM *as she takes her position and the first notes are struck by the musicians present.* LOTUS BLOSSOM *performs for them a traditional dance of infinite grace and delicacy. She finishes, concluding her performance in front of* FISBY, *who rises and bows to her.*) What a lovely little thing you are! This belongs to you. (*He returns the chrysanthemum with a flourish.* LOTUS BLOSSOM *accepts it and seats herself quickly on a mat and hides her head.*)

SAKINI. Oh, boss . . . you know what you do!

FISBY. It called for flowers.

SAKINI. That mean you give your heart to her.

FISBY (*lightly*). Well, I do. We all do. (*Turns to* MC LEAN.) Wasn't that beautiful, Mac!

MC LEAN. She can dance in my cha ya any day.

SAKINI. You sit beside Lotus Blossom now, boss. You guest of honor and referee.

FISBY (*starts to sit down*). Referee! I thought this was a birthday party.

SAKINI. Lotus Blossom now putting on wrestling match for you, boss.

FISBY. *Wrestling* match?

LOTUS BLOSSOM (*stands and claps hands*). Sa, osumo hajime mashoyo.

(*Immediately two men bring in four poles which they set up downstage center to mark a square. Each pole has colored cloth hanging from it.*)

MC LEAN. Who is wrestling? (*He sits next to* FISBY.)

SAKINI. Wrestling match between Chief of Agriculture and Chief of Police.

FISBY (*to* LOTUS BLOSSOM). Hokaida and Seiko? (*She nods.*)

SAKINI. Grudge fight, boss.

FISBY. Really?

SAKINI. Whoever win match get to haul sweet potatoes for Lotus Blossom.

FISBY (*watching the poles being set up, he indicates them to* LOTUS BLOSSOM). Why have they wrapped colored cloth around the poles?

LOTUS BLOSSOM. Kuro wa fuyu, Ao wa haru, Akaga natsu de, Shirowa akiyo. Wakkatta?

SAKINI. She explain, boss, that black cloth remind us of winter, green cloth remind us of spring, red is the summer and white the autumn.

LOTUS BLOSSOM (*claps her hands*). Osumo, osumo!

(MR. HOKAIDA, *bare except for a pair of black shorts, enters and crosses to one corner of the ring, where he squats on his heels. An outburst of approval greets his entrance. He smiles with fatuous pleasure, and makes a desperate effort to hold in his fat stomach.*)

MC LEAN. Do his black shorts mean anything?

SAKINI. Just easy to clean.

(LOTUS BLOSSOM *claps her dainty hands again.* MR. SEIKO *enters, lean and wiry, also wearing black shorts and a sweat shirt reading* U.S.S. Princeton.)

FISBY. Where did he get *that?*

SAKINI. Sailor at naval base. Some class, eh? (MR. SEIKO *peels off the shirt to great applause and squats in the opposite corner. He glares across at* HOKAIDA, *who thrusts his jaw forward.*) They waiting on you to give signal now, boss.

FISBY. Waiting on *me?*

SAKINI. Oh, yes . . . you are Honorable Referee.

LOTUS BLOSSOM (*hands her fan to* FISBY). Korede aizu shite kudasai.

FISBY. What do I do with this?

SAKINI. Now you cover face with fan.

FISBY. Why?

SAKINI. That mean you not take sides. Now you go to center of ring and drop fan from face.

MC LEAN. And get the hell out in a hurry.

FISBY. How many falls?

SAKINI. No falls, boss. First one to throw other out of ring—winner. (FISBY *covers his face with the fan and walks down center. The two wrestlers crouch, poised to leap, their eyes on the fan.* FISBY *whips the fan away from his face and dashes back out of range. The protagonists circle each other slowly. Suddenly all hell breaks loose. The teahouse guests cheer their favorite. The fat* MR. HOKAIDA *picks up* MR. SEIKO *and subjects him to a series of head spins and thumpings. But he exhausts himself; and it is* SEIKO *who ends by tossing* HOKAIDA *out of the ring. A cheer rises from the guests.* FISBY *sighs with relief.*) Now the judges must decide who win.

FISBY. Decide! Is there any doubt?

(*The three judges confer. They then turn to* MR. HOKAIDA *and bow.*)

SAKINI. Mr. Hokaida! The winner . . .

(*This startling announcement is greeted with approval.* SEIKO *beats his head and wails.*)

FISBY. How *could* he be the winner! He was thrown out of the ring.

SAKINI. Maybe so, but judges all cousins of Mr. Hokaida.

FISBY. But the judges are wrong.

SAKINI (*confidentially*). We know who really win . . . but this way nobody lose face.

(SEIKO *and* HOKAIDA *exit.*)

LOTUS BLOSSOM. Sa kondo wa Fu-san no ban yo.

SAKINI. Lotus Blossom say guests now wish *you* to perform.

FISBY. Perform what?

SAKINI. They like now for you and doctor to sing song or something.

FISBY. Sing!

SAKINI. Must do, boss. Bad manners to refuse.

FISBY (*repeats in alarm*). Sing! (*He turns to* MC LEAN.) Get on your feet, Mac, we've got to sing something.

MC LEAN. What?

FISBY. We could sing the national anthem.

MC LEAN. No, we couldn't—I don't know the words.

FISBY. How about "Deep in the Heart of Texas"?

MC LEAN. Why not? There're no Texans here. (*They step forward.*)

FISBY. Mac, let's have some fun. (*He turns to* SAKINI.) Sakini, you tell them they must all help us. They must clap and sing "Deep in the Heart of Texas" every time *we* do.

SAKINI (*beaming*). Tewo tataite Deep in the Heart of Texas. (*Demonstrates clapping.*) Koshte, Deep in the Heart of Texas.

(*The* VILLAGERS *chatter and agree with enthusiasm.* FISBY *and* MC LEAN *stand close together and begin singing. Each time they come to the designated phrase,* SAKINI *gives a signal and the* VILLAGERS *join in lustily. Lost in their eager concentration, no one observes the entrance of* COLONEL PURDY. *He looks from the "kimono"-clad figures of* FISBY *and* MC LEAN *to the assemblage. As he shouts at* FISBY, *his voice is drowned out by the chorus of "Deep in the Heart of Texas." The song continues.* PURDY *signals offstage.* GREGOVICH *enters and is instructed by* COLONEL PURDY *to end the objectionable noises.*)

GREGOVICH. Captain Fisby!

(*Again the voice coincides with the shouts of "Deep in the Heart of Texas" and is lost.* COLONEL PURDY *stalks downstage center, followed by* GREGOVICH.)

PURDY. Captain Fisby! What in the name of Occupation is going on here?

(FISBY *gasps and backs away. Suddenly aware of his bathrobe, he stoops down to cover his bare legs.* MC LEAN *surrenders completely to panic. He runs to hide behind guests. The* GUESTS, *alarmed by the sudden intrusion, scatter in all directions. In the midst of this bedlam—*

THE PANELS ARE LOWERED

SCENE TWO

SCENE: *Office of Captain Fisby.*

TIME: *Next morning.*

AT RISE: *The four bamboo panels are down.* SAKINI *enters from the wings right and crosses down to the footlights.*

SAKINI

(*Bows*)
When present is blackest,
Future can only be brighter.
Okinawa invaded many times.
Not sink in ocean yet.

Survive Chinese.

Survive Japanese.

Survive missionaries and Americans.

Invaded by typhoon.

Invaded by locust.

Invaded by cockroach and sweet-potato moth.

Tobiki now invaded by Honorable Colonel.

Not sink in ocean.

(*He goes to the left side of the stage and raises the panels in front of Fisby's office. He then exits.* COLONEL PURDY *is seated at Fisby's desk going through his papers.* FISBY *stands behind him nervously watching.* MC LEAN *sits on the cot biting his nails. He rises.*)

PURDY (*without looking up*). Sit down! (MC LEAN *sits down again.* PURDY *turns to* FISBY *and glares at him.*) Where are your bimonthly Progress Reports?

FISBY. I—I think they should be right here under the cricket cage, sir.

PURDY (*takes some papers from under the cage and glances at them*). These are all completely blank. (*He turns to* FISBY.) Fisby, you can't convince me that you've been down here for two months doing absolutely nothing.

FISBY. Oh, no, sir. I mean yes, sir, I have not been doing "nothing."

PURDY. You're beginning to sound like a native.

MC LEAN (*rises*). The tendency is always to descend to the level of the environment, sir. It's a primary postulate of psychology.

PURDY (*turns on him*). Well, it's a primary regulation of the Army to make out reports! (*Back to* FISBY.) Now, I want to know exactly what you've accomplished here from the moment you arrived.

FISBY. Well, let me think. . . .

MC LEAN. Could I—

PURDY. Sit down! (*He turns to* FISBY.) How many lectures have you delivered to the village children on democratic theory?

FISBY. Well, let me see.

PURDY. Four-five?

FISBY (*thinks*). Not that many, sir.

PURDY. Three?

MC LEAN (*hopefully*). Two?

FISBY. N-no.

PURDY. You only delivered *one* lecture?

FISBY. None, sir.

PURDY. Don't tell me you haven't de-

livered a single lecture!

FISBY. Yes, sir, I haven't delivered no lecture. I mean . . . any lecture.

PURDY. Did you organize a Ladies' League for Democratic Action?

FISBY (*beaming*). Yes, sir. I sure did. I did that all right!

PURDY. And how many lectures on democratic theory have you given *them?*

FISBY (*deflated again*). None, sir.

PURDY. You can't mean none. You must mean one or two.

FISBY. No, sir, none.

PURDY. I refuse to believe it.

FISBY. I'm glad, sir.

MC LEAN (*rises in desperation*). Sir, I *must* go.

PURDY. Where!

MC LEAN. My *seedlings* are wilting. I have to transplant them.

PURDY. Captain, you will pack your gear and transplant yourself to your unit at once.

MC LEAN. Yes, sir. (*He turns to* FISBY.) They'll die. It's murder. (*He goes to the door and turns sadly to* FISBY *again.*) Please take care of my beans. (*He exits.*)

PURDY (*turns back to* FISBY). Now! Is the schoolhouse finished?

FISBY (*sighs*). No, sir.

PURDY. *Why* isn't it finished?

FISBY. It isn't finished, sir, because it isn't started.

PURDY. I have a splitting headache, Fisby. I ask you not to provoke me needlessly. Now, where is the schoolhouse?

FISBY. I never built it.

PURDY. Don't stand there and tell me you never built it. I sent the lumber down two months ago.

FISBY (*impressed*). Is it *that* long, sir?

PURDY. What did you do with the lumber I sent?

FISBY. Well, I built a teahouse.

PURDY (*stares at him*). I don't suppose you have any aspirin here?

FISBY. No, sir, I haven't.

PURDY. Now, sit down. Fisby. I want to be fair. (FISBY *sits down.*) I'm a patient man. When I run into something that defies reason, I like to find the reason. (*Explodes.*) What in the name of Occupation do you mean by saying you built a *teahouse* instead of a *schoolhouse!*

FISBY. It's a little hard to explain, sir. Everybody in the village wanted one . . . and Lotus Blossom needed it for her work.

PURDY. And just what is your relationship with this woman?

FISBY. Well, she was a present. So to speak. She's a geisha girl—after a fashion.

PURDY. You built this teahouse—this place for her to ply her trade—with lumber belonging to the Army of Occupation of the United States Government?

FISBY. Well, it just seemed like lumber at the time.

PURDY. Fisby, are you operating a house of prostitution here on Government rice?

FISBY. No, sir! Geishas aren't what you think.

PURDY. Don't tell me what to think. Army Intelligence warned me I'd find something mighty peculiar going on in Tobiki.

FISBY. What's Army Intelligence got to do with it, sir?

PURDY. You're not very cunning, Fisby. With all the Occupation money on the island finding its way to this village, did you think it wouldn't come to the attention of Intelligence?

FISBY. Oh.

PURDY. Why did you do it, Fisby, why!

FISBY. Well, Lotus Blossom had to have a place to teach the Ladies' League how to become geishas and—

PURDY. Fisby! You mean to say you've turned all the decent women of this village into professional . . . (*He slumps into the chair.*) How could you sink to such depths, man!

FISBY. I was only giving in to what the majority wanted, sir.

PURDY. I don't doubt that statement—not at all. It is a sad thing that it took a war to convince me that most of the human race is degenerate. Thank God I come from a country where the air is clean, where the wind is fresh, where—

FISBY (*interrupts*). For heaven's sake, sir, would you please listen to me instead of yourself! There is not a thing goes on in that teahouse that your mother couldn't watch.

PURDY (*leaps to his feet and points a warning finger*). You be careful how you use my mother's name, Fisby.

FISBY. Well, *my* mother then. I swear there's nothing immoral about our tea-house.

PURDY. Then answer me this. What is bringing all that Occupation money to this particular village? There is only one thing that attracts that kind of money.

FISBY. Well, evidently there are two things.

PURDY. And if it isn't honor that you sell here, what is it?

FISBY (*sighs unhappily*). We . . . make things.

PURDY. What?

FISBY. Mats . . . and hats . . . and cricket cages.

PURDY. One hundred and fifty thousand yen finds its way to this village every month. You can't convince me that the American soldier is spending that much on "cricket cages."

FISBY. Well, naturally . . . not all of it. (*The telephone rings.* FISBY *looks at it apprehensively.*)

PURDY. Answer it.

FISBY (*pauses*). It's nothing important, sir.

PURDY. It might be for me. Answer it.

FISBY (*airily*). Oh, it rings all day, sir. Pay no attention.

PURDY. Then I'll *answer* it! (*He picks up the telephone.* FISBY *covers his face.*) Hello? *What* do you want? Who is this? Well, Commander Myers, I think you have the wrong connection. This is not a brewery. Yes . . . yes . . . yes! (*He turns to look at* FISBY.) Oh . . . I see. I see. I see. (*He hangs up. He turns to* FISBY, *who smiles weakly.*)

FISBY. It was the only thing we could make that anyone wanted to buy, sir.

PURDY. Brandy! (*Sadly.*) I don't know which is worse. Putting your country in the white slave trade or the wholesale liquor business. Congress will have to decide.

FISBY. We've the most prosperous village on the island, sir.

PURDY. This ends my Army career. I promised Mrs. Purdy I'd come out a general. You've broken a fine woman's heart, Fisby.

FISBY. You said to make the village self-supporting, sir.

PURDY. I didn't tell you to encourage lewdness and drunkenness. You've sullied the reputation of your nation and all the tears—

FISBY. All right, sir, shall I kill myself?

PURDY. Oh, don't minimize this. You don't know the enemy's genius for propaganda.

FISBY. Does anyone have to know, sir? We're doing all right.

PURDY (*explodes*). Yes, they have to know! I requested an investigation myself. I've notified the Inspector General. Now I'll have to radio the whole story to Washington.

FISBY. Oh.

PURDY (*calmer*). Well, what have you done with all this money you've made so dishonestly?

FISBY. Banked it in Seattle.

PURDY. Oh, that's despicable—making a personal fortune off the labor of these ignorant people.

FISBY. I haven't touched a cent for myself, sir. It's been deposited in the name of the Tobiki Cooperative. The whole village are equal partners. Share and share alike.

PURDY (*leaps up*). That's *Communism!*

FISBY. Is it?

PURDY (*sinks down again*). I'll be lucky to get out of this war a private. (*He is a beaten man.*) Well, there is only one thing for me to do.

FISBY. What is that, sir?

PURDY. First, you are to consider yourself under technical arrest. You will proceed to H.Q. at once to await court-martial.

FISBY. Yes, sir.

PURDY (*steps to the door*). Gregovich! (*He turns back to* FISBY.) I must go on to Awasi this afternoon on an inspection tour. But before I leave, I intend to wipe this stain from our country's honor.

(SERGEANT GREGOVICH *enters and salutes.*)

GREGOVICH. You called, sir?

PURDY. I did. We have some business to attend to here before going on to Awasi.

GREGOVICH. Yes, sir. I'm glad to hear it. (*He turns to* FISBY.) May I congratulate you on what you've done to this village, sir. It's a dream.

FISBY. Thank you, Sergeant.

PURDY. It is an alcoholic dream. It is one vast distillery. I want you to take a detail and some axes and smash every still in this village.

GREGOVICH. Destroy them?

PURDY. Beyond repair. I want you take another detail and rip down that teahouse.

GREGOVICH. But, Colonel—

PURDY. Pile the lumber beside the warehouse. That is an order. Do you understand?

GREGOVICH. Yes, sir! (*As he turns to follow orders,* FISBY *sinks into his chair and the scene blacks out quickly.*)

CURTAIN

SCENE THREE

SCENE: *Teahouse of the August Moon.*
TIME: *A few hours later.*
AT RISE: *All the panels are down. Behind the sceens can be heard the destruction of the stills and the dismantling of the teahouse.* SAKINI *comes out from the wings and crosses down to the footlights. He flinches at the sound of an ax falling on wood.*

————

SAKINI
(*Sadly*)
Oh, no comment.
(*He walks back into the wings as all the panels are raised simultaneously. Only the frame of the teahouse has been spared. The paper panels have disappeared, the pagoda roof is gone with its tinkling bells. There are no colored lanterns and no dwarf pines to grace the path. The bare supports stand stark and ugly. Resting at the edge of the frame is a wheelbarrow.* LOTUS BLOSSOM *is collecting the last of her possessions. She takes a brass brazier down to place in the wheelbarrow. Then she stands with her back to the audience surveying all that remains of the teahouse.* FISBY *comes on, and, seeing* LOTUS BLOSSOM, *hesitates. Then he crosses to stand beside her. He takes her hand, and the two of them stand looking at the ruins.* LOTUS BLOSSOM *walks to the center of the teahouse and sits on the bare floor.* FISBY *comes up and sits on the floor facing her. She goes through the ceremony of pouring him an imaginary cup of tea.* FISBY *accepts with mock formality. As he takes the cup and pretends to drink it,* LOTUS BLOSSOM *covers her face with her hands.* FISBY *sits watching her mutely.*)

SAKINI (*entering*). Jeep all loaded, boss.
FISBY. I'll be along in a minute.
SAKINI. Oh, pretty soon have nice

schoolhouse here.

FISBY (*bitterly*). Pentagon-shaped.

SAKINI. Not be too bad. You take Lotus Blossom with you?

FISBY. No.

SAKINI. What happen to her then?

FISBY. What would have happened to her if we'd never come along?

SAKINI. Not know. Maybe someday she meet nice man and give up Geisha Guild.

FISBY. Ask her if there is anything I can do for her before I go.

SAKINI (*comes up to stand behind them*). Nanika iitai?

LOTUS BLOSSOM (*softly*). Fu-san, watashi-hito kekkon shite chodai.

SAKINI (*scolding*). Sonna bakana koto.

LOTUS BLOSSOM (*persistent*). Iikara hay-aku itte!

FISBY. What does she want?

SAKINI. Oh, that crazy Lotus Blossom. She want you to marry her.

FISBY. Why should she want to marry me?

SAKINI. She think you nicest man she ever see, boss.

FISBY. Tell her that I am clumsy, that I seem to have a gift for destruction. That I'd disillusion her as I have disillusioned her people.

SAKINI. Kokai suruyo.

LOTUS BLOSSOM. Ikitai noyo. Amerika ni. Ikitai noyo.

SAKINI. She say she think she like to go to America. There everybody happy. Sit around and drink tea while machines do work.

FISBY. She wouldn't like it, Sakini. I should hate to see her wearing sweaters and sport shoes and looking like an American looking like an Oriental.

SAKINI. But she want to be an American, boss. She never see an American she not like, boss.

FISBY. Some of them wouldn't like her. Sakini. In the small town where I live, there'd be some who would make her unhappy.

SAKINI. Why, boss?

FISBY. She'd be different.

SAKINI. Dame dayo.

LOTUS BLOSSOM (*takes Fisby's hand*). Sonna koto naiwa, Amerikatte minshu shugi desumono ne.

SAKINI. She say not believe that. In America everybody love everybody. Everybody help everybody; that's democracy.

FISBY. No. That's faith. Explain to her that democracy is only a method—an ideal system for people to get together. But that unfortunately . . . the people who get together . . . are not always ideal.

SAKINI. That's very hard to explain, boss. She girl in love. She just want to hear pretty things.

FISBY. Then tell her that I love what she is, and that it would be wrong to change that. To impose my way of life on her.

SAKINI. Tassha dene!

FISBY. Tell her that I shall never forget her. Nor this village. Tell her that in the autumn of my life on the other side of the world—when an August moon rises from the east, I will remember what was beautiful in my youth, and what I was wise enough to leave beautiful.

SAKINI. Issho wasurenai kara ne. Mangetsu no yoru niwa anata o omoidashimasu.

LOTUS BLOSSOM (*remains silent a moment*). Watashi mo Fu-san no koto issho wasurenaiwa. Fu-san no koto uta ni shite, Okinawaju ni hirome masu.

SAKINI. She say she always remember you, boss. She say she guess maybe she be what she is—first-class geisha girl. She want you to know she make up long song-story about you to sing in teahouse. And maybe hundred years from now, you be famous all over Okinawa.

FISBY (*rises*). I'd like that.

LOTUS BLOSSOM (*rises*). Iinoyo. Fu-san damedemo Seiko-san ga irun dakara.

SAKINI. She say, since you not marry her, maybe you suggest somebody here. (FISBY *laughs*.) She say that Mr. Seiko been looking at her like sick goat. She say what you think of him?

FISBY. Well, he took an awful beating just so he could carry her sweet potatoes.

LOTUS BLOSSOM. Fu-san, Seiko-san iito omouno?

SAKINI. She say you think she ought to marry him?

FISBY. I think she ought to decide for herself.

(*And* MR. SEIKO *enters. He is dressed in his white suit and his hair is slicked down tight. He crosses to* LOTUS BLOSSOM. *They all turn to look at him.*)

SEIKO (*bows to* LOTUS BLOSSOM).A, boku, oshimasho.

SAKINI (*to* FISBY). Mr. Seiko tell Lotus Blossom he sure like to push her wheelbarrow for her.

LOTUS BLOSSOM. Iikara sakini itte cho-dai.

SAKINI. She say, oh, all right, but not to think that means she's his property.

(MR. SEIKO *beams like a schoolboy and, picking up the handles of the wheelbarrow, he trots off stage with* LOTUS BLOSSOM'S *possessions. She turns to* FISBY *and hands him her fan.*)

LOTUS BLOSSOM. Korede aizu shite cho-dai. Soremade watashi dokonimo ikima-sen kara.

SAKINI. She say she go now, but you still her boss. She not go until you give signal.

(FISBY *takes the fan and puts it before his eyes. Without waiting for him to drop it,* LOTUS BLOSSOM *runs off right. When he lowers the fan, he knows she's gone. He sits down on the platform that had been the teahouse veranda.*)

SAKINI. You go now, boss?

FISBY. Shortly.

SAKINI. Since you not take Lotus Blossom, maybe you take me, boss?

FISBY. Major McEvoy is coming down to take charge. You'll work with him.

SAKINI. Would rather work with you.

FISBY. You'll like Major McEvoy.

SAKINI. I'll work for you for half price, boss.

FISBY. Major McEvoy will need your help in getting this village on its feet again.

SAKINI. You very hard man to bargain with, boss. If you want, I work for rice rations only.

FISBY. No.

SAKINI. You mean you going to make me work for *nothing*, boss?

FISBY. I mean *yes*, you're *not* going to work for me at all. And you belong here.

SAKINI. You know what I think happen when Americans leave Okinawa?

FISBY. What?

SAKINI (*grins*). I think maybe we use pentagon-shaped schoolhouse for tea-house.

(FISBY *laughs. He gives* SAKINI *a slap on the shoulder.*)

FISBY. Good-bye, Sakini, you're a rare rascal and I'll miss you.

SAKINI. Good-bye, boss. (FISBY *starts off left. He has gone halfway when* SAKINI *calls.*) Boss—

FISBY (*stops*). Yes?

SAKINI. You not failure.

FISBY (*laughs*). I'll tell you something,

SAKINI. I used to worry a lot about not being a big success. I must have felt as you people felt at always being conquered. Well, now I'm not so sure who's the conqueror and who the conquered.

SAKINI. Not understand, boss.

FISBY. It's just that I've learned from Tobiki the wisdom of gracious acceptance. I don't want to be a world leader. I'm making peace with myself somewhere between my ambitions and my limitations.

SAKINI. That's good?

FISBY. It's a step backward in the right direction. (*He throws* SAKINI *a salute.*) Take care.

(*He walks off and* SAKINI *watches him go. Then, with a sigh,* SAKINI *turns to survey the skeleton of the teahouse. The silence is broken by the stormy entrance of* COLONEL PURDY.)

PURDY. Sakini! Where is Captain Fisby?

SAKINI (*points*). Just leaving, boss.

PURDY (*shouts*). Fisby! Fisby! (*Gestures frantically.*) Come back here at once! (*He goes to the platform and sinks down gasping.*) I'm not in shape— too much paper work. (FISBY *returns from the left.*) Where in hell have you been, Fisby? I've been looking all over for you.

FISBY. I'm ready to leave, sir.

PURDY. You can't leave. You've got to stay here. You've got to help me, Fisby.

FISBY. Help doing what, sir?

PURDY. Pulling this village back together again. All hell has broken loose, Fisby. (*He sits down to wipe his brow.*) Where is Gregovich!

FISBY. Breaking up the last of the stills, sir.

PURDY. Oh, *no!* (*He holds his head.*)

FISBY. What's happened, sir?

PURDY. I radioed the report to Washington. Some fool senator misunderstood. He's using this village as an example of American "get-up-and-go" in the recovery program. The Pentagon is boasting. Congress is crowing. We're all over the papers.

FISBY. But that's wonderful, sir.

PURDY. No, it's not wonderful. A Congressional Committee is flying over to study our methods. They are bringing in photographers for a magazine spread. Today, Fisby, today!

FISBY. Oh, that's bad, sir.

PURDY (*wails*). Gregovich!

FISBY. Isn't there any way to stall

them off, sir? Quarantine the place or something?

PURDY. You can't quarantine a congressman. They have immunity or something. (*He takes* FISBY *by the jacket.*) Fisby, help me. I don't ask for my sake. I ask for Mrs. Purdy. I could be a brigadier yet.

(*Before* FISBY *can answer,* GREGOVICH *comes in from the left and salutes.*)

GREGOVICH. You called, sir?

PURDY (*hurries over to him*). Gregovich! Gregovich! You haven't destroyed all the stills, have you, Gregovich? No, of course you haven't.

GREGOVICH. Yes, sir, I have. I carried out orders to the letter.

PURDY (*turns away shouting*). Why can't someone disobey orders once in a while! What has happened to the American spirit of rebellion! (GREGOVICH *hiccups, smiles sillily and folds up on the floor.* FISBY *and* PURDY *race over to kneel beside him.*) Sunstroke?

FISBY. Potato brandy.

PURDY. Sergeant, wake up. Do you hear me? That's an order.

FISBY. I'm afraid he's passed out, sir.

PURDY. It's desertion. I need every man. Gregovich, get to your feet!

(*With* FISBY's *help he gets* GREGOVICH *to his feet.*)

GREGOVICH. Sorry, sir.

PURDY. I want to ask you some questions. Stop weaving.

GREGOVICH. *You're* weaving, sir. *I'm* perfectly still.

PURDY. You smell like a brewery.

GREGOVICH. I fell in a vat.

PURDY. You got drunk.

GREGOVICH. No, sir. I fell in a vat. Naturally, I had to open my mouth to yell for help.

PURDY. Go to the office and sober up at once.

GREGOVICH. Yes, sir. (*He salutes with a happy smile, jogs off.*)

PURDY. I'm a sinking ship . . . scuttled by my own men.

(*He sinks.* SAKINI, *who has been sitting with arms folded and a fatuous grin on his face, speaks up.*)

SAKINI. Colonel Purdy?

PURDY. Don't bother me.

SAKINI. Stills not all destroyed.

PURDY. I haven't got time to . . . What did you say?

SAKINI. We not born yesterday. Get sergeant drunk . . . and give him water

barrels to break.

PURDY. Sakini, my friend, you're not just saying that to make me feel better?

SAKINI. Oh, stills all good as ever. Production not cease yet.

FISBY (*fondly*). You really are a rogue, Sakini.

PURDY. No . . . he's really an American. He has get-up-and-go.

FISBY. Sakini, if everybody in the village worked together . . . how long would it take to rebuild the teahouse?

PURDY. We don't ask the impossible.

SAKINI. Oh, maybe three minutes . . . maybe five.

PURDY. That's impossible.

SAKINI. We not destroy. Just take away and hide. You watch now, boss. (*He turns and calls.*) Oi, mo iiyo, mo iiyo. (*From the wings, right and left, the* VILLAGERS *step out.*) Oi, haba, haba. (*The* VILLAGERS *respond with happy cries and dash off.*) Country that has been invaded many times soon master art of hiding things.

PURDY. You think we can pull it off, Sakini?

SAKINI. You watch now.

(*And even as he speaks, the sections of the teahouse are carried in and the swift work of putting them together progresses before our eyes. Music is heard in the background. The pagoda roof with its tinkling bells is lowered. The dwarf pines and the arched bridge are brought back. The colored panels are slipped into place and the lanterns are hung.* LOTUS BLOSSOM *comes on with flowers which she arranges.* SAKINI *snaps his fingers and the August moon is magically turned on in the sky. When the final lantern is hung,* MC LEAN *comes in. He stops. His mouth falls open.*)

PURDY. Close your mouth, Captain—haven't you ever seen a cha ya before? (*He turns back to* FISBY.) Fisby, this is a land of adventure . . . a land of jade and spices . . . of Chinese junks and river pirates. . . . Makes a man's blood pound.

FISBY. Colonel . . . I consider what you just said pure . . . (*He pauses.*) . . . poetry.

PURDY. Thank you . . . thank you, boy. (*He sighs ecstatically.*) It's the mystery of the Orient.

FISBY. It's beautiful. Simply beautiful.

PURDY. There's only one thing wrong. It needs a sign to tell people what it is. And I think we ought to put a sign up over there naming this Grace Purdy Avenue. And another sign . . .

FISBY. Colonel Purdy. Won't you have

a cup of tea? (*He takes his arm. As he propels him toward the teahouse, he speaks over his shoulder to* SAKINI.) Twenty Star for the colonel, Sakini.

(*As the bamboo panels begin to descend on the teahouse,* SAKINI *steps down to the audience.*)

Little story now concluded.
History of world unfinished.
Lovely ladies . . . kind gentlemen—
Go home to ponder.

What was true at the beginning remains
   true.
Pain makes man think.
Thought makes man wise.
Wisdom makes life endurable.
Our play has ended.
May August moon bring gentle sleep.
   (*He bows.*)

THE CURTAIN FALLS

THE DIARY OF ANNE FRANK

Dramatized by

Frances Goodrich and *Albert Hackett*

(based upon the book, *Anne Frank: Diary of a Young Girl*)

The Diary of Anne Frank was first presented by Kermit Bloomgarden at the Cort Theatre, New York City, on October 5, 1955. It was staged by Garson Kanin, with setting designed by Boris Aronson. The cast was as follows:

MR. FRANK . . . . Joseph Schildkraut
MIEP . . . . Gloria Jones
MRS. VAN DAAN . . . . Dennie Moore
MR. VAN DAAN . . . . Lou Jacobi
PETER VAN DAAN . . . . David Levin
MRS. FRANK . . . . Gusti Huber
MARGOT FRANK . . . . . . Eva Rubinstein
ANNE FRANK . . . . Susan Strasberg
MR. KRALER . . . . Clinton Sundberg
MR. DUSSEL . . . . Jack Gilford

THE TIME: During the years of World War II and immediately thereafter. THE PLACE: Amsterdam. There are two acts.

Copyright as an unpublished work 1954 and 1956, and © Copyright 1956 by Albert Hackett, Frances Goodrich Hackett and Otto Frank. Reprinted by permission of Random House, Inc.

All rights including the right of reproduction in whole or in part, in any form, are reserved under International and Pan-American Copyright Conventions. Published in New York by Random House, Inc., and simultaneously in Toronto, Canada, by Random House of Canada, Limited.

CAUTION: *The Diary of Anne Frank* is the sole property of the dramatists and is fully protected by copyright. It may not be acted by professionals or amateurs without written permission and the payment of a royalty. All rights, including professional, amateur, stock, radio broadcasting, television, motion picture, recitation, lecturing, public reading, and the rights of translation into foreign languages, are reserved. All inquiries should be addressed to the dramatists' agent: Leah Salisbury, 234 West 44th Street, New York, N.Y.

The Diary of Anne Frank, one of the outstanding productions of the American stage in the 1950's, is in every respect a work of collaboration. It is based on the posthumous book *Anne Frank: The Diary of a Young Girl*, an intensely moving record of a young girl's life while hiding with her family in Amsterdam before the Nazi conquerors of the Netherlands herded them off to a German concentration camp. The book itself is the product of an individual situation and a social reality; Anne Frank's sensibility collaborated with the crisis of the Nazi occupation of Europe in producing the *Diary*. Then Frances Goodrich and Albert Hackett collaborated on a dramatization authorized by the girl-author's father, Otto Frank, the sole survivor of the family.

The playwrights started collaborating successfully in 1930, married a year later, and became a permanent literary partnership, accounting for *Up Pops the Devil* (1930), *Bridal Wise*, and *The Great Big Doorstep* as well as for numerous motion pictures, including *The Thin Man, Father of the Bride*, and *Lady in the Dark*. Miss Goodrich, born in Belleville, New York, came to the theatre after exposure to the stage at Vassar, where the celebrated Hallie Flanagan Davis conducted her Vassar Experimental Theatre courses with distinction. Miss Goodrich also took postgraduate work at the New York School of Social Service, but became an actress rather then a social worker.

Albert Hackett, who was born in New York in 1900, began his career as actor at the age of six and attended the Professional Children's School, a suitable start for the son of a theatrical family that ran and performed in the Lubin Stock Company of Philadelphia.

Mr. Hackett summarized the inception of his career delightfully in an article in the January 4, 1961 issue of *Variety*. "Fifty-five years ago," he wrote, "when *Variety* was starting, I was starting. I was playing in *Lottie the Poor Saleslady, or Death before Dishonor. Variety* has changed a lot since. So have I. I was playing a little girl." He added to this reminiscence that he died in the second act, and after extricating himself from the leading lady (presumably the stage mother), who had collapsed on top of him with simulated grief, he would rush offstage, adjust wings over his night-gown, reappear on the kitchen table, and wing his way to heaven against a background of moving clouds. On tour, during one-night stands, he would also assist the stage crew, hold a smoke pot in the fire scene, roll buckshot on a drumhead in the storm scene, and perform other necessary chores, before he joined the ranks of unemployed actors at the age of nine and was sent to a convent school. One season, if his memory is accurate, he played three hundred one-night stands.

Nothing the collaborators had accomplished proved to be so distinguished and materially successful as their work on the *Diary*. Louis Kronenberger's comment is especially true and relevant: "They brought off, by a right approach, what might easily have been ruined through a lachrymose or stagy one. They took an adolescent girl's real-life chronicle of Jews hiding out in an Amsterdam garret and contrived vivid stage pictures of their huddled, muffled, strangely commingled existence. They portrayed it as a weird blend of the brightly ordinary and the hideously abnormal . . . of comic fault-finding and heroic adjustment."

In the New York production, impeccably staged for Kermit Bloomgarden by Garson Kanin, the collaborators' efforts received noteworthy support from Joseph Schildkraut's Otto Frank, Gusti Huber's Mrs. Frank, Eva Rubinstein's young Margot Frank (Anne's elder sister), and Susan Strasberg's immensely appealing Anne. Rising from little human realities to nobility in the Friday evening lighting-of-the-candles scene, and to controlled heroism in the next to the last scene when the elder Frank fetches the bags he has kept in readiness for the time when the Nazis would discover them, declaring, "For the past two years we have lived in fear. Now we can live in hope," the dramatization made a profound impression on audiences on both sides of the Atlantic, and perhaps nowhere more strongly than in postwar Germany itself.

It may be niggling to try to apportion credit to the play as distinct from the stage production, or as distinct from its appeal as an historical document. Creative imagination as well as craftmanship entered into the work, and there is no reason to treat a living document as a second-class citizen in the realm of art. As for the collaborators, the adaptation brought them to the ranks of our most successful playwrights, and it was of little consequence to the public to what degree they got to their destination on their own steam. In playwriting, success is usually determined by circumstance and luck as well as by intrinsic merit, and it does not matter to audiences whether or not the achievement is exclusively the playwright's.

The Diary of Anne Frank was indeed an event rather than ordinary play. The *Diary*, begun by Anne when she was thirteen and discovered in 1945 after its young author's death at the age of fifteen in the concentration camp, was published in 19 languages. The play founded on it, though with much independent creation and organization by the adapting team, was performed in more than twenty countries. It was seen by some two million playgoers in Germany alone. It opened simultaneously in seven German cities, and the awed silence of the audiences as they filed out of the theatres was a tribute to the compelling reality of the play as well as the humanity of the gifted girl whose unmarked remains lay buried in one of the mass graves of Bergen-Belsen, about eighty miles from Hamburg.

A Berlin reviewer described the effect of the Berlin premiere in one typically sesquipedalian German sentence that nevertheless reflects the awesome experience: "When, after three hours, as if awakening from deepest embarrassment, the people in the stalls can hardly rise from their seats, will not permit applause, and leave silently with bowed heads, that marks the greatness of a moment which must rouse the slowest hearts and which must shake the most indifferent nerves." (*New York Times*, October 14, 1956.)

The adapters, aware of the importance of their assignment, made as many as eight drafts of their dramatization. Garson Kanin staged the work with a sense of dignified dedication which was reflected in the memorable New York production that started the wave of productions throughout the rest of the world.

ACT ONE

Scene One

The scene remains the same throughout the play. It is the top floor of a warehouse and office building in Amsterdam, Holland. The sharply peaked roof of the building is outlined against a sea of other rooftops, stretching away into the distance. Nearby is the belfry of a church tower, the Westertoren, whose carillon rings out the hours. Occasionally faint sounds float up from below: the voices of children playing in the street, the tramp of marching feet, a boat whistle from the canal.

The three rooms of the top floor and a small attic space above are exposed to our view. The largest of the rooms is in the center, with two small rooms, slightly raised, on either side. On the right is a bathroom, out of sight. A narrow steep flight of stairs at the back leads up to the attic. The rooms are sparsely furnished with a few chairs, cots, a table or two. The windows are painted over, or covered with makeshift blackout curtains. In the main room there is a sink, a gas ring for cooking and a woodburning stove for warmth.

The room on the left is hardly more than a closet. There is a skylight in the sloping ceiling. Directly under this room is a small steep stairwell, with steps leading down to a door. This is the only entrance from the building below. When the door is opened we see that it has been concealed on the outer side by a bookcase attached to it.

The curtain rises on an empty stage. It is late afternoon November, 1945.

The rooms are dusty, the curtains in rags. Chairs and tables are overturned.

The door at the foot of the small stairwell swings open. MR. FRANK *comes up the steps into view. He is a gentle, cultured European in his middle years. There is still a trace of a German accent in his speech.*

He stands looking slowly around, making a supreme effort at self-control. He is weak, ill. His clothes are threadbare.

After a second he drops his rucksack on the couch and moves slowly about. He opens the door to one of the smaller rooms, and then abruptly closes it again, turning away. He goes to the window at the back, looking off at the Westertoren as its carillon strikes the hour of six, then he moves restlessly on.

From the street below we hear the sound of a barrel organ and children's voices at play. There is a many-colored scarf hanging from a

nail. MR. FRANK *takes it, putting it around his neck. As he starts back for his rucksack, his eye is caught by something lying on the floor. It is a woman's white glove. He holds it in his hand and suddenly all of his self-control is gone. He breaks down, crying.*

We hear footsteps on the stairs. MIEP GIES *comes up, looking for* MR. FRANK. MIEP *is a Dutch girl of about twenty-two. She wears a coat and hat, ready to go home. She is pregnant. Her attitude toward* MR. FRANK *is protective, compassionate.*

MIEP. Are you all right, Mr. Frank?

MR. FRANK (*quickly controlling himself*). Yes, Miep, yes.

MIEP. Everyone in the office has gone home . . . It's after six. (*Then pleading.*) Don't stay up here, Mr. Frank. What's the use of torturing yourself like this?

MR. FRANK. I've come to say good-by . . . I'm leaving here, Miep.

MIEP. What do you mean? Where are you going? Where?

MR. FRANK. I don't know yet. I haven't decided.

MIEP. Mr. Frank, you can't leave here! This is your home! Amsterdam is your home. Your business is here, waiting for you . . . You're needed here . . . Now that the war is over, there are things that . . .

MR. FRANK. I can't stay in Amsterdam, Miep. It has too many memories for me. Everywhere there's something . . . the house we lived in . . . the school . . . that street organ playing out there . . . I'm not the person you used to know, Miep. I'm a bitter old man. (*Breaking off.*) Forgive me. I shouldn't speak to you like this . . . after all that you did for us . . . the suffering . . .

MIEP. No. No. It wasn't suffering. You can't say we suffered. (*As she speaks, she straightens a chair which is overturned.*)

MR. FRANK. I know what you went through, you and Mr. Kraler. I'll remember it as long as I live. (*He gives one last look around.*) Come, Miep. (*He starts for the steps, then remembers his rucksack, going back to get it.*)

MIEP (*hurrying up to a cupboard*). Mr. Frank, did you see? There are some of your papers here. (*She brings a bundle of papers to him.*) We found them in a heap of rubbish on the floor after . . . after you left.

MR. FRANK. Burn them. (*He opens his*

rucksack to put the glove in it.)

MIEP. But, Mr. Frank, there are letters, notes . . .

MR. FRANK. Burn them. All of them.

MIEP. Burn *this?* (*She hands him a paper-bound notebook.*)

MR. FRANK (*quietly*). Anne's diary. (*He opens the diary and begins to read.*) "Monday, the sixth of July, nineteen forty-two." (*To* MIEP.) Nineteen forty-two. Is it possible, Miep? . . . Only three years ago. (*As he continues his reading, he sits down on the couch.*) "Dear Diary, since you and I are going to be great friends, I will start by telling you about myself. My name is Anne Frank. I am thirteen years old. I was born in Germany the twelfth of June, nineteen twenty-nine. As my family is Jewish, we emigrated to Holland when Hitler came to power."

(*As* MR. FRANK *reads on, another voice joins his, as if coming from the air. It is* ANNE'S VOICE.)

MR. FRANK AND ANNE. "My father started a business, importing spice and herbs. Things went well for us until nineteen forty. Then the war came, and the Dutch capitulation, followed by the arrival of the Germans. Then things got very bad for the Jews."

(MR. FRANK'S VOICE *dies out.* ANNE'S VOICE *continues alone. The lights dim slowly to darkness. The curtain falls on the scene.*)

ANNE'S VOICE. You could not do this and you could not do that. They forced Father out of his business. We had to wear yellow stars. I had to turn in my bike. I couldn't go to a Dutch school any more. I couldn't go to the movies, or ride in an automobile, or even on a streetcar, and a million other things. But somehow we children still managed to have fun. Yesterday Father told me we were going into hiding. Where, he wouldn't say. At five o'clock this morning Mother woke me and told me to hurry and get dressed. I was to put on as many clothes as I could. It would look too suspicious if we walked along carrying suitcases. It wasn't until we were on our way that I learned where we were going. Our hiding place was to be upstairs in the building where Father used to have his business. Three other people were coming in with us . . . the Van Daans and their son Peter . . . Father knew the Van Daans but we had never met them . . .

(*During the last lines the curtain rises on*

the scene. The lights dim on. ANNE'S VOICE fades out.)

SCENE TWO

It is early morning, July, 1942. The rooms are bare, as before, but they are now clean and orderly.

MR. VAN DAAN, *a tall, portly man in his late forties, is in the main room, pacing up and down, nervously smoking a cigarette. His clothes and overcoat are expensive and well cut.*

MRS. VAN DAAN *sits on the couch, clutching her possessions, a hatbox, bags, etc. She is a pretty woman in her early forties. She wears a fur coat over her other clothes.*

PETER VAN DAAN *is standing at the window of the room on the right, looking down at the street below. He is a shy, awkward boy of sixteen. He wears a cap, a raincoat, and long Dutch trousers, like "plus fours." At his feet is a black case, a carrier for his cat.*

The yellow Star of David is conspicuous on all of their clothes.

———

MRS. VAN DAAN (*rising, nervous, excited*). Something's happened to them! I know it!

MR. VAN DAAN. Now, Kerli!

MRS. VAN DAAN. Mr. Frank said they'd be here at seven o'clock. He said . . .

MR. VAN DAAN. They have two miles to walk. You can't expect . . .

MRS. VAN DAAN. They've been picked up. That's what's happened. They've been taken . . .

(MR. VAN DAAN *indicates that he hears someone coming.*)

MR. VAN DAAN. You see?

(PETER *takes up his carrier and his schoolbag, etc., and goes into the main room as* MR. FRANK *comes up the stairwell from below.* MR. FRANK *looks much younger now. His movements are brisk, his manner confident. He wears an overcoat and carries his hat and a small cardboard box. He crosses to the* VAN DAANS, *shaking hands with each of them.*)

MR. FRANK. Mrs. Van Daan, Mr. Van Daan, Peter. (*Then, in explanation of their lateness.*) There were too many of the Green Police on the streets . . . we had to take the long way around.

(*Up the steps come* MARGOT FRANK, MRS. FRANK, MIEP (*not pregnant now*), *and* MR. KRALER. *All of them carry bags, packages, and so forth. The Star of David is conspicuous on all of the* FRANKS' *clothing.* MARGOT *is eighteen, beautiful, quiet, shy.* MRS. FRANK *is a young mother, gently bred, reserved. She, like* MR. FRANK, *has a slight German accent.* MR. KRALER *is a Dutchman, dependable, kindly.*

As MR. KRALER *and* MIEP *go upstage to put down their parcels,* MRS. FRANK *turns back to call* ANNE.)

MRS. FRANK. Anne?

(ANNE *comes running up the stairs. She is thirteen, quick in her movements, interested in everything, mercurial in her emotions. She wears a cape, long wool socks and carries a schoolbag.*)

MR. FRANK (*introducing them*). My wife, Edith. Mr. and Mrs. Van Daan (MRS. FRANK *hurries over, shaking hands with them.*) . . . their son, Peter . . . my daughters, Margot and Anne.

(ANNE *gives a polite little curtsy as she shakes* MR. VAN DAAN'S *hand. Then she immediately starts off on a tour of investigation of her new home, going upstairs to the attic room.*

MIEP *and* MR. KRALER *are putting the various things they have brought on the shelves.*)

MR. KRALER. I'm sorry there is still so much confusion.

MR. FRANK. Please. Don't think of it. After all, we'll have plenty of leisure to arrange everything ourselves.

MIEP (*to* MRS. FRANK). We put the stores of food you sent in here. Your drugs are here . . . soap, linen here.

MR. FRANK. Thank you, Miep.

MIEP. I made up the beds . . . the way Mr. Frank and Mr. Kraler said. (*She starts out.*) Forgive me. I have to hurry. I've got to go to the other side of town to get some ration books for you.

MRS. VAN DAAN. Ration books? If they see our names on ration books, they'll know we're here.

MR. KRALER. There isn't anything . . .

MIEP. Don't worry. Your names won't be on them. (*As she hurries out.*) I'll be up later.

} (*Together.*)

MR. FRANK. Thank you, Miep.

MRS. FRANK (*to* MR. KRALER). It's illegal, then, the ration books? We've never done anything illegal.

MR. FRANK. We won't be living here exactly according to regulations.

(*As* MR. KRALER *reassures* MRS. FRANK, *he takes various small things, such as matches, soap, etc., from his pockets, handing them to her.*)

MR. KRALER. This isn't the black market, Mrs. Frank. This is what we call the white market . . . helping all of the hundreds and hundreds who are hiding out in Amsterdam.

(*The carillon is heard playing the quarter-hour before eight.* MR. KRALER *looks at his watch.* ANNE *stops at the window as she comes down the stairs.*)

ANNE. It's the Westertoren!

MR. KRALER. I must go. I must be out of here and downstairs in the office before the workmen get here. (*He starts for the stairs leading out.*) Miep or I, or both of us, will be up each day to bring you food and news and find out what your needs are. Tomorrow I'll get you a better bolt for the door at the foot of the stairs. It needs a bolt that you can throw yourself and open only at our signal. (*To* MR. FRANK.) Oh . . . You'll tell them about the noise?

MR. FRANK. I'll tell them.

MR. KRALER. Good-by then for the moment. I'll come up again, after the workmen leave.

MR. FRANK. Good-by, Mr. Kraler.

MRS. FRANK (*shaking his hand*). How can we thank you?

(*The others murmur their good-bys.*)

MR. KRALER. I never thought I'd live to see the day when a man like Mr. Frank would have to go into hiding. When you think—

(*He breaks off, going out.* MR. FRANK *follows him down the steps, bolting the door after him. In the interval before he returns,* PETER *goes over to* MARGOT, *shaking hands with her. As* MR. FRANK *comes back up the steps,* MRS. FRANK *questions him anxiously.*)

MRS. FRANK. What did he mean, about the noise?

MR. FRANK. First let us take off some of these clothes.

(*They all start to take off garment after garment. On each of their coats, sweaters, blouses, suits, dresses, is another yellow Star of David.* MR. *and* MRS. FRANK *are underdressed quite simply. The others wear several things, sweaters, extra dresses, bathrobes, aprons, nightgowns, etc.*)

MR. VAN DAAN. It's a wonder we weren't arrested, walking along the streets . . . Petronella with a fur coat in July . . . and that cat of Peter's crying all the way.

ANNE (*as she is removing a pair of panties*). A cat?

MRS. FRANK (*shocked*). Anne, please!

ANNE. It's all right. I've got on three more.

(*She pulls off two more. Finally, as they have all removed their surplus clothes, they look to* MR. FRANK, *waiting for him to speak.*)

MR. FRANK. Now. About the noise. While the men are in the building below, we must have complete quiet. Every sound can be heard down there, not only in the workrooms, but in the offices too. The men come at about eight-thirty, and leave at about five-thirty. So, to be perfectly safe, from eight in the morning until six in the evening we must move only when it is necessary, and then in stockinged feet. We must not speak above a whisper. We must not run any water. We cannot use the sink, or even, forgive me, the w.c. The pipes go down through the workrooms. It would be heard. No trash . . . (MR. FRANK *stops abruptly as he hears the sound of marching feet from the street below. Everyone is motionless, paralyzed with fear.* MR. FRANK *goes quietly into the room on the right to look down out of the window.* ANNE *runs after him, peering out with him. The tramping feet pass without stopping. The tension is relieved.* MR. FRANK, *followed by* ANNE, *returns to the main room and resumes his instructions to the group.*) . . . No trash must ever be thrown out which might reveal that someone is living up here . . . not even a potato paring. We must burn everything in the stove at night. This is the way we must live until it is over, if we are to survive.

(*There is silence for a second.*)

MRS. FRANK. Until it is over.

MR. FRANK (*reassuringly*). After six we can move about . . . we can talk and laugh and have our supper and read and play games . . . just as we would at home. (*He looks at his watch.*) And now I think it would be wise if we all went to our rooms, and were settled before eight o'clock. Mrs. Van Daan, you and your husband will be upstairs. I regret that there's no place up there for Peter. But he will be here, near us. This will be our common room, where we'll meet to talk and eat and read, like one family.

MR. VAN DAAN. And where do you and Mrs. Frank sleep?

MR. FRANK. This room is also our bedroom.

MRS. VAN DAAN. That isn't right. We'll sleep here and you take the room upstairs. ⎱ (*Together.*)

MR. VAN DAAN. It's your place. ⎰

MR. FRANK. Please. I've thought this out for weeks. It's the best arrangement. The only arrangement.

MRS. VAN DAAN (*to* MR. FRANK). Never, never can we thank you. (*Then to* MRS. FRANK.) I don't know what would have happened to us, if it hadn't been for Mr. Frank.

MR. FRANK. You don't know how your husband helped me when I came to this country . . . knowing no one . . . not able to speak the language. I can never repay him for that. (*Going to* VAN DAAN.) May I help you with your things?

MR. VAN DAAN. No. No. (*To* MRS. VAN DAAN.) Come along, *liefje.*

MRS. VAN DAAN. You'll be all right, Peter? You're not afraid?

PETER (*embarrassed*). Please, Mother.

(*They start up the stairs to the attic room above.* MR. FRANK *turns to* MRS. FRANK.)

MR. FRANK. You too must have some rest, Edith. You didn't close your eyes last night. Nor you, Margot.

ANNE. I slept, Father. Wasn't that funny? I knew it was the last night in my own bed, and yet I slept soundly.

MR. FRANK. I'm glad, Anne. Now you'll be able to help me straighten things in here. (*To* MRS. FRANK *and* MARGOT.) Come with me . . . You and Margot rest in this room for the time being. (*He picks up their clothes, starting for the room on the right.*)

MRS. FRANK. You're sure . . . ? I could help . . . And Anne hasn't had her milk . . .

MR. FRANK. I'll give it to her. (*To* ANNE *and* PETER.) Anne, Peter . . . it's best that you take off your shoes now, before you forget. (*He leads the way to the room, followed by* MARGOT.)

MRS. FRANK. You're sure you're not tired, Anne?

ANNE. I feel fine. I'm going to help Father.

MRS. FRANK. Peter, I'm glad you are to be with us.

PETER. Yes, Mrs. Frank.

(MRS. FRANK *goes to join* MR. FRANK *and* MARGOT.)

(*During the following scene* MR. FRANK

helps MARGOT *and* MRS. FRANK *to hang up their clothes. Then he persuades them both to lie down and rest. The* VAN DAANS *in their room above settle themselves. In the main room* ANNE *and* PETER *remove their shoes.* PETER *takes his cat out of the carrier.*)

ANNE. What's your cat's name?

PETER. Mouschi.

ANNE. Mouschi! Mouschi! Mouschi! (*She picks up the cat, walking away with it. To* PETER.) I love cats. I have one . . . a darling little cat. But they made me leave her behind. I left some food and a note for the neighbors to take care of her . . . I'm going to miss her terribly. What is yours? A him or a her?

PETER. He's a tom. He doesn't like strangers. (*He takes the cat from her, putting it back in its carrier.*)

ANNE (*unabashed*). Then I'll have to stop being a stranger, won't I? Is he fixed?

PETER (*startled*). Huh?

ANNE. Did you have him fixed?

PETER. No.

ANNE. Oh, you ought to have him fixed—to keep him from—you know, fighting. Where did you go to school?

PETER. Jewish Secondary.

ANNE. But that's where Margot and I go! I never saw you around.

PETER. I used to see you . . . sometimes . . .

ANNE. You did?

PETER. . . . in the school yard. You were always in the middle of a bunch of kids. (*He takes a penknife from his pocket.*)

ANNE. Why didn't you ever come over?

PETER. I'm sort of a lone wolf. (*He starts to rip off his Star of David.*)

ANNE. What are you doing?

PETER. Taking it off.

ANNE. But you can't do that. They'll arrest you if you go out without your star.

(*He tosses his knife on the table.*)

PETER. Who's going out?

ANNE. Why, of course! You're right! Of course we don't need them any more. (*She picks up his knife and starts to take her star off.*) I wonder what our friends will think when we don't show up today?

PETER. I didn't have any dates with anyone.

ANNE. Oh, I did. I had a date with Jopie to go and play ping-pong at her

house. Do you know Jopie deWaal?

PETER. No.

ANNE. Jopie's my best friend. I wonder what she'll think when she telephones and there's no answer? . . . Probably she'll go over to the house . . . I wonder what she'll think . . . we left everything as if we'd suddenly been called away . . . breakfast dishes in the sink . . . beds not made . . . (*As she pulls off her star the cloth underneath shows clearly the color and form of the star.*) Look! It's still there! (PETER *goes over to the stove with his star.*) What're you going to do with yours?

PETER. Burn it.

ANNE (*she starts to throw hers in, and cannot*). It's funny, I can't throw mine away. I don't know why.

PETER. You can't throw . . . ? Something they branded you with . . .? That they made you swear so they could spit on you?

ANNE. I know. I know. But after all, it *is* the Star of David, isn't it?

(*In the bedroom, right,* MARGOT *and* MRS. FRANK *are lying down.* MR. FRANK *starts quietly out.*)

PETER. Maybe it's different for a girl.

(MR. FRANK *comes into the main room.*)

MR. FRANK. Forgive me, Peter. Now let me see. We must find a bed for your cat. (*He goes to a cupboard.*) I'm glad you brought your cat. Anne was feeling so badly about hers. (*Getting a used small washtub.*) Here we are. Will it be comfortable in that?

PETER (*Gathering up his things*). Thanks.

MR. FRANK (*opening the door of the room on the left*). And here is your room. But I warn you, Peter, you can't grow any more. Not an inch, or you'll have to sleep with your feet out of the skylight. Are you hungry?

PETER. No.

MR. FRANK. We have some bread and butter.

PETER. No, thank you.

MR. FRANK. You can have it for luncheon then. And tonight we will have a real supper . . . our first supper together.

PETER. Thanks. Thanks.

(*He goes into his room. During the following scene he arranges his possessions in his new room.*)

MR. FRANK. That's a nice boy, Peter.

ANNE. He's awfully shy, isn't he?

MR. FRANK. You'll like him, I know.

ANNE. I certainly hope so, since he's the only boy I'm likely to see for months and months.

(MR. FRANK *sits down, taking off his shoes.*)

MR. FRANK. Annele, there's a box there. Will you open it?

(*He indicates a carton on the couch.* ANNE *brings it to the center table. In the street below there is the sound of children playing.*)

ANNE (*as she opens the carton*). You know the way I'm going to think of it here? I'm going to think of it as a boarding house. A very peculiar summer boarding house, like the one that we—(*She breaks off as she pulls out some photographs.*) Father! My movie stars! I was wondering where they were! I was looking for them this morning . . . and Queen Wilhelmina! How wonderful!

MR. FRANK. There's something more. Go on. Look further.

(*He goes over to the sink, pouring a glass of milk from a thermos bottle.*)

ANNE (*pulling out a pasteboard-bound book*). A diary! (*She throws her arms around her father.*) I've never had a diary. And I've always longed for one. (*She looks around the room.*) Pencil, pencil, pencil. (*She starts down the stairs.*) I'm going down to the office to get a pencil.

MR. FRANK. Anne! No!

(*He goes after her, catching her by the arm and pulling her back.*)

ANNE (*startled*). But there's no one in the building now.

MR. FRANK. It doesn't matter. I don't want you ever to go beyond that door.

ANNE (*sobered*). Never . . . ? Not even at nighttime, when everyone is gone? Or on Sundays? Can't I go down to listen to the radio?

MR. FRANK. Never. I am sorry, Anneke. It isn't safe. No, you must never go beyond that door.

(*For the first time* ANNE *realizes what "going into hiding" means.*)

ANNE. I see.

MR. FRANK. It'll be hard, I know. But always remember this, Anneke. There are no walls, there are no bolts, no locks that anyone can put on your mind. Miep will bring us books. We will read history, poetry, mythology. (*He gives her the glass of milk.*) Here's your milk. (*With his arm about her, they go over to the couch, sitting down side by side.*) As a matter of fact, between us, Anne, being here has certain advantages for you. For instance, you remember the battle you had with your mother the other day on the subject of overshoes? You said you'd rather die than wear overshoes? But in the end you had to wear them? Well now, you see, for as long as we are here you will never have to wear overshoes! Isn't that good? And the coat that you inherited from Margot, you won't have to wear that any more. And the piano! You won't have to practice on the piano. I tell you, this is going to be a fine life for you!

ANNE's *panic is gone.* PETER *appears in the doorway of his room, with a saucer in his hand. He is carrying his cat.*)

PETER. I . . . I . . . I thought I'd better get some water for Mouschi before . . .

MR. FRANK. Of course.

(*As he starts toward the sink the carillon begins to chime the hour of eight. He tiptoes to the window at the back and looks down at the street below. He turns to* PETER, *indicating in pantomime that it is too late.* PETER *starts back for his room. He steps on a creaking board. The three of them are frozen for a minute in fear. As* PETER *starts away again,* ANNE *tiptoes over to him and pours some of the milk from her glass into the saucer for the cat.* PETER *squats on the floor, putting the milk before the cat.* MR. FRANK *gives* ANNE *his fountain pen, and then goes into the room at the right. For a second* ANNE *watches the cat, then she goes over to the center table, and opens her diary.*

In the room at the right, MRS. FRANK *has sat up quickly at the sound of the carillon.* MR. FRANK *comes in and sits down beside her on the settee, his arm comfortingly around her.*

Upstairs, in the attic room, MR. *and* MRS. VAN DAAN *have hung their clothes in the closet and are now seated on the iron bed.* MRS. VAN DAAN *leans back exhausted.* MR. VAN DAAN *fans her with a newspaper.*

ANNE *starts to write in her diary. The lights dim out, the curtain falls.*

In the darkness ANNE'S VOICE *comes to us again, faintly at first, and then with growing strength.*)

ANNE'S VOICE. I expect I should be describing what it feels like to go into hiding. But I really don't know yet myself. I only know it's funny never to be able to go outdoors . . . never to breathe fresh air . . . never to run and shout and jump. It's the silence in the nights that frightens me most. Every time I hear a creak in the house, or a step on the street outside, I'm sure they're coming for us. The days aren't so bad. At least we know that Miep and Mr. Kraler are down there below us in the office. Our protectors, we call them. I asked Father what would happen to them if the Nazis found out they were hiding us. Pim said that they would suffer the same fate that we would . . . Imagine! They know this, and yet when they come up here, they're always cheerful and gay as if there were nothing in the world to bother them . . . Friday, the twenty-first of August, nineteen forty-two. Today I'm going to tell you our general news. Mother is unbearable. She insists on treating me like a baby, which I loathe. Otherwise things are going better. The weather is . . .

(*As* ANNE'S VOICE *is fading out, the curtain rises on the scene.*)

Scene Three

It is a little after six o'clock in the evening, two months later.

MARGOT *is in the bedroom at the right, studying.* MR. VAN DAAN *is lying down in the attic room above.*

The rest of the "family" is in the main room. ANNE *and* PETER *sit opposite each other at the center table, where they have been doing their lessons.* MRS. FRANK *is on the couch.* MRS. VAN DAAN *is seated with her fur coat, on which she has been sewing, in her lap. None of them are wearing their shoes.*

Their eyes are on MR. FRANK, *waiting for him to give them the signal which will release them from their day-long quiet.* MR. FRANK, *his shoes in his hand, stands looking down out of the window at the back, watching to be sure that all of the workmen have left the building below.*

After a few seconds of motionless silence, MR. FRANK *turns from the window.*

MR. FRANK (*quietly, to the group*). It's safe now. The last workman has left.

(*There is an immediate stir of relief.*)

ANNE (*her pent-up energy explodes*). WHEE!

MRS. FRANK (*startled, amused*). Anne!

MRS. VAN DAAN. I'm first for the w.c.

(*She hurries off to the bathroom.* MRS. FRANK *puts on her shoes and starts up to the sink to prepare supper.* ANNE *sneaks* PETER'S *shoes from under the table and hides them behind her back.* MR. FRANK *goes in to* MARGOT'S *room.*)

MR. FRANK (*to* MARGOT). Six o'clock. School's over.

(MARGOT *gets up, stretching.* MR. FRANK *sits down to put on his shoes. In the main room* PETER *tries to find his.*)

PETER (*to* ANNE). Have you seen my shoes?

ANNE (*innocently*). Your shoes?

PETER. You've taken them, haven't you?

ANNE. I don't know what you're talking about.

PETER. You're going to be sorry!

ANNE. Am I?

(PETER *goes after her.* ANNE, *with his shoes in her hand, runs from him, dodging behind her mother.*)

MRS. FRANK (*protesting*). Anne, dear!

PETER. Wait till I get you!

ANNE. I'm waiting! (PETER *makes a lunge for her. They both fall to the floor.* PETER *pins her down, wrestling with her to get the shoes.*) Don't! Don't! Peter, stop it. Ouch!

MRS. FRANK. Anne! . . . Peter!

(*Suddenly* PETER *becomes self-conscious. He grabs his shoes roughly and starts for his room.*)

ANNE (*following him*). Peter, where are you going? Come dance with me.

PETER. I tell you I don't know how.

ANNE. I'll teach you.

PETER. I'm going to give Mouschi his dinner.

ANNE. Can I watch?

PETER. He doesn't like people around while he eats.

ANNE. Peter, please.

PETER. No!

(*He goes into his room.* ANNE *slams his door after him.*)

MRS. FRANK. Anne, dear, I think you shouldn't play like that with Peter. It's not dignified.

ANNE. Who cares if it's dignified? I don't want to be dignified.

(MR. FRANK *and* MARGOT *come from the room on the right.* MARGOT *goes to help her mother.* MR. FRANK *starts for the center table to correct* MARGOT'S *school papers.*)

MRS. FRANK (*to* ANNE). You complain that I don't treat you like a grownup. But when I do, you resent it.

ANNE. I only want some fun . . . someone to laugh and clown with . . . After you've sat still all day and hardly moved, you've got to have some fun. I don't know what's the matter with that boy.

MR. FRANK. He isn't used to girls. Give him a little time.

ANNE. Time? Isn't two months time? I could cry. (*Catching hold of* MARGOT.) Come on, Margot . . . dance with me. Come on, please.

MARGOT. I have to help with supper.

ANNE. You know we're going to forget how to dance . . . When we get out we won't remember a thing.

(*She starts to sing and dance by herself.* MR. FRANK *takes her in his arms, waltzing with her.* MRS. VAN DAAN *comes in from the bathroom.*)

MRS. VAN DAAN. Next? (*She looks around as she starts putting on her shoes.*) Where's Peter?

ANNE (*as they are dancing*). Where would he be!

MRS. VAN DAAN. He hasn't finished his lessons, has he? His father'll kill him if he catches him in there with that cat and his work not done. (MR. FRANK *and* ANNE *finish their dance. They bow to each other with extravagant formality.*) Anne, get him out of there, will you?

ANNE (*at* PETER'S *door*). Peter? Peter?

PETER (*opening the door a crack*). What is it?

ANNE. Your mother says to come out.

PETER. I'm giving Mouschi his dinner.

MRS. VAN DAAN. You know what your father says.

(*She sits on the couch, sewing on the lining of her fur coat.*)

PETER. For heaven's sake, I haven't even looked at him since lunch.

MRS. VAN DAAN. I'm just telling you, that's all.

ANNE. I'll feed him.

PETER. I don't want you in there.

MRS. VAN DAAN. Peter!

PETER (*to* ANNE). Then give him his dinner and come right out, you hear?

(*He comes back to the table.* ANNE *shuts the door of* PETER'S *room after her and disappears behind the curtain covering his closet.*)

MRS. VAN DAAN (*to* PETER). Now is that any way to talk to your little girl friend?

PETER. Mother . . . for heaven's sake . . . will you please stop saying that?

MRS. VAN DAAN. Look at him blush! Look at him!

PETER. Please! I'm not . . . anyway . . . let me alone, will you?

MRS. VAN DAAN. He acts like it was something to be ashamed of. It's nothing to be ashamed of, to have a little girl friend.

PETER. You're crazy. She's only thirteen.

MRS. VAN DAAN. So what? And you're sixteen. Just perfect. Your father's ten years older than I am. (*To* MR. FRANK.) I warn you, Mr. Frank, if this war lasts much longer, we're going to be related and then . . .

MR. FRANK. *Mazeltov!*

MRS. FRANK (*deliberately changing the conversation*). I wonder where Miep is. She's usually so prompt.

(*Suddenly everything else is forgotten as they hear the sound of an automobile coming to a screeching stop in the street below. They are tense, motionless in their terror. The car starts away. A wave of relief sweeps over them. They pick up their occupations again.* ANNE *flings open the door of* PETER'S *room, making a dramatic entrance. She is dressed in* PETER'S *clothes.* PETER *looks at her in fury. The others are amused.*)

ANNE. Good evening, everyone. Forgive me if I don't stay. (*She jumps up on a chair.*) I have a friend waiting for me in there. My friend Tom. Tom Cat. Some people say that we look alike. But Tom has the most beautiful whiskers, and I have only a little fuzz. I am hoping . . . in time . . .

PETER. All right, Mrs. Quack Quack!

ANNE (*outraged—jumping down*). Peter!

PETER. I heard about you . . . How you talked so much in class they called you Mrs. Quack Quack. How Mr. Smitter made you write a composition . . . " 'Quack, quack,' said Mrs. Quack Quack."

ANNE. Well, go on. Tell them the rest. How it was so good he read it out loud to the class and then read it to all his other classes!

PETER. Quack! Quack! Quack . . . Quack . . . Quack . . .

(ANNE *pulls off the coat and trousers.*)

ANNE. You are the most intolerable, insufferable boy I've ever met!

(*She throws the clothes down the stairwell.* PETER *goes down after them.*)

PETER. Quack, quack, quack!

MRS. VAN DAAN (*to* ANNE). That's right, Anneke! Give it to him!

ANNE. With all the boys in the world . . . Why I had to get locked up with one like you! . . .

PETER. Quack, quack, quack, and from now on stay out of my room!

(*As* PETER *passes her,* ANNE *puts out her foot, tripping him. He picks himself up, and goes on into his room.*)

MRS. FRANK (*quietly*). Anne, dear . . . your hair. (*She feels* ANNE's *forehead.*) You're warm. Are you feeling all right?

ANNE. Please, Mother.

(*She goes over to the center table, slipping into her shoes.*)

MRS. FRANK (*following her*). You haven't a fever, have you?

ANNE (*pulling away*). No. No.

MRS. FRANK. You know we can't call a doctor here, ever. There's only one thing to do . . . watch carefully. Prevent an illness before it comes. Let me see your tongue.

ANNE. Mother, this is perfectly absurd.

MRS. FRANK. Anne, dear, don't be such a baby. Let me see your tongue. (*As* ANNE *refuses,* MRS. FRANK *appeals to* MR. FRANK.) Otto . . . ?

MR. FRANK. You hear your mother, Anne.

(ANNE *flicks out her tongue for a second, then turns away.*)

MRS. FRANK. Come on—open up! (*As* ANNE *opens her mouth very wide.*) You seem all right . . . but perhaps an aspirin . . .

MRS. VAN DAAN. For heaven's sake, don't give that child any pills. I waited for fifteen minutes this morning for her to come out of the w.c.

ANNE. I was washing my hair!

MR. FRANK. I think there's nothing the matter with our Anne that a ride on her bike, or a visit with her friend Jopie deWaal wouldn't cure. Isn't that so, Anne?

(MR. VAN DAAN *comes down into the room. From outside we hear faint sounds of bombers going over and a burst of ack-ack.*)

MR. VAN DAAN. Miep not come yet?

MRS. VAN DAAN. The workmen just left, a little while ago.

MR. VAN DAAN. What's for dinner to-night?

MRS. VAN DAAN. Beans.

MR. VAN DAAN. Not again!

MRS. VAN DAAN. Poor Putti! I know. But what can we do? That's all that Miep brought us.

(MR. VAN DAAN *starts to pace, his hands behind his back.* ANNE *follows behind him, imitating him.*)

ANNE. We are now in what is known as the "bean cycle." Beans boiled, beans en casserole, beans with strings, beans without strings . . .

(PETER *has come out of his room. He slides into his place at the table, becoming immediately absorbed in his studies.*)

MR. VAN DAAN (*to* PETER). I saw you . . . in there, playing with your cat.

MRS. VAN DAAN. He just went in for a second, putting his coat away. He's been out here all the time, doing his lessons.

MR. FRANK (*looking up from the paper*). Anne, you got an excellent in your history paper today . . . and very good in Latin.

ANNE (*sitting beside him*). How about algebra?

MR. FRANK. I'll have to make a confession. Up until now I've managed to stay ahead of you in algebra. Today you caught up with me. We'll leave it to Margot to correct.

ANNE. Isn't algebra *vile*, Pim!

MR. FRANK. Vile!

MARGOT (*to* MR. FRANK). How did I do?

ANNE (*getting up*). Excellent, excellent, excellent, excellent!

MR. FRANK (*to* MARGOT). You should have used the subjunctive here . . .

MARGOT. Should I? . . . I thought . . . look here . . . I didn't use it here . . .

(*The two become absorbed in the papers.*)

ANNE. Mrs. Van Daan, may I try on your coat?

MRS. FRANK. No, Anne.

MRS. VAN DAAN (*giving it to* ANNE). It's all right . . . but careful with it. (ANNE *puts it on and struts with it.*) My father gave me that the year before he died. He always bought the best that money could buy.

ANNE. Mrs. Van Daan, did you have a lot of boy friends before you were married?

MRS. FRANK. Anne, that's a personal question. It's not courteous to ask personal questions.

MRS. VAN DAAN. Oh I don't mind. (*To* ANNE.) Our house was always swarming with boys. When I was a girl we had . . .

MR. VAN DAAN. Oh, God. Not again!

MRS. VAN DAAN (*good-humored*). Shut up! (*Without a pause, to* ANNE. MR. VAN DAAN *mimics* MRS. VAN DAAN, *speaking the first few words in unison with her.*) One summer we had a big house in Hilversum. The boys came buzzing round like bees around a jam pot. And when I was sixteen! . . . We were wearing our skirts very short those days and I had good-looking legs. (*She pulls up her skirt, going to* MR. FRANK.) I still have 'em. I may not be as pretty as I used to be, but I still have my legs. How about it, Mr. Frank?

MR. VAN DAAN. All right. All right. We see them.

MRS. VAN DAAN. I'm not asking you. I'm asking Mr. Frank.

PETER. Mother, for heaven's sake.

MRS. VAN DAAN. Oh, I embarrass you, do I? Well, I just hope the girl you marry has as good. (*Then to* ANNE.) My father used to worry about me, with so many boys hanging round. He told me, if any of them gets fresh, you say to him . . . "Remember, Mr. So-and-So, remember I'm a lady."

ANNE. "Remember, Mr. So-and-So, remember I'm a lady."

(*She gives* MRS. VAN DAAN *her coat.*)

MR. VAN DAAN. Look at you, talking that way in front of her! Don't you know she puts it all down in that diary?

MRS. VAN DAAN. So, if she does? I'm only telling the truth!

(ANNE *stretches out, putting her ear to the floor, listening to what is going on below. The sound of the bombers fades away.*)

MRS. FRANK (*setting the table*). Would you mind, Peter, if I moved you over to the couch?

ANNE (*listening*). Miep must have the radio on.

(PETER *picks up his papers, going over to the couch beside* MRS. VAN DAAN.)

MR. VAN DAAN (*accusingly, to* PETER). Haven't you finished yet?

PETER. No.

MR. VAN DAAN. You ought to be ashamed of yourself.

PETER. All right. All right. I'm a dunce. I'm a hopeless case. Why do I go on?

MRS. VAN DAAN. You're not hopeless. Don't talk that way. It's just that you haven't anyone to help you, like the girls have. (*To* MR. FRANK.) Maybe you could help him, Mr. Frank?

MR. FRANK. I'm sure that his father . . . ?

MR. VAN DAAN. Not me. I can't do anything with him. He won't listen to me. You go ahead . . . if you want.

MR. FRANK (*going to* PETER). What about it, Peter? Shall we make our school coeducational?

MRS. VAN DAAN (*kissing* MR. FRANK). You're an angel, Mr. Frank. An angel. I don't know why I didn't meet you before I met that one there. Here, sit down, Mr. Frank . . . (*She forces him down on the couch beside* PETER.) Now, Peter, you listen to Mr. Frank.

MR. FRANK. It might be better for us to go into Peter's room.

(PETER *jumps up eagerly, leading the way.*)

MRS. VAN DAAN. That's right. You go in there, Peter. You listen to Mr. Frank. Mr. Frank is a highly educated man.

(*As* MR. FRANK *is about to follow* PETER *into his room,* MRS. FRANK *stops him and wipes the lipstick from his lips. Then she closes the door after them.*)

ANNE (*on the floor, listening*). Shh! I can hear a man's voice talking.

MR. VAN DAAN (*to* ANNE). Isn't it bad enough here without your sprawling all over the place?

(ANNE *sits up.*)

MRS. VAN DAAN (*to* MR. VAN DAAN). If you didn't smoke so much, you wouldn't be so bad-tempered.

MR. VAN DAAN. Am I smoking? Do you see me smoking?

MRS. VAN DAAN. Don't tell me you've used up all those cigarettes.

MR. VAN DAAN. One package. Miep only brought me one package.

MRS. VAN DAAN. It's a filthy habit anyway. It's a good time to break yourself.

MR. VAN DAAN. Oh, stop it, please.

MRS. VAN DAAN. You're smoking up all our money. You know that, don't you?

MR. VAN DAAN. Will you shut up?. (*During this,* MRS. FRANK *and* MARGOT *have studiously kept their eyes down. But* ANNE, *seated on the floor, has been following the discussion interestedly.* MR. VAN DAAN *turns to see her staring up at him.*) And what are you staring at?

ANNE. I never heard grownups quarrel before. I thought only children quarreled.

MR. VAN DAAN. This isn't a quarrel! It's a discussion. And I never heard children so rude before.

ANNE (*rising, indignantly*). I, rude!

MR. VAN DAAN. Yes!

MRS. FRANK (*quickly*). Anne, will you get me my knitting? (ANNE *goes to get it.*) I must remember, when Miep comes, to ask her to bring me some more wool.

MARGOT (*going to her room*). I need some hairpins and some soap. I made a list.

(*She goes into her bedroom to get the list.*)

MRS. FRANK (*to* ANNE). Have you some library books for Miep when she comes?

ANNE. It's a wonder that Miep has a life of her own, the way we make her run errands for us. Please, Miep, get me some starch. Please take my hair out and have it cut. Tell me all the latest news, Miep. (*She goes over, kneeling on the couch beside* MRS. VAN DAAN.) Did you know she was engaged? His name is Dirk, and Miep's afraid the Nazis will ship him off to Germany to work in one of their war plants. That's what they're doing with some of the young Dutchmen . . . they pick them up off the streets—

MR. VAN DAAN (*interrupting*). Don't you ever get tired of talking? Suppose you try keeping still for five minutes. Just five minutes.

(*He starts to pace again. Again* ANNE *follows him, mimicking him.* MRS. FRANK *jumps up and takes her by the arm up to the sink, and gives her a glass of milk.*)

MRS. FRANK. Come here, Anne. It's time for your glass of milk.

MR. VAN DAAN. Talk, talk, talk. I never heard such a child. Where is my . . . ? Every evening it's the same, talk, talk, talk. (*He looks around.*) Where is my . . . ?

MRS. VAN DAAN. What're you looking for?

MR. VAN DAAN. My pipe. Have you seen my pipe?

MRS. VAN DAAN. What good's a pipe? You haven't got any tobacco.

MR. VAN DAAN. At least I'll have something to hold in my mouth! (*Opening* MARGOT'S *bedroom door.*) Margot, have you seen my pipe?

MARGOT. It was on the table last night.

(ANNE *puts her glass of milk on the table and picks up his pipe, hiding it behind her back.*)

MR. VAN DAAN. I know. I know. Anne, did you see my pipe? . . . Anne!

MRS. FRANK. Anne, Mr. Van Daan is speaking to you.

ANNE. Am I allowed to talk now?

MR. VAN DAAN. You're the most aggravating . . . The trouble with you is, you've been spoiled. What you need is a good old-fashioned spanking.

ANNE (*mimicking* MRS. VAN DAAN). "Remember, Mr. So-and-So, remember I'm a lady."

(*She thrusts the pipe into his mouth, then picks up her glass of milk.*)

MR. VAN DAAN (*restraining himself with difficulty*). Why aren't you nice and quiet like your sister Margot? Why do you have to show off all the time? Let me give you a little advice, young lady. Men don't like that kind of thing in a girl. You know that? A man likes a girl who'll listen to him once in a while . . . a domestic girl, who'll keep her house shining for her husband . . . who loves to cook and sew and . . .

ANNE. I'd cut my throat first! I'd open my veins! I'm going to be remarkable! I'm going to Paris . . .

MR. VAN DAAN (*scoffingly*). Paris!

ANNE. . . . to study music and art.

MR. VAN DAAN. Yeah! Yeah!

ANNE. I'm going to be a famous dancer or singer . . . or something wonderful.

(*She makes a wide gesture, spilling the glass of milk on the fur coat in* MRS. VAN DAAN'S *lap.* MARGOT *rushes quickly over with a towel.* ANNE *tries to brush the milk off with her skirt.*)

MRS. VAN DAAN. Now look what you've done . . . you clumsy little fool! My beautiful fur coat my father gave me . . .

ANNE. I'm so sorry.

MRS. VAN DAAN. What do you care? It isn't yours . . . So go on, ruin it! Do you know what that coat cost? Do you? And now look at it! Look at it!

ANNE. I'm very, very sorry.

MRS. VAN DAAN. I could kill you for this. I could just kill you!

(MRS. VAN DAAN *goes up the stairs, clutching the coat.* MR. VAN DAAN *starts after her.*)

MR. VAN DAAN. Petronella . . . *liefje! Liefje!* . . . Come back . . . the supper . . . come back!

MRS. FRANK. Anne, you must not behave in that way.

ANNE. It was an accident. Anyone can have an accident.

MRS. FRANK. I don't mean that. I mean the answering back. You must not answer back. They are our guests. We must always show the greatest courtesy to them. We're all living under terrible tension. (*She stops as* MARGOT *indicates that* VAN DAAN *can hear. When he is gone, she continues.*) That's why we must control ourselves . . . You don't hear Margot getting into arguments with them, do you? Watch Margot. She's always courteous with them. Never familiar. She keeps her distance. And they respect her for it. Try to be like Margot.

ANNE. And have them walk all over me, the way they do her? No, thanks!

MRS. FRANK. I'm not afraid that anyone is going to walk all over you, Anne. I'm afraid for other people, that you'll walk on them. I don't know what happens to you, Anne. You are wild, self-willed. If I had ever talked to my mother as you talk to me . . .

ANNE. Things have changed. People aren't like that any more. "Yes, Mother." "No, Mother." "Anything you say, Mother." I've got to fight things out for myself! Make something of myself!

MRS. FRANK. It isn't necessary to fight to do it. Margot doesn't fight, and isn't she . . . ?

ANNE (*violently rebellious*). Margot! Margot! Margot! That's all I hear from everyone . . . how wonderful Margot is . . . "Why aren't you like Margot?"

MARGOT (*protesting*). Oh, come on, Anne, don't be so . . .

ANNE (*paying no attention*). Everything she does is right, and everything I do is wrong! I'm the goat around here! . . . You're all against me! . . . And you worst of all!

(*She rushes off into her room and throws herself down on the settee, stifling her sobs.* MRS. FRANK *sighs and starts toward the stove.*)

MRS. FRANK (*to* MARGOT). Let's put the soup on the stove . . . if there's anyone who cares to eat. Margot, will you take the bread out? (MARGOT *gets the bread from the cupboard.*) I don't know how we can go on living this way . . . I can't say a word to Anne . . . she flies at me . . .

MARGOT. You know Anne. In half an hour she'll be out here, laughing and joking.

MRS. FRANK. And . . . (*She makes a motion upwards, indicating the* VAN DAANS.) . . . I told your father it wouldn't work .. but no . . . no . . . he had to ask them, he said . . . he owed it to him, he said. Well, he knows now that I was right! These quarrels! . . . This bickering!

MARGOT (*with a warning look*). Shush. Shush.

(*The buzzer for the door sounds.* MRS. FRANK *gasps, startled.*)

MRS. FRANK. Every time I hear that sound, my heart stops!

MARGOT (*starting for* PETER'S *door*). It's Miep. (*She knocks at the door.*) Father?

(MR. FRANK *comes quickly from* PETER'S *room.*)

MR. FRANK. Thank you, Margot. (*As he goes down the steps to open the outer door.*) Has everyone his list?

MARGOT. I'll get my books. (*Giving her mother a list.*) Here's your list. (MARGOT *goes into her and* ANNE's *bedroom on the right.* ANNE *sits up, hiding her tears, as* MARGOT *comes in.*) Miep's here.

(MARGOT *picks up her books and goes back.* ANNE *hurries over to the mirror, smoothing her hair.*)

MR. VAN DAAN (*coming down the stairs*). Is it Miep?

MARGOT. Yes. Father's gone down to let her in.

MR. VAN DAAN. At last I'll have some cigarettes!

MRS. FRANK (*to* MR. VAN DAAN.) I can't tell you how unhappy I am about Mrs. Van Daan's coat. Anne should never have touched it.

MR. VAN DAAN. She'll be all right.

MRS. FRANK. Is there anything I can do?

MR. VAN DAAN. Don't worry.

(*He turns to meet* MIEP. *But it is not* MIEP *who comes up the steps. It is* MR. KRALER, *followed by* MR. FRANK. *Their faces are grave.* ANNE *comes from the bedroom.* PETER *comes from his room.*)

MRS. FRANK. Mr. Kraler!

MR. VAN DAAN. How are you, Mr. Kraler?

MARGOT. This is a surprise.

MRS. FRANK. When Mr. Kraler comes, the sun begins to shine.

MR. VAN DAAN. Miep is coming?

MR. KRALER. Not tonight.

(KRALER *goes to* MARGOT *and* MRS. FRANK *and* ANNE, *shaking hands with them.*)

MRS. FRANK. Wouldn't you like a cup of coffee? . . . Or, better still, will you have supper with us?

MR. FRANK. Mr. Kraler has something to talk over with us. Something has happened, he says, which demands an immediate decision.

MRS. FRANK (*fearful*). What is it?

(MR. KRALER *sits down on the couch. As he talks he takes bread, cabbages, milk, etc., from his briefcase, giving them to* MARGOT *and* ANNE *to put away.*)

MR. KRALER. Usually, when I come up here, I try to bring you some bit of good news. What's the use of telling you the bad news when there's nothing that you can do about it? But today something has happened . . . Dirk . . . Miep's Dirk, you know, came to me just now. He tells me that he has a Jewish friend living near him. A dentist. He says he's in trouble. He begged me, could I do anything for this man? Could I find him a hiding place? . . . So I've come to you . . . I know it's a terrible thing to ask of you, living as you are, but would you take him in with you?

MR. FRANK. Of course we will.

MR. KRALER (*rising*). It'll be just for a night or two . . . until I find some other place. This happened so suddenly that I didn't know where to turn.

MR. FRANK. Where is he?

MR. KRALER. Downstairs in the office.

MR. FRANK. Good. Bring him up.

MR. KRALER. His name is Dussel . . . Jan Dussel.

MR. FRANK. Dussel . . . I think I know him.

MR. KRALER. I'll get him.

(*He goes quickly down the steps and out.* MR. FRANK *suddenly becomes conscious of the others.*)

MR. FRANK. Forgive me. I spoke without consulting you. But I knew you'd feel as I do.

MR. VAN DAAN. There's no reason for you to consult anyone. This is your place. You have a right to do exactly as you please. The only thing I feel . . . there's so little food as it is . . . and to take in another person . . .

(PETER *turns away, ashamed of his father.*)

MR. FRANK. We can stretch the food a little. It's only for a few days.

MR. VAN DAAN. You want to make a bet?

MRS. FRANK. I think it's fine to have him. But, Otto, where are you going to put him? Where?

PETER. He can have my bed. I can sleep on the floor. I wouldn't mind.

MR. FRANK. That's good of you, Peter. But your room's too small . . . even for *you.*

ANNE. I have a much better idea. I'll come in here with you and Mother, and Margot can take Peter's room and Peter can go in our room with Mr. Dussel.

MARGOT. That's right. We could do that.

MR. FRANK. No, Margot. You mustn't sleep in that room . . . neither you nor Anne. Mouschi has caught some rats in there. Peter's brave. He doesn't mind.

ANNE. Then how about *this?* I'll come in here with you and Mother, and Mr. Dussel can have my bed.

MRS. FRANK. No. No. *No!* Margot will come in here with us and he can have her bed. It's the only way. Margot, bring your things in here. Help her, Anne.

(MARGOT *hurries into her room to get her things.*)

ANNE (*to her mother*). Why Margot? Why can't I come in here?

MRS. FRANK. Because it wouldn't be proper for Margot to sleep with a . . . Please, Anne. Don't argue. Please.

(ANNE *starts slowly away.*)

MR. FRANK (*to* ANNE). You don't mind sharing your room with Mr. Dussel, do you, Anne?

ANNE. No. No, of course not.

MR. FRANK. Good. (ANNE *goes off into her bedroom, helping* MARGOT. MR. FRANK *starts to search in the cupboards.*) Where's the cognac?

MRS. FRANK. It's there. But, Otto, I was saving it in case of illness.

MR. FRANK. I think we couldn't find a better time to use it. Peter, will you get five glasses for me?

(PETER *goes for the glasses.* MARGOT *comes out of her bedroom, carrying her possessions, which she hangs behind a curtain in the main room.* MR. FRANK *finds the cognac and pours it into the five glasses that* PETER *brings him.* MR. VAN DAAN *stands looking on sourly.* MRS. VAN DAAN *comes downstairs and looks around at all the bustle.*)

MRS. VAN DAAN. What's happening? What's going on?

MR. VAN DAAN. Someone's moving in with us.

MRS. VAN DAAN. In here? You're joking.

MARGOT. It's only for a night or two . . . until Mr. Kraler finds him another place.

MR. VAN DAAN. Yeah! Yeah!

(MR. FRANK *hurries over as* MR. KRALER *and* DUSSEL *come up.* DUSSEL *is a man in his late fifties, meticulous, finicky . . . bewildered now. He wears a raincoat. He carries a briefcase, stuffed full, and a small medicine case.*)

MR. FRANK. Come in, Mr. Dussel.

MR. KRALER. This is Mr. Frank.

DUSSEL. Mr. Otto Frank?

MR. FRANK. Yes. Let me take your things. (*He takes the hat and briefcase, but* DUSSEL *clings to his medicine case.*) This is my wife Edith . . . Mr. and Mrs. Van

Daan . . . their son, Peter . . . and my daughters, Margot and Anne.

(DUSSEL *shakes hands with everyone.*)

MR. KRALER. Thank you, Mr. Frank. Thank you all. Mr. Dussel, I leave you in good hands. Oh . . . Dirk's coat.

(DUSSEL *hurriedly takes off the raincoat, giving it to* MR. KRALER. *Underneath is his white dentist's jacket, with a yellow Star of David on it.*)

DUSSEL (*to* MR. KRALER). What can I say to thank you . . . ?

MRS. FRANK (*to* DUSSEL). Mr. Kraler and Miep . . . They're our life line. Without them we couldn't live.

MR. KRALER. Please, Please. You make us seem very heroic. It isn't that at all. We simply don't like the Nazis. (*To* MR. FRANK, *who offers him a drink.*) No, thanks. (*Then going on.*) We don't like their methods. We don't like . . .

MR. FRANK (*smiling*). I know. I know. "No one's going to tell us Dutchmen what to do with our damn Jews!"

MR. KRALER (*to* DUSSEL). Pay no attention to Mr. Frank. I'll be up tomorrow to see that they're treating you right. (*To* MR. FRANK.) Don't trouble to come down again. Peter will bolt the door after me, won't you, Peter?

PETER. Yes, sir.

MR. FRANK. Thank you, Peter. I'll do it.

MR. KRALER. Good night. Good night.

GROUP. Good night, Mr. Kraler. We'll see you tomorrow, etc., etc.

(MR. KRALER *goes out with* MR. FRANK. MRS. FRANK *gives each one of the "grownups" a glass of cognac.*)

MRS. FRANK. Please, Mr. Dussel, sit down.

(MR. DUSSEL *sinks into a chair.* MRS. FRANK *gives him a glass of cognac.*)

DUSSEL. I'm dreaming. I know it. I can't believe my eyes. Mr. Otto Frank here! (*To* MRS. FRANK.) You're not in Switzerland then? A woman told me . . . She said she'd gone to your house . . . the door was open, everything was in disorder, dishes in the sink. She said she found a piece of paper in the wastebasket with an address scribbled on it . . . an address in Zurich. She said you must have escaped to Zurich.

ANNE. Father put that there purposely . . . just so people would think that very thing!

DUSSEL. And you've been *here* all the time?

MRS. FRANK. All the time . . . ever since July.

(ANNE *speaks to her father as he comes back.*)

ANNE. It worked, Pim . . . the address you left! Mr. Dussel says that people believe we escaped to Switzerland.

MR. FRANK. I'm glad. . . . And now let's have a little drink to welcome Mr. Dussel. (*Before they can drink*, MR. DUSSEL *bolts his drink.* MR. FRANK *smiles and raises his glass.*) To Mr. Dussel. Welcome. We're very honored to have you with us.

MRS. FRANK. To Mr. Dussel, welcome.

(*The* VAN DAANS *murmur a welcome. The "grownups" drink.*)

MRS. VAN DAAN. Um. That was good.

MR. VAN DAAN. Did Mr. Kraler warn you that you won't get much to eat here? You can imagine . . . three ration books among the seven of us . . . and now you make eight.

(PETER *walks away, humiliated. Outside a street organ is heard dimly.*)

DUSSEL (*rising*). Mr. Van Daan, you don't realize what is happening outside that you should warn me of a thing like that. You don't realize what's going on . . . (*As* MR. VAN DAAN *starts his characteristic pacing,* DUSSEL *turns to speak to the others.*) Right here in Amsterdam every day hundreds of Jews disappear . . . They surround a block and search house by house. Children come home from school to find their parents gone. Hundreds are being deported . . . people that you and I know . . . the Hallensteins . . . the Wessels . . .

MRS. FRANK (*in tears*). Oh, no. No!

DUSSEL. They get their call-up notice . . . come to the Jewish theatre on such and such a day and hour . . . bring only what you can carry in a rucksack. And if you refuse the call-up notice, then they come and drag you from your home and ship you off to Mauthausen. The death camp!

MRS. FRANK. We didn't know that things had got so much worse.

DUSSEL. Forgive me for speaking so.

ANNE (*coming to* DUSSEL). Do you know the deWaals? . . . What's become of them? Their daughter Jopie and I are in the same class. Jopie's my best friend.

DUSSEL. They are gone.

ANNE. Gone?

DUSSEL. With all the others.

ANNE. Oh, no. Not Jopie!

(*She turns away, in tears.* MRS. FRANK *motions to* MARGOT *to comfort her.* MARGOT *goes to* ANNE, *putting her arms comfortingly around her.*)

MRS. VAN DAAN. There were some people called Wagner. They lived near us . . . ?

MR. FRANK (*interrupting, with a glance at* ANNE). I think we should put this off until later. We all have many questions we want to ask . . . But I'm sure that Mr. Dussel would like to get settled before supper.

DUSSEL. Thank you. I would. I brought very little with me.

MR. FRANK (*giving him his hat and briefcase*). I'm sorry we can't give you a room alone. But I hope you won't be too uncomfortable. We've had to make strict rules here . . . a schedule of hours . . . We'll tell you after supper. Anne, would you like to take Mr. Dussel to his room?

ANNE (*controlling her tears*). If you'll come with me, Mr. Dussel?

(*She starts for her room.*)

DUSSEL (*shaking hands with each in turn*). Forgive me if I haven't really expressed my gratitude to all of you. This has been such a shock to me. I'd always thought of myself as Dutch. I was born in Holland. My father was born in Holland, and my grandfather. And now . . . after all these years . . . (*He breaks off.*) If you'll excuse me.

(DUSSEL *gives a little bow and hurries off after* ANNE. MR. FRANK *and the others are subdued.*)

ANNE (*turning on the light*). Well, here we are.

(DUSSEL *looks around the room. In the main room* MARGOT *speaks to her mother.*)

MARGOT. The news sounds pretty bad, doesn't it? It's so different from what Mr. Kraler tells us. Mr. Kraler says things are improving.

MR. VAN DAAN. I like it better the way Kraler tells it.

(*They resume their occupations, quietly.* PETER *goes off into his room. In* ANNE's *room,* ANNE *turns to* DUSSEL.)

ANNE. You're going to share the room with me.

DUSSEL. I'm a man who's always lived alone. I haven't had to adjust myself to others. I hope you'll bear with me until I learn.

ANNE. Let me help you. (*She takes his briefcase.*) Do you always live all alone? Have you no family at all?

DUSSEL. No one.

(*He opens his medicine case and spreads his bottles on the dressing table.*)

ANNE. How dreadful. You must be terribly lonely.

DUSSEL. I'm used to it.

ANNE. I don't think I could ever get used to it. Didn't you even have a pet? A cat, or a dog?

DUSSEL. I have an allergy for fur-bearing animals. They give me asthma.

ANNE. Oh, dear. Peter has a cat.

DUSSEL. Here? He has it here?

ANNE. Yes. But we hardly ever see it. He keeps it in his room all the time. I'm sure it will be all right.

DUSSEL. Let us hope so. (*He takes some pills to fortify himself.*)

ANNE. That's Margot's bed, where you're going to sleep. I sleep on the sofa there. (*Indicating the clothes hooks on the wall.*) We cleared these off for your things. (*She goes over to the window.*) The best part about this room . . . you can look down and see a bit of the street and the canal. There's a houseboat . . . you can see the end of it . . . a bargeman lives there with his family . . . They have a baby and he's just beginning to walk and I'm so afraid he's going to fall into the canal some day. I watch him. . . .

DUSSEL (*interrupting*). Your father spoke of a schedule.

ANNE (*coming away from the window*). Oh, yes. It's mostly about the times we have to be quiet. And times for the w.c. You can use it now if you like.

DUSSEL (*stiffly*). No, thank you.

ANNE. I suppose you think it's awful, my talking about a thing like that. But you don't know how important it can get to be, especially when you're frightened . . . About this room, the way Margot and I did . . . she had it to herself in the afternoons for studying, reading . . . lessons, you know . . . and I took the mornings. Would that be all right with you?

DUSSEL. I'm not at my best in the morning.

ANNE. You stay here in the mornings then. I'll take the room in the afternoons.

DUSSEL. Tell me, when you're in here, what happens to me? Where am I spending my time? In there, with all the people?

ANNE. Yes.

DUSSEL. I see. I see.

ANNE. We have supper at half past six.

DUSSEL (*going over to the sofa*). Then, if you don't mind . . . I like to lie down quietly for ten minutes before eating. I find it helps the digestion.

ANNE. Of course. I hope I'm not going to be too much of a bother to you. I seem to be able to get everyone's back up.

(DUSSEL *lies down on the sofa, curled up, his back to her.*)

DUSSEL. I always get along very well with children. My patients all bring their children to me, because they know I get on well with them. So don't you worry about that.

(ANNE *leans over him, taking his hand and shaking it gratefully.*)

ANNE. Thank you. Thank you, Mr. Dussel.

(*The lights dim to darkness. The curtain falls on the scene.* ANNE'S VOICE *comes to us faintly at first, and then with increasing power.*)

ANNE'S VOICE. . . . And yesterday I finished Cissy Van Marxvelt's latest book. I think she is a first-class writer. I shall definitely let my children read her. Monday the twenty-first of September, nineteen forty-two. Mr. Dussel and I had another battle yesterday. Yes, Mr. Dussel! According to him, nothing, I repeat . . . nothing, is right about me . . . my appearance, my character, my manners. While he was going on at me I thought . . . sometime I'll give you such a smack that you'll fly right up to the ceiling! Why is it that every grownup thinks he knows the way to bring up children? Particularly the grownups that never had any. I keep wishing that Peter was a girl instead of a boy. Then I would have someone to talk to. Margot's a darling, but she takes everything too seriously. To pause for a moment on the subject of Mrs. Van Daan. I must tell you that her attempts to flirt with father are getting her nowhere. Pim, thank goodness, won't play.

(*As she is saying the last lines, the curtain rises on the darkened scene.* ANNE'S VOICE *fades out.*)

SCENE FOUR

It is the middle of the night, several months later. The stage is dark except for a little light which comes through the skylight in PETER'S *room.*

Everyone is in bed. MR. *and* MRS. FRANK *lie on the couch in the main room, which has been pulled out to serve as a makeshift double bed.*

MARGOT *is sleeping on a mattress on the floor in the main room, behind a curtain stretched across for privacy. The others are all in their accustomed rooms.*

From outside we hear two drunken soldiers singing "Lili Marlene." A girl's high giggle is heard. The sound of running feet is heard coming closer and then fading in the distance. Throughout the scene there is the distant sound of airplanes passing overhead.

A match suddenly flares up in the attic. We dimly see MR. VAN DAAN. *He is getting his bearings. He comes quickly down the stairs, and goes to the cupboard where the food is stored. Again the match flares up, and is as quickly blown out. The dim figure is seen to steal back up the stairs.*

There is quiet for a second or two, broken only by the sound of airplanes, and running feet on the street below.

Suddenly, out of the silence and the dark, we hear ANNE *scream.*

———

ANNE (*screaming*). No! No! Don't . . . don't take me!

(*She moans, tossing and crying in her sleep. The other people wake, terrified.* DUSSEL *sits up in bed, furious.*)

DUSSEL. Shush! Anne! Anne, for God's sake, shush!

ANNE (*still in her nightmare*). Save me! Save me!

(*She screams and screams.* DUSSEL *gets out of bed, going over to her, trying to wake her.*)

DUSSEL. For God's sake! Quiet! Quiet! You want someone to hear?

(*In the main room* MRS. FRANK *grabs a shawl and pulls it around her. She rushes in to* ANNE, *taking her in her arms.* MR. FRANK *hurriedly gets up, putting on his overcoat.* MARGOT *sits up, terrified.* PETER'S *light goes on in his room.*)

MRS. FRANK (*to* ANNE, *in her room*). Hush, darling, hush. It's all right. It's all right. (*Over her shoulder to* DUSSEL.) Will you be kind enough to turn on the light, Mr. Dussel? (*Back to* ANNE.) It's nothing, my darling. It was just a dream.

(DUSSEL *turns on the light in the bedroom.* MRS. FRANK *holds* ANNE *in her arms. Gradually* ANNE *comes out of her nightmare, still trembling with horror.* MR. FRANK *comes into the room, and goes quickly to the window, looking out to be sure that no one outside has heard* ANNE'S *screams.* MRS. FRANK *holds* ANNE, *talking softly to her. In the main room* MARGOT *stands on a chair, turning on the center hanging lamp. A light goes on in the* VAN DAANS' *room overhead.* PETER *puts his robe on, coming out of his room.*)

DUSSEL (*to* MRS. FRANK, *blowing his nose*). Something must be done about that child, Mrs. Frank. Yelling like that! Who knows but there's somebody on the streets? She's endangering all our lives.

MRS. FRANK. Anne, darling.

DUSSEL. Every night she twists and turns. I don't sleep. I spend half my night shushing her. And now it's nightmares!

(MARGOT *comes to the door of* ANNE'S *room, followed by* PETER. MR. FRANK *goes to them, indicating that everything is all right.* PETER *takes* MARGOT *back.*)

MRS. FRANK (*to* ANNE). You're here, safe, you see? Nothing has happened. (*To* DUSSEL.) Please, Mr. Dussel, go back to bed. She'll be herself in a minute or two. Won't you, Anne?

DUSSEL (*picking up a book and a pillow*). Thank you, but I'm going to the w.c. The one place where there's peace!

(*He stalks out.* MR. VAN DAAN, *in underwear and trousers, comes down the stairs.*)

MR. VAN DAAN (*to* DUSSEL). What is it? What happened?

DUSSEL. A nightmare. She was having a nightmare!

MR. VAN DAAN. I thought someone was murdering her.

DUSSEL. Unfortunately, no.

(*He goes into the bathroom.* MR. VAN DAAN *goes back up the stairs.* MR. FRANK, *in the main room, sends* PETER *back to his own bedroom.*)

MR. FRANK. Thank you, Peter. Go back to bed.

(PETER *goes back to his room.* MR. FRANK *follows him, turning out the light and looking out the window. Then he goes back to the main room, and gets up on a chair, turning out the center hanging lamp.*)

MRS. FRANK (*to* ANNE). Would you like some water? (ANNE *shakes her head.*) Was it a very bad dream? Perhaps if you told me . . . ?

ANNE. I'd rather not talk about it.

MRS. FRANK. Poor darling. Try to sleep then. I'll sit right here beside you until you fall asleep. (*She brings a stool over, sitting there.*)

ANNE. You don't have to.

MRS. FRANK. But I'd like to stay with you . . . very much. Really.

ANNE. I'd rather you didn't.

MRS. FRANK. Good night, then. (*She leans down to kiss* ANNE. ANNE *throws her arm up over her face, turning away.* MRS. FRANK, *hiding her hurt, kisses* ANNE'S *arm.*) You'll be all right? There's nothing that you want?

ANNE. Will you please ask Father to come.

MRS. FRANK (*after a second*). Of course, Anne dear. (*She hurries out into the other room.* MR. FRANK *comes to her as she comes in.*) *Sie verlangt nach Dir!*

MR. FRANK (*sensing her hurt*). Edith, Liebe, schau . . .

MRS. FRANK. *Es macht nichts! Ich danke dem lieben Herrgott, dass sie sich wenigstens an Dich wendet, wenn sie Trost braucht! Geh hinein, Otto, sie ist ganz hysterisch vor Angst.* (*As* MR. FRANK *hesitates.*) *Geh zu ihr.* (*He looks at her for a second and then goes to get a cup of water for* ANNE. MRS. FRANK *sinks down on the bed, her face in her hands, trying to keep from sobbing aloud.* MARGOT *comes over to her, putting her arms around her.*) She wants nothing of me. She pulled away when I leaned down to kiss her.

MARGOT. It's a phase . . . You heard Father . . . Most girls go through it . . . they turn to their fathers at this age . . . they give all their love to their fathers.

MRS. FRANK. You weren't like this. You didn't shut me out.

MARGOT. She'll get over it . . .

(*She smooths the bed for* MRS. FRANK *and sits beside her a moment as* MRS. FRANK *lies down. In* ANNE'S *room* MR. FRANK *comes in, sitting down by* ANNE. ANNE *flings her arms around him, clinging to him. In the distance we hear the sound of ack-ack.*)

ANNE. Oh, Pim. I dreamed that they came to get us! The Green Police! They broke down the door and grabbed me and started to drag me out the way they did Jopie.

MR. FRANK. I want you to take this pill.

ANNE. What is it?

MR. FRANK. Something to quiet you.

(*She takes it and drinks the water. In the main room* MARGOT *turns out the light and goes back to her bed.*)

MR. FRANK (*to* ANNE). Do you want me to read to you for a while?

ANNE. No. Just sit with me for a minute. Was I awful? Did I yell terribly loud? Do you think anyone outside could have heard?

MR. FRANK. No. No. Lie quietly now. Try to sleep.

ANNE. I'm a terrible coward. I'm so disappointed in myself. I think I've conquered my fear . . . I think I'm really grown-up . . . and then something happens . . . and I run to you like a baby . . . I love you, Father. I don't love anyone but you.

MR. FRANK (*reproachfully*). Annele!

ANNE. It's true. I've been thinking about it for a long time. You're the only one I love.

MR. FRANK. It's fine to hear you tell me that you love me. But I'd be happier if you said you loved your mother as well . . . She needs your help so much . . . your love . . .

ANNE. We have nothing in common. She doesn't understand me. Whenever I try to explain my views on life to her she asks me if I'm constipated.

MR. FRANK. You hurt her very much now. She's crying. She's in there crying.

ANNE. I can't help it. I only told the truth. I didn't want her here . . . (*Then, with sudden change.*) Oh, Pim, I was horrible, wasn't I? And the worst of it is, I can stand off and look at myself doing it and know it's cruel and yet I can't stop doing it. What's the matter with me? Tell me. Don't say it's just a phase! Help me.

MR. FRANK. There is so little that we parents can do to help our children. We can only try to set a good example . . . point the way. The rest you must do yourself. You must build your own character.

ANNE. I'm trying. Really I am. Every night I think back over all of the things I did that day that were wrong . . . like putting the wet mop in Mr. Dussel's bed . . . and this thing now with Mother. I say to myself, that was wrong. I make up my mind, I'm never going to do that again. Never! Of course I may do something worse . . . but at least I'll never do *that* again! . . . I have a nicer side, Father . . . a sweeter, nicer side. But I'm scared to show it. I'm afraid that people are going to laugh at me if I'm serious. So the mean Anne comes to the outside and the good Anne stays on the inside, and I keep on trying to switch them around and have the good Anne outside and the bad Anne inside and be what I'd like to be . . . and might be . . . if only . . . only . . .

(*She is asleep.* MR. FRANK *watches her for a moment and then turns off the light, and starts out. The lights dim out. The curtain falls on the scene.* ANNE'S VOICE *is heard dimly at first, and then with growing strength.*)

ANNE'S VOICE. . . . The air raids are getting worse. They come over day and night. The noise is terrifying. Pim says it should be music to our ears. The more planes, the sooner will come the end of the war. Mrs. Van Daan pretends to be a fatalist. What will be, will be. But when the planes come over, who is the most frightened? No one else but Petronella! . . . Monday, the ninth of November, nineteen forty-two. Wonderful news! The Allies have landed in Africa. Pim says that we can look for an early finish to the war. Just for fun he asked each of us what was the first thing we wanted to do when we got out of here. Mrs. Van Daan longs to be home with her own things, her needle-point chairs, the Beckstein piano her father gave her . . . the best that money could buy. Peter would like to go to a movie. Mr. Dussel wants to get back to his dentist's drill. He's afraid he is losing his touch. For myself, there are so many things . . . to ride a bike again . . . to laugh till my belly aches . . . to have new clothes from the skin out . . . to have a hot tub filled to overflowing and wallow in it for hours . . . to be back in school with my friends . . .

(*As the last lines are being said, the curtain rises on the scene. The lights dim on as* ANNE'S VOICE *fades away.*)

SCENE FIVE

It is the first night of the Hanukkah celebration. MR. FRANK *is standing at the head of the table on which is the Menorah. He lights the Shamos, or servant candle, and holds it as he says the blessing. Seated listening is all of the "family," dressed in their best. The men wear hats,* PETER *wears his cap.*

MR. FRANK (*reading from a prayer book*). "Praised be Thou, oh Lord our God, Ruler of the universe, who has sanctified us with Thy commandments and bidden us kindle the Hanukkah lights. Praised be Thou, oh Lord our God, Ruler of the universe, who has wrought wondrous deliverances for our fathers in days of old. Praised be Thou, oh Lord our God, Ruler of the universe, that Thou has given us life and sustenance and brought us to this happy season." (MR. FRANK *lights the one candle of the Menorah as he continues.*) "We kindle this Hanukkah light to celebrate the great and wonderful deeds wrought through the zeal with which God filled the hearts of the heroic Maccabees, two thousand years ago. They fought against indifference, against tyranny and oppression, and they restored our Temple to us. May these lights remind us that we should ever look to God, whence cometh our help." Amen. [Pronounced O-mayn.]

ALL. Amen.

(MR. FRANK *hands* MRS. FRANK *the prayer book.*)

MRS. FRANK (*reading*). "I lift up mine eyes unto the mountains, from whence cometh my help. My help cometh from the Lord who made heaven and earth. He will not suffer thy foot to be moved. He that keepeth thee will not slumber. He that keepeth Israel doth neither slumber nor sleep. The Lord is thy keeper. The Lord is thy shade upon thy right hand. The sun shall not smite thee by day, nor the moon by night. The Lord shall keep thee from all evil. He shall keep thy soul. The Lord shall guard thy going out and thy coming in, from this time forth and forevermore." Amen.

ALL. Amen.

(MRS. FRANK *puts down the prayer book and goes to get the food and wine.* MARGOT *helps her.* MR. FRANK *takes the men's hats and puts them aside.*)

DUSSEL (*rising*). That was very moving.

ANNE (*pulling him back*). It isn't over yet!

MRS. VAN DAAN. Sit down! Sit down!

ANNE. There's a lot more, songs and presents.

DUSSEL. Presents?

MRS. FRANK. Not this year, unfortunately.

MRS. VAN DAAN. But always on Hanukkah everyone gives presents . . . everyone!

DUSSEL. Like our St. Nicholas' Day.

(*There is a chorus of "no's" from the group.*)

MRS. VAN DAAN. No! Not like St. Nicholas! What kind of a Jew are you that you don't know Hanukkah?

MRS. FRANK (*as she brings the food*). I remember particularly the candles . . . First one, as we have tonight. Then the second night you light two candles, the next night three . . . and so on until you have eight candles burning. When there are eight candles it is truly beautiful.

MRS. VAN DAAN. And the potato pancakes.

MR. VAN DAAN. Don't talk about them!

MRS. VAN DAAN. I make the best *latkes* you ever tasted!

MRS. FRANK. Invite us all next year . . . in your own home.

MR. FRANK. God willing!

MRS. VAN DAAN. God willing.

MARGOT. What I remember best is the presents we used to get when we were little . . . eight days of presents . . . and each day they got better and better.

MRS. FRANK (*sitting down*). We are all here, alive. That is present enough.

ANNE. No, it isn't. I've got something . . . (*She rushes into her room, hurriedly puts on a little hat improvised from the lamp shade, grabs a satchel bulging with parcels and comes running back.*)

MRS. FRANK. What is it?

ANNE. Presents!

MRS. VAN DAAN. Presents!

DUSSEL. Look!

MRS. VAN DAAN. What's she got on her head?

PETER. A lamp shade!

ANNE (*she picks out one at random*). This is for Margot. (*She hands it to* MARGOT, *pulling her to her feet.*) Read it out loud.

MARGOT (*reading*).
"You have never lost your temper.
  You never will, I fear,
  You are so good.
  But if you should,
  Put all your cross words here."
(*She tears open the package.*) A new crossword puzzle book! Where did you get it?

ANNE. It isn't new. It's one that you've done. But I rubbed it all out, and if you wait a little and forget, you can do it all over again.

MARGOT (*sitting*). It's wonderful, Anne. Thank you. You'd never know it wasn't new.

(*From outside we hear the sound of a streetcar passing.*)

ANNE (*with another gift*). Mrs. Van Daan.

MRS. VAN DAAN (*taking it*). This is awful . . . I haven't anything for anyone . . . I never thought . . .

MR. FRANK. This is all Anne's idea.

MRS. VAN DAAN (*holding up a bottle*). What is it?

ANNE. It's hair shampoo. I took all the odds and ends of soap and mixed them with the last of my toilet water.

MRS. VAN DAAN. Oh, Anneke!

ANNE. I wanted to write a poem for all of them, but I didn't have time. (*Offering a large box to* MR. VAN DAAN.) Yours, Mr. Van Daan, is *really* something . . . something you want more than anything. (*As she waits for him to open it.*) Look! Cigarettes!

MR. VAN DAAN. Cigarettes!

ANNE. Two of them! Pim found some old pipe tobacco in the pocket lining of his coat . . . and we made them . . . or rather, Pim did.

MRS. VAN DAAN. Let me see . . . Well, look at that! Light it, Putti! Light it.

(MR. VAN DAAN *hesitates*.)

ANNE. It's tobacco, really it is! There's a little fluff in it, but not much.

(*Everyone watches as* MR. VAN DAAN *cautiously lights it. The cigarette flares up. Everyone laughs.*)

PETER. It works!

MRS. VAN DAAN. Look at him.

MR. VAN DAAN (*spluttering*). Thank you, Anne. Thank you.

(ANNE *rushes back to her satchel for another present.*)

ANNE (*handing her mother a piece of paper*). For Mother, Hanukkah greeting.

(*She pulls her mother to her feet.*)

MRS. FRANK (*She reads*). "Here's an I.O.U. that I promise to pay.
Ten hours of doing whatever you say.
Signed, Anne Frank." (MRS. FRANK, *touched, takes* ANNE *in her arms, holding her close.*)

DUSSEL (*to* ANNE). Ten hours of doing what you're told? *Anything* you're told?

ANNE. That's right.

DUSSEL. You wouldn't want to sell that, Mrs. Frank?

MRS. FRANK. Never! This is the most precious gift I've ever had!

(*She sits, showing her present to the others.* ANNE *hurries back to the satchel and pulls out a scarf, the scarf that* MR. FRANK *found in the first scene.*)

ANNE (*offering it to her father*). For Pim.

MR. FRANK. Anneke . . . I wasn't supposed to have a present!

(*He takes it, unfolding it and showing it to the others.*)

ANNE. It's a muffler . . . to put round your neck . . . like an ascot, you know. I made it myself out of odds and ends . . . I knitted it in the dark each night, after I'd gone to bed. I'm afraid it looks better in the dark!

MR. FRANK (*putting it on*). It's fine. It fits me perfectly. Thank you, Anneke.

(ANNE *hands* PETER *a ball of paper, with a string attached to it.*)

ANNE. That's for Mouschi.

PETER (*rising to bow*). On behalf of Mouschi, I thank you.

ANNE (*hesitant, handing him a gift*). And . . . this is yours . . . from Mrs. Quack Quack. (*As he holds it gingerly in his hands.*) Well . . . open it . . . Aren't you going to open it?

PETER. I'm scared to. I know something's going to jump out and hit me.

ANNE. No. It's nothing like that, really.

MRS. VAN DAAN (*as he is opening it*). What is it, Peter? Go on. Show it.

ANNE (*excitedly*). It's a safety razor!

DUSSEL. A what?

ANNE. A razor!

MRS. VAN DAAN (*looking at it*). You didn't make that out of odds and ends.

ANNE (*to* PETER). Miep got it for me. It's not new. It's second-hand. But you really do need a razor now.

DUSSEL. For what?

ANNE. Look on his upper lip . . . you can see the beginning of a mustache.

DUSSEL. He wants to get rid of that? Put a little milk on it and let the cat lick if off.

PETER (*starting for his room*). Think you're funny, don't you.

DUSSEL. Look! He can't wait! He's going in to try it!

PETER. I'm going to give Mouschi his present!

(*He goes into his room, slamming the door behind him.*)

MR. VAN DAAN (*disgustedly*). Mouschi, Mouschi, Mouschi.

(*In the distance we hear a dog persistently barking.* ANNE *brings a gift to* DUSSEL.)

ANNE. And last but never least, my roommate, Mr. Dussel.

DUSSEL. For me? You have something for me? (*He opens the small box she gives him.*)

ANNE. I made them myself.

DUSSEL (*puzzled*). Capsules! Two capsules!

ANNE. They're ear-plugs!

DUSSEL. Ear-plugs?

ANNE. To put in your ears so you won't hear me when I thrash around at night. I saw them advertised in a magazine. They're not real ones . . . I made them out of cotton and candle wax. Try them . . . See if they don't work . . . see if you can hear me talk . . .

DUSSEL (*putting them in his ears*). Wait now until I get them in . . . so.

ANNE. Are you ready?

DUSSEL. Huh?

ANNE. Are you ready?

DUSSEL. Good God! They've gone inside! I can't get them out! (*They laugh as* MR. DUSSEL *jumps about, trying to shake the plugs out of his ears. Finally he gets them out. Putting them away.*) Thank you, Anne! Thank you!

MR. VAN DAAN. A real Hanukkah!

MRS. VAN DAAN. Wasn't it cute of her?

MRS. FRANK. I don't know when she did it.

MARGOT. I love my present.

⎫ (*Together.*)

ANNE (*sitting at the table*). And now let's have the song, Father . . . please . . . (*To* DUSSEL.) Have you heard the Hanukkah song, Mr. Dussel? The song is the whole thing! (*She sings.*) "Oh, Hanukkah! Oh Hanukkah! The sweet celebration . . ."

MR. FRANK (*quieting her*). I'm afraid, Anne, we shouldn't sing that song tonight. (*To* DUSSEL.) It's a song of jubilation, of rejoicing. One is apt to become too enthusiastic.

ANNE. Oh, please, please. Let's sing the song. I promise not to shout!

MR. FRANK. Very well. But quietly now . . . I'll keep an eye on you and when . . .

(*As* ANNE *starts to sing, she is interrupted by* DUSSEL, *who is snorting and wheezing.*)

DUSSEL (*pointing to* PETER). You . . . You! (PETER *is coming from his bedroom, ostentatiously holding a bulge in his coat as if he were holding his cat, and dangling* ANNE's *present before it.*) How many times . . . I told you . . . Out! Out!

MR. VAN DAAN (*going to* PETER). What's the matter with you? Haven't you any sense? Get that cat out of here.

PETER (*innocently*). Cat?

MR. VAN DAAN. You heard me. Get it out of here!

PETER. I have no cat. (*Delighted with his joke, he opens his coat and pulls out a bath towel. The group at the table laugh, enjoying the joke.*)

DUSSEL (*still wheezing*). It doesn't need to be the cat . . . his clothes are enough . . . when he comes out of that room . . .

MR. VAN DAAN. Don't worry. You won't be bothered any more. We're getting rid of it.

DUSSEL. At last you listen to me.

(*He goes off into his bedroom.*)

MR. VAN DAAN (*calling after him*). I'm not doing it for you. That's all in your mind . . . all of it! (*He starts back to his place at the table.*) I'm doing it because I'm sick of seeing that cat eat all our food.

PETER. That's not true! I only give him bones . . . scraps . . .

MR. VAN DAAN. Don't tell me! He gets fatter every day! Damn cat looks better than any of us. Out he goes tonight!

PETER. No! No!

ANNE. Mr. Van Daan, you can't do that! That's Peter's cat. Peter loves that cat.

MRS. FRANK (*quietly*). Anne.

PETER (*to* MR. VAN DAAN). If he goes, I go.

MR. VAN DAAN. Go! Go!

MRS. VAN DAAN. You're not going and the cat's not going! Now please . . . this is Hanukkah . . . Hanukkah . . . this is the time to celebrate . . . What's the matter with all of you? Come on, Anne. Let's have the song.

ANNE (*singing*).

"Oh, Hanukkah! Oh, Hanukkah!
  The sweet celebration."

MR. FRANK (*rising*). I think we should first blow out the candle . . . then we'll have something for tomorrow night.

MARGOT. But, Father, you're supposed to let it burn itself out.

MR. FRANK. I'm sure that God understands shortages. (*Before blowing it out.*) "Praised be Thou, oh Lord our God, who hast sustained us and permitted us to celebrate this joyous festival."

(*He is about to blow out the candle when suddenly there is a crash of something falling below. They all freeze in horror, motionless. For a few seconds there is complete silence.* MR. FRANK *slips off his shoes. The others noiselessly follow his example.* MR. FRANK turns out a light near him. He motions to PETER to turn off the center lamp. PETER tries to reach it, realizes he cannot and gets up on a chair. Just as he is touching the lamp he loses his balance. The chair goes out from under him. He falls. The iron lamp shade crashes to the floor. There is a sound of feet below, running down the stairs.)

MR. VAN DAAN (under his breath). God Almighty! (The only light left comes from the Hanukkah candle. DUSSEL comes from his room. MR. FRANK creeps over to the stairwell and stands listening. The dog is heard barking excitedly.) Do you hear anything?

MR. FRANK (in a whisper). No. I think they've gone.

MRS. VAN DAAN. It's the Green Police. They've found us.

MR. FRANK. If they had, they wouldn't have left. They'd be up here by now.

MRS. VAN DAAN. I know it's the Green Police. They've gone to get help. That's all. They'll be back!

MR. VAN DAAN. Or it may have been the Gestapo, looking for papers . . .

MR. FRANK (interrupting). Or a thief, looking for money.

MRS. VAN DAAN. We've got to do something . . . Quick! Quick! Before they come back.

MR. VAN DAAN. There isn't anything to do. Just wait.

(MR. FRANK holds up his hand for them to be quiet. He is listening intently. There is complete silence as they all strain to hear any sound from below. Suddenly ANNE begins to sway. With a low cry she falls to the floor in a faint. MRS. FRANK goes to her quickly, sitting beside her on the floor and taking her in her arms.)

MRS. FRANK. Get some water, please! Get some water!

(MARGOT starts for the sink.)

MR. VAN DAAN (grabbing MARGOT). No! No! No one's going to run water!

MR. FRANK. If they've found us, they've found us. Get the water. (MARGOT starts again for the sink. MR. FRANK, getting a flashlight.) I'm going down.

(MARGOT rushes to him, clinging to him. ANNE struggles to consciousness.)

MARGOT. No, Father, no! There may be someone there, waiting . . . It may be a trap!

MR. FRANK. This is Saturday. There is no way for us to know what has happened until Miep or Mr. Kraler comes on Monday morning. We cannot live with this uncertainty.

MARGOT. Don't go, Father!

MRS. FRANK. Hush, darling, hush. (MR. FRANK slips quietly out, down the steps and out through the door below.) Margot! Stay close to me.

(MARGOT goes to her mother.)

MR. VAN DAAN. Shush! Shush!

(MRS. FRANK whispers to MARGOT to get the water. MARGOT goes for it.)

MRS. VAN DAAN. Putti, where's our money? Get our money. I hear you can buy the Green Police off, so much a head. Go upstairs quick! Get the money!

MR. VAN DAAN. Keep still!

MRS. VAN DAAN (kneeling before him, pleading). Do you want to be dragged off to a concentration camp? Are you going to stand there and wait for them to come up and get you? Do something, I tell you!

MR. VAN DAAN (pushing her aside). Will you keep still!

(He goes over to the stairwell to listen. PETER goes to his mother, helping her up onto the sofa. There is a second of silence, then ANNE can stand it no longer.)

ANNE. Someone go after Father! Make Father come back!

PETER (starting for the door). I'll go.

MR. VAN DAAN. Haven't you done enough?

(He pushes PETER roughly away. In his anger against his father PETER grabs a chair as if to hit him with it, then puts it down, burying his face in his hands. MRS. FRANK begins to pray softly.)

ANNE. Please, please, Mr. Van Daan. Get Father.

MR. VAN DAAN. Quiet! Quiet!

(ANNE is shocked into silence. MRS. FRANK pulls her closer, holding her protectively in her arms.)

MRS. FRANK (softly, praying). "I lift up mine eyes unto the mountains, from whence cometh my help. My help cometh from the Lord who made heaven and earth. He will not suffer thy foot to be moved . . . He that keepeth thee will not slumber . . ."

(She stops as she hears someone coming. They all watch the door tensely. MR. FRANK comes quietly in. ANNE rushes to him, holding him tight.)

MR. FRANK. It was a thief. That noise must have scared him away.

MRS. VAN DAAN. Thank God.

MR. FRANK. He took the cash box. And

the radio. He ran away in such a hurry that he didn't stop to shut the street door. It was swinging wide open. (*A breath of relief sweeps over them.*) I think it would be good to have some light.

MARGOT. Are you sure it's all right?

MR. FRANK. The danger has passed. (MARGOT *goes to light the small lamp.*) Don't be so terrified, Anne. We're safe.

DUSSEL. Who says the danger has passed? Don't you realize we are in greater danger than ever?

MR. FRANK. Mr. Dussel, will you be still!

(MR. FRANK *takes* ANNE *back to the table, making her sit down with him, trying to calm her.*)

DUSSEL (*pointing to* PETER). Thanks to this clumsy fool, there's someone now who knows we're up here! Someone now knows we're up here, hiding!

MRS. VAN DAAN (*going to* DUSSEL). Someone knows we're here, yes. But who is the someone? A thief! A thief! You think a thief is going to go to the Green Police and say . . . I was robbing a place the other night and I heard a noise up over my head? You think a thief is going to do that?

DUSSEL. Yes. I think he will.

MRS. VAN DAAN (*hysterically*). You're crazy!

(*She stumbles back to her seat at the table.* PETER *follows protectively, pushing* DUSSEL *aside.*)

DUSSEL. I think some day he'll be caught and then he'll make a bargain with the Green Police . . . if they'll let him off, he'll tell them where some Jews are hiding!

(*He goes off into the bedroom. There is a second of appalled silence.*)

MR. VAN DAAN. He's right.

ANNE. Father, let's get out of here! We can't stay here now . . . Let's go . . .

MR. VAN DAAN. Go! Where?

MRS. FRANK (*sinking into her chair at the table*). Yes. Where?

MR. FRANK (*rising, to them all*). Have we lost all faith? All courage? A moment ago we thought that they'd come for us. We were sure it was the end. But it wasn't the end. We're alive, safe. (MR. VAN DAAN *goes to the table and sits.* MR. FRANK *prays.*) "We thank Thee, oh Lord our God, that in Thy infinite mercy Thou hast again seen fit to spare us." (*He blows out the candle, then turns to* ANNE.)

Come on, Anne. The song! Let's have the song! (*He starts to sing.* ANNE *finally starts falteringly to sing, as* MR. FRANK *urges her on. Her voice is hardly audible at first.*)

ANNE (*singing*).
"Oh, Hanukkah! Oh, Hanukkah!
The sweet . . . celebration . . ."

(*As she goes on singing, the others gradually join in, their voices still shaking with fear.* MRS. VAN DAAN *sobs as she sings.*)

GROUP.
"Around the feast . . . we . . . gather
In complete . . . jubilation . . .
Happiest of sea . . . sons
Now is here.
Many are the reasons for good cheer."

(DUSSEL *comes from the bedroom. He comes over to the table, standing beside* MARGOT, *listening to them as they sing.*)
"Together
We'll weather
Whatever tomorrow may bring."

(*As they sing on with growing courage, the lights start to dim.*)
"So hear us rejoicing
And merrily voicing
The Hanukkah song that we sing.
Hoy!"

(*The lights are out. The curtain starts slowly to fall.*)
"Hear us rejoicing
And merrily voicing
The Hanukkah song that we sing."

(*They are still singing, as the curtain falls.*)

CURTAIN

ACT TWO

SCENE ONE

In the darkness we hear ANNE'S VOICE, *again reading from the diary.*

———

ANNE'S VOICE. Saturday, the first of January, nineteen forty-four. Another new year has begun and we find ourselves still in our hiding place. We have been here now for one year, five months and twenty-five days. It seems that our life is at a standstill.

(*The curtain rises on the scene. It is afternoon. Everyone is bundled up against the cold. In the main room* MRS. FRANK *is taking down the laundry, which is hung across the back.* MR. FRANK *sits in the chair down left, reading.* MARGOT *is lying on the couch with a blanket over her and the many-colored knitted scarf around her throat.* ANNE *is seated at the center table, writing in her diary.* PETER, MR. *and* MRS. VAN DAAN, *and* DUSSEL *are all in their own rooms, reading or lying down.*

As the lights dim on, ANNE'S VOICE *continues, without a break.*)

ANNE'S VOICE. We are all a little thinner. The Van Daan's "discussions" are as violent as ever. Mother still does not understand me. But then I don't understand her either. There is one great change, however. A change in myself. I read somewhere that girls of my age don't feel quite certain of themselves. That they become quiet within and begin to think of the miracle that is taking place in their bodies. I think that what is happening to me is so wonderful . . . not only what can be seen, but what is taking place inside. Each time it has happened I have a feeling that I have a sweet secret. (*We hear the chimes and then a hymn being played on the carillon outside.*) And in spite of any pain, I long for the time when I shall feel that secret within me again.

(*The buzzer of the door below suddenly sounds. Everyone is startled;* MR. FRANK *tiptoes cautiously to the top of the steps and listens. Again the buzzer sounds, in* MIEP'S *V-for-Victory signal.*)

MR. FRANK. It's Miep! (*He goes quickly down the steps to unbolt the door.* MRS. FRANK *calls upstairs to the* VAN DAANS *and then to* PETER.)

MRS. FRANK. Wake up, everyone! Miep is here! (ANNE *quickly puts her diary away.* MARGOT *sits up, pulling the blanket around her shoulders.* MR. DUSSEL *sits on the edge of his bed, listening, disgruntled.* MIEP *comes up the steps, followed by* MR. KRALER. *They bring flowers, books, newspapers, etc.* ANNE *rushes to* MIEP, *throwing her arms affectionately around her.*) Miep . . . and Mr. Kraler . . . What a delightful surprise!

MR. KRALER. We came to bring you New Year's greetings.

MRS. FRANK. You shouldn't . . . you should have at least one day to yourselves. (*She goes quickly to the stove and brings down teacups and tea for all of them.*)

ANNE. Don't say that, it's so wonderful to see them! (*Sniffing at* MIEP'S *coat.*) I can smell the wind and the cold on your clothes.

MIEP (*giving her the flowers*). There you are. (*Then to* MARGOT, *feeling her forehead.*)

How are you, Margot? . . . Feeling any better?

MARGOT. I'm all right.

ANNE. We filled her full of every kind of pill so she won't cough and make a noise.

(*She runs into her room to put the flowers in water.* MR. *and* MRS. VAN DAAN *come from upstairs. Outside there is the sound of a band playing.*)

MRS. VAN DAAN. Well, hello, Miep. Mr. Kraler.

MR. KRALER (*giving a bouquet of flowers to* MRS. VAN DAAN). With my hope for peace in the New Year.

PETER (*anxiously*). Miep, have you seen Mouschi? Have you seen him anywhere around?

MIEP. I'm sorry, Peter. I asked everyone in the neighborhood had they seen a gray cat. But they said no.

(MRS. FRANK *gives* MIEP *a cup of tea.* MR. FRANK *comes up the steps, carrying a small cake on a plate.*)

MR. FRANK. Look what Miep's brought for us!

MRS. FRANK (*taking it*). A cake!

MR. VAN DAAN. A cake! (*He pinches* MIEP'S *cheeks gaily and hurries up to the cupboard.*) I'll get some plates.

(DUSSEL, *in his room, hastily puts a coat on and starts out to join the others.*)

MRS. FRANK. Thank you, Miepia. You shouldn't have done it. You must have used all of your sugar ration for weeks. (*Giving it to* MRS. VAN DAAN.) It's beautiful, isn't it?

MRS. VAN DAAN. It's been ages since I even saw a cake. Not since you brought us one last year. (*Without looking at the cake, to* MIEP.) Remember? Don't you remember, you gave us one on New Year's Day? Just this time last year? I'll never forget it because you had "Peace in nineteen forty-three" on it. (*She looks at the cake and reads.*) "Peace in nineteen forty-four!"

MIEP. Well, it has to come sometime, you know. (*As* DUSSEL *comes from his room.*) Hello, Mr. Dussel.

MR. KRALER. How are you?

MR. VAN DAAN (*bringing plates and a knife*). Here's the knife, *liefje.* Now, how many of us are there?

MIEP. None for me, thank you.

MR. FRANK. Oh, please. You must.

MIEP. I couldn't.

MR. VAN DAAN. Good! That leaves one

. . . two . . . three . . . seven of us.

DUSSEL. Eight! Eight! It's the same number as it always is!

MR. VAN DAAN. I left Margot out. I take it for granted Margot won't eat any.

ANNE. Why wouldn't she!

MRS. FRANK. I think it won't harm her.

MR. VAN DAAN. All right! All right! I just didn't want her to start coughing again, that's all.

DUSSEL. And please, Mrs. Frank should cut the cake.

MR. VAN DAAN. What's the difference? ⎫

MRS. VAN DAAN. It's not Mrs. Frank's cake, is it, Miep? It's for all of us. ⎬ (*Together.*)

DUSSEL. Mrs. Frank divides things better. ⎭

MRS. VAN DAAN (*going to* DUSSEL). What are you trying to say? ⎫

MR. VAN DAAN. Oh, come on! Stop wasting time! ⎬ (*Together.*)

MRS. VAN DAAN (*to* DUSSEL). Don't I always give everybody exactly the same? Don't I?

MR. VAN DAAN. Forget it, Kerli.

MRS. VAN DAAN. No. I want an answer! Don't I?

DUSSEL. Yes. Yes. Everybody gets exactly the same . . . except Mr. Van Daan always gets a little bit more.

(VAN DAAN *advances on* DUSSEL, *the knife still in his hand.*)

MR. VAN DAAN. That's a lie!

(DUSSEL *retreats before the onslaught of the* VAN DAANS.)

MR. FRANK. Please, please! (*Then to* MIEP.) You see what a little sugar cake does to us? It goes right to our heads!

MR. VAN DAAN (*handing* MRS. FRANK *the knife*). Here you are, Mrs. Frank.

MRS. FRANK. Thank you. (*Then to* MIEP *as she goes to the table to cut the cake.*) Are you sure you won't have some?

MIEP (*drinking her tea*). No, really, I have to go in a minute.

(*The sound of the band fades out in the distance.*)

PETER (*to* MIEP). Maybe Mouschi went back to our house . . . they say that cats . . . Do you ever get over there . . . ? I mean . . . do you suppose you could . . . ?

MIEP. I'll try, Peter. The first minute I get I'll try. But I'm afraid, with him gone a week . . .

DUSSEL. Make up your mind, already

someone has had a nice big dinner from that cat!

(PETER *is furious, inarticulate. He starts toward* DUSSEL *as if to hit him.* MR. FRANK *stops him.* MRS. FRANK *speaks quickly to ease the situation.*)

MRS. FRANK (*to* MIEP). This is delicious, Miep!

MRS. VAN DAAN (*eating hers*). Delicious!

MR. VAN DAAN (*finishing it in one gulp*). Dirk's in luck to get a girl who can bake like this!

MIEP (*putting down her empty teacup*). I have to run. Dirk's taking me to a party tonight.

ANNE. How heavenly! Remember now what everyone is wearing, and what you have to eat and everything, so you can tell us tomorrow.

MIEP. I'll give you a full report! Goodby, everyone!

MR. VAN DAAN (*to* MIEP). Just a minute. There's something I'd like you to do for me.

(*He hurries off up the stairs to his room.*)

MRS. VAN DAAN (*sharply*). Putti, where are you going? (*She rushes up the stairs after him, calling hysterically.*) What do you want? Putti, what are you going to do?

MIEP (*to* PETER). What's wrong?

PETER (*his sympathy is with his mother*). Father says he's going to sell her fur coat. She's crazy about that old fur coat.

DUSSEL. Is it possible? Is it possible that anyone is so silly as to worry about a fur coat in times like this?

PETER. It's none of your darn business . . . and if you say one more thing . . . I'll, I'll take you and I'll . . . I mean it . . . I'll . . .

(*There is a piercing scream from* MRS. VAN DAAN *above. She grabs at the fur coat as* MR. VAN DAAN *is starting downstairs with it.*)

MRS. VAN DAAN. No! No! No! Don't you dare take that! You hear? It's mine! (*Downstairs* PETER *turns away, embarrassed, miserable.*) My father gave me that! You didn't give it to me. You have no right. Let go of it . . . you hear?

(MR. VAN DAAN *pulls the coat from her hands and hurries downstairs.* MRS. VAN DAAN *sinks to the floor, sobbing. As* MR. VAN DAAN *comes into the main room the others look away, embarrassed for him.*)

MR. VAN DAAN (*to* MR. KRALER). Just a little—discussion over the advisability of selling this coat. As I have often reminded Mrs. Van Daan, it's very selfish of her to keep it when people outside are in such desperate need of clothing . . . (*He gives the coat to* MIEP.) So if you will please to sell it for us? It should fetch a good price. And by the way, will you get me cigarettes. I don't care what kind they are . . . get all you can.

MIEP. It's terribly difficult to get them, Mr. Van Daan. But I'll try. Good-by.

(*She goes.* MR. FRANK *follows her down the steps to bolt the door after her.* MRS. FRANK *gives* MR. KRALER *a cup of tea.*)

MRS. FRANK. Are you sure you won't have some cake, Mr. Kraler?

MR. KRALER. I'd better not.

MR. VAN DAAN. You're still feeling badly? What does your doctor say?

MR. KRALER. I haven't been to him.

MRS. FRANK. Now, Mr. Kraler! . . .

MR. KRALER (*sitting at the table*). Oh, I tried. But you can't get near a doctor these days . . . they're so busy. After weeks I finally managed to get one on the telephone. I told him I'd like an appointment . . . I wasn't feeling very well. You know what he answers . . . over the telephone . . . Stick out your tongue! (*They laugh. He turns to* MR. FRANK *as* MR. FRANK *comes back.*) I have some contracts here . . . I wonder if you'd look over them with me . . .

MR. FRANK (*putting out his hand*). Of course.

MR. KRALER (*he rises*). If we could go downstairs . . . (MR. FRANK *starts ahead,* MR. KRALER *speaks to the others.*) Will you forgive us? I won't keep him but a minute. (*He starts to follow* MR. FRANK *down the steps.*)

MARGOT (*with sudden foreboding*). What's happened? Something's happened! Hasn't it, Mr. Kraler?

(MR. KRALER *stops and comes back, trying to reassure* MARGOT *with a pretense of casualness.*)

MR. KRALER. No, really. I want your father's advice . . .

MARGOT. Something's gone wrong! I know it!

MR. FRANK (*coming back, to* MR. KRALER). If it's something that concerns us here, it's better that we all hear it.

MR. KRALER (*turning to him, quietly*). But . . . the children . . . ?

MR. FRANK. What they'd imagine would be worse than any reality. (*As* MR. KRALER *speaks, they all listen with intense apprehension.* MRS. VAN DAAN *comes down the stairs and sits on the bottom step.*)

MR. KRALER. It's a man in the storeroom . . . I don't know whether or not you remember him . . . Carl, about fifty, heavy-set, nearsighted . . . He came with us just before you left.

MR. FRANK. He was from Utrecht?

MR. KRALER. That's the man. A couple of weeks ago, when I was in the storeroom, he closed the door and asked me . . . how's Mr. Frank? What do you hear from Mr. Frank? I told him I only knew there was a rumor that you were in Switzerland. He said he'd heard that rumor too, but he thought I might know something more. I didn't pay any attention to it . . . but then a thing happened yesterday . . . He'd brought some invoices to the office for me to sign. As I was going through them, I looked up. He was standing staring at the bookcase . . . your bookcase. He said he thought he remembered a door there . . . Wasn't there a door there that used to go up to the loft? Then he told me he wanted more money. Twenty guilders more a week.

MR. VAN DAAN. Blackmail!

MR. FRANK. Twenty guilders? Very modest blackmail.

MR. VAN DAAN. That's just the beginning.

DUSSEL (*coming to* MR. FRANK). You know what I think? He was the thief who was down there that night. That's how he knows we're here.

MR. FRANK (*to* MR. KRALER). How was it left? What did you tell him?

MR. KRALER. I said I had to think about it. What shall I do? Pay him the money? . . . Take a chance on firing him . . . or what? I don't know.

DUSSEL (*frantic*). For God's sake don't fire him! Pay him what he asks . . . keep him here where you can have your eye on him.

MR. FRANK. Is it so much that he's asking? What are they paying nowadays?

MR. KRALER. He could get it in a war plant. But this isn't a war plant. Mind you, I don't know if he really knows . . . or if he doesn't know.

MR. FRANK. Offer him half. Then we'll soon find out if it's blackmail or not.

DUSSEL. And if it is? We've got to pay it, haven't we? Anything he asks we've got to pay!

MR. FRANK. Let's decide that when the time comes.

MR. KRALER. This may be all imagination. You get to a point, these days, where you suspect everyone and everything. Again and again . . . on some simple look or word, I've found myself . . .

(*The telephone rings in the office below.*)

MRS. VAN DAAN (*hurrying to* MR. KRALER). There's the telephone! What does that mean, the telephone ringing on a holiday?

MR. KRALER. That's my wife. I told her I had to go over some papers in my office . . . to call me there when she got out of church. (*He starts out.*) I'll offer him half then. Good-by . . . we'll hope for the best!

(*The group call their good-bys half-heartedly.* MR. FRANK *follows* MR. KRALER, *to bolt the door below. During the following scene,* MR. FRANK *comes back up and stands listening, disturbed.*)

DUSSEL (*to* MR. VAN DAAN). You can thank your son for this . . . smashing the light! I tell you, it's just a question of time now.

(*He goes to the window at the back and stands looking out.*)

MARGOT. Sometimes I wish the end would come . . . whatever it is.

MRS. FRANK (*shocked*). Margot!

(ANNE *goes to* MARGOT, *sitting beside her on the couch with her arms around her.*)

MARGOT. Then at least we'd know where we were.

MRS. FRANK. You should be ashamed of yourself! Talking that way! Think how lucky we are! Think of the thousands dying in the war, every day. Think of the people in concentration camps.

ANNE (*interrupting*). What's the good of that? What's the good of thinking of misery when you're already miserable? That's stupid!

MRS. FRANK. Anne!

(*As* ANNE *goes on raging at her mother,* MRS. FRANK *tries to break in, in an effort to quiet her.*)

ANNE. We're young, Margot and Peter and I! You grownups have had your chance! But look at us . . . If we begin thinking of all the horror in the world, we're lost! We're trying to hold onto some kind of ideals . . . when everything . . . ideals, hopes . . . everything, are being destroyed! It isn't our fault that the world is in such a mess! We weren't around when all this started! So don't try to take it out on us! (*She rushes off to*

her room, slamming the door after her. She picks up a brush from the chest and hurls it to the floor. Then she sits on the settee, trying to control her anger.*)

MR. VAN DAAN. She talks as if we started the war! Did we start the war?

(*He spots* ANNE'S *cake. As he starts to take it,* PETER *anticipates him.*)

PETER. She left her cake. (*He starts for* ANNE'S *room with the cake. There is silence in the main room.* MRS. VAN DAAN *goes up to her room, followed by* VAN DAAN. DUSSEL *stays looking out the window.* MR. FRANK *brings* MRS. FRANK *her cake. She eats it slowly, without relish.* MR. FRANK *takes his cake to* MARGOT *and sits quietly on the sofa beside her.* PETER *stands in the doorway of* ANNE'S *darkened room, looking at her, then makes a little movement to let her know he is there.* ANNE *sits up, quickly, trying to hide the signs of her tears.* PETER *holds out the cake to her.*) You left this.

ANNE (*dully*). Thanks.

(PETER *starts to go out, then comes back.*)

PETER. I thought you were fine just now. You know just how to talk to them. You know just how to say it. I'm no good . . . I never can think . . . especially when I'm mad . . . That Dussel . . . when he said that about Mouschi . . . someone eating him . . . all I could think is . . . I wanted to hit him. I wanted to give him such a . . . a . . . that he'd . . . That's what I used to do when there was an argument at school . . . That's the way I . . . but here . . . And an old man like that . . . it wouldn't be so good.

ANNE. You're making a big mistake about me. I do it all wrong. I say too much. I go too far. I hurt people's feelings . . .

(DUSSEL *leaves the window, going to his room.*)

PETER. I think you're just fine . . . What I want to say . . . if it wasn't for you around here, I don't know. What I mean . . .

(PETER *is interrupted by* DUSSEL'S *turning on the light.* DUSSEL *stands in the doorway, startled to see* PETER. PETER *advances toward him forbiddingly.* DUSSEL *backs out of the room.* PETER *closes the door on him.*)

ANNE. Do you mean it, Peter? Do you really mean it?

PETER. I said it, didn't I?

ANNE. Thank you, Peter!

(*In the main room* MR. *and* MRS. FRANK *collect the dishes and take them to the sink, washing them.* MARGOT *lies down again on the couch.* DUSSEL, *lost, wanders into* PETER'S *room and takes up a book, starting to read.*)

PETER (*looking at the photographs on the wall*). You've got quite a collection.

ANNE. Wouldn't you like some in your room? I could give you some. Heaven knows you spend enough time in there . . . doing heaven knows what . . .

PETER. It's easier. A fight starts, or an argument . . . I duck in there.

ANNE. You're lucky, having a room to go to. His lordship is always here . . . I hardly ever get a minute alone. When they start in on me, I can't duck away. I have to stand there and take it.

PETER. You gave some of it back just now.

ANNE. I get so mad. They've formed their opinions . . . about everything . . . but we . . . we're still trying to find out . . . We have problems here that no other people our age have ever had. And just as you think you've solved them, something comes along and bang! You have to start all over again.

PETER. At least you've got someone you can talk to.

ANNE. Not really. Mother . . . I never discuss anything serious with her. She doesn't understand. Father's all right. We can talk about everything . . . everything but one thing. Mother. He simply won't talk about her. I don't think you can be really intimate with anyone if he holds something back, do you?

PETER. I think your father's fine.

ANNE. Oh, he is, Peter! He is! He's the only one who's ever given me the feeling that I have any sense. But anyway, nothing can take the place of school and play and friends of your own age . . . or near your age . . . can it?

PETER. I suppose you miss your friends and all.

ANNE. It isn't just . . . (*She breaks off, staring up at him for a second.*) Isn't it funny, you and I? Here we've been seeing each other every minute for almost a year and a half, and this is the first time we've ever really talked. It helps a lot to have someone to talk to, don't you think? It helps you to let off steam.

PETER (*going to the door*). Well, any time you want to let off steam, you can come into my room.

ANNE (*following him*). I can get up an awful lot of steam. You'll have to be careful how you say that.

PETER. It's all right with me.

ANNE. Do you mean it?

PETER. I said it, didn't I?

(*He goes out.* ANNE *stands in her doorway looking after him. As* PETER *gets to his door he stands for a minute looking back at her. Then he goes into his room.* DUSSEL *rises as he comes in, and quickly passes him, going out. He starts across for his room.* ANNE *sees him coming, and pulls her door shut.* DUSSEL *turns back toward* PETER'S *room.* PETER *pulls his door shut.* DUSSEL *stands there, bewildered, forlorn.*

The scene slowly dims out. The curtain falls on the scene. ANNE'S VOICE *comes over in the darkness . . . faintly at first, and then with growing strength.*)

ANNE'S VOICE. We've had bad news. The people from whom Miep got our ration books have been arrested. So we have had to cut down on our food. Our stomachs are so empty that they rumble and make strange noises, all in different keys. Mr. Van Daan's is deep and low, like a bass fiddle. Mine is high, whistling like a flute. As we all sit around waiting for supper, it's like an orchestra tuning up. It only needs Toscanini to raise his baton and we'd be off in the Ride of the Valkyries. Monday, the sixth of March, nineteen forty-four. Mr. Kraler is in the hospital. It seems he has ulcers. Pim says we are his ulcers. Miep has to run the business and us too. The Americans have landed on the southern tip of Italy. Father looks for a quick finish to the war. Mr. Dussel is waiting every day for the warehouse man to demand more money. Have I been skipping too much from one subject to another? I can't help it. I feel that spring is coming. I feel it in my whole body and soul. I feel utterly confused. I am longing . . . so longing . . . for everything . . . for friends . . . for someone to talk to . . . someone who understands . . . someone young, who feels as I do . . .

(*As these last lines are being said, the curtain rises on the scene. The lights dim on.* ANNE'S VOICE *fades out.*)

SCENE TWO

It is evening, after supper. From outside we hear the sound of children playing. The "grownups," with the exception of MR. VAN DAAN, *are all in the main room.* MRS. FRANK *is doing some mending,* MRS. VAN DAAN *is reading a fashion magazine.* MR. FRANK *is going over business accounts.* DUSSEL, *in his dentist's jacket, is pacing up and down, impatient to get into his bedroom.* MR. VAN DAAN *is upstairs working on a piece of embroidery in an embroidery frame.*

In his room PETER *is sitting before the mirror, smoothing his hair. As the scene goes on, he puts on his tie, brushes his coat and puts it on, preparing himself meticulously for a visit from* ANNE. *On his wall are now hung some of* ANNE'S *motion picture stars.*

In her room ANNE *too is getting dressed. She stands before the mirror in her slip, trying various ways of dressing her hair.* MARGOT *is seated on the sofa, hemming a skirt for* ANNE *to wear.*

In the main room DUSSEL *can stand it no longer. He comes over, rapping sharply on the door of his and* ANNE'S *bedroom.*

ANNE (*calling to him*). No, no, Mr. Dussel! I am not dressed yet. (DUSSEL *walks away, furious, sitting down and burying his head in his hands.* ANNE *turns to* MARGOT.) How is that? How does that look?

MARGOT (*glancing at her briefly*). Fine.

ANNE. You didn't even look.

MARGOT. Of course I did. It's fine.

ANNE. Margot, tell me, am I terribly ugly?

MARGOT. Oh, stop fishing.

ANNE. No. No. Tell me.

MARGOT. Of course you're not. You've got nice eyes . . . and a lot of animation, and . . .

ANNE. A little vague, aren't you?

(*She reaches over and takes a brassière out of* MARGOT'S *sewing basket. She holds it up to herself, studying the effect in the mirror. Outside,* MRS. FRANK, *feeling sorry for* DUSSEL, *comes over, knocking at the girls' door.*)

MRS. FRANK (*outside*). May I come in?

MARGOT. Come in, Mother.

MRS. FRANK (*shutting the door behind her*). Mr. Dussel's impatient to get in here.

ANNE (*still with the brassière*). Heavens, he takes the room for himself the entire day.

MRS. FRANK (*gently*). Anne, dear, you're not going in again tonight to see Peter?

ANNE (*dignified*). That is my intention.

MRS. FRANK. But you've already spent a great deal of time in there today.

ANNE. I was in there exactly twice.

Once to get the dictionary, and then three-quarters of an hour before supper.

MRS. FRANK. Aren't you afraid you're disturbing him?

ANNE. Mother, I have some intuition.

MRS. FRANK. Then may I ask you this much, Anne. Please don't shut the door when you go in.

ANNE. You sound like Mrs. Van Daan! (*She throws the brassière back in* MARGOT'S *sewing basket and picks up her blouse, putting it on.*)

MRS. FRANK. No. No. I don't mean to suggest anything wrong. I only wish that you wouldn't expose yourself to criticism . . . that you wouldn't give Mrs. Van Daan the opportunity to be unpleasant.

ANNE. Mrs. Van Daan doesn't need an opportunity to be unpleasant!

MRS. FRANK. Everyone's on edge, worried about Mr. Kraler. This is one more thing . . .

ANNE. I'm sorry, Mother. I'm going to Peter's room. I'm not going to let Petronella Van Daan spoil our friendship.

(MRS. FRANK *hesitates for a second, then goes out, closing the door after her. She gets a pack of playing cards and sits at the center table, playing solitaire. In* ANNE'S *room* MARGOT *hands the finished skirt to* ANNE. *As* ANNE *is putting it on,* MARGOT *takes off her high-heeled shoes and stuffs paper in the toes so that* ANNE *can wear them.*)

MARGOT (*to* ANNE). Why don't you two talk in the main room? It'd save a lot of trouble. It's hard on Mother, having to listen to those remarks from Mrs. Van Daan and not say a word.

ANNE. Why doesn't she say a word? I think it's ridiculous to take it and take it.

MARGOT. You don't understand Mother at all, do you? She can't talk back. She's not like you. It's just not in her nature to fight back.

ANNE. Anyway . . . the only one I worry about is you. I feel awfully guilty about you. (*She sits on the stool near* MARGOT, *putting on* MARGOT'S *high-heeled shoes.*)

MARGOT. What about?

ANNE. I mean, every time I go into Peter's room, I have a feeling I may be hurting you. (MARGOT *shakes her head.*) I know if it were me, I'd be wild. I'd be desperately jealous, if it were me.

MARGOT. Well, I'm not.

ANNE. You don't feel badly? Really? Truly? You're not jealous?

MARGOT. Of course I'm jealous . . . jealous that you've got something to get up in the morning for . . . But jealous of you and Peter? No.

(ANNE *goes back to the mirror.*)

ANNE. Maybe there's nothing to be jealous of. Maybe he doesn't really like me. Maybe I'm just taking the place of his cat . . . (*She picks up a pair of short white gloves, putting them on.*) Wouldn't you like to come in with us?

MARGOT. I have a book.

(*The sound of the children playing outside fades out. In the main room* DUSSEL *can stand it no longer. He jumps up, going to the bedroom door and knocking sharply.*)

DUSSEL. Will you please let me in my room!

ANNE. Just a minute, dear, dear Mr. Dussel. (*She picks up her Mother's pink stole and adjusts it elegantly over her shoulders, then gives a last look in the mirror.*) Well, here I go . . . to run the gauntlet. (*She starts out, followed by* MARGOT.)

DUSSEL (*as she appears — sarcastic*). Thank you so much.

(DUSSEL *goes into his room.* ANNE *goes toward* PETER'S *room, passing* MRS. VAN DAAN *and her parents at the center table.*)

MRS. VAN DAAN. My God, look at her! (ANNE *pays no attention. She knocks at* PETER'S *door.*) I don't know what good it is to have a son. I never see him. He wouldn't care if I killed myself. (PETER *opens the door and stands aside for* ANNE *to come in.*) Just a minute, Anne. (*She goes to them at the door.*) I'd like to say a few words to my son. Do you mind? (PETER *and* ANNE *stand waiting.*) Peter, I don't want you staying up till all hours tonight. You've got to have your sleep. You're a growing boy. You hear?

MRS. FRANK. Anne won't stay late. She's going to bed promptly at nine. Aren't you, Anne?

ANNE Yes, Mother . . . (*To* MRS. VAN DAAN.) May we go now?

MRS. VAN DAAN. Are you asking me? I didn't know I had anything to say about it.

MRS. FRANK. Listen for the chimes, Anne dear.

(*The two young people go off into* PETER'S *room, shutting the door after them.*)

MRS. VAN DAAN (*to* MRS. FRANK). In my day it was the boys who called on the girls. Not the girls on the boys.

MRS. FRANK. You know how young

people like to feel that they have secrets. Peter's room is the only place where they can talk.

MRS. VAN DAAN. Talk! That's not what they called it when I was young.

(MRS. VAN DAAN *goes off to the bathroom.* MARGOT *settles down to read her book.* MR. FRANK *puts his papers away and brings a chess game to the center table. He and* MRS. FRANK *start to play. In* PETER'S *room,* ANNE *speaks to* PETER, *indignant, humiliated.*)

ANNE. Aren't they awful? Aren't they impossible? Treating us as if we were still in the nursery. (*She sits on the cot.* PETER *gets a bottle of pop and two glasses.*)

PETER. Don't let it bother you. It doesn't bother me.

ANNE. I suppose you can't really blame them . . . they think back to what *they* were like at our age. They don't realize how much more advanced we are . . . When you think what wonderful discussions we've had! . . . Oh, I forgot. I was going to bring you some more pictures.

PETER. Oh, these are fine, thanks.

ANNE. Don't you want some more? Miep just brought me some new ones.

PETER. Maybe later. (*He gives her a glass of pop and, taking some for himself, sits down facing her.*)

ANNE (*looking up at one of the photographs*). I remember when I got that . . . I won it. I bet Jopie that I could eat five ice-cream cones. We'd all been playing ping-pong . . . We used to have heavenly times . . . we'd finish up with ice cream at the Delphi, or the Oasis, where Jews were allowed . . . there'd always be a lot of boys . . . we'd laugh and joke . . . I'd like to go back to it for a few days or a week. But after that I know I'd be bored to death. I think more seriously about life now. I want to be a journalist . . . or something. I love to write. What do you want to do?

PETER. I thought I might go off some place . . . work on a farm or something . . . some job that doesn't take much brains.

ANNE. You shouldn't talk that way. You've got the most awful inferiority complex.

PETER. I know I'm not smart.

ANNE. That isn't true. You're much better than I am in dozens of things . . . arithmetic and algebra and . . . well, you're a million times better than I am in algebra. (*With sudden directness.*) You like Margot, don't you? Right from the start you liked her, liked her much better than me.

PETER (*uncomfortably*). Oh, I don't know.

(*In the main room* MRS. VAN DAAN *comes from the bathroom and goes over to the sink, polishing a coffeepot.*)

ANNE. It's all right. Everyone feels that way. Margot's so good. She's sweet and bright and beautiful and I'm not.

PETER. I wouldn't say that.

ANNE. Oh, no, I'm not. I know that. I know quite well that I'm not a beauty. I never have been and never shall be.

PETER. I don't agree at all. I think you're pretty.

ANNE. That's not true!

PETER. And another thing. You've changed . . . from at first, I mean.

ANNE. I have?

PETER. I used to think you were awful noisy.

ANNE. And what do you think now, Peter? How have I changed?

PETER. Well . . . er . . . you're . . . quieter.

(*In his room* DUSSEL *takes his pajamas and toilet articles and goes into the bathroom to change.*)

ANNE. I'm glad you don't just hate me.

PETER. I never said that.

ANNE. I bet when you get out of here you'll never think of me again.

PETER. That's crazy.

ANNE. When you get back with all of your friends, you're going to say . . . now what did I ever see in that Mrs. Quack Quack.

PETER. I haven't got any friends.

ANNE. Oh, Peter, of course you have. Everyone has friends.

PETER. Not me. I don't want any. I get along all right without them.

ANNE. Does that mean you can get along without me? I think of myself as your friend.

PETER. No. If they were all like you, it'd be different.

(*He takes the glasses and the bottle and puts them away. There is a second's silence and then* ANNE *speaks, hesitantly, shyly.*)

ANNE. Peter, did you ever kiss a girl?

PETER. Yes. Once.

ANNE (*to cover her feelings*). That picture's crooked. (PETER *goes over, straightening the photograph.*) Was she pretty?

PETER. Huh?

ANNE. The girl that you kissed.

PETER. I don't know. I was blindfolded. (*He comes back and sits down again*). It was at a party. One of those kissing games.

ANNE (*relieved*). Oh. I don't suppose that really counts, does it?

PETER. It didn't with me.

ANNE. I've been kissed twice. Once a man I'd never seen before kissed me on the cheek when he picked me up off the ice and I was crying. And the other was Mr. Koophuis, a friend of Father's who kissed my hand. You wouldn't say those counted, would you?

PETER. I wouldn't say so.

ANNE. I know almost for certain that Margot would never kiss anyone unless she was engaged to them. And I'm sure too that Mother never touched a man before Pim. But I don't know . . . things are so different now . . . What do you think? Do you think a girl shouldn't kiss anyone except if she's engaged or something? It's so hard to try to think what to do, when here we are with the whole world falling around our ears and you think . . . well . . . you don't know what's going to happen tomorrow and . . . What do you think?

PETER. I suppose it'd depend on the girl. Some girls, anything they do's wrong. But others . . . well . . . it wouldn't it wouldn't necessarily be wrong with them. (*The carillon starts to strike nine o'clock.*) I've always thought that when two people . . .

ANNE. Nine o'clock. I have to go.

PETER. That's right.

ANNE (*without moving*). Good night.

(*There is a second's pause, then* PETER *gets up and moves toward the door.*)

PETER. You won't let them stop you coming?

ANNE. No. (*She rises and starts for the door.*) Sometime I might bring my diary. There are so many things in it that I want to talk over with you. There's a lot about you.

PETER. What kind of thing?

ANNE. I wouldn't want you to see some of it. I thought you were a nothing, just the way you thought about me.

PETER. Did you change your mind, the way I changed my mind about you?

ANNE. Well . . . You'll see . . .

(*For a second* ANNE *stands looking up at* PETER, *longing for him to kiss her. As he makes no move she turns away. Then suddenly* PETER *grabs her awkwardly in his arms, kissing her on the cheek.* ANNE *walks out dazed. She stands for a minute, her back to the people in the main room. As she regains her poise she goes to her mother and father and* MARGOT, *silently kissing them. They murmur their good nights to her. As she is about to open her bedroom door, she catches sight of* MRS. VAN DAAN. *She goes quickly to her, taking her face in her hands and kissing her first on one cheek and then on the other. Then she hurries off into her room.* MRS. VAN DAAN *looks after her, and then looks over at* PETER'S *room. Her suspicions are confirmed.*)

MRS. VAN DAAN (*She knows*). Ah hah!

(*The lights dim out. The curtain falls on the scene. In the darkness* ANNE'S VOICE *comes faintly at first and then with growing strength.*)

ANNE'S VOICE. By this time we all know each other so well that if anyone starts to tell a story, the rest can finish it for him. We're having to cut down still further on our meals. What makes it worse, the rats have been at work again. They've carried off some of our precious food. Even Mr. Dussel wishes now that Mouschi was here. Thursday, the twentieth of April, nineteen forty-four. Invasion fever is mounting every day. Miep tells us that people outside talk of nothing else. For myself, life has become much more pleasant. I often go to Peter's room after supper. Oh, don't think I'm in love, because I'm not. But it does make life more bearable to have someone with whom you can exchange views. No more tonight. P.S. ... I must be honest. I must confess that I actually live for the next meeting. Is there anything lovelier than to sit under the skylight and feel the sun on your cheeks and have a darling boy in your arms? I admit now that I'm glad the Van Daans had a son and not a daughter. I've outgrown another dress. That's the third. I'm having to wear Margot's clothes after all. I'm working hard on my French and am now reading *La Belle Nivernaise.*

(*As she is saying the last lines— the curtain rises on the scene. The lights dim on, as* ANNE'S VOICE *fades out.*)

Scene Three

It is night, a few weeks later. Everyone is in bed. There is complete quiet. In the VAN DAANS' *room a match flares up for a moment and then is quickly put out.* MR. VAN DAAN, *in bare feet, dressed in underwear and trousers, is dimly seen coming stealthily down the stairs and into the main room, where* MR. *and* MRS. FRANK *and* MARGOT *are sleeping. He goes to the food safe and again lights a match. Then he cautiously opens the safe, taking out a half-loaf of bread. As he closes the safe, it creaks. He stands rigid.* MRS. FRANK *sits up in bed. She sees him.*

———

MRS. FRANK (*screaming*). Otto! Otto! Komme schnell!

(*The rest of the people wake, hurriedly getting up.*)

MR. FRANK. Was ist los? Was ist passiert?

(DUSSEL, *followed by* ANNE, *comes from his room.*)

MRS. FRANK (*as she rushes over to* MR. VAN DAAN). Er stiehlt das Essen!

DUSSEL (*grabbing* MR. VAN DAAN). You! You! Give me that.

MRS. VAN DAAN (*coming down the stairs*). Putti ... Putti ... what is it?

DUSSEL (*his hands on* VAN DAAN'S *neck*). You dirty thief ... stealing food ... you good-for-nothing ...

MR. FRANK. Mr. Dussel! For God's sake! Help me, Peter!

(PETER *comes over, trying, with* MR. FRANK, *to separate the two struggling men.*)

PETER. Let him go! Let go!

(DUSSEL *drops* MR. VAN DAAN, *pushing him away. He shows them the end of a loaf of bread that he has taken from* VAN DAAN.)

DUSSEL. You greedy, selfish ... !

(MARGOT *turns on the lights.*)

MRS. VAN DAAN. Putti ... what is it?

(*All of* MRS. FRANK'S *gentleness, her self-control, is gone. She is outraged, in a frenzy of indignation.*)

MRS. FRANK. The bread! He was stealing the bread!

DUSSEL. It was you, and all the time we thought it was the rats!

MR. FRANK. Mr. Van Daan, how could you!

MR. VAN DAAN. I'm hungry.

MRS. FRANK. We're all of us hungry! I see the children getting thinner and thinner. Your own son Peter ... I've heard him moan in his sleep, he's so hungry. And you come in the night and steal food that should go to them ... to the children!

MRS. VAN DAAN (*going to* MR. VAN DAAN *protectively*). He needs more food than the rest of us. He's used to more. He's a big man.

(MR. VAN DAAN *breaks away, going over and sitting on the couch.*)

MRS. FRANK (*turning on* MRS. VAN DAAN). And you . . . you're worse than he is! You're a mother, and yet you sacrifice your child to this man . . . this . . . this . . .

MR. FRANK. Edith! Edith!

(MARGOT *picks up the pink woolen stole, putting it over her mother's shoulders.*)

MRS. FRANK (*paying no attention, going on to* MRS. VAN DAAN). Don't think I haven't seen you! Always saving the choicest bits for him! I've watched you day after day and I've held my tongue. But not any longer! Not after this! Now I want him to go! I want him to get out of here!

MR. FRANK. Edith! ⎫
MR. VAN DAAN. Get out ⎬ (*Together.*)
of here? ⎭

MRS. VAN DAAN. What do you mean?

MRS. FRANK. Just that! Take your things and get out!

MR. FRANK (*to* MRS. FRANK). You're speaking in anger. You cannot mean what you are saying.

MRS. FRANK. I mean exactly that!

(MRS. VAN DAAN *takes a cover from the* FRANKS' *bed, pulling it about her.*)

MR. FRANK. For two long years we have lived here, side by side. We have respected each other's rights . . . we have managed to live in peace. Are we now going to throw it all away? I know this will never happen again, will it, Mr. Van Daan?

MR. VAN DAAN. No. No.

MRS. FRANK. He steals once! He'll steal again!

(MR. VAN DAAN, *holding his stomach, starts for the bathroom.* ANNE *puts her arms around him, helping him up the step.*)

MR. FRANK. Edith, please. Let us be calm. We'll all go to our rooms . . . and afterwards we'll sit down quietly and talk this out . . . we'll find some way . . .

MRS. FRANK. No! No! No more talk! I want them to leave!

MRS. VAN DAAN. You'd put us out, on the streets?

MRS. FRANK. There are other hiding places.

MRS. VAN DAAN. A cellar . . . a closet. I know. And we have no money left even to pay for that.

MRS. FRANK. I'll give you money. Our of my own pocket I'll give it gladly.

(*She gets her purse from a shelf and comes back with it.*)

MRS. VAN DAAN. Mr. Frank, you told Putti you'd never forget what he'd done for you when you came to Amsterdam. You said you could never repay him, that you . . .

MRS. FRANK (*counting out money*). If my husband had any obligation to you, he's paid it, over and over.

MR. FRANK. Edith, I've never seen you like this before. I don't know you.

MRS. FRANK. I should have spoken out long ago.

DUSSEL. You can't be nice to some people.

MRS. VAN DAAN (*turning on* DUSSEL). There would have been plenty for all of us, if *you* hadn't come in here!

MR. FRANK. We don't need the Nazis to destroy us. We're destroying ourselves.

(*He sits down, with his head in his hands.* MRS. FRANK *goes to* MRS. VAN DAAN.)

MRS. FRANK (*giving* MRS. VAN DAAN *some money*). Give this to Miep. She'll find you a place.

ANNE. Mother, you're not putting Peter out. Peter hasn't done anything.

MRS. FRANK. He'll stay, of course. When I say I must protect the children, I mean Peter too.

(PETER *rises from the steps where he has been sitting.*)

PETER. I'd have to go if Father goes.

(MR. VAN DAAN *comes from the bathroom.* MRS. VAN DAAN *hurries to him and takes him to the couch. Then she gets water from the sink to bathe his face.*)

MRS. FRANK (*while this is going on*). He's no father to you . . . that man! He doesn't know what it is to be a father!

PETER (*starting for his room*). I wouldn't feel right. I couldn't stay.

MRS. FRANK. Very well, then. I'm sorry.

ANNE (*rushing over to* PETER). No, Peter! No! (PETER *goes into his room, closing the door after him.* ANNE *turns back to her mother, crying.*) I don't care about the food. They can have mine! I don't want it! Only don't send them away. It'll be daylight soon. They'll be caught . . .

MARGOT (*putting her arms comfortingly around* ANNE). Please, Mother!

MRS. FRANK. They're not going now. They'll stay here until Miep finds them a place. (*To* MRS. VAN DAAN.) But one thing I insist on! He must never come down here again! He must never come to this room where the food is stored! We'll divide what we have . . . an equal share for each! (DUSSEL *hurries over to get a sack of potatoes from the food safe.* MRS. FRANK *goes on, to* MRS. VAN DAAN.) You can cook it here and take it up to him.

(DUSSEL *brings the sack of potatoes back to the center table.*)

MARGOT. Oh, no. No. We haven't sunk so far that we're going to fight over a handful of rotten potatoes.

DUSSEL (*Dividing the potatoes into piles*). Mrs. Frank, Mr. Frank, Margot, Anne, Peter, Mrs. Van Daan, Mr. Van Daan, myself . . . Mrs. Frank . . .

(*The buzzer sounds in* MIEP's *signal.*)

MR. FRANK. It's Miep! (*He hurries over, getting his overcoat and putting it on.*)

MARGOT. At this hour?

MRS. FRANK. It is trouble.

MR. FRANK (*as he starts down to unbolt the door*). I beg you, don't let her see a thing like this!

MR. DUSSEL (*counting without stopping*). . . . Anne, Peter, Mrs. Van Daan, Mr. Van Daan, myself . . .

MARGOT (*to* DUSSEL). Stop it! Stop it!

DUSSEL. . . . Mr. Frank, Margot, Anne, Peter, Mrs. Van Daan, Mr. Van Daan, myself, Mrs. Frank . . .

MRS. VAN DAAN. You're keeping the big ones for yourself! All the big ones . . . Look at the size of that! . . . And that! . . .

(DUSSEL *continues on with his dividing.* PETER, *with his shirt and trousers on, comes from his room.*)

MARGOT. Stop it! Stop it!

(*We hear* MIEP's *excited voice speaking to* MR. FRANK *below.*

MIEP. Mr. Frank . . . the most wonderful news! . . . The invasion has begun!

MR. FRANK. Go on, tell them! Tell them!

(MIEP *comes running up the steps, ahead of* MR. FRANK. *She has a man's raincoat on over her nightclothes and a bunch of orange-colored flowers in her hand.*)

MIEP. Did you hear that, everybody? Did you hear what I said? The invasion has begun! The invasion!

(*They all stare at* MIEP, *unable to grasp what she is telling them.* PETER *is the first to recover his wits.*)

PETER. Where?

MRS. VAN DAAN. When? When, Miep?

MIEP. It began early this morning . . .

(*As she talks on, the realization of what she has said begins to dawn on them. Everyone goes crazy. A wild demonstration takes place.* MRS. FRANK *hugs* MR. VAN DAAN.)

MRS. FRANK. Oh, Mr. Van Daan, did you hear that?

(DUSSEL *embraces* MRS. VAN DAAN. PETER *grabs a frying pan and parades around the room, beating on it, singing the Dutch National Anthem.* ANNE *and* MARGOT *follow him, singing, weaving in and out among the excited grownups.* MARGOT *breaks away to take the flowers from* MIEP *and distribute them to everyone. While this pandemonium is going on* MRS. FRANK *tries to make herself heard above the excitement.*)

MRS. FRANK (*to* MIEP). How do you know?

MIEP. The radio . . . The B.B.C.! They said they landed on the coast of Normandy!

PETER. The British?

MIEP. British, Americans, French, Dutch, Poles, Norwegians . . . all of them! More than four thousand ships! Churchill spoke, and General Eisenhower! D-Day they call it!

MR. FRANK. Thank God, it's come!

MRS. VAN DAAN. At last!

MIEP (*starting out*). I'm going to tell Mr. Kraler. This'll be better than any blood transfusion.

MR. FRANK (*stopping her*). What part of Normandy did they land, did they say?

MIEP. Normandy . . . that's all I know now . . . I'll be up the minute I hear some more! (*She goes hurriedly out.*)

MR. FRANK (*to* MRS. FRANK). What did I tell you? What did I tell you?

(MRS. FRANK *indicates that he has forgotten to bolt the door after* MIEP. *He hurries down the steps.* MR. VAN DAAN, *sitting on the couch, suddenly breaks into a convulsive sob. Everybody looks at him, bewildered.*)

MRS. VAN DAAN (*hurrying to him*). Putti! Putti! What is it? What happened?

MR. VAN DAAN. Please. I'm so ashamed.

(MR. FRANK *comes back up the steps.*)

DUSSEL. Oh, for God's sake!

MRS. VAN DAAN. Don't, Putti.

MARGOT. It doesn't matter now!

MR. FRANK (*going to* MR. VAN DAAN). Didn't you hear what Miep said? The invasion has come! We're going to be liberated! This is a time to celebrate! (*He embraces* MRS. FRANK *and then hurries to the cupboard and gets the cognac and a glass.*)

MR. VAN DAAN. To steal bread from children!

MRS. FRANK. We've all done things that we're ashamed of.

ANNE. Look at me, the way I've treated Mother . . . so mean and horrid to her.

MRS. FRANK. No, Anneke, no.

(ANNE *runs to her mother, putting her arms around her.*)

ANNE. Oh, Mother, I was. I was awful.

MR. VAN DAAN. Not like me. No one is as bad as me!

DUSSEL (*to* MR. VAN DAAN). Stop it now! Let's be happy!

MR. FRANK (*giving* MR. VAN DAAN *a glass of cognac*). Here! Here! *Schnapps! Locheim!*

(VAN DAAN *takes the cognac. They all watch him. He gives them a feeble smile.* ANNE *puts up her fingers in a V-for-Victory sign. As* VAN DAAN *gives an answering V-sign, they are startled to hear a loud sob from behind them. It is* MRS. FRANK, *stricken with remorse. She is sitting on the other side of the room.*)

MRS. FRANK (*through her sobs*). When I think of the terrible things I said . . .

(MR. FRANK, ANNE *and* MARGOT *hurry to her, trying to comfort her.* MR. VAN DAAN *brings her his glass of cognac.*)

MR. VAN DAAN. No! No! You were right!

MRS. FRANK. That I should speak that way to you! . . . Our friends! . . . Our guests! (*She starts to cry again.*)

DUSSEL. Stop it, you're spoiling the whole invasion!

(*As they are comforting her, the lights dim out. The curtain falls.*)

ANNE'S VOICE (*faintly at first and then with growing strength*). We're all in much better spirits these days. There's still excellent news of the invasion. The best part about it is that I have a feeling that friends are coming. Who knows? Maybe I'll be back in school by fall. Ha, ha! The joke is on us! The warehouse man doesn't know a thing and we are paying him all that money! . . . Wednesday, the second of July, nineteen forty-four. The invasion seems temporarily to be bogged down. Mr. Kraler has to have an operation, which looks bad. The Gestapo have found the radio that was stolen. Mr. Dussel says they'll trace it back and back to the thief, and then, it's just a matter of time till they get to us. Everyone is low. Even poor Pim can't raise their spirits. I have often been downcast myself . . .

but never in despair. I can shake off everything if I write. But . . . and that is the great question . . . will I ever be able to write well? I want to so much. I want to go on living even after my death. Another birthday has gone by, so now I am fifteen. Already I know what I want. I have a goal, an opinion.

(*As this is being said—the curtain rises on the scene, the lights dim on, and* ANNE'S VOICE *fades out.*)

SCENE FOUR

It is an afternoon a few weeks later . . . Everyone but Margot is in the main room. There is a sense of great tension.

Both MRS. FRANK *and* MR. VAN DAAN *are nervously pacing back and forth,* DUSSEL *is standing at the window, looking down fixedly at the street below.* PETER *is at the center table, trying to do his lessons.* ANNE *sits opposite him, writing in her diary.* MRS. VAN DAAN *is seated on the couch, her eyes on* MR. FRANK *as he sits reading.*

The sound of a telephone ringing comes from the office below. They all are rigid, listening tensely. MR. DUSSEL *rushes down to* MR. FRANK.

DUSSEL. There it goes again, the telephone! Mr. Frank, do you hear?

MR. FRANK (*quietly*). Yes. I hear.

DUSSEL (*pleading, insistent*). But this is the third time, Mr. Frank! The third time in quick succession! It's a signal! I tell you it's Miep, trying to get us! For some reason she can't come to us and she's trying to warn us of something!

MR. FRANK. Please. Please.

MR. VAN DAAN (*to* DUSSEL). You're wasting your breath.

DUSSEL. Something has happened, Mr. Frank. For three days now Miep hasn't been to see us! And today not a man has come to work. There hasn't been a sound in the building!

MRS. FRANK. Perhaps it's Sunday. We may have lost track of the days.

MR. VAN DAAN (*to* ANNE). You with the diary there. What day is it?

DUSSEL (*going to* MRS. FRANK). I don't lose track of the days! I know exactly what day it is! It's Friday, the fourth of August. Friday, and not a man at work. (*He rushes back to* MR. FRANK, *pleading with him, almost in tears.*) I tell you Mr. Kraler's dead. That's the only explanation. He's dead and they've closed down the building, and Miep's trying to tell us!

MR. FRANK. She'd never telephone us.

DUSSEL (*frantic*). Mr. Frank, answer that! I beg you, answer it!

MR. FRANK. No.

MR. VAN DAAN. Just pick it up and listen. You don't have to speak. Just listen and see if it's Miep.

DUSSEL (*speaking at the same time*). For God's sake . . . I ask you.

MR. FRANK. No. I've told you, no. I'll do nothing that might let anyone know we're in the building.

PETER. Mr. Frank's right.

MR. VAN DAAN. There's no need to tell us what side you're on.

MR. FRANK. If we wait patiently, quietly, I believe that help will come.

(*There is silence for a minute as they all listen to the telephone ringing.*)

DUSSEL. I'm going down. (*He rushes down the steps.* MR. FRANK *tries ineffectually to hold him.* DUSSEL *runs to the lower door, unbolting it. The telephone stops ringing.* DUSSEL *bolts the door and comes slowly back up the steps.*) Too late. (MR. FRANK *goes to* MARGOT *in* ANNE's *bedroom.*)

MR. VAN DAAN. So we just wait here until we die.

MRS. VAN DAAN (*hysterically*). I can't stand it! I'll kill myself! I'll kill myself!

MR. VAN DAAN. For God's sake, stop it!

(*In the distance, a German military band is heard playing a Viennese waltz.*)

MRS. VAN DAAN. I think you'd be glad if I did! I think you want me to die!

MR. VAN DAAN. Whose fault is it we're here? (MRS. VAN DAAN *starts for her room. He follows, talking at her.*) We could've been safe somewhere . . . in America or Switzerland. But no! No! You wouldn't leave when I wanted to. You couldn't leave your things. You couldn't leave your precious furniture.

MRS. VAN DAAN. Don't touch me!

(*She hurries up the stairs, followed by* MR. VAN DAAN. PETER, *unable to bear it, goes to his room.* ANNE *looks after him, deeply concerned.* DUSSEL *returns to his post at the window.* MR. FRANK *comes back into the main room and takes a book, trying to read.* MRS. FRANK *sits near the sink, starting to peel some potatoes.* ANNE *quietly goes to* PETER's *room, closing the door after her.* PETER *is lying face down on the cot.* ANNE *leans over him, holding*

him in her arms, trying to bring him out of his despair.)

ANNE. Look, Peter, the sky. (*She looks up through the skylight.*) What a lovely, lovely day! Aren't the clouds beautiful? You know what I do when it seems as if I couldn't stand being cooped up for one more minute? I *think* myself out. I think myself on a walk in the park where I used to go with Pim. Where the jonquils and the crocus and the violets grow down the slopes. You know the most wonderful part about *thinking* yourself out? You can have it any way you like. You can have roses and violets and chrysanthemums all blooming at the same time . . . It's funny . . . I used to take it all for granted . . . and now I've gone crazy about everything to do with nature. Haven't you?

PETER. I've just gone crazy. I think if something doesn't happen soon . . . if we don't get out of here . . . I can't stand much more of it!

ANNE (*softly*). I wish you had a religion, Peter.

PETER. No, thanks! Not me!

ANNE. Oh, I don't mean you have to be Orthodox . . . or believe in heaven and hell and purgatory and things . . . I just mean some religion . . . it doesn't matter what. Just to believe in something! When I think of all that's out there . . . the trees . . . and flowers . . . and seagulls . . . when I think of the dearness of you, Peter, . . . and the goodness of the people we know . . . Mr. Kraler, Miep, Dirk, the vegetable man, all risking their lives for us every day . . . When I think of these good things, I'm not afraid any more . . . I find myself, and God, and I . . .

(PETER *interrupts, getting up and walking away.*)

PETER. That's fine! But when I begin to think, I get mad! Look at us, hiding out for two years. Not able to move! Caught here like . . . waiting for them to come and get us . . . and all for what?

ANNE. We're not the only people that've had to suffer. There've always been people that've had to . . . sometimes one race . . . sometimes another . . . and yet . . .

PETER. That doesn't make me feel any better!

ANNE (*going to him*). I know it's terrible,

trying to have any faith . . . when people are doing such horrible . . . But you know what I sometimes think? I think the world may be going through a phase, the way I was with Mother. It'll pass, maybe not for hundreds of years, but some day . . . I still believe, in spite of everything, that people are really good at heart.

PETER. I want to see something now . . . Not a thousand years from now!

(*He goes over, sitting down again on the cot.*)

ANNE. But, Peter, if you'd only look at it as part of a great pattern . . . that we're just a little minute in the life . . . (*She breaks off.*) Listen to us, going at each other like a couple of stupid grownups! Look at the sky now. Isn't it lovely? (*She holds out her hand to him.* PETER *takes it and rises, standing with her at the window looking out, his arms around her.* Some day, when we're outside again, I'm going to . . .

(*She breaks off as she hears the sound of a car, its brakes squealing as it comes to a sudden stop. The people in the other rooms also become aware of the sound. They listen tensely. Another car roars up to a screeching stop.* ANNE *and* PETER *come from* PETER'S *room.* MR. *and* MRS. VAN DAAN *creep down the stairs.* DUSSEL *comes out from his room. Everyone is listening, hardly breathing. A doorbell clangs again and again in the building below.* MR. FRANK *starts quietly down the steps to the door.* DUSSEL *and* PETER *follow him. The others stand rigid, waiting, terrified.*

In a few seconds DUSSEL *comes stumbling back up the steps. He shakes off* PETER'S *help and goes to his room.* MR. FRANK *bolts the door below, and comes slowly back up the steps. Their eyes are all on him as he stands there for a minute. They realize that what they feared has happened.* MRS. VAN DAAN *starts to whimper.* MR. VAN DAAN *puts her gently in a chair, and then hurries off up the stairs to their room to collect their things.* PETER *goes to comfort his mother. There is a sound of violent pounding on a door below.*)

MR. FRANK (*quietly*). For the past two years we have lived in fear. Now we can live in hope.

(*The pounding below becomes more insistent. There are muffled sounds of voices, shouting commands.*)

MEN'S VOICES. *Auf machen! Da drinnen! Auf machen! Schnell! Schnell! Schnell! etc., etc.*

(*The street door below is forced open. We*

hear the heavy tread of footsteps coming up. MR. FRANK *gets two school-bags from the shelves, and gives one to* ANNE *and the other to* MARGOT. *He goes to get a bag for* MRS. FRANK. *The sound of feet coming up grows louder.* PETER *comes to* ANNE, *kissing her good-by, then he goes to his room to collect his things. The buzzer of their door starts to ring.* MR. FRANK *brings* MRS. FRANK *a bag. They stand together, waiting. We hear the thud of gun butts on the door, trying to break it down.*

ANNE *stands, holding her school satchel, looking over at her father and mother with a soft, reassuring smile. She is no longer a child, but a woman with courage to meet whatever lies ahead.*

The lights dim out. The curtain falls on the scene. We hear a mighty crash as the door is shattered. After a second ANNE'S *voice is heard.*)

ANNE'S VOICE. And so it seems our stay is over. They are waiting for us now. They've allowed us five minutes to get our things. We can each take a bag and whatever it will hold of clothing. Nothing else. So, dear Diary, that means I must leave you behind. Good-by for a while. P.S. Please, please, Miep, or Mr. Kraler, or anyone else. If you should find this diary, will you please keep it safe for me, because some day I hope . . .

(*Her voice stops abruptly. There is silence. After a second the curtain rises.*)

SCENE FIVE

It is again the afternoon in November, 1945. The rooms are as we saw them in the first scene. MR. KRALER *has joined* MIEP *and* MR. FRANK. *There are coffee cups on the table. We see a great change in* MR. FRANK. *He is calm now. His bitterness is gone. He slowly turns a few pages of the diary. They are blank.*

MR. FRANK. No more. (*He closes the diary and puts it down on the couch beside him.*)

MIEP. I'd gone to the country to find food. When I got back the block was surrounded by police . . .

MR. KRALER. We made it our business to learn how they knew. It was the thief . . . the thief who told them.

(MIEP *goes up to the gas burner, bringing back a pot of coffee.*)

MR. FRANK (*after a pause*). It seems strange to say this, that anyone could be happy in a concentration camp. But Anne was happy in the camp in Holland where they first took us. After two years of being shut up in these rooms, she could be out . . . out in the sunshine and the fresh air that she loved.

MIEP (*offering the coffee to* MR. FRANK). A little more?

MR. FRANK (*holding out his cup to her*). The news of the war was good. The British and Americans were sweeping through France. We felt sure that they would get to us in time. In September we were told that we were to be shipped to Poland . . . The men to one camp. The women to another. I was sent to Auschwitz. They went to Belsen. In January we were freed, the few of us who were left. The war wasn't yet over, so it took us a long time to get home. We'd be sent here and there behind the lines where we'd be safe. Each time our train would stop . . . at a siding, or a crossing . . . we'd

all get out and go from group to group . . . Where were you? Were you at Belsen? At Buchenwald? At Mauthausen? Is it possible that you knew my wife? Did you ever see my husband? My son? My daughter? That's how I found out about my wife's death . . . of Margot, the Van Daans . . . Dussel. But Anne . . . I still hoped . . . Yesterday I went to Rotterdam. I'd heard of a woman there . . . She'd been in Belsen with Anne . . . I know now.

(*He picks up the diary again, and turns the pages back to find a certain passage. As he finds it we hear* ANNE'S VOICE.)

ANNE'S VOICE. In spite of everything, I still believe that people are really good at heart.

(MR. FRANK *slowly closes the diary.*)

MR. FRANK. She puts me to shame.

(*They are silent.*)

The CURTAIN *falls.*

LOOK HOMEWARD, ANGEL

Ketti Frings

Based on the novel by THOMAS WOLFE

Presented by Kermit Bloomgarden and Theatre 200, Inc.,
at the Ethel Barrymore Theatre, New York, on November 28th, 1957,
with the following cast:

BEN GANT	Arthur Hill	FLORRY MANGLE	Elizabeth Lawrence
MRS. MARIE "FATTY" PERT		MRS. SNOWDEN	Julia Johnston
	Florence Sundstrom	MR. FARREL	Dwight Marfield
HELEN GANT BARTON	Rosemary Murphy	MISS BROWN	Susan Torrey
HUGH BARTON	Leonard Stone	LAURA JAMES	Frances Hyland
ELIZA GANT	Jo Van Fleet	W. O. GANT	Hugh Griffith
WILL PENTLAND	Tom Flatley Reynolds	DR. MAGUIRE	Victor Kilian
EUGENE GANT	Anthony Perkins	TARKINTON	Jack Sheehan
JAKE CLATT	Joseph Bernard	MADAME ELIZABETH	Bibi Osterwald
MRS. CLATT	Mary Farrell	LUKE GANT	Arthur Storch

Directed by George Roy Hill
Settings and lighting by Jo Mielziner
Costumes by Motley

The town of Altamont, in the State of North Carolina, in the fall of the
year nineteen hundred and sixteen.

ACT ONE. SCENE 1: The Dixieland Boarding House; a fall afternoon.
SCENE 2: The same; that evening.

ACT TWO. SCENE 1: Gant's marble yard and shop; one week later.
SCENE 2: The Dixieland Boarding House; the next night.

ACT THREE. The Dixieland Boarding House; two weeks later.

Copyright ©, 1958, by Edward C. Aswell, as Administrator, C.T.A.,
of the Estate of Thomas Wolfe, and/or Fred Wolfe and Ketti Frings.

Reprinted by permission of Ketti Frings and the Estate of Thomas Wolfe.
All rights reserved.

CAUTION: Professionals and amateurs are hereby warned that this play, being fully
protected under the copyright laws of the United States of America, the British Empire,
including the Dominion of Canada and all other countries of the Copyright Union,
is subject to a royalty. All rights, including professional, amateur, motion pictures,
recitation, public reading, radio broadcasting, television, and the rights of translation
into foreign languages are strictly reserved. In its present form the play is
dedicated to the reading public only.

Where the play is available for amateur production royalty will be quoted on application to Samuel French, Inc., at 25 West 45th Street, New York 36, N. Y., or at 7623 Sunset Boulevard, Hollywood 46, Calif., or to Samuel French (Canada), Ltd., 27 Grenville Street, Toronto 5, Ontario, Canada, one week before the date when the play is given.

Stock royalty quoted on application to Samuel French, Inc.

For all other rights than those stipulated above, apply to Pincus Berner, Administrator, C.T.A., of the Estate of Thomas Wolfe, 25 West 43rd Street, New York 36, N. Y., and Friend & Reiskind, 375 Park Avenue, New York, N. Y.

Particular emphasis is laid on the question of amateur or professional readings, permission for which must be secured in writing from Samuel French, Inc.

CAUTION: These songs, the lyrics of which appear in this play, are fully copyrighted and may not be used in connection with any performance of *Look Homeward, Angel* unless permission is first obtained from the firms indicated below.

"My Pony Boy," words by Bobby Heath, music by Charles O'Donnell. Copyright, 1909. Copyright renewed 1936 and assigned to Jerry Vogel Music Co., Inc. Used by permission of the copyright owner solely for the purpose of printing in this edition.

"K-K-K-Katy," words and music by Geoffrey O'Hara © 1918, copyright renewal 1945 Leo Feist, Inc., Used by permission of the copyright owner.

"Just a Baby's Prayer at Twilight," words by Sam M. Lewis and Joe Young, music by M. K. Jerome, © 1918. Copyright renewal 1946. Mills Music, Inc., 1619 Broadway, New York 19, N. Y., and Warlock Music, Inc. Used by permission of the copyright owners.

IT WOULD have been difficult to believe that so effective a dramatization of Thomas Wolfe's *Look Homeward, Angel* could have been made without distortion of that comprehensively detailed novel of a sensitive young giant and his turbulent family. Even if there would be no distortion for the sake of dramatic cohesion, the dramatization was bound to produce an effect of amputation; surely one would be aware of missing events in any playwright's effort to pack a huge novel into a two-hour play. That, except for some loss of language (compensated for by good acting and by excision of the novelist-narrator's occasional fustian), the dramatization proved to be so satisfactory may be attributed to the skill of the adapter, Ketti Frings, an author of fiction herself who, like Thomas Wolfe, had been attracted to the theatre as a playwright. She first attracted attention during World War II with *Mr. Sycamore,* a dramatization which the Theatre Guild produced at some risk, since the subject of this delicate little play, which dealt with a mailman's transformation into a tree, was more suitable for inclusion in Ovid's *Metamorphoses* than for presentation in a Shubert playhouse. Mrs. Frings returned to Hollywood after the short, unhappy run of *Mr. Sycamore,* which was one of the Theatre Guild's and the present editor's mistakes; and it was there she remained, turning out reputable screen adaptations of William Inge's *Come Back, Little Sheba* and Joseph Kramm's Broadway success *The Shrike,* before her intrepid dramatization of *Look Homeward, Angel* settled down for a long run at the Ethel Barrymore Theatre under the expert guardianship of Kermit Bloomgarden. Mrs. Frings met with the approval of the New York Drama Critics Circle and the Pulitzer Prize board, both of which gave awards to her dramatization as the best American play of the year.

It is to be hoped the ghost of Thomas Wolfe was somewhat appeased. Like Henry James this natural novelist had hoped to succeed as a playwright, and he had studied the craft under Frederick H. Koch at the University of North Carolina and for three years under George Pierce Baker in his Workshop 47 at Harvard. Wolfe wrote a number of short and long plays, one of which, *Welcome to Our City,* was held under option by the Theatre Guild of New York in 1923. But his only dramatic success was a posthumous one, when his family drama *Mannerhouse* was translated and produced in Germany.

A factor in the success of the dramatization that should not be overlooked is Jo Mielziner's setting, which made it possible to play different scenes simultaneously. But the feat of unifying the action of the novel started with Mrs. Frings' ability to condense it into a period of a few weeks and to relate the gangling seventeen-year-old protagonist's development to the events of that period. It is a testimony to the adapter's craftsmanship that she was able to crowd together with barely an indication of contrivance, as the late Wolcott Gibbs put it, "such diverse material as a boy's first love, a shocking death in the family, the final disintegration of a marriage, and the culmination not only of a woman's fierce conflict between greed and her need to be loved but of her son's equally agonized struggle to escape from the surroundings that are destroying him both as a man and as an artist." The least the novel became in Mrs. Frings' capable hands is a workable family drama, although it is more than that—a young artist's discovery of reality. In one respect it is even an improvement on the autobiographical flamboyance, the self-centeredness, of the novelist.

ACT ONE

SCENE ONE

SCENE: *The Dixieland Boarding House; a fall afternoon. The house is a flimsily constructed frame house of fifteen draughty, various-sized rooms. It has a rambling, unplanned gabular appearance, and is painted a dirty yellow. Most of its furniture is badly worn and out of style. The beds are chipped enamel-covered iron. There are accordion hat trees, cracked mirrors, an occasional plant. On the typically Southern veranda which embraces the front and one side of the house, there are chairs, rockers, and a woodbox. There is a sign above the door, electrically lighted at night:* DIXIELAND— ROOMS AND BOARD. *In the center of the house, slightly raised, is a turntable on which all the bedroom scenes are played. At the back of the house a walk approaches the rear of the veranda. There is a side door and near it a circular yard seat. Also down front of the bedroom is a table and a chair. The street itself has a feeling of great trees hanging over it. Occasionally during the play, the stillness is broken by the rustle of autumn leaves, and the poignant wail of a train whistle. The Curtain rises in darkness. After a moment we hear* EUGENE'S *voice coming from his room. Seated, he is glimpsed, writing, surrounded by books.*

EUGENE. "Ben" by Eugene Gant. . . . My brother Ben's face is like a piece of slightly yellow ivory. (*Lights come up on the veranda where* BEN GANT, *30, delicate and sensitive, the most refined of the Gants, and forever a stranger among them, is seated on the front steps reading a newspaper. He is sometimes scowling and surly, but he is the hero protector of those he loves, with quiet authority and a passion for home which is fundamental. At times he speaks to the side over his shoulder, in a peculiar mannerism of speech, as though he were addressing a familiar unseen presence.*)
His high, white forehead is knotted fiercely by an old man's scowl.
His mouth is like a knife.
His smile the flicker of light across the blade.
His face is like a blade, and a knife, and a flicker of light.

And when he fastens his hard white fingers
And his scowling eyes upon a thing he wants to fix,
He sniffs with sharp and private concentration.
(*Lights now reveal* MARIE "FATTY" PERT, *43, seated near* BEN *in her rocker. She is a generous, somewhat boozy woman, knitting a pair of men's socks and tenderly regarding* BEN.)
Thus women looking, feel a well of tenderness
For his pointed, bumpy, always scowling face. . . .
(EUGENE *continues writing.*)
BEN. Somebody's got to drive the Huns from the skies. Poor old England can't be expected to do it alone.
MRS. PERT. It's their mess, isn't it?
BEN. It says here there's an American flying corps forming in Canada.
MRS. PERT. Ben Gant, what are you thinking of?
BEN. All my life in this one little burg, Fatty! Besides getting away, I'd be doing my bit.
MRS. PERT. Would they take you so old?
BEN. This article says eighteen to thirty-two.
MRS. PERT. Aren't the physical standards pretty high?
BEN. Listen to her! I'm in good condition!
MRS. PERT. You're twenty pounds underweight! I never saw anyone like you for not eating.
BEN. Maguire gave me a thorough checkup this spring!
MRS. PERT. How would your family feel if you went?
BEN. What family? The batty boarders? (*Takes her hand.*) Apologies, Fatty. I never associate you with them. Except for Gene, nobody'd know I was gone. (*Looks up, dreamily.*) To fly up there in the wonderful world of the sky. Up with the angels.
(HELEN GANT BARTON *and her husband* HUGH *enter from the house.* HELEN *is gaunt, raw-boned, in her middle twenties, often nervous, intense, irritable and abusive, though basically generous, the hysteria of excitement constantly lurking in her. It is a spiritual and physical necessity for her to exhaust herself in service to others, though her grievances, especially*)

in her service to her mother, are many. HUGH *is a cash-register salesman, simple, sweet, extremely warmhearted. He carries a newspaper, a tray with a coffee pot and cups and saucers, which* HELEN *helps him set on a table. They have been arguing.*)

HUGH. We should never have agreed to live here for one day—that's the answer. You work yourself to the bone—for what?

HELEN (*busy putting cups in saucers*). Mrs. Pert, the other boarders have almost finished dinner!

MRS. PERT. What's the dessert, Helen?

HELEN. Charlotte Russe.

HUGH. They're like children with a tapeworm. (*Crosses and sits woodbox down right.*)

BEN. Fatty, I told you you'd better get in there!

MRS. PERT. I was trying to do without, but I'm afraid that calls me. (*Rises.*) See you later, Ben. (*She leaves her knitting on the chair, exits inside.*)

HELEN. Ben, where is Mama?

BEN. How should I know?

HELEN. I've had to serve the entire dinner alone!

HUGH. Look at me, holes in my socks, a trouser button missing—and before I married you I had the reputation of being "dapper."

HELEN. I bet she's off somewhere with Uncle Will, and *I'm* left in the kitchen to slave for a crowd of old cheap boarders! That's her tactic!

HUGH. "Dapper Hugh Barton"—it said so in the newspaper when we were married.

HELEN (*crosses to* BEN, *who pays no attention*). You know that, don't you, *don't you?* And do I ever hear her say a word of thanks? Do I get—do I get as much as a go-to-hell for it? No. "Why, pshaw, child," she'll say, "I work more than anybody!" And most times, damn her, she does.

BOARDERS (*offstage, calling, ringing the service bell*). Helen. Helen!

HELEN. You come in, Hugh, and help me! (*Exits into the house.*)

BEN. How are the cash registers selling, Hugh?

HUGH. Putting the cigar box out of business. I got a good order in Raleigh last week. I've already put away nine

hundred dollars toward our own little house.

BEN (*rises*). You ought to have one, Hugh. You and Helen. (*Crossing toward wicker unit down left where he has left his coat.*)

HUGH (*looking at part of newspaper*). I guess they don't have to advertise the good jobs, do they? The really big jobs—they wouldn't be here in the newspaper, would they?

BEN. Why?

HUGH. If there was something good here in town—not on the road so much—maybe then I could talk Helen into moving away. Ben— (*Rises.*) you hear things around the paper—

HELEN (*off*). Hugh! Hugh!

BEN. I'll keep my ears open, Hugh.

HUGH. Well, I guess I don't want to make Helen any madder at me. Thanks, Ben. (*Exits inside.*)

(*An automobile is heard off, driving up, stopping.* BEN *moves down to the yard seat, reads his newspaper. The car door slams.*)

ELIZA (*off*). I'll vow I never saw such a man. What little we have got, I've had to fight for tooth and nail, tooth and nail! (ELIZA GANT *enters with* WILL PENTLAND, *her brother.* ELIZA, *57, is of Scotch descent, with all the acquisitiveness and fancied premonitions of the Scotch. She is mercurial, with dauntless energy, greed and love. She has an odd way of talking, pursing her lips, and she characteristically uses her right hand in a point-making gesture, fist enclosed, forefinger extended. These mannerisms are often imitated by those who hate and love her.* ELIZA *is carrying some fall leaves, a real estate circular and two small potted plants.* WILL *is paunchy, successful, secure, a real estate broker. He carries a small tray with several flower pots, geranium cuttings, and a can of peat moss therein, which he places on woodbox. They do not notice* BEN.) Like the fellow says, there's no fool like an old fool! Of course Mr. Gant's been a fool all his life. Pshaw! If I hadn't kept after him all these years we wouldn't have a stick to call our own.

WILL. You had to have an "artistic" husband. (*Places flower pots on table above* PERT'S *rocker.*)

ELIZA (*crosses to left of* WILL). Artistic. I have my opinion about that. Why, Will, the money that man squanders every year on liquor alone would buy all kinds of good downtown property, to say nothing of paying off this place. We could be well-to-do people now if we'd started at the very beginning.

WILL (*he fixes a cutting into one of the pots and places it on the porch rail right*). You've given him every opportunity.

ELIZA. He's always hated the idea of owning anything—couldn't bear it, he told me once—'cause of some bad trade he made when he was a young man up in Pennsylvania. If I'd been in the picture then, you can bet your bottom dollar there'd been no loss.

WILL (*chuckling*). Or the loss'd been on the other side.

ELIZA (*moving him front of her to the steps*). That's a *good* one! You know us Pentlands! Well, I'm going to get after Mr. Gant right today about that bank offer.

WILL (*in yard right of right porch pillar*). Let me know when you've warmed him up enough for me to talk to him.

ELIZA (*on porch step*). It'll take a good deal of warming up, I can tell you. He's so blamed stubborn about that precious old marble yard, but I'll do it!

WILL. Give me a jingle when you want to look at that farm property. (*Exiting*) I'll drive you out there.

ELIZA. Thanks, Will! I appreciate it. (*Places leaves, brochure and purse on left porch pillar. Sees* BEN.) Ben! What are you doing home at this hour?

BEN. I'm working afternoons this week.

ELIZA. Oh. (*Somewhat worriedly. Crossing onto porch for two small flower pots.*) Will you get dinner downtown?

BEN. I usually do.

ELIZA (*crossing into yard to right of center table*). You always sound so short with me, Ben. Why is that? You don't even look at me. You know I can't stand not being looked at by the person I'm talking to. Don't you feel well?

BEN. I feel good.

(*A train whistle is heard in the distance.*)

ELIZA. Oh, pshaw, there's the midday train now! Has Eugene gone to the station?

BEN. How should I know?

ELIZA (*crossing left. Calling up to* EUGENE's *room*). Eugene, are you up in your room? Eugene? (EUGENE, *hearing his mother's voice, rises from his chair, turns toward the window, but he doesn't answer, and* ELIZA *does not see him.* EUGENE *is 17, the youngest of the Gants, tall, awkward, with a craving for knowledge and love. During the following he leaves his room. Crossing toward porch right*) Eugene! I'll vow, that boy! Just when I need him— (*Notices* MRS. PERT's *knitting.*) Ben, I hope you haven't been lying around here wasting time with that Mrs. Pert again?

BEN. Listen to her! It's the nicest time I spend.

ELIZA (*crossing to right of him*). I tell you what: it doesn't look right, Ben. What must the other boarders think? A woman her age—a drinking woman—married. Can't you find someone young and pretty and free to be with? I don't understand it. You're the best looking boy I've got.

BEN (*more pleasantly*). If it'll make you feel better, Mama, I'll look around.

ELIZA (*relieved by the change in his mood, smiles. She also notices the sprawled newspaper. Crossing to right of center table*). That's Mr. Clatt's newspaper. You know he's finicky about reading it first. Fold it up before you go. (*During the above,* EUGENE *is seen coming down the stairs from his room. Now limping slightly, he starts to sneak out the side door, but* ELIZA *spots him.*) Eugene, where are you sneaking to? Come out here.

EUGENE (*comes out to left of center table*). Yes, Mama?

ELIZA. The train's just coming in. Now you hurry over to that depot.

EUGENE. Today? I did it yesterday.

ELIZA. Every day until every room is filled. The advertising cards are on the hall table. Go get them. (EUGENE, *disgruntled, goes into the entry hall to get the cards from a small stand.* ELIZA *strips some dead leaves off a plant.*) I declare, seventeen is an impossible age. I don't know why he complains. He hasn't anything else to do. Spending his time up there scribbling, dreaming.

BEN. The other boarding houses send their porters to the trains.

ELIZA. Never you mind, Ben Gant, you used to do it. It's little enough I've ever asked of you boys. (*To* EUGENE *as he comes from the hall.*) Have you got the cards? (*Crosses onto porch to flower tray.*)

EUGENE (*crossing left*). In my pocket.

ELIZA (*holding out her hand*). Let me see them. Let me see them!

EUGENE (*in yard front of left pillar. Takes cards from pocket, reads*). "Stay at Dixieland, Altamont's Homiest Boarding House."—It should be homeliest.

ELIZA. Eugene!

EUGENE. I hate drumming up trade! It's deceptive and it's begging.

ELIZA. Oh, my—my! Dreamer Eugene Gant, what do you think the world is all about? We are all—all of us—selling something. Now you get over to the depot right this minute. And for heaven's sake, boy, spruce up, shoulders back! Look like you *are* somebody! (EUGENE *starts off.*) And smile! Look pleasant! (EUGENE *grins, maniacally.*)

BEN (*suddenly, as he watches* EUGENE *limping*). Gene! What are you walking like that for?

EUGENE. Like what?

BEN (*rises*). What are you limping for? My God, those are my shoes you've got on! I threw them out yesterday!

ELIZA (*busy at flower tray*). They're practically brand new.

BEN. They're too small for *me*, they must be killing him.

EUGENE. Ben, please!

ELIZA (*takes flower tray to up right table*). Maybe you can afford to throw out brand-new shoes.

BEN. Mama, for God's sake, you ask him to walk straight, how can he? His toes must be like pretzels!

EUGENE. They're all right. I'll get used to them.

BEN (*throwing down his paper*). My God, it's a damned disgrace, sending him out on the streets like a hired man. Gene should be *on* that train, going to college!

ELIZA (*crossing to right of center table with can of peat moss*). That's enough—that's just enough of that! You haven't a family to provide for like I have, Ben Gant. Now I don't want to hear another word about it! Gene will go to college when we can afford it. This year he can help Papa at the shop.

BEN. I thought you were going to "warm up" Papa, so he'll sell the shop.

ELIZA. Ben Gant, that wasn't intended

for your ears. I'd appreciate it if you wouldn't mention it to Mr. Gant until I have. Hurry off now, son, get us a customer!

EUGENE (*crossing to left of center table*). Why should Papa sell his shop?

ELIZA (*packing moss in flower pots*). Now, you're too young to worry about my business. You tend to yours.

EUGENE. What business do I have to attend to, Mama?

ELIZA. Well, get busy, get busy! Help your Papa at the shop.

EUGENE. I don't want to be a stonecutter.

ELIZA. Well, go back to delivering newspapers. Work for Uncle Will in his real estate office. But keep the ball rolling, child. Now hurry on or you'll be late! (EUGENE *exits.*)

HELEN (*entering from hall right*). Mama, dinner's practically over! I'm no slave!

ELIZA. I'll be right in, Helen. (HELEN *exits, slamming door.* ELIZA *sighs. For a moment, left alone with* BEN, *she becomes herself, a deeply troubled woman.*) What's the matter with him, Ben? What's wrong with that boy? (*Crosses to pillar for purse, leaves and brochure.*) What's the matter with all of you? I certainly don't know. I tell you what, sometimes I get frightened. Seems as if every one of you's at the end of something, dissatisfied, and wants something else. But it just can't be. A house divided against itself cannot stand. I'll vow, I don't know what we're all coming to. (*Approaches side door left, pauses.*) If you like, this once, as long as you're home, why don't you eat here? I'm sure there's plenty left over.

BEN. No, thank you, Mama. (*He starts off.*)

ELIZA. A good hot meal!

BEN (*tosses paper on center table*). I've got to get over there.

ELIZA. Ben, are you sure you feel all right?

BEN. I feel fine.

ELIZA. Well, have a nice day at the paper, son.

(BEN *exits,* ELIZA *looks after him, then hearing the voices of the boarders, exits into the house by the side door. The boarders, ushered by* HELEN, *enter through the front door. They are:* JAKE CLATT, *30, an insensitive boor.* MRS. CLATT,

60, JAKE's *mother, with a coarse smile and dyed hair. She is deaf and carries a cane.* FLORRY MANGLE, *29, wistful, humorless, interested in* JAKE. MRS. SNOWDEN, *50, quiet, unobtrusive, lonely. Takes her coffee, sits up right.* MISS BROWN, *36, prim on the surface, but with the marks of the amateur prostitute.* MR. FARREL, *60, a retired dancing master, new to Dixieland.*)

MRS. CLATT. I ate too much again.

HELEN (*loudly to* MRS. CLATT, *as she crosses to table with fresh pot of coffee*). Help yourself to coffee, please, Mrs. Clatt. I'm short-handed today.

MRS. CLATT (*brandishing her cane at* MR. FARREL, *who is about to sit chair down right*). Not there, that's my chair! That one's free, since the school teacher left.

MISS BROWN (*at front of porch door*). You're a teacher too, aren't you, Mr. Farrel?

MR. FARREL. Of the dance. Retired.

MISS BROWN. I hope you'll stay with us for a while. Where are you from?

MR. FARREL. Tampa.

MISS BROWN. Do you know the Castle Walk, Mr. Farrel? I'd love to learn it! (*They stroll down to the yard seat left.*)

MRS. CLATT. I don't know what Mrs. Gant makes this coffee of. (*Crosses, sits down right.*) There isn't a bean invented tastes like this.

JAKE (*on porch up right center*). Couldn't you make it for us sometime, Helen?

HELEN. My mother always make the coffee here.

(HUGH *and* MRS. PERT *enter. The others seat themselves.*)

MRS. PERT. That was scrumptious dessert, but oh dear! (*Sits in her rocker.*)

JAKE (*down right center on porch*). Yes, it was good, if only the servings were bigger.

MRS. CLATT. I'm told the best boarding house food in town is down the street at Mrs. Haskell's.

JAKE. That's right, Mother. That's what I heard.

HUGH (*crossing to yard to left of* MRS. PERT). Then move in to Mrs. Haskell's!

HELEN (*with a shove*). Hugh! (*She exits.*)

MISS MANGLE (*seated right of door*). I spent one season there, but I prefer it here. It's more informal and entertaining.

JAKE (*seated woodbox*). Not lately. It's been over a month since Mrs. Gant had to have Mr. Molasses Edward, and his two Dixie Ramblers evicted for not paying their rent. She certainly loves to see the police swarm around!

LAURA JAMES, *23, carrying a suitcase, and a Dixieland advertising card, enters. She is attractive, but not beautiful. She advances to the steps.*)

MISS MANGLE. Don't you?

JAKE. I like excitement—why shouldn't I?

MISS MANGLE. Other people's excitement. Don't you ever want excitement of your own? I do.

(MRS. CLATT *sees* LAURA; *nudges her son into attention.* HUGH *turns to her.*)

LAURA. Good afternoon!

HUGH. Good afternoon!

LAURA. Is the proprietor here?

HUGH. I'll call her. (*Calls inside.*) Mrs. Gant! Customer! (*To* LAURA) Please come right up.

JAKE (*leaping to* LAURA). Here, let me take that suitcase. It must be heavy for you.

LAURA. Thank you.

(JAKE *takes* LAURA's *suitcase. Puts it on porch right of right pillar. The other boarders look her over, whisper.* ELIZA, *wearing an apron, places the leaves in a vase, on the hall table, enters. At first raking glance she doubts that* LAURA, *so young and different, is a true prospect.*)

ELIZA. Yes?

LAURA. Are you the proprietor?

ELIZA. Mrs. Eliza Gant—that's right.

LAURA (*crossing to left of* ELIZA *on porch*). I found this card on the sidewalk.

ELIZA (*takes card*). On the sidewalk! And you're looking for a room?

LAURA. If you have one for me.

ELIZA (*taking her to chair left of center table which* HUGH *has pulled out for her*). Of course I have, dear—a nice quiet room. You just sit down here and have yourself a cup of my *good* coffee, while I go and open it up, so I can show it to you. Hugh, you take care of the young lady. This is Mr. Barton, my son-in-law.

LAURA. How do you do, Mr. Barton? I'm Laura James.

ELIZA (*turns at steps*). Laura—why that's a *good* Scotch name. Are you Scotch?

LAURA. On one side.

ELIZA (*crosses back to her*). Pshaw! I could have told you were the Scotch the minute I laid eyes on you. I'm Scotch too. Well, isn't that nice? (*Makes introductions.* HUGH *crosses porch for coffee.*) Miss James, Mr. Clatt—(*Each acknowledges the introduction according to his personality.*) His mother, Mrs. Clatt, Mrs. Snowden, Miss Mangle, Mr. Farrel—(*Disapprovingly notices* MISS BROWN *flirting with* MR. FARREL.) Miss Brown—Miss Brown! and Mrs. Pert. Where do you come from, dear?

LAURA. I live in Richmond.

(MISS BROWN *and* MR. FARREL *exit down right practicing the Castle Walk, eventually reappear at the rear of the veranda up right.*)

ELIZA. Richmond! Now that's a pleasant city—but hot! Not like it is here, cool and refreshing in these hills. You haven't come to Altamont for a cure, have you, dear?

LAURA. I'm healthy, if that's what you mean. But I've been working hard and I need a rest.

ELIZA (*as* HUGH *approaches with coffee*). Here's your coffee.

LAURA (*takes coffee*). Thank you, Mr. Barton. What are your rates, Mrs. Gant?

EUGENE (*off*). Mama! (*Runs up the back walk, around the veranda.*)

ELIZA. Suppose I show you the room first.

EUGENE. Mama!

ELIZA (*crossing above* LAURA *to right of her*). I declare that child either crawls like a snail or speeds like a fire engine—

EUGENE (*pulls* ELIZA *off left away from the others*). Can I speak to you, Mama?

ELIZA. I don't see you limping *now*, when you're not trying to get sympathy. Don't think I don't know your little tricks to—

EUGENE (*urgently*). Mama, Papa's been at Laughran's again. Doctor Maguire is trying to steer him home now.

ELIZA (*momentarily stabbed*). The doctor? Is he sick or is he drunk?

EUGENE. He's rip roaring! He's awful. He kicked Uncle Will again!

(HUGH *and* JAKE *have seated* LAURA *left of center table*—LAURA *removes her hat. Offstage are the sounds of a small riot approaching. The occasional bull yell of* GANT, *children chanting "Old Man Gant came home drunk," a dog barking,* etc.)

ELIZA (*weakly*). I don't think I can stand it again. A *new* young lady, too. (EUGENE *turns to see* LAURA, *who, with the other boarders, have heard the approaching* GANT.) Oh, Eugene, why do they keep bringing him home? Take him to a state institution, throw him in the gutter, I don't care. I don't know what to do any more. What'll I do, child?

EUGENE. At least it's been a month this time.

GANT (*off*). Mountain Grills! Stay away from me!

JAKE CLATT. My God, Mr. Gant's on the loose again! (*Crosses onto porch.*)

MISS MANGLE. Oh dear, oh dear—

MRS. CLATT. What? What is it?

JAKE CLATT (*shouting*). The old boy's on the loose again!

EUGENE (*crossing up to the boarders*). Would you go inside, all of you, please?

MRS. CLATT. I haven't finished my coffee.

EUGENE. You can wait in the parlor. Please, just until we get him upstairs!

JAKE CLATT (*crosses porch up right*). And miss the show?

MISS BROWN. Come along, Mr. Farrel. Let's clear the deck for the old geezer.

MR. FARREL. Perhaps there is some way I can help?

MISS BROWN. I wouldn't recommend it, Mr. Farrel.

JAKE CLATT. Look at him, he's really got a snootful this time!

(EUGENE *urges several of the boarders inside, where they cram in the hallway.* JAKE *and* MRS. CLATT *remain on the porch.* LAURA, *not knowing where to go, remains with* HUGH *outside.*)

GANT (*from up the walk in the back, bellowing like a wounded bull. Off*). Mountain Grills! Mountain Grills! Fiends, not friends! Don't push me! *Get away from me!*

DR. MAGUIRE (*off*). All right then, Gant, if you can walk, walk! (ELIZA *stands downstage, stiff and straight.* W. O. GANT, *60, clatters up the back veranda steps, his arms flailing. At heart he is a far wanderer and a minstrel but he has degraded his life with libertinism and drink. In him still, though, there is a monstrous fumbling for life. He is accompanied by* DR. MAGUIRE, *unkempt but kind, and by* TARKINTON, *disreputably dressed, a crony, also drunk but navigating, and by* WILL

PENTLAND.) Here we are, Gant; let's go in the back way.

(WILL *precedes* GANT *and crosses to yard down right.* GANT *pushes the* DOCTOR *aside, plunges headlong along the veranda, scattering rockers, flower pots, etc.*)

GANT. Where are you? Where are you? The lowest of the low—boarding house swine! Merciful God, what a travesty! That it should come to this! (*Stumbles, almost falls, bursts into maniacal laughter.*)

EUGENE. Papa, come on—Papa, please! (EUGENE *tries to take* GANT *by the arm;* GANT *flings him aside.*)

GANT (*with a sweeping gesture*). "Waken lords and ladies gay On the mountain dawns the day—" (*Stumbles,* GENE *catches him.* MRS. CLATT *screams and dashes into the hall.*) Don't let me disturb your little tete-a-tete. Go right ahead, help yourself. (*Tosses* GENE *toward* PERT's *rocker.*) Another helping of mashed potatoes, Mrs. Clatt? Put another tire around your middle— (EUGENE *tries to catch* GANT's *flailing arms.*)

ELIZA (*crossing to left of left pillar*). Mr. Gant, I'd be ashamed, I'd be ashamed.

GANT. Who speaks?

ELIZA. I thought you were sick.

GANT. I am not sick, Madame; I am in a wild, blind fury. (*Raises a chair aloft, threatening* ELIZA. EUGENE *and the* DOCTOR *grab it away from him.* LAURA, *urged by* HUGH, *retreats to down left unit.*)

ELIZA. Dr. Maguire, get him in the house.

DR. MAGUIRE (*right of* GANT). Come on, Gant, let me help you.

GANT. Just one moment! You don't think I know my own home when I see it? This is not where I live. I reside at 92 *Woodson Street.*

DR. MAGUIRE. That was some years ago. This is your home now, Gant.

GANT. This barn? This damnable, this awful, this murderous and bloody barn—home? Holy hell, what a travesty on nature! A-h-h-h! (*He maniacally lunges to the yard after* ELIZA. GENE *halts him.*)

WILL. Why don't we carry him in?

DR. MAGUIRE. You keep out of this, Pentland. You're the one who enrages him.

GANT (*tossing* GENE *onto steps*). Pentland—now that's a name for you! (*Pivots, searching for him.*) Where are you, Will

Pentland? (*Sees him, staggers toward him.*) You're a Mountain Grill! Your father was a Mountain Grill and a horse thief, and he was hanged in the public square.

(*While* HUGH *holds* GANT, EUGENE *brings a cup of coffee.*)

EUGENE (*left of* GANT). Papa, wouldn't you like some coffee? There's some right here.

GANT. Hah! Some of Mrs. Gant's *good* coffee? (*He kicks at the coffee cup.* EUGENE *backs away.*) Ahh! I'll take some of that *good* bourbon, if you have it, son.

DR. MAGUIRE (*crosses, puts bag on* PERT *rocker*). Get him a drink! Maybe he'll pass out.

GANT. Drink!

ELIZA (*stopping* GENE *at door*). Gene! Dr. Maguire, you know there isn't a drop of alcohol in this house!

LAURA. I have some. (LAURA *quickly opens her handbag, takes from it a small vial, crosses to the* DOCTOR.) I always carry it in case of a train accident.

GANT (*lunges toward her*). Well, what are we waiting for, let's have it!

DR. MAGUIRE (*taking the vial*). Good God, this won't fill one of his teeth.

GANT (*roars*). Well, let's have it! (LAURA *backs away in fear.*)

DR. MAGUIRE. You can have it, Gant—but you'll have to come up onto the veranda to drink it—

GANT. Mountain Grills! Vipers! Lowest of the low! I'll stand here until you take me home. (HELEN *enters from up right.*) Isn't anybody going to take me home?

HELEN (*crossing to right of* GANT). Papa! Why have you been drinking again when you know what it does to you?

GANT (*weakens, leans against her*). Helen—I have a pain right here.

HELEN. Of course you do. Come with me now. I'll put you to bed, and bring you some soup. (HELEN *takes the huge man's arm, leads him toward the veranda.* HELEN's *success with* GANT *etches itself deeply into* ELIZA's *face.*)

GANT (*weakly*). Got to sit down— (*Sits on edge of porch, left of left pillar, pats space beside him.*) Sit down, Helen, you and me. (*She sits step right of* GANT. GENE *sits table left of* GANT.) Sit and talk. Would you like to hear some Keats—beautiful Keats?

ELIZA (*crossing up to veranda, angrily*).

He's got his audience now. That's all he wants.

EUGENE. Mama, he's sick!

ELIZA (*on porch step*). Mr. Gant, if you feel so bad, why don't you act nice and go inside? The whole neighborhood's watching you.

GANT (*wildly sings*). "Old man Gant came home drunk—" (TARKINTON *joins him.*) "Old man Gant came home drunk—"

TARKINTON (*singing, waving his arms. Seated chair which* GENE *had taken from* GANT *and placed left of woodbox*). "Old man Gant came home—" (*His joy fades as he sees* ELIZA *glaring at him.*)

ELIZ. Were you drinking with him too, Mr. Tarkinton?

TARKINTON. Sev-ereral of us were, Mrs. Gant, I regret to say.

ELIZA (*pulling* TARKINTON *to his feet*). I'll have Tim Laughran thrown in jail for this.

TARKINTON. He started out so peaceable like—

ELIZA (*pushing him toward rear exit of veranda*). I've warned him for the last time.

TARKINTON. Just on beer!

ELIZA. *Get off my premises!*

(TARKINTON *exits.* GANT *groans.* DOCTOR *to yard right of* HELEN.)

HELEN. Dr. Maguire's here to give you something for your pain, Papa.

GANT. Doctors! Thieves and bloodsuckers! (DOCTOR *crosses to bag.*) "The paths of glory lead but to the grave."—Gray's Elegy. Only four cents a letter on any tombstone you choose, by the master carver— Any orders? (*He groans with pain.*) It's the devil's own pitchfork. Don't let them put me under the knife— promise me, daughter. Promise me! (HELEN *nods. With a giant effort,* GANT *pulls himself up.*) "Over the stones, rattle his bones! He's only a beggar that nobody owns."

DR. MAGUIRE. Good God, he's on his feet again.

EUGENE. Hugh, let's get him in the house.

GANT (*throwing off* HUGH *and* EUGENE). I see it! I see it! Do you see the Dark Man's shadow? There! There he stands— the Grim Reaper—as I always knew he would. So you've come at last to take the old man home? Jesus, have mercy on my soul! (GANT *falls to the ground. There is an agonized silence.* EUGENE, THE DOCTOR, *and* HUGH *rush to him.*)

ELIZA (*anxiously, above right pillar*). Dr. Maguire.

DR. MAGUIRE (*feels* GANT'S *heart*). He's just passed out, Mrs. Gant. Men, let's carry him up!

(HUGH, WILL, MAGUIRE *and* EUGENE *lift the heavy body, quickly carry* GANT *inside.* HELEN *follows.* ELIZA, *saddened and miserable, starts to gather the coffee cups.* LAURA *picks up her suitcase and starts off.* ELIZA *turns, sees her.*)

ELIZA. Oh, Miss James. I was going to show you that room, wasn't I? (*Crosses, seizes* LAURA'S *suitcase.*)

LAURA. Hmmmmmm?

ELIZA (*right center*). I think you'll enjoy it here. It's quiet and peaceful—oh, nobody pays any mind to Mr. Gant. I'll tell you: we don't have occurrences like this every day.

LAURA. Well, how much is it?

ELIZA. Twenty—fifteen dollars a week. Three meals a day, and the use of electricity and the bath. Do you want me to show it to you?

LAURA. No, I'm sure it will be all right.

ELIZA (*starting in, turns back*). That's in advance, that is.

LAURA (*opens her purse, takes out a roll of one-dollar bills, puts them one by one into* ELIZA'S *outstretched hand.*) One, two, three—I always keep my money in one-dollar bills—it feels like it's more.

ELIZA (*almost cheerful again*). Oh, I know what you mean. (MR. FARREL *enters by the side door with his suitcase. He is hoping to sneak out.* ELIZA *sees him as the paying business continues. Crossing to left of* LAURA.) Mr. Farrel! Where are you going? Mr. Farrel, you've paid for a week in advance! (MR. FARREL *wordlessly gestures that it's all too much for him, exits.*) Well, they come and they go. And you're here now, isn't that nice?

LAURA. . . . Nine . . . ten. . . .

BEN (*enters from the other direction, hurriedly*). I heard about Father—how is he? (*Crosses to porch.*)

ELIZA. Drunk. Dr. Maguire's taking care of him now. Ben, this is Miss James —this is my son, Ben Gant.

BEN (*impressed by her looks, nods*). Miss James.

LAURA (*barely looking at* BEN, *nods*).

—fourteen, fifteen. There.

ELIZA (*puts the money in bosom of her dress*). Thank you, dear. Miss James is going to stay with us a while, we hope! I'll take you up, dear. You'll be cozy and comfortable here. (*They start inside.*) I'll show you the rest of the house later.

LAURA (*turning in doorway*). Nice to have met you, Mr. Gant. (ELIZA *and* LAURA *exit.*)

BEN (*imitating* LAURA's *disinterest, as he picks up cup of coffee*). Nice to have met you, Mr. Gant. (*Shrugs, sits woodbox and lights cigarette.*)

WILL (*enters from the house, still sweating. Left of* BEN). That father of yours. Do you know he kicked me? I don't want to tell you where. Why don't you watch out for him more, Ben? It's up to you boys, for your mother's sake—for Dixieland. I warned her about him—a born wanderer like he is, and a widower. But you can't advise women—not when it comes to love and sex. (*He starts off, stops up right.*) You might thank me for my help. No one else has.

BEN. Thank you, Uncle Will.

WILL. Bunch of ungrateful Gants. You're the only one of them who has any class. (*Exits up right.*)

EUGENE (*enters*). Did you hear about it, Ben?

BEN. There isn't a soul in town who hasn't.

EUGENE (*crossing into yard*). What's it all about? It doesn't make sense. Can you figure it out, Ben? Why does he do it?

BEN. How should I know? (*Drinks his coffee.*) Is Maguire almost through?

EUGENE (*hurt, not understanding* BEN's *preoccupation*). Ben, remember in the morning when we used to walk together and you were teaching me the paper route? We talked a lot then.

BEN. Listen to him! We're talking.

EUGENE (*crosses, sits step*). If he hates it so much here, why does he stay?

BEN. You stupid little fool, it's like being caught in a photograph. Your face is there, and no matter how hard you try, how are you going to step out of a photograph? (DOCTOR MAGUIRE *enters.*) Shut up now, will you. Hello, Doc. (*Rises, leaves coffee on woodbox.*)

DR. MAGUIRE (*entering, putting on cap*). Your sister sure can handle that old goat like a lamb! The funny thing though is that people like him. He's a good man, when sober.

BEN. Is he all right?

DR. MAGUIRE (*taking bag, crossing to yard down right*). He's going to be.

BEN (*crossing yard to left of down right*). Can I speak to you a minute about me? If you have a minute.

DR. MAGUIRE. Shoot, Ben.

BEN (*to* EUGENE, *who has seated himself right of door*). Haven't you got something else to do?

EUGENE. No.

(BEN *crosses to right of center table.*)

DR. MAGUIRE (*crossing to right of* BEN). What's the matter—you got pyorrhea of the toenails or is it something more private?

BEN. I'm tired of pushing daisies here. I want to push them somewhere else.

DR. MAGUIRE. What's that supposed to mean?

BEN. I suppose you've heard there's a war going on in Europe? I've decided to enlist in Canada.

EUGENE (*rises*). What do you want to do that for?

BEN (*to* EUGENE). You keep out of this.

DR. MAGUIRE. It is a good question, Ben. Do you want to save the world? This world?

BEN. In Christ's name, Maguire, you'll recommend me, won't you? You examined me just a couple of months ago.

DR. MAGUIRE (*crosses, puts down his bag on right pillar*). Well, let's see, for a war the requirements are somewhat different. Stick out your chest. (BEN *does so; the* DOCTOR *looks him over.*) Feet? Good arch, but pigeon-toed.

BEN. Since when do you need toes to shoot a gun?

DR. MAGUIRE (*crossing to him*). How're your teeth, son?

BEN. Aren't you overdoing it, Doc? (BEN *draws back his lips and shows two rows of hard white grinders. Unexpectedly* MAGUIRE *prods* BEN's *solar plexus with a strong yellow finger and* BEN's *distended chest collapses. He sinks to the veranda edge, coughing.*)

EUGENE. What did you do that for?

DR. MAGUIRE (*crosses for bag*). They'll have to save this world without you, Ben.

BEN (*rises, grabs the* DOCTOR). What do you mean?

DR. MAGUIRE. That's all. That's all.

BEN. You're saying I'm not all right?

DR. MAGUIRE (*turns to him*). Who said you weren't all right?

BEN (*left of down right*). Quit your kidding.

DR. MAGUIRE. What's the rush? We may get into this war ourselves before too long. Wait a bit. (*To* EUGENE.) Isn't that right, son? (*Turns for bag.*)

BEN (*grabs his right arm*). I want to know. Am I all right or not?

DR. MAGUIRE. Yes, Ben, you're all right. Why, you're one of the most all right people I know. (*Carefully, as he feels* BEN'S *arm.*) You're a little run down, that's all. You need some meat on those bones. (BEN *breaks from him, moves away left.*) You can't exist with a cup of coffee in one hand and a cigarette in the other. Besides, the Altamont air is good for you. Stick around. Big breaths, Ben, big breaths. (*Picks up his bag.*)

BEN. Thanks. As a doctor, you're a fine first baseman.

DR. MAGUIRE. Take it easy. Try not to care too much. (*Exits down right.* BEN *puts out cigarette in coffee cup on center table.*)

EUGENE (*crosses to right of* BEN). He's right. You should try to look after yourself more, Ben. (*Tries to comfort* BEN. BEN *avoids his touch, lurches away.*)

BEN. He doesn't have any spirit about this war, that's all that's the matter with him. (*Recovers his coffee, drinks.* EUGENE *studies him.*)

EUGENE. I didn't know you wanted to get away from here so badly.

BEN (*looks over at* EUGENE, *puts down coffee on right pillar. Crosses to yard*). Come here, you little bum. (EUGENE *approaches close.*) My God, haven't you got a clean shirt? (*He gets out some money.*) Here, take this and go get that damn long hair cut off, and get some shoes that fit, for God's sake, you look like a lousy tramp—

EUGENE (*backing away left*). Ben, I can't keep taking money from you.

BEN. What else have you got me for? (*The brothers roughhouse playfully with the money,* EUGENE *giggling. Then with sudden intense ferocity* BEN *seizes* EUGENE'S *arms, shakes him.*) You listen to me. You go to college, understand? Don't settle for anyone or anything—

learn your lesson from me! I'm a hack on a hick paper—I'll never be anything else. You can be. Get money out of them, any way you can! Beg it, take it, steal it, but get it from them somehow. Get it and get away from them. To hell with them all! (BEN *coughs.* EUGENE *tries to help him.* BEN *escapes, sits tiredly on the veranda's edge.* EUGENE *disconsolately sinks into nearby chair left of center table.*) Neither Luke, nor Stevie, nor I made it. But you can, Gene. I let her hold on and hold on until it was too late. Don't let that happen to you. And Gene, don't try to please everyone—please yourself. (BEN *studies* EUGENE, *realizes his confusion and depression. Then, noticing* LAURA'S *hat which she has left on the yard table, points to it.*) Where's she from?

EUGENE (*follows* BEN'S *gaze to* LAURA'S *hat, picks it up, sniffs it*). I don't know. I don't even know her name.

BEN. Miss James. I'll have to announce her arrival in my "society" column. (*Takes hat from* EUGENE, *admires it.*) The firm young line of spring—budding, tender, virginal. "Like something swift, with wings, which hovers in a wood— among the feathery trees, suspected, but uncaught, unseen." Exquisite. (*Returns hat to table, rises.*) Want to walk downtown with me? I'll buy you a cup of mocha.

EUGENE. Maybe I ought to stay here.

BEN (*ruffling* EUGENE'S *hair. Crossing for coffee*). With her around I don't blame you. I dream of elegant women myself, all the time.

EUGENE (*rising*). You do? But, Ben, if you dream of elegant women, how is it, well—

BEN (*on porch*). Mrs. Pert? Fatty's a happy woman—there's no pain in her she feels she has to unload onto someone else. Besides she's as adorable as a duck; don't you think so?

EUGENE. I guess you're right. I like her —myself—sure.

BEN (*replaces coffee cup on tray, crosses to yard down right*). Some day you'll find out what it means. I've got to get back to work.

EUGENE (*front of left pillar*). Ben, I'm glad they won't take you in Canada.

BEN (*with that upward glance*). Listen to him! I was crazy to think of going. I have to bring you up first, don't I? (BEN *exits*.)

MISS BROWN (*dressed for a stroll, carrying a parasol, she enters from the house*). Gene! You haven't even said hello to me today.

EUGENE. Hello, Miss Brown.

MISS BROWN (*crosses to yard down right*). My, everything's quiet again. Lovely warm day, isn't it? (MISS BROWN *sings and dances sensuously for* EUGENE.)*
"Pony boy, pony boy,
Won't you be my pony boy?
Don't say no, can't we go
Right across the plains?"
(MISS BROWN *approaches* EUGENE, *he backs away from her, stumbling against the table. She starts out through rear veranda.*)
"Marry me, carry me—
Far away with you!
Giddy-ap, giddy-ap, giddy-ap. Oh!
My pony boy!"
(MISS BROWN *exits.* EUGENE *sits in the yard, takes off one shoe and rubs his aching toes.* LAURA *enters, picks up her hat, sees* EUGENE. EUGENE *hides his shoeless foot.* MISS BROWN'S VOICE *from offstage, receding in distance.*)
"Pony boy, pony boy
Mmmm, mmm, mmm—Mmmm, mmm, mmm,
Marry me, carry me
Giddy-ap, giddy-ap, giddy-ap. Oh!
My pony boy."
(*At the door,* LAURA *looks again at* EUGENE, *smiles, exits.*)

CURTAIN

SCENE Two

SCENE: *The same; that evening. The night is sensuous, warm. A light storm is threatening. Long, swaying tree shadows project themselves on the house. Seated on the side veranda are* JAKE, MRS. CLATT, FLORRY, MISS BROWN, *and* MRS. SNOWDEN. MRS. PERT *is seated in her rocker,* BEN *left of her. They are drinking beer.* MRS. PERT *measures the socks she is knitting against* BEN'S *shoe.* JAKE CLATT *softly plays the ukulele and sings.* EUGENE *is*

* "My Pony Boy" used by special permission Inc., New York 36, N. Y.
of copyright owner, Jerry Vogel Music Co.,
Far away with you

sitting on the side door steps, lonely, yearning. Glasses of lemonade have replaced the noontime coffee cups. And a phonograph replaces the flower tray on the up right center table on the porch.

JAKE (*singing "K-K-Katy"*).* "K-K-K-aty, K-K-Katy," etc. (*As* JAKE *finishes,* FLORRY *gently applauds.* JAKE *starts softly strumming something else.*)

MRS. PERT (*to* BEN, *quietly*). I know you talked to the doctor today. What did he say? Tell Fatty.

BEN. I'm out before I'm in. Oh, I know you're pleased, but you don't know how it feels to be the weakling. All the other members of this family—they're steers, mountain goats, eagles. Except Father, lately—unless he's drunk. Do you know, though, I still think of him as I thought of him as a little boy—a Titan! The house on Woodson Street that he built for Mama with his own hands, the great armloads of food he carried home—the giant fires he used to build. The women he loved at Madame Elizabeth's. Two and three a night, I heard.

MRS. PERT. It's nice for parents to have their children think of them as they were young. (*As* BEN *chuckles*) I mean, that's the way I'd like my children to think of me. Oh, you know what I mean.

BEN (*laughs with his typical glance upward*). Listen to her!

MRS. PERT. Ben, who are you always talking to, like that? (*Imitates* BEN *looking up over his shoulder.*)

BEN. Who, him? (*She nods.*) That's Grover, my twin. It was a habit I got into, while he was still alive.

MRS. PERT. I wish you'd known me when I was young. I was some different.

BEN. I bet you weren't half as nice and warm and round as you are now.

MRS. PERT. Ben, don't ever let your mother hear you say those things. What could she think?

BEN. Who cares what she thinks?

MRS. PERT. Dear, I only hope when the right girl comes along you won't be sorry for the affection you've lavished on me.

* "K-K-K-Katy," words and music by Geoffrey O'Hara © 1918, copyright renewal 1945 Leo Feist, Inc. Used by permission of the copyright owner solely for the purpose of printing in this edition. CAUTION: Permission to include this song in any performance of this play must be obtained from Leo Feist, Inc., 1540 Broadway, New York 36, N. Y.

BEN. I don't want the "right girl." Like some more beer? I've got another bottle.

MRS. PERT. Love some more, honey.

(BEN *rises, searches under the yard table for the bottle he has hidden, realizes it's not there, suspiciously looks at* EUGENE. EUGENE *innocently gestures, then reaches behind him and tosses the beer bottle to* BEN. BEN *and* FATTY *laugh.* BEN *returns with the beer to* FATTY *as* LAURA *enters from the house.*)

JAKE (*rising expectantly*). Good evening, Miss James.

LAURA. Good evening.

JAKE. Won't you sit down? (*Indicates woodbox where he has been sitting.*)

MRS. CLATT (*as* LAURA *seems about to choose a chair*). That's Mr. Farrel's. Yours is back there!

JAKE (*loudly. Moves up left of her*). Mr. Farrel has left, Mother.

MRS. CLATT. What?

JAKE. Never mind. (*To* LAURA.) No sense in being formal. Won't you sing with me, Miss James?

LAURA. I love music, but I have no talent for it. (*Moves toward rear of veranda, away from the others.* JAKE *places uke on woodbox.*)

FLORRY (*to* JAKE). I love to sing.

(JAKE *ignores* FLORRY, *follows after* LAURA, FLORRY *tugging at* JAKE's *coat.*)

MRS. SNOWDEN (*to* JAKE *as he passes*). Do you know Indiana Lullaby? It's a lovely song.

(JAKE *and* LAURA *exit.*)

BEN. I'm comfortable when I'm with you, Fatty.

MRS. PERT. That's good, so'm I.

BEN. People don't understand. Jelly roll isn't everything, is it?

MRS. PERT. Ben Gant, what kind of a vulgar phrase is that?

BEN. It's a Stumptown word. I used to deliver papers there. Sometimes those negra women don't have money to pay their bill, so they pay you in jelly roll.

MRS. PERT. Ben—your little brother's right over there listening!

BEN (*glances toward* EUGENE). Gene knows all about jelly roll, don't you? Where do you think he's been all his life —in Mama's front parlor?

EUGENE. Oh, come on, Ben. (*Embarrassed laugh.*)

BEN (*laughs*). There's another word I remember in the eighth grade. We had a thin, anxious-looking teacher. The boys had a poem about her. (*Quotes.*)
"Old Miss Groody
Has good toody."

MRS. PERT. Ben, stop it! (*They both laugh.* EUGENE *joins in.* LAURA *has managed to lose* JAKE, *has strolled around the back of the house. She enters to* EUGENE *from the side door.*)

LAURA. Good evening.

EUGENE. What!

LAURA. I said good evening.

EUGENE (*flustered*). Goodyado. (*Rises, moves down left of her.*)

LAURA. I beg your pardon?

EUGENE. I mean—I meant to say good evening, how do you do?

LAURA. Goodyado! I like that much better. Goodyado! (*They shake hands,* LAURA *reacting to* EUGENE's *giant grip.* EUGENE *sits left on unit.*) Don't you think that's funny?

EUGENE. It's about as funny as most things I do.

LAURA. May I sit down?

EUGENE (*leaping up*). Please.

LAURA (*as she sits*). I'm Laura James.

EUGENE. I know. My name's Eugene Gant.

LAURA. You know, I've seen you before.

EUGENE. Yes, earlier this afternoon.

LAURA. I mean before that. I saw you throw those advertising cards in the gutter.

EUGENE. You did?

LAURA. I was coming from the station. You know where the train crosses the street? You were just standing there staring at it. I walked right by you and smiled at you. I never got such a snub before in my whole life. My, you must be crazy about trains.

EUGENE (*sits left of her*). You stood right beside me? (BEN *plays a record on the phonograph.*) Where are you from?

LAURA. Richmond, Virginia.

EUGENE. Richmond! That's a big city, isn't it?

LAURA. It's pretty big.

EUGENE. How many people?

LAURA. Oh, about a hundred and twenty thousand, I'd say.

EUGENE. Are there a lot of pretty parks and boulevards?

LAURA. Oh, yes—

EUGENE. And fine tall buildings, with elevators?

LAURA. Yes, it's quite a metropolis.

EUGENE. Theatres and things like that?

LAURA. A lot of good shows come to Richmond. Are you interested in shows?

EUGENE. You have a big library. Did you know it has over a hundred thousand books in it?

LAURA. No, I didn't know that.

EUGENE. Well, it does. I read that somewhere. It would take a long time to read a hundred thousand books, wouldn't it?

LAURA. Yes, it would.

EUGENE. I figure about twenty years. How many books do they let you take out at one time?

LAURA. I really don't know.

EUGENE. They only let you take out two here!

LAURA. That's too bad.

EUGENE. You have some great colleges in Virginia. Did you know that William and Mary is the second oldest college in the country?

LAURA. Is it? What's the oldest?

EUGENE. Harvard! I'd like to study there! First Chapel Hill. That's our state university. Then Harvard. I'd like to study all over the world, learn all its languages. I love words, don't you?

LAURA. Yes; yes, I do.

EUGENE. Are you laughing at me?

LAURA. Of course not.

EUGENE. You are smiling a lot!

LAURA. I'm smiling because I'm enjoying myself. I like talking to you.

EUGENE. I like talking to you, too. I always talk better with older people.

LAURA. Oh!

EUGENE. They know so much more.

LAURA. Like me?

EUGENE. Yes. You're very interesting.

LAURA. Am I?

EUGENE. Oh yes! You're very interesting!

(JACK CLATT *approaches*, FLORRY MANGLE *hovering anxiously on the veranda*.)

JAKE. Miss James?

LAURA. Yes, Mr. Platt?

JAKE. Clatt.

LAURA. Clatt.

JAKE. Jake Clatt! It's a lovely evening. Would you like to take a stroll?

LAURA. It feels to me like it's going to rain.

JAKE (*looking at the sky*). Oh, I don't know.

EUGENE (*rising, moving in between* LAURA *and* JAKE). It's going to rain, all right.

JAKE. Oh, I wouldn't be so sure!

LAURA. Perhaps some other time, Mr. Clatt.

JAKE. Certainly. Good night, Miss James. Good night, sonny.

(EUGENE *glares after* JAKE, *who returns to the veranda under* FLORRY's *jealous stare. The other boarders have disappeared.* JAKE *and* FLORRY *exit*, FLORRY *hugging* JAKE's *ukulele in her arms. Only* FATTY *and* BEN *still sit on the steps. A train whistle moans mournfully in the distance.* EUGENE *cocks an ear, listens.*)

LAURA. You do like trains, don't you?

EUGENE. Mama took us on one to St. Louis to the Fair, when I was only five. Have you ever touched one?

LAURA. What?

EUGENE. A locomotive. Have you put your hand on one? You have to feel things to fully understand them.

LAURA. Aren't they rather hot?

EUGENE. Even a cold one, standing in a station yard. You know what you feel? You feel the shining steel rails under it— and the rails send a message right into your hand—a message of all the mountains that engine ever passed—all the flowing rivers, the forests, the towns, all the houses, the people, the washlines flapping in the fresh cool breeze—the beauty of the people in the way they live and the way they work—a farmer waving from his field, a kid from the school yard —the faraway places it roars through at night, places you don't even know, can hardly imagine. Do you believe it? You feel the rhythm of a whole life, a whole country clicking through your hand.

LAURA (*impressed*). I'm not sure we all would. I believe *you* do.

(*There is a moment while* LAURA *looks at* EUGENE. BEN *moves up to the veranda and the phonograph plays another record.* EUGENE *and* LAURA *speak simultaneously.*)

EUGENE. How long do you plan to stay here—?

LAURA. How old are you, Gene?

EUGENE. I'm sorry—please. (*Draws a chair close to* LAURA, *straddles it, facing her.*)

LAURA. No, you.

EUGENE. How long do you plan to stay here, Miss James?

LAURA. My name is Laura. I wish you'd call me that.

EUGENE. Laura. It's a lovely name. Do you know what it means?

LAURA. No.

EUGENE. I read a book once on the meaning of names. Laura is the laurel. The Greek symbol of victory.

LAURA. Victory. Maybe some day I'll live up to that! (*After a second*) What does Eugene mean?

EUGENE. Oh, I forget.

LAURA. *You,* forget?

EUGENE. It means "well born."

LAURA. How old are you?

EUGENE. Why?

LAURA. I'm always curious about people's ages.

EUGENE. So am I. How old are you?

LAURA. I'm twenty-one. You?

EUGENE. Nineteen. Will you be staying here long?

LAURA. I don't know exactly.

EUGENE. You're only twenty-one?

LAURA. How old did you think I was?

EUGENE. Oh, about that. About twenty-one, I'd say. That's not old at all!

LAURA (*laughs*). I don't feel it is!

EUGENE. I was afraid you might think I was too young for you to waste time with like this!

LAURA. I don't think nineteen is young at all!

EUGENE. It isn't, really, is it?

LAURA (*rises*). Gene, if we keep rushing together like this, we're going to have a collision.

(LAURA *moves away from* EUGENE. *He follows her. They sit together on the side steps, reaching with whispers toward each other. The turntable revolves, removing* EUGENE'S *room and revealing* GANT'S *room. As it does so:*)

FATTY. Ben, what's your full name?

BEN. Benjamin Harrison Gant. Why?

FATTY. I though Ben was short for benign.

BEN. Benign! Listen to her!

(*They laugh. The lights come up in* GANT'S *bedroom.* ELIZA, *carrying a pitcher and a glass, enters.* GANT *is in bed, turned away from her.*)

GANT. Helen?

ELIZA (*bitterly*). No, it's not Helen, Mr. Gant. (*She pours a glass of water.*)

GANT (*without turning*). If that's water, take it away. (*She leaves glass and pitcher on dresser.*)

ELIZA. Why aren't you asleep? Do you have any pain?

GANT. None but the everyday pain of thinking. You wouldn't know what that is.

ELIZA. I wouldn't know? (*She starts picking up* GANT'S *strewn socks and shoes.*)

GANT. How could you? You're always so busy puttering.

ELIZA. All the work I do around here, and you call it puttering?

GANT. Some people are doers, some are thinkers.

ELIZA (*neatly rearranging his vest on the back of the chair*). Somebody has to *do,* Mr. Gant. Somebody has to. Oh! I know you look on yourself as some kind of artist fella—but personally, a man who has to be brought maudlin through the streets—screaming curses—if you call that artistic!

GANT. The hell hound is at it again. Shut up, woman!

ELIZA. Mr. Gant, I came in here to see if there was something I could do for you. Only pity in my heart. Now will you please turn over and look at me when I talk to you? You know I can't stand being turned away from!

GANT. You're a bloody monster, you would drink my heart's blood!

ELIZA. You don't mean that—we've come this far together; I guess we can continue to the end. (*Picks up socks she has placed on bed.*) You know I was thinking only this morning about that first day we met. Do you realize it was thirty-one years ago, come July?

GANT (*groaning*). Merciful God, thirty-one long miserable years!

ELIZA. I can remember like it was yesterday. I'd just come down from Cousin Sally's and I passed by your shop and there you were. I'll vow you looked as big as one of your tombstones—and as dusty —with a wild and dangerous look in your eye. You were romantic in those days— like the fellow says, a regular courtin' fool—"Miss Pentland," you said, "you have come into this hot and grubby shop like a cooling summer shower—like a cooling summer shower." That's just what you said!

GANT. And you've been a wet blanket ever since.

ELIZA. I forgive you your little jokes, Mr. Gant. I forgive your little jokes. (*She sits chair. Starts to fold his nightgown.*)

GANT. Do you? (*Slowly turns towards her and looks at her finally.*) Do you ever forgive me, Eliza? If I could make you understand something. I was such a strong man. I was dozing just now, dreaming of the past. The far past. The people and the place I came from. Those great barns of Pennsylvania. The order, the thrift, the plenty. It all started out so right, there. There I was a man who set out to get order and position in life. And what have I come to? Only rioting and confusion, searching and wandering. There was so much before, so much. Now it's all closing in. My God, Eliza, where has it all gone? Why am I here, now, at the rag end of my life? The years are all blotted and blurred—my youth a red waste —I've gotten old, an old man. But why here? Why here?

ELIZA. You belong here, Mr. Gant, that's why! You belong here. (*She touches his hand.*)

GANT (*throws away her hand*). And as I get weaker and weaker, you get stronger and stronger!

ELIZA (*rise, puts folded nightgown in dresser*). Pshaw! If you feel that way, it's because you have no position in life. If you'd ever listened to me once, things would have been different. You didn't believe me, did you, when I told you that little, old marble shop of yours would be worth a fortune some day? Will and I happened to be downtown this morning— (GANT *groans. Picks up his robe from bed.*)—and old Mr. Beecham from the bank stopped us on the street and he said, "Mrs. Gant, the bank is looking for a site to build a big new office building, and do you know the one we have our eye on?" And I said, "No." "We have our eye on Mr. Gant's shop, and we're willing to pay twenty thousand dollars for it!" Now what do you think of that? (*She sits chair, starts to mend robe.*)

GANT. And you came in here with only pity in your heart!

ELIZA. Well, I'll tell you what, twenty thousand dollars is a lot of money! Like the fellow says, "It ain't hay!"

GANT. And my angel, my Carrara angel? You were going to sell her too?

ELIZA. The angel, the angel, the angel! I'm so tired of hearing about that angel!

GANT. You always have been. Money dribbled from your honeyed lips. But never a word about my angel. I've started twenty pieces of marble trying to capture her. But my life's work doesn't interest you.

ELIZA. If you haven't been able to do it in all these years, don't you think your gift as a stone cutter may be limited?

GANT. Yes, Mrs. Gant, it may be limited. It may be limited.

ELIZA. Then why don't you sell the shop? We can pay off the mortgage at Dixieland and then just set back big as you please and live off the income from the boarders the rest of our lives!

GANT (*furiously, he all but leaps from the bed*). Oh, holy hell; Wow-ee! The boarders! That parade of incognito pimps and prostitutes, calling themselves penniless dancing masters, pining widows, part-time teachers and God knows what all! Woman, have mercy! That shop is my last refuge on earth. I beg you—let me die in peace! You won't have long to wait. You can do what you please with it after I'm gone. But give me a little comfort now. *And leave me my work!* At least my first wife understood what it meant to me. (*He sentimentally seeks the plump pillow.*) Cynthia, Cynthia . . .

ELIZA (*coldly*). You promised me you would never mention her name to me again. (*There is a long silence.* ELIZA *bites the sewing thread, rises and tosses robe on bed.*) Mr. Gant, I guess I never will understand you. I guess that's just the way it is. Good night. Try to get some sleep. (*She tucks the bed clothes about him.*) I reckon it's like the fellow says, some people never get to understand each other—not in this life. (*Exits and stands outside* GANT'S *door, trying to pull herself together.*)

GANT (*moans*). Oh-h-h, I curse the day I was given life by that blood-thirsty monster up above. Oh-h-h, Jesus! I beg of you. I know I've been bad. Forgive me. Have mercy and pity upon me. Give me another chance in Jesus' name. . . . Oh-h-h!

(*The turntable removes* GANT'S *room, replacing it with* EUGENE'S *room. Lights come up on the veranda.* LAURA *and* EUGENE *still sit on the side steps.* FATTY *and* BEN, *seated as earlier, are softly laughing.* ELIZA, *bitterly warped by her scene with* GANT, *enters. She starts gathering up the boarders' lemonade glasses.*)

MRS. PERT (*a little giddy*). Why, if it

isn't Mrs. Gant! Why don't you sit down and join us for a while?

ELIZA (*her sweeping glance takes in the beer glasses*). I've told you before, Mrs. Pert, I don't tolerate drinking at Dixieland!

BEN. Oh, Mama, for God's sake—

ELIZA. You two can be heard all over the house with your carrying on.

BEN. Carrying on—listen to her!

ELIZA (*angrily turns off phonograph*). You're keeping the boarders awake.

BEN. They just went in!

ELIZA. As I came past your door just now, Mrs. Pert, there was a light under it. If you're going to spend all night out here, there's no sense in wasting electricity.

BEN. The Lord said, "Let there be light," even if it's only 40 watts.

ELIZA. Don't you get on your high horse with me, Ben Gant. You're not the one who has to pay the bills! If you did, you'd laugh out of the other side of your mouth. I don't like any such talk. You've squandered every penny you've ever earned because you've never known the value of a dollar!

BEN. The value of a dollar! (*Rises, goes into hall to get his jacket.*) Oh what the hell's the use of it, anyway? Come on, Fatty, let's go for a stroll.

FATTY (*rises. Crosses to yard right of right pillar*). Whatever you say, Ben, old Fatty's willing.

ELIZA (*attacking* FATTY; *on step left of her*). I don't want any butt-ins from you, do you understand? You're just a paying boarder here. That's all. You're not a member of my family, and never will be, no matter what low methods you try!

EUGENE (*leaving* LAURA, *miserably*). Mama, please.

ELIZA (*crosses to* EUGENE). I'm only trying to keep decency and order here, and this is the thanks I get! You should all get down on your knees and be grateful to me!

BEN (*coming out of hall, slamming the screen door*). What am I supposed to be grateful for? For what?

FATTY (*trying to stop it*). Ben, Ben, come on.

BEN (*on step right of* ELIZA). For selling the house that Papa built with his own hands and moving us into this drafty barn where we share our roof, our food, our pleasures, our privacy so that you

can be Queen Bee? Is that what I'm supposed to be grateful for?

ELIZA (*picks up bottle and glasses from left of left pillar*). It's that vile liquor that's talking!

EUGENE. Let's stop it! For God's sake, let's stop it! Mama, go to bed, please. Ben— (*Sees that* LAURA *has exited into the house. He frantically looks after her.*)

BEN. Look at your kid there! You've had him out on the streets since he was eight years old—collecting bottles, selling papers —anything that would bring in a penny.

ELIZA. Gene is old enough to earn his keep!

BEN. Then he's old enough for you to let go of him! But no, you'd rather hang on to him like a piece of property! Maybe he'll grow in value, you can turn a quick trade on him, make a profit on him. He isn't a son, he's an investment! You're so penny-mad that— (*Shifting the bottles and glasses into one hand,* ELIZA *slaps* BEN. *There is a long silence. They stare at each other.*) Come on, Fatty. (BEN *exits, past* FATTY, *down the street.*)

FATTY. He didn't mean it, Mrs. Gant. (*She follows* BEN.) Ben? Ben, wait for Fatty! (*Exits.*)

EUGENE (*quietly, miserably*). Mama. Mama. Mama!

ELIZA. Well, she put him up to it! He never used to talk to me like that. You stood right there and saw it. Now I'll just ask you: was it my fault? Well, was it?

EUGENE (*looks after* LAURA). Mama, Mama, in God's name go to bed, won't you? Just go to bed and forget about it, won't you?

ELIZA (*crossing porch, placing bottles, glasses on tray*). All of you. Every single one of you. Your father, then Ben, now you—you all blame me. And not one of you has any idea, any idea—you don't know what I've had to put up with all these years.

EUGENE. Oh Mama, stop! Please stop!

ELIZA (*sinking onto the steps left of right pillar*). I've done the best I could. I've done the best I could. Your father's never given me a moment's peace. Nobody knows what I've been through with him. Nobody knows, child, nobody knows.

EUGENE (*sits beside her*). I know, Mama. I do know. Forget about it! It's all right.

ELIZA. You just can't realize. You don't

know what a day like this does to me. Ben and I used to be so close—especially after little Grover died. I don't think a mother and son were ever closer. You don't remember when he was a youngster, the little notes he was always writing me. I'd find them slipped under my door, when he got up early to go on his paper route. . . . "Good morning, Mama!" . . . "Have a nice day; Mama." We were so close . . .

EUGENE (*gently*). It's late. You're tired.

ELIZA (*managing to pull herself together*). Well, like the fellow says, it's no use crying over *that* spilt milk. I have all those napkins and towels to iron for tomorrow.

EUGENE (*rises, looking toward* LAURA's *room*). The boarders can get along without new napkins tomorrow. Mama, why don't you get some sleep?

ELIZA (*rises*). Well, I tell you what: I'm not going to spend my life slaving away here for a bunch of boarders. They needn't think it. I'm going to sit back and take things as easy as any of them. One of these days you may just find us Gants living in a big house in Doak Park. I've got the lot—the best lot out there. I made the trade with old Mr. Doak himself the other day. What about that? (*She laughs.*) He said, "Mrs. Gant, I can't trust any of my agents with you. If I'm to make anything on this deal, I've got to look out. You're the sharpest trader in this town!" "Why, pshaw, Mr. Doak," I said (I never let on I believed him or anything), "all I want is a fair return on my investment. I believe in everyone making his profit and giving the other fellow a chance. Keep the ball a-rolling," I said, laughing as big as you please! (*She laughs again in recollection.*) "You're the sharpest trader in this town." That's exactly his words. Oh, dear— (EUGENE *joins her laughter.*) Well—I'd better get at those napkins. Are you coming in, child?

EUGENE (*rises, looks toward* LAURA's *room*). In a little while.

ELIZA. Don't forget to turn off the sign. Good night, son. (EUGENE *returns to* ELIZA. *She kisses him.*) Get a *good* night's sleep, boy. You mustn't neglect your health. (*She starts in.*)

EUGENE. Don't work too late. (*Starts toward the side door.*)

ELIZA. Gene, you know where Sunset Terrace runs up the hill? At the top of the rise? Right above Dick Webster's place. That's my lot. You know where I mean, don't you?

EUGENE. Yes, Mama.

ELIZA. And that's where we'll build— right on the very top. I tell you what, though, in another five years that lot'll bring twice the value. You mark my words!

EUGENE. Yes, Mama. Now, for God's sake, go and finish your work so you can get to sleep!

ELIZA. No sir, they needn't think I'm going to slave away all my life. I've got plans, same as the next fellow! You'll see. (*Offstage, the church chimes start to sound the midnight hour.*) Well, good night, son.

EUGENE. Good night, Mama. . . . (ELIZA *exits.* EUGENE *calls with desperate softness.*) Laura—Laura! (*Gives up, turns away.* LAURA *enters through the side door.* EUGENE *turns, sees her.*) Did you hear all that? I'm sorry, Laura.

LAURA. What's there to be sorry about?

EUGENE. Would you like to take a walk?

LAURA. It's a lovely evening.

EUGENE. It might rain.

LAURA. I love the rain.

(EUGENE *and* LAURA *hold out their hands to each other.* EUGENE *approaches her, takes her hand. They go off together D. L. For a moment the stage is silent.* ELIZA *enters with an envelope in her hand.*)

ELIZA. See, looky here—I made a map of it. Sunset Terrace goes— (*She looks around.*) Gene? Eugene? (*She looks up towards* EUGENE's *room.*) Gene, I asked you to turn out the sign! That boy. I don't know what I'm going to do with him. (*Goes into the hall, turns out the sign and stands for a moment. Offstage, a passerby is whistling "Genevieve."* ELIZA *comes down to the edge of the veranda and looks out into the night in the direction taken by* BEN *and* FATTY.) Ben? Ben?

SLOW CURTAIN

ACT TWO

SCENE ONE

SCENE: GANT's *marble yard and shop, a week later. Under a high wide shed is the sign:* W. O. GANT—STONE CARVER. *The shed is on a back street, behind the town square. In the distance can be seen the outline of Dixieland. Inside the shed, are slabs of marble and granite and some finished monuments—an urn, a couchant lamb and several angels. The largest and most prominent monument is a delicately carved angel of a lustrous white Carrara marble, with an especially beautiful smiling countenance. There is a cutting area down right, protected from the sun by a shade, where* EUGENE, *wearing one of his father's aprons, is discovered operating a pedalled emery wheel. At the other side of the shed is an office with a grimy desk, a telephone, and a curtain into another room beyond. A sidewalk runs between the shed and a picket fence upstage. Near the office is a stone seat, bearing the inscription, "Rest here in peace."* ELIZA *enters from the street right. The prim shabbiness of her dress is in contrast to her energetic mood and walk.*

ELIZA (*crosses to office, calls inside*). Mr. Gant! Mr. Gant!

EUGENE (*stops wheel, calls*). Papa's not here now, Mama.

ELIZA (*approaches* EUGENE *just as he accidentally blows some marble dust in her face*). Where is he? Gene, you know I can't stand that marble dust—will you step out here where I can talk to you? Besides, I can't stand not to see the face I'm talking to. My goodness, spruce up, boy—how many times do I have to tell you? Shoulders back—like you *are* somebody. And smile, look pleasant. (EUGENE *gives that idiotic grin.* ELIZA *indicates Laughran is off up left.*) O pshaw! I hope your father's not over at you-know-where again.

EUGENE. He went to buy a newspaper for the obituaries.

ELIZA. How enterprising of him! But he won't follow up on it. Oh no, he says it's ghoulish to contact the bereaved ones right off. I declare, tombstones are no business anyway, any more—in this day and age people die too slowly. (EUGENE *crosses with stencil letter and chalk to left of center table.* ELIZA *sinks onto stone seat, leans back; for a brief instant seems actually to rest.*) I tell you what, this feels good. I wish I had as much time as some folks and could sit outside and enjoy the air. (*Notices* EUGENE *looking at her dress,*

as he works lettering a marble slab.) What are you looking at? I don't have a rent, do I?

EUGENE. I was just noticing you have on your dealing and bargaining costume again.

ELIZA. Eugene Gant, whatever do you mean by that? Don't I look all right? Heaven knows, I always try to look neatly respectable.

EUGENE (*crosses to right unit for chalk*). Come on, Mama.

ELIZA. What! I declare! I might have a better dress than this, but law's sake, there's some places it don't pay to advertise it! Oh, Gene, you're smart, smart, I tell you! You've got a future ahead of you, child.

EUGENE (*crossing to left of center table*). Mama, what kind of a future have I got if I can't get an education?

ELIZA. Pshaw, boy, you'll get your education if my plans work out! I'll tell you what, though—in the meantime, it wouldn't hurt you to work in Uncle Will's office, would it?

EUGENE (*working*). I don't know anything about real estate, Mama.

ELIZA. What do you have to know? Buying and selling is an instinct, and you've got it. You've got my eye for looking and seeing and remembering, and that's what's important. Why there isn't a vital statistic about a soul in Altamont I don't carry right in my head. What they make, what they owe—what they're hiding, what they show! (GENE *crosses to right unit for stencil letter and then back to Center table. She laughs, enjoying her cleverness.*) You see, Eugene, I'm a poet, too—"a poet and I don't know it, but my feet show it—they're longfellows!" (*She leans back, chuckles.*) Oh dear, I can't get a smile out of you this morning. You've been so strange all this last week. (*Rises, slaps him on his back.*) Gene, stand with your shoulders back. If you go humped over, you'll get lung trouble sure as you're born. (*Moves upstage, looks toward the town center where she presumes* GANT *is.*) That's one thing about your papa: he always carried himself straight as a rod. Of course, he's not as straight now as he used to be— Gene, *what* in the world are you standing on one foot and then the other for? Do you have to go to the bathroom?

EUGENE. Mama! Asking me that at my age!

ELIZA. Then why are you fidgeting? It's not often we have a nice chance to chat like this.

EUGENE. Papa's paying me thirty cents an hour!

ELIZA. Paying you? How did you manage that?

EUGENE. I told him I needed the money.

ELIZA. For heaven's sake, what for? You've got your room and board.

EUGENE. Don't you think I need new clothes for one thing?

ELIZA. Pshaw! The way you're still growing? It doesn't pay. (EUGENE *returns to work. She purses her lips, looks at him significantly.*) Has my baby gone and got himself a girl?

EUGENE (*exasperated, sits on table*). What of it? What if it were true? Haven't I as much right as anyone?

ELIZA. Pshaw! You're too young to think of girls, especially that Miss James. She's practically a mature woman compared to you. I don't think you realize how young you are, just because you're tall and read a lot of books. (*Sounds of car off right.* ELIZA *looks off.*) Pshaw! That's your Uncle Will come for me. Say, how long does it take your father to buy a newspaper, anyway?

EUGENE. He said he'd be right back. Is it something important?

ELIZA (*crosses for purse and stole she has left on bench*). Oh, I've got plans, Gene, for him, plans for all of us. Well, tell him I'll be back. Second thought, don't tell him, I'll just catch him. I want you to be here, too. Work hard, child!

(ELIZA *exits, the car leaves.* EUGENE *approaches the Carrara angel, touches the draped folds over her breast.* GANT *enters upper left, watches smiling. He has had a few beers, but he is not drunk.* EUGENE *becomes aware of* GANT's *presence, starts guiltily. Crosses down right.*)

GANT (*crossing to angel*). I've done that myself many a time, son. Many a time. Well, what did your mother have to say?

EUGENE. Did you see her?

GANT (*crossing to unit left for apron*). I've been sitting over at Laughran's waiting for her to leave. What a long-winded bag!

EUGENE. You promised the doctor you wouldn't go to Laughran's.

GANT (*putting on his apron*). What difference does it make? A couple of beers won't hurt what I've got. Was that Will Pentland she went off with?

EUGENE. Yes.

GANT (*upper left center*). Aha! And she said she'd be back?

EUGENE. Yes.

GANT. I have a mind what she's up to. She'll be back with freshly drawn-up papers tucked in her bosom. Yes, when you touch the breast of Miss Eliza, you feel the sharp crackle of bills of sale— (*Crosses to angel.*) not like the bosom of this angel. She begins to look better after a bath, doesn't she? I've been neglecting her lately. My, how she gleams!

EUGENE (*sits below angel*). Papa, you were young when you got married, weren't you?

GANT. What?

EUGENE. When did you get married?

GANT (*crossing to left of center table to work*). It was thirty-one bitter years ago when your mother first came wriggling around that corner at me like a snake on her belly—

EUGENE. I don't mean Mama. How old were you when you were first married? To Cynthia?

GANT. By God, you better not let your mother hear you say that name!

EUGENE. I want to know—how old were you?

GANT (*crossing down right center*). Well, I must have been twenty-eight. Ah, Cynthia, Cynthia!

EUGENE. You loved her, didn't you, Papa?

GANT. She had a real glowing beauty. Sweet, noble, proud, and yet soft, soft— she died in her bloom.

EUGENE. She was older than you, wasn't she?

GANT. Yes. Ten years.

EUGENE. Ten years! But it didn't make any difference, did it?

GANT (*confidingly*). She was a skinny, mean, tubercular old hag who nearly drove me out of my mind! (*Crosses to center table to work.*)

EUGENE (*shocked*). Then why do you talk about her the way you do? To Mama?

GANT. Because I'm a bastard, Gene. I'm a bastard! (LAURA *enters upper right carrying a picnic basket, her mood some-*

what restless.) Say, isn't this a pretty little somebody looking for you?

EUGENE (*crosses to her*). Laura!

LAURA (*left of* GANT). Hello, Mr. Gant.

GANT. Hello!

LAURA (*crossing to right of angel*). Hello, Gene. So this is your shop?

GANT (*a step toward her*). This is a real pleasure. It's not often I see *smiling* people around here. Haven't you got fed up with our little resort, young lady?

LAURA. I'm really just beginning to enjoy it here.

GANT. What do you find to enjoy about it?

LAURA. Oh, the countryside is beautiful. Gene and I have had lots of pleasant walks in the hills.

GANT. Oh, so it's Gene who makes it pleasant for you, hey?

EUGENE. Come on, Papa! Hah, hah— (*Embarrassed laugh and turns away.*)

GANT. You're fond of Gene, aren't you?

LAURA. He's very nice and intelligent.

GANT. Gene's a good boy—our best.

LAURA (*looking around*). My, isn't this shop interesting? How did you happen to become a stone cutter, Mr. Gant?

(EUGENE *puts apron on bench, studies* LAURA *during this, sensing her evasiveness to him.*)

GANT. Well, I guess you'd call it a passion with some people. When I was a boy Gene's age, I happened to pass a shop something like this. (*Of the angel*) And this very angel was there. She's Carrara marble— (*Sits right on center table.*) from Italy. And as I looked at her smiling face, I felt, more than anything in the world, I wanted to carve delicately with a chisel. It was as though, if I could do that, I could bring something of me out onto a piece of marble. Oh, the reminiscences of the old always bore the young.

LAURA. No, they don't.

GANT. So I walked into that shop, and asked the stone cutter if I could become an apprentice. Well, I worked there for five years. When I left, I bought the angel. (*He looks at the angel with longing.*) I've hardly had her out of my sight, since. I bet I've started twenty pieces of marble, but I've never been able to capture her. . . . I guess there's no use trying any more— (*He becomes silent, morose. Sensitively* EUGENE *touches* GANT's *shoulder, looks at* LAURA.)

EUGENE. Would you like to look around, Laura?

LAURA. I'm afraid I'm bothering you at your work.

GANT (*looks at* EUGENE, *coming out of his distant thought and mood*). No, no. Show her about, Gene. (*Suddenly decisive.*) I have some other things I must do—(*Starts toward office, pauses.*)—though some people find looking at tombstones depressing. Still we all come to them in the end. (GANT *exits.*)

EUGENE. Why do you think you might be bothering me?

LAURA. You are supposed to be working.

EUGENE (*a step to her*). You came here to see me. What's happened, Laura? Something's different today.

LAURA (*crossing left, puts picnic basket on marble slab down right*). Oh, don't pay any attention to me. I just—I don't know.

EUGENE. What's in the basket?

LAURA. I asked Helen to pack us a picnic lunch.

EUGENE (*crosses for basket and takes her hand*). Good! Let's go!

LAURA (*pulling away*). Not now.

EUGENE (*puts his arm around her*). What is it, Laura? What's the matter? Have I done something wrong?

LAURA (*shakes her head*). Gene, Helen knows about us! And your father too. He—

EUGENE. I don't care—I want the whole world to know. (*Picks up basket.*) Here, let's go.

LAURA (*pulling away*). No. Let's not talk about it. (*Sits on stool, near slab.*) This is pretty marble. Where's it from?

EUGENE. Laura, you don't give a damn where that marble came from!

LAURA (*starts to cry*). Oh, Gene, I'm so ashamed, so ashamed.

EUGENE (*sits beside her on slab*). Laura, my darling, what is it?

LAURA. Gene, I lied to you—I'm twenty-three years old.

EUGENE. Is that all?

LAURA. You're not nineteen either. You're seventeen.

EUGENE. I'm a thousand years old, all the love I've stored up for you. (*Again puts his arms around her.*)

LAURA (*struggling away*). I'm an older woman—

EUGENE. In God's name, what does that have to do with us?

LAURA. There have to be rules!

EUGENE. Rules are made by jealous people. They make rules to love by so even those with no talent for it can at least pretend. We don't need rules. We don't have to pretend. Oh, Laura, my sweet, what we have is so beautiful, so rare . . . how often in life can you find it?

LAURA (*escaping his arms, rises, crosses down right center and turns to him*). Eugene, you're a young boy, a whole world just waiting for you.

EUGENE. You are my world, Laura. You always will be. Don't let anything destroy us. Don't leave me alone. I've always been alone.

LAURA. It's what you want, dear. It's what you'll always want. You couldn't stand anything else. You'd get so tired of me. You'll forget—you'll forget.

EUGENE. I'll never forget. I won't live long enough. (*Takes her in his arms, kisses her.*) Will you forget?

LAURA (*as he holds her*). Oh my darling, every word, every touch, how could I?

EUGENE. Then nothing has changed. Has it? Has it?

MADAME ELIZABETH'S VOICE (*off*). Good morning! (MADAME ELIZABETH, *38, the town madame, enters along the street upper left. She is well-clad, carries herself stylishly. She sees* EUGENE *and* LAURA, *stops as they break from each other.*)

EUGENE. Good morning, Madame Elizabeth.

MADAME ELIZABETH (*closing her parasol*). Is Mr. Gant here?

EUGENE. He's inside.

MADAME ELIZABETH. Well, don't let me keep you from what you're doing. (*Approaches office, calls.*) Mr. Gant! (*Places parasol down left of bench. Crosses to angel.*)

(LAURA *and* EUGENE *exit into yard down right.* GENE *carrying off down right stool.* GANT, *changed into another, better pair of trousers, tying his tie, enters.*)

GANT. Elizabeth, my dear Elizabeth! Well, this is a surprise! (*Seizes her hands.*)

MADAME ELIZABETH (*sentimentally looking him over*). Six years, W.O. Six years —except to nod to. Time, what a thief you are.

GANT. He hasn't stolen from you— you're still as handsome and stylish as ever. Won't you sit down?

MADAME ELIZABETH (*crossing to bench down left center*). Oh, W.O.—you and your gallant manners. But I'm no chicken any more, and no one knows it better than I do. If you only knew how often we talk about you up on Eagle Crescent. What a man you were! Wild! Bacchus himself. You remember the song you used to sing?

GANT. Life was many songs in those days, Elizabeth.

MADAME ELIZABETH. But when you got liquored up enough—don't you remember? Of course I can't boom it out like you do. (*Sings, imitating* GANT. GANT *joins her.*)
"Up in that back room, boys,
Up in *that* back room
All those kisses and those hugs
Among the fleas and bugs
In the evening's gloom, boys,
I pity your sad doom.
Up in that back room, boys,
Up in *that* back room."
(*Both laugh.* GANT *gives her an affectionate fanny slap.*)

GANT. The loss of all that, that's the worst, Elizabeth.

MADAME ELIZABETH (*sitting on the bench downstage*). Oh, W.O., W.O.! We do miss you.

GANT (*joining her on the bench*). How are all the girls, Elizabeth?

MADAME ELIZABETH (*suddenly distressed*). That's what I came to see you about. I lost one of them last night. (*Takes handkerchief from her pocket, quietly cries into it.*)

GANT. Oh. I'm sorry to hear that.

MADAME ELIZABETH. Sick only three days. I'd have done anything in the world for her. A doctor and two trained nurses by her all the time.

GANT. Too bad. Too bad. Which one was it?

MADAME ELIZABETH. Since your time, W.O. We called her Lily.

GANT. Tch—tch—tch! Lily.

MADAME ELIZABETH. I couldn't have loved her more if she had been my own daughter. Twenty-two. A child, a mere child. And not a relative who would do anything for her. Her mother died when she was thirteen, and her father is a mean old bastard who wouldn't even come to her death-bed.

GANT. He will be punished.

MADAME ELIZABETH. As sure as there's a God in heaven—the old bastard! I hope he rots! Such a fine girl, such a bright future for her. She had more opportunities than I ever had—and you know what I've done here. I'm a rich woman today, W.O. Why, not even your wife owns more property than I do. I beg your pardon—I hope you don't mind my speaking of her— (GANT *gestures to go right ahead.*) Mrs. Gant and I both understand that property is what makes a person hold one's head up! And Lily could have had all that too. Poor Lily! No one knows how much I'll miss her. (*A moment's quiet.* GANT *is respecting her grief.*)

GANT. There! There! (*As he comfortingly pats her hand*) I suppose you'll be wanting something for her grave? (*As* MADAME ELIZABETH *nods, he rises, crossing to left of lamb.*) Here's a sweet lamb—*couchant* lamb, it's called. "Couchant" means lying-down in French. That should be appropriate.

MADAME ELIZABETH. No, I've already made up my mind— (*Rises, moves toward the Carrara angel.*) I want that angel.

GANT (*crosses to left of her*). You don't want *her*, Elizabeth. Why, she's a white elephant. Nobody can afford to buy her!

MADAME ELIZABETH. I can and I want her.

GANT (*crossing right*). My dear Elizabeth, I have other fine angels. What about this one? My own carving.

MADAME ELIZABETH. No. Ever since I first saw that angel, I thought, when somebody who means something to me goes, she's going to be on the grave.

GANT. That angel's not for sale, Elizabeth.

MADAME ELIZABETH. Then why should you have her out here?

GANT. The truth is, I've promised her to someone.

MADAME ELIZABETH (*crossing to bench for her purse then back to angel*). I'll buy her from whoever you promised and give them a profit. Cash on the line. Who did you sell it to?

GANT (*crossing to right of her with urn*). My dear Madame Elizabeth, here is a nice expensive Egyptian urn. Your beloved Lily would like that.

MADAME ELIZABETH. Egyptian urns—pah! Pee pots! I want the angel!

GANT (*with growing intensity, angrily replaces urn on unit*). It's not for sale! Anything you like—*everything* you like—I'll give it to you—I'll make you a present, for old times' sake. But not my angel!

MADAME ELIZABETH. Now, let's not waste any more time over this. How much, W.O.?

GANT. She's Carrara marble from Italy, and too good for any whore! (*He calls.*) Eugene—Eugene!

MADAME ELIZABETH (*furious*). Why you old libertine, how dare you speak to me like that?

EUGENE (*entering, with* LAURA). What is it, Father? What's the matter?

MADAME ELIZABETH. Your father's a stubborn old nut, that's what!

GANT (*crosses toward office, turns*). I'm sorry if I've offended you.

MADAME ELIZABETH. You have, W.O., deeply!

GANT. Gene, will you be so kind and see if you can wait upon the Madame? (*Exits into the inner room of the office.*)

MADAME ELIZABETH (*crossing left*). I've heard the trouble your mother has with the old terror—now I believe it! All I'm asking is that he sells me that angel—for one of my dear girls who's gone—a dear, young girl in the flower of her life—(*Of* LAURA) like this young girl here—

EUGENE (*upper center*). Madame Elizabeth, I believe Papa is saving that angel for his own grave.

MADAME ELIZABETH (*sits on bench*). Oh-h-h, why didn't he say so? Why didn't he tell me? Poor, poor W.O. Well, of course in that case— (*She partially recovers; to* LAURA.) If you were to think of *your* death, dear—if you can, I mean, and we never know, we never know—is there something here that would appeal to you?

LAURA (*crosses to right of center table. Looks around*). I like the little lamb.

MADAME ELIZABETH. Lambs are for children, aren't they?

EUGENE (*stoops left of lamb*). Lambs are for anybody. Put your hand on it. Feel it. (MADAME ELIZABETH's *hand strokes across the lamb.*) Isn't it cool and content and restful? And you could have a poem engraved on the base.

MADAME ELIZABETH. A poem—

EUGENE. Let's see if we can find something you'd like. (*Picks up book from desk.*) Here's a book of Fifty Fine Memorial Poems. (MADAME ELIZABETH *still strokes the lamb;* EUGENE *finds a poem.*) See if you like this— (*Reads.*)
"She went away in beauty's flower,
Before her youth was spent;
Ere life and love had lived their hour,
God called her—and she went."
(MADAME ELIZABETH *sobs.*)
"Yet whispers faith upon the wind;
No grief to her was given.
She left your love and went to find
A greater one in heaven."

MADAME ELIZABETH (*quoting, through her heartfelt tears*). "She left *your* love and went to find a greater one in heaven. . . ." (*Rises, addresses* EUGENE.) I hope you never lose someone you love, boy. (*Gets parasol.*) Well, let me know when the little lying-down lamb is ready. (*She nods with majestic dignity to* LAURA, *exits.* WILL *and* ELIZA *enter, look off in the direction taken by* MADAME ELIZABETH.)

ELIZA. Don't stare after her, Will! You know who that is. (*To* EUGENE) Was that shameless woman here to see your father?

EUGENE. One of the girls at Eagle Crescent died. She bought a monument.

ELIZA. Oh she did! She bought one! Well, your father certainly has to deal with all kinds of people. Will, go in and tell Mr. Gant that we're here. (WILL *exits.* ELIZA *looks at* LAURA.) Oh, Miss James, it's five minutes to dinner time at Dixieland, and you know the rules about being late.

EUGENE (*crosses to pick up basket*). Laura and I are going on a picnic.

ELIZA. Not now, you're not. (*To* LAURA) My dear, I want to talk privately to Mr. Gant—to Eugene, too, and I've asked Ben to join us.

EUGENE. We've made plans, Mama.

ELIZA (*beside bench*). Son, this is a family conference.

LAURA. Gene, please—I'll wait for you over at Woodruff's. Please. (LAURA *and* EUGENE *stroll off up right whispering.* WILL *enters from office paring his nails.*)

ELIZA. Is he in there?

WILL. He's there. We've got him cornered. (*They chuckle.* BEN, *looking feverish and ill, enters up left.*)

BEN. Hello, Uncle Will. Hello, Mama—you look like you just swallowed fifty or a hundred acres. What did you buy today?

ELIZA. Now, Ben, it just happens that today we're selling—I hope we are, anyway.

BEN. What's it all about?

ELIZA (*crossing to center*). You just sit down there. I may not need you, but I want you to be here.

BEN (*sits beneath the angel*). I hope it won't take long.

GANT (*enters. He wears a coat of carefully brushed black wool, a tie, and carries his hat which he leaves just inside the office*). Good morning, Miss Eliza.

ELIZA. My, how elegant! Aren't we burning a river this morning?

GANT (*places hat on office stool, crosses to left of center table*). I heard you were out here, Miss Eliza. I so seldom have a visit from you! (*He gestures the tribute.*)

ELIZA. That's most gracious. You may all sit down now. Gene! Will! (EUGENE *enters, sits on center table.* WILL *sits on office step.* GANT *moves a chair to center.*) Now, Mr. Gant—

GANT (*as he places chair left of center table and sits*). This isn't one of your temperance meetings?

ELIZA (*a bit surprised. Putting stole and purse on bench*). Our private temperance problem—that's a part of it, yes. Mr. Gant, how old are you?

GANT. I've lost track.

ELIZA. You're sixty years old in December. And if Dr. Maguire were here, he could tell you—

GANT. I've heard what Doc Maguire has to tell me. I shouldn't be lifting these marbles. I shouldn't be drinking liquor. I should take a nice long rest.

ELIZA. Then you save me a great deal of argument about that. Now, Gene— (*Crosses over to* EUGENE *above center table.*)

EUGENE. Yes, Mama? (*Rises.*)

ELIZA. You want to go to college, don't you?

EUGENE. Very much.

ELIZA. Well, I figure that four years at Chapel Hill will cost thirty-four hundred dollars—but of course you'll have to wait on table. Otherwise it would be forty-four hundred dollars, which is ridiculous

—at the moment we don't even have thirty-four hundred dollars—

GANT. Oh, for God's sake, get to the point, Miss Eliza. Have you got the papers from the bank?

ELIZA (*crosses to left of him*). Why, what do you mean, what papers?

GANT. You know what I mean. Fish for them, woman! (*Pointing to her bosom.*) *Go ahead, fish for them.* (ELIZA *turns her back, from her bosom fishes out a large envelope.* GANT *laughs, a roaring bitter laugh, leaps up to* EUGENE *who joins the laughter.*)

ELIZA (*angrily*). What in the world are you two hyenas laughing at?

GANT. Oh, as you would say, Miss Eliza, that's a good one, that's a *good* one.

ELIZA. Well, I am glad to see you in a *good* mood.

GANT (*crossing down right center*). So the bank wants this little old lot, here? That's what you told me, didn't you? Though I can't for the life of me see why.

WILL. There's a new business street going through here in a few months.

GANT (*crosses to right of her*). Let me see the check.

ELIZA (*takes check from envelope, hands it to him*). Well, it's for twenty thousand dollars. Will had to guarantee it personally for me to bring it here. Did you ever see anything like it? Two, zero, coma, zero—zero—zero—decimal—zero—zero!

GANT. "W. O. Gant." It seems to be in good order, all right.

ELIZA. Well—it is—and Will's looked over this deed, and it's all in order too, isn't it, Will? (*Hands the deed to* GANT.) Give me your pen, Will.

WILL (*hands* ELIZA *the pen*). And I just had it filled.

GANT (*examining the deed. Crosses, sits center*). This fine print—I really do need glasses.

ELIZA. You can trust Will. (*Puts pen on work table.*) He's been all over it, Mr. Gant!

WILL (*looks at angel*). What about the marble stock and the monuments?

ELIZA. They're not included.

EUGENE. Papa—the years you've spent here—all your fine work. Please don't give it up.

ELIZA. Now, Gene, your father knows what he's doing.

EUGENE. But he's such a fine stone cutter!

GANT. You think my work is fine, son?

EUGENE. Isn't it, Ben? (GANT *crosses down right into the marble yard, looking about.*)

ELIZA. Your father knows his duty to all of us—and to himself—

EUGENE. There isn't a cemetery in the state that isn't filled with his work—you can always recognize it. Clean, and pure and beautiful. Why should he give it up?

ELIZA. Why, law, I don't say he should give it up entirely. He can have another little shop further out of town!

EUGENE. But he's too old to transplant now, Mama. This is his street. Everyone knows him here. People pass by. Mr. Jannadeau's shop next door, and Woodruff's across the way—All the people and places Papa knows!

GANT. And Tim Laughran's down the block!

ELIZA (*crosses down to* GANT). Oh, yes. That's another reason for getting rid of this place. Put yourself out of temptation's way, Mr. Gant.

GANT (*sits on slab*). I certainly do love it here.

EUGENE. Don't give it up, Papa.

BEN. What do you want to do to him, Mama?

ELIZA. Now, looky here—you are a fine stone cutter—why, haven't I always said so? But it's time you rested. You want to live a long time, don't you? (*Sits beside him on slab.*)

GANT. Well, sometimes, I'm not sure.

ELIZA. Well, you do—and I want you to live a long time—we all want to! People can talk about a short but sweet life, but we all want to live! Look at me, I'm fifty-seven years old. I've borne nine children, raised six of them, and worked hard all my life. I'd like to back up and rest a little myself. And we can, Mr. Gant. If you'll just sign that little slip of paper. I guarantee, in a year from now, you'll have completely forgotten this dingy, crooked, dusty yard. Won't he, Ben? Won't he? Ben!

BEN. Some people have trouble forgetting some things, Mama.

ELIZA. Why, pshaw, I'm going to *see* to it that he forgets it. I'll have time to look after you. Won't I, Mr. Gant?

GANT. You're right about one thing, Miss Eliza—that I can't dispute. You have worked hard. (*Rises, moves to center work table.*)

EUGENE. Papa, please, don't do it. (GANT *sits at work table, signs the deed.* ELIZA *crosses to him, picks it up.*)

ELIZA. Thank you, Mr. Gant. Now the check. You know what I'm going to do? I'm going to plan a great, glorious celebration. (*Gives the deed to* WILL, *speaks to* EUGENE.) We'll ask your brother Luke to come home, if the Navy will let him out. And we'll invite Stevie, and Daisy and her husband, too, except if she brings those whiny children of hers. (*Notices* GANT *just looking at the check.*) Turn it over, Mr. Gant. Sign it on the back.

GANT. Why do I have to sign it?

ELIZA. Endorse it, that's all. "W. O. Gant," like it's written on the front of the check.

GANT. That can wait until I offer it, can't it?

ELIZA. To clear the check, Mr. Gant!

GANT. I'm not used to these things. How do you clear it?

ELIZA. You sign it—I'll deposit it in the Dixieland account, then we draw checks on it.

GANT. We?

ELIZA. Yes. You draw what you want. I'll draw what we need for Gene's college —for Dixieland, and for anything else we need.

GANT (*rises, crosses to office*). I think I'll wait to cash it until I get to Chapel Hill. The bank has a branch there, doesn't it, Will? (*Gives* WILL *his pen.*)

ELIZA. Why would you want to cash it in Chapel Hill?

GANT. This is my check, isn't it? I'm the one who had the foresight to buy this little pie-cornered lot thirty-one years ago for four hundred dollars—money from the estate of Cynthia L. Gant, deceased. I guess I'm entitled to the profit.

ELIZA. Now, Mr. Gant, if you're thinking to get my dander up!

GANT (*picks up hat, puts it on*). Miss Eliza, I've been wanting to get away from here for a long time. I'm taking Gene with me. (*Crosses to* EUGENE.) I'm going to put him in that college there at Chapel Hill.

EUGENE. Now?

GANT. Now! And then I'm going to travel—and when Gene's free in the summer, we'll travel together. (*Crosses back to* ELIZA.) And there's nothing in this whole wide world that you're going to do to stop me. And I can just see the word Dixieland forming on your cursed lips. What about Dixieland? Nothing for Dixieland? *No, not one god-damn red cent!* You've plenty of property of your own you can sell. If it's rest and comfort you really want, sell it, woman, sell it! But I think you like working hard, because then that makes us all feel sorry for you. And I do feel sorry for you too, from the bottom of my heart. (*Puts check in pocket.*) Well, Eugene!

EUGENE. Papa, I can't go now.

GANT. Why not? You haven't got any better clothes . . . so you might as well go as you are. I guess we'll say our good-byes. (*Addresses the angel.*) So long, dear Carrara angel. I'll arrange for us to be together again some day. Good-bye, Ben— Tell Helen—tell Helen I'll write to her. (*Shakes hands with* BEN.)

ELIZA (*leaping at* GANT). I won't let you do this. I won't let you.

EUGENE. MAMA!

ELIZA (*seizes check from* GANT's *pocket, tears it up, flings it on the ground*). All right, all right, all right! There's your check. I guess there's nothing to prevent you from going to the bank and trying to get another check, but it won't work because I'm going to put an injunction against you. I'll prove you're not responsible to sell this property, or even to own it. I'll get guardianship over you! Everyone knows the times you've been to the cure—the threats you've made to me —the times you've tried to kill me—I'll tell them. You're a madman, Mr. Gant, a madman. You're not going to get away with this. I'll fight you tooth and nail, tooth and nail. And I'll win. (*Trembling, she picks up her handbag from the stone seat.*)

GANT. All the things you've said about me are true, Eliza. I've only brought you pain. Why don't you let me go?

ELIZA. Because you're my husband, Mr. Gant! You're my husband. Thirty-one years together and we'll go on—we must go on. A house divided against itself cannot stand. We must try to understand and love each other. We must try. . . . (*Exits up right.*)

GANT (*quietly*). Take her home, will you, Will? (WILL *hurries after* ELIZA. *A long moment.* BEN, *weak and feverish, dries his forehead with his handkerchief.* GANT *sinks into a chair.*) Eugene, go over to Laughran's and get me a bottle. You heard me.

EUGENE. No, Papa.

GANT. Are you still paddling along after your mother?

BEN. Leave Gene alone. If you want to get sick, do it yourself.

GANT. Ungrateful sons! Oh, the sad waste of years, the red wound of all our mistakes. (*Rises, exits up left.* EUGENE *looks after him.*)

BEN. The fallen Titan. He might have succeeded if he hadn't tried to take you. He could still make it, but he won't try again.

EUGENE. They loved each other once. They must have had one moment in time that was perfect. What happened? It frightens me, Ben; how can something so perfect turn into this torture?

BEN. They're strangers. They don't know each other. No one ever really comes to know anyone.

EUGENE (*sits center table*). That's not true. I know you—I know Laura.

BEN. Listen to him! No matter what arms may clasp us, what heart may warm us, what mouth may kiss us, we remain strangers. We never escape it. Never, never, never. (*Closes eyes, leans back.*)

EUGENE. Ben! Hey, Ben? (*Worriedly crosses down to* BEN, *feels his face.*) Ben, you're burning up! Come on— (*Tries to lift him.*) Put your arms around me. I'm going to take you home.

BEN (*sinks back*). Can't. It's all right, I'm just tired.

EUGENE (*takes* BEN's *coat from his lap and puts it around his shoulders*). Why didn't you tell somebody you're sick, you crazy idiot! (*Again tries to lift* BEN.)

BEN. To hell with them, Gene. To hell with them all. Don't give a damn for anything. Nothing gives a damn for you. There are a lot of bad days, there are a lot of good ones— (EUGENE *rushes into the office, picks up the telephone.*) That's all there is . . . a lot of days . . . My God, is there no freedom on this earth?

EUGENE (*into telephone*). Get me Dr. Maguire quickly. *It's my brother Ben!*

BEN (*stirs, in anguish, looks up at the Carrara angel*). And still you smile. . . .

CURTAIN

ACT TWO

SCENE TWO

SCENE: *The Dixieland Boarding House; the next night. A painful tenseness grips the house.* LAURA *and* EUGENE *sit together on the yard seat down left.* MRS. PERT *sits motionless in a rocker near the front door.* HUGH *slowly walks about. The inside hall is lighted; as is* BEN's *room, which we see for the first time. There* DR. MAGUIRE *and* HELEN *are hovering over* BEN's *still body.* GANT *is at the hall telephone.*

GANT (*shouting into telephone*). Second class seaman, Luke Gant. G-A-N-T— Gant! (*Angrily*) I don't know why you can't hear me.

HUGH (*crosses to door*). W.O., you don't have to shout because it's long distance.

GANT. Shut up, Hugh, I know what I'm doing. (*Into telephone*) Do what? I am standing back from the telephone. All right, all right. . . . (*Moves telephone away from him, lower.*) Can you hear me now? Of all the perversities. Very well, I will repeat. Yesterday I sent a telegram to my son, Luke Gant, to come home, that his brother Ben has pneumonia. Can you tell me if—oh, he did leave? Why didn't he let us know? All right! Thank you. Thank you very much. (*Hangs up, joins the others on the veranda.*)

HUGH. They gave him leave?

GANT. If he made good connections he ought to be here by now.

HUGH. Ben'll be all right, W.O.

GANT (*crosses to sit wicker stool down right.* HUGH *sits woodbox*). I remember when little Grover was ill in St. Louis, and Eliza sent for me. I didn't get there on time.

ELIZA (*enters from the house*). Did you reach him?

GANT. He's on his way.

ELIZA (*at center on porch*). It's all nonsense, of course. Ben is far from dying. But you do like to dramatize, Mr. Gant. Still, it will be good to see Luke—

EUGENE (*crosses to* ELIZA). Mama, when can I see Ben?

ELIZA. When the doctor says. I'll tell

you what: when you go in there, don't make out like Ben is sick. Just make a big joke of it—laugh as big as you please—

EUGENE (*groans, sits left of left pillar*). Mama!

ELIZA. Well, it's the sick one's frame of mind that counts. I remember when I was teaching school in Hominy township, I had pneumonia. Nobody expected me to live, but I—did—I got through it somehow. I remember one day I was sitting down—I reckon I was convalescing as the fella says. Old Doc Fletcher had been there—and as he left I saw him shake his head at my cousin Sally. "Why, Eliza, what on earth," she says, just as soon as he had gone, "he tells me you're spitting up blood every time you cough; you've got consumption as sure as you live!" "Pshaw!" I said. I remember I was just determined to make a big joke of it. "I don't believe a word of it," I said. "Not one single word." And it was because I didn't believe it that *I got well.*

GANT (*quietly*). Eliza, don't run on so.

HELEN (*appears on veranda*). The doctor says Mama can come in for a few minutes, but no one else yet.

EUGENE (*rises, take* HELEN's *hand*). How is he?

HELEN. You know Dr. Maguire. If you can get anything out of him. . . . (ELIZA *takes a big breath; she and* HELEN *go in.*)

GANT (*moans worriedly*). Oh God, I don't like the feel of it. I don't like the feel of it.

BEN (*weakly*). Maguire, if you don't stop hanging over me I'll smother to death.

MAGUIRE (*to the women as they enter*). With both of you in here soaking up oxygen, leave that door open. (ELIZA *advances slowly to* BEN, *swallows a gasp at the sight of the tortured, wasted body.* BEN's *eyes are closed.*)

HELEN (*foot of bed*). Mama's here, Ben.

ELIZA (*speaking as though to a baby*). Why hello, son—did you think I wasn't ever coming in to see you?

HELEN (*after a pause*). Ben, Mama's here.

ELIZA (*to* MAGUIRE). Can't he talk? Why doesn't he look at me?

MAGUIRE (*head of bed*). Ben, you can hear what's going on, can't you?

BEN (*quietly, his eyes still closed*). I wish you'd all get out and leave me alone.

ELIZA. What kind of talk is that? You have to be looked after, son!

BEN. Then let Mrs. Pert look after me.

HELEN. Ben!

BEN. Maguire, where's Fatty? I want to see Fatty.

HELEN (*crosses center of bed.* ELIZA *turns away up left*). Ben, how can you talk that way? Your mother and your sister? If it weren't for that woman you wouldn't be sick now. Drinking, carousing with her night after night—

BEN (*yells with dwindling strength*). Fatty! Fatty! (*On the veranda* MRS. PERT *stands quickly, then enters house toward* BEN's *room.*)

HELEN (*to* BEN). You ought to be ashamed of yourself!

DR. MAGUIRE. Mrs. Gant, we need some more cold cloths. Why don't you—

HELEN (*crosses angrily to* MAGUIRE). Fiend! Do you have to add to her misery? When you need something, ask me. (ELIZA *starting out of* BEN's *room, meets* FATTY *in doorway.* FATTY *hesitates.*)

DR. MAGUIRE. That's all right, Mrs. Pert.

BEN (*immediately turns toward her*). Fatty?

DR. MAGUIRE. Ben seems to want you here, that's all I care about. (*To* HELEN) You'll be called if you're needed.

HELEN. This is the last time you come into this house, Dr. Maguire!

(HELEN *leaves the room. Outside* BEN's *door* ELIZA *hands some cold cloths to* HELEN.)

BEN. Fatty, stay by me. Sing to me. "A Baby's Prayer at Twilight."

FATTY (*sitting beside him*). Sh-h-h, Ben. Be quiet, dear. Save yourself.

BEN. Hold my hand, Fatty.

FATTY (*takes his hand, sings*).*
"Just a baby's prayer at twilight
When lights are low
A baby's years
Are filled with tears
Hmmmmm hmmmmm hmmmmmm."

---

* "Just a Baby's Prayer at Twilight," words by Sam M. Lewis and Joe Young, music by M. K. Jerome. © 1918. Copyright renewal 1946. Mills Music, Inc., and Warlock Music, Inc. Used by permission of the copyright owners solely for the purpose of printing in this edition. CAUTION: Permission to include this song in any performance of this play must be obtained from Mills Music, Inc., 1619 Broadway, New York 19, N. Y.

(HELEN *re-enters* BEN's *room. Places cloths on bureau. Hearing the voice,* EUGENE *stands, looks up toward* BEN's *room.* HELEN *and* ELIZA *appear on the veranda,* HELEN *comforting her mother.*)

EUGENE. How does he seem, Mama?

ELIZA (*right of* HELEN). He couldn't stand to see me worrying. That's what it was, you know. He couldn't stand to see me worrying about him.

GANT (*groaning*). Oh Jesus, it's fearful—that this should be put on me, old and sick as I am—

HELEN (*in blazing fury. Crosses to left of him*). You shut your mouth this minute, you damned old man! I've spent my life taking care of you! Everything's been done for you—everything—and you'll be here when we're all gone—so don't let us hear anything about your sickness, you selfish old man—it makes me furious!

DR. MAGUIRE (*appearing on veranda*). If any of you are interested, Ben is a little better.

EUGENE. Thank God!

HELEN. Ben is better? Why didn't you say so before?

ELIZA. I could have told you! I could have told you! I had a feeling all along!

DR. MAGUIRE (*crosses down steps*). I'll be back in a little while.

GANT. Well! We can all relax now.

DR. MAGUIRE (*motions* EUGENE *away from the others to down left*). Eugene, it's both lungs now. I can't tell them. But see to it that they stay around. I'm going next door and phone for some oxygen. It may ease it a little for him. It won't be long. (*He gives* EUGENE *a fond, strengthening touch, exits.*)

GANT (*in doorway*). What about Luke? Luke'll be furious when he finds out he came all this way for nothing!

ELIZA (*R. of him*). For nothing? You call Ben's getting well "for nothing"?

GANT. Oh, you know what I mean, Miss Eliza. I'm going to take a little nap.

ELIZA. You're going to take a little nip, that's what you mean.

GANT. You can come up and search my room if you don't believe me. (*Exits into house.*)

(EUGENE *stands, dazed and miserable, forces himself during the following scene.* JAKE *and* FLORRY *enter from rear veranda where* HELEN *and* HUGH *have moved to.*)

ELIZA (*excitedly*). Mr. Clatt, Miss Mangle—did you hear? Ben is getting better! The crisis is past!

JAKE. We're so happy for you, Mrs. Gant.

ELIZA. I knew all along—something told me. Oh, not that he didn't have a very high fever—I admit that—but my second sense—

LUKE (*off right*). Hello—o—o there!

ELIZA (*peering off*). Luke. (*Rushes down steps.*) Luke! Luke Gant!

(*The boarders melt into the background as* LUKE GANT *enters, wearing a Navy uniform and carrying a lightly packed duffle bag, which he places on wicker stool down right. He is attractive, slight, lighted by an enormous love of humor and life, and adored by everyone. He is the son who got away early, but he still carries the marks of a distressing childhood; he sometimes stutters.*)

LUKE. Mama, Mama! (*Swings her around.*)

HUGH (*right of him in yard*). Well, if it isn't the sailor himself! How are you?

LUKE (*shaking hands with* HUGH). I'm fine, Hugh! How goes it?

ELIZA. Aren't you going to kiss your old mother?

LUKE. Old? You're getting younger and stronger by the minute. (*Kisses her.*)

ELIZA. I am, I am, son. I feel it—now that Ben's going to get well.

LUKE. The old boy is better?

HELEN (R. of R. *pillar*). Luke!

LUKE. Helen!

HELEN (*leaps into his arms from porch*). How's my boy?

LUKE. S-s-slick as a puppy's belly. I thought you all might need cheering up. I brought you some ice cream from Woodruff's! (*Gives carton of ice cream to* HELEN.)

HELEN. Naturally; you wouldn't be Luke Gant if you didn't!

EUGENE (*crosses to center*). Welcome home, Luke!

LUKE (*crosses to him. They shake hands*). My God, doesn't anybody buy you any clothes—and look at that hair. Mama, he looks like an orphan! Cut off those damn big feet of his, he'd go up in the air!

EUGENE. How long have you got, Luke?

LUKE. Can you s-s-stand me for twenty-four hours? (*Sees* LAURA, *crosses to her.*) Who's this?

ELIZA (*following*). That's Miss James from Virginia. Laura, this is another of my sons, Luke Gant.

LAURA (*shaking hands*). How do you do, Mr. Gant?

LUKE. How do you do?

ELIZA (*drawing* LUKE *away*). All right, just come along here, and behave yourself.

HELEN. I'd better dish up the ice cream before it melts. (*Exits into house.*)

LUKE (*calling after* HELEN *from porch*). Maybe Ben would like some. I got pistachio especially for him.

ELIZA (*to* HELEN, *left of left pillar*). Tell your father the admiral is here!

LUKE. Can I see Ben, now?

ELIZA. Well, the truth is, that Mrs. Pert is in there with him now.

LUKE. Mrs. Pert is? (*Looks at the others.*)

HUGH (*crosses onto porch with duffle bag. Sits woodbox*). I wouldn't go into it, Luke. It's a somewhat "fraught" subject.

LUKE. Oh boy, oh boy, I know what that is! Still the same old happy household? (LUKE *and* ELIZA *sit on the veranda edge.*)

ELIZA. Nonsense. I have nothing against the woman except she's getting too many ideas that she's a fixture here. First thing in the morning I'm going to ask her to move.

LUKE. Doesn't she pay her rent?

ELIZA. Oh, she pays it.

LUKE (*laughs*). Then you're never going to ask her to move—don't kid me! The paying customers are what counts around here! Aren't they, Mama?

ELIZA. Luke Gant, there are certain standards I have to keep up, for the reputation of Dixieland!

LUKE (*never unkindly*). What kind of standards? The old dope fiend who hung himself in the same bedroom where Ben had to sleep for eight years after he cut him down? And all those amateur femme fatales who bask under your protection here, waylaying us in the hall, the bathroom—Mama, we never had a s-s-safe moment! And people think you find out about life in the Navy!

ELIZA (*playfully*). I'm warning you, Luke! It's a good thing I know you're teasing.

(HELEN *enters with plates, dishes up ice cream.*)

LUKE. Remember the early mornings when Ben and Gene and I used to take the paper route together, remember, Gene? Old Ben used to make up stories for us about all the sleeping people in all the sleeping houses! He always used to throw the papers as lightly as he could because he hated to wake them. Remember, Gene?

HELEN (*offering* HUGH *ice cream*). And that book of baseball stories Ben used to read to us by the hour—what was it, Gene?

EUGENE (*in tears*). You Know Me, Al, by Ring Lardner.

ELIZA (*leaping to* EUGENE). Eugene. Child, what is it? What is it!

MRS. PERT (*enters hurriedly*). Mrs. Gant! Mrs. Gant!

HELEN. What is it, Mrs. Pert?

MRS. PERT. He can't get his breath!

HUGH. Gene, get the doctor! (HELEN *and* ELIZA *follow* MRS. PERT *into the house.*)

ELIZA. You ridiculous woman! The doctor said he was better. (EUGENE *exits to get* DR. MAGUIRE. GANT *enters side door.*)

GANT. What the hell's all the commotion about? (*Sees* LUKE.) Luke! Welcome home!

LUKE (*as they shake hands right center*). Papa—Ben's not doing so well.

GANT (*crosses to right pillar*). Jesus, have mercy! That I should have to bear this in my old age. Not another one—first Grover, now Ben . . .

LUKE (*on porch above him*). For God's sake, Papa, try to behave decently, for Ben's sake! (EUGENE *and* DR. MAGUIRE *enter hurriedly.*)

GANT (*seizing* DR. MAGUIRE). Maguire, you got to save him—you got to save him. (DR. MAGUIRE *pushes past* GANT *into the house, enters* BEN's *room where the three women are gathered,* MRS. PERT *standing nearest* BEN *at the head of the bed.*)

DR. MAGUIRE. You women step back, give him air. (*Bends over* BEN.)

GANT (*collapsing on to the porch right of right pillar*). When the old die, no one cares. But the young . . . the young . . .

EUGENE (*sits left of him on steps.* LUKE *sits rocker*). I would care, Papa.

BEN. It's one way—to step out of—

the photograph—isn't it, Fatty?

FATTY. Hush, Ben, don't say that!

HELEN (*to* DR. MAGUIRE; *right of him*). There must be something you can do!

DR. MAGUIRE (*straightens up*). Not all the king's horses, not all the doctors in the world can help him now.

HELEN. Have you tried everything? Everything?

DR. MAGUIRE (*turns upstage*). My dear girl! He's drowning! Drowning!

ELIZA (*in deep pain, moving from foot of bed*). Mrs. Pert, you're standing in my place— (FATTY *moves away.* ELIZA *steps close to* BEN, *sits.*) Ben—son.

(*She reaches to touch him. His head turns toward her, drops. There is a last rattling, drowning sound.* BEN *dies.* DR. MAGUIRE *checks his heart.*)

DR. MAGUIRE. It's over. It's all over.

HELEN (*racked, exits to veranda; tries to stifle her sobs*). He's gone. Ben's gone.

(ELIZA *sits stool and takes* BEN'S *hand.* FATTY *puts the socks she has been knitting at* BEN'S *feet and exits upstairs.* HELEN *falls into* EUGENE'S *arms.* DR. MAGUIRE, *carrying his doctor's bag, appears in the hall, puts a match to his chewed cigar.*)

EUGENE (*crossing to right of* DR. MAGUIRE). Did he say anything? Did he say anything at the end?

DR. MAGUIRE. What were you expecting him to say?

EUGENE. I don't know. I just wondered.

DR. MAGUIRE. If he found what he was looking for? I doubt that, Gene. At least he didn't say anything.

(EUGENE *leaves and goes into* BEN'S *room.* DR. MAGUIRE *comes out into the veranda.*)

LUKE. How long have you known, Doc?

DR. MAGUIRE. For two days—from the beginning. Since I first saw him at three in the morning in the Uneeda Lunch with a cup of coffee in one hand and a cigarette in the other.

GANT. Was there nothing to be done?

DR. MAGUIRE. My dear, dear Gant, we can't turn back the days that have gone. We can't turn back to the hours when our lungs were sound, our blood hot, our bodies young. We are a flash of fire—a brain, a heart, a spirit. And we are three cents' worth of lime and iron—which we cannot get back. (*He shakes his head.*) We can believe in the nothingness of life. We can believe in the nothingness of death, and of a life after death. But who can believe in the nothingness of Ben?

HELEN. Come on, Papa, there's nothing more to sit up for. Let me put you to bed. Come along.

(*She takes the old man and leads him gently into the house, as* DR. MAGUIRE *exits.* HUGH *and* LUKE *exit after* HELEN *and* GANT. *Only* LAURA *is left, still sitting on the yard seat.* EUGENE, *who has been standing in the corner in* BEN'S *room, goes to his mother, who is holding* BEN'S *hand tightly.*)

EUGENE. Mama?

ELIZA. He doesn't turn away from me any more.

EUGENE (*takes her hand, tries gently to disengage* BEN'S). Mama, you've got to let go. You've got to let go, Mama! (ELIZA *shakes her head, her rough clasp tightening.* EUGENE *leaves the room, comes out to the veranda. There, slowly, he sinks to his knees, prays.* LAURA *watches him, her heart going out to him.*) Whoever You are, be good to Ben tonight. Whoever You are, be good to Ben tonight . . . Whoever You are . . . be good to Ben tonight . . . be good to Ben tonight . . .

SLOW CURTAIN

ACT THREE

SCENE: *The Dixieland Boarding House; two weeks later. The house is seen in a soft early light. From offstage, a newsboy, whistling, throws four tightly wadded newspapers onto the veranda—plop—plop—plop—plop. The whistling and his steps fade away. The lights come up dimly in* LAURA'S *room.* LAURA *is in bed in her nightgown.* EUGENE *is at the foot of the bed by the window, looking out. He takes his shirt from the bedpost, puts it on.*

LAURA (*stirring*). Gene? What was that?

EUGENE (*head of* LAURA'S *bed*). Soaks Baker with the morning papers. Plop-plop-plop-plop—how I used to love that sound. Every time the heavy bag getting lighter. I'll always feel sorry for people who have to carry things. (*Sighs.*) It's getting light, it's nearly dawn.

LAURA. Don't go yet. (*Reaches for his hand.*)

EUGENE. Do you think I want to on your last morning here? Mama gets up so early. Do you know that every morning before she cooks breakfast she visits Ben's grave? (*Sits on bed, takes her in his arms.*)

LAURA. Gene, Gene.

EUGENE. Oh Laura, I love you so. When I'm close to you like this, it's so natural. Are all men like me? Tell me.

LAURA. I've told you I've never known anyone like you.

EUGENE (*as* LAURA *turns away*). But you have known men? It would be strange if you hadn't. A woman so beautiful, so loving. You make me feel like I only used to dream of feeling. I've hardly thought to daydream in weeks—except about us.

LAURA. What did you used to dream?

EUGENE. I always wanted to be the winner, the general, the spearhead of victory! Then following that I wanted to be loved. Victory and love! Unbeaten and beloved. And I am that now, truly! Laura, will you marry me?

LAURA (*moving away*). Oh, darling!

EUGENE. You knew I was going to ask you, didn't you? You knew I couldn't let you go even for a day.

LAURA. Yes, I knew.

EUGENE. You're happy with me. You know I make you happy. And I'm so complete with you. Do you know that three hundred dollars Ben left me? He would want me to use it for us. I'll go with you to Richmond today. I'll meet your parents, so they won't think I'm an irresponsible fool who's stolen you. That may be a little hard to prove—but there is a job I can get. Would you mind living in Altamont?

LAURA (*moving into his arms*). I don't care where I live. Just keep holding me.

EUGENE. I am going to have to tell Mama first.

LAURA. Let's not worry about that now. Tell me about us.

EUGENE. All the treasures the world has in store for us? We'll see and know them all. . . . All the things and the places I've read about. There isn't a state in this country we won't know. The great names of Arizona, Texas, Colorado, California— we'll ride the freights to get there if we have to. And we'll go to Europe, and beyond—the cool, green land of Shakespeare, the gloomy forests of Gaul, the great Assyrian plains where Alexander feasted—the crumbling walls of Babylon,

the palaces of the kings of Egypt, the towering white crags of Switzerland. My God, Laura, there might not be time enough for all!

LAURA. There will be time enough, darling.

(*From a far distance, they hear the whistle of a train as it passes.*)

EUGENE. The Richmond train leaves at noon. I'll have to get packed.

LAURA. You do love trains, don't you?

EUGENE. I love only you. Will you have confidence in me, the unbeaten and beloved?

LAURA. Yes, darling, I will have confidence in you.

EUGENE. I'll never have to sneak out of this room again. (*Rises, moves to the door.* LAURA, *on her knees, reaches toward him.*)

LAURA. Eugene! (*He comes back to her.*) I will love you always. (*They kiss.* EUGENE *exits.* LAURA *leaps from the bed, hurries after him.*) Gene!

(ELIZA *has come out the side door, putting on sweater, takes flowers out of a bucket preparing to take them to* BEN's *grave.* EUGENE *enters the hallway, lifts the phone receiver. He doesn't see* ELIZA. *Lights dim down on* LAURA's *room as she gets slippers and exits.*)

EUGENE (*into telephone*). Good morning. Three-two, please— Hello, Uncle Will? This is Eugene— Yes, I know how early it is— You know that position you offered me? I've decided to take it.

ELIZA (*pleased, to herself*). Well, can you imagine!

EUGENE (*into telephone*). I've thought it over, and that's what I'd like to do, for a while anyway— That's right— That's fine— Well, you see, I'm getting married— (ELIZA *freezes in pain at center.*) Yes, married—to Miss James. We're going to Richmond for a few days. We're leaving on the noon train— Thanks, Uncle Will. Thanks a lot. (*Hangs up and starts to go back upstairs.*)

ELIZA. Eugene!

EUGENE (*coming out to her slowly*). Well, now—with your second sense, I thought you would have guessed it, Mama.

ELIZA (*sits left of left pillar*). Why didn't I know, why didn't I see?

EUGENE (*kneels at pillar*). I'm sorry, Mama, but we couldn't wait any longer.

ELIZA. Gene, child, don't make this mistake. She's so much older than you. Don't throw yourself away, boy!

EUGENE. Mama, there's no use arguing. Nothing you can say will change my mind.

ELIZA (*desperately*). And my plans for you? What of my plans for you?

EUGENE. Mama, I don't want your plans, I've got my own life to live! (*Moves to right on porch.* ELIZA *follows.*)

ELIZA. But you don't know! Gene, listen, you know that Stumptown property of mine? I sold it just yesterday so you could go to Chapel Hill— You know I've always wanted you to have an education. You can have it now, child, you can have it.

EUGENE. It's too late, Mama, it's too late!

ELIZA. Why law, child, it's never too late for anything! It's what Ben wanted, you know.

EUGENE. Laura and I are leaving, Mama. I'm going up to get packed. (*She turns away from his kiss and he exits into house.*)

ELIZA. Gene! (ELIZA *stands looking after him a moment, then quickly enters the hall, lifts the telephone receiver.*) Three-two, please. (*Waits.*)

HELEN (*enters from the kitchen, with a broom with which she sweeps the veranda*). What are you calling Uncle Will so early for?

ELIZA (*into phone*). Will? No, no, I know—I heard— Yes, I know it's early— Listen, Will, I want you to do something for me. You know my Stumptown property? I want you to sell it— Now, this morning— Will, don't argue with me— I don't care what it's worth. Call Cash Rankin, he's been after me for weeks to sell— Well, I know what I want to do— I'll explain it to you later— Just do what I say and let me know. (*She hangs up.*)

(LAURA *re-enters her bedroom.*)

HELEN. Well, it's never too early in the morning to turn a trade, is it? What are you selling?

ELIZA. Some property I own.

HELEN. Maybe you can put a little of that money into getting somebody else to help you at that altar of yours, the kitchen stove.

ELIZA (*puts sweater on hall chair*). Helen, get breakfast started, will you? I'll be in later. And if Gene comes down,

keep him in there, will you?

HELEN. Oh, all right. You let me know when I can let him out! (*Exits into house.*)

(ELIZA *appears at door of* LAURA's *room.* LAURA *is dressed and is packing her suitcase on the bed.*)

LAURA. Oh, Mrs. Gant. I've been expecting you. Come in. (*As* ELIZA *enters.*)

ELIZA. I should think you would.

LAURA. Mrs. Gant, before you say anything—

ELIZA. I'll vow I can't believe a mature woman—at a time of trouble like this— would take advantage of a child, a mere child—

LAURA. Mrs. Gant, will you please listen?

ELIZA (*tossing her nightgown from head of bed into suitcase*). I will listen to nothing. You just pack your things and get out of this house. I should have known what you were from the first minute I set eyes on you . . . "I'm looking for a room, Mrs. Gant . . ." Why, butter wouldn't melt in your mouth—

LAURA (*slowly, distinctly*). Mrs. Gant, I am not marrying Eugene. I'm not. I wish with all my heart I could!

ELIZA (*turning to dresser*). You can't lie out of it. Gene just told me.

LAURA. I am engaged to be married to a young man in Richmond.

ELIZA. What kind of a wicked game are you playing with my child?

LAURA (*sits bed.* ELIZA *sits chair left*). Mrs. Gant, this isn't easy. I should have told Gene long ago—but I didn't. A girl about to get married suddenly finds herself facing responsibilities. I never liked responsibilities. Gene knows how I am. I like music, I like to walk in the woods, I like—to dream. I know I'm older than Gene, but in many ways I'm younger. The thought of marriage frightened me. I told my fiancé I needed time to think it over. I fell in love with Eugene. I found the kind of romance I'd never known before, but I've also found that it isn't the answer. Gene is a wonderful boy, Mrs. Gant. He must go to college. He must have room to expand and grow, to find himself. He mustn't be tied down at this point in his life. He needs the whole world to wander in—and I know now that I need a home, I need children —I need a husband. (*Rises, closes bag.*) For people like me there are rules, very good rules for marriage and for happi-

ness—and I've broken enough of them.
I telephoned Philip last night. He's arriving at the depot on that early train. We're
going on to Charleston together, and we'll
be married there. He loves me, and I
will love him too after a while. (*Takes
note from desk.*) I left this note for
Eugene. I couldn't just tell him. (*Gives
it to* ELIZA. *Crosses for bag, puts it down
left of head of bed. Gets hat and purse
from bureau.*) Will you say good-bye to
Mr. Gant for me, and tell him I hope
he feels better? And my good-byes to
Mr. Clatt and the others? And to Helen.
Especially to Helen. She works so hard.
(*Looks around.*) Good-bye, little room.
I've been happy here. (*Picks up suitcase,
faces* ELIZA.) Some day you're going to
let him go, too. Good-bye, Mrs. Gant.
(*She exits.*)

(*During the above* HUGH *has entered
the veranda, is seated, reading the newspaper.* LAURA *enters from the house, looks
back lingeringly, then, hearing the approaching train, hurries off toward the
station down left.* HELEN *enters, drinking
coffee.*)

HELEN. Mama? Now, where on earth!
Hugh, have you seen Mama?

HUGH. Umph.

HELEN (*crosses upstage on porch*). Do
you know she was on the phone just now
selling some property? Imagine—at this
hour! And she leaves me to slave in the
kitchen. . . . Do you know where she is?

HUGH. You know, they don't advertise
the good jobs in here, not the really big
ones.

GANT (*entering in his suspenders, sleep-
ily rubbing his jaw*). Isn't breakfast ready
yet?

HELEN. Papa, how many times has
Mama told you, you wait until the
boarders have had theirs! And don't you
dare appear in front of them in your
suspenders, do you hear?

GANT. Merciful God! What a way to
greet the day! (*He exits.*)

HELEN (*calling after* GANT). Papa, do
you know where Mama is?

(HELEN *exits after* GANT. EUGENE *enters
downstairs, carrying his suitcase, stops
at* LAURA's *door, knocks.* ELIZA *has just
laid* LAURA's *letter on the bed.*)

EUGENE. Laura? Laura? (*Enters to*
ELIZA.) Mama! Where's Laura? Where
is she?

ELIZA. She's gone.

EUGENE. Gone? Where?

ELIZA. She just walked out on you,
child. Just walked out on you. (*Shakes
her finger at him.*) I could have told
you, the minute I laid eyes on her—

EUGENE (*seizing* ELIZA's *hand*). You
sent her away.

ELIZA. I never did. She just walked
out on you, child. (EUGENE *breaks for the
door.* ELIZA *picks up the letter, runs after
him.*) Gene! Eugene! Wait!

EUGENE (*runs down to the veranda*).
Laura— (*Looks up street.*) Laura— (*As*
HUGH *points toward station, starts off
that way.*) Laura—

ELIZA (*entering, waving the letter*).
Wait! Wait! She left you this. Gene! (EU-
GENE *turns, sees the letter.*) She left you
this. Read it, child. (EUGENE *crosses to*
ELIZA, *takes the letter, reads it as the train
is heard leaving station.*) You see, it's no
use. It's no use. (EUGENE *crosses slowly
to the yard seat, sits.* ELIZA *watches him.*
HELEN *enters through the front door.*)

HELEN. Mama, there you are! Where
have you been? We've got to start getting
breakfast. (*As* ELIZA *waves her to silence*)
What's the matter?

ELIZA. That Miss James. She and
Eugene—

HELEN (*laughs*). Oh my God, Mama,
have you just found out about that? What
about it?

ELIZA. She's gone.

HELEN. What?

ELIZA. She just walked out on him.

HELEN (*crosses to* EUGENE). Oh ho, so
that's it, is it? Has your girl gone and
left you, huh? Huh? (*Tickles his ribs;
he turns, clasps her knees.*) Why, Gene,
forget about it! You're only a kid yet.
She's a grown woman.

ELIZA (*crossing above to left of* EUGENE).
Helen's right. Why, child, I wouldn't
let a girl get the best of me. She was
just fooling you all the time, just leading you on, wasn't she, Helen?

HELEN. You'll forget her in a week,
Gene.

ELIZA. Why, of course you will. Pshaw,
this was just puppy love. Like the fellow
says, there's plenty good fish in the sea,
as ever came out of it.

HELEN. Cheer up, you're not the only
man got fooled in his life!

HUGH (*from behind his paper*). By

God, that's the truth! (HELEN *and* ELIZA *glare at him.*)

ELIZA. Helen, go inside, I'll be in in a minute.

HELEN. Oh, all right. Hugh, you come in and help me. (HELEN *exits, followed by* HUGH.)

ELIZA (*sits beside* EUGENE, *his back still turned to her*). Gene. You know what I'd do if I were you? I'd just show her I was a good sport, that's what! I wouldn't let on to her that it affected me one bit. I'd write her just as big as you please and laugh about the whole thing.

EUGENE. Oh, God, Mama, please, leave me alone, leave me alone!

ELIZA. Why, I'd be ashamed to let any girl get my goat like that. When you get older, you'll just look back on this and laugh. You'll see. You'll be going to college next year, and you won't remember a thing about it. (EUGENE *turns, looks at her.*) I told you I'd sold that Stumptown property, and I have. This year's term has started already but next year—

EUGENE. Mama, *now! Now!* I've wasted enough time!

ELIZA. What are you talking about? Why you're a child yet, there's plenty of time yet—

EUGENE (*rises, walks about her, beggingly*). Mama, Mama, what is it? What more do you want from me? Do you want to strangle and drown me completely? Do you want more string? Do you want me to collect more bottles? Tell me what you want! Do you want more property? Do you want the town? Is that it?

ELIZA. Why, I don't know what you're talking about, boy. If I hadn't tried to accumulate a little something, none of you would have had a roof to call your own.

EUGENE (*right center*). A roof to call our own? Good God, I never had a bed to call my own! I never had a room to call my own! I never had a quilt to call my own that wasn't taken from me to warm the mob that rocks on that porch and grumbles.

ELIZA (*rises, looking for an escape*). Now you may sneer at the boarders if you like—

EUGENE. No, I can't. There's not breath or strength enough in me to sneer at them all I like. Ever since I was this

high, and you sent me to the store for the groceries, I used to think, "This food is not for us—it's for them!" Mama, making us wait until they've eaten, all these years—feeding us on *their* leftovers —do you know what it does to us?— when it's you we wanted for us, *you* we needed for us. Why? Why?

ELIZA (*trembling*). They don't hurt me like the rest of you do—they wouldn't talk to me like you are, for one thing. (*Starts toward side door.*)

EUGENE. Because they don't care— they're strangers. They don't give a damn about you! They'll talk like this about you behind your back—I've heard them do that plenty!

ELIZA (*turns*). What? What? What kind of things do they say about me?

EUGENE. What does it matter what they say—*they* say! Doesn't it matter to you what I say? (*Takes her in his arms, holds her.*)

ELIZA (*beginning to weep*). I don't understand.

EUGENE (*releases her, moves away*). Oh, it's easy to cry now, Mama, but it won't do you any good! I've done as much work for my wages as you deserve. I've given you fair value for your money, I thank you for nothing. (*Crosses up to the veranda.*)

ELIZA (*crosses to left of left pillar*). What's that? What are you saying!

EUGENE. I said I thank you for nothing, but I take that back. Yes, I have a great deal to be thankful for. I give thanks for every hour of loneliness I've had here, for every dirty cell you ever gave me to sleep in, for the ten million hours of indifference, and for these two minutes of cheap advice.

ELIZA. You will be punished if there's a just God in Heaven.

EUGENE. Oh, there is! I'm sure there is! Because I have been punished. By God, I shall spend the rest of my life getting my heart back, healing and forgetting every scar you put upon me when I was a child. The first move I ever made after the cradle was to crawl for the door. And every move I ever made since has been an effort to escape. And now, at last I am free from all of you. And I shall get me some order out of this chaos. I shall find my way out of it yet, though it takes me twenty years more—alone. (*Starts for door.*)

ELIZA. Gene! Gene, you're not leaving?

EUGENE. Ah, you were not looking, were you? I've already gone.

(EUGENE *exits into the house.* ELIZA *sits on the veranda edge, stunned.* GANT, *wearing a vest over his suspenders, enters.*)

GANT. Now do you suppose I can get some breakfast? (ELIZA *doesn't answer.*) Well, do you mind if I make a fire in the fireplace? (*Goes to woodbox, muttering.*) If I can't get any food to keep me alive, I can get a little warmth out of this drafty barn! (*Starts collecting wood from box.*) Some day I'm going to burn up this house—just pile in all the logs that old grate'll hold—and all the furniture—and all the wooden-headed people around here —and some kerosene—till this old barn takes off like a giant cinder blazing through the sky. That would show them —all fifteen miserable rooms—burning, blistering—

ELIZA. I wish you would, Mr. Gant. I just wish you would.

GANT. You think I'm joking.

ELIZA. No, I don't.

GANT. If I just get drunk enough, I will!

ELIZA (*rises, faces house*). Serve it right —miserable, unholy house!

GANT. Why, Miss Eliza!

ELIZA. I'll do it myself— (*With demoniacal strength she shakes the left pillar by the steps.*) I'll tear you down! I'll kill you, house, kill you! I'll shake you to pieces!

GANT. Let me help you, Mrs. Gant! (*Picks up* MRS. PERT'S *rocker, crashes it.*)

HELEN (*entering hurriedly*). Eliza Gant, have you gone mad!

GANT (*drops wood, starts tearing at the other post.*) God-damned barn! Thief! Travesty on nature

ELIZA. God-damned barn!—(*Hits latticed panels under the veranda left with stick of wood.*)

HELEN (*calls inside*). Hugh, come out here!

WILL (*entering from rear of veranda*). My God, what are they doing?

GANT (*screaming up at house. Brandishing torn pillar*). Clatt—Mangle—Brown— Come out of there, you rats, all of you —come out, come out, wherever you are!

(*The boarders begin to yell and squeal from inside.*)

ELIZA (*hysterically imitating* GANT; *crossing left*). Come out, come out, wherever you are!

HUGH (*entering*). What's going on?

GANT (*breaking off the newel post; crosses to right center*). We're tearing down this murderous trap, that's what. Hand me the hatchet, Hugh. It's in the woodbox.

HUGH. Fine! Fine! (*Dashes to woodbox, takes out hatchet.*)

(*Boarders enter downstairs in various stages of undress.*)

MISS BROWN. Call the police.

MRS. CLATT. Let's get to Mrs. Haskell's!

JAKE. Gant's off his nut!

GANT (*chasing them off left, threatening the boarders*). Squeal, you croaking bastards. Croak and run! Run for your lives!

BOARDERS (*ad lib as they scurry off.*) The house is falling down!—It's a tornado! —Ladies' Temperance Society, humph!— Has anyone called the police?—(*etc.*)

HUGH (*yard right center*). Here's the hatchet, W.O.

GANT (*leaping for it. Tossing pillar up right center*). Give it to me.

WILL (*right of* HUGH, *grabbing for hatchet*). Stop it, Gant—stop this! Have you all lost your minds?

ELIZA (*throwing flower pot after the boarders.*) Go to Mrs. Haskell's!

HELEN. Mama!

GANT (*brandishing hatchet at* JAKE *and* MRS. CLATT *as they exit porch up right*). Look at 'em run! And they haven't even had breakfast. Run, scatterbrains, empty-bellies!

JAKE. I'll sue you for this, Gant, I'll sue you for this! (*Exits.*)

(MRS. SNOWDEN *enters through front door,* GANT *whirls on her.*)

GANT. So you don't like the food here? So you don't like my wife's coffee! (MRS. SNOWDEN, *screaming, hastily retreats.*)

ELIZA (*lifting a chair to hurl after the boarders*). Why, law, that's good coffee! (HELEN *seizes* ELIZA'S *arms, stops her.* ELIZA'S *sensibilities slowly return.*)

GANT. Look at 'em run! Oh, Miss Eliza, what a woman you are! (*Roaring with laughter, he crosses down to* ELIZA, *is about to embrace her, sees her sober, shocked face.*)

ELIZA (*picking up broken pillar*). Mr. Gant, Mr. Gant, what have you done? What have you done?

GANT. What have I done? What have

I— Merciful God, woman!

ELIZA (*tosses pillar onto porch left*). Just look at this mess! And the boarders have all gone!

HELEN (*left of* ELIZA). I don't know what got into you, Papa.

GANT (*speechless, turns to* HUGH *on porch right*). Merciful God! What got into me? Didn't she just stand there herself and—

ELIZA. Helen, go get the boarders, tell them he's been drinking, tell them anything, but get them back!

WILL (*down right*). I never saw such an exhibition.

ELIZA. Will, go with Helen. Tell them we all apologize. They'll listen to you. Hugh, help me clean up this mess. (HELEN *and* WILL *exit after the boarders up right*.)

GANT. Let them go, Miss Eliza. *Let the boarders go!* (ELIZA *stands rigid.* GANT *waits anxiously.*)

ELIZA (*on porch center*). I just don't know what came over me.

GANT (*crosses—flings the hatchet in the woodbox.* ELIZA *crosses to see damage to veranda lattice.*) Merciful God! (EUGENE *enters with his suitcase.*) Where are you going?

EUGENE. I'm going to school at Chapel Hill, Papa.

GANT. You are? (*He looks at* ELIZA.)

EUGENE. Mama promised me the money. She sold her Stumptown property.

GANT (*crosses to right of her*). Oh? By God, maybe it isn't going to be such a god-damned miserable day, after all! Got any money, son?

EUGENE (*in yard, right of* GANT). I've got Ben's money. Thanks, Papa.

GANT (*takes money from his pocket, tucks it into* EUGENE's *pocket*). Well, go, Gene. Go for both of us. Keep right on going.

EUGENE. I will, Papa. Good-bye.

GANT (*as they shake hands*). Good-bye, Gene. (*Starts into house, turns.*) You're going to bust loose, boy—you're going to bust loose, all over this dreary planet!

(GANT *exits.* EUGENE *crosses to right of* ELIZA, *who starts picking up the debris.*)

ELIZA. I reckon you've made up your mind all right.

EUGENE. Yes, Mama, I have. (*Crosses down left.*)

ELIZA (*crosses to porch, slamming wood in woodbox*). Well, I'll deposit the money in the Chapel Hill Bank for you. I tell you what! It looks mighty funny, though, that you can't just stay a day or two more with Ben gone and all. It seems you'll do anything to get away from me. That's all right, I know your mind's made up and I'm not complaining! It seems all I've ever been fit for around here is to cook and sew. That's all the use any of you have ever had for me—

EUGENE. Mama, don't think you can work on my feelings here at the last minute.

ELIZA. It seems I've hardly laid eyes on you all summer long— (*Replacing wood in woodbox and picking up rocker.* EUGENE *turns to her.*) Well, when you get up there, you want to look up your Uncle Emerson and Aunt Lucy. Your Aunt Lucy took a great liking to you when they were down here, and when you're in a strange town it's mighty good sometimes to have someone you know. And say, when you see your Uncle Emerson, you might just tell him not to be surprised to see me any time now. (*She nods pertly at him.*) I reckon I can pick right up and light out the same as the next fellow when I get ready. I'm not going to spend all my days slaving away for a lot of boarders—it don't pay. If I can turn a couple of trades here this fall, I just may start out to see the world like I always intended to. I was talking to Cash Rankin the other day—he said, "Why, Mrs. Gant," he said, "if I had your head for figures, I'd be a rich man in—" (*Her talk drifts off.* EUGENE *stands looking at her. There is another terrible silence between them. She points at him with her finger, finally her old loose masculine gesture. Crossing to left on porch.*) Here's the thing I'm going to do. You know that lot of mine on Sunset Terrace, right above Dick Webster's place? Well, I been thinking. If we started to build there right away, we could be in our own house by spring. I've been thinking about it a lot lately. . . . (*There is another silence.*) I hate to see you go, son.

EUGENE. Good-bye, Mama.

ELIZA. Try to be happy, child, try to be a little more happy. . . . (*She turns and, with unsteady step, starts into the house.*)

EUGENE. MAMA! (*He drops the valise, takes the steps in a single bound, catching*

ELIZA's *rough hands, which she had held clasped across her body, and drawing them to his breast.*) GOOD-BYE . . . GOOD-BYE . . . GOOD-BYE . . . MAMA . . .

ELIZA (*holding him*). Poor child . . . poor child . . . poor child. (*Huskily, faintly*) We must try to love one another. (*Finally* EUGENE *moves from her, picks up the valise, as the lights start dimming, holding a spot on her.* ELIZA *seems to recede in the distance as into his memory.*) Now for Heaven's sake, spruce up, boy, spruce up! Throw your shoulders back! And smile, look pleasant! Let them know up there that you *are* somebody!

(ELIZA's *voice fades, the set is black. A spot holds on* EUGENE.)

EPILOGUE

BEN's VOICE. So you're finally going, Gene?

EUGENE. Ben? Is that you, Ben?

BEN's VOICE. Who did you think it was, you little idiot? Do you know why you're going, or are you just taking a ride on a train?

EUGENE (*looking up and front right*). I know. Of course I know why I'm going. There's nothing here for me. Ben, what really happens? Everything is going. Everything changes and passes away. Can you remember some of the things I do?

I've already forgotten the old faces. I forget the names of people I knew for years. I get their faces mixed. I get their heads stuck on other people's bodies. I think one man has said what another said. And I forget. There is something I have lost and can't remember.

BEN's VOICE. The things you have forgotten and are trying to remember is the child that you were. He's gone, Gene, as I am gone. And will never return. No matter where you search for him, in a million streets, in a thousand cities.

EUGENE. Then I'll search for an end to hunger, and the happy land!

BEN's VOICE. Ah, there is no happy land. There is no end to hunger!

EUGENE. Ben, help me! You must have an answer. Help me, and I won't go searching for it.

BEN's VOICE. You little fool, what do you want to find out there?

EUGENE. *I want to find the world. Where is the world?*

BEN's VOICE (*fading*). The world is nowhere, Gene. . . .

EUGENE. Ben, wait! Answer me!

BEN's VOICE. The world is nowhere, no one, Gene. *You* are your world.

(*The train whistle sounds. Lights reveal Dixieland in dim silhouette.* EUGENE, *without looking back, exits.*)

CURTAIN

TWO FOR THE SEESAW

William Gibson

Presented by Fred Coe at the Booth Theatre, New York,
on January 16, 1958, with the following cast:

JERRY RYAN Henry Fonda   GITTEL MOSCA Anne Bancroft

The action takes place this past year, between fall and spring, in two
rooms—Jerry's and Gittel's—in New York City.

ACT ONE. SCENE 1: Both rooms. September, late afternoon. SCENE 2:
   Gittel's room. Midnight, the same day. SCENE 3: Both rooms. Day-
   break following.
ACT TWO. SCENE 1: Jerry's room. October, dusk. SCENE 2: Both rooms.
   December, noon. SCENE 3: Gittel's room. February, a Saturday night.
ACT THREE. SCENE 1: Gittel's room. March, midday. SCENE 2: Jerry's
   room. May, dusk. SCENE 3: Both rooms. A few days later, afternoon.

Directed by Arthur Penn
Settings by George Jenkins
Costumes by Virginia Volland

© Tamarack Productions, Ltd., 1959
Copyright 1956 by William Gibson, 1959 by Tamarack Productions, Ltd. All rights reserved.
Reprinted by permission of Alfred A. Knopf, Inc.

CAUTION: *Two for the Seesaw* is the sole property of the author and
is fully protected by copyright. All rights, including professional,
amateur, stock, radio broadcasting, television, motion picture, recitation,
lecturing, public reading, and the rights of translation into foreign languages, are
reserved and may not be used without written permission and payment of
royalty. All inquiries should be addressed to the author's agent: Leah Salisbury,
Inc., 234 West 44th Street, New York 36, N. Y.

WILLIAM GIBSON had apparently been getting along in the world very nicely as an independent writer. He had published verse, and he had made reputation as well as money on a novel, *The Cobweb,* which was bought after publication by a motion-picture company. He was also living peacefully in Stockbridge, Massachusetts, where his wife, a psychoanalyst, was attached to the celebrated Austen Riggs Center —happily remote from New York City, where he had spent his first twenty years, and where he had attended the City College and dreamed of becoming a college teacher. But he incautiously wrote a two-character comedy, *Two for the Seesaw,* entrusted it to the producing hands of that able drama graduate from Yale Fred Coe, now a successful producer, who in turn entrusted it to Arthur Penn, one of the country's ablest stage directors. Even worse luck! The producers enlisted the aid of Henry Fonda, an actor who has a way of appearing in "hit" films and plays, and Anne Bancroft, a hitherto unknown young lady who acquired the habit of performing her role so well that she became one of the country's leading actresses almost effortlessly and has since won all sorts of prizes in leading roles.

There was no help for it!—*Two for the Seesaw* simply had to become a hit, and Mr. Gibson was snared for Broadway even before the run of that play was over. With Miss Anne Bancroft in mind he proceeded to develop a second play, *The Miracle Worker,* out of a television script he had written about Annie Sullivan, the woman who opened the world that had been closed to little Helen Keller when she became blind, deaf, and consequently virtually mute, too, in infancy. *The Miracle Worker,* the pulsing drama of a young teacher's heroic struggle with a refractory child close to savagery who later became a distinguished woman despite her handicap, proved to be an even greater success on the stage and the screen than *Two for the Seesaw.*

Publication of the last-mentioned play by the firm of Alfred A. Knopf was, however, a double victory for the author. The reader was treated not only to a Broadway success in print, but to a fierce and funny anti-Broadway crusade under the title of *The Seesaw Log,* which makes excellent reading. In it Mr. Gibson describes a playwright's dismay at the mills of Broadway production which grind out successes and failures with equal indifference to an author's sensibilities, nerves, and integrity for the sake of ensuring a commercial success. (It was an honest and touching cry one heard in the author's comment that "The play grew more and more effective and I felt less and less fulfilled as a writer.") And Mr. Gibson's puzzlement grew amusingly, though without actually resolving any problems, when he reflected that his yielding to pressure had brought good results—"that the hammering my script and head had undergone . . . had issued in a much better play." This autobiographical chronicle did not, however, inhibit the author's next collaboration with the same producer and director in the fabrication of a hit. Mr. Gibson was trapped into becoming a successful Broadway author even though, just to square things, he became an unsuccessful off-Broadway one with a satiric fantasy called *Dinny and the Witches.* And Mr. Gibson, who was unusual among playwrights in resenting Broadway success, proved to be unusual as well in attaining it in mid-Manhattan and not attaining it in Greenwich Village.

Comment on *Two for the Seesaw,* one of the most enjoyable Broadway comedies of any season and especially noteworthy for the original characterization of Gittel, the heroine, would be superfluous here. Let the reader enjoy himself—and let the buyer beware only if he goes out shopping not for fun and felicity but for profundity and sociology.*

---

* For the reader who wants to involve himself in somber exercises, the editor unblushingly recommends his own essay, *"Two for the Seesaw* and *The Seesaw Log"* in his book *Theatre at the Crossroads,* pages 211-217 (Holt, Rinehart and Winston, 1960) and the broadside delivered with pyrotechnical skill by John Simon in the August 1960 issue (Number 15) of The Mid-Century, published by the Mid-Century Book Society, pages 15-22; see also Sol Stein's note in the same issue, pages 1-3.

THE SET *consists of two rooms, angled toward each other, but in no way related; they are in different buildings, a few miles apart, in New York.*

The room on stage right is JERRY RYAN'S *and is the tiny living room of a bleak two-room flat in a lower East Side tenement. It contains principally a narrow couch with a kitchen chair at its side, and at the beginning has the depressing air of having been moved into recently and minimally; the telephone for instance sits on the bare floor. In the right wall is a window through which we see nearby rooftops. In the rear wall is a doorway which opens into a kitchen so dark it is practically indecipherable; in this kitchen is a gas range, a covered bathtub, and the entrance door of the flat. The left wall of the room towards stage center is omitted or fragmented, so as not to obstruct our view of the other room on the stage.*

The room on stage left is GITTEL MOSCA'S *and is the living room of a flat in a run-down brownstone in midtown. It is on a lower level than Jerry's, is larger and lighter, and has a pleasantly untidy and cluttered air of having been lived in for some time; though furnished in very ordinary taste, it speaks of human comfort and warmth. Downstage in the left wall is the entrance door, and upstage a doorway into the kitchen, which is partly visible. The room contains among other things a studio double bed, a night table with lamp and phone, a bureau, chairs, and a dress dummy and sewing machine in the corner; there is also a window which looks out upon the street.*

ACT ONE

SCENE ONE

Both rooms. It is a late afternoon in September; the windows of both rooms are open, and the sounds of traffic float in. GITTEL'S *room is empty.*

In the other room JERRY *is sitting on his couch, cigarette in hand, searching with his finger down the phone book open between his feet.* JERRY *is a long fellow in his thirties, attractive, with an underlayer of melancholy and, deeper, a lurking anger; his manner of dress, which is casually conservative, is too prosperous*

for this drab and disorderly room. The couch is unmade, the kitchen chair next to it has a typewriter on it and is hung with clothes, a handsome suitcase is open on the unswept floor, and the dust is gathering in bunches along the baseboard. Now JERRY *finds the number he wants, and dials.*

The phone in GITTEL'S *room rings.*

On the fourth ring JERRY *hangs up. Simultaneously there has been a rattle of key and knob at* GITTEL'S *door; she runs in, not stopping to set down her bag of groceries, and grabs the phone.*

GITTEL (*out of breath*). Yeah, hello? (*She waits a second.*) Oh, hell. (*She hangs up. She is a dark, thin girl of indeterminate age, too eccentric to be called pretty, nervous, uncouth, and engaging by virtue of some indestructible cheerfulness in her; all her clothes—denim skirt, peasant blouse, sandals—are somehow misfits, and everything she does has the jerky and lightweight intensity of a bird on the ground.*

Now she and JERRY *go about their separate business.*

JERRY *lifts the suitcase onto the couch, and taking out his clothes—a fine jacket, a fine suit, a fine topcoat—begins hanging them on a clothes rod set catty-corner between two walls; while he is putting some shoes down, the rod slips out of one support and everything falls on his head.*)

JERRY. Oh, you son of a bitch. (*He lets it all lie, and returns into the kitchen. He comes back with a block of wood, hammer, and nails; he nails the block any which way under the socket on one wall, puts the rod back in place, and hangs the clothes up again; this time the rod holds.*

Meanwhile GITTEL, *on her way to the kitchen with her bag of groceries, has stopped in front of the dress dummy and looks critically at a gaudy bodice pinned together on it; she stands unmoving for a minute, then with her free hand unpins the collar and commences to work. After a while she steps back, and is disgusted.*)

GITTEL. Oh, for Christ sakes. (*She gives up, slaps the pins down, and continues on to the kitchen, where we see her pour out a panful of milk and set it to warm on a gas burner; she puts the other groceries away in cupboard and icebox.* JERRY *finishes with his clothes, turns to regard the phone, sits on the couch, checks the* same number, and dials it once more. *The phone in* GITTEL's *room rings.* GITTEL *runs back and answers it just as* JERRY *is about to hang up after two rings.*) Yeah, hello?

(JERRY's *voice when we hear it now is well-educated, with a deadpan mockery in it that is essentially detached.*)

JERRY. Gittel Mosca, please.

GITTEL. It's me, who's this?

JERRY. This is Jerry Ryan. We met across eight or nine unidentified bodies last night at Oscar's. I'm a slight acquaintance of his from back home.

GITTEL. Oh?

JERRY. I say slight, about 170 pounds. Six one. (*Waits; then elaborately*) Red beard—

GITTEL. Oh, you were the fella in the dark hat that didn't say anything!

JERRY. You must know some very bright hats. I overheard you talk about a frigidaire you want to sell. Be all right if I stop by for a look?

GITTEL. At that frigidaire?

JERRY. It's all I had in mind, to begin with.

GITTEL. It's not a frigidaire, it's an icebox.

JERRY. Good enough. No electric bill, a product of American know-how. I could be there in about—

GITTEL. I gave it away!

JERRY (*a pause, stymied*). Oh. Not very kind of you.

GITTEL. I just helped him lug it home. Some jerk I never saw in my life, Sophie sent him over, so I let him have it just to get rid of the goddam thing. Why didn't you ask me last night?

JERRY. I didn't want to be among the quick. Last night.

GITTEL. Huh?

JERRY. I changed my mind and life today, great day, I thought I'd start by putting my nose in on you for a look.

GITTEL. It just isn't here.

JERRY. So you said. (*A pause, both waiting.*) Yes. Thanks anyway.

GITTEL. Sure. (JERRY *hangs up.*) Oh, hell. (*She hangs up too.* JERRY *after a morose moment gets up, fingers in his pack of cigarettes, finds it empty. En route to the window with it he bumps his knee against the couch; he lifts his foot and shoves it back, it jars the wall, the clothes rod is jogged out of the other*

support, *and the clothes fall on the floor.*)

JERRY. Agh, you son of a bitch! (*He grabs the rod and brings it down over his knee; it only bends, flies up in his face. He attacks it again, can't break it, trips over it, and doesn't know where to get rid of it, in a rage which is comic, until suddenly he throws a short punch into the window, not comic; the glass flies. He stands, grimly considers his fist, his surroundings, his state of mind, gets away from the window, walks into the phone on the floor, regards it, gathers it up, and dials. Meanwhile* GITTEL's *milk boils over as she is removing her sandals. She jumps up, and is hurrying toward the kitchen when her phone rings.*)

GITTEL. Oh, for Christ sakes. (*She is undecided, then hurries back and grabs up the phone.*) Just a minute, will you, I'm boiling over. (*She lays it down, hurries into the kitchen, turns the milk off, and comes back to the phone.*) Milk all over the goddam stove, yeah? (JERRY *sits with his eyes closed, the mouthpiece against his eyebrows.*) Hello? (JERRY *separates his face and the mouthpiece.*) Hello, is anybody on this line?

JERRY. No.

GITTEL. Huh? (JERRY *hangs up.*) Hey! (*She stares at the phone in her hand, then replaces it. She decides to shrug it off and go back to her milk, which she cools off by adding more from the container; but she stands in the doorway sipping it for only a second, then makes for the phone. She dials, and waits.* JERRY *walking in his room finds his hand is bleeding a bit, wraps it in his handkerchief, and has a private argument, not liking himself.*)

JERRY. You brokenhearted fly, begin. (*He gazes around the bare room, answers himself mordantly.*) Begin what? The conquest of the Sunday *Times*? (*He shoves the suitcase off the couch, lies down and extracts section after section of newspaper from under him, flinging them away.* GITTEL *gets an answer.*)

GITTEL. Sophie. Is Oscar there? . . . Well, listen, that hat-type friend of his last night, the long one, what's his number? . . . Look, girl, will you drag your mind up out of your girdle and go see if Oscar's got it written down?

(JERRY's *legs are overhanging, he moves back, but now his head bumps the wall. He gets to his feet and considers the couch grimly, muttering.*)

JERRY. Six feet of man, five feet of couch, calls for a new man. (*He stands the suitcase on end at the couch foot, lies down again with his feet out upon it, and extracts and flings away a final section of newspaper.* GITTEL *scribbles.*)

GITTEL. 69 what? Yeah, yeah, yeah, very funny. (*She clicks down, and immediately dials it.* JERRY's *phone rings. His head lifts to regard it, and he lets it ring another time before he leans over to pick it up.*)

JERRY (*guardedly*). Yes?

GITTEL (*quickly, a little nervous*). Look, I been thinking here about that icebox, what we could do is I could take you around the corner where this character lives, if you offer him a buck or two he might turn loose of it, and it's worth five easy, what do you say? (JERRY *on his elbow mulls her over.*) Hey, you still with me?

JERRY. I don't know yet, I might be against you. I'm not in the book, how did you get my number?

GITTEL. Sophie gave me it. Now about this icebox, I mean for nothing I let this kid have a real bargain, you could afford to make it worth his while, what do you think?

JERRY. I think you can't be calling about an icebox you had to help someone carry through the streets to get rid of.

GITTEL. What do you mean?

JERRY. You're calling either because like me you have nothing better to do, or because you're under the misap—

GITTEL (*indignantly*). I got eleven different things I could be doing!

JERRY. Different isn't better, why aren't we doing them? Or because you're under the misapprehension it was me who just hung up on you.

GITTEL (*confused*). Uh—it wasn't?

JERRY. Whoever it was had a reason. Question now is what's yours? If a man calls up to say he's not calling up, a girl who calls him back can be either lonely, solicitous, prying, a help or a nuisance—

GITTEL. Look, how'd I get in the wrong here?

JERRY. —and I'm curious to know which.

GITTEL. Did you call me up about this icebox or not?

JERRY. Not.

(GITTEL *bangs the phone down, gets up, and tears her scrap of paper with his number into bits; she throws them into the wastebasket.* JERRY *after a surprised moment finds this somewhat amusing, smiles in spite of himself, clicks down, and dials back.* GITTEL's *phone rings, and she comes to answer it;* JERRY's *manner now is rather teasing.*)

GITTEL. Yeah, hello?

JERRY. I said I didn't call you about an icebox.

GITTEL (*darkly*). Whaat?

JERRY. It seems I did, but I didn't.

GITTEL. Look, I can't follow this whole conversation. You called—

JERRY. I called because the only female voice I've heard on this phone is the robot lady with the correct time, and I'm going off my nut in solitary here. I called to make contact.

GITTEL. Oh!

JERRY. With someone of the weaker sex who's weaker.

GITTEL (*pause*). Okay, here I am. (JERRY *ponders it.*) Contact!

JERRY. I called to invite you to dinner tonight. And a show.

GITTEL. So why didn't you?

JERRY. I was afraid you'd say yes or no.

GITTEL. Huh? I would of said sure.

JERRY. See what I mean? All right, which show? It's Sunday, we'll have to see what—

GITTEL. Well, now I'm *not* so sure.

JERRY. Why?

GITTEL. I don't know if I want to get involved now, you sound awful complicated to me!

JERRY. How? Man calls to invite you to dinner via the icebox, you say there isn't any icebox, he waits to be invited in without the icebox, you show no interest in anything but the icebox, you call him back to invite him to invite you via the icebox again, he expresses interest in your personality, not your icebox, you're so devoted to the icebox you hang up. What's complicated?

GITTEL (*a pause*). Look, what's your point?

JERRY (*dryly*). I'm kind of pointless, how are you?

GITTEL. I mean I'm the girl, right? You're the man, make up your mind. *Then* ask me to dinner, and I'll make up my mind.

JERRY. My point is I've been trying to make up my mind for a month here.

GITTEL. What, to ask me to dinner?

JERRY. To climb off a certain piece of flypaper. It's a beginning. (*Pause*) I mean once you break a leg in five places you hesitate to step out.

GITTEL. Oh!

JERRY. It's one night in the year I don't want to eat alone. (*Another pause*) The reason I hung up was I didn't want to say please. Help me.

GITTEL. Well. How'd you expect to pick me up?

JERRY. How far east are you?

GITTEL. Off Second.

JERRY. I'll be there in half an hour.

GITTEL. Maybe you shouldn't, is it okay enough to?

JERRY. Is what okay enough to?

GITTEL. Your leg.

JERRY. What leg? Oh. (*He is deadpan.*) I don't know, it seems to have affected my head. I'll see you. (*He hangs up, replaces the phone on his couch. GITTEL stares, shakes her head, glances at an alarm clock on the night table, hangs up hurriedly, and darts out her door into the hall, where from another room we hear the bathtub water being turned on. Meanwhile JERRY's mood has lightened; he picks up his fallen clothes and lays them across the couch, brushes his jacket off, and slips into it. He is on his way out with his hat when the phone rings, and he comes back to answer it, thinking it is GITTEL and speaking dryly into the mouthpiece.*) I'm as sane as you are, stop worrying. (*Then his faces changes, becomes guarded.*) Yes, this is Mr. Ry— (*His mouth sets. After a second*) Who's calling from Omaha? (*Suddenly he hangs up. He stands over the phone, his hand upon it, until it begins to ring again; then he puts his hat on slowly, and walks out of the room. He pulls the kitchen light out, and leaves, closing the outer door. The phone continues to ring.*)

Scene Two

GITTEL's *room. It is close to midnight the same day, and both rooms are dark, except for the lights of the city in the sky beyond their open windows. The faint sounds of metropolitan night are audible.*

Under GITTEL's *door there is a line of yellow light from the hall, where presently we hear voices and footsteps; the door is unlocked, and* GITTEL *comes in with* JERRY *behind her, both silhouetted. Their mood is light, though* JERRY's *manner remains essentially ironic and preoccupied.*

GITTEL. Look out for the furniture. Got to be a bat to find your way around *this* goddam room in the dark.

JERRY. Some of my best friends are bats. And the rest are cuckoos. The— Oogh!

GITTEL. There. (*She clicks on a lamp which gives a cozy light, and tosses her purse and a theater program on the bed.* JERRY *is holding a carton of cokes and a bag, and rubbing his shin with his bandaged hand;* GITTEL *comes back, grinning.*) So whyn't you listen?

JERRY (*surrenders the things*). No place like home, be it ever so deadly. Sixty per cent of the accidents in this country occur in the home. (GITTEL *takes the things into her kitchen.*) Doesn't include ruptured marriages. Be safe, be homeless.

GITTEL (*calling in, amused*). What'll you have, coke or beer, Jerry?

JERRY. Anything you're having that's wet.

GITTEL. I'm having warm milk.

JERRY (*with doubt*). Warm milk. (*He considers it, putting his hat on the dress dummy while* GITTEL *in the kitchen lights the gas under a potful.*) I think I'm too old for you. I'll have a hell-bent coke.

GITTEL. Coke's got caffeine in it, maybe I'll give you a beer better, huh?

JERRY. Better for what?

GITTEL. It's more relaxing. You had three cups of coffee at dinner, a coke now makes—

JERRY. Gittel, call off the St. Bernards. I mean let's not nurse me, I've been taken care of to shreds. (GITTEL *is brought back to the doorway by his tone, which has an edge.*) Coke, and damn the torpedoes.

GITTEL. You said you don't sleep. So you *won't* sleep. (*She goes back into the kitchen.* JERRY *thinks it over, dryly.*)

JERRY. It's a non-income-producing habit. If you guarantee I'll sleep with beer, you can give me beer.

(GITTEL *comes back into the doorway.*)

GITTEL. Look, let's start all over, on

your own. Coke or beer?

JERRY. Warm milk.

GITTEL. Now listen—

JERRY. If I'm relaxing I don't want to be *casual* about it.

(GITTEL, *shaking her head, goes back into the kitchen; she continues from there, while* JERRY *explores the room.*)

GITTEL. What kind of bed you got you don't sleep?

JERRY. A couch I got at the Salvation Army, eight dollars.

GITTEL. Well, my God, no wonder! Take a feel of that bed. (*She comes into the doorway, points with a mug;* JERRY *stops to eye the bed.*) You know how much I paid for that mattress alone? Fifty-nine bucks! Sears' best.

JERRY. Six lovely feet long and wide enough for two, isn't it?

GITTEL. Yeah, well, that's one thing I'd never be without is a good bed, you just got to get yourself a good bed. (*She goes back into the kitchen.*) I mean figure it out, you're in it a third of your life.

JERRY (*dryly*). You lead a very puritanical life, by that estimate.

GITTEL. How come? Oh. Okay, half!

JERRY (*interested*). Hm. Well, I've been spending most of my nights here on the jewel-like bridges. I can't afford fifty-nine dollars just to make my bedbugs comfy.

GITTEL. You got bedbugs? (*She comes in frowning, with a box of cookies and two mugs of milk, and hands him one.*)

JERRY. Among other things eating me at night.

GITTEL. You out of work, Jerry?

JERRY (*inspecting his milk*). I know why I'm drinking this, why are you?

GITTEL. Oh, I got an ulcer. (*She indicates her chest, explains.*) In the duodenum.

JERRY. Serious? (GITTEL *shrugging wags her head, makes herself comfortable on the bed, her legs under her.*) I thought ulcers in women went out with the bicycle built for two, isn't it a man's disease nowadays?

GITTEL (*philosophically*). Well, I got it!

JERRY. Well, which are you, the old-fashioned type or the manly type?

GITTEL. Why, what's the difference?

JERRY. Present difference might be whether I drink this and go, or stay all night. (*He cocks an eye at her, and* GITTEL *eyes him back unperturbed, a moment of frank speculation, both ways.*)

GITTEL. You don't exactly lead up to things, do you?

JERRY. Oh, I've been *up* for hours, pawing the ground. The only question is which way to run. (*He moves away from this subject, which leaves her perplexed; he stops to regard the gaudy bodice on the dress dummy, his manner dry and light.*) Speaking of blind as a bat, who is this for?

GITTEL. Dance costume, some kid she's at the Education Alliance next Sunday.

JERRY. Has no bottom part, this kid she has no bottom parts?

GITTEL. Goes with tights, natch!

JERRY (*at the sewing machine*). Good idea. And here you earn an immodest living, hm?

GITTEL (*dubiously*). Mmm. Half and half.

JERRY. Why, what's the other half?

GITTEL. The other half I'm unemployed!

JERRY (*at photos on a wall*). Well, the answer is simple, longer costumes. Aha, acrobats. Who's the black beauty with cramps?

GITTEL. That's me.

JERRY. You?

GITTEL. Yeah, don't act so surprised! I'm dancing.

JERRY. Oh. Yes, I see. I had the impression you'd given up that line of work, or vice versa.

GITTEL (*indignant*). No! That's what I *am*. Ye gods, I studied with Jose for years.

JERRY. Jose who?

GITTEL (*staring*). Are you serious?

JERRY. Good question. You mean this is the real you.

GITTEL. Well, if it isn't I sure wasted a lot of seven-fifties a week!

JERRY. And Mr. America here would be your ex-mistake?

GITTEL. Who?

JERRY. Your husband.

GITTEL. Nah, Wally wasn't around long enough to *snap* a picture. That's Larry.

JERRY (*sagely*). Oh. The present mistake. (*He contemplates the photos.*) Somehow there's more *of* the real you. Do you have such nice legs?

GITTEL. Sure! Well, I mean I did, but that's some time back, before I got sick,

I lost a lot of weight since then.

JERRY (*on tiptoe at one photo's neck-line*). With your old-fashioned duo-denum? Can almost make it out in this one—

GITTEL. No, ulcers you put *on* weight. That diet, ye gods, six meals a day, the last hemorrhage I had I put on eighteen pounds. I looked very good. (JERRY *turns to her with a frown*.) Everybody said!

JERRY. The last.

GITTEL. Yeah, I hope it's the last. I got just so much blood!

JERRY. It is serious. How many hemor-rhages have you had?

GITTEL. Two. Then when I never looked healthier in my life, they had to operate on me.

JERRY. For the ulcer?

GITTEL. Appendicitis! (*She becomes self-conscious under his continued gaze; she laughs*.) No kidding, I'm a physical wreck, practically.

(*After a moment* JERRY *raises his milk to her*.)

JERRY. To your physique. As is, with-out appendix. I couldn't resist another ounce. (*He drinks to her, and* GITTEL *cheerfully acknowledges it with a sip of her own*.)

GITTEL. So okay, that's what's wrong with me, what's wrong with you?

JERRY. Me? Not a thing.

GITTEL. How'd you break your leg in five places?

JERRY. Oh, my leg. It broke with grief. (*He empties the mug, sets it down, stops at her radio and clicks it on, sees that it lights up, clicks it off, and moves on, taking out a cigar*.)

GITTEL. Look, whyn't you settle down and rest up? (JERRY *turns to her, she an-ticipates him*.) I'm not nursing, it just makes me nervous to watch!

JERRY (*dryly*). I have two rates of mo-tion, the other is collapse. The last lady who invited me to settle down I couldn't get up for nine years. (*He drops in a chair apart from her, unwrapping the cigar;* GITTEL *stares*.)

GITTEL. Who was that?

JERRY. Her name escapes me. The question at hand is how we're to make up our mind.

GITTEL. About what?

JERRY. About my staying over. I appre-ciate the invitation, but I'm not sure you should insist. On the other hand, it's very pleasant here and I can't plead any prior engagements.

GITTEL (*a pause*). I don't get you, Jerry.

JERRY. I only sound hard to get. No one's had much trouble.

GITTEL. I mean first you can't say if you even want to eat with me, the next min-ute, bing, into bed. Only it's all talk, how come?

JERRY. It's exploratory talk. Like the old lady who said how do I know what I think till I hear what I say.

GITTEL. Ahuh. Is that the way you de-cide everything?

JERRY. How?

GITTEL. In your head?

JERRY. Well, I have a little gray thing-amajig in there supposed to save me false moves. Where do you decide things?

GITTEL. Well, that one not in my head! I mean a couple of false moves might get you further.

JERRY (*studies her for a moment*). Don't rush me. I think I should examine what I'm getting into.

GITTEL (*eyebrows up*). Who said yes, yet?

JERRY. And so should you. What if all I can afford is a—(*He waves a hand at the photos*.)—lady on a picture, not a whole human being with hemorrhages and so on?

GITTEL (*indignantly*). So who's giving them to you?

JERRY. Well. I'm burning my bridges before me. Maybe we could have a little music to obscure the future, I've missed that too.

GITTEL. My God, you haven't got a radio even?

JERRY. No, why?

GITTEL. Everybody's got a radio! (*He lights the cigar.* GITTEL *stares at him, till the radio comes in under her hand; she dials around to some music*.) Listen, are you really broke?

JERRY (*inspecting the cigar*). What kind of a name is Gittel? Has an exotic ring, Eskimo or—

GITTEL. Polish. Are you?

JERRY. Polish?

GITTEL. Broke!

JERRY. Why do you ask?

GITTEL. I just want to know if that's what's keeping you up nights, and if so what'd we eat out and go to a show for?

I mean we could of gone Dutch at least.

JERRY (*deadpan*). I thought you were Italian.

GITTEL. Who, me? Jewish!

JERRY. Mosca?

GITTEL. Oh, *that's* exotic. It's my stage name.

JERRY. What stage are you in?

GITTEL. Huh?

JERRY. What's your real name?

GITTEL. Too long. For the marquees, Moscowitz.

JERRY. So you became a witzless Italian. Is that where you were born?

GITTEL. Italy?

JERRY. Poland.

GITTEL (*indignantly*). I was born in the Bronx. Listen, why'n't you get unemployed insurance? It's what I do.

JERRY. Well. For one thing, I'm not a legal resident of this state.

GITTEL. Oh. (*She considers it.*) So what state are you from, legally?

JERRY. Nebraska.

GITTEL. Nebraska. That's somewhere out in California, isn't it?

JERRY. I think it's Nevada that's in California.

GITTEL. I mean, you're a long ways from home. You don't know anybody here you can borrow from?

(JERRY *in his chair appraises her steadily.*)

JERRY. Only you. (*A quiet moment, their eyes not leaving each other.* GITTEL *then picks up his mug, to refill it, debating.*)

GITTEL. How much do you need?

JERRY (*eyes down*). You're a very generous girl. (*Then he gets to his feet, his voice flattening; he walks away from her.*) Much too generous. Don't play the fairy godmother, the wolf will eat you up.

GITTEL. You said you were broke!

JERRY. No, you said I was broke. The unromantic fact is that last year I made fifteen thousand dollars.

GITTEL (*staring*). Doing what?

JERRY. I'm an attorney.

GITTEL. You mean a lawyer?

JERRY. Attorney. To be exotic.

GITTEL (*indignant*). I got eighteen bucks to get me through the month, what am I helping you out for?

JERRY (*indifferent, at the window*). Offhand I think you enjoy feeding stray wolves.

GITTEL. What?

JERRY. I think you're a born victim.

GITTEL. Of who?

JERRY. Yourself.

GITTEL (*staring*). Am I wrong or have you got a nerve? I felt sorry for you, what's so terrible?

JERRY (*turning*). For me.

GITTEL. Sure.

JERRY. How old are you?

GITTEL. Twenty-nine, so?

JERRY. So. Don't talk like twenty-eight. At thirty you're over the hill, half a life gone, there's very little in this room to show for it. I think it's time you worried about your worries.

GITTEL (*scowling*). I do! I got plans!

JERRY. What plans?

GITTEL. Several! I'm starting right away with this Larry, we're going to work up a whole goddam dance recital, why shouldn't we be the new Humphrey and Weidman? I'm hunting everywhere for a cheap loft to fix up a studio, I can rent it out for classes too. Not to mention I'll probably do the costumes for a show downtown, Oscar's in a new theater bunch there, he says he can—

JERRY (*flatly*). None of this will happen. (*This is true enough to take the wind out of* GITTEL *for a moment.*)

GITTEL (*incensed*). So I'll think up something else! Why are you riding me for?

JERRY. Seriously?

GITTEL. Yeah!

JERRY (*evenly*). Because I enjoy you, life is short, and if you're spending it like a sailor on a spree you might as well spend some on me, but all I probably mean is trouble, I can be here today and gone tomorrow, and I'd rather not be responsible for an ingenuous little nitwit like you. In one word.

GITTEL (*scowling*). What's ingenuous mean, smart?

JERRY. Dumb. Naïve.

GITTEL. Oh, for Christ sakes. I had a room of my own in the Village at sixteen, what do you think, to play potsy? All those reasons, I think you're just scared!

JERRY (*a pause, levelly*). Do you sleep with him?

GITTEL. Who?

JERRY. Mr. America. Larry.

GITTEL. He's a *dancer*.

JERRY. So you said.

GITTEL. I mean we're very good friends and all that, but my God. You think I'm peculiar or something? (*Her eyes widen.*) Are you?

JERRY. Am I what?

GITTEL. Queer?

JERRY (*a pause, shakes his head*). Oh, you've gone too far. (*He puts down the cigar.*) No one's in your life now?

GITTEL. No, I'm free as a bird, goddam it.

JERRY. I'm free as a worm. We can keep it as simple as that, an item of diet. (*His hands gesture for her, and* GITTEL *readily comes;* JERRY *kisses her. It begins temperately enough, but as* GITTEL *co-operates it becomes a wholehearted and protracted undertaking. It is* GITTEL *who slides out of it, leaving* JERRY *with his hands trembling; she is a bit jittery herself.*)

GITTEL. Brother. How long you been on the wagon?

JERRY. A year.

GITTEL (*staring*). Where you been, in jail? (JERRY *reaches, grasping her arms this time inexorably. He kisses her again; she resists weakly, responds, resists very weakly, and gives up, hanging loosely in his hands until they part mouths for air.*) Look, let's not get all worked up if we're not going to finish it, huh?

JERRY. Who's not going to, huh.

GITTEL. I mean you just have another cookie to calm down, and then maybe you better go.

JERRY. Go!

GITTEL. Please.

(JERRY *releases her. A silence.*)

JERRY. Is that what you meant by a false move would get me further?

GITTEL. No, I—

JERRY. Go where? (*He turns away, very annoyed, finds himself at the radio, and mocks her.*) Back to a room without a radio?

GITTEL (*weakly*). Radio costs nineteen ninety-five—

JERRY. That's cheap enough. I had the impression you'd been inviting me all night. To buy a radio? (*He snaps the radio off, and walks.*)

GITTEL (*defensive*). I got an ironclad rule I wouldn't sleep with God Almighty on the first date, you want me to be *promiscuous*? In the second place you—walk around too much—(*She works up some indignation.*)—and in the third place I can't stand cigars in the first place, and in the fourth place I tell you my whole life practically and what do I hear out of you, no news at all, why should I hit the hay right away with someone I don't know if he's— (JERRY *wheels on her so bitingly it stops her like a blow.*)

JERRY. *Because I'm drowning in cement here!*

GITTEL. Where?

JERRY. This town! (*He paces, talking through his teeth, more to himself than to her.*) I haven't passed a word with a living soul for a month, until I called Oscar—and we never liked one another! Everyone else I knew here has moved to Connecticut, Vermont, the Arctic Circle. I've worn out a pair of shoes in the museums. And a pair of pants in bad movies. And if I hike over another beautiful bridge here by my lonesome, so help me, I'll jump off! So I go back to my cell, twenty-one dollars a month, with garbage pails in the hall they'll find me gassed to death by some morning. (*He turns on her.*) And I can't *spend* nineteen ninety-five on a radio!

GITTEL (*the neighbors*). Sssh! Why?

JERRY (*hissing*). Because I came east with five hundred dollars. I'm living on three-fifty a day here now.

GITTEL (*hissing*). You spent about sixteen-eighty on me tonight!

JERRY (*hissing*). I splurged.

GITTEL. What, on me?

JERRY. On me. I was thirty-three years old today. (GITTEL *is speechless. He lifts up his cigar, dourly.*) So, I bought myself a dollar cigar.

GITTEL. It's your *birthday*?

JERRY. Sorry it—exploded. (*He crushes it out in the ash tray.*)

GITTEL (*alarmed*). So don't ruin it! You got to buy yourself a present on your birthday, my God? Whyn't you tell me?

JERRY. Why, you'd like to give me one?

GITTEL. Sure!

JERRY. Thank you. (*He retrieves his hat from the dummy.*) I'm not hinting for handouts, from crackpot lovable waifs. Just don't tell a man go when you've been indicating come all night, it's not ladylike. (*He walks toward the door.*)

GITTEL (*stung*). So what do you think

you been doing right along?

JERRY (*stops*). What?

GITTEL. Hinting for handouts! It's what *you* been doing all night!

JERRY. Are you talking to me?

GITTEL. Sure. All these hints, unhappy, bedbugs, broke—

JERRY. Unhappy bedbugs!

GITTEL. Unhappy! Bedbugs!

JERRY. What in God's name are you dreaming—

GITTEL. Like this minute, if I don't sleep with you they'll find you dead?

JERRY (*astonished*). Who said that?

GITTEL. You did. With the garbage?

JERRY. Oh, cut it out. I—

GITTEL. Or off a bridge, you're so lonely? That's the *last* thing you said?

JERRY. I was—I— (*But he breaks off, staring at her in less disbelief.*) That was —campaign oratory. You call that all night?

GITTEL. The *first* thing you said was help me. On the phone. Right?

(JERRY *stares, almost speechless, though he makes one more convictionless try.*)

JERRY. I—said I *wouldn't* say that, I—

GITTEL. Oh, come on! You said help me, I said sure. (JERRY *cannot remove his eyes from her, at a loss for words.*) I'm not complaining, I'm used to all kinds, but what do you call me names, you want it both ways? (JERRY *still stares at her, but something has opened in him that now takes him away from her, downstage, his fingers at his brow, almost in a daze.* GITTEL *becomes concerned.*) Hey. I say something hurt your feelings?

JERRY (*with an effort*). Yes, slightly. I— (*He shakes his head, abandons the attempt at irony. Low*) I'm remembering. Something from—(*It comes from far away, his tone now simple and vulnerable.*)—thirteen years ago yesterday. I was walking across the campus of Nebraska U, with a beautiful auburn-haired girl whose father was a sizable wheel in the state. The girl and I were—intimate that summer, and I was telling her I'd have to leave school, no family to help me. The next day—my birthday—was the luckiest in my life, I got the George Norris scholarship. It kept me in school, and I became a lawyer. The girl and I— continued. (*He stops.* GITTEL *waits.*)

GITTEL. That's the whole story?

JERRY. I married her.

GITTEL (*darkly*). You got a *wife?*

JERRY. Had a wife. She's divorcing me out there.

GITTEL (*contrite*). Oh. You too, huh?

JERRY. Me too. It was just before we married I learned that Lucian—her father —had wangled that scholarship for me. You know what I said?

GITTEL. What?

JERRY. Nothing. (*He opens his hands, helplessly.*) It's absolutely true, the— point you made, you made your point.

GITTEL. Which?

JERRY. I ask for handouts. I never *saw* it happening before, right under my nose. (*He shakes his head, finds his hat again, and walks once more to the door.*)

GITTEL. So where you going now?

JERRY. Back to solitary. (*Beset*) There I go again!

GITTEL. So don't. Ye gods, if you hate it so much you don't want to go back there on your birthday, stay over. I got a couch in the back room, you take the bed. Maybe a good night's sleep you'll feel better in the morning, huh? (JERRY *stares unseeing.*) You want to stay?

JERRY. Stay?

GITTEL. So you'll get a good night's sleep. You'll feel better in the morning.

JERRY. You mean, put you out?

GITTEL. It's not out, I fit that couch. I mean you got—long legs, you know?

JERRY. Yes. (GITTEL *is eyeing his legs, with interest. When their eyes meet it is as though for the first time, really: something warmer passes between them, they are both shy about it.*) Both of them.

GITTEL. Yeah, well, I— You mind my sheets? (*She yanks the bedspread down, takes a pillow, gathers things up.*) I put them on clean yesterday and I had a bath.

JERRY. No. It's kind of you to offer, kind of absurd, but kind—

GITTEL. What do you mean absurd? You got a lousy bed, tomorrow you'll get some kerosene and see where they come out of the wall.

JERRY. Gittel. You're a very sweet girl—

GITTEL (*embarrassed*). Well—you're a very sweet girl, too. The john's right out there behind you—

JERRY. —but all I proposed was a change of bedmates.

GITTEL. Listen, all *I* got in mind is a good night's sleep you'll feel better in the morning—

JERRY (*simultaneously with her*). —feel better in the morning. No doubt.

GITTEL (*all settled*). So okay! (*She turns with her armful into the kitchen, puts out the light there.*)

JERRY. Gittel!.

GITTEL (*within*). What?

JERRY. I can't.

GITTEL (*within*). I'm all packed!

JERRY (*a pause*). Crazy. (*Nevertheless, the bed attracts his eye; he turns back from it.*) Gittel! (GITTEL *reappears, still with her armful.*) Look, agree with me. It would be an act of—frailty to stay after—

GITTEL. What, on your birthday? (*She goes back in. JERRY considers this argument for a long moment, contemplates the bed and the room around it, and sighs.*)

JERRY. Gittel. (GITTEL *reappears; his tone is humble.*) Should I really stay?

GITTEL. Look, don't nudya me! You want to stay?

JERRY (*a pause*). I haven't been in a place that smelled of—human living in a month. Of course I want to stay.

GITTEL. So stay! (GITTEL *takes the hat out of his hand, drops it on the bed, gives him a towel, and disappears beyond the kitchen again. When JERRY opens the towel, it has a large hole in it. He shakes his head, amused, and rather forlorn.*)

JERRY. I feel ridiculous. (*He walks out into the hall, leaving the door open. After a moment GITTEL comes back through the kitchen, still with her armful.*)

GITTEL. Listen, I— (*She sees the room is empty, stops, stares at his hat on the bed. She scowls at it, debating. Then she shakes her head, no, no, and walks back toward the kitchen with her armful. But on the threshold she halts. After a second she turns back, and stands to give the hat another stare. Finally she sighs, and with an air of disgusted resignation mutters to herself.*) Oh, what the hell, happy birthday. (*And she puts everything back, her clothes back in the drawer, the clock back on the table, the pillow back in place alongside the other on the bed. She unbuttons and takes off her blouse, hangs it dangling on a chair, sits on the bed to remove her sandals, stands to slip her skirt off, walks in her half-slip and bra to a drawer again, takes out pajama-tops,*

and at this moment hears JERRY *in the hall; she skedaddles with the pajama-tops into the darkness beyond the kitchen.*

JERRY *returns, and walks around, restive. It is a moment before he accidentally kicks one of GITTEL's sandals, stares at them, then at her skirt on the floor, then at her pillow next to his, and looking toward the kitchen, comprehends her intention. He takes up her blouse in his fingers. Bringing it to his face, he inhales the odor of woman again; he rubs it against his cheek, thinking, scowling. At last he comes out of the other end of some maze, and tells himself grittily:*)

JERRY. It's, not, a, *beginning.* (*He hangs the blouse back on the chair, turns, picks up his hat from the bed, and walks straight out into the hall, closing the door behind him.*)

After a moment GITTEL peers in from the kitchen, clad in the pajama-tops and carrying her underthings; she sees the room is still empty and comes in. Quickly she clicks off the lamp, turns down the sheet, has her knee up to get in, remembers, and kneels around to the foot of the bed with her hand outstretched for JERRY's hat. It is not there. She searches, baffled, then sees the door is now closed; she scrambles over the bed to it, looks along the hall to the john and then down over the bannister. Two stories down, there is the closing of the street door.

GITTEL *comes back into her doorway, where she stands silhouetted; after a perplexed moment she slaps her thigh, in resignation.*)

SCENE THREE

Both rooms. It is several hours later, and the first light of dawn is just beginning to pick out the furniture in both rooms.

GITTEL *is in her bed, asleep, with the blanket and sheet pulled up over her ears.*

JERRY's *room is empty, but after a moment we hear JERRY letting himself in at his door. When he opens it, he spies and bends to pick up a telegram waiting inside the threshold. He comes into his living room staring at it, unkempt, needing a shave, weary from walking all night, but relatively lighthearted. He takes the telegram to the broken window, tears the envelope open, then pauses in*

*the act of lifting the message out, and
presently shoves it back in, tosses it onto
his couch, and lights a cigarette. He walks
around a few steps, then stands deliberating between the telegram and the phone,
and suddenly sits to the phone. He dials,
waits.*

The phone in GITTEL's *room rings.*
GITTEL *rolls around before she is altogether
awake, her hand fumbling till it finds
the phone.*

GITTEL (*eyes closed*). Yeah, h'lo. (JERRY
considers how to begin.) H'lo!

JERRY (*dryly*). About that icebox. I
think you let that other jerk have it too
cheap.

GITTEL. Whah?

JERRY. If you keep handing things out
to the first comer, judgment day will
find you without an icebox to your name,
morally speaking.

GITTEL (*jerking up*). Jerry! Hey, you
all right? I called you two three times,
no answer.

JERRY. I tried another bridge. Queens-
boro, it opens a vast new territory to—
(*He catches himself, breaks off.*) I was
about to say get lost in, but that's my last
hint. I walked out on you, Gittel.

GITTEL. Yeah. I noticed!

JERRY. What changed your ironclad
rule?

GITTEL. Oh—I couldn't resist your goddam hat!

JERRY. I should have left it for you. I
thought it was something else.

GITTEL. Like what?

JERRY. Charity. I think your trouble is
running the community chest.

GITTEL. Huh?

JERRY. My trouble is my wife does
understand me. You lit a fair-sized birthday candle under me tonight, it cast a
light backwards all the way to Omaha,
Nevada.

GITTEL. How?

JERRY. Tess—her name is Tess, it comes
back to me from time to time—also
smothered me in loving kindnesses. But
my God, if I hinted for them it's not all
her fault. I needn't have gone into her
father's law office. I needn't have let him
set us up in a handsome house in Fair-
acres. It poisoned the well.

GITTEL (*scowling*). Well?

JERRY. Well—we had running water,
but not much monogamy. I had to be

heroic with some wife, no matter whose,
and Tess now is marrying someone else,
a colleague of mine who— (*He breaks
this off.*) That's another chapter. I
wanted to say only that tonight half my
like looks like a handout, and I finally
walked out on one. From you.

GITTEL. Oh. *I* thought it was something
else.

JERRY. Such as?

GITTEL. I figured you figured I wasn't—
(*She takes a breath.*) I mean maybe you
didn't think I was— You know.

JERRY. No.

GITTEL. Attractive!

JERRY (*a pause*). Oh, God. And you
still called me two or three times?

GITTEL (*she has her pride*). *Two* times.

JERRY. Why?

GITTEL. Well, you disappear like that, I
got worried about you.

JERRY. Gittel. (*His tone is gentle, very
affectionate, for the first time genuinely
heedful of her; the relationship is taking
on a quite different color.*) Gittel, I'll
tell you two truths. One, you're attractive,
two, you don't look out for yourself.

GITTEL. Sure I do.

JERRY. No. If you did you'd object
more.

GITTEL. What to?

JERRY. So many things. This minute,
this very minute, why aren't you taking
my head off about the time?

GITTEL. Why, what time is it?

JERRY. Little before five. It takes practice, go ahead.

GITTEL. Go ahead what?

JERRY. Practice. Protest. Enter an objection.

GITTEL. Huh?

JERRY. *Holler* at me!

GITTEL. What for?

JERRY. It's a hell of an hour to phone
anyone. Who do I think I am, waking
you up this time of night, my father-in-
law? It shows no respect for you, you
resent it, say so!

GITTEL. Look, what are you hollering at
me for?

JERRY (*mildly*). Your own good.

GITTEL. I don't like to holler at people,
it makes me nervous. Anyway, I'm glad
you phoned.

JERRY. Why?

GITTEL (*exasperated*). What makes you
so dumb? *I was worried about you!*

JERRY. That's better.

GITTEL. Better!

JERRY. All you need is practice. Go ahead.

GITTEL (*irately*). Who's practicing? What do you think, I'm nuts, you know what time it is, is that what you call me up five o'clock in the morning to practice hollering?

JERRY (*amused*). No, I called to say don't give anything else away. Until I see you.

GITTEL. What?

JERRY. I'm asking whether you'd— care to try being half of a pair?

GITTEL (*a pause*). Look, let's not go through all *that* again!

JERRY. On my terms, this time. And I don't mean as a handout.

GITTEL. So what do you mean?

JERRY. That *I'd*—like to look out for you. Hemorrhages notwithstanding. (GITTEL *stares at the phone.*) Will you let me? (GITTEL *shakes her head, too uncertain about her feelings to know what to say; she is touched, and also wants to snicker.*)

GITTEL. I'm—I— Why?

JERRY. I think you can use me. Not that I'll be such a bargain, a lot of me is still tied up in the—civil wars. I thought I'd tell you the whole mess, if you'd have breakfast with me.

GITTEL. Where?

JERRY. Here. Will you come?

GITTEL. Well, I'm having a tooth pulled out eight-fifteen. I mean I'll be spitting a lot of goddam blood, we won't be able to *do* anything.

JERRY. Will you come?

GITTEL. Sure I'll come.

JERRY (*a pause, gently*). I'll look for you. (*He is about to hang up, when he has an afterthought.*) Gittel.

GITTEL. Yeah?

JERRY. What do you do when a tooth bleeds?

GITTEL (*concerned*). Why, you got one?

JERRY. Oh, you're a character. I'm talking about *yours*.

GITTEL. Oh. Let it bleed, why? It dries up.

JERRY. I knew I'd have a use for that icebox. I'll have a cake of ice in the sink.

GITTEL. What for?

JERRY. For the ice bag I'll buy for your tooth.

GITTEL (*a pause, amused*). You're start-ing right in, huh?

JERRY. Not a minute to lose. It's a new day, in my thirty-fourth year, and I feel like a rising lark. Get some sleep, now. (*He hangs up.* GITTEL *sits for a moment, then also hangs up and shakes her head in a kind of wonderment.*)

GITTEL. Sonofabitch. (*Presently she gets up and goes into her kitchen, pours herself some milk from the pot, and comes back; she settles in bed with it.*)

(JERRY *sets his phone on the floor and remains smiling, until his eyes again encounter the telegram. He picks it up, fingers it. Finally he draws it out, takes it to the window, and reads it. He goes over it twice in silence; the third time he reads it aloud to himself, without expression.*)

JERRY. "I called to say happy birthday you stinker don't shut me out God help both of us but will you remember I love you I do Tess." (*After a second he perceives the telegram is trembling. He crumples it in his hand, and drops it slowly out the broken window. He returns to his couch, transfers his clothes to the chair, and lies down to finish his cigarette.*

Each lies alone with his thoughts in the bleak light of daybreak, JERRY *smoking and* GITTEL *sipping her milk; the only sound is some distant church clock ringing five.*)

ACT TWO

SCENE ONE

JERRY's *room. It is October now, early evening, dusk.*

GITTEL's *room is much the same, with her bed unmade and two pillows rumpled; but a transformation has overtaken* JERRY's. *It has been fixed up inexpensively, and now is tidy, pleasant, livable, with bedspread, wall lamp, throw rugs, burlap drapes, stained fruit crates for shelving—all improvements in the peasant style of* GITTEL's *garb. Near the window there is a bridge table with two chairs, set for dinner.* GITTEL's *little radio is playing on a shelf, WNYC, symphonic music.*

The light in the kitchen is on, now agreeably shaded; out here GITTEL, *wearing a dishtowel for an apron, is preparing dinner. She comes in carrying a bowlful of salad, sets it on the table, and stands listening thoughtfully to the music; she then has a kind of slow convulsion, which after a moment we see is a modern-dance movement, because she stops, is dissatisfied, scratches her head, tries another, gives it up, and returns to the kitchen. Here she opens the gas-range oven to peer in, does some basting, closes it. In the middle of her next turn she halts, listens towards the door, then skedaddles back in and hastily begins lighting two candles on the table. We then see* JERRY *opening the outer door.*

GITTEL (*calling happily*). Hiya, baby.

JERRY. Hi. (*He stops to sniff the oven, looks in.*) Hmm. Smells good, who's in here? Chicken!

GITTEL. And salad, and potatoes, and wine's on the ice.

JERRY. Wine, well. (*Coming into the doorway he leans there, just taking her in at the candles; he is in street clothes and hat, with a legal tome or two under his arm, and some parcels.*) What are we launching, me?

GITTEL. I got a bargain, sixty-nine cents a bottle. Must of been getting kind of old. (*She comes to kiss his amused face above her, and his arm draws her in.*) What's so funny?

JERRY. You are, infant. (*He spies the window over her shoulder.*) You put up curtains for me!

GITTEL. Sure, what do you think I come over for, just to see you?

JERRY. Very cozy. Last couple of weeks you've turned this into the show place of the nation. You're better than wine, you improve with age.

GITTEL. What's in the bag?

JERRY. Everything's in the bag.

GITTEL. I mean this bag.

JERRY. Don't move!

GITTEL (*alarmed*). Huh?

JERRY. Careful. Back in one inch.

GITTEL. Why?

JERRY (*soberly*). Because all afternoon I've been totally surrounded by lawbooks, and I like it much better being totally surrounded by you. I got your thread. (*He jiggles a bag at her ear.*)

GITTEL. Oh, good. You see Frank Taubman, Jerry?

JERRY. I did. And dessert. (*He jiggles another bag.*) Soya cake. Salt-free, butter-free, flavor-free.

GITTEL. Well, what'd he say?

JERRY. You'll hear. And a piece of the moon. From me, to you. (*He deposits the third bag in her hand.*)

GITTEL. A present?

JERRY. Just a piece of the moon. (GITTEL *unwraps it at the candles, while* JERRY *gets rid of his books and hat, takes off his jacket.*)

GITTEL. I can't wait to see what's in it, what's in it?

JERRY (*deadpan*). Well, it turns out this way, she opens this box from her lover thinking it's candy but it's really the preserved brains of her unfaithful father, who has run away to join this gang of juvenile delinquents, she recognizes him instantly and lets out an unearthly shriek—

GITTEL (*blankly, lifts it*). A cake of soap?

JERRY (*approaching*). Supposed to be the preserved brains of—

GITTEL. What's the matter, I smell?

JERRY. Good idea, let's investigate. (*He puts his nose in her hair from behind, his arms around her waist.*)

GITTEL. I mean what kind of present is a cake of soap, I need a bath?

JERRY. What kind of present is a— Did you look at the box?

GITTEL. No.

JERRY. Read the soap.

GITTEL (*by candlelight*). Channel number—

JERRY. Channel number five, it's a TV sample. Chanel number five, girl, you're holding a two-fifty soap bubble there.

GITTEL (*aghast*). Two-fif— For *one* cake of soap?

JERRY. Don't you dare take a bath with that. We're going to eat it, spoonful by spoonful. Instead of that soya cake.

GITTEL. You know sometimes I think the nutty one of this twosome some of us think I am is you? Two-fifty, we won't eat!

JERRY. We'll eat, it will be a feast. How's your belly?

GITTEL. Oh, fine. I took some banthine, it went away.

JERRY. Didn't all go away. Here's some.

GITTEL. Some what?

JERRY. Belly.

GITTEL. Oh. You think I'm too fat.

JERRY. Good God, no.

GITTEL. You think I'm too skinny?

JERRY (*dryly*). I think you're a sacred vessel of womanhood.

GITTEL. Ahuh. Sexy as all get-out, that's why you buy me a hunk of soap.

JERRY. Buoyant in the bow, swively in the stern, and spicy in the hatch, how's that?

GITTEL. S'pretty good. (*They have been kissing; now* GITTEL *cocks her head back.*) You think I'm *too* sexy?

JERRY. Hm?

GITTEL. I mean oversexed?

JERRY. I think you're a mixed-up girl. Calmly considered, your bottom is tops.

GITTEL. Some vessel. Sounds like a shipwreck. (*She kisses him again. When they come up for air, she slides out of his hands.*) Anyway! You're getting a phone call soon. Long-distance.

JERRY. Who from?

GITTEL (*brightly*). Your wife. (*She inhales at the soap again.*) This her kind, Jerry?

JERRY (*a pause*). No. And I seldom gave her gifts, she was—amply supplied.

GITTEL. Okay. (*She takes the soap out into the kitchen, busies herself at the oven.* JERRY *stands alone, not moving, for a long moment; then he calls out, sounding casual.*)

JERRY. When did she call?

GITTEL (*calling in*). Soon's I got here. Said she'd call back eight o'clock. (*JERRY looks at his wristwatch, stares at the phone, clears the litter off the table, glances again at the phone, and goes to his window, to gaze out.* GITTEL *comes back in, bearing a casserole of chicken and a bowlful of French fries to the table, with cheerful chatter.*) She must have money to burn, huh? I mean *two* long-distant phone calls, ye gods. You know I only made one long-distant phone call in my whole life? (*She stands serving out their portions.*) Tallahassee, that's in Florida, right after we were married. Wally had a job there. I mean he said he had a job, when I found out it was really a redhead he went back to I didn't drop dead either, but I called him up—

JERRY. I don't think I care to talk to her. (GITTEL *continues serving, but frowning over it.*) Gittel.

GITTEL. So don't. Anyway I got the bill,

that's when I did drop dead.

JERRY. I won't answer.

GITTEL (*presently*). All right. You want to get the wine?

JERRY. With pleasure. (*He turns the radio on, and goes into the kitchen.*) Let's drink life to the dregs, the whole sixty-nine cents worth. I have something for us to toast. I had a long session this afternoon with Frank—(GITTEL *meanwhile stares at the phone, then switches the radio off; the mood in the room changes, and the phone now begins to haunt what they do and say.* JERRY *returns with the wine and a corkscrew.*) What's the matter, honey?

GITTEL (*sits*). I don't see any crowd.

JERRY. That I said I wouldn't answer?

GITTEL. Nothing's the matter!

JERRY. It's dead and buried. (*He uncorks the bottle.*) Six feet under, the coffin is sealed, the headstone is paid for, I'd rather not open it all up again. (*Lightly*) Let's change the subject to something pleasant. How are you making out on your recital?

GITTEL. That's pleasant? I looked at that loft again—the goddam bastard still wants a two-year lease and won't come down a cent. I mean I haven't got that kind of gelt. It's a very fine dance studio, for Rockefeller.

JERRY. You don't need Rockefeller, you have Fort Knox here.

GITTEL. Where?

JERRY (*taps his brow*). I had a long session with Frank Taubman this afternoon.

GITTEL. So what'd he tell you? (*But her look is on the phone.*)

JERRY. That if I'm not a member of the New York Bar he could offer me only some briefs to prepare.

GITTEL. Oh.

JERRY. I'll go down with you in the morning and we'll give this goddam bastard two months rent.

GITTEL. Out of what?

JERRY. I accepted them. It pays per brief, we'll be papering the walls with gelt.

GITTEL. I'll get the loft when *I* get a job. (*Her look again is on the phone; this time* JERRY *notices.*)

JERRY (*a pause*). It didn't say anything.

GITTEL. Huh?

JERRY. The phone.

GITTEL. Yeah. I heard Schrafft's was putting on girls, I'm going to see about it tomorrow.

JERRY. Schrafft's. Waiting on table?

GITTEL. Whatever they got. I worked the candy counter for them last year, I put on seven pounds. It's very good candy.

JERRY. Do me a small favor, let me do you a small favor?

GITTEL. Sure. Like what?

JERRY. Like stake you to Loft's instead of Schrafft's. You know how much I can earn doing briefs? A hundred a week, I'll *buy* you candy. It's absurd for you to work at Schrafft's.

GITTEL. What have you got against Schrafft's?

JERRY. I'm afraid someone there will eat *you* up. No Schrafft's, the prosecution rests. (*They eat again.*) You know this chicken is fabulous? What makes it taste like gin?

GITTEL. Gin.

JERRY. Fabulous. You can sew, you can cook, you—(*He suddenly takes note, ominously.*) What are we doing eating French fries?

GITTEL. You like them.

JERRY. Not after you were up half the night with a bellyache.

GITTEL (*indignant*). You said they were your favorite.

JERRY (*mildly*). My favorite will put holes in *your* stomach lining. And your stomach lining is my favorite, how many did you eat?

GITTEL. Three.

JERRY (*rises*). Three too many.

GITTEL. I love them.

JERRY (*hesitates*). Four is all you get. (*He lifts the potatoes from her plate in his fingers, drops one back and takes the bowlful out into the kitchen.*)

GITTEL. Hey! (*But the protest is weak, she contents herself with snaring others from* JERRY's *plate in his absence, and pops them into her mouth. He comes back with a slice or two of bread.*)

JERRY. Here. Instead. You need starch to soak up the acids, honey, I've been reading up on the whole pathology of ulcers and you simply don't know what to do with your acids. In medical parlance we call this a half-acid diagnosis. Let's stick to what *you* can eat, hm?

GITTEL (*her mouth full*). Certainly!

(JERRY *about to sit consults his wristwatch, frowns, glances at the phone; then, sitting, finds* GITTEL's *eyes on him.*) It didn't say anything!

JERRY. What?

GITTEL. The phone.

JERRY. Not going to, either. I was just thinking I'd forgotten the sound of her voice. How did she sound?

GITTEL (*scowling*). What do you mean how did she sound?

JERRY (*bored*). Only how did she sound, don't—

GITTEL. Lovely, she sounded lovely! You want to hear how she sounds, talk to her. What are you scared of? (JERRY *puts down his fork, and contemplates her.*)

JERRY (*evenly*). You really want me to answer it, don't you?

GITTEL. Who, me?

JERRY. Why?

GITTEL. Why not?

JERRY. Because I'm in a state of grace here in a garden of Eden with you and a stuffed chicken. Adam and Eve, and you know what that twelve hundred miles of phone cable is? the snake. Why let it in, it was enough work getting rid of the bedbugs.

GITTEL. Why do you hate her so?

JERRY. I don't, let's change the subject. (*They eat again.*) I'll go with you about this loft tomorrow. Tell the man I'm your lawyer, I handle nothing but your leases, I'll negotiate the whole transaction. I'll even bring my brief case.

GITTEL. What kind of bread is this?

JERRY. Health bread. For our health.

GITTEL. Gee, they must cut this right off a *stump*, huh? (JERRY *sits back and enjoys her.*)

JERRY. You're a bug. A water bug, this way, that, what did I do to have you in my blood stream? Look. I'm saying if you're a dancer it's time to do something about it, the days are going—

GITTEL (*vehemently*). Of course I'm a dancer, it's driving me crazy! Everybody else is getting famous, all I'm getting is repair bills from Singer's!

JERRY. All right then, I can lead a hand with the loft. You go to work on the recital, I go to work on the briefs.

GITTEL. What's doing briefs?

JERRY. Researching a case for precedents. (GITTEL *is uncomprehending, so he clarifies it.*) When one cuke brings suit against another cuke, the court can't decide which cuke is cukier until it hears how two other cukes made out in *another* court in 1888.

GITTEL. So is that fun?

JERRY. Not unless you have a nose-in-the-book talent. But I needn't be writing briefs for the rest of my life, I can practice in court here any time I take the state Bar exam.

GITTEL. So whyn't you take it?

JERRY (*smiles*). It makes me nervous.

GITTEL. Aah. You'd knock them dead.

JERRY. What makes you think so?

GITTEL (*serenely*). I got my impressions.

JERRY. I barely know the traffic laws here. Statutory law *varies*, from state to state, I—

GITTEL. So what, you could study up.

JERRY (*dryly*). I'm a little old to go back to school.

GITTEL. Every day you read in the paper, some grandma going to NYU, eleven grandchildren, seventy years—

JERRY. Do I look like somebody's grandma? I'm not *that* old, but I've been a practicing—(*But he breaks off and leans back to regard her for a moment. Then*) How do you do it?

GITTEL. What?

JERRY. We begin with my saying I'll lend a hand, and end one minute later with you putting me through college.

GITTEL. I don't need a hand, I'll make out! (*JERRY is displeased with this, and after a moment lowers his face to his plate.*) You got to take the exam sometime, no?

JERRY. No.

GITTEL. So what'll you be here in your old age?

JERRY. Don't rush me into the grave. I'm not living that far ahead.

(GITTEL *is displeased with this, and after a moment lowers her face to her plate. They eat.* GITTEL *then bounces up, marches into the kitchen, returns with the bowl of potatoes, and drops a fistful into her plate.*)

GITTEL. What are you, on vacation here? (*She sits.* JERRY *reaches over, puts the fistful back into the bowl, rises, and carries it out again to the kitchen. He returns without it.*)

JERRY. Not necessarily, but I *might* die somewhere else. Be a shame to go to all

the trouble of taking the Bar exam in New York and die in New Jersey. I'd have to commute. (*He sits.* GITTEL *rises, and marches toward the kitchen again; but* JERRY *catches her wrist, pulls her onto his lap.*) Look, look. (*He reaches a long arm out to the couch, catches up one of the legal tomes, and deposits it open on* GITTEL's *thighs. She scowls at the text.*)

GITTEL. What?

JERRY. This is Clevenger. Civil Practice Act of New York, what I don't know fills this little volume and a library full besides. To take the Bar exam here. For two days in this state they lift open the top of your skull and stare in. Now—

GITTEL. Jerry, you know what I think you got too much of? Lack of confidence!

JERRY. Oh, great.

GITTEL. I mean ye gods, you were such a popular lawyer in Nevada, what's the difference?

JERRY. Nebraska, dear. (*He kisses her neck.*)

GITTEL. Nebraska, so what's the difference?

JERRY. About a thousand miles. You know you have a two-fifty smell without that damned soap?

GITTEL (*squirms*). Giving me goose-pimples. Jerry, now I'm talking seri—(JERRY *turns her face, kisses her; after a moment she comes up for breath.*) —ous, how come you were so popular there if—

JERRY (*kissing her throat*). I shot in the mid-seventies.

GITTEL (*stares*). Shot what?

JERRY (*kissing her chin*). Birdies.

GITTEL. That made you *popular*?

JERRY. In the butterfly set. (*He kisses her mouth; this time she comes up with her eyes closed, takes a breath, and gives up.*)

GITTEL. Oh, damn you. (*She seizes his ears and kisses him fiercely; Clevenger slides to the floor, unnoticed, and the kiss goes on. Now the phone rings.* GITTEL's *head comes up. After a second* JERRY *draws it down with his hand, but the next ring brings her up scowling at it.*) Phone's ringing.

JERRY (*lightly*). I don't want the world in. (*He draws her to him again; it rings again.*)

GITTEL. I can't!

(JERRY *puts her aside on her feet, gets*

*up, crosses, takes the phone off the hook,
drops it to hang and comes back.*)

JERRY. Better?

GITTEL. Oh, for Christ sakes. (*She ducks
past him, and picks up the phone, com-
bative.*) Yeah, hello. . . .

JERRY (*outraged*). Put down that
phone!

GITTEL. . . . So whyn't you call sooner—
. . . (*JERRY coming swiftly snatches the
phone from her, ready to slam it down.*)
It's *Larry!* (*JERRY stares at her, lifts the
phone to his ear, listens, then hands it
to her, and walks away.*) Hello? . . . No,
we thought it was the—landlord. So
what'd the Y say? . . . *How much?* . . .
(*JERRY stands staring out the window,
which is now dark with night;* GITTEL's
eyes are on him.) Well, listen, I can't—
. . . No, maybe we'll try Henry Street, but
I can't think about it now. . . . I'm in the
middle of eating, Larry, I'll call you back
later. . . . No, I can't swing the loft yet,
but I can't go into all that now. (*She
hangs up and stands over the phone.* JERRY
*leaves the window; at the table he drains
his tumbler of wine in one swallow, sets
it down. They stand silent for a moment,*
GITTEL *not taking her eyes from him.*)

JERRY (*curtly*). I'm sorry I shouted.

GITTEL. What did that bitch do to you?

JERRY (*rounding*). Bitch? (*Grimly,
then*) Married me, helped put me
through law school, stood by me in
pinches. Loved me, if anyone did or
could. She was never a bitch, don't call
her that again.

GITTEL (*nettled*). That's why you left
Nebraska, she was so nice?

JERRY. I left because I couldn't take
being in the same town with her and her
fiancé.

GITTEL. So you ran away.

JERRY. If that's what you call starting
over from bedrock, yes, I ran away.

GITTEL. So stop running, it's the Atlantic
Ocean already.

JERRY. No one's running now.

GITTEL. You're running, why can't you
talk to her on the phone?

(*JERRY turns to look at her.*)

JERRY. Ask it of me. Don't do it for
me, ask it of me, perhaps I'll do it for
you. Do you want me to?

GITTEL. She's your wife.

JERRY. Do you want me to?

GITTEL. It's your phone.

JERRY. Do *you* want me to? Yes or no!

GITTEL. No!

JERRY (*a pause*). You want me to work
here for Frank Taubman?

GITTEL. No.

JERRY. What *do* you want from me?

GITTEL. Not a goddam thing. (*She
lights a cigarette, takes a drag.* JERRY
passing removes it from her lips, and
GITTEL, *very annoyed, shakes another from
his pack while he is stubbing the first
out.*)

JERRY. Why do you smoke, you know
it's not good for your stomach.

GITTEL. I'll keep track of my own
stomach, we been together almost thirty
years now, we get by! (*She strikes the
match to the new cigarette and* JERRY
*turns. He observes her, not moving a
muscle, until it comes in an outburst.*)

JERRY. Don't be such a damfool tower
of strength!

GITTEL. What!

JERRY. I'm sick of it too, idiotic act of
taking care of you and your weak
stomach. Weak, you're as tough as wire.

GITTEL. So one of us better be!

(*JERRY stares at her grimly; when he
speaks now it is level, but unsparing.*)

JERRY. And one of us better not be.
You don't get by, you only tell yourself
lies. From day to day, sure, job to job,
man to man, you get by. And nothing
sticks, they take off to Tallahassee. Did
you pay his train fare? (*This is a mock
question, but* GITTEL's *open mouth is a
real answer.*) My God, you did! You pay
the freight, and every bum climbs on for
a free ride. And you never know why the
ride is over, do you? I'll tell you why,
when a man offers you a hand up when you
put a donation into it. Why don't you
spit in it? So they use you and walk out.
How many of them have you slept with
on their way through, twenty-five? (*He
waits.*) Fifty? (GITTEL *only stares, now
he is inexorable.*) Five hundred? It's not
a lark any more, you're not a kid, you're
on the edge of a nightmare, and you're all
alone. Who cares, but me? Don't spit in
my hand, Gittel, whether you know it
or not you need it. And make one claim,
one real claim on a man, he just might
surprise you. (*He waits:* GITTEL *continues
to stare, palely, not answering.* JERRY's
voice is hard:) Do you get my point?

GITTEL (*shaken*). Sure. (*Then she re-*

acts, leap-frogging over her own feelings)
You're a *terrific* lawyer, what are you
bashful about?

JERRY. You didn't understand one
word I—

GITTEL. Sure I did, and if I was the jury
I'd send me up for five years, no kidding.
(*She rises, escaping toward the kitchen;*
JERRY *catches her wrists.*)

JERRY. *I'm* not kidding!

GITTEL. So what do you want? Let go
my—

JERRY. Need someone!

GITTEL. Let me go, Jerry, you're hurting—

JERRY. Need someone!

GITTEL. For what? Let go my arms or
I'll yell!

JERRY. You won't yell. Now you—

GITTEL. *Help!* (JERRY *drops her wrists.*
She stumbles away from him, tears of
pain in her eyes, and inspects her wrists.)

JERRY. You little lunatic, someone will
come.

GITTEL. Nobody'll come, it's New York.
(*But her voice is trembling as she shows*
her arm.) Look, I'm going to be all black
and blue, you big ape! I ought to get out
of here before you slug me.

JERRY. Slug you. Is that something
you've learned to expect from your ro-
mances?

GITTEL. I expect the worst! When it
comes to men I expect the worst! (*Now*
she is struggling against the tears.)
Whyn't you pick up the phone if you're
so goddam strong?

JERRY. Do you want me to?

GITTEL. I don't know where I stand
here, it's a big question mark, why should
I stick my neck out?

JERRY (*inexorably*). Do you want me
to?

GITTEL. I *will* get a job too, what's
such a crime, just—cause I—won't—(*And*
finally the tears come; helpless with sobs
she turns away, trying to keep her weep-
ing as private as she can, and failing.)

JERRY (*moved*). Gittel, I—shouldn't
have said all that—

GITTEL (*wheeling on him*). All right,
all right, I can scream my head off here
and nobody comes, who can I count on
besides me?

JERRY. Me, Gittel. (*The phone rings.*
JERRY *alone turns his eyes to it; he stands*
unmoving. GITTEL *gets her sobbing in*

hand, and waits on his decision. It rings
again, and at last she speaks.*)

GITTEL. You. Lean on you I'll fall in a
big hole in Nevada somewhere. (*She*
comes to the table to crush the cigarette,
but JERRY *stops her hand; he takes the*
cigarette from her, goes with it to the
phone, and lifts the receiver.)

JERRY. Yes? . . . Yes, speaking. . . . (*A*
pause, while the connection is made; GIT-
TEL *stands, and* JERRY *takes a much-*
needed drag. His head comes up with
the voice at the other end.) Hello, Tess.
. . . (*His own voice starts out deliberately*
casual.) No, I didn't care to talk to you
the other times, I'm doing it now by
special request. . . . What's that, woman's
intuition? . . . Yes, she is. . . . (GITTEL
now moves to clear the dishes from the
table, very quietly; she takes a stack out
to the kitchen.) Her name's Gittel . . . I
do, very much. . . . I didn't plan to be
celibate the rest of my days, wouldn't do
you any good. . . . And a year of it in
your house didn't do me any good. . . .
(*Sardonically*) Oh, I'll be glad to represent you in the divorce. If your father
will represent me, I need a good lawyer
to help take him to the cleaners. . . .
(*Now more irritable*) Oh, tell him to
stuff it up his—safe-deposit box, if I need
money I can earn it . . . I have a job, I
accepted one today. A girl, an apartment,
a job adds up to a life, I'm beginning.
. . . I have no intention of contesting
the divorce, tell Lucian he can file any
time, I'll enter a voluntary appearance.
The sooner the better . . . I'm not interested in being *friends* with you and your
fiancé, you'll have to put up with each
other. . . . (*Now through his teeth:*) Tess,
you can't sink a knife in me and hope to
leave a tender afterglow. . . . (*Watching*
him with the cigarette we see what this
conversation is coming to cost him; he
controls himself. Now weary:) Tess, are
you calling me halfway across the continent to talk about the furniture? . . . If
the house is haunted burn it, we'll split
the insurance. . . . (GITTEL *comes back in*
to clear what remains on the table. Now
shakily) I'm not unfeeling, *I* don't want
to be haunted either, my God, you made
a choice, get your hand out of my bowels!
. . . (GITTEL *stiffens at this.* JERRY *closes*
his eyes in pain.) Tess. . . . Don't. . . .
Please—plea— . . . (TESS *hangs up.* JERRY

looks at the phone, and slowly replaces it; he is drenched in sweat, and sudden tears confuse his eyes; when he lifts his hand for a prolonged drag, the cigarette is shaking. He does not look at GITTEL. *She reaches with her fingers and pinches out each of the candles; the room goes dark except for the light from the kitchen.* GITTEL *without a word lies face down on the couch, and does not stir.*) Gittel. (GITTEL *is silent.* JERRY *comes to stand above her, puts a hand on her hair; she huddles away.*) Gittel, I—

GITTEL (*suddenly*). It's not what you think!

JERRY. What isn't?

GITTEL. Larry says the Y wants six hundred and twenty-five bucks for one night, that's where we been saying we'd give it. I can't even get up sixty-five a month for a lousy loft! (*Another silence.*)

JERRY (*shakily*). No. Let's look at the snake. (*He tugs the string to the overhead bulb, and its naked light floods the room. He stands, unsteady.*) Gittel. Turn around. Please. (*She lies unmoving.*) Look at me! (*She rolls half around now, to face him with her eyes smouldering.*) Don't pretend. It hurts, let me see it hurts—

GITTEL. What, what?

JERRY. How I can—drown in that well. I need you.

GITTEL. For what?

JERRY. Give me something to hold onto! How do I climb out, where do I get a— foothold here, who do I work *for*, what do I build on? I'm in limbo here and I'm— shaking inside. Gittel. Need *me* for something, if it's only a lousy loft.

(GITTEL *keeps her eyes on him for a long moment; then she comes through in kind, almost inaudibly.*)

GITTEL. Sure it hurts. I'll never hear you tell me that.

JERRY. What?

GITTEL. That I got a—hand inside you.

JERRY (*a pause*). Meet me halfway.

(*Presently* GITTEL *smiles, wryly.*)

GITTEL. You mean in that loft, huh? Okay. Now put out that goddam light, will you? (JERRY *tugs it out.*) C'mere, you—French fry potato. (*He comes, she clasps him around the neck, and pulls him down upon her; and they lie in the haven, rack, forcing-bed of each other's arms.*)

SCENE TWO

Both rooms. It is several weeks later, noon, a cold December day. In both rooms the heat is now on—in GITTEL's *from a gas heater affixed to the wall, in* JERRY's *from a new kerosene stove in the center of the floor.*

GITTEL's *room is empty, the door ajar.* JERRY *is in his room, lying in a spread of legs and legal papers on the couch, with the telephone receiver tucked at his shoulder, in the middle of a conversation.*

JERRY. . . . Yes. . . . Well, that was the issue in McCuller *v.* Iowa Transfer, if a claimant not the consignee enters— . . . That's right, they appealed and it was reversed. This outfit doesn't stand a Chinaman's chance of collecting out there, Mr. Taubman, I don't— . . . Hm? . . . All right: Frank. I don't think we should even consider a settlement . . . It's not going out on a limb. Though many a lawyer would have a fresh view of things from the end of a limb, I— . . . Why, thank you. . . . No, the surprise is finding myself such an expert here on Midwest jurisprudence. . . . I see what it proves, it proves an expert is a damn fool a long way from home. . . . (*The phone in* GITTEL's *room rings.*) No, taking the Bar exam is something I need about as badly as a brain operation, what for? . . . Why should they admit me to the Bar on motion? . . . I'm familiar with the procedure, you sponsor me and I deliver a truckload of Nebraska affidavits. Maybe I can get the affidavits, I'm doubtful about the truck. . . . If it saves me taking the Bar exam why not, but why should you sponsor— . . . Full time. I see. . . . How much would you pay me?—just to keep it symbolic. . . . 6500 what, two-dollar bills? . . . Not enough, Mr.—Frank. If I'm useful to have around full time I'm worth at least 7500, and to nail me down will take eight, so we'd have to begin talking at nine. . . . (GITTEL's *phone rings again.*) I might be very serious, I'm interested in being nailed down. . . . But not to the cross, by a Bar exam. If you'll sponsor me on motion, I'll certainly see what affidavits I can dig out of Omaha— . . .

(GITTEL *meanwhile runs in from the hall, to answer her phone; she is clad in a nondescript wrap, and we see her coun-*

tenance is adorned with a white mustache-smear and goatee-dab of bleaching cream. Her mood is listless.)

GITTEL. Yeah, hello? . . . Oh, Sophie, hiya. . . .

JERRY (*glancing at wristwatch*). . . . Yes, I can take a cab up. . . .

GITTEL. . . . Good thing you called, how long am I supposed to leave this stuff on? I look like a goddam Kentucky colonel here. . . .

JERRY. . . . No, I was going to bring this Wharton brief in after lunch anyway. . . .

GITTEL. . . . It itches. . . .

JERRY. . . . All right, men's grill at the St. Regis, quarter past. . . .

GITTEL. . . . What old friend? . . . Sam? . . .

JERRY. . . . Yes. See you. (*He clicks down, again consults his watch, and dials.*)

GITTEL. . . . What'd you tell him I'm going steady for? I mean how do *you* know I'm going steady if I don't know? . . . So let *me* shoo them off. . . . I don't know what I sound worried about, I sound worried? . . .

JERRY (*busy signal*). Come on, Sophie, get off that damned line. (*He hangs up, and without collecting his things walks out of his flat.*)

GITTEL. . . . Well, my stomach's been giving me a pain in the behind. . . . No, everything's peachy. . . . Oh, she's going to marry someone else. . . . I don't *know* how I get involved in such a mix-up, anyway it's not such a mix-up. . . . No, Wally was different. . . . Milton was different. . . . Which Max? . . . (*She locates her mug of milk, and takes a swallow.*) Look, did anybody ever buy me a loft before? . . . Yeah, *he* used to bring me a Mr. Goodbar, that one still owes me seventy-two bucks I'll never see again. The fact is I'm a born victim! Here I am, practically thirty years old, I'm just finding it out. . . . (JERRY *returns with a fistful of mail, among which is a feminine blue envelope; it stops him. He discards the others, rips it open and reads it, troubledly.*) So who's *against* going steady? . . . What do you think, I'm crazy? Take him home to meet Momma he'll leave New York in a balloon. . . . You don't understand—he plays *golf*, for instance. I never knew anybody per-

sonally played golf. . . . Oh, what do *you* know? . . . He's got a lot on the ball! He busts his brains all day over these briefs he's doing, then he comes down the loft and sweeps up for me, what do you think of that? . . . Sure! I made twenty-two bucks on that loft this month, and Molly's got this kids' class she's going to move in this week. . . .

(JERRY *consults his watch again; he returns to the phone and dials, one digit.*)

JERRY. Operator, I want to call Omaha, Nebraska, Atlantic 5756. . . .

GITTEL (*dispirited*). . . . Yeah, I been working on my recital. Well, trying to. . . .

JERRY. . . . Algonquin 4-6099. . . .

GITTEL. . . . It's hard to get started again after so long, you know? . . .

JERRY. . . . Call me back, please. (*He hangs up, then slowly lifts the letter to his nostrils, in a faraway nostalgia.*)

GITTEL. . . . Maybe I'll take up golf instead. . . . Sure he talks to her. . . . About the divorce, she won't get off the pot! . . . Sophie, I *told* him talk to her, he *has* to talk with her, what are you bending my ear about? . . . Sophie, you're getting me mad. . . . Cause you're pestering me! . . . So don't be such a friend, be an enemy and don't pester me! (*She hangs up irately, and commences to dial again. Before she completes the round,* JERRY's *phone rings; he answers it.*)

JERRY. Yes? . . . All right. . . .

GITTEL (*busy signal*). Oh, nuts. (*She hangs up, gathers some clothes, and goes into her back room.*)

JERRY. . . . Hi, Ruth, is your boss in? . . . Tell him it's his son-in-law. The retiring one. . . . Thank you, Ruth, I miss you folks too. . . . Hello, Lucian, how are you, don't answer that question. . . . (*He moves the phone out from his ear.*) No, I have a job, thanks, in fact I'm applying for admission to the New York Bar on motion. . . . Sure, tell Tess. She thinks the only feet I can stand on are hers. . . . I'm calling about her. I have a letter from her here, it has a St. Joe postmark. What's she doing in St. Joe? . . . (*He moves the phone out from his ear.*) Well, it didn't walk down there and mail itself. I've had a call in to her since Wednesday, there's nobody in the house. When did you see her, Lucian? . . . Drives where for three days? . . .

Just drives? . . . I wish you'd spend more time around her, you're better than nothing . . . I mean your idea of solicitude is a loud voice, Lucian, just talking to you on the phone is like a workout with dumbbells. . . . (*He moves the phone out from his ear.*) Money isn't enough. I have too much to say on that, though, sometime I'll call you collect. . . . She's not all right, I can smell it between the lines here. . . . What girl? . . . Of course I have a girl here, I told Tess so. . . . You mean it's since *then* she's so— . . . Devastated by what? . . . My God, Lucian, I waited for a year, a solid year, till I didn't have an ounce of self-respect left in me! One ounce, I packed with it. . . . Is that her word, abandoned? Tell me how I can abandon another man's bride, I'll come to the wedding. . . . Lucian, listen. Keep an eye on her, will you? That's all I called to say. . . . And give her my best. (GITTEL *comes out of her back room, dressed for the street.* JERRY *hangs up, collects his topcoat, hat, and brief case, consults his watch, then hurries to dial.* GITTEL *picks up her phone, commences to dial, and* JERRY *gets a busy signal.*) Oh, hell. (*He hangs up, as* GITTEL *completes dialing, and hastens out of his flat. His phone now rings once, twice, while* GITTEL *in her room stares at her phone with mounting indignation. On the third ring* JERRY *comes running back in, and grabs up his phone just in time to hear* GITTEL *addressing hers.*)

GITTEL. Ye gods, you were just there!

JERRY. I'm here.

GITTEL. Oh, Jerry!

JERRY. I called twice. Hasn't Sophie got anything better to do than to talk to you?

GITTEL. No. I called *three* times, who you been yakking with?

JERRY. I was talking to Omaha.

GITTEL. What, *again*?

(*A pause.*)

JERRY. What does that mean? I had a peculiar letter from Tess, she—

GITTEL. You ask her about the divorce?

JERRY. No. It was Lucian, I didn't get to the divorce. Tess seems sunk, her father says she—

GITTEL (*hastily*). Jerry, I'm on my way to the loft, I got to hurry, what are you calling me about?

JERRY. I thought you were calling me.

GITTEL. Who?

JERRY. Never mind. I called Lucian because I had to know what's going on out there, he says Tess has shut herself off from—

GITTEL (*interrupting*). Jerry, I got to run, you give me a ring tomorrow.

JERRY (*staring*). What about tonight?

GITTEL. It's Friday, after the loft I'm going to Momma's.

JERRY. What's special about Friday?

GITTEL. Gefüllte fish, good-bye.

JERRY (*protesting*). Hey, we had a dinner—(*But* GITTEL *hangs up.* JERRY *looks at the empty phone, his voice dying.*)— date. (*After a moment he also hangs up.* GITTEL *backs away from her phone, while* JERRY *glances at his watch; each is reluctant to leave.* GITTEL *halts,* JERRY *hesitates over his phone, both are tempted to try again; but neither does. After a melancholy moment they turn and leave, in opposite directions.*)

SCENE THREE

GITTEL's *room. It is February now, a Saturday night, late. Both rooms are dark, and the glow of the city plays in the snowy night outside the windows.*

For a moment there is no movement in either room.

Then there is the sound of a key at GITTEL's *and the door swings open.* GITTEL *is silhouetted in the doorway, alone and motionless, resting against the jamb from brow to pelvis; then she pushes away, and comes unsteadily in. There is a sprinkling of snow on her hair and overcoat. She lets her purse drop on the floor, weaves her way around the bed without light except from the hall, and in the kitchen gets herself a glass of water at the sink; she drinks it, fills another, brings it in, and sits on the bed, with head bowed in her hand. After a moment she reaches to click on the lamp, takes up her address book, and searches for a number. She dials it, and waits; when she speaks her voice is tired and tipsy.*

GITTEL. Dr. Segen there? . . . *I'm* calling, who are you? I mean are you really there or are you one of these answering nuisances? . . . So can you reach Dr. Segen for me? . . . Yeah, it's an emergency. . . . Gittel Mosca, I used to be a patient of his, will you tell him I'm very sick? . . . Canal 6-2098. . . . Thanks. (*She gets rid of the phone, and still in her overcoat, drops back onto the bed. The lamplight is in her eyes, and she puts up a fumbling hand to click it off. She lies in the dark, an arm over her face. After a second* JERRY *in topcoat and hat comes silently up, around the bannister in the hall, and into the doorway, where he stands. The snow has accumulated thickly on him. He sees* GITTEL's *purse on the floor, picks it up, sees the key still in the lock, and draws it out; it is this sound that brings* GITTEL *up on her elbow, startled, apprehensive.*) Oh! Hiya, Jerry. Where'd you blow in from? (JERRY *regards her, his manner is heavy and grim, and hers turns light.*) How was *your* party, have a good time?

JERRY. Not as good as you. Are you drunk, at least?

GITTEL (*with a giggle*). I had a couple, yeah. I had this terrible thirst all night, you know, I didn't stop to think. I mean think to stop.

(JERRY *drops the key in her purse, tosses it on the bed, and closes the door; he walks to the window, silent, where he leans against the casing, not removing his hat.*)

JERRY (*then*). Let's get it over with, who was the wrestler?

GITTEL. What wrestler?

JERRY. The fat-necked one who brought you home just now.

GITTEL. Jake? (*She sits up.*) He's not a wrestler, he's a very modern painter.

JERRY. That's why you kiss him goodnight, you're a patroness of the arts?

GITTEL (*staring*). Where were you?

JERRY. One jump behind you. In more ways than one.

GITTEL. I didn't kiss him, he kissed me. Didn't you go to Frank Taubman's party —(*She pushes herself to her feet, changes her mind, and sits again, shivering.*) Light the gas, will you, honey, I'm awful cold.

(JERRY *after a moment takes out matches, and kneels to the gas heater. When it comes on, it illuminates* GITTEL *drinking the glass of water in one gulp;* JERRY *rising sees her, and comes over to grip her wrist.*)

JERRY. You've drunk enough.

GITTEL. It's water! (JERRY *pries her fingers loose, and tastes it. He gives it back.* GITTEL *grins.*) What's the matter, you don't trust me?

JERRY. Trust you. You were in his cellar in Bleecker Street for an hour.

GITTEL (*staring*). How do you know?

JERRY. What was he showing you, great paintings, great wrestling holds, what? (GITTEL *does not answer, and* JERRY *yanks on the lamp, sits opposite her on the bed, and turns her face into the light.*) What? (*She only reads his eyes and* JERRY *reads hers, a long moment in which she might almost cry on his shoulder, but she ends it with a rueful little snigger.*)

GITTEL. So what do you see, your fortune?

JERRY. Yours. And not one I want to see. You look trampled, is that what you're in training to be?

GITTEL (*irked*). Ye gods, I had about six drinks, you think I'm ruined for life?

JERRY. I don't mean anything so wholesome as drink. You slept with him, didn't you?

GITTEL. Whyn't you take off your hat and stay awhile? (*She pushes his hat back from his eyes, then touches his temple and cheek.*) Poor Jerry, you—

JERRY (*puts her hand down*). You slept with him.

GITTEL. You want to cry? I want to cry.

JERRY (*grimly*). Differences aren't soluble in tears, this city would be one flat mud pie. *Did* you sleep with him? (*But* GITTEL *rolls away into a pillow, her back to him.*)

GITTEL. We both know I'm dumb, whyn't you talk plain words a normal dumb person could understand?

JERRY. How plain, one syllable?

GITTEL. Yeah.

JERRY. Fine. Did he lay you? (GITTEL *lies averted in silence, her eyes open.*) I asked did he—

GITTEL. So what if he did, that's the end of the world? (*Now she does rise, to get away from him, though she is wobbly, and soon drops into a chair.* JERRY *puts his fingers to his eyes, and remains on the bed; it takes him time to come to terms with this.*)

JERRY. Maybe. Of this world. (*But he can't hold the anger in, he smacks the glass off the night table and is on his feet, bewildered and savage, to confront her.*) Why? *Why?*

GITTEL (*wearily*). What's it matter?

JERRY. It matters because I'm at a cross-

roads and which way I send my life packing turns on you! And so are you, you
want to watch *your* life float down the
sewer out to sea? You care so little?

GITTEL. I don't know, I—

JERRY. For me?

GITTEL. Oh, Jerry, I—

JERRY. For yourself?

GITTEL. Myself, I got other things to
worry—

JERRY. Why did you *want* to?

GITTEL. I don't *know* why! Anyway
who said I did?

JERRY (*glaring at her*). You'll drive *me*
to drink. *Did you or didn't you?*

GITTEL. Well, he may of slept with me,
but I didn't sleep with him.

(*JERRY stares at her, tight-lipped for
patience.*)

JERRY. All right, let's go back. Why did
you go home with him?

GITTEL. It's a long story, I used to go
with Jake two three years ago—

JERRY. Not that far back. Get to tonight.

GITTEL. So tonight I had a couple of
drinks too many, I guess it was—just a
case of old lang syne.

JERRY. Old lang syne—

GITTEL. *You* know.

JERRY. Yes, I'm an expert in it, especially tonight. Why did you drink?

GITTEL (*bored*). You're supposed to be
at the Taubman's having a good time.

JERRY. Is that why?

GITTEL. Nah, who wants to go there,
for God's sake.

JERRY. I went about this trouble with
the affidavits. I left as soon as I could to
pick you up at Sophie's, you were just coming out with him, giggling like a pony.

GITTEL (*indignantly*). I was plastered,
I said so, you want a *written* confession?

JERRY. You don't get plastered and
flush us down the drain for no reason,
and Taubman's party isn't it. I'm after
the—(*She gets up wearily, again to move
away from him.*) Don't walk away from
me! I'm talking to you.

GITTEL. So go ahead, talk. Lawyers, boy.

JERRY. Because when something happens to me *twice* I like to know why.
I'm after the reason, what did I do this
time, what's your complaint?

GITTEL. Who's complaining? *You* are!

JERRY. My God, I have no right?

GITTEL. Don't get off the subject.

JERRY. It's the subject, I'm talking
about you and me.

GITTEL. Well, I'm talking about your
wife!

(*A silence. GITTEL walks, rubbing her
stomach with the heel of her hand. JERRY
quiets down, then:*)

JERRY. All right, let's talk about her.
She's interested in you too, I feel like an
intercom. What about her?

GITTEL. I saw your last month's phone
bill. Omaha Neb 9.81, Omaha Neb 12.63
—Whyn't you tell me you were the
world's champion talkers?

JERRY. I like to keep in touch, Gittel,
she's having a very rough time.

GITTEL. So who isn't? I got a headache,
lemme alone.

JERRY. What's your case, I'm unfaithful to you with my wife over the phone,
it's the phone bill pushes you into bed
with this what's his name jerk?

GITTEL. Jake.

JERRY. Jerk! It could be you're pushing
me into Grand Central for a ticket back,
has that thought struck you? Is that what
you want, to cut me loose? So you can
try anything in pants in New York
you've overlook—(*But GITTEL has flopped
across the bed, face down, and lies still
and miserable. JERRY contemplates her,
his anger going, compassion coming, until he resigns himself with a sigh.*) All
right. All right, it can wait till tomorrow. We'll battle it out when you're on
your feet. (*He drops his hat on a chair,
comes over to the bed, kneels and begins
untying her shoes. This kindness sends
GITTEL off into a misery, her shoulders
quiver, and she whimpers.*)

GITTEL. Oh, Jerry—

JERRY. What's the matter?

GITTEL. You don't like me any more.

JERRY. I hate you, isn't that passionate enough? Turn over. (*GITTEL turns
over, and he starts to unbutton her overcoat; her hands come up, his ignore
them.*)

GITTEL. I can do it.

JERRY. It's a huge favor, have the grace
not to, hm?

GITTEL (*desisting*). You don't hate me.

JERRY. I wouldn't say so.

GITTEL. You just feel sorry for me.

JERRY. What makes you think you're so
pathetic? Pull.

GITTEL (*freeing one arm*). Ever saw

me dancing around that loft, boy, you'd think I was pathetic. I been sitting on that goddam floor so many hours I'm getting a callus, I wait for ideas to show up like I'm—*marooned* or something. So the dawn came, after all these years, you know what's wrong?

JERRY (*pausing, gently*). You're not a dancer?

GITTEL (*staring*). How'd you know?

JERRY. I didn't. I meant that loft as a help, not just to puncture a bubble.

GITTEL. So if I'm not a dancer, what am I?

JERRY. Is that why you got crocked? Turn over. (GITTEL *turns back over, and he slips the coat from her other arm and off; he begins to unbutton her blouse in back.*) Will you drink coffee if I make some?

GITTEL (*shuddering*). No.

JERRY. Or an emetic? Get the stuff off your stomach?

GITTEL. You mean vomit?

JERRY. Yes.

(GITTEL *now, breaking away from his fingers in sudden vexation, rolls up to glare at his face.*)

GITTEL. Why we always talking about my stomach? I got no other charms? (JERRY *reaches again.*) Get away! (*She pulls the still-buttoned blouse over her head, gets stuck, and struggles blindly.*)

JERRY (*compassionately*). Gittel. (*His hands come again, but when she feels them she kicks out fiercely at him.*)

GITTEL (*muffled*). I don't want your goddam favors! (*One of her kicks lands in his thigh, and stops him.* GITTEL *then yanks the blouse off with a rip, slings it anywhere, which happens to be at him, drags the coat over her head on her way down, and lies still. A silence.*)

JERRY (*then*). I'm sorry you don't. I could use it. (*He retrieves the blouse, draws the sleeves right side out, and hangs it over a chair, then stands regarding her.*) That's how you intend to sleep it off? (GITTEL *under the coat neither moves nor answers.*) Gittel? (*Again no answer*) You want me to stay or go? (*After a wait* JERRY *walks to his hat, picks it up.*) Go. (*He looks at the gas heater, pauses.*) Shall I leave the gas on? (*No response from under* GITTEL's *coat.*) Yes. You need me for anything? (*He waits.*) No. Of course not. (*Presently he*

puts the lamp out, walks around the bed to the door, and opens it. But he stands. Then he bangs it shut again, throws his hat back at the chair and walks in again after it. GITTEL *then sits up to see the closed door, and gives a wail of abandonment.*)

GITTEL. Jerry—Jerry—

JERRY (*behind her*). What? (GITTEL *rolls around, to see him staring out the window.*)

GITTEL (*indignant*). What are you still here?

JERRY. I *can't* put it off till tomorrow. (*He catches up a newspaper and rolls it in his hands as he paces, grimly.* GITTEL *kneels up on the bed and regards him.*)

GITTEL. What's ailing *you*?

JERRY. I have to talk. I called home today.

GITTEL. So what'd she say for herself this time?

JERRY. I didn't talk to her. (*He paces.*) I can't get the court affidavits I need there unless I ask her father to pull strings for me. I called to ask, and couldn't get my tongue in the old groove.

GITTEL. So hooray.

JERRY. Yes, hooray. It means the Appellate Division here won't admit me, on motion. I want my day in court. I've got to get out from behind that pile of books into a courtroom, and I'm at a dead end here. With one way out, the March Bar exam.

GITTEL. So take it.

JERRY. I'm *scared*. I've been under Lucian's wing all my professional life, I'm not sure myself what's in my skull besides his coattails, if I take that exam I'm putting everything I am in the scales. If I flunk it, what?

GITTEL. What else can you do?

JERRY (*slowly*). I can live where I *am* a member of the Bar.

(GITTEL *stares at him, and neither moves; then she sits back on her heels.*)

GITTEL (*unbelieving*). You want to go back. (*The phone rings.* GITTEL *glances at it with sharp nervousness, knowing who it is, then back at* JERRY.) Go on.

JERRY. Answer it.

GITTEL. No. Go on. (*It rings again, and* JERRY *walks to it, the roll of newspaper in his hand.*) Let it ring! I won't talk to anybody. (*Her alarmed vehemence stops* JERRY, *he stares at her. The phone rings a few times throughout the following, then ceases.*)

JERRY (*sharply*). Who is it, this late, him?

GITTEL. I don't know. So you going or not?

JERRY (*angered*). Why not? I can make three times the money I earn here, to do the work I'm starved for, it tempts me and what's so tempting here, Jake? Beat my head against a Bar exam when I'm building here on what, Jake, kicks in the belly, quicksand? (GITTEL *offers no answer. He turns back to the window.* GITTEL *now digs in her purse for a bottle of banthine tablets.*)

GITTEL. What do you think *I'm* up to my neck in here, not quicksand? (*She goes out into the kitchen, where she puts on the light and sets a pot of milk up to warm;* JERRY *turns after her.*)

JERRY. All right, then tell me that! If something sticks in your throat you can't spit it out? It's so much quicker to hop in with the first gorilla you meet instead? How *dare* you treat yourself like a hand-me-down snotrag any bum can blow his nose in? (GITTEL *is shaken by this; but she avoids him and comes back in, cool as metal, unscrewing her bottle of tablets.*)

GITTEL. Okay. When?

JERRY. When what?

GITTEL. When you going?

JERRY (*heavily*). Look. Don't rush *me* off to Tallahassee. I don't turn loose so easy.

GITTEL. Well, I got to make my plans.

JERRY. What plans, now?

GITTEL (*unconcernedly*). I'll probably hook up with Jake again. He's got a lot to give a girl, if you know what I mean, you'd be surprised. (JERRY *stands like a statue,* GITTEL *with a not unmalicious twinkle gazing back at him. Then his arm leaps up with the roll of newspaper to crack her across the side of the head, it knocks her off balance and the bottle of tablets flies out of her hand in a shower; she falls on the bed.*)

JERRY (*furious*). That's not all I mean to you! *Now tell the truth, once!* (GITTEL *holds her cheek, never taking her eyes from him.* JERRY *then looks around, stoops and picks up the tablets and bottle, reads the label, sees what it is. He goes into the kitchen. He pours her milk into the*

mug, and brings it back in. He hands her the mug, which GITTEL *takes, still staring at his face while he weighs the tablets in his palm.*) How many?

GITTEL. Two. (JERRY *gives her two, and she swallows them with a mouthful of milk. He replaces the others in the bottle.*)

JERRY. If your stomach's bothering you, why don't you go to a doctor?

GITTEL. What do I want to go to the doctor? He tells me don't have emotions. (JERRY *screws the cap back on the bottle, tosses it on the bed, and regards her.*)

JERRY. How bad is it?

GITTEL. It's not bad!

JERRY. Did I hurt you?

GITTEL. Sure you hurt me. What do you think my head's made, out of tin? (*She waits.*) You didn't say you're sorry.

JERRY. You had it coming. Didn't you?

GITTEL. Sure.

JERRY. I'm sorry.

(GITTEL *now takes a sip of milk, holding it in both hands like a child; then she looks up at him with a grin.*)

GITTEL. You see? I said you'd slug me and you did.

JERRY. Makes you so happy I'll oblige every hour.

GITTEL (*ruefully*). Who's happy? Boy, what a smack. (*She explores her cheek, tentatively, with one palm.*) Okay, so you're *not* going! (*She eyes him cheerfully, but* JERRY *turns away from her.*)

JERRY. I didn't finish. (*He stands at the window, to gaze down at the street.*) Now the divorce plea is in, Tess is in a—tailspin. Lucian thinks she won't remarry.

(*This is worse than being hit, and* GITTEL *can only sit and stare.*)

GITTEL (*at last*). Oh, brother. You stand a chance?

JERRY. Maybe. (*But he shakes his head, suddenly wretched at the window.*) I don't know what or where I stand, what to put behind me, what's ahead, am I coming or going, so help me, I— (*He breaks it off.* GITTEL *hugs her shoulders together, she is cold; it takes her a moment to find desperation enough to try to go over the edge.*)

GITTEL. All right, Jerry, I'll tell you the truth. I— (*She looks for where to begin.*) About tonight and Jake, I—did want to go to Frank Taubman's. Only I don't fit in with your classy friends. Like she would.

(JERRY *turns and looks at her.*)

JERRY. What?

GITTEL. What do you think, I don't know? (*She is hugging herself, shivering a little as she makes herself more naked, but trying to smile.*) I mean all I am is what I am. Like Wally, he wanted me to get braces on my teeth, I said so face it, I got a couple of buck teeth, what did I keep it, such a secret? I said you got to take me the way I am, I got these teeth.

JERRY. You're a beautiful girl. Don't you know that?

GITTEL. But I'm not her. And she's all you been thinking about since the minute we met.

JERRY. No.

GITTEL. Yes. So what's Jake, a—piece of penny candy. It's like when I was a kid, we used to neck in the vestibule, she's inside you and I'm always in the vestibule! You never gave me a chance. Okay, but then you say need you. I need you, I *need* you, who has to say everything in black and white? (*She rises to confront him, pressing the heel of her hand into her stomach.*) But if you want I should of just laid down and said jump on me, no, Jerry. No. Cause I knew all the time you had it in the back of your head to—prove something to her—

JERRY. To myself.

GITTEL. To her. Everything you gave me was to show her, you couldn't wait for a goddam *letter* to get to her. So when *you*—ask *me* to—hand myself over on a platter— (*She has endeavored to be dispassionate, but now it is welling up to a huge accusatory outcry:*) For what? For *what?* What'll I *get?* Jake, I pay a penny, get a penny candy, but you, you're a—big ten-buck box and all I'll get is the cellophane! *You shortchange people, Jerry!* (JERRY *takes this indictment moveless, but rocked, staring at her.* GITTEL *hugs herself, tense, waiting till she has hold of herself.*) And that's the truth. That's what you did *this* time. (*A silence. She waits upon him, intent, still tense, so much hangs on this; while he absorbs it painfully in his entire anatomy.*)

JERRY (*then*). You mean I want a—complete surrender. And don't give one.

GITTEL. Yeah. Is that all I said?

(JERRY *closes his eyes on her.*)

JERRY. This time. And last time too. Because I shortchanged her also, didn't I?

GITTEL (*desperate*). I'm not talking about *her* now, that's exactly what I'm talking about! (*But it takes* JERRY *unhearing away from her to the bureau, averted.* GITTEL *gives up, sits, slaps her chair, and puts her head in her hands.*)

JERRY. It's true. God help me, it's true, half of me isn't in this town.

GITTEL. So I tried Jake.

JERRY. Of course.

GITTEL. Okay, a snotrag. So we're both flops.

JERRY. Both? (*And presently he nods. But when he turns his gaze to her, and takes in her forlorn figure, his eyes moisten.*) No. Not altogether. (*He comes to stand behind her; she does not lift her head.*) All these months I've been telling you one thing, infant, you live wrong. I wanted to make you over. Now I'll tell you the other thing, how you live right. (*He gazes down at her hair, moves his hand to touch it, refrains.*) You're a gift. Not a flop, a gift. Out of the blue. God knows there aren't many like you, so when he makes one it's for many poor buggers. Me among many. (*He shakes his head, slowly.*) The men don't matter. I promise you, *the men don't matter.* If they use you and walk out, they walk out with something of you, in them, that helps. Forget them, not one of them has dirtied you. Not one has possessed you, nobody's even got close. I said a beautiful girl, I didn't mean skin deep, there you're a delight. Anyone can see. And underneath is a street brawler. That some can see. But under the street brawler is something as fresh and crazy and timid as a colt, and virginal. No one's been there, not even me. And why you lock them out is—not my business. (*He finds his hat, stands with it, not looking at her now.*) What you've given me is—something I can make out with, from here on. And more. More. But what I've given you has been—What? A gift of *me*, but half of it's a fraud, and it puts you in bed with bums. That colt needs an unstinting hand, infant. Not Jake, not me. (*He walks to the door, opens it, pauses, looking for a final word, and gives it across his shoulder.*) I love your buck teeth. (*After a moment he starts out, and* GITTEL'S *head comes up.* JERRY *is on the stairs when she stumbles around her chair, and cries out the doorway after him.*)

GITTEL. Jerry! Don't go! (JERRY *halts, not turning.*) The main thing *I* did in Jake's was—faint in the john. That's when I found I— (*Her voice breaks, the tremor in it is out as a sob.*) I'm bleeding, Jerry!

JERRY (*wheels on the stairs*). What!

GITTEL. It's why I was so thirsty, I'm—scared, Jerry, this time I'm scared to be bleeding—

JERRY. Gittel! (*He runs back in, to grip her up by the arms; she leans on him.*)

GITTEL. Help me, Jerry!

JERRY (*stricken*). Who's your doctor?

GITTEL. It's all right, you just got to get me to the hospital—

JERRY. *Who's* your doctor?

GITTEL. Segen. In my book, it was him calling, I didn't want you to know—

JERRY. You *lunatic.* Lie down, you—crazy, crazy—nitwit— (*He turns her to the bed, where she lies down;* JERRY *sits with her, and looks for the number in her book.*)

GITTEL (*weeping*). Jerry, don't hate my guts.

JERRY. Why didn't you *tell* me?

GITTEL. I didn't want to trap you—trap you in anything you—

JERRY. Trap me? *Trap* me?

GITTEL. I hate my goddam guts, I'm so ashamed, but don't leave—

JERRY. Oh God, shut up, you—lunatic girl—

GITTEL. Don't leave me, don't leave me—

JERRY. I'm not leaving! (*He finds the number, bends to her face on his knee.*) I'm *here,* infant. Take it easy, can't you see I'm here? (*He kisses her; then he commences to dial with his free hand,* GITTEL *pressing the other to her cheek.*)

ACT THREE

SCENE ONE

GITTEL'S *room. It is March now, midday, sunny and warm.*

JERRY'S *room has an unused look—the window is closed and the shade pulled down, a pillow in its bare ticking lies on the couch, the curtain drawn back on the clothes-closet corner reveals chiefly empty hangers.*

In GITTEL'S *room the window is open and the sunlight streams in. The furniture has been rearranged.* JERRY'S *suitcase is in a corner. The sewing machine and dress dummy are gone, and in their place is a table littered with lawbooks, mimeographed sheets and syllabuses, notebooks, pencils in a jar, a desk lamp,* JERRY'S *portable typewriter, a coffee cup, a dirty plate or two, a saucer full of butts. The night table by* GITTEL'S *bed has become a medicine table, studded with bottles and glasses, including one of milk; a new and more expensive radio is also on it, playing softly.*

GITTEL *herself in a cotton nightgown is in bed, pale, thin, and glum. She lies with her head turned to gaze out the window. The hefty book she has been trying to read rests on her lap, her finger in it, and she is not hearing the radio, until the music stops and the announcer begins, cheerfully. What he has to say is that this is WQXR, the radio station of* The New York Times, *to be fully informed read* The New York Times, *and wouldn't she like to have* The New York Times *delivered every morning before breakfast so she could enjoy its worldwide coverage while sipping her coffee, join the really smart people who—*

GITTEL (*disgusted*). Aah, shut up, what do you know. (*She dials him out, and gets some music elsewhere; but she is in no mood to listen, and clicks it off altogether. She then opens the book again, and scowls with an effort of concentration over the page. But she heaves first a gloomy sigh, and next the book: it hits the floor and almost hits a flinching* JERRY, *who is opening the door with his foot, his arms laden with lawbooks and groceries, his topcoat over his shoulder, his hat back on his head.* GITTEL *brightens at once.*)

JERRY. Hold your fire, I'm unarmed!

GITTEL. Jerry, honey, I thought you'd never be home.

(JERRY *bends to kiss her, then drops his lawbooks and coat and a gift box on the table. Throughout the scene he attends to a variety of chores in an unpausing flow, without leisure really to stop once; he is in something of a fever of good spirits. He indicates the gift box.*)

JERRY. I came home a roundabout way, to bring you something from China. Though they met me more than half-way.

GITTEL. You don't have to bring presents.

JERRY. After lunch. I got in a tangle with old Kruger on this Lever contract, I have to be back by one. (*He bears the groceries out to the kitchen.*)

GITTEL (*darkly*). That's two minutes ago.

JERRY. Yes, if I hurry I'll be late. I had a great morning though, I bore down on the old barracuda and he only opened his mouth like a goldfish. All those barracudas seem to be shrinking, lately, must be the humidity. What kind of morning did you have?

GITTEL. So so.

JERRY (*not approving*). Just lay here?

GITTEL. I almost got up to go to the john.

JERRY. Ah, that will be the day, won't it?

GITTEL. Yeah. Be in all the newsreels. (JERRY *in silence in the kitchen lights the oven, unwraps a small steak, slides it under the broiler.*) I'll try for the john tomorrow, Jerry, I'm pretty wobbly.

JERRY. What do you expect the first time, to climb Mount Everest?

GITTEL (*a pause*). *That's* what they go up there for? (*She gazes out the open window, while* JERRY *opens a can of potatoes, and dumps them in a pot to warm.*) You know where I'd like to be this minute?

JERRY. In bed, or you'd be out of it.

GITTEL. Central Park. On the grass. I don't get any *use* out of Central Park, you know? Specially a day like this, I mean here spring isn't even here and spring is here.

(JERRY *comes back in, unknotting his tie, en route to the bureau to rummage in its drawers.*)

JERRY. I'll make you a proposition, will you shoot for the stairs by Friday afternoon?

GITTEL (*uneasily*). Why?

JERRY. I called Dr. Segen again this morning, he emphatically recommended a change of venue. I'll take you to Central Park in a cab Friday afternoon, is it a date?

GITTEL. What's Friday afternoon?

JERRY. The exam's over, I'd like to collapse in Central Park myself. Be down to get you in a taxi, honey, straight from the Bar exam. Date?

GITTEL (*evading it*). One thing I'll be glad when that exam's over, maybe you'll stop running long enough to say hello.

JERRY (*obliges, with a smile*). Hello. Date?

GITTEL (*scowling*). I just sit on the edge here, I feel like my stomach's a—cracked egg or something. I don't want any more leaks.

(JERRY *gives her a severe eye while he hangs his jacket over a chair and takes a batch of mail out of its pocket.*)

JERRY. Doctor says if you don't get out of bed this week all your blood will rust. I really couldn't afford that hello, I didn't have a minute yet to look into who's writing me what here. (*He hurries through the envelopes, discarding them one by one onto the bed.*) Harper's wants me to buy their complete works, haven't time to read why. Hospital bill, ouch. Smoke it after dinner, on the gas stove. Clerk of the District Court, Omaha— (*But this one stops him short. He carries it away from her, rips it open, unfolds a legal document, in blue backing distinctive enough to be remembered later, and stares at it.*)

GITTEL. Anything?

JERRY (*a silence*). Legal stuff. Coming out of my ears these days, I— (*He finds it difficult to lift his eyes from it, it takes him an effort, but he drops document and envelope on the table and gets back into stride.*) Here, before I forget. (*From his jacket he brings a check out and over to* GITTEL.) I let Molly's class in the loft, she gave me a check for you. She'll leave the key over the door, I'll pick it up before cram-school.

GITTEL. Gee, Jerry, you shouldn't take time. (*She takes his hand as well as the check, and puts her cheek to it.*) You're okay.

JERRY. It's your money I'm after, infant.

GITTEL (*brightly*). Yeah, it pays to be a big fat capitalist, huh? Lay here, it just rolls in.

JERRY (*stooping*). And this rolls out.

Get up today or forever hold your peas. (*He comes up with a bedpan from under the bed, and bears it into the back room, while* GITTEL *stares.*)

GITTEL. Hey, what's the—My God, I lost a quart of blood!

JERRY. I bought you three pints, that's a handsome enough profit. Capitalists who aren't satisfied with fifty per cent end up in the federal hoosegow. (*On his way back he picks up the book and a mimeographed exam sheet that has fallen out of it.*) What are you doing with this exam, boning up for me?

GITTEL. Just looking.

JERRY (*scanning*). '53, I'll have to go through this one tonight. (*He drops the novel and exam sheet back on the bed, strips to the waist, now at last removes his hat and sets it on the desk lamp, and collects the dirty plates and saucer of butts, while* GITTEL *watches him.*)

GITTEL. When you going to get some sleep? You're getting skinny!

JERRY. Muscle, I'm all muscle these days. And that reminds me, if you don't get off your rear end soon I'll be advertising in the Sunbathers Gazette for one that works. (*He bears the plates into the kitchen, where he next opens the oven and turns the steak over.*)

GITTEL (*scowling*). Mine works.

JERRY. Unemployed. You think unemployed insurance can go on in perpetuity? (*This is only kidding, while he proceeds to splash water into his face at the sink; but* GITTEL *staring into the future is so despondent she has to shake it off.*)

GITTEL. So when have you got any time, *now?*

JERRY. Three-thirty Friday after the battle, mother. Date?

GITTEL. In Central Park?

JERRY (*not hearing*). And at your service, from then on in.

GITTEL (*glumly*). For how long?

JERRY. Hey?

GITTEL. I said for how long.

JERRY. Can't hear you. (*He turns off the water and comes in, drying his face with a towel.*) Hm?

GITTEL. I said I love you. (JERRY *stands absolutely still for a long moment. Then* GITTEL *lowers her eyes.*) Hell, I don't have to say it, do I? You know it.

JERRY (*gently*). Yes.

GITTEL. I'll try not to say it too often.

Twice a week.

JERRY. You can't say it too often, it's part of my new muscle.

GITTEL. Maybe getting sick was the biggest favor I ever did you, huh?

JERRY. I think we can manage without. The big favor is to get back on your feet, Gittel. (GITTEL's *eyes are down.* JERRY *glances at his watch, bends to kiss her cheek, and crosses to the bureau.*)

GITTEL (*low*). What's the percentage?

(JERRY *opening a drawer frowns. He then takes out a laundered shirt, removes the cardboard, and slips into the shirt.*)

JERRY. The percentage is ∩ne hundred.

GITTEL. I don't mean to get better, I mean—

JERRY. I know what you mean. When I said I'd like to look out for you what do you think *I* meant, a thirty-day option? (*Buttoning his shirt he goes back into the kitchen, where he turns the potatoes off and puts a plate in the oven to warm.*) You ready for lunch?

GITTEL. You eat already?

JERRY. I'll take a sandwich into the office. You wouldn't care to spring to your feet and run around the plate three times, work up an appetite? (*He waits on her in the doorway; she does not meet his eyes.*)

GITTEL. I got an appetite.

JERRY. A hm. (*Presently he turns back into the kitchen, where he prepares a tray —tumbler of milk, paper napkin, silverware, and the meal on a plate.*)

GITTEL. You ought to have more than a sandwich, Jerry, you get sick too we'll really be up the goddam creek. Get a malted, too, huh? And tell him make it a guggle-muggle while he's at it.

JERRY. A what?

GITTEL. It's with a beat-up egg. I mean two whole days of exam, you got to keep your strength up for those cruds.

(JERRY *brings in the tray, and places it on her lap in bed.*)

JERRY. The condemned man ate a hearty guggle-muggle and lived another thirty-four years. I don't intend to get sick, infant, even to get you up. (*He collects papers and books on the table, slipping them into his brief case, and pauses over the legal document he has dropped there; he takes it up, and with his back to* GITTEL *reads it again, grimly.*)

GITTEL. Jerry.

JERRY. Yes.

GITTEL (*painfully*). I'm not just taking advantage, you know, I'm—I mean since you been living here I'm—Nobody ever took care of me so good, it sort of weakens your will power, you know? (JERRY *looks over his shoulder at her, then back at the document; he is deliberating between them.*)

JERRY. Strengthens mine.

GITTEL. I mean I'm kind of in the habit of—seeing your neckties around, now. I'll miss them.

(*A silence,* JERRY *weighing the document and something else, much heavier, in himself.*)

JERRY (*then*). Why do you think I'm taking this Bar exam, you boob, to lift legal dumbbells? I intend to live here, work here, be used. Lot of my life I've been cold from being unused.

GITTEL. I'm scared of afterwards, Jerry.

JERRY. What's afterwards?

GITTEL. I get up out of here, all the goddam neckties go back to your place. I'm scared to—live alone, again. Now.

(JERRY *stands for a long moment with the document. Then abruptly and decisively he wads it into his briefcase, sits, thrusts books and papers away to clear space, and writes.*)

JERRY. Eat your lunch.

(GITTEL *obeys, for a mouthful or two, but watches him perplexedly.*)

GITTEL. What are you writing?

JERRY. A promissory note. I promise you, conversation at meals. (*When he is finished he folds the paper; standing, he takes up the gift box.*) And other items, less elevating. (*He lifts out a Chinese bed jacket of brocaded silk.* GITTEL *drops her fork.*)

GITTEL. Hey! That's *beautiful*, what is it?

JERRY. Something to remember me by, till six o'clock.

GITTEL. A bed jacket! Ye gods, I'll never get up. (*She wiggles her fingers for it, but* JERRY *holds up the folded paper.*)

JERRY. This is a letter to my landlord. (*He slips it into the pocket of the bed jacket.*) For *you* to mail. By hand.

GITTEL. Huh?

JERRY. At the corner. As soon as you're on your feet to make it down there.

GITTEL. Why, what's it say? (*Her eyes widen.*) Get a new tenant! Huh?

JERRY. See for yourself.

GITTEL. You'll move the neckties in for keeps?

JERRY. See for yourself. (*From across the room he holds the bed jacket ready for her, the letter poking out prominently.*)

GITTEL (*reproachfully*). Jerry.

JERRY. Come and get it.

GITTEL (*reproachfully*). Jerry, I got to be on my feet to get you?

JERRY. Maybe. Better find out, hm? (GITTEL *shakes her head.*) Is it so out of the question that I want to keep the goddam neckties here? Come on. (GITTEL *just gazes at him, her eyes moist.*) Come. Come and get it.

(GITTEL *puts the tray aside, moves her legs to the edge, and sits still.*) Come on, honey. (GITTEL *stands, unsteady for a moment, then moves toward him, afraid of her belly, afraid of her legs, the progress of someone who hasn't walked in a month; but she gets to him and the letter, unfolds it, and reads.*)

GITTEL. You're giving up your flat.

JERRY. Save rent.

GITTEL (*a pause*). You're really ruining me, Jerry! (*She keeps her face averted, on the verge of tears.*) I didn't use to be a —bitch of a—lousy blackmailer. (*Another pause.*) And I'm not going to be either! Enough is enough! (*And with sudden resolution she tears the letter into pieces.*)

JERRY (*equably*). That's how you waste forest resources? Now I'll have to write another.

GITTEL. Not unless you want to!

JERRY. I want to. (*His arms wrap her in the bed jacket, and hold her. He kisses her, studies her eyes; she searches his. Then he glances at his watch, pats her cheek, and reaches for his brief case.*) Don't overdo a good thing. Lie down soon. Chew your lunch before swallowing. Take your medicine. Don't tackle the stairs alone. Button up your overcoat, you belong to me. (*He is on his way to the door, when her small voice stops him.*)

GITTEL. Jerry. I do. You know I do, now?

JERRY. Yes. I know that, infant.

GITTEL. I love you. (JERRY *stands inarticulate, until she releases him:*) That's twice, there, I used up the whole week!

JERRY (*lightly*). I may need to hear it

again before that Bar exam. For muscle.

GITTEL. You'll pass.

JERRY. Hell, I'll blow all the answers out of my brilliant nose. (*He blows her a kiss and is out the door, gone, leaving her on her feet in the room, shaking her head after him, in her Chinese silk, like a rainbow, half radiance, half tears. She fingers his coat, sits, and brings it to her face; she is much troubled.*)

SCENE TWO

JERRY'S *room. It is May, almost summer now, a hot muggy dusk, and eight months since this affair began. Once again the windows of both rooms are open—*JERRY'S *from the top—and the sounds of traffic float in.*

In GITTEL'S *room the only change is that the table is cleared of all* JERRY'S *exam preparations, the night table is cleared of medicines, the bed is made.*

JERRY'S *flat however is a shambles. Packing is in progress, nothing is in its place, cartons stand here and there. In the kitchen* JERRY *in his shirt sleeves is slowly wrapping dishware in newspaper; in the living room* GITTEL—*barefoot and back to normal, but with a stratum of gloom underneath—is folding linens into a carton. This separate activity goes on for an interval of silence, until* JERRY *calls in; his voice is rather dispirited, and so is hers.*

JERRY. What about these pots, honey? You want them packed separate?

GITTEL. Separate from what?

JERRY. Dishes.

GITTEL. Guess so. I mean, sure. (*They go back to packing in silence. Both are sweaty with the prosaic drudgery of packing, and depressed, but neither is admitting this; there is an atmosphere of something being avoided. Then* GITTEL *stands on a chair to take down the clothes-closet curtain, and in the process jogs one support of the rod with its remaining clothes; it falls.* GITTEL *grabs it.*) Help! (JERRY *drops what he is doing, and comes at once, on the run.*)

JERRY. What's wrong?

GITTEL. This cruddy pole. S'all.

JERRY (*relieved*). Oh, I thought you— (*He stops himself, takes the rod and clothes off her hands, and lays them on the couch.*) Never did get around to fixing that thing permanently. Guess I never believed it was permanent, all it takes is two screws and a—(*He becomes aware of her eyes moody on him.*) Hm?

GITTEL. Nothing. (*They gaze at each other a moment, something unsaid between them. Then* JERRY *grips her at the waist, and lifts her down.*)

JERRY. You stay on the ground, squirrel.

GITTEL (*irked*). Why?

JERRY. Because I've climbed Long's Peak four times. I'm used to these rare altitudes. (*He climbs the chair, and begins to unhook the curtain.*)

GITTEL. What'd you think, I was doing a nose dive? No such luck.

JERRY (*another gaze*). What kind of cheery remark is that?

GITTEL. I mean *bad* luck.

JERRY. Oh. I thought you meant good bad luck.

GITTEL. What's Long's Peak?

JERRY. Mountain. Front Range, Colorado. Fourteen thousand feet, up on all fours, down on all fives.

GITTEL (*a pause*). I been up the Empire State nineteen times, so what?

(JERRY *smiles, shakes his head, and turns to hand her the curtain.*)

JERRY. Here. (*But* GITTEL *is on her way out to the kitchen, in a mood.* JERRY *stares, tosses the curtain onto the couch mattress, bare in its ticking, and considers the window drapes.*) You want this other one down?

GITTEL (*out of sight*). What other one?

JERRY. Window curtain.

GITTEL. D'you want it down?

JERRY (*puzzled*). Yes, I want it down.

GITTEL. So take it down!

JERRY (*frowning*). What's eating you?

GITTEL. A banana!

JERRY. What?

GITTEL. A banana. (*She comes in again, eating a banana.*) Want a bite?

JERRY. I said, what's eating *you*. (*He moves the chair to the window, gets up again, and works on the burlap drapes.*)

GITTEL. Oh, *me*. What's eating you.

JERRY. I asked you first.

GITTEL. I mean what's eating me is figuring out what's eating you.

JERRY. I see. Well, what's eating me is figuring out what's eating you. Which just about exhausts that investigation. Be altogether fruitless except for the banana.

Want these brackets too? (GITTEL *not re-plying bites at the banana, and* JERRY *looks from the brackets down to her.*) Hm?

GITTEL. *I* don't want a goddam thing. D'*you* want them?

JERRY (*a pause*). Correction. Do *we* want them?

GITTEL. We sure do. Cost good money, can always use them.

JERRY. That's right, ten cents a pair. I'll get a screwdriver. (*He comes down, to head for the kitchen.*)

GITTEL. So then don't!

JERRY. I mean what do we need *all* this junk for? We have your curtains there, we're not going to—

GITTEL. What junk? (*She is handling the drapes, pinches up a piece.*) That's good stuff, forty-seven cents a yard reduced, I could make eleven different things out of it.

JERRY. Name ten.

GITTEL. Anything. Bedspread, cushions, pocketbook, I was even thinking I'd make you some neckties.

JERRY (*very dubious*). Well.

GITTEL. You don't want?

JERRY. I just don't see myself appearing in court in a red burlap necktie. (*He goes into the kitchen.* GITTEL *takes up the banana again for a last bite, slings the peel straight across the room out the open window, and sits gloomily on the couch.* JERRY *returning with the screwdriver studies her as he passes.*) Maybe we ought to knock off for tonight, infant. You look tired.

GITTEL (*testily*). I'm not tired!

JERRY. Then why so down?

GITTEL. *Who's* down? I'm in sixth heaven! (JERRY *stops to eye her before mounting the chair.*) Just don't rush to the rescue. You're killing me with kindness. (JERRY *after a moment plunges the screwdriver by the handle straight into the chair, and lets it stand;* GITTEL's *eyes widen. But* JERRY *shows no further vehemence, and when he speaks it is calmly enough.*)

JERRY. That's in exchange for all the little needles.

GITTEL (*sullen*). I'm sorry.

JERRY. We're supposed to be joyfully packing to be together. Why act as though—

GITTEL. Nobody around here's *enjoying*

this. Every frigging towel I put in that box I feel worse.

JERRY (*dryly*). It's a chore, who likes to break up a happy home? (*He fishes in his shirt pocket for cigarettes.*) Though in a peculiar way it has been. I won't forget *this* first-aid station in a hurry.

GITTEL. There's always the next one.

JERRY. What next one?

GITTEL. The one we're fixing up for me. (JERRY *looks at her, lights the cigarette, and to avoid the topic mounts the chair again with the screwdriver.* GITTEL *takes a fresh breath and dives in, very brightly.*) Look, Jerry, whyn't we just, sort of, get married and get the goddam thing over with, huh?

(JERRY *half-turns, to gaze at her over his shoulder.*)

JERRY. Bigamy? Big of you, I mean, I have one wife now.

GITTEL. I mean *after* the divorce. I'm not going to be just a ball and chain, now you passed that Bar exam you know the first thing I'm going to do? Take up shorthand!

JERRY. Shorthand is the one thing this romance has lacked from the beginning.

GITTEL. So when you open your law office, there I am! A goddam secretary, you're really going to save dough on me. And soon as I make enough out of that loft I'm going to fix up the flat for us, real nice.

JERRY. It's real nice.

GITTEL. Stinks.

JERRY. What stinks about it?

GITTEL. It's a dump, you think I don't know that? My God, how can you entertain somebody a cockroach committee comes out of the sink to see who's here? Hasn't been an exterminator in there since Babe Ruth.

JERRY. Who are we exterminating?

GITTEL. Huh?

JERRY. I meant to say entertaining.

GITTEL. Well, anybody you need to. Customers! Partners, the Taubmans, maybe *criminals*, you don't know who yet, but you can't have a dump for them. Can you?

JERRY (*a pause*). No. I couldn't think of representing some dope addict who'd just murdered his mother and have him see a cockroach. Here's the brackets. (*But* GITTEL *is folding the drapes to put in the carton, and he steps down with them.*)

GITTEL. Who knows, maybe later on we'll move to a real apartment house even. You know one thing I always wanted to live in a house with?

JERRY. Me?

GITTEL. An elevator! With an elevator you can invite anybody.

(JERRY *drops the brackets in her purse, next to her little radio. The radio stops him, he contemplates it, rubs it with his thumb, and then finds* GITTEL's *eye on him.*)

JERRY (*smiles*). Remembering the day you left this at the door. We kept each other company many a wee hour, I hate to see it end up all alone in some closet.

GITTEL. Nah, we'll use it.

JERRY (*mildly*). If you have in mind plastic neckties, they're also out. I have room for it in with the pots. (*He takes the radio out into the kitchen.* GITTEL *on her knees begins on another carton, loading in books, papers, a miscellany.*)

GITTEL (*calling out*). What about this stuff, Jerry, bills? Gas, phone—

JERRY (*out of sight*). Leave them out where I'll see them, I don't think I paid those yet.

GITTEL (*discarding them*). What do you want to pay them, all they can do is shut it off if you do or you don't. Letters—(*She unfolds one, on feminine blue stationery.*) "Jerry dearest, I—" Whoops. (*She shuts in a hurry, not reading it, but as she puts it away she comes to a legal document in blue backing that tickles her memory: the last time she saw it was in her room, in* JERRY's *hands. She reads, frowning, her lips moving at first soundlessly, then becoming audible.*) "—although the plaintiff has conducted herself as a true and faithful wife to the defendant, the said defendant has been guilty. Of acts of cruelty toward the plaintiff, destroying the—" (*Now* JERRY *is standing in the doorway, a cup in his hand.*) "—peace of mind of the plaintiff and the objects of—matrimony. It is hereby ordered, adjudged—"

(JERRY *completes it from memory.*)

JERRY (*slowly*). —and decreed by the Court that the bonds of matrimony heretofore existing are severed and held for naught. And that the said plaintiff is granted an absolute divorce from the defendant. Unquote.

(*A silence*)

GITTEL. So why didn't you tell me, Jerry.

JERRY (*a pause*). I had to live with it. A while longer. Digest it. Let it grow out with my fingernails, till I was—rid of it.

(*Another pause*)

GITTEL. You didn't want me to know.

JERRY. Not till I was—on top of it. Do you know what the sense of never is? Never again, not even once? Never is a deep hole, it takes time to—close over.

GITTEL. Then what'll you do?

JERRY. Then?

GITTEL. Yeah. Then.

JERRY (*a pause, gently*). I think I'll do one thing at a time.

GITTEL. What?

JERRY. Pack this cup. (*He comes to the carton with it, kneeling near her.*)

GITTEL. You sonofabitch. (JERRY *wheels on his knee to confront her.*) You tell her about *me*? That you moved in?

JERRY (*whitely*). Yes.

GITTEL. Because I had a hemorrhage?

JERRY. I'm *not* a sonofabitch—

GITTEL. *Did you tell her I had a hemorrhage?*

JERRY. Yes.

GITTEL. And you didn't tell me about this (*She slings the decree straight into his face.* JERRY *squats, rigid.* GITTEL *then scrambles up and makes for her shoes.* JERRY *rising slams the cup into the carton of crockery.*) Smash them all, who needs them?

JERRY. What are you off on this time?

GITTEL. I'm getting out of here, you— you goddam—(*But the grief breaks through, and she wails to him out of loss:*) Jerry, *why* didn't you *tell* me?

JERRY. I couldn't.

(GITTEL *gazing at him takes this in; then she finishes putting her shoes on, and makes a beeline for her bag.*)

GITTEL. Yeah. You only tell her about me. My God, even when you *divorce* her it's a secret you have with her! One of these days you'll marry me, she'll know it and I won't! (*But when she turns to the doorway,* JERRY *is planted in it, blocking her.*)

JERRY. You're not leaving.

GITTEL. Jerry, look out!

JERRY. Sit down.

GITTEL. You look out or I'll let you

have it, Jerry!

JERRY. Go ahead, street brawler. (GITTEL *slaps him across the face, he is unmoving; she slaps him again backhand, he is like a statue; she then wheels looking for a weapon, comes up from the carton with the broken cup, and charges his face, but hesitates.* JERRY *stands moveless, waiting.*) Do. I'll beat your behind off. (GITTEL *flinging the cup past him throws herself averted on the couch, tearful with rage.*)

GITTEL. Sonofabitch, all my life I never yet could beat up one goddam man, it's just *no* fair!

JERRY. Why do you think I told her about the hemorrhage?

GITTEL. To prove something to her on *me,* now.

JERRY. Like what?

GITTEL. How you're so wonderful, looking after me, you don't need her help.

JERRY. I told her because she asked *my* help. She wants me home.

(GITTEL *rolls over, to stare at him.*)

GITTEL. She does.

JERRY. When at last she really needs me, and I'm enough my own man to help, I had to say no. And why.

GITTEL (*a deep breath*). Okay, Jerry. You said make a claim, right?

JERRY. Yes.

GITTEL. So I'm going to make it.

JERRY. All right.

GITTEL. I want you here. I want *all* of you here. I don't want half a hunk of you, I want—I mean it's—(*With difficulty.*) It's leap year, Jerry, tell the truth. *Would* you—ever say—I love you? Once.

JERRY (*pained*). It's a lifetime promise, infant, I've only said it once. (*But the moment he turns again to the kitchen, her voice rises after him:*)

GITTEL. Jerry, Jerry, give me a break, will you? Don't kid me along. Is that a friend? (*This word nails him, he turns back with his eyes moist.*) I'll tell you straight, you move in I just—won't give up on you marrying me. You—you let me have it straight, too. (*He stands, gazing at her.*) Jerry, you my friend?

JERRY (*finally*). I'm your friend. Here it is, straight. You say love, I think you mean *in* love. I mean so much more by that word now—

GITTEL. I mean wanting. Somebody. So bad—

JERRY. Not wanting. Love is having, having had, having had so—deeply, daily, year in and out, that a man and woman exchange—guts, minds, memories, exchange—eyes. Love is seeing through the other's eyes. So because she likes bridges I never see a bridge here without grief, that her eyes are not looking. A hundred things like that. Not simply friend, some ways my mortal enemy, but *wife,* and ingrown. (*He looks down at the decree.*) What *could* I tell you about this—piece of paper, that the bonds of matrimony are *not* severed? Why would I—love my right hand, if I lost it? That's what love is. To me, now.

(GITTEL *keeps her eyes on him for a long moment, then she closes them.*)

GITTEL. You ever tell her that?

JERRY. No. I should have told her years ago. I didn't know it then.

(GITTEL *rolls up; she climbs the chair at the window and hangs gazing out, to find her way through this.*)

GITTEL. You'll never marry me, Jerry.

JERRY. I can't, infant.

GITTEL. So what kind of competition can I give her, have a hemorrhage twice a year? Trap you that way, be *more* of a cripple, one month to another? Get half of you by being a wreck on your hands, will that keep you around?

JERRY. As long as you need me, I'll be around.

(GITTEL *turns on the chair, staring at him, as it dawns on her.*)

GITTEL. And you'll move in. Even now.

JERRY. What's in me to give, without shortchanging, I'll give—

GITTEL. My God, *I'm* in a goddam trap! (*A pause; then* JERRY *nods.*) You're one, all right, I could—lose a leg or something in you.

JERRY. Yes, you could lose—a lot of time. You're a growing girl, and of the two things I really want, one is to see you grow. And bear your fruit.

GITTEL. And the other is—

JERRY. Tess.

GITTEL. Jerry, Jerry, Jerry. (*She regards him, her eyes blinking; this is hard to say.*) I don't *want* the short end. I want somebody'll—say to me what you just said about her. (*She gets down, retrieving her bag, and stands not looking at him.*) What do you say we—give each other the gate, huh, Jerry? (*She moves to pass him in the doorway; but he stops her, to take her face between his palms, and search her eyes.*)

JERRY. For whose sake?

GITTEL. Jerry, I haven't taken one happy breath since that hemorrhage. I want to get out of here and *breathe.* (*After a moment* JERRY *lets her go. She brushes quickly past him, through the kitchen and out of the flat. He turns in the doorway, looking after her, with his hands up on the jambs, unmoving as the lights dim.*)

SCENE THREE

Both rooms. It is a few days later, a gray afternoon.

JERRY'S *room is cleaned out, altogether bare except for his suitcase and portable typewriter standing there, and the phone on the floor near them.* JERRY *is not in sight, though we may hear him in the kitchen.*

GITTEL *is in her room, taking the dance photos of herself down from the wall. She is engaged in this without feeling, almost without awareness; it is something to do while she waits. What she is waiting for is the phone, as we see from her eyes. She takes the photos to her night table and drops them in a drawer, then walks nervously round and round her room, eyeing her alarm clock, eyeing her phone.*

Meanwhile a match has been lighted in JERRY'S *dark kitchen,* JERRY *making a last survey of it. When he comes in, he is in street clothes and hat; he is shaking the match out, his other arm cradles a few last toilet articles, shaving cream, brush, razor. He kneels at the typewriter case, and fits these articles carefully in. Then he consults his wrist watch. He stands over the phone a heavy moment, picks it up, and dials.*

The phone in GITTEL'S *room rings, and she flies to sit on her bed.*

GITTEL. Yeah, hello?

JERRY (*a pause*). Honey, I'm—all packed here, I—

GITTEL (*softly*). Hiya, Jerry.

JERRY (*a pause*). Some cartons of—odds and ends in the kitchen here, the key will be with the janitor. If you want anything.

GITTEL. I won't want anything.

JERRY. If you do. (*A pause*) Look, if you do, I mean anything—important, Gittel, I'm at the Commodore Hotel in Lincoln, I don't have the number, long-distance will give it to you. Lincoln, Nebraska. *Not* Nevada.

GITTEL. Not Nevada.

JERRY. And not Omaha, I'm not walking back into that mistake, ever again. As soon as I get an office and a phone I'll send you the number. Now if you—if you need anything in a hurry, I mean instantly, will you call Frank Taubman? You won't have to explain anything, it's taken care of, just call him.

GITTEL (*a pause*). Yeah.

JERRY. No. Promise.

GITTEL. I promise. (*A pause*) Jerry, I'm all right now. You just—you just get what you want out there, huh?

JERRY. I'll try. It's back to the wars. My terms are steep, I won't work for Lucian, I won't live in Omaha, and all we'll have is what I earn. I'm beginning very—modestly, a desk and a phone and a pencil. And what's in my head.

GITTEL. It's a lot.

JERRY. But I won't shortchange her. It has to be a new deal, on both sides.

GITTEL. I'm rooting for you, Jerry.

JERRY. No backsliding. By you either, Gittel, don't you give up either, hm?

GITTEL. Oh, I don't! I bounce up, like a —jack in the box, you know?

JERRY. I'm rooting for you, too. It's a big city and you're the salt of the earth, just don't waste it, he's around some corner. You'll find him.

GITTEL. I'm looking. I got a better opinion of myself now, I'm going to propose more often. I'll send you a birthday card now and then, huh?

JERRY. Now and then.

GITTEL. Twice a week!

(JERRY *pinches his eyes, he is shaky.*)

JERRY. Gittel. What am I doing, I— moments here I think I—

GITTEL. You're doing right, Jerry. I mean *I* don't want any handouts either, you know? That's no favor.

JERRY. If I know anything I know that.

GITTEL. And I'm not going to be just giving them out, from now on. I want somebody'll take care of me who's all mine. You taught me that. And nobody like Sam or Jake, between them they couldn't take care of a chiclet. I mean, things look a lot different to me, Jerry, you did me a world of good.

JERRY. Did I really? Golly, if I could think each of us—helped somehow, helped a bit—

GITTEL. You been a great help, Jerry, it's the first affair I—come out with more than I went in. I mean, wherever this guy is, he'll owe you!

JERRY (*a pause, humbly*). Thank you for that. And she'll owe you more than she'll know. After—(*He tries to recall it.*) After the verb to love, to help is—

GITTEL (*a pause*). What, Jerry?

JERRY. —the sweetest in the tongue. Somebody said it. Well. (*He looks at his watch.*) Well. So long, infant.

(GITTEL *tries to say it, but her eyes are full, her heart is in her mouth, and she struggles to keep it from overflowing there; she cannot.*)

GITTEL. *I love you, Jerry!* (JERRY *is rigid; it takes her a moment to go on.*) Long as you *live* I want you to remember the last thing you heard out of me was I love you!

JERRY (*long pause*). I love you too, Gittel. (*He hangs up, and for a moment there is no movement.*

Then JERRY *puts the phone down, and lights himself a cigarette; his first drag tells us how much he needs it. After another, he kneels again, shuts the typewriter case, stands with it and the suitcase in either hand, and gives the room a final check.*

GITTEL *meanwhile has not hung up; she clicks down, then rapidly dials again. But the minute it rings once, she claps the phone down.*

JERRY *is on his way out with typewriter and suitcase when the single ring comes. He stops, not putting either down, just staring at the phone for a long minute.*

GITTEL *sits, head high, eyes closed. Neither moves.*

Then GITTEL *takes her hand off the phone. And* JERRY *turns, and walks out of his flat.*)

OH DAD, POOR DAD, MAMMA'S HUNG YOU IN THE CLOSET AND I'M FEELIN' SO SAD

A Pseudoclassical Tragifarce in a Bastard French Tradition

Arthur L. Kopit

Presented at the Phoenix Theatre, New York, by arrangement with Roger L. Stevens, on February 26, 1962, with the following cast:

MADAME ROSEPETTLE	Jo Van Fleet	BELLBOYS	Jaime Sanchez
JONATHAN	Austin Pendleton		Anthony Ponzini
ROSALIE	Barbara Harris		Ernesto Gonzalez
COMMODORE ROSEABOVE	Sandor Szabo		Louis Waldon
HEAD BELLBOY	Tony Lo Bianco		David Faulkner
			Barry Primus

Directed by Jerome Robbins
Scenery by William and Jean Eckart
Costumes by Patricia Zipprodt
Lighting by Thomas Skelton
Music by Robert Prince

SCENE. The action takes place in Port Royale, a city somewhere in the Caribbean. The play is in three scenes without intermission.

Broadway production:

Presented by Roger L. Stevens and T. Edward Hambleton, by arrangement with the Phoenix Theatre, at the Morosco Theatre in New York on August 27, 1963, with the following cast:

MADAME ROSEPETTLE	Hermione Gingold	BELLBOYS	Jaime Sanchez
JONATHAN	Sam Waterston		Thom Koutsoukos
ROSALIE	Alix Elias		Gary Garth
COMMODORE ROSEABOVE	Sandor Szabo		Ernesto Aponte
HEAD BELLBOY	John Hallow		Peter Lenahan
			Carl Guttenberger

(Other production credits same as for original production.)

Copyright ©, as an Unpublished Work, 1959, by Arthur L. Kopit.
Copyright ©, 1960, by Arthur L. Kopit.

All rights reserved.

Reprinted by permission of Hill & Wang, Inc., and the author, who introduced hitherto unpublished alterations into the text.

CAUTION: Professionals and amateurs are hereby warned that *Oh Dad, Poor Dad, Mamma's Hung You in the Closet and I'm Feelin' So Sad* is subject to a royalty.
It is fully protected under the copyright laws of the United States of America, the British Empire, including the Dominion of Canada, and all other countries of the Copyright Union. All rights, including professional, amateur, motion pictures, recitation, lecturing, public reading, radio broadcasting, television and the rights of translation into foreign languages are strictly reserved.

Oh Dad, Poor Dad, Mamma's Hung You in the Closet and I'm Feelin' So Sad is slightly restricted. Where available, this play may be given stage presentation by amateurs upon payment of a royalty to Samuel French, Inc., at 25 West 45th Street, New York 36, N. Y., or at 7623 Sunset Boulevard, Hollywood 46, Calif., or to Samuel French (Canada), Ltd., 27 Grenville Street, Toronto 5, Ontario, Canada. Royalty of the required amount must be paid whether the play is presented for charity or gain and whether or not admission is charged. Stock royalty quoted on application to Samuel French, Inc.

For all other rights than those stipulated above, apply to Audrey Wood, c/o Ashley Steiner, Inc., 555 Madison Avenue, New York 22, N. Y.

Particular emphasis is laid on the question of amateur or professional readings, permission and terms for which must be secured in writing from Samuel French, Inc.

FOR some time before the production of *Oh Dad, Poor Dad, Mamma's Hung You in the Closet and I'm Feelin' So Sad,* the reputation of the play was being dubiously established by persistent reports about a Harvard prodigy who was heading for New York with a play bearing the longest title in the theatre. That the respected Phoenix Theatre, one of New York's experimental—you might call it "off-Broadway" —groups had put it on its production schedule made the reputation less dubious, as did the fact that the firm of Hill and Wang had listed it for publication. The Phoenix Theatre, headed by T. Edward Hambleton and Norris Houghton, we knew, was not an irresponsible group of dilettantes, and Arthur Wang and Larry Hill had one of the youngest but also one of the most reputable companies in the publishing business. The play opened in New York about a year after the advance publicity reached its peak, and a strange thing happened—the play looked as good as it was supposed to be (and perhaps even better) in the Phoenix production staged by the choreographer Jerome Robbins. There were indeed skeptics who insisted on regarding it as a piece of juvenile self-indulgence, but playgoers kept on filling the pleasant little theatre in the Seventies that had become the new home of the Phoenix. And more than that, opinions of the play kept on improving. It was no longer about a stunt but about an engrossing entertainment that people spoke.

People even got used to the title; it had ceased to be fashionable to quip about it, as had a New York wit who declared that he had already read Kopit's play but hadn't yet gone through the title. It was even possible that playgoers who paid the work its proper tribute of laughter were laughing with considerable uncertainty. The play projected youthful anxiety—call it "castration anxiety" if you are not averse to employing psychoanalytical jargon. Mr. Kopit expressed in jocular and fantastic terms a widespread fear of the voracious woman or even nymphet who figuratively devours the male—an observation not exclusively Strindbergian or altogether subjective. The form and style of the work agreed, in fact, with the ambivalence present in this confection of the bizarre and the romantic on which serious studies may yet be written. The work was fantastic and clinical, entertaining and disconcerting, and technically both a comedy and a grotesque melodrama. And its ultra-skeptical view of love, romance, domesticity, and mother-son relationships, all in one respect or another associated with the "norms" of life, enrolled the play in the recently fashionable "Theatre of the Absurd" imported from the Left Bank theatre of Ionesco and Genet.

Arthur L. Kopit, the author of the so-called Absurdist play that was so very funny yet so disturbing below the surface, was born in New York City on May 10, 1937.

After attending the Lawrence High School on Long Island, he went to Harvard and started writing plays, nine of which were produced by academic theatrical groups. *Oh Dad . . .* was one of these, and was first performed by Harvard undergraduates in January, 1960. The play had its professional premiere during the summer of 1961 in England. It was hardly a success there, but the New York production half a year later (ɪ ɪuary 26, 1962), presented by the Phoenix Theatre in association with Roger L. :vens, established itself quickly as something no true-blue follower of the arts could afford to miss. Even a reserved critic of the work such as Alan Downer, to whom it was essentially an expanded revue skit, was willing to admit that it had a "vitality" or "an enthusiasm for audacious play that the contemporary theatre can ill spare (*Quarterly Journal of Speech,* October, 1962, p. 269).

Meanwhile, Kopit had graduated from Harvard in 1959 and won a Shaw Travelling Fellowship for a year's sojourn in Europe. His further and reputable career was yet to be determined. *Oh Dad . . . ,* translated into French by Marcel Aymé, was scheduled to open early in the fall of 1963 in Paris; it would be interesting and it might be instructive to know what the Left Bank of Ionesco, Adamov, and Genet would think of the play. Mr. Kopit was, however, bent upon other business; he was working on a new comedy bearing the extravagant title *Asylum or What the Gentlemen Are Up To Not To Mention the Ladies,* withdrawn by him after a brief initial presentation at the Theatre de Lys in Greenwich Village in 1963.

Kopit's rich farcicality may not be sufficiently apparent in the text of *Oh Dad . . . ,* which is a thoroughly theatrical one, depending upon dexterity by the director and his cast, rather than a literary piece; and this is quite remarkable in the work of a young Phi Beta Kappa from Harvard, as well as fortunate since the theme of Momism would have otherwise been tiresomely overfamiliar. The bizarreness of the work, a quality that cannot be insisted on too much (and the author agrees), must become evident as a subject for laughter rather than of morbid interest, regardless of what psychological interpretation is put upon it by those who are undaunted by the author's statement (to his interviewer, Frances Herridge of the New York *Post,* March 9, 1962), that his own family is "quite the opposite" of the voraciously overprotective mother of the play.

It does appear, however, that an attitude toward women not without the ambivalence of a youthful artist was an undercurrent in the writing. It clearly affects the treatment of the boy-girl affair in the play and gives depth and macabre humor to the work while disturbing its unity. Kopit gave vent to this feeling himself in declaring in his *Post* interview that he did think "it's difficult to have any free relationship with a woman," since "a woman's social needs are different from a man's" and "the more feminine she is the more permanently she wants him"—which "makes tension between them." At the same time it must be noted that the difficult marriage of overt farce and inner anxiety in the play results in an imperfect blending of moods in *Oh Dad. . . .* Unkind critics may blame this defect, which stage production cannot be expected to eradicate, on a young writer's inexperience and penchant for improvisation and attribute to him a self-conscious effort to imitate fashionable Absurdist drama in the free-wheeling manner of Ionesco's extravaganzas. The present editor believes there is more to the play than undergraduate recklessness and imitativeness.

As restaged by Jerome Robbins, the director of the original "off-Broadway" Phoenix Theatre production, *Oh Dad, Poor Dad . . .* reopened on Broadway at the Morosco Theatre on August 27, 1963, for a limited run prior to a national tour under the auspices of Roger L. Stevens and T. Edward Hambleton. The new production, which featured Hermione Gingold as Madame Rosepettle, was broader than the original one. The new staging, combined with Miss Gingold's stylization of her role as the mother and the swivel-hipped caricature of a nymphet by Alix Elias, whose voice became as imperious as the virago-mother's, pointed up the cartoon-like qualities of the play. One reviewer, Mr. Richard Watts, Jr., of the New York *Post,* actually enjoyed it most this time as a travesty of Tennessee Williams, while regretting that the obviousness of the new production deprived the play of some of its odd fascination. Those who found the play alternately weird and funny or ghoulish and loony did not have to reach for definitions of the style, but for those who prefer an exact label the term "surrealistic farce" was readily available.

SCENE ONE

SCENE: *A lavish hotel suite somewhere in the Caribbean.*

AT RISE: *As the curtain goes up a platoon of* BELLBOYS *is seen hurrying about. Some are opening the shades on the windows, others are dusting. A group of* BELLBOYS *enter with extravagant luggage. They march to the master bedroom. Another group enters with duplicate luggage, only smaller. They march to the other bedroom in the suite. Enter* BELLBOYS ONE *and* TWO, *carrying a coffin. They look about the room nervously.*

———

WOMAN'S VOICE (*offstage*). Put it in the bedroom!

BELLBOYS ONE AND TWO. The bedroom. (BELLBOY ONE *goes toward the bedroom at stage left.* BELLBOY TWO *starts toward the bedroom at stage right. The handles come off the coffin. It falls to the floor as* MADAME ROSEPETTLE *enters, dressed in black, a veil covering her face, with* JONATHAN *trailing behind her. The* BELLBOYS *are frozen with terror.*)

MADAME ROSEPETTLE. *Fools!*

HEAD BELLBOY. Uh—*which* bedroom, madame?

MADAME ROSEPETTLE. *Which* bedroom? Why the *master* bedroom, of course. Which bedroom did you think? (*The* BELLBOYS *smile ashamedly, bow, pick up the coffin and carry it toward the master bedroom.*) Gently! (*They open the bedroom doors.* MADAME ROSEPETTLE *lowers her eyes as the blinding rays of sunlight stream from the room.*) People have no respect for coffins nowadays. They think nothing of the dead. (*Short pause*) I wonder what the dead think of them? (*Short pause*) Agh! The world is growing dismal.

(*The door to the master bedroom opens and* BELLBOYS ONE *and* TWO *reappear, coffin still in hand.*)

BELLBOY ONE. Uh—begging madame's pardon.

BELLBOY TWO. Sorry to interrupt.

MADAME ROSEPETTLE. Speak up! Speak up!

BELLBOY ONE. Well—you see—

BELLBOY TWO. Yes, you see—

BELLBOY ONE. We were curious.

BELLBOY TWO. Yes. Curious.

BELLBOY ONE. Uh—just *where* in ma-

dame's bedroom would she like it to be put?

MADAME ROSEPETTLE. Next to the *bed,* of course!

BELLBOYS ONE AND TWO. Of course. (*Exit,* BELLBOYS ONE *and* TWO.)

MADAME ROSEPETTLE. Morons!—*Imbeciles.* (*Enter two* BELLBOYS *carrying two large black-draped plants before them. They look about the room, then nod and walk out to the porch.*) Ah, my plants! (*They set the plants down.*) Uh—not so close together. They fight. (*The* BELLBOYS *move the plants apart.*)

(BELLBOY THREE *enters carrying a dictaphone on a silver tray and black drapes under his arm.* BELLBOYS ONE *and* TWO *exit fearfully from the master bedroom.*)

HEAD BELLBOY. The dictaphone, madame.

MADAME ROSEPETTLE. Ah, splendid.

HEAD BELLBOY. Where would madame like it to be put?

MADAME ROSEPETTLE. Oh, great gods, are you all the same? The center table, naturally. One never dictates one's memoirs from *anywhere* but the center of a room. Any nincompoop knows that.

HEAD BELLBOY. It must have slipped my mind.

MADAME ROSEPETTLE. You flatter yourself.

HEAD BELLBOY. Will there be something else?

MADAME ROSEPETTLE. Will there be something else, he asks? *Will there be something else?* Of course there'll be something else. There's *always* something else. That's one of the troubles with Life.

HEAD BELLBOY. Sorry, madame.

MADAME ROSEPETTLE. Yes, so am I. (*Pause*) Oh, this talk is getting us nowhere. Words are precious. On bellboys they're a waste. And so far you have thoroughly wasted my time. Now to begin:—

HEAD BELLBOY. Madame, I'm afraid this must end.

MADAME ROSEPETTLE (*incredulously*). I —beg your pardon?

HEAD BELLBOY. I said this must end! I and *not a common* bellboy, madame—I'm a lieutenant. (Notice the stripes if you will.) I am a lieutenant, madame. And being a lieutenant am in charge of other bellboys and therefore entitled, I think, to a little more respect from you.

MADAME ROSEPETTLE. Well—*you* may consider yourself a lieutenant, lieutenant, but *I* consider you a *bore!* If you're going to insist upon pulling rank, however, I'll have you know that I am a Tourist. (Notice the money if you will.) I am a Tourist, my boy.—And being a Tourist am in charge of you. Remember that and I'll mail you another stripe when I leave. As for "respect," we'll have no time for *that* around here. We've got too many important things to do. Right, Albert?

JONATHAN. Ra-ra-ra-rrrright.

MADAME ROSEPETTLE. Now, to begin: you may pick up the drapes which were so ingeniously dropped in a lump on my table, carry them into the master bedroom and tack them over my window panes. I don't wear black in the tropics for my health, my boy. I'm in mourning. And while I'm here in Port Royale, no single speck of sunlight shall enter and brighten the mournful gloom of my heart —at least, not while I'm in my bedroom. Well, go on, lieutenant, go on. Forward to the field of battle, head high. Tack the drapes across my windows and when my room is black, call me in.

HEAD BELLBOY (*weakly*). Yes, madame. (*He picks up the drapes and leaves.*)

MADAME ROSEPETTLE. In Buenos Aires the lieutenant clicked his heels when leaving. That's the trouble with these revolutionaries. No regard for the duties of rank. Remind me, Edward, to have this man fired, first thing in the morning. He'll never do.

(JONATHAN *takes a pad of paper out of his pocket and writes with a pencil he has tied on a chain about his neck. Enter* BELLBOYS ONE *and* FIVE *carrying miniature treasure chests.*)

BELLBOY FIVE. The stamp collection, madame.

MADAME ROSEPETTLE. Ah, Robinson! Your fantastic stamp collection. Look! It's arrived.

BELLBOY ONE. Where would madame like it put?

MADAME ROSEPETTLE. Where would you like it put, my love?

JONATHAN. Uh—uh—uh—

MADAME ROSEPETTLE. Now—now, let's not start stammering again. You know what I think of it.

JONATHAN. Ummmm—

MADAME ROSEPETTLE. My dear, what is wrong with your tongue?

JONATHAN. Uhhhh—

MADAME ROSEPETTLE. But they're *only* bellboys.

JONATHAN. Ummmm—

(*Enter* BELLBOYS TWO *and* THREE, *also with miniature treasure chests.*)

BELLBOY TWO. The coin collection, madame. Where would you like it put?

MADAME ROSPETTLE. Edward, your fabulous collection of coins has just arrived as well. *Now*—where would you like it put?

JONATHAN. Ummmm—

MADAME ROSEPETTLE. Oh, great gods! Can't you for once talk like a normal human being without showering the room with your inarticulate spit!?

JONATHAN. I-I-I—I—da—da—

MADAME ROSEPETTLE. Oh, very well. Very well— If you can't muster the nerve to answer—stick out your paw and point.

(*He thrusts out his trembling hand and points to a large set of transparent drawers held by an elegant gold frame.*)

JONATHAN. If—if—they would—be so kind.

MADAME ROSEPETTLE. Of course they would! They're *bellboys*. Remember that. It's your first Lesson in Life for the day. (*To the* BELLBOYS.) No! Don't get the stamps in with the coins. They stick!

HEAD BELLBOY (*he returns from the master bedroom*). I'm terribly sorry to disturb you, madame, but I find that— that I don't seem to have a—uh—

MADAME ROSEPETTLE. I wondered when you'd ask. (*She takes a huge hammer out of her purse and hands it to him.*)

HEAD BELLBOY (*ashamedly*). Thank you —madame. (*He turns nervously and starts to leave.*)

MADAME ROSEPETTLE (*cuttingly*). Bellboy? (*He stops.*) The nails.

HEAD BELLBOY. Yes, of course. How foolish of me.

MADAME ROSEPETTLE (*she reaches into her purse again and takes out a fistful of nails which she promptly dumps in his hands*). Keep the extras. (*He exits, once more, into the master bedroom.*) In Buenos Aires the lieutenant came equipped with a pneumatic drill. *That's* what I call service. Remind me, Robinson darling, to have this man barred from all hotels, everywhere. *Everywhere.* (JONATHAN *scratches a large "X" on his pad.*

The other BELLBOYS *have now finished putting the stamps and coins away.* MADAME ROSEPETTLE *goes over and dips her hand in the box. To* BELLBOY TWO) Here, for your trouble: a little something. It's a Turkish piaster—1876. Good year for piasters. (*To* BELLBOY FIVE) And for you a—a 1739 Danzig gulden. Worth a fortune, my boy. A *small* fortune, I will admit, but nevertheless a fortune. (*To* BELLBOY THREE) And for you we have a—a—1962 DIME!! *Edward*—what is a dime doing in here? Fegh! (*She flings the dime to the ground as if it had been handled by lepers. The* BELLBOYS *leap to get it.*)

JONATHAN (*sadly*). Some—some—some day—it will be—as rare as the others.

MADAME ROSEPETTLE. Some day! *Some day!* That's the trouble with you, Robinson. Always an optimist. I trust you have no more such currency contaminating your fabulous collection. H'm, Albert? Do I assume correctly? H'm? Do I? H'm? Do I? H'm? Do I?

JONATHAN. Ya—yes.

MADAME ROSEPETTLE. Splendid. Then I'll give you your surprise for the day.

JONATHAN. Na—now?

MADAME ROSEPETTLE. Yes, now.

JONATHAN. In—in—front of—*them?*

MADAME ROSEPETTLE. Turn your backs, bellboys. (*She digs into her handbag and picks out a coin in a velvet box.*) Here, Edward, my sweet. The rarest of all coins for your rarest of all collections. A 1572 Javanese Yen-Sen.

JONATHAN (*excitedly*). How—how many—were—were minted?

MADAME ROSEPETTLE. None.

JONATHAN. Na—none?

MADAME ROSEPETTLE. I made it myself. (*She squeezes his hand.*) ·So glad you like it. (*To the* BELLBOYS.) You may turn around now. (*The sound of a hammer is heard offstage.*) If you must bang like that, my boy, then please bang with some sort of rhythm. Oh, the lieutenant in Buenos Aires, remember him, Robinson? How he shook when he drilled. I fairly danced that day. (*She begins to dance, the other* BELLBOYS *clapping in rhythm.*) That's enough. That's enough. (*She stops.*)

BELLBOY FOUR (*he enters pushing a huge treasure chest, on rollers*). The, uh —book collection, madame.

(JONATHAN *leaps up in glee.*)

MADAME ROSEPETTLE. Albert, *look.* Albert! *Look!* Your unbelievable collection of books. *It's arrived.*

JONATHAN. Ca—ca—could they—open it—I—I-I wonder?

MADAME ROSEPETTLE. You want to see them, eh Albert? You really want to see them again? That badly? You really want to see them again, that badly?

JONATHAN Yyyyyyessssss.

MADAME ROSEPETTLE. Then let the trunk be opened.

(*They open the trunk. Hundreds of books fall onto the floor.* JONATHAN *falls on top of them like a starved man upon food.*)

JONATHAN (*emotionally*). Tra-Tra-Trollope — Ha-Haggard — Daudet — Ga-Ga-Gautier—ma-mmmmy old—fffriends. La—lllook at them all. Sh-Sh-Sholokhov—Alain-Fournier — Alighieri — Turturturgenev. My—old friends. (*He burrows into them, reading to himself in wild abandon.*)

MADAME ROSEPETTLE (*coldly*). All right, Albert, that's enough.

(*He looks up bewildered. She stares at him disapprovingly.*)

JONATHAN. But—

MADAME ROSEPETTLE. That's enough— Get up, get up— Come, off your knees. Rise from your books and sing of love.

JONATHAN. But I—I can't sing.

MADAME ROSEPETTLE. Well, stand up anyway. (*He rises sadly. Short pause*) All right! Now where's Rosalinda.

THE NEAREST BELLBOY. Who?

MADAME ROSEPETTLE. My fish. I want my fish. Who has my fish?

A VOICE (*from outside the door*). I have it, madame.

(*Enter* BELLBOY TWO *carrying, at arms' length, an object covered by a black cloth. He wears large, thick, well-padded gloves —the sort a snake trainer might wear when handling a newly caught cobra.*)

MADAME ROSEPETTLE. Ah, splendid. Bring it here. Put it here, by the dictaphone. Near my memoirs. Bring it here, bellboy. But set it gently, if you will. (*He sets it down.*) Now. The black shawl of mourning, bellboy. Remove it, if you will. But gently. Gently. Gently as she goes. (*The* BELLBOY *lifts off the shawl. Revealed is a fish bowl with a fish and a cat's skeleton inside.*) Ah, I see you fed it today. (*She reaches into her handbag and extracts a pair of long tongs. She plucks the skeleton from the fish bowl.*) Siamese, I presume.

BELLBOY TWO. No, madame. Alley.

MADAME ROSEPETTLE. *WHAT!?* A common alley cat? Just who do you think I am? What kind of fish do you think I have? *Alley cat? Alley cat? Indeed.* In Buenos Aires, I'll have you know, Rosalinda was fed nothing but Siamese *kittens,* which are even more tender than Siamese cats. *That's* what I call consideration! Edward, make note: we will dismiss this creature from the bellboy squad *first thing in the morning!*

(JONATHAN *scribbles on his pad.*)

BELLBOY TWO. Madame, please, there were no Siamese cats.

MADAME ROSEPETTLE. There are *always* Siamese cats!

BELLBOY TWO. Not in Port Royale.

MADAME ROSEPETTLE. Then you should have flown to Buenos Aires. I would have paid the way. Give me back your Turkish piaster. (*He hands back the coin.*) No. Never mind. Keep it. It's not worth a thing except in Istanbul, and hardly a soul uses anything but traveler's checks there anyhow! Shows you should never trust me.

BELLBOY TWO. Madame, *please.* I have a wife.

MADAME ROSEPETTLE. And *I* have a fish. I dare say there are half a million men in Port Royale with wives. But show me one person with a silver piranha fish and then you'll be showing me something. Your marital status does not impress me, sir. You are common, do you hear? Common! While my piranha fish is *rare.*

ROSALINDA THE FISH (*sadly*). Glump.

MADAME ROSEPETTLE. Oh, dear thing. You can just tell she's not feeling up to snuff. *Someone will pay for this!*

HEAD BELLBOY (*enters from the bedroom*). Well, I'm finished.

MADAME ROSEPETTLE. You certainly are.

HEAD BELLBOY. I beg your pardon?

MADAME ROSEPETTLE. Edward, make note. First thing in the morning we speak to the chef. Subject: Siamese cats—kittens if possible, though I seriously doubt it here. And make a further note, Albert my darling. Let's see if we can't get our cats on the American plan, while we're at it.

(JONATHAN *scribbles on his pad of paper.*)

HEAD BELLBOY. Madame, is there something I can—

MADAME ROSEPETTLE. QUIET! And put that hammer down. (*He puts it down. She puts it back in her purse.*) You have all behaved rudely. If the sunset over Guanabacoa Bay were not so full of magenta and wisteria blue I'd leave this place tonight. But the sunset *is* full of magenta and wisteria blue, and so I think I'll stay. Therefore, beware. Madame Rosepettle will have much to do. She won't have time for hiring and firing people like you. Right, Robinson? (JONATHAN *opens his mouth to speak but no words come out.*) I said, *right, Robinson?* (*Again he tries to speak, and again no words come out.*) RIGHT, ROBINSON!? (*He nods.*) There's your answer. Now get out and leave us alone. (*They start to exit.*) No. Wait. (*They stop.*) A question before you go. That yacht in the harbor.

HEAD BELLBOY. *Which* yacht in the harbor?

MADAME ROSEPETTLE The pink one, of course—187 feet long, I'd judge. Who owns it?

HEAD BELLBOY. Why, Commodore Roseabove, madame. It's a pretty sloop.

MADAME ROSEPETTLE (*distantly.*) Roseabove. *Roseabove*—I like that name.

HEAD BELLBOY. Madame realizes, of course, it's the largest yacht at the island.

MADAME ROSEPETTLE. It's also the largest yacht in Haiti, Puerto Rico, Bermuda, the Dominican Republic and West Palm Beach. I haven't checked the Virgin Islands yet. I thought I'd leave them till last. But I doubt if I'll find a larger one there. I take great pleasure, you see, in measuring yachts. My hobby, you might say. (*The* BELLBOYS *exit.*) Edward, make note. First thing in the morning we re-staff this hotel. (JONATHAN *scribbles on his pad of paper.* MADAME ROSEPETTLE *walks over to the French windows and stares wistfully out. There is a short silence before she speaks. Dreamily, with a slight smile*) Roseabove. I like that name.

ROSALINDA THE FISH (*gleefully*). Gleep.

MADAME ROSEPETTLE (*fondly*). Ah, listen. My lovely little fish. She, too, is feeling better already. She, too. You can tell—you can tell. (MADAME ROSEPETTLE *who is now standing beside her fish, picks up the mouthpiece of her dicta-phone.) My Memoirs.* Port Royale—Part One—The Arrival. (*Pause, while she thinks of what to say*) Sorry to say, once again, nothing unusual to report.

(*The lights now begin to fade on* MA-DAME ROSEPETTLE *as* JONATHAN, *standing alone by the porch, sneaks out a little ways and peeks down at the streets below. As carnival music is heard, the lights fade.*)

SCENE TWO

The place is the same. The time, two weeks later. JONATHAN *is in the room with* ROSALIE, *a girl some two years older than he and dressed in sweet girlish pink.*

———

ROSALIE. But if you've been here two weeks, why haven't I seen you?

JONATHAN. I've—I've been in my room.

ROSALIE. All the time?

JONATHAN. Yes—all the time.

ROSALIE. Well, you must get out some-times. I mean, sometimes you simply must get out. You just couldn't stay in-side all the time—could you?

JONATHAN. Yyyyyes.

ROSALIE. You never get out at all? I mean, never at all?

JONATHAN. Some-sometimes, I do go out on the porch. M-Ma-Mother has some—Venus'-flytraps which she bra-brought back from the rain forests of Va-Va-Va-Venezuela. They're va-very rrrrare and need a—a lot of sunshine. Well, sir, she ka-keeps them on the porch and I—I feed them. Twice a day, too.

ROSALIE. Oh.

JONATHAN. Ma-Ma-Mother says everyone must have a vocation in life. (*With a slight nervous laugh*) I ga-guess that's—my job.

ROSALIE. I don't think I've ever met anyone before who's fed—uh—Venus'-flytraps.

JONATHAN. Ma-Ma-Mother says I'm va-very good at it. I—don't know—if—I am, but—that's—what she says so I—guess I am.

ROSALIE. Well, uh, what do you—feed them? You see, I've never met anyone before who's fed Venus'-flytraps so—that's why I don't know what—you're supposed to feed them.

JONATHAN (*happy that she asked*). Oh, I fa-feed them—l-l-lots of things. Ga-ga-green peas, chicken feathers, rubber bands. They're—not very fussy. They're—nice, that way. Ma-Ma-Mother says it it it ga-gives me a feeling of a-co-co-complish-ment. Ifffff you would—like to to see them I—could show them to you. It's—almost fa-feeding time. It is, and—and I could show them to you.

ROSALIE. No. That's all right. (JONATHAN *looks away, hurt.*) Well, how about later?

JONATHAN. Do-do-do you ra-really ww-wwwwant to see them?

ROSALIE. Yes. Yes, I really think I would like to see them—later. If you'll show them to me then, I'd really like that. (JONATHAN *looks at her and smiles. There is an awkward silence while he stares at her thankfully.*) I still don't understand why you never go out. How can you just sit in—?

JONATHAN.   SometimeswhenI'monthe-porchIdootherthings.

ROSALIE. *What?*

JONATHAN. Sa-sa-sometimes, when I'm—on the porch, you know, when I'm on the porch? Ssssssssome-times I—do *other things,* too.

ROSALIE. What sort of things? (JONA-THAN *giggles.*) What sort of things do you do?

JONATHAN. Other things.

ROSALIE (*coyly.*) What do you mean, "Other things?"

JONATHAN. Other things besides feed-ing my mother's plants. Other things be-sides that. That's what I mean. Other things besides that.

ROSALIE. What kind of things—*in par-ticular?*

JONATHAN. Oh, watching.

ROSALIE. Watching?

JONATHAN. Yes. Like—watching.

ROSALIE. Watching what? (*He giggles.*) *Watching what?*

JONATHAN. You.

(*Short pause. She inches closer to him on the couch.*)

ROSALIE. What do you mean—watching me?

JONATHAN. I—watch you from the porch. That's what I mean. I watch you from the porch. I watch you a lot, too. Every day. It's—it's the truth. I—I swear it—is. I watch you ev'ry day. Do you believe me?

ROSALIE. Of course I believe you, Albert. Why—

JONATHAN. Jonathan!

ROSALIE. What?

JONATHAN. Jonathan. Ca-ca-call me Ja-Jonathan. That's my name.

ROSALIE. But your mother said your name was—

JONATHAN. Nooooo! Call—me Jonathan. Pa-pa-please?

ROSALIE. All right—Jonathan.

JONATHAN (*excitedly*). You *do* believe me! You rrrreally do believe me. I-I can tell!

ROSALIE. Of course I believe you. Why shouldn't—?

JONATHAN. You want me to tell you how I watch you? You want me to tell you? I'll bet you'll na-never guess.

ROSALIE. How?

JONATHAN. *Guess.*

ROSALIE. (*ponders*). Through a telescope?

JONATHAN. How did you guess?

ROSALIE. I—I don't know. I was just joking. I didn't really think that was—

JONATHAN. I'll bet everyone watches you through a telescope. I'll bet everyone you go out with watches you through a telescope. That's what I'll bet.

ROSALIE. No. Not at all.

JONATHAN. Well, that's how I watch you. Through a telescope.

ROSALIE. I never would have guessed that.

JONATHAN. I thought you were—ga-going to say I—I watch you with—with love in my eyes or some—thing like that. I didn't think you were going to guess that I—watch you through a telescope. I didn't think you were going to guess that I wa-watch you through a telescope on the fa-first guess, anyway. Not on the *first guess.*

ROSALIE. Well, it was just a guess.

JONATHAN (*hopefully*). Do you watch *me* through a telescope?

ROSALIE. I never knew where your room was.

JONATHAN. Now you know. Now will you watch me?

ROSALIE. Well, I—don't have a telescope.

JONATHAN (*getting more elated and excited*). You can make one. That's how I got mine. I made it. Out of lenses and tubing. That's all you need. Lenses and tubing. Do you have any lenses?

ROSALIE. No.

JONATHAN. Do you have any tubing?

ROSALIE. No.

JONATHAN. Oh. (*Pause*) Well, would you like me to tell you how I made mine in case you find some lenses and tubing? Would you like that?

ROSALIE (*disinterestedly*). Sure, Jonathan. I think that would be nice.

JONATHAN. Well, I made it out of lenses and tubing. The lenses I had because Ma-Ma-Mother gave me a set of lenses so I could see my stamps better. I have a fabulous collection of stamps, as well as a fantastic collection of coins and a simply unbelievable collection of books. Well, sir, Ma-Ma-Mother gave me these lenses so I could see my stamps better. She suspected that some were fake so she gave me the lenses so I might be—able to see. You see? Well, sir, I happen to have nearly a billion sta-stamps. So far I've looked closely at 1,352,769. I've discovered three actual fakes! Number 1,352,767 was a fake. Number 1,352,768 was a fake, and number 1,352,769 was a fake. They were stuck together. Ma-Mother made me feed them immediately to her flytraps. Well— (*He whispers.*) one day, when Mother wasn't looking—that is, when she was out, I heard an airplane flying. An airplane—somewhere—far away. It wasn't very loud, but still I heard it. An airplane. Flying—somewhere, far away. And I ran outside to the porch so that I might see what it looked like. The airplane. With hundreds of people inside it. Hundreds and hundreds and hundreds of people. And I thought to myself, if I could just see—if I could just see what they looked like, the people, sitting at their windows, looking out—and flying. If I could see— just once—if I could see *just once* what they looked like—then I might—know what I—what I . . . (*Slight pause*) So I —built a telescope in case the plane ever—came back again. The tubing came from an old blowgun. (*He reaches behind the bureau and produces a huge blowgun, easily a foot larger than he.*) Mother brought it back from her last hunting trip to Zanzibar. The lenses were the lenses she had given me for my stamps. So I built it. My telescope. A telescope so I might be able to see. And— (*He walks out to the porch.*) and—and I *could* see!

I could! I COULD! I really could. For miles and miles I could see. For miles and miles and *miles!* (*He begins to lift it up to look through but stops, for some reason, before he's brought it up to his eye.*) Only . . . (*He hands it to* ROSALIE. *She takes it eagerly and scans the horizon and the sky. She hands it back to him.*)

ROSALIE (*with annoyance*). There's nothing out there to see.

JONATHAN (*sadly*). I know. That's the trouble. You take the time to build a telescope that can sa-see for miles, then there's nothing out there to see. Ma-Mother says it's a Lesson in Life. (*Pause*) But I'm not sorry I built my telescope. And you know why? Because I saw you. Even if I didn't see anything else, I did see you. And—and I'm—very glad. (ROSALIE *moves slightly closer to him on the couch. She moistens her lips.*) I—I remember, you were standing across the way in your penthouse garden playing blind man's buff with ten little children. (*After a short pause, fearfully*) Are—are they by any chance—*yours?*

ROSALIE (*sweetly*). Oh, I'm not married.

JONATHAN. Oh!

ROSALIE. I'm a baby sitter.

JONATHAN (*with obvious relief*). Oh.

ROSALIE. I work for the people who own the penthouse.

JONATHAN. I've never seen them around.

ROSALIE. I've never seen them, either. They're never home. They just mail me a check every week and tell me to make sure I keep the children's names straight.

JONATHAN. If you could tell me which way they went I could find them with my telescope. It can see for miles.

ROSALIE. They must love children very much, to have so many, I mean. What a remarkable woman she must be. (*Pause*) There's going to be another one, too! Another child is coming! I got a night letter last night.

JONATHAN. By airplane?

ROSALIE. I don't know.

JONATHAN. I bet it was. I can't see at night. Ma-Mother can but I can't. I'll bet that's when the planes fly.

ROSALIE (*coyly*). If you like, I'll read you the letter. I have it with me. (*She unbuttons the top of her blouse and turns around in a coquettish manner to take the letter from her brassiere. Reading*) "Have had another child. Sent it yester-day. Will arrive tomorrow. Call it Cynthia."

JONATHAN. That will make eleven. That's an awful lot of children to take care of. I'll bet it must be wonderful.

ROSALIE. Well, they do pay very well.

JONATHAN. They pay you?

ROSALIE. Of course— What did you think? (*Pause. Softly, seductively*) Jonathan? (*He does not answer but seems lost in thought. With a feline purr*) Jonathan?

JONATHAN. Yyyyyes?

ROSALIE. It gets very lonesome over there. The children go to sleep early and the parents are never home so I'm always alone. Perhaps—well, Jonathan, I thought that perhaps you might—visit me.

JONATHAN. Well—well—well, you—you see—I—I——

ROSALIE. We could spend the evenings together—at my place. It gets so lonesome there, you know what I mean? I mean, I don't know what to do. I get so lonesome there.

JONATHAN. Ma-ma-ma-maybe you—you can—come over—here? Maybe you you can do—that.

ROSALIE. Why are you trembling so?

JONATHAN. I'm—I'm—I'm—I'm—

ROSALIE. Are you afraid?

JONATHAN. Nnnnnnnnnnnnnnnnnnnnno. Whaaaaaaaaaa—why—should I—be—a-fraid?

ROSALIE. Then why won't you come visit me?

JONATHAN. I—I—I—I—

ROSALIE. I don't think you're allowed to go out. That's what I think.

JONATHAN. Nnnn-o. I—I can—can—can—

ROSALIE. Why can't you go out, Jonathan? I want to know.

JONATHAN. Nnnnnnnnn—

ROSALIE. Tell me, Jonathan!

JONATHAN. I—I—

ROSALIE. I said I want to know! *Tell me.*

JONATHAN. I—I don't know. I don't know why. I mean. I've—nnnnnnnnever really thought—about going out. I—guess it's—just natural for me to—stay inside. (*He laughs nervously as if that explained everything.*) You see—I've got so much to do. I mean, all my sssssstamps and—ca-coins and books. The pa-pa-plane might fffffly overhead while I was was

going downstairs. And then thhhhere are
—the plants ta-to feeeeeeed. And I enjoy
vvvery much wa—watching you and all
yyyyyyour chil-dren. I've—really got so
ma-many things—to—do. Like—like my
future, for instance. Ma-Mother says I'm
going to be great. That's—that's—that's
what she—says. I'm going to be great. I
sssswear. Of course, she doesn't know
ex-actly what I'm—going to be great in—
so she sits every afternoon for—for two
hours and thinks about it. Na-na-natu-
rally I've—got to be here when she's
thinking in case she—thinks of the answer. Otherwise she might forget and I'd
never know—what I'm ga-going to be
great in. You—see what I mean? I mean,
I've—I've ggggggot so many things to do
I—just couldn't possibly get *anything*
done if I ever—went—outside. (*There is
a silence.* JONATHAN *stares at* ROSALIE *as
if he were hoping that might answer her
question sufficiently. She stares back at
him as if she knows there is more.*) Besides, Mother locks the front door.

ROSALIE. I thought so.

JONATHAN. No! You-you don't understand. It's not what you think. She doesn't
lock the door to ka-ka-keep me in, which
would be malicious. She—locks the door
so I can't get out, which is for my own
good and therefore—beneficent.

CUCKOO CLOCK (*from the master bedroom*). Cuckoo! Cuckoo! Cuckoo!

ROSALIE. What's that?

JONATHAN (*fearfully*). A warning.

ROSALIE. What do you mean, a warning?

JONATHAN. A warning that you have
to go. Your time is up.

ROSALIE. My time is what?

JONATHAN. Your time is up. You have
to go. Now. At once. Right away. You
can't stay any longer. You've got to go!

ROSALIE. Why?

JONATHAN (*puzzled; as if this were the
first time the question had ever occurred
to him*). I don't really know.

CUCKOO CLOCK (*louder*). Cuckoo!
Cuckoo! Cuckoo!

(JONATHAN *freezes in terror.* ROSALIE
looks at him calmly.)

ROSALIE. Why did your mother ask me
to come up here?

JONATHAN. What?

ROSALIE. Why did your mother ask
me—?

JONATHAN. So I—I could meet you.

ROSALIE. Then why didn't you ask me
yourself? Something's wrong around
here, Jonathan. I don't understand why
you didn't ask me yourself.

JONATHAN. Ma-Mother's so much better at those things.

CUCKOO CLOCK (*very loudly*). CUCK-
OO! CUCKOO! CUCKOO!

JONATHAN. You've got to get out of
here! That's the third warning. (*He
starts to push her toward the door.*)

ROSALIE. Will you call me on the
phone?

JONATHAN. Please, you've got to go!

ROSALIE. Instead of your mother telling
me to come, will you come and get me
yourself? Will you at least call me? Wave
to me?

JONATHAN. Yes-yes—I'll do that. Now
get out of here!

ROSALIE. I want you to promise to come
and see me again.

JONATHAN. Get out!

ROSALIE (*coyly*). Promise me.

JONATHAN. GET OUT! (*He pushes her
toward the door.*)

ROSALIE. Why do you keep looking at
that door?

JONATHAN (*almost in tears*). Please.

ROSALIE. Why do you keep looking at
that door?

JONATHAN. *Please! You've* got to go before it's too late!

ROSALIE. There's something very wrong
here. I want to see what's behind that
door. (*She starts toward the master bedroom.* JONATHAN *throws his arms about
her legs and collapses at her feet, his face
buried against her thighs.*)

JONATHAN (*sobbing uncontrollably*). I
love you.

(ROSALIE *stops dead in her tracks and
stares down at* JONATHAN.)

ROSALIE. What did you say?

JONATHAN. I-I-I llllllove you. I love
you, I love you, I love you, I— (*The
CUCKOO CLOCK screams, cackles, and goes
out of its mind, its call ending in a
crazed, strident rasp as if it had broken
all its springs, screws and innards. The
door to the master bedroom opens.
MADAME ROSEPETTLE appears. Weakly*)
Too late.

MADAME ROSEPETTLE. Two warnings are
enough for any man. Three are enough
for any woman. The cuckoo struck three

times and then a fourth and still she's here. May I ask why?

ROSALIE. You've been listening at the keyhole, haven't you!

MADAME ROSEPETTLE. I'm talking to my son, harlot!

ROSALIE. What did you say!

MADAME ROSEPETTLE. Harlot, I called you! Slut, scum, sleazy prostitute catching and caressing children and men. Stroking their hearts. I've seen you.

ROSALIE. What are you talking about?

MADAME ROSEPETTLE. Blind man's buff with the children in the garden. The red-headed one—fifteen, I think. Behind the bush while the others cover their eyes. Up with the skirt, one-two-three and it's done. Don't try to deny it. I've seen you in action. I know your kind.

ROSALIE. That's a lie!

MADAME ROSEPETTLE. Life is a lie, my sweet. Not words but Life itself. Life in all its ugliness. It builds green trees that tease your eyes and draw you under them. Then when you're there in the shade and you breathe in and say, "Oh God, how beautiful," that's when the bird on the branch lets go his droppings and hits you on the head. Life, my sweet, beware. It isn't what it seems. I've seen what it can do. I've watched you dance.

ROSALIE. What do you mean by that?

MADAME ROSEPETTLE. Last night in the ballroom. I've watched you closely and I know what I see. You danced too near those men and you let them do too much. Don't try to deny it. Words will only make it worse. It would be best for all concerned if you left at once and never came again. Good day. (MADAME ROSE-PETTLE *turns to leave.* ROSALIE *does not* MOVE.)

ROSALIE. Why don't you let Jonathan out of his room?

MADAME ROSEPETTLE. Who?

ROSALIE. Jonathan.

MADAME ROSEPETTLE. Who?

ROSALIE. Your son.

MADAME ROSEPETTLE. You mean Albert? Is that who you mean? Albert?

JONATHAN. Pa-pa-please do-don't.

MADAME ROSEPETTLE. Is that who you mean, slut? H'm? Speak up? Is that who you mean?

ROSALIE. I mean your son.

MADAME ROSEPETTLE. *I don't let him out because he is my son.* I don't let him

out because his skin is as white as fresh snow and he would burn if the sun struck him. I don't let him out because outside there are trees with birds sitting on their branches waiting for him to walk beneath. I don't let him out because you're there, waiting behind the bushes with your skirt up. I don't let him out because he is *susceptible.* That's why. Because he is *susceptible.* Susceptible to trees and to sluts and to sunstroke.

ROSALIE. Then why did you come and get me?

MADAME ROSEPETTLE. Because, my dear, my stupid son has been watching you through that stupid telescope he made. Because, in short, he wanted to meet you and I, in short, wanted him to know what you were really like. Now that he's seen, you may go.

ROSALIE. And if I choose to stay?

(*Pause.*)

MADAME ROSEPETTLE (*softly; slyly*). Can you cook?

ROSALIE. Yes.

MADAME ROSEPETTLE. How well?

ROSALIE. Fairly well.

MADAME ROSEPETTLE. Not good enough! My son is a connoisseur. A connoisseur, do you hear? I cook him the finest foods in the world. Recipes no one knows exist. Food, my sweet, is the finest of arts. And since you can't cook you are artless. You nauseate my son's aesthetic taste. Do you like cats?

ROSALIE. Yes.

MADAME ROSEPETTLE. What kind of cats?

ROSALIE. Any kind of cats.

MADAME ROSEPETTLE. Alley cats?

ROSALIE. Especially alley cats.

MADAME ROSEPETTLE. I thought so. Go, my dear. Find yourself some weeping willow and set yourself beneath it. Cry of your lust for my son and wait, for a mocking bird waits above to deposit his verdict on your whorish head. My son is as white as fresh snow and you are tainted with sin. You are garnished with garlic and turn our tender stomachs in disgust.

ROSALIE. Why did you come to Port Royale?

MADAME ROSEPETTLE. To find *you!*

ROSALIE. And now that you've found me—?

MADAME ROSEPETTLE. I throw you out!

I toss you into the garbage can! I heard everything, you know. So don't try to call. The phone is in my room—*and no one goes into my room but me.* (*She stares at* ROSALIE *for a moment, then exits with a flourish.* ROSALIE *and* JONATHAN *move slowly toward each other. When they are almost together,* MADAME ROSE-PETTLE *reappears.*) One more thing. If, by some chance, the eleventh child named Cynthia turns out to be a Siamese cat, give it to me. I, too, pay well.

(MADAME ROSEPETTLE *turns toward her room.* ROSALIE *starts toward the door.* JONATHAN *grabs her hand in desperation.*)

JONATHAN (*in a whisper*). Come back again. Pa-please—come back again.

(*For a moment* ROSALIE *stops and looks at* JONATHAN. *But* MADAME ROSEPETTLE *stops too, and turning, looks back at both of them, a slight smile on her lips.* ROSA-LIE, *sensing her glance, walks toward the door, slipping from* JONATHAN'S *outstretched hands as she does. The lights fade about* JONATHAN, *alone in the center of the room.*)

CURTAIN

SCENE THREE

The hotel room at night, one week later. JONATHAN *is alone in the living room. He is sitting in a chair near the fish bowl, staring at nothing in particular with a particularly blank expression on his face. A clock is heard ticking softly in the distance. For an interminably long time it continues to tick while* JONATHAN *sits in his chair, motionless. After a while the ticking speeds up almost imperceptibly and soon after, laughter is heard. At first it is a giggle from the rear of the theatre, then a cough from the side, then a self-conscious laugh from the other side, then a full, gusty belly-roar from all corners of the theatre. Soon the entire world is hysterical. Cuban drums begin to beat. Fireworks explode. Orgiastic music is heard.* JONATHAN *continues to sit, motionless. Only his eyes have begun to move. The clock continues to tick. The laughter grows louder: the laughter of the insane. Suddenly* JONATHAN *leaps up and rushes to the French windows, his*

fingers pressed against his ears. He slams the French windows shut. The noises stop. JONATHAN *closes his eyes and sighs with relief. The French windows sway unsteadily on their hinges. They tip forward. They fall to the floor. They shatter. The laughter returns.* JONATHAN *stares down at them in horror. The* VENUS'-FLY-TRAPS *grow larger and growl.*

VENUS'-FLYTRAPS (*viciously*). Grrrrrrrr.

(*The piranha fish stares hungrily from its bowl.*)

ROSALINDA THE FISH (*more viciously*). Grarrgh!

(*The* FLYTRAPS *lunge at* JONATHAN *but he walks dazedly past, unaware of their snapping petals, and goes out to the edge of the balcony. He stares out in complete bewilderment. The laughter and music of a carnival, the sounds of* PEOPLE *dancing in the streets fill the air. He looks down at them sadly. Meekly he waves. The sounds immediately grow softer and the* PEOPLE *begin to drift away. He watches as they leave. Behind him the* FLYTRAPS *keep growing and reaching out for him, but of this he is unaware. He only stands at the railing, looking down. A last lingering laugh is heard somewhere in the distance, echoing. The door to the suite opens. The* BELLBOYS *enter and set a small table, two small chairs, a champagne bottle and ice bucket, and a small vase with one wilting rose. They spray the room with an atomizer. They exit, except for a* VIOLINIST. *The lights fade in the room and only the table is lit. The music grows in brilliance. The* COMMODORE *and* MADAME ROSEPETTLE *waltz into the room. A spot of light follows them about the floor.*)

THE COMMODORE. How lovely it was this evening, madame, don't you think? (*She laughs softly and demurely and discreetly lowers her eyes. They waltz about the floor.*) How gentle the wind was, madame. And the stars, how clear and bright they were, don't you think? (*She turns her face away and smiles softly. They begin to whirl about the floor.*) Ah, the waltz. How exquisite it is, madame, don't you think? One-two-three, one-two-three, one-two-three. Ahhhhh, madame, how classically simple. How stark; how strong—how romantic—how sublime. (*She giggles girlishly. They whirl madly about the floor.*) Oh, if only madame knew how I've waited for this moment. If only madame knew how long. How this week, these nights, the nights we shared together on my yacht; the warm, wonderful nights, the almost-perfect nights, the would-have-been-perfect nights had it not been for the crew peeking through the portholes. Ah, those nights, madame, those nights; almost alone but never quite; but now, tonight, at last, we *are* alone. And now, madame, now we are ready for romance. For the night was made for love. And tonight, madame— we will love.

MADAME ROSEPETTLE (*with the blush of innocence*). Oh, Commodore, how you do talk.

(*They whirl about the room as the lilting rhythm of the waltz grows and sweeps on and on.*)

THE COMMODORE (*suavely*). Madame, may I kiss you?

MADAME ROSEPETTLE. Why?

THE COMMODORE (*after recovering from the abruptness of the question*). Your lips . . . are a thing of beauty.

MADAME ROSEPETTLE. My lips, Commodore, are the color of blood. (*She smiles at him. He stares blankly ahead. They dance on.*) I must say, you dance exceptionally well, Commodore—for a man your age.

THE COMMODORE (*bristling*). I dance with *you*, madame. That is why I dance well. For to dance with you, madame— is to hold you.

MADAME ROSEPETTLE. Well, I don't mind your holding me, Commodore, but at the moment you happen to be holding me too tight.

THE COMMODORE. I hold you too dear to hold you too tight, madame. I hold you close, that is all. And I hold you close in the hope that my heart may feel your heart beating.

MADAME ROSEPETTLE. *One*-two-three, *one*-two-three. You're not paying enough attention to the music, Commodore. I'm afraid you've fallen out of step.

THE COMMODORE. Then lead me, madame. Take my hand and lead me wherever you wish. For I would much rather think of my words than my feet.

MADAME ROSEPETTLE (*with great sweetness*). Why certainly, Commodore. Certainly. If that is what you want—it will be my pleasure to oblige. (*They switch*

hands and she begins to lead him about the floor. They whirl wildly about, spinning faster than they had when the COMMODORE led.*) Beautiful, isn't it, Commodore? The waltz. The Dance of Lovers. I'm so glad you enjoy it so much. (*With a gay laugh she whirls him around the floor. Suddenly he puts his arms about her shoulders and leans close to kiss her. She pulls back.*) Commodore! You were supposed to spin just then. When I squeeze you in the side it means *spin!*

THE COMMODORE (*flustered*). I—I thought it was a sign of affection.

(*She laughs.*)

MADAME ROSEPETTLE. You'll learn. (*She squeezes him in the side. He spins about under her arm.*) Ah, you're learning.

(*He continues to spin, around and around, faster and faster like a runaway top while MADAME ROSEPETTLE, not spinning at all, leads him about the floor, a wild smile of ecstasy spreading over her face.*)

THE COMMODORE. Ho-ho, ho-ho. Stop. I'm dizzy. Dizzy. Stop, please. Stop. Ho-ho. Stop. Dizzy. Ho-ho. Stop. Too fast. Slow. Slower. Stop. Ho-ho. Dizzy. Too dizzy. Weeeeeeee! (*And then, without any warning at all, she grabs him in the middle of a spin, and kisses him. Her back is to the audience, so the COMMODORE'S face is visible. At first he is too dizzy to realize that his motion has been stopped. But shortly he does, and his first expression is that of shock. But the kiss is long and the shock turns into perplexity and then, finally, into panic; into fear. He struggles desperately and breaks free from her arms, gasping wildly for air. He points weakly to his chest, gasping.*) Asthma. (*His chest heaves as he gulps in air.*) Couldn't breathe. Asthmatic. Couldn't get any air. (*He gasps for air. She starts to walk toward him, slowly.*) Couldn't get any . . . air. (*She nears him. Instinctively he backs away.*) You—you surprised me—you know. Out —of breath. Wasn't—ready for that. Didn't—expect you to kiss me.

MADAME ROSEPETTLE. I know. That's why I did it. (*She laughs and puts her arm tenderly about his waist.*) Perhaps you'd prefer to sit down for a while, Commodore? Catch your breath, so to speak. Dancing can be so terribly tiring—

when you're growing old. Well, if you like, Commodore, we could just sit and talk. And perhaps—sip some pink champagne, eh? Champagne?

THE COMMODORE. Ah, champagne.

MADAME ROSEPETTLE (*she begins to walk with him toward the table*). And just for the two of us.

THE COMMODORE. Yes. The two of us. Alone.

MADAME ROSEPETTLE (*with a laugh*). Yes. All alone.

(*Exit, the* VIOLINIST.)

THE COMMODORE. At last.

MADAME ROSEPETTLE. With music in the distance.

THE COMMODORE. A waltz.

MADAME ROSEPETTLE. A *Viennese* waltz.

THE COMMODORE. The Dance of Lovers.

MADAME ROSEPETTLE (*she takes his hand, tenderly*). Yes, Commodore. The Dance of Lovers. (*They look at each other in silence.*)

THE COMMODORE. Madame, you have won my heart. And easily.

MADAME ROSEPETTLE. No, Commodore. You have lost it. *Easily.* (*She smiles seductively. The room darkens till only a single spot of light falls upon the table set in the middle of the room. The waltz plays on.* MADAME ROSEPETTLE *nods to the* COMMODORE *and he goes to sit. But before he can pull his chair out, it slides out under its own power. He places himself and the chair slides back in, as if some invisible waiter had been holding it in his invisible hands.* MADAME ROSEPETTLE *smiles sweetly and, pulling out her chair herself, sits. They stare at each other in silence. The waltz plays softly. The* COMMODORE *reaches across the table and touches her hand. A thin smile spreads across her lips. When finally they speak, their words are soft; the whispered thoughts of lovers.*) Champagne?

THE COMMODORE. Champagne.

MADAME ROSEPETTLE. Pour?

THE COMMODORE. Please.

(*She lifts the bottle out of the ice bucket and pours with her right hand, her left being clasped firmly in the* COMMODORE'S *passionate hands. They smile serenely at each other. She lifts her glass. He lifts his. The music swells.*)

MADAME ROSEPETTLE. A toast?

THE COMMODORE. To you.

MADAME ROSEPETTLE. No, Commodore, to you.

THE COMMODORE. No, madame. To us.

MADAME ROSEPETTLE *and* THE COMMODORE (*together*). To us. (*They raise their glasses. They gaze wistfully into each other's eyes. The music builds to brilliance. The* COMMODORE *clicks his glass against* MADAME ROSEPETTLE'S *glass. The glasses break.*)

THE COMMODORE (*furiously mopping up the mess*). Pardon, madame! Pardon!

MADAME ROSEPETTLE (*flicking some glass off her bodice*). Pas de quoi, monsieur.

THE COMMODORE. J'étais emporté par l'enthousiasme du moment.

MADAME ROSEPETTLE (*extracting pieces of glass from her lap*). Pas de quoi. (*She snaps her fingers gaily. Immediately a* WAITER *appears from the shadows with a table in his hands. It is already covered with a table cloth, two champagne glasses, two candelabras* [*the candles already flickering in them*], *and a vase with one wilting rose protruding. Another* WAITER *whisks the wet table away. The new table is placed. The* WAITERS *disappear into the shadows.* MADAME ROSEPETTLE *lifts the bottle of champagne out of the ice bucket.*) Encore?

THE COMMODORE. S'il vous plaît. (*She pours. They lift their glasses in toast. The music swells again.*) To us.

MADAME ROSEPETTLE. To us, Monsieur —Commodore. (*They clink their glasses lightly. The* COMMODORE *closes his eyes and sips.* MADAME ROSEPETTLE *holds her glass before her lips, poised but not touching; waiting. She watches him. Softly*) Tell me about yourself.

THE COMMODORE. My heart is speaking, madame. Doesn't it tell you enough?

MADAME ROSEPETTLE. Your heart, monsieur, is growing old. It speaks with a murmur. Its words are too weak to understand.

THE COMMODORE. But the feeling, madame, is still strong.

MADAME ROSEPETTLE. Feelings are for animals, monsieur. Words are the specialty of Man. Tell me what your heart has to say.

THE COMMODORE. My heart says it loves you.

MADAME ROSEPETTLE. And how many others, monsieur, has your heart said this to?

THE COMMODORE. None but you, madame. None but you.

MADAME ROSEPETTLE. And pray, monsieur, just what is it that I've done to make you love me so?

THE COMMODORE. Nothing, madame. And that is why. You are a strange woman, you see. You go out with me and you know how I feel. Yet, I know nothing of you. You disregard me, madame, but never discourage. You treat my love with indifference—but never disdain. You've led me on, madame. That is what I mean to say.

MADAME ROSEPETTLE. I've led you to my room, monsieur. That is all.

THE COMMODORE. To me, that is enough.

MADAME ROSEPETTLE. I know. That's why I did it.

(*The music swells. She smiles distantly. There is a momentary silence.*)

THE COMMODORE (*with desperation*). Madame, I must ask you something. Why are you here? (*Short pause.*)

MADAME ROSEPETTLE. Well, I have to be somewhere, don't I?

THE COMMODORE. But why here, where I am? Why in Port Royale?

MADAME ROSEPETTLE. You flatter yourself, monsieur. I am in Port Royale only because Port Royale was in my way. . . . I think I'll move on tomorrow.

THE COMMODORE. For—home?

MADAME ROSEPETTLE (*laughing slightly*). Only the very young and the very old have homes. I am neither. So I have none.

THE COMMODORE. But—surely you must come from somewhere.

MADAME ROSEPETTLE. Nowhere you've ever been.

THE COMMODORE. I've been many places.

MADAME ROSEPETTLE (*softly*). But not many enough. (*She picks up her glass of champagne and sips, a distant smile on her lips.*)

THE COMMODORE (*with sudden, overwhelming and soul-rending passion*). Madame, don't go tomorrow. Stay. My heart is yours.

MADAME ROSEPETTLE. How much is it worth?

THE COMMODORE. A fortune, madame.

MADAME ROSEPETTLE. Good. I'll take it in cash.

THE COMMODORE. But the heart goes with it, madame.

MADAME ROSEPETTLE. And you with the heart, I suppose?

THE COMMODORE. Forever.

MADAME ROSEPETTLE. Sorry, monsieur. The money's enticing and the heart would have been nice, but you, I'm afraid, are a bit too bulky to make it all worth while.

THE COMMODORE. You jest, madame.

MADAME ROSEPETTLE. I never jest, monsieur. There isn't enough time.

THE COMMODORE. Then you make fun of my passion, madame, which is just as bad.

MADAME ROSEPETTLE. But, monsieur, I've never taken your passion seriously enough to make fun of it.

THE COMMODORE (*there is a short pause. The* COMMODORE *sinks slowly back in his seat. Weakly, sadly*). Then why have you gone out with me?

MADAME ROSEPETTLE. So that I might drink champagne with you tonight.

THE COMMODORE. That makes no sense.

MADAME ROSEPETTLE. It makes *perfect* sense.

THE COMMODORE. Not to me.

MADAME ROSEPETTLE. It does to me.

THE COMMODORE. But *I* don't understand. And I *want* to understand.

MADAME ROSEPETTLE. Don't worry, Commodore. You will.

THE COMMODORE. When?

MADAME ROSEPETTLE. Soon.

THE COMMODORE. How soon?

MADAME ROSEPETTLE. Very soon. (*He stares at her in submissive confusion. Suddenly, with final desperation, he grabs her hands in his and, leaning across the table, kisses them passionately, sobbingly. In a scarcely audible whisper*) Now.

THE COMMODORE. Madame—I love you. Forever. Don't you understand? (*He kisses her hands again. A smile of triumph spreads across her face.*) Oh, your husband— He must have been—a wonderful man—to have deserved a woman such as you. (*He sobs and kisses her hands again.*)

MADAME ROSEPETTLE (*nonchalantly*). Would you like to see him?

THE COMMODORE. A snapshot?

MADAME ROSEPETTLE. No. My husband. He's inside in the closet. I had him stuffed. Wonderful taxidermist I know. H'm? What do you say, Commodore?

Wanna peek? He's my very favorite trophy. I take him with me wherever I go.

THE COMMODORE (*shaken. Not knowing what to make of it*). Hah-hah, hah-hah. Yes. Very good. Very funny. Sort of a—um—*white elephant,* you might say.

MADAME ROSEPETTLE. *You* might say.

THE COMMODORE. Well, it's—certainly very—courageous of you, a—a woman still in mourning, to—to be able to laugh at what most other women wouldn't find —well, shall we say—funny.

MADAME ROSEPETTLE. Life, my dear Commodore, is never funny. It's grim! It's there every morning breathing in your face the moment you open your red baggy eyes. Life, Mr. Roseabove, is a husband hanging from a hook in the closet. Open the door too quickly and your whole day's shot to hell. But open the door just a little ways, sneak your hand in, pull out your dress and your day is made. Yet he's still there, and waiting—and sooner or later the moth balls are gone and you have to clean house. Oh, it's a bad day, Commodore, when you have to stare Life in the face, and you will find he doesn't smile at all; just hangs there—with his tongue sticking out.

THE COMMODORE. I—don't find this— very funny.

MADAME ROSEPETTLE. Sorry. I was hoping it would give you a laugh.

THE COMMODORE. I don't think it's funny at all. And the reason that I don't think it's funny at all is that it's not my kind of joke. One must respect the dead.

MADAME ROSEPETTLE. Then tell me, Commodore—why not the living, too? (*Pause. She lifts out the bottle of champagne and pours herself some more.*)

THE COMMODORE (*weakly, with a trace of fear*). How—how did he die?

MADAME ROSEPETTLE. Why, I killed him, of course. Champagne? (*She smiles sweetly and fills his glass. She raises hers in toast.*) To your continued good health. (*He stares at her blankly. The music swells in the background.*) Ah, the waltz, monsieur. Listen. The waltz. The Dance of Lovers. Beautiful—*don't you think?*

(*She laughs and sips some more champagne. The music grows to brilliance. The* COMMODORE *starts to rise from his chair.*)

THE COMMODORE. Forgive me, madame. But—I find I must leave. Urgent business calls. Good evening. (*He tries to push his chair back, but for some reason it will not move. He looks about in panic. He pushes frantically. It does not move. It is as if the invisible waiter who had come and slid the chair out when he went to sit down, now stood behind the chair and held it in so he could not get up. And as there are arms on the chair, the* COMMODORE *cannot slide out at the sides.* MADAME ROSEPETTLE *smiles.*)

MADAME ROSEPETTLE. Now you don't *really* want to leave—do you, Commodore? After all, the night is still so young—and you haven't even seen my husband yet. Besides, there's a little story I still must tell you. A bedtime story. A fairy tale full of handsome princes and enchanted maidens; full of love and joy and music; tenderness and charm. It's my very favorite story, you see. And I never leave a place without telling it to at least one person. So please, Commodore, won't you stay? . . . *Just for a little while?* (*He stares at her in horror. He tries once more to push his chair back. But the chair does not move. He sinks down into it weakly. She leans across the table and tenderly touches his hand.*) Good. I knew you'd see it my way. It would have been such a shame if you'd had to leave. For you see, Commodore, we are, in a way, united. We share something in common—you and I. We share desire. For you desire me, with love in your heart. While I, my dear Commodore—desire your heart. (*She smiles sweetly and sips some more champagne.*) How simple it all is, in the end. (*She rises slowly from her chair and walks over to him. She runs her hands lovingly through his hair and down the back of his neck. The light on the table dims slightly.* MADAME ROSEPETTLE *walks slowly away. A spot of light follows her as she goes. Light on the table fades more. The* COMMODORE *sits, motionless.*) His name was Albert Edward Robinson Rosepettle III. How strange and sad he was. All the others who had come to see me had been tall, but he was short. They had been rich, while he was poor. The others had been handsome, but Albert, poor Albert, he was as ugly as a humid day . . . (*She laughs sadly, distantly.*) and just about as wet, too. Oh, he was a fat bundle of sweat, Mr. Roseabove. He was nothing but one great torrent of perspiration. Winter and summer, spring and fall, Albert was dripping wet. Yes, he was round and wet and hideous and I never could figure out how he ever got such a name as Albert Edward Robinson Rosepettle III.

Oh, I must have been very susceptible indeed to have married Albert. I *was* twenty-eight and that *is* a susceptible year in a woman's life. And of course I *was* a virgin, but still I— Oh, stop blushing, Mr. Roseabove. I'm not lying. It's all true. Part of the cause of my condition, I will admit, was due to the fact that I still hadn't gone out with a man. But I am certain, Mr. Roseabove, I am certain that despite your naughty glances my virtue would have remained unsoiled, no matter what. You see, I had spoken to men. (Their voices are gruff.) And in crowded streets I had often brushed against them. (Their bodies, I found, are tough and bony.) I had observed their ways and habits, Mr. Roseabove. Even at that tender age I had the foresight to realize I must know what I was up against. So I watched them huddled in hallways, talking in nervous whispers and laughing when little girls passed by. I watched their hands in crowded buses and even felt their feeling elbows on crowded streets. And then, one night, when I was walking home I saw a man standing in a window. I saw him take his contact lenses out and his hearing aid out of his ear. I saw him take his teeth out of his thin-lipped mouth and drop them into a smiling glass of water. I saw him lift his snow-white hair off of his wrinkled white head and place it on a gnarled wooden hat tree. And then I saw him take his clothes off. And when he was done and didn't move but stood and stared at a full-length mirror whose glass he had covered with towels, then I went home and wept.

And so one day I bolted the door to my room. I locked myself inside, bought a small revolver just in case, then sat at my window and watched what went on below. It was not a pretty sight. Some men came up to see me. I did not let them in.

"Hello in there," they said.

"Hello in there,
My name is Steven.
Steven S. (for Steven) Steven.

One is odd
But two is even.
I know you're hot
So I'm not leavin'."

. . . or something like that.

(*Short pause*) But they all soon left anyway. I think they caught the scent of a younger woman down the hall. And so I listened to the constant sound of feet disappearing down the stairs. I watched a world walk by my window; a world of lechery and lies and greed. I watched a world walk by and I decided not to leave my room until this world came to me, *exactly* as I wanted it.

One day Albert came toddling up the stairs. He waddled over to my room, scratched on the door and said, in a frail and very frightened voice, "Will you please marry me?" And so I did. It was as simple as that. (*Pause. Then distantly*) I still wonder why I did it though. I still wonder why. (*Short pause. Then with a laugh of resignation*) I don't know. . . . Yes, maybe it's because one look at Albert's round, sad face and I knew he could be mine . . . that no matter where he went, or whom he saw, or what he did, Albert could be mine, my husband, my lover, my own—mine to love, mine to live with, mine to kill. . . .

And so we were wed. That night I went to bed with a man for the first time in my life. The next morning I picked up my mattress and moved myself into another room. Oh, how easily is Man satisfied. How easily is his porous body saturated with "fun." All he asks is a little sex and a little food and there he is, asleep with a smile and snoring. Never the slightest regard for you, lying in bed next to him, your eyes open wide. No, he stretches his legs and kicks you in the shins; stretches his arms and smacks you in the eye. Oh, how noble, how magical, how marvelous is Love.

So you see, Mr. Roseabove, I *had* to leave his room. For as long as I stayed there I was not safe. After all, we'd only met the day before and I knew far too little about him. But now that we were married I had time to find out more. A few of the things I thought I should know were: what had he done before we'd met, what had he wanted to do, what did he *still* want to do, what was he doing about it? What did he dream about while he slept? What did he think about when he stared out the window? What did he think about when I wasn't near?

These were the things that concerned me most. And so I began to watch him closely.

My plan worked best at night, for that was when he slept. . . . I would listen at my door until I heard his door close. Then I'd tiptoe out and watch him through his keyhole. When his lights went out I'd open up his door and creep across the floor to his bed, and then I'd listen more. My ear became a stethoscope that recorded the fluctuations of his dream life. For I was waiting for him to speak, waiting for the slightest word that might betray his sleeping, secret thoughts. . . . But no, Albert only snored, and smiled, and slept on and on. And that, Mr. Roseabove, is how I spent my nights! —next to him, my husband, my "Love." I never left his side, never took my eyes from his sleeping face. I dare you to find me a wife who's as devoted as that. (*She laughs. Short pause.*)

A month later I found that I was pregnant. It had happened that first horrible night. How like Albert to do something like that. I fancy he knew it was going to happen all the time, too. I do believe he planned it that way. One night, one shot, one chance in a lifetime and bham! you've had it. It takes an imaginative man to miss. It takes someone like Albert to do something like that. But yet, I never let on. Oh, no. Let him think I'm simply getting fat, I said. And that's the way I did it, too. I, nonchalantly putting on weight; Albert nonchalantly watching my belly grow. If he knew what was happening to me he never let me know it. He was as silent as before. (*Pause.*)

Twelve months later my son was born. He was so overdue that when he came out he was already teething. He bit the index finger off the poor doctor's hand and snapped at the nurse till she fainted. I took him home and put him in a cage in the darkest corner of my room. But still I—

THE COMMODORE. Was it a large cage?

MADAME ROSEPETTLE. What?

THE COMMODORE. Was his cage large? I hope it was. Otherwise it wouldn't be very comfortable.

MADAME ROSEPETTLE. I'm sorry. Did I say cage? I meant crib. I put him in a crib and set the crib in a corner of my room where my husband would not see him. For until I found out exactly why he'd married me, I would not tell him that a son had been born. (*Pause.*)

Shortly after that, Rosalinda came. She was one of Albert's many secretaries. You know, I've always felt there was something star-crossed about those two, for she was the only person I ever met who was equally as ugly as he.

Well, naturally I never let on that I knew she had come. I simply set an extra place at the table and cooked a little bit more. And at night, instead of preparing one, I prepared two beds. Instead of fluffing one pillow I fluffed up two and straightened an extra pair of sheets. I said good night as politely as I could and left them alone—the monster and my husband, two soulmates expressing their souls through sin. And while they lay in bed I listened at the keyhole. And when they slept I crept in and listened more. Albert had begun to speak!

After months of listening for some meager clue he suddenly began to talk in torrents. Words poured forth and I, like some listening sponge, soaked them up and stayed for more. At last he was talking in his sleep! He told her things he never told to me. Words of passion and love. He told her how he worshiped the way she cooked; how he worshiped the way she talked; how he'd worshiped the way she'd looked when he'd first met her; even the way she looked now. And this to a hideous, twisted slut of a woman sleeping in sin with him! Words he never told to me. I ask you, Mr. Roseabove, I ask you, how much is a woman supposed to take?

Ah, but the signs of regret were beginning to show. And oh, how I laughed when I found out: when I saw how tired he'd begun to look, when I noticed how little he ate; how little he spoke; how slowly he seemed to move. It's funny, but he never slept any more. I could tell by his breathing. And through the keyhole at night I could see his large, round, empty eyes shining sadly in the dark. (*Pause.*)

Then one night he died. One year

after she had come he passed on. The doctors don't know why. His heart, they said, seemed fine. It was as large a heart as they'd ever seen. And yet he died. At one o'clock in the morning his heart stopped beating. (*She laughs softly.*) But it wasn't till dawn that she discovered he was dead. (*She starts to laugh louder.*)

Well, don't you get it? Don't you catch the irony, the joke? What's wrong with you!? He died at one. At ONE O'CLOCK IN THE MORNING!! Dead!! Yet she didn't know he was dead till dawn. (*She laughs again, loudly.*)

Well don't you get the point? The point of this whole story? What is wrong with you? He was lying with her in bed for nearly six hours, *dead,* and she never knew it. What a lover he must have been! WHAT A LOVER! (*She laughs uproariously but stops when she realizes he's not laughing with her.*)

Well don't you see? Their affair, their sinfulness—it never even existed! He tried to make me jealous but there was nothing to be jealous of. He was *mine!* Mine all the time, even when he was in bed with another, even in death . . . *he was mine!* (THE COMMODORE *climbs up in his chair and crawls over his arm rest. He begins to walk weakly toward the door.*) Don't tell me you're leaving, Commodore. Is there something wrong? (THE COMMODORE *walks weakly toward the door, then runs the last part of the way. In panic he twists the doorknob. The doorknob comes off. He falls to the ground.*) Why Commodore, you're on your knees! *How romantic.* Don't tell me you're going to ask me to marry you again? Commodore, you're trembling. What's wrong? Don't tell me you're afraid that I'll accept?

THE COMMODORE (*weakly*). I . . . I-I . . . feel . . . sa-sorry for your . . . sssssson . . . that's . . . all I can . . . sssssay.

MADAME ROSEPETTLE. And I feel sorrier for you! For you are *nothing!* While my son is mine. His skin is the color of fresh snow, his voice is like the music of angels, and his mind is pure. For he is safe, Mr. Roseabove, and it is *I* who have saved him. Saved him from the world beyond that door. The world of you. The world of his father. A world waiting to devour those who trust in it; those who love. A world vicious under

the hypocrisy of kindness, ruthless under the falseness of a smile. Well, go on, Mr. Roseabove. Leave my room and enter your world again—your sex-driven, dirt-washed waste of cannibals eating each other up while they pretend they're kissing. Go, Mr. Roseabove, enter your blind world of darkness. My son shall have only light!

(*She turns with a flourish and enters her bedroom.* THE COMMODORE *stares helplessly at the door knob in his hand. Suddenly the door swings open, under its own power.* THE COMMODORE *crawls out. The door closes behind him, under its own power. From outside can be heard the sound of a church bell chiming. The bedroom door reopens and* MADAME ROSE-PETTLE *emerges wearing an immense straw hat, sun glasses, tight toreador pants and a short beach robe. She carries a huge flashlight. She is barefoot. She tiptoes across the floor and exits through the main door. The church bell chimes thirteen times.* JONATHAN *emerges from behind the* VENUS'-FLYTRAPS. *He runs to the door, puts his ear to it then races back to the balcony and stares down at the street below. Carnival lights flash weirdly against the night sky and laughter drifts up. The* VENUS'-FLYTRAPS *reach out to grab him but somehow he senses their presence and leaps away in time.*)

VENUS'-FLYTRAPS (*gruffly*). Grrrrrrrr!

(JONATHAN *backs up, staring in horror at the now huge leaves which snap at him hungrily, reaching for him. He backs, accidentally, into the table on which the fish and the dictaphone lie. He jars the table in doing so. The dictaphone makes a strange noise and begins to speak.*)

THE DICTAPHONE (MADAME ROSEPETTLE'S *voice*). ". . . And of course, could one ever forget those lovely seaside shops—"

(JONATHAN *slams the buttons on the machine. The tape stops and starts to play backwards. The* PLANTS *grow.* JONATHAN, *in horror, slams the buttons again. The tape whirls at the wrong speed. The voice shrieks wildly.* JONATHAN *stares at it in horror as the tape runs out and turns, clicking on its spool. He hits the right button and the machine stops. The* FISH *giggles.* JONATHAN *stares at it in horror. The* PLANTS *snarl.* JONATHAN *runs to the wall and smashes the glass case that* covers the fire axe. He takes out the axe. He advances cautiously toward the FLY-TRAPS. He feints and attacks; they follow his movements. He bobs, they weave. It is a cat-and-mouse game of death. Suddenly JONATHAN leaps upon them and hacks them apart till they fall to the floor, writhing, then dead. JONATHAN stands above them, victorious, panting, but somehow seeming to breathe easier. Slowly he turns and looks at the fish bowl. His eyes seem glazed, his expression insanely determined. He walks slowly toward the bowl. There are three knocks on the door to the suite. He does not hear them. He raises his axe. The door opens. ROSALIE enters, pursued by a group of gayly drunken BELLBOYS. She laughs and closes the door on them. She herself is dressed in an absurdly childish pink party dress, complete with crinolines and frills—the portrait of a girl ten years old at her first "staying-up-late party." Her shoes are black leather pumps and she wears short pink socks. Her cheeks have round circles of rouge on them—like a young girl might have who had never put on make-up before. She carries masks and party favors.)

ROSALIE. Jonathan! Jonathan! What have you done? (JONATHAN stops. He does not look at her but continues to stare at the fish bowl.) Jonathan! Put down that silly old axe. You might hurt yourself. (He still does not answer but only stares at the bowl. He does not lower the axe.) Jonathan! (Slowly he turns and faces her.)

JONATHAN. I killed it.

ROSALIE. Ssh. Not so loudly. Where'd you put her body?

JONATHAN (pointing to the plants). There.

ROSALIE. Where? I don't see a body. Where is she?

JONATHAN. Who?

ROSALIE. Your mother.

JONATHAN. I haven't killed my mother. I've killed her plants. The ones I used to feed. I've chopped their hearts out.

ROSALIE (with an apologetic laugh). I thought you'd—killed your mother. (The PIRANHA FISH giggles. JONATHAN turns and stares at it again. He starts to move towards it, slowly.) Jonathan, stop. (He hesitates, as if he were uncertain about what to do. Slowly he raises the axe.) Jonathan! (He smashes the axe against

the fish bowl. It breaks. The fish screams.)

ROSALINDA THE FISH (fearfully). AAIE-EEEEEEEEEEEEE!!!

ROSALIE. Now look at the mess you've made.

JONATHAN. Do you think it can live without water?

ROSALIE. What will your mother say when she gets back?

JONATHAN. Maybe I should hit it again. Just in case. (He strikes it again.)

ROSALINDA THE FISH (mournfully). UGHHHHHHHH!

(JONATHAN stares in horror at the dead fish. He drops the axe and turns away, sickened and weak. ROSALIE walks over and touches him gently, consolingly on the arm.)

ROSALIE. There's something bothering you, isn't there?

(Pause. JONATHAN does not answer at first, but stares off into space frightened, bewildered.)

JONATHAN (weakly). I never thought I'd see you again. I never thought I'd talk to you again. I never thought you'd come.

ROSALIE. Did you really think that?

JONATHAN. She told me she'd never let you visit me again. She said no one would ever visit me again. She told me I had seen enough.

ROSALIE. But I had a key made.

JONATHAN. She—she hates me.

ROSALIE. What?

JONATHAN. She doesn't let me do anything. She doesn't let me listen to the radio. She took the tube out of the television set. She doesn't let me use her phone. She makes me show her all my letters before I seal them. She doesn't—

ROSALIE. Letters? What letters are you talking about?

JONATHAN. Just—letters I write.

ROSALIE. To whom?

JONATHAN. To people.

ROSALIE. Other girls? Could they be to other girls by any chance?

JONATHAN. No. They're just to people. No people in particular. Just people in the phone book. Just names. So far I've covered all the "A's" and "B's" up to Barrera.

ROSALIE. What is it you say to them? Can you tell me what you say to them—or is it private? Jonathan, just what do you say to them!?

JONATHAN. Mostly I just ask them what they look like. (*Pause. Suddenly he starts to sob in a curious combination of laughter and tears.*) But I don't think she ever mails them. She reads them, then takes them out to mail. But I don't think she ever does. I'll bet she just throws them away. Well, if she's not going to mail them, why does she say she will? I—I could save the stamps.

ROSALIE. Guess why I had this key made.

JONATHAN. I'll bet she's never even mailed one. From Abandono to Barrera, not one.

ROSALIE. Do you know why I had this key made? Do you know why I'm wearing this new dress?

JONATHAN. She tells me I'm brilliant. She makes me read and re-read books no one's ever read. She smothers me with blankets at night in case of a storm. She tucks me in so tight I can't even get out till she comes and takes my blankets off.

ROSALIE. Try and guess why I'm all dressed up.

JONATHAN. She says she loves me. Every morning, before I even have a chance to open my eyes, there she is, leaning over my bed, breathing in my face and saying, "I love you, I love you."

ROSALIE. Jonathan, isn't my dress pretty?

JONATHAN. But I heard everything tonight. I heard it all when she didn't know I was here. (*He stares off into space, bewildered.*)

ROSALIE. What's the matter? (*He does not answer.*) Jonathan, what's the matter?

JONATHAN. But she must have known I was here. She *must* have known! I mean —where could I have gone? (*Pause*) But—if that's the case—*why did she let me hear?*

ROSALIE. Jonathan, I do wish you'd pay more attention to me. Here, look at my dress. You can even touch it if you like. Guess how many crinolines I have on. Guess why I'm wearing such a pretty, new dress. *Jonathan!*

JONATHAN (*distantly*). Maybe—it didn't make any difference to her—whether I heard or not. (*He turns suddenly to her and hugs her closely. She lets him hold her, then she steps back and away from him. Her face looks strangely old and determined under her girlish powder and pinkness.*)

ROSALIE. Come with me.

JONATHAN. What?

ROSALIE. Leave and come with me.

JONATHAN (*fearfully*). Where?

ROSALIE. Anywhere.

JONATHAN. Wha'—wha'—what do you mean?

ROSALIE. I mean, let's leave. Let's run away. Far away. Tonight. Both of us, together. Let's run and run. Far, far away.

JONATHAN. You—mean, leave?

ROSALIE. Yes. Leave.

JONATHAN. Just like that?

ROSALIE. Just like that.

JONATHAN. But—but—but—

ROSALIE. You want to leave, don't you?

JONATHAN. I—I don't—don't know. I—I—

ROSALIE. What about the time you told me how much you'd like to go outside, how you'd love to walk by yourself, anywhere you wanted?

JONATHAN. I—I don't—know.

ROSALIE. Yes, you do. Come. Give me your hand. Stop trembling so. Everything will be all right. Give me your hand and come with me. Just through the door. Then we're safe. Then we can run far away, somewhere where she'll never find us. Come, Jonathan. It's time to go.

JONATHAN. There are others you could take.

ROSALIE. But I don't love them. (*Pause.*)

JONATHAN. You—you *love* me?

ROSALIE. Yes, Jonathan. I love you.

JONATHAN. Wha-wha-why?

ROSALIE. Because you watch me every night.

JONATHAN. Well—can't we stay here?

ROSALIE. No!

JONATHAN. Wha-wha-whhhhy?

ROSALIE. *Because I want you alone.* (JONATHAN *turns from her and begins to walk about the room in confusion.*) I want you, Jonathan. Do you understand what I said? *I want you for my husband.*

JONATHAN. I—I—can't, I mean, I—I want to go—go with you very much but I—I don't think—I can. I'm—sorry. (*He sits down and holds his head in his hands, sobbing quietly.*)

ROSALIE. What time will your mother be back?

JONATHAN. Na—not for a while.

ROSALIE. Are you sure?

JONATHAN. Ya-yes.

ROSALIE. Where is she?

JONATHAN. The usual place.

ROSALIE. What do you mean, "the usual place"?

JONATHAN (*with a sad laugh*). The beach. (ROSALIE *looks at* JONATHAN *quizzically.*) She likes to look for people making love. Every night at midnight she walks down to the beach searching for people lying on blankets and making love. When she finds them she kicks sand in their faces and walks on. Sometimes it takes her as much as three hours to chase everyone away. (ROSALIE *smiles slightly and walks toward the master bedroom.* JONATHAN *freezes in fear. She puts her hand on the door knob.*) WHAT ARE YOU DOING!? (*She smiles at him over her shoulder. She opens the door.*) STOP!! You can't go in there!!! STOP!!

ROSALIE (*she opens the door completely and beckons him to come*). Come.

JONATHAN. Close it. Quickly!

ROSALIE. Come, Jonathan. Let's go inside.

JONATHAN. Close the door!

ROSALIE (*with a laugh*). You've never been in here, have you?

JONATHAN. No. And you can't go in, either. No one can go in there but Mother. It's her room. Now close the door!

ROSALIE (*she flicks on the light switch. No lights go on*). What's wrong with the lights?

JONATHAN. There are none. Mother's in mourning. (ROSALIE *walks into the room and pulls the drapes from off the windows. Weird colored lights stream in and illuminate the bedroom in wild, distorted, nightmarish shadows and lights. They blink on and off, on and off. It's all like some strange, macabre fun house in an insane amusement park. Even the furniture in the room seems grotesque and distorted. The closet next to the bed seems peculiarly prominent. It almost seems to tilt over the bed. Still in the main room*) What have you done!? (ROSALIE *walks back to the door and smiles to him from within the master bedroom.*) What have you done?

ROSALIE. Come in, Jonathan.

JONATHAN. GET OUT OF THERE!

ROSALIE. Will you leave with me?

JONATHAN. I can't!

ROSALIE. But you want to, don't you?

JONATHAN. Yes, yes, I want to, but I told you—I—I—I can't. I can't! Do you understand? I can't! Now come out of there.

ROSALIE. Come in and get me.

JONATHAN. Rosalie, *please*.

ROSALIE (*bouncing on the bed*). My, what a comfortable bed.

JONATHAN. GET OFF THE BED!!!

ROSALIE. What soft, fluffy pillows. I think I'll take a nap.

JONATHAN. Rosalie, *please listen to me.* Come out of there. You're not supposed to be in that room. Please come out. Rosalie, *please*.

ROSALIE. Will you leave with me if I do?

JONATHAN. Rosalie—? I'll—I'll show you my stamp collection if you'll promise to come out.

ROSALIE. Bring it in here.

JONATHAN. Will you come out then?

ROSALIE. Only if you bring it in here.

JONATHAN. But I'm not allowed to go in there.

ROSALIE (*poutingly*). Then I shan't come out!

JONATHAN. You've got to!

ROSALIE. Why?

JONATHAN. Mother will be back.

ROSALIE. She can sleep out there. (ROSALIE *yawns.*) I think I'll take a little nap. This bed is so comfortable. Really, Jonathan, you should come in and try it.

JONATHAN. MOTHER WILL BE BACK SOON!!

ROSALIE. Give her your room then if you don't want her to sleep on the couch. I find it very nice in here. Good night. (*Pause.*)

JONATHAN. If I come in, will you come out?

ROSALIE. If you don't come in I'll never come out.

JONATHAN. And if I do?

ROSALIE. Then I may.

JONATHAN. What if I bring my stamps in?

ROSALIE. Bring them and find out.

JONATHAN (*he goes to the dresser and takes out the drawer of stamps. Then he takes out the drawer of coins*). I'm bringing the coins, too.

ROSALIE. How good you are, Jonathan.

JONATHAN (*he takes a shelf full of books*). My books, too. How's that? I'll show you my books and my coins and my stamps. I'll show you them all. Then will you leave?

ROSALIE. Perhaps. (*He carries them all into the bedroom and sets them down next to the bed. He looks about fearfully.*) What's wrong?

JONATHAN. I've never been in here before.

ROSALIE. It's nothing but a room. There's nothing to be afraid of.

JONATHAN (*he looks about doubtfully.*) Well, let me show you my stamps. I have one billion, five—

ROSALIE. Later, Jonathan. We'll have time. Let me show you something first.

JONATHAN. What's that?

ROSALIE. You're trembling.

JONATHAN. What do you want to show me?

ROSALIE. There's nothing to be nervous about. Come. Sit down.

JONATHAN. What do you want to show me?

ROSALIE. I can't show you if you won't sit down.

JONATHAN. I don't want to sit down!

(*She takes hold of his hand. He pulls it away.*)

ROSALIE. Jonathan!

JONATHAN. You're sitting on Mother's bed.

ROSALIE. Then let's pretend it's my bed.

JONATHAN. It's not your bed!

ROSALIE. Come, Jonathan. Sit down here next to me.

JONATHAN. We've got to get out of here. Mother might come.

ROSALIE. Don't worry. We've got plenty of time. The beach is full of lovers.

JONATHAN. How do you know?

ROSALIE. I checked before I came.

(*Pause.*)

JONATHAN. Let—let me show you my coins.

ROSALIE. Why are you trembling so?

JONATHAN. Look, we've got to get out! Something terrible will happen if we don't.

ROSALIE. Then leave with me.

JONATHAN. The bedroom?

ROSALIE. The hotel. The island. Your mother. Leave with me, Jonathan. Leave with me now, before it's too late.

JONATHAN. I—I—I—

ROSALIE. I love you, Jonathan, and I won't give you up. I want you . . . all for myself. Not to share with your mother,

but for me, alone—to love, to live with, to have children by. I want you, Jonathan. You, whose skin is softer and whiter than anyone's I've ever known. Whose voice is quiet and whose love is in every look of his eye. I want you, Jonathan, and I won't give you up.

(*Short pause.*)

JONATHAN (*softly, weakly*). What do you want me to do?

ROSALIE. Forget about your mother. Pretend she never existed and look at me. Look at my eyes, Jonathan; my mouth, my hands, my skirt, my legs. Look at me, Jonathan. Are you still afraid?

JONATHAN. I'm not afraid. (*She smiles and starts to unbutton her dress.*) What are you doing!? No!

ROSALIE (*she continues to unbutton her dress*). Your mother is strong, but I am stronger. (*She rises and her skirt falls about her feet. She stands in a slip and crinolines.*) I don't look so pink and girlish any more, do I? (*She laughs.*) But you want me anyhow. You're ashamed but you want me anyhow. It's written on your face. And I'm very glad. Because I want you. (*She takes off a crinoline.*)

JONATHAN. PUT IT ON! *Please,* put it back on!

ROSALIE. Come, Jonathan. (*She takes off another crinoline.*) Lie down. Let me loosen your shirt.

JONATHAN. No . . . NO . . . NO! STOP! *Please,* stop!

(*She takes her last crinoline off and reaches down to take off her socks. The lights outside blink weirdly. Wild, jagged music with a drum beating in the background is heard.*)

ROSALIE. Don't be afraid, Jonathan. Come. Lie down. Everything will be wonderful. (*She takes her socks off and lies down in her slip. She drops a strap over one shoulder and smiles.*)

JONATHAN. Get off my mother's bed!

ROSALIE. I want you, Jonathan, all for my own. Come. The bed is soft. Lie here by my side. (*She reaches up and takes his hand. Meekly he sits down on the edge of the bed. The closet door swings open suddenly and the corpse of Albert Edward Robinson Rosepettle III tumbles forward stiffly and onto the bed, his stone-stiff arms falling across* ROSALIE'S *legs, his head against her side.* JONATHAN, *too terrified to scream, puts his hand across his mouth and sinks down onto the bed, almost in a state of collapse. Outside the music screams.)* Who the hell is this!

JONATHAN. It-it-it-it—it—it's—

ROSALIE. What a stupid place to keep a corpse. *(She pushes him back in the closet and shuts the door.)* Forget it, Jonathan. I put him back in the closet. Everything's fine again.

JONATHAN. It's—it's—it's my—my—my—

ROSALIE *(kneeling next to him on the bed and starting to unbutton his shirt).* It's all right, Jonathan. It's all right. Sshh. Come. Let me take off your clothes.

JONATHAN *(still staring dumbly into space).* It's—it's my—ffffather.

(The closet door swings open again and the CORPSE falls out, this time his arms falling about ROSALIE's neck. JONATHAN almost swoons.)

ROSALIE. Oh, for God's sake. *(She pushes him off the bed and onto the floor.)* Jonathan . . . ? LISTEN TO ME, JONATHAN! STOP LOOKING AT HIM AND LOOK AT ME! *(He looks away from his father, fearfully, his mouth open in terror.)* I love you, Jonathan, and I want you *now.* Not later and not as partner with your mother but now and by myself. I want you, Jonathan, as my husband. I want you to lie with me, to sleep with me, to be with me, to kiss me and touch me, to live with me, *forever.* Stop looking at him! He's dead! Listen to me. I'm alive. I want you for my husband! Now help me take my slip off. Then you can look at my body and touch me. Come, Jonathan. Lie down. I want you forever.

JONATHAN. Ma-Mother was right! You *do* let men do anything they want to you.

ROSALIE. Of course she was right! Did you really think I was that sweet and pure? Everything she said was right. *(She laughs.)* Behind the bushes and it's done. One-two-three and it's done. Here's the money. Thanks. Come again. Hah-hah! Come again! *(Short pause)* So what!? It's only you I love. They make no difference.

JONATHAN. You're dirty! *(He tries to get up but can't, for his father is lying in front of his feet.)*

ROSALIE. No, I'm not dirty. I'm full of love and womanly feelings. I want chil-dren. Tons of them. I want a husband. Is that dirty? Take off your clothes.

JONATHAN. NO!!

ROSALIE. Forget about your father. Drop your pants on top of him, then you won't see his face. Forget about your mother. She's gone. Forget them both and look at me. Love is so beautiful, Jonathan. Come and let me love you; tonight and forever. Come and let me keep you mine. Mine to love when I want, mine to kiss when I want, mine to have when I want. Mine. All mine. So come, Jonathan. Come and close your eyes. It's better that way. Close your eyes so you can't see. Close your eyes and let me lie with you. Let me show you how beautiful it is . . . love.

(She lies back in bed and slowly starts to raise her slip. JONATHAN stares at her legs in horror. Then, suddenly, he seizes her crumpled skirt and throws it over her face, and smothers her to death. At last he rises and, picking up his box of stamps, dumps the stamps over her limp body. He does the same with his coins and finally, his books, until at last she is buried. Then, done, he throws his hands over his eyes and and turns to run. But as he staggers past the corpse of his father, his father's lifeless arms somehow come to life for an instant and, reaching out, grab JONATHAN by the feet. JONATHAN falls to the floor. For a moment he lies there, stretched across his father's body, too terrified to move. But a soft, ethereal-green light begins to suffuse the room and heavenly harp music is heard in the air. As if his body had suddenly become immortal and weightless JONATHAN rises up from the floor and with long, slow, dream-like steps [like someone walking under water], he floats through the bedroom door and drifts across the living room, picking up his telescope on the way. He floats out to the balcony and begins to scan the sky. The harp music grows louder and more paradisiacal: Debussy in Heaven. While under the harp music, soft, muffled laughter can be heard; within the bedroom, within the living room, from the rear of the theatre, laughter all about. His MOTHER tiptoes into the living room. Her hair is awry, her hat is on crooked, her blouse hangs wrinkled and out of her pants. Her legs are covered with sand.)

MADAME ROSEPETTLE. Twenty-three couples. I annoyed twenty-three couples, all of them coupled in various positions, all equally distasteful. It's a record, that's what it is. It's a record! (*Breathing heavily from excitement she begins to tuck in her blouse and straighten her hair. She notices the chaotic state of the room. She shrieks slightly.*) What has happened!? (*She notices the plants.*) My plants! (*She notices the fish.*) Rosalinda! Great gods, my fish has lost her water! ALBERT! ALBERT! (*She searches about the room for her son. She sees him standing on the porch.*) Ah, there you are, Edward; what has been going on during my brief absence? What are you doing out here when Roslinda is lying in there dead? DEAD!? Oh, God, dead. (*She gives her fish artificial respiration, but alas, it does not work.*) Robinson, answer me. What are you looking for? I've told you there's nothing out there. This place is a mad-house. That's what it is. A madhouse. (*She turns and walks into her bedroom. An airplane is heard flying in the distance.* JONATHAN *scans the horizon frantically. The plane grows nearer.* JONATHAN *follows it with his telescope. It flies overhead. It begins to circle about. Wildly, desperately,* JONATHAN *waves his arms to the plane. It flies away.* MADAME ROSE-PETTLE *re-enters the room.*) ROBINSON! I went to lie down and I stepped on your father! I lay down and I lay on some girl. Robinson, there is a woman on my bed and I do believe she's stopped breathing. What is more, you've buried her under your fabulous collection of stamps, coins and books. I ask you, Robinson. As a mother to a son I ask you. *What is the meaning of this?*

BLACKOUT

CURTAIN

WHO'S AFRAID OF VIRGINIA WOOLF?

Edward Albee

First presented by Richard Barr and Clinton Wilder for Theatre 1963
at the Billy Rose Theatre, New York, on October 13, 1962,
with the following cast:

MARTHA Uta Hagen   NICK   George Grizzard
GEORGE Arthur Hill   HONEY Melinda Dillon

Original matinee cast:

MARTHA Kate Reid   NICK   Bill Berger
GEORGE Sheppard Strudwick HONEY Avra Tetrides

NOTE: Nancy Kelly substituted for Uta Hagen during the summer of
1963; and later played the role of Martha in the national touring company.

Directed by Alan Schneider
Designed by William Ritmar

Copyright © 1962 by Edward Albee.
All rights reserved.

Reprinted by permission of Atheneum Publishers.

CAUTION: Professionals and amateurs are hereby warned that WHO'S AFRAID OF
VIRGINIA WOOLF?, being fully protected under the Copyright Laws of the
United States of America, the British Empire, including the Dominion of Canada,
and all other countries of the Berne and Universal Copyright Conventions, is subject
to royalty. All rights, including professional, amateur, motion picture, recitation, lecturing,
public reading, radio and television broadcasting, and the rights of translation into
foreign languages, are strictly reserved. Particular emphasis is laid on the question of
readings, permission for which must be secured from the author's agent in writing.
All inquiries should be addressed to the William Morris Agency, 1740 Broadway,
New York, N.Y.

THE DETAILS of Edward Franklin Albee's life, his being the adopted child of a well-to-do family well known in show business, his having been sent to the Hotchkiss private school, his having had a difficult childhood and kept himself going with odd jobs as a short-order cook, copy boy, and clerk, his having perhaps more than his share of problems attendant upon youth—all this I pass by, resolved to provide no grist to the amateur analysts who infest the world of theatre. (Though I like Jerry Tallmer's saying in the New York *Post* that "Albee writes from his own interior in metaphor.") So far as the present editor is concerned, our present business is only to know that Edward Albee was born on March 12, 1928, that he spent much of his early youth writing poetry and fiction, and then turned to writing plays.

His first produced play, written in his thirtieth year, was the remarkable long one-act piece, *The Zoo Story,* the theme of which is loneliness carried to the point of desperation. The subject was brilliantly evoked if perhaps melodramatically resolved in a nevertheless distinctly original climactic scene. Due to the circuitous circulation of the manuscript among friends in Europe, *The Zoo Story* was first produced in Berlin on September 28, 1959. The American premiere came several months later, on January 14, 1960, when the play was produced at the Provincetown Playhouse in Greenwich Village on a twin bill with Samuel Beckett's *Krapp's Last Tape,* by Richard Barr, a former member of John Houseman and Orson Welles' famous Mercury Theatre of the late 1930's. Barr and his Broadway-seasoned partner, Clinton Wilder, subsequently presented Mr. Albee's *surréaliste* one-act satire on conformity, *The American Dream,* in 1960. To this Ionesco-like play (clever and, I believe, also moving), they ultimately added another Albee one-acter, *The Death of Bessie Smith,* which had also had its world premiere in Berlin (in 1959), a too loosely organized yet uncommonly piercing piece. The two playlets made up a well-attended off-Broadway attraction and won for their author a citation and cash prize in June, 1961, the Lola D'Annunzio Award, from a jury of critics. Another one-acter, the fourteen-minute miniature drama, *The Sandbox,* written for the Spoleto "Festival of Two Worlds" (but not produced at Spoleto), proved to be completely entrancing yet meaningful when presented on the stage and on a television program in 1960.

Harold Clurman, in covering *The Zoo Story* for *The Nation,* wrote that "Albee's play is the introduction to what could prove to be an important talent of the American stage." When *Who's Afraid of Virginia Woolf?* opened October 13, 1962, under the Richard Barr and Clinton Wilder ("Theatre 1963") management, Mr. Clurman proved to be a good prophet, as did the Lola D'Annunzio jury that had singled out Albee as the most promising newcomer to the American stage. The success of the lengthy and taxing new play (so taxing, in fact, that a different cast was assembled for the matinee performances) was an unmistakable triumph for the author, especially since this trenchant three-and-a-half hour drama had to overcome public uneasiness caused by its uncongenial subject matter and the vigor and occasionally disconcerting language with which it was treated. In view of the excellence of the Broadway production staged by Alan Schneider with Uta Hagen and Arthur Hill in the evening performances, Mr. Albee could share his honors with them. But there were enough of these to spare. They came with impressive frequency toward the end of the 1962-63 season. Virtually the only available award the play did not receive was the Pulitzer Prize recommended by the Pulitzer Prize jury of John Mason Brown and John Gassner, who promptly resigned when their recommendation was rejected by the Pulitzer Prize Advisory Board.

Because the play also encountered some determined resistance, and since both its structure and texture appear to have been insufficiently appreciated even by admirers, I reproduce passages from my long review of an excellent Columbia recording in 1963 which appeared in the June 29 issue of *The Saturday Review.*

"Entire episodes exist as verbal structures in Albee's play and the phrases mesh with each other not so much as logically connected statements but as spontaneous utterances carrying pertinent moods, attitudes, or intentions. Albee's short phrases and sentences make up a series of musico-dramatic movements perhaps even more distinctly related than they could be in a visual production because the text comes at us naked, so to speak—that is, as pure sound.

"In Act III, for example, there are several of these movements. The first is Martha's desperation, expressed in a drunken soliloquy (it has its own unique broken rhythm); the second is her disillusionment with men, starting with a teasing colloquy with her would-be but ultimately inadequate lover Nick and culminating in a monologue the keynote of which is 'I am the Earth Mother, and you're all flops. . . . I pass my life in crummy, totally pointless infidelities . . . *would*-be infidelities.' A new rhythm is established in a second, rather analytical, conversation with Nick concerning her attitude toward her husband George, 'who has made the hideous, the hurting, the insulting mistake of loving me and must be punished for it.' It is followed by the teasing rhythms of reducing Nick to the lowly status of a 'houseboy' in compelling him to answer the doorbell, and of herself being teased and insulted by the mounting aggressiveness of her nearly cuckolded husband George. Then the beat quickens, the pulse grows uneven, and the voices strain toward a climax of violence as Martha strives to preserve her illusion of motherhood while George endeavors to strip her of it, the struggle culminating in the strong counterpoint of Martha's dramatizing the illusioned son while her husband recites the Latin prayers for the dead—that is, for the son who had never existed except in their imagination and whom he now proposes to 'kill.' Finally, there is the denouement or 'falling action' starting with the ominous quietness of George's 'I am afraid our boy isn't coming home for his birthday' and concluding with the fragmented sentences with which Martha reluctantly relinquishes her hitherto fiercely defended illusion. After that episode, when the two guests, Nick and his wife, depart, the lines assigned to the emotionally drained Martha and George rarely exceed two-word speeches of 'I'm cold' and 'It's late,' and the play closes with Martha's dully spoken monosyllabic response to the 'Who's Afraid of Virginia Woolf?' ditty sung by her husband 'I . . . am . . . George . . . I . . . am. . . .'

"It is not particularly space-consuming to point out that, in spite of its great length and almost musical fluidity, *Who's Afraid of Virginia Woolf?* is a notably concentrated and carefully constructed drama.

"An irritable middle-aged couple, notably articulate but also inebriated, comes home from a party, and before long the husband and wife, George and Martha, are slashing away at each other, mercilessly exposing themselves and two guests, a younger and seemingly happier but actually just as miserable couple. The battle attains sensational intensity because the principals are not only sufficiently aroused but, as Albee declares in the Columbia Records brochure, 'intelligent and sensitive enough to build proper weapons for their war with each other.' The struggle fluctuates, with dubious victory falling first to one side, then to the other, until the antagonists are sufficiently self-revealed and purged to arrive at a tentative reconciliation. Hosts and their guests in conventional American society (which Albee satirized previously in *The American Dream*) go in for 'fun and games,' and it is under the pretense of 'fun and games' that the action proceeds. One movement is a 'Get the Host' game in which Martha is the aggressor against George in the presence of the visitors. A second movement, a 'get the guests' game, is directed against the visitors by the humiliated George, who resents the smugness of his guest and university colleague, the biologist Nick, on personal and general grounds. Nick, infuriated by revelations of his own unsatisfactory domestic life, and Martha, who is also out for vengeance, collaborate on the third game, in which Nick supposedly makes a cuckold of George—that is, 'gets' the hostess, Martha. In the final movement, George counterattacks with a climactic 'bringing up baby' game that 'brings up' the crucial fact that Martha and he have never had a son and could not have a child. After all the devastating 'fun' they have been having and the 'games' the history professor George and his wife have been playing from midnight to dawn they are brought to the point of renouncing the game they have been playing privately for some twenty-three years. The time for illusions is over, at last, and the husband and wife will have to make the best of whatever reality there is for them, facing life together, even if the thought of 'Just . . . us?' fills Martha with misgivings.

"An exegesis on this conclusion, and indeed on the entire play, is a distinct possibility. It is perhaps even a necessity for those who sense that a larger gambit than Martha's

365

and George's 'games' is being played and would like to have it spelled out for them once the 'fun' (and there is plenty of comedy in the text) becomes grim. Symbol or image hunters can have a field day with the play." *

Also, since I believe readers and playgoers able to leave their barbed-wire defenses of right- or left-wing moralism for a while will profit from an analysis written by a professed "layman" for his own and his friends' pleasure, I am pleased to be able to reprint an article written by Dr. Harold Lamport of Westport, who—I hasten to add— is not a practicing psychoanalyst or psychologist but research associate in *physiology* at the Yale University Medical Center in New Haven. I am grateful to Dr. Lamport for permission to reprint his fine essay virtually intact, and I expect that the reader will be too—as he will also be by a statement by Albee especially relevant to the resolution of the play. He is reported to have said to Jerry Tallmer, interviewing him in the *Post* (Nov. 4, 1962), *"We must try to claw our way into compassion."* This is a true insight into a play which was originally called *Exorcism* and culminates in an act bearing the same title.

WHO'S AFRAID OF VIRGINIA WOOLF?

by Harold Lamport

(December 22, 1962)

"It is easy to accept Albee's play as a drama of marital conflict, concerned primarily with deep character development, the portrayal by a misogynist of Strindberg stripe of the mutual destructiveness of a couple ill-suited to marriage. Some critics have regarded the homosexual components of the history professor husband as the primary element in the raging battle between the sexes shown by Albee on the stage and regard Albee's goal in this play that of the naturalist, the description of this battle and its protagonists. Such purpose seems to me better exemplified in *The Shrike,* a play seen on Broadway several years earlier, in which a mordantly destructive woman works the ruin of her husband and his permanent incarceration within a mental institution.

"That Albee meant more by his play is revealed in its title. From the advance publicity we learned that other titles were considered before production because of possible legal objections to the use of the name of an author who died recently. Albee is said to have insisted on retaining the title if at all possible because of its importance to the play and Leonard Woolf, his wife's executor, gave permission.

" 'Who's afraid of Virginia Woolf?' are the words of a humorous song danced and sung by faculty wives at a faculty party. Several times the two faculty wives of the two couples joke about this song-and-dance and sing snatches of it, regarding it as extremely hilarious, more so than the men. Later, it becomes the battle song of the historian whenever he is moved to defy his destructive wife. One is constrained to regard these words with deep curiosity; they must contain in condensed form much of what Albee's play is about, perhaps telling even more than Albee himself is aware. Of course, in seeking the profounder meaning of such a nonsense phrase (a little reminiscent of the single-sentence irrational problems of Zen Buddhism), one examines one's own associations in the hope that they will duplicate, after subtraction of the purely personal, what Albee meant and—if he succeeded as a playwright—what he communicated to his audience even if inchoate in their minds.

"Superficially, 'Who's afraid of Virginia Woolf?' suggests to me: Who's afraid of the intellectual woman, since Virginia Woolf in the English-speaking literary world represents such a woman, able to lead as a critic and a writer among the most cerebral of men. As sung by the faculty wives, the refrain seems dual and ambivalent: we faculty wives—witness our light-hearted song-and-dance—are really not so intellectual as Virginia Woolf and we are a little jealous and afraid of the intellectual type whom our husbands may prefer; and, less clearly, speaking for our men, though intellectuals (mostly), they are often insecure as males in the presence of the intellectually out-

* Reprinted from *The Saturday Review* (June 29, 1963) by permission of the editors.

standing woman and *they* are afraid of the Virginia Woolf in us, since we are not as unintellectual as our song-and-dance may make us seem—we could compete effectively with them if we permitted ourselves to. My guess is that the first statement is what the audience hears, particularly the women, and the second is what the men hear, particularly the two professors in the play, who didn't think the skit funny.

"Virginia Woolf might be replaced by other famous women of intellectual stamp (but offhand a good substitute is hard to find), yet Albee was insistent. The reason, I think, is that the phrase is a parody of the nursery song from the fable of the piglets: 'Who's afraid of the big bad wolf?' As we know, the piglets were very *much* afraid of the wolf—and with good reason: Their song certainly was a whistling-in-the-dark to keep up their courage. Certainly the success of the wolf in the fable is known to us all. The allusive pun on Virginia Woolf's name adds zest to the words of the song-and-dance routine and to the title of Albee's play.

"Various means of expressing hostility, aside from the most overt—the historian's abortive attempt to choke his wife—are employed in the play. But the method that draws blood, that shatters each character, one by one, is the statement of an unpleasant, hidden truth either to the concerned individual alone or before others where its impact is to castigate that individual without mercy.

"The crowning betrayal, the last salvo that so utterly unhinges his sadistic wife, is the historian's disclosure to his guests that their son is imaginary, a delusion he had permitted his wife and shared with her only so long as their agreed *folie-à-deux* rule of keeping it secret was honored. Strangely, after all the in-fighting in which she was the aggressor, disregarding his repeated warnings of retribution, she pleads to be allowed to keep this delusion, but he has been too sorely tried and for him resolution of their violent encounter requires this final victory after so many prior defeats.

"The young biologist's wife has been finally exposed, not as the sweet young thing she first seemed, but as an alcoholic, the wealthy heiress of a peculating preacher, an hysteric who vomits with little provocation and whose false pregnancy before marriage at first was offered by her husband to the historian as the pretext for his spuriously magnanimous marriage. However, the young biologist is shown to be a go-getter who wanted the help of a rich wife in getting to the top, one who accepts the role of a gigolo (gratuitously revealed to his wife) and toady to gain advancement.

"The historian's academic failure has been related before all to a character defect obviously derived from his great guilt over his fantasies of killing his parents (to what extent there is a basis in fact is not clear). And the historian's wife, the daughter of the president of the college, she more than any lays herself bare and is bared as she attacks all. Her inordinate love of her father is said to be unreciprocated, her desire to marry a man who vicariously would fulfill her desire to inherit her father's power and position are found to have been frustrated by the wrong choice of mate. It is she who burns with unhappiness, who has leaned on the invention of a son to provide her a way to satisfy some of her drive towards the role of masculinity.

"The penchant of the intellectual for introspection and for learning the truths about others' inner thoughts is a dangerous sport, terribly destructive when the truths so discovered are wantonly revealed. In *Who's Afraid of Virginia Woolf?* the devastating impact of publicly exposing the truth, whether already known or not to those most intimately concerned, is made frightfully clear. Is not the cruel exposure of the secret truth (or falsehood) on which our self-respect rests the villain of the play? Is he not the wolf we foolishly or sadistically release without adequate realization of the consequences? . . .

"The relationship between the history professor and his wife is fascinating. Slowly, it becomes apparent that along with their headlong hate there is also love. Why else are they still together? They understand and appreciate one another even though each is a tortured person. They play the same games, they say—and it is true. The professor rejects the wet smacky kiss tendered by his wife because it would excite him too much sexually when the biologist and wife are momentarily expected. Later, sourly regarding the fiasco of her seduction of the not-so-potent biologist, she compliments her husband on his greater virility. There is a healthy carnal element in their marriage. And when almost mortally wounded by her husband's killing off the fantasy of the son, she still turns to him for compassion and support. He provides them. Their relationship is an incredible inferno of sado-masochism: their most violent attacks are not without a loving component and each provides the other with the opportunity for expressing these ambivalent feelings. With brief insight, she says it well:

" 'George who is good to me, and whom I revile; who understands me, and whom I push off; who can make me laugh, and I choke it back in my throat; who can hold me, at night, so that it's warm, and whom I will bite so there's blood; who keeps learning the games we play as quickly as I can change the rules; who can make me happy and I do not wish to be happy . . . who has made the hideous, the hurting, the insulting mistake of loving me and must be punished for it . . . who tolerates, which is intolerable; who is kind, which is cruel; who understands, which is beyond comprehension. . . .' "

THE SCENE. The living room of a house on the campus of a small New England college.

ACT ONE:

FUN AND GAMES

Set in darkness. Crash against front door. MARTHA's *laughter heard. Front door opens, lights are switched on.* MARTHA *enters, followed by* GEORGE.

———

MARTHA. *Jesus.* . . .

GEORGE. . . . Shhhhhhh. . . .

MARTHA. . . . H. Christ. . . .

GEORGE. For God's sake, Martha, it's two o'clock in the. . . .

MARTHA. Oh, George!

GEORGE. Well, I'm *sorry*, but. . . .

MARTHA. What a cluck! What a cluck you are.

GEORGE. It's late, you know? Late.

MARTHA (*looks about the room. Imitates Bette Davis*). What a dump. Hey, what's that from? "What a dump!"

GEORGE. How would I know what. . . .

MARTHA. Aw, come on! What's it from? *You* know. . . .

GEORGE . . . Martha. . . .

MARTHA. WHAT'S IT FROM, FOR CHRIST'S SAKE?

GEORGE (*wearily*). What's what from?

MARTHA. I just told you; I just did it. "What a dump!" Hunh? What's that from?

GEORGE. I haven't the faintest idea what. . . .

MARTHA. Dumbbell! It's from some goddamn Bette Davis picture . . . some goddamn Warner Brothers epic. . . .

GEORGE. *I* can't remember all the pictures that. . . .

MARTHA. Nobody's asking you to remember every single goddamn Warner Brothers epic . . . just one! One single little epic! Bette Davis gets peritonitis in the end . . . she's got this big black fright wig she wears all through the picture and she gets peritonitis, and she's married to Joseph Cotten or something. . . .

GEORGE . . . Some*body*. . . .

MARTHA . . . some*body* . . . and she wants to go to Chicago all the time, 'cause she's in love with that actor with the scar. . . . But she gets sick, and she sits down in front of her dressing table. . . .

GEORGE. What actor? What scar?

MARTHA. *I* can't remember his name, for God's sake. What's the name of the *picture?* I want to know what the name of the *picture* is. She sits down in front of her dressing table . . . and she's got this peritonitis . . . and she tries to put her lipstick on, but she can't . . . and she gets it all over her face . . . but she decides to go to Chicago anyway, and. . . .

GEORGE. *Chicago!* It's called *Chicago.*

MARTHA. Hunh? What . . . what is?

GEORGE. The picture . . . it's called *Chicago.* . . .

MARTHA. Good grief! Don't you know *anything?* Chicago was a 'thirties musical, starring little Miss Alice *Faye*. Don't you know *anything?*

GEORGE. Well, that was probably before my *time*, but. . . .

MARTHA. Can it! Just cut that out! This picture . . . Bette Davis comes home from a hard day at the grocery store. . . .

GEORGE. She works in a grocery store?

MARTHA. She's a housewife; she buys things . . . and she comes home with the groceries, and she walks into the modest living room of the modest cottage modest Joseph Cotten has set her up in. . . .

GEORGE. Are they married?

MARTHA (*impatiently*). Yes. They're married. To each other. Cluck! And she comes in, and she looks around, and she puts her groceries down, and she says, "What a dump!"

GEORGE (*pause*). Oh.

MARTHA (*pause*). She's discontent.

GEORGE (*pause*). Oh.

MARTHA (*pause*). Well, what's the name of the picture?

GEORGE. I really don't know, Martha. . . .

MARTHA. Well, think!

GEORGE. I'm tired, dear . . . it's late . . . and besides. . . .

MARTHA. I don't know what you're so tired about . . . you haven't *done* anything all day; you didn't have any classes, or anything. . . .

GEORGE. Well, I'm tired. . . . If your father didn't set up these goddamn Saturday night orgies all the time. . . .

MARTHA. Well, that's too bad about you, George. . . .

GEORGE (*grumbling*). Well, that's how it is, anyway.

MARTHA. You didn't *do* anything; you never *do* anything; you never *mix*. You just sit around and *talk*.

GEORGE. What do you want me to do? Do you want me to act like you? Do you want me to go around all night *braying* at everybody, the way you do?

MARTHA (*braying*). I DON'T BRAY!

GEORGE (*softly*). All right . . . you don't bray.

MARTHA (*hurt*). I do not *bray*.

GEORGE. All right. I said you didn't bray.

MARTHA (*pouting*). Make me a drink.

GEORGE. What?

MARTHA (*still softly*). I said, make me a drink.

GEORGE (*moving to the portable bar*). Well, I don't suppose a nightcap'd kill either one of us. . . .

MARTHA. A nightcap! Are you kidding? We've got guests.

GEORGE (*disbelieving*). We've got what?

MARTHA. Guests. GUESTS.

GEORGE. GUESTS!

MARTHA. Yes . . . guests . . . people. . . . We've got guests coming over.

GEORGE. When?

MARTHA. NOW!

GEORGE. Good Lord, Martha . . . do you know what time it. . . . *Who's* coming over?

MARTHA. What's-their-name.

GEORGE. Who?

MARTHA. WHAT'S-THEIR-NAME!

GEORGE. Who what's-their-name?

MARTHA. I don't know what their name is, George. . . . You met them tonight . . . they're new . . . he's in the math department, or something. . . .

GEORGE. Who . . . who are these people?

MARTHA. You met them tonight, George.

GEORGE. I don't remember meeting anyone tonight. . . .

MARTHA. Well you did . . . Will you give me my drink, please. . . . He's in the math department . . . about thirty, blond, and. . . .

GEORGE . . . and good-looking. . . .

MARTHA. Yes . . . and good-looking. . . .

GEORGE. It figures.

MARTHA . . . and his wife's a mousey little type, without any hips, or anything.

GEORGE (*vaguely*). Oh.

MARTHA. You remember them now?

GEORGE. Yes, I guess so, Martha. . . . But why in God's name are they coming over here now?

MARTHA (*in a so-there voice*). Because Daddy said we should be nice to them, that's why.

GEORGE (*defeated*). Oh, Lord.

MARTHA. May I have my drink, please? Daddy said we should be nice to them. Thank you.

GEORGE. But why now? It's after two o'clock in the morning, and. . . .

MARTHA. Because Daddy said we should be nice to them!

GEORGE. Yes. But I'm sure your father didn't mean we were supposed to stay up all *night* with these people. I mean, we could have them over some Sunday or something. . . .

MARTHA. Well, never mind. . . . Besides, it *is* Sunday. Very early Sunday.

GEORGE. I mean . . . it's ridiculous. . . .

MARTHA. Well, it's *done*!

GEORGE (*resigned and exasperated*). All right. Well . . . where are they? If we've got guests, where are they?

MARTHA. They'll be here soon.

GEORGE. What did they do . . . go home and get some sleep first, or something?

MARTHA. They'll *be* here!

GEORGE. I wish you'd *tell* me about something sometime. . . . I wish you'd stop *springing* things on me all the time.

MARTHA. I don't *spring* things on you all the time.

GEORGE. Yes, you do . . . you really do . . . you're always *springing* things on me.

MARTHA (*friendly-patronizing*). Oh, George!

GEORGE. Always.

MARTHA. Poor Georgie-Porgie, put-upon pie! (*As he sulks*) Awwwwww . . . what are you doing? Are you sulking? Hunh? Let me see . . . are you sulking? Is that what you're doing?

GEORGE (*very quietly*). Never mind, Martha. . . .

MARTHA. AWWWWWWWWWW!

GEORGE. Just don't bother yourself. . . .

MARTHA. AWWWWWWWWWW! (*No reaction.*) Hey! (*No reaction.*) HEY! (GEORGE *looks at her, put-upon.*) Hey. (*She sings.*)
Who's afraid of Virginia Woolf,
　　　　　Virginia Woolf,
　　　　　Virginia Woolf. . . .

Ha, ha, ha, HA! (*No reaction.*) What's the matter . . . didn't you think that was funny? Hunh? (*Defiantly*) I thought it was a scream . . . a real scream. You didn't like it, hunh?

GEORGE. It was all right, Martha. . . .

MARTHA. You laughed your head off when you heard it at the party.

GEORGE. I smiled. I didn't laugh my head off . . . I smiled, you know? . . . it was all right.

MARTHA (*gazing into her drink*). You laughed your goddamn head off.

GEORGE. It was all right. . . .

MARTHA (*ugly*). It was a scream!

GEORGE (*patiently*). It was very funny; yes.

MARTHA (*after a moment's consideration*). You make me puke!

GEORGE. What?

MARTHA. Uh . . . you make me puke!

GEORGE (*thinks about it . . . then . . .*) That wasn't a very nice thing to say, Martha.

MARTHA. That wasn't *what*?

GEORGE . . . a very nice thing to say.

MARTHA. I like your anger. I think that's what I like about you most . . . your anger. You're such a . . . such a simp! You don't even have the . . . the what? . . .

GEORGE. . . . guts? . . .

MARTHA. PHRASEMAKER! (*Pause . . . then they both laugh.*) Hey, put some more ice in my drink, will you? You never put any ice in my drink. Why is that, hunh?

GEORGE (*takes her drink*). I always put ice in your drink. You eat it, that's all. It's that habit you have . . . chewing your ice cubes . . . like a cocker spaniel. You'll crack your big teeth.

MARTHA. THEY'RE MY BIG TEETH!

GEORGE. Some of them . . . some of them.

MARTHA. I've got more teeth than you've got.

GEORGE. Two more.

MARTHA. Well, two more's a lot more.

GEORGE. I suppose it is. I suppose it's pretty remarkable . . . considering how old you are.

MARTHA. YOU CUT THAT OUT! (*Pause.*) You're not so young yourself.

GEORGE (*with boyish pleasure . . . a chant*). I'm six years younger than you are. . . . I always have been and I always

will be.

MARTHA (*glumly*). Well . . . you're going bald.

GEORGE. So are you. (*Pause . . . they both laugh.*) Hello, honey.

MARTHA. Hello. C'mon over here and give your Mommy a big sloppy kiss.

GEORGE. . . . oh, now. . . .

MARTHA. I WANT A BIG SLOPPY KISS!

GEORGE (*preoccupied*). I don't *want* to kiss you, Martha. Where *are* these people? Where are these *people* you invited over?

MARTHA. They stayed on to talk to Daddy. . . . They'll be here. . . . *Why* don't you want to kiss me?

GEORGE (*too matter-of-fact*). Well, dear, if I kissed you I'd get all excited . . . I'd get beside myself, and I'd take you, by force, right here on the living room rug, and then our little guests would walk in, and . . . well, just think what your father would say about *that*.

MARTHA. You pig!

GEORGE (*haughtily*). Oink! Oink!

MARTHA. Ha, ha, ha, HA! Make me another drink . . . lover.

GEORGE (*taking her glass*). My God, you can swill it down, can't you?

MARTHA (*imitating a tiny child*). I'm firsty.

GEORGE. Jesus!

MARTHA (*swinging around*). Look, sweetheart, I can drink you under any goddamn table you want . . . so don't worry about me!

GEORGE. Martha, I gave you the prize years ago. . . . There isn't an abomination award going that you. . . .

MARTHA. I swear . . . if you existed I'd divorce you. . . .

GEORGE. Well, just stay on your feet, that's all. . . . These people are your guests, you know, and. . . .

MARTHA. I can't even see you . . . I haven't been able to see you for years. . . .

GEORGE. . . . if you pass out, or throw up, or something. . . .

MARTHA. . . . I mean, you're a blank, a cipher. . . .

GEORGE. . . . and try to keep your clothes on, too. There aren't many more sickening sights than you with a couple of drinks in you and your skirt up over your head, you know. . . .

MARTHA. . . . a zero. . . .

GEORGE. . . . your *head*s, I should

say. . . .

(*The front doorbell chimes.*)

MARTHA. Party! Party!

GEORGE (*murderously*). I'm really looking forward to this, Martha. . . .

MARTHA (*same*). Go answer the door.

GEORGE (*not moving*). You answer it.

MARTHA. Get to that door, you. (*He does not move.*) I'll fix you, you. . . .

GEORGE (*fake-spits*). . . . to you. . . .

(*Door chime again.*)

MARTHA (*shouting . . . to the door*). C'MON IN! (*To* GEORGE, *between her teeth*) I said, get over there!

GEORGE (*moves a little toward the door, smiling slightly*). All right, love . . . whatever love wants. (*Stops.*) Just don't start on the bit, that's all.

MARTHA. The bit? The bit? What kind of language is that? What are you talking about?

GEORGE. The bit. Just don't start in on the bit.

MARTHA. You imitating one of your students, for God's sake? What are you trying to do? WHAT BIT?

GEORGE. Just don't start in on the bit about the kid, that's all.

MARTHA. What do you take me for?

GEORGE. Much too much.

MARTHA (*really angered*). Yeah? Well, I'll start in on the kid if I want to.

GEORGE. Just leave the kid out of this.

MARTHA (*threatening*). He's mine as much as he is yours. I'll talk about him if I want to.

GEORGE. I'd advise against it, Martha.

MARTHA. Well, good for you. (*Knock.*) C'mon in. Get over there and open the door!

GEORGE. You've been advised.

MARTHA. Yeah . . . sure. Get over there!

GEORGE (*moving toward the door*). All right, love . . . whatever love wants. Isn't it nice the way some people have manners, though, even in this day and age? Isn't it nice that some people won't just come breaking into other people's houses even if they *do* hear some sub-human monster yowling at 'em from inside . . . ?

MARTHA. SCREW YOU!

(*Simultaneously with* MARTHA's *last remark,* GEORGE *flings open the front door.* HONEY *and* NICK *are framed in the entrance. There is a brief silence, then. . . .*)

GEORGE (*ostensibly a pleased recognition of* HONEY *and* NICK, *but really satisfaction at having* MARTHA's *explosion overheard*). Ahhhhhhhhh!

MARTHA (*a little too loud . . . to cover*). HI! Hi, there . . . c'mon in!

HONEY *and* NICK (*ad lib*). Hello, here we are . . . hi . . . etc.

GEORGE (*very matter-of-factly*). You must be our little guests.

MARTHA. Ha, ha, ha, HA! Just ignore old sour-puss over there. C'mon in, kids . . . give your coats and stuff to sour-puss.

NICK (*without expression*). Well, now, perhaps we shouldn't have come. . . .

HONEY. Yes . . . it *is* late, and. . . .

MARTHA. Late! Are you kidding? Throw your stuff down anywhere and c'mon in.

GEORGE (*vaguely . . . walking away*). Anywhere . . . furniture, floor . . . doesn't make any difference around this place.

NICK (*to* HONEY). I told you we shouldn't have come.

MARTHA (*stentorian*). I said c'mon in! Now c'mon!

HONEY (*giggling a little as she and* NICK *advance*). Oh, dear.

GEORGE (*imitating* HONEY's *giggle*). Hee, hee, hee, hee.

MARTHA (*swinging on* GEORGE). Look, muckmouth . . . you cut that out!

GEORGE (*innocence and hurt*). Martha! (*To* HONEY *and* NICK) Martha's a devil with language; she really is.

MARTHA. Hey, *kids* . . . sit down.

HONEY (*as she sits*). Oh, isn't this lovely!

NICK (*perfunctorily*). Yes indeed . . . very handsome.

MARTHA. Well, thanks.

NICK (*indicating the abstract painting*). Who . . . who did the . . . ?

MARTHA. That? Oh, that's by. . . .

GEORGE. . . . some Greek with a mustache Martha attacked one night in. . . .

HONEY (*to save the situation*). Oh, ho, ho, ho, HO.

NICK. It's got a . . . a. . . .

GEORGE. A quiet intensity?

NICK. Well, no . . . a. . . .

GEORGE. Oh. (*Pause*) Well, then a certain noisy relaxed quality, maybe?

NICK (*knows what* GEORGE *is doing, but stays grimly, coolly polite*). No. What I meant was. . . .

GEORGE. How about . . . uh . . . a quietly noisy relaxed intensity.

HONEY. Dear! You're being joshed.

NICK (*cold*). I'm aware of that.

(*A brief, awkward silence.*)

GEORGE (*truly*). I *am* sorry.

(NICK *nods condescending forgiveness.*)

GEORGE. What it is, actually, is it's a pictorial representation of the order of Martha's mind.

MARTHA. Ha, ha, ha, HA! Make the kids a drink, George. What do you want, kids? What do you want to drink, hunh?

NICK. Honey? What would you like?

HONEY. I don't know, dear . . . A little brandy, maybe. "Never mix—never worry." (*She giggles.*)

GEORGE. Brandy? Just brandy? Simple; simple. (*Moves to the portable bar.*) What about you . . . uh. . . .

NICK. Bourbon on the rocks, if you don't mind.

GEORGE (*as he makes drinks*). Mind? No, I don't mind. I don't think I mind. Martha? Rubbing alcohol for you?

MARTHA. Sure. "Never mix—never worry."

GEORGE. Martha's tastes in liquor have come down . . . simplified over the years . . . crystallized. Back when I was courting Martha—well, don't know if that's exactly the right word for it—but back when I was courting Martha. . . .

MARTHA (*cheerfully*). Screw, sweetie!

GEORGE (*returning with* HONEY *and* NICK's *drinks*). At any rate, back when I was courting Martha, she'd order the damnedest things! You wouldn't believe it! We'd go into a bar . . . you know, a *bar* . . . a whiskey, beer, and bourbon *bar* . . . and what she'd do would be, she'd screw up her face, think real hard, and come up with . . . brandy Alexanders, creme de cacao frappes, gimlets, flaming punch bowls . . . seven-layer liqueur things.

MARTHA. They were good . . . I liked them.

GEORGE. Real lady-like little drinkies.

MARTHA. Hey, where's my rubbing alcohol?

GEORGE (*returning to the portable bar*). But the years have brought to Martha a sense of essentials . . . the knowledge that cream is for coffee, lime juice for pies . . . and alcohol (*Brings* MARTHA *her drink.*) pure and simple . . . here you are, angel . . . for the pure and simple. (*Raises his glass.*) For the mind's blind eye, the heart's ease, and the liver's craw.

Down the hatch, all.

MARTHA (*to them all*). Cheers, dears. (*They all drink.*) You have a poetic nature, George . . . a Dylan Thomas-y quality that gets me right where I live.

GEORGE. Vulgar girl! With guests here!

MARTHA. Ha, ha, ha, HA! (*To* HONEY *and* NICK) Hey; hey! (*Sings, conducts with her drink in her hand.* HONEY *joins in toward the end.*)

Who's afraid of Virginia Woolf,
Virginia Woolf,
Virginia Woolf,
Who's afraid of Virginia Woolf. . . .

(MARTHA *and* HONEY *laugh;* NICK *smiles.*)

HONEY. Oh, wasn't that funny? That was so funny. . . .

NICK (*snapping to*). Yes . . . yes, it was.

MARTHA. I thought I'd bust a gut; I really did. . . . I really thought I'd bust a gut laughing. George didn't like it. . . . George didn't think it was funny at all.

GEORGE. Lord, Martha, do we have to go through this again?

MARTHA. I'm trying to shame you into a sense of humor, angel, that's all.

GEORGE (*over-patiently, to* HONEY *and* NICK). Martha didn't think I laughed loud enough. Martha thinks that unless . . . as she demurely puts it . . . that unless you "bust a gut" you aren't amused. You know? Unless you carry on like a hyena you aren't having any fun.

HONEY. Well, I certainly had fun . . . it was a *wonderful* party.

NICK (*attempting enthusiasm*). Yes . . . it certainly was.

HONEY (*to* MARTHA). And your father! Oh! He is so marvelous!

NICK (*as above*). Yes . . . yes, he is.

HONEY. Oh, I tell you.

MARTHA (*genuinely proud*). He's quite a guy, isn't he? Quite a guy.

GEORGE (*at* NICK). And you'd better believe it!

HONEY (*admonishing* GEORGE). Ohhhh-hhhhh! He's a wonderful man.

GEORGE. I'm not trying to tear him down. He's a God, we all know that.

MARTHA. You lay off my father!

GEORGE. Yes, love. (*To* NICK.) All I mean is . . . when you've had as many of these faculty parties as I have. . . .

NICK (*killing the attempted rapport*). I rather appreciated it. I mean, aside from enjoying it, I appreciated it. You know, when you're new at a place . . . (GEORGE *eyes him suspiciously.*) Meeting everyone, getting introduced around . . . getting to know some of the men. . . . When I was teaching in Kansas. . . .

HONEY. You won't believe it, but we had to make our way all by *ourselves* . . . isn't that right, dear?

NICK. Yes, it is. . . . We. . . .

HONEY. . . . We had to make our own way. . . . I had to go up to wives . . . in the library, or at the supermarket . . . and say, "Hello, I'm new here . . . you must be Mrs. So-and-so, Doctor So-and-so's wife." It really wasn't very nice at all.

MARTHA. Well, *Daddy* knows how to run things.

NICK (*not enough enthusiasm*). He's a remarkable man.

MARTHA. You bet your sweet life.

GEORGE (*to NICK . . . a confidence, but not whispered*). Let me tell you a secret, baby. There are easier things in the world, if you happen to be teaching at a university, there are easier things than being married to the daughter of the president of that university. There are easier things in this world.

MARTHA (*loud . . . to no one in particular*). It *should* be an extraordinary opportunity . . . for *some* men it would be the chance of a lifetime!

GEORGE (*to NICK . . . a solemn wink*). There are, believe me, easier things in this world.

NICK. Well, I can understand how it might make for some . . . awkwardness, perhaps . . . conceivably, but. . . .

MARTHA. *Some* men would give their right arm for the chance!

GEORGE (*quietly*). Alas, Martha, in reality it works out that the sacrifice is usually of a somewhat more private portion of the anatomy.

MARTHA (*a snarl of dismissal and contempt*). NYYYYAAAAHHHHH!

HONEY (*rising quickly*). I wonder if you could show me where the . . . (*Her voice trails off.*)

GEORGE (*to MARTHA, indicating HONEY*). Martha. . . .

NICK (*to HONEY*). Are you all right?

HONEY. Of course, dear. I want to . . . put some powder on my nose.

GEORGE (*as MARTHA is not getting up*).

Martha, won't you show her where we keep the . . . euphemism?

MARTHA. Hm? What? Oh! Sure! (*Rises.*) I'm sorry, c'mon. I want to show you the house.

HONEY. I think I'd like to. . . .

MARTHA. . . . wash up? Sure . . . c'mon with me. (*Takes HONEY by the arm. To the men*) You two do some men talk for a while.

HONEY (*to NICK*). We'll be back, dear.

MARTHA (*to GEORGE*). Honestly, George, you burn me up!

GEORGE (*happily*). All right.

MARTHA. You really do, George.

GEORGE. O.K. Martha . . . O.K. Just . . . trot along.

MARTHA. You really do.

GEORGE. Just don't shoot your mouth off . . . about . . . you-know-what.

MARTHA (*surprisingly vehement*). I'll talk about any goddamn thing I want to, George!

GEORGE. O.K. O.K. Vanish.

MARTHA. Any goddamn thing I want to! (*Practically dragging HONEY out with her*) C'mon. . . .

GEORGE. Vanish. (*The women have gone.*) So? What'll it be?

NICK. Oh, I don't know . . . I'll stick to bourbon, I guess.

GEORGE (*takes NICK's glass, goes to portable bar*). That what you were drinking over at Parnassus?

NICK. Over at. . . ?

GEORGE. Parnassus.

NICK. I don't understand. . . .

GEORGE. Skip it. (*Hands him his drink.*) One bourbon.

NICK. Thanks.

GEORGE. It's just a private joke between li'l ol' Martha and me. (*They sit.*) So? (*Pause*) So . . . you're in the math department, eh?

NICK. No . . . uh, no.

GEORGE. Martha said you were. I think that's what she said. (*Not too friendly*) What made you decide to be a teacher?

NICK. Oh . . . well, the same things that . . . uh . . . motivated you, I imagine.

GEORGE. What were they?

NICK (*formal*). Pardon?

GEORGE. I said, what were they? What were the things that motivated me?

NICK (*laughing uneasily*). Well . . . I'm sure I don't know.

GEORGE. You just finished saying that the things that motivated you were the same things that motivated me.

NICK (*with a little pique*). I said I *imagined* they were.

GEORGE. Oh. (*Off-hand*) Did you? (*Pause*) Well. . . . (*Pause*) You like it here?

NICK (*looking about the room*). Yes . . . it's . . . it's fine.

GEORGE. I mean the University.

NICK. Oh. . . . I thought you meant. . . .

GEORGE. Yes . . . I can see you did. (*Pause*) I meant the University.

NICK. Well, I . . . I like it . . . fine. (*As* GEORGE *just stares at him*) Just fine. (*Same*) You . . . you've been here quite a long time, haven't you?

GEORGE (*absently, as if he had not heard*). What? Oh . . . yes. Ever since I married . . . uh, What's-her-name . . . uh, Martha. Even before that. (*Pause*) Forever. (*To himself*) Dashed hopes, and good intentions. Good, better, best, bested. (*Back to* NICK) How do you like that for a declension, young man? Eh?

NICK. Sir, I'm sorry if we. . . .

GEORGE (*with an edge in his voice*). You didn't answer my question.

NICK. Sir?

GEORGE. Don't you condescend to me! (*Toying with him*) I asked you how you liked that for a declension: Good; better; best; bested. Hm? Well?

NICK (*with some distaste*). I really don't know what to say.

GEORGE (*feigned incredulousness*). You really don't know what to *say*?

NICK (*snapping it out*). All right . . . what do you want me to say? Do you want me to say it's funny, so you can contradict me and say it's sad? or do you want me to say it's sad so you can turn around and say no, it's funny. You can play that damn little game any way you want to, you know!

GEORGE (*feigned awe*). Very good! Very good!

NICK (*even angrier than before*). And when my wife comes back, I think we'll just. . . .

GEORGE (*sincere*). Now, now . . . calm down, my boy. Just . . . calm . . . down. (*Pause*) All right? (*Pause*) You want another drink? Here, give me your glass.

NICK. I still have one. I *do* think that

when my wife comes downstairs. . . .

GEORGE. Here . . . I'll freshen it. Give me your glass. (*Takes it.*)

NICK. What I mean is . . . you two . . . you and your wife . . . seem to be having *some* sort of a. . . .

GEORGE. Martha and I are having . . . nothing. Martha and I are merely . . . exercising . . . that's all . . . we're merely walking what's left of our wits. Don't pay any attention to it.

NICK (*undecided*). Still. . . .

GEORGE (*an abrupt change of pace*). Well, now . . . let's sit down and talk, hunh?

NICK (*cool again*). It's just that I don't like to . . . become involved . . . (*An afterthought*) uh . . . in other people's affairs.

GEORGE (*comforting a child*). Well, you'll get over that . . . small college and all. Musical beds is the faculty sport around here.

NICK. Sir?

GEORGE. I said, musical beds is the faculty. . . . Never mind. I wish you wouldn't go "Sir" like that . . . not with the question mark at the end of it. You know? Sir? I know it's meant to be a sign of respect for your (*Winces*) elders . . . but . . . uh . . . the way you do it. . . . Sir? . . . Madam?

NICK (*with a small, noncommittal smile*). No disrespect intended.

GEORGE. How old *are* you?

NICK. Twenty-eight.

GEORGE. I'm forty something. (*Waits for reaction . . . gets none.*) Aren't you surprised? I mean . . . don't I look older? Doesn't this . . . *gray* quality suggest the fifties? Don't I sort of fade into backgrounds . . . get lost in the cigarette smoke? Hunh?

NICK (*looking around for an ashtray*). I think you look . . . fine.

GEORGE. I've always been lean . . . I haven't put on five pounds since I was your age. I don't have a paunch, either. . . . What I've got . . . I've got this little distension just below the belt . . . but it's hard . . . It's not soft flesh. I use the handball courts. How much do *you* weigh?

NICK. I. . . .

GEORGE. Hundred and fifty-five, sixty . . . something like that? Do you play handball?

NICK. Well, yes . . . no . . . I mean, not

very well.

GEORGE. Well, then . . . we shall play some time. Martha is a hundred and eight . . . years *old*. She weighs somewhat more than that. How old is *your* wife?

NICK (*a little bewildered*). She's twenty-six.

GEORGE. Martha is a remarkable woman. I would imagine she weighs around a hundred and ten.

NICK. Your . . . wife . . . weighs . . . ?

GEORGE No, no, my boy. Yours! *Your* wife. My wife is Martha.

NICK. Yes . . . I know.

GEORGE. If you were married to Martha you would know what it means. (*Pause*) But then, if I were married to your wife I would know what that means, too . . . wouldn't I?

NICK (*after a pause*). Yes.

GEORGE Martha says you're in the Math Department, or something.

NICK (*as if for the hundredth time*). No . . . I'm not.

GEORGE. Martha is seldom mistaken . . . maybe you *should* be in the Math Department, or something.

NICK. I'm a biologist. I'm in the Biology Department.

GEORGE (*after a pause*). Oh. (*Then, as if remembering something*) OH!

NICK. Sir?

GEORGE. You're the one! You're the one's going to make all that trouble . . . making everyone the same, rearranging the chromozones, or whatever it is. Isn't that right?

NICK (*with that small smile*). Not exactly: chromo*somes*.

GEORGE. I'm very mistrustful. Do you believe . . . (*Shifting in his chair*) . . . do you believe that people learn nothing from history? Not that there is nothing to learn, mind you, but that people learn nothing? I am in the History Department.

NICK. Well. . . .

GEORGE. I am a Doctor. A.B. . . . M.A. . . . PH.D. . . . ABMAPHID! Abmaphid has been variously described as a wasting disease of the frontal lobes, and as a wonder drug. It is actually both. I'm really very mistrustful. Biology, hunh? (NICK *does not answer . . . nods . . . looks.*) I read somewhere that science fiction is really not fiction at all . . . that you people are arranging my genes, so that everyone will be like everyone else. Now, I won't have that! It would be a . . . shame. I mean . . . look at me! Is it really such a good idea . . . if everyone was forty something and looked fifty-five? You didn't answer my question about history.

NICK. This genetic business you're talking about. . . .

GEORGE. Oh, that. (*Dismisses it with a wave of his hand.*) That's very upsetting . . . very . . . disappointing. But history is a great deal more . . . disappointing. I am in the History Department.

NICK. Yes . . . you told me.

GEORGE. I know I told you. . . . I shall probably tell you several more times. Martha tells me often, that I am *in* the History Department . . . as opposed to *being* the History Department . . . in the sense of *running* the History Department. I do not run the History Department.

NICK. Well, I don't run the Biology Department.

GEORGE. You're twenty-one!

NICK. Twenty-eight.

GEORGE. Twenty-eight! Perhaps when you're forty something and look fifty-five, you will run the History Department. . . .

NICK. . . . Biology. . . .

GEORGE. . . . the Biology Department. I *did* run the History Department, for four years, during the war, but that was because everybody was away. Then . . . everybody came back . . . because nobody got killed. That's New England for you. Isn't that amazing? Not one single man in this whole place got his head shot off. That's pretty irrational. (*Broods.*) Your wife *doesn't* have any hips . . . has she . . . does she?

NICK. What?

GEORGE. I don't mean to suggest that I'm hip-happy. . . . I'm not one of those thirty-six, twenty-two, seventy-eight men. No-siree . . . not me. Everything in proportion. I was implying that your wife is . . . slim-hipped.

NICK. Yes . . . she is.

GEORGE (*looking at the ceiling*). What are they *doing* up there? I assume that's where they are.

NICK (*false heartiness*). You know women.

GEORGE (*gives* NICK *a long stare, of feigned incredulity . . . then his attention moves*). Not one son-of-a-bitch got killed. Of course, nobody bombed Washington. No . . . that's not fair. You have any kids?

NICK. Uh . . . no . . . not yet. (*Pause*) You?

GEORGE (*a kind of challenge*). That's for me to know and you to find out.

NICK. Indeed?

GEORGE. No kids, hunh?

NICK. Not yet.

GEORGE. People do . . . uh . . . have kids. That's what I meant about history. You people are going to make them in test tubes, aren't you? You biologists. Babies. Then the rest of us . . . them as wants to . . . can screw to their heart's content. What will happen to the tax deduction? Has anyone figured that out yet? (NICK, *who can think of nothing better to do, laughs mildly.*) But you *are* going to have kids . . . anyway. In spite of history.

NICK (*hedging*). Yes . . . certainly. We . . . want to wait . . . a little . . . until we're settled.

GEORGE. And this . . . (*With a handsweep taking in not only the room, the house, but the whole countryside*) . . . this is your heart's content—Illyria . . . Penguin Island . . . Gomorrah. . . . You think you're going to be happy here in New Carthage, eh?

NICK (*a little defensively*). I hope we'll stay here.

GEORGE. And every definition has its boundaries, eh? Well, it isn't a bad college, I guess. I mean . . . it'll do. It isn't M.I.T. . . . . it isn't U.C.L.A. . . . . it isn't the Sorbonne . . . or Moscow U. either, for that matter.

NICK. I don't mean . . . forever.

GEORGE. Well, don't you let that get bandied about. The old man wouldn't like it. Martha's father expects loyalty and devotion out of his . . . staff. I was going to use another word. Martha's father expects his . . . staff . . . to cling to the walls of this place, like the ivy . . . to come here and grow old . . . to fall in the line of service. One man, a professor of Latin and Elocution, actually fell in the cafeteria line, one lunch. He was buried, as many of us have been, and as many more of us will be, under the shrubbery around the chapel. It is said . . . and I have no reason to doubt it . . . that we make excellent fertilizer. But the old man is not going to be buried under the shrubbery . . . the old man is not going to die. Martha's father has the staying power of one of those Micronesian tortoises. There are rumors . . . which you must not breathe in front of Martha, for she foams at the mouth . . . that the old man, her father, is over two hundred years old. There is probably an irony involved in this, but I am not drunk enough to figure out what it is. How many kids you going to have?

NICK. I . . . I don't know. . . . My wife is. . . .

GEORGE. Slim-hipped. (*Rises*) Have a drink.

NICK. Yes.

GEORGE. MARTHA! (*No answer*) DAMN IT! (*To* NICK) You asked me if I knew women. . . . Well, one of the things I do *not* know about them is what they talk about while the men are talking. (*Vaguely*) I must find out some time.

MARTHA'S VOICE. WHADD'YA WANT?

GEORGE (*to* NICK). Isn't that a wonderful sound? What I mean is . . . what do you think they really *talk* about . . . or don't you care?

NICK. Themselves, I would imagine.

MARTHA'S VOICE. GEORGE?

GEORGE (*to* NICK). Do you find women . . . puzzling?

NICK. Well . . . yes and no.

GEORGE (*with a knowing nod*). Unhhunh. (*Moves toward the hall, almost bumps into* HONEY, *re-entering.*) Oh! Well, here's one of you, at least. (HONEY *moves toward* NICK. GEORGE *goes to the hall.*)

HONEY (to GEORGE). She'll be right down. (*To* NICK) You must see this house, dear . . . this is such a wonderful old house.

NICK. Yes, I. . . .

GEORGE. MARTHA!

MARTHA'S VOICE. FOR CHRIST'S SAKE, HANG ON A MINUTE, WILL YOU?

HONEY (*to* GEORGE). She'll be right down . . . she's changing.

GEORGE (*incredulous*). She's *what*? She's changing?

HONEY. Yes.

GEORGE. Her clothes?

HONEY. Her dress.

GEORGE (*suspicious*). Why?

HONEY (*with a nervous little laugh*). Why, I imagine she wants to be . . . comfortable.

GEORGE (*with a threatening look toward the hall*). Oh, she does, does she?

HONEY. Well, heavens, I should think. . . .

GEORGE. YOU DON'T KNOW!

NICK (*as* HONEY *starts*). You feel all right?

HONEY (*reassuring, but with the echo of a whine. A long-practiced tone*). Oh, yes, dear . . . perfectly fine.

GEORGE (*fuming . . . to himself*). So she wants to be comfortable, does she? Well, we'll see about that.

HONEY (*to* GEORGE, *brightly*). I didn't know until just a minute ago that you had a *son*.

GEORGE (*wheeling, as if struck from behind*). WHAT?

HONEY. A son! I hadn't known.

NICK. You to know and me to find out. Well, he must be quite a big. . . .

HONEY. Twenty-one . . . twenty-one tomorrow . . . tomorrow's his birthday.

NICK (*a victorious smile*). Well!

GEORGE (*to* HONEY). She told you about him?

HONEY (*flustered*). Well, *yes*. Well, I mean. . . .

GEORGE (*nailing it down*). She told you about him.

HONEY (*a nervous giggle*). Yes.

GEORGE (*strangely*). You say she's changing?

HONEY. Yes.

GEORGE. And she mentioned . . . ?

HONEY (*cheerful, but a little puzzled*). . . . your son's birthday . . . yes.

GEORGE (*more or less to himself*). O.K., Martha . . . O.K.

NICK. You look pale, Honey. Do you want a . . . ?

HONEY. Yes, dear . . . a little more brandy, maybe. Just a drop.

GEORGE. O.K., Martha.

NICK. May I use the . . . uh . . . bar?

GEORGE. Hm? Oh, yes . . . yes . . . by all means. Drink away . . . you'll need it as the years go on. (*For* MARTHA, *as if she were in the room*) You goddam destructive. . . .

HONEY (*to cover*). What time is it, dear?

NICK. Two-thirty.

HONEY. Oh, it's so late . . . we *should* be getting home.

GEORGE (*nastily, but he is so preoccupied he hardly notices his own tone*). For what? You keeping the babysitter up, or something?

NICK (*almost a warning*). I told you we didn't have children.

GEORGE. Hm? (*Realizing*) Oh, I'm sorry. I wasn't even listening . . . or thinking . . . (*With a flick of his hand*) . . . whichever one applies.

NICK (*softly, to* HONEY). We'll go in a little while.

GEORGE (*driving*). Oh no, now . . . you mustn't. Martha is changing . . . and Martha is not changing for *me*. Martha hasn't changed for *me* in years. If Martha is changing, it means we'll be here for . . . days. You are being accorded an honor, and you must not forget that Martha is the daughter of our beloved boss. She is his . . . right ball, you might say.

NICK. You might not understand this . . . but I wish you wouldn't talk that way in front of my wife.

HONEY. Oh, now. . . .

GEORGE (*incredulous*). Really? Well, you're quite right . . . We'll leave that sort of talk to Martha.

MARTHA (*entering*). What sort of talk? (MARTHA *has changed her clothes, and she looks, now, more comfortable and . . . and this is most important . . . most voluptuous*)

GEORGE. There you are, my pet.

NICK (*impressed; rising*). Well, now. . . .

GEORGE. Why, Martha . . . your Sunday chapel dress!

HONEY (*slightly disapproving*). Oh, that's most attractive.

MARTHA (*showing off*). You like it? Good! (*To* GEORGE) What the hell do you mean screaming up the stairs at me like that?

GEORGE. We got lonely, darling . . . we got lonely for the soft purr of your little voice.

MARTHA (*deciding not to rise to it*). Oh. Well, then, you just trot over to the barie-poo. . . .

GEORGE (*taking the tone from her*). . . . and make your little mommy a gweat big dwink.

MARTHA (*giggles*). That's right (*To*

NICK) Well, did you two have a nice little talk? You men solve the problems of the world, as usual?

NICK. Well, no, we. . .

GEORGE (*quickly*). What we did, actually, if you really want to know, what we did actually is try to figure out what you two were talking about.

(HONEY *giggles,* MARTHA *laughs.*)

MARTHA (*to* HONEY). Aren't they something? Aren't these . . . (*Cheerfully disdainful*) . . . *men* the absolute end? (*To* GEORGE) Why didn't you sneak upstairs and listen in?

GEORGE. Oh, I wouldn't have *listened,* Martha. . . . I would have *peeked.*

(HONEY *giggles,* MARTHA *laughs.*)

NICK (*to* GEORGE, *with false heartiness*). It's a conspiracy.

GEORGE. And now we'll never know. Shucks!

MARTHA (*to* NICK, *as* HONEY *beams*). Hey, you must be quite a boy, getting your Masters when you were . . . what? . . . twelve? You hear that, George?

NICK. Twelve-and-a-half, actually. No, nineteen really. (*To* HONEY) Honey, you needn't have mentioned that. It. . . .

HONEY. Ohhh . . . I'm *proud* of you. . . .

GEORGE (*seriously, if sadly*). That's very . . . impressive.

MARTHA (*aggressively*). You're damned right!

GEORGE (*between his teeth*). I said I was impressed, Martha. I'm beside myself with jealousy. What do you want me to do, throw up? (*To* NICK) That really is very impressive. (*To* HONEY) You should be right proud.

HONEY (*coy*). Oh, he's a pretty nice fella.

GEORGE (*to* NICK). I wouldn't be surprised if you *did* take over the History Department one of these days.

NICK. The Biology Department.

GEORGE. The *Biology* Department . . . of course. I seem preoccupied with history. Oh! What a remark. (*He strikes a pose, his hand over his heart, his head raised, his voice stentorian.*) "I am preoccupied with history."

MARTHA (*as* HONEY *and* NICK *chuckle*). Ha, ha, ha, HA!

GEORGE (*with some disgust*). I think I'll make *myself* a drink.

MARTHA. George is not preoccupied with history. . . . George is preoccupied with the *History Department.* George is preoccupied with the History Department because. . . .

GEORGE. . . . because he is *not* the History Department, but is only *in* the History Department. We know, Martha . . . we went all through it while you were upstairs . . . getting up. There's no need to go through it again.

MARTHA. That's right, baby . . . keep it clean. (*To the others*) George is bogged down in the History Department. He's an old bog in the History Department, that's what George is. A bog. . . . A fen. . . . A G.D. swamp Ha, ha, ha, HA! A SWAMP! Hey, swamp! Hey SWAMPY!

GEORGE (*with a great effort controls himself . . then as if she had said nothing more than "George, dear". . . .*) Yes, Martha? Can I get you something?

MARTHA (*amused at his game*). Well . . . uh . . . sure, you can light my cigarette, if you're of a mind to.

GEORGE (*considers, then moves off*). No . . . there are limits. I mean, man can put up with only so much without he descends a rung or two on the old evolutionary ladder . . . (*Now a quick aside to* NICK) . . . which is up your line . . . (*Then back to* MARTHA) . . . sinks, Martha, and it's a funny ladder . . . you can't reverse yourself . . . start back up once you're descending. (MARTHA *blows him an arrogant kiss.*) Now . . . I'll hold your hand when it's dark and you're afraid of the bogey man, and I'll tote your gin bottles out after midnight, so no one'll see . . . but I will not light your cigarette. And that, as they say, is that.

(*Brief silence*)

MARTHA (*under her breath*). Jesus! (*Then, immediately, to* NICK) Hey, you played football, hunh?

HONEY (*as* NICK *seems sunk in thought*). Dear. . . .

NICK. Oh! Oh, yes . . . I was a . . . quarterback . . . but I was much more . . . adept . . . at boxing, really.

MARTHA (*with great enthusiasm*). BOXING! You hear that, George?

GEORGE (*resignedly*). Yes, Martha.

MARTHA (*to* NICK, *with peculiar intensity and enthusiasm*). You musta been pretty good at it . . . I mean, you don't look like you got hit in the face at all.

HONEY (*proudly*). He was intercollegiate state middleweight champion.

NICK (*embarrassed*). Honey. . . .

HONEY. Well, you were.

MARTHA You look like you still got a pretty good body *now,* too . . . is that right? Have you?

GEORGE (*intensely*). Martha . . . decency forbids. . . .

MARTHA (*to* GEORGE . . . *still staring at* NICK, *though*). SHUT UP! (*Now, back to* NICK) Well, have you? Have you kept your body?

NICK (*unselfconscious . . . almost encouraging her*). It's still pretty good. I work out.

MARTHA (*with a half-smile*). Do you!

NICK. Yeah.

HONEY. Oh, yes . . . he has a very . . . firm body.

MARTHA (*still with that smile . . . a private communication with* NICK). Have you! Oh, I think that's very nice.

NICK (*narcissistic, but not directly for* MARTHA). Well, you never know . . . (*Shrugs.*) . . . you know . . . once you have it. . . .

MARTHA. . . . you never know when it's going to come in handy.

NICK. I was going to say . . . why give it up until you have to.

MARTHA I couldn't agree with you more. (*They both smile, and there is a rapport of some unformed sort, established.*) I couldn't agree with you more.

GEORGE. Martha, your obscenity is more than. . . .

MARTHA. George, here, doesn't cotton much to body talk . . . do you sweetheart? (*No reply*) George isn't too happy when we get to muscle. You know . . . flat bellies, pectorals. . . .

GEORGE (*to* HONEY). Would you like to take a walk around the garden?

HONEY (*chiding*). Oh, now. . . .

GEORGE (*incredulous*). You're amused? (*Shrugs.*) All right.

MARTHA. Paunchy over there isn't too happy when the conversation moves to muscle. How much do you weigh?

NICK. A hundred and fifty-five, a hundred and. . . .

MARTHA. Still at the old middleweight limit, eh? That's pretty good. (*Swings around.*) Hey George, tell 'em about the boxing match *we* had.

GEORGE (*slamming his drink down, moving toward the hall*). Christ!

MARTHA. George! Tell 'em about it!

GEORGE (*with a sick look on his face*). You tell them, Martha. You're good at it. (*Exits.*)

HONEY. Is he . . . all right?

MARTHA (*laughs*). Him? Oh, sure. George and I had this boxing match . . . Oh, Lord, twenty years ago . . . a couple of years after we were married.

NICK. A boxing match? The two of you?

HONEY. Really?

MARTHA. Yup . . . the two of us . . . really.

HONEY (*with a little shivery giggle of anticipation*). I can't magine it.

MARTHA. Well, like I say, it was twenty years ago, and it wasn't in a ring, or anything like that, you know what I mean. It was wartime, and Daddy was on this physical fitness kick . . . Daddy's always admired physical fitness . . . says a man is only part brain . . . he has a body, too, and it's his responsibility to keep both of them up . . . you know?

NICK. Unh-hunh.

MARTHA. Says the brain can't work unless the body's working, too.

NICK. Well, that's not exactly so. . . .

MARTHA. Well, maybe that *isn't* what he says . . . something like it. *But* . . . it was wartime, and Daddy got the idea all the men should learn how to box . . . self-defense. I suppose the idea was if the Germans landed on the coast, or something, the whole faculty'd go out and punch 'em to death. . . . I don't know.

NICK. It was probably more the principle of the thing.

MARTHA. No kidding. Anyway, so Daddy had a couple of us over one Sunday and we went out in the back, and Daddy put on the gloves himself. Daddy's a strong man. . . . Well, *you* know.

NICK. Yes . . . yes.

MARTHA And he asked George to box with him Aaaaannnnd . . . George didn't *want* to . . . probably something about not wanting to bloody-up his meal ticket. . . .

NICK. Unh-hunh.

MARTHA. . . . Anyway, George said he didn't want to, and Daddy was saying, "Come on, young man . . . what sort of son-in-law *are* you?" . . . and stuff like that.

NICK. Yeah.

MARTHA. So, while this was going on . . . I don't know why I *did* it . . . I got into a pair of gloves myself . . . you know, I didn't lace 'em up, or anything . . . and I snuck up behind George, just kidding, and I yelled "Hey George!" and at the same time I let go sort of a round-house right . . . just kidding, you know?

NICK. Unh-hunh.

MARTHA. . . . and George wheeled around real quick, and he caught it right in the jaw . . . POW! (NICK *laughs.*) I hadn't meant it . . . honestly. Anyway . . . POW! Right in the jaw . . . and he was off balance . . . he must have been . . . and he stumbled back a few steps, and then, CRASH, he landed . . . flat . . . in a huckleberry bush! (NICK *laughs.* HONEY *goes tsk, tsk, tsk, tsk, and shakes her head.*) It was awful, really. It was funny, but it was awful. (*She thinks, gives a muffled laugh in rueful contemplation of the incident.*) I think it's colored our whole life. Really I do! It's an excuse, anyway. (GEORGE *enters now, his hands behind his back. No one sees him.*) It's what he uses for being bogged down, anyway . . . why he hasn't *gone* anywhere.

(GEORGE *advances.* HONEY *sees him.*)

MARTHA. And it was an *accident* . . . a real, goddamn accident!

(GEORGE *takes from behind his back a short-barreled shotgun, and calmly aims it at the back of* MARTHA's *head.* HONEY *screams . . . rises.* NICK *rises, and, simultaneously,* MARTHA *turns her head to face* GEORGE. GEORGE *pulls the trigger.*)

GEORGE. POW!!! (*Pop! From the barrel of the gun blossoms a large red and yellow Chinese parasol.* HONEY *screams again, this time less, and mostly from relief and confusion.*) You're dead! Pow! You're dead!

NICK (*laughing*). Good Lord. (HONEY *is beside herself.* MARTHA *laughs too . . . almost breaks down, her great laugh booming.* GEORGE *joins in the general laughter and confusion. It dies, eventually.*)

HONEY. Oh! My goodness!

MARTHA (*joyously*). Where'd you get that, you bastard?

NICK (*his hand out for the gun*). Let me see that, will you?

(GEORGE *hands him the gun.*)

HONEY. I've never been so frightened in my life! Never!

GEORGE (*a trifle abstracted*). Oh, I've had it awhile. Did you like that?

MARTHA (*giggling*). You bastard.

HONEY (*wanting attention*). I've *never* been so frightened . . . never.

NICK. This is quite a gadget.

GEORGE (*leaning over* MARTHA). You liked that, did you?

MARTHA. Yeah . . . that was pretty good. (*Softer*) C'mon . . . give me a kiss.

GEORGE (*indicating* NICK *and* HONEY). Later, sweetie. (*But* MARTHA *will not be dissuaded. They kiss,* GEORGE *standing, leaning over* MARTHA's *chair. She takes his hand, places it on her stage-side breast. He breaks away.*) Oh-ho! That's what you're after, is it? What are we going to have . . . blue games for the guests? Hunh? Hunh?

MARTHA (*angry-hurt*). You . . . prick!

GEORGE (*a Pyrrhic victory*). Everything in its place, Martha . . . everything in its own good time.

MARTHA (*an unspoken epithet*). You....

GEORGE (*over to* NICK, *who still has the gun*). Here, let me show you . . . it goes back in, like this. (*Closes the parasol, reinserts it in the gun.*)

NICK. That's damn clever.

GEORGE (*puts the gun down*). Drinks now! Drinks for all! (*Takes* NICK's *glass without question . . . goes to* MARTHA.)

MARTHA (*still angry-hurt*). I'm not finished.

HONEY (*as* GEORGE *puts out his hand for her glass*). Oh, I think I need *something.*

(*He takes her glass, moves back to the portable bar.*)

NICK. Is that Japanese?

GEORGE. Probably.

HONEY (*to* MARTHA). I was never so frightened in my life. Weren't you frightened? Just for a second?

MARTHA (*smothering her rage at* GEORGE). I don't remember.

HONEY. Ohhhh, now . . . I bet you were.

GEORGE. Did you really think I was going to kill you, Martha?

MARTHA (*dripping contempt*). You? . . . Kill me? . . . That's a laugh.

GEORGE. Well, now, I might . . . some day.

MARTHA. Fat chance.

NICK (*as* GEORGE *hands him his drink*). Where's the john?

GEORGE. Through the hall there . . . and down to your left.

HONEY. Don't you come back with any guns, or anything, now.

NICK (*laughs*). Oh, no.

MARTHA. You don't need any props, do you, baby?

NICK. Unh-unh.

MARTHA (*suggestive*). I'll bet not. No fake Jap gun for you, eh?

NICK (*smiles at* MARTHA. *Then, to* GEORGE, *indicating a side table near the hall*). May I leave my drink here?

GEORGE (*as* NICK EXITS *without waiting for a reply*). Yeah . . . sure . . . why not? We've got half-filled glasses everywhere in the house, wherever Martha forgets she's left them . . . in the linen closet, on the edge of the bathtub. . . . . I even found one in the freezer, once.

MARTHA (*amused in spite of herself*). You did not!

GEORGE. *Yes* I did.

MARTHA (*ibid*). You did *not!*

GEORGE (*giving* HONEY *her brandy*). Yes I *did*. (*To* HONEY.) Brandy doesn't give you a hangover?

HONEY. I never mix. And then, I don't drink very much, either.

GEORGE (*grimaces behind her back*). Oh . . . that's good. Your . . . your husband was telling me all about the . . . chromosomes.

MARTHA (*ugly*). The what?

GEORGE. The chromosomes, Martha . . . the genes, or whatever they are. (*To* HONEY) You've got quite a . . . terrifying husband.

HONEY (*as if she's being joshed*). Ohhhhhhhhh. . . .

GEORGE. No, really. He's quite terrifying, with his chromosomes, and all.

MARTHA. He's in the Math Department.

GEORGE. No, Martha . . . he's a biologist.

MARTHA (*her voice rising*). He's in the *Math* Department!

HONEY (*timidly*). Uh . . . biology.

MARTHA (*unconvinced*). Are *you* sure?

HONEY (*with a little giggle*). Well, I ought to. (*Then as an afterthought*) Be.

MARTHA (*grumpy*). I suppose *so*. I don't know who said he was in the Math Department.

GEORGE. You did, Martha.

MARTHA (*by way of irritable explana-tion*). Well, I can't be expected to re-member *everything*. I meet fifteen new teachers and their goddamn wives . . . present company outlawed, of course . . . (HONEY *nods, smiles sillily.*) . . . and I'm supposed to remember *everything*. (*Pause*) So? He's a biologist. Good for him. Biology's even better. It's less . . . abstruse.

GEORGE. Abstract.

MARTHA. ABSTRUSE! In the sense of rec-ondite. (*Sticks her tongue out at* GEORGE.) Don't you tell me words. Biology's even better. It's . . . right at the *meat* of things. (NICK *reenters*.) You're right at the meat of things, baby.

NICK (*taking his drink from the side table*). Oh?

HONEY (*with that giggle*). They thought you were in the Math Department.

NICK. Well, maybe I ought to be.

MARTHA. You stay right where you are . . . you stay right at the . . . *meat* of things.

GEORGE. You're obsessed with that phrase, Martha. . . . It's ugly.

MARTHA (*ignoring* GEORGE . . . *to* NICK). You stay right there. (*Laughs.*) Hell, you can take over the History De-partment just as easy from there as any-where else. God knows, *some*body's going to take over the History Department, *some* day, and it ain't going to be Georgie-boy, there . . . that's for sure. Are ya, swampy . . . are ya, hunh?

GEORGE. In my mind, Martha, you are buried in cement, right up to your neck. (MARTHA *giggles*.) No . . . right up to your nose . . . that's much quieter.

MARTHA (*to* NICK). Georgie-boy, here, says you're terrifying. Why are you terri-fying?

NICK (*with a small smile*). I didn't know I was.

HONEY (*a little thickly*). It's because of your chromosomes, dear.

NICK. Oh, the chromosome business. . . .

MARTHA (*to* NICK). What's all this about chromosomes?

NICK. Well, chromosomes are. . . .

MARTHA. I know what chromosomes are, sweetie, I love 'em.

NICK. Oh. . . . Well, then.

GEORGE. Martha eats them . . . for break-fast . . . she sprinkles them on her cereal. (*To* MARTHA, *now*) It's very simple, Martha, this young man is working on a system whereby chromosomes can be altered . . . well not all by himself—he probably has one or two co-conspirators—the genetic makeup of a sperm cell changed, reordered . . . *to* order, actually . . . for hair and eye color, stature, potency . . . I imagine . . . hairiness, features, health . . . and *mind*. Most important . . . Mind. All imbalances will be corrected, sifted out . . . propensity for various diseases will be gone, longevity assured. We will have a race of men . . . test-tube-bred . . . incubator-born . . . superb and sublime.

MARTHA (*impressed*). Hunh!

HONEY. How exciting!

GEORGE. *But!* Everyone will tend to be rather the same. . . . Alike. Everyone . . . and I'm sure I'm not wrong here . . . will tend to look like this young man *here*.

MARTHA. *That's* not a bad idea.

NICK (*impatient*). All right, now. . . .

GEORGE. It will, on the surface of it, be all rather pretty . . . quite jolly. But of course there will be a dank side to it, too. A certain amount of regulation will be necessary . . . uh . . . for the experiment to succeed. A certain number of sperm tubes will have to be cut.

MARTHA. Hunh! . . .

GEORGE. Millions upon millions of them . . . millions of tiny little slicing operations that will leave just the smallest scar, on the underside of the scrotum (MARTHA *laughs.*) but which will assure the sterility of the imperfect . . . the ugly, the stupid . . . the . . . unfit.

NICK (*grimly*). Now look . . . !

GEORGE. . . . with this, we will have, in time, a race of glorious men.

MARTHA. Hunh!

GEORGE. I suspect we will not have much music, much painting, but we will have a civilization of men, smooth, blond, and right at the middleweight limit.

MARTHA. Awww. . . .

GEORGE. . . . a race of scientists and mathematicians, each dedicated to and working for the greater glory of the super-civilization.

MARTHA. Goody.

GEORGE. There will be a certain . . . loss of liberty, I imagine, as a result of this experiment . . . but diversity will no longer be the goal. Cultures and races will eventually vanish . . . the ants will take over the world.

NICK. Are you finished?

GEORGE (*ignoring him*). And I, naturally, am rather opposed to all this. History, which is my field . . . history, of which I am one of the most famous bogs. . . .

MARTHA. Ha, ha, HA!

GEORGE. . . . will lose its glorious variety and unpredictability. I, and with me the . . . the surprise, the multiplexity, the sea-changing rhythm of . . . history, will be eliminated. There will be order and constancy . . . and I am unalterably opposed to it. I will not give up Berlin!

MARTHA. You'll give up Berlin, sweetheart. You going to defend it with your paunch?

HONEY. I don't see what Berlin has to *do* with anything.

GEORGE. There is a saloon in West Berlin where the barstools are five feet high. And the earth . . . the floor . . . is . . . so . . . far . . . below you. I will not give up things like that. No . . . I won't. I will fight you, young man . . . one hand on my scrotum, to be sure . . . but with my free hand I will battle you to the death.

MARTHA (*mocking, laughing*). Bravo!

NICK (*to* GEORGE). That's right. And I am going to be the wave of the future.

MARTHA. You bet you are, baby.

HONEY (*quite drunk—to* NICK). I don't see why you want to do all those things, dear. You never told me.

NICK (*angry*). Oh for God's sake!

HONEY (*shocked*). OH!

GEORGE. The most profound indication of a social malignancy . . . no sense of humor. None of the monoliths could take a joke. Read history. I know something about history.

NICK (*to* GEORGE, *trying to make light of it all*). You . . . you don't know much about science, do you?

GEORGE. I know something about history. I know when I'm being threatened.

MARTHA (*salaciously—to* NICK). So, everyone's going to look like you, eh?

NICK. Oh, sure. I'm going to be a personal screwing machine!

MARTHA. Isn't that nice.

HONEY (*her hands over her ears*). Dear, you mustn't . . . you mustn't . . . you mustn't.

NICK (*impatiently*). I'm sorry, Honey.

HONEY. Such language. It's. . . .

NICK. I'm *sorry*. All right?

HONEY (*pouting*). Well . . . all right. (*Suddenly she giggles insanely, subsides. To* GEORGE) . . . When is your son? (*Giggles again.*)

GEORGE. What?

NICK (*distastefully*). Something about your son.

GEORGE. SON!

HONEY. When is . . . where is your son . . . coming home? (*Giggles.*)

GREORGE. Ohhhh. (*Too formal*) Martha? When is our son coming home?

MARTHA. Never mind.

GEORGE. No, no . . . I want to know . . . you brought it out into the open. When is he coming home, Martha?

MARTHA. I said never mind. I'm sorry I brought it up.

GEORGE. Him up . . . not it. You brought *him* up. Well, more or less. When's the little bugger going to appear, hunh? I mean isn't tomorrow meant to be his birthday, or something?

MARTHA. I don't want to talk about it!

GEORGE (*falsely innocent*). But Martha. . . .

MARTHA. I DON'T WANT TO TALK ABOUT IT!

GEORGE. I'll bet you don't. (*To* HONEY *and* NICK) Martha does not want to talk about it . . . him. Martha is sorry she brought it up . . . him.

HONEY (*idiotically*). When's the little bugger coming home? (*Giggles.*)

GEORGE. Yes, Martha . . . since you had the bad taste to bring the matter up in the first place . . . when *is* the little bugger coming home?

NICK. Honey, do you think you . . . ?

MARTHA. George talks disparagingly about the little bugger because . . . well, because he has problems.

GEORGE. The little bugger has problems? What problems has the little bugger got?

MARTHA. Not the little bugger . . . stop calling him that! You! You've got problems.

GEORGE (*feigned disdain*). I've never heard of anything more ridiculous in my life.

HONEY. Neither have I!

NICK. Honey.'. . . .

MARTHA. George's biggest problem about the little . . . ha, ha, ha, HA! . . .

about our son, about our great big son, is that deep down in the private-most pit of his gut, he's not completely sure it's his own kid.

GEORGE (*deeply serious*). My God, you're a wicked woman.

MARTHA. And I've told you a million times, baby . . . I wouldn't conceive with anyone but you . . . you know that, baby.

GEORGE. A deeply wicked person.

HONEY (*deep in drunken grief*). My, my, my, my. Oh, my.

NICK. I'm not sure that this is a subject for. . . .

GEORGE. Martha's lying. I want you to know that, right now. Martha's lying. (MARTHA *laughs*.) There are very few things in this world that I *am* sure of . . . national boundaries, the level of the ocean, political allegiances, practical morality . . . none of these would I stake my stick on any more . . . but the one thing in this whole sinking world that I am sure of is my partnership, my chromosomological partnership in the . . . creation of our . . . blond-eyed, blue-haired . . . son.

HONEY. Oh, I'm so glad!

MARTHA. That was a very pretty speech, George.

GEORGE. Thank you, Martha.

MARTHA. You rose to the occasion . . . good. Real good.

HONEY. Well . . . real well.

NICK. Honey. . . .

GEORGE. Martha knows . . . she knows better.

MARTHA (*proudly*). I know better. I been to college like everybody else.

GEORGE. Martha been to college. Martha been to a convent when she were a little twig of a thing, too.

MARTHA. And I was an atheist. (*Uncertainly*) I still am.

GEORGE. Not an atheist, Martha . . . a pagan. (*To* HONEY *and* NICK) Martha is the only true pagan on the eastern seaboard. (MARTHA *laughs*.)

HONEY. Oh, that's nice. Isn't that nice, dear?

NICK (*humoring her*). Yes . . . wonderful.

GEORGE. And Martha paints blue circles around her things.

NICK. You do?

MARTHA (*defensively, for the joke's sake*). Sometimes. (*Beckoning*) You wanna see?

GEORGE (*admonishing*). Tut, tut, tut.

MARTHA. Tut, tut yourself . . . you old floozie!

HONEY. He's not a floozie . . . he can't be a floozie . . . you're a floozie. (*Giggles.*)

MARTHA (*shaking a finger at* HONEY). Now you watch yourself!

HONEY (*cheerfully*). All right. I'd like a nipper of brandy, please.

NICK. Honey, I think you've had enough, now. . . .

GEORGE. Nonsense! Everybody's ready, I think. (*Takes glasses, etc.*)

HONEY (*echoing* GEORGE). Nonsense.

NICK (*shrugging*). O.K.

MARTHA (*to* GEORGE). Our son does *not* have blue hair . . . or blue eyes, for that matter. He has green eyes . . . like me.

GEORGE. He has blue eyes, Martha.

MARTHA (*determined*). Green.

GEORGE (*patronizing*). Blue, Martha.

MARTHA (*ugly*). GREEN! (*To* HONEY *and* NICK.) He has the loveliest green eyes . . . they aren't all flaked with brown and gray, you know . . . hazel . . . they're real green . . . deep, pure green eyes . . . like mine.

NICK (*peers*). Your eyes are . . . brown, aren't they?

MARTHA. Green! (*A little too fast*) Well, in some lights they look brown, but they're green. Not green like his . . . more hazel. George has watery blue eyes . . . milky blue.

GEORGE. Make up your mind, Martha.

MARTHA. I was giving you the benefit of the doubt. (*Now back to the others*) Daddy has green eyes, too.

GEORGE. He does not! Your father has tiny red eyes . . . like a white mouse. In fact, he *is* a white mouse.

MARTHA. You wouldn't dare say a thing like that if he was here! You're a coward!

GEORGE (*to* HONEY *and* NICK). You know . . . that great shock of white hair, and those little beady red eyes . . . a great big white mouse.

MARTHA. George hates Daddy . . . not for anything Daddy's done to him, but for his own. . . .

GEORGE (*nodding . . . finishing it for her*). . . . inadequacies.

MARTHA (*cheerfully*). That's right. You hit it . . . right on the snout. (*Seeing* GEORGE *exiting.*) Where do you think you're going?

GEORGE. We need some more booze, angel.

MARTHA. Oh. (*Pause*) So, go.

GEORGE (*exiting*). Thank you.

MARTHA (*seeing that* GEORGE *has gone*). He's a good bartender . . . a good bar nurse. The S.O.B., he hates my father. You know that?

NICK (*trying to make light of it*). Oh, come on.

MARTHA (*offended*). You think I'm kidding? You think I'm joking? I never joke . . . I don't have a sense of humor. (*Almost pouting*) I have a fine sense of the ridiculous, but no sense of humor. (*Affirmatively*) I have no sense of humor!

HONEY (*happily*). I haven't, either.

NICK (*half-heartedly*). Yes, you have, Honey . . . a quiet one.

HONEY (*proudly*). Thank you.

MARTHA. You want to know *why* the S.O.B. hates my father? You want me to tell you? All right. . . . I will now tell you why the S.O.B. hates my father.

HONEY (*swinging to some sort of attention*). Oh, good!

MARTHA (*sternly, to* HONEY). *Some* people feed on the calamities of others.

HONEY (*offended*). They do not!

NICK. Honey. . . .

MARTHA. All right! Shut up! Both of you! (*Pause*) All right, now. Mommy died early, see, and I sort of grew up with Daddy. (*Pause—thinks.*) . . . I went away to school, and stuff, but I more or less grew up with him. Jesus, I admired that guy! I worshipped him . . . I absolutely worshipped him. I still do. And he was pretty fond of me, too . . . you know? We had a real . . . rapport going . . . a real rapport.

NICK. Yeah, yeah.

MARTHA. And Daddy built this college . . . I mean, he built it up from what it was . . . it's his whole life. He *is* the college.

NICK. Unh-hunh.

MARTHA. The college is him. You know what the endowment was when he took over, and what it is *now*? You look it up some time.

NICK. I know . . . I read about it. . . .

MARTHA. Shut up and listen . . . (*As an afterthought*) . . . cutie. So after I got done with college and stuff, I came back here and sort of . . . sat around, for a while. I wasn't married, or anything. Wellllll, I'd *been* married . . . sort of . . . for a week, my sophomore year at Miss Muff's Academy for Young Ladies . . . college. A kind of junior Lady Chatterly arrangement, as it turned out . . . the marriage. (NICK *laughs.*) He mowed the lawn at Miss Muff's, sitting up there, all naked, on a big power mower, mowing away. But Daddy and Miss Muff got together and put an end to that . . . real quick . . . annulled . . . which is a laugh . . . because theoretically you can't get an annullment if there's entrance. Ha! Anyway, so I was revirginized, finished at Miss Muff's . . . where they had one less gardener's boy, and a real shame, that was . . . and I came back here and sort of sat around for a while. I was hostess for Daddy and I took care of him . . . and it was . . . nice. It was very nice.

NICK. Yes . . . yes.

MARTHA. What do you mean, yes, yes? How would you know? (NICK *shrugs helplessly.*) Lover. (NICK *smiles a little.*) And I got the idea, about then, that I'd marry into the college . . . which didn't seem to be quite as stupid as it turned out. I mean, Daddy had a sense of history . . . of . . . continuation. . . . Why don't you come over here and sit by me?

NICK (*indicating* HONEY, *who is barely with it*). I . . . don't think I . . . should. . . . I. . . .

MARTHA. Suit yourself. A sense of continuation . . . history . . . and he'd always had it in the back of his mind to . . . *groom* someone to take over . . . some time, when he quit. A succession . . . you know what I mean?

NICK. Yes, I do.

MARTHA. Which is natural enough. When you've made something, you want to pass it on, to somebody. So, I was sort of on the lookout, for . . . prospects with the new men. An heir-apparent. (*Laughs.*) It wasn't *Daddy's* idea that I had to necessarily marry the guy. I mean, I wasn't the albatross . . . you didn't have to take me to get the prize, or anything like that. It was something *I* had in the back of *my* mind. And a lot of the new men were married . . . naturally.

NICK. Sure.

MARTHA (*with a strange smile*). Like you, baby.

HONEY (*a mindless echo*). Like you, baby.

MARTHA (*ironically*). But then George came along . . . along come George.

GEORGE (*reentering, with liquor*). And along came George, bearing hooch. What are you doing now, Martha?

MARTHA (*unfazed*). I'm telling a story. Sit down . . . you'll learn something.

GEORGE (*stays standing. Puts the liquor on the portable bar*). All rightie.

HONEY. You've come back!

GEORGE. That's right.

HONEY. Dear! He's come back!

NICK. Yes, I see . . . I see.

MARTHA. Where was I?

HONEY. I'm *so* glad.

NICK. Shhhhh.

HONEY (*imitating him*). Shhhhh.

MARTHA. Oh yeah. And along came George. That's right. WHO was young . . . intelligent . . . and . . . bushy-tailed, and . . . sort of cute . . . if you can imagine it. . . .

GEORGE. . . . and younger than you. . . .

MARTHA. . . . and younger than me. . . .

GEORGE. . . . by six years. . . .

MARTHA. . . . by six years. . . . It doesn't bother me, George. . . . And along he came, bright-eyed, into the History Department. And you know what I did, dumb cluck that I am? You know what I did? I fell for him.

HONEY (*dreamy*). Oh, that's nice.

GEORGE. Yes, she did. You should have seen it. She'd sit outside of my room, on the lawn, at night, and she'd howl and claw at the turf . . . I couldn't work.

MARTHA (*laughs, really amused*). I actually fell for him . . . it . . . that, there.

GEORGE. Martha's a Romantic at heart.

MARTHA. That I am. So, I actually fell for him. And the match seemed . . . practical, too. You know, Daddy was looking for someone to. . . .

GEORGE. Just a minute, Martha. . . .

MARTHA. . . . take over, some time, when he was ready to. . . .

GEORGE (*stony*). Just a minute, Martha.

MARTHA. . . . retire, and so I thought. . . .

GEORGE. STOP IT, MARTHA!

MARTHA (*irritated*). Whadda you want?

GEORGE (*too patiently*). I'd thought you were telling the story of our courtship, Martha . . . I didn't know you were going to start in on the other business.

MARTHA (*so-thereish*). Well, I am!

GEORGE. I wouldn't, if I were you.

MARTHA. Oh . . . you wouldn't? Well, you're not!

GEORGE. Now, you've already sprung a leak about you-know-what. . . .

MARTHA (*a duck*). What? What?

GEORGE. . . . about the apple of our eye . . . the sprout . . . the little bugger . . . (*Spits it out.*) . . . our *son* . . . and if you start in on this other business, I warn you, Martha, it's going to make me angry.

MARTHA (*laughing at him*). Oh, it is, is it?

GEORGE. I warn you.

MARTHA (*incredulous*). You *what?*

GEORGE (*very quietly*). I warn you.

NICK. Do you really think we have to go through . . . ?

MARTHA. I stand warned! (*Pause . . . then, to* HONEY *and* NICK) So, anyway, I married the S.O.B., and I had it all planned out. . . . He was the groom . . . he was going to be groomed. He'd take over some day . . . first, he'd take over the History Department, and then, when Daddy retired, he'd take over the college . . . you know? That's the way it was supposed to be. (*To* GEORGE, *who is at the portable bar with his back to her*) You getting angry, baby? Hunh? (*Now back*) That's the way it was *supposed* to be. Very simple. And Daddy seemed to think it was a pretty good idea, too. For a while. Until he watched for a couple of years! (*To* GEORGE *again*) You getting angrier? (*Now back*) Until he watched for a couple of years and started thinking maybe it wasn't such a good idea after all . . . that maybe Georgie-boy didn't have the stuff . . . that he didn't have it in him!

GEORGE (*still with his back to them all*). Stop it, Martha.

MARTHA (*viciously triumphant*). The hell I will! You see, George didn't have much . . . push . . . he wasn't particularly . . . aggressive. In fact he was sort of a . . (*Spits the word at* GEORGE's *back.*) . . . a FLOP! A great . . . big . . . fat . . . FLOP!

(CRASH! *Immediately after* Flop! GEORGE *breaks a bottle against the portable bar and stands there, still with his back to them all, holding the remains of the bottle by the neck. There is a silence, with*

everyone frozen. Then. . . .)

GEORGE (*almost crying*). I said stop, Martha.

MARTHA (*after considering what course to take*). I hope that was an empty bottle, George. You don't want to waste good liquor . . . not on your salary. (GEORGE *drops the broken bottle on the floor, not moving.*) Not on an Associate Professor's salary. (*To* NICK *and* HONEY) I mean, he'd be . . . no good . . . at trustees' dinners, fund raising. He didn't have any . . . personality, you know what I mean? Which was disappointing to Daddy, as you can imagine. So, here I am, stuck with this flop. . . .

GEORGE (*turning around*). . . . . don't go on, Martha. . . .

MARTHA. . . . this BOG in the History Department. . . .

GEORGE. . . . . don't, Martha, don't. . . .

MARTHA (*her voice rising to match his*). . . . . who's married to the President's daughter, who's expected to *be* somebody, not just some nobody, some bookworm, somebody who's so damn . . . contemplative, he can't make anything out of himself, somebody without the *guts* to make anybody proud of him . . . ALL RIGHT, GEORGE!

GEORGE (*under her, then covering, to drown her*). I said, don't. All right . . . all right: (*Sings.*)
Who's afraid of Virginia Woolf,
Virginia Woolf,
Virginia Woolf,
Who's afraid of Virginia Woolf,
early in the morning.

GEORGE *and* HONEY (*who joins him drunkenly*).
Who's afraid of Virginia Woolf,
Virginia Woolf,
Virginia Woolf . . . (*etc.*)

MARTHA. STOP IT!

(*A brief silence.*)

HONEY (*rising, moving toward the hall*). I'm going to be sick . . . I'm going to be sick . . . I'm going to vomit. (*Exits.*)

NICK (*going after her*). Oh, for God's sake! (*Exits.*)

MARTHA (*going after them, looks back at* GEORGE, *contemptuously*). Jesus! (*Exits.* GEORGE *is alone on stage.*)

CURTAIN

ACT TWO:

WALPURGISNACHT

GEORGE, *by himself: NICK reenters.*

———

NICK (*after a silence*). I . . . guess . . . she's all right. (*No answer*) She . . . really shouldn't drink. (*No answer*) She's . . . frail. (*No answer*) Uh . . . slim-hipped, as you'd have it. (GEORGE *smiles vaguely.*) I'm really very sorry.

GEORGE (*quietly*). Where's my little yum yum? Where's Martha?

NICK. She's making coffee . . . in the kitchen. She . . . gets sick quite easily.

GEORGE (*preoccupied*). Martha? Oh no, Martha hasn't been sick a day in her life, unless you count the time she spends in the rest home. . . .

NICK (*he, too, quietly*). No, no; *my* wife . . . *my* wife gets sick quite easily. Your wife is Martha.

GEORGE (*with some rue*). Oh, yes . . . I know.

NICK (*a statement of fact*). She doesn't really spend any time in a rest home.

GEORGE. Your wife?

NICK. No. Yours.

GEORGE. Oh! Mine. (*Pause*) No, no, she doesn't . . . *I* would; I mean if I were . . . her . . . she . . . *I* would. But I'm not . . . and so I don't. (*Pause*) I'd like to, though. It gets pretty bouncy around here sometimes.

NICK (*coolly*). Yes . . . I'm sure.

GEORGE. Well, you saw an example of it.

NICK. I try not to. . . .

GEORGE. Get involved. Um? Isn't that right?

NICK. Yes . . . that's right.

GEORGE. I'd imagine not.

NICK. I find it . . . embarrassing.

GEORGE (*sarcastic*). Oh, you do, hunh?

NICK. Yes. Really. Quite.

GEORGE (*mimicking him*). Yes. Really. Quite (*Then aloud, but to himself*) IT'S DISGUSTING!

NICK. Now look! I didn't have anything. . . .

GEORGE. DISGUSTING! (*Quietly, but with great intensity*) Do you think I like having that . . . whatever-it-is . . . ridiculing me, tearing me down, in front of . . . (*Waves his hand in a gesture of contemptuous dismissal.*) YOU? Do you think I *care* for it?

NICK (*cold—unfriendly*). Well, no . . . I don't imagine you care for it at all.

GEORGE. Oh, you don't imagine it, hunh?

NICK (*antagonistic*). No . . . I don't. I don't imagine you do!

GEORGE (*withering*). Your sympathy disarms me . . . your . . . your compassion makes me weep! Large, salty, unscientific tears!

NICK (*with great disdain*). I just don't see why you feel you have to subject *other* people to it.

GEORGE. *I?*

NICK. If you and your . . . wife . . . want to go at each other, like a couple of. . . .

GEORGE. *I?* Why *I* want to!

NICK. . . . animals, I don't see why you don't do it when there aren't any. . . .

GEORGE (*laughing through his anger*). Why, you smug, self-righteous little. . . .

NICK (*a genuine threat*). CAN . . . IT . . . MISTER! (*Silence*) Just . . . watch it!

GEORGE. . . . scientist.

NICK. I've never hit an older man.

GEORGE (*considers it*). Oh. (*Pause*) You just hit younger men . . . and children . . . women . . . birds. (*Sees that* NICK *is not amused.*) Well, you're quite right, of course. It isn't the prettiest spectacle . . . seeing a couple of middle-age types hacking away at each other, all red in the face and winded, missing half the time.

NICK. Oh, you two don't miss . . . you two are pretty good. Impressive.

GEORGE. And impressive things impress you, don't they? You're . . . easily impressed . . . sort of a . . . pragmatic idealism.

NICK (*a tight smile*). No, it's that sometimes I can admire things that I don't admire. Now, flagellation isn't my idea of good times, but. . . .

GEORGE. . . . but you can admire a good flagellator . . . a real pro.

NICK. Unh-hunh . . . yeah.

GEORGE. Your wife throws up a lot, eh?

NICK. I didn't say that. . . . I said she gets sick quite easily.

GEORGE. Oh. I thought by sick you meant. . . .

NICK. Well, it's true. . . . She . . . she does throw up a lot. Once she starts . . . there's practically no stopping her. . . . I mean, she'll go right on . . . for hours.

Not all the time, but . . . regularly.

GEORGE. You can tell time by her, hunh?

NICK. Just about.

GEORGE. Drink?

NICK. Sure. (*With no emotion, except the faintest distaste, as* GEORGE *takes his glass to the bar*) I married her because she was pregnant.

GEORGE. (*Pause*) Oh? (*Pause*) But you said you didn't have any children . . . When I asked you, you said. . . .

NICK. She wasn't . . . really. It was a hysterical pregnancy. She blew up, and then she went down.

GEORGE. And while she was up, you married her.

NICK. And then she went down. (*They both laugh, and are a little surprised that they do.*)

GEORGE. Uh . . . Bourbon *is* right.

NICK. Uh . . . yes, Bourbon.

GEORGE (*at the bar, still*). When I was sixteen and going to prep school, during the Punic Wars, a bunch of us used to go into New York on the first day of vacations, before we fanned out to our homes, and in the evening this bunch of us used to go to this gin mill owned by the gangster-father of one of us—for this was during the Great Experiment, or Prohibition, as it is more frequently called, and it was a bad time for the liquor lobby, but a fine time for the crooks and the cops—and we would go to this gin mill, and we would drink with the grown-ups and listen to the jazz. And one time, in the bunch of us, there was this boy who was fifteen, and he had killed his mother with a shotgun some years before—accidentally, completely accidentally, without even an unconscious motivation, I have no doubt, no doubt at all—and this one evening this boy went with us, and we ordered our drinks, and when it came his turn he said, I'll have bergin . . . give me some bergin, please . . . bergin and water. Well, we all laughed . . . he was blond and he had the face of a cherub, and we all laughed, and his cheeks went red and the color rose in his neck, and the assistant crook who had taken our order told people at the next table what the boy had said, and then they laughed, and then more people were told and the laughter grew, and more laughter, and no one

was laughing more than us, and none of us more than the boy who had shot his mother. And soon, everyone in the gin mill knew what the laughter was about, and everyone started ordering bergin, and laughing when they ordered it. And soon, of course, the laughter became less general, but it did not subside, entirely, for a very long time, for always at this table or that someone would order bergin and a new area of laughter would rise. We drank free that night, and we were bought champagne by the management, by the gangster-father of one of us. And, of course, we suffered the next day, each of us, alone, on his train, away from New York, each of us with a grown-up's hangover . . . but it was the grandest day of my . . . youth. (*Hands* NICK *a drink on the word.*)

NICK (*very quietly*). Thank you. What . . . what happened to the boy . . . the boy who had shot his mother?

GEORGE. I won't tell you.

NICK. All right.

GEORGE. The following summer, on a country road, with his learner's permit in his pocket and his father on the front seat to his right, he swerved the car, to avoid a porcupine, and drove straight into a large tree.

NICK (*faintly pleading*). No.

GEORGE. He was not killed, of course. And in the hospital, when he was conscious and out of danger, and when they told him that his father *was* dead, he began to laugh, I have been told, and his laughter grew and he would not stop, and it was not until after they jammed a needle in his arm, not until after that, until his consciousness slipped away from him, that his laughter subsided . . . stopped. And when he was recovered from his injuries enough so that he could be moved without damage should he struggle, he was put in an asylum. That was thirty years ago.

NICK. Is he . . . still there?

GEORGE. Oh, yes. And I'm told that for these thirty years he has . . . not . . . uttered . . . one . . . sound. (*A rather long silence: five seconds, please.*) MARTHA! (*Pause*) MARTHA!

NICK. I told you . . . she's making coffee.

GEORGE. For your hysterical wife, who goes up and down.

NICK. Went. Up and down.

GEORGE. Went. No more?

NICK. No more. Nothing.

GEORGE (*after a sympathetic pause*). The saddest thing about men. . . . Well, no, one of the saddest things about men is the way they age . . . some of them. Do you know what it is with insane people? Do you? . . . the quiet ones?

NICK. No.

GEORGE. They don't change . . . they don't grow old.

NICK. They must.

GEORGE. Well, eventually, probably, yes. But they don't . . . in the usual sense. They maintain a . . . a firm-skinned serenity . . . the . . . the under-use of everything leaves them . . . quite whole.

NICK Are you recommending it?

GEORGE No. Some things are sad, though. (*Imitates a pep-talker.*) But ya jest gotta buck up an' face 'em, 'at's all. Buck up! (*Pause*) Martha doesn't have hysterical pregnancies.

NICK. My wife had *one*.

GEORGE. Yes. Martha doesn't have pregnancies at all.

NICK. Well, no . . . I don't imagine so . . . now. Do you have any other kids? Do you have any daughters, or anything?

GEORGE (*as if it's a great joke*). Do we have any *what*?

NICK. Do you have any . . . I mean, do you have only one . . . kid . . . uh . . . your son?

GEORGE (*with a private knowledge*). Oh no . . . just one . . . one boy . . . our son.

NICK. Well . . . (*Shrugs.*) . . . that's nice.

GEORGE. Oh ho, ho. Yes, well, he's a . . . comfort, a bean bag.

NICK. A what?

GEORGE. A bean bag. Bean bag. You wouldn't understand. (*Over-distinct*) Bean . . . bag.

NICK. I *heard* you . . . I didn't say I was deaf . . . I said I didn't understand.

GEORGE. You didn't say that at all.

NICK. I meant I was *implying* I didn't understand. (*Under his breath*) For Christ's sake!

GEORGE. You're getting testy.

NICK (*testy*). I'm sorry.

GEORGE. All I said was, our son . . . the apple of our three eyes, Martha being a Cyclops . . . our son is a bean bag, and you get testy.

NICK. I'm sorry! It's late, I'm tired, I've been drinking since nine o'clock, my wife is vomiting, there's been a lot of screaming going on around here. . . .

GEORGE. And so you're testy. Naturally. Don't . . . worry about it. Anybody who comes here ends up getting . . . testy. It's expected . . . don't be upset.

NICK (*testy*) I'm not upset!

GEORGE. You're testy.

NICK. Yes.

GEORGE. I'd like to set you straight about something . . . while the little ladies are out of the room . . . I'd like to set you straight about what Martha said.

NICK. I don't . . . make judgments, so there's no need, really, unless you. . . .

GEORGE. Well, I want to. I know you don't like to become involved . . . I know you like to . . . preserve your scientific detachment in the face of—for lack of a better word—Life . . . and all . . . but still, I want to tell you.

NICK (*a tight, formal smile*). I'm a . . . guest. You go right ahead.

GEORGE (*mocking appreciation*). Oh . . . well, thanks. Now! That makes me feel all warm and runny inside.

NICK. Well, if you're going to . . .

MARTHA'S VOICE. HEY!

NICK. . . . if you're going to start that kind of stuff again. . . .

GEORGE. Hark! Forest sounds.

NICK. Hm?

GEORGE. Animal noises.

MARTHA (*sticking her head in*). Hey!

NICK. Oh!

GEORGE. Well, here's nursie.

MARTHA (*to* NICK). We're sitting up . . . we're having coffee, and we'll be back in.

NICK (*not rising*). Oh . . . is there anything I should do?

MARTHA. Nayh. You just stay here and listen to George's side of things. Bore yourself to death.

GEORGE. Monstre!

MARTHA. Cochon!

GEORGE. Bête!

MARTHA. Canaille!

GEORGE. Putain!

MARTHA (*with a gesture of contemptuous dismissal*). Yaaahhh! You two types amuse yourselves . . . we'll be in. (*As she goes*) You clean up the mess you made, George?

GEORGE (MARTHA *goes.* GEORGE *speaks to the empty hallway*). No, Martha, I did not clean up the mess I made. I've been trying for years to clean up the mess I made.

NICK. Have you?

GEORGE. Hm?

NICK. *Have* you been trying for years?

GEORGE (*after a long pause . . . looking at him*). Accommodation, malleability, adjustment . . . those do seem to be in the order of things, don't they?

NICK. Don't try to put me in the same class with you!

GEORGE (*pause*). Oh. (*Pause*) No, of course not. Things are simpler with you . . . you marry a woman because she's all blown up . . . while I, in my clumsy, old-fashioned way. . . .

NICK. There was more to it than that!

GEORGE. Sure! I'll bet she has money, too!

NICK (*looks hurt. Then, determined, after a pause*). Yes.

GEORGE. Yes? (*Joyfully*) YES! You mean I was right? I hit it?

NICK. Well, you see. . . .

GEORGE. My God, what archery! First try, too. How about that!

NICK. You see. . . .

GEORGE. There were other things.

NICK. Yes.

GEORGE. To compensate.

NICK. Yes.

GEORGE. There always are. (*Sees that* NICK *is reacting badly*.) No, I'm sure there are. I didn't mean to be . . . flip. There are *always* compensating factors . . . as in the case of Martha and myself. . . . Now, on the surface of it. . . .

NICK. We sort of grew up together, you know. . . .

GEORGE. . . . it looks to be a kind of knock-about, drag-out affair, on the *surface* of it. . . .

NICK. We knew each other from, oh God, I don't know, when we were *six,* or something. . . .

GEORGE. . . . but somewhere back there, at the beginning of it, right when I first came to New Carthage, back then. . . .

NICK (*with some irritation*). I'm *sorry.*

GEORGE. Hm? Oh. No, no . . . *I'm* sorry.

NICK. No . . . it's . . . it's all right.

GEORGE. No . . . you go ahead.

NICK. No . . . please.

GEORGE. I insist. . . . You're a guest. You go first.

NICK. Well, it seems a little silly . . . now.

GEORGE. Nonsense! (*Pause*) But if you were six, she must have been four, or something.

NICK. Maybe I was eight . . . she was six. We . . . we used to play . . . doctor.

GEORGE. That's a good healthy heterosexual beginning.

NICK (*laughing*). Yup.

GEORGE. The scientist even then, eh?

NICK (*laughs*). Yeah. And it was . . . always taken for granted . . . you know . . . by our families, and by us, too, I guess. And . . . so, we did.

GEORGE. (*Pause*) Did what?

NICK. We got married.

GEORGE. When you were eight?

NICK. No. No, of course not. Much later.

GEORGE. I wondered.

NICK. I wouldn't say there was any . . . particular *passion* between us, even at the beginning . . . of our marriage, I mean.

GEORGE. Well, certainly no surprise, no earth-shaking discoveries, after doctor, and all.

NICK (*uncertainly*). No. . . .

GEORGE. Everything's all pretty much the same, anyway . . . in *spite* of what they say about Chinese women.

NICK. What is that?

GEORGE. Let me freshen you up. (*Takes* NICK'S *glass.*)

NICK. Oh, thanks. After a while you don't get any drunker, do you?

GEORGE. Well, you *do* . . . but it's different . . . everything slows down. . . . you get sodden. . . . unless you can upchuck . . . like your wife . . . then you can sort of start all over again.

NICK. Everybody drinks a lot here in the East. (*Thinks about it.*) Everybody drinks a lot in the Middle West, too.

GEORGE. We drink a great deal in this country, and I suspect we'll be drinking a great deal more, too . . . if we survive. We should be Arabs or Italians . . . the Arabs don't drink, and the Italians don't get drunk much, except on religious holidays. We should live on Crete, or something.

NICK (*sarcastically . . . as if killing a joke*). And that, of course, would make us cretins.

GEORGE (*mild surprise*). So it would. (*Hands* NICK *his drink.*) Tell me about your wife's money.

NICK (*suddenly suspicious*). Why?

GEORGE. Well . . . don't, then.

NICK. What do you want to know about my wife's money for? (*Ugly*) Hunh?

GEORGE. Well, I thought it would be nice.

NICK. No you didn't.

GEORGE (*still deceptively bland*). All right. . . . I want to know about your wife's money because . . . well, because I'm fascinated by the methodology . . . by the pragmatic accommodation by which you wave-of-the-future boys are going to take over.

NICK. You're starting in again.

GEORGE. Am I? No I'm not. Look . . . Martha has money too. I mean, her father's been robbing this place blind for years, and. . . .

NICK. No, he hasn't. He has not.

GEORGE. He hasn't?

NICK. No.

GEORGE (*shrugs*). Very well. . . . Martha's father has *not* been robbing this place blind for years, and Martha does not have any money. O.K.?

NICK. We were talking about *my* wife's money . . . not yours.

GEORGE. O.K. . . . talk.

NICK. No. (*Pause*) My father-in-law . . . was a man of the Lord, and he was very rich.

GEORGE. What faith?

NICK. He . . . my father-in-law . . . was called by God when he was six, or something, and he started preaching, and he baptized people, and he saved them, and he traveled around a lot, and he became pretty famous . . . not like some of them, but he became pretty famous . . . and when he died he had a lot of money.

GEORGE. God's money.

NICK. No . . . his own.

GEORGE. What happened to God's money?

NICK. He spent God's money . . . and he saved his own. He built hospitals, and he sent off Mercy ships, and he brought the outhouses indoors, and he brought the people outdoors, into the sun, and he built three churches, or whatever they were, and two of them burned down . . .

and he ended up pretty rich.

GEORGE (*after considering it*). Well, I think that's very nice.

NICK. Yes. (*Pause. Giggles a little.*) And so, my wife's got some money.

GEORGE. But not God's money.

NICK. No. Her own.

GEORGE. Well, I think that's very nice. (NICK *giggles a little.*) *Martha's* got money because Martha's father's second wife . . . not Martha's mother, but after Martha's mother died . . . was a very old lady with warts who was very rich.

NICK. She was a witch.

GEORGE. She was a *good* witch, and she married the white mouse . . . (NICK *begins to giggle.*) . . . with the tiny red eyes . . . and he must have nibbled her warts, or something like that, because she went up in a puff of smoke almost immediately. POUF!

NICK. POUF!

GEORGE. POUF! And all that was left, aside from some wart medicine, was a big fat will. . . . A peach pie, with some for the township of New Carthage, some for the college, some for Martha's daddy, and just this much for Martha.

NICK (*quite beside himself*). Maybe . . . maybe my father-in-law and the witch with the warts should have gotten together, because he was a mouse, too.

GEORGE (*urging* NICK *on*). He was?

NICK (*breaking down*). Sure . . . he was a church mouse! (*They both laugh a great deal, but it is sad laughter . . . eventually they subside, fall silent.*) Your wife never mentioned a stepmother.

GEORGE (*considers it*). Well . . . maybe it isn't true.

NICK (*narrowing his eyes*). And maybe it is.

GEORGE. Might be . . . might not. Well, I think your story's a lot nicer . . . about your pumped-up little wife, and your father-in-law who was a priest. . . .

NICK. He was not a priest . . . he was a man of God.

GEORGE. Yes.

NICK. And my wife wasn't pumped up . . . she blew up.

GEORGE. Yes, yes.

NICK (*giggling*). Get things straight.

GEORGE. I'm sorry . . . I will. I'm sorry.

NICK. O.K.

GEORGE. You realize, of course, that I've been drawing you out on this stuff, not because I'm interested in your terrible lifehood, but only because you represent a direct and pertinent threat to my lifehood, and I want to get the goods on you.

NICK (*still amused*). Sure . . . sure.

GEORGE. I mean . . . I've warned you . . . you stand warned.

NICK. I stand warned. (*Laughs.*) It's you sneaky types worry me the most, you know. You ineffectual sons of bitches . . . you're the worst.

GEORGE. Yes . . . we are. Sneaky. An elbow in your steely-blue eye . . . a knee in your solid gold groin . . . we're the worst.

NICK. Yup.

GEORGE. Well, I'm glad you don't believe me. . . . I know you've got history on your side, and all. . . .

NICK. Unh-unh. *You've* got history on *your* side. . . . I've got biology on mine. History, biology.

GEORGE. I know the difference.

NICK. You don't act it.

GEORGE. No? I thought we'd decided that you'd take over the History Department first, before you took over the whole works. You know . . . a step at a time.

NICK (*stretching . . . luxuriating . . . playing the game*). Nyaah . . . what I thought I'd do is . . . I'd sort of insinuate myself generally, play around for a while, find all the weak spots, shore 'em up, but with my own name plate on 'em . . . become sort of a fact, and then turn into a . . . a what . . . ?

GEORGE. An inevitability.

NICK. Exactly. . . . An inevitability. You know. . . . Take over a few courses from the older men, start some special groups for myself . . . plow a few pertinent wives. . . .

GEORGE. Now that's it! You can take over all the courses you want to, and get as much of the young elite together in the gymnasium as you like, but until you start plowing pertinent wives, you really aren't working. The way to a man's heart is through his wife's belly, and don't you forget it.

NICK (*playing along*). Yeah. . . . I know.

GEORGE. And the women around here are no better than puntas—you know, South American ladies of the night. You know what they do in South America

. . . in Rio? The puntas? Do you know? They hiss . . . like geese. . . . They stand around in the street and they hiss at you . . . like a bunch of geese.

NICK. Gangle.

GEORGE. Hm?

NICK. Gangle . . . gangle of geese . . . not bunch . . . gangle.

GEORGE. Well, if you're going to get all cute about it, all ornithological, it's gaggle . . . not gangle, *gaggle*.

NICK. Gaggle? Not gangle?

GEORGE. Yes, gaggle.

NICK (*crestfallen*). Oh.

GEORGE. Oh. Yes. . . . Well they stand around on the street and they hiss at you, like a bunch of geese. All the faculty wives, downtown in New Carthage, in front of the A&P, hissing away like a bunch of geese. That's the way to power —plow 'em all!

NICK (*still playing along*). I'll bet you're right.

GEORGE. Well, I am.

NICK. And I'll bet your wife's the biggest goose in the gangle, isn't she . . . ? Her father president, and all.

GEORGE. You bet your historical inevitability she is!

NICK. Yessirree. (*Rubs his hands together.*) Well now, I'd just better get her off in a corner and mount her like a goddam dog, eh?

GEORGE. Why, you'd certainly better.

NICK (*looks at* GEORGE *a minute, his expression a little sick*). You know, I almost think you're serious.

GEORGE (*toasting him*). No, baby . . . *you* almost think you're serious, and it scares the hell out of you.

NICK (*exploding in disbelief*). ME!

GEORGE (*quietly*). Yes . . . you.

NICK. You're kidding!

GEORGE (*like a father*). I wish I were. . . . I'll give you some good advice if you want me to. . . .

NICK. Good advice! From you? Oh boy! (*Starts to laugh.*)

GEORGE. You haven't learned yet. . . . Take it whenever you can get it. . . . Listen to me, now.

NICK. Come off it!

GEORGE. I'm giving you good advice, now.

NICK. Good God . . . !

GEORGE. There's quicksand here, and you'll be dragged down, just as. . . .

NICK. Oh boy . . . !

GEORGE. . . . before you know it . . . sucked down. . . . (NICK *laughs derisively*.) You disgust me on principle, and you're a smug son of a bitch personally, but I'm trying to give you a survival kit. DO YOU HEAR ME?

NICK (*still laughing*). I hear you. You come in loud.

GEORGE. ALL RIGHT!

NICK. Hey, Honey.

GEORGE (*silence. Then quietly*). All right . . . O.K. You want to play it by ear, right? Everything's going to work out anyway, because the time-table's history, right?

NICK. Right . . . right. You just tend to your knitting, grandma. . . . I'll be O.K.

GEORGE (*after a silence*). I've tried to . . . tried to reach you . . . to. . . .

NICK (*contemptuously*). . . . make contact?

GEORGE. Yes.

NICK (*still*). . . . communicate?

GEORGE. Yes. Exactly.

NICK. Aw . . . that *is* touching . . . is . . . downright moving . . . that's what it is. (*With sudden vehemence*) UP YOURS!

GEORGE (*brief pause*). Hm?

NICK (*threatening*). You heard me!

GEORGE (*at NICK, not to him*). You take the trouble to construct a civilization . . . to . . . to build a society, based on the principles of . . . of principle . . . you endeavor to make communicable sense out of natural order, morality out of the unnatural disorder of man's mind . . . you make government and art, and realize that they are, must be, both the same . . . you bring things to the saddest of all points . . . to the point where there *is* something to lose . . . then all at once, through all the music, through all the sensible sounds of men building, attempting, comes the *Dies Irae*. And what is it? What does the trumpet sound? Up yours. I suppose there's justice to it, after all the years. . . . Up yours.

NICK (*brief pause . . . then applauding*). Ha, ha! Bravo! Ha, ha! (*Laughs on.*)

(*And* MARTHA *reenters, leading* HONEY, *who is wan but smiling bravely.*)

HONEY (*grandly*). Thank you . . . thank you.

MARTHA. Here we are, a little shaky, but on our feet.

GEORGE. Goodie.

NICK. What? Oh . . . OH! Hi, Honey . . . you better?

HONEY. A little bit, dear. . . . I'd better sit down, though.

NICK. Sure . . . c'mon . . . you sit by me.

HONEY. Thank you, dear.

GEORGE (*beneath his breath*). Touching . . . touching.

MARTHA (*to GEORGE*). Well? Aren't you going to apologize?

GEORGE (*squinting*). For what, Martha?

MARTHA. For making the little lady throw up.

GEORGE. I did not make her throw up.

MARTHA. You most certainly did!

GEORGE. I did not!

HONEY (*papal gesture*). No, now . . . no.

MARTHA (*to GEORGE*). Well, who do you think did . . . Sexy over there? You think he made his *own* little wife sick?

GEORGE (*helpfully*). Well, you make *me* sick.

MARTHA. THAT'S DIFFERENT!

HONEY. No, now. I . . . I throw up . . . I mean, I get sick . . . occasionally, all by myself . . . without any reason.

GEORGE. Is that a fact?

NICK. You're . . . you're delicate, Honey.

HONEY (*proudly*). I've always done it.

GEORGE. Like Big Ben.

NICK (*a warning*). Watch it!

HONEY. And the doctors say there's nothing wrong with me . . . organically. You know?

NICK. Of course there isn't.

HONEY. Why, just before we got married, I developed . . . appendicitis . . . or everybody *thought* it was appendicitis . . . but it turned out to be . . . it was a . . . (*Laughs briefly.*) . . . false alarm.

(GEORGE *and* NICK *exchange glances.*)

MARTHA (*to GEORGE*). Get me a drink. (GEORGE *moves to the bar.*) George makes everybody sick. . . . When our son was just a little boy, he used to. . . .

GEORGE. Don't, Martha. . . .

MARTHA. . . . he used to throw up all the time, because of George. . . .

GEORGE. I said, don't!

MARTHA. It got so bad that whenever

George came into the room he'd start right in retching, and. . . .

GEORGE. . . . the real reason (*Spits out the words.*) our son . . . used to throw up all the time, wife and lover, was nothing more complicated than that he couldn't stand you fiddling at him all the time, breaking into his bedroom with your kimono flying, fiddling at him all the time, with your liquor breath on him, and your hands all over his. . . .

MARTHA. YEAH? And I suppose that's why he ran away from home twice in one month, too. (*Now to the guests*) Twice in one month! Six times in one year!

GEORGE (*also to the guests*). Our son ran away from home all the time because Martha here used to corner him.

MARTHA (*braying*). I NEVER CORNERED THE SON OF A BITCH IN MY LIFE!

GEORGE (*handing* MARTHA *her drink*). He used to run up to me when I'd get home, and he'd say, "Mama's always coming at me." That's what he'd say.

MARTHA. Liar!

GEORGE (*shrugging*). Well, that's the way it was . . . you were always coming at him. I thought it was very embarrassing.

NICK. If you thought it was so embarrassing, what are you talking about it for?

HONEY (*admonishing*). Dear . . . !

MARTHA. Yeah! (*To* NICK) Thanks, sweetheart.

GEORGE (*to them all*). I didn't want to talk about him at all . . . I would have been perfectly happy not to discuss the whole subject. . . . I never want to talk about it.

MARTHA. Yes you do.

GEORGE. When we're alone, maybe.

MARTHA. We're alone!

GEORGE. Uh . . . no, love . . . we've got guests.

MARTHA (*with a covetous look at* NICK). We sure have.

HONEY. Could I have a little brandy? I think I'd like a little brandy.

NICK. Do you think you should?

HONEY. Oh yes . . . yes, dear.

GEORGE (*moving to the bar again*). Sure! Fill 'er up!

NICK. Honey, I don't think you. . . .

HONEY (*petulance creeping in*). It will steady me, *dear*. I feel a little unsteady.

GEORGE. Hell, you can't walk steady on half a bottle . . . got to do it right.

HONEY. Yes. (*To* MARTHA) I love brandy . . . I really do.

MARTHA (*somewhat abstracted*). Good for you.

NICK (*giving up*). Well, if you think it's a good idea. . . .

HONEY (*really testy*). I know what's best for me, dear.

NICK (*not even pleasant*). Yes . . . I'm sure you do.

HONEY (GEORGE *hands her a brandy*). Oh, goodie! Thank you. (*To* NICK) Of course I do, dear.

GEORGE (*pensively*). I used to drink brandy.

MARTHA (*privately*). You used to drink bergin, too.

GEORGE (*sharp*). Shut up, Martha!

MARTHA (*her hand over her mouth in a little-girl gesture*). Oooooops.

NICK (*something having clicked, vaguely*). Hm?

GEORGE (*burying it*). Nothing . . . nothing.

MARTHA (*she, too*). You two men have it out while we were gone? George tell you his side of things? He bring you to tears, hunh?

NICK. Well . . . no. . . .

GEORGE. No, what we did, actually, was . . . we sort of danced around.

MARTHA. Oh, yeah? Cute!

HONEY. Oh, I love dancing.

NICK. He didn't mean that, Honey.

HONEY. Well, I didn't think he did! Two grown men dancing . . . heavens!

MARTHA. You mean he didn't start in on how he would have amounted to something if it hadn't been for Daddy? How his high moral sense wouldn't even let him *try* to better himself? No?

NICK (*qualified*). No. . . .

MARTHA. And he didn't run on about how he tried to publish a goddam book, and Daddy wouldn't let him.

NICK. A book? No.

GEORGE. Please, Martha. . . .

NICK (*egging her on*). A book? What book?

GEORGE (*pleading*). Please. Just a book.

MARTHA (*mock incredulity*). Just a book!

GEORGE. *Please,* Martha!

MARTHA (*almost disappointed*). Well, I guess you didn't get the whole sad story.

What's the matter with you, George?
You given up?

GEORGE (*calm . . . serious*). No . . . no.
It's just I've got to figure out some new
way to fight you, Martha. Guerilla tac-
tics, maybe . . . internal subversion . . .
I don't know. Something.

MARTHA. Well, you figure it out, and
let me know when you do.

GEORGE (*cheery*). All right, love.

HONEY. Why don't we dance? I'd love
some dancing.

NICK. Honey. . . .

HONEY. I would! I'd love some dancing.

NICK. Honey. . . .

HONEY. I *want* some! I want some
dancing!

GEORGE. All right . . . ! For heaven's
sake . . . we'll have some dancing.

HONEY (*all sweetness again; to* MAR-
THA). Oh, I'm so glad . . . I just love
dancing. Don't you?

MARTHA (*with a glance at* NICK). Yeah
. . . yeah, that's not a bad idea.

NICK (*genuinely nervous*). Gee.

GEORGE. Gee.

HONEY. I dance like the wind.

MARTHA (*without comment*). Yeah?

GEORGE (*picking a record*). Martha had
her daguerrotype in the paper once . . .
oh, 'bout twenty-five years ago. . . .
Seems she took second prize in one o'
them seven-day dancin' contest things
. . . biceps all bulging, holding up her
partner.

MARTHA. Will you put a record on and
shut up?

GEORGE. Certainly, love. (*To all*) How
are we going to work this? Mixed dou-
bles?

MARTHA. Well, you certainly don't think
I'm going to dance with *you,* do you?

GEORGE (*considers it*). Noooooo . . . not
with him around . . . that's for sure. And
not with twinkle-toes here, either.

HONEY. I'll dance with anyone. . . . I'll
dance by myself.

NICK. Honey. . . .

HONEY. I dance like the wind.

GEORGE. All right, kiddies . . . choose
up and hit the sack.

(*Music starts. . . . Second movement,
Beethoven's 7th Symphony*)

HONEY (*up, dancing by herself*). De,
de de *da* da, da-da de, da *da*-da de da
. . . wonderful . . . !

NICK. Honey. . . .

MARTHA. All right, George . . . cut that
out!

HONEY. Dum, de de da da, da-da de,
dum de *da* da da. . . . Wheeeee . . . !

MARTHA. Cut it out, George!

GEORGE (*pretending not to hear*). What,
Martha? What?

NICK. Honey. . . .

MARTHA (*as* GEORGE *turns up the volume*). CUT IT OUT, GEORGE!

GEORGE. WHAT?

MARTHA (*gets up, moves quickly,
threateningly, to* GEORGE). All right, you
son of a bitch. . . .

GEORGE (*record off, at once. Quietly*).
What did you say, love?

MARTHA. You son of a. . . .

HONEY (*in an arrested posture*). You
stopped! Why did you stop?

NICK. Honey. . . .

HONEY (*to* NICK, *snapping*). Stop that!

GEORGE. I thought it was fitting, Martha.

MARTHA. Oh you did, hunh?

HONEY. You're always *at* me when I'm
having a good time.

NICK (*trying to remain civil*). I'm sorry,
Honey.

HONEY. Just . . . leave me alone!

GEORGE. Well, why don't *you* choose,
Martha? (*Moves away from the phonograph . . . leaves it to* MARTHA.) Martha's
going to run things . . . the little lady's
going to lead the band.

HONEY. I like to dance and you don't
want me to.

NICK. *I* like you to dance.

HONEY. Just . . . leave me alone. (*She
sits . . . takes a drink.*)

GEORGE. Martha's going to put on some
rhythm she understands . . . Sacre du
Printemps, maybe. (*Moves . . . sits by*
HONEY.) Hi, sexy.

HONEY (*a little giggle-scream*).
Oooooohhhhh!

GEORGE (*laughs mockingly*). Ha, ha,
ha, ha, ha. Choose it, Martha . . . do
your stuff!

MARTHA (*concentrating on the machine*). You're damn right!

GEORGE (*to* HONEY). You want to dance
with me, angel-tits?

NICK. What did you call my wife?

GEORGE (*derisively*). Oh boy!

HONEY (*petulantly*). No! If I can't do
my interpretive dance, I don't want to
dance with anyone. I'll just sit here and.

. . . (*Shrugs . . . drinks.*)

MARTHA (*record on . . . a jazzy slow pop tune*). O.K. stuff, let's go. (*Grabs* NICK.)

NICK. Hm? Oh . . . hi.

MARTHA. Hi. (*They dance, close together, slowly.*)

HONEY (*pouting*). We'll just sit here and watch.

GEORGE. That's *right!*

MARTHA (*to* NICK). Hey, you *are* strong, aren't you?

NICK. Unh-hunh.

MARTHA. I like that.

NICK. Unh-hunh.

HONEY. They're dancing like they've danced before.

GEORGE. It's a familiar dance . . . they both know it. . . .

MARTHA. Don't be shy.

NICK. I'm . . . not. . . .

GEORGE (*to* HONEY). It's a very old ritual, monkey-nipples . . . old as they come.

HONEY. I . . . I don't know what you mean.

NICK *and* MARTHA *move apart now, and dance on either side of where* GEORGE *and* HONEY *are sitting; they face each other, and while their feet move but little, their bodies undulate congruently. . . . It is as if they were pressed together.*)

MARTHA. I like the way you move.

NICK. I like the way you move, too.

GEORGE (*to* HONEY). They like the way they move.

HONEY (*not entirely with it*). That's nice.

MARTHA (*to* NICK). I'm surprised George didn't give you his side of things.

GEORGE (*to* HONEY). Aren't they cute?

NICK. Well, he didn't.

MARTHA. That surprises me. (*Perhaps* MARTHA's *statements are more or less in time to the music.*)

NICK. Does it?

MARTHA. Yeah . . . he usually does . . . when he gets the chance.

NICK. Well, what do you know.

MARTHA. It's really a very sad story.

GEORGE. You have ugly talents, Martha.

NICK. Is it?

MARTHA. It would make you weep.

GEORGE. Hideous gifts.

NICK. Is that so?

GEORGE. Don't encourage her.

MARTHA. Encourage me.

NICK. Go on.

(*They may undulate toward each other and then move back.*)

GEORGE. I warn you . . . don't encourage her.

MARTHA. He warns you . . . don't encourage me.

NICK. I heard him . . . tell me more.

MARTHA (*consciously making rhymed speech*).

Well, Georgie-boy had lots of big ambitions

In spite of something funny in his past. . . .

GEORGE (*quietly warning*). Martha. . . .

MARTHA.

Which Georgie-boy here turned into a novel. . . .

His first attempt and also his last. . . .

Hey! I rhymed! I rhymed!

GEORGE. I warn you, Martha.

NICK. Yeah . . . you rhymed. Go on, go on.

MARTHA. But Daddy took a look at Georgie's novel. . . .

GEORGE. You're looking for a punch in the mouth. . . . You know that, Martha.

MARTHA. Do tell . . . and he was very shocked by what he read.

NICK. He was?

MARTHA. Yes . . . he was. . . . A novel all about a naughty boychild. . . .

GEORGE (*rising*). I will not tolerate this!

NICK (*offhand, to* GEORGE). Oh, can it.

MARTHA. . . . ha, ha!

naughty boychild

who . . . uh . . . who killed his mother and his father dead.

GEORGE. STOP IT, MARTHA!

MARTHA. And Daddy said . . . Look here, I will not let you publish such a thing. . . .

GEORGE (*rushes to phonograph . . . rips the record off*). That's it! The dancing's over. That's it. Go on now!

NICK. What do you think you're doing, hunh?

HONEY (*happily*). Violence! Violence!

MARTHA (*loud: a pronouncement*). And Daddy said . . . Look here, kid, you don't think for a second I'm going to let you publish this crap, do you? Not on your life, baby . . . not while you're teaching here. . . . You publish that goddam book and you're out . . . on your ass!

GEORGE. DESIST! DESIST!

MARTHA. Ha, ha, ha, HA!

NICK (*laughing*). De . . . sist!

HONEY. Oh, violence . . . violence!

MARTHA. Why, the idea! A teacher at a respected, conservative institution like this, in a town like New Carthage, publishing a book like that? If you respect your position here, young man, young . . . whippersnapper, you'll just withdraw that manuscript. . . .

GEORGE. I will not be made mock of!

NICK. He will not be made mock of, for Christ's sake. (*Laughs.*)

(HONEY *joins in the laughter, not knowing exactly why.*)

GEORGE. I will not! (*All three are laughing at him. Infuriated*) THE GAME IS OVER!

MARTHA (*pushing on*). Imagine such a thing! A book about a boy who murders his mother and kills his father, and pretends it's all an accident!

HONEY (*beside herself with glee*). An accident!

NICK (*remembering something related*). Hey . . . wait a minute. . . .

MARTHA (*her own voice now*). And you want to know the clincher? You want to know what big brave Georgie said to Daddy?

GEORGE. NO! NO! NO! NO!

NICK. Wait a minute now. . . .

MARTHA. Georgie said . . . but Daddy . . . I mean . . . ha, ha, ha, ha . . . but *Sir* it isn't a *novel* at all. . . . (*Other voice*) Not a novel? (*Mimicking* GEORGE's *voice*) No, sir . . . it isn't a novel at all. . . .

GEORGE (*advancing on her*). You will not say this!

NICK (*sensing the danger*). Hey.

MARTHA. The hell I won't. Keep away from me, you bastard! (*Backs off a little . . . uses* GEORGE's *voice again.*) No, sir, this isn't a novel at all . . . this is the truth . . . this really happened. . . . TO ME!

GEORGE (*on her*). I'LL KILL YOU! (*Grabs her by the throat. They struggle.*)

NICK. HEY! (*Comes between them.*)

HONEY (*wildly*). VIOLENCE! VIOLENCE!

(GEORGE, MARTHA, *and* NICK *struggle . . . yells, etc.*)

MARTHA. IT HAPPENED! TO ME! TO ME!

GEORGE. YOU SATANIC BITCH!

NICK. STOP THAT! STOP THAT!

HONEY. VIOLENCE! VIOLENCE!

(*The other three struggle.* GEORGE's *hands are on* MARTHA's *throat.* NICK *grabs him, tears him from* MARTHA, *throws him on the floor.* GEORGE, *on the floor;* NICK *over him;* MARTHA *to one side, her hand on her throat.*)

NICK. That's enough now!

HONEY (*disappointment in her voice*). Oh . . . oh . . . oh. . . .

GEORGE *drags himself into a chair. He is hurt, but it is more a profound humiliation than a physical injury.*)

GEORGE (*they watch him . . . a pause. . . .*) All right . . . all right . . . very quiet now . . . we will all be . . . very quiet.

MARTHA (*softly, with a slow shaking of her head*). Murderer. Mur . . . der . . . er.

NICK (*softly to* MARTHA). O.K. now . . . that's enough.

(*A brief silence. They all move around a little, self-consciously, like wrestlers flexing after a fall.*)

GEORGE (*composure seemingly recovered, but there is a great nervous intensity*). Well! That's one game. What shall we do now, hunh? (MARTHA *and* NICK *laugh nervously.*) Oh come on . . . let's think of something else. We've played Humiliate the Host . . . we've gone through that one . . . what shall we do now?

NICK. Aw . . . look. . . .

GEORGE. AW LOOK! (*Whines it.*) Awww . . . looooook. (*Alert*) I mean, come on! We must know other games, college-type types like us . . . that can't be the . . . limit of our vocabulary, can it?

NICK. I think maybe. . . .

GEORGE. Let's see now . . . what else can we do? There are other games. How about . . . how about . . . Hump the Hostess? HUNH?? How about that? How about Hump the Hostess? (*To* NICK) You wanna play that one? You wanna play Hump the Hostess? HUNH? HUNH?

NICK (*a little frightened*). Calm down, now.

(MARTHA *giggles quietly.*)

GEORGE. Or is that for later . . . mount her like a goddamn dog?

HONEY (*wildly toasting everybody*). Hump the Hostess!

NICK (*to* HONEY . . . *sharply*). Just shut up . . . will you?

(HONEY *does, her glass in mid-air.*)

GEORGE. You don't wanna play that

now, hunh? You wanna save that game till later? Well, what'll we play now? We gotta play a game.

MARTHA (*quietly*). Portrait of a man drowning.

GEORGE (*affirmatively, but to none of them*). I am not drowning.

HONEY (*to* NICK, *tearfully indignant*). You told me to shut up!

NICK (*impatiently*). I'm sorry.

HONEY (*between her teeth*). No you're not.

NICK (*to* HONEY, *even more impatiently*). I'm sorry.

GEORGE (*claps his hands together, once, loud*). I've got it! I'll tell you what game we'll play. We're done with Humiliate the Host . . . this round, anyway . . . we're done with that . . . and we don't want to play Hump the Hostess, yet . . . not yet . . . so I know what we'll play. . . . We'll play a round of Get the Guests. How about that? How about a little game of Get the Guests?

MARTHA (*turning away, a little disgusted*). Jesus, George.

GEORGE. Book dropper! Child mentioner!

HONEY. I don't like these games.

NICK. Yeah. . . . I think maybe we've had enough of games, now. . . .

GEORGE. Oh, no . . . oh, no . . . we haven't. We've had only one game. . . . Now we're going to have another. You can't fly on one game.

NICK. I think maybe. . . .

GEORGE (*with great authority*). SILENCE! (*It is respected.*) Now, how are we going to play Get the Guests?

MARTHA. For God's sake, George. . . .

GEORGE. You be quiet! (MARTHA *shrugs.*) I wonder. . . . I wonder. (*Puzzles . . . then. . . .*) O.K.! Well . . . Martha . . . in her indiscreet way . . . well, not really indiscreet, because Martha is a naïve, at heart . . . anyway, Martha told you all about my first novel. True or false? Hunh? I mean, true or false that there ever was such a thing. HA! But, Martha told you about it . . . my first novel, my . . . memory book . . . which I'd sort of preferred she hadn't, but hell, that's blood under the bridge. BUT! what she didn't do . . . what Martha didn't tell you about is she didn't tell us all about my *second* novel. (MARTHA *looks at him with puzzled curiosity.*) No,

you didn't know about that, did you, Martha? About my second novel, true or false. True or false?

MARTHA (*sincerely*). No.

GEORGE. *No.* (*He starts quietly but as he goes on, his tone becomes harsher, his voice louder.*) Well, it's an allegory, really —probably—but it can be read as straight, cozy prose . . . and it's all about a nice young couple who come out of the Middle West. It's a bucolic you see. AND, this nice young couple comes out of the Middle West, and he's blond and about thirty, and he's a scientist, a teacher, a scientist . . . and his mouse is a wifey little type who gargle. brandy all the time . . . and. . . .

NICK. Just a minute here. . . .

GEORGE. . . .and they got to know each other when they was only teensie little types, and they used to get under the vanity table and poke around, and. . . .

NICK. I said JUST A MINUTE!

GEORGE. This is my game! You played yours . . . you people. This is my game!

HONEY (*dreamy*). I want to hear the story. I love stories.

MARTHA. George, for heaven's sake. . . .

GEORGE. AND! And Mousie's father was a holy man, see, and he ran sort of a traveling clip joint, based on Christ and all those girls, and he took the faithful . . . that's all . . . just took 'em. . . .

HONEY (*puzzling*). This is familiar.

NICK (*voice shaking a little*). No kidding!

GEORGE. . . . and he died eventually, Mousie's pa, and they pried him open, and all sorts of money fell out. . . . Jesus money, Mary money. . . . LOOT!

HONEY (*dreamy, puzzling*). I've heard this story before.

NICK (*with quiet intensity . . . to waken her*). Honey. . . .

GEORGE. But that's in the backwash, in the early part of the book. Anyway, Blondie and his frau out of the plain states came. (*Chuckles.*)

MARTHA. Very funny, George. . . .

GEORGE. . . . thank you . . . and settled in a town just like nouveau Carthage here. . . .

NICK (*threatening*). I don't think you'd better go on, mister. . . .

GEORGE. Do you not!

NICK (*less certainly*). No. I . . . I don't think you'd better.

HONEY. I love familiar stories . . . they're the best.

GEORGE. How right you are. But Blondie was in disguise, really, all got up as a teacher, 'cause his baggage ticket had bigger things writ on it . . . H.I. HI! Historical inevitability.

NICK. There's no need for you to go any further, now. . . .

HONEY (*puzzling to make sense out of what she is hearing*). Let them go on.

GEORGE. We shall. And he had this baggage with him, and part of this baggage was in the form of his mouse. . . .

NICK. We don't have to listen to this!

HONEY. Why not?

GEORGE. Your bride has a point. And one of the things nobody could understand about Blondie was his baggage . . . his mouse, I mean, here he was, pan-Kansas swimming champeen, or something, and he had this mouse, of whom he was solicitous to a point that faileth human understanding . . . given that she was sort of a simp, in the long run. . . .

NICK. This isn't fair of you. . . .

GEORGE. Perhaps not. Like, as I said, his mouse, she tooted brandy immodestly and spent half of her time in the upchuck. . . .

HONEY (*focussing*). I know these people. . . .

GEORGE. Do you! . . . But she was a money baggage amongst other things . . . Godly money ripped from the golden teeth of the unfaithful, a pragmatic extension of the big dream . . . and she was put up with. . . .

HONEY (*some terror*). I don't like this story. . . .

NICK (*surprisingly pleading*). Please . . . please don't.

MARTHA. Maybe you better stop, George. . . .

GEORGE. . . . and she was put up with. . . . STOP? Ha-ha.

NICK. Please . . . please don't.

GEORGE. Beg, baby.

MARTHA. George. . . .

GEORGE. . . . and . . . oh, we get a flashback here, to How They Got Married.

NICK. NO!

GEORGE (*triumphant*). YES!

NICK (*almost whining*). Why?

GEORGE. How They Got Married. Well, how they got married is this. . . . The Mouse got all puffed up one day, and she went over to Blondie's house, and she stuck out her puff, and she said . . . look at me.

HONEY (*white . . . on her feet*). I . . . don't . . . like this.

NICK (*to* GEORGE). Stop it!

GEORGE. Look at me . . . I'm all puffed up. Oh my goodness, said Blondie. . . .

HONEY (*as from a distance*). . . . and so they were married. . . .

GEORGE. . . . and so they were married. . . .

HONEY. . . . and then. . . .

GEORGE. . . . and then. . . .

HONEY (*hysteria*). WHAT? . . . and then, WHAT?

NICK. NO! No!

GEORGE (*as if to a baby*). . . . and then the puff went *away* . . . like magic . . . pouf!

NICK (*almost sick*). Jesus God. . . .

HONEY. . . . the puff went away. . . .

GEORGE (*softly*). . . . pouf.

NICK. Honey . . . I didn't mean to . . . honestly, I didn't mean to. . . .

HONEY. You . . . you told them. . . .

NICK. Honey . . . I didn't mean to. . . .

HONEY (*with outlandish horror*). You . . . told them! You told them! oooooHHHH! Oh, no, no, no, no! You couldn't have told them . . . oh, noooo!

NICK. Honey, I didn't mean to. . . .

HONEY (*grabbing at her belly*). Ohhhhh . . . nooooo.

NICK. Honey . . . baby . . . I'm sorry . . . I didn't mean to. . . .

GEORGE (*abruptly and with some disgust*). And that's how you play Get the Guests.

HONEY. I'm going to . . . I'm going to be . . . sick. . . .

GEORGE. Naturally!

NICK. Honey. . . .

HONEY (*hysterical*). Leave me alone . . . I'm going . . . to . . . be . . . sick. (*She runs out of the room.*)

MARTHA (*shaking her head, watching* HONEY's *retreating form*). God Almighty.

GEORGE (*shrugging*). The patterns of history.

NICK (*quietly shaking*). You shouldn't have done that . . . you shouldn't have done that at all.

GEORGE (*calmly*). I hate hypocrisy.

NICK. That was cruel . . . and vicious. . . .

GEORGE. . . . she'll get over it. . . .

NICK. . . . and damaging . . . !

GEORGE. . . . she'll recover. . . .

NICK. DAMAGING!! TO ME!!

GEORGE (*with wonder*). To you!

NICK. TO ME!!

GEORGE. To you!!

NICK. YES!!

GEORGE. Oh beautiful . . . beautiful. By God, you gotta have a swine to show you where the truffles are. (*So calmly*) Well, you just rearrange your alliances, boy. You just pick up the pieces where you can . . . you just look around and make the best of things . . . you scramble back up on your feet.

MARTHA (*quietly, to* NICK). Go look after your wife.

GEORGE. Yeah . . . go pick up the pieces and plan some new strategy.

NICK (*to* GEORGE, *as he moves toward the hall*). You're going to regret this.

GEORGE. Probably. I regret everything.

NICK. I mean, I'm going to make you regret this.

GEORGE (*softly*). No doubt. Acute embarrassment, eh?

NICK. I'll play the charades like you've got 'em set up. . . . I'll play in your language. . . . I'll be what you say I am.

GEORGE. You are already . . . you just don't know it.

NICK (*shaking within*). No . . . no. Not really. But I'll *be* it, mister. . . . I'll show you something come to life you'll wish you hadn't set up.

GEORGE. Go clean up the mess.

NICK (*quietly . . . intensely*). You just wait, mister. (*He exits. Pause.* GEORGE *smiles at* MARTHA.)

MARTHA. Very good, George.

GEORGE. Thank you, Martha.

MARTHA. Really good.

GEORGE. I'm glad you liked it.

MARTHA. I mean. . . . You did a good job . . . you really fixed it.

GEORGE. Unh-hunh.

MARTHA. It's the most . . . life you've shown in a long time.

GEORGE. You bring out the best in me, baby.

MARTHA. Yeah . . . pigmy hunting!

GEORGE. PIGMY!

MARTHA. You're really a bastard.

GEORGE. I? I?

MARTHA. Yeah . . . you.

GEORGE. Baby, if quarterback there is a pigmy, you've certainly changed your style. What are you after now . . . giants?

MARTHA. You make me sick.

GEORGE. It's perfectly all right for you. . . . I mean, you can make your own rules . . . you can go around like a hopped-up Arab, slashing away at everything in sight, scarring up half the world if you want to. But somebody else try it . . . no sir!

MARTHA. You miserable. . . .

GEORGE (*mocking*). Why baby, I did it all for you. I thought you'd like it, sweetheart . . . it's sort of to your taste . . . blood, carnage and all. Why, I thought you'd get all excited . . . sort of heave and pant and come running at me, your melons bobbling.

MARTHA. You've really screwed up, George.

GEORGE (*spitting it out*). Oh, for God's sake, Martha!

MARTHA. I mean it . . . you really have.

GEORGE (*barely contained anger now*). You can sit there in that chair of yours, you can sit there with the gin running out of your mouth, and you can humiliate me, you can tear me apart . . . ALL NIGHT . . . and that's perfectly all right . . . that's O.K. . . .

MARTHA. YOU CAN STAND IT!

GEORGE. I CANNOT STAND IT!

MARTHA. YOU CAN STAND IT!! YOU MARRIED ME FOR IT!!

(*A silence*)

GEORGE (*quietly*). That is a desperately sick lie.

MARTHA. DON'T YOU KNOW IT, EVEN YET?

GEORGE (*shaking his head*). Oh . . . Martha.

MARTHA. My arm has gotten tired whipping you.

GEORGE (*stares at her in disbelief*). You're mad.

MARTHA. For twenty-three years!

GEORGE. You're deluded . . . Martha, you're deluded.

MARTHA. IT'S NOT WHAT I'VE WANTED!

GEORGE. I thought at least you were . . . on to yourself. I didn't know. I . . . didn't know.

MARTHA (*anger taking over*). I'm on to myself.

GEORGE (*as if she were some sort of bug*). No . . . no . . . you're . . . sick.

MARTHA (*rises—screams*). I'LL SHOW YOU WHO'S SICK!

GEORGE. All right, Martha . . . you're going too far.

MARTHA (*screams again*). I'LL SHOW YOU WHO'S SICK. I'LL SHOW YOU.

GEORGE (*he shakes her*). Stop it! (*Pushes her back in her chair.*) Now, stop it!

MARTHA (*calmer*). I'll show you who's sick. (*Calmer*) Boy, you're really having a field day, hunh? Well, I'm going to finish you . . . before I'm through with you. . . .

GEORGE. . . . you and the quarterback . . . you both gonna finish me . . . ?

MARTHA. . . . before I'm through with you you'll wish you'd died in that automobile, you bastard.

GEORGE (*emphasizing with his forefinger*). And you'll wish you'd never mentioned our son!

MARTHA (*dripping contempt*). You. . . .

GEORGE. Now, I said I warned you.

MARTHA. I'm impressed.

GEORGE. I warned you not to go too far.

MARTHA. I'm just beginning.

GEORGE (*calmly, matter-of-factly*). I'm numbed enough . . . and I don't mean by liquor, though maybe that's been part of the process—a gradual, over-the-years going to sleep of the brain cells—I'm numbed enough, now, to be able to take you when we're alone. I don't listen to you . . . or when I *do* listen to you, I sift everything, I bring everything down to reflex response, so I don't really *hear* you, which is the only way to manage it. But you've taken a new tack, Martha, over the past couple of centuries—or however long it's been I've lived in this house with you—that makes it just too much . . . too much. I don't mind your dirty underthings in public . . . well, I *do* mind, but I've reconciled myself to that . . . but you've moved bag and baggage into your own fantasy world now, and you've started playing variations on your own distortions, and, as a result. . . .

MARTHA. Nuts!

GEORGE. Yes . . . you have.

MARTHA. Nuts!

GEORGE. Well, you can go on like that as long as you want to. And, when you're done. . . .

MARTHA. Have you ever listened to your sentences, George? Have you ever listened to the way you talk? You're so frigging . . . convoluted . . . that's what you are.

You talk like you were writing one of your stupid papers.

GEORGE. Actually, I'm rather worried about you. About your mind.

MARTHA. Don't you worry about my mind, sweetheart!

GEORGE. I think I'll have you committed.

MARTHA. You WHAT?

GEORGE (*quietly . . . distinctly*). I think I'll have you committed.

MARTHA (*breaks into long laughter*). Oh baby, aren't you something!

GEORGE. I've got to find some way to really get at you.

MARTHA. You've got at me, George . . . you don't have to do anything. Twenty-three years of you has been quite enough.

GEORGE. Will you go quietly, then?

MARTHA. You know what's happened, George? You want to know what's *really happened*? (*Snaps her fingers.*) It's snapped, finally. Not me . . . *it*. The whole arrangement. You can go along . . . forever, and everything's . . . manageable. You make all sorts of excuses to yourself . . . *you* know . . . this is life . . . the hell with it . . . maybe tomorrow he'll be dead . . . maybe tomorrow *you'll* be dead . . . all sorts of excuses. But then, one day, one night, something happens . . . and SNAP! It breaks. And you just don't give a damn anymore. I've tried with you, baby . . . really, I've tried.

GEORGE. Come off it, Martha.

MARTHA. I've tried . . . I've really tried.

GEORGE (*with some awe*). You're a monster . . . you *are*.

MARTHA. I'm loud, and I'm vulgar, and I wear the pants in this house because somebody's got to, but I am *not* a monster. I am *not*.

GEORGE. You're a spoiled, self-indulgent, willful, dirty-minded, liquor-ridden. . . .

MARTHA. SNAP! It went snap. Look, I'm not going to try to get through to you any more. . . . I'm not going to try. There was a second back there, maybe, there was a second, just a second, when I could have gotten through to you, when maybe we could have cut through all this crap. But that's past, and now I'm not going to try.

GEORGE. Once a month, Martha! I've gotten used to it . . . once a month and we get misunderstood Martha, the good-hearted girl underneath the barnacles, the little Miss that the touch of kindness'd bring to bloom again. And I've believed it more times than I want to remember, because I don't want to think I'm that much of a sucker. I don't believe you . . . I just don't believe you. There is no moment . . . there is no moment any more when we could . . . come together.

MARTHA (*armed again*). Well, maybe you're right, baby. You can't come together with nothing, and you're nothing! SNAP! It went snap tonight at Daddy's party. (*Dripping contempt, but there is fury and loss under it.*) I sat there at Daddy's party, and I watched you . . . I watched you sitting there, and I watched the younger men around you, the men who were going to go somewhere. And I sat there and I watched you, and *you* weren't *there!* And it snapped! It finally snapped! And I'm going to howl it out, and I'm not going to give a damn what I do, and I'm going to make the damned biggest explosion you ever heard.

GEORGE (*very pointedly*). You try it and I'll beat you at your own game.

MARTHA (*hopefully*). Is that a threat, George? Hunh?

GEORGE. That's a threat, Martha.

MARTHA (*fake-spits at him*). You're going to get it, baby.

GEORGE. Be careful, Martha . . . I'll rip you to pieces.

MARTHA. You aren't man enough . . . you haven't got the guts.

GEORGE. Total war?

MARTHA. Total.

(*Silence. They both seem relieved . . . elated.* NICK *reenters.*)

NICK (*brushing his hands off*). Well . . . she's . . . resting.

GEORGE (*quietly amused at* NICK's *calm, off-hand manner*). Oh?

MARTHA. Yeah? She all right?

NICK. I think so . . . now. I'm . . . terribly sorry. . . .

MARTHA. Forget about it.

GEORGE. Happens all the time around here.

NICK. She'll be all right.

MARTHA. She lying down? You put her upstairs? On a bed?

NICK (*making himself a drink*). Well, no, actually. Uh . . . may I? She's . . . in the bathroom . . . on the bathroom floor . . . she's lying there.

GEORGE (*considers it*). Well . . . that's

not very nice.

NICK. She likes it. She says it's . . . cool.

GEORGE. Still, I don't think. . . .

MARTHA (*overruling him*). If she wants to lie on the bathroom floor, let her. (*To* NICK, *seriously*) Maybe she'd be more comfortable in the tub?

NICK (*he, too, seriously*). No, she says she likes the floor . . . she took up the mat, and she's lying on the tiles. She . . . she lies on the floor a lot . . . she really does.

MARTHA (*pause*). Oh.

NICK. She . . . she gets lots of headaches and things, and she always lies on the floor. (*To* GEORGE) Is there . . . ice?

GEORGE. What?

NICK. Ice. Is there ice?

GEORGE (*as if the word were unfamiliar to him*). Ice?

NICK. Ice. Yes.

MARTHA. Ice.

GEORGE (*as if he suddenly understood*). Ice!

MARTHA. Attaboy.

GEORGE (*without moving*). Oh, yes . . . I'll get some.

MARTHA. Well, go. (*Mugging . . . to* NICK) Besides, we want to be alone.

GEORGE (*moving to take the bucket*). I wouldn't be surprised, Martha . . . I wouldn't be surprised.

MARTHA (*as if insulted*). Oh, you wouldn't, hunh?

GEORGE. Not a bit, Martha.

MARTHA (*violent*). NO?

GEORGE (*he too*). NO! (*Quietly again*) You'll try anything, Martha. (*Picks up the ice bucket.*)

NICK (*to cover*). Actually, she's very . . . frail, and. . . .

GEORGE. . . . . slim-hipped.

NICK (*remembering*). Yes . . . exactly.

GEORGE (*at the hallway . . . not kindly*). That why you don't have any kids? (*He exits.*)

NICK (*to* GEORGE's *retreating form*). Well, I don't know that that's . . . (*Trails off.*) . . . if that has anything to do with any . . . thing.

MARTHA. Well, if it does, who cares? Hunh?

NICK. Pardon?

(MARTHA *blows him a kiss.*)

NICK (*still concerned with* GEORGE's *remark*). I . . . what? . . . I'm sorry.

MARTHA. I said . . . (*Blows him an-other kiss.*)

NICK (*uncomfortable*). Oh . . . yes.

MARTHA. Hey . . . hand me a cigarette . . . lover. (NICK *fishes in his pocket.*) That's a good boy. (*He gives her one.*) Unh . . . thanks. (*He lights it for her. As he does, she slips her hand between his legs, somewhere between the knee and the crotch, bringing her hand around to the outside of his leg.*) Ummmmmmmm. (*He seems uncertain, but does not move. She smiles, moves her hand a little.*) Now, for being such a good boy, you can give me a kiss. C'mon.

NICK (*nervously*). Look . . . I don't think we should. . . .

MARTHA. C'mon, baby . . . a friendly kiss.

NICK (*still uncertain*). Well. . . .

MARTHA. . . . you won't get hurt, little boy. . . .

NICK. . . . not so little. . . .

MARTHA. I'll bet you're not. C'mon. . . .

NICK (*weakening*). But what if he should come back in, and . . . or . . . ?

MARTHA (*all the while her hand is moving up and down his leg*). George? Don't worry about him. Besides, who could object to a friendly little kiss? It's all in the faculty. (*They both laugh, quietly . . .* NICK *a little nervously.*) We're a close-knit family here . . . Daddy always says so. . . . Daddy wants us to get to know each other . . . that's what he had the party for tonight. So c'mon . . . let's get to know each other a little bit.

NICK. It isn't that I don't want to . . . believe me. . . .

MARTHA. You're a scientist, aren't you? C'mon . . . make an experiment . . . make a little experiment. Experiment on old Martha.

NICK (*giving in*). . . . not very old. . . .

MARTHA. That's right, not very old, but lots of good experience . . . lots of it.

NICK. I'll . . . I'll bet.

MARTHA (*as they draw slowly closer*). It'll be a nice change for you, too.

NICK. Yes, it would.

MARTHA. And you could go back to your little wife all refreshed.

NICK (*closer . . . almost whispering*). She wouldn't know the difference.

MARTHA. Well, nobody else's going to know, either. (*They come together. What might have been a joke rapidly becomes*

serious, with MARTHA *urging it in that direction. There is no frenetic quality, but rather a slow, continually involving intertwining. Perhaps* MARTHA *is still more or less in her chair, and* NICK *is sort of beside and on the chair.*

(GEORGE *enters . . . stops . . . watches a moment . . . smiles . . . laughs silently, nods his head, turns, exits, without being noticed.*)

(NICK, *who has already had his hand on* MARTHA'S *breast, now puts his hand inside her dress.*)

MARTHA (*slowing him down*). Hey . . . hey. Take it easy, boy. Down, baby. Don't rush it, hunh?

NICK (*his eyes still closed*). Oh, c'mon, now. . . .

MARTHA (*pushing him away*). Unh-unh. Later, baby . . . later.

NICK. I told you . . . I'm a biologist.

MARTHA (*soothing him*). I know. I can tell. Later, hunh?

(GEORGE *is heard off-stage, singing "Who's afraid of Virginia Woolf?"* MARTHA *and* NICK *go apart,* NICK *wiping his mouth,* MARTHA *checking her clothes. Safely later,* GEORGE *reenters with the ice bucket.*)

GEORGE. . . . of Virginia Woolf, Virginia Woolf, Virginia. . . .

. . . ah! Here we are . . . ice for the lamps of China, Manchuria thrown in. (*To* NICK) You better watch those yellow bastards, my love . . . they aren't amused. Why don't you come on over to our side, and we'll blow the hell out of 'em. Then we can split up the money between us and be on Easy Street. What d'ya say?

NICK (*not at all sure what is being talked about*). Well . . . sure. Hey! Ice!

GEORGE (*with hideously false enthusiasm*). Right! (*Now to* MARTHA, *purring*) Hello, Martha . . . my dove. . . . You look . . . radiant.

MARTHA (*off-hand*). Thank you.

GEORGE (*very cheerful*). Well now, let me see. I've got the ice. . . .

MARTHA. . . . gotten.

GEORGE. *Got*, Martha. Got is perfectly correct . . . it's just a little . . . archaic, like you.

MARTHA (*suspicious*). What are you so cheerful about?

GEORGE (*ignoring the remark*). Let's

see now . . . I've got the ice. Can I make someone a drink? Martha, can I make you a drink?

MARTHA (*bravura*). Yeah, why not?

GEORGE (*taking her glass*). Indeed . . . why not? (*Examines the glass.*) Martha! You've been nibbling away at the glass.

MARTHA. I have not!

GEORGE (*to* NICK, *who is at the bar*). I see you're making your own, which is fine . . . fine. I'll just hootch up Martha, here, and then we'll be all set.

MARTHA (*suspicious*). All set for what?

GEORGE (*pause . . . considers*). Why, I don't know. We're having a party, aren't we? (*To* NICK, *who has moved from the bar*) I passed your wife in the hall. I mean, I passed the john and I looked in on her. Peaceful . . . so peaceful. Sound asleep . . . and she's actually . . . sucking her thumb.

MARTHA. Awwwwww!

GEORGE. Rolled up like a fetus, sucking away.

NICK (*a little uncomfortably*). I suppose she's all right.

GEORGE (*expansively*). Of course she is! (*Hands* MARTHA *her drink.*) There you are.

MARTHA (*still on her guard*). Thanks.

GEORGE. And now one for me. It's my turn.

MARTHA. Never, baby . . . it's never your turn.

GEORGE (*too cheerful*). Oh, now, I wouldn't say that, Martha.

MARTHA. You moving on the principle the worm turns? Well, the worm part's O.K. . . . cause that fits you fine, but the turning part . . . unh-unh! You're in a straight line, buddy-boy, and it doesn't lead anywhere . . . (*A vague afterthought*) . . . except maybe the grave.

GEORGE (*chuckles, takes his drink*). Well, you just hold that thought, Martha . . . hug it close . . . run your hands over it. Me, I'm going to sit down . . . if you'll excuse me. . . . I'm going to sit down over there and read a book. (*He moves to a chair facing away from the center of the room, but not too far from the front door.*)

MARTHA. You're gonna do *what?*

GEORGE (*quietly, distinctly*). I am going to read a book. Read. Read. Read? You've heard of it? (*Picks up a book.*)

MARTHA (*standing*). Whaddya mean you're gonna read? What's the matter with you?

GEORGE (*too calmly*). There's nothing the matter with me, Martha. . . . I'm going to read a book. That's all.

MARTHA (*oddly furious*). We've got company!

GEORGE (*over-patiently*). I know, my dear . . . (*Looks at his watch.*) . . . but . . . it's after four o'clock, and I always read around this time. Now, you . . . (*Dismisses her with a little wave.*) . . . go about your business. . . . I'll sit here very quietly. . . .

MARTHA. You read in the afternoon! You read at four o'clock in the afternoon . . . you don't read at four o'clock in the morning! Nobody reads at four o'clock in the morning!

GEORGE (*absorbing himself in his book*). Now, now, now.

MARTHA (*incredulously, to* NICK). He's going to read a book. . . . The son of a bitch is going to read a book!

NICK (*smiling a little*). So it would seem. (*Moves to* MARTHA, *puts his arm around her waist.* GEORGE *cannot see this, of course.*)

MARTHA (*getting an idea*). Well, we can amuse ourselves, can't we?

NICK. I imagine so.

MARTHA. We're going to amuse ourselves, George.

GEORGE (*not looking up*). Unh-hunh. That's nice.

MARTHA. You might not like it.

GEORGE (*never looking up*). No, no, now . . . you go right ahead . . . you entertain your guests.

MARTHA. I'm going to entertain myself, too.

GEORGE. Good . . . good.

MARTHA. Ha, ha. You're a riot, George.

GEORGE. Unh-hunh.

MARTHA. Well, I'm a riot, too, George.

GEORGE. Yes you are, Martha.

(NICK *takes* MARTHA's *hand, pulls her to him. They stop for a moment, then kiss, not briefly.*)

MARTHA (*after*). You know what I'm doing, George?

GEORGE. No, Martha . . . what are you doing?

MARTHA. I'm entertaining. I'm entertaining one of the guests. I'm necking with one of the guests.

GEORGE (*seemingly relaxed and pre-*

occupied, never looking). Oh, that's nice. Which one?

MARTHA (*livid*). Oh, by God you're funny. (*Breaks away from* NICK . . . *moves into* GEORGE'S *side-line of vision by herself. Her balance is none too good, and she bumps into or brushes against the door chimes by the door. They chime.*)

GEORGE. Someone at the door, Martha.

MARTHA. Never mind that. I said I was necking with one of the guests.

GEORGE. Good . . . good. You go right on.

MARTHA (*pauses . . . not knowing quite what to do*). Good?

GEORGE. Yes, good . . . good for you.

MARTHA (*her eyes narrowing, her voice becoming hard*). Oh, I see what you're up to, you lousy little. . . .

GEORGE. I'm up to page a hundred and. . . .

MARTHA. Cut it! Just cut it out! (*She hits against the door chimes again; they chime.*) Goddam bongs.

GEORGE. They're chimes, Martha. Why don't you go back to your necking and stop bothering me? I want to read.

MARTHA. Why, you miserable. . . . I'll show you.

GEORGE (*swings around to face her . . . says, with great loathing*). No . . . show him, Martha . . . he hasn't seen it. *Maybe* he hasn't seen it. (*Turns to* NICK.) You haven't seen it yet, have you?

NICK (*turning away, a look of disgust on his face*). I . . . I have no respect for you.

GEORGE. And none for yourself, either. . . . (*Indicating* MARTHA) I don't know what the younger generation's coming to.

NICK. You don't . . . you don't even. . . .

GEORGE. Care? You're quite right. . . . I couldn't care less. So, you just take this bag of laundry here, throw her over your shoulder, and. . . .

NICK. You're disgusting.

GEORGE (*incredulous*). Because *you're* going to hump Martha, *I'm* disgusting? (*He breaks down in ridiculing laughter.*)

MARTHA (*to* GEORGE). You Mother! (*To* NICK.) Go wait for me, hunh? Go wait for me in the kitchen. (*But* NICK *does not move.* MARTHA *goes to him, puts her arms around him.*) C'mon, baby . . . please. Wait for me . . . in the kitchen . . . be a good baby. (NICK *takes her kiss,*

glares at GEORGE . . . *who has turned his back again . . . and exits.* MARTHA *swings around to* GEORGE.) Now you listen to me. . . .

GEORGE. I'd rather read, Martha, if you don't mind. . . .

MARTHA (*her anger has her close to tears, her frustration to fury*). Well, I do mind. Now, you pay attention to me! You come off this kick you're on, or I swear to God I'll do it. I swear to God I'll follow that guy into the kitchen, and then I'll take him upstairs, and. . . .

GEORGE (*swinging around to her again . . . loud . . . loathing*). SO WHAT, MARTHA?

MARTHA (*considers him for a moment . . . then, nodding her head, backing off slowly*). O.K. . . . O.K. . . . You asked for it . . . and you're going to get it.

GEORGE (*softly, sadly*). Lord, Martha, if you want the boy that much . . . have him . . . but do it honestly, will you? Don't cover it over with all this . . . all this . . . footwork.

MARTHA (*hopeless*). I'll make you sorry you made me want to marry you. (*At the hallway*) I'll make you regret the day you ever decided to come to this college. I'll make you sorry you ever let yourself down. (*She exits.*)

(*Silence.* GEORGE *sits still, staring straight ahead. Listening . . . but there is no sound. Outwardly calm, he returns to his book, reads a moment, then looks up . . . considers. . . .*)

GEORGE. "And the west, encumbered by crippling alliances, and burdened with a morality too rigid to accommodate itself to the swing of events, must . . . eventually . . . fall." (*He laughs, briefly, ruefully . . . rises, with the book in his hand. He stands still . . . then, quickly, he gathers all the fury he has been containing within himself . . . he shakes . . . he looks at the book in his hand and, with a cry that is part growl, part howl, he hurls it at the chimes. They crash against one another, ringing wildly. A brief pause, then* HONEY *enters.*)

HONEY (*the worse for wear, half asleep, still sick, weak, still staggering a little . . . vaguely, in something of a dream world*). Bells. Ringing. I've been hearing bells.

GEORGE. Jesus!

HONEY. I couldn't sleep . . . for the bells. Ding-ding, bong . . . it woke me up. What time is it?

GEORGE (*quietly beside himself*). Don't bother me.

HONEY (*confused and frightened*). I was asleep, and the bells started . . . they BOOMED! Poe-bells . . . they were Poe-bells . . . Bing-bing-bong-BOOM!

GEORGE. BOOM!

HONEY. I was asleep, and I was dreaming of . . . something . . . and I heard the sounds coming, and I didn't know what it was.

GEORGE (*never quite to her*). It was the sound of bodies. . . .

HONEY. And I didn't want to wake up, but the sound kept coming. . . .

GEORGE. . . . go back to sleep. . . .

HONEY. . . . and it FRIGHTENED ME!

GEORGE (*quietly . . . to* MARTHA, *as if she were in the room*). I'm going to get you . . . Martha.

HONEY. And it was so . . . cold. The wind was . . . the wind was so cold! And I was lying somewhere, and the covers kept slipping away from me, and I didn't want them to. . . .

GEORGE. Somehow, Martha.

HONEY. . . . and there was someone there . . . !

GEORGE. There was no one there.

HONEY (*frightened*). And I didn't want someone there. . . . I was . . . naked . . . !

GEORGE. You don't know what's going on, do you?

HONEY (*still with her dream*). I DON'T WANT ANY . . . NO . . . !

GEORGE. You don't know what's been going on around here while you been having your snoozette, do you?

HONEY. NO! . . . I DON'T WANT ANY . . . I DON'T WANT THEM. . . . GO 'WAY. . . . (*Begins to cry.*) I DON'T WANT . . . ANY . . . CHILDREN. . . . I . . . don't . . . want . . . any . . . children. I'm afraid! I don't want to be hurt. . . . PLEASE!

GEORGE (*nodding his head . . . speaks with compassion*). I should have known.

HONEY (*snapping awake from her reverie*). What! What?

GEORGE. I should have known . . . the whole business . . . the headaches . . . the whining . . . the. . . .

HONEY (*terrified*). What are you talking about?

GEORGE (*ugly again*). Does *he* know that? Does that . . . stud you're married to know about that, hunh?

HONEY. About what? Stay away from me!

GEORGE. Don't worry, baby . . . I wouldn't. . . . Oh, my God, that *would* be a joke, wouldn't it! But don't worry, baby. HEY! How you do it? Hunh? How do you make your secret little murders stud-boy doesn't know about, hunh? Pills? PILLS? You got a secret supply of pills? Or what? Apple jelly? WILL POWER?

HONEY. I feel sick.

GEORGE. You going to throw up again? You going to lie down on the cold tiles, your knees pulled up under your chin, your thumb stuck in your mouth . . . ?

HONEY (*panicked*). Where is he?

GEORGE. Where's who? There's nobody here, baby.

HONEY. I want my husband! I want a drink!

GEORGE. Well, you just crawl over to the bar and make yourself one. (*From offstage comes the sound of* MARTHA'S *laughter and the crashing of dishes. Yelling.*) That's right! Go at it!

HONEY. I want . . . something. . . .

GEORGE. You know what's going on in there, little Miss? Hunh? You hear all that? You know what's going on in there?

HONEY. I don't want to know anything!

GEORGE. There are a couple of people in there. . . . (MARTHA'S *laughter again.*) . . . they are in there, in the kitchen. . . . Right there, with the onion skins and the coffee grounds . . . sort of . . . sort of a . . . sort of a dry run for the wave of the future.

HONEY (*beside herself*). I . . . don't . . . understand . . . you. . . .

GEORGE (*a hideous elation*). It's very simple. . . . When people can't abide things as they are, when they can't abide the present, they do one of two things . . . either they . . . either they turn to a contemplation of the past, as I have done, or they set about to . . . alter the future. And when you want to change something . . . you BANG! BANG! BANG! BANG!

HONEY. Stop it!

GEORGE. And you, you simpering bitch . . . you don't want *children*?

HONEY. You leave me . . . alone. Who . . . WHO RANG?

GEORGE. What?

HONEY. What were the bells? Who

rang?

GEORGE. You don't want to know, do you? You don't want to listen to it, hunh?

HONEY (*shivering*). I don't want to listen to you. . . . I want to know who rang.

GEORGE. Your husband is . . . and you want to know who *rang*?

HONEY. Who rang? Someone rang!

GEORGE (*his jaw drops open . . . he is whirling with an idea*). . . . Someone. . . .

HONEY. RANG!

GEORGE. . . . someone . . . rang . . . yes . . . yessss. . . .

HONEY. The . . . bells . . . rang. . . .

GEORGE (*his mind racing ahead*). The bells rang . . . and it was someone. . . .

HONEY. Somebody. . . .

GEORGE (*he is home, now*). . . . somebody rang . . . it was somebody . . . with . . . I'VE GOT IT! I'VE GOT IT, MARTHA . . . ! Somebody with a message . . . and the message was . . . our son . . . OUR SON! (*Almost whispered*) It was a message . . . the bells rang and it was a message, and it was about . . . our son . . . and the message . . . was . . . and the message was . . . our . . . son . . . is . . . DEAD!

HONEY (*almost sick*). Oh . . . no.

GEORGE (*cementing it in his mind*). Our son is . . . dead. . . . And . . . Martha doesn't know. . . . I haven't told . . . Martha.

HONEY. No . . . no . . . no.

GEORGE (*slowly, deliberately*). Our son is dead, and Martha doesn't know.

HONEY. Oh. God in heaven . . . no.

GEORGE (*to* HONEY . . . *slowly, deliberately, dispassionately*). And you're not going to tell her.

HONEY (*in tears*). Your son is dead.

GEORGE. I'll tell her myself . . . in good time. I'll tell her myself.

HONEY (*so faintly*). I'm going to be sick.

GEORGE (*turning away from her . . . he, too, softly*). Are you? That's nice. (MARTHA's *laugh is heard again.*) Oh, listen to that.

HONEY. I'm going to die.

GEORGE (*quite by himself now*). Good . . . good . . . you go right ahead. (*Very softly, so* MARTHA *could not possibly hear*) Martha? Martha? I have some . . . terrible news for you. (*There is a strange half-smile on his lips.*) It's about our . . .

son. He's dead. Can you hear me, Martha? Our boy is dead. (*He begins to laugh, very softly . . . it is mixed with crying.*)

CURTAIN

ACT THREE:

THE EXORCISM

MARTHA *enters, talking to herself.*

———

MARTHA. Hey, hey. . . . Where is everybody . . . ? (*It is evident she is not bothered.*) So? Drop me; pluck me like a goddamn . . . whatever-it-is . . . creeping vine, and throw me over your shoulder like an old shoe . . . George? (*Looks about her.*) George? (*Silence*) George! What are you doing: Hiding, or something? (*Silence*) GEORGE!! (*Silence*) Oh, fa Chri . . . . . . (*Goes to the bar, makes herself a drink and amuses herself with the following performance.*) Deserted! Abandon-ed! Left out in the cold like an old pussycat. HA! Can I get you a drink, Martha? Why, thank you, George; that's very kind of you. No, Martha, no; why I'd do anything for you. Would you, George? Why, I'd do anything for you, too. Would you, Martha? Why, certainly, George. Martha, I've misjudged you. And I've misjudged you, too, George. WHERE IS EVERYBODY!!! Hump the Hostess! (*Laughs greatly at this, falls into a chair; calms down, looks defeated, says, softly.*) Fat chance. (*Even softer*) Fat chance. (*Baby-talk now.*) Daddy? Daddy? Martha is abandon-ed. Left to her own vices at . . . (*Peers at a clock.*) . . . something o'clock in the old A.M. Daddy White-Mouse; do you really have red eyes? Do you? Let me see. Ohhhhh! You do! You do! Daddy, you have red eyes . . . because you cry all the time, don't you, Daddy. Yes; you do. You cry alllll the time. I'LL GIVE ALL YOU BASTARDS FIVE TO COME OUT FROM WHERE YOU'RE HIDING!! (*Pause*) I cry all the time too, Daddy. I cry alllll the time; but deep inside, so no one can see me. I cry all the time. And Georgie cries all the time, too. We both cry all the time, and then, what we do, we cry, and we take our tears, and we put 'em in the ice box, in the goddamn ice trays (*Begins to laugh.*) until they're all frozen

(*Laughs even more.*) and then . . . we put them . . . in our . . . drinks. (*More laughter, which is something else, too. After sobering silence*) Up the drain, down the spout, dead, gone and forgotten. . . . Up the spout, not down the spout; *up* the spout: THE POKER NIGHT. Up the spout. . . . (*Sadly*) I've got windshield wipers on my eyes, because I married you . . . baby! . . . Martha, you'll be a song-writer yet. (*Jiggles the ice in her glass.*) CLINK! (*Does it again.*) CLINK! (*Giggles, repeats it several times.*) CLINK! . . . CLINK! . . . CLINK! . . . CLINK!

(NICK *enters while* MARTHA *is clinking; he stands in the hall entrance and watches her; finally he comes in.*)

NICK. My God, you've gone crazy too.

MARTHA. Clink?

NICK. I said, you've gone crazy too.

MARTHA (*considers it*). Probably . . . probably.

NICK. You've all gone crazy: I come downstairs, and what happens. . . .

MARTHA. What happens?

NICK. . . . my wife's gone into the can with a liquor bottle, and she winks at me . . . winks at me! . . .

MARTHA (*sadly*). She's never wunk at you; what a shame. . . .

NICK. She is lying down on the floor again, the tiles, all curled up, and she starts peeling the label off the liquor bottle, the brandy bottle. . . .

MARTHA. . . . we'll never get the deposit back that way. . . .

NICK. . . . and I ask her what she's doing, and she goes: shhhhhh!, nobody knows I'm here; and I come back in here, and you're sitting there going Clink!, for God's sake. Clink!

MARTHA. CLINK!

NICK. You've all gone crazy.

MARTHA. Yes. Sad but true.

NICK. Where is your husband?

MARTHA. He is vanish-ed. Pouf!

NICK. You're all crazy: nuts.

MARTHA (*affects a brogue*). Awww, 'tis the refuge we take when the unreality of the world weighs too heavy on our tiny heads. (*Normal voice again*) Relax; sink into it; you're no better than anybody else.

NICK (*wearily*). I think I am.

MARTHA (*her glass to her mouth*). You're certainly a flop in some departments.

NICK (*wincing*). I beg your pardon . . . ?

MARTHA (*Unnecessarily loud*). I said, you're certainly a flop in some. . . .

NICK (*he, too, too loud*). I'm sorry you're disappointed.

MARTHA (*braying*). I didn't say I was disappointed! Stupid!

NICK. You should try me some time when we haven't been drinking for ten hours, and maybe. . . .

MARTHA (*still braying*). I wasn't talking about your potential; I was talking about your goddamn performance.

NICK (*softly*). Oh.

MARTHA (*she softer, too*). Your potential's fine. It's dandy. (*Wiggles her eyebrows.*) Absolutely dandy. I haven't seen such a dandy potential in a long time. Oh, but baby, you sure are a flop.

NICK (*snapping it out*). Everybody's a flop to you! Your husband's a flop, *I'm a flop.* . . .

MARTHA (*dismissing him*). You're all flops. I am the Earth Mother, and you're all flops. (*More or less to herself*) I disgust me. I pass my life in crummy, totally pointless infidelities . . . (*Laughs ruefully.*) *would*-be infidelities. Hump the Hostess? That's a laugh. A bunch of boozed-up . . . impotent lunk-heads. Martha makes goo-goo eyes, and the lunk-heads grin, and roll their beautiful, beautiful eyes back, and grin some more, and Martha licks her chops, and the lunk-heads slap over to the bar to pick up a little courage *and* they pick up a little courage, and they bounce back over to old Martha, who does a little dance for them, which heats them all up . . . mentally . . . and so they slap over to the bar again, and pick up a little more courage, and their wives and sweethearts stick their noses up in the air . . . right through the ceiling, sometimes . . . which sends the lunk-heads back to the soda fountain again where they fuel up some more, while Martha-poo sits there with her dress up over her head . . . suffocating—you don't know how *stuffy* it is with your dress up over your head—suffocating! waiting for the lunk-heads; so, *finally* they get their courage up . . . but that's all, baby! Oh my, there is sometimes some very nice potential, but, oh my! My, my, my. (*Brightly*) But that's how it is in a civilized society. (*To herself again*) All the gorgeous lunk-heads.

Poor babies. (*To* NICK, *now; earnestly*) There is only one man in my life who has ever . . . made me happy. Do you know that? One!

NICK. The . . . the what-do-you-call-it? . . . uh . . . the lawn mower, or something?

MARTHA. No; I'd forgotten him. But when I think about him and me it's almost like being a voyeur. Hunh. No; I didn't mean him; I meant George, of course. (*No response from* NICK) Uh . . . George; my husband.

NICK (*disbelieving*). You're kidding.

MARTHA. Am I?

NICK. You must be. Him?

MARTHA. Him.

NICK (*as if in on a joke*). Sure; sure.

MARTHA. You don't believe it.

NICK (*mocking*). Why, of course I do.

MARTHA. You always deal in appearances?

NICK (*derisively*). Oh, for God's sake. . . .

MARTHA. . . . George who is out somewhere there in the dark. . . . George who is good to me, and whom I revile; who understands me, and whom I push off; who can make me laugh, and I choke it back in my throat; who can hold me, at night, so that it's warm, and whom I will bite so there's blood; who keeps learning the games we play as quickly as I can change the rules; who can make me happy and I do not wish to be happy, and yes I do wish to be happy. George and Martha: sad, sad, sad.

NICK (*echoing, still not believing*). Sad.

MARTHA. . . . whom I will not forgive for having come to rest; for having seen me and having said: yes, this will do; who has made the hideous, the hurting, the insulting mistake of loving me and must be punished for it. George and Martha: sad, sad, sad.

NICK (*puzzled*). Sad.

MARTHA. . . . who tolerates, which is intolerable; who is kind, which is cruel; who understands, which is beyond comprehension. . . .

NICK. George and Martha: sad, sad, sad.

MARTHA. Some day . . . hah! some *night* . . . some stupid, liquor-ridden night . . . I will go too far . . . and I'll either break the man's back . . . or push him off for good . . . which is what I deserve.

NICK. I don't think he's got a vertebra

intact.

MARTHA (*laughing at him*). You don't, huh? You don't think so. Oh, little boy, you got yourself hunched over that microphone of yours. . . .

NICK. Microscope. . . .

MARTHA. . . . yes . . . and you don't see anything, do you? You see everything but the goddamn mind; you see all the little specs and crap, but you don't see what goes on, do you?

NICK. I know when a man's had his back broken; I can see that.

MARTHA. Can you!

NICK. You're damn right.

MARTHA. Oh . . . you know so little. And you're going to take over the world, hunh?

NICK. All right, now. . . .

MARTHA. You think a man's got his back broken 'cause he makes like a clown and walks bent, hunh? Is that *really* all you know?

NICK. I said, all *right!*

MARTHA. Ohhhh! The stallion's mad, hunh. The gelding's all upset. Ha, ha, ha, HA!

NICK (*softly; wounded*). You . . . you swing wild, don't you.

MARTHA (*triumphant*). HAH!

NICK. Just . . . anywhere.

MARTHA. HAH! I'm a Gatling gun. Hahahahahahahahaha!

NICK (*in wonder*). Aimless . . . butchery. Pointless.

MARTHA. Aw! You poor little bastard.

NICK. Hit out at everything.

(*The door chimes chime.*)

MARTHA. Go answer the door.

NICK (*amazed*). What did you say?

MARTHA. I said, go answer the door. What are you, deaf?

NICK (*trying to get it straight*). You . . . want me . . . to go answer the door?

MARTHA. That's right, lunk-head; answer the door. There must be something you can do well; or, are you too drunk to do that, too? Can't you get the latch up, either?

NICK. Look, there's no need. . . .

(*Door chimes again*)

MARTHA (*shouting*). Answer it! (*Softer*) You can be houseboy around here for a while. You can start off being houseboy right now.

NICK. Look, lady, I'm no flunky to you.

MARTHA (*cheerfully*). Sure you are!

You're ambitious, aren't you, boy? You didn't chase me around the kitchen and up the goddamn stairs out of mad, driven passion, did you now? You were thinking a little bit about your career, weren't you? Well, you can just houseboy your way up the ladder for a while.

NICK. There's no limit to you, is there? (*Door chimes again*)

MARTHA (*calmly, surely*). No, baby; none. Go answer the door. (NICK *hesitates*.) Look, boy; once you stick your nose in it, you're not going to pull out just whenever you feel like it. You're in for a while. Now, git!

NICK. Aimless . . . wanton . . . pointless. . . .

MARTHA. Now, now, now; just do what you're told; show old Martha there's something you *can* do. Hunh? Atta boy.

NICK (*considers, gives in, moves toward the door. Chimes again*). I'm coming, for Christ's sake!

MARTHA (*claps her hands*). Ha HA! Wonderful; marvelous. (*Sings.*) "Just a gigolo, everywhere I go, people always say. . . ."

NICK. STOP THAT!

MARTHA (*giggles*). Sorry, baby; go on now; open the little door.

NICK (*with great rue*). Christ. (*He flings open the door, and a hand thrusts into the opening a great bunch of snapdragons; they stay there for a moment.* NICK *strains his eyes to see who is behind them.*)

MARTHA. Oh, how lovely!

GEORGE (*appearing in the doorway, the snapdragons covering his face; speaks in a hideously cracked falsetto*). Flores; flores para los muertos. Flores.

MARTHA. Ha, ha, ha HA!

GEORGE (*A step into the room; lowers the flowers; sees* NICK; *his face becomes gleeful; he opens his arms*). Sonny! You've come home for your birthday! At last!

NICK (*backing off*). Stay away from me.

MARTHA. Ha, ha, ha, HA! That's the houseboy, for God's sake.

GEORGE. Really? That's not our own little sonny-Jim? Our own little all-American something-or-other?

MARTHA (*giggling*). Well, I certainly hope not; he's been acting awful funny, if he is.

GEORGE (*almost manic*). Ohhhh! I'll bet! Chippie-chippie-chippie, hunh? (*Affecting embarrassment*) I . . . I brungya dese flowers, Mart'a, 'cause I . . . wull, 'cause you'se . . . awwwwww hell. Gee.

MARTHA. Pansies! Rosemary! Violence! My wedding bouquet!

NICK (*starting to move away*). Well, if you two kids don't mind, I think I'll just. . . .

MARTHA. Ach! You just stay where you are. Make my hubby a drink.

NICK. I don't think I will.

GEORGE. No, Martha, no; that would be too much; he's your houseboy, baby, not mine.

NICK. I'm nobody's houseboy. . . .

GEORGE *and* MARTHA. . . . Now! (*Sing.*) I'm nobody's houseboy now. . . . (*Both laugh.*)

NICK. Vicious. . . .

GEORGE (*finishing it for him*). . . . children. Hunh? That right? Vicious children, with their oh-so-sad games, hop-scotching their way through life, etcetera, etcetera. Is that it?

NICK. Something like it.

GEORGE. Screw, baby.

MARTHA. Him can't. Him too fulla booze.

GEORGE. Weally? (*Handing the snapdragons to* NICK) Here; dump these in some gin. (NICK *takes them, looks at them, drops them on the floor at his feet.*)

MARTHA (*sham dismay*). Awwwwww.

GEORGE. What a terrible thing to do . . . to Martha's snapdragons.

MARTHA. Is that what they are?

GEORGE. Yup. And here I went out into the moonlight to pick 'em for Martha tonight, and for our sonny-boy tomorrow, for his birfday.

MARTHA (*passing on information*). There is no moon now. I saw it go down from the bedroom.

GEORGE (*feigned glee*). From the bedroom! (*Normal tone*) Well, there was a moon.

MARTHA (*too patient; laughing a little*). There couldn't have been a moon.

GEORGE. Well, there was. There is.

MARTHA. There is no moon; the moon went down.

GEORGE. There is a moon; the moon is up.

MARTHA (*straining to keep civil*). I'm afraid you're mistaken.

GEORGE (*too cheerful*). No; no.

MARTHA (*between her teeth*). There is no goddamn moon.

GEORGE. My dear Martha . . . I did not pick snapdragons in the stony dark. I did not go stumbling around Daddy's greenhouse in the pitch.

MARTHA. Yes . . . you did. You would.

GEORGE. Martha, I do not pick flowers in the blink. I have never robbed a hothouse without there is a light from heaven.

MARTHA (*with finality*). There is no moon; the moon went down.

GEORGE (*with great logic*). That may very well be, Chastity; the moon may very well have gone down . . . but it came back up.

MARTHA. The moon does *not* come back up; when the moon has gone down it stays down.

GEORGE (*getting a little ugly*). You don't know anything. IF the moon went down, then it came back up.

MARTHA. BULL!

GEORGE. Ignorance! Such . . . ignorance.

MARTHA. Watch who you're calling ignorant!

GEORGE. Once . . . once, when I was sailing past Majorca, drinking on deck with a correspondent who was talking about Roosevelt, the moon went down, thought about it for a little . . . considered it, you know what I mean? . . . and then, POP, came up again. Just like that.

MARTHA. That is not true! That is such a lie!

GEORGE. You must not call everything a lie, Martha. (*To* NICK) Must she?

NICK. Hell, I don't know when you people are lying, or what.

MARTHA. You're damned right!

GEORGE. You're not supposed to.

MARTHA. Right!

GEORGE. At any rate, I was sailing past Majorca. . . .

MARTHA. You never sailed past Majorca. . . .

GEORGE. Martha. . . .

MARTHA. You were never in the goddamn Mediterranean at all . . . ever. . . .

GEORGE. I certainly was! My Mommy and Daddy took me there as a college graduation present.

MARTHA. Nuts!

NICK. Was this after you killed them?

(GEORGE *and* MARTHA *swing around and look at him; there is a brief, ugly pause.*)

GEORGE (*defiantly*). Maybe.

MARTHA. Yeah; maybe not, too.

NICK. Jesus!

(GEORGE *swoops down, picks up the bunch of snapdragons, shakes them like a feather duster in* NICK's *face, and moves away a little.*)

GEORGE. HAH!

NICK. Damn you.

GEORGE (*to* NICK). Truth and illusion. Who knows the difference, eh toots? Eh?

MARTHA. You were never in the Mediterranean . . . truth or illusion . . . either way.

GEORGE. If I wasn't in the Mediterranean, how did I get to the Aegean? Hunh?

MARTHA. OVERLAND!

NICK. Yeah!

GEORGE. Don't you side with her, houseboy.

NICK. I am not a houseboy.

GEORGE. Look! I know the game! You don't make it in the sack, you're a houseboy.

NICK. I AM NOT A HOUSEBOY!

GEORGE. No? Well, then you must have made it in the sack. Yes? (*He is breathing a little heavy; behaving a little manic.*) Yes? Someone's lying around here; somebody isn't playing the game straight. Yes? Come on; come on; who's lying? Martha? Come on!

NICK (*after a pause; to* MARTHA, *quietly with intense pleading*). Tell him I'm not a houseboy.

MARTHA (*after a pause, quietly, lowering her head*). No; you're not a houseboy.

GEORGE (*with great, sad relief*). So be it.

MARTHA (*pleading*). Truth and illusion, George; you don't know the difference.

GEORGE. No; but we must carry on as though we did.

MARTHA. Amen.

GEORGE (*flourishing the flowers*). SNAP WENT THE DRAGONS!! (NICK *and* MARTHA *laugh weakly.*) Hunh? Here we go round the mulberry bush, hunh?

NICK (*tenderly, to* MARTHA). Thank you.

MARTHA. Skip it.

GEORGE (*loud*). I said, here we go

round the mulberry bush!

MARTHA (*impatiently*). Yeah, yeah; we know; snap go the dragons.

GEORGE (*taking a snapdragon, throwing it, spearlike, stem-first at* MARTHA). SNAP!

MARTHA. Don't, George.

GEORGE (*throws another*). SNAP!

NICK. Don't do that.

GEORGE. Shut up, stud.

NICK. I'm not a stud!

GEORGE (*throws one at* NICK). SNAP! Then you're a houseboy. Which is it? Which are you? Hunh? Make up your mind. Either way. . . . (*Throws another at him.*) SNAP! . . . you disgust me.

MARTHA. Does it matter to you, George!?

GEORGE (*throws one at her*). SNAP! No, actually, it doesn't. Either way . . . I've had it.

MARTHA. Stop throwing those goddamn things at me!

GEORGE. Either way. (*Throws another at her.*) SNAP!

NICK (*to* MARTHA). Do you want me to . . . do something to him?

MARTHA. You leave him alone!

GEORGE. If you're a houseboy, baby, you can pick up after me; if you're a stud, you can go protect your plow. Either way. Either way. . . . Everything.

NICK. Oh for God's. . . .

MARTHA (*a little afraid*). Truth or illusion, George. Doesn't it matter to you . . . at all?

GEORGE (*without throwing anything*). SNAP! (*Silence*) You got your answer, baby?

MARTHA (*sadly*). Got it.

GEORGE. You just gird your blue-veined loins, girl. (*Sees* NICK *moving toward the hall.*) Now; we got one more game to play. And it's called bringing up baby.

NICK (*more-or-less under his breath*). Oh, for Lord's sake. . . .

MARTHA. George. . . .

GEORGE. I don't want any fuss. (*To* NICK) You don't want any scandal around here, do you, big boy? You don't want to wreck things, do you? Hunh? You want to keep to your time table, don't you? Then sit! (NICK *sits. To* MARTHA) And you, pretty Miss, you like fun and games, don't you? You're a sport from way back, aren't you?

MARTHA (*quietly, giving in*). All right, George; all right.

GEORGE (*seeing them both cowed; purrs*). Goooooooood; gooooood. (*Looks about him.*) But, we're not all here. (*Snaps his fingers a couple of times at* NICK.) You; you . . . uh . . . you; your little wifelet isn't here.

NICK. Look; she's had a rough night, now; she's in the can, and she's. . . .

GEORGE. Well, we can't play without everyone here. Now that's a fact. We gotta have your little wife. (*Hog-calls toward the hall.*) SOOOWWWIIIEEE!! SOOOWWWIIIEEE!!

NICK (*as* MARTHA *giggles nervously*). Cut that!

GEORGE (*swinging around, facing him*). Then get your butt out of that chair and bring the little dip back in here. (*As* NICK *does not move*) Now be a good puppy. Fetch, good puppy, go fetch. (NICK *rises, opens his mouth to say something, thinks better of it, exits.*) One more game.

MARTHA (*after* NICK *goes*). I don't like what's going to happen.

GEORGE (*surprisingly tender*). Do you know what it is?

MARTHA (*pathetic*). No. But I don't like it.

GEORGE. Maybe you will, Martha.

MARTHA. No.

GEORGE. Oh, it's a real fun game, Martha.

MARTHA (*pleading*). No more games.

GEORGE (*quietly triumphant*). One more, Martha. One more game, and then beddie-bye. Everybody pack up his tools and baggage and stuff and go home. And you and me, well, we gonna climb them well-worn stairs.

MARTHA (*almost in tears*). No, George; no.

GEORGE (*soothing*). Yes, baby.

MARTHA. No, George; please?

GEORGE. It'll all be done with before you know it.

MARTHA. No, George.

GEORGE. No climb stairs with Georgie?

MARTHA (*a sleepy child*). No more games . . . please. It's games I don't want. No more games.

GEORGE. Aw, sure you do, Martha . . . original game-girl and all, 'course you do.

MARTHA. Ugly games . . . ugly. And now this new one?

GEORGE (*stroking her hair*). You'll love it, baby.

MARTHA. No, George.

GEORGE. You'll have a ball.

MARTHA (*tenderly; moves to touch him*). Please, George, no more games; I. . . .

GEORGE (*slapping her moving hand with vehemence*). Don't you touch me! You keep your paws clean for the undergraduates!

MARTHA (*a cry of alarm, but faint*).

GEORGE (*grabbing her hair, pulling her head back*). Now, you listen to me, Martha; you have had quite an evening . . . quite a night for yourself, and you can't just cut it off whenever you've got enough blood in your mouth. We are going on, and I'm going to have at you, and it's going to make your performance tonight look like an Easter pageant. Now I want you to get yourself a little alert. (*Slaps her lightly with his free hand.*) I want a little life in you, baby. (*Again*)

MARTHA (*struggling*). Stop it!

GEORGE (*again*). Pull yourself together! (*Again*) I want you on your feet and slugging, sweetheart, because I'm going to knock you around, and I want you up for it. (*Again; he pulls away, releases her; she rises.*)

MARTHA. All right, George. What do you want, George?

GEORGE. An equal battle, baby; that's all.

MARTHA. You'll get it!

GEORGE. I want you mad.

MARTHA. I'M MAD!!

GEORGE. Get madder!

MARTHA. DON'T WORRY ABOUT IT!

GEORGE. Good for you, girl; now we're going to play this one to the death.

MARTHA. Yours!

GEORGE. You'd be surprised. Now, here come the tots; you be ready for this.

MARTHA (*she paces, actually looks a bit like a fighter*). I'm ready for you.

(NICK *and* HONEY *re-enter;* NICK *supporting* HONEY, *who still retains her brandy bottle and glass.*)

NICK (*unhappily*). Here we are.

HONEY (*cheerfully*). Hip, hop. Hip, hop.

NICK. You a bunny, Honey? (*She laughs greatly, sits.*)

HONEY. I'm a bunny, Honey.

GEORGE (*to* HONEY). Well, now, how's the bunny?

HONEY. Bunny funny! (*She laughs again.*)

NICK (*under his breath*). Jesus.

GEORGE. Bunny funny? Good for bunny!

MARTHA. Come on, George!

GEORGE (*to* MARTHA). Honey funny bunny! (HONEY *screams with laughter.*)

NICK. Jesus God. . . .

GEORGE (*slaps his hands together, once*). All right! Here we go! Last game! All sit. (NICK *sits.*) Sit down, Martha. This is a civilized game.

MARTHA (*cocks her fist, doesn't swing. Sits*). Just get on with it.

HONEY (*to* GEORGE). I've decided I don't remember anything. (*To* NICK) Hello, dear.

GEORGE. Hunh? What?

MARTHA. It's almost dawn, for God's sake. . . .

HONEY (*ibid*). I don't remember anything, and you don't remember anything, either. Hello, dear.

GEORGE. You what?

HONEY (*ibid, an edge creeping into her voice*). You heard me, nothing. Hello, dear.

GEORGE (*to* HONEY, *referring to* NICK). You do know that's your husband, there, don't you?

HONEY (*with great dignity*). Well, I certainly know *that*.

GEORGE (*close to* HONEY's *ear*). It's just some things you can't remember . . . hunh?

HONEY (*a great laugh to cover; then quietly, intensely to* GEORGE). Don't remember; not *can't*. (*At* NICK, *cheerfully*) Hello, dear.

GEORGE (*to* NICK). Well, speak to your little wifelet, your little bunny, for God's sake.

NICK (*softly, embarrassed*). Hello, Honey.

GEORGE. Awww, that was nice. I think we've been having a . . . a real good evening . . . all things considered. . . . We've sat around, and got to know each other, and had fun and games . . . curl-up-on-the-floor, for example. . . .

HONEY. . . . the tiles. . . .

GEORGE. . . . the tiles. . . . Snap the Dragon.

HONEY. . . . peel the label. . . .

GEORGE. . . . peel the . . . what?

MARTHA. Label. Peel the label.

HONEY (*apologetically, holding up her brandy bottle*). I peel labels.

GEORGE. We all peel labels, sweetie; and when you get through the skin, all three layers, through the muscle, slosh aside the organs (*An aside to* NICK) them which is still sloshable—(*Back to* HONEY) and get down to bone . . . you know what you do then?

HONEY (*terribly interested*). No.

GEORGE. When you get down to bone, you haven't got all the way, yet. There's something inside the bone . . . the marrow . . . and that's what you gotta get at. (*A strange smile at* MARTHA)

HONEY. Oh! I see.

GEORGE. The marrow. But bones are pretty resilient, especially in the young. Now, take our son. . . .

HONEY (*strangely*). Who?

GEORGE. Our son. . . . Martha's and my little joy!

NICK (*moving toward the bar*). Do you mind if I . . . ?

GEORGE. No, no; you go right ahead.

MARTHA. George. . . .

GEORGE (*too kindly*). Yes, Martha?

MARTHA. Just what are you doing?

GEORGE. Why love, I was talking about our son.

MARTHA. Don't.

GEORGE. Isn't Martha something? Here we are, on the eve of our boy's homecoming, the eve of his twenty-first birfday, the eve of his majority . . . and Martha says don't talk about him.

MARTHA. Just . . . don't.

GEORGE. But I want to, Martha! It's very important we talk about him. Now bunny and the . . . well, whichever he is . . . here don't know much about junior, and I think they should.

MARTHA. Just . . . don't.

GEORGE. (*snapping his fingers at* NICK). You. Hey, you! You want to play bringing up baby, don't you!

NICK (*hardly civil*). Were you snapping at me?

GEORGE. That's right. (*Instructing him*) *You* want to hear about our bouncey boy.

NICK (*pause; then shortly*). Yeah; sure.

GEORGE (*to* HONEY). And you, my dear? You want to hear about him, too, don't you.

HONEY (*pretending not to understand*).

Whom?

GEORGE. Martha's and my son.

HONEY (*nervously*). Oh, you have a child?

(MARTHA *and* NICK *laugh uncomfortably.*)

GEORGE. Oh, indeed; do we ever! Do you want to talk about him, Martha, or shall I? Hunh?

MARTHA (*a smile that is a sneer*). Don't, George.

GEORGE. All rightie. Well, now; let's see. He's a nice kid, really, in spite of his home life; I mean, most kids'd grow up neurotic, what with Martha here carrying on the way she does: sleeping 'till four in the P.M., climbing all over the poor bastard, trying to break the bathroom door down to wash him in the tub when he's sixteen, dragging strangers into the house at all hours.

MARTHA (*rising*). O.K. YOU!

GEORGE (*mock concern*). Martha!

MARTHA. That's enough!

GEORGE. Well, do you want to take over?

HONEY (*to* NICK). Why would anybody want to wash somebody who's sixteen years old?

NICK (*slamming his drink down*). Oh, for Christ's sake, Honey!

HONEY (*stage whisper*). Well, why?!

GEORGE. Because it's her baby-poo.

MARTHA. ALL RIGHT!! (*By rote; a kind of almost-tearful recitation*) Our son. You want our son? You'll have it.

GEORGE. You want a drink, Martha?

MARTHA (*pathetically*). Yes.

NICK (*to* MARTHA *kindly*). We don't have to hear about it . . . if you don't want to.

GEORGE. Who says so? You in a position to set the rules around here?

NICK (*pause; tight-lipped*). No.

GEORGE. Good boy; you'll go far. All right, Martha; your recitation, please.

MARTHA (*from far away*). What, George?

GEORGE (*prompting*). "Our son. . . ."

MARTHA. All right. Our son. Our son was born in a September night, a night not unlike tonight, though tomorrow, and twenty . . . one . . . years ago.

GEORGE (*beginning of quiet asides*). You see? I told you.

MARTHA. It was an easy birth. . . .

GEORGE. Oh, Martha; no. You labored

. . . how you labored.

MARTHA. It was an easy birth . . . once it had been . . . accepted, relaxed into.

GEORGE. Ah . . . yes. Better.

MARTHA. It was an easy birth, once it had been accepted, and I was young.

GEORGE. And I was younger. . . . (*Laughs quietly to himself.*)

MARTHA. And I was young, and he was a healthy child, a red, bawling child, with slippery firm limbs. . . .

GEORGE. . . . Martha thinks she saw him at delivery. . . .

MARTHA. . . . with slippery, firm limbs, and a full head of black, fine, fine hair which, oh, later, later, became blond as the sun, our son.

GEORGE. He was a healthy child.

MARTHA. And I had wanted a child . . . oh, I had wanted a child.

GEORGE (*prodding her*). A son? A daughter?

MARTHA. A child! (*Quieter*) A child. And I had my child.

GEORGE. Our child.

MARTHA (*with great sadness*). Our child. And we raised him . . . (*Laughs, briefly, bitterly.*) yes, we did; we raised him. . . .

GEORGE. With teddy bears and an antique bassinet from Austria . . . and *no nurse.*

MARTHA. . . . with teddy bears and transparent floating goldfish, and a pale blue bed with cane at the headboard when he was older, cane which he wore through . . . finally . . . with his little hands . . . in his . . . sleep. . . .

GEORGE. . . . nightmares. . . .

MARTHA. . . . *sleep.* . . . He was a restless child. . . .

GEORGE (*soft chuckle, head-shaking of disbelief*). . . . Oh Lord . . .

MARTHA. . . . sleep . . . and a croup tent . . . a pale green croup tent, and the shining kettle hissing in the one light of the room that time he was sick . . . those four days . . . and animal crackers, and the bow and arrow he kept under his bed. . . .

GEORGE. . . . the arrows with rubber cups at their tip. . . .

MARTHA. . . . at their tip, which he kept beneath his bed. . . .

GEORGE. Why? Why, Martha?

MARTHA. . . . for fear . . . for fear of. . . .

GEORGE. For fear. Just that: for fear.

MARTHA (*vaguely waving him off; going on*). . . . and . . . and sandwiches on Sunday night, and Saturdays . . . (*Pleased recollection*) . . . and Saturdays the banana boat, the whole peeled banana, scooped out on top, with green grapes for the crew, a double line of green grapes, and along the sides, stuck to the boat with toothpicks, orange slices. . . . SHIELDS.

GEORGE. And for the oar?

MARTHA (*uncertainly*). A . . . carrot?

GEORGE. Or a swizzle stick, whatever was easier.

MARTHA. No. A carrot. And his eyes were green . . . green with . . . if you peered so deep into them . . . so deep . . . bronze . . . bronze parentheses around the irises . . . such green eyes!

GEORGE. . . . blue, green, brown. . . .

MARTHA. . . . and he loved the sun! . . . He was tan before and after everyone . . . and in the sun his hair . . . became . . . fleece.

GEORGE (*echoing her*). . . . fleece. . . .

MARTHA. . . . beautiful, beautiful boy.

GEORGE. Absolve, Domine, animas, omnium fidelium defunctorum ab omni vinculo delictorum.

MARTHA. . . . and school . . . and summer camp . . . and sledding . . . and swimming. . . .

GEORGE. Et gratia tua illis succurrente, mereantur evadere judicium ultionis.

MARTHA (*laughing, to herself*). . . . and how he broke his arm . . . how funny it was . . . oh, no, it hurt him! . . . but, oh, it was funny . . . in a field, his very first cow, the first he'd ever seen . . . and he went into the field, to the cow, where the cow was grazing, head down, busy . . . and he moo'd at it! (*Laughs ibid.*) He moo'd at it . . . and the beast, oh, surprised, swung its head up and moo'd at him, all three years of him, and he ran, startled, and he stumbled . . . fell . . . and broke his poor arm. (*Laughs, ibid.*) Poor lamb.

GEORGE. Et lucis aeternae beatitudine perfrui.

MARTHA. George cried! Helpless . . . George . . . cried. I carried the poor lamb. George snuffling beside me. I carried the child, having fashioned a sling . . . and across the great fields.

GEORGE. In Paradisum deducant te Angeli.

MARTHA. And as he grew . . . and as he grew . . . oh! so wise! . . . he walked evenly between us . . . (*She spreads her hands.*) . . . a hand out to each of us for what we could offer by way of support, affection, teaching, even love . . . and these hands, still, to hold us off a bit, for mutual protection, to protect us all from George's . . . weakness . . . and my . . . necessary greater strength . . . to protect himself . . . and *us*.

GEORGE. In memoria aeterna erit justus: ab auditione mala non timebit.

MARTHA. So wise; so wise.

NICK (*to* GEORGE). What is this? What are you doing?

GEORGE. Shhhhh.

HONEY. Shhhhh.

NICK (*shrugging*). O.K.

MARTHA. So beautiful; so wise.

GEORGE (*laughs quietly*). All truth being relative.

MARTHA. It was true! Beautiful; wise; perfect.

GEORGE. There's a real mother talking.

HONEY (*suddenly; almost tearfully*). I want a child.

NICK. Honey. . . .

HONEY (*more forcefully*). I want a child!

GEORGE. On principle?

HONEY (*in tears*). I want a child. I want a baby.

MARTHA (*waiting out the interruption, not really paying it any mind*). Of course, this state, this perfection . . . couldn't last. Not with George . . . not with George around.

GEORGE (*to the others*). There; you see? I knew she'd shift.

HONEY. Be still!

GEORGE (*mock awe*). Sorry . . . mother.

NICK. Can't you be still?

GEORGE (*making a sign at* NICK). Dominus vobiscum.

MARTHA. Not with George around. A drowning man takes down those nearest. George tried, but, oh, God, how I fought him. God, how I fought him.

GEORGE (*a satisfied laugh*). Ahhhhhhh.

MARTHA. Lesser states can't stand those above them. Weakness, imperfection cries out against strength, goodness and innocence. And George tried.

GEORGE. How did I try, Martha? How did I try?

MARTHA. How did you . . . what? . . . No! No . . . he grew . . our son grew . . . up; he is grown up; he is away at school, college. He is fine, everything is fine.

GEORGE (*mocking*). Oh, come on, Martha!

MARTHA. No. That's all.

GEORGE. Just a minute! You can't cut a story off like that, sweetheart. You started to say something . . . now you say it!

MARTHA. No!

GEORGE. Well, I will.

MARTHA. No!

GEORGE. You see, Martha, here, stops just when the going gets good . . . just when things start getting a little rough. Now, Martha here, is a misunderstood little girl; she really is. Not only does she have a husband who is a bog . . . a younger-than-she-is bog albeit . . . not only does she have a husband who is a bog, she has as well a tiny problem with spiritous liquors—like she can't get enough. . . .

MARTHA (*without energy*). No more, George.

GEORGE. . . . and on top of all that, poor weighed-down girl, PLUS a father who really doesn't give a damn whether she lives or dies, who couldn't care less *what* happens to his only daughter . . . on top of all that she has a *son*. She has a son who fought her every inch of the way, who didn't want to be turned into a weapon against his father, who didn't want to be used as a goddamn club whenever Martha didn't get things like she wanted them!

MARTHA (*rising to it*). Lies! Lies!

GEORGE. Lies? All right. A son who would *not* disown his father, who came to him for advice, for information, for love that wasn't mixed with sickness—and you know what I mean, Martha!—who could not tolerate the slashing, braying residue that called itself his MOTHER. MOTHER? HAH!!

MARTHA (*cold*). All right, you. A son who was so ashamed of his father he asked me once if it—possibly—wasn't true, as he had heard, from some cruel boys, maybe, that he was not our child; who could not tolerate the shabby failure his father had become. . . .

GEORGE. Lies!

MARTHA. Lies? Who would not bring his girl friends to the house. . . .

GEORGE. . . . in shame of his mother. . . .

MARTHA. . . . of his father! Who writes letters only to me!

GEORGE. Oh, so you think! To me! At my office!

MARTHA. Liar!

GEORGE. I have a stack of them!

MARTHA. YOU HAVE NO LETTERS!

GEORGE. And you have?

MARTHA. He has no letters. A son . . . a son who spends his summers away . . . away from his family . . . ON ANY PRETEXT . . . because he can't stand the shadow of a man flickering around the edges of a house. . . .

GEORGE. . . . who spends his summers away . . . and he does! . . . who spends his summers away because there isn't room for him in a house full of empty bottles, lies, strange men, and a harridan who. . . .

MARTHA. Liar!!

GEORGE. Liar?

MARTHA. . . . A son who I have raised as best I can against . . . vicious odds, against the corruption of weakness and petty revenges. . . .

GEORGE. . . . A son who is, deep in his gut, sorry to have been born. . . .

(*Both together*)

MARTHA. I have tried, oh God I have tried; the one thing . . . the one thing I've tried to carry pure and unscathed through the sewer of this marriage; through the sick nights, and the pathetic, stupid days, through the derision and the laughter . . . *God,* the laughter, through one failure after another, one failure compounding another failure, each attempt more sickening, more numbing than the one before; the one thing, the one *person* I have tried to protect, to raise above the mire of this vile, crushing marriage; the one light in all this hopeless . . . *darkness* . . . our SON.

GEORGE. Libera me, Domine, de morte aeterna, in die illa tremenda; Quando caei movendi sunt et terra: Dum veneris judicare saeculum per ignem. Tremens factus sum ego, et timeo, dum discussio venerit, atque ventura ira. Quando caeli movendi sunt et terra. Dies illa, dies irae, calamitatis et miseriae; dies magna et amara valde. Dum veneris judicare

saeculum per ignem. Requiem aeternam dona eis, Domine: et lux perpetua luceat eis. Libera me Domine de morte aeterna in die illa tremenda: quando caeli movendi sunt et terra; Dum veneris judicare saeculum per ignem.

(*End together*)

HONEY (*her hands to her ears*). STOP IT!! STOP IT!!

GEORGE (*with a hand sign*). Kyrie, eleison. Christe, eleison. Kyrie, eleison.

HONEY. JUST STOP IT!!

GEORGE. Why, baby? Don't you like it?

HONEY (*quite hysterical*). You . . . can't . . . do . . . this!

GEORGE (*triumphant*). Who says!

HONEY. I! Say!

GEORGE. Tell us why, baby.

HONEY. No!

NICK. Is this game over?

HONEY. Yes! Yes, it is.

GEORGE. Ho-ho! Not by a long shot. (*To* MARTHA) We got a little surprise for you, baby. It's about sunny-Jim.

MARTHA. No more, George.

GEORGE. YES!

NICK. Leave her be!

GEORGE. I'M RUNNING THIS SHOW! (*To* MARTHA) Sweetheart, I'm afraid I've got some bad news for you . . . for us, of course. Some rather sad news.

(HONEY *begins weeping, head in hands.*)

MARTHA (*afraid, suspicious*). What is this?

GEORGE (*oh, so patiently*). Well, Martha, while you were out of the room, while the . . . two of you were out of the room . . . I mean, I don't know where, hell, you both must have been somewhere (*Little laugh*). . . . While you were out of the room, for a while . . . well, Missey and I were sittin' here havin' a little talk, you know: a chaw and a talk . . . and the doorbell rang. . . .

HONEY (*head still in hands*). Chimed.

GEORGE. Chimed . . . and . . . well, it's hard to tell you, Martha. . . .

MARTHA (*a strange throaty voice*). Tell me.

HONEY. Please . . . don't.

MARTHA. Tell me.

GEORGE. . . . and . . . what it was . . . it was good old Western Union, some little boy about seventy.

MARTHA (*involved*). Crazy Billy?

GEORGE. Yes, Martha, that's right . . .

crazy Billy . . . and he had a telegram, and it was for us, and I have to tell you about it.

MARTHA (*as if from a distance*). Why didn't they phone it? Why did they bring it; why didn't they telephone it?

GEORGE. Some telegrams you have to deliver, Martha; some telegrams you can't phone.

MARTHA (*rising*). What do mean?

GEORGE. Martha. . . . I can hardly bring myself to say it. . . .

HONEY. Don't.

GEORGE (*to* HONEY). Do you want to do it?

HONEY (*defending herself against an attack of bees*). No no no no no.

GEORGE (*sighing heavily*). All right. Well, Martha . . . I'm afraid our boy isn't coming home for his birthday.

MARTHA. Of course he is.

GEORGE. No, Martha.

MARTHA. Of course he is. I say he is!

GEORGE. He . . . can't.

MARTHA. He is! I say so!

GEORGE. Martha . . . (*Long pause*) . . . our son is . . . dead. (*Silence*) He was . . . killed . . . late in the afternoon. . . . (*Silence. A tiny chuckle*) on a country road, with his learner's permit in his pocket, he swerved, to avoid a porcupine, and drove straight into a. . . .

MARTHA (*rigid fury*). YOU . . . CAN'T . . . DO . . . THAT!

GEORGE. . . . . large tree.

MARTHA. YOU CANNOT DO THAT!

NICK (*softly*). Oh, my God. (HONEY *is weeping louder*.)

GEORGE (*quietly, dispassionately*). I thought you should know.

NICK. Oh my God; no.

MARTHA (*quivering with rage and loss*). NO! NO! YOU CANNOT DO THAT! YOU CAN'T DECIDE THAT FOR YOURSELF! I WILL NOT LET YOU DO THAT!

GEORGE. We'll have to leave around noon, I suppose. . . .

MARTHA. I WILL NOT LET YOU DECIDE THESE THINGS!

GEORGE. . . . . because there are matters of identification, naturally, and arrangements to be made. . . .

MARTHA (*leaping at* GEORGE, *but ineffectual*). YOU CAN'T DO THIS! (NICK *rises, grabs hold of* MARTHA, *pins her arms behind her back*.) I WON'T LET YOU DO THIS, GET YOUR HANDS OFF ME!

GEORGE (*as* NICK *holds on, right in* MARTHA's *face*). You don't seem to understand, Martha; I haven't done anything. Now, pull yourself together. Our son is DEAD! Can you get that into your head?

MARTHA. YOU CAN'T DECIDE THESE THINGS.

NICK. Lady, please.

MARTHA. LET ME GO!

GEORGE. Now listen, Martha; listen carefully. We got a telegram; there was a car accident, and he's dead. POUF! Just like that! Now, how do you like it?

MARTHA (*a howl which weakens into a moan*). NOOOOOOoooooo.

GEORGE (*to* NICK). Let her go. (MARTHA *slumps to the floor in a sitting position*.) She'll be all right now.

MARTHA (*pathetic*). No; no, he is *not* dead; he is not *dead*.

GEORGE. He is dead. Kyrie, eleison. Christe, eleison. Kyrie, eleison.

MARTHA. You *cannot*. You may not decide these things.

NICK (*leaning over her; tenderly*). He hasn't decided anything, lady. It's not his doing. He doesn't have the power. . . .

GEORGE. That's right, Martha; I'm not a God. I don't have the power over life and death, do I?

MARTHA. YOU CAN'T KILL HIM! YOU CAN'T HAVE HIM DIE!

HONEY. Lady . . . please. . . .

MARTHA. YOU CAN'T! ·

GEORGE. There was a telegram, Martha.

MARTHA (*up; facing him*). Show it to me! Show me the telegram!

GEORGE (*long pause; then, with a straight face*). I ate it.

MARTHA (*a pause; then with the greatest disbelief possible, tinged with hysteria*). What did you just say to me?

GEORGE (*barely able to stop exploding with laughter*). I . . . ate . . . it.

(MARTHA *stares at him for a long moment, then spits in his face*.)

GEORGE (*with a smile*). Good for you, Martha.

NICK (*to* GEORGE). Do you think that's the way to treat her at a time like this? Making an ugly goddamn joke like that? Hunh?

GEORGE (*snapping his fingers at* HONEY). Did I eat the telegram or did I not?

HONEY (*terrified*). Yes; yes, you ate it. I watched . . . I watched you . . . you

. . . you ate it all down.

GEORGE (*prompting*). . . . like a good boy.

HONEY. . . . like a . . . g-g-g-good . . . boy. Yes.

MARTHA (*to* GEORGE, *coldly*). You're not going to get away with this.

GEORGE (*with disgust*). YOU KNOW THE RULES, MARTHA! FOR CHRIST'S SAKE, YOU KNOW THE RULES!

MARTHA. NO!

NICK. (*with the beginnings of a knowledge he cannot face*). What are you two talking about?

GEORGE. I can kill him, Martha, if I want to.

MARTHA. HE IS OUR CHILD!

GEORGE. Oh yes, and you bore him, and it was a good delivery. . . .

MARTHA. HE IS OUR CHILD!

GEORGE. AND I HAVE KILLED HIM!

MARTHA. NO!

GEORGE. YES!

(*Long silence*)

NICK (*very quietly*). I think I understand this.

GEORGE (*ibid*). Do you?

NICK (*ibid*). Jesus Christ, I think I understand this.

GEORGE (*ibid*). Good for you, buster.

NICK (*violently*). JESUS CHRIST I THINK I UNDERSTAND THIS!

MARTHA (*great sadness and loss*). You have no right . . . you have no right at all. . . .

GEORGE (*tenderly*). I have the right, Martha. We never spoke of it; that's all. I could kill him any time I wanted to.

MARTHA. But why? Why?

GEORGE. You broke our rule, baby. You mentioned him . . . you mentioned him to someone else.

MARTHA (*tearfully*). I did *not*. I never did.

GEORGE. Yes, you did.

MARTHA. Who? WHO?!

HONEY (*crying*). To me. You mentioned him to me.

MARTHA (*crying*). I FORGET! Sometimes . . . sometimes when it's night, when it's late, and . . . and everybody else is . . . talking . . . I forget and I . . . want to mention him . . . but I . . . HOLD ON . . . I hold on . . . but I've wanted to . . . so often . . . oh, George, you've *pushed* it . . . there was no need . . . there was no need for *this*. I *men*tioned him . . . all

right . . . but you didn't have to push it over the EDGE. You didn't have to . . . kill him.

GEORGE. Requiescat in pace.

HONEY. Amen.

MARTHA. You didn't have to have him die, George.

GEORGE. Requiem aeternam dona eis, Domine.

HONEY. Et lux perpetua luceat eis.

MARTHA. That wasn't . . . needed.

(*A long silence*)

GEORGE (*softly*). It will be dawn soon. I think the party's over.

NICK (*to* GEORGE; *quietly*). You couldn't have . . . any?

GEORGE. *We* couldn't.

MARTHA (*a hint of communion in this*). *We* couldn't.

GEORGE (*to* NICK *and* HONEY). Home to bed, children; it's way past your bedtime.

NICK (*his hand out to* HONEY). Honey?

HONEY (*rising, moving to him*). Yes.

GEORGE (MARTHA *is sitting on the floor by a chair now*). You two go now.

NICK. Yes.

HONEY. Yes.

NICK. I'd like to. . . .

GEORGE. Good night.

NICK (*pause*). Good night.

(NICK *and* HONEY *exit;* GEORGE *closes the door after them; looks around the room; sighs, picks up a glass or two, takes it to the bar.*)

(*This whole last section very softly, very slowly.*)

GEORGE. Do you want anything, Martha?

MARTHA (*still looking away*). No . . . nothing.

GEORGE. All right. (*Pause*) Time for bed.

MARTHA. Yes.

GEORGE. Are you tired?

MARTHA. Yes.

GEORGE. I am.

MARTHA. Yes.

GEORGE. Sunday tomorrow; all day.

MARTHA. Yes. (*a long silence between them*) Did you . . . did you . . . have to?

GEORGE (*pause*). Yes.

MARTHA. It was . . . ? You had to?

GEORGE (*pause*). Yes.

MARTHA. I don't know.

GEORGE. It was . . . time.

MARTHA. Was it?

GEORGE. Yes.

MARTHA (*pause*). I'm cold.

GEORGE. It's late.

MARTHA. Yes.

GEORGE (*long silence*). It will be better.

MARTHA (*long silence*). I don't . . . know.

GEORGE. It will be . . . maybe.

MARTHA. I'm . . . not . . . sure.

GEORGE. No.

MARTHA. Just. . . . us?

GEORGE. Yes.

MARTHA. I don't suppose, maybe, we could. . . .

GEORGE. No, Martha.

MARTHA. Yes. No.

GEORGE. Are you all right?

MARTHA. Yes. No.

GEORGE (*puts his hand gently on her shoulder; she puts her head back and he sings to her, very softly*).

Who's afraid of Virginia Woolf

Virginia Woolf

Virginia Woolf,

MARTHA. I . . . am . . . George. . . .

GEORGE. Who's afraid of Virginia Woolf. . . .

MARTHA. I . . . am . . . George. . . . I . . . am. . . .

(GEORGE *nods, slowly.*)

(*Silence; tableau*)

CURTAIN

THE ODD COUPLE

Neil Simon

---

*THE ODD COUPLE was first presented by Saint Subber on March 10, 1965,
at the Plymouth Theatre in New York City, with the following cast:*

(In order of appearance)

SPEED Paul Dooley

MURRAY Nathaniel Frey

ROY Sidney Armus

VINNIE John Fiedler

OSCAR MADISON Walter Matthau

FELIX UNGAR Art Carney

GWENDOLYN PIGEON Carole Shelley

CECILY PIGEON Monica Evans

Written by Neil Simon
Directed by Mike Nichols
Set designed by Oliver Smith
Lighting by Jean Rosenthal
Costumes by Ann Roth

SYNOPSIS OF SCENES

The action takes place in an apartment on Riverside Drive in New York City.
ACT ONE. A hot summer night.
ACT TWO. SCENE 1: Two weeks later, about eleven at night. SCENE 2: A few
days later, about eight P.M.
ACT THREE. The next evening, about seven-thirty.

© *Copyright, 1966, by Nancy Enterprises, Inc.*
Reprinted by permission of Random House, Inc.
All rights including the right of reproduction in whole or in part, in any form, are reserved
under International and Pan-American Copyright Conventions. Published in New York
by Random House, Inc., and simultaneously in Toronto, Canada, by Random House of
Canada Limited.

CAUTION: Professionals and amateurs are hereby warned that *The Odd Couple* is fully protected under the Universal Copyright Convention, Berne Convention and Pan-American Copyright Convention and is subject to royalty. All rights are strictly reserved, including professional, amateur, motion picture, television, radio, recitation, lecturing, public reading and foreign language translation, and none of such rights can be exercised or used without written permission from the copyright owner. All inquiries for licenses and permissions should be addressed to:—

International Authors Society, Ltd.
c/o Albert I. DaSilva
4 West 56th Street
New York, N.Y. 10019

Neil Simon was born with success in his mouth rather than a silver spoon, and it has never hurt him a bit. He was also born, just like Yankee Doodle Dandy, on the Fourth of July—the Fourth of July in question coming in 1927. He started to write with his brother Danny, and produced revue sketches and the like, to say nothing of a widely acclaimed first play, *Come Blow Your Horn,* first given in 1961.

From then onward Mr. Simon has never looked sideways, let alone back. He has become one of the most successful comedy writers of all time, and the natural inheritor of the old Broadway writers of the twenties and thirties.

In a way Mr. Simon was the first writer to cut his teeth artistically in television. It gave him two things—one good and one bad. The good thing was his ear for the speech of the people, his total empathy with their wit, his perhaps dangerously accurate assessment of the joke and sentiment that will corral in the ratings. What was bad in fact was merely a mirror image of what was good. His very adroitness played enemy to his brilliance.

What at first perhaps happened was that his humanity never quite lived up to his wit. He has a simply god-given talent to make jokes. His situations are funny enough in all conscience, but he can back it up with a crackling wit that obtains its crackle simply from its unassailable likelihood. One of Mr. Simon's most popular plays was the brilliantly, almost indecently, funny *Plaza Suite.* In the first play, where a Peter Pan suburban husband tries to find a lost youth with his secretary rather than recognizing reality with his wife, he aims dead center at life. He misses, not because his people are not real—they are, they even chatter with the red blood of life—but because the situation itself is so real it is a cliché.

Simon's problem is not that he is not as good as his glorious predecessors in the history of American comedy, but that he is so much better. In plays like *Barefoot in the Park,* or musicals such as the woefully underrated *Little Me,* the surprisingly overrated *Sweet Charity,* and the altogether blissful *Promises, Promises,* Simon has set up a standard of verbal wit and sheer literacy that almost seems its own worst enemy.

He is so sharp—the jokes have such a beautiful, seemingly machine-made precision—that you wonder what lies behind the superficial glitter. And frankly, if you are human and you envy any man that funny, you probably presume but little. Only serious men get themselves taken seriously, which is probably why they are serious. But Neil Simon is not just content to stand up and make jokes, to tease and titillate a loyal public into delightedly shocked laughter. Mr. Simon wants, deserves, and needs to be taken seriously.

The first play of *Plaza Suite,* with its derelict marriage floating out to a lost sea, is an example of this very important element in Simon's playwrighting. Even at its most outrageously witty, when the jokes are falling like snow in December, Mr. Simon's play itself takes more pride in its humanity than in its humor.

Of all Simon's many plays and musical books, *The Odd Couple* is very possibly his best. The jokes and wisecracks are, of course, all present and correct and only waiting to be counted. But, more surprisingly, this comedy of two grass widowers setting up house together has a great deal more than its wit to keep it warm. In this story of a man and his maladjustment with another man—that historic encounter between the social slob and the social saint—Simon creates a genuine comedy of manners. It would be easy to say "Go and Enjoy," but beyond your immediate enjoyment note the strange intensity of the writing, and the delicacy of the situations as well as the sharpness of the wit. Mr. Simon has written a comedy so perfectly of its time and place that it seems safe to say that it will survive every change of fashion, as have the best of the old Broadway comedies of the past.

C.B.

ACT ONE

It is a warm summer night in OSCAR
MADISON's *apartment. This is one of those
large eight-room affairs on Riverside Drive
in the upper eighties. The building is
about thirty-five years old and still has
vestiges of its glorious past—high ceilings,
walk-in closets and thick walls. We are in
the living room with doors leading off to
the kitchen, a bedroom and a bathroom,
and a hallway to the other bedrooms.*

*Although the furnishings have been
chosen with extreme good taste, the room
itself, without the touch and care of a
woman these past few months, is now a
study in slovenliness. Dirty dishes, dis-
carded clothes, old newspapers, empty bottles, glasses filled and unfilled, opened and
unopened laundry packages, mail and dis-
arrayed furniture abound. The only cheerful note left in this room is the lovely view
of the New Jersey Palisades through its
twelfth-floor window. Three months ago
this was a lovely apartment.*

*As the curtain rises, the room is filled
with smoke. A poker game is in progress.
There are six chairs around the table but
only four men are sitting. They are* MUR-
RAY, ROY, SPEED *and* VINNIE. VINNIE, *with
the largest stack of chips in front of him,
is nervously tapping his foot; he keeps
checking his watch.* ROY *is watching* SPEED
and SPEED *is glaring at* MURRAY *with incredulity and utter fascination.* MURRAY *is
the dealer. He slowly and methodically
tries to shuffle. It is a ponderous and painful business.* SPEED *shakes his head in disbelief. This is all done wordlessly.*

SPEED (*cups his chin in his hand and
looks at* MURRAY). Tell me, Mr. Maverick,
is this your first time on the riverboat?

MURRAY (*with utter disregard*). You
don't like it, get a machine.

(*He continues to deal slowly.*)

ROY. Geez, it stinks in here.

VINNIE (*looks at his watch*). What time
is it?

SPEED. Again what time is it?

VINNIE (*whining*). My watch is slow.
I'd like to know what time it is.

SPEED (*glares at him*). You're winning
ninety-five dollars, that's what time it is.
Where the hell are you running?

VINNIE. I'm not running anywhere. I

just asked what time it was. Who said
anything about running?

ROY (*looks at his watch*). It's ten-thirty.

(*There is a pause.* MURRAY *continues to
shuffle.*)

VINNIE (*after the pause*). I got to leave
by twelve.

SPEED (*looks up in despair*). Oh, Christ!

VINNIE. I told you that when I sat
down. I got to leave by twelve. Murray,
didn't I say that when I sat down? I said
I got to leave by twelve.

SPEED. All right, don't talk to him. He's
dealing. (*To* MURRAY.) Murray, you wanna
rest for a while? Go lie down, sweetheart.

MURRAY. You want speed or accuracy,
make up your mind.

(*He begins to deal slowly.* SPEED *puffs
on his cigar angrily.*)

ROY. Hey, you want to do me a really
big favor? Smoke toward New Jersey.

(SPEED *blows smoke at* ROY.)

MURRAY. No kidding, I'm really worried
about Felix. (*Points to an empty chair.*)
He's never been this late before. Maybe
somebody should call. (*Yells off.*) Hey,
Oscar, why don't you call Felix?

ROY (*waves his hand through the
smoke*). Listen, why don't we chip in
three dollars apiece and buy another window. How the hell can you breathe in
here?

MURRAY. How many cards you got,
four?

SPEED. Yes, Murray, we all have four
cards. When you give us one more, we'll
all have five. If you were to give us two
more, we'd have six. Understand how it
works now?

ROY (*yells off*). Hey, Oscar, what do
you say? In or out?

(*From offstage we hear* OSCAR's *voice.*)

OSCAR (*offstage*). Out, pussycat, out!

(SPEED *opens and the others bet.*)

VINNIE. I told my wife I'd be home by
one the latest. We're making an eight
o'clock plane to Florida. I told you that
when I sat down.

SPEED. Don't cry, Vinnie. You're forty-
two years old. It's embarrassing. Give me
two . . .

(*He discards.*)

ROY. Why doesn't he fix the air conditioner? It's ninety-eight degrees, and it
sits there sweating like everyone else. I'm
out.

(*He goes to the window and looks out.*)

MURRAY. Who goes to Florida in July?

VINNIE. It's off-season. There's no crowds and you get the best room for one-tenth the price. No cards . . .

SPEED. Some vacation. Six cheap people in an empty hotel.

MURRAY. Dealer takes four . . . Hey, you think maybe Felix is sick? (*He points to the empty chair.*) I mean he's never been this late before.

ROY (*takes a laundry bag from an armchair and sits*). You know, it's the same garbage from last week's game. I'm beginning to recognize things.

MURRAY (*throwing his cards down*). I'm out . . .

SPEED (*showing his hand*). Two kings . . .

VINNIE. Straight . . .

(*He shows his hand and takes in the pot.*)

MURRAY. Hey, maybe he's in his office locked in the john again. Did you know Felix was once locked in the john overnight. He wrote out his entire will on a half a roll of toilet paper! Heee, what a nut!

(VINNIE *is playing with his chips.*)

SPEED (*glares at him as he shuffles the cards*). Don't play with your chips. I'm asking you nice; don't play with your chips.

VINNIE (*to* SPEED). I'm not playing. I'm counting. Leave me alone. What are you picking on me for? How much do you think I'm winning? Fifteen dollars!

SPEED. Fifteen dollars? You dropped more than that in your cuffs!

(SPEED *deals a game of draw poker.*)

MURRAY (*yells off*). Hey, Oscar, what do you say?

OSCAR (*enters carrying a tray with beer, sandwiches, a can of peanuts, and opened bags of pretzels and Fritos*). I'm in! I'm in! Go ahead. Deal!

(OSCAR MADISON *is forty-three. He is a pleasant, appealing man who seems to enjoy life to the fullest. He enjoys his weekly poker game, his friends, his excessive drinking and his cigars. He is also one of those lucky creatures in life who even enjoys his work—he's a sports-writer for the New York* Post. *His carefree attitude is evident in the sloppiness of his household, but it seems to bother others*

more than it does OSCAR. *This is not to say that* OSCAR *is without cares or worries. He just doesn't seem to have any.*)

VINNIE. Aren't you going to look at your cards?

OSCAR (*sets the tray on a side chair*). What for? I'm gonna bluff anyway. (*Opens a bottle of Coke.*) Who gets the Coke?

MURRAY. I get a Coke.

OSCAR. My friend Murray the policeman gets a warm Coke.

(*He gives him the bottle.*)

ROY (*opens the betting*). You still didn't fix the refrigerator? It's been two weeks now. No wonder it stinks in here.

OSCAR (*picks up his cards*). Temper, temper. If I wanted nagging I'd go back with my wife. (*Throws them down.*) I'm out. Who wants food?

MURRAY. What have you got?

OSCAR (*looks under the bread*). I got brown sandwiches and green sandwiches. Well, what do you say?

MURRAY. What's the green?

OSCAR. It's either very new cheese or very old meat.

MURRAY. I'll take the brown.

(OSCAR *gives* MURRAY *a sandwich.*)

ROY (*glares at* MURRAY). Are you crazy? You're not going to eat that, are you?

MURRAY. I'm hungry.

ROY. His refrigerator's been broken for two weeks. I saw milk standing in there that wasn't even in the bottle.

OSCAR (*to* ROY). What are you, some kind of a health nut? Eat, Murray, eat!

ROY. I've got six cards . . .

SPEED. That figures—I've got three aces. Misdeal.

(*They all throw their cards in.* SPEED *begins to shuffle.*)

VINNIE. You know who makes very good sandwiches? Felix. Did you ever taste his cream cheese and pimento on date-nut bread?

SPEED (*to* VINNIE). All right, make up your mind, poker or menus. (OSCAR *opens a can of beer, which sprays in a geyser over the players and the table. There is a hubbub as they all yell at* OSCAR. *He hands* ROY *the overflowing can and pushes the puddle of beer under the chair. The players start to go back to the game only to be sprayed again as* OSCAR *opens another beer can. There is another outraged cry as they try to stop* OSCAR *and mop up the beer on the table with a towel which was hanging on the standing lamp.* OSCAR, *undisturbed, gives them the beer and the bags of refreshments, and they finally sit back in their chairs.* OSCAR *wipes his hands on the sleeve of* ROY's *jacket which is hanging on the back of the chair.*) Hey, Vinnie, tell Oscar what time you're leaving.

VINNIE (*like a trained dog*). Twelve o'clock.

SPEED (*to the others*). You hear? We got ten minutes before the next announcement. All right, this game is five card stud. (*He deals and ad libs calling the cards, ending with* MURRAY's *card.*) . . . And a bullet for the policeman. All right, Murray, it's your bet. (*No answer.*) Do something, huh.

OSCAR (*getting a drink at the bar*). Don't yell at my friend Murray.

MURRAY (*throwing in a coin*). I'm in for a quarter.

OSCAR (*proudly looks in* MURRAY's *eyes*). Beautiful, baby, beautiful.

(*He sits down and begins to open the can of peanuts.*)

ROY. Hey, Oscar, let's make a rule. Every six months you have to buy fresh potato chips. How can you live like this? Don't you have a maid?

OSCAR (*shakes his head*). She quit after my wife and kids left. The work got to be too much for her. (*He looks on the table.*) The pot's shy. Who didn't put in a quarter?

MURRAY (*to* OSCAR). You didn't.

OSCAR (*puts in money*). You got a big mouth, Murray. Just for that, lend me twenty dollars.

(SPEED *deals another round.*)

MURRAY. I just loaned you twenty dollars ten minutes ago.

(*They all join in a round of betting.*)

OSCAR. You loaned me *ten* dollars *twenty* minutes ago. Learn to count, pussycat.

MURRAY. Learn to play poker, chicken licken! Borrow from somebody else. I keep winning my own money back.

ROY (*to* OSCAR). You owe everybody in the game. If you don't have it, you shouldn't play.

OSCAR. All right, I'm through being the nice one. You owe me six dollars apiece for the buffet.

SPEED (*dealing another round of cards*). Buffet? Hot beer and two sandwiches left over from when you went to high school?

OSCAR. What do you want at a poker game, a tomato surprise? Murray, lend me twenty dollars or I'll call your wife and tell her you're in Central Park wearing a dress.

MURRAY. You want money, ask Felix.

OSCAR. He's not here.

MURRAY. Neither am I.

ROY (*gives him money*). All right, here. You're on the books for another twenty.

OSCAR. How many times are you gonna keep saying it?

(*He takes the money.*)

MURRAY. When are you gonna call Felix?

OSCAR. When are we gonna play poker?

MURRAY. Aren't you even worried? It's the first game he's missed in over two years.

OSCAR. The record is fifteen years set by Lou Gehrig in 1939! I'll call! I'll call!

ROY. How can you be so lazy?

(*The phone rings.*)

OSCAR (*throwing his cards in*). Call me irresponsible, I'm funny that way.

(*He goes to the phone.*)

SPEED. Pair of sixes . . .

VINNIE. Three deuces . . .

SPEED (*throws up his hands in despair*). This is my last week. I get all the aggravation I need at home.

(OSCAR *picks up the phone.*)

OSCAR. Hello! Oscar the Poker Player!

VINNIE (*to* OSCAR). If it's my wife tell her I'm leaving at twelve.

SPEED (*to* VINNIE). You look at your watch once more and you get the peanuts in your face. (*To* ROY.) Deal the cards!

(*The game continues during* OSCAR's *phone conversation, with* ROY *dealing a game of stud.*)

OSCAR (*into the phone*). Who? Who did you want, please? *Dabby?* Dabby who? No, there's no Dabby here. Oh, *Daddy!* (*To the others.*) For crise sakes, it's my kid. (*Back into the phone, he speaks with great love and affection.*) Brucey, hello, baby. Yes, it's Daddy! (*There is a general outburst of ad libbing from the poker players. To the others.*) Hey, come on, give me a break, willya? My five-year-old kid is calling from California. It must be costing him a fortune. (*Back into the phone.*) How've you been, sweetheart? Yes, I finally got your letter. It took three weeks. Yes, but next time you tell Mommy to give you a stamp. I know, but you're not supposed to draw it on. (*He laughs. To the others.*) You hear?

SPEED. We hear. We hear. We're all thrilled.

OSCAR (*into the phone*). What's that, darling? What goldfish? Oh, in your room! Oh, sure. Sure, I'm taking care of them. (*He holds the phone over his chest*). Oh, God, I killed my kid's goldfish! (*Back into the phone.*) Yes, I feed them every day.

ROY. Murderer!

OSCAR. Mommy wants to speak to me? Right. Take care of yourself, soldier. I love you.

VINNIE (*beginning to deal a game of stud*). Ante a dollar . . .

SPEED (*to* OSCAR). Cost you a dollar to play. You got a dollar?

OSCAR. Not after I get through talking to this lady. (*Into the phone with false cheerfulness.*) Hello, Blanche. How are you? Err, yes, I have a pretty good idea why you're calling. I'm a week behind with the check, right? *Four* weeks? That's not possible. Because it's not possible. Blanche, I keep a record of every check and I *know* I'm only *three* weeks behind! Blanche, I'm trying the best I can. Blanche, don't threaten me with jail because it's not a threat. With my expenses and my alimony, a prisoner takes home more pay than I do! Very nice, in front of the kids. Blanche, don't tell me you're going to have my salary attached, just say goodbye! Goodbye! (*He hangs up. To the players.*) I'm eight hundred dollars behind in alimony so let's up the stakes.

(*He gets his drink from the poker table.*)

ROY. She can do it, you know.

OSCAR. What?

ROY. Throw you in jail. For nonsupport of the kids.

OSCAR. Never. If she can't call me once a week to aggravate me, she's not happy.

(*He crosses to the bar.*)

MURRAY. It doesn't bother you? That you can go to jail? Or that maybe your kids don't have enough clothes or enough to eat?

OSCAR. Murray, *Poland* could live for a year on what my kids leave over from lunch! Can we play cards?

(*He refills his drink.*)

ROY. But that's the point. You shouldn't *be* in this kind of trouble. It's because you don't know how to manage anything. I should know; I'm your accountant.

OSCAR (*crossing to the table*). If you're my accountant, how come I need money?

ROY. If you need money, how come you play poker?

OSCAR. Because I need money.

ROY. But you always lose.

OSCAR. That's why I need the money! Listen, *I'm* not complaining. *You're* complaining. I get along all right. I'm living.

ROY. Alone? In eight dirty rooms?

OSCAR. If I win tonight, I'll buy a broom.

(MURRAY *and* SPEED *buy chips from* VINNIE, *and* MURRAY *begins to shuffle the deck for a game of draw.*)

ROY. That's not what you need. What you need is a wife.

OSCAR. How can I afford a wife when I can't afford a broom?

ROY. Then don't play poker.

OSCAR (*puts down his drink, rushes to* ROY *and they struggle over the bag of potato chips, which rips, showering everyone. They all begin to yell at one another*). Then don't come to my house and eat my potato chips!

MURRAY. What are you yelling about? We're playing a friendly game.

SPEED. Who's *playing?* We've been sitting here talking since eight o'clock.

VINNIE. Since *seven.* That's why I said I was going to quit at *twelve.*

SPEED. How'd you like a stale banana right in the mouth?

MURRAY (*the peacemaker*). All right, all right, let's calm down. Take it easy. I'm a cop, you know. I could arrest the whole lousy game. (*He finishes dealing the cards.*) Four . . .

OSCAR (*sitting at the table*). My friend Murray the Cop is right. Let's just play cards. And please hold them up; I can't see where I marked them.

MURRAY. You're worse than the kids from the PAL.

OSCAR. But you still love me, Roy, sweety, right?

ROY (*petulant*). Yeah, yeah.

OSCAR. That's not good enough. Come on, say it. In front of the whole poker game. "I love you, Oscar Madison."

ROY. You don't take any of this seriously, do you? You owe money to your wife, your government, your friends . . .

OSCAR (*throws his cards down*). What do you want me to do, Roy, jump in the garbage disposal and grind myself to death? (*The phone rings. He goes to answer it.*) Life goes on even for those of us who are divorced, broke and sloppy. (*Into the phone.*) Hello? Divorced, Broke and Sloppy. Oh, hello, sweetheart. (*He becomes very seductive, pulls the phone to the side and talks low, but he is still audible to the others, who turn and listen.*) I told you not to call me during the game. I can't talk to you now. You *know* I do, darling. All right, just a minute. (*He turns.*) Murray, it's your wife.

(*He puts the phone on the table and sits on the sofa.*)

MURRAY (*nods disgustedly as he crosses to the phone*). I wish you *were* having an affair with her. Then she wouldn't bother *me* all the time. (*He picks up the phone.*) Hello, Mimi, what's wrong?

(SPEED *gets up, stretches and goes into the bathroom.*)

OSCAR (*in a woman's voice, imitating* MIMI). What time are you coming home? (*Then imitating* MURRAY.) I don't know, about twelve, twelve-thirty.

MURRAY (*into the phone*). I don't know, about twelve, twelve-thirty! (ROY *gets up and stretches.*) Why, what did you want, Mimi? "A corned beef sandwich and a strawberry malted!"

OSCAR. Is she pregnant again?

MURRAY (*holds the phone over his chest*). No, just fat! (*There is the sound of a toilet flushing, and after* SPEED *comes out of the bathroom,* VINNIE *goes in. Into the phone again.*) What? How could you hear that, I had the phone over my chest? Who? Felix? No, he didn't show up tonight. What's wrong? You're kidding! How should I know? All right, all right, goodbye. (*The toilet flushes again, and after* VINNIE *comes out of the bathroom,* ROY *goes in.*) Goodbye, Mimi. Goodbye. (*He hangs up. To the others.*) Well, what did I tell you? I knew it!

ROY. What's the matter?

MURRAY (*pacing by the couch*). Felix is missing!

OSCAR. Who?

MURRAY. Felix! Felix Ungar! The man who sits in that chair every week and cleans ashtrays. I told you something was up.

SPEED (*at the table*). What do you mean, missing?

MURRAY. He didn't show up for work today. He didn't come home tonight. No one knows where he is. Mimi just spoke to his wife.

VINNIE (*in his chair at the poker table*). Felix?

MURRAY. They looked everywhere. I'm telling you he's missing.

OSCAR. Wait a minute. No one is missing for one day.

VINNIE. That's right. You've got to be missing for forty-eight hours before you're missing. The worst he could be is lost.

MURRAY. How could he be lost? He's forty-four years old and lives on West End Avenue. What's the matter with you?

ROY (*sitting in an armchair*). Maybe he had an accident.

OSCAR. They would have heard.

ROY. If he's laying in a gutter somewhere? Who would know who he is?

OSCAR. He's got ninety-two credit cards in his wallet. The minute something happens to him, America lights up.

VINNIE. Maybe he went to a movie. You know how long those pictures are today.

SPEED (*looks at* VINNIE *contemptuously*). No wonder you're going to Florida in July! Dumb, dumb, dumb!

ROY. Maybe he was mugged?

OSCAR. For thirty-six hours? How much money could he have on him?

ROY. Maybe they took his clothes. I knew a guy who was mugged in a doctor's office. He had to go home in a nurse's uniform.

(OSCAR *throws a pillow from the couch at* ROY.)

SPEED. Murray, you're a cop. What do you think?

MURRAY. I think it's something real bad.

SPEED. How do you know?

MURRAY. I can feel it in my bones.

SPEED (*to the others*). You hear? Bulldog Drummond.

ROY. Maybe he's drunk. Does he drink?

OSCAR. Felix? On New Year's Eve he has Pepto-Bismol. What are we guessing? I'll call his wife.

(*He picks up the phone.*)

SPEED. Wait a minute! Don't start anything yet. Just 'cause we don't know where he is doesn't mean somebody else doesn't. Does he have a girl?

VINNIE. A what?

SPEED. A girl? You know. Like when you're through work early.

MURRAY. Felix? Playing around? Are you crazy? He wears a vest and galoshes.

SPEED (*gets up and moves toward* MURRAY). You mean you automatically know who has and who hasn't got a girl on the side?

MURRAY (*moves to* SPEED). Yes, I automatically know.

SPEED. All right, you're so smart. Have I got a girl?

MURRAY. No, you haven't got a girl. What you've got is what *I've* got. What you *wish* you got and what you *got* is a whole different civilization! *Oscar* maybe has a girl on the side.

SPEED. That's different. He's divorced. That's not on the side. That's in the middle.

(*He moves to the table.*)

OSCAR (*to them both as he starts to dial*). You through? 'Cause one of our poker players is missing. I'd like to find out about him.

VINNIE. I thought he looked edgy the last couple of weeks. (*To* SPEED.) Didn't you think he looked edgy?

SPEED. No. As a matter of fact, I thought *you* looked edgy.

(*He moves down to the right.*)

OSCAR (*into the phone*). Hello? Frances? Oscar. I just heard.

ROY. Tell her not to worry. She's probably hysterical.

MURRAY. Yeah, you know women.

(*He sits down on the couch.*)

OSCAR (*into the phone*). Listen, Frances, the most important thing is not to worry. Oh! (*To the others.*) She's not worried.

MURRAY. Sure.

OSCAR (*into the phone*). Frances, do you have *any* idea where he could be? He what? You're kidding? Why? No, I didn't know. Gee, that's too bad. All right, listen, Frances, you just sit tight and the minute I hear anything I'll let you know. Right. G'bye.

(*He hangs up. They all look at him expectantly. He gets up wordlessly and crosses to the table, thinking. They all watch him a second, not being able to stand it any longer.*)

MURRAY. Ya gonna tell us or do we hire a private detective?

OSCAR. They broke up!

ROY. Who?

OSCAR. Felix and Frances! They broke up! The entire marriage is through.

VINNIE. You're kidding!

ROY. I don't believe it.

SPEED. After twelve years?

(OSCAR *sits down at the table.*)

VINNIE. They were such a happy couple.

MURRAY. Twelve years doesn't mean you're a *happy* couple. It just means you're a *long* couple.

SPEED. Go figure it. Felix and Frances.

ROY. What are you surprised at? He used to sit there every Friday night and tell us how they were fighting.

SPEED. I know. But who believes Felix?

VINNIE. What happened?

OSCAR. She wants out, that's all.

MURRAY. He'll go to pieces. I know Felix. He's going to try something crazy.

SPEED. That's all he ever used to talk about. "My beautiful wife. My wonderful wife." What happened?

OSCAR. His beautiful, wonderful wife can't stand him, that's what happened.

MURRAY. He'll kill himself. You hear what I'm saying? He's going to go out and try to kill himself.

SPEED (*to* MURRAY). Will you shut up, Murray? Stop being a cop for two minutes. (*To* OSCAR.) Where'd he go, Oscar?

OSCAR. He went out to kill himself.

MURRAY. What did I tell you?

ROY (*to* OSCAR). Are you serious?

OSCAR. That's what she said. He was going out to kill himself. He didn't want to do it at home 'cause the kids were sleeping.

VINNIE. Why?

OSCAR. Why? Because that's Felix, that's why. (*He goes to the bar and refills his drink.*) You know what he's like. He sleeps on the window sill. "Love me or I'll jump." 'Cause he's a nut, that's why.

MURRAY. That's right. Remember he tried something like that in the army? She wanted to break off the engagement so he started cleaning guns in his mouth.

SPEED. I don't believe it. Talk! That's all Felix is, talk.

VINNIE (*worried*). But is that what he

said? In those words? "I'm going to kill myself?"

OSCAR (*pacing about the table*). I don't know in what words. She didn't read it to me.

ROY. You mean he left her a note?

OSCAR. No, he sent a telegram.

MURRAY. A *suicide telegram*? Who sends a suicide telegram?

OSCAR. Felix, the nut, that's who! Can you imagine getting a thing like that? She even has to tip the kid a quarter.

ROY. I don't get it. If he wants to kill himself, why does he send a telegram?

OSCAR. Don't you see how his mind works? If he sends a note, she might not get it till Monday and he'd have no excuse for not being dead. This way, for a dollar ten, he's got a chance to be saved.

VINNIE. You mean he really doesn't want to kill himself? He just wants sympathy.

OSCAR. What he'd really like is to go to the funeral and sit in the back. He'd be the biggest crier there.

MURRAY. He's right.

OSCAR. Sure I'm right.

MURRAY. We get these cases every day. All they want is attention. We got a guy who calls us every Saturday afternoon from the George Washington Bridge.

ROY. I don't know. You never can tell what a guy'll do when he's hysterical.

MURRAY. Nahhh. Nine out of ten times they don't jump.

ROY. What about the tenth time?

MURRAY. They jump. He's right. There's a possibility.

OSCAR. Not with Felix. I know him. He's too nervous to kill himself. He wears his seatbelt in a drive-in movie.

VINNIE. Isn't there someplace we could look for him?

SPEED. Where? Where would you look? Who knows where he is?

(*The doorbell rings. They all look at* OSCAR.)

OSCAR. Of course! If you're going to kill yourself, where's the safest place to do it? With your friends!

(VINNIE *starts for the door*.)

MURRAY (*stopping him*). Wait a minute! The guy may be hysterical. Let's play it nice and easy. If *we're* calm, maybe *he'll* be calm.

ROY (*getting up and joining them*).

That's right. That's how they do it with those guys out on the ledge. You talk nice and soft.

(SPEED *rushes over to them, and joins in the frenzied discussion*.)

VINNIE. What'll we say to him?

MURRAY. We don't say nothin'. Like we never heard a thing.

OSCAR (*trying to get their attention*). You through with this discussion? Because he already could have hung himself out in the hall. (*To* VINNIE.) Vinnie, open the door!

MURRAY. Remember! Like we don't know nothin'.

(*They all rush back to their seats and grab up cards, which they concentrate on with the greatest intensity.* VINNIE *opens the door.* FELIX UNGAR *is there. He's about forty-four. His clothes are rumpled as if he had slept in them, and he needs a shave. Although he tries to act matter-of-fact, there is an air of great tension and nervousness about him.*)

FELIX (*softly*). Hi, Vin! (VINNIE *quickly goes back to his seat and studies his cards.* FELIX *has his hands in his pockets, trying to be very nonchalant. With controlled calm.*) Hi, fellas. (*They all mumble hello, but do not look at him. He puts his coat over the railing and crosses to the table.*) How's the game going? (*They all mumble appropriate remarks, and continue staring at their cards.*) Good! Good! Sorry I'm late. (FELIX *looks a little disappointed that no one asks "What?" He starts to pick up a sandwich, changes his mind and makes a gesture of distaste.*) Any Coke left?

OSCAR (*looking up from his cards*). Coke? Gee, I don't think so. I got a Seven-Up!

FELIX (*bravely*). No, I felt like a Coke. I just don't feel like Seven-Up tonight!

(*He stands watching the game.*)

OSCAR. What's the bet?

SPEED. You bet a quarter. It's up to Murray. Murray, what do you say? (MURRAY *is staring at* FELIX.) Murray! Murray!

ROY (*to* VINNIE). Tap his shoulder.

VINNIE (*taps* MURRAY'S *shoulder*). Murray!

MURRAY (*startled*). What? What?

SPEED. It's up to you.

MURRAY. Why is it always up to me?

SPEED. It's not always up to you. It's up

to you now. What do you do?

MURRAY. I'm in. I'm in.

(*He throws in a quarter.*)

FELIX (*moves to the bookcase*). Anyone call about me?

OSCAR. Er, not that I can remember. (*To the others.*) Did anyone call for Felix? (*They all shrug and ad lib "No."*) Why? Were you expecting a call?

FELIX (*looking at the books on the shelf*). No! No! Just asking.

(*He opens a book and examines it.*)

ROY. Er, I'll see his bet and raise it a dollar.

FELIX (*without looking up from the book*). I just thought someone might have called.

SPEED. It costs me a dollar and a quarter to play, right?

OSCAR. Right!

FELIX (*still looking at the book, in a sing-song*). But, if no one called, no one called.

(*He slams the book shut and puts it back. They all jump at the noise.*)

SPEED (*getting nervous*). What does it cost me to play again?

MURRAY (*angry*). A dollar and a quarter! *A dollar and a quarter!* Pay attention, for crise sakes!

ROY. All right, take it easy. Take it easy.

OSCAR. Let's calm down, everyone, heh?

MURRAY. I'm sorry. I can't help it. (*Points to* SPEED.) He makes me nervous.

SPEED. I make *you* nervous. You make *me* nervous. You make *everyone* nervous.

MURRAY (*sarcastic*). I'm sorry. Forgive me. I'll kill myself.

OSCAR. Murray!

(*He motions with his head to* FELIX.)

MURRAY (*realizes his error*). Oh! Sorry.

(SPEED *glares at him. They all sit in silence a moment, until* VINNIE *catches sight of* FELIX, *who is now staring out an upstage window. He quickly calls the others' attention to* FELIX.)

FELIX (*looking back at them from the window*). Gee, it's a pretty view from here. What is it, twelve floors?

OSCAR (*quickly crossing to the window and closing it*). No. It's only eleven. That's all. Eleven. It says twelve but it's really only eleven. (*He then turns and closes the other window as* FELIX *watches him.* OSCAR *shivers slightly.*) Chilly in here. (*To the others.*) Isn't it chilly in here?

(*He crosses back to the table.*)

ROY. Yeah, that's much better.

OSCAR (*to* FELIX). Want to sit down and play? It's still early.

VINNIE. Sure. We're in no rush. We'll be here till three, four in the morning.

FELIX (*shrugs*). I don't know; I just don't feel much like playing now.

OSCAR (*sitting at the table*). Oh! Well, what *do* you feel like doing?

FELIX (*shrugs*). I'll find *something*. (*He starts to walk toward the other room.*) Don't worry about me.

OSCAR. Where are you going?

FELIX (*stops in the doorway. He looks at the others who are all staring at him*). To the john.

OSCAR (*looks at the others, worried, then at* FELIX). Alone?

FELIX (*nods*). I always go alone! Why?

OSCAR (*shrugs*). No reason. You gonna be in there long?

FELIX (*shrugs, then says meaningfully, like a martyr*). As long as it takes.

(*Then he goes into the bathroom and slams the door shut behind him. Immediately they all jump up and crowd about the bathroom door, whispering in frenzied anxiety.*)

MURRAY. Are you crazy? Letting him go to the john alone?

OSCAR. What did you want me to do?

ROY. Stop him! Go in with him!

OSCAR. Suppose he just has to go to the john?

MURRAY. Supposing he does? He's better off being embarrassed than dead!

OSCAR. How's he going to kill himself in the john?

SPEED. What do you mean, how? Razor blades, pills. Anything that's in there.

OSCAR. That's the kids' bathroom. The worst he could do is brush his teeth to death.

ROY. He could jump.

VINNIE. That's right. Isn't there a window in there?

OSCAR. It's only six inches wide.

MURRAY. He could break the glass. He could cut his wrists.

OSCAR. He could also flush himself into the East River. I'm telling you he's not going to try anything!

(*He moves to the table.*)

ROY (*goes to the doorway*). Shhh! Listen! He's crying. (*There is a pause as all listen as* FELIX *sobs.*) You hear that. He's crying.

MURRAY. Isn't that terrible? For God's sakes, Oscar, do something! Say something!

OSCAR. What? What do you say to a man who's crying in your bathroom?

(*There is the sound of the toilet flushing and* ROY *makes a mad dash back to his chair.*)

ROY. He's coming!

(*They all scramble back to their places.* MURRAY *gets mixed up with* VINNIE *and they quickly straighten it out.* FELIX *comes back into the room. But he seems calm and collected, with no evident sign of having cried.*)

FELIX. I guess I'll be running along.

(*He starts for the door.* OSCAR *jumps up. So do the others.*)

OSCAR. Felix, wait a second.

FELIX. No! No! I can't talk to you. I can't talk to anyone.

(*They all try to grab him, stopping him near the stairs.*)

MURRAY. Felix, please. We're your friends. Don't run out like this.

(FELIX *struggles to pull away.*)

OSCAR. Felix, sit down. Just for a minute. Talk to us.

FELIX. There's nothing to talk about. There's nothing to say. It's over. Over. Everything is over. Let me go!

(*He breaks away from them and dashes into the stage-right bedroom. They start to chase him and he dodges from the bedroom through the adjoining door into the bathroom.*)

ROY. Stop him! Grab him!

FELIX (*looking for an exit*). Let me out! I've got to get out of here!

OSCAR. Felix, you're hysterical.

FELIX. Please let me out of here!

MURRAY. The john! Don't let him get in the john!

FELIX (*comes out of the bathroom with* ROY *hanging onto him, and the others trailing behind*). Leave me alone. Why doesn't everyone leave me alone?

OSCAR. All right, Felix, I'm warning you. Now cut it out!

(*He throws a half-filled glass of water, which he has picked up from the bookcase, into* FELIX's *face.*)

FELIX. It's *my* problem. I'll work it out. Leave me alone. Oh, my stomach.

(*He collapses in* ROY's *arms.*)

MURRAY. What's the matter with your stomach?

VINNIE. He looks sick. Look at his face.

(*They all try to hold him as they lead him over to the couch.*)

FELIX. I'm not sick. I'm all right. I didn't take anything. I swear. Ohh, my stomach.

OSCAR. What do you mean you didn't take anything? What did you take?

FELIX (*sitting on the couch*). Nothing! Nothing! I didn't take anything. Don't tell Frances what I did, please! Oohh, my stomach.

MURRAY. He took something! I'm telling you he took something!

OSCAR. What, Felix? *What?*

FELIX. Nothing! I didn't take anything.

OSCAR. Pills? Did you take pills?

FELIX. No! No!

OSCAR (*grabbing* FELIX). Don't lie to me, Felix. Did you take pills?

FELIX. No, I didn't. I didn't take anything.

MURRAY. Thank God he didn't take pills.

(*They all relax and take a breath of relief.*)

FELIX. Just a few, that's all.

(*They all react in alarm and concern over the pills.*)

OSCAR. He took pills.

MURRAY. How many pills?

OSCAR. What kind of pills?

FELIX. I don't know what kind. Little green ones. I just grabbed anything out of her medicine cabinet. I must have been crazy.

OSCAR. Didn't you look? Didn't you see what kind?

FELIX. I couldn't see. The light's broken. Don't call Frances. Don't tell her. I'm so ashamed. So ashamed.

OSCAR. Felix, how many pills did you take?

FELIX. I don't know. I can't remember.

OSCAR. I'm calling Frances.

FELIX (*grabs him*). No! Don't call her. Don't call her. If she hears I took a whole bottle of pills . . .

MURRAY. A whole bottle? *A whole bottle of pills?* (*He turns to* VINNIE.) My God, call an ambulance!

(VINNIE *runs to the front door.*)

OSCAR (*to* MURRAY). You don't even know what *kind!*

MURRAY. What's the difference? He took

a whole bottle!

OSCAR. Maybe they were vitamins. He could be the healthiest one in the room! Take it easy, will you?

FELIX. Don't call Frances. Promise me you won't call Frances.

MURRAY. Open his collar. Open the window. Give him some air.

SPEED. Walk him around. Don't let him go to sleep.

(SPEED *and* MURRAY *pick* FELIX *up and walk him around, while* ROY *rubs his wrists.*)

ROY. Rub his wrists. Keep his circulation going.

VINNIE (*running to the bathroom to get a compress*). A cold compress. Put a cold compress on his neck.

(*They sit* FELIX *in the armchair, still chattering in alarm.*)

OSCAR. One doctor at a time, heh? All the interns shut the hell up!

FELIX. I'm all right. I'll be all right. (*To* OSCAR *urgently.*) You didn't call Frances, did you?

MURRAY (*to the others*). You just gonna stand here? No one's gonna do anything? I'm calling a doctor.

(*He crosses to the phone.*)

FELIX. No! No doctor.

MURRAY. You *gotta* have a doctor.

FELIX. I don't need a doctor.

MURRAY. You gotta get the pills out.

FELIX. I got them out. I threw up before! (*He sits back weakly.* MURRAY *hangs up the phone.*) Don't you have a root beer or a ginger ale?

(VINNIE *gives the compress to* SPEED.)

ROY (*to* VINNIE). Get him a drink.

OSCAR (*glares angrily at* FELIX). He threw up!

VINNIE. Which would you rather have, Felix, the root beer or the ginger ale?

SPEED (*to* VINNIE). Get him the drink! Just get him the drink.

(VINNIE *runs into the kitchen as* SPEED *puts the compress on* FELIX's *head.*)

FELIX. Twelve years. Twelve years we were married. Did you know we were married twelve years, Roy?

ROY (*comforting him*). Yes, Felix. I knew.

FELIX (*with great emotion in his voice*). And now it's over. Like that, it's over. That's hysterical, isn't it?

SPEED. Maybe it was just a fight. You've had fights before, Felix.

FELIX. No, it's over. She's getting a lawyer tomorrow. My cousin. She's using *my* cousin! (*He sobs.*) Who am *I* going to get?

(VINNIE *comes out of the kitchen with a glass of root beer.*)

MURRAY (*patting his shoulder*). It's okay, Felix. Come on. Take it easy.

VINNIE (*gives the glass to* FELIX). Here's the root beer.

FELIX. I'm all right, honestly. I'm just crying.

(*He puts his head down. They all look at him helplessly.*)

MURRAY. All right, let's not stand around looking at him. (*Pushes* SPEED *and* VINNIE *away.*) Let's break it up, heh?

FELIX. Yes, don't stand there looking at me. Please.

OSCAR (*to the others*). Come on, he's all right. Let's call it a night.

(MURRAY, SPEED *and* ROY *turn in their chips at the poker table, get their coats and get ready to go.*)

FELIX. I'm so ashamed. Please, fellas, forgive me.

VINNIE (*bending to* FELIX). Oh, Felix, we—we understand.

FELIX. Don't say anything about this to anyone, Vinnie. Will you promise me?

VINNIE. I'm going to Florida tomorrow.

FELIX. Oh, that's nice. Have a good time.

VINNIE. Thanks.

FELIX (*turns away and sighs in despair*). We were going to go to Florida next winter. (*He laughs, but it's a sob.*) Without the kids! Now they'll go without me.

(VINNIE *gets his coat and* OSCAR *ushers them all to the door.*)

MURRAY (*stopping at the door*). Maybe one of us should stay?

OSCAR. It's all right, Murray.

MURRAY. Suppose he tries something again?

OSCAR. He won't try anything again.

MURRAY. How do you *know* he won't try anything again?

FELIX (*turns to* MURRAY). I won't try anything again. I'm very tired.

OSCAR (*to* MURRAY). You hear? He's very tired. He had a busy night. Good night, fellows.

(*They all ad lib goodbyes and leave.*

The door closes, but opens immediately and ROY *comes back in.*)

ROY. If anything happens, Oscar, just call me.

(*He exits, and as the door starts to close, it reopens and* SPEED *comes in.*)

SPEED. I'm three blocks away. I could be here in five minutes.

(*He exits, and as the door starts to close, it reopens and* VINNIE *comes back in.*)

VINNIE. If you need me I'll be at the Meridian Motel in Miami Beach.

OSCAR. You'll be the first one I'll call, Vinnie.

(VINNIE *exits. The door closes and then reopens as* MURRAY *comes back.*)

MURRAY (*to* OSCAR). You're sure?

OSCAR. I'm sure.

MURRAY (*loudly to* FELIX, *as he gestures to* OSCAR *to come to the door*). Good night, Felix. Try to get a good night's sleep. I guarantee you things are going to look a lot brighter in the morning. (*To* OSCAR, *sotto voce.*) Take away his belt and his shoe laces.

(*He nods and exits.* OSCAR *turns and looks at* FELIX *sitting in the armchair and slowly moves across the room. There is a moment's silence.*)

OSCAR (*he looks at* FELIX *and sighs*). Ohh, Felix, Felix, Felix, Felix!

FELIX (*sits with his head buried in his hands. He doesn't look up*). I know, I know, I know, I know! What am I going to do, Oscar?

OSCAR. You're gonna wash down the pills with some hot, black coffee. (*He starts for the kitchen, then stops.*) Do you think I could leave you alone for two minutes?

FELIX. No, I don't think so! Stay with me, Oscar. Talk to me.

OSCAR. A cup of black coffee. It'll be good for you. Come on in the kitchen. I'll sit on you.

FELIX. Oscar, the terrible thing is, I think I still love her. It's a lousy marriage but I still love her. I didn't want this divorce.

OSCAR (*sitting on the arm of the couch*). How about some Ovaltine? You like Ovaltine? With a couple of fig newtons or chocolate mallomars?

FELIX. All right, so we didn't get along. But we had two wonderful kids, and a beautiful home. Didn't we, Oscar?

OSCAR. How about vanilla wafers? Or Vienna fingers? I got everything.

FELIX. What more does she want? What does *any* woman want?

OSCAR. I want to know what *you* want. Ovaltine, coffee or tea. Then we'll get to the divorce.

FELIX. It's not fair, damn it! It's just not fair! (*He bangs his fist on the arm of the chair angrily, then suddenly winces in great pain and grabs his neck.*) Oh! Ohh, my neck. My neck!

OSCAR. What? What?

FELIX (*he gets up and paces in pain. He is holding his twisted neck*). It's a nerve spasm. I get it in the neck. Oh! Ohh, that hurts.

OSCAR (*rushing to help*). Where? Where does it hurt?

FELIX (*stretches out an arm like a half-back*). Don't touch me! Don't touch me!

OSCAR. I just want to see where it hurts.

FELIX. It'll go away. Just let me alone a few minutes. Ohh! Ohh!

OSCAR (*moving to the couch*). Lie down; I'll rub it. It'll ease the pain.

FELIX (*in wild contortions*). You don't know how. It's a special way. Only Frances knows how to rub me.

OSCAR. You want me to ask her to come over and rub you?

FELIX (*yells*). No! No! We're getting divorced. She wouldn't want to rub me anymore. It's tension. I get it from tension. I must be tense.

OSCAR. I wouldn't be surprised. How long does it last?

FELIX. Sometimes a minute, sometimes hours. I once got it while I was driving. I crashed into a liquor store. Ohhh! Ohhh!

(*He sits down, painfully, on the couch*).

OSCAR (*getting behind him*). You want to suffer or do you want me to rub your stupid neck?

(*He starts to massage it.*)

FELIX. Easy! Easy!

OSCAR (*yells*). Relax, damn it: relax!

FELIX (*yells back*). Don't yell at me! (*Then quietly.*) What should I do? Tell me nicely.

OSCAR (*rubbing the neck*). Think of warm jello!

FELIX. Isn't that terrible? I can't do it. I can't relax. I sleep in one position all night. Frances says when I die on my tombstone it's going to say, "Here Stands

Felix Ungar." (*He winces.*) Oh! Ohh!

OSCAR (*stops rubbing*). Does that hurt?

FELIX. No, it feels good.

OSCAR. Then say so. You make the same sound for pain or happiness.

(*Starts to massage his neck again.*)

FELIX. I know. I know. Oscar—I think I'm crazy.

OSCAR. Well, if it'll make you feel any better, I think so too.

FELIX. I mean it. Why else do I go to pieces like this? Coming up here, scaring you to death. Trying to kill myself. What is that?

OSCAR. That's panic. You're a panicky person. You have a low threshold for composure.

(*He stops rubbing.*)

FELIX. Don't stop. It feels good.

OSCAR. If you don't relax I'll break my fingers. (*Touches his hair.*) Look at this. The only man in the world with clenched hair.

FELIX. I do terrible things, Oscar. You know I'm a cry baby.

OSCAR. Bend over.

(FELIX *bends over and* OSCAR *begins to massage his back.*)

FELIX (*head down*). I tell the whole world my problems.

OSCAR (*massaging hard*). Listen, if this hurts just tell me, because I don't know what the hell I'm doing.

FELIX. It just isn't nice, Oscar, running up here like this, carrying on like a nut.

OSCAR (*finishes massaging*). How does your neck feel?

FELIX (*twists his neck*). Better. Only my back hurts. (*He gets up and paces, rubbing his back.*)

OSCAR. What you need is a drink.

(*He starts for the bar.*)

FELIX. I can't drink. It makes me sick. I tried drinking last night.

OSCAR (*at the bar*). Where *were* you last night?

FELIX. Nowhere. I just walked.

OSCAR. All night?

FELIX. All night.

OSCAR. In the rain?

FELIX. No. In a hotel. I couldn't sleep. I walked around the room all night. It was over near Times Square. A dirty, depressing room. Then I found myself looking out the window. And suddenly, I began to think about jumping.

OSCAR (*he has two glasses filled and crosses to* FELIX). What changed your mind?

FELIX. Nothing. I'm still thinking about it.

OSCAR. Drink this.

(*He hands him a glass, crosses to the couch and sits.*)

FELIX. I don't want to get divorced, Oscar. I don't want to suddenly change my whole life. (*He moves to the couch and sits next to* OSCAR.) Talk to me, Oscar. What am I going to do? What am I going to do?

OSCAR. You're going to pull yourself together. And then you're going to drink that Scotch, and then you and I are going to figure out a whole new life for you.

FELIX. Without Frances? Without the kids?

OSCAR. It's been done before.

FELIX (*paces around*). You don't understand, Oscar. I'm nothing without them. I'm—*nothing*!

OSCAR. What do you mean, nothing? You're something! (FELIX *sits in the armchair.*) A person! You're flesh and blood and bones and hair and nails and ears. You're not a fish. You're not a buffalo. You're *you*! You walk and talk and cry and complain and eat little green pills and send suicide telegrams. No one else does that, Felix. I'm telling you, *you're the only one of its kind in the world!* (*He goes to the bar.*) Now drink that.

FELIX. Oscar, you've been through it yourself. What did you do? How did you get through those first few nights?

OSCAR (*pours a drink*). I did exactly what you're doing.

FELIX. Getting hysterical!

OSCAR. No, drinking! *Drinking!* (*He comes back to the couch with the bottle and sits.*) I drank for four days and four nights. And then I fell through a window. I was bleeding but I was forgetting.

(*He drinks again.*)

FELIX. How can you forget your kids? How can you wipe out twelve years of marriage?

OSCAR. You can't. When you walk into eight empty rooms every night it hits you in the face like a wet glove. But those are the facts, Felix. You've got to face it. You can't spend the rest of your life crying. It annoys people in the movies! Be a good boy and drink your Scotch.

(*He stretches out on the couch with his head near* FELIX.)

FELIX. I can imagine what Frances must be going through.

OSCAR. What do you mean, what *she's* going through?

FELIX. It's much harder on the woman, Oscar. She's all alone with the kids. Stuck there in the house. She can't get out like me. I mean where is she going to find someone now at her age? With two kids. Where?

OSCAR. I don't know. Maybe someone'll come to the door! Felix, there's a hundred thousand divorces a year. There must be *something* nice about it. (FELIX *suddenly puts both his hands over his ears and hums quietly.*) What's the matter now?

(*He sits up.*)

FELIX. My ears are closing up. I get it from the sinus. It must be the dust in here. I'm allergic to dust.

(*He hums. Then he gets up and tries to clear his ears by hopping first on one leg then the other as he goes to the window and opens it.*)

OSCAR (*jumping up*). What are you doing?

FELIX. I'm not going to jump. I'm just going to breathe. (*He takes deep breaths.*) I used to drive Frances crazy with my allergies. I'm allergic to perfume. For a while the only thing she could wear was my after-shave lotion. I was impossible to live with. It's a wonder she took it this long.

(*He suddenly bellows like a moose. He makes this strange sound another time.* OSCAR *looks at him dumbfounded.*)

OSCAR. What are you doing?

FELIX. I'm trying to clear my ears. You create a pressure inside and then it opens it up.

(*He bellows again.*)

OSCAR. Did it open up?

FELIX. A little bit. (*He rubs his neck.*) I think I strained my throat.

(*He paces about the room.*)

OSCAR. Felix, why don't you leave yourself alone? Don't tinker.

FELIX. I can't help myself. I drive everyone crazy. A marriage counselor once kicked me out of his office. He wrote on my chart, "Lunatic!" I don't blame her. It's impossible to be married to me.

OSCAR. It takes two to make a rotten marriage.

(*He lies back down on the couch.*)

FELIX. You don't know what I was like at home. I bought her a book and made her write down every penny we spent. Thirty-eight cents for cigarettes; ten cents for a paper. Everything had to go in the book. And then we had a big fight because I said she forgot to write down how much the book was. Who could live with anyone like that?

OSCAR. An accountant! What do I know? We've not perfect. We all have faults.

FELIX. Faults? Heh! Faults. We have a maid who comes in to clean three times a week. And on the other days, Frances does the cleaning. And at night, after they've both cleaned up, I go in and clean the whole place again. I can't help it. I like things clean. Blame it on my mother. I was toilet-trained at five months old.

OSCAR. How do you remember things like that?

FELIX. I loused up the marriage. Nothing was ever right. I used to recook everything. The minute she walked out of the kitchen I would add salt or pepper. It's not that I didn't trust her, it's just that I was a better cook. Well, I cooked myself out of a marriage. (*He bangs his head with the palm of his hand three times.*) *God damned idiot!*

(*He sinks down in the armchair.*)

OSCAR. Don't do that; you'll get a headache.

FELIX. I can't stand it, Oscar. I hate me. Oh, boy, do I hate me.

OSCAR. You don't hate you. You love you. You think no one has problems like you.

FELIX. Don't give me that analyst jazz. I happen to know I hate my guts.

OSCAR. Come on, Felix; I've never *seen* anyone so in love.

FELIX (*hurt*). I thought you were my friend.

OSCAR. That's why I can talk to you like this. Because I love you almost as much as *you* do.

FELIX. Then help me.

OSCAR (*up on one elbow*). How can I help you when I can't help myself? You think *you're* impossible to live with? Blanche used to say, "What time do you want dinner?" And I'd say, "I don't know. I'm not hungry." Then at three o'clock in the morning I'd wake her up and say, "Now!" I've been one of the highest paid sports-writers in the East for the past fourteen years, and we saved eight and a half dollars—in pennies! I'm never home, I gamble, I burn cigar holes in the furniture, drink like a fish and lie to her every chance I get. And for our tenth wedding anniversary, I took her to see the New York Rangers-Detroit Red Wings hockey game where she got hit with a puck. And I *still* can't understand why she left me. That's how impossible *I* am!

FELIX. I'm not like you, Oscar. I couldn't take it living all alone. I don't know how I'm going to work. They've got to fire me. How am I going to make a living?

OSCAR. You'll go on street corners and cry. They'll throw nickels at you! You'll work, Felix; you'll work.

(*He lies back down.*)

FELIX. You think I ought to call Frances?

OSCAR (*about to explode*). What for? (*He sits up.*)

FELIX. Well, talk it out again.

OSCAR. You've *talked* it all out. There are no words left in your entire marriage. When are you going to face up to it?

FELIX. I can't help it, Oscar; I don't know what to do.

OSCAR. Then listen to me. Tonight you're going to sleep here. And tomorrow you're going to get your clothes and your electric toothbrush and you'll move in with me.

FELIX. No. no. It's your apartment. I'll be in the way.

OSCAR. There's eight rooms. We could go for a year without seeing each other. Don't you understand? I *want* you to move in.

FELIX. Why? I'm a pest.

OSCAR. I *know* you're a pest. You don't have to keep telling me.

FELIX. Then why do you want me to live with you?

OSCAR. Because I can't stand living alone, that's why! For crying out loud, I'm proposing to you. What do you want, a ring?

FELIX (*moves to* OSCAR). Well, Oscar, if you really mean it, there's a lot I can do around here. I'm very handy around the house. I can fix things.

OSCAR. You don't have to fix things.

FELIX. I want to do *something,* Oscar.

Let me do something.

OSCAR (*nods*). All right, you can take my wife's initials off the towels. Anything you want.

FELIX (*beginning to tidy up*). I can cook. I'm a terrific cook.

OSCAR. You don't have to cook. I eat cold cuts for breakfast.

FELIX. Two meals a day at home, we'll save a fortune. We've got to pay alimony, you know.

OSCAR (*happy to see* FELIX'*s new optimism*). All right, you can cook.

(*He throws a pillow at him.*)

FELIX (*throws the pillow back*). Do you like leg of lamb?

OSCAR. Yes, I like leg of lamb.

FELIX. I'll make it tomorrow night. I'll have to call Frances. She has my big pot.

OSCAR. *Will you forget Frances!* We'll get our own pots. Don't drive me crazy before you move in. (*The phone rings.* OSCAR *picks it up quickly.*) Hello? Oh, hello, Frances!

FELIX (*stops cleaning and starts to wave his arms wildly. He whispers screamingly*). I'm not here! I'm not here! You didn't see me. You don't know where I am. I didn't call. I'm not here. I'm not here.

OSCAR (*into the phone*). Yes, he's here.

FELIX (*pacing back and forth*). How does she sound? Is she worried? Is she crying? What is she saying? Does she want to speak to me? I don't want to speak to her.

OSCAR (*into the phone*). Yes, he is!

FELIX. You can tell her I'm not coming back. I've made up my mind. I've had it there. I've taken just as much as she has. You can tell her for me if she thinks I'm coming back she's got another think coming. Tell her. Tell her.

OSCAR (*into the phone*). Yes! Yes, he's fine.

FELIX. Don't tell her I'm fine! You heard me carrying on before. What are you telling her that for? I'm not fine.

OSCAR (*into the phone*). Yes, I understand, Frances.

FELIX (*sits down next to* OSCAR). Does she want to speak to me? Ask her if she wants to speak to me?

OSCAR (*into the phone*). Do you want to speak to him?

FELIX (*reaches for the phone*). Give me

the phone. I'll speak to her.

OSCAR (*into the phone*). Oh. You don't want to speak to him.

FELIX. She doesn't want to speak to me?

OSCAR (*into the phone*). Yeah, I see. Right. Well, goodbye.

(*He hangs up.*)

FELIX. She didn't want to speak to me?

OSCAR. No!

FELIX. Why did she call?

OSCAR. She wants to know when you're coming over for your clothes. She wants to have the room repainted.

FELIX. Oh!

OSCAR (*pats* FELIX *on the shoulder*). Listen, Felix, it's almost one o'clock.

(*He gets up.*)

FELIX. Didn't want to speak to me, huh?

OSCAR. I'm going to bed. Do you want a cup of tea with Fruitanos or Raisinettos?

FELIX. She'll paint it pink. She always wanted it pink.

OSCAR. I'll get you a pair of pajamas. You like stripes, dots, or animals?

(*He goes into the bedroom.*)

FELIX. She's really heartbroken, isn't she? I want to kill myself, and she's picking out colors.

OSCAR (*in the bedroom*). Which bedroom do you want? I'm lousy with bedrooms.

FELIX (*gets up and moves toward the bedroom*). You know, I'm glad. Because she finally made me realize—it's over. It didn't sink in until just this minute.

OSCAR (*comes back with pillow, pillowcase, and pajamas*). Felix, I want you to go to bed.

FELIX. I don't think I believed her until just now. My marriage is *really* over.

OSCAR. Felix, go to bed.

FELIX. Somehow it doesn't seem so bad now. I mean, I think I can live with this thing.

OSCAR. Live with it tomorrow. Go to bed tonight.

FELIX. In a little while. I've got to think. I've got to start rearranging my life. Do you have a pencil and paper?

OSCAR. Not in a little while. Now! It's my house; I make up the bedtime.

(*He throws the pajamas to him.*)

FELIX. Oscar, please. I have to be alone for a few minutes. I've got to get organized. Go on, you go to bed. I'll—I'll clean up.

(*He begins picking up debris from the floor.*)

OSCAR (*putting the pillow into the pillowcase*). You don't have to clean up. I pay a dollar fifty an hour to clean up.

FELIX. It's all right, Oscar. I wouldn't be able to sleep with all this dirt around anyway. Go to bed. I'll see you in the morning.

(*He puts the dishes on the tray.*)

OSCAR. You're not going to do anything big, are you, like rolling up the rugs?

FELIX. Ten minutes, that's all I'll be.

OSCAR. You're sure?

FELIX (*smiles*). I'm sure.

OSCAR. No monkey business?

FELIX. No monkey business. I'll do the dishes and go right to bed.

OSCAR. Yeah.

(*Crosses up to his bedroom, throwing the pillow into the downstage bedroom as he passes. He closes his bedroom door behind him.*)

FELIX (*calls him*). Oscar! (OSCAR *anxiously comes out of his bedroom and crosses to* FELIX.) I'm going to be all right! It's going to take me a couple of days, but I'm going to be all right.

OSCAR (*smiles*). Good! Well, good night, Felix.

(*He turns to go toward the bedroom as* FELIX *begins to plump up a pillow from the couch.*)

FELIX. Good night, Frances.

(OSCAR *stops dead.* FELIX, *unaware of his error, plumps another pillow as* OSCAR *turns and stares at* FELIX *with a troubled expression.*)

ACT TWO

SCENE ONE

Two weeks later, about eleven at night. The poker game is in session again. VINNIE, ROY, SPEED, MURRAY *and* OSCAR *are all seated at the table.* FELIX's *chair is empty.*

There is one major difference between this scene and the opening poker-game scene. It is the appearance of the room. It is immaculately clean. No, not clean. Sterile! Spotless! Not a speck of dirt can be seen under the ten coats of Johnson's Glo-Coat that have been applied to the floor in the last three weeks. No laundry bags, no dirty dishes, no half-filled glasses.

Suddenly FELIX *appears from the kitchen. He carries a tray with glasses and food—and napkins. After putting the tray down, he takes the napkins one at a time, flicks them out to full length and hands one to every player. They take them with grumbling and put them on their laps. He picks up a can of beer and very carefully pours it into a tall glass, measuring it perfectly so that not a drop spills or overflows. With a flourish he puts the can down.*

FELIX (*moves to* MURRAY). An ice-cold glass of beer for Murray.

(MURRAY *reaches up for it.*)

MURRAY. Thank you, Felix.

FELIX (*holds the glass back*). Where's your coaster?

MURRAY. My what?

FELIX. Your coaster. The little round thing that goes under the glass.

MURRAY (*looks around on the table*). I think I bet it.

OSCAR (*picks it up and hands it to* MURRAY). I knew I was winning too much. Here!

FELIX. Always try to use your coasters, fellows. (*He picks up another drink from the tray.*) Scotch and a little bit of water?

SPEED (*raises his hand*). Scotch and a little bit of water. (*Proudly.*) And I have my coaster.

(*He holds it up for inspection.*)

FELIX (*hands him the drink*). I hate to be a pest but you know what wet glasses do?

(*He goes back to the tray and picks up and wipes a clean ashtray.*)

OSCAR (*coldly and deliberately*). They leave little rings on the table.

FELIX (*nods*). Ruins the finish. Eats right through the polish.

OSCAR (*to the others*). So let's watch those little rings, huh?

FELIX (*takes an ashtray and a plate with a sandwich from the tray and crosses to the table*). And we have a clean ashtray for Roy (*handing* ROY *the ashtray*). Aaaaand—a sandwich for Vinnie.

(*Like a doting headwaiter, he skillfully places the sandwich in front of* VINNIE.)

VINNIE (*looks at* FELIX, *then at the sandwich*). Gee, it smells good. What is it?

FELIX. Bacon, lettuce and tomato with mayonnaise on pumpernickle toast.

VINNIE (*unbelievingly*). Where'd you get it?

FELIX (*puzzled*). I made it. In the kitchen.

VINNIE. You mean you put in toast and cooked bacon? Just for me?

OSCAR. If you don't like it, he'll make you a meat loaf. Takes him five minutes.

FELIX. It's no trouble. Honest. I love to cook. Try to eat over the dish. I just vacuumed the rug. (*He goes back to the tray, then stops.*) Oscar!

OSCAR (*quickly*). Yes, sir?

FELIX. I forgot what you wanted. What did you ask me for?

OSCAR. Two three-and-a-half-minute eggs and some petit fours.

FELIX (*points to him*). A double gin and tonic. I'll be right back. (FELIX *starts out, then stops at a little box on the bar.*) Who turned off the Pure-A-Tron?

MURRAY. The what?

FELIX. The Pure-A-Tron! (*He snaps it back on.*) Don't play with this, fellows. I'm trying to get some of the grime out of the air.

(*He looks at them and shakes his head disapprovingly, then exits. They all sit in silence a few seconds.*)

OSCAR. Murray, I'll give you two hundred dollars for your gun.

SPEED (*throws his cards on the table and gets up angrily*). I can't take it any more. (*With his hand on his neck.*) I've had it up to here. In the last three hours we played four minutes of poker. I'm not giving up my Friday nights to watch cooking and housekeeping.

ROY (*slumped in his chair, head hanging down*). I can't breathe. (*He points to the Pure-A-Tron.*) That lousy machine is sucking everything out of the air.

VINNIE (*chewing*). Gee, this is delicious. Who wants a bite?

MURRAY. Is the toast warm?

VINNIE. Perfect. And not too much mayonnaise. It's really a well-made sandwich.

MURRAY. Cut me off a little piece.

VINNIE. Give me your napkin. I don't want to drop any crumbs.

SPEED (*watches them, horrified, as* VIN-NIE *carefully breaks the sandwich over* MURRAY's *napkin. Then he turns to* OSCAR).

Are you listening to this? Martha and Gertrude at the Automat. (*Almost crying in despair.*) What the hell happened to our poker game?

ROY (*still choking*). I'm telling you that thing could kill us. They'll find us here in the morning with our tongues on the floor.

SPEED (*yells at* OSCAR). Do something! Get him back in the game.

OSCAR (*rises, containing his anger*). Don't bother me with your petty little problems. You get this one stinkin' night a week. I'm cooped up here with Dione Lucas twenty-four hours a day.

(*He moves to the window.*)

ROY. It was better before. With the garbage and the smoke, it was better before.

VINNIE (*to* MURRAY). Did you notice what he does with the bread?

MURRAY. What?

VINNIE. He cuts off the crusts. That's why the sandwich is so light.

MURRAY. And then he only uses the soft, green part of the lettuce. (*Chewing.*) It's really delicious.

SPEED (*reacts in amazement and disgust*). I'm going out of my mind.

OSCAR (*yells toward the kitchen*). Felix! Damn it, *Felix!*

SPEED (*takes the kitty box from the bookcase, puts it on the table, and puts the money in*). Forget it. I'm going home.

OSCAR. Sit down!

SPEED. I'll buy a book and I'll start to read again.

OSCAR. Siddown! Will you siddown! (*Yells.*) Felix!

SPEED. Oscar, it's all over. The day his marriage busted up was the end of our poker game. (*He takes his jacket from the back of the chair and crosses to the door.*) If you find some real players next week, call me.

OSCAR (*following him*). You can't run out now. I'm a big loser.

SPEED (*with the door open*). You got no one to blame but yourself. It's all your fault. You're the one who stopped him from killing himself.

(*He exits and slams the door.*)

OSCAR (*stares at the door*). He's right! The man is absolutely right.

(*He moves to the table.*)

MURRAY (*to* VINNIE). Are you going to eat that pickle?

VINNIE. I wasn't thinking of it. Why? Do you want it?

MURRAY. Unless you want it. It's your pickle.

VINNIE. No, no. Take it. I don't usually eat pickle.

(VINNIE *holds the plate with the pickle out to* MURRAY. OSCAR *slaps the plate, which sends the pickle flying through the air.*)

OSCAR. Deal the cards!

MURRAY. What did you do that for?

OSCAR. Just deal the cards. You want to play poker, deal the cards. You want to eat, go to Schrafft's. (*To* VINNIE.) Keep your sandwich and your pickles to yourself. I'm losing ninety-two dollars and everybody's getting fat! (*He screams.*) Felix!

(FELIX *appears in the kitchen doorway.*)

FELIX. What?

OSCAR. Close the kitchen and sit down. It's a quarter to twelve. I still got an hour and a half to win this month's alimony.

ROY (*sniffs*). What is that smell? Disinfectant! (*He smells the cards.*) It's the cards. *He washed the cards!*

(*He throws down the cards, takes his jacket from the chair, and moves past the table to put his money into the kitty box.*)

FELIX (*comes to the table with* OSCAR'S *drink, which he puts down; then he sits in his own seat*). Okay. What's the bet?

OSCAR (*hurrying to his seat*). I can't believe it. We're gonna play cards again. (*He sits.*) It's up to Roy. Roy, baby, what are you gonna do?

ROY. I'm going to get in a cab and go to Central Park. If I don't get some fresh air, you got yourself a dead accountant.

(*He moves toward the door.*)

OSCAR (*follows him*). What do you mean? It's not even twelve o'clock.

ROY (*turns back to* OSCAR). Look, I've been sitting here breathing Lysol and ammonia for four hours! Nature didn't intend for poker to be played like that. (*He crosses to the door.*) If you wanna have a game next week (*He points to* FELIX.) either Louis Pasteur cleans up *after* we've gone, or we play in the Hotel Dixie! Good night!

(*He goes and slams the door. There is a moment's silence.* OSCAR *goes back to the table and sits.*)

OSCAR. We got just enough for handball!

FELIX. Gee, I'm sorry. Is it my fault?

VINNIE. No, I guess no one feels like playing much lately.

MURRAY. Yeah. I don't know what it is, but something's happening to the old gang.

(*He goes to a side chair, sits and puts on his shoes.*)

OSCAR. Don't you know what's happening to the old gang? It's breaking up. Everyone's getting divorced. I swear, we used to have better games when we couldn't get out at night.

VINNIE (*getting up and putting on his jacket*). Well. I guess I'll be going too. Bebe and I are driving to Asbury Park for the weekend.

FELIX. Just the two of you, heh? Gee, that's nice! You always do things like that together, don't you?

VINNIE (*shrugs*). We have to. I don't know how to drive! (*He takes all the money from the kitty box and moves to the door.*) You coming, Murray?

MURRAY (*gets up, takes his jacket and moves toward the door*). Yeah, why not? If I'm not home by one o'clock with a hero sandwich and a frozen éclair, she'll have an all-points out on me. Ahhh, you guys got the life.

FELIX. Who?

MURRAY (*turns back*). Who? You! The Marx Brothers! Laugh, laugh laugh. What have you got to worry about? If you suddenly want to go to the Playboy Club to hunt Bunnies, who's gonna stop you?

FELIX. I don't belong to the Playboy Club.

MURRAY. I know you don't, Felix, it's just a figure of speech. Anyway, it's not such a bad idea. Why don't you join?

FELIX. Why?

MURRAY. Why! Because for twenty-five dollars they give you a key—and you walk into Paradise. *My* keys cost thirty cents— and you walk into corned beef and cabbage. (*He winks at him.*) Listen to me.

(*He moves to the door.*)

FELIX. What are you talking about, Murray? You're a happily married man.

MURRAY (*turns back on the landing*). I'm not talking about *my* situation. (*He puts on his jacket.*) I'm talking about *yours!* Fate has just played a cruel and rotten trick on you, so enjoy it! (*He turns to go, revealing "PAL" letters sewn on the back of his jacket.*) C'mon, Vinnie.

(VINNIE *waves goodbye and they both exit.*)

FELIX (*staring at the door*). That's funny, isn't it, Oscar? They think we're happy. They really think we're enjoying this. (*He gets up and begins to straighten up the chairs.*) They don't know, Oscar. They don't know what it's like.

(*He gives a short, ironic laugh, tucks the napkins under his arm and starts to pick up the dishes from the table.*)

OSCAR. I'd be immensely grateful to you, Felix, if you didn't clean up just now.

FELIX (*puts dishes on the tray*). It's only a few things. (*He stops and looks back at the door.*) I can't get over what Murray just said. You know I think they really envy us. (*He clears more stuff from the table.*)

OSCAR. Felix, leave everything alone. I'm not through dirtying-up for the night.

(*He drops some poker chips on the floor.*)

FELIX (*putting stuff on the tray*). But don't you see the irony of it? Don't you see it, Oscar?

OSCAR (*sighs heavily*). Yes, I see it.

FELIX (*clearing the table*). No, you don't. I really don't think you do.

OSCAR. Felix, I'm telling you I see the irony of it.

FELIX (*pauses*). Then tell me. What is it? What's the irony?

OSCAR (*deep breath*). The irony is—unless we can come to some other arrangement, I'm gonna kill you! That's the irony.

FELIX. What's wrong?

(*He crosses back to the tray and puts down all the glasses and other things.*)

OSCAR. There's something wrong with this system, that's what's wrong. I don't think that two single men living alone in a big eight-room apartment should have a cleaner house than my mother.

FELIX (*gets the rest of the dishes, glasses and coasters from the table*). What are you talking about? I'm just going to put the dishes in the sink. You want me to leave them here all night?

OSCAR (*takes his glass, which* FELIX *has put on the tray, and crosses to the bar for a refill*). I don't care if you take them to bed with you. You can play Mr. Clean all you want. But don't make *me* feel guilty.

FELIX (*takes the tray into the kitchen, leaving the swinging door open*). I'm not asking you to do it, Oscar. You don't have to clean up.

OSCAR (*moves up to the door*). That's why you make me feel guilty. You're always in my bathroom hanging up my towels. Whenever I smoke you follow me around with an ashtray. Last night I found you washing the kitchen floor, shaking your head and moaning, "Footprints, footprints!"

(*He paces around the room.*)

FELIX (*comes back to the table with a silent butler. He dumps the ashtrays, then wipes them carefully*). I didn't say they were yours.

OSCAR (*angrily sits down in the wing chair*). Well, they *were* mine, damn it. I have feet and they make prints. What do you want me to do, climb across the cabinets?

FELIX. No! I want you to walk on the floor.

OSCAR. I appreciate that! I really do.

FELIX (*crosses to the telephone table and cleans the ashtray there*). I'm just trying to keep the place livable. I didn't realize I irritated you that much.

OSCAR. I just feel *I* should have the right to decide when my bathtub needs a going over with Dutch Cleanser. It's the democratic way!

FELIX (*puts the silent butler and his rag down on the coffee table and sits down glumly on the couch*). I was wondering how long it would take.

OSCAR. How long *what* would take?

FELIX. Before I got on your nerves.

OSCAR. I didn't say you get on my nerves.

FELIX. Well, it's the same thing. You said I irritated you.

OSCAR. *You* said you irritated me. *I* didn't say it.

FELIX. Then what *did* you say?

OSCAR. I don't know *what* I said. What's the difference what I said?

FELIX. It doesn't make any difference. I was just repeating what I thought you said.

OSCAR. Well, don't repeat what you *thought* I said. Repeat what I *said!* My God, that's irritating!

FELIX. You see! You *did* say it!

OSCAR. I don't believe this whole conversation.

(*He gets up and paces by the table.*)

FELIX (*pawing with a cup*). Oscar, I'm —I'm sorry. I don't know what's wrong with me.

OSCAR (*still pacing*). And don't pout. If you want to fight, we'll fight. But don't pout! Fighting *I* win. Pouting *you* win!

FELIX. You're right. Everything you say about me is absolutely right.

OSCAR (*really angry, turns to* FELIX). And don't give in so easily. I'm *not* always right. Sometimes *you're* right.

FELIX. You're right. I do that. I always figure I'm in the wrong.

OSCAR. Only this time you *are* wrong. And I'm right.

FELIX. Oh, leave me alone.

OSCAR. And don't sulk. That's the same as pouting.

FELIX. I know. I know. (*He squeezes his cup with anger.*) Damn me, why can't I do one lousy thing right?

(*He suddenly stands up and cocks his arm back, about to hurl the cup angrily against the front door. Then he thinks better of it, puts the cup down and sits.*)

OSCAR (*watching this*). Why didn't you throw it?

FELIX. I almost did. I get so insane with myself sometimes.

OSCAR. Then why don't you throw the cup?

FELIX. Because I'm trying to control myself.

OSCAR. Why?

FELIX. What do you mean, why?

OSCAR. Why do you have to control yourself? You're angry, you felt like throwing the cup, why don't you throw it?

FELIX. Because there's no point to it. I'd still be angry and I'd have a broken cup.

OSCAR. How do you *know* how you'd feel? Maybe you'd feel *wonderful*. Why do you have to control every single thought in your head? Why don't you let loose *once* in your life? Do something that you *feel* like doing—and not what you *think* you're supposed to do. Stop keeping books, Felix. Relax. Get drunk. Get angry. C'mon, *break the goddamned cup!*

(FELIX *suddenly stands up and hurls the cup against the door, smashing it to pieces. Then he grabs his shoulder in pain.*)

FELIX. Oww! I hurt my arm!

(*He sinks down on the couch, massag-*

ing his arm.)

OSCAR (*throws up his hands*). You're hopeless! You're a hopeless mental case!

(*He paces around the table.*)

FELIX (*grimacing with pain*). I'm not supposed to throw with that arm. What a stupid thing to do.

OSCAR. Why don't you live in a closet? I'll leave your meals outside the door and slide in the papers. Is that safe enough?

FELIX (*rubbing his arm*). I used to have bursitis in this arm. I had to give up golf. Do you have a heating pad?

OSCAR. How can you hurt your arm throwing a cup? If it had coffee in it, that's one thing. But an empty cup . . .

(*He sits in the wing chair.*)

FELIX. All right, cut it out, Oscar. That's the way I am. I get hurt easily. I can't help it.

OSCAR. You're not going to cry, are you? I think all those tears dripping on the arm is what gave you bursitis.

FELIX (*holding his arm*). I once got it just from combing my hair.

OSCAR (*shaking his head*). A world full of room-mates and I pick myself the Tin Man. (*He sighs.*) Oh, well, I suppose I could have done worse. Here

FELIX (*moves the rag and silent butler to the bar. Then he takes the chip box from the bar and crosses to the table*). You're darn right, you could have. A *lot* worse.

OSCAR. How?

FELIX. What do you mean, how? How'd you like to live with ten-thumbs Murray or Speed and his complaining? (*He gets down on his knees, picks up the chips and puts them into the box.*) Don't forget I cook and clean and take care of this house. I save us a lot of money, don't I?

OSCAR. Yeah, but then you keep me up all night counting it.

FELIX (*goes to the table and sweeps the chips and cards into the box*). Now wait a minute. We're not always going at each other. We have some fun too, don't we?

OSCAR (*crosses to the couch*). Fun? Felix, getting a clear picture on Channel Two isn't my idea of whoopee.

FELIX. What are you talking about?

OSCAR. All right, what do you and I do every night?

(*He takes off his sneakers and drops them on the floor.*)

FELIX. What do we do? You mean after dinner?

OSCAR. That's right. After we've had your halibut steak and the dishes are done and the sink has been Brillo'd and the pans have been S.O.S.'d and the leftovers have been Saran-Wrapped—what do we do?

FELIX (*finishes clearing the table and puts everything on top of the bookcase*). Well, we read, we talk . . .

OSCAR (*takes off his pants and throws them on the floor*). No, no. I read and *you* talk! I try to work and you talk. I take a bath and you talk. I go to sleep and you talk. We've got your life arranged pretty good but I'm still looking for a little entertainment.

FELIX (*pulling the kitchen chairs away from the table*). What are you saying? That I talk too much?

OSCAR (*sits on the couch*). No, no. I'm not complaining. You have a lot to say. What's worrying me is that I'm beginning to listen.

FELIX (*pulls the table into the alcove*). Oscar, I told you a hundred times, just tell me to shut up. I'm not sensitive.

(*He pulls the love seat down into the room, and centers the table between the windows in the alcove.*)

OSCAR. I don't think you're getting my point. For a husky man, I think I've spent enough evenings discussing tomorrow's menu. The night was made for other things. ⟶F

FELIX. Like what?

(*He puts two dining chairs neatly on one side of the table.*)

OSCAR. Like unless I get to touch something soft in the next two weeks, I'm in big trouble.

FELIX. You mean women?

(*He puts two other dining chairs neatly on the other side of the table.*)

OSCAR. If you want to give it a name, all right, women!

FELIX (*picks up the two kitchen chairs and starts toward the landing*). That's funny. You know I haven't even *thought* about women in weeks.

OSCAR. I fail to see the humor.

FELIX (*stops*). No, that's really strange. I mean when Frances and I were happy, I don't think there was a girl on the street I didn't stare at for ten minutes. (*He crosses to the kitchen door and pushes it open with his back.*) I used to take the wrong subway home just following a pair of legs. But since we broke up, I don't even know what a woman looks like.

(*He takes the chairs into the kitchen.*)

OSCAR. Well, either I could go downstairs and buy a couple of magazines—or I could make a phone call.

FELIX (*from the kitchen, as he washes the dishes*). What are you saying?

OSCAR (*crosses to a humidor on a small table and takes out a cigar*). I'm saying let's spend one night talking to someone with higher voices than us.

FELIX. You mean go out on a date?

OSCAR. Yah . . .

FELIX. Oh, well, I—I can't.

OSCAR. Why not?

FELIX. Well, it's all right for you. But I'm still married.

OSCAR (*paces toward the kitchen door*). You can *cheat* until the divorce comes through!

FELIX. It's not that. It's just that I have no—no *feeling* for it. I can't explain it.

OSCAR. Try!

FELIX (*comes to the doorway with a brush and dish in his hand*). Listen, I intend to go out. I get lonely too. But I'm just separated a few weeks. Give me a little time.

(*He goes back to the sink.*)

OSCAR. There isn't any time left. I saw *TV Guide* and there's nothing on this week! (*He paces into and through the kitchen and out the kitchen door onto the landing.*) What am I asking you? All I want to do is have dinner with a couple of girls. You just have to eat and talk. It's not hard. You've eaten and talked before.

FELIX. Why do you need me? Can't you go out yourself?

OSCAR. Because I may want to come back here. And if we walk in and find you washing the windows, it puts a damper on things.

(*He sits down.*)

FELIX (*pokes his head out of the kitchen*). I'll take a pill and go to sleep.

(*He goes back into the kitchen.*)

OSCAR. Why take a pill when you can take a girl?

FELIX (*comes out with an aerosol bomb held high over his head and circles around the room, spraying it*). Because I'd feel guilty, that's why. Maybe it doesn't make any sense to you, but that's the way I feel.

(*He puts the bomb on the bar and takes the silent butler and rag into the kitchen. He places them on the sink and busily begins to wipe the refrigerator.*)

OSCAR. Look, for all I care you can take her in the kitchen and make a blueberry pie. But I think it's a lot healthier than sitting up in your bed every night writing Frances' name all through the crossword puzzles. Just for one night, talk to another girl.

FELIX (*pushes the love seat carefully into position and sits, weakening*). But who would I call? The only single girl I know is my secretary and I don't think she likes me.

OSCAR (*jumps up and crouches next to FELIX*). Leave that to me. There's two sisters who live in this building. English girls. One's a widow; the other's a divorcée. They're a barrel of laughs.

FELIX. How do you know?

OSCAR. I was trapped in the elevator with them last week. (*Runs to the telephone table, puts the directory on the floor, and gets down on his knees to look for the number.*) I've been meaning to call them but I didn't know which one to take out. This'll be perfect.

FELIX. What do they look like?

OSCAR. Don't worry. Yours is very pretty.

FELIX. I'm not worried. Which one is mine?

OSCAR (*looking in the book*). The divorcée.

FELIX (*goes to* OSCAR). Why do I get the divorcée?

OSCAR. I don't care. You want the widow?

(*He circles a number on the page with a crayon.*)

FELIX (*sitting on the couch*). No, I don't want the widow. I don't even want the divorcée. I'm just doing this for you.

OSCAR. Look, take whoever you want. When they come in the door, point to the sister of your choice. (*Tears the page out of the book, runs to the bookcase and hangs it up.*) I don't care. I just want to have some laughs.

FELIX. All right. All right.

OSCAR (*crosses to the couch and sits next to* FELIX). Don't say all right. I want you to promise me you're going to try to have a good time. Please, Felix. It's important. Say, "I promise."

FELIX (*nods*). I promise.

OSCAR. Again!

FELIX. I promise!

OSCAR. And no writing in the book, a dollar thirty for the cab.

FELIX. No writing in the book.

OSCAR. No one is to be called Frances. It's Gwendolyn and Cecily.

FELIX. No Frances.

OSCAR. No crying, sighing, moaning or groaning.

FELIX. I'll smile from seven to twelve.

OSCAR. And this above all, no talk of the past. Only the present.

FELIX. And the future.

OSCAR. That's the new Felix I've been waiting for. (*Leaps up and prances around.*) Oh, is this going to be a night. Hey, where do you want to go?

FELIX. For what?

OSCAR. For dinner. Where'll we eat?

FELIX. You mean a restaurant? For the four of us? It'll cost a fortune.

OSCAR. We'll cut down on laundry. We won't wear socks on Thursdays.

FELIX. But that's throwing away money. We can't afford it, Oscar.

OSCAR. We have to eat.

FELIX (*moves to* OSCAR). We'll have dinner here.

OSCAR. *Here?*

FELIX. I'll cook. We'll save thirty, forty dollars.

(*He goes to the couch, sits and picks up the phone.*)

OSCAR. What kind of a double date is that? You'll be in the kitchen all night.

FELIX. No, I won't. I'll put it up in the afternoon. Once I get my potatoes in, I'll have all the time in the world.

(*He starts to dial.*)

OSCAR (*pacing back and forth*). What happened to the new Felix? Who are you calling?

FELIX. Frances. I want to get her recipe for London broil. The girls'll be crazy about it.

(*He dials as* OSCAR *storms off toward his bedroom.*)

CURTAIN

SCENE TWO

It is a few days later, about eight o'clock.

No one is on stage. The dining table looks like a page out of House and Garden. *It is set for dinner for four, complete with linen tablecloth, candles and wine glasses. There is a floral centerpiece and flowers about the room, and crackers and dip on the coffee table. There are sounds of activity in the kitchen.*

The front door opens and OSCAR *enters with a bottle of wine in a brown paper bag, his jacket over his arm. He looks about gleefully as he listens to the sounds from the kitchen. He puts the bag on the table and his jacket over a chair.*

———

OSCAR (*calls out in a playful mood*). I'm home, dear! (*He goes into his bedroom, taking off his shirt, and comes skipping out shaving with a cordless razor, with a clean shirt and a tie over his arm. He is joyfully singing as he admires the table.*) Beautiful! Just beautiful! (*He sniffs, obviously catching the aroma from the kitchen.*) Oh, yeah. Something wonderful is going on in that kitchen. (*He rubs his hands gleefully.*) No, sir. There's no doubt about it. I'm the luckiest man on earth. (*He puts the razor into his pocket and begins to put on the shirt.* FELIX *enters slowly from the kitchen. He's wearing a small dish towel as an apron. He has a ladle in one hand. He looks silently and glumly at* OSCAR, *crosses to the armchair and sits.*) I got the wine. (*He takes the bottle out of the bag and puts it on the table.*) Batard Montrachet. Six and a quarter. You don't mind, do you, pussycat? We'll walk to work this week. (FELIX *sits glumly and silently.*) Hey, no kidding, Felix, you did a great job. One little suggestion? Let's come down a little with the lights (*he switches off the wall brackets*) —and up very softly with the music. (*He crosses to the stereo set in the bookcase and picks up some record albums.*) What do you think goes better with London broil, Mancini or Sinatra? (FELIX *just stares ahead.*) Felix? What's the matter? (*He puts the albums down.*) Something's wrong. I can tell by your conversation. (*He goes into the bathroom, gets a bottle of after-shave lotion and comes out putting it on.*) All right, Felix, what is it?

FELIX (*without looking at him*). What is it? Let's start with what time do you think it is?

OSCAR. What time? I don't know. Seven thirty?

FELIX. Seven thirty? Try eight o'clock.

OSCAR (*puts the lotion down on the small table*). All right, so it's eight o'clock. So? (*He begins to fix his tie.*)

FELIX. So? You said you'd be home at seven.

OSCAR. Is that what I said?

FELIX (*nods*). That's what you said. "I will be home at seven" is what you said.

OSCAR. Okay, I said I'd be home at seven. And it's eight. So what's the problem?

FELIX. If you knew you were going to be late, why didn't you call me?

OSCAR (*pauses while making the knot in his tie*). I couldn't call you. I was busy.

FELIX. Too busy to pick up a phone? Where were you?

OSCAR. I was in the office, working.

FELIX. Working? Ha!

OSCAR. Yes. Working!

FELIX. I called your office at seven o'clock. You were gone.

OSCAR (*tucking in his shirt*). It took me an hour to get home. I couldn't get a cab.

FELIX. Since when do they have cabs in Hannigan's Bar?

OSCAR. Wait a minute. I want to get this down on a tape recorder, because no one'll believe me. You mean now I have to call you if I'm coming home late for dinner?

FELIX (*crosses to* OSCAR). Not *any* dinner. Just the ones I've been slaving over since two o'clock this afternoon—to help save *you* money to pay your wife's alimony.

OSCAR (*controlling himself*). Felix, this is no time to have a domestic quarrel. We have two girls coming down any minute.

FELIX. You mean you told them to be here at eight o'clock?

OSCAR (*takes his jacket and crosses to the couch, then sits and takes some dip from the coffee table*). I don't remember what I said. Seven thirty, eight o'clock. What differences does it make?

FELIX (*follows* OSCAR). I'll tell you what difference. You told me they were coming at seven thirty. You were going to be here at seven to help me with the hors d'oeuvres. At seven thirty they arrive and we have cocktails. At eight o'clock we have dinner. It is now eight o'clock. *My London broil is finished!* If we don't eat now the whole damned thing'll be *dried out!*

OSCAR. Oh, God, help me.

FELIX. Never mind helping *you*. Tell Him to save the meat. Because we got nine dollars and thirty-four cents worth drying up in there right now.

OSCAR. Can't you keep it warm?

FELIX (*pacing*). What do you think I am, the Magic Chef? I'm lucky I got it to come out at eight o'clock. What am I going to do?

OSCAR. I don't know. Keep pouring gravy on it.

FELIX. What gravy?

OSCAR. Don't you have any gravy?

FELIX (*storms over to* OSCAR). Where the hell am I going to get gravy at eight o'clock?

OSCAR (*getting up*). I thought it comes when you cook the meat.

FELIX (*follows him*). When you *cook the meat?* You don't know the first thing you're talking about. You have to make gravy. It doesn't come!

OSCAR. You asked my advice, I'm giving it to you. (*He puts on his jacket.*)

FELIX. Advice? (*He waves the ladle in his face.*) You didn't know where the kitchen was till I came here and showed you.

OSCAR. You wanna talk to me, put down the spoon.

FELIX (*exploding in rage, again waving the ladle in his face*). Spoon? You dumb ignoramus. It's a ladle. You don't even know it's a ladle.

OSCAR. All right, Felix, get a hold of yourself.

FELIX (*pulls himself together and sits on the love seat*). You think it's so easy? Go on. The kitchen's all yours. Go make a London broil for four people who come a half hour late.

OSCAR (*to no one in particular*). Listen to me. I'm arguing with him over gravy. (*The bell rings.*)

FELIX (*jumps up*). Well, they're here. Our dinner guests. I'll get a saw and cut the meat. (*He starts for the kitchen.*)

OSCAR (*stopping him*). Stay where you are!

FELIX. I'm not taking the blame for this dinner.

OSCAR. Who's blaming you? Who even *cares* about the dinner?

FELIX (*moves to* OSCAR). *I* care. I take *pride* in what I do. And you're going to explain to them exactly what happened.

OSCAR. All right, you can take a Polaroid picture of me coming in at eight o'clock! Now take off that stupid apron because I'm opening the door.

(*He rips the towel off* FELIX *and goes to the door.*)

FELIX (*takes his jacket from a dining chair and puts it on*). I just want to get one thing clear. This is the last time I ever cook for you. Because people like you don't even appreciate a decent meal. That's why they have TV dinners.

OSCAR. You through?

FELIX. I'm through!

OSCAR. Then smile. (OSCAR *smiles and opens the door. The girls poke their heads through the door. They are in their young thirties and somewhat attractive. They are undoubtedly British.*) Well, hello.

GWENDOLYN (*to* OSCAR). Hallo!

CECILY (*to* OSCAR). Hallo.

GWENDOLYN. I do hope we're not late.

OSCAR. No, no. You timed it perfectly. Come on in. (*He points to them as they enter.*) Er, Felix, I'd like you to meet two very good friends of mine, Gwendolyn and Cecily . . .

CECILY (*pointing out his mistake*). Cecily and Gwendolyn.

OSCAR. Oh, yes. Cecily and Gwendolyn . . . er (*trying to remember their last name*). Er . . . Don't tell me. Robin? No, no. Cardinal?

GWENDOLYN. Wrong both times. It's Pigeon!

OSCAR. Pigeon. Right. Cecily and Gwendolyn Pigeon.

GWENDOLYN (*to* FELIX). You don't spell it like Walter Pidgeon. You spell it like "Coo-Coo" Pigeon.

OSCAR. We'll remember that if it comes up. Cecily and Gwendolyn, I'd like you to meet my room-mate, and our chef for the evening, Felix Ungar.

CECILY (*holding her hand out*). Heh d'yew dew?

FELIX (*moving to her and shaking her hand*). How do you do?

GWENDOLYN (*holding her hand out*). Heh d'yew dew?

FELIX (*stepping up on the landing and shaking her hand*). How do you do you?

(*This puts him nose to nose with* OSCAR, *and there is an awkward pause as they look at each other.*)

OSCAR. Well, we did that beautifully. Why don't we sit down and make ourselves comfortable?

(FELIX *steps aside and ushers the girls down into the room. There is ad libbing and a bit of confusion and milling about as they all squeeze between the armchair and the couch, and the* PIGEONS *finally seat themselves on the couch.* OSCAR *sits in the armchair, and* FELIX *sneaks past him to the love seat. Finally all have settled down.*)

CECILY. This is ever so nice, isn't it, Gwen?

GWENDOLYN (*looking around*). Lovely. And much nicer than our flat. Do you have help?

OSCAR. Er, yes. I have a man who comes in every night.

CECILY. Aren't you the lucky one?

(CECILY, GWENDOLYN *and* OSCAR *all laugh at her joke.* OSCAR *looks over at* FELIX *but there is no response.*)

OSCAR (*rubs his hands together*). Well, isn't this nice? I was telling Felix yesterday about how we happened to meet.

GWENDOLYN. Oh? Who's Felix?

OSCAR (*a little embarrassed, he points to* FELIX). He is!

GWENDOLYN. Oh, yes, of course. I'm so sorry.

(FELIX *nods that it's all right.*)

CECILY. You know it happened to us again this morning.

OSCAR. What did?

GWENDOLYN. Stuck in the elevator again.

OSCAR. Really? Just the two of you?

CECILY. And poor old Mr. Kessler from the third floor. We were in there half an hour.

OSCAR. No kidding? What happened?

GWENDOLYN. Nothing much, I'm afraid.

(CECILY *and* GWENDOLYN *both laugh at her latest joke, joined by* OSCAR. *He once again looks over at* FELIX, *but there is no response.*)

OSCAR (*rubs his hands again*). Well, this really is nice.

CECILY. And ever so much cooler than our place.

GWENDOLYN. It's like equatorial Africa on our side of the building.

CECILY. Last night it was so bad Gwen and I sat there in nature's own cooling ourselves in front of the open fridge. Can you imagine such a thing?

OSCAR. Er, I'm working on it.

GWENDOLYN. Actually, it's impossible to get a night's sleep. Cec and I really don't know what to do.

OSCAR. Why don't you sleep with an air conditioner?

GWENDOLYN. We haven't got one.

OSCAR. I know. But we have.

GWENDOLYN. Oh, you! I told you about that one, didn't I, Cec?

FELIX. They say it may rain Friday.

(*They all stare at* FELIX.)

GWENDOLYN. Oh?

CECILY. That should cool things off a bit.

OSCAR. I wouldn't be surprised.

FELIX. Although sometimes it gets hotter after it rains.

GWENDOLYN. Yes, it does, doesn't it?

(*They continue to stare at* FELIX.)

FELIX (*jumps up and, picking up the ladle, starts for the kitchen*). Dinner is served!

OSCAR (*stopping him*). No, it isn't!

FELIX. Yes, it is!

OSCAR. No, it isn't! I'm sure the girls would like a cocktail first. (*To the girls.*) Wouldn't you, girls?

GWENDOLYN. Well, I wouldn't put up a struggle.

OSCAR. There you are. (*To* CECILY.) What would you like?

CECILY. Oh, I really don't know. (*To* OSCAR.) What have you got?

FELIX. London broil.

OSCAR (*to* FELIX). She means to drink. (*To* CECILY.) We have everything. And what we don't have, I mix in the medicine cabinet. What'll it be?

(*He crouches next to her.*)

CECILY. Oh, a double vodka.

GWENDOLYN. Cecily, not before dinner.

CECILY (*to the men*). My sister. She watches over me like a mother hen. (*To* OSCAR.) Make it a *small* double vodka.

OSCAR. A small double vodka! And for the beautiful mother hen?

GWENDOLYN. Oh, I'd like something cool. I think I would like to have a double

Drambuie with some crushed ice, unless you don't have the crushed ice.

OSCAR. I was up all night with a sledge hammer. I shall return!

(*He goes to the bar and gets bottles of vodka and Drambuie.*)

FELIX (*going to him*). Where are you going?

OSCAR. To get the refreshments.

FELIX (*starting to panic*). Inside? What'll *I* do?

OSCAR. You can finish the weather report.

(*He exits into the kitchen.*)

FELIX (*calls after him*). Don't forget to look at my meat! (*He turns and faces the girls. He crosses to a chair and sits. He crosses his legs nonchalantly but he is ill at ease and he crosses them again. He is becoming aware of the silence and he can no longer get away with just smiling.*) Er, Oscar tells me you're sisters.

CECILY. Yes. That's right.

(*She looks at* GWENDOLYN.)

FELIX. From England.

GWENDOLYN. Yes. That's right.

(*She looks at* CECILY.)

FELIX. I see. (*Silence. Then, his little joke.*) We're not brothers.

CECILY. Yes. We know.

FELIX. Although I am a brother. I have a brother who's a doctor. He lives in Buffalo. That's upstate in New York.

GWENDOLYN (*taking a cigarette from her purse*). Yes, we know.

FELIX. You know my brother?

GWENDOLYN. No. We know that Buffalo is upstate in New York.

FELIX. Oh!

(*He gets up, takes a cigarette lighter from the side table and moves to light* GWENDOLYN'*s cigarette.*)

CECILY. We've been there! Have you?

FELIX. No! Is it nice?

CECILY. Lovely.

(FELIX *closes the lighter on* GWENDO-LYN'*s cigarette and turns to go back to his chair, taking the cigarette, now caught in the lighter, with him. He notices the cigarette and hastily gives it back to* GWENDOLYN, *stopping to light it once again. He puts the lighter back on the table and sits down nervously. There is a pause.*)

FELIX. Isn't that interesting? How long have you been in the United States of

America?

CECILY. Almost four years now.

FELIX (*nods*). Uh huh. Just visiting?

GWENDOLYN (*looks at* CECILY). No! We live here.

FELIX. And you work here too, do you?

CECILY. Yes. We're secretaries for Slenderama.

GWENDOLYN. You know. The health club.

CECILY. People bring us their bodies and we do wonderful things with them.

GWENDOLYN. Actually, if you're interested, we can get you ten per cent off.

CECILY. Off the price, not off your body.

FELIX. Yes, I see. (*He laughs. They all laugh. Suddenly he shouts toward the kitchen.*) Oscar where's the drinks?

OSCAR (*offstage*). Coming! Coming!

CECILY. What field of endeavor are you engaged in?

FELIX. I write the news for CBS.

CECILY. Oh! Fascinating!

GWENDOLYN. Where do you get your ideas from?

FELIX (*he looks at her as though she's a Martian*). From the news.

GWENDOLYN. Oh, yes, of course. Silly me . . .

CECILY. Maybe you can mention Gwen and I in one of your news reports.

FELIX. Well, if you do something spectacular, maybe I will.

CECILY. Oh, we've done spectacular things but I don't think we'd want it spread all over the telly, do you, Gwen?

(*They both laugh.*)

FELIX (*he laughs too, then cries out almost for help*). Oscar!

OSCAR (*offstage*). Yeah, yeah!

FELIX (*to the girls*). It's such a large apartment, sometimes you have to shout.

GWENDOLYN. Just you two baches live here?

FELIX. Baches? Oh, bachelors! We're not bachelors. We're divorced. That is, Oscar's divorced. I'm *getting* divorced.

CECILY. Oh. Small world. We've cut the dinghy loose too, as they say.

GWENDOLYN. Well, you couldn't have a *better* matched foursome, could you?

FELIX (*smiles weakly*). No. I suppose not.

GWENDOLYN. Although technically I'm a widow. I was divorcing my husband, but he died before the final papers came through.

FELIX. Oh, I'm awfully sorry. (*Sighs.*) It's a terrible thing, isn't it? Divorce.

GWENDOLYN. It can be—if you haven't got the right solicitor.

CECILY. That's true. Sometimes they can drag it out for months. I was lucky. Snip, cut and I was free.

FELIX. I mean it's terrible what it can do to people. After all, what is divorce? It's taking two happy people and tearing their lives completely apart. It's inhuman, don't you think so?

CECILY. Yes, it can be an awful bother.

GWENDOLYN. But of course, that's all water under the bridge now, eh? Er, I'm terribly sorry, but I think I've forgotten your name.

FELIX. Felix.

GWENDOLYN. Oh, yes. Felix.

CECILY. Like the cat.

(FELIX *takes his wallet from his jacket pocket.*)

GWENDOLYN. Well, the Pigeons will have to beware of the cat, won't they?

(*She laughs.*)

CECILY (*nibbles on a nut from the dish*). Mmm, cashews. Lovely.

FELIX (*takes a snapshot out of his wallet*). This is the worst part of breaking up.

(*He hands the picture to* CECILY.)

CECILY (*looks at it*). Childhood sweethearts, were you?

FELIX. No, no. That's my little boy and girl. (CECILY *gives the picture to* GWENDOLYN, *takes a pair of glasses from her purse and puts them on.*) He's seven, she's five.

CECILY (*looks again*). Oh! Sweet.

FELIX. They live with their mother.

GWENDOLYN. I imagine you must miss them terribly.

FELIX (*takes back the picture and looks at it longingly*). I can't stand being away from them. (*Shrugs.*) But—that's what happens with divorce.

CECILY. When do you get to see them?

FELIX. Every night. I stop there on my way home! Then I take them on the weekends, and I get them on holidays and July and August.

CECILY. Oh! Well, when is it that you miss them?

FELIX. Whenever I'm not there. If they didn't have to go to school so early, I'd go over and make them breakfast. They love my French toast.

GWENDOLYN. You're certainly a devoted father.

FELIX. It's Frances who's the wonderful one.

CECILY. She's the little girl?

FELIX. No. She's the mother. My wife.

GWENDOLYN. The one you're divorcing?

FELIX (*nods*). Mm! She's done a terrific job bringing them up. They always look so nice. They're so polite. Speak beautifully. Never, "Yeah." Always, "Yes." They're such good kids. And she did it all. She's the kind of woman who— Ah, what am I saying? You don't want to hear any of this.

(*He puts the picture back in his wallet.*)

CECILY. Nonsense. You have a right to be proud. You have two beautiful children and a wonderful ex-wife.

FELIX (*containing his emotions*). I know. I know. (*He hands* CECILY *another snapshot.*) That's her. Frances.

GWENDOLYN (*looking at the picture*). Oh, she's pretty. Isn't she pretty, Cecy?

CECILY. Oh, yes. Pretty. A pretty girl. Very pretty.

FELIX (*takes the picture back*). Thank you. (*Shows them another snapshot.*) Isn't this nice?

GWENDOLYN (*looks*). There's no one in the picture.

FELIX. I know. It's a picture of our living room. We had a beautiful apartment.

GWENDOLYN. Oh, yes. Pretty. Very pretty.

CECILY. Those are lovely lamps.

FELIX. Thank you! (*Takes the picture.*) We bought them in Mexico on our honeymoon. (*He looks at the picture again.*) I used to love to come home at night. (*He's beginning to break.*) That was my whole life. My wife, my kids—and my apartment.

(*He breaks down and sobs.*)

CECILY. Does she have the lamps now too?

FELIX (*nods*). I gave her everything. It'll never be like that again. Never! I— I—(*He turns his head away.*) I'm sorry. (*He takes out a handkerchief and dabs his eyes.* GWENDOLYN *and* CECILY *look at each other with compassion.*) Please forgive me. I didn't mean to get emotional. (*Trying to pull himself together, he picks up a bowl from the side table and offers it to the girls.*) Would you like some potato chips?

(CECILY *takes the bowl.*)

GWENDOLYN. You mustn't be ashamed I think it's a rare quality in a man to be able to cry.

FELIX (*puts a hand over his eyes*). Please. Let's not talk about it.

CECILY. I think it's sweet. Terribly, terribly sweet.

(*She takes a potato chip.*)

FELIX. You're just making it worse.

GWENDOLYN (*teary-eyed*). It's so refreshing to hear a man speak so highly of the woman he's divorcing! Oh, dear. (*She takes out her handkerchief.*) Now you've got me thinking about poor Sydney.

CECILY. Oh, Gwen. Please don't.

(*She puts the bowl down.*)

GWENDOLYN. It was a good marriage at first. Everyone said so. Didn't they, Cecily? Not like you and George.

CECILY (*the past returns as she comforts* GWENDOLYN). That's right. George and I were never happy. Not for one single, solitary day.

(*She remembers her unhappiness, grabs her handkerchief and dabs her eyes. All three are now sitting with handkerchiefs at their eyes.*)

FELIX. Isn't this ridiculous?

GWENDOLYN. I don't know what brought this on. I was feeling so good a few minutes ago.

CECILY. I haven't cried since I was fourteen.

FELIX. Just let it pour out. It'll make you feel much better. I always do.

GWENDOLYN. Oh, dear; oh, dear; oh, dear.

(*All three sit sobbing into their handkerchiefs. Suddenly* OSCAR *bursts happily into the room with a tray full of drinks. He is all smiles.*)

OSCAR (*like a corny M.C.*). Is ev-rybuddy happy? (*Then he sees the maudlin scene.* FELIX *and the girls quickly try to pull themselves together.*) What the hell happened?

FELIX. Nothing! Nothing!

(*He quickly puts his handkerchief away.*)

OSCAR. What do you mean, nothing? I'm gone three minutes and I walk into a funeral parlor. What did you say to them?

FELIX. I didn't say anything. Don't start in again, Oscar.

OSCAR. I can't leave you alone for five seconds. Well, if you really want to cry, go inside and look at your London broil.

FELIX (*he rushes madly into the kitchen*). Oh, my gosh! Why didn't you call me? I told you to call me.

OSCAR (*giving a drink to* CECILY). I'm sorry, girls. I forgot to warn you about Felix. He's a walking soap opera.

GWENDOLYN. I think he's the dearest thing I ever met.

CECILY (*taking the glass*). He's so sensitive. So fragile. I just want to bundle him up in my arms and take care of him.

OSCAR (*holds out* GWENDOLYN's *drink. At this, he puts it back down on the tray and takes a swallow from his own drink*). Well, I think when he comes out of that kitchen you may have to.

(*Sure enough,* FELIX *comes out of the kitchen onto the landing looking like a wounded puppy. With a protective kitchen glove, he holds a pan with the exposed London broil. Black is the color of his true love.*)

FELIX (*very calmly*). I'm going down to the delicatessen. I'll be right back.

OSCAR (*going to him*). Wait a minute. Maybe it's not so bad. Let's see it.

FELIX (*shows him*). Here! Look! Nine dollars and thirty-four cents worth of ashes! (*Pulls the pan away. To the girls.*) I'll get some corned beef sandwiches.

OSCAR (*trying to get a look at it*). Give it to me! Maybe we can save some of it.

FELIX (*holding it away from* OSCAR). There's nothing to save. It's all black meat. Nobody likes black meat!

OSCAR. Can't I even look at it?

FELIX. No, you can't look at it!

OSCAR. Why can't I look at it?

FELIX. If you looked at your watch before, you wouldn't have to look at the black meat now! Leave it alone!

(*He turns to go back into the kitchen.*)

GWENDOLYN (*going to him*). Felix! Can *we* look at it?

CECILY (*turning to him, kneeling on the couch*). Please? (FELIX *stops in the kitchen doorway. He hesitates for a moment. He likes them. Then he turns and wordlessly holds the pan out to them.* GWENDOLYN *and* CECILY *inspect it wordlessly, and then turn away sobbing quietly. To* OSCAR) How about Chinese food?

OSCAR. A wonderful idea.

GWENDOLYN. I've got a better idea. Why don't we just make pot luck in the kitchen?

OSCAR. A *much* better idea.

FELIX. I used up all the pots!

(*He crosses to the love seat and sits, still holding the pan.*)

CECILY. Well, then we can eat up in *our* place. We have tons of Horn and Hardart's.

OSCAR (*gleefully*). That's the best idea I ever heard.

GWENDOLYN. Of course it's awfully hot up there. You'll have to take off your jackets.

OSCAR (*smiling*). We can always open up a refrigerator.

CECILY (*gets her purse from the couch*). Give us five minutes to get into our cooking things.

(GWENDOLYN *gets her purse from the couch.*)

OSCAR. Can't you make it four? I'm suddenly starving to death.

(*The girls are crossing to the door.*)

GWENDOLYN. Don't forget the wine.

OSCAR. How could I forget the wine?

CECILY. And a corkscrew.

OSCAR. *And* a corkscrew.

GWENDOLYN. And Felix.

OSCAR. No, I won't forget Felix.

CECILY. Ta, ta!

OSCAR. Ta, ta!

GWENDOLYN. Ta, ta!

(*The girls exit.*)

OSCAR (*throws a kiss at the closed door*). You bet your sweet little crumpets, "Ta, Ta!" (*He wheels around beaming and quickly gathers up the corkscrew from the bar, and picks up the wine and the records.*) Felix, I love you. You've just overcooked us into one hell of a night. Come on, get the ice bucket. Ready or not, here we come.

(*He runs to the door.*)

FELIX (*sitting motionless*). I'm not going!

OSCAR. What?

FELIX. I said I'm not going.

OSCAR (*crossing to* FELIX). Are you out of your mind? Do you know what's waiting for us up there? You've just been invited to spend the evening in a two-bedroom hothouse with the Coo-Coo Pigeon Sisters! What do you mean you're not going?

FELIX. I don't know how to talk to them. I don't know what to say. I already told them about my brother in Buffalo. I've used up my conversation.

OSCAR. Felix, they're crazy about you. They told me! One of them wants to wrap you up and make a bundle out of you. You're doing better than I am! Get the ice bucket.

(*He starts for the door.*)

FELIX. Don't you understand? I cried! I cried in front of two women.

OSCAR (*stops*). And they *loved* it! I'm thinking of getting hysterical. (*Goes to the door.*) Will you get the ice bucket?

FELIX. But why did I cry? Because I felt guilty. Emotionally I'm still tied to Frances and the kids.

OSCAR. Well, untie the knot just for tonight, will you!

FELIX. I don't want to discuss it any more. (*Starts for the kitchen.*) I'm going to scrub the pots and wash my hair.

(*He goes into the kitchen and puts the pan in the sink.*)

OSCAR (*yelling*). Your greasy pots and your greasy hair can wait. You're coming upstairs with me!

FELIX (*in the kitchen*). I'm not! *I'm not!*

OSCAR. What am I going to do with two girls? Felix, don't do this to me. I'll never forgive you!

FELIX. I'm not going!

OSCAR (*screams*). All right, damn you, I'll go without you! (*And he storms out the door and slams it. Then it opens and he comes in again.*) Are you coming?

FELIX (*comes out of the kitchen looking at a magazine*). No.

OSCAR. You mean you're not going to make any effort to change? This is the person you're going to be—until the day you die?

FELIX (*sitting on the couch*). We are what we are.

OSCAR (*nods, then crosses to a window, pulls back the drapes and opens the window wide. Then he starts back to the door.*) It's twelve floors, not eleven.

(*He walks out as* FELIX *stares at the open windows.*)

CURTAIN

ACT THREE

The next evening about 7:30 P.M. *The room is once again set up for the poker game, with the dining table pulled down, the chairs set about it, and the love seat moved back beneath the windows in the alcove.* FELIX *appears from the bedroom with a vacuum cleaner. He is doing a thorough job on the rug. As he vacuums around the table, the door opens and* OSCAR *comes in wearing a summer hat and carrying a newspaper. He glares at* FELIX, *who is still vacuuming, and shakes his head contemptuously. He crosses behind* FELIX, *leaving his hat on the side table next to the armchair, and goes into his bedroom.* FELIX *is not aware of his presence. Then suddenly the power stops on the vacuum, as* OSCAR *has obviously pulled the plug in the bedroom.* FELIX *tries switching the button on and off a few times, then turns to go back into the bedroom. He stops and realizes what's happened as* OSCAR *comes back into the room.* OSCAR *takes a cigar out of his pocket and as he crosses in front of* FELIX *to the couch, he unwraps it and drops the wrappings carelessly on the floor. He then steps up on the couch and walks back and forth mashing down the pillows. Stepping down, he plants one foot on the armchair and then sits on the couch, taking a wooden match from the coffee table and striking it on the table to light his cigar. He flips the used match onto the rug and settles back to read his newspaper.* FELIX *has watched this all in silence, and now carefully picks up the cigar wrappings and the match and drops them into* OSCAR's *hat. He then dusts his hands and takes the vacuum cleaner into the kitchen, pulling the cord in after him.* OSCAR *takes the wrappings from the hat and puts them in the butt-filled ashtray on the coffee table. Then he takes the ashtray and dumps it on the floor. As he once more settles down with his newspaper,* FELIX *comes out of the kitchen carrying a tray with a steaming dish of spaghetti. As he crosses behind* OSCAR *to the table, he indicates that it smells delicious and passes it close to* OSCAR *to make sure* OSCAR *smells the fantastic dish he's missing. As* FELIX *sits and begins to eat,* OSCAR *takes a can of aerosol spray from the bar, and circling the table, sprays all around* FELIX, *then puts the can down next to him and goes back to his newspaper.*

———

FELIX (*pushing the spaghetti away*). All right, how much longer is this gonna go on?

OSCAR (*reading his paper*). Are you talking to me?

FELIX. That's right, I'm talking to you.

OSCAR. What do you want to know?

FELIX. I want to know if you're going to spend the rest of your life not talking to me. Because if you are, I'm going to buy a radio. (*No reply.*) Well? (*No reply.*) All right. Two can play at this game. (*Pause.*) If you're not going to talk to me, I'm not going to talk to you. (*No reply.*) I can act childish too, you know. (*No reply.*) I can go on without talking just as long as you can.

OSCAR. Then why the hell don't you shut up?

FELIX. Are you talking to me?

OSCAR. You had your chance to talk last night. I begged you to come upstairs with me. From now on I never want to hear a word from that shampooed head as long as you live. That's a warning, Felix.

FELIX (*stares at him*). I stand warned. Over and out!

OSCAR (*gets up, takes a key out of his pocket and slams it on the table*). There's a key to the back door. If you stick to the hallway and your room, you won't get hurt.

(*He sits back down on the couch.*)

FELIX. I don't think I gather the entire meaning of that remark.

OSCAR. Then I'll explain it to you. Stay out of my way.

FELIX (*picks up the key and moves to the couch*). I think you're serious. I think you're really serious. Are you serious?

OSCAR. This is my apartment. Everything in my apartment is mine. The only thing here that's yours is you. Just stay in your room and speak softly.

FELIX. Yeah, you're serious. Well, let me remind you that I pay half the rent and I'll go into any room I want.

(*He gets up angrily and starts toward the hallway.*)

OSCAR. Where are you going?

FELIX. I'm going to walk around your bedroom.

OSCAR (*slams down his newspaper*). You stay out of there.

FELIX (*steaming*). Don't tell me where to go. I pay a hundred and twenty dollars a month.

OSCAR. That was off-season. Starting tomorrow the rates are twelve dollars a day.

FELIX. All right. (*He takes some bills out of his pocket and slams them down on the table.*) There you are. I'm paid up for today. Now I'm going to walk in your bedroom.

(*He starts to storm off.*)

OSCAR. Stay out of there! Stay out of my room!

(*He chases after him.* FELIX *dodges around the table as* OSCAR *blocks the hallway.*)

FELIX (*backing away, keeping the table between them*). Watch yourself! Just watch yourself, Oscar!

OSCAR (*with a pointing finger*). I'm warning you. You want to live here, I don't want to see you, I don't want to hear you and I don't want to smell your cooking. Now get this spaghetti off my poker table.

FELIX. Ha! Ha, ha!

OSCAR. What the hell's so funny?

FELIX. It's not spaghetti. It's linguini!

(OSCAR *picks up the plate of linguini, crosses to the doorway and hurls it into the kitchen.*)

OSCAR. Now it's garbage!

(*He paces by the couch.*)

FELIX (*looks at* OSCAR *unbelievingly: what an insane thing to do*). You are crazy! I'm a neurotic nut but *you are crazy!*

OSCAR. *I'm* crazy, heh? That's really funny coming from a fruitcake like you.

FELIX (*goes to the kitchen door and looks in at the mess. Turns back to* OSCAR). I'm not cleaning that up.

OSCAR. Is that a promise?

FELIX. Did you hear what I said? I'm not cleaning it up. It's your mess. (*Looking into the kitchen again.*) Look at it. Hanging all over the walls.

OSCAR (*crosses to the landing and looks in the kitchen door*). I like it.

(*He closes the door and paces around.*)

FELIX (*fumes*). You'd just let it lie there, wouldn't you? Until it turns hard and brown and . . . Yich, it's disgusting. I'm cleaning it up.

(*He goes into the kitchen.* OSCAR *chases after him. There is the sound of a struggle and falling pots.*)

OSCAR. *Leave it alone!* You touch one strand of that linguini—and I'm gonna punch you right in your sinuses.

FELIX (*dashes out of the kitchen with* OSCAR *in pursuit. He stops and tries to calm* OSCAR *down*). Oscar, I'd like you to take a couple of phenobarbital.

OSCAR (*points*). Go to your room! Did you hear what I said? *Go to your room!*

FELIX. All right, let's everybody just settle down, heh? (*He puts his hand on* OSCAR's *shoulder to calm him but* OSCAR *pulls away violently from his touch.*)

OSCAR. If you want to live through this night, you'd better tie me up and lock your doors and windows.

FELIX (*sits at the table with a great pretense of calm*). All right, Oscar, I'd like to know what's happened?

OSCAR (*moves toward him*). What's *happened?*

FELIX (*hurriedly slides over to the next chair*). That's right. Something must have caused you to go off the deep end like this. What is it? Something I said? Something I did? Heh? What?

OSCAR (*pacing*). It's nothing you said. It's nothing you did. It's *you!*

FELIX. I see. Well, that's plain enough.

OSCAR. I could make it plainer but I don't want to hurt you.

FELIX. What is it, the cooking? The cleaning? The crying?

OSCAR (*moving toward him*). I'll tell you exactly what it is. It's the cooking, cleaning and crying. It's the talking in your sleep, it's the moose calls that open your ears at two o'clock in the morning. I can't take it any more, Felix. I'm crackin' up. Everything you do irritates me. And when you're not here, the things I know you're gonna do when you come in irritate me. You leave me little notes on my pillow. I told you a hundred times, I can't stand little notes on my pillow. "We're all out of Corn Flakes. F.U." It took me three hours to figure out that F.U. was Felix Ungar. It's not your fault, Felix. It's a rotten combination.

FELIX. I get the picture.

OSCAR. That's just the frame. The picture I haven't even painted yet. I got a typewritten list in my office of the "Ten Most Aggravating Things You Do That Drive Me Berserk." But last night was the topper. Oh, that was the topper. Oh, that was the ever-loving lulu of all times.

FELIX. What are you talking about, the London broil?

OSCAR. No, not the London broil. I'm talking about those two lamb chops. (*He points upstairs.*) I had it all set up with that English Betty Boop and her sister, and I wind up drinking tea all night and telling them *your* life story.

FELIX (*jumps up*). Oho! So *that's* what's bothering you. That I loused up your evening!

OSCAR. After the mood you put them in, I'm surprised they didn't go out to Rockaway and swim back to England.

FELIX. Don't blame me. I warned you not to make the date in the first place.

(*He makes his point by shaking his finger in* OSCAR's *face.*)

OSCAR. Don't point that finger at me unless you intend to use it!

FELIX (*moves in nose to nose with* OSCAR). All right, Oscar, get off my back. Get off! Off!

(*Startled by his own actions,* FELIX *jumps back from* OSCAR, *warily circles him, crosses to the couch and sits.*)

OSCAR. What's this? A display of temper? I haven't seen you really angry since the day I dropped my cigar in your pancake batter.

(*He starts toward the hallway.*)

FELIX (*threateningly*). Oscar, you're asking to hear something I don't want to say. But if I say it, I think you'd better hear it.

OSCAR (*comes back to the table, places both hands on it and leans toward* FELIX). If you've got anything on your chest besides your chin, you'd better get it off.

FELIX (*strides to the table, places both hands on it and leans toward* OSCAR. *They are nose to nose*). All right, I warned you. You're a wonderful guy, Oscar. You've done everything for me. If it weren't for you, I don't know what would have happened to me. You took me in here, gave me a place to live and something to live for. I'll never forget you for that. You're tops with me, Oscar.

OSCAR (*motionless*). If I've just been told off, I think I may have missed it.

FELIX. It's coming now! You're also one

of the biggest slobs in the world.

OSCAR. I see.

FELIX. And completely unreliable.

OSCAR. Finished?

FELIX. Undependable.

OSCAR. Is that it?

FELIX. And irresponsible.

OSCAR. Keep going. I think you're hot.

FELIX. That's it. I'm finished. *Now* you've been told off. How do you like that?

(*He crosses to the couch.*)

OSCAR (*straightening up*). Good. Because now I'm going to tell *you* off. For six months I lived alone in this apartment. All alone in eight rooms. I was dejected, despondent, and disgusted. Then *you* moved in—my dearest and closest friend. And after three weeks of close, personal contact—I am about to have a nervous breakdown! Do me a favor. Move into the kitchen. Live with your pots, your pans, your ladle and your meat thermometer. When you want to come out, ring a bell and I'll run into the bedroom. (*Almost breaking down.*) I'm asking you nicely, Felix—as a friend. Stay out of my way!

(*And he goes into the bedroom.*)

FELIX (*is hurt by this, then remembers something. He calls after him*). Walk on the paper, will you? The floors are wet. (OSCAR *comes out of the door. He is glaring maniacally, as he slowly strides back down the hallway.* FELIX *quickly puts the couch between him and* OSCAR.) Awright, keep away. Keep away from me.

OSCAR (*chasing him around the couch*). Come on. Let me get in one shot. You pick it. Head, stomach or kidneys.

FELIX (*dodging about the room*). You're gonna find yourself in one sweet law suit, Oscar.

OSCAR. It's no use running, Felix. There's only eight rooms and I know the short cuts.

(*They are now poised at opposite ends of the couch.* FELIX *picks up a lamp for protection.*)

FELIX. Is this how you settle your problems, Oscar? Like an animal?

OSCAR. All right. You wanna see how I settle my problems. I'll show you. (*Storms off into* FELIX's *bedroom. There is the sound of falling objects and he returns with a suitcase.*) I'll show you how

I settle them. (*Throws the suitcase on the table.*) There! That's how I settle them!

FELIX (*bewildered, looks at the suitcase*). Where are you going?

OSCAR (*exploding*). Not me, you idiot! You. You're the one who's going. I want you out of here. Now! Tonight!

(*He opens the suitcase.*)

FELIX. What are you talking about?

OSCAR. It's all over, Felix. The whole marriage. We're getting an annulment! Don't you understand? I don't want to live with you any more. I want you to pack your things, tie it up with your Saran Wrap and get out of here.

FELIX. You mean actually move out?

OSCAR. Actually, physically and immediately. I don't care where you go. Move into the Museum of Natural History. (*Goes into the kitchen. There is the crash of falling pots and pans.*) I'm sure you'll be very comfortable there. You can dust around the Egyptian mummies to your heart's content. But I'm a human, living person. (*Comes out with a stack of cooking utensils which he throws into the open suitcase.*) All I want is my freedom. Is that too much to ask for? (*Closes it.*) There, you're all packed.

FELIX. You know, I've got a good mind to really leave.

OSCAR (*looking to the heavens*). Why doesn't he ever listen to what I say? Why doesn't he hear me? I know I'm talking —I recognize my voice.

FELIX (*indignantly*). Because if you really want me to go, I'll go.

OSCAR. Then go. I want you to go, so go. When are you going?

FELIX. When am I going, huh? Boy, you're in a bigger hurry than Frances was.

OSCAR. Take as much time as she gave you. I want you to follow your usual routine.

FELIX. In other words, you're throwing me out.

OSCAR. Not in other words. Those are the perfect ones. (*Picks up the suitcase and holds it out to* FELIX.) I am throwing you out.

FELIX. All right, I just wanted to get the record straight. Let it be on *your* conscience.

(*He goes into his bedroom.*)

OSCAR. What? What? (*Follows him to the bedroom doorway.*) Let what be on my conscience?

FELIX (*comes out putting on his jacket and passing by* OSCAR). That you're throwing me out. (*Stops and turns back to him.*) I'm perfectly willing to stay and clear the air of our differences. But you refuse, right?

OSCAR (*still holding the suitcase*). Right! I'm sick and tired of you clearing the air. That's why I want you to leave!

FELIX. Okay, as long as I heard you say the words, "Get out of the house." Fine. But remember, what happens to me is your responsibility. Let it be on *your* head.

(*He crosses to the door.*)

OSCAR (*follows him to the door and screams*). Wait a minute, damn it! Why can't you be thrown out like a decent human being? Why do you have to say things like, "Let it be on your head"? I don't want it on my head. I just want you out of the house.

FELIX. What's the matter, Oscar? Can't cope with a little guilt feelings?

OSCAR (*pounding the railing in frustration*). Damn you. I've been looking forward to throwing you out all day long, and now you even take the pleasure out of that.

FELIX. Forgive me for spoiling your fun. I'm leaving now—according to your wishes and desires.

(*He starts to open the door.*)

OSCAR (*pushes by* FELIX *and slams the door shut. He stands between* FELIX *and the door.*) You're not leaving here until you take it back.

FELIX. Take what back?

OSCAR. "Let it be on your head." What the hell is that, the Curse of the Cat People?

FELIX. Get out of my way, please.

OSCAR. Is this how you left that night with Frances? No wonder she wanted to have the room repainted right away. (*Points to* FELIX's *bedroom.*) I'm gonna have yours dipped in bronze.

FELIX (*sits on the back of the couch with his back to* OSCAR). How can I leave if you're blocking the door?

OSCAR (*very calmly*). Felix, we've been friends a long time. For the sake of that friendship, please say, "Oscar, we can't stand each other; let's break up."

FELIX. I'll let you know what to do about my clothes. Either I'll call—or some-one else will. (*Controlling great emotion.*) I'd like to leave now.

(OSCAR, *resigned, moves out of the way.* FELIX *opens the door.*)

OSCAR. Where will you go?

FELIX (*turns in the doorway and looks at him*). Where? (*He smiles.*) Oh, come on, Oscar. You're not really interested, are you?

(*He exits.* OSCAR *looks as though he's about to burst with frustration. He calls after* FELIX.)

OSCAR. All right, Felix, you win. (*Goes out into the hall.*) We'll try to iron it out. Anything you want. Come back, Felix. Felix? *Felix?* Don't leave me like this— you louse! (*But* FELIX *is gone.* OSCAR *comes back into the room closing the door. He is limp. He searches for something to ease his enormous frustration. He throws a pillow at the door, and then paces about like a caged lion.*) All right, Oscar, get a hold of yourself! He's gone! Keep saying that over and over. He's gone. He's really gone! (*He holds his head in pain.*) He did it. He put a curse on me. It's on my head. I don't know what it is, but something's on my head. (*The doorbell rings and he looks up hopefully.*) Please let it be him. Let it be Felix. Please give me one more chance to kill him.

(*Putting the suitcase on the sofa, he rushes to the door and opens it.* MURRAY *comes in with* VINNIE.)

MURRAY (*putting his jacket on a chair at the table*). Hey, what's the matter with Felix? He walked right by me with that "human sacrifice" look on his face again.

(*He takes off his shoes.*)

VINNIE (*laying his jacket on the love seat*). What's with him? I asked him where he's going and he said, "Only Oscar knows. Only Oscar knows." Where's he going, Oscar?

OSCAR (*sitting at the table*). How the hell should I know? All right, let's get the game started, heh? Come on, get your chips.

MURRAY. I have to get something to eat. I'm starving. Mmm, I think I smell spaghetti.

(*He goes into the kitchen.*)

VINNIE. Isn't he playing tonight?

(*He takes two chairs from the dining alcove and puts them at the table.*)

OSCAR. I don't want to discuss it. I don't

even want to hear his name.

VINNIE. Who? Felix?

OSCAR. I told you not to mention his name.

VINNIE. I didn't know what name you meant.

(*He clears the table and places what's left of* FELIX's *dinner on the bookcase.*)

MURRAY (*comes out of the kitchen*). Hey, did you know there's spaghetti all over the kitchen?

OSCAR. Yes, I know, and it's not spaghetti; it's linguini.

MURRAY. Oh. I thought it was spaghetti. (*He goes back into the kitchen.*)

VINNIE (*taking the poker stuff from the bookcase and putting it on the table*). Why shouldn't I mention his name?

OSCAR. Who?

VINNIE. Felix. What's happened? Has something happened?

(SPEED *and* ROY *come in the open door.*)

SPEED. Yeah, what's the matter with Felix?

(SPEED *puts his jacket over a chair at the table.* ROY *sits in the armchair.* MURRAY *comes out of the kitchen with a six-pack of beer and bags of pretzels and chips. They all stare at* OSCAR *waiting for an answer. There is a long pause and then he stand up.*)

OSCAR. We broke up! I kicked him out. It was my decision. I threw him out of the house. All right? I admit it. Let it be on my head.

VINNIE. Let what be on your head?

OSCAR. How should I know? *Felix put it there!* Ask him! (*He paces around to the right.*)

MURRAY. He'll go to pieces. I know Felix. He's gonna try something crazy.

OSCAR (*turns to the boys*). Why do you think I did it? (MURRAY *makes a gesture of disbelief and moves to the couch, putting down the beer and the bags.* OSCAR *moves to him.*) You think I'm just selfish? That I wanted to be cruel? I did it for you—I did it for all of us.

ROY. What are you talking about?

OSCAR (*crosses to* ROY). All right, we've all been through the napkins and the ashtrays and the bacon, lettuce and tomato sandwiches. But that was just the beginning. Just the beginning. Do you know what he was planning for next Friday night's poker game? As a change of pace.

Do you have any idea?

VINNIE. What?

OSCAR. A Luau! An Hawaiian Luau! Spareribs, roast pork and fried rice. They don't play poker like that in Honolulu.

MURRAY. One thing has nothing to do with the other. We all know he's impossible, but he's still our friend, and he's still out on the street, and I'm still worried about him.

OSCAR (*going to* MURRAY). And I'm not, heh? I'm not concerned? I'm not worried? Who do you think sent him out there in the first place?

MURRAY. Frances!

OSCAR. What?

MURRAY. Frances sent him out in the first place. *You* sent him out in the second place. And whoever he lives with next will send him out in the third place. Don't you understand? It's Felix. He does it to himself.

OSCAR. Why?

MURRAY. I don't know why. *He* doesn't know why. There are people like that. There's a whole tribe in Africa who hit themselves on the head all day long.

(*He sums it all up with an eloquent gesture of resignation.*)

OSCAR (*a slow realization of a whole new reason to be angry*). I'm not going to worry about him. Why should I? He's not worrying about me. He's somewhere out on the streets sulking and crying and having a wonderful time. If he had a spark of human decency he would leave us all alone and go back to Blanche.

(*He sits down at the table.*)

VINNIE. Why should he?

OSCAR (*picks up a deck of cards*). Because it's his wife.

VINNIE. No, Blanche is your wife. His wife is Frances.

OSCAR (*stares at him*). What are you, some kind of wise guy?

VINNIE. What did I say?

OSCAR (*throws the cards in the air*). All right, the poker game is over. I don't want to play any more.

(*He paces around on the right.*)

SPEED. Who's playing? We didn't even start.

OSCAR (*turns on him*). Is that all you can do is complain? Have you given one single thought to where Felix might be?

SPEED. I thought you said you're not

worried about him.

OSCAR (*screams*). I'm not worried, damn it. I'm not worried. (*The doorbell rings. A gleeful look passes over* OSCAR's *face.*) It's him. I bet it's him! (*The boys start to go for the door.* OSCAR *stops them.*) Don't let him in; he's not welcome in this house.

MURRAY (*moves toward the door*). Oscar, don't be childish. We've got to let him in.

OSCAR (*stopping him and leading him to the table*). I won't give him the satisfaction of knowing we've been worrying about him. Sit down. Play cards. Like nothing happened.

MURRAY. But, Oscar . . .

OSCAR. Sit down. Everybody. Come on, sit down and play poker.

(*They sit and* SPEED *begins to deal out cards.*)

VINNIE (*crossing to the door*). Oscar . . .

OSCAR. All right, Vinnie, open the door.

(VINNIE *opens the door. It is* GWENDOLYN *standing there.*)

VINNIE (*surprised*). Oh, hello. (*To* OSCAR.) It's not him, Oscar.

GWENDOLYN. How do you do.

(*She walks into the room.*)

OSCAR (*crosses to her*). Oh, hello, Cecily. Boys, I'd like you to meet Cecily Pigeon.

GWENDOLYN. Gwendolyn Pigeon. Please don't get up. (*To* OSCAR.) May I see you for a moment, Mr. Madison?

OSCAR. Certainly, Gwen. What's the matter?

GWENDOLYN. I think you know. I've come for Felix's things.

(OSCAR *looks at her in shock and disbelief. He looks at the boys, then back at* GWENDOLYN.)

OSCAR. Felix? My Felix?

GWENDOLYN. Yes. Felix Ungar. That sweet, tortured man who's in my flat at this moment pouring his heart out to my sister.

OSCAR (*turns to the boys*). You hear? I'm worried to death and he's up there getting tea and sympathy.

(CECILY *rushes in dragging a reluctant* FELIX *with her.*)

CECILY. Gwen, Felix doesn't want to stay. Please tell him to stay.

FELIX. Really, girls, this is very embarrassing. I can go to a hotel. (*To the boys.*)

Hello, fellas.

GWENDOLYN (*overriding his objections*). Nonsense. I told you, we've plenty of room, and it's a very comfortable sofa. Isn't it, Cecy?

CECILY (*joining in*). Enormous. And we've rented an air conditioner.

GWENDOLYN. And we just don't like the idea of you wandering the streets looking for a place to live.

FELIX. But I'd be in the way. Wouldn't I be in the way?

GWENDOLYN. How could you possibly be in anyone's way?

OSCAR. You want to see a typewritten list?

GWENDOLYN (*turning on him*). Haven't you said enough already, Mr. Madison? (*To* FELIX.) I won't take no for an answer. Just for a few days, Felix.

CECILY. Until you get settled.

GWENDOLYN. Please. Please say, "Yes," Felix.

CECILY. Oh, please—we'd be so happy.

FELIX (*considers*). Well, maybe just for a few days.

GWENDOLYN (*jumping with joy*). Oh, wonderful.

CECILY (*ecstatic*). Marvelous!

GWENDOLYN (*crosses to the door*). You get your things and come right up.

CECILY. And come hungry. We're making dinner.

GWENDOLYN (*to the boys*). Good night, gentlemen; sorry to interrupt your bridge game.

CECILY (*to* FELIX). If you'd like, you can invite your friends to play in our flat.

GWENDOLYN (*to* FELIX). Don't be late. Cocktails in fifteen minutes.

FELIX. I won't.

GWENDOLYN. Ta, ta.

CECILY. Ta, ta.

FELIX. Ta, ta.

(*The girls leave.* FELIX *turns and looks at the fellows and smiles as he crosses the room into the bedroom. The five men stare dumbfounded at the door without moving. Finally* MURRAY *crosses to the door.*)

SPEED (*to the others*). I told you. It's always the quiet guys.

MURRAY. Gee, what nice girls.

(*He closes the door.* FELIX *comes out of the bedroom carrying two suits in a plastic cleaner's bag.*)

ROY. Hey, Felix, are you really gonna move in with them?

FELIX (*turns back to them*). Just for a few days. Until I find my own place. Well, so long, fellows. You can drop your crumbs on the rug again.

(*He starts toward the door.*)

OSCAR. Hey, Felix. Aren't you going to thank me?

FELIX (*stopping on the landing*). For what?

OSCAR. For the two greatest things I ever did for you. Taking you in and throwing you out.

FELIX (*lays his suits over the railing and goes to* OSCAR). You're right, Oscar. Thanks a lot. Getting kicked out twice is enough for any man. In gratitude, I remove the curse.

OSCAR (*smiles*). Oh, bless you and thank you, Wicked Witch of the North.

(*They shake hands. The phone rings.*)

FELIX. Ah, that must be the girls.

MURRAY (*picking up the phone*). Hello?

FELIX. They hate it so when I'm late for cocktails. (*Turning to the boys.*) Well, so long.

MURRAY. It's your wife.

FELIX (*turning to* MURRAY). Oh? Well, do me a favor, Murray. Tell her I can't speak to her now. But tell her I'll be calling her in a few days, because she and I have a lot to talk about. And tell her if I sound different to her, it's because I'm not the same man she kicked out three weeks ago. Tell her, Murray; tell her.

MURRAY. I will when I see her. This is Oscar's wife.

FELIX. Oh!

MURRAY (*into the phone*). Just a minute, Blanche.

(OSCAR *crosses to the phone and sits on the arm of the couch.*)

FELIX. Well, so long, fellows.

(*He shakes hands with the boys, takes his suits and moves to the door.*)

OSCAR (*into the phone*). Hello? Yeah, Blanche. I got a pretty good idea why you're calling. You got my checks, right? Good. (FELIX *stops at the door, caught by* OSCAR'*s conversation. He slowly comes back*

into the room to listen, putting his suits on the railing, and sitting down on the arm of the armchair.*) So now I'm all paid up. No, no, I didn't win at the track. I've just been able to save a little money. I've been eating home a lot. (*Takes a pillow from the couch and throws it at* FELIX.*) Listen, Blanche, you don't have to thank me. I'm just doing what's right. Well, that's nice of you too. The apartment? No, I think you'd be shocked. It's in surprisingly good shape. (FELIX *throws the pillow back at* OSCAR.*) Say, Blanche, did Brucey get the goldfish I sent him? Yeah, well, I'll speak to you again soon, huh? Whenever you want. I don't go out much any more.

FELIX (*gets up, takes his suits from the railing and goes to the door*). Well, good night, Mr. Madison. If you need me again, I get a dollar-fifty an hour.

OSCAR (*makes a gesture to stop* FELIX *as he talks on the phone*). Well, kiss the kids for me. Good night, Blanche. (*Hangs up and turns to* FELIX.*) Felix?

FELIX (*at the opened door*). Yeah?

OSCAR. How about next Friday night? You're not going to break up the game, are you?

FELIX. Me? Never! Marriages may come and go, but the game must go on. So long, Frances.

(*He exits, closing the door.*)

OSCAR (*yelling after him*). So long, Blanche. (*The boys all look at* OSCAR *a moment.*) All right, are we just gonna sit around or are we gonna play poker?

ROY. We're gonna play poker.

(*There is a general hubbub as they pass out the beer, deal the cards and settle around the table.*)

OSCAR (*standing up*). Then let's play poker. (*Sharply, to the boys.*) And watch your cigarettes, will you? This is my house, not a pig sty.

(*He takes the ashtray from the side table next to the armchair, bends down and begins to pick up the butts. The boys settle down to play poker.*)

CURTAIN

FIDDLER ON THE ROOF

Joseph Stein

Based on Sholom Aleichem's Stories
Presented by Harold Prince at the Imperial Theatre, New York City, on September 22, 1964, with the following cast:

TEVYE, *a dairyman* Zero Mostel
GOLDE, *his wife* Maria Karnilova

TZEITEL
HODEL
CHAVA }*their daughters*{ Joanna Merlin
SHPRINTZE   Julia Migenes
BIELKE   Tanya Everett
   Marilyn Rogers
   Linda Ross

YENTE, *a matchmaker* Beatrice Arthur
MOTEL KAMZOIL, *a tailor* Austin Pendleton
SHANDEL, *his mother* Helen Verbit
PERCHIK, *a student* Bert Convy
LAZAR WOLF, *a butcher* Michael Granger
MORDCHA, *an innkeeper* Zvee Scooler
RABBI Gluck Sandor
MENDEL, *his son* Leonard Frey
AVRAM, *a bookseller* Paul Lipson
NAHUM, *a beggar* Maurice Edwards
GRANDMA TZEITEL, *Golde's grandmother*
  Sue Babel

FRUMA-SARAH, *Lazar Wolf's first wife*
  Carol Sawyer
YUSSEL, *a hatter* Mitch Thomas
CONSTABLE Joseph Sullivan
FYEDKA, *a young man* Joe Ponazecki
SASHA, *his friend* Robert Berdeen
THE FIDDLER Gino Conforti
VILLAGERS Tom Abbott, John C. Attle, Sue Babel, Sammy Bayes, Robert Berdeen, Lorenzo Bianco, Duane Bodin, Robert Currie, Sarah Felcher, Tony Gardell, Louis Genevrino, Ross Gifford, Dan Jasin, Sandra Kazan, Thom Koutsoukos, Sharon Lerit, Sylvia Mann, Peff Modelski, Irene Paris, Charles Rule, Carol Sawyer, Roberta Senn, Mitch Thomas, Helen Verbit

Music by Jerry Bock
Lyrics by Sheldon Harnick
Entire production directed and choreographed by Jerome Robbins
Settings by Boris Aronson
Costumes by Patricia Zipprodt
Lighting by Jean Rosenthal
Orchestrations by Don Walker
Musical Direction and Vocal Arrangements by Milton Greene
Dance Music arranged by Betty Walberg
Production Stage Manager, Ruth Mitchell

© 1964 by Joseph Stein
Music and Lyrics © 1964 by Sunbeam Music Corp.
Produced by special permission of the Estate of Olga Rabinowitz, Arnold Perl,
and Crown Publishers, Inc.

CAUTION: Professionals and amateurs are hereby warned that *Fiddler on the Roof* is fully
protected by the laws of copyright and is subject to royalty. All rights, including professional,
amateur, motion picture, recitation, lecturing, public reading, radio and television
broadcasting, the rights of translation into foreign languages, and quotation are strictly
reserved. No part of this work may be used in any way without the written consent of the
copyright holders. All inquiries concerning rights in the book should be addressed to
the William Morris Agency, 1740 Broadway, New York, N.Y. 10019, and all inquiries
concerning rights in the music and lyrics should be addressed to the Sunbeam Music Corp.,
22 West 48th Street, New York, N.Y. 10036.

A musical is always an act of collaboration, like a film or a ballet, rather than the product of one, or perhaps two, men. Also, by and large, the musical is more of a musical form than a literary form. There have been examples of musicals winning the Pulitzer Prize (*Of Thee I Sing* by George and Ira Gershwin was one), but normally people leave a musical humming the tunes rather than pondering on the story.

Another songwriting team to win a Pulitzer, however, was that of Jerry Bock (the music) and Sheldon Harnick (the lyrics), who achieved the distinction in 1959 with their smash-hit musical *Fiorello!* A few years after this they had the idea of basing a musical on the stories of the great Yiddish writer, Sholom Aleichem. They turned to the playwright Joseph Stein to provide the book, as they had worked with him on an earlier musical, *The Body Beautiful*.

It was Stein's task to adapt the Yiddish humor of Sholom Aleichem and his great character Tevye the milkman, and make it acceptable to a Broadway audience. This he undoubtedly achieved although admirers of the original Sholom Aleichem stories—most of the incidents here are taken from the book *Tevye's Daughters*—have occasionally suggested that the musical is a vulgarization of the original. But of course such objections are always raised when literature is used as a basis for a musical play—I have no doubt that Charles Gounod was more than once informed that *Faust* was a vulgarization of Goethe. What matters is not what has been lost, but what has been retained, and what has been created out of that.

Bock, Harnick, and Stein were not the only creative minds on this musical that came to be known as *Fiddler on the Roof*. Although he had no special creative function, the director and choreographer Jerome Robbins played a vital part in the shaping of the show.

It was Robbins, helped by the scenery of Boris Aronson and the costumes of Patricia Zipprodt, who was largely responsible for providing the musical with its remarkable ethnic atmosphere, and for re-creating the feeling of the small Russian village of Anatevka, where the musical is set.

Perhaps the most interesting aspect of *Fiddler on the Roof* was its lack of familiar commercial attributes. Here was a musical not only without its chorus line of pretty girls, but a musical stained with genuine tragedy, and ending on a note, at best, no more cheerful than pathos. .

Yet there is real feeling here. Tevye's hot line to God, which he never ceases to use, his passion and humanity, his relationship with his daughters, and, most of all perhaps, his compassion and understanding for the world around him make him the most unforgettable character in the modern musical theatre.

Stein has done his work very smoothly and adroitly, but so too has Harnick. The lyrics are an integral part with the book, they both carry the action forward, and they go together with Bock's music to give the piece its authentic Yiddish feel. For example, how neat it is for the lyrics to introduce a Yiddish word, such as l'chaim or mazeltov, but in the same musical phrase also to provide it with its translation.

Fiddler on the Roof has shown—as did in a less original context the Shavian adaptation *My Fair Lady*—that a musical comedy can be possessed of marked literary value. It is revealing perhaps that this is the only musical to be included in this "crème de la crème," as Miss Jean Brodie would have said in her prime, of the American theatre. It is also ironic that *Fiddler* did not become the sixth musical in history to win a Pulitzer Prize. That is life, as Tevye would be the first to recognize.

C. B.

ACT ONE

THE PLACE: Anatevka, a village in Russia.
THE TIME: 1905, on the eve of the revolutionary period.

PROLOGUE

The exterior of TEVYE's *house. A* FIDDLER *is seated on the roof, playing.* TEVYE *is outside the house.*

———

TEVYE. A fiddler on the roof. Sounds crazy, no? But in our little village of Anatevka, you might say everyone of us is a fiddler on the roof, trying to scratch out a pleasant, simple tune without breaking his neck. It isn't easy. You may ask, why do we stay up here if it's so dangerous? We stay because Anatevka is our home. And how do we keep our balance? That I can tell you in a word—tradition!
VILLAGERS (*enter, singing*).
Tradition, tradition—Tradition.
Tradition, tradition—Tradition.
TEVYE. Because of our traditions, we've kept our balance for many, many years. Here in Anatevka we have traditions for everything—how to eat, how to sleep, how to wear clothes. For instance, we always keep our heads covered and always wear a little prayer shawl. This shows our constant devotion to God. You may ask, how did this tradition start? I'll tell you—I don't know! But it's a tradition. Because of our traditions, everyone knows who he is and what God expects him to do.
TEVYE *and* PAPAS *sing:*
["Tradition"]

Who, day and night,
Must scramble for a living,
Feed a wife and children,
Say his daily prayers?
And who has the right,
As master of the house,
To have the final word at home?
ALL.
The papa, the papa—Tradition.
The papa, the papa—Tradition.
GOLDE *and* MAMAS.
Who must know the way to make
a proper home,
A quiet home, a kosher home?
Who must raise a family and run
the home

So Papa's free to read the Holy
Book?
ALL.
The mama, the mama—Tradition.
The mama, the mama—Tradition.
SONS.
At three I started Hebrew school,
At ten I learned a trade.
I hear they picked a bride for me.
I hope she's pretty.
ALL.
The sons, the sons—Tradition.
The sons, the sons—Tradition.
DAUGHTERS.
And who does Mama teach
To mend and tend and fix,
Preparing me to marry
Whoever Papa picks?
ALL.
The daughters, the daughters—
Tradition.
The daughters, the daughters—
Tradition.
(*They repeat the song as a round.*)
PAPAS.
The papas.
MAMAS.
The mamas.
SONS.
The sons.
DAUGHTERS.
The daughters.
ALL.
Tradition.
PAPAS.
The papas.
MAMAS.
The mamas.
SONS.
The sons.
DAUGHTERS.
The daughters.
ALL.
Tradition.
TEVYE. And in the circle of our little village, we have always had our special types. For instance, Yente, the matchmaker . . .
YENTE. Avram, I have a perfect match for your son. A wonderful girl.
AVRAM. Who is it?
YENTE. Ruchel, the shoemaker's daughter.
AVRAM. Ruchel? But she can hardly see. She's almost blind.

YENTE. Tell the truth, Avram, is your son so much to look at? The way she sees and the way he looks, it's a perfect match. (*All dance.*)

TEVYE. And Reb Nahum, the beggar . . .

NAHUM. Alms for the poor, alms for the poor.

LAZAR. Here, Reb Nahum, is one kopek.

NAHUM. One kopek? Last week you gave me two kopeks.

LAZAR. I had a bad week.

NAHUM. So if you had a bad week, why should I suffer? (*All dance.*)

TEVYE. And, most important, our beloved rabbi . . .

MENDEL. Rabbi, may I ask you a question?

RABBI. Certainly, my son.

MENDEL. Is there a proper blessing for the Tsar?

RABBI. A blessing for the Tsar? Of course. May God bless and keep the Tsar —far away from us! (*All dance.*)

TEVYE. Then, there are the others in our village. They make a much bigger circle. (*The* PRIEST, *the* CONSTABLE, *and other* RUSSIANS *cross the stage. The two groups nod to each other.*)

TEVYE. His Honor the Constable, his Honor the Priest, and his Honor—many others. We don't bother them, and, so far, they don't bother us. And among ourselves we get along perfectly well. Of course, there was the time (*pointing to the* TWO MEN) when he sold him a horse and he delivered a mule, but that's all settled now. Now we live in simple peace and harmony and— (*The* TWO MEN *begin an argument, which is taken up by the entire group.*)

FIRST MAN. It was a horse.

SECOND MAN. It was a mule.

FIRST MAN. It was a horse!

SECOND MAN. It was a mule, I tell you!

VILLAGERS. Horse!

VILLAGERS. Mule!

VILLAGERS. Horse!

VILLAGERS. Mule!

VILLAGERS. Horse!

VILLAGERS. Mule!

VILLAGERS. Horse!

VILLAGERS. Mule!

EVERYONE.
  Tradition, tradition—Tradition.
  Tradition, tradition—Tradition.

TEVYE (*quieting them*). Tradition. Without our traditions, our lives would be as shaky as—as a fiddler on the roof! (*The* VILLAGERS *exit, and the house opens to show its interior.*)

SCENE ONE

The kitchen of TEVYE'*s house.* GOLDE, TZEITEL, *and* HODEL *are preparing for the Sabbath.* SHPRINTZE *and* BIELKE *enter from outside, carrying logs.*

———

SHPRINTZE. Mama, where should we put these?

GOLDE. Put them on my head! By the stove, foolish girl. Where is Chava?

HODEL. She's in the barn, milking.

BIELKE. When will Papa be home?

GOLDE. It's almost Sabbath and he worries a lot when he'll be home! All day long riding on top of his wagon like a prince.

TZEITEL. Mama, you know that Papa works hard.

GOLDE. His horse works harder! And you don't have to defend your papa to me. I know him a little longer than you. He could drive a person crazy. (*Under her breath.*) He should only live and be well. (*Out loud.*) Shprintze, bring me some more potatoes. (CHAVA *enters, carrying a basket, with a book under her apron.*) Chava, did you finish milking?

CHAVA. Yes, Mama. (*She drops the book.*)

GOLDE. You were reading again? Why does a girl have to read? Will it get her a better husband? Here. (*Hands* CHAVA *the book.*) (CHAVA *exits into the house.* SHPRINTZE *enters with a basket of potatoes.*)

SHPRINTZE. Mama, Yente's coming. She's down the road.

HODEL. Maybe she's finally found a good match for you, Tzeitel.

GOLDE. From your mouth to God's ears.

TZEITEL. Why does she have to come now? It's almost Sabbath.

GOLDE. Go finish in the barn. I want to talk to Yente alone.

SHPRINTZE. Mama, can I go out and play?

GOLDE. You have feet? Go.

BIELKE. Can I go too?

GOLDE. Go too.

(SHPRINTZE *and* BIELKE *exit.*)

TZEITEL. But Mama, the men she finds. The last one was so old and he was bald. He had no hair.

GOLDE. A poor girl without a dowry can't be so particular. You want hair, marry a monkey.

TZEITEL. After all, Mama, I'm not yet twenty years old, and—

GOLDE. Shah! (*Spits between her fingers.*) Do you have to boast about your age? Do you want to tempt the Evil Eye? Inside.

(TZEITEL *leaves the kitchen as* YENTE *enters from outside.*)

YENTE. Golde darling, I had to see you because I have such news for you. And not just every-day-in-the-week news—once-in-a-lifetime news. And where are your daughters? Outside, no? Good. Such diamonds, such jewels. You'll see, Golde, I'll find every one of them a husband. But you shouldn't be so picky. Even the worst husband, God forbid, is better than no husband, God forbid. And who should know better than me? Ever since my husband died I've been a poor widow, alone, nobody to talk to, nothing to say to anyone. It's no life. All I do at night is think of him, and even thinking of him gives me no pleasure, because you know as well as I, he was not much of a person. Never made a living, everything he touched turned to mud, but better than nothing.

MOTEL (*entering*). Good evening. Is Tzeitel in the house?

GOLDE. But she's busy. You can come back later.

MOTEL. There's something I'd like to tell her.

GOLDE. Later.

TZEITEL (*entering*). Oh, Motel, I thought I heard you.

GOLDE. Finish what you were doing. (TZEITEL *goes out. To* MOTEL.) I said later.

MOTEL (*exiting*). All right!

YENTE. What does that poor little tailor, Motel, want with Tzeitel?

GOLDE. They have been friends since they were babies together. They talk, they play . . .

YENTE (*suspiciously*). They play? What do they play?

GOLDE. Who knows? They're just children.

YENTE. From such children, come other children.

GOLDE. Motel, he's a nothing. Yente, you said—

YENTE. Ah, children, children! They are your blessing in your old age. But my Aaron, may he rest in peace, couldn't give me children. Believe me, he was good as gold, never raised his voice to me, but otherwise he was not much of a man, so what good is it if he never raised his voice? But what's the use complaining. Other women enjoy complaining, but not Yente. Not every woman in the world is a Yente. Well, I must prepare my poor Sabbath table, so good-bye, Golde, and it was a pleasure taking our hearts out to each other. (*She starts to exit.*)

GOLDE. Yente, you said you had news for me.

YENTE (*returning*). Oh, I'm losing my head. One day it will fall off altogether, and a horse will kick it into the mud, and good-bye, Yente. Of course, the news. It's about Lazar Wolf, the butcher. A good man, a fine man. And I don't have to tell you that he's well off. But he's lonely, the poor man. After all, a widower . . . You understand? Of course you do. To make it short, out of the whole town, he's cast his eye on Tzeitel.

GOLDE. My Tzeitel?

YENTE. No, the Tsar's Tzeitel! Of course your Tzeitel.

GOLDE. Such a match, for my Tzeitel. But Tevye wants a learned man. He doesn't like Lazar.

YENTE. Fine. So he won't marry him. Lazar wants the daughter, not the father. Listen to me, Golde, send Tevye to him. Don't tell him what it's about. Let Lazar discuss it himself. He'll win him over. He's a good man, a wealthy man—true? Of course true! So you'll tell me how it went, and you don't have to thank me, Golde, because aside from my fee—which anyway Lazar will pay—it gives me satisfaction to make people happy—what better satisfaction is there? So good-bye, Golde, and you're welcome.

(*She goes out. Enter* TZEITEL.)

TZEITEL. What did she want, Mama?

GOLDE. When I want you to know, I'll tell you. Finish washing the floor.

(*She exits.* HODEL *and* CHAVA *enter with wash mop and bucket.*)

HODEL. I wonder if Yente found a husband for you?

TZEITEL. I'm not anxious for Yente to find me a husband.

CHAVA (*teasing*). Not unless it's Motel, the tailor.

TZEITEL. I didn't ask you.

HODEL. Tzeitel, you're the oldest. They have to make a match for you before they can make one for me.

CHAVA. And then after her, one for me.

HODEL. So if Yente brings—

TZEITEL. Oh, Yente! Yente!

HODEL. Well, somebody has to arrange the matches. Young people can't decide these things for themselves.

CHAVA. She might bring someone wonderful—

HODEL. Someone interesting—

CHAVA. And well off—

HODEL. And important—

["Matchmaker, Matchmaker"]

Matchmaker, Matchmaker,
Make me a match,
Find me a catch.
Catch me a catch.
Matchmaker, Matchmaker,
Look through your book
And make me a perfect match.
CHAVA.
Matchmaker, Matchmaker,
I'll bring the veil,
You bring the groom,
Slender and pale.
Bring me a ring for I'm longing
    to be
The envy of all I see.
HODEL.
For Papa,
Make him a scholar.
CHAVA.
For Mama,
Make him rich as a king.
CHAVA *and* HODEL.
For me, well,
I wouldn't holler
If he were as handsome as any-
    thing.
Matchmaker, Matchmaker,
Make me a match,
Find me a find,
Catch me a catch.
Night after night in the dark I'm
    alone,
So find me a match
Of my own.

TZEITEL. Since when are you interested in a match, Chava? I thought you just had your eye on your books. (HODEL *chuckles.*) And you have your eye on the rabbi's son.

HODEL. Why not? We only have one rabbi and he only has one son. Why shouldn't I want the best?

TZEITEL. Because you're a girl from a poor family. So whatever Yente brings, you'll take. Right? Of course right. (*Sings.*)
Hodel, oh Hodel,
Have I made a match for you!
He's handsome, he's young!
All right, he's sixty-two,
But he's a nice man, a good catch
    —true? True.
I promise you'll be happy.
And even if you're not,
There's more to life than that—
Don't ask me what.
Chava, I found him.
Will you be a lucky bride!
He's handsome, he's tall—
That is, from side to side.
But he's a nice man, a good catch
    —right? Right.
You heard he has a temper.
He'll beat you every night,
But only when he's sober,
So you're all right.
Did you think you'd get a prince?
Well, I do the best I can.
With no dowry, no money, no
    family background
Be glad you got a man.
CHAVA.
Matchmaker, Matchmaker,
You know that I'm
Still very young.
Please, take your time.
HODEL.
Up to this minute
I misunderstood
That I could get stuck for good.
CHAVA *and* HODEL.
Dear Yente,
See that he's gentle.
Remember,
You were also a bride.
It's not that
I'm sentimental.
CHAVA, HODEL, *and* TZEITEL.
It's just that I'm terrified!
Matchmaker, Matchmaker,
Plan me no plans,
I'm in no rush.

Maybe I've learned
Playing with matches
A girl can get burned.
So,
Bring me no ring,
Groom me no groom,
Find me no find,
Catch me no catch,
Unless he's a matchless match.

SCENE Two

The exterior of TEVYE's *house.* TEVYE
*enters, pulling his cart. He stops, and sits
on the wagon seat, exhausted.*

———

TEVYE. Today I am a horse. Dear God,
did you have to make my poor old horse
lose his shoe just before the Sabbath? That
wasn't nice. It's enough you pick on me,
Tevye, bless me with five daughters, a life
of poverty. What have you got against my
horse? Sometimes I think when things are
too quiet up there, You say to Yourself:
"Let's see, what kind of mischief can I
play on my friend Tevye?"

GOLDE (*entering from house*). You're
finally here, my breadwinner.

TEVYE (*to heaven*). I'll talk to You later.

GOLDE. Where's your horse?

TEVYE. He was invited to the black-
smith's for the Sabbath.

GOLDE. Hurry up, the sun won't wait for
you. I have something to say to you. (*Exits
into the house.*)

TEVYE. As the Good Book says, "Heal
us, O Lord, and we shall be healed." In
other words, send us the cure, we've got
the sickness already. (*Gestures to the door.*)
I'm not really complaining—after all, with
Your help, I'm starving to death. You
made many, many poor people. I realize,
of course, that it's no shame to be poor, but
it's no great honor either. So what would
have been so terrible if I had a small fortune?

["If I Were a Rich Man"]

If I were a rich man
Daidle deedle daidle
Digguh digguh deedle daidle
    dum,
All day long I'd biddy biddy
    bum,
If I were a wealthy man.

Wouldn't have to work hard,
Daidle deedle daidle
Digguh digguh deedle daidle
    dum,
If I were a biddy biddy rich
Digguh digguh deedle daidle
    man.

I'd build a big, tall house with
    rooms by the dozen
Right in the middle of the town,
A fine tin roof and real wooden
    floors below.
There would be one long stair-
    case just going up,
And one even longer coming
    down,
And one more leading nowhere
    just for show.

I'd fill my yard with chicks and
    turkeys and geese
And ducks for the town to see
    and hear,
Squawking just as noisily as they
    can.
And each loud quack and cluck
    and gobble and honk
Will land like a trumpet on the
    ear,
As if to say, here lives a wealthy
    man.

(*Sighs.*)

If I were a rich man,
Daidle deedle daidle
Digguh digguh deedle daidle
    dum,
All day long I'd biddy biddy
    bum,
If I were a wealthy man.

Wouldn't have to work hard,
Daidle deedle daidle
Digguh digguh deedle daidle
    dum,
If I were a biddy biddy rich
Digguh digguh deedle daidle
    man.

I see my wife, my Golde, looking
    like a rich man's wife,
With a proper double chin,
Supervising meals to her heart's
    delight.

I see her putting on airs and strut-
ting like a peacock,
Oi! what a happy mood she's in,
Screaming at the servants day and
night.

The most important men in town
will come to fawn on me.
They will ask me to advise them
like a Solomon the Wise,
"If you please, Reb Tevye. Pardon
me, Reb Tevye,"
Posing problems that would cross
a rabbi's eyes.
(*He chants.*)

And it won't make one bit of dif-
f'rence
If I answer right or wrong.
When you're rich they think you
really know!

If I were rich I'd have the time
that I lack
To sit in the synagogue and pray,
And maybe have a seat by the
eastern wall,
And I'd discuss the Holy Books
with the learned men
Seven hours every day.
That would be the sweetest thing
of all.
(*Sighs.*)

If I were a rich man,
Daidle deedle daidle
Digguh digguh deedle daidle
dum,
All day long I'd biddy biddy
bum,
If I were a wealthy man.

Wouldn't have to work hard,
Daidle deedle daidle
Digguh digguh deedle daidle
dum,
Lord, who made the lion and the
lamb,
You decreed I should be what I
am,
Would it spoil some vast, eternal
plan—
If I were a wealthy man?

(*As the song ends,* MORDCHA, MENDEL,
PERCHIK, AVRAM, *and other* TOWNSPEOPLE
enter.)

MORDCHA. There he is! You forgot my
order for the Sabbath!

TEVYE. Reb Mordcha, I had a little accident with my horse.

MENDEL. Tevye, you didn't bring the
rabbi's order.

TEVYE. I know, Reb Mendel.

AVRAM. Tevye, you forgot my order for
the Sabbath.

TEVYE. This is bigger news than the
plague in Odessa.

AVRAM (*waving the newspaper that he
holds*). Talking about news, terrible news
in the outside world—terrible!

MORDCHA. What is it?

MENDEL. What does it say?

AVRAM. In a village called Rajanka, all
the Jews were evicted, forced to leave their
homes.

(*They all look at each other.*)

MENDEL. For what reason?

AVRAM. It doesn't say. Maybe the Tsar
wanted their land. Maybe a plague . . .

MORDCHA. May the Tsar have his own
personal plague.

ALL. Amen.

MENDEL (*to* AVRAM). Why don't you ever
bring us some good news?

AVRAM. I only read it. It was an edict
from the authorities.

MORDCHA. May the authorities start itch-
ing in places that they can't reach.

ALL. Amen.

PERCHIK (*has quietly entered during
above and sat down to rest*). Why do you
curse them? What good does your cursing
do? You stand around and curse and chatter and don't do anything. You'll all chatter your way into the grave.

MENDEL. Excuse me, you're not from this
village.

PERCHIK. No.

MENDEL. And where are you from?

PERCHIK. Kiev. I was a student in the
university there.

MORDCHA. Aha! The university. Is that
where you learned to criticize your elders?

PERCHIK. That's where I learned that
there is more to life than talk. You should
know what's going on in the outside world.

MORDCHA. Why should I break my head
about the outside world? Let them break
their own heads.

TEVYE. He's right. As the Good Book
says, "If you spit in the air, it lands in your

face."

PERCHIK. That's nonsense. You can't close your eyes to what's happening in the world.

TEVYE. He's right.

AVRAM. He's right and he's right? How can they both be right?

TEVYE. You know, you're also right.

MORDCHA. He's right! He's still wet behind the ears! Good Sabbath, Tevye.

VILLAGERS. Good Sabbath, Tevye.

(*They take their orders and leave.* MENDEL *remains.*)

MENDEL. Tevye, the rabbi's order. My cheese!

TEVYE. Of course. So you're from Kiev, Reb . . .

PERCHIK. Perchik.

TEVYE. Perchik. So, you're a newcomer here. As Abraham said, "I am a stranger in a strange land."

MENDEL. Moses said that.

TEVYE (*to* MENDEL). Forgive me. As King David put it, "I am slow of speech and slow of tongue."

MENDEL. That was also Moses.

TEVYE. For a man with a slow tongue, he talked a lot.

MENDEL. And the cheese!

(TEVYE *notices that* PERCHIK *is eying the cheese hungrily.*)

TEVYE. Here, have a piece.

PERCHIK. I have no money. And I am not a beggar.

TEVYE. Here—it's a blessing for me to give.

PERCHIK. Very well—for your sake! (*He takes the cheese and devours it.*)

TEVYE. Thank you. You know, it's no crime to be poor.

PERCHIK. In this world, it's the rich who are the criminals. Someday their wealth will be ours.

TEVYE. That would be nice. If they would agree, I would agree.

MENDEL. And who will make this miracle come to pass?

PERCHIK. People. Ordinary people.

MENDEL. Like you?

PERCHIK. Like me.

MENDEL. Nonsense!

TEVYE. And until your golden day comes, Reb Perchik, how will you live?

PERCHIK. By giving lessons to children. Do you have children?

TEVYE. I have five daughters.

PERCHIK. Five?

TEVYE. Daughters.

PERCHIK. Girls should learn too. Girls are people.

MENDEL. A radical!

PERCHIK. I would be willing to teach them. Open their minds to great thoughts.

TEVYE. What great thoughts?

PERCHIK. Well, the Bible has many lessons for our times.

TEVYE. I am a very poor man. Food for lessons? (PERCHIK *nods.*) Good. Stay with us for the Sabbath. Of course, we don't eat like kings, but we don't starve, either. As the Good Book says, "When a poor man eats a chicken, one of them is sick."

MENDEL. Where does the Book say that?

TEVYE. Well, it doesn't exactly say that, but someplace it has something about a chicken. Good Sabbath.

MENDEL. Good Sabbath.

PERCHIK. Good Sabbath.

(MENDEL *exits as* TEVYE *and* PERCHIK *enter the house.*)

SCENE THREE

The interior of TEVYE'*s house.* TEVYE'*s daughters are there.* TEVYE *and* PERCHIK *enter.*

———

TEVYE. Good Sabbath, children.

DAUGHTERS (*running to him*). Good Sabbath, Papa.

TEVYE. Children! (*They all stop.*) This is Perchik. Perchik, this is my oldest daughter.

PERCHIK. Good Sabbath.

TZEITEL. Good Sabbath.

PERCHIK. You have a pleasant daughter.

TEVYE. I have five pleasant daughters. (*He beckons to the girls, and they run into his arms, eagerly, and* TEVYE *kisses each.*) This is mine . . . this is mine . . . this is mine . . . this is mine . . . this is mine . . .

(MOTEL *enters.* TEVYE *almost kisses him in sequence.*) This is not mine. Perchik, this is Motel Kamzoil and he is—

GOLDE (*entering*). So you did me a favor and came in.

TEVYE. This is also mine. Golde, this is Perchik, from Kiev, and he is staying the Sabbath with us. He is a teacher. (*To* SHPRINTZE *and* BIELKE.) Would you like to take lessons from him? (*They giggle.*)

PERCHIK. I am really a good teacher, a very good teacher.

HODEL. I heard once, the rabbi who must praise himself has a congregation of one.

PERCHIK. Your daughter has a quick and witty tongue.

TEVYE. The wit she gets from me. As the Good Books says—

GOLDE. The Good Book can wait. Get washed!

TEVYE. The tongue she gets from her mother.

GOLDE. Motel, you're also eating with us? (MOTEL *gestures, "Yes, if I may."*) Of course, another blessing. Tzeitel, two more. Shprintze, Bielke, get washed. Get the table.

TZEITEL. Motel can help me.

GOLDE. All right. Chava, you go too. (*To* PERCHIK.) You can wash outside at the well.

(*Exit the* DAUGHTERS, PERCHIK, *and* MOTEL.) Tevye, I have something to say to you.

TEVYE. Why should today be different? (*He starts to pray.*)

GOLDE. Tevye, I have to tell you—

TEVYE. Shhh. I'm praying. (*Prays.*)

GOLDE (*having waited a moment*). Lazar Wolf wants to see you.

(TEVYE *begins praying again, stopping only to respond to* GOLDE, *then returning to prayer.*)

TEVYE. The butcher? About what? (*Prays.*)

GOLDE. I don't know. Only that he says it is important.

TEVYE. What can be important? I have nothing for him to slaughter. (*Prays.*)

GOLDE. After the Sabbath, see him and talk to him.

TEVYE. Talk to him about what? If he is thinking about buying my new milk cow (*prays*) he can forget it. (*Prays.*)

GOLDE. Tevye, don't be an ox. A man sends an important message, at least you can talk to him.

TEVYE. Talk about what? He wants my new milk cow! (*Prays.*)

GOLDE (*insisting*). Talk to him!

TEVYE. All right. After the Sabbath, I'll talk to him.

(TEVYE *and* GOLDE *exit. He is still praying.* MOTEL, TZEITEL, *and* CHAVA *bring in the table.* CHAVA *exits.*)

TZEITEL. Motel, Yente was here.

MOTEL. I saw her.

TZEITEL. If they agree on someone, there will be a match and then it will be too late for us.

MOTEL. Don't worry, Tzeitel. I have found someone who will sell me his used sewing machine, so in a few weeks I'll have saved up enough to buy it, and then your father will be impressed with me and . . .

TZEITEL. But, Motel, a few weeks may be too late.

MOTEL. But what else can we do?

TZEITEL. You could ask my father for my hand tonight. Now!

MOTEL. Why should he consider me now? I'm only a poor tailor.

TZEITEL. And I'm only the daughter of a poor milkman. Just talk to him.

MOTEL. Tzeitel, if your father says no, that's it, it's final. He'll yell at me.

TZEITEL. Motel!

MOTEL. I'm just a poor tailor.

TZEITEL. Motel, even a poor tailor is entitled to some happiness.

MOTEL. That's true.

TZEITEL (*urgently*). Will you talk to him? Will you talk to him?

MOTEL. All right, I'll talk to him.

TEVYE (*entering*). It's late! Where is everybody? Late.

MOTEL (*following him*). Reb Tevye—

TEVYE (*disregarding him*). Come in, children, we're lighting the candles.

MOTEL. Reb Tevye. (*Summoning courage.*) Reb Tevye, Reb Tevye.

TEVYE. Yes? What is it? (*Loudly.*) Well, Motel, what is it?

MOTEL (*taken aback*). Good Sabbath, Reb Tevye.

TEVYE (*irritated with him*). Good Sabbath, Good Sabbath. Come, children, come.

(TEVYE'*s family,* PERCHIK, *and* MOTEL *gather around the table.* GOLDE *lights the candles and says a prayer under her breath.*)

TEVYE *and* GOLDE (*sing to* DAUGHTERS).
["Sabbath Prayer"]

May the Lord protect and defend
    you,
May He always shield you from
    shame,
May you come to be
In Yisroel a shining name.

May you be like Ruth and like
 Esther,
May you be deserving of praise.
Strengthen them, O Lord,
And keep them from the stran-
 ger's ways.

May God bless you
And grant you long lives.
(*The lights go up behind them, showing other families, behind a transparent curtain, singing over Sabbath candles.*)

GOLDE.
 May the Lord fulfill our Sabbath
  prayer for you.
TEVYE *and* GOLDE.
 May God make you
 Good mothers and wives.
TEVYE.
 May He send you husbands who
  will care for you.
TEVYE *and* GOLDE.
 May the Lord protect and defend
  you,
 May the Lord preserve you from
  pain.
 Favor them, O Lord,
 With happiness and peace.
 O hear our Sabbath prayer.
 Amen.

SCENE FOUR

The inn, the following evening. AVRAM, LAZAR, MENDEL, *and several other people are sitting at tables.* LAZAR *is waiting impatiently, drumming on the tabletop, watching the door.*

——

LAZAR. Reb Mordcha.

MORDCHA. Yes, Lazar Wolf.

LAZAR. Please bring me a bottle of your best brandy and two glasses.

AVRAM. "Your best brandy," Reb Lazar?

MORDCHA. What's the occasion? Are you getting ready for a party?

LAZAR. There might be a party. Maybe even a wedding.

MORDCHA. A wedding? Wonderful. And I'll be happy to make the wedding merry, lead the dancing, and so forth. For a little fee, naturally.

LAZAR. Naturally, a wedding is no wedding without you—and your fee.

(FYEDKA *enters with several other* RUS-

SIANS.)

FIRST RUSSIAN. Good evening, Innkeeper.

MORDCHA. Good evening.

FIRST RUSSIAN. We'd like a drink. Sit down, Fyedka.

MORDCHA. Vodka? Schnapps?

FYEDKA. Vodka.

MORDCHA. Right away.

(TEVYE *enters.* LAZAR, *who has been watching the door, turns away, pretending not to be concerned.*)

TEVYE. Good evening.

MORDCHA. Good evening, Tevye.

MENDEL. What are you doing here so early?

TEVYE (*aside to* MENDEL). He wants to buy my new milk cow. Good evening, Reb Lazar.

LAZAR. Ah, Tevye. Sit down. Have a drink. (*Pours a drink.*)

TEVYE. I won't insult you by saying no. (*Drinks.*)

LAZAR. How goes it with you, Tevye?

TEVYE. How should it go?

LAZAR. You're right.

TEVYE. And you?

LAZAR. The same.

TEVYE. I'm sorry to hear that.

LAZAR (*pours a drink*). So how's your brother-in-law in America?

TEVYE. I believe he is doing very well.

LAZAR. He wrote you?

TEVYE. Not lately.

LAZAR. Then how do you know?

TEVYE. If he was doing badly, he would write. May I? (*Pours himself another drink.*)

LAZAR. Tevye, I suppose you know why I wanted to see you.

TEVYE (*drinks*). Yes, I do, Reb Lazar, but there is no use talking about it.

LAZAR (*upset*). Why not?

TEVYE. Why yes? Why should I get rid of her?

LAZAR. Well, you have a few more without her.

TEVYE. I see! Today you want one. Tomorrow you may want two.

LAZAR (*startled*). Two? What would I do with two?

TEVYE. The same as you do with one!

LAZAR (*shocked*). Tevye! This is very important to me.

TEVYE. Why is it so important to you?

LAZAR. Frankly, because I am lonesome.

TEVYE (*startled*). Lonesome? What are

you talking about?

LAZAR. You don't know?

TEVYE. We're talking about my new cow. The one you want to buy from me.

LAZAR (*stares at* TEVYE, *then bursts into laughter*). A milk cow! So I won't be lonesome! (*He howls with laughter.* TEVYE *stares at him.*)

TEVYE. What's so funny?

LAZAR. I was talking about your daughter. Your daughter, Tzeitel! (*Bursts into laughter.* TEVYE *stares at him, upset.*)

TEVYE. My daughter, Tzeitel?

LAZAR. Of course, your daughter, Tzeitel! I see her in my butcher shop every Thursday. She's made a good impression on me. I like her. And as for me, Tevye, as you know, I'm pretty well off. I have my own house, a good store, a servant. Look, Tevye, why do we have to try to impress each other? Let's shake hands and call it a match. And you won't need a dowry for her. And maybe you'll find something in your own purse, too.

TEVYE (*shouting*). Shame on you! Shame! (*Hiccups.*) What do you mean, my purse? My Tzeitel is not the sort that I would sell for money!

LAZAR (*calming him*). All right! Just as you say. We won't talk about money. The main thing is, let's get it done with. And I will be good to her, Tevye. (*Slightly embarrassed.*) I like her. What do you think?

TEVYE (*to the audience*). What do I think? What do I think? I never liked him! Why should I? You can have a fine conversation with him, if you talk about kidneys and livers. On the other hand, not everybody has to be a scholar. If you're wealthy enough, no one will call you stupid. And with a butcher, my daughter will surely never know hunger. Of course, he has a problem—he's much older than her. That's her problem. But she's younger. That's his problem. I always thought of him as a butcher, but I misjudged him. He is a good man. He likes her. He will try to make her happy. (*Turns to* LAZAR.) What do I think? It's a match!

LAZAR (*delighted*). You agree?

TEVYE. I agree.

LAZAR. Oh, Tevye, that's wonderful. Let's drink on it.

TEVYE. Why not? To you.

LAZAR. No, my friend, to you.

TEVYE. To the both of us.

LAZAR. To our agreement.

TEVYE. To our agreement. To our prosperity. To good health and happiness. (*Enter* FIDDLER.) And, most important (*sings*):

["To Life"]

To Life, to Life, L'Chaim.

TEVYE *and* LAZAR.
    L'Chaim, L'Chaim, To Life.

TEVYE.
    Here's to the father I've tried to
        be.

LAZAR.
    Here's to my bride to be.

TEVYE *and* LAZAR.
    Drink, L'Chaim,
    To Life, to Life, L'Chaim.
    L'Chaim, L'Chaim to Life.

TEVYE.
    Life has a way of confusing us,

LAZAR.
    Blessing and bruising us,

TEVYE *and* LAZAR.
    Drink, L'Chaim, to Life.

TEVYE.
    God would like us to be joyful,
    Even when our hearts lie panting
        on the floor.

LAZAR.
    How much more can we be joyful
    When there's really something
    To be joyful for!

TEVYE *and* LAZAR.
    To Life, to Life, L'Chaim.

TEVYE.
    To Tzeitel, my daughter.

LAZAR.
    My wife.
    It gives you something to think
        about,

TEVYE.
    Something to drink about,

TEVYE *and* LAZAR.
    Drink, L'Chaim, to Life.

LAZAR. Reb Mordcha.

MORDCHA. Yes, Lazar Wolf.

LAZAR. Drinks for everybody.

MENDEL. What's the occasion?

LAZAR. I'm taking myself a bride.

VILLAGERS. Who? Who?

LAZAR. Tevye's eldest, Tzeitel.

VILLAGERS. Mazeltov. . . . Wonderful. . . . Congratulations. . . . (*Sing.*)
    To Lazar Wolf.

TEVYE.
To Tevye.

VILLAGERS.
To Tzeitel, your daughter.

LAZAR.
My wife.

ALL.
May all your futures be pleasant
    ones,
Not like our present ones.
Drink, L'Chaim, to Life,
To Life, L'Chaim,
L'Chaim, L'Chaim, to Life.
It takes a wedding to make us
    say,
"Let's live another day,"
Drink, L'Chaim, to Life.
We'll raise a glass and sip a drop
    of schnapps
In honor of the great good luck
That favored you.
We know that
When good fortune favors two
    such men
It stands to reason we deserve it,
    too.
To us and our good fortune.
Be happy, be healthy, long life!
And if our good fortune never
    comes,
Here's to whatever comes.
Drink, L'Chaim, to Life.
Dai-dai-dai-dai-dai-dai-dai.
(*They begin to dance. A* RUSSIAN *starts
to sing, and they stop, uncomfortable.*)

RUSSIAN.
Za va sha, Zdarovia,
Heaven bless you both, Nazdro-
    via,
To your health, and may we live
    together in peace.
Za va sha, Zdarovia,
Heaven bless you both, Nazdro-
    via,
To your health, and may we live
    together in peace.

OTHER RUSSIANS.
May you both be favored with the
    future of your choice.
May you live to see a thousand
    reasons to rejoice.
Za va sha, Zdarovia,
Heaven bless you both, Nazdro-
    via,
To your health, and may we live
    together in peace.

Hey!
(*The* RUSSIANS *begin to dance, the*
OTHERS *join in and they dance to a wild
finale pileup on the bar.*)
TEVYE (*from the pileup*).
To Life!
(*Blackout.*)

SCENE FIVE

*The street outside the inn. Entering
through the inn door are the* FIDDLER,
LAZAR, TEVYE, *the other* VILLAGERS, *and the*
RUSSIANS, *singing "To Life."*

LAZAR. You know, Tevye, after the marriage, we will be related. You will be my
papa.

TEVYE. Your papa! I always wanted a
son, but I wanted one a little younger
than myself.

(*The* CONSTABLE *enters.*)

CONSTABLE. Good evening.

FIRST RUSSIAN. Good evening, Constable.

CONSTABLE. What's the celebration?

FIRST RUSSIAN. Tevye is marrying off his
oldest daughter.

CONSTABLE. May I offer my congratulations, Tevye?

TEVYE. Thank you, your Honor.

(*All but* TEVYE *and the* CONSTABLE *exit.*)

CONSTABLE. Oh, Tevye, I have a piece of
news that I think I should tell you, as a
friend.

TEVYE. Yes, your Honor?

CONSTABLE. And I'm giving you this
news because I like you. You are a decent,
honest person, even though you are a
Jewish dog.

TEVYE. How often does a man get a
compliment like that? And your news?

CONSTABLE. We have received orders
that sometime soon this district is to have
a little unofficial demonstration.

TEVYE (*shocked*). A pogrom? Here?

CONSTABLE. No—just a little unofficial
demonstration.

TEVYE. How little?

CONSTABLE. Not too serious—just some
mischief, so that if an inspector comes
through, he will see that we have done
our duty. Personally, I don't know why
there has to be this trouble between people, but I thought I should tell you, and
you can tell the others.

TEVYE. Thank you, your Honor. You're a good man. If I may say so, it's too bad you're not a Jew.

CONSTABLE (*amused*). That's what I like about you, Tevye, always joking. And congratulations again, for your daughter.

TEVYE. Thank you, your Honor. Goodbye. (*The* CONSTABLE *exits.* TEVYE *turns to heaven.*) Dear God, did You have to send me news like that, today of all days? It's true that we are the Chosen People. But once in a while can't You choose someone else? Anyway, thank You for sending a husband for my Tzeitel. L'Chaim.

(*The* FIDDLER *enters, he circles* TEVYE, *and they dance off together.*)

SCENE SIX

Outside TEVYE's *house.* PERCHIK *is teaching* SHPRINTZE *and* BIELKE *while they peel potatoes at a bench.* HODEL *is cleaning pails at the pump.*

———

PERCHIK. Now, children, I will tell you the story from the Bible, of Laban and Jacob, and then we will discuss it together. All right? (*They nod.*) Good. Now Laban had two daughters, Leah and the beautiful Rachel. And Jacob loved the younger, Rachel, and he asked Laban for her hand. Laban agreed, if Jacob would work for him for seven years.

SHPRINTZE. Was Laban a mean man?

PERCHIK (*dryly*). He was an employer! Now, after Jacob worked seven years, do you know what happened? Laban fooled him, and gave him his ugly daughter, Leah. So, to marry Rachel, Jacob was forced to work another seven years. You see, children, the Bible clearly teaches us, you must never trust an employer. Do you understand?

SHPRINTZE. Yes, Perchik.

BIELKE. Yes, Perchik.

PERCHIK. Good, now—

GOLDE (*entering from the barn*). Papa isn't up yet?

HODEL. No, Mama.

GOLDE. Then enough lessons. We have to do Papa's work today. How long can he sleep? He staggered home last night and fell into bed like a dead man. I couldn't get a word out of him. Put that away and clean the barn. (SHPRINTZE *and* BIELKE *exit into the barn. To* HODEL.) Call me when Papa gets up. (GOLDE *exits.* HODEL *pumps a bucket of water.*)

HODEL. That was a very interesting lesson, Perchik.

PERCHIK. Do you think so?

HODEL. Although I don't know if the rabbi would agree with your interpretation.

PERCHIK. And neither, I suppose, would the rabbi's son.

HODEL. My little sisters have big tongues.

PERCHIK. And what do you know about him, except that he is the rabbi's son? Would you be interested in him if he were the shoemaker's son, or the tinsmith's son?

HODEL. At least I know this, he does not have any strange ideas about turning the world upside down.

PERCHIK. Certainly. Any new idea would be strange to you. Remember, the Lord said, "Let there be light."

HODEL. Yes, but He was not talking to you personally. Good day. (*Starts off.*)

PERCHIK. You have spirit. Even a little intelligence, perhaps.

HODEL. Thank you.

PERCHIK. But what good is your brain? Without curiosity it is a rusty tool. Good day, Hodel.

HODEL. We have an old custom here. A boy acts respectfully to a girl. But, of course, that is too traditional for an advanced thinker like you.

PERCHIK. Our traditions! Nothing must change! Everything is perfect exactly the way it is!

HODEL. We like our ways.

PERCHIK. Our ways are changing all over but here. Here men and women must keep apart. Men study. Women in the kitchen. Boys and girls must not touch, should not even look at each other.

HODEL. I am looking at you!

PERCHIK. You are very brave! Do you know that in the city boys and girls can be affectionate without permission of a matchmaker? They hold hands together, they even dance together—new dances—like this. (*He seizes her and starts dancing, humming.*) I learned it in Kiev. Do you like it?

HODEL (*startled*). It's very nice.

PERCHIK (*stops dancing*). There. We've just changed an old custom.

HODEL (*bewildered*). Yes. Well, you're welcome—I mean, thank you—I mean, good day.

PERCHIK. Good day!

(TEVYE *enters, suffering from a headache.*)

TEVYE. Bielke, Shprintze, what's your name?

HODEL. Hodel, Papa.

TEVYE. Where is Tzeitel?

HODEL. She's in the barn.

TEVYE. Call her out. (HODEL *exits into the barn.*) Reb Perchik. How did the lesson go today?

PERCHIK (*watching* HODEL's *exit*). I think we made a good beginning.

(*Enter* GOLDE.)

GOLDE. Ah, he's finally up. What happened last night, besides your drinking like a peasant? Did you see Lazar Wolf? What did he say? What did you say? Do you have news?

TEVYE. Patience, woman. As the Good Book says, "Good news will stay and bad news will refuse to leave." And there's another saying that goes—

GOLDE (*exasperated*). You can die from such a man!

(TZEITEL *enters from the barn.* HODEL *and* CHAVA *follow her.*)

TEVYE. Ah, Tzeitel, my lamb, come here. Tzeitel, you are to be congratulated. You are going to be married!

GOLDE. Married!

TZEITEL. What do you mean, Papa?

TEVYE. Lazar Wolf has asked for your hand.

GOLDE (*thrilled*). I knew it!

TZEITEL (*bewildered*). The butcher?

GOLDE (*enraptured*). My heart told me this was our lucky day. O dear God, I thank Thee, I thank Thee.

TEVYE. And what do you say, Tzeitel?

GOLDE. What can she say? My first-born, a bride! May you grow old with him in fortune and honor, not like Fruma-Sarah, that first wife of his. She was a bitter woman, may she rest in peace. Not like my Tzeitel. And now I must thank Yente. My Tzeitel, a bride! (*She hurries off.*)

HODEL *and* CHAVA (*subdued*). Mazeltov, Tzeitel.

TEVYE. You call that a Mazeltov? (HODEL *and* CHAVA *exit.*) And you, Reb Perchik, aren't you going to congratulate her?

PERCHIK (*sarcastic*). Congratulations,

Tzeitel, for getting a rich man.

TEVYE. Again with the rich! What's wrong with being rich?

PERCHIK. It is no reason to marry. Money is the world's curse.

TEVYE. May the Lord smite me with it! And may I never recover! Tzeitel knows I mean only her welfare. Am I right, Tzeitel?

TZEITEL. Yes, Papa.

TEVYE. You see.

PERCHIK. I see. I see very well. (*He exits.*)

TEVYE. Well, Tzeitel, my child, why are you so silent? Aren't you happy with this blessing?

TZEITEL (*bursts into tears*). Oh, Papa, Papa.

TEVYE. What is it? Tell me.

TZEITEL. Papa, I don't want to marry him. I can't marry him. I can't—

TEVYE. What do you mean, you can't? If I say you will, you will.

TZEITEL. Papa, if it's a matter of money, I'll do anything. I'll hire myself out as a servant. I'll dig ditches, I'll haul rocks, only don't make me marry him, Papa, please.

TEVYE. What's wrong with Lazar? He likes you.

TZEITEL. Papa, I will be unhappy with him. All my life will be unhappy. I'll dig ditches, I'll haul rocks.

TEVYE. But we made an agreement. With us an agreement is an agreement.

TZEITEL (*simply*). Is that more important that I am, Papa? Papa, don't force me. I'll be unhappy all my days.

TEVYE. All right. I won't force you.

TZEITEL. Oh, thank you, Papa.

TEVYE. It seems it was not ordained that you should have all the comforts of life, or that we should have a little joy in our old age after all our hard work.

(*Enter* MOTEL, *breathless.*)

MOTEL. Reb Tevye, may I speak to you?

TEVYE. Later, Motel. Later.

MOTEL. I would like to speak to you.

TEVYE. Not now, Motel. I have problems.

MOTEL. That's what I want to speak to you about. I think I can help.

TEVYE. Certainly. Like a bandage can help a corpse. Good-bye, Motel. Good-bye.

TZEITEL. At least listen to him, Papa.

TEVYE. All right. You have a tongue, talk.

MOTEL. Reb Tevye, I hear you are arranging a match for Tzeitel.

TEVYE. He also has ears.

MOTEL. I have a match for Tzeitel.

TEVYE. What kind of match?

MOTEL. A perfect fit.

TEVYE. A perfect fit.

MOTEL. Like a glove.

TEVYE. Like a glove.

MOTEL. This match was made exactly to measure.

TEVYE. A perfect fit. Made to measure. Stop talking like a tailor and tell me who it is.

MOTEL. Please, don't shout at me.

TEVYE. All right. Who is it?

MOTEL. Who is it?

TEVYE (*pauses*). Who is it?

MOTEL. Who is it?

TEVYE. Who is it?

MOTEL. It's me—myself.

TEVYE (*stares at him, then turns to the audience, startled and amused*). Him? Himself? (*To* MOTEL.) Either you're completely out of your mind or you're crazy. (*To the audience.*) He must be crazy. (*To* MOTEL.) Arranging a match for yourself. What are you, everything? The bridegroom, the matchmaker, the guests all rolled into one? I suppose you'll even perform the ceremony. You must be crazy!

MOTEL. Please don't shout at me, Reb Tevye. As for being my own matchmaker, I know it's a little unusual.

TEVYE. Unusual? It's crazy.

MOTEL. Times are changing, Reb Tevye. The thing is, your daughter Tzeitel and I gave each other our pledge more than a year ago that we would marry.

TEVYE (*stunned*). You gave each other your pledge?

TZEITEL. Yes, Papa, we gave each other our pledge.

TEVYE (*looks at them, turns to the audience. Sings*).

["Tradition" Reprise]

They gave each other a pledge.
Unheard of, absurd.
You gave each other a pledge?
Unthinkable.
Where do you think you are?
In Moscow?
In Paris?
Where do they think they are?
America?

What do you think you're doing?
You stitcher, you nothing!
Who do you think you are?
King Solomon?
This isn't the way it's done,
Not here, not now.
Some things I will not, I cannot,
    allow.
Tradition—
Marriages must be arranged by
    the papa.
This should never be changed.
One little time you pull out a
    prop,
And where does it stop?
Where does it stop?

(*Speaks.*) Where does it stop? Do I still have something to say about my daughter, or doesn't anyone have to ask a father anymore?

MOTEL. I have wanted to ask you for some time, Reb Tevye, but first I wanted to save up for my own sewing machine.

TEVYE. Stop talking nonsense. You're just a poor tailor.

MOTEL (*bravely*). That's true, Reb Tevye, but even a poor tailor is entitled to some happiness. (*Looks at* TZEITEL *triumphantly.*) I promise you, Reb Tevye, your daughter will not starve.

TEVYE (*impressed, turns to the audience*). He's beginning to talk like a man. On the other hand, what kind of match would that be, with a poor tailor? On the other hand, he's an honest, hard worker. On the other hand, he has absolutely nothing. On the other hand, things could never get worse for him, they could only get better. (*Sings.*)

They gave each other a pledge—
Unheard of, absurd.
They gave each other a pledge—
Unthinkable.
But look at my daughter's face—
She loves him, she wants him—
And look at my daughter's eyes,
So hopeful.

(*Shrugs. To the audience.*)
Tradition!

(*To* TZEITEL *and* MOTEL.) Well, children, when shall we make the wedding?

TZEITEL. Thank you, Papa.

MOTEL. Reb Tevye, you won't be sorry.

TEVYE. I won't be sorry? I'm sorry already!

TZEITEL. Thank you, Papa.

MOTEL. Thank you, Papa.

TEVYE. Thank you, Papa! They pledged their troth! (*Starts to exit, then looks back at them.*) Modern children! (*Has a sudden thought.*) Golde! What will I tell Golde? What am I going to do about Golde? (*To heaven.*) Help! (*Exits.*)

TZEITEL. Motel, you were wonderful!

MOTEL. It was a miracle! It was a miracle. (*Sings.*)

["Miracle of Miracles"]

Wonder of wonders, miracle of
    miracles,
God took a Daniel once again,
Stood by his side, and miracle of
    miracles,
Walked him through the lion's
    den.
Wonder of wonders, miracle of
    miracles,
I was afraid that God would
    frown.
But, like He did so long ago in
    Jericho,
God just made a wall fall down.
When Moses softened Pharoah's
    heart,
That was a miracle.
When God made the waters of
    the Red Sea part,
That was a miracle, too.
But of all God's miracles large
    and small,
The most miraculous one of all
Is that out of a worthless lump
    of clay
God has made a man today.
Wonder of wonders, miracle of
    miracles,
God took a tailor by the hand,
Turned him around, and, miracle
    of miracles,
Led him to the Promised Land.
When David slew Goliath, yes!
That was a miracle.
When God gave us manna in the
    wilderness,
That was a miracle, too.
But of all God's miracles, large
    and small,
The most miraculous one of all
Is the one I thought could never
    be—
God has given you to me.

SCENE SEVEN

TEVYE's *bedroom. The room is in complete darkness. A groan is heard, then another, then a scream.*

———

TEVYE. Aagh! Lazar! Motel! Tzeitel!

GOLDE. What is it? What?

TEVYE. Help! Help! Help!

GOLDE. Tevye, wake up! (GOLDE *lights the lamp. The light reveals* TEVYE *asleep in bed.*)

TEVYE (*in his sleep*). Help! Help!

GOLDE (*shaking him*). Tevye! What's the matter with you? Why are you howling like that?

TEVYE (*opening his eyes, frightened*). Where is she? Where is she?

GOLDE. Where is who? What are you talking about?

TEVYE. Fruma-Sarah. Lazar Wolf's first wife, Fruma-Sarah. She was standing here a minute ago.

GOLDE. What's the matter with you, Tevye? Fruma-Sarah has been dead for years. You must have been dreaming. Tell me what you dreamt, and I'll tell you what it meant.

TEVYE. It was terrible.

GOLDE. Tell me.

TEVYE. All right—only don't be frightened!

GOLDE (*impatiently*). Tell me!

TEVYE. All right, this was my dream. In the beginning I dreamt that we were having a celebration of some kind. Everybody we knew was there, and musicians too.

(*As he speaks,* MEN, *including a* RABBI, WOMEN, *and* MUSICIANS *enter the bedroom.* TEVYE, *wearing a nightshirt, starts to get out of bed to join the dream.*) In the middle of the dream, in walks your Grandmother Tzeitel, may she rest in peace.

GOLDE (*alarmed*). Grandmother Tzeitel? How did she look?

TEVYE. For a woman who is dead thirty years, she looked very good. Naturally, I went up to greet her. She said to me—

(GRANDMA TZEITEL *enters, and* TEVYE *approaches her and greets her in pantomime.* GRANDMA *sings.*)

["The Tailor, Motel Kamzoil"]

GRANDMA TZEITEL.
    A blessing on your head,

RABBI.

    Mazeltov, Mazeltov.

GRANDMA TZEITEL.

    To see a daughter wed.

RABBI.

    Malzeltov, Mazeltov.

GRANDMA TZEITEL.

    And such a son-in-law,

    Like no one ever saw,

    The tailor Motel Kamzoil.

GOLDE (*bewildered*). Motel?

GRANDMA TZEITEL.

    A worthy boy is he,

RABBI.

    Mazeltov, Mazeltov.

GRANDMA TZEITEL.

    Of pious family.

RABBI. ~

    Mazeltov, Mazeltov.

GRANDMA TZEITEL.

    They named him after my

    Dear Uncle Mordecai,

    The tailor Motel Kamzoil.

GOLDE. A tailor! She must have heard wrong. She meant a butcher.

(TEVYE, *who has returned to* GOLDE, *listens to this, then runs back to* GRANDMA TZEITEL.)

TEVYE.

    You must have heard wrong,

      Grandma,

    There's no tailor,

    You mean a butcher, Grandma,

    By the name of Lazar Wolf.

GRANDMA TZEITEL (*flies into the air, screaming angrily*). No!!

(*Sings.*)

    I mean a tailor, Tevye.

    My great grandchild,

    My little Tzeitel, who you named

      for me,

    Motel's bride was meant to be.

    For such a match I prayed.

CHORUS.

    Mazeltov, Mazeltov,

GRANDMA TZEITEL.

    In heaven it was made.

CHORUS.

Mazeltov, Mazeltov,

GRANDMA TZEITEL.

    A fine upstanding boy,

    A comfort and a joy,

    The tailor Motel Kamzoil.

GOLDE (*from bed*). But we announced it already. We made a bargain with the butcher.

TEVYE.

    But we announced it, Grandma,

    To our neighbors.

    We made a bargain, Grandma,

    With the butcher, Lazar Wolf.

GRANDMA TZEITEL (*Again flies into the air, screaming angrily*). No!!

(*Sings.*)

    So you announced it, Tevye,

      That's your headache.

    But as for Lazar Wolf, I say to

      you,

    Tevye, that's your headache, too.

CHORUS.

    A blessing on your house, Mazel-

      tov, Mazeltov,

    Imagine such a spouse, Mazeltov,

      Mazeltov,

    And such a son-in-law,

    Like no one ever saw,

    The tailor Motel Kamzoil.

TEVYE (*speaks*). It was a butcher!

CHORUS.

    The tailor Motel Kamzoil.

TEVYE (*speaks*). It was Lazar Wolf.

(*Sings.*)

    The tailor Motel Kam . . .

CHORUS.

        Shah! shah!

        Look!

        Who is this?

        Who is this?

        Who comes here?

    Who? who? who? who? who?

        What woman is this

    By righteous anger shaken?

SOLO VOICES.

        Could it be?

        Sure!

        Yes, it could!

        Why not?

    Who could be mistaken?

CHORUS.

    It's the butcher's wife come from

      beyond the grave.

    It's the butcher's dear, darling,

      departed wife,

    Fruma-Sarah, Fruma-Sarah.

    Fruma-Sarah, Fruma-Sarah, Fru-

      ma-Sarah.

FRUMA-SARAH.

        Tevye! Tevye!

    What is this about your daugh-

      ter marrying my husband?

CHORUS.

        Yes, her husband.

FRUMA-SARAH.
  Would you do this to your friend
    and neighbor,
        Fruma-Sarah?
CHORUS.
        Fruma-Sarah.
FRUMA-SARAH.
  Have you no consideration for a
    woman's feelings?
CHORUS.
        Woman's feelings.
FRUMA-SARAH.
  Handing over my belongings to
    a total stranger.
CHORUS.
        Total stranger.
FRUMA-SARAH.
    How can you allow it, how?
  How can you let your daughter
    take my place?
  Live in my house, carry my keys,
  And wear my clothes, pearls—
    how?
CHORUS.
  How can you allow your daughter
    To take her place?
FRUMA-SARAH.
        Pearls!
CHORUS.
        House!
FRUMA-SARAH.
        Pearls!
CHORUS.
        Keys!
FRUMA-SARAH.
        Pearls!
CHORUS.
        Clothes!
FRUMA-SARAH.
        Pearls!
CHORUS.
        How?
FRUMA-SARAH.
        Tevye!!
CHORUS.
        Tevye!!
FRUMA-SARAH.
  Such a learned man as Tevye
    wouldn't let it happen.
CHORUS.
        Let it happen.
FRUMA-SARAH.
  Tell me that it isn't true, and
    then I wouldn't worry.
CHORUS.
        Wouldn't worry.
FRUMA-SARAH.
  Say you didn't give your blessing

to your daughter's
    marriage.
CHORUS.
        Daughter's marriage.
FRUMA-SARAH.
  Let me tell you what would fol-
    low such a fatal wedding.
CHORUS.
        Fatal wedding.
          Shh!
FRUMA-SARAH.
    If Tzeitel marries Lazar Wolf,
        I pity them both.
  She'll live with him three weeks,
  And when three weeks are up,
    I'll come to her by night,
  I'll take her by the throat, and

        . . .
    This I'll give your Tzeitel,
    That I'll give your Tzeitel,
    This I'll give your Tzeitel,
(*Laughs wildly.*) Here's my wedding present if she marries Lazar Wolf!
(*She starts choking Tevye. The* CHORUS
exits screaming.)
  GOLDE (*while* TEVYE *is being choked*).
It's an evil spirit: May it fall into the
river; may it sink into the earth. Such a
dark and horrible dream! And to think
it was brought on by that butcher. If my
Grandmother Tzeitel, may she rest in
peace, took the trouble to come all the
way from the other world to tell us about
the tailor, all we can say is that it is all
for the best, and it couldn't possibly be
any better. Amen.
  TEVYE. Amen.
  GOLDE (*sings*).
    A blessing on my head, Mazel-
      tov, Mazeltov,
    Like Grandma Tzeitel said, Maz-
      eltov, Mazeltov.
      We'll have a son-in-law,
      Like no one ever saw,
    The tailor Motel Kamzoil.
  TEVYE.
    We haven't got the man,
  GOLDE.
      Mazeltov, Mazeltov.
  TEVYE.
    We had when we began.
  GOLDE.
      Mazeltov, Mazeltov.
  TEVYE.
  But since your Grandma came,

She'll marry what's his name?
GOLDE.
    The tailor Motel Kamzoil.
TEVYE *and* GOLDE.
    The tailor Motel Kamzoil,
    The tailor Motel Kamzoil,
    The tailor Motel Kamzoil.
(GOLDE *goes back to sleep.* TEVYE *mouths the words "Thank You" to God, and goes to sleep.*)

SCENE EIGHT

The village street and the interior of MOTEL's *tailor shop.* MOTEL *and* CHAVA *are in the shop.* VILLAGERS *pass by.*

———

MAN. Bagels, fresh bagels.
WOMAN (*excited*). Did you hear? Did you hear? Tevye's Tzeitel is marrying Motel, not Lazar Wolf.
VILLAGERS. No!
WOMAN. Yes.
MENDEL. Tzeitel is marrying Motel?
WOMAN. Yes!
VILLAGERS. No! (*They rush into the shop and surround* MOTEL. MORDCHA *enters the street.*) Mazeltov, Motel. Congratulations.
MORDCHA. What's all the excitement?
AVRAM. Tevye's Tzeitel is going to marry—
MORDCHA. I know. Lazar Wolf, the butcher. It's wonderful.
AVRAM. No. Motel, the tailor.
MORDCHA. Motel, the tailor, that's terrible! (*Rushes into the shop.*) Mazeltov, Motel.
WOMAN (*to* SHANDEL, *exiting from the shop*). Imagine! Tzeitel is marrying Motel. I can't believe it!
SHANDEL (*outraged*). What's wrong with my son, Motel?
WOMAN. Oh, excuse me, Shandel. Mazeltov.
VILLAGERS (*inside the shop*). Mazeltov, Mazeltov.
MOTEL. Yussel, do you have a wedding hat for me?
YUSSEL. Lazar Wolf ordered a hat but it's not cheap.
MOTEL. I got his bride, I can get his hat!
YUSSEL. Then come, Motel, come.
MOTEL. Chava, can you watch the shop for a few minutes? I'll be back soon.

CHAVA. Of course.
MOTEL. Thank you, Chava. (*They all exit from the shop, calling Mazeltovs.*)
VILLAGERS (*to* CHAVA). We just heard about your sister. . . . Mazeltov, Chava. . . . Mazeltov, Chava.
CHAVA. Thanks—thank you very much. (*All but* CHAVA *exit.* FYEDKA, SASHA, *and another* RUSSIAN *enter at the same time. They cross to* CHAVA, *blocking her way into the shop.*)
SASHA *and* RUSSIAN (*mockingly, imitating others, with a slight mispronunciation*). Mazeltov, Chava. Mazeltov, Chava.
CHAVA. Please may I pass.
SASHA (*getting in her way*). Why? We're congratulating you.
RUSSIAN. Mazeltov, Chava.
FYEDKA (*calmly*). All right, stop it.
SASHA. What's wrong with you?
FYEDKA. Just stop it.
SASHA. Now listen here, Fyedka—
FYEDKA. Good-bye, Sasha. (SASHA *and the* RUSSIAN *hesitate.*) I said good-bye! (*They look at* FYEDKA *curiously, then exit.*) I'm sorry about that. They mean no harm.
CHAVA. Don't they? (*She enters shop. He follows her.*) Is there something you want?
FYEDKA. Yes. I'd like to talk to you.
CHAVA. I'd rather not. (*She hesitates.*)
FYEDKA. I've often noticed you at the bookseller's. Not many girls in this village like to read. (*A sudden thought strikes him. He extends the book he is holding.*) Would you like to borrow this book? It's very good.
CHAVA. No, thank you.
FYEDKA. Why? Because I'm not Jewish? Do you feel about us the way they feel about you? I didn't think you would. And what do you know about me? Let me tell you about myself. I'm a pleasant fellow, charming, honest, ambitious, quite bright, and very modest.
CHAVA. I don't think we should be talking this way.
FYEDKA. I often do things I shouldn't. Go ahead, take the book. It's by Heinrich Heine. Happens to be Jewish, I believe.
CHAVA. That doesn't matter.
FYEDKA. You're quite right. (*She takes the book.*) Good. After you return it, I'll ask you how you like it, and we'll talk about it for a while. Then we'll talk about life, how we feel about things, and it can

all turn out quite pleasant.

(CHAVA *puts the book on the table as*
MOTEL *enters.*)

MOTEL. Oh, Fyedka! Can I do something for you?

FYEDKA. No, thank you. (*Starts to
leave.*)

MOTEL. Oh, you forgot your book.

CHAVA. No, it's mine.

MOTEL. Thank you, Chava. (CHAVA
takes the book and leaves the shop with
FYEDKA.)

FYEDKA (*outside*). Good day, Chava.

CHAVA. Good day.

FYEDKA (*pleasantly*). Fyedka.

CHAVA. Good day, Fyedka. (*They exit.*
MOTEL *puts on his wedding hat.*)

SCENE NINE

Part of TEVYE's *yard. Night.* TZEITEL, *in
a bridal gown, enters, followed by* TEVYE,
GOLDE, HODEL, BIELKE, CHAVA, SHPRINTZE,
and RELATIONS. MOTEL *enters, followed by
his* PARENTS *and* RELATIONS. *Many* GUESTS
*enter, carrying lit candles. The men take
their places on the right, as a group, the
women on the left;* TZEITEL *and* MOTEL
stand in the center. MOTEL *places a veil
over* TZEITEL's *head.* FOUR MEN *enter, carrying a canopy. They are followed by the*
RABBI. *The canopy is placed over* MOTEL
and TZEITEL. GUESTS *start singing.*

———

["Sunrise, Sunset"]

TEVYE.
  Is this the little girl I carried?
  Is this the little boy at play?
GOLDE.
  I don't remember growing older.
        When did they?
TEVYE.
  When did she get to be a beauty?
  When did he grow to be so tall?
GOLDE.
  Wasn't it yesterday when they
    were small?
MEN.
        Sunrise, sunset,
        Sunrise, sunset,
      Swiftly flow the days.
  Seedlings turn overnight to sun-
    flowers,
  Blossoming even as we gaze.

WOMEN.
      Sunrise, sunset,
      Sunrise, sunset,
    Swiftly fly the years.
  One season following another,
  Laden with happiness and tears.
TEVYE.
  What words of wisdom can I
    give them?
  How can I help to ease their
    way?
GOLDE.
  Now they must learn from one
    another
        Day by day.
PERCHIK.
  They look so natural together.
HODEL.
  Just like two newlyweds should
    be.
PERCHIK *and* HODEL.
  Is there a canopy in store for me?
ALL.
      Sunrise, sunset,
      Sunrise, sunset,
    Swiftly fly the years.
  One season following another,
  Laden with happiness and tears.
(*During the song, the following mime
is performed. The* RABBI *lifts* TZEITEL's *veil.
He prays over a goblet of wine and hands
it to the bride and groom. They each sip
from it.* TZEITEL *slowly walks in a circle
around* MOTEL. MOTEL *places a ring on*
TZEITEL's *finger. The* RABBI *places a wine-
glass on the floor. The song ends. A moment's pause.* MOTEL *treads on the glass.*)

ALL (*at the moment the glass breaks*).
Mazeltov!

SCENE TEN

*The set opens to show the entire yard
of* TEVYE's *house. Part of it is divided
down the center by a short partition. Several tables are set up at the rear of each
section. The* MUSICIANS *play, and all dance
and then seat themselves on benches at
the tables. The women are on the left, the
men on the right. As the dance concludes,*
MORDCHA *mounts a stool and signals for
silence. The noise subsides.*

———

ALL. Shah. Shah. Quiet. Reb Mordcha.
Shah. Shah.

MORDCHA. My friends, we are gathered here to share the joy of the newlyweds, Motel and Tzeitel. May they live together in peace to a ripe old age. Amen.

ALL. Amen.

(*The* RABBI *slowly makes his way to the table, assisted by* MENDEL.)

MORDCHA. Ah, here comes our beloved rabbi. May he be with us for many, many years.

RABBI (*ahead of the others*). Amen.

ALL. Amen.

MORDCHA. I want to announce that the bride's parents are giving the newlyweds the following: a new featherbed, a pair of pillows—

GOLDE (*shouting from the women's side*). Goose pillows.

MORDCHA. Goose pillows. And this pair of candlesticks.

ALL. Mazeltov!

MORDCHA. Now let us not in our joy tonight forget those who are no longer with us, our dear departed, who lived in pain and poverty and hardship and who died in pain and poverty and hardship. (*All sob. He pauses a moment.*) But enough tears. (*The mourning stops immediately.*) Let's be merry and content, like our good friend, Lazar Wolf, who has everything in the world, except a bride. (*Laughter.*) But Lazar has no ill feelings. In fact, he has a gift for the newlyweds that he wants to announce himself. Come, Lazar Wolf.

LAZAR (*rising*). Like he said, I have no ill feelings. What's done is done. I am giving the newlyweds five chickens, one for each of the first five Sabbaths of their wedded life. (*Murmurs of appreciation from all.*)

TEVYE (*rising*). Reb Lazar, you are a decent man. In the name of my daughter and her new husband, I accept your gift. There is a famous saying that—

LAZAR. Reb Tevye, I'm not marrying your daughter. I don't have to listen to your sayings.

TEVYE. If you would listen a second, I was only going to say—

LAZAR. Why should I listen to you? A man who breaks an agreement!

(*Murmurs by the assemblage.*)

MENDEL. Not now, Lazar, in the middle of a wedding.

LAZAR. I have a right to talk.

TEVYE (*angry*). What right? This is not your wedding.

LAZAR. It should have been!

(*Murmurs by the assemblage.*)

MENDEL. Reb Lazar, don't shame Reb Tevye at his daughter's wedding.

LAZAR. But he shamed me in front of the whole village!

(*An argument breaks out. Everyone takes sides.*)

ALL. That's true. . . . The rabbi said . . . It was a shame . . . He has no feelings . . . This is not the place—

MENDEL. Shah. Shah. Quiet. The rabbi. The rabbi, the rabbi.

RABBI (*rising, as the noise subsides*). I say—Let's sit down. (*Sits.*)

TEVYE. We all heard the wise words of the rabbi.

(*Everyone returns to his seat.*)

MORDCHA. Now, I'd like to sing a little song that—

TEVYE (*bursting out*). You can keep your diseased chickens!

LAZAR. Leave my chickens out of this. We made a bargain.

TEVYE. The terms weren't settled.

LAZAR. We drank on it—

FIRST MAN. I saw them, they drank on it.

SECOND MAN. But the terms weren't settled.

SHANDEL. What's done is done.

TEVYE. Once a butcher, always a butcher.

GOLDE. I had a sign. My own grandmother came to us from the grave.

YENTE. What sign? What grandmother? My grandfather came to me from the grave and told me that her grandmother was a big liar.

LAZAR. We drank on it.

(*Bedlam.* MORDCHA *tries to quiet the guests.* PERCHIK *climbs onto a stool, banging two tin plates together.*)

MORDCHA. Quiet, I'm singing.

TEVYE. The terms weren't settled.

GOLDE. I had a sign.

YENTE. An agreement is an agreement.

PERCHIK (*silences them*). Quiet! Quiet! What's all the screaming about? "They drank on it—" "An agreement—" "A sign." It's all nonsense. Tzeitel wanted to marry Motel and not Lazar.

MENDEL. A young girl decides for herself?

PERCHIK. Why not? Yes! They love

each other.

AVRAM. Love!

LAZAR. Terrible!

MENDEL. He's a radical!

YENTE. What happens to the match-maker?

(*Another violent argument breaks out.*)

RABBI. I say—I say—(*They all turn to him.*)

TEVYE. Let's sit down? (*Rabbi nods.*)

MORDCHA. Musicians, play. A dance, a dance! (*The music starts, but no one dances.*) Come on, dance. It's a wedding.

YENTE. Some wedding!

(*PERCHIK crosses to the women's side.*)

AVRAM. What's he doing?

TEVYE. Perchik!

FIRST MAN. Stop him!

PERCHIK (*to* HODEL). Who will dance with me?

MENDEL. That's a sin!

PERCHIK. It's no sin to dance at a wed-ding.

AVRAM. But with a girl?

LAZAR. That's what comes from bring-ing a wild man into your house.

TEVYE (*signaling* PERCHIK *to return to the men's side*). He's not a wild man. His ideas are a little different, but—

MENDEL. It's a sin.

PERCHIK. It's no sin. Ask the rabbi. Ask him. (*They all gather around the* RABBI.)

TEVYE. Well, Rabbi?

RABBI (*thumbs through a book, finds the place*). Dancing—Well, it's not exactly forbidden, but—

TEVYE. There, you see? It's not forbid-den.

PERCHIK (*to* HODEL). And it's no sin. Now will someone dance with me? (HO-DEL *rises to dance.*)

GOLDE. Hodel!

HODEL. It's only a dance, Mama.

PERCHIK. Play! (PERCHIK *and* HODEL *dance.*)

LAZAR. Look at Tevye's daughter.

MENDEL. She's dancing with a man.

TEVYE. I can see she's dancing. (*Starts toward them as if to stop them. Changes his mind.*) And I'm going to dance with my wife. Golde! (*Golde hesitates, then dances with him.*)

SHANDEL. Golde! (MOTEL *crosses to* TZEI-TEL.) Motel!

(TZEITEL *dances with* MOTEL. *Others join them. They all dance, except for* LAZAR

and YENTE, *who storm off. As the dance reaches a wild climax, the* CONSTABLE *and his* MEN *enter, carrying clubs. The dancers see them and slowly stop.*)

CONSTABLE. I see we came at a bad time, Tevye. I'm sorry, but the orders are for to-night. For the whole village. (*To the* MUSI-CIANS.) Go on, play, play. All right, men.

(*The* RUSSIANS *begin their destruction, turning over tables, throwing pillows, smashing dishes and the window of the house. One of them throws the wedding-gift candlesticks to the ground, and* PER-CHIK *grapples with him. But he is hit with a club and falls to the ground. The* GUESTS *leave.*)

HODEL (*rushes to* PERCHIK). No, Per-chik!

(*The* GUESTS *have left during the above action.*)

CONSTABLE (*to his* MEN). All right, enough! (*To* TEVYE.) I am genuinely sorry. You understand. (TEVYE *does not answer. To his* MEN.) Come. (*The* CONSTA-BLE *and his* MEN *exit.*)

GOLDE. Take him in the house. (HODEL *helps* PERCHIK *into the house.*)

TEVYE (*quietly*). What are you stand-ing around for? Clean up. Clean up.

(*They start straightening up, picking up broken dishes, bringing bedding back to the house.* TZEITEL *picks up candlesticks, one of which is broken. They freeze at sudden sounds of destruction in a nearby house, then continue straightening up as the curtain falls.*)

ACT TWO

PROLOGUE. *The exterior of* TEVYE'*s house.* TEVYE *is sitting on a bench.*

———

TEVYE (*to heaven*). That was quite a dowry You gave my daughter Tzeitel at her wedding. Was that necessary? Any-way, Tzeitel and Motel have been mar-ried almost two months now. They work very hard, they are as poor as squirrels in winter. But they are both so happy they don't know how miserable they are. Motel keeps talking about a sewing machine. I know You're very busy—wars and revo-lutions, floods, plagues, all those little things that bring people to You—couldn't You take a second away from Your catastrophes and get it for him? How much trouble would it be? Oh, and while You're in the neighborhood, my horse's left leg—Am I bothering You too much? I'm sorry. As the Good Book says—Why should I tell You what the Good Book says? (*Exits.*)

SCENE ONE

The exterior of TEVYE'S *house. After-noon.* HODEL *enters, petulantly, followed by* PERCHIK.

———

PERCHIK. Please don't be upset, Hodel.

HODEL. Why should I be upset? If you must leave, you must.

PERCHIK. I do have to. They expect me in Kiev tomorrow morning.

HODEL. So you told me. Then good-bye.

PERCHIK. Great changes are about to take place in this country. Tremendous changes. But they can't happen by them-selves.

HODEL. So naturally you feel that you personally have to—

PERCHIK. Not only me. Many people. Jews, Gentiles, many people hate what is going on. Don't you understand?

HODEL. I understand, of course. You want to leave. Then good-bye,

PERCHIK. Hodel, your father, the others here, think what happened at Tzeitel's wedding was a little cloudburst and it's over and everything will now be peaceful again. It won't. Horrible things are hap-pening all over the land—pogroms, vio-lence—whole villages are being emptied of their people. And it's reaching every-where, and it will reach here. You under-stand?

HODEL. Yes, I—I suppose I do.

PERCHIK. I have work to do. The great-est work a man can do.

HODEL. Then good-bye, Perchik.

PERCHIK. Before I go (*he hesitates, then summons up courage*), there is a certain question I wish to discuss with you.

HODEL. Yes?

PERCHIK. A political question.

HODEL. What is it?

PERCHIK. The question of marriage.

HODEL. This is a political question?

PERCHIK (*awkwardly*). In a theoretical

sense, yes. The relationship between a man and woman known as marriage is based on mutual beliefs, a common atti-tude and philosophy toward society—

HODEL. And affection.

PERCHIK. And affection. This relation-ship has positive social values. It reflects a unity and solidarity—

HODEL. And affection.

PERCHIK. Yes. And I personally am in favor of it. Do you understand?

HODEL. I think you are asking me to marry you.

PERCHIK. In a theoretical sense, yes, I am.

HODEL. I was hoping you were.

PERCHIK. Then I take it you approve? And we can consider ourselves engaged, even though I am going away? (*She nods.*) I am very happy, Hodel. Very happy.

HODEL. So am I, Perchik.

PERCHIK (*sings*).

["Now I Have Everything"]

I used to tell myself
That I had everything,
But that was only half true.
I had an aim in life,
And that was everything,
But now I even have you.
I have something that I would
die for,
Someone that I can live for, too.
Yes, now I have everything—
Not only everything,
I have a little bit more—
Besides having everything,
I know what everything's for.
I used to wonder,
Could there be a wife
To share such a difficult, wand-
'ring kind of life.

HODEL.
I was only out of sight,
Waiting right here.

PERCHIK.
Who knows tomorrow
Where our home will be?

HODEL.
I'll be with you and that's
Home enough for me.

PERCHIK.
Everything is right at hand.

HODEL *and* PERCHIK.
Simple and clear.

PERCHIK.

 I have something that I would
  die for,
 Someone that I can live for, too.
 Yes, now I have everything—
  Not only everything,
  I have a little bit more—
 Besides having everything,
 I know what everything's for.

HODEL. And when will we be married,
Perchik?

PERCHIK. I will send for you as soon
as I can. It will be a hard life, Hodel.

HODEL. But it will be less hard if we
live it together.

PERCHIK. Yes.

(TEVYE *enters.*)

TEVYE. Good evening.

PERCHIK. Good evening. Reb Tevye, I
have some bad news. I must leave this
place.

TEVYE. When?

PERCHIK. Right away.

TEVYE. I'm sorry, Perchik. We will all
miss you.

PERCHIK. But I also have some good
news. You can congratulate me.

TEVYE. Congratulations. What for?

PERCHIK. We're engaged.

TEVYE. Engaged?

HODEL. Yes, Papa, we're engaged. (*Takes*
PERCHIK's *hand.*)

TEVYE (*pleasantly, separating them*). No,
you're not. I know, you like him, and he
likes you, but you're going away, and
you're staying here, so have a nice trip,
Perchik. I hope you'll be very happy, and
my answer is no.

HODEL. Please, Papa, you don't understand.

TEVYE. I understand. I gave my permission to Motel and Tzeitel, so you feel
that you also have a right. I'm sorry,
Perchik. I like you, but you're going
away, so go in good health and my answer is still no.

HODEL. You don't understand, Papa.

TEVYE (*patiently*). You're not listening.
I say no. I'm sorry, Hodel, but we'll find
someone else for you, here in Anatevka.

PERCHIK. Reb Tevye.

TEVYE. What is it?

PERCHIK. We are not asking for your
permission, only for your blessing. We are
going to get married.

TEVYE (*to* HODEL). You're not asking

for my permission?

HODEL. But we would like your blessing, Papa.

TEVYE.

["Tradition" Reprise]

 I can't believe my own ears. My
  blessing? For What?
 For going over my head? Impos-
  sible.
 At least with Tzeitel and Motel,
  they asked me,
 They begged me.
 But now, if I like it or not,
 She'll marry him.
 So what do you want from me?
  Go on, be wed.
 And tear out my beard and un-
  cover my head.
 Tradition!
 They're not even asking permis-
  sion
 From the papa.
 What's happening to the tradi-
  tion?
 One little time I pulled out a
  thread
 And where has it led? Where has
  it led?
 Where has it led? To this! A man
  tells me he is getting mar-
  ried.
 He doesn't ask me, he tells me.
  But first, he abandons her.

HODEL. He is not abandoning me, Papa.

PERCHIK. As soon as I can, I will send
for her and marry her. I love her.

TEVYE (*mimicking him*). "I love her."
Love. It's a new style. On the other hand,
our old ways were once new, weren't they?
On the other hand, they decided without parents, without a matchmaker. On
the other hand, did Adam and Eve have
a matchmaker? Yes, they did. Then it
seems these two have the same matchmaker. (*Sings.*)

 They're going over my head—
 Unheard of, absurd.
 For this they want to be
  blessed?—
 Unthinkable.
 I'll lock her up in her room.
 I couldn't—I should!—
 But look at my daughter's eyes.
 She loves him.
 Tradition!

(*Shrugs.*) Very well, children, you have my blessing and my permission.

HODEL. Oh, thank you, Papa. You don't know how happy that makes me.

TEVYE (*to the audience*). What else could I do?

PERCHIK. Thank you, Papa.

TEVYE (*worried*). "Thank you, Papa." What will I tell your mother? Another dream?

PERCHIK. Perhaps if you tell her something—that I am going to visit a rich uncle—something like that.

TEVYE. Please, Perchik. I can handle my own wife. (PERCHIK *and* HODEL *exit. He calls aggressively.*) Golde! Golde! (*She enters from the house. He speaks timidly.*) Hello, Golde. I've just been talking to Perchik and Hodel.

GOLDE. Well?

TEVYE. They seem to be very fond of each other—

GOLDE. Well?

TEVYE. Well, I have decided to give them my permission to become engaged. (*Starts into the house.*)

GOLDE (*stopping him*). What? Just like this? Without even asking me?

TEVYE (*roaring*). Who asks you? I'm the father.

GOLDE. And who is he? A pauper. He has nothing, absolutely nothing!

TEVYE (*hesitating*). I wouldn't say that. I hear he has a rich uncle, a very rich uncle. (*Changes the subject.*) He is a good man, Golde. I like him. He is a little crazy, but I like him. And what's more important, Hodel likes him. Hodel loves him. So what can we do? It's a new world, a new world. Love. (*Starts to go, then has a sudden thought.*) Golde—(*Sings.*)
["Do You Love Me?"]

Do you love me?
GOLDE.
Do I what?
TEVYE.
Do you love me?
GOLDE.
Do I love you?
With our daughters getting married
And this trouble in the town,
You're upset, you're worn out,
Go inside, go lie down.
Maybe it's indigestion.
TEVYE. Golde, I'm asking you a question—
Do you love me?
GOLDE.
You're a fool.
TEVYE. I know—
But do you love me?
GOLDE.
Do I love you?
For twenty-five years I've washed
your clothes,
Cooked your meals, cleaned your
house,
Given you children, milked the
cow.
After twenty-five years, why talk
about
Love right now?
TEVYE.
Golde, the first time I met you
Was on our wedding day.
I was scared.
GOLDE.
I was shy.
TEVYE.
I was nervous.
GOLDE.
So was I.
TEVYE.
But my father and my mother
Said we'd learn to love each other.
And now I'm asking, Golde,
Do you love me?
GOLDE.
I'm your wife.
TEVYE. I know—
But do you love me?
GOLDE.
Do I love him?
For twenty-five years I've lived
with him,
Fought with him, starved with
him.
Twenty-five years my bed is his.
If that's not love, what is?
TEVYE.
Then you love me?
GOLDE.
I suppose I do.
TEVYE.
And I suppose I love you, too.
TEVYE *and* GOLDE.
It doesn't change a thing,
But even so,
After twenty-five years,
It's nice to know.

Scene Two

The village street. YENTE, TZEITEL, *and other villagers cross.* YENTE *and* TZEITEL *meet.*)

———

FISH SELLER. Fish! Fresh fish!

YENTE. Oh, Tzeitel, Tzeitel darling. Guess who I just saw! Your sister Chava with that Fyedka! And it's not the first time I've seen them together.

TZEITEL. You saw Chava with Fyedka?

YENTE. Would I make it up? Oh, and Tzeitel, I happened to be at the post office today and the postman told me there was a letter there for your sister Hodel.

TZEITEL. Wonderful, I'll go get it. (*Starts off.*)

YENTE. I got it! It's from her intended, Perchik. (*Hands letter to* TZEITEL.)

TZEITEL. Hodel will be so happy, she's been waiting—But it's open.

YENTE. It happened to be open. (TZEITEL *exits.* YENTE *watches her leave, then turns to a group of* VILLAGERS.) Rifka, I have such news for you.

["I Just Heard"]

Remember Perchik, that crazy
    student?
Remember at the wedding,
When Tzeitel married Motel
And Perchik started dancing
With Tevye's daughter Hodel?
Well, I just learned
That Perchik's been arrested, in
    Kiev.

VILLAGERS.
  No!
YENTE.
  Yes!

(YENTE *and the* FIRST GROUP *exit. A* WOMAN *crosses to a* SECOND GROUP.)

FIRST WOMAN. Shandel, Shandel! Wait till I tell you—
Remember Perchik, that crazy
    student?
Remember at the wedding,
He danced with Tevye's Hodel?
Well,
I just heard
That Hodel's been arrested, in
    Kiev.

VILLAGERS.
  No! Terrible, terrible!

(*The* SECOND GROUP *exits. A* SECOND WOMAN *crosses to a* THIRD GROUP.)

SECOND WOMAN. Mirila!
Do you remember Perchik,
That student, from Kiev?
Remember how he acted
When Tzeitel married Motel?
Well, I just heard
That Motel's been arrested
For dancing at the wedding.

VILLAGERS.
  No!
SECOND WOMAN.
  In Kiev!

(*The* THIRD GROUP *exits.* MENDEL *crosses to a* FOURTH GROUP.)

MENDEL. Rabbi! Rabbi!
Remember Perchik, with all his
    strange ideas?
Remember Tzeitel's wedding
Where Tevye danced with Golde?
Well I just heard
That Tevye's been arrested
And Golde's gone to Kiev.

VILLAGERS.
  No!
MENDEL.
  God forbid.
VILLAGERS.
  She didn't.
MENDEL.
  She did.

(*The* FOURTH GROUP *exits.* AVRAM *crosses to the* FIFTH GROUP. YENTE *enters and stands at the edge of the* GROUP *to listen.*)

AVRAM. Listen, everybody, terrible news —terrible—
Remember Perchik,
Who started all the trouble?
Well, I just heard, from someone
    who should know,
That Golde's been arrested,
And Hodel's gone to Kiev.
Motel studies dancing,
And Tevye's acting strange.
Shprintze has the measles,
And Bielke has the mumps.

YENTE.
And that's what comes from men
    and women dancing!

Scene Three

The exterior of the railroad station. Morning. HODEL *enters and walks over to a bench.* TEVYE *follows, carrying her suit-case.*

HODEL. You don't have to wait for the train, Papa. You'll be late for your customers.

TEVYE. Just a few more minutes. Is he in bad trouble, that hero of yours? (*She nods.*) Arrested? (*She nods.*) And convicted?

HODEL. Yes, but he did nothing wrong. He cares nothing for himself. Everything he does is for humanity.

TEVYE. But if he did nothing wrong, he wouldn't be in trouble.

HODEL. Papa, how can you say that, a learned man like you? What wrongs did Joseph do, and Abraham, and Moses? And they had troubles.

TEVYE. But why won't you tell me where he is now, this Joseph of yours?

HODEL. It is far, Papa, terribly far. He is in a settlement in Siberia.

TEVYE. Siberia! And he asks you to leave your father and mother and join him in that frozen wasteland, and marry him there?

HODEL. No, Papa, he did not ask me to go. I want to go. I don't want him to be alone. I want to help him in his work. It is the greatest work a man can do.

TEVYE. But, Hodel, baby—

HODEL. Papa—(*Sings.*)
["Far From the Home I Love"]

How can I hope to make you understand
Why I do what I do,
Why I must travel to a distant land
Far from the home I love?
Once I was happily content to be
As I was, where I was,
Close to the people who are close to me
Here in the home I love.
Who could see that a man would come
Who would change the shape of my dreams?
Helpless, now, I stand with him
Watching older dreams grow dim.
Oh, what a melancholy choice this is,
Wanting home, wanting him,
Closing my heart to every hope

but his,
Leaving the home I love.
There where my heart has settled long ago
I must go, I must go.
Who could imagine I'd be wand'ring so
Far from the home I love?
Yet, there with my love, I'm home.

TEVYE. And who, my child, will there be to perform a marriage, there in the wilderness?

HODEL. Papa, I promise you, we will be married under a canopy.

TEVYE. No doubt a rabbi or two was also arrested. Well, give him my regards, this Moses of yours. I always thought he was a good man. Tell him I rely on his honor to treat my daughter well. Tell him that.

HODEL. Papa, God alone knows when we shall see each other again.

TEVYE. Then we will leave it in His hands. (*He kisses* HODEL, *starts to go, stops, looks back, then looks to heaven.*) Take care of her. See that she dresses warm. (*He exits, leaving* HODEL *seated on the station platform.*)

SCENE FOUR

The village street, some months later. The VILLAGERS *enter.*

AVRAM. Reb Mordcha, did you hear the news? A new arrival at Motel and Tzeitel's.

MORDCHA. A new arrival at Motel and Tzeitel's? I must congratulate him.

AVRAM. Rabbi, did you hear the news? A new arrival at Motel and Tzeitel's.

RABBI. Really?

MENDEL. Mazeltov.

FIRST MAN. Mazeltov.

SECOND MAN. Mazeltov.

(SHANDEL *crosses quickly, meeting a* WOMAN.)

WOMAN. Shandel, where are you running?

SHANDEL. To my boy, Motel. There's a new arrival there.

VILLAGERS. Mazeltov, Mazeltov, Mazeltov, Shandel.

SCENE FIVE

MOTEL's *tailor shop.* MOTEL *and* CHAVA *are in the shop.* GOLDE *and the* VILLAGERS *crowd around* MOTEL, *congratulating him. They fall back, revealing a used sewing machine.*

———

VILLAGERS. Mazeltov, Motel. We just heard. Congratulations. Wonderful.

MOTEL. Thank you, thank you very much.

(TZEITEL *enters.*)

AVRAM. Mazeltov, Tzeitel.

TZEITEL (*ecstatic*). You got it!

MOTEL. I got it!

TZEITEL. It's beautiful.

MOTEL. I know!

TZEITEL. Have you tried it yet?

MOTEL (*holds up two different-colored pieces of cloth sewn together*). Look.

TZEITEL. Beautiful.

MOTEL. I know. And in less than a minute. And see how close and even the stiches are.

TZEITEL. Beautiful.

MOTEL. I know. From now on, my clothes will be perfect, made by machine. No more handmade clothes.

(*The* RABBI *enters.*)

MORDCHA. The rabbi, the rabbi.

MOTEL. Look, Rabbi, my new sewing machine.

RABBI. Mazeltov.

TZEITEL. Rabbi, is there a blessing for a sewing machine?

RABBI. There is a blessing for everything. (*Prays.*) Amen.

VILLAGERS. Amen. . . . Mazeltov. (VILLAGERS, RABBI *exit.*)

GOLDE. And the baby? How is the baby?

TZEITEL. He's wonderful, Mama.

(FYEDKA *enters. There is an awkward pause.*)

FYEDKA. Good afternoon.

MOTEL. Good afternoon, Fyedka.

FYEDKA. I came for the shirt.

MOTEL. It's ready.

TZEITEL. See, it's my new sewing machine.

FYEDKA. I see. Congratulations.

MOTEL. Thank you.

FYEDKA (*after another awkward moment*). Good day. (*Leaves the shop.*)

MOTEL. Good day.

GOLDE. How does it work?

MOTEL. See, it's an amazing thing. You work it with your foot and your hand.

(CHAVA *exits from the shop and meets* FYEDKA *outside.*)

FYEDKA. They still don't know about us? (*She shakes her head.*) You must tell them.

CHAVA. I will, but I'm afraid.

FYEDKA. Chava, let me talk to your father.

CHAVA. No, that would be the worst thing, I'm sure of it.

FYEDKA. Let me try.

CHAVA. No, I'll talk to him. I promise.

(TEVYE *enters.*)

FYEDKA (*extending his hand*). Good afternoon.

TEVYE (*takes the hand limply*). Good afternoon.

FYEDKA (*looks at* CHAVA). Good day. (*Exits.*)

TEVYE. Good day. What were you and he talking about?

CHAVA. Nothing, we were just talking. (TEVYE *turns to go into* MOTEL's *shop.*) Papa, Fyedka, and I have known each other for a long time and—and

TEVYE (*turning back*). Chava, I would be much happier if you would remain friends from a distance. You must not forget who you are and who that man is.

CHAVA. He has a name, Papa.

TEVYE. Of course. All creatures on earth have a name.

CHAVA. Fyedka is not a creature, Papa. Fyedka is a man.

TEVYE. Who says that he isn't? It's just that he is a different kind of man. As the Good Book says, "Each shall seek his own kind." Which, translated, means, "A bird may love a fish, but where would they build a home together?" (*He starts toward the shop, but* CHAVA *seizes his arm.*)

CHAVA. The world is changing, Papa.

TEVYE. No. Some things do not change for us. Some things will never change.

CHAVA. We don't feel that way.

TEVYE. We?

CHAVA. Fyedka and I. We want to be married.

TEVYE. Are you out of your mind? Don't you know what this means, marrying outside of the faith?

CHAVA. But, Papa—

TEVYE. No, Chava! I said no! Never talk about this again! Never mention his name again! Never see him again! Never! Do you understand me?

CHAVA. Yes, Papa. I understand you.

(GOLDE *enters from the shop, followed* by SHPRINTZE *and* BIELKE.)

GOLDE. You're finally here? Let's go home. It's time for supper.

TEVYE. I want to see Motel's new machine.

GOLDE. You'll see it some other time. It's late.

TEVYE. Quiet, woman, before I get angry. And when I get angry, even flies don't dare to fly.

GOLDE. I'm very frightened of you. After we finish supper, I'll faint. Come home.

TEVYE (*sternly*). Golde. I am the man in the family. I am head of the house. I want to see Motel's new machine, now! (*Strides to the door of the shop, opens it, looks in, closes the door, turns to* GOLDE.) Now, let's go home! (*They exit.* CHAVA *remains looking after them.*)

SCENE SIX

A road. Late afternoon. TEVYE *is pushing his cart.*

———

TEVYE (*sinks down on the cart*). How long can that miserable horse of mine complain about his leg? (*Looks up.*) Dear God, if I can walk on two legs, why can't he walk on three? I know I shouldn't be too upset with him. He is one of Your creatures and he has the same rights as I have: the right to be sick, the right to be hungry, the right to work like a horse. And, dear God, I'm sick and tired of pulling this cart. I know, I know, I should push it a while. (*He starts pushing the cart.*)

GOLDE (*offstage*). Tevye! (*She enters, upset.*) Tevye!

TEVYE (*struck by her manner*). What? What it is?

GOLDE. It's Chava. She left home this morning. With Fyedka.

TEVYE. What?

GOLDE. I looked all over for her. I even went to the priest. He told me—they were married.

TEVYE. Married! (*She nods.*) Go home, Golde. We have other children at home. Go home, Golde. You have work to do. I

have work to do.

GOLDE. But, Chava—

TEVYE. Chava is dead to us! We will forget her. Go home. (GOLDE *exits.* TEVYE *sings.*)

["Chavaleh"]

Little bird, little Chavaleh,
I don't understand what's happening today.
Everything is all a blur.
All I can see is a happy child,
The sweet little bird you were,
Chavaleh, Chavaleh.
Little bird, little Chavaleh,
You were always such a pretty little thing.
Everybody's fav'rite child,
Gentle and kind and affectionate,
What a sweet little bird you were,
Chavaleh, Chavaleh.

(CHAVA *enters.*)

CHAVA. Papa, I want to talk with you. Papa, stop. At least listen to me. Papa, I beg you to accept us.

TEVYE (*to heaven*). Accept them? How can I accept them? Can I deny everything I believe in? On the other hand, can I deny my own child? On the other hand, how can I turn my back on my faith, my people? If I try to bend that far, I will break. On the other hand . . . there is no other hand. No Chava. No—no—no!

CHAVA. Papa. Papa.

VILLAGERS (*seen behind a transparent curtain, sing as* CHAVA *exits slowly*).

Tradition. Tradition. Tradition.

SCENE SEVEN

TEVYE'S *barn.* YENTE *enters with two* BOYS, *teen-age students, who are obviously uncomfortable in the situation.*

———

YENTE. Golde, are you home? I've got the two boys, the boys I told you about.

(GOLDE *enters, followed by* SHPRINTZE *and* BIELKE.) Golde darling, here they are, wonderful boys, both learned boys, Golde, from good families, each of them a prize, a jewel. You couldn't do better for your girls—just right. From the top of the tree.

GOLDE. I don't know, Yente. My girls are still so young.

YENTE. So what do they look like, grandfathers? Meanwhile they'll be engaged, nothing to worry about later, no looking around, their future all signed and sealed.

GOLDE. Which one for which one?

YENTE. What's the difference? Take your pick.

GOLDE. I don't know, Yente. I'll have to talk with—

(*Enter* LAZAR WOLF, AVRAM, MENDEL, MORDCHA, *and other* VILLAGERS.)

AVRAM. Golde, is Reb Tevye home?

GOLDE. Yes, but he's in the house. Why, is there some trouble?

AVRAM (*to* BIELKE *and* SHPRINTZE). Call your father. (*They exit.*)

YENTE (*to the* BOYS). Go home. Tell your parents I'll talk to them. (*They exit.*)

GOLDE. What is it? Why are you all gathered together like a bunch of goats? What's—

(TEVYE *enters.*)

AVRAM. Reb Tevye, have you seen the constable today?

TEVYE. No. Why?

LAZAR. There are some rumors in town. We thought because you knew him so well, maybe he told you what is true and what is not.

TEVYE. What rumors?

AVRAM. Someone from Zolodin told me that there was an edict issued in St. Petersburg that all—Shh. Shh.

(*He stops as the* CONSTABLE *enters with* TWO MEN.)

TEVYE. Welcome, your Honor. What's the good news in the world?

CONSTABLE. I see you have company.

TEVYE. They are my friends.

CONSTABLE. It's just as well. What I have to say is for their ears also. Tevye, how much time do you need to sell your house and all your household goods? (*There is a gasp from the* VILLAGERS. *They are stunned. They look to* TEVYE.)

TEVYE. Why should I sell my house? Is it in anybody's way?

CONSTABLE. I came here to tell you that you are going to have to leave Anatevka.

TEVYE. And how did I come to deserve such an honor?

CONSTABLE. Not just you, of course, but all of you. At first I thought you might be spared, Tevye, because of your daughter Chava, who married—

TEVYE. My daughter is dead!

CONSTABLE. I understand. At any rate, it affects all of you. You have to leave.

TEVYE. But this corner of the world has always been our home. Why should we leave?

CONSTABLE (*irritated*). I don't know why. There's trouble in the world. Troublemakers.

TEVYE (*ironically*). Like us!

CONSTABLE. You aren't the only ones. Your people must leave all the villages— Zolodin, Rabalevka. The whole district must he emptied. (*Horrified and amazed exclamations from the* VILLAGERS.) I have an order here, and it says that you must sell your homes and be out of here in three days.

VILLAGERS. Three days! . . . Out in three days!

TEVYE. And you who have known us all your life, you'd carry out this order?

CONSTABLE. I have nothing to do with it, don't you understand?

TEVYE (*bitterly*). We understand.

FIRST MAN. And what if we refuse to go?

CONSTABLE. You will be forced out.

LAZAR. We will defend ourselves.

VILLAGERS. Stay in our homes . . . Refuse to leave . . . Keep our land.

SECOND MAN. Fight!

CONSTABLE. Against our army? I wouldn't advise it!

TEVYE. I have some advice for you. Get off my land! (*The* VILLAGERS *crowd toward the* CONSTABLE *and his* MEN.) This is still my home, my land. Get off my land! (*The* CONSTABLE *and his men start to go. The* CONSTABLE *turns.*)

CONSTABLE. You have three days! (*Exits.*)

FIRST MAN. After a lifetime, a piece of paper and get thee out.

MORDCHA. We should get together with the people of Zolodin. Maybe they have a plan.

FIRST MAN. We should defend ourselves. An eye for an eye, a tooth for a tooth.

TEVYE. Very good. And that way, the whole world will be blind and toothless.

MENDEL. Rabbi, we've been waiting for the Messiah all our lives. Wouldn't this be a good time for him to come?

RABBI. We'll have to wait for him someplace else. Meanwhile, let's start packing. (*The* VILLAGERS *start to go, talking together.*)

VILLAGERS. He's right. . . . I'll see you

before I go.

FIRST MAN. Three days!

MORDCHA. How will I be able to sell my shop? My merchandise?

THIRD MAN. Where can I go with a wife, her parents, and three children?

(*Exit all but* YENTE, GOLDE, AVRAM, LAZAR, MENDEL, *and* TEVYE.)

YENTE. Well, Anatevka hasn't been exactly the Garden of Eden.

AVRAM. That's true.

GOLDE. After all, what've we got here? (*Sings.*)

["Anatevka"]

A little a bit of this,
A little bit of that,

YENTE.

A pot,

LAZAR.

A pan,

MENDEL.

A broom,

AVRAM.

A hat.

TEVYE.

Someone should have set a match to this place long ago.

MENDEL.

A bench,

AVRAM.

A tree,

GOLDE.

So what's a stove?

LAZAR.

Or a house?

MENDEL (*speaks*). People who pass through Anatevka don't even know they've been here.

GOLDE.

A stick of wood,

YENTE.

A piece of cloth.

ALL.

What do we leave?
Nothing much,
Only Anatevka. . . .
Anatevka, Anatevka,
Underfed, overworked Anatevka,
Where else could Sabbath be so
    sweet?
Anatevka, Anatevka,
Intimate, obstinate Anatevka,
Where I know everyone I meet.
Soon I'll be a stranger in a strange
    new place,

Searching for an old familiar face
From Anatevka.
I belong in Anatevka,
Tumbledown, workaday Ana-
    tevka,
Dear little village, little town of
    mine.

GOLDE. Eh, it's just a place.

MENDEL. And our forefathers have been, forced out of many, many places at a moment's notice.

TEVYE (*shrugs*). Maybe that's why we always wear our hats.

SCENE EIGHT

Outside TEVYE's *house.* MOTEL *and* TZEITEL *are packing baggage into a cart and a wagon.* SHPRINTZE *and* BIELKE *enter with bundles.*

———

SHPRINTZE. Where will we live in America?

MOTEL. With Uncle Abram, but he doesn't know it yet.

SHPRINTZE. I wish you and the baby were coming with us.

TZEITEL. We'll be staying in Warsaw until we have enough money to join you.

GOLDE (*entering, with goblets*). Motel, be careful with these. My mother and father, may they rest in peace, gave them to us on our wedding day.

TZEITEL (*to* BIELKE *and* SHPRINTZE). Come, children, help me pack the rest of the clothes. (*They exit into house.*)

YENTE (*enters*). Golde darling, I had to see you before I left because I have such news for you. Golde darling, you remember I told you yesterday I didn't know where to go, what to do with these old bones? Now I know! You want to hear? I'll tell you. Golde darling, all my life I've dreamed of going to one place and now I'll walk, I'll crawl, I'll get there. Guess where. You'll never guess. Every year at Passover, what do we say? "Next year in Jerusalem, next year in the Holy Land."

GOLDE. You're going to the Holy Land!

YENTE. You guessed! And you know why? In my sleep, my husband, my Aaron, came to me and said, "Yente, go to the Holy Land." Usually, of course, I wouldn't listen to him, because, good as he was, too much brains he wasn't blessed with. But in my sleep it's a sign. Right? So, somehow or other, I'll get to the Holy Land. And you want to know what I'll do there? I'm a matchmaker, no? I'll arrange marriages, yes? Children come from marriages, no? So I'm going to the Holy Land to help our people increase and multiply. It's my mission. So good-bye, Golde.

GOLDE. Good-bye, Yente. Be well and go in peace. (*They embrace.*)

YENTE (*exiting*). Maybe next time, Golde, we will meet on happier occasions. Meanwhile, we suffer, we suffer, we suffer in silence! Right? Of course, right. (*She exits.* GOLDE *sits on a large straw trunk, sadly wrapping a pair of silver goblets.* TEVYE *enters, carrying a bundle of books, and puts them on the wagon.*)

TEVYE. We'll have to hurry, Golde. (*She is looking at the goblets.*) Come, Golde, we have to leave soon.

GOLDE. Leave. It sounds so easy.

TEVYE. We'll all be together soon. Motel, Tzeitel, and the baby, they'll come too, you'll see. That Motel is a person.

GOLDE. And Hodel and Perchik? When will we ever see them?

TEVYE. Do they come visiting us from Siberia every Sabbath? You know what she writes. He sits in prison, and she works, and soon he will be set free and together they will turn the world upside down. She couldn't be happier. And the other children will be with us.

GOLDE (*quietly*). Not all.

TEVYE (*sharply*). All. Come, Golde, we have to get finished.

GOLDE. I still have to sweep the floor.

TEVYE. Sweep the floor?

GOLDE. I don't want to leave a dirty house. (*She exits behind the house as* LAZAR *enters, carrying a large suitcase.*)

LAZAR. Well, Tevye, I'm on my way.

TEVYE. Where are you going?

LAZAR. Chicago. In America. My wife, Fruma-Sarah, may she rest in peace, has a brother there.

TEVYE. That's nice.

LAZAR. I hate him, but a relative is a relative! (*They embrace.*) Good-bye, Tevye. (LAZAR *exits.* TEVYE *enters the house, passing* TZEITEL, *who enters with a blanket and a small bundle.*)

TEVYE. Tzeitel, are they finished inside?

TZEITEL. Almost, Papa. (TZEITEL *puts the blanket on* MOTEL'S *wagon, kneels down, and begins rummaging in the bundle.* CHAVA *and* FYEDKA *enter.* TZEITEL *turns to enter the house, and sees them.*) Chava! (CHAVA *runs to her. They embrace.* TZEITEL *looks toward the house.*) Papa will see you.

CHAVA. I want him to. I want to say good-bye to him.

TZEITEL. He will not listen.

CHAVA. But at least he will hear.

TZEITEL. Maybe it would be better if I went inside and told Mama that— (GOLDE *comes round the side of the house.*)

GOLDE. Chava!

(*She starts toward her as* TEVYE *enters from the house with a length of rope. He sees them, turns, reenters house, returns, and bends down to tie up the straw trunk, his back to* CHAVA *and* FYEDKA.)

CHAVA. Papa, we came to say good-bye. (TEVYE *does not respond, but goes on working.*) We are also leaving this place. We are going to Cracow.

FYEDKA. We cannot stay among people who can do such things to others.

CHAVA. We wanted you to know that. Good-bye, Papa, Mama. (*She waits for an answer, gets none, and turns to go.*)

FYEDKA. Yes, we are also moving. Some are driven away by edicts, others by silence. Come, Chava.

TZEITEL. Good-bye, Chava, Fyedka.

TEVYE (*to* TZEITEL, *prompting her under his breath as he turns to another box*). God be with you!

TZEITEL (*looks at him, then speaks to Chava, gently*). God be with you!

CHAVA. We will write to you in America. If you like.

GOLDE. We will be staying with Uncle Abram.

CHAVA. Yes, Mama. (CHAVA *and* FYEDKA *exit.* TEVYE *turns and watches them leave. There is a moment of silence; then he turns on* GOLDE.)

TEVYE (*with mock irritation*). We will be staying with Uncle Abram! We will be staying with Uncle Abram! The whole world has to know our business!

GOLDE. Stop yelling and finish packing. We have a train to catch.

(MOTEL, SHPRINTZE, *and* BIELKE *enter from the house.*)

TEVYE. I don't need your advice, Golde. Tzeitel, don't forget the baby. We have to catch a train, and a boat. Bielke, Shprintze, put the bundles on the wagon.

(TEVYE *moves the wagon to the center of the stage, and* MOTEL *puts the trunk on it.* TZEITEL *brings the baby out of the house. They turn to one another for good-byes.*)

TZEITEL. Good-bye, Papa. (*They embrace.*)

GOLDE. Good-bye, Motel.

MOTEL. Good-bye, Mama.

(TZEITEL *and* GOLDE *embrace.*)

TEVYE. Work hard, Motel. Come to us soon.

MOTEL. I will, Reb Tevye. I'll work hard. (TEVYE *takes one last look at the baby, then* TZEITEL *and* MOTEL *exit with their cart. When they are gone,* TEVYE *turns to the wagon.*)

TEVYE (*picking up pots*). Come, children. Golde, we can leave these pots.

GOLDE. No, we can't.

TEVYE. All right, we'll take them. (*Puts them back.*)

BIELKE (*childishly, swinging around with* SHPRINTZE). We're going on a train and a boat. We're going on a—

GOLDE (*sharply*). Stop that! Behave yourself! We're not in America yet!

TEVYE. Come, children. Let's go.

(*The stage begins to revolve, and* TEVYE *begins to pull the wagon in the opposite direction. The other* VILLAGERS, *including the* FIDDLER, *join the circle. The revolve stops. There is a last moment together, and the* VILLAGERS *exit, at different times and in opposite directions, leaving the family on stage.* TEVYE *begins to pull his wagon upstage, revealing the* FIDDLER, *playing his theme.* TEVYE *stops, turns, beckons to him. The* FIDDLER *tucks his violin under his arm and follows the family upstage as the curtain falls.*)